D1809130

AUSTRALIAN
INTELLECTUAL PROPERTY

COMMENTARY, LAW AND PRACTICE

AUSTRALIAN
INTELLECTUAL PROPERTY

COMMENTARY, LAW AND PRACTICE

SECOND EDITION

KATHY BOWREY

MICHAEL HANDLER

DIANNE NICOL

KIMBERLEE WEATHERALL

OXFORD
UNIVERSITY PRESS
AUSTRALIA & NEW ZEALAND

OXFORD
UNIVERSITY PRESS

Oxford University Press is a department of the University of Oxford.
It furthers the University's objective of excellence in research, scholarship,
and education by publishing worldwide. Oxford is a registered trademark
of Oxford University Press in the UK and in certain other countries.

Published in Australia by
Oxford University Press
253 Normanby Road, South Melbourne, Victoria 3205, Australia

© Kathy Bowrey, Michael Handler, Dianne Nicol and Kimberlee Weatherall 2015

The moral rights of the authors have been asserted.

First edition published 2010

All rights reserved. No part of this publication may be reproduced, stored in a retrieval
system, or transmitted, in any form or by any means, without the prior permission in
writing of Oxford University Press, or as expressly permitted by law, by licence, or under
terms agreed with the appropriate reprographics rights organisation. Enquiries concerning
reproduction outside the scope of the above should be sent to the Rights Department,
Oxford University Press, at the address above.

You must not circulate this work in any other form and you must impose this same
condition on any acquirer.

National Library of Australia Cataloguing-in-Publication entry

Author: Bowrey, Kathy, author.
Title: Australian intellectual property: commentary, law and practice / Kathy Bowrey,
    Michael Handler, Dianne Nicol, Kimberlee Weatherall.
Edition: 2nd edition.
ISBN: 9780195598469 (paperback)
Notes: Includes index.
Subjects: Intellectual property—Australia.
        Industrial property—Australia.
Other Authors/Contributors: Handler, Michael, author.
                    Nicol, Dianne, author.
                    Weatherall, Kimberlee, author.
Dewey Number: 346.94048

Reproduction and communication for educational purposes
The Australian *Copyright Act 1968* (the Act) allows a maximum of one chapter
or 10% of the pages of this work, whichever is the greater, to be reproduced
and/or communicated by any educational institution for its educational purposes
provided that the educational institution (or the body that administers it) has
given a remuneration notice to Copyright Agency Limited (CAL) under the Act.

For details of the CAL licence for educational institutions contact:

Copyright Agency Limited
Level 15, 233 Castlereagh Street
Sydney NSW 2000
Telephone: (02) 9394 7600
Facsimile: (02) 9394 7601
Email: info@copyright.com.au

Edited by Natasha Broadstock
Text design by Denise Lane
Typeset by diacriTech, Chennai, India
Proofread by Roz Edmond
Indexed by Glenda Browne
Tables by Jon Jermey
Printed by Markono Print Media Pte Ltd, Singapore

*Links to third party websites are provided by Oxford in good faith and for information only. Oxford
disclaims any responsibility for the materials contained in any third party website referenced in this work.*

CONTENTS

TABLE OF CASES

Bold entries indicate case extracts.

TABLE OF STATUTES

BRITAIN

PREFACE

Given the dynamic nature of intellectual property (IP) law, it is entirely unsurprising there have been a number of significant developments in Australian IP law since the publication of the first edition of this book in late 2010. These form the major changes that are contained in this second edition.

In the area of copyright, we have seen new decisions on emerging technologies, considering the potential liability of internet service providers for the acts of their subscribers, and of providers of novel video-streaming services (Chapter 6). We have seen new cases on whether copyright subsists in newspaper headlines and Imperial Stormtrooper helmets (Chapter 4). But perhaps the most complex development in copyright has related to the law on 'authorship' and 'originality' in light of the High Court's decision in *IceTV Pty Ltd v Nine Network Pty Ltd* [2009] HCA 14; (2009) 239 CLR 458, which has raised difficult questions about the protection of computer-generated and computer-assisted works. To address the magnitude of this last change, we have split the issues that were addressed in Chapter 2 of the first edition across Chapters 2 and 3 of this edition.

In patent law, the *Intellectual Property Laws Amendment (Raising the Bar) Act 2012* (Cth) has brought about fundamental changes to the *Patents Act 1990* (Cth), in particular to the key criteria of 'inventive step' and 'usefulness' (Chapter 11) and to the disclosure and claiming requirements (Chapter 12). There have also been groundbreaking new cases on patentable subject matter, both in Australia and the USA, on issues as diverse as human genetic material and computer-implemented business methods (Chapter 10).

In the field of trade marks and passing off, there have been new and somewhat controversial decisions on the legal protection of product appearance (Chapter 16) and on the longstanding test for assessing the distinctiveness of a trade mark (Chapter 17).

The most significant change in the second edition is, however, one of personnel. Kathy, Dianne and Michael are delighted to welcome Kimberlee Weatherall to the team of authors. Kimberlee has been a leading copyright law scholar for many years, having published extensively on the topic in Australia and internationally. Kimberlee has been primarily responsible for updating Chapters 2–8 of this edition, with Dianne being responsible for Chapters 9–13 and Michael being responsible for Chapters 1 and 14–19; and with Kathy having oversight of the entire edition. The text is current as at 13 February 2015.

We owe a very large debt of gratitude to all of our colleagues who have commented and provided helpful feedback on both the first edition and drafts of this edition. We would like to thank, in particular, Isabella Alexander, Tanya Aplin, Catherine Bond, Rob Clark, Angus Lang and Dilan Thampapillai. We would also like to thank all of our students who have used and engaged with the first edition, especially the University of New South Wales LLB and JD students in 'Intellectual Property 1' and 'Intellectual Property 2' between 2011 and 2014, whose feedback has helped us reshape the book for this edition.

Finally, we wish to thank our partners, families and friends for their love and ongoing support. Without them, a project of this magnitude would simply not be possible.

Kathy Bowrey
Michael Handler
Dianne Nicol
Kimberlee Weatherall
February 2015

ACKNOWLEDGMENTS

The author and the publisher wish to thank the following copyright holders for reproduction of their material.

Australian Law Reform Commission for extract from *Copyright and the Digital Economy* (2014); Commonwealth of Australia for extracts from the *ACIP Review of the Designs System: Options Paper* (2014), *Designs Act, Copyright Act* 1968, *Explanatory Memorandum to the Intellectual Property Laws Amendment (Raising the Bar) Bill* 2011, *Patents Act, Plant Breeders Rights Act, Pharmaceutical Patents Review, Productivity Commission Inquiry Report, Trade Marks Act*. This legislative material is reproduced by permission, but is not the official or authorised version. It is subject to Commonwealth of Australia copyright; Bass Gabrielle for Bass Gabrielle logo image; Court of Justice of the European Union for extracts from *the European Court Report* (ECR); Edward Elgar Publishing for extract from *Trademark Law and Theory: A Handbook of Contemporary Research* by G Dinwoodie and M Janis, 2008; © EMI Songs Australia Pty Limited (ABN 85 000 063 267) for *Down Under* – C.Hay/R. Stryker, Locked Bag 7300, Darlinghurst, NSW 1300, Australia. International copyright secured. All rights reserved. Used by Permission. With thanks to Jonathan Carter for his assistance; European Patents Office for extract from *Official journal of the European Patents Office* (OJEPO) 545; Federal Court of Australia for case extracts; High Court of Australia for case extracts; Incorporated Council of Law Reporting (ICLR) for extract from *Chancery Law Report* (CH) *Weekly Law Report* (WLR); LexisNexis Australia for extracts from *Australian Law Reports* (ALR), *Intellectual Property Reports* (IPR), *New Zealand Law Reports* (NZLR), *Queensland Reports* (Qd R), *Victorian Reports* (VR); LexisNexis UK for extract from *All England Law Reports* (All ER); Lloyds Reports for extract; Music Sales Pty Ltd for *Kookaburra* lyrics by Marion Sinclair; Oxford Journals for extracts from *Reports of Patent Design and Trade*; Shutterstock/360b/urbanbuzz for the superman logo; Star Reality for Star Reality logo image; Starr Partners for Starr Partners logo image; Supreme Court of Canada for case extract; The John Marshall Law School for extract from *Review of Intellectual Property Law*; The Yale Law Journal for extract from *Breakfast with Batman: The Public Interest in the Advertising Age* by J Bitman (1999); Thomson Reuters (Professional) Australia Limited for extracts from *Commonwealth Law Reports* (CLR), *Federal Law Reports* (FLR), *NSW Law Reports* (NSWLR) www.thomsonreuters.com.au; Thomson Reuters (Professional) UK Limited for extracts from *Fleet Street Reports* (FLR), *Entertainment & Media Law Reports, European Copyright and Design Report, Fleet Street Report, Intellectual Property Quarterly*; Thomson Reuters Canada for extract from *Canadian Rights Reporter* (CPR); World Trade Organization for extracts from *Agreement on Trade Related Aspects of Intellectual Property Rights (TRIPS Agreement)* 1994.

Every effort has been made to trace the original source of copyright material contained in this book. The publisher will be pleased to hear from copyright holders to rectify any errors or omissions.

— 1 —

INTRODUCTION: AUSTRALIAN INTELLECTUAL PROPERTY LAW IN THE GLOBAL MARKETPLACE

INTRODUCTION

Over the past 30 years intellectual property (IP) has evolved from being an intellectual curiosity seldom seen in undergraduate law school curricula to becoming a front-rank and popular legal subject. An understanding of IP laws is central to the sciences, manufacturing and the arts, and increasingly important to mainstream legal practice. IP has also become a more controversial and politicised area of study in light of its emergence as a specialisation within international trade law, and the fast-paced development of the information economy. IP laws impact on our daily lives in much more obvious ways than in the past, and affect the way we access or engage with technology, medicine, nature, education and entertainment.

There have been statutes and regulations that we now recognise as IP laws dating from the seventeenth century, and specific international agreements since the late nineteenth: the *Paris Convention for the Protection of Industrial Property* (1883) and the *Berne Convention for the Protection of Literary and Artistic Works* (1886). These instruments, developed to address 'international piracy' between dominant political powers, arranged IP into two related but distinct fields: manufacturing and the arts. The term 'industrial property' covered patents over inventions, design rights and trade marks. 'Literary and artistic works' were defined broadly to encompass written texts, drawings, paintings, architecture, sculptures, engravings, lithography and sheet music. The conventions marked out certain standards for the protection and treatment of such subject matter, but the protection conferred depended upon the technicalities of the respective domestic laws of the signatories to these conventions.

This separation of art and science still underpins commonsense intuitions about IP laws today. Regulation of the culture industries and education is perceived as requiring essentially different considerations from that of industry and manufacturing, and perhaps also as requiring different kinds of legal skills. Notwithstanding that, it is still also common to find the terms 'copyright', 'patent' and 'trade mark' being used colloquially and in the media as imprecise and often confusing catch-all phrases in relation to debates about what intangible subject matter 'should' or 'should not' be protected.

It is important for law students to appreciate that despite the way IP laws might commonly come to be discussed in the broader community, as a subject of legal knowledge, IP is a problematic term.

Considered as an overarching concept, the idea of a unified IP system, or IP regime, leads to the conflation of vastly different subject matters and divergent approaches to regulation itself.

IP is an artificial construct and, as a matter of law, it is made up of a number of distinctive categories, most with underlying statutes that define the particulars of the property and limits to the rights. Each area of IP has its own history, rationales and technicalities. These 'knowledge laws' only fit together in a very loose and rather uncoordinated way. Accordingly, the categories need to be studied and understood as discrete legal and political constructs.

IP LEGISLATION

Australian IP laws today include:

- *Copyright Act 1968* (Cth), *Copyright Regulations 1969* (Cth) and *Copyright (International Protection) Regulations 1969* (Cth);
- *Designs Act 2003* (Cth) and *Designs Regulations 2004* (Cth);
- *Patents Act 1990* (Cth) and *Patents Regulations 1991* (Cth);
- *Trade Marks Act 1995* (Cth) and *Trade Marks Regulations 1995* (Cth);
- *Competition and Consumer Act 2010* (Cth), Sch 2 (the 'Australian Consumer Law');
- *Resale Royal Right for Visual Artists Act 2009* (Cth);
- *Circuit Layouts Act 1989* (Cth);
- *Plant Breeder's Rights Act 1994* (Cth);
- *Australian Grape and Wine Authority Act 2013* (Cth);
- the common law tort of passing off;
- the equitable action to prevent the breach of confidence (used to regulate trade secrets); and
- cultural protocols for the protection of Indigenous cultural and intellectual property.

A broad survey approach to the main categories of law allows students to grasp the nature and scope of the relevant legislation and administration applicable in each area. This book is designed as an introduction to:

- equip law students with legal knowledge appropriate for entry-level legal practice in IP;
- develop basic rights and commercialisation awareness for scientists, creators and managers of IP rights and their administration; and
- provide a foundation to enable students to progress to more specialised postgraduate study of IP law.

In relation to each main area of Australian IP law this book covers:

- a policy overview of the legal category, its history and emerging trends;
- an explanation of the structure of the legislation and associated rights; and
- leading case extracts to elucidate key legal principles and tensions.

METHODOLOGY

Our methodology, which we developed in the first edition of this text, utilises a new approach to the selection of cases. Where material and space permits, and especially in relation to difficult or controversial concepts, we provide different types of case materials and indicate their nature with tabs in the margin:

- A precedent chosen to give context to an enduring authority or to highlight a contrast with the reasoning in current law is marked with the tab PRECEDENT.
- A current leading authority is marked with the tab CURRENT LAW.
- A counterpoint (comparative perspective) precedent is marked with the tab COMPARATIVE LAW.

Case books perform an important role in organising legal knowledge. There are, however, limits to their usefulness as stand-alone texts. On the one hand, if case selection is too narrow (which may occur in an effort to present the law in tidy, easily digested snippets), the impression given may be misleading. The question of selection is especially problematic in IP, as principal legislation is complex and often confusingly drafted, with key concepts sometimes not defined in relevant legislation (instead requiring reference to regulations or 'practice and procedure' manuals). Also, there are very few legal principles that do not require significant qualification or analytical work so that they can be applied to new situations. On the other hand, the inclusion of too many cases in a text makes it unwieldy and unsuitable as an introduction because there is too much information to be appreciated and not enough opportunity for it to be synthesised, particularly by readers who are new to the area.

Our case selection provides students with tools to move away from both a simplistic and an overly dense treatment of the law, and recognises the fluidity of the law and related policy changes. This provides a mechanism for covering the basics while keeping policy challenges and international perspectives at the fore. This approach does not compromise the traditional role of the case book in exposing students to the field and its key principles, but it does allow for a more critical and engaged discussion of those principles. While the primary focus is Australian law, an awareness of comparative law—especially US law and UK law (the latter increasingly influenced by EU developments)—is vitally important in legal practice today.

AUSTRALIAN IP POLICY MANAGEMENT IN A GLOBAL CONTEXT

A number of agencies have an international agenda-setting role in IP policy, and four key agencies are considered below. The claim that IP rights are central to economic development has been much scrutinised of late, with considerable debate revolving around the politics of world trade, development, economics, and biological and cultural diversity.[1]

INTERNATIONAL ORGANISATIONS
WORLD INTELLECTUAL PROPERTY ORGANIZATION (WIPO)

WIPO is an intergovernmental organisation established in 1967 as a specialised agency of the United Nations (UN). It is the successor to the *United International Bureaux for the Protection of Intellectual Property* (BIRPI), established in 1893 to administer the *Paris Convention for the*

---

1 Some of these issues are explored further in K Bowrey, M Handler and D Nicol, eds, *Emerging Challenges in Intellectual Property*, Oxford University Press, Melbourne, 2011.

Protection of Industrial Property (1883) and the *Berne Convention for the Protection of Literary and Artistic Works* (1886). As set out in the *Convention Establishing the World Intellectual Property Organization* (1967), WIPO has two main objectives:

- to promote the protection of IP worldwide; and
- to ensure administrative cooperation among the intellectual property unions established by the treaties that WIPO administers.

WIPO now administers over 25 treaties. It also engages in policy development and offers a range of education and dispute resolution services. WIPO's principal sources of income are fees paid by private users of the international registration services and contributions paid by the governments of member states.[2]

WORLD TRADE ORGANIZATION (WTO)

The WTO administers the *Agreement on Trade-Related Aspects of Intellectual Property Rights* (the 'TRIPS Agreement') (1994).[3] The TRIPS Agreement was negotiated in the 1986–94 Uruguay Round of the General Agreement on Tariffs and Trade, and is Annex 1C to the *Agreement Establishing the World Trade Organization* (1994). It introduced IP rules into the multilateral trading system for the first time by setting minimum levels of protection that each WTO member must provide across most fields of IP, as well as requiring adherence to most of the substantive provisions of the Paris Convention and the Berne Convention. Developed countries were given until 1995 to ensure that their laws and practices conformed with the TRIPS Agreement. Developing countries and transition economies were given until 2000 (with a further five years to implement product patent protection). Least-developed countries initially had until 2006, since extended to 2021, to implement their TRIPS obligations. As well as setting minimum standards of protection in many areas, the TRIPS Agreement also established general principles applicable to all intellectual property enforcement. Disputes between WTO members about adherence to the TRIPS obligations are subject to WTO dispute settlement procedures. As TRIPS is a minimum-standards agreement, members may provide more extensive protection and determine the appropriate method of implementing the provisions of the Agreement within their own legal systems. TRIPS led to the reform of many provisions of Australian IP law and continues to affect Australian law in contentious areas such as access to pharmaceuticals and rights to genetic material.

UNITED NATIONS EDUCATIONAL, SCIENTIFIC AND CULTURAL ORGANIZATION (UNESCO)

UNESCO was founded on 16 November 1945. It facilitates universal access to information and knowledge, and its primary role in IP relates to setting ethical standards that encourage global information sharing, including providing information about the advantages and disadvantages of using free and open source or proprietary software.

---

2   See www.wipo.int.
3   See www.wto.org/english/tratop_e/trips_e/trips_e.htm.

CONVENTION ON BIOLOGICAL DIVERSITY (CBD), CONFERENCE OF PARTIES (COP)

The CBD, signed at the 1992 Rio Earth Summit, is dedicated to promoting sustainable development. Australia ratified the Convention in 1993. The Convention's governing body is the COP, consisting of all 193 governments and regional economic integration organisations that have ratified the Convention (but not the USA). The CBD impacts on IP rights by raising issues surrounding ownership and control over plant genetic resources, bioprospecting and Indigenous rights to equitable benefits derived from the utilisation of IP.[4]

AUSTRALIAN ORGANISATIONS

Domestically, IP policy development is fragmented among a number of federal departments. To observers, little coordination of these efforts is apparent. This is partly a historical problem dating from our colonial heritage and a longstanding bureaucratic separation of responsibility for the arts, education and the sciences. It is also a consequence of contemporary politics, where different government departments react to IP reform agendas emanating from Europe or the USA. It is also quite difficult to identify any distinctively Australian element in our contemporary IP policy (even though highly distinctive approaches to particular IP issues are taken in Australian IP legislation, which further increases the complexity of this area of law).

DEPARTMENT OF FOREIGN AFFAIRS AND TRADE (DFAT)

DFAT supports the development of strong IP rights and the harmonisation of rights with major trading partners, arguing that internationally consistent IP regimes allow Australian producers and manufacturers to take advantage of global supply chains by protecting important IP in foreign markets when parts of their business operations are offshore. DFAT has a role in managing TRIPS-related matters (e.g. in bringing disputes against allegedly non-compliant parties, or defending such actions). It also has the central role in negotiating preferential trade agreements with key trading partners, which include IP chapters. The most important of these is the *Australia–US Free Trade Agreement* (AUSFTA) (2004), with more recent agreements negotiated with Korea and Japan.[5] At the time of writing, DFAT is also involved in negotiations for a regional trade agreement known as the *Trans-Pacific Partnership Agreement* (TPP) with Japan, the USA, Singapore, New Zealand, Malaysia, Brunei, Canada, Chile, Mexico, Peru and Vietnam. The IP negotiations in the TPP have proved to be particularly contentious. It is apparent that countries like the USA and Japan are seeking high levels of IP protection, especially in relation to pharmaceutical patents and related rights; while developing countries and countries like Australia and New Zealand—which provide subsidised access to pharmaceuticals—are concerned about the potential impact on the cost of, and access to, medicines. Detailed provisions on the enforcement of IP rights are also proving to be controversial.

DFAT's relatively recent role in developing Australian IP policy has been considered contentious in some circles, with concern that the international trade agenda has advanced protection of IP rights

---

4   See www.cbd.int/convention.
5   See www.dfat.gov.au/trade/topics/intellectual-property/

without due regard to the impact these reforms will have on the Australian public, our cultural and educational rights, and our public health policy.[6]

COMMONWEALTH ATTORNEY-GENERAL'S DEPARTMENT

The Attorney-General's Department has a key role in developing policy on a miscellaneous range of copyright and related issues. At the time of writing, it is looking into such issues as online copyright infringement, the role of 'safe harbours' for carriage service providers, and the domestic implementation of the *Marrakesh Treaty to Facilitate Access to Published Works for Persons Who Are Blind, Visually Impaired or Otherwise Print Disabled* (2013).[7] Formerly, the *Copyright Law Review Committee* (CLRC) was part of the Attorney-General's Department: this was a part-time committee appointed to consider and report on specific copyright matters referred to it. The CLRC published a number of significant reports from 1959 (the Spicer Report,[8] which formed the foundation of the *Copyright Act 1968* (Cth)) to 2005, when it was abolished. The Attorney-General also makes occasional requests to the independent Australian Law Reform Commission (ALRC) to inquire into particular areas of the law. In 2012 the then Attorney-General made a reference to the ALRC to consider reform of Australian copyright exceptions, which led to Report No 122, *Copyright in the Digital Economy* (2013).

COMMONWEALTH DEPARTMENT OF INDUSTRY

The Department of Industry develops policies to support a national innovation system with the goal of driving knowledge creation, cutting-edge science and research, international competitiveness and greater productivity. The Department also releases Annual Innovation System Reports, which assess the performance of the Australian innovation system by comparing it to that of other OECD countries, looking at issues such as patent filing figures and trade in IP-protected goods and services.

IP AUSTRALIA

IP Australia is an independent government agency under the Department of Industry. It administers the grant of patents, designs, trade marks and plant breeder's rights (PBR), and provides policy advice to government. Since 2012 IP Australia has had an office of the Chief Economist, which conducts and commissions IP research and policy analysis. IP Australia is self-funding, with revenue (mainly from fees paid by applicants for registration and renewal of registration) of over $178 million for the 2013–14 financial year. IP Australia also promotes IP awareness and basic

---

6   See R Burrell and K Weatherall, 'Exporting Controversy? Reactions to the Copyright Provisions of the US–Australia Free Trade Agreement: Lessons for US Trade Policy' [2008] *University of Illinois Journal of Law, Technology & Policy* 259; K Weatherall, 'Of Copyright Bureaucracies and Incoherence: Stepping Back from Australia's Recent Copyright Reforms' (2007) 31 *Melbourne University Law Review* 967; P Drahos et al, 'Pharmaceuticals, Intellectual Property and Free Trade: The Case of the US–Australia Free Trade Agreement' (2004) 22 *Prometheus* 243; K Weatherall, 'The Australia–US Free Trade Agreement's Impact on Australia's Copyright Trade Policy' (2015) *Australian Journal of International Affairs* (forthcoming).

7   See www.ag.gov.au/RightsAndProtections/IntellectualProperty/Pages/default.aspx.

8   Copyright Law Review Committee (the 'Spicer Committee'), *Report of the Committee appointed by the Attorney-General of the Commonwealth to Consider what Alterations are Desirable in the Copyright Law of the Commonwealth* (1959).

IP education to business and the public. IP Australia's searchable databases of patents, designs and trade marks are an important free public resource providing access to a wide array of technical information. The agency also publishes practice and procedure manuals that are used as reference tools for examiners within their patents, designs, trade marks and PBR sections. These guides set out procedural and legal matters relevant to the examination of applications under each of the relevant Acts and are helpful for those seeking a practical understanding of the operation of the relevant law.[9]

IP Australia also provides secretariat services to the Advisory Council on Intellectual Property (ACIP). ACIP is an independent body appointed by the government to advise on IP matters and the strategic administration of IP Australia. ACIP recently completed reviews into the innovation patent system, and collaborations between the public and private sectors involving IP.[10] It has been announced that ACIP will be disbanded on completion of its current review into the operation of the designs system.

LEGAL FOUNDATIONS: THE CONSTITUTION

Section 51 of the *Commonwealth of Australia Constitution Act 1900* (Imp), which is headed 'Legislative powers of the Parliament', provides:

> The Parliament shall, subject to this Constitution, have power to make laws for the peace, order, and good government of the Commonwealth with respect to:
>
> ...
>
> (v) postal, telegraphic, telephonic, and other like services;
>
> ...
>
> (xviii) copyrights, patents of inventions and designs, and trade marks;
>
> ...
>
> (xxix) external affairs.

The Australian Constitution offers little indication of the nature or purpose of our IP laws. The specificity of s 51(xviii) once supported a conservative approach to the federal power to make new laws that might expand on the subject matter originally covered. This interpretation sat oddly with an area of law which might, by its nature, be expected to be forward-looking and innovative in ambition. Following the *Union Label* case (*Attorney-General for New South Wales v Brewery Employees' Union of New South Wales* (1908) 6 CLR 469, extracted first below) it was subsequently questioned whether the constitutional provision could support reforms relating to performers' rights, moral rights for authors, circuit layouts protection, plant variety rights and trade marks for services. However, in addition to adopting a more generous interpretative approach to s 51(xviii), there was potential to enact some IP legislation by relying upon the postal and telegraphic power in s 51(v) and the external affairs power in s 51(xxix).

The uncertainties over the scope of s 51(xviii), and the extent to which it could be used to support the enactment of laws covering novel forms of IP, remained unresolved until a

---

9 See www.ipaustralia.gov.au.
10 See http://acip.gov.au.

challenge to the constitutionality of the *Plant Variety Rights Act 1987* (Cth) and the subsequent *Plant Breeder's Rights Act 1994* (Cth) in *Grain Pool of Western Australia v Commonwealth* [2000] HCA 14; (2000) 202 CLR 479, extracted second below. This decision has somewhat settled the scope of s 51(xviii) today.

It has been recommended that the Constitution should be amended to simply permit laws with respect to 'intellectual property'—a term more current now than it was at Federation. Alternatively, Australia could consider the value of a US-style provision that provides a foundation for constitutional challenges with reference to the overriding public purpose of IP laws. In *Grain Pool* the High Court noted the comparative breadth of the Australian IP power compared with that of the USA. However, while the US Constitution creates a 'system' of copyright and patent laws that promotes the 'Progress of Science and useful Arts', in a constitutional challenge in 2003 the US Supreme Court determined that it is generally the role of Congress—and not for the courts— to decide how best to pursue that objective and achieve the delicate balance of interests to be served (see *Eldred v Ashcroft* 537 US 186 (2003), extracted third below).

The Australian approach to the constitutional power places few limits on the freedom of Parliament to make laws about 'intellectual effort'. It encourages an IP jurisprudence that is particularly attentive to the detail of particular provisions without necessarily requiring much analysis of the politics of IP as a system of law supportive of innovation overall.[11]

PRECEDENT

CASE EXTRACT: PRECEDENT

Attorney-General for New South Wales v Brewery Employees' Union of New South Wales (the 'Union Label case')

(1908) 6 CLR 469
High Court of Australia

[The *Trade Marks Act 1905* (Cth) provided for registration of 'workers' trade marks' which indicated that the goods were made by an individual Australian worker or members of a trade union. The marks were politically controversial,[12] and two years after their introduction the Part of the Act dealing with workers' trade marks was challenged as not being supported by s 51(xviii) of the Constitution.]

Griffith CJ (at 500–518): The plaintiffs contend that the 'workers' trade mark' authorized by Part VII to be registered by an association of workers is not a trade mark at all in the sense in which that word is used in the Constitution. The defendants answer that the mark in question is a mark; that it is to be used in connection with trade, which includes manufacture and production; and that this is sufficient to bring the Act within the power. Now, while there is no doubt that within the ambit of its powers the Parliament is supreme, it has no authority whatever beyond that ambit. It is necessary, therefore, to consider the nature of the authority conferred by s 51(xviii) ...

---

11   For a rare case where the High Court took into account the politics surrounding IP reform, see *Stevens v Kabushiki Kaisha Sony Computer Entertainment* [2005] HCA 58; (2005) 224 CLR 193.
12   See S Ricketson, 'The Union Label Case: An Early Australian IP Story' in A Kenyon, M Richardson and S Ricketson, eds, *Landmarks in Australian Intellectual Property Law*, Cambridge University Press, Melbourne, 2009.

The meaning of the terms used in that instrument must be ascertained by their signification in 1900. The Parliament cannot enlarge its powers by calling a matter with which it is not competent to deal by the name of something else which is within its competence. On the other hand, it must be remembered that with advancing civilization new developments, now unthought of, may arise with respect to many subject matters. So long as those new developments relate to the same subject matter the powers of the Parliament will continue to extend to them. For instance, I cannot doubt that the powers of the legislature as to posts and telegraphs extend to wireless telegraphy and to any future discoveries of a like kind, although in detail they may be very different from posts and telegraphs and telephones as known in the nineteenth century ...

We have then to choose between these two conflicting lines of reasoning, and to say whether the term 'trade marks' used as defining a subject matter of legislation is to be taken in the wider or more limited sense. Apart from any light thrown on the question by the history of the use of the word in legislation or otherwise, it might be contended with much force that the term means 'a mark used in connection with trade,' the term 'trade' being, perhaps, limited to the exchange of vendible articles by way of commerce. If this view is accepted, the Parliament has absolute authority to prescribe:

(1) whether any marks may be so used at all;
(2) what marks may be so used;
(3) whether certain marks must be so used;
(4) by whom any marks may be so used;
(5) by whom any marks must be so used;
(6) the signification to be given to any particular mark;
(7) the conditions of the particular trade upon which the right or obligation to use the mark shall depend.

Such authority would undoubtedly involve a very large power of interference with the conditions of domestic trade, but that is no objection if the authority is given.

If, on the other hand, the term 'trade mark' is interpreted strictly according to the definitions which had been given in English Courts before the year 1900, the result would be that, although new kinds of marks and new purposes to which marks of the old kind may be applied may be, and indeed have been, devised since that time, the authority of Parliament is limited to dealing with the particular kind of trade mark then known, and to the use of trade marks for the particular purposes then recognized, with the result that all new developments of the subject matter would fall within the domain of State legislation.

... In my opinion it follows, from a consideration both of the Statute law of England and the Australian Colonies up to 1900 and of the authoritative expositions of the law with respect to trade marks in British Courts of Justice, that, whether the term 'trade mark' as used in s 51 (xviii) of the Constitution is to be regarded as a term of art or as a word used in popular language, it did not in that year denote every kind of mark which might be used in trade or in connection with articles of trade and commerce, but meant a mark which is the visible symbol of a particular kind of incorporeal or industrial property consisting in the right of a person engaged in trade to distinguish by a special mark goods in which he deals, or with which he has dealt, from the goods of other persons.

This concept includes in my opinion five distinct elements:

(1) A right which is in the nature of property;

(2) The owner of the right must be a person, natural or artificial, engaged in trade;

(3) The right is appurtenant or incident to the dealing with goods in the course of his trade;

(4) The owner has such an independent dominion over the goods to which the mark is to be affixed as to entitle him to affix it to them; (It is not material whether this right is incident to his possession of the goods or arises under an agreement with the owner of them.)

(5) The mark distinguishes the goods as having been dealt with by some particular person or persons engaged in trade; (I use the word 'particular' not as meaning that the person in question is indicated *nominatim*, but as indicating that he is a person who has an independent individual right with respect to the goods in question, and who is capable of ascertainment upon inquiry).

With regard to this species of property the power of the Parliament is absolute. They can prescribe the conditions on which it may be acquired, retained, or enjoyed; they may possibly even prohibit its enjoyment altogether; but they cannot, by calling something else by the name of 'trade mark,' create a new and different kind of industrial property.

...

In my opinion, therefore, the workers' trade mark does not conform in any respect to the concept of a trade mark as used in the Constitution.

Higgins J (dissenting) (at 600–614): The case as put for the plaintiffs is short and simple. They say that, though the Federal Parliament has power to legislate about 'trade marks' a 'workers' trade mark' was not a 'trade mark' within the accepted definition in 1900, the date of the Constitution, and that therefore the Parliament has no power to make any law as to 'workers' trade marks.' It is said that, though the mark is to be used by or with the consent of a trader, for the purposes of pushing trade, it is not a trade mark.

If the argument for the plaintiffs is right—if the powers of the Commonwealth Parliament are so rigidly and narrowly circumscribed as is contended—there will be some curious results, not merely as to trade marks, but as to most, if not all, of the subjects of legislation in s 51. No matter how circumstances may change, no matter what may be the developments of science, of the arts, of business enterprise, and of society to the end of time, the Parliament is confined for ever (unless there be an alteration in the Constitution) to such trade marks as the Court enforced in the year 1900. Even since that year the class of trade marks which the Court will enforce has been extended in Great Britain and Ireland so as to include marks such as the plaintiffs deny to be 'trade marks' (English *Trade Marks Act 1905*, ss 3, 62); and s 62 has been incorporated in our *Trade Marks Act 1905* (s 22). But though the British legislation is, of course, valid, the Commonwealth legislation, to the same effect, for Australia, is to be treated as invalid. The Commonwealth is to be tied down to the practice in 1900. According to the plaintiffs' argument, the Federal Parliament having covered all the ground for trade marks as enforced by the law in 1900, the State Parliaments may, each for its own State, make such laws as they think fit, varying in character and in machinery, as to any marks to be used for purposes of trade, excepting only such trade marks as the Courts enforced in 1900. The several State Parliaments may, it is said, legislate even for 'workers' trade marks,' may create any new kinds of enforceable trade marks; and if the plaintiffs' argument be successful, we shall have as a result a position which must be confusing and baneful to traders and to the public—we shall have seven different bodies of law makers in Australia laying down laws as to marks used for trade purposes. But, if the plaintiffs are right, it cannot be helped. It is a flaw in the Constitution.

This doctrine of the plaintiffs, if it is to be accepted, cannot be confined to the subject of trade marks. It means that the Federal Parliament cannot give validity to any kinds of patents, or to any kinds of copyrights, which were not recognized in 1900. Copyright in designs is a recent and useful development in the law of copyright. If it had not been accepted before 1900, it could not—according to the plaintiffs—be now adopted by the Federal Parliament. Nor, if the developments of industry should render a further extension of copyright expedient, is it possible for the Federal Parliament to meet the want—if the plaintiffs are right … [T]he case of trade marks contains excellent illustrations within its own bounds. Text-writers have found themselves compelled to include in their treatises on 'trade marks' dissertations on mere 'trade names,' and on 'passing off' cases; for these matters are treated by the Courts on the same principles as those trade marks which satisfy the plaintiffs' definition; but, according to the plaintiffs, these matters have still to be left to the States …

If the plaintiffs are right in their argument, the Court is bound to treat the boundaries of the class of trade marks, and the boundaries of the other subjects, as finally settled and stereotyped in 1900, so far as the Federal Parliament is concerned. There may be development everywhere else; but so far as Australia and its Federal Parliament is concerned, there is an arrested development. In place of Australia having by its Constitution acquired for the Australian Parliament the power of dealing with the whole subject of marks used for the purposes of trade, it turns out that the Federal Parliament can deal only with the trade marks enforced by the Courts as property in 1900, and that each of the States separately must deal with the other parts of the subject …

What is committed to the Federal Parliament is not the *class* of things called trade marks, but the whole *subject* of trade marks. No doubt, we are to ascertain the meaning of 'trade marks' as in 1900. But having ascertained that meaning, we have then to find the extent of the power to deal with the subject of trade marks—or, what is the same thing, to find the meaning of the 'power to make laws with respect to trade marks.' The usage in 1900 gives us the central type; it does not give us the circumference of the power …

It is not necessary for the purpose of the decision of this case to decide precisely what is the outer limit, the ring fence, of this power. But at present I am strongly inclined to the view that the grant of such a power, made by the British Parliament to the Federal Parliament, confers on the Federal Parliament as wide a power, with regard to Australia, as the British Parliament could itself have exercised, provided that the laws made would come fairly under the description of 'trade mark laws,' in ordinary parlance, if made by the British Parliament. It will also be found, I believe, ultimately, that the phrase under which powers are granted to the Federal Parliament gives to that Parliament even wider scope for its action than is given to the United States Congress by the corresponding grants of power in the United States Constitution.

CASE EXTRACT: CURRENT LAW

Grain Pool of Western Australia v Commonwealth

[2000] HCA 14; (2000) 202 CLR 479
High Court of Australia

Gleeson CJ, Gaudron, McHugh, Gummow, Hayne and Callinan JJ (some footnotes omitted):
16. The general principles which are to be applied to determine whether a law is with respect to a head of legislative power such as s 51(xviii) are well settled. They include the following. First, the constitutional text is to be construed 'with all the generality which the words used admit'. Here the words used are 'patents of inventions'. This, by 1900, was 'a recognised category of legislation (as taxation, bankruptcy)', and when the validity of such legislation is in question the task is to consider whether it 'answers the description, and to disregard purpose or object'. Secondly, the character of the law in question must be determined by reference to the rights, powers, liabilities, duties and privileges which it creates. Thirdly, the practical as well as the legal operation of the law must be examined to determine if there is a sufficient connection between the law and the head of power. Fourthly, as Mason and Deane JJ explained in *Re F; Ex parte F* [(1986) 161 CLR 376 at 388]:

> In a case where a law fairly answers the description of being a law with respect to two subject-matters, one of which is and the other of which is not a subject-matter appearing in s 51, it will be valid notwithstanding that there is no independent connexion between the two subject-matters.

Finally, if a sufficient connection with the head of power does exist, the justice and wisdom of the law, and the degree to which the means it adopts are necessary or desirable, are matters of legislative choice.

17. In a passage in the joint judgment of the Court in *Nintendo Co Ltd v Centronics Systems Pty Ltd* [(1994) 181 CLR 134 at 160] upholding the validity of the *Circuit Layouts Act 1989* (Cth) ('the Circuit Layouts Act'), the Court attended to the first of these matters, the construction of the terms of s 51(xviii) with the generality admitted by the words used. Their Honours said:

> The grant of Commonwealth legislative power which sustains the [Circuit Layouts Act] is that contained in s 51(xviii) of the Constitution with respect to 'Copyrights, patents of inventions and designs, and trade marks' [cf, eg, *R v Brislan; Ex parte Williams* (1935) 54 CLR 262; *Jones v Commonwealth [No 2]* (1965) 112 CLR 206]. It is of the essence of that grant of legislative power that it authorizes the making of laws which create, confer, and provide for the enforcement of, intellectual property rights in original compositions, inventions, designs, trade marks and other products of intellectual effort.

In the present case, the plaintiff contends that the final phrase in this passage should not be read so as to treat as sufficient to attract this head of power *any* product of intellectual effort. Those supporting validity contend that the legislation here is valid without such a wide reading of the power. That which constitutes the invention for the [Plant] Varieties Act is 'the origination' of the 'new plant variety' (s 5(a)) and for the [Plant] Breeder's Rights Act it is 'the breeding' of the plant variety (s 10(b)). It will be necessary to return to these submissions.

18. What is of immediate significance for present purposes is the reference in *Nintendo* by their Honours to *R v Brislan; Ex parte Williams* and *Jones v Commonwealth [No 2]*. Those authorities dealt with the inherent scope for expansion of the application of the power with respect to postal, telegraphic, telephonic 'and other like services' in s 51(v) of the Constitution. This serves to emphasise a point of significance in the present case. Later developments in scientific methods for the provision of telegraphic and telephonic services were contemplated by s 51(v). Likewise, it would be expected that what might answer the description of an invention for the purpose of s 51(xviii) would change to reflect developments in technology.

19. Consistently with the general principles which we have identified above, an appropriate approach to the interpretation of s 51(xviii) is that appearing in what was then the dissenting judgment of Higgins J in *Attorney-General for NSW v Brewery Employees' Union of NSW* ('the *Union Label Case*').

...

22. The judgment of the Court in *Nintendo* and [that] of Higgins J, ... delivered across the lifespan of the Court, exemplify the first of the general principles of constitutional interpretation to which reference has been made. They reflect what the foundation members of the Court had intended by their adoption in *Baxter v Commissioners of Taxation (NSW)* [(1907) 4 CLR 1087 at 1105] of a passage of the judgment of Story J delivering the opinion of the Court in *Martin v Hunter's Lessee* [14 US 141 at 151]. In that well-known statement with respect to the interpretation of the United States Constitution, Story J had stressed that the legislative powers of the Congress were expressed 'in general terms', so as 'to provide [not] merely for the exigencies of a few years, but ... to endure through a long lapse of ages, the events of which were locked up in the inscrutable purposes of Providence'.

23. These words do not suggest, and what follows in these reasons does not give effect to, any notion that the boundaries of the power conferred by s 51(xviii) are to be ascertained solely by identifying what in 1900 would have been treated as a copyright, patent, design or trade mark. No doubt some submissions by the plaintiff would fail even upon the application of so limited a criterion. However, other submissions, as will appear, fail because they give insufficient allowance for the dynamism which, even in 1900, was inherent in any understanding of the terms used in s 51(xviii).

24. The collocation in s 51(xviii) represents a classification of the various species of intellectual or industrial property which had developed in the United Kingdom in the second half of the nineteenth century. This development had been encouraged by the publication of what became standard treatises on copyright, trade marks and patents [Sherman and Bently, *The Making of Modern Intellectual Property Law: The British Experience, 1760–1911* (1999) at 138]. These works had dealt with the appearance of the modern statutory regimes in legislation such as the *Patents, Designs, and Trade Marks Act 1883* (UK) ('the 1883 Act'). The scheme of the 1883 Act had been followed in Queensland, Victoria, Tasmania and Western Australia. These works also had dealt with the international movements which culminated in the Union for the Protection of Industrial Property established by the Paris Convention of 1883, and in the Berne Convention of [1886] for the protection of the rights of authors over their literary and artistic works.

...

26. ... [I]t is important to note that, within the terms used by Higgins J in ... the *Union Label Case* ... it would be wrong to regard the legislative grant of monopoly rights in new plant varieties as being,

in 1900, outside the 'central type' of the subject of patents of inventions. In his recent judgment for the Court of Appeals for the Federal Circuit in *Imazio Nursery, Inc v Dania Greenhouses* [69 F 3d 1560 (1995)], Judge Rich explained legislative proposals before the Congress more than a century ago. His Honour said [at 1562–1563]:

> At least as early as 1892, legislation was proposed to grant patent rights for plant-related inventions. Plant patent legislation was supported by such prominent individuals as Thomas Edison who stated that '[n]othing that Congress could do to help farming would be of greater value and permanence than to give to the plant breeder the same status as the mechanical and chemical inventors now have through the law.' It was also supported by Luther Burbank, a leading plant breeder of the day … whose widow stated that her late husband 'said repeatedly that until Government made some such provision [for plant patent protection] the incentive to create work with plants was slight and independent research and breeding would be discouraged to the great detriment of horticulture.'

Such views would have been at the time apposite to the position of Australian wheat breeders such as William Farrer, whose Federation cultivar of wheat was named in 1901.

27. Whilst the plaintiff accepts much of what would follow from these considerations, it submits that not every plant variety may be the subject of a patent in accordance with what it contends are traditional principles of patent law which are reflected in s 51(xviii) and limit its operation …

THE EVOLUTION OF COMMON LAW AND STATUTE

33. The plaintiff emphasises that not all of what might be termed intellectual or industrial property, even as understood in 1900, was embraced by the collection of terms in s 51(xviii). This circumstance is said to caution against an over-broad construction of the term 'patents of inventions'. The first proposition may be accepted but a consideration of the common law does not support the second proposition.

34. Many of the established categories referred to in s 51(xviii) had common law antecedents. Here, as elsewhere, the common law had been dynamic rather than static. In *Pacific Film Laboratories Pty Ltd v Federal Commissioner of Taxation* [(1970) 121 CLR 154 at 166], Windeyer J explained that, whilst by the nineteenth century copyright had become the creature of statute, there had been in the century before great dispute as to the nature of common law copyright, particularly in unpublished literary works. Again, in *Interfirm Comparison (Australia) Pty Ltd v Law Society of New South Wales* [[1975] 2 NSWLR 104 at 118–119], Bowen CJ in Eq observed that the earlier decisions relating to copyright in unpublished literary works have an affinity with the development of equitable principles relating to confidential communications.

35. The remedy of injunction, provided by statute for over a century, to prevent the infringement of registered trade marks reflects the equity decisions which protected and established a property right in the goodwill of trade marks before they were recognised by statute. In *Colbeam Palmer Ltd v Stock Affiliates Pty Ltd* [(1968) 122 CLR 25 at 33], Windeyer J remarked:

> The jurisdiction of courts of equity in relation to trade marks did not begin with the protection of statutory trade marks. It began with what have been called common law trade marks. These, notwithstanding their somewhat misleading name, were the creatures of equity which established a form of property in a mark gained by use and reputation.

It should be noted that, at the time of the adoption of the Constitution and for many years thereafter, both in the United Kingdom and Australia, whilst 'service marks' might be protected by a passing-off action, the statutory systems did not permit their registration. The statutory systems were concerned with marks used to indicate a connection in the course of trade in goods between the goods and the person entitled to use the mark.

36. The modern classification of copyright into literary, dramatic, musical and artistic works dated in Australia from the *Copyright Act 1905* (Cth) [This was repealed by s 4 of the *Copyright Act 1912* (Cth)]. In the United Kingdom, the changes were made by the *Copyright Act 1911* (Imp) ('the 1911 Act') ... A striking departure in the 1911 Act was that it had no registration system. The 1911 Act also (in s 31) abolished common law copyright in unpublished works. This common law copyright was still recognised in 1900. However, perhaps as a reflection of the state of technology at the time, the 1911 Act did not provide for distinct copyright protection in respect of sound recordings, cinematograph films or broadcasts. That circumstance, however, would not deny to those provisions in the *Copyright Act 1968* (Cth), which now protect such subject-matter, the character of laws with respect to copyright.

37. In the United Kingdom, the first comprehensive legislation for the registration of trade marks was the *Trade Marks Registration Act 1875* (UK). The first of a series of statutes providing for the administration of patent law on a modern footing had been the *Patent Law Amendment Act 1852* (UK) ... In 1900, the United Kingdom statutory regimes with respect to copyright, trade marks, patents and designs were of recent origin and, like the common law, they were plainly still in various stages of development. This was true also of the legislation in force in the Australian colonies before displacement by federal law. That development has continued to the present day.

...

40. There were in 1900 unresolved issues respecting the interrelation of the various intellectual property regimes. A legislative attempt to deal with the overlap between copyright and registered design law later was made in s 22 of the 1911 Act. This provision in turn gave rise to much uncertainty and litigation. In the case law at the end of the nineteenth century attempts were made to differentiate the nature of the protection afforded under the patent law and that with respect to registered designs. Efforts also were made in that period ... to distinguish the distinct conceptual bases of copyright and patent law ...

41. Given these cross-currents and uncertainties in the common law and statute at the time of federation, it plainly is within the head of power in s 51(xviii) to resolve them. It also is within power, as the legislation upheld in *Nintendo* demonstrates, to determine that there be fresh rights in the nature of copyright, patents of inventions and designs and trade marks.

42. The broad term 'intellectual effort' used in *Nintendo* embraces a variable rather than a fixed constitutional criterion ... The 'origination' or 'breeding' required respectively by the Varieties Act and the Breeder's Rights Act involves sufficient 'intellectual effort' in the sense of that term in *Nintendo*.

[The Court concluded that the *Plant Variety Rights Act 1987* (Cth) and the *Plant Breeder's Rights Act 1994* (Cth) were both supported by s 51(xviii) of the Constitution.]

CASE EXTRACT: COMPARATIVE LAW

Eldred v Ashcroft

537 US 186 (2003)
Supreme Court of the United States

Ginsburg J (delivering the Opinion of the majority of the Court) (at 192–213) (footnotes omitted):
This case concerns the authority the Constitution assigns to Congress to prescribe the duration of
copyrights. The Copyright and Patent Clause of the *Constitution*, Art I, §8, cl 8, provides as to copyrights:
'Congress shall have Power … [t]o promote the Progress of Science … by securing [to Authors]
for limited Times … the exclusive Right to their … Writings.' In 1998, in the measure here under
inspection, Congress enlarged the duration of copyrights by 20 years. *Copyright Term Extension Act*
(CTEA), Pub L 105–298, §§102(b) and (d), 112 Stat 2827–2828 (amending 17 USC §§302, 304). As
in the case of prior extensions, principally in 1831, 1909, and 1976, Congress provided for application
of the enlarged terms to existing and future copyrights alike.

Petitioners are individuals and businesses whose products or services build on copyrighted works
that have gone into the public domain. They seek a determination that the CTEA fails constitutional
review under both the Copyright Clause's 'limited Times' prescription and the First Amendment's
free speech guarantee. Under the 1976 *Copyright Act*, copyright protection generally lasted from the
work's creation until 50 years after the author's death. Under the CTEA, most copyrights now run
from creation until 70 years after the author's death. 17 USC §302(a). Petitioners do not challenge the
'life-plus-70-years' timespan itself … Congress went awry, petitioners maintain, not with respect to
newly created works, but in enlarging the term for published works with existing copyrights. The 'limited
Tim[e]' in effect when a copyright is secured, petitioners urge, becomes the constitutional boundary,
a clear line beyond the power of Congress to extend …

In accord with the District Court and the Court of Appeals, we reject petitioners' challenges to the
CTEA. In that 1998 legislation, as in all previous copyright term extensions, Congress placed existing
and future copyrights in parity. In prescribing that alignment, we hold, Congress acted within its authority
and did not transgress constitutional limitations.

… The measure at issue here, the CTEA, installed the fourth major duration extension of federal
copyrights. Retaining the general structure of the 1976 Act, the CTEA enlarges the terms of all existing
and future copyrights by 20 years … This standard harmonizes the baseline United States copyright
term with the term adopted by the European Union in 1993 … For anonymous works, pseudonymous
works, and works made for hire, the term is 95 years from publication or 120 years from creation,
whichever expires first. 17 USC §302(c) …

A

We address first the determination of the courts below that Congress has authority under the Copyright
Clause to extend the terms of existing copyrights. Text, history, and precedent, we conclude, confirm
that the Copyright Clause empowers Congress to prescribe 'limited Times' for copyright protection and
to secure the same level and duration of protection for all copyright holders, present and future.

COMPARATIVE LAW

The CTEA's baseline term of life plus 70 years, petitioners concede, qualifies as a 'limited Tim[e]' as applied to future copyrights. Petitioners contend, however, that existing copyrights extended to endure for that same term are not 'limited.' Petitioners' argument essentially reads into the text of the Copyright Clause the command that a time prescription, once set, becomes forever 'fixed' or 'inalterable.' The word 'limited,' however, does not convey a meaning so constricted. At the time of the Framing, that word meant what it means today: 'confine[d] within certain bounds,' 'restrain[ed],' or 'circumscribe[d].' ... Thus understood, a timespan appropriately 'limited' as applied to future copyrights does not automatically cease to be 'limited' when applied to existing copyrights ...

To comprehend the scope of Congress' power under the Copyright Clause, 'a page of history is worth a volume of logic.' *New York Trust Co v Eisner*, 256 US 345, 349 (1921) (Holmes, J). History reveals an unbroken congressional practice of granting to authors of works with existing copyrights the benefit of term extensions so that all under copyright protection will be governed evenhandedly under the same regime ... [T]he First Congress accorded the protections of the Nation's first federal copyright statute to existing and future works alike. 1790 Act §1. Since then, Congress has regularly applied duration extensions to both existing and future copyrights. 1831 Act §§1, 16; 1909 Act §§23–24; 1976 Act §§302–303; 17 USC §§302–304.

Because the Clause empowering Congress to confer copyrights also authorizes patents, congressional practice with respect to patents informs our inquiry. We count it significant that early Congresses extended the duration of numerous individual patents as well as copyrights ... The courts saw no 'limited Times' impediment to such extensions; renewed or extended terms were upheld in the early days, for example, by Chief Justice Marshall and Justice Story sitting as circuit justices ...

Congress' consistent historical practice of applying newly enacted copyright terms to future and existing copyrights reflects a judgment stated concisely by Representative Huntington at the time of the 1831 Act: '[J]ustice, policy, and equity alike forb[id]' that an 'author who had sold his [work] a week ago, be placed in a worse situation than the author who should sell his work the day after the passing of [the] act.' 7 Cong Deb 424 (1831) ... The CTEA follows this historical practice by keeping the duration provisions of the 1976 Act largely in place and simply adding 20 years to each of them. Guided by text, history, and precedent, we cannot agree with petitioners' submission that extending the duration of existing copyrights is categorically beyond Congress' authority under the Copyright Clause.

... Satisfied that the CTEA complies with the 'limited Times' prescription, we turn now to whether it is a rational exercise of the legislative authority conferred by the Copyright Clause. On that point, we defer substantially to Congress. *Sony* [*Corp of America v Universal City Studios, Inc*], 464 US, at 429, 104 S Ct 774 ('[I]t is Congress that has been assigned the task of defining the scope of the limited monopoly that should be granted to authors ... in order to give the public appropriate access to their work product.').

The CTEA reflects judgments of a kind Congress typically makes, judgments we cannot dismiss as outside the Legislature's domain. As respondent describes ..., a key factor in the CTEA's passage was a 1993 European Union (EU) directive instructing EU members to establish a copyright term of life plus 70 years. EU Council Directive 93/98, Art 1(1), p 11; see 144 Cong Rec S12377–S12378 (daily ed Oct 12, 1998) (statement of Sen Hatch). Consistent with the Berne Convention, the EU directed its members to deny this longer term to the works of any non-EU country whose laws did not secure the same extended term. See Berne Conv Art 7(8); P Goldstein, *International Copyright* §5.3, p 239 (2001). By extending the baseline United States copyright term to life plus 70 years, Congress sought to ensure that American authors would receive the same copyright protection in Europe as their European counterparts. The CTEA may also provide greater incentive for American and other authors to create and disseminate their work in the United States ...

In addition to international concerns, Congress passed the CTEA in light of demographic, economic, and technological changes ..., and rationally credited projections that longer terms would encourage copyright holders to invest in the restoration and public distribution of their works ... see H R Rep No 105–452, p 4 (1998) (term extension 'provide[s] copyright owners generally with the incentive to restore older works and further disseminate them to the public').

In sum, we find that the CTEA is a rational enactment; we are not at liberty to second-guess congressional determinations and policy judgments of this order, however debatable or arguably unwise they may be. Accordingly, we cannot conclude that the CTEA—which continues the unbroken congressional practice of treating future and existing copyrights in parity for term extension purposes— is an impermissible exercise of Congress' power under the Copyright Clause.

B

Petitioners' Copyright Clause arguments rely on several novel readings of the Clause. We next address these arguments and explain why we find them unpersuasive.

1

Petitioners contend that even if the CTEA's 20-year term extension is literally a 'limited Tim[e],' permitting Congress to extend existing copyrights allows it to evade the 'limited Times' constraint by creating effectively perpetual copyrights through repeated extensions. We disagree.

As the Court of Appeals observed, a regime of perpetual copyrights 'clearly is not the situation before us.' 239 F 3d, at 379. Nothing before this Court warrants construction of the CTEA's 20-year term extension as a congressional attempt to evade or override the 'limited Times' constraint. Critically, we again emphasize, petitioners fail to show how the CTEA crosses a constitutionally significant threshold with respect to 'limited Times' that the 1831, 1909, and 1976 Acts did not. See ... Austin, ['Does the Copyright Clause Mandate Isolationism?' 26 Colum VLA J L & Arts 17] at 56 ('If extending copyright protection to works already in existence is constitutionally suspect,' so is 'extending the protections of US copyright law to works by foreign authors that had already been created and even first published when the federal rights attached.'). Those earlier Acts did not create perpetual copyrights, and neither does the CTEA.

2

Petitioners dominantly advance a series of arguments all premised on the proposition that Congress may not extend an existing copyright absent new consideration from the author. They pursue this main theme under three headings. Petitioners contend that the CTEA's extension of existing copyrights (1) overlooks the requirement of 'originality,' (2) fails to 'promote the Progress of Science,' and (3) ignores copyright's *quid pro quo.*

... More forcibly, petitioners contend that the CTEA's extension of existing copyrights does not 'promote the Progress of Science' as contemplated by the preambular language of the Copyright Clause. Art I, §8, cl 8. To sustain this objection, petitioners do not argue that the Clause's preamble is an independently enforceable limit on Congress' power. See 239 F 3d, at 378 (Petitioners acknowledge

COMPARATIVE LAW

that 'the preamble of the Copyright Clause is not a substantive limit on Congress' legislative power.' (internal quotation marks omitted)). Rather, they maintain that the preambular language identifies the sole end to which Congress may legislate; accordingly, they conclude, the meaning of 'limited Times' must be 'determined in light of that specified end.' Brief for Petitioners 19. The CTEA's extension of existing copyrights categorically fails to 'promote the Progress of Science,' petitioners argue, because it does not stimulate the creation of new works but merely adds value to works already created.

As petitioners point out, we have described the Copyright Clause as 'both a grant of power and a limitation,' *Graham v John Deere Co of Kansas City*, 383 US 1, 5 (1966), and have said that '[t]he primary objective of copyright' is '[t]o promote the Progress of Science,' *Feist* [*Publications, Inc v Rural Telephone Service Co*], 499 US, at 349 ... The 'constitutional command,' we have recognized, is that Congress, to the extent it enacts copyright laws at all, create[s] a 'system' that 'promote[s] the Progress of Science.' *Graham*, 383 US, at 6.

We have also stressed, however, that it is generally for Congress, not the courts, to decide how best to pursue the Copyright Clause's objectives. See *Stewart v Abend*, 495 US, at 230 ('Th[e] evolution of the duration of copyright protection tellingly illustrates the difficulties Congress faces ... [I]t is not our role to alter the delicate balance Congress has labored to achieve.'); *Sony*, 464 US at 429 ('[I]t is Congress that has been assigned the task of defining the scope of [rights] that should be granted to authors or to inventors in order to give the public appropriate access to their work product.'); *Graham*, 383 US, at 6 ('Within the limits of the constitutional grant, the Congress may, of course, implement the stated purpose of the Framers by selecting the policy which in its judgment best effectuates the constitutional aim.'). The justifications we earlier set out for Congress' enactment of the CTEA, supra, at 781–782, provide a rational basis for the conclusion that the CTEA 'promote[s] the Progress of Science.'

In the US Supreme Court's subsequent decision in *Golan v Holder*, 132 S Ct 873 (2012), a constitutional challenge was brought to domestic legislation that made international works that had previously been unprotected in the USA subject to US copyright protection (following the USA's accession to the Berne Convention). The petitioners' key argument was that removing works from the public domain violated the 'limited [t]imes' restriction in the Copyright Clause. Ginsburg J, again delivering the opinion of the Court, rejected this argument, holding that it was incorrect to say that the term of protection had been 'limited' to zero for previously unprotected works. Her Honour also disagreed with the argument that the legislation did not 'promote the Progress of Science', on the basis that this phrase was not confined to 'incentives for creation', and could also encompass incentives for the dissemination of existing cultural goods.

PHILOSOPHICAL JUSTIFICATIONS AND SLIPPERY CONCEPTS

Contemporary policy debates around Western IP are generally grounded in political and philosophical arguments about the naturalness and public benefits of private property rights, and their social costs.[13] Philosophical justifications for IP rights include discussions of natural

---

13   See generally R Merges, *Justifying Intellectual Property*, Harvard University Press, Cambridge, MA, 2011.

rights elaborated by nineteenth-century philosophers, especially Locke,[14] Hegel[15] and Kant.[16] Twentieth-century theories of kinds of unjust enrichment have also been influential, contributing to reflection on the need to balance the rights of creators with the rights of others.[17] Neoclassical economic analyses have substantially extended this discourse, questioning the market efficiency of strong IP protection, the incentives created by IP law reforms, and the divergence between private and social advantage that may follow from strong proprietary rights.[18] Human rights dialogues have also emerged as another possible foundation for IP,[19] especially in relation to protection of Indigenous cultural rights.[20]

As will be evident from the discussion of constitutional foundations above, international conventions and domestic statutes, rather than political philosophy or ideology, usually frame contemporary discussion in Australia. However, in the course of contemporary IP commentary a number of 'loaded terms' that draw upon politics, philosophy and jurisprudence are worth noting here. They disclose contested ideologies related to seemingly uncomplicated deployments of notions of *property* and of *right* in IP discourse.

Rights created under authority of statutes such as those covering copyright, design, patents and trade marks are a form of *private property* capable of being assigned or licensed to third parties. However, most IP rights are *positive rights*. These are not natural rights, and what is legally recognised is not property in the lay sense of involving an exclusive right to exert control over a thing or object. In other words, in IP the *exclusive rights* are not absolute rights. IP is *intangible property* and most rights are subject to statutory forms of *limitation*—in duration; by criteria concerning what acts do (and do not) constitute infringement; and, for patents, designs and trade marks, administrative and substantive registration requirements that must be met. These limitations in turn construct the *public domain* of unrestricted activity and content, reflecting the larger public interest, particularly in education, research and access to information.

The matrix of statutory limitations affecting IP rights is usually referred to, by way of shorthand, as the *intellectual property balance*. The notion of 'balance' suggests that any underlying tension between sponsoring innovation through providing private incentives and the public interest in access to knowledge can be ameliorated by the legislature (and in turn, the judiciary) making the right policy choices. However, it is important to recognise that not all limitations relate to a well-articulated public purpose, and that the notion of the 'public' is quite fragmentary and residual, rather than omnipresent, in Australian IP legislation.

---

14 See H Breakey, *Intellectual Liberty: Natural Rights and Intellectual Property*, Ashgate, Farnham, 2012.

15 See P Drahos, *A Philosophy of Intellectual Property*, Ashgate, Dartmouth, 1996.

16 MC Pievatolo, 'Freedom, Ownership and Copyright: Why Does Kant Reject the Concept of Intellectual Property?' in *Società Italiana di Filosofia Politica* (2010), at http://eprints.sifp.it/243/1/kantcmp.pdf.

17 S Ricketson, 'Reaping Without Sowing: Unfair Competition and Intellectual Property Rights in Anglo-Australian Intellectual Property Law' [1984] *University of New South Wales Law Journal* 1; W Gordon, 'An Inquiry Into the Merits of Copyright: The Challenges of Consistency, Consent, and Encouragement Theory' (1989) 41 *Stanford Law Review* 1345.

18 W Landes and R Posner, *The Economic Structure of Intellectual Property Law*, The Belknap Press of Harvard University Press, Cambridge, MA, 2003.

19 L Helfer and G Austin, *Human Rights and Intellectual Property: Mapping the Global Interface*, Cambridge University Press, Cambridge, 2011.

20 J Gibson, 'UDHR and the Group: Individual and Community Rights to Culture' (2008) 30 *Hamline Journal of Public Law & Policy* 85.

It is important to be attentive to the specificity of the rights and the particular fact situations at stake in IP discussions. There is often a tendency to generalise the nature and extent of private rights and public interests, and this can be misleading. The problem is further complicated when IP discourse borrows terminology and concepts from other jurisdictions. IP terminology from other jurisdictions will usually have 'something' in common with our legal concepts, but our rights are nonetheless technically different. Thus, legal precision is an important skill to develop in coming to grips with this rapidly developing area of law.

2

COPYRIGHT LAW: HISTORY, JUSTIFICATIONS AND BASIC PRINCIPLES

INTRODUCTION

Copyright is an IP right generally familiar to the community as a body of law affecting the world of art and entertainment by providing financial reward to those who make and distribute literature, art, music and other forms of entertainment. However, this area of law does more than just provide monetary rewards to artists and entertainers. It also regulates the creation and use of cultural goods, and affects a broad sweep of cultural, commercial, technological and educational activity. Depending on the circumstances, you may need copyright permission to do everyday things, such as copy a transport timetable, download a podcast and transfer it to your mobile phone, watch a short clip on YouTube or photocopy educational materials for school. The fact that permission may be required will not be readily apparent for some or all of these transactions, and ascertaining what permissions are needed, and from whom, can be quite perplexing.[1]

Copyright is an unwieldy and complex body of law that has been expanding since the eighteenth century, with a large amount of legislative reform in the past two decades. Understanding copyright obligations requires paying close attention to matters of legal categorisation, technical definitions, legislative presumptions and statutory exceptions. There are a large number of provisions and few short cuts that can be taken in conveying the essential aspects of the subject. In practice, copyright lawyers often specialise in particular industries such as book publishing, film and television, music, education or information technology. Rather than being across every part of the *Copyright Act 1968* (Cth), lawyers develop a deeper understanding of the law and convention in their particular industry, and a good understanding of how copyright in their area works in conjunction with other forms of IP protection available.

This chapter continues with a brief historical overview of the origin of copyright and some of its basic principles. Chapter 3 addresses criteria for the subsistence of copyright. Chapter 4 provides an understanding of the various categories of works and other subject matter protected. Chapter 5 describes rules on the ownership and exploitation of copyright. Chapter 6 considers how copyright is infringed and the scope of possible defences to infringement. Chapter 7 surveys additional rights

---

1   See K Weatherall, 'IP in a Changing Information Environment' in K Bowrey, M Handler and D Nicol, eds, *Emerging Challenges in Intellectual Property*, Oxford University Press, Melbourne, 2011.

of creators and related schemes that provide other kinds of protection and income for artists. There is also a need to consider the overlap between copyright and design law in Chapter 8, because in some circumstances copyright protection is lost, and only design protection is available.[2]

Generally, copyright cases are not especially difficult to understand in terms of their facts or legal reasoning. But some core concepts are sufficiently open-textured that more than one interpretation is possible: understanding why one interpretation prevailed requires a grasp of the rationales and purposes of copyright. In addition, working out how the various pieces of the jigsaw fit together—mapping the legal logic across the whole, and working through the implications of the law for others who may be affected, or extrapolating from one case to related scenarios—can be challenging.

HISTORY AND JUSTIFICATIONS

THE ORIGINS OF COPYRIGHT

The early origins of copyright law lie with the development of literary culture and attempts to contain the impact of a new and disruptive communications technology: the printing press.

It is commonly argued that the printing press led to the emergence of a literary culture, and that this made individual claims to 'own culture' possible. In these discussions historians and communications theorists often distinguish between oral and literary cultures.[3] Oral culture is transmitted in the form of stories, tales, legends and myths, from person to person. Works so told are often claimed to represent the deep history of the people who transmit them, with stories reflecting eternal values and certain truths about the people, or the meaning of God. The author of oral stories is not generally known or acknowledged. Asserting ownership of truth, myth or legend would disrupt the grounding of the meaning and authority of the work in tradition, custom, God or community. By contrast, print culture enables individual ownership of expressions to be documented and the origin of ideas attributed to distinctive authors. Some suggest that, though not an inevitable development, it was this capacity for documentation and attribution that eventually led to the birth of the modern author and the emergence of copyright.[4] The distinction between oral and literary cultures remains of legal significance in copyright today, with exclusive rights awarded to fixed expressions such as those in writing, whereas unfixed oral expressions and ideas generally remain part of the public domain—'common property', free for all to access and use.

THE FIRST LITERARY PROPERTY STATUTE

The author did not become a formal holder of rights in works of authorship until the passing of what is known as the first Anglo literary property law, the *Statute of Anne 1710* (8 Anne, c 19). However,

---

2   For details of what is covered in the other chapters of this text, see p 376 (for Chapters 9–13), p 570 (for Chapter 14), p 604 (for Chapters 15–18) and p 809 (for Chapter 19).

3   S Wright, *International Human Rights, Decolonisation and Globalisation: Becoming Human*, Routledge, London, 2001, pp 123–127.

4   E Eisenstein, *The Printing Revolution in Early Modern Europe*, Cambridge University Press, Cambridge, 1983; M Rose, *Authors and Owners: The Invention of Copyright*, Harvard University Press, Cambridge, MA, 1993; M Woodmansee and P Jaszi, eds, *The Construction of Authorship: Textual Appropriation in Law and Literature*, Duke University Press, Durham, NC, 1994.

prior to that Act a number of practical methods for securing exclusive publication rights had developed. These 'pre-modern' rights were primarily exclusive rights claimed by printers, publishers and booksellers.

Crown Patents were granted in a range of subject matter, including books, from the fifteenth century. It was not until the seventeenth century that the conditions of these grants came under review, with the complaint that they were unfair monopolies and a restraint on liberty and free trade,[5] and throughout the seventeenth and eighteenth centuries patents in literary works remained lucrative. Rights were granted in essential titles such as bibles, prayer books and alphabet books, and valuable interests were divided up and often traded as 'shares'. For the time, these patent rights were relatively secure forms of guaranteed future income and the interest was assumed to be perpetual.

There were also rights granted to the members of the Stationers' Company of London, which was established by Royal Charter in 1557. In exchange for the exclusive right to print books in England, the Stationers' Company provided the Crown with assistance in censorship. As part of this process, the printers registered their 'sole right' to a copy of a manuscript in an official register (referred to as the 'copy right' or 'stationers' copyright'). Even when the political climate around censorship changed in the late seventeenth century, and laws requiring licensing of presses lapsed, the Stationers' monopolies remained a useful and valued economic tool for regulating the English book trade. A small group of London printers could control book supply, distribution and prices for England as the market for works continued to expand and the book trade grew.

Private contracts between printers and publishers (and less commonly between publishers and authors) recognising exclusive rights were also utilised. These contracts could be enforced in Chancery with recourse to equity and conscience, as well as in the Common Law courts in accordance with broader notions of natural justice. At the time, enforcement did not necessitate legal inquiry into the precise legal origin or status of the exclusive literary property right claimed by the plaintiff.[6] Despite ongoing concerted efforts to stamp out piracy, as the printing industry and book trade expanded and transportation across England improved, works came to be distributed from further afield.[7] There remained a large, legitimate and (though hard to ascertain) clearly significant unlicensed book trade. This led to agitation for reform.

The legal situation of the London Stationers was also formally altered after the Union with Scotland (1707). Scottish printers were unaffected by the arrangements of the London trade and began to print and sell titles encroaching on established markets. This led to the London Stationers successfully petitioning for a law recognising the exclusive right to literary property: the *Statute of Anne*.

The text of this first Anglo literary property statute is instructive. The subtitle describes it as an 'act for the encouragement of learning, by vesting the copies of printed books in the authors or purchasers of such copies, during the times therein mentioned', and the text continues:

---

5   See discussion of the *Statute of Monopolies 1623* (21 Jac 1, c 3) in Chapter 9.

6   C Hesse, 'The Rise of Intellectual Property 700 BC–AD 2000: An Idea in Balance' (2002) 131 *Dædalus* 26;
J Feather and P Lindebaum, 'Milton's Contract' (1992) 10 *Cardozo Arts & Entertainment Law Journal* 439;
J Loewenstein, 'The Script in the Marketplace' (1985) 12 *Representations* 101; M Rose, *Authors and Owners: The Invention of Copyright*, Harvard University Press, Cambridge, MA, 1993; H Tomás Gómez-Arostegui, 'What History Teaches Us about Copyright Injunctions and the Inadequate-Remedy-At-Law Requirement' (2008) 81 *Southern California Law Review* 1197.

7   J Feather, *Publishing, Piracy and Politics: An Historical Study of Copyright in Britain*, Mansell, London, 1994.

Whereas printers, booksellers, and other persons have of late frequently taken the liberty of printing, reprinting, and publishing, or causing to be printed, reprinted, and published, books and other writings, without the consent of the authors or proprietors of such books and writings, to their very great detriment, and too often to the ruin of them and their families: for preventing therefore such practices for the future, and for the encouragement of learned men to compose and write useful books; may it please your Majesty, that it may be enacted ...; That from and after the tenth day of April, one thousand seven hundred and ten, the author of any book or books already printed, who hath not transferred to any other the copy or copies of such book or books, share or shares thereof, or the bookseller or booksellers, printer or printers, or other person or persons, who hath or have purchased or acquired the copy or copies of any book or books, in order to print or reprint the same, shall have the sole right and liberty of printing such book and books for the term of one and twenty years, to commence from the said tenth day of April, and no longer.[8]

Three points are worth noting. The first is the justification given for literary property. It was a right granted in the public interest: an incentive was created in order to encourage production and supply of 'useful books'. Second, the author was acknowledged as the original owner of the literary property right, but the interests of the author and printer were somewhat conflated. Third, the right granted was only for a limited term.

THE LITERARY PROPERTY DEBATE

The *Statute of Anne* had its origins in the Enlightenment, a philosophical movement of the eighteenth century in which reason was advocated as the primary source and legitimacy for authority.[9] Enlightenment policies sought to encourage the pursuit of truth, which belonged to Man and God, to foster the progress of Art and Science (which were not then seen as separate pursuits) and to raise the education levels of the population. There was no widespread idea of literary property as a perpetual natural right of individuals at the time of drafting of the *Statute of Anne*. Limited private rights were thought to provide an incentive that could advance the public interest. There is a notion of proportionality and balance in this justification—the private right should be tailored to serve the public end. A private right to this form of intangible property is not inherently in public interest.[10]

Though John Locke was also an Enlightenment philosopher, his *Two Treatises on Government* (1689), celebrating the political importance of private property and natural right to own the fruits of one's labour, became increasingly influential by the late eighteenth century. The virtue of property ownership and theories of natural right were also celebrated in William Blackstone's *Commentaries on the Law of England* (1765–69). Blackstone extended Locke's claim for landed property and intangible rights into a case for the natural right of authors to perpetual copyright. This view led to arguments for a perpetual common law right of literary property.

---

8   L Bently and M Kretschmer, eds, *Primary Sources on Copyright* (1450–1900) at www.copyrighthistory.org. This resource provides a wealth of information and commentary about the early history of UK copyright (unfortunately excluding reference to the Australian colonies).

9   J Schmidt, ed, *What is Enlightenment? Eighteenth Century Answers to Twentieth Century Questions*, University of California Press, Berkeley, CA, 1996.

10   For a contemporary restatement of incentive theories of copyright, see Y Benkler, *The Wealth of Networks: How Social Production Transforms Markets and Freedom*, Yale University Press, New Haven, CT, 2006.

Romanticism was also becoming an increasingly influential artistic and intellectual movement throughout the late eighteenth century, reaching its heyday in the nineteenth century.[11] Unlike the rationalism of the Enlightenment era, Romantic art focused on the importance of conveying feelings in works—emphasising passion, the senses and the sensual, as well as imagination. This led to a preoccupation with the creative genius of the modern author. Romanticism leads to presumptions that copyright rewards original creative endeavours, as opposed to merely useful works, although the legislation of the nineteenth century had no formal requirement of originality.

These different philosophical traditions and justifications for literary property rights came into play in two key cases in the mid-to-late eighteenth century, together known as the 'Literary Property Debate'. The questions in these cases were whether a perpetual common law right of authors to literary property existed, and what the relationship was between any pre-existing authorial rights and the *Statute of Anne*.

In *Millar v Taylor* (1769) 4 Burr 2303; 98 ER 201, a London printer, Millar, claimed he had purchased rights to *The Seasons*, a work of the Scottish romantic poet James Thomson, and consequently had obtained a perpetual common law right to publish this work. A Scottish printer, Taylor, claimed that under the *Statute of Anne* copyright had expired and thus there was no infringement. Blackstone acted as counsel for Millar.

The Court of King's Bench found in favour of Millar. Willes J found that the records of Chancery proved the existence of a common law right of the author. He reasoned that the time limitations in the statute were not general provisions affecting pre-existing common law rights, and that the enactment was primarily of application to other situations such as university publishing. He further argued that Taylor was a stranger attempting to reap the benefit of another man's labour and that a perpetual monopoly was essential to encourage the 'painful researches of learned men'. Aston J and Lord Mansfield agreed, with the latter adding:

> it is just that an Author should reap the pecuniary Profits of his own Ingenuity and Labour
> ...
> It is agreeable to the Principles of Right and Wrong, the Fitness of Things, Convenience and Policy, and therefore to the common law, to protect the copy before Publication.

The dissent of Yates J is worth noting, as it proved influential in the later case of *Donaldson v Beckett* (1774) 4 Burr 2408; 98 ER 257. He argued that to succeed, Millar needed to prove that compositions of authors were property. Yates J defined property with reference to established general principles of real property, and found that:

> the dominion of a Proprietor can not extend beyond the Duration of the Property: No Man can have that Right beyond the just Bounds of his Property.

That is, one can have property in a book, but cannot have property rights beyond the actual pages between the covers, extending to rights to reproduce that book. The only reason for such an extension of the right would be to protect 'mere value', but:

> [t]he Air, the Light, the Sun are of Value inestimable: But Who can claim a Property in them?

---

11 M Woodmansee, *The Author, Art, and the Market*, Columbia University Press, New York, NY, 1994; M Rose, *Authors and Owners: The Invention of Copyright*, Harvard University Press, Cambridge, MA, 1993.

Yates J rejected the possibility of acquiring property by labour alone because this claim presumes that the object is capable of sustaining a private right simply by labouring upon it. He argued that the only reason real property could be acquired by labour was because in law occupation founded the claim to the land. However:

> [t]he occupancy of a Thought would be a new kind of occupancy indeed. By what outward Mark must the Property denote Appropriation? ... At what Time, and by what Act does the Author's common law property attach?

He pointed out the absurdity of reckoning this at the time of publication because it would mean that another person who had the same ideas as an author could not presume to publish them—the ideas already being 'pre-occupied' and therefore private property. He rejected the presumption of justice in Blackstone's Locke-inspired justification—preventing another reaping what they have not sown—because it begs the very question in dispute. It presumes that ideas are capable of being exclusively owned. Any determination of injustice depended upon a determination of the extent and duration of the author's property.

The finding for exclusive common law literary property that survived the *Statute of Anne* in *Millar v Taylor* was soon effectively overruled by the House of Lords in *Donaldson v Beckett* (1774) 4 Burr 2408, 98 ER 257, another case concerning Thomson's *The Seasons*.[12]

The *Donaldson* debate followed the same arguments as in *Millar v Taylor*, sketched above, but the recorded decision is somewhat unsatisfactory as a 'leading case' as it does little to determine the precise legal origins of copyright authoritatively. For the modern reader, the report of the reasoning is very disjointed. The problem is compounded because there was also confusion arising from the recording of the decision, which was subsequently misreported in later commentaries and cases. This has led to ongoing debate about whether there ever had been a common law right of the author, and the matter remains somewhat unclear.[13]

Notwithstanding this confusion, *Donaldson* is generally understood as affirming the existence of copyright at common law, but finding that the natural authorial property right had been supplanted by the *Statute of Anne 1710* for published books. Echoes of the philosophical debates in *Millar v Taylor* and *Donaldson v Beckett* persist today: similar competing arguments are used to promote (or oppose) copyright reforms in the legislature, or interpretations of the law by courts.

THE DEVELOPMENT OF MODERN COPYRIGHT

The rights in the *Statute of Anne* were limited. First, the term of copyright was 21 years for existing works, and 14 years from first publication of new works with the privilege of renewal for a further 14 years if the author survived the first term. Second, the *Statute of Anne* only provided for rights in 'books'. Third, copyright was limited to works first published in Britain.[14] Last, the Act gave a 'right to copy'.

---

12 The case is thoroughly discussed in R Deazley, *On the Origin of the Right to Copy: Charting the Movement of Copyright Law in Eighteenth Century Britain (1695–1775)*, Hart Publishing, Oxford, 2004.

13 K Bowrey and N Fowell, 'Digging up Fragments and Building IP Franchises' (2009) 31 *Sydney Law Review* 185. Deazley's interpretation of *Donaldson v Beckett* as rejecting common law literary property, ibid, has been challenged recently in H Tomás Gómez-Arostegui, 'Copyright at Common Law in 1774' (2014) 47 *Connecticut Law Review* 1.

14 See *Jeffreys v Boosey* (1854) 4 HLC 815; *Routledge v Low* (1868) LR 3 HL 100.

These limits soon came under pressure. There was judicial debate about whether 'books' included newspapers, pamphlets, advertising, sheet music and so on, and at the same time protected subject matters were expanded through legislation, via a myriad of subject-specific copyright-like laws throughout the eighteenth and nineteenth centuries.[15] Uncertainty over the copyright status of unpublished works and the lack of protection for the works of colonial authors first published outside Britain led to dissatisfaction. There were significant debates over the meaning and the scope of the right to 'copy', including the status of 'colourably altered' works, adaptations, abridgments and translations, and associated notions of 'piracy'.[16]

Copyright law underwent major rationalisation in the early twentieth century. The *Copyright Act 1911* (UK) amalgamated the piecemeal legislation of the nineteenth century into one law, albeit one which still drew some distinctions between subject matters.[17] The 1911 Act extended the term of copyright to the life of the author plus 50 years; it was also part of a major effort to deal with copyright in a harmonised way throughout the British Empire. Australia played an active role in this process, and 'replaced' its own *Copyright Act 1905* (Cth) with the 1911 British Act via the *Copyright Act 1912* (Cth). This Act, with various amendments, governed copyright in Australia until the *Copyright Act 1968* (Cth).

The UK revised its copyright law mid-century through the *Copyright Act 1956* (UK), which was preceded by a comprehensive consideration by the Gregory Committee. Australia followed with its own review, published in 1959 by the Spicer Committee, and, after some delay, the 1968 Act. A key reason for both reviews was the perceived need to address technologies for distributing content which had emerged in the first half of the twentieth century: in particular, sound recordings (known, at that time, as phonographs), cinematograph films, and radio and television broadcasts. It was clear under the 1911/1912 Acts that authors' works could be disseminated (and infringed) through films, sound recordings and broadcasts, and provisions in the 1911/1912 Acts had included making mechanical records of work as an exclusive right of the author. Both sound recordings and films were afforded some protection under the 1911/1912 Act, but uncomfortably: films, for example, were treated in part as a series of photographs.

Incorporation of these subject matters into copyright was not straightforward. There was international debate about whether such productions should be protected in their own right as objects of author-like creativity or of significant investment. On the one hand, offering full copyright protection would seem to move away from a focus on authors, and towards protection of straightforward investment. On the other hand, it could be argued that the people who made sound recordings and films and curated broadcasts were engaged in creative acts. The Spicer Committee noted, for example, that 'the making of a record [phonogram or sound recording] involves a

---

15 For example, *Engravers' Copyright Acts 1735* and *1766*; *Calico Printers' Acts 1787* and *1794*; *Sculpture Copyright Acts 1798* and *1814*; *Dramatic Copyright Act 1833*; *Copyright of Designs Act 1839*; *Ornamental Designs Act 1842*; *Fine Art Copyright Act 1862*.

16 For consideration of this period, see R Deazley, *Rethinking Copyright: History, Theory, Language*, Edward Elgar, Cheltenham, 2006; I Alexander, *Copyright Law and the Public Interest in the Nineteenth Century*, Hart Publishing, Oxford, 2010.

17 B Sherman and L Bently, *The Making of Modern Intellectual Property Law: The British Experience, 1760–1911*, Cambridge University Press, Cambridge, 1999.

considerable amount of artistic and technical skill'.[18] The issue was resolved, to a large extent, by drawing a distinction in the international conventions between 'authors' rights' (*droit d'auteur*; sometimes referred to simply as 'copyright') and 'neighbouring rights' (*droits voisins*; also referred to as 'entrepreneurial works'). The *Berne Convention for the Protection of Literary and Artistic Works* (1886) protects authors' rights; the *Rome Convention for the Protection of Performers, Producers of Phonograms and Broadcasting Organizations* (1961) addresses neighbouring rights.

In Australian law, the 1968 Act was divided into two distinct parts: a structure which persists today. Part III deals with traditional works of authorship. Part IV incorporates films, sound recordings, broadcasts and published editions as 'subject matter other than works'. Part IV establishes different, and in some ways lesser, protection. As the Spicer Committee noted:[19]

> Insofar as those subject matters involve the use of original works, copyright in them is ancillary to the fundamental rights of the author of those works, that is to say, none of the rights which we recommend in this part of the Report is intended, unless otherwise expressly stated, to affect or detract from the rights which we have recommended should be enjoyed by the authors of original literary, dramatic, musical or artistic works.

The differences between Part III and Part IV protection are further explored in Chapters 4 and 6.

The 1968 Act still governs copyright in Australia, but has undergone further, significant waves of reform to address subsequent developments in media and technology. This has included reforms dealing with the development of photocopying in the 1970s, computer programs and early digital technology in the 1980s, and then, in the 1990s, the rise of the internet and World Wide Web, which led to the *Copyright Amendment (Digital Agenda) Act 2000* (Cth). In addition, new kinds of rights have been introduced. Performers have been recognised as another holder of neighbouring rights: first through the introduction in Part XIA of 'anti-bootlegging' rights to prevent recording or broadcast of live performances without their consent in 1989, and later, in 2004, full economic rights in sound recordings of live performances. In 2000, Australia also finally adopted specific 'moral rights' laws through a new Part IX, which protect the connection between authors and their works. Moral rights include a right to be recognised as the author of a work, and the right of an author to protect the integrity of their work. Moral rights were further extended to performers in 2007. These other rights of creators are discussed further in Chapter 7. Major reforms to Australia's copyright law were also introduced via the *Copyright Amendment Act 2006* (Cth), which, among other reforms, expanded criminal liability for copyright infringement, and introduced a series of new copyright exceptions.

The evolution of reproductive technologies and practices, and the expansion of copyright to recognise different kinds of creative contributions, have generated more and more law, but have not necessarily made the law any simpler to understand, or comprehensive. There has been a tendency to add ever more provisions in response to particular conceptual weaknesses as they become apparent in litigation. To appreciate the significance of these reforms courts often need to refer to the rather

---

18 Copyright Law Review Committee (the 'Spicer Committee'), *Report of the Committee appointed by the Attorney-General of the Commonwealth to Consider what Alterations are Desirable in the Copyright Law of the Commonwealth* (1959) at [241].

19 Ibid at [226].

general Explanatory Memoranda and, frequently, to parliamentary debates relating to individual pieces of amending legislation.

Anglo-derived copyright is commonly described as a creature of positive law, and s 8 of the *Copyright Act 1968* prescribes that 'copyright does not subsist otherwise than by virtue of this Act'. But the 1968 Act continues to draw extensively on previous Australian and UK legislation, and precedent from the nineteenth and early twentieth century is generally presumed to be authoritative (when this is convenient).[20] There is no preamble to the Act to assist with context. Key concepts are not clearly defined in the Act and so have been developed through case law, which adds to interpretative complexity by allowing reference to a wide range of legal and cultural meanings to influence interpretation.

PHILOSOPHICAL JUSTIFICATIONS

Throughout the history outlined above, a number of different rationales have been used to justify the existence, reform and expansion of copyright. One set of rationales is utilitarian, and is embodied in the title and preamble of the *Statute of Anne*. A utilitarian justification sees the grant of exclusive rights as a tool to achieve certain social purposes: copyright provides an incentive to encourage the production and dissemination of works of literature, art and other cultural products for the benefit of the broader public. Utilitarian rationales find a modern form in economic justifications for copyright protection. Law and economics analysis of copyright recognises that the creation of cultural products, such as books or movies, can require significant upfront investment of time and resources.[21] Once created, however, such products are relatively easy to duplicate. Without exclusive rights, creators will be forced to compete with copyists who can produce duplicates cheaply and who do not have to recover the costs of initial production. It is important to recognise that on a utilitarian rationale, it is the broader benefit to the public through increased access to a larger range of high-quality content that justifies the grant of private rights.

Today, a different kind of economic argument is made for copyright, with increasing emphasis placed on the 'economic contribution' of copyright to the broader economy. Copyright is said to be justified because it supports copyright-intensive industries, which create economic output and employment, and spillover benefits for other industries, which provide goods and services to the copyright industries or sell associated goods (such as businesses that sell computers or televisions necessary to enjoy content). It is difficult to obtain reliable statistics about the net worth, costs and benefits of the copyright sector as a whole. For example, the commonly cited report commissioned by the Australian Copyright Council, PricewaterhouseCoopers' *The Economic Contribution of Australia's Copyright Industries 1996–7 to 2010–11* (2012), has little hard economic data supporting its conclusions about the economic benefits of copyright protection.[22] There are, however, agreed

---

20 For discussion, see I Alexander, '"Manacles upon Science": Re-evaluating Copyright in Informational Works in Light of Eighteenth Century Case Law' (2014) 38 *Melbourne University Law Review* 317.

21 W Landes and R Posner, 'An Economic Analysis of Copyright Law' (1989) 18 *Journal of Legal Studies* 325.

22 See also the report commissioned by a group of copyright collecting societies to evaluate the benefits of extending the copyright term: Allens Consulting, *Copyright Term Extension: Australian Benefits and Costs* (2003). See further K Weatherall, 'Of Copyright Bureaucracies and Incoherence: Stepping Back from Australia's Recent Copyright Reforms' (2007) 31 *Melbourne University Law Review* 967.

statistics in relation to royalty earnings for audio-visual trade (imports and exports of cinema films, television content and video). Since 1991–92, when data began to be evaluated by the Australian Bureau of Statistics, Australia has recorded a net deficit in earnings (with the one exception of the Olympics year, where SOCOG audio-visual earnings provided a trade surplus of $552 million). Data for 2008–09 shows a trade deficit in copyright royalties for audio-visual items of $654 million (comprising imports of $1.359 billion and exports of $234 million), with the USA receiving a 50 per cent share of Australia's copyright royalties paid overseas.[23] There is usually little attempt to link statistics about copyright's contribution with specific rules or reforms to copyright.

Another rationale for copyright is the argument, articulated by philosopher John Locke, that creators have a natural right to own the fruits of their labour. Such thinking finds voice in arguments that infringers have 'misappropriated' the labour of others, or are trying to 'reap where they have not sown'. Although this kind of thinking is influential in copyright cases, the High Court has cautioned against focusing too closely on misappropriation. Gummow, Hayne and Heydon JJ in *IceTV Pty Ltd v Nine Network Pty Ltd* [2009] HCA 14; (2009) 239 CLR 458 at [131]–[132] warned against:

> the dangers when applying the Act of adopting the rhetoric of 'appropriation' of 'skill and labour'. A finding that one party has 'appropriated' skill and labour, of itself, is not determinative of the issue of infringement of a copyright work. The Act does not provide for any general doctrine of 'misappropriation' and does not afford protection to skill and labour alone.
>
> ... To speak of the 'appropriation' of '[the company's] skill and labour', rather than attending to the relevant 'original' work of the author or authors, [is] to take a fundamental departure from the text and structure of the Act.

Another rationale for copyright protection may be found in the philosophies of Immanuel Kant and Georg Hegel, who, to various extents, argued that cultural products are an emanation of the personality of the author. On this view, copyright is a form of legal protection for the author's own personhood, and exclusive rights in cultural products recognise the vital and ongoing connection between author and work.[24] The recognition of property rights in works of authorship is recognised as a fundamental human right of the author: see, for example, Art 27(2) of the *Universal Declaration of Human Rights* (1948). Aspects of these author-centric philosophies have been more influential in continental or *droit d'auteur* systems, but are also embodied in Anglo-Australian copyright law, especially through moral rights and the way copyright duration is tied to the lifespan of the author.

No one of these justifications affords a complete explanation for modern copyright law. It is often hard to identify any incentive effect of specific copyright reforms, and a strict utilitarian perspective would grant only sufficient exclusive rights to provide incentives for a desirable (or, in economic terms, optimal) level of investment in creation. It is hard to argue that current copyright law is so finely calibrated. Similarly, many copyright rules (such as the way that copyright rights are readily and fully transferable) are inconsistent with a focus on the protection of authors' personhood.

---

23 Australian Bureau of Statistics, *Arts and Culture in Australia: A Statistical Overview* (2011).
24 J Hughes, 'The Philosophy of Intellectual Property' (1988) 77 *Georgetown Law Journal* 287.

A mixture of justifications for copyright may be seen at different times in debates around copyright interpretation and reform.[25]

Another concept frequently used in copyright policy discussions is 'balance'. The Preamble to the *WIPO Copyright Treaty* (1996), for example, recognises 'the need to maintain a balance between the rights of authors and the larger public interest'. The idea of balance may be useful to the extent that it makes clear that no single goal—whether access on the part of the public, or the promotion of the interests of authors—governs copyright. However, different interest groups will disagree where the balance should be struck, and the concept can be problematic to the extent, first, that it suggests that the interests of authors and of the broader public are necessarily antagonistic, and second, if it is understood as meaning that whenever changes are made to strengthen one set of interests in copyright, then further reform is necessary to protect 'the other side'.

INTERNATIONAL INFLUENCES

While the Attorney-General's Department has responsibility for the *Copyright Act*, Australian legislation has been increasingly affected by the ongoing internationalisation of rights. This reflects the increased importance of IP in global trade.

Multilateral treaties have helped shape copyright law since the late nineteenth century.[26] Three leading multilateral treaties define the broad structure of copyright law: the *Berne Convention for the Protection of Literary and Artistic Works* (1886), the *Rome Convention for the Protection of Performers, Producers of Phonograms and Broadcasting Organizations* (1961) and the *Agreement on Trade-Related Aspects of Intellectual Property Rights* (the 'TRIPS Agreement') (1994). The Berne Convention provides the underlying framework for authors' copyright and the Rome Convention underpins neighbouring rights. The TRIPS Agreement is part of the suite of agreements establishing the World Trade Organization (WTO). The TRIPS Agreement incorporates, and extends, many of the substantive provisions of the Berne and Rome Conventions, applies these rules to all WTO members and allows states to use the WTO's dispute settlement processes to raise complaints about other members' implementation of copyright law. There have been several disputes over IP law, including an important dispute between Europe and the USA over copyright exceptions.[27]

In 1996, two treaties, the *WIPO Copyright Treaty* and the *WIPO Phonograms and Performances Treaty*, were concluded with the aim of updating multilateral rules to take account of digital technologies and the rise of the internet. These treaties introduced a new, technology-neutral right of 'communication to the public' (discussed in Chapter 6), and also additional requirements for countries to protect technological measures used by copyright owners in an attempt to control content online (discussed in Chapter 7).

---

25 See, for example, the 'guiding principles for reform' adopted by the Australian Law Reform Commission (ALRC) in its recent review of copyright exceptions, which refers to several of these justifications: ALRC, Report No 122, *Copyright and the Digital Economy* (2013).

26 See S Ricketson and J Ginsburg, *International Copyright and Neighbouring Rights: The Berne Convention and Beyond*, 2nd ed, Oxford University Press, Oxford, 2005.

27 Panel Report, *United States—Section 110(5) of the US Copyright Act,* WT/DS160/R, adopted 27 July 2000, DSR 2000: VIII, 3769 (discussed in Chapter 6).

Detailed rules relating to copyright and its enforcement are also increasingly incorporated into bilateral and regional trade agreements. The *Australia–US Free Trade Agreement* (AUSFTA) (2004) was a watershed in Australian copyright law, requiring an extension of the term of copyright for 20 additional years; extensive changes to Australia's digital copyright enforcement provisions, including new 'safe harbours' for online intermediaries and a different scheme for protecting technological measures used by copyright owners; as well as a whole new regime of performers' economic and moral rights.[28] In addition to the reforms required by the treaty text itself, AUSFTA catalysed a further round of domestic reform in 2006, including new exceptions to 'balance' the extensions of copyright that had occurred in 2004.[29]

At the time of writing, international lawmaking continues in multilateral, regional and bilateral fora. WIPO is conducting ongoing work on the rights of broadcasting organisations and exceptions. A new treaty addressing the access of visually impaired persons to copyright content— the *Marrakesh Treaty to Facilitate Access to Published Works for Persons Who Are Blind, Visually Impaired or Otherwise Print Disabled*—was concluded in 2013 and was significant for being the first multilateral convention focused mostly on exceptions rather than rights. Australia is also involved in negotiations for a regional trade agreement known as the *Trans-Pacific Partnership Agreement* (TPP) with Japan, the USA, Singapore, New Zealand, Malaysia, Brunei, Canada, Chile, Mexico, Peru and Vietnam. It is expected that if the TPP is concluded, among the chapters dealing with a full range of trade issues it will contain a chapter on IP, including copyright and IP enforcement. Australia is also engaged in various bilateral trade negotiations, and in 2013–14 concluded negotiations with South Korea, Japan and China. The agreements with South Korea and Japan both contain commitments on copyright. It seems likely that Australian copyright policymaking will continue to be heavily influenced by international developments.

The discussion above reveals a series of competing influences on copyright law: history; the claims of stakeholder groups; competing philosophies, rationales and goals; and the impact of international commitments. That all of these factors are relevant in both explaining and reforming copyright was recognised by the Australian Law Reform Commission in its Report No 122, *Copyright and the Digital Economy* (2013), which identified five framing principles for copyright reform:[30]

- acknowledging and respecting authorship and creation;
- maintaining incentives for creation and dissemination;
- promoting fair access to content;
- providing rules that are flexible, clear and adaptive; and
- providing rules consistent with international obligations.

---

28 For more detail and a history of how these developments were received, see R Burrell and K Weatherall, 'Exporting Controversy? Reactions to the Copyright Provisions of the US–Australia Free Trade Agreement: Lessons for US Trade Policy' [2008] *University of Illinois Journal of Law, Technology and Policy* 259.

29 The details are discussed in K Weatherall, 'Of Copyright Bureaucracies and Incoherence: Stepping Back from Australia's Recent Copyright Reforms' (2007) 31 *Melbourne University Law Review* 967.

30 Australian Law Reform Commission, Report No 122, *Copyright and the Digital Economy* (2013), ch 1.

COPYRIGHT PRINCIPLES

The *Copyright Act* is complex legislation. The level of technical detail can make it difficult to generalise about its principles. There are, however, some general principles that underpin copyright logic. These include concepts of:

- original expression as the object of protection;
- the author;
- the public domain;
- the nature of copyright as intangible property, separate from physical property in which it is embodied; and
- the idea/expression dichotomy.

Originality and authorship are key criteria for subsistence of copyright for 'works' under Part III of the Act, and are addressed in detail in Chapter 3. The other three principles in this list are introduced in the remainder of this chapter.

PUBLIC DOMAIN

The terms 'public domain' and 'information commons' are often used to provide a reference point that defines the public's interest in copyright.[31] The public domain is the sum of things *not* protected by copyright and hence, in positive terms, is a resource on which the public can freely draw. Legally, however, the public domain is ascertained primarily against the backdrop of the positive rights of owners. The public domain thus has the character of a negative presence necessary to frame the state grant of monopoly rights. The Australian public domain clearly includes:

- works in which copyright has expired;
- productions not protected (e.g. because of jurisdictional complications or the type of subject matter); and
- ideas, information and facts (but note that protection is available for compilations of facts).

Some commentators include within the concept of the public domain other circumstances in which users can access works without permission:

- where the resource fails to meet minimum threshold standards for protection (e.g. the work lacks originality);
- where a user takes an insubstantial portion of a copyright work (the test of infringement requires a 'substantial' taking); and
- where a user exercises fair dealing rights.

The impact of extensions of copyright can be measured with reference to their impact on the public domain, such as books that cannot be reproduced without permission and accessed by the public at no cost (e.g. at Project Gutenberg) when the term of copyright is extended.[32] The case below, dealing with a claim to 'quasi-property' in spectacles, illustrates the role the public domain plays in structuring legal reasoning.

---

31   See the breadth of the term in C Waelde and H MacQueen, eds, *Intellectual Property: The Many Faces of the Public Domain*, Edward Elgar, Cheltenham, 2007.

32   See http://gutenberg.net.au.

CASE EXTRACT: PRECEDENT

Victoria Park Racing and Recreation Grounds Co Ltd v Taylor

(1937) 58 CLR 479
High Court of Australia

[The owner of land adjoining a racecourse erected an elevated platform on his land from which it was possible to overlook the course and (among other things) read information as to starters, scratchings and race results appearing on noticeboards at the racecourse. In return for payment, the landowner permitted an employee of a broadcaster to use the platform during race meetings, and broadcast descriptions of races and results. The racecourse proprietor sought an injunction to restrain this use of the adjoining land.]

Latham CJ (at 496–497): It has been argued that by the expenditure of money the plaintiff has created a spectacle, and that he therefore has what is described as a quasi-property in the spectacle which the law will protect. The vagueness of this proposition is apparent upon its face. What it really means is that there is some principle (apart from contract or confidential relationship) which prevents people in some circumstances from opening their eyes and seeing something and then describing what they see. The court has not been referred to any authority in English law which supports the general contention that if a person chooses to organise an entertainment or to do anything else which other persons are able to see, he has a right to obtain from a court an order that they shall not describe to anybody what they see. If the claim depends upon interference with a proprietary right it is difficult to see how it can be material to consider whether the interference is large or small—whether the description is communicated to many persons by broadcasting or by a newspaper report, or only to a few persons in conversation or correspondence. Further, as I have already said, the mere fact that damage results to a plaintiff from such a description cannot be relied upon as a cause of action.

I find difficulty in attaching any precise meaning to the phrase 'property in a spectacle'. A 'spectacle' cannot be 'owned' in any ordinary sense of that word. Even if there were any legal principle which prevented one person from gaining an advantage for himself or causing damage to another by describing a spectacle produced by that other person, the rights of the latter person could be described as property only in a metaphorical sense. Any appropriateness in the metaphor would depend upon the existence of the legal principle. The principle cannot itself be based upon such a metaphor.

Even if, on the other hand, a spectacle could be said to exist as a subject matter of property, it would still be necessary, in order to provide the plaintiff in this case with a remedy, to show that the description of such property is wrongful, or that such description is wrongful when it is widely disseminated. No authority has been cited to support such a proposition.

COPYRIGHT AS PROPERTY

With copyright works there are usually two associated property rights:

- the rights to the original work in its *tangible* form, such as a manuscript; and
- the copyright—the *intangible* right to make copies of the work.

Though the two arise conjointly when, for example, an author writes their manuscript, there is no necessity for their continued coexistence. Copyright can quite feasibly continue well after the tangible original has been destroyed. For example, the destruction of a painting does not affect the survival of any copyrights associated with that artwork. However, as a practical matter, reproducing the work often requires access to the tangible property. The issue can become complicated when different parties hold the two kinds of property rights.

CASE EXTRACT: PRECEDENT

In re Dickens; Dickens v Hawksley

[1935] Ch 267
Court of Appeal of England and Wales

[Charles Dickens died in 1870, bequeathing 'all my private papers whatsoever and wheresoever' to his sister-in-law, Georgina Hogarth. The residue, which expressly included Dickens' 'copyrights', went to his children. Among the author's private papers was the manuscript of an unpublished work, known as 'The Life of Christ'. When the right to publish the work was eventually sold in 1934 to Associated Newspapers, the question arose as to who was entitled to the proceeds: the beneficiaries claiming through the residue of Dickens' estate (i.e. through his children) or those claiming through the will of Georgina Hogarth.]

Romer LJ (at 291–294): The next question is whether there passed to Georgina Hogarth, together with the manuscript, what has been called the common law 'copyright' in the work, that is to say, the sole right of first printing and publishing the same for sale. That such a right was vested in Dickens at the date of his death is clearly established by numerous authorities of which it is sufficient to mention *Millar v Taylor* [(1769) 4 Burr 2303; 98 ER 201] ... But there is no doubt that in the case of an unpublished literary work the author and those claiming through him had the sole right of publication. In cases where the author himself retains possession of the manuscript, it matters not whether this right flows from such possession or from a right in the literary composition apart from and independent of such possession. But the question is one of vital importance where the manuscript is in the possession of some person other than the author. This, of course, usually happens in the case of letters. The manuscript is in the physical possession of the recipient of the letter. It has nevertheless been established by numerous authorities that the writer of the letters may restrain publication. This right exists quite independently of there being any such breach of trust or confidence in making the publication as would induce a Court of equity to interfere. The publication is a breach of a common law right. In *Millar v Taylor*, Willes J said this in speaking of the manuscript of a literary work: 'Suppose the original, or a transcript, was given or lent to a man to read, for his own use; and he publishes it; it would be a violation of the author's common law right to the copy. This never was doubted; and has often been determined.' He then referred to four cases in Chancery that had been cited in argument which included that of *Pope v Curl* [(1741) 2 Atk 342] ... [He continued:] 'It has all along been expressly admitted "that by the common law an author is entitled to the copy of his own work until it has been once printed and published by his authority," and "that the four cases in Chancery, cited for that purpose, are agreeable to the common law; and the relief was properly given, in consequence of the legal right." The property in the copy, thus abridged, is equally an incorporeal right to print a set of intellectual ideas or modes of thinking, communicated in a set of words and sentences and modes of expression. It is equally detached from the manuscript, or any other physical existence whatsoever,' and he added a little later: 'No disposition, no transfer of paper upon which the composition is written, marked, or impressed, (though it gives the power to print and publish) can be construed a conveyance of the copy without the author's express consent "to print and publish"; much less against his will. The property of the copy, thus narrowed, may equally go down from generation to generation, and possibly continue for ever: though neither the author nor his representatives should have any manuscript whatsoever of the work, original duplicate, or transcript.' It is plain that the words 'though it gives the power to print and publish' in this passage means 'though it gives the opportunity to print and publish.'

... [I]t is difficult to see why the copy should pass with a gift of the manuscript unless it is in terms expressly made to do so. Confirmation of this view seems to me to be afforded by *Caird v Sime* [(1887) 12 AC 326], in which the right of a professor to restrain the publication of lectures delivered by him in his class room was upheld by the House of Lords. In that case Lord Watson said: 'The author of a lecture on moral philosophy, or of any other original composition, retains a right of property in his work which entitles him to prevent its publication by others until it has, with his consent, been communicated to the public.' If such consent is not to be implied by the delivery of a lecture in a class room I cannot see why it should be implied by the delivery of the manuscript of a literary composition to some friend or acquaintance of the author ...

In view of these authorities I am of opinion that the bequest to Miss Georgina Hogarth of the manuscript of 'The Life of Christ' did not pass to her the incorporeal right of Charles Dickens in the composition. That right would, therefore, have passed under the gift in his will of his residuary estate even though such estate had been referred to merely in general terms.

Note: While the result was that copyright in the work belonged to the residuary estate of Charles Dickens, publication was possible only by use of the physical manuscript, owned by those claiming through Georgina Hogarth. Therefore, the Court of Appeal determined that proceeds of sale of the copyright should be equally divided between beneficiaries claiming through the will of Hogarth and persons interested in the residuary estate of Dickens.

The decision also makes clear that the common law right of the author in unpublished works was unaffected by *Donaldson v Beckett* (1774) 4 Burr 2408; 98 ER 257. This situation changed when statutory copyright in unpublished works came into operation in the *Copyright Act 1911* (UK), which became Australian law under the *Copyright Act 1912* (Cth). Section 198 of the *Copyright Act 1968* (Cth) provides that unless there is a contrary intention, a bequest of an unpublished literary, dramatic or musical work or of an artistic work also includes transfer of the copyright (although Dickens' will, by referring expressly to 'copyrights', might have indicated such an intention, leading to the same result under the current law).

CASE EXTRACT: CURRENT LAW

Pacific Film Laboratories Pty Ltd v Federal Commissioner of Taxation

(1970) 121 CLR 154
High Court of Australia

[This litigation involved a tax applied to the sale of goods. The taxpayer company received film from customers, developed the film and supplied prints to the customers for payment. The taxpayer company argued that because copyright in the print was held by the customer, the company was not selling goods to the customer and thus not liable to pay the tax in question.]

Barwick CJ (at 162–164): But it is objected that there could not in any case be a sale of a print or duplicate either to the photographer or to any other person because of the provisions of the *Copyright Act 1912*. It has been assumed in argument that the person ordering the print was the owner of the copyright in the negative or transparency. This may or may not be so, but I am prepared to assume it as fact. Because the negative or transparency was the subject of copyright it is said that the appellant as the producer of the print or duplicate as a reproduction of the negative or transparency could not have any general property in the print which he could transfer by sale to any person including the owner of the copyright. It is submitted that it would have no more than a lien for the amount agreed to be paid for the production of the print or duplicate. The fact that he owned the sensitized paper or the film on which the print or duplicate was made to appear and such of the chemicals as remained on the paper or film at the end of the process of making the print or duplicate did not give him any general property in the print or duplicate as reproductions of the copyright work, the negative or transparency as the case may be ...

There are, in my opinion, several clear answers to this submission. In the first place, there is authority for the proposition that the property in a chattel may be in one person and the copyright in another: *In re Dickens; Dickens v Hawksley* [1935] Ch 267. In the second place, an authority to reproduce a copyright work given by the owner of the copyright allows the authorized person to produce the copy as his own property and indeed unless the authority to reproduce it provides otherwise, he is free to dispose of the reproduction, cf. *Copinger and Skone James' Law of Copyright,* 10th ed (1965), p 378, s 1027. In the third place, whilst of course the *Copyright Act* enables the copyright owner to recover possession of infringing copies of the copyright work or damages for the conversion of such infringing copies there were in this case no infringing copies, the owner of the copyright on the supposition made, authorized the making of the copy and its delivery to himself. It seems to me that even if the agreement between the owner of the copyright and the appellant had been no more than an agreement for the rendering of services the print produced by the appellant could not have been claimed by the owner of the copyright as his own nor could he have recovered it in detinue before it had been delivered to him but if as I think the agreement was an agreement for the sale of the print or duplicate by the appellant to the owner of the copyright it seems to me necessarily to follow that not only was there no property in the owner of the copyright in the print viewed as a chattel at any time before the delivery of the print to the owner of the copyright but that it was intended that property in the print or duplicate should pass on delivery of the print or duplicate ...

In my opinion, the delivery of the prints or duplicates by the appellant for an agreed sum was a sale of those prints or transparencies ... Accordingly, in my opinion, the sale value of those sales was rightly included in an assessment by the respondent Commissioner of the appellant.

EXPRESSION VERSUS IDEAS, FACTS, SYSTEMS AND METHODS OF OPERATION

The eighteenth century literary property cases about the status of common law copyright did not agree on any particular way of defining what it was in a work that deserved protection. Successive Acts also failed to define the precise limits to the protected expressions. Courts soon found that to confine protection to an exact unauthorised reproduction of a copyright work offered insufficient protection to owners. Slowly, some kinds of adaptations, abridgments and less-than-exact copies came within the ambit of copyright. However, it remained difficult to define the boundaries of the protected expression in copyright with precision.

When required to arbitrate on the limits to protection afforded by statute, judges formulated the principle of the idea/expression dichotomy. Out of respect for competing interests and the notion that owners' rights are limited in order to maintain the public domain, it is said that *ideas*, and facts, are free for all to use, and only the *expression* (fixed in some material form) is capable of receiving protection.

Some of the rationales for excluding ideas and facts from copyright protection include:

- copyright's Enlightenment origins and the belief that knowledge belongs to the 'information commons', which should be open to all to draw upon;
- democratic beliefs that full participation in society requires access to ideas without censorship arising through too-expansive protection;
- a value for competition suggesting that in order for works to continue to be produced there must be sufficient protection to provide an incentive to producers, but that monopolies need to be limited to ensure new players are not blocked from entry to the marketplace; and
- evidentiary concerns that require a monopoly to be clearly defined.

The idea/expression dichotomy is embodied in a number of treaty provisions, including Art 2 of the *WIPO Copyright Treaty* and Art 9 of the TRIPS Agreement, which both state that '[c]opyright protection extends to expressions and not to ideas, procedures, methods of operation or mathematical concepts as such'. *Hollinrake v Truswell* [1894] 3 Ch 420, extracted below, represents one attempt to use copyright to protect a 'procedure' or 'method of operation'. In justifying denial of protection, the Court evoked the idea/expression dichotomy.

CASE EXTRACT: PRECEDENT

PRECEDENT

Hollinrake v Truswell

[1894] 3 Ch 420
Court of Appeal of England and Wales

[Section 2 of the *Copyright Act 1842* (UK) conferred protection on a 'map, chart, or plan'. The plaintiff was assignee under an assignment in writing of 1 February 1891, from one Edmund George Kendall, 'of the copyright in a book, to wit, a map, chart, or plan' entitled the 'Cosmopolitan Sleeve Chart, 1886'. The chart was in fact a cardboard device used by tailors to accurately measure and cut inner sleeves.]

Lord Herschell LC (at 423–424): Now, I have to observe, in the first place, that no one could claim a monopoly of the use of such a sentence as 'measure round the thick part of the arm,' or of a half-inch scale. And the words and figures found on the 'chart' do not in combination convey any intelligible idea, nor could they be of the slightest use to any one, apart from the cardboard upon which they are printed. The object of the *Copyright Act* was to prevent any one publishing a copy of the particular form of expression in which an author conveyed ideas or information to the world.

These may be retained by any one, though the book, map, or chart which embodied them has passed out of his possession. If he were to commit to memory the contents of the book, or the information disclosed by the map or chart, he would be as much in possession of the author's ideas or information as if the book, map, or chart were physically in his hands. But this is not the case with the words or figures upon the sleeve chart. They are intended to be used, and can only be of use, in connection with that upon which they are inscribed. They are not merely directions for the use of the cardboard, which is in truth a measuring apparatus, but they are a part of that very apparatus itself, without which it cannot be used, and except in connection with which they are absolutely useless.

I think it is clear, therefore, that what the Plaintiff has sought to protect under the Act for the protection of literary productions is not a literary production, but an apparatus for the use of which certain words and figures must necessarily be inscribed upon it. It is quite true that, notwithstanding the words of the preamble, the protection of copyright may be obtained for works which cannot be said, in the ordinary sense of the term, to have literary merit. Compilations, such as the Post Office Directory, have, no doubt, properly been held to be the subject of copyright; but there is, as I have pointed out, a marked distinction between these and the claim of protection under the *Copyright Act* for words and figures inscribed on and necessarily forming part of an apparatus or tool.

Lindley LJ (at 426–427): I am not aware of any English authority which throws any real light on the applicability of the *Copyright Act* to such a thing as this ...

The character of what is published is the test of copyright. If what is published is not separately published, is not a publication complete in itself, but is only a direction on a tool or machine, to be understood and used with it, such direction cannot, in my opinion, be severed from the tool or machine of which it is really part, and cannot be monopolized by its inventor under the *Copyright Act* ...

The Defendant may have got her own idea from the Plaintiff's chart, but the Defendant has not copied more than the Plaintiff's method of measuring. Copyright, however, does not extend to ideas, or schemes, or systems, or methods; it is confined to their expression; and if their expression is not copied the copyright is not infringed ... *Baker v Selden*, [101 US 99 (1879)] illustrates this very well. It was there held that the author of a system of book-keeping was not entitled to any monopoly in the system, but was only entitled to prevent other persons from copying his description of it.

This is an attempt to use the *Copyright Act* for a purpose to which it is not properly applicable, and the appeal must be allowed, with costs here and below.

A significant modern Australian case touching on the distinction between facts and expression is *IceTV Pty Ltd v Nine Network Australia Pty Ltd* [2009] HCA 14; (2009) 239 CLR 458, extracted below. This is also a key case on originality and authorship, which are considered further in Chapter 3. This extract deals with the relationship between copyright and facts.

CASE EXTRACT: CURRENT LAW

IceTV Pty Ltd v Nine Network Australia Pty Ltd

[2009] HCA 14; (2009) 239 CLR 458
High Court of Australia

[Nine Network Australia is a television broadcaster. Employees of Nine decided what television programs would be shown and when; the results of this work were recorded in a 'Master Paper Grid' and in an internal Nine database. One of Nine's employees would generate a 'Weekly Schedule' from the database and send it out to third party companies which published aggregated television guides. The Weekly Schedule was a document in tabular form, recording the time, title of the show, assorted information (e.g. classification) and a synopsis of the program. IceTV produced an electronic program guide (EPG) suitable for use in digital personal video recorders (PVRs). Rather than copy the whole television program directly, IceTV arranged for someone to watch television for a period of time and record what programs were shown and when. To produce the EPG thereafter, this information was updated by IceTV employees using the published television guides derived from Nine's Weekly Schedule. Nine alleged that the copying of time and title information to update the EPG infringed copyright in Nine's Weekly Schedule.]

French CJ, Crennan and Kiefel JJ (footnotes omitted): 24. ... Copyright legislation strikes a balance of competing interests and competing policy considerations. Relevantly, it is concerned with rewarding authors of original literary works with commercial benefits having regard to the fact that literary works in turn benefit the reading public.

25. In both its title and opening recitals, the *Statute of Anne* of [1710] echoed explicitly the emphasis on the practical or utilitarian importance that certain seventeenth century philosophers attached to knowledge and its encouragement in the scheme of human progress. The 'social contract' envisaged by the *Statute of Anne*, and still underlying the present Act, was that an author could obtain a monopoly, limited in time, in return for making a work available to the reading public.

26. Whilst judicial and academic writers may differ on the precise nature of the balance struck in copyright legislation in different places, there can be no doubt that copyright is given in respect of 'the particular form of expression in which an author convey[s] ideas or information to the world'.

27. The particular form of expression here was the Weekly Schedule (or the Nine Database). The balance spoken of above is important in the present context because, generally speaking, no copyright could be claimed in a programme title alone and the time at which a programme will be broadcast is a single item of quotidian information.

28. Copyright does not protect facts or information. Copyright protects the particular form of expression of the information, namely the words, figures and symbols in which the pieces of information are expressed, and the selection and arrangement of that information. That facts are not protected is a crucial part of the balancing of competing policy considerations in copyright legislation. The information/expression dichotomy, in copyright law, is rooted in considerations of social utility. Copyright, being an exception to the law's general abhorrence of monopolies, does not confer a monopoly on facts or information because to do so would impede the reading public's access to and use of facts and information. Copyright is not given to reward work distinct from the production of a particular form of expression.

The joint judgment of Gummow, Hayne and Heydon JJ also addressed the relevance of the distinction between facts and expression in assessing infringement of copyright (an issue addressed in Chapter 6). Their Honours noted at [170] that:

> [I]n assessing the quality of the time and title information, as components of the weekly schedule, baldly stated matters of fact or intention are inseparable from and co-extensive with their expression. It is difficult to discern the expression of thought in statements of which programmes will be broadcast and when this will occur. If the facts be divorced from the other elements constituting the compilation in suit, as is the case with the use by IceTV of the time and title information, then it is difficult to treat the IceGuide as the reproduction of a substantial part of the weekly schedule in the qualitative sense required by the case law.

These comments highlight that although 'copyright does not protect facts', it does protect works comprised of factual material. Copyright lies in the expression of the facts, and where facts can be expressed in a multitude of different ways, it will be infringement to copy a writer's particular choices of expression. For example, *Sanofi-Aventis Australia Pty Ltd v Apotex Pty Ltd (No 3)* [2011] FCA 846; (2011) 92 IPR 320 concerned a Product Information document (PI) required by the *Therapeutic Goods Act 1989* (Cth). PIs are required to contain, in broadly prescribed form, a scientific, objective account of a medicine's usefulness and limitations as shown by the data supporting the application. Jagot J found that the PI was protected by copyright, as there were many different ways the facts could have been selected for inclusion, organised and expressed. (The legislature has since created a new copyright exception to allow reproduction of PIs: s 44BA).

Another Federal Court case in which the idea/expression dichotomy was invoked is extracted below.

CURRENT LAW

CASE EXTRACT: CURRENT LAW

Victoria v Pacific Technologies (Australia) Pty Ltd (No 2)

[2009] FCA 737; (2009) 177 FCR 61
Federal Court of Australia

[Pacific Technologies claimed to be the owner of copyright in the phrase 'Help-Help-Driver-in-Danger-Call-Police-Ph.000' (referred to as the 'Help Words'), to be displayed on the outside of a taxi when a driver duress alarm was activated by the driver. The phrase was included in Pacific Technologies' patent specifications. The State of Victoria made regulations requiring taxi owners/licence holders to fit duress alarms using the phrase. Pacific Technologies sought equitable remuneration for use of the phrase in the Copyright Tribunal; the tribunal proceedings were adjourned to allow the Federal Court to determine whether copyright subsisted in the phrase. Emmett J rejected the claim, in part on the basis that the phrase was 'too insubstantial' to constitute a copyright work, but also invoking the idea/expression dichotomy.]

Emmett J: 17. Copyright is concerned with the protection of the *expression* of ideas and not with the protection of ideas as such. Literary work comprises more than mere ideas. Many things that have no pretensions to literary style can be the subject of copyright. A literary work may be expressed in print or writing, irrespective of the question whether the quality or style is high: see *University of London Press Ltd v University Tutorial Press Ltd* [1916] 2 Ch 601 at 608; 1B IPR 186 at 190–1 (*University of London Press*). However, there must be some work involved in its production of a literary work, in the sense that it is necessary for the author to add something of substance in the form of the expression of ideas. Whether or not what the author adds is sufficient may be a question of degree in any given case.

18. The originality that is required concerns the expression of the idea or thought and not the inventiveness of the idea: see *University of London Press* at Ch 608; IPR 190–1. While the required skill or labour necessary for the creation of a literary work in which copyright may subsist is not large, it must not be insubstantial. For example, as a rule, a title does not involve literary composition and is not sufficiently substantial to justify claims of copyright protection. However, that does not mean that in a particular case the title may not be so extensive and of such a significant character as to attract the protection of copyright: see *Francis Day and Hunter Ltd v Twentieth Century Fox Corporation* [1940] AC 112 at 123 ...

22. The Help Words are not a form of literary expression, but a setting down of several simple words in the nature of saying something in ordinary parlance. They are no more than a simple instruction. The Help Words do no more than state the obvious words for use in drawing attention to a taxi driver requiring urgent assistance. They are not words that should be afforded monopoly protection.

23. The Help Words simply indicate a desire to convey the notion that a taxi driver in duress seeks urgent assistance. They do no more than state an idea. The expression is inseparable from the fundamental idea that is being conveyed by the words. When the expression of an idea is inseparable from its function it forms part of the idea and is not entitled to the protection of copyright: see *Autodesk Inc v Dyason* (1992) 173 CLR 330 at 345 ...

24. It would be inappropriate for the Help Words not to be available for use by anybody without the consent of Pacific Technologies, lest infringement occurred by a taxi driver or a passer-by using the words. In all of the circumstances, I consider that copyright under the *Copyright Act* does not subsist in the Help Words.

— 3 —

CRITERIA FOR SUBSISTENCE OF COPYRIGHT

INTRODUCTION

This chapter considers several criteria for the subsistence of copyright under the *Copyright Act 1968* (Cth):

1 the requirement (for Part III works) of originality;
2 the requirement (for Part III works) of a human author;
3 the requirement for copyright subject matter to be fixed in material form (Part III) or 'made' (Part IV); and
4 associated 'country of origin' requirements.

Since copyright only subsists for a limited time period, this chapter also considers the duration of copyright rights. For copyright to subsist material must also fall within one of the categories of protected subject matter, discussed in Chapter 4.

There is no registration requirement for copyright (and, as a result of the *Berne Convention for the Protection of Literary and Artistic Works* (1886), Australia may not seek to introduce registration as a precondition for protection). Protection is automatically conferred on meeting the minimum threshold requirements for subsistence. In this regard copyright is quite different from design, patent and trade mark law, all of which require registration in accordance with set criteria and payment of fees, administered by IP Australia. Creators of efforts that may not meet the legislative criteria for award of these other schemes may try to evoke copyright law if they can claim to fall within the categories of copyright subject matter.

While reading this chapter it is important to remember the distinction, mentioned in Chapter 2, between traditional works of authorship protected under Part III of the Act, and subject matter other than works protected through Part IV of the Act. As we will see, the criteria for subsistence differs between the two parts of the Act.

ORIGINALITY

Under s 32 of the *Copyright Act 1968* (Cth), copyright subsists in 'original' works of authorship. Originality is not just a criterion for subsistence. It is a core concept in copyright, relevant to determining whether infringement has occurred (the originality of what has been copied is relevant in determining whether an alleged infringer has taken 'too much'), and to allocating ownership among competing potential authors.

Originality became a criterion for subsistence in the *Copyright Act 1911* (UK) and the *Copyright Act 1912* (Cth). But the term itself has never been defined in legislation. The concept has a number of possible meanings. 'Original work' could be a reference to the origins of the work; that is, the bare fact of its creation through the labour of the author. On this meaning, a work is original if it has not been copied from anything. Alternatively, confining copyright protection to original works could mean requiring claimants to show novelty or artistic quality, or that the work is the product of investment (of labour, and/or skill, and/or judgment).

Courts in both Australia and the UK were quick to reject the idea that a work had to be novel or inventive in order to be 'original'. This is not surprising, since courts are naturally uncomfortable sitting in judgment over the artistic quality of a work. A commonly cited authority establishing that novelty is not required is *University of London Press Ltd v University Tutorial Press* Ltd [1916] 2 Ch 601, where Peterson J held at 608:

> The word 'original' does not in this connection mean that the work must be the expression of original or inventive thought. Copyright Acts are not concerned with the originality of ideas, but with the expression of thought. But the Act does not require that the expression must be in an original or novel form, but that the work must not be copied from another work—that it should originate from the author.

The rejection of a standard requiring creative or inventive expression was also consistent with the longstanding recognition by the Anglo-Australian courts of proprietary rights in a very wide range of written work, extending beyond works of fiction, poetry and scholarly essays to include useful (but mundane) material such as calendars, directories, almanacs and maps. In Australia, the High Court in *Sands & McDougall Pty Ltd v Robinson* (1917) 23 CLR 49 took a similar approach, determining that the new requirement of originality intended no change to the existing position: the concept of an 'original work' was 'correlative' with that of the 'author'. In that case, a map was sufficiently original as it was created by drawing on the common stock of information, in circumstances where the map's author had applied 'independent intellectual effort' to create a map with distinct differences from existing maps.

Most of the case law is explicit about what 'originality' *does not* involve. It does not require the display of novelty or a particularly high aesthetic or cultural quality. Explaining what is included *in* the category of the 'original' has proved much harder. 'Expressing thought' is required. But how do you know when an expression is sufficient? What kinds of contributions count?

The most difficult cases have involved compilations of fact, especially 'whole of universe' comprehensive collections of fact where extensive effort, but no creativity, judgment or selection is involved in their production. The Full Federal Court decision *Desktop Marketing Systems Pty Ltd v Telstra Corporation Ltd* [2002] FCAFC 112; (2002) 119 FCR 491, extracted below, set a very low threshold of originality: deciding, in effect, that mere labour or investment of effort was sufficient. This is known colloquially as a 'sweat of the brow' standard.

CASE EXTRACT: PRECEDENT

Desktop Marketing Systems Pty Ltd v Telstra Corporation Ltd

[2002] FCAFC 112; (2002) 119 FCR 491
Federal Court of Australia, Full Court

[Desktop Marketing Systems produced searchable marketing and residential directories on CD-ROM using data and categories from Telstra's White and Yellow Pages telephone directories. Telstra sued for copyright infringement, and succeeded at first instance. A question in the case was whether 'industrious collection' was sufficient to establish 'originality'; such that copyright subsisted in comprehensive sets of data like Telstra's telephone directories which exhibited no creativity or judgment in selection or arrangement of the information. The US Supreme Court had held, in *Feist Publications, Inc v Rural Telephone Service Co*, 499 US 340 (1991), that copyright did not subsist in a telephone directory: at least a 'modicum of creativity' (at 362) or some 'minimal creative spark' (at 363) was needed.]

Sackville J: 335. The principal issue in this case concerns the 'innovation threshold' which must be satisfied if a compilation of the names, addresses and telephone numbers of subscribers to a telephone service is to be accorded copyright protection: see S Ricketson, *The Law of Intellectual Property Copyright, Designs and Confidential Information* (2001) at [7.35], citing a comment by Professor James Lahore. The resolution of this issue and the related question of infringement ultimately depends on the proper construction of the *Copyright Act* since, as noted earlier, copyright in Australia cannot subsist otherwise than by virtue of the Act: s 8. It is, however, difficult to approach the task of construction without reference to the older authorities which predate the passage of the first comprehensive copyright legislation, namely the *Copyright Act 1911* (UK) (the '*1911 Act*') declared to operate in Australia, subject to minor modifications, by the *Copyright Act 1912* (Cth) (the '*1912 Act*'). Indeed, the written and oral submissions on the appeal referred to numerous authorities decided both before and after 1911.

336. The earlier authorities may be important, especially if they have been followed or approved in more recent cases based on modern legislation. ...

337. Even so, some caution is necessary when reading the earlier authorities. There are significant differences between the nineteenth century law of copyright and the more modern law. At the time the much-cited case of *Kelly v Morris* (1866) LR 1 Eq 697 was decided (upholding copyright in the 'Post-Office London Directory'), the legislation in the UK made no explicit provision for a literary work to include a compilation. A provision to that effect was first introduced by s 35 of the *1911 Act*. The reasoning in other cases depends, at least in part, on provisions that have no exact counterpart in modern legislation. In *Chilton v Progress Printing and Publishing Co* [1895] 2 Ch 29, for example, the Court of Appeal held that there was no copyright in a list of the plaintiff's selection of horses tipped to win at races to be held in the ensuing week. Lord Halsbury pointed out that the object of the *Literary Copyright Act 1842* (UK), as stated in the preamble, was 'to afford greater encouragement to the production of literary works of lasting benefit to the world'. That object was, in his Lordship's view (at 32), not served by regarding the plaintiff's opinion as to likely winners as a 'literary composition such as intended to be protected by the *Copyright Act*'. The *Copyright Act* currently in force in Australia makes specific provision for copyright in compilations, but has no preamble or statement of objects corresponding to the provisions relied on by Lord Halsbury.

PRECEDENT

338. It is also important to bear in mind that copyright protection extends to many different kinds of work. Each particular category of copyright presents its own issues as to the subsistence and infringement of copyright. It ought not to be assumed that the concepts applicable to one form of copyright work necessarily apply, without modification, to others …

…

340. The Supreme Court of the US pointed out in *Feist* that there is an 'undeniable tension' between the 'fundamental axiom' of copyright law, that no author may have copyright in the facts narrated (*Victoria Park Racing & Recreation Grounds Co Ltd v Taylor* (1937) 58 CLR 479 at 498 per Latham CJ), and the principle, enshrined in statute in Australia as elsewhere, that compilations of facts may be the subject-matter of copyright. The present case provides a nice illustration. Since compilations, consisting exclusively of a record of facts, can be the subject matter of copyright, does it not follow that Telstra should be rewarded for its substantial investment of time and resources by being accorded copyright protection in the directory information recorded in the White Pages and Yellow Pages? And if that protection is to be meaningful, should it not protect Telstra not merely against a competitor who produces more or less identical publications, but also against one who uses Telstra's directory information to create a rather different commercial product? On the other hand, if Telstra is entitled to prevent use of its directory information by a competitor, regardless of whether the final product is structured and presented in the same way as the White Pages and the Yellow Pages, is this not, in effect, conferring copyright protection in respect of facts? …

[Sackville J surveyed the authorities on copyright in compilations then continued:]

404. This survey of the authorities shows that English and Australian courts have long grappled with the special difficulties created by claims of copyright in compilations. Well before legislation accorded compilations express recognition as 'literary works', English and Scottish cases accepted that compilations of factual information, such as directories and catalogues, could be the subject matter of copyright. The underlying rationale, stated in early cases such as *Kelly v Morris* and *Morris v Ashbee* [(1868) 7 LR Eq 34] but repeated in many later cases, was that the compiler should be rewarded for the labour and expense involved in collecting and presenting the information. The first copyright statute, 8 Anne c 19 ([1710]), had included among its objects the encouragement of learning and the prevention of ruin to authors and proprietors of books by unauthorised reprinting and publishing: see the preamble, set out in S Ricketson, *The Law of Intellectual Property* (2001), at par 3.125. The nineteenth century authorities extended the rationale beyond the authors of 'literary' works in the traditional sense to the less creative, but not necessarily less useful endeavours of compilers of factual information.

405. Some of the earlier judgments, reflecting the prevailing enthusiasm to protect the labour and expense of compilers, gave an expansive interpretation to the scope of copyright in compilations. Hence the famous but excessive admonition to the defendant in *Kelly v Morris*, that he was not entitled to take a single line of the plaintiff's directory for the purpose of saving himself labour and trouble in getting his information. Later cases recognised the difficulty of reconciling an admonition in these terms with the principle that the 'law of copyright does not … give any person an exclusive right to state or describe particular facts': *Victoria Park v Taylor* at 498 per Latham CJ.

406. The need to reconcile apparently conflicting imperatives led to two important qualifications or refinements of the approach taken in the early cases. The first was to impose a threshold requirement to be satisfied before the compiler's labour and expense could support copyright in a particular compilation.

Cases such as *Leslie v Young* [*& Sons* [1894] AC 335]; [*GA*] *Cramp* [*& Sons Ltd v Frank Smythson Ltd* [1944] AC 329] and *Victoria Park v Taylor* are illustrations of a compiler's failure to satisfy the threshold requirement. Second, later authorities emphasised the significance of the statutory requirement that, in order to establish infringement, the copyright owner must show that a substantial part of the work has been taken: s 14(1) of the *Copyright Act*. This requirement has become more onerous for the copyright owner in Australia by reason of the High Court's rejection, in *Data Access* [*Corporation*] *v Powerflex* [*Services Pty Ltd* (1999) 202 CLR 1], of the so-called 'but for' test of substantiality and the substitution of a test requiring reference to the originality of that part of the copyright work taken by the alleged infringer.

407. Despite these qualifications, the course of authority in the UK and Australia recognises that originality in a factual compilation may lie in the labour and expense involved in collecting the information recorded in the work, as distinct from the 'creative' exercise of skill or judgment, or the application of intellectual effort. The formulations, for example, of Dixon J in *Victoria Park v Taylor* and of the members of the House of Lords in *Ladbroke* [*(Football) Ltd v William Hill (Football) Ltd* [1964] 1 WLR 27] support this proposition. So too do the authorities which have approved the reasoning in *Blacklock* [*& Co Ltd v C Arthur Pearson Ltd* [1915] 2 Ch 376]. That case is very difficult to interpret except as a decision upholding copyright in a compilation which involved much work and effort in collecting information, but which required no particular judgment or skill. Moreover, much-cited cases such as *Football League* [*Ltd*] *v Littlewoods* [*Pools Ltd* [1959] 1 Ch 637] and *Ladbroke v William Hill* have rejected the view that, in assessing the originality of a compilation, only skill, judgment or labour associated with the presentation of the compilation (as distinct from skill, judgment or labour at an earlier stage) can be taken into account.

...

409. In summary, the authorities support these propositions:

(i) A compilation will ordinarily be an *original* literary work for copyright purposes if the compiler has exercised skill, judgment or knowledge in selecting the material for inclusion in the compilation (as with a collection of commentaries) or in presenting or arranging the material (as with the births and deaths column in *John Fairfax* [*& Sons Pty Ltd v Australian Consolidated Press Ltd* [1960] SR (NSW) 413]).

(ii) In addition, a compilation of factual information will ordinarily be an *original* literary work for copyright purposes if the compiler has undertaken substantial labour or incurred substantial expense in collecting the information recorded in the compilation.

(iii) In order for copyright to subsist in a factual compilation, on the basis of the labour or expense required to collect the information, the compiler must show that the labour or expense exceeds a minimum threshold: *Cramp v Smythson*; *Victoria Park v Taylor*. Various formulations have been advanced to describe the threshold requirement (see *Kalamazoo (Aust) Pty Ltd v Compact Business Systems Pty Ltd* (1985) 84 FLR 101 at 120ff per Thomas J), but it is not necessary to pursue the issue further in this case. In this sense, the question of whether a factual compilation is original is a matter of fact and degree (compare *Ladbroke v William Hill*).

(iv) In assessing whether a factual compilation is an original work, the labour or expense required to collect the information can be taken into account regardless of whether the labour or expense was directly related to the preparation or presentation of the compilation in material form, provided it was for the purpose of producing the compilations: *Football League v Littlewoods*; *Ladbroke v William Hill*.

(v) Copyright in a factual compilation will be infringed only where the alleged infringer takes a substantial part of the copyright work. Substantiality is to be determined by reference to the originality of that part of the work taken by the alleged infringer: *Data Access v Powerflex*. Where originality in a factual compilation is found, in whole or in part, in the compiler's labour or expense required to collect the information, infringement depends on the extent to which the collected information has been appropriated by the alleged infringer. To this extent, too, the issue of infringement may involve matters of fact and degree.

(vi) These principles apply to 'whole of universe' compilations. ...

[Sackville J discussed the decision in *Feist* and continued:]

423. ... [T]he significance of *Feist* for present purposes is whether the reasoning, shorn of issues peculiar to the US, convincingly establishes a 'unitary concept of creative originality for copyright law': JC Ginsburg, 'No "Sweat"? Copyright and Other Protection of Works of Information After *Feist v Rural Telephone*' (1992) 92 *Colum L Rev* 338 at 341. The opinion shows that the concept of 'originality' in copyright law is capable of being understood as incorporating a 'creative spark' requirement. But this is not the only view that can be taken. The English and Australian authorities, to which reference has already been made, demonstrate that the concept of originality can equally be understood as embracing a compilation that is the product of substantial labour or expense, provided that it goes beyond the mere copying of other works. On this approach, originality does not always involve the 'creative spark' identified as essential in *Feist*. This view of originality also accommodates the special characteristics of factual compilations which, by statute, can be the subject matter of copyright.

424. Doubtless there would be good reasons to follow *Feist* in Australia if, from a policy perspective, its approach offers clear advantages over one which protects industrious compilations. The policy question essentially revolves around the means of resolving the tension between providing incentives to produce potentially useful works and encouraging free access to information or 'raw facts'. In an article cited by the Supreme Court in *Feist*, Professor Denicola [in 'Copyright in Collections of Facts: A Theory for the Protection of Nonfiction Literary Works' (1981) 81 *Colum L Rev* 516 at 542] argues in favour of recognising that a

> *particular collection of facts* appearing in a work is *itself* a work of authorship. [Emphasis in original]

Professor Denicola criticises as too limited the 'traditional approach' (later affirmed in *Feist*) which insists on some creativity in the selection or arrangement of data. He argues (at 530) that the:

> effort of authorship can be effectively encouraged and rewarded only by linking the existence and extent of protection to the total labor of production. To focus on the superficial form of the final product to the exclusion of the effort expended in collecting the data presented in the work is to ignore the central contribution of the compiler.

This analysis, of course, reflects the policy considerations informing the nineteenth century authorities on copyright in factual compilations. The danger in refusing copyright protection to an industrious compilation is that a potential compiler will be deprived of the incentive to undertake work that may prove to be of great value. It is doubtless for this reason that the UK, in accordance with the 1996 directive issued by the European Union, has established a separate regime for databases, including a *sui generis* property right called a 'database right', which applies regardless of whether the database is a copyright work: see reg 13 of the *Databases Regulations* (UK); K Garnett, J James and G Davies, *Copinger and Skone James on Copyright* (14th ed, 1999), paras 3-88, 3-96, 180-03ff. (UK law now provides that a database receives protection under the copyright regime only if 'by reason of the selection or arrangement of the contents of the database the database constitutes the author's own intellectual creation': reg 5 of the *Databases Regulations* (UK); s 3A of the *Copyright, Designs and Patents Act 1988* (UK)).

425. Professor Denicola addresses the argument, subsequently given much emphasis by the Supreme Court, that copyright protection for industrious compilations would effectively confer monopoly rights in relation to facts. He argues (at 531) that unfettered access to individual facts would be protected by the requirement of substantial similarity:

> Since it is the collection as a whole that represents the original work of authorship, only copying
> sufficient to produce a substantially similar collection would generate potential liability.

He also argues that the fair use doctrine provides a mechanism to moderate the effect of recognised property interests in collections of data: at 532. In short, he rejects the suggestion that copyright protection for industrious compilations amounts to granting copyright over facts as such. A competitor is free to gather facts from whatever source he or she wishes, so long as the product (in Australian terms) does not reproduce in a material form a substantial part of the compiler's work. It is the collection in respect of which copyright subsists, not the facts collected by the compiler.

...

427. I do not suggest that the policy issues raised by *Feist* and indeed by the present case are easy to resolve. The point is that policy considerations by no means compel the conclusion that the approach in *Feist* should be followed in Australia. The general propositions I have derived from the authorities can be supported by cogent policy arguments.

428. This is not to say that affording copyright protection to the compiler of a factual compilation, who happens to enjoy monopoly privileges that facilitate the making of the compilation, is necessarily a satisfactory state of affairs. This was an issue raised, but not pursued in depth, in the course of argument. It is striking that Telstra in the present case, like Rural in *Feist*, was able, for at least part of the relevant period, to compile the information incorporated into its White Pages by virtue of monopoly powers granted to it by law. (Telstra's position changed from 1 July 1997, when the *Telecommunications Act* came into force and the extent of its monopoly thereafter was not made entirely clear). There may be powerful reasons, in such circumstances, for requiring the owner of copyright in the compilation to submit to a compulsory licensing regime. Such schemes are established by statute in other areas: see, for example, *Copyright Act*, s 108, providing that copyright in a recording is not infringed by a public performance if equitable remuneration is paid. A compulsory licensing regime might appropriately reward the monopolist's labour and expense, yet leave room for innovative competitors who cannot gain access to the basic information required to establish databases of potential commercial value.

429. A court is ill-equipped to undertake the inquiries and make the policy assessments necessary to resolve these issues. The questions are for parliament to consider. In the meantime, Australian

PRECEDENT

law recognises copyright in so-called industrious compilations, even in the case of whole of universe compilations prepared by monopolists.

...

431. The primary judge pointed out that it is necessary, for the purpose of determining whether a work is protected by copyright to look at the work as a whole. As Lord Reid said in *Ladbroke v William Hill* at 277, the correct approach

> is first to determine whether the plaintiffs' work as a whole is 'original' and protected by copyright, and then to inquire whether the part taken by the defendant is substantial.

Given that a compilation may constitute an original literary work if the compiler has undertaken substantial labour or incurred substantial expense in collecting the information recorded in the compilation, there is no difficulty in concluding that the primary judge was correct to hold that Telstra had copyright in the White Pages and Yellow Pages directories.

The High Court of Australia refused special leave to appeal from this decision in *Desktop Marketing Systems Pty Ltd v Telstra Corporation Ltd* [2003] HCATrans 796. The decision appeared to establish 'sweat of the brow' as the standard for originality in Australia. However, the subsequent High Court decision in *IceTV Pty Ltd v Nine Network Australia Pty Ltd* [2009] HCA 14; (2009) 239 CLR 458 only a few years later, extracted next, threw this position into doubt. Although subsistence of copyright was conceded in the case, it was necessary to consider the originality of parts copied from the television program guide in question, in determining whether they constituted a 'substantial part' and hence a copyright infringement. Both judgments made important comments about the nature and standard of originality in the context of subsistence.

CASE EXTRACT: CURRENT LAW

CURRENT LAW

IceTV Pty Ltd v Nine Network Australia Pty Ltd

[2009] HCA 14; (2009) 239 CLR 458
High Court of Australia

[An extract from this case discussing the idea/expression dichotomy, and a detailed statement of key facts, were included in Chapter 2, p 41.]

French CJ, Crennan and Kiefel JJ (some footnotes omitted):

ORIGINALITY IN THE CONTEXT OF SUBSISTENCE OF COPYRIGHT

33. The requirement for copyright subsistence that a literary work be 'original' was first introduced into the *Copyright Act 1911* (Imp), although it had already been recognised at common law. Originality for this purpose requires that the literary work in question *originated* with the author and that it was not merely copied from another work. It is the author or joint authors who bring into existence the work protected by the Act. In that context, originality means that the creation (ie the production) of the work required some independent intellectual effort, but neither literary merit nor novelty or inventiveness as required in patent law.

34. There has been a long held assumption in copyright law that 'authorship' and 'original work' are correlatives; the legislation does not impose double conditions.

ORIGINALITY IN THE CONTEXT OF INFRINGEMENT

35. In this appeal, the question of 'originality' arises not in the context of subsistence, but in the context of infringement, in particular the determination of the quality of the part of the Weekly Schedules (or the Nine Database) alleged to have been reproduced.

36. A Weekly Schedule (and the Nine Database) contains both 'information' and 'creative' material. The material may have been confidential before being provided to the Aggregators or released to the public. For the purposes of copyright law, that confidentiality does not matter. In terms of the distinction between information and creative material, the time and title information is information about Nine's intended future conduct. It is, however, contained within a whole, a collocation (ie the Weekly Schedule or the Nine Database), which also contains creative material such as the synopses of programmes to be broadcast.

37. In *Ladbroke (Football) Ltd v William Hill (Football) Ltd* [[1964] 1 WLR 273 at 293], Lord Pearce spoke of the situation where reproduction of an unoriginal part of an original whole will not be an infringement when he said:

> The reproduction of a part which by itself has no originality will not normally be a substantial part of the copyright and therefore will not be protected. For that which would not attract copyright except by reason of its collocation will, when robbed of that collocation, not be a substantial part of the copyright and therefore the courts will not hold its reproduction to be an infringement. (emphasis added).

This means that where the part reproduced did not originate with the author, so that the author would not have copyright in the part standing alone, the part reproduced will not be a substantial part. Here, however, the predetermination of future broadcasts was done by employees of Nine, at least some of whom may be the authors of the works in suit. For that reason, it cannot be said that the part reproduced did not originate with the author or authors of the works in suit.

38. However, the fact that a part reproduced originates from the author (as here) does not, of itself, mean that it is necessarily a substantial part of the whole work. Originality in the context of infringement has a broader aspect. The point was pursued in *Autodesk Inc v Dyason [No 2]* [(1993) 176 CLR 300] and *Data Access Corporation v Powerflex Services Pty Ltd* [(1999) 202 CLR 1]. In *Autodesk [No 2]*, though the whole of a computer program originated from the author, Mason CJ (in dissent [at 306]) considered that reproducing part of the program containing data may not be reproduction of a substantial part because it: 'may conceivably be akin to the reproduction of the material simpliciter in a table or compilation or the reproduction of something that is itself largely unoriginal.'

39. In *Data Access*, Gleeson CJ, McHugh, Gummow and Hayne JJ approved Mason CJ's view and said that, in the case of a computer program, 'the originality of what was allegedly taken from a computer program must be assessed with respect to the originality with which it expresses [the] algorithmic or logical relationship [between the function desired to be performed by a device and the device] or part thereof' [at 33 [85]] and its 'inherent originality' [at 33–34 [87]]. Their Honours concluded that the 'Reserved Words' under consideration, which were user inputs associated in the program with certain functions, were not a substantial part of the computer program. This was, first,

CURRENT LAW

because the Reserved Words were 'irrelevant to the structure, choice of commands and combination and sequencing of the commands in source code' [at 34 [88]]. Secondly, since the Reserved Words consisted of ordinary English words suggestive of their function or words common in other computer languages (or combinations thereof), 'they d[id] not possess sufficient originality as data to constitute a substantial part of the computer program' [at 34 [92]].

40. These cases direct attention to the degree of originality in the *expression* of the part of the work reproduced. The same point is made in the current edition of *Copinger and Skone James on Copyright* [15th ed (2005)]:

> [T]he more simple or lacking in substantial originality the copyright work, the greater the degree of taking will be needed before the substantial part test is satisfied.

41. The Weekly Schedule (and the Nine Database) as a whole involves orderly arrangement of its various elements and the evidence showed choices were made about what programmes were included or excluded. As a whole, it is an original (ie not copied) collocation of both information and creative material.

42. However, the expression of the time and title information, in respect of each programme, is not a form of expression which requires particular mental effort or exertion. The way in which the information can be conveyed is very limited. Expressing a title of a programme to be broadcast merely requires knowledge of the title, generally bestowed by the producer of the programme rather than by a broadcaster of it. Expressing the time at which a programme is broadcast, for public consumption, can only practically be done in words or figures relating to a twelve or twenty-four hour time cycle for a day. The authors of the Weekly Schedule (or the Nine Database) had little, if any, choice in the particular form of expression adopted, as that expression was essentially dictated by the nature of the information. That expression lacks the requisite originality (in the sense explained) for the part to constitute a substantial part.

43. Counsel for Nine sought to place importance upon the reproduction not only of time and title information in respect of each programme, but also of the chronological arrangement of the time and title information for various programmes. Whether a selection or arrangement of elements constitutes a substantial part of a work depends on the degree of originality of that selection or arrangement. In this case, a chronological arrangement of times at which programmes will be broadcast is obvious and prosaic, and plainly lacks the requisite originality.

44. These considerations lead to the conclusion that the part of the Weekly Schedule (or the Nine Database) alleged to have been reproduced was not a substantial part. Something must be said, then, of the relevance of 'skill and labour' to this question and how it may lead to error.

SKILL AND LABOUR IN THE CONTEXT OF SUBSISTENCE

45. Not every piece of printing or writing which conveys information will be subject to copyright. For a long time, and precisely because compilations often contain facts, it has been commonplace to inquire what skill and labour was required in the preparation of a compilation. That question has arisen in the context of considering whether copyright subsists at all in a compilation as well as being relevant to a later inquiry as to the 'quality' of any material taken from a copyrighted work.

46. In *Feist Publications Inc v Rural Telephone Service Co Inc* [499 US 340 (1991)] the Supreme Court of the United States considered the compatibility of two propositions: first, that compilations of

facts are generally copyrightable, and secondly, that facts were not copyrightable. This case involves the same tension between those two propositions. 'Originality' was a constitutional requirement that was the source of Congress's power to 'secur[e] for limited Times to Authors ... the exclusive Right to their respective Writings'. It was recognised, however, that copyright in a factual compilation is necessarily 'thin' because the standard for originality should not be such that copyright owners have a monopoly on facts or information. Ultimately the decision turned in a significant degree on the view that '[t]he primary objective of copyright is not to reward the labor of authors, but "[t]o promote the Progress of Science and useful Arts"' [at 349]. The exclusion of ideas and information from copyright protection has been codified in the United States.

47. Much has been written about differing standards of originality in the context of the degree or kind of 'skill and labour' said to be required before a work can be considered an 'original' work in which copyright will subsist. 'Industrious collection' or 'sweat of the brow', on the one hand, and 'creativity', on the other, have been treated as antinomies in some sort of mutually exclusive relationship in the mental processes of an author or joint authors. They are, however, kindred aspects of a mental process which produces an object, a literary work, a particular form of expression which copyright protects. A complex compilation or a narrative history will almost certainly require considerable skill and labour, which involve both 'industrious collection' and 'creativity', in the sense of requiring original productive thought to produce the expression, including selection and arrangement, of the material.

48. It may be that too much has been made, in the context of subsistence, of the kind of skill and labour which must be expended by an author for a work to be an 'original' work. The requirement of the Act is only that the work originates with an author or joint authors from some independent intellectual effort. Be that as it may, as noted previously, since the subsistence of copyright need not be considered in this appeal, the relevance of skill and labour to that inquiry need not be considered further.

SKILL AND LABOUR IN THE CONTEXT OF INFRINGEMENT

49. In the context of infringement, in particular the determination of whether a part reproduced is a 'substantial part', a matter often referred to is whether there has been an 'appropriation' of the author's skill and labour. As already noted, both the primary judge and the Full Court adopted that approach in this case. However, it is always necessary to focus on the nature of the skill and labour, and in particular to ask whether it is directed to the originality of the particular form of expression.

...

52. Rewarding skill and labour in respect of compilations without any real consideration of the productive effort directed to coming up with a particular form of expression of information can lead to error. The error is of a kind which might enable copyright law to be employed to achieve anti-competitive behaviour of a sort not contemplated by the balance struck in the Act between the rights of authors and the entitlements of the reading public. The Act mandates an inquiry into the substantiality of the part of the work which is reproduced. A critical question is the degree of originality of the particular form of expression of the part. Consideration of the skill and labour expended by the author of a work may assist in addressing that question: that the creation of a work required skill and labour may indicate that the particular form of expression adopted was highly original. However, focusing on the 'appropriation' of the author's skill and labour must not be allowed to distract from the inquiry mandated by the Act. To put aside the particular form of expression can cause difficulties, as evidenced by *Desktop Marketing Systems Pty Ltd v Telstra Corporation Ltd.*

53. It is not seriously in dispute that skill and labour was expended on producing the Weekly Schedules (and the Nine Database). The evidence disclosed considerable skill and labour involved in programming decisions. There was a contest about whether it mattered if some of the skill and labour expended was directed to business considerations. Plainly, the skill and labour was highly relevant to matters such as advertising revenue. It is not difficult to understand that questions of the timing of particular broadcasts are crucial for advertising revenues. The fact that business considerations inform the decision to adopt a particular form of expression will not necessarily detract from the originality of that form of expression.

54. However, the critical question is whether skill and labour was directed to the particular form of expression of the time and title information, including its chronological arrangement. The skill and labour devoted by Nine's employees to programming decisions was not directed to the originality of the particular form of expression of the time and title information. The level of skill and labour required to express the time and title information was minimal. That is not surprising, given that, as explained above, the particular form of expression of the time and title information is essentially dictated by the nature of that information.

Gummow, Hayne and Heydon JJ also criticised the Full Federal Court's emphasis on the 'misappropriation' of 'Nine's' skill and labour, stating at [132] that this approach was 'a fundamental departure from the text and structure of the Act'. Instead, 'the originality of the compilation being the Weekly Schedule lay not in the provision of time and title information, but in the selection and presentation of that information together with additional programme information and synopses, to produce a composite whole' (at [152]). *Desktop Marketing*, the judgment stated, should be treated 'with particular care' given that there had been no attempt in the case to identify the author or authors of the work in suit (at [134]). In response to an intervener's submission that the Court should affirm, contrary to *Desktop Marketing*, that 'there must be some 'creative spark' or 'exercise of skill and judgment' before a work is sufficiently 'original' for the subsistence of copyright, the justices suggested at [188]:

> It is by no means apparent that the law even before the 1911 Act was to any different effect to that for which the Digital Alliance contends. It may be that the reasoning in *Desktop Marketing* with respect to compilations is out of line with the understanding of copyright law over many years. These reasons explain the need to treat with some caution the emphasis in *Desktop Marketing* upon 'labour and expense' per se and upon misappropriation. However, in the light of the admission of Ice that the Weekly Schedule was an original literary work, this is not an appropriate occasion to take any further the subject of originality in copyright works.

IceTV did not authoritatively rule on the standard of originality for the purposes of subsistence, and, as the extracts above suggest, the two judgments differed on this point.[1]

One common theme between the judgments, however, was the need to focus on identification of the *author* and any *original expression* contributed by that author. We return to authorship below (see 'The author', p 61). Before doing so, it is worth noting references in the French CJ et al judgment to

---

1   Note that only six justices sat in this case.

the importance of an author making 'some independent intellectual effort' in producing an original work (at [33]). Gummow J et al also spoke at [99] about 'sufficient effort of a literary nature' as giving rise to authorship. First instance judges are now treating these phrases as the standard of originality in Australia.[2] With limited case law, however, it is not clear what will be sufficient to constitute 'intellectual' effort or 'sufficient effort of a literary [or musical, or dramatic, or artistic] nature'. Can cases overseas provide any guidance? The difficulty is that the 'innovation threshold' for copyright varies between countries. As noted in the extracts above, the US Supreme Court in *Feist* stated that for copyright to subsist, some 'modicum of creativity' or 'minimal creative spark' was required. In Europe, the Court of Justice in Case C-5/08, *Infopaq International A/S v Danske Dagblades Forening* [2009] ECR I-6569, in considering the scope of the reproduction right under harmonised EU law, held that such a right 'is liable to apply only in relation to a subject-matter which is original in the sense that it is its author's own intellectual creation' (at [37]). *Infopaq* concerned whether 11-word extracts from newspaper articles, when copied by a media monitoring service, were sufficient to constitute copyright infringement. The Court of Justice held:

> 45. Regarding the elements of such works covered by the protection, it should be observed that they consist of words which, considered in isolation, are not as such an intellectual creation of the author who employs them. It is only through the choice, sequence and combination of those words that the author may express his creativity in an original manner and achieve a result which is an intellectual creation.
>
> 46. Words as such do not, therefore, constitute elements covered by the protection.
>
> 47. That being so, given the requirement of a broad interpretation of the scope of the protection ... the possibility may not be ruled out that certain isolated sentences, or even certain parts of sentences in the text in question, may be suitable for conveying to the reader the originality of a publication such as a newspaper article, by communicating to that reader an element which is, in itself, the expression of the intellectual creation of the author of that article ...

In its subsequent decision in Joined Cases C-403/08 and C-429/08, *Football Association Premier League Ltd v QC Leisure and Karen Murphy v Media Protection Services Ltd* [2011] ECR I-9083 the Court of Justice confirmed at [97] that the *Infopaq* standard of 'author's own intellectual creation' is the standard of originality required for copyright to subsist in all works under EU law. What this standard means is elusive. In *Football Association* it was suggested that a spectacle such as a football match would not meet this standard because, being subject to rules of the game, there was 'no room for creative freedom' (at [98]), while in Case C-145/10, *Painer v Standard VerlagsGmbH* [2011] ECR I-12533, involving portrait photography, the Court considered that the making of choices by which the photographer would 'stamp the work created with his "personal touch"' would be sufficient (at [92]).[3] UK courts have had to grapple with the impact of the 'intellectual creation' standard on

---

2   See, for example, *Sports Data Pty Ltd v Sports Australia Pty Ltd* [2014] FCA 595; (2014) 107 IPR 1 at [76]; *QS Holdings SARL v Paul's Retail Pty Ltd* [2011] FCA 853; (2011) 92 IPR 460 at [63], [68]; *Dynamic Supplies Pty Ltd v Tonnex International Pty Ltd* [2011] FCA 362; (2011) 91 IPR 488 at [49]. See also, in obiter, *EMI Songs Australia Pty Ltd v Larrikin Music Publishing Pty Ltd* [2011] FCAFC 47; (2011) 191 FCR 444 at [55], [263].

3   For discussion, see A Rahmatian, 'Originality in UK Copyright Law: The Old "Skill and Labour" Doctrine under Pressure' (2013) 44 *International Review of Intellectual Property and Competition Law* 4.

older UK cases which emphasised the 'skill and labour' of the author. In *The Newspaper Licensing Agency Ltd v Meltwater Holding BV* [2010] EWHC 3099 (Ch); [2011] RPC 7, Proudman J held at [81] that the test of quality had been 're-stated but [for the purposes of that case] not significantly altered by *Infopaq*'. The headlines in that case were original where they 'demonstrate[d] the stamp of individuality reflecting of the creation of the author or authors of the article' (at [83]). Many of the relevant headlines and extracts did express the author's intellectual creation, in that they were not mere commonplace arrangements of words: they provided the tone of the article, and drew the reader in to the work as a whole. In *SAS Institute v World Programming Ltd* [2013] EWCA Civ 1482; [2014] RPC 8, Lewison LJ stated for the Court of Appeal at [31] that:

> the essence of the term ['intellectual creation'] is that the person in question has exercised expressive and creative choices in producing the work. The more restricted the choices, the less likely it is that the product will be the intellectual creation (or the expression of the intellectual creation) of the person who produced it.

The Canadian Supreme Court has used language to describe the standard of originality similar to that of the High Court in *IceTV*, in the extract below.

CASE EXTRACT: COMPARATIVE LAW

CCH Canadian Ltd v Law Society of Upper Canada

[2004] 1 SCR 339
Supreme Court of Canada

[CCH published law reports and other legal materials. In these proceedings they alleged that a photocopy-on-demand service, offered by a research and reference library operated by the Law Society of Upper Canada, infringed copyright in their copyright works, namely headnotes, case summaries, topical indexes and compilations of reported judicial decisions. One issue in the case was subsistence of copyright in the pleaded works.]

McLachlin CJ (delivering the judgment of the Court): 15. There are competing views on the meaning of 'original' in copyright law. Some courts have found that a work that originates from an author and is more than a mere copy of a work is sufficient to ground copyright. See, for example, *University of London Press Ltd v University Tutorial Press Ltd* [1916] 2 Ch 601; *U & R Tax Services Ltd v H & R Block Canada Inc* (1995) 62 CPR (3d) 257 (FCTD). This approach is consistent with the 'sweat of the brow' or 'industriousness' standard of originality, which is premised on a natural rights or Lockean theory of 'just desserts', namely that an author deserves to have his or her efforts in producing a work rewarded. Other courts have required that a work must be creative to be 'original' and thus protected by copyright. See, for example, *Feist Publications Inc v Rural Telephone Service Co*, 499 US 340 (1991); *Tele-Direct (Publications) Inc v American Business Information, Inc* [1998] 2 FC 22 (CA). This approach is also consistent with a natural rights theory of property law; however it is less absolute in that only those works that are the product of creativity will be rewarded with copyright protection. It has been suggested that the 'creativity' approach to originality helps ensure that copyright protection only extends to the expression of ideas as opposed to the underlying ideas or facts. See *Feist, supra*, at p 353.

16. I conclude that the correct position falls between these extremes. For a work to be 'original' within the meaning of the *Copyright Act*, it must be more than a mere copy of another work. At the same time, it need not be creative, in the sense of being novel or unique. What is required to attract copyright protection in the expression of an idea is an exercise of skill and judgment. By skill, I mean the use of one's knowledge, developed aptitude or practised ability in producing the work. By judgment, I mean the use of one's capacity for discernment or ability to form an opinion or evaluation by comparing different possible options in producing the work. This exercise of skill and judgment will necessarily involve intellectual effort. The exercise of skill and judgment required to produce the work must not be so trivial that it could be characterized as a purely mechanical exercise. For example, any skill and judgment that might be involved in simply changing the font of a work to produce 'another' work would be too trivial to merit copyright protection as an 'original' work.

...

36. In summary, the headnotes, case summary, topical index and compilation of reported judicial decisions are all works that have originated from their authors and are not mere copies. They are the product of the exercise of skill and judgment that is not trivial. As such, they are all 'original' works in which copyright subsists ...

ORIGINALITY, 'SLAVISH COPYING' AND PHOTOGRAPHS

Courts frequently state that originality does not arise where a work has been 'slavishly copied' from another, even if significant skill and effort has been expended in producing the copy. Small changes during the copying will, however, often be sufficient to confer a 'fresh copyright'. This issue was considered by the Federal Court of Australia in *Interlego AG v Croner Trading Pty Ltd* (1993) 25 IPR 65. That case concerned drawings of Lego and Duplo toy bricks. In producing the drawing used as a representative example, a Lego employee had sat down with an earlier drawing of a Lego brick and copied it, using a different scale and making some small changes to the appearance of the brick in the drawing. The process had taken between half a day and two days for each drawing. The trial judge concluded that the new drawings were not original, being copies with only small changes. This ruling was overturned on appeal, with Gummow J noting the 'great skill' involved, and that the changes were sufficient to make the new drawings 'visually distinctive'.

Similar questions about originality have also arisen in relation to photographs. Although photographs are specifically listed as 'artistic works' in s 10(1) of the *Copyright Act*, and s 10(1) further identifies the 'author' of a photograph as 'the person who took the photograph',[4] courts have considered whether a photograph is sometimes 'just a copy'.

---

4   Cf *Nottage v Jackson* (1883) 11 QBD 627 at 632: 'It is difficult to say who is the author of the photograph. Neither of them make the picture because, after all, that is done by the sun'.

CASE EXTRACT: COMPARATIVE LAW

Antiquesportfolio.com Plc v Rodney Fitch & Co Ltd

[2001] FSR 345
High Court of England and Wales, Chancery Division

Neuberger J (at 352–354): [T]he real issue between the parties is the extent to which a photograph of a single static item, such as a jug or candelabra or sofa, can be said to be protected by copyright. That is a point which is not entirely easy and appears to be free of direct authority ...

The Claimant in this case has to contend that a photograph is an 'original ... artistic work'; and, if not every photograph is within that definition, that the circumstances in which these photographs were taken were such that they were, or at least may have been, within that definition.

In Laddie, Prescott and Vitoria, on the *Modern Law of Copyright and Designs* (2nd ed, 1995), one finds this at para 3.56:

> Originality presupposes the exercise of substantial independence, skill, labour, judgment and so forth. For this reason it is submitted that a person makes a photograph merely by placing a drawing or painting on the glass of a photocopying machine and pressing the button gets no copyright at all ... It will be evident that in photography there is room for originality in three respects. First, there may be originality which does not depend on creation of the scene or object to be photographed, or anything remarkable about its capture, and which resides in such specialities as angle of shot, light and shade, exposure, effects achieved by means of filters, developing techniques ... Secondly, there may be creation of the scene or subject to be photographed ... Thirdly, a person may create a worthwhile photograph by being at the right place at the right time. Here his merit consists of capturing and recording a scene unlikely to recur ...

The problem is also considered in *Copinger and Skone James on Copyright* (14th ed, 1999). At para 3.104 there is this:

> In terms of what is original, for the purpose of determining whether copyright subsists in a photograph, the requirement of originality is low, and may be satisfied by little more than the opportunistic pointing of the camera and the pressing of the shutter button. There seems no reason of principle why there should be any distinction between the photograph which is the result of such a process and a photograph which is intended to reproduce a work of art, such as a painting or another photograph. Provided that the author can demonstrate that he expended some small degree of time, skill and labour in producing the photograph, (which may be demonstrated by the exercise of judgment as to such matters as the angle from which to take the photograph, the lighting, the correct film speed, what filter to use, et cetera) the photograph ought to be entitled to copyright protection, irrespective of its subject matter. What is the extent of protection afforded by the copyright in a photograph is a different matter.

I have also been referred to a United States work on the subject, *Nimmer on Copyright*, where there is this at paragraph 2.130:

> Any, or (as will be indicated below) almost any, photograph may claim the necessary originality to support a copyright merely by virtue of the photographer's personal choice of subject matter,

angle of photograph, lighting and determination of the precise time when the photograph is to be taken.

Two exceptional situations are dealt with a little later.

> The first such situation will arise where a photograph or other printed matter is made that amounts to nothing more than a slavish copying. If no originality can be claimed in making an additional print from a photographic negative, there should be no finding of a greater originality where the same effect is achieved by photographing a print rather than printing a negative. In neither case is a distinguishable variation reproduced ... The other situation in which copyright may be denied to a photograph of lack of originality arises where the photographer in choosing a subject matter, camera angle, lighting, et cetera, copies and attempts to duplicate all of such elements as contained in a prior photograph. Here the second photographer has been photographing a live subject rather than the first photograph; but, in so far as the original elements contained in the first photograph are concerned, there is no meaningful distinction.

In my judgment, the views expressed in the two latter works represent the law of England. The only possible difference between the view in the two latter works and that in Laddie, Prescott and Vitoria, might be said to arise in the case of a purely representational photograph of a two-dimensional object such as a photograph or a painting.

In such a case, a United States court, which concluded that the English law, in particular the 1988 Act, applied in a particular case, held that there would be no copyright under the 1988 Act in relation to such a photograph—see *Bridgeman Art Library Ltd v Correll Corporation* at 25 Fed Supp 2d 421 per District Judge Kaplan at 426 to 428.

However, as is suggested in *Nimmer*, it may well be that, if the photographer in such a case could show that he had in fact used some degree of skill and care in taking the photograph, he could claim originality in, and, therefore, intellectual property rights in respect of, such a photograph. That is not a point I need to decide.

In the case of photographs of a three-dimensional object, with which I am concerned in the present case, it can be said that the positioning of the object (unless it is a sphere), the angle at which it is taken, the lighting and the focus, and matters such as that, could all be matters of aesthetic or even commercial judgment, albeit in most cases at a very basic level.

Further, the instant photographs appear to have been taken with a view to exhibiting particular qualities, including the colour (in the case of some items), their features (eg the glaze in pottery) and, in the case of almost all the items, the details. It may well be that, in those circumstances, some degree of skill was involved in the lighting, angling and judging the positioning.

It may also be relevant that the photographer chose the particular item in order to find a typical example of a certain type of artefact, or a particularly fine example of a certain type of artefact, and that may be a relevant factor.

English authority is not much of assistance here. Both parties relied on *Bauman v Fussell*, decided in 1953 but only reported at 1978 RPC, but, to my mind, that case was concerned with whether a substantial part of a particular photograph had been reproduced—see the discussion in Laddie, Prescott and Vitoria at para 3.59. If anything of relevance to the question of copyright in the present case can be gained from the judgments in that case, it appears to me that all three judgments in the

Court of Appeal proceeded on the assumption that a wholesale lifting of a photograph would be a breach of copyright.

…

In my judgment, therefore, copyright does exist in the photographs.

THE AUTHOR

The High Court judgment in *IceTV* highlighted the importance of identifying both the particular expression in which copyright is claimed, and the author responsible for that expression. Owing to its literary heritage, the *Copyright Act 1968* (Cth) uses the generic term 'author' in s 32 as the term for identifying the creator of all (Part III) copyright works—literary, dramatic, artistic or musical. Sound recordings, films, broadcasts and published editions (subject matter other than works protected under Part IV of the Act) do not have 'authors', but rather have 'makers'. This is discussed further under 'Material form' below, p 73.

HUMAN AUTHORS

Identifying the author is rarely a difficult legal issue. Authorship, as a matter of law, is usually apparent from the conditions of the production of the manuscript and the application of the material form requirement. A rare exception, where the conditions of authorship were disputed, was a rather astonishing case: *Cummins v Bond* [1927] 1 Ch 167, extracted below. The sincere desire of both plaintiff, Miss Cummins (a spiritualist medium), and defendant, Mr Bond (her client), was to attribute authorship of the work to someone other than a living human. In the period following the First World War there was a strong interest in spiritualism, possibly related to the multitudes affected by personal losses arising from that conflict where the location of loved ones was not known. Cummins was a highly regarded and experienced medium, whose talent for automatic writing had been scrutinised by researchers of psychic phenomena. As well as reflecting her—and others'— beliefs in her ability, the reluctance to attribute human authorship to the resultant work perhaps also reflects the religious nature of the writings in issue. The notion of allowing copyright in religious writing was once quite controversial.

CASE EXTRACT: PRECEDENT

PRECEDENT

Cummins v Bond

[1927] 1 Ch 167
High Court of England and Wales, Chancery Division

Eve J (at 172–175): The issue in this action is reduced to the simple question who, if any one, is the owner of the copyright in this work. Prima facie it is the author, and so far as this world is concerned there can be no doubt who is the author here, for it has been abundantly proved that the plaintiff is the writer of every word to be found in this bundle of original script. But the plaintiff and her witness and the defendant are all of opinion—and I do not doubt that the opinion is an honest one—that the true originator of all that is to be found in these documents is some being no longer inhabiting this world, and who has been out of it for a length of time sufficient to justify the hope that he has no reasons for wishing to return to it.

According to the case put forward by those entertaining the opinion I have referred to the individual in question is particularly desirous of assisting in further discoveries relating to the ancient Abbey of Glastonbury, and he chooses the Brompton Road as the locality in which, and the plaintiff as the medium through whom, his views as to further works to be undertaken on the site of the Abbey shall be communicated to the persons engaged in the work of excavation. He is sufficiently considerate not to do so in language so antiquated as not to be understood by the excavators and others engaged in the interesting operations, but in order not to appear of too modern an epoch he selects a medium capable of translating his messages into language appropriate to a period some sixteen or seventeen centuries after his death. I am not impugning the honesty of persons who believe, and of the parties to this action who say that they believe, that this long departed being is the true source from which the contents of these documents emanate; but I think I have stated enough with regard to the antiquity of the source and the language in which the communications are written to indicate that they could not have reached us in this form without the active co-operation of some agent competent to translate them from the language in which they were communicated to her into something more intelligible to persons of the present day. The plaintiff claims to be this agent and to possess, and the defendant admits that she does possess, some qualification enabling her, when in a more or less unconscious condition, to reproduce in language understandable by those who have the time and inclination to read it, information supplied to her from the source referred to in language with which the plaintiff has no acquaintance when fully awake.

From this it would almost seem as though the individual who has been dead and buried for some 1900 odd years and the plaintiff ought to be regarded as the joint authors and owners of the copyright, but inasmuch as I do not feel myself competent to make any declaration in his favour, and recognizing as I do that I have no jurisdiction extending to the sphere in which he moves, I think I ought to confine myself when inquiring who is the author to individuals who were alive when the work first came into existence and to conditions which the legislature in 1911 may reasonably be presumed to have contemplated. So doing it would seem to be clear that the authorship rests with this lady, to whose gift of extremely rapid writing coupled with a peculiar ability to reproduce in archaic English matter communicated to her in some unknown tongue we owe the production of these documents. But the defendant disputes the plaintiff's right to be considered the sole author, alleging that he was an element and a necessary element in the production, and claiming, if the authorship is to be confined to persons resident in this world, that he is entitled to the rights incident to authorship jointly with the plaintiff.

.... His claim to be considered a joint author is suggestive of an hallucination, for it is based upon the assertion that by his presence at the seances where the writing took place he in some way transmitted from his brain to the unconscious brain of the medium the classical and historical references which are to be found in these documents. He frankly admits that he does not appreciate how it was done, or to what extent he did it; but he has evidently brought himself to believe that he did contribute materially to the composition of the work and that his contribution was made by means of some silent transfer from his brain to that of the unconscious medium of phrases and allusions with which he was familiar but of which she knew nothing. But inasmuch as the medium is credited

PRECEDENT

with a power to translate language of which she knew nothing into archaic English, of which she was almost equally ignorant, and at a phenomenal pace, it does not appear necessary to fall back on the defendant's presence in order to explain the classical and historical references which he maintains must have emanated from his brain. They may well have originated in the brain of the medium herself. In these circumstances I am quite unable to hold that the defendant has made out any case entitling him to be treated as a joint author. I think he is labouring under a complete delusion in thinking that he in any way contributed to the production of these documents.

Alternatively failing to establish any claim on his own behalf he submits that there is no copyright in the work at all, that it has come from a far off locality which I cannot specify, and that the plaintiff is the mere conduit pipe by which it has been conveyed to this world. I do not think that is a fair appreciation of the plaintiff's activities, they obviously involved a great deal more than mere repetition; but, apart altogether from these considerations, the conclusion which the defendant invites me to come to in this submission involves the expression of an opinion I am not prepared to make, that the authorship and copyright rest with some one already domiciled on the other side of the inevitable river. That is a matter I must leave for solution by others more competent to decide it than I am. I can only look upon the matter as a terrestrial one, of the earth earthy, and I propose to deal with it on that footing. In my opinion the plaintiff has made out her case, and the copyright rests with her.

A more important scenario in which identifying an 'author' has become decisive in determining copyright subsistence relates to works wholly, or partially, generated through automated processes. *IceTV*'s emphasis on human authorship, as seen in the extract below, has rendered subsistence of such works uncertain under Australian law.

CASE EXTRACT: CURRENT LAW

CURRENT LAW

IceTV Pty Ltd v Nine Network Australia Pty Ltd

[2009] HCA 14; (2009) 239 CLR 458
High Court of Australia

[An extract from this case and a detailed statement of key facts were included in Chapter 2, p 41. A further extract appears above, p 51.]

French CJ, Crennan and Kiefel JJ (some footnotes omitted): 22. The 'author' of a literary work and the concept of 'authorship' are central to the statutory protection given by copyright legislation, including the Act.

23. Undoubtedly, the classical notion of an individual author was linked to the invention of printing and the technical possibilities thereafter for the production of texts otherwise than by collective efforts, such as those made in mediaeval monasteries. The technological developments of today throw up new challenges in relation to the paradigm of an individual author. A 'work of joint authorship', as recognised under the Act, requires that the literary work in question 'has been produced by the collaboration of two or more authors and in which the contribution of each author is not separate from the contribution of

the other author or the contributions of the other authors'. As in other cases where the facts resemble those under consideration here, the Weekly Schedules (and the Nine Database) were the result of both a collaborative effort and an evolutionary process of development, involving in this instance both manpower and the use of computers. However, nothing in these reasons turns on any conclusion as to the precise identity of the author or authors of those works.

24. In assessing the centrality of an author and authorship to the overall scheme of the Act, it is worth recollecting the longstanding theoretical underpinnings of copyright legislation. Copyright legislation strikes a balance of competing interests and competing policy considerations. Relevantly, it is concerned with rewarding authors of original literary works with commercial benefits having regard to the fact that literary works in turn benefit the reading public.

...

26. Whilst judicial and academic writers may differ on the precise nature of the balance struck in copyright legislation in different places, there can be no doubt that copyright is given in respect of 'the particular form of expression in which an author convey[s] ideas or information to the world.'

Gummow, Hayne and Heydon JJ: 95. Something should be said respecting two fundamental principles of copyright law and their treatment in the course of the litigation. The concession by Ice of the subsistence of copyright in the Weekly Schedule appears to have distracted attention from the necessary part these principles must play in any resolution of the dispute between the parties.

96. The first principle concerns the significance of 'authorship'. The subject matter of the Act now extends well beyond the traditional categories of original works of authorship, but the essential source of original works remains the activities of authors. While, by assignment or by other operation of law, a party other than the author may be owner of the copyright from time to time, original works emanate from authors. So it was that in *Victoria Park Racing and Recreation Grounds Co Ltd v Taylor* [(1937) 58 CLR 479 at 510], Dixon J observed:

> Perhaps from the facts a presumption arises that the plaintiff company is the owner of the copyright but, as corporations must enlist human agencies to compose literary, dramatic, musical and artistic works, it cannot found its title on authorship. No proof was offered that the author or authors was or were in the employment of the company under a contract of service and that the book was compiled or written in the course of such employment.

97. Key provisions of Pt III of the Act fix on 'the author'. Examples include the requirement for the author of unpublished works to be a 'qualified person' for copyright to subsist (s 32(1)), the fixing of copyright duration by reference to the death of the author (s 33), and the conferral of copyright upon the author subject to the terms of employment or contractual arrangements under which the author labours (s 35) ...

98. Like the *Copyright Act 1956* (UK) ('the 1956 Act') in its original form, the Act does not define the term 'author' beyond the statement that in relation to a photograph it is the person who took that photograph. As a result of changes made by the 1988 UK Act, in relation to a work 'author' means the person 'who creates it'; in the case of a 'computer-generated' work this is taken to be 'the person by whom the arrangements necessary for the creation of the work are undertaken'. No such provision is made in the Australian statute, but the notion of 'creation' conveys the earlier understanding of an 'author' as 'the person who brings the copyright work into existence in its material form'.

99. Where a literary work is brought into such existence by the efforts of more than one individual, it will be a question of fact and degree which one or more of them have expended sufficient effort of a literary nature to be considered an author of that work within the meaning of the Act. If the work be protected as a 'compilation', the author or authors will be those who gather or organise the collection of material and who select, order or arrange its fixation in material form. May there be joint authors of the one original work, rather than several authors each of a distinct work?

100. While the Act speaks of 'the author', the Act affords protection to works of joint authorship by force of Div 9 of Pt III (ss 78-83). The expression 'work of joint authorship' means (s 10(1)):

> a work that has been produced by the collaboration of two or more authors and in which the contribution of each author is not separate from the contribution of the other author or the contributions of the other authors.

101. In the present case, the primary judge and the Full Court each recorded in their reasons that there was no dispute that 'the authors' of the Weekly Schedule were 'qualified persons'. However, neither at trial nor in the Full Court was there any finding of the identity of those persons or any finding that the Weekly Schedule was a 'work of joint authorship' within the meaning of the Act.

The significance of identifying authors, and authorship, in order to ground subsistence of copyright arose in the subsequent case of *Telstra Corporation Ltd v Phone Directories Co Pty Ltd* [2010] FCAFC 149; (2010) 194 FCR 142 (below). This case appeared to raise the question whether *Desktop Marketing* was still good law following the High Court's decision in *IceTV*, by asking whether copyright subsisted in telephone directories as original works. The case is one of several which has explored the implications of *IceTV* for computer-generated works. Others include *Acohs Pty Ltd v Ucorp Pty Ltd* [2012] FCAFC 16; (2012) 201 FCR 173 and *Dynamic Supplies Pty Ltd v Tonnex International Pty Ltd* [2011] FCA 362; (2011) 91 IPR 488.[5]

CASE EXTRACT: CURRENT LAW

Telstra Corporation Ltd v Phone Directories Co Pty Ltd

[2010] FCAFC 149; (2010) 194 FCR 142
Federal Court of Australia, Full Court

[The case concerned whether copyright subsisted under s 32 in two kinds of telephone directory published by Telstra through its subsidiary Sensis: the *White Pages Directory* (WPD) and *Yellow Pages Directory* (YPD). Each WPD and YPD listed the names, addresses, telephone numbers and other information in relation to residential or business customers for a particular geographic area. Numerous individuals contributed to work preparatory to each phone directory, which was managed by a database of a computer system known as the Genesis Computer System. There was no claim to infringement

---

5   The cases are discussed in J McCutcheon, 'The Vanishing Author in Computer-Generated Works: A Critical Analysis of Recent Australian Cases' (2013) 36 *Melbourne University Law Review* 915.

in Genesis or the database per se. The claim was to infringement of the final, published
directories. The production process for the directories consisted, broadly, of three key phases:

1   Collection Phase: This involved the maintenance, updating and editing of the data in the
database. Sensis employees created initial listing records, updated information, and dealt with
customers to determine the features of the listing desired—checking listings and verifying
information prior to publication.

2   The Book Extract Phase: This was where a software routine was run over the Genesis database
to generate an electronic file containing all the listings to appear in the designated directory, in
order (and, in the case of the YPD, the Headings which had listings attached). This file was then
used (again by running it through software) to create an automatic, electronic proof of the directory
known as the galley file. The galley file contained all the listings, and in-column advertisements, in
the format and sequence in which they would appear in the directory, but without certain 'display
advertisements'. The galley file would be manually checked and late changes would be incorporated
by employees.

3   The Book Production Phase: This involved automated pagination (determining the final structure and
number of pages) and typesetting (involving automated incorporation of display advertisements),
followed by manual checking and editing by employees.

Every stage of this production process was controlled by 'the Rules': a set of prescriptive guidelines that
controlled, dictated, restricted and/or prohibited the content and presentation of listings in the WPD and
YPD. The Rules regulated the font, the proper abbreviations, colour schemes, spacing between words
and entries, and the acceptability of particular words or phrases. The Rules were directly automated,
in that information could only be entered in the Genesis system in a form compliant with the Rules,
and the Rules were written into the software routines that created the Book Extract and galley file, and
undertook pagination and typesetting. The Rules were also applied by human intervention during the
production process at each stage of manual checking and editing. The whole process was engineered
to ensure that decisions violating the Rules were as rare as possible.]

Keane CJ: 89. The compilation of the directories was overwhelmingly the work of the Genesis Computer
System or its predecessors. The selection of data and its arrangement in the form presented in each
directory occurred only at 'the book extract' or 'book production' process. The compilations which
emerged from the operation of the computer system do not originate from an individual or group of
individuals. Indeed, none of the individuals who contributed to the production of the directories had any
conception of the actual form in which they were finally expressed.

90. In my respectful opinion, the decision of the trial judge [that copyright did not subsist] must be
upheld on the basis that the findings of primary fact made by her Honour establish that the WPDs and
YPDs are not compiled by individuals but by the automated processes of the Genesis Computer System
or its predecessors. That being so, it is neither necessary nor relevant to seek to come to a conclusion
as to the sufficiency of the intellectual effort deployed by those individuals who provide data input into
the computerised database. Their activities are not part of the activity of compilation: they do not select,
arrange and present that data in the form in which it is published.

. . .

Perram J: ...

RELEVANCE OF SKILL AND LABOUR NOT DIRECTED TO THE CREATION OF THE MATERIAL FORM

101. ... The information in the directories was collected through processes which I would accept involved human industry and the results of which were stored in a substantial and sophisticated database. However, the creation of the material form of the directories was carried out by a computer program overseen by persons who had no substantive input into those forms. The questions which arise are, therefore, two. *First*, granted that there must be independent intellectual effort or sufficient effort of a literary nature, is that effort required to be directed at the creation of the material form of the work (here the form of the directories) or does it suffice that the effort was directed at some anterior activity (here the collection of information presented in the directories)? *Secondly*, if the intellectual effort must be directed at the creation of the material form of the directories, was there sufficient human effort involved in that process in this case to mean that the directories were reduced to a material form by an author or authors?

102. Those questions inevitably necessitate an appreciation of just how these telephone directories were composed. The learned primary judge was burdened by a great weight of evidence about the manner in which two of the directories were created (and those two directories served as representative examples for a larger number of other directories). Her Honour considered all of this body of material and made detailed findings of fact none of which were challenged before this Court. At the risk of oversimplification there were, in effect, three processes involved. The first involved the maintenance, updating and editing of a database containing customer details (the Collection Phase). The second involved the extraction from that database of information for each directory and the sublimation of that information into an electronic form which constituted substantially the form of the ensuing directory (the Extraction Phase). The third process involved the typesetting of that form and the physical production of the directories (the Production Phase). One may, I think, dispense with the Production Phase at the outset. There will be cases where the layout of a document is, in fact, itself a literary work. One well-known example of the truth of that proposition is afforded by the example of the football coupons in *Ladbroke (Football) Ltd v William Hill (Football) Ltd* [1964] 1 WLR 273. However, in such cases, originality in the layout must be evidenced and this will require the demonstration of some independent intellectual effort or sufficient effort of a literary nature. I do not think that the organisation of the pages of a telephone directory exhibits activity of that kind. There may be cases where the typesetting of one literary work involves the creation of another (the layout of a newspaper may be one example). However, the layout of a telephone directory is essentially dictated by the material form of the work being printed.

103. I would accept, however, that there was intellectual effort at the Collection Phase. The evidence showed that the business structure of the appellant Sensis (which was responsible for the production of the directories) was complex and that a significant number of employees worked away on a daily basis updating the very many entries in the directory. Many others were involved in quality control. Some of this work was ministerial; other parts of it involved seeking to persuade customers to enlarge or embellish their entries. What was involved was the full panoply of activities which one might expect to attend the collection and maintenance of customer information for telephone directories prepared for a country of twenty or so million people. Much of this activity, but by no means all of it, was automated. Computers and databases were ever-present but on no view would the Collection Phase have been able to proceed without the involvement of significant human activity.

104. The question then is whether that human industry is relevant to the issue of the directories' originality. I think the answer to that question is that it is not. Whatever else might be said of the kind of efforts required of an author, they must be efforts which result in the material form of the work. The important creative steps which involve the fashioning of the ideas on which a literary work's ultimate form rests are not actions which the Act counts as authorial and this is because what is protected by the copyright monopoly is the form of a work and not the ideas which presage or prefigure it. And this is so even if those ideas can plainly be discerned in the fabric of the material form. The travels reduced to a touring guide, the toils in the library underpinning a substantive work of history and the life led which finally results in an autobiography are not authorial activities however essential they might be to the creation of the work in question. No doubt the quality of many literary works will be much enhanced if their form reflects ideas of sophistication or merit but those ideas go not to the work's originality for copyright purposes save only to the limited extent that they show that the work is not copied from elsewhere. Much skill and hard work—'sweat of the brow'—may be involved in the steps preparatory to the making of the material form of a work but those labours are not what is protected by copyright and are relevant only to show that the work is not copied.

105. That is not, however, to put at nought such ideas but only to emphasise that the skill and labour in a copyright context must always be fixed upon the creation of forms and not ideas: 'The essence of literary copyright is proprietary protection (in the form of exclusive rights to do acts restricted by the copyright in the work) for a literary work in recognition of the investment of effort, time and skill *in reducing it into material form*, such as words, signs and symbols': *Baigent v Random House Group Ltd* (2007) 72 IPR 195 at [141] per Mummery LJ, cited with approval in *IceTV* at [49] per French CJ, Crennan and Kiefel JJ (my emphasis). Subject to one matter, the same perspective on the connexion between authorship and reduction into material form may be observed in the reasons of Gummow, Hayne and Heydon JJ in *IceTV* who thought (at [98]) that the word 'author' conveyed the notion of 'the person who brings the copyright work into existence in its material form'.

...

112. Once one accepts that the focus of the copyright is on the creation of the material form by an author it is analytically difficult to identify any role for labour or skill in the collection of material beyond the question posed by the statute, namely, whether the work is 'original' in the sense of not being copied from elsewhere. Any role for skill and labour in the process of collection which extends beyond that is inconsistent with the emphasis given in *IceTV* to the reduction of a work into a material form. It follows that, beyond showing that the directories were original in the sense of not having been copied, the activities in the Collection Phase are not relevant to assessing whether those who reduced the directories to material form did so with sufficient independent intellectual or literary effort. To the extent that *Desktop* requires a contrary conclusion it should be overruled. It is inconsistent with considered dicta of a majority of the High Court which bind this Court: *Farah Constructions Pty Ltd v Say-Dee Pty Ltd* (2007) 230 CLR 89 at [134] per the Court.

AUTHORSHIP AND COMPUTERS

113. Who were the people who reduced these directories to their material form? Material form matters because a work is made when it is first reduced to writing or 'some other material form' (s 22(1) of the Act). Further, 'material form' by s 10 includes 'any form (whether visible or not) of storage of the work

CURRENT LAW

...' which, plainly enough, will cover the situation where a work is first assembled as a computer file. In this case, there is no doubt that the directories first took on a material form when a computer file known as the 'galley file' was generated which contained the full listing as it would appear for each directory (without the art work). This occurred as a result of the Extraction Phase. I have no doubt if the galley file (or some physical analogue of it) had been generated by humans this would have meant that the directories were original works. Since the Act stipulates that compilations are literary works it follows generally that those who reduce a compilation to material form are likely to be its authors provided there is sufficient intellectual or literary effort involved in the process of reduction. In this case, the putting together of each directory required the application of a large number of internal house rules, the extraction of relevant customer entries from a much larger database of all customers and the sorting into relevant formats. The work involved might not be regarded as highly creative but that is not the test, particularly where the literary effort required must be that which attends the creation of a compilation rather than, for example, a novel or a history. Had the tasks been attended to manually an original work would have ensued.

114. The difficulty in this case is not that the efforts which might have gone into the production of the galley file could not be sufficient acts of an appropriate quality to count as acts of authorship. Rather, the difficulty is that those tasks were not carried out by humans but by computer programs. The trial judge found—and it is not disputed—that the production of the galley file was almost entirely automated. There were some minor aspects of checking which subsequently occurred after the production of the galley file but even these too were largely automated.

...

117. There is, no doubt, that if any humans can be said to have reduced these directories to material form it is Messrs Vormwald and Cooper [two employees who ran the Book Extract routine]. It is correct to say that they were in control of the software. But that control did not involve Mr Vormwald or Mr Cooper in shaping or guiding the material form of the directories. They were not using the software, as perhaps a novelist uses a word processor, to give form to an idea already conceived. Instead, they were giving instructions at the very highest level about the principal parameters of the directories, namely, the year and the location to which each related. Neither gentleman conceived the material form of the directories; neither had the need, for the Book Extract routine was designed to relieve humans of that, no doubt, tedious task. It is true that intellectual effort went into the operation of the software by these two gentlemen but that effort was not directed to the incarnation of the material form of the directories.

118. The Act does not presently deal explicitly with the impact of software on authorship (although this is not so in the United Kingdom: s 9(3) *Copyright, Designs and Patents Act 1988* (UK)). But a computer program is a tool and it is natural to think that the author of a work generated by a computer program will ordinarily be the person in control of that program. However, care must taken to ensure that the efforts of that person can be seen as being directed to the reduction of a work into a material form. Software comes in a variety of forms and the tasks performed by it range from the trivial to the substantial. So long as the person controlling the program can be seen as directing or fashioning the material form of the work there is no particular danger in viewing that person as the work's author. But there will be cases where the person operating a program is not controlling the nature of the material form produced by it and in those cases that person will not contribute sufficient independent intellectual

effort or sufficient effort of a literary nature to the creation of that form to constitute that person as its author: a plane with its autopilot engaged is flying itself. In such cases, the performance by a computer of functions ordinarily performed by human authors will mean that copyright does not subsist in the work thus created. Those observations are important to this case because they deny the possibility that Mr Vormwald or Mr Cooper were the authors of the directories. They did not guide the creation of the material form of the directories using the programs and their efforts were not, therefore, sufficient for the purposes of originality.

119. The consequence of those conclusions is that the directories were not copied from elsewhere but neither were they created by a human author or authors. Although humans were certainly involved in the Collection Phase that process antedated the reduction of the collected information into material form and was not relevant to the question of authorship (other than to show that the works were not copied). Whilst humans were ultimately in control of the software which did reduce the information to a material form, their control was over a process of automation and they did not shape or direct the material form themselves (that process being performed by the software). The directories did not, therefore, have an author and copyright cannot subsist in them.

    . . .

Yates J: 137. Recognising that authorship denotes human authorship, two further presently-relevant concepts emerge. First, the test for originality is whether the work originated from the author in the sense that it was not copied by the author: *Robinson v Sands & McDougall Pty Ltd* (1916) 22 CLR 124 at 132–133; *Sands & McDougall Pty Ltd v Robinson* (1917) 23 CLR 49 at 52; *Ladbroke (Football) Ltd v William Hill (Football) Ltd* [1964] 1 WLR 273 at 291; *Bookmakers' Afternoon Greyhound Services Ltd v Wilf Gilbert (Staffordshire) Ltd* [1994] FSR 723 at 731. As Lindgren J observed in *Desktop Marketing Systems Pty Ltd v Telstra Corporation Ltd* (2002) 119 FCR 491 at [92] the test must be applied to the thing to which the legislation attaches copyright protection. In this case this means the identified compilations represented in the published form of each regional directory as a WPD or a YPD: does each compilation originate from an author or authors? Secondly, the origination must involve human intellectual endeavour. This is not to say that originality means novelty as, say, understood in the law respecting patents for inventions. It does mean, however, that the creation of the work must be the product of a human intellectual process. These propositions were not disputed by the appellants.

138. In *IceTV*, Gummow, Hayne and Heydon JJ described the nature of authorship in compilations. Their Honours said at [99]:

> Where a literary work is brought into such existence by the efforts of more than one individual, it will be a question of fact and degree which one or more of them have expended sufficient effort of a literary nature to be considered an author of that work within the meaning of the Act. If the work be protected as a 'compilation', the author or authors will be those who gather or organise the collection of material and who select, order or arrange its fixation in material form . . .

139. It is plain that their Honours, in that passage, were describing the scope of relevant activity encompassing authorial contribution. However, the context in which their Honours described those activities shows that 'fixation', as an act or event, is a sine qua non for copyright to subsist. In that

CURRENT LAW

connection their Honours, quoting from *Network Ten Pty Ltd v TCN Channel Nine Pty Ltd* (2004) 218 CLR 273 at [51], said (at [102] omitting references):

> The second principle is related to the first and concerns the requirement for the subsistence of copyright of 'fixation' of the original work in a material form. It is well established that copyright does not subsist in a work unless and until the work takes some material form, so that protection:
>
>> does not extend to the ideas or information contained in the work and a balance is struck between the interests of authors and those of society in free and open communication.

140. Thus whilst activities such as gathering or organising the collection of material may be relevant authorial activities for copyright purposes, those activities are not of themselves, once engaged in, the subject matter of copyright protection. It is the fixation in material form of the 'work' that attains copyright protection for the 'work' in that particular form. In *IceTV* French CJ, Crennan and Kiefel JJ remarked at [28]:

> Copyright is not given to reward work distinct from the production of a particular form of expression …

143. *IceTV* underscores the centrality of authorship to copyright subsistence in works. Authorship is an essential characteristic of originality for copyright purposes. This was correctly recognised by the primary judge in the present case.

…

CONSIDERATION

164. The starting point must be the identification of the alleged copyright work. That starting point is critical because it is only at that point that one can ask and then consider the question: is this an *original* work? It is only by looking back from that vantage point that one can identify and assess the nature and quality of the acts that can be said to contribute to the material form of the work for which copyright is claimed. In the case of a compilation the relevant acts are of those who gather or organise the collection of material and who select, order or arrange its fixation in material form: *IceTV* at [99]; see also *Waterlow Publishers Ltd v Rose* (1989) 17 IPR 493 at 500. Of necessity, those acts must be the acts of an author or authors.

165. I would not, therefore, accept, without qualification, the respondents' submission that the extraction of the list of entries for particular directories is the first relevant step for the purpose of considering authorship and the originality of the works in question. Undoubtedly extraction was an essential step in the making of the relevant compilation in each case. However, the respondents' posited first step initiates a process of inquiry that looks forward to an end-point that is the reduction to material form of the claimed copyright work, whereas the identification of the claimed copyright work must be the starting-point for the inquiry. If that starting-point is not taken then the inquiry is skewed by ignoring antecedent acts that may be relevant acts of authorship in relation to the work in question.

166. In my view the work of the second appellant's [Sensis'] employees is relevant to the consideration of whether each work, as a compilation, was an original literary work for copyright purposes. However, as I have noted, this work was more in the nature of collecting, entering and manipulating data to provide the fabric (the Genesis Computer System database) out of which each identified compilation in the WPDs and YPDs was to be fashioned. In this sense it can be seen that

CURRENT LAW

those activities contributed to the making of each claimed copyright work. However, significantly, the selection, ordering and arrangement of information to fix the compilation in its material form was computer-generated by the Genesis Computer System.

167. Contrary to the appellants' submission, the Genesis Computer System was not a mere tool utilised by the second appellant's employees for this purpose. To describe the functioning of the system in this way obscures the fact that the activities carried out by the Genesis Computer System in the 'Book Extract' process were transformative steps that were obviously fundamental to the making of the compilation in each case. It was those activities that resulted in each compilation taking the form that it did. Those activities replaced what would otherwise have been, no doubt, the extensive work of individuals deploying their respective intellectual resources and capacities to select, order and arrange the listings as they appeared in each WPD or YPD, albeit in accordance with specifically mandated rules and procedures. When carried out by individuals, activities of this kind undoubtedly would have been of an authorial nature and would have been counted as an essential contribution to the making of the compilation in each case. However, in the present case, these activities, essentially, were not those of an author for copyright purposes. The appellants, no doubt for good commercial reasons, effectively supplanted the involvement of authors in carrying out those transformative steps.

168. In this connection it is not to the point that the second appellant's employees were also involved (as the appellants submitted) in selecting, customising, maintaining and operating the computer systems that were deployed in the production of the directories, including particularly in relation to the 'Book Extract' process. Those activities are akin to educating, training or instructing individuals, and maintaining a sufficient number of them, to carry out the discrete activities of selecting, ordering and arranging material to create the individual compilations. However, the two bodies of activity should not be confused for one another. It may well be, of course, that the activities of the second appellant's employees, in this regard, have resulted in the creation of other works (for example, a computer program or a compilation of computer programs) that are protected by copyright. However, no such claims have been made in this proceeding.

169. No doubt questions of fact and degree are involved in forming a judgment about whether a work is an original work for copyright purposes: see, for example, the effect of the authorities summarised in *Desktop Marketing* by Lindgren J at [160] (proposition 7). Similar questions arise in forming a judgment about authorship: *IceTV* at [99]. Leaving aside the possibility of non-authorial contributions that are, overall, and in context, insignificant or inconsequential, it is essential to a finding of originality for copyright purposes that the work be one that is properly characterised as originating from an author or authors. In my view, the compilations claimed in this case cannot bear that characterisation. The contribution of the essentially computer-generated 'Book Extract' process was of such overwhelming significance to the expression in material form of each compilation that none of the compilations can be properly characterised, overall, as a work that originates from an author or authors, even though elements of authorial contribution are present. It follows, in my view, that none of the works can be an original work for copyright purposes. Thus copyright cannot subsist in those works.

170. This conclusion makes it unnecessary to consider the additional contribution of other computer-generated activities (such as the rollover process) to the making of each compilation.

Although Telstra sought to rely on the Full Federal Court decision in *Desktop Marketing* (extracted above, p 46), all three judges in *Telstra v Phone Directories* noted that there had been no consideration, in that earlier case, of the impact of automated processes on authorship. There are comments in the Full Federal Court decision in *Telstra v Phone Directories* suggesting that some activities undertaken by the Genesis Computer System *would* have been sufficient for originality and subsistence if undertaken by human authors.

MATERIAL FORM

The judgments in *IceTV* and in *Telstra v Phone Directories* place importance on the point in time when a copyright work is first fixed in material form. Copyright subsists in a work from the time it is 'made' (for unpublished works: s 32(1)) or 'published' (for published works: ss 32(2) and 29).

A work is 'made' when it is reduced to writing or some other material form (s 22(1)). One potentially difficult current issue in Australian copyright law relates to the relationship between fixation in material form and authorship. The High Court in *IceTV* seemed to suggest that an author must be a person who reduces a work to material form. This has, however, been strongly criticised by Adeney who has pointed out that focusing on the physical act of fixation rather than the conceptually distinct act of forming copyrightable expression (e.g. putting words or sounds together) would be inconsistent with the position in other jurisdictions and with the purposes of copyright law.[6]

It is often easy to identify the fixation of a work: it is the time when the letter or manuscript is written, the canvas painted, the words of the literary work typed into a word processor and saved, or the musical work first recorded in a sound recording (see s 22(2)). However, the literary model—with its attendant assumptions about the temporality and materiality of production and reproduction leading to the manuscript becoming a printed book—does not fit all kinds of works. It is much harder to ascertain the fixation of other kinds of cultural productions, especially where technology more complex than a pen is used. Technological developments have led to the need for additional legislative clarification. 'Material form' is defined expansively in s 10(1), to include any form of storage, whether visible or not. This includes fixation in computer memory, whether permanent or temporary. Note that copyright still subsists in a work even if the only copy is destroyed, although it may be difficult to prove infringement.

In fashioning protection for cinematograph films, sound recordings and broadcasts, the 1968 Act introduced provisions to clarify some of the ambiguities surrounding their fixation and to more efficiently determine subsistence. Thus, copyright subsists in sound recordings that have been made (ss 89(1)–(2) and 22(3)–(3C)) or published (ss 89(3) and 29); in cinematograph films that have been made (ss 90(1)–(2) and 22(4)) or published (ss 90(2) and 29); and in television and sound broadcasts made from a place in Australia (ss 91 and 22(5)).

---

6   E Adeney, 'Authorship and Fixation in Copyright Law: A Comparative Comment' (2011) 35 *Melbourne University Law Review* 677.

QUALIFICATION

AUSTRALIAN SUBJECT MATTER

In the case of original literary, dramatic, musical and artistic works, copyright subsists in Australia in one of three scenarios:

1   if the work is unpublished, the author must be a 'qualified person' at the time the work was made, meaning an Australian citizen or a person resident in Australia: s 32(1), (4); or
2   if the work is published, then the work needs to be first published in Australia, or the author must have been a qualified person at the time the work was first published (or, if the author died before that time, was a qualified person at the time at the time of his or her death): s 32(2), (4); or
3   if the work is a building or an artistic work attached to a building, the building must be situated in Australia: s 32(3).

In the case of subject matter other than works, detailed rules are set out in ss 89–92, as interpreted in accordance with ss 22 and 29. For sound recordings, and cinematograph films, these embody similar requirements that either the maker/publisher be a qualified person, or the subject matter be made in Australia or first published in Australia. For broadcasts, those made by qualified broadcasters (public broadcasters and holders of commercial broadcasting licences) are protected. For published editions, either first publication must take place in Australia or the publisher must be a qualified person. Who or what constitutes a maker is considered in Chapter 5 below (p 175).

FOREIGN SUBJECT MATTER

Under the principle of 'national treatment' in international copyright treaties, the copyright of foreign nationals is protected in Australia. Section 184 permits the extension of protection under the Act to foreign works and other subject matter, and this has been given effect through the *Copyright (International Protection) Regulations 1969* (Cth). Whether a foreign work or subject matter is protected will depend on whether the relevant country is a member of a relevant international copyright treaty as specified in the Regulations, and, in some limited cases, on whether that country extends similar protection to Australian copyright owners.

DURATION

The *Statute of Anne 1710* (8 Anne, c 19) limited the term of copyright to 14–21 years. This was expanded to the author's life plus seven years, or a maximum of 42 years, under the *Copyright Act 1842* (UK). The *Copyright Act 1911* (UK) introduced a further extension of the term to life plus 50 years for most works, consistent with Berne Convention requirements. The 'life plus 50 years' term for works was adopted in Australia in the *Copyright Act 1912* and continued under the *Copyright Act 1968*.

The term of copyright for both works and some other subject matter was extended under the *US Free Trade Agreement Implementation Act 2004* (Cth), with effect from 1 January 2005. For published works, the term is now 70 years from the end of the year in which the author died (s 33(2)). Special rules apply for anonymous and pseudonymous works (s 34), unless the author is generally known or can be ascertained by reasonable inquiry. For sound recordings and cinematograph films, the term is 70 years from the end of the year in which the recording or film was first published (ss 93, 94). The term of protection for broadcasts (50 years from the first broadcast: s 95) and published editions (25 years from first publication: s 96) remained unchanged, as did copyright in material made or first published by the Crown (50 years from first publication: ss 180–181). However, the extended terms do not have retrospective application so as to put works and other subject matters previously in the public domain (i.e. where copyright had expired before the new duration provisions came into effect on 1 January 2005) back in copyright. Table 3.1 sets out a useful guide to duration.

Works (other than artistic works) that have not been 'made public' (by publication, performance, recording, broadcast or offer for sale) and unpublished films and sound recordings remain in copyright indefinitely (s 33(3), (5) for works, s 93 for sound recordings and s 94 for films).

As there is no registration system for published works, it can often be very difficult to determine whether or not copyright has expired.

TABLE 3.1 GENERAL RULES OF COPYRIGHT DURATION[7]

Note: This table does not apply where a government owns or would have owned copyright.

SECTION	WORK	PUBLICATION STATUS	DURATION	EXPIRED IF ...
33	Literary work (other than a computer program), dramatic or musical work	Published, performed, broadcast or offered for sale during author's lifetime	70 years after calendar year in which author died	Author died before 1 January 1955
		Published, performed, broadcast or offered for sale after author's lifetime	70 years after calendar year in which publication, performance, broadcast or offer for sale first takes place	Published, performed, broadcast or offered for sale before 1 January 1955
		Has never been published, performed, broadcast or offered for sale	Indefinite	-
	Artistic work not including engraving, and computer program	Published or unpublished (subject to special provisions for photographs)	70 years after calendar year in which author died	Author died before 1 January 1955
	Photograph	Published before 1 January 1955		Copyright in all such photographs has expired
	Engraving	Published	70 years after expiration of calendar year in which engraving first published	Author died before 1 January 1955
		Unpublished	Effectively indefinite	-

(continued)

---

7   Sources: Copyright Council Information Sheet GO23v17; E Hudson and A Kenyon, *Copyright and Cultural Institutions: Guidelines for Digitisation*, Melbourne Law School Legal Studies Research Paper No 140, February 2006.

TABLE 3.1 GENERAL RULES OF COPYRIGHT DURATION (*continued*)

SECTION	WORK	PUBLICATION STATUS	DURATION	EXPIRED IF ...
34	Work published anonymously or under a pseudonym	N/A	70 years after the expiration of the calendar year in which the work was first published	Published before 1 January 1955
80	Work of joint authorship	N/A	As under s 33, but calculated from death of author who died last	Author who died last died before 1 January 1955
93	Sound recording	Published	70 years after expiration of calendar year in which recording first published	Made before 1 January 1955
		Unpublished	Effectively indefinite	-
94	Cinematograph film	Has been published and was made on or after 1 May 1969	70 years after expiration of calendar year in which the film first published	None yet expired; will start expiring 1 January 2040
		Has been published and was made before 1 May 1969	70 years after calendar year in which author (of images and/or dramatic work) died	Author who died last died before 1 January 1955
		Unpublished	Effectively indefinite	-
95	Television or sound broadcast	Made on or after 1 May 1969	50 years after expiration of calendar year in which broadcast first made	None yet expired; will start expiring 1 January 2020
96	Published edition	Published	25 years after expiration of calendar year in which edition first published	Published more than 25 years ago

— 4 —

COPYRIGHT SUBJECT MATTER

INTRODUCTION

In addition to the criteria associated with originality, authorship and material form outlined in the previous chapter, in order to be protected, creative efforts also need to take the form of recognised copyright subject matter.

Throughout the twentieth century there was considerable growth in protected subject matter. Copyright expanded in response to changes in technologies of media delivery and demands from various industries for better protection of their intangible assets.

As noted in Chapter 2, the *Copyright Act 1968* (Cth) distinguishes between different kinds of creations. 'Works' include creations that were originally found in nineteenth-century subject-specific legislation: literary, dramatic, artistic and musical works. The imaginatively named 'subject matter other than works' includes productions that were first recognised only in the 1968 Act (although aspects of these productions were already partly protected through the existence of underlying literary, dramatic, artistic and musical works). They are sound recordings, cinematograph films, sound and television broadcasts, and published editions.

The list of subject matters in Parts III and IV of the *Copyright Act* is exhaustive: to qualify for copyright protection, authors' or makers' efforts need to come under at least one of the categories of subject matter. However, the legal categories are generally inclusive, not exclusive. This means it may be possible for different aspects of a product to be protected in multiple categories, and for rights to overlap. It is important to identify *all* the relevant rights in order to license copyright uses appropriately and plead infringement comprehensively. Identifying copyright subject matter is not simply a case of thinking about the most obvious category of protection.

DEFINITIONS AND INTERPRETIVE APPROACHES

It can be quite difficult to keep track of the diversity of interests recognised as copyright subject matter, not least because some definitions stick more closely than others to general cultural expectations of the meaning of terms. In short, some legal definitions follow common sense or dictionary definitions, while others adopt literal and more technical meanings. It can become quite confusing once 'common sense' and 'copyright sense' part company. Much of our current case law on copyright subject matter pushes the boundaries of protection, perhaps well beyond what was originally expected to fall within copyright legislation. Some judgments more openly acknowledge the broader strategic pressures and motives at play in litigation than others.

One cause for some of the difficulties in interpretation lies with courts' discomfort in making decisions about aesthetic quality. There is a clear preference for 'objective' criteria. As discussed in Chapter 3, the requirement of originality in copyright is not a test of aesthetic quality: the work need not be the expression of novel or inventive thought. This logic developed through the cases but is carried through into the legislation, particularly the definition of 'artistic work', which states that paintings, drawings, sculptures, engravings, photographs and buildings are protected whether they are 'of artistic quality or not' (s 10). In combination with the low standard for originality, the tendency to eschew judgments about quality suggests that any bare efforts expressed in the medium of writing or drawing satisfy the requirements for subsistence of rights. However, to award copyright protection so readily might be thought to confound everyday expectations that copyright should protect genuine works of culture and serve the arts, whereas design, patent and trade mark protection are more appropriate to the needs of industry. If copyright is conferred too readily, it undermines the policy balances of the other categories of IP.

Another difficulty with the definition of copyright subject matter relates to the need to anticipate future innovation. Technical definitions of subject matter tie copyright protection to the innovations of the past. Over the past 35 years there has been a revolution in information and communications technologies. The pace of change has led to a commitment to adopt a 'technologically neutral' approach to copyright legislation and interpretation, where possible. However, coupled with the fluid nature of new communication media, this can create a level of imprecision regarding when protected works arise, and with what boundaries. For example, most computer programs are very technically complex, made up of thousands of individual bits of programming and routines. How large need the stream of code be before it qualifies for protection, and are all the subparts separate works? Sound and television broadcasts are a continuous signal—or may sometimes be streamed as stand-alone programs—so, in addition to the rights in any film and/or script (a dramatic work) contained in the broadcast, where does copyright in the broadcast signal itself begin and end?

Determining the boundaries of protection relies on policy decisions about the foundations and basic rationales of copyright in general, and for the particular category of rights. However, these rationales are contested, and they change over time. In application, the court often wants it both ways: to depart, when necessary, from the limits created by the technological detail of a definition; and, conversely, to use technological facts about the creation of subject matter to draw the line between what is and isn't protected, as appropriate to the circumstances or as justice dictates. In your reading it is worth noting the degree to which the courts routinely rely on copyright rationales, as well as copyright principles—such as the idea/expression dichotomy, authorship, originality and material form—for guidance (or justification) in determining the ambit of protected subject matter. Copyright lawyers learn to use these tools in argumentation to construct a convincing narrative of the appropriate bounds of protection.

PART III OF THE *COPYRIGHT ACT*: COPYRIGHT IN ORIGINAL LITERARY, DRAMATIC, MUSICAL AND ARTISTIC WORKS

Section 10(1) of the *Copyright Act* provides that 'work' means a literary, dramatic, musical or artistic work. Each of these four categories will be considered in turn.

LITERARY WORKS

The category of 'literary work' includes the kinds of things you would expect to be protected, such as novels, essays and works of non-fiction. In accordance with the low standards of originality required for subsistence, this category also includes mundane, everyday items such as instruction manuals, short emails, advertising copy, university examination papers and technical documentation. Further, s 10(1) of the *Copyright Act* expands the concept of literary work to include:

(a) a table, or compilation, expressed in words, figures or symbols; and

(b) a computer program or compilation of computer programs.

In defining what counts as a literary work, courts have asserted that it is something that is 'expressed in print or writing, irrespective of the question whether the quality or style is high' (*University of London Press Ltd v University Tutorial Press Ltd* [1916] 2 Ch 601 at 608), or 'something which was intended to afford either information and instruction or pleasure in the form of literary enjoyment' (*Hollinrake v Truswell* [1894] 3 Ch 420 at 428). One difficult issue in defining literary works has been how small, or short, can a work be and still count: is a phrase a work? A few lines of advertising material?[1] A title or headline? Plaintiffs have incentives to define the boundaries of their work as narrowly as possible in order to make proving infringement more straightforward: as discussed in Chapter 6, infringement occurs when the whole or a substantial part of a work is reproduced.

The two cases extracted below illustrate the difficulty courts have excluding short works from protection; they also demonstrate the importance courts have placed on thinking through the consequences of different definitions of works. Note also how considerations of originality and the idea/expression dichotomy interact with arguments about whether there is a literary work.

CASE EXTRACT: PRECEDENT

PRECEDENT

Exxon Corp v Exxon Insurance Consultants International Ltd

[1982] Ch 119
Court of Appeal of England and Wales

[The plaintiffs claimed copyright in an invented word, 'Exxon', as an 'original literary work' entitled to copyright protection.]

Stephenson LJ (at 139–143): The question, therefore, is whether this word 'Exxon' is an 'original literary work.' It was invented, as the statement of claim alleges, after research and testing to find a suitable word, apparently over a period of more than a year. It is therefore difficult, if not impossible, to say that it is not original. It was invented and devised by and originated with the first plaintiff. Is it an 'original literary work'? Mr Price submitted that it is. He said that the Act of 1842, by its preamble, was concerned to protect literary works of lasting benefit to the world, but such literary works were confined

---

1   *Budget Eyewear Australia Pty Ltd v Specsavers Pty Ltd* [2010] FCA 507; (2010) 86 IPR 479.

PRECEDENT

by the Act, as is clear from all its sections, to printed books; there is no such limitation in copyright in literary works since 1911 in this country. What is now protected as an original literary work is anything which can be, and has been, written down for the first time; any combination of letters thought out and written down; any tangible product of intellectual endeavour. Mr Price referred us to *Webster's Dictionary*, in which 'work' is defined in one place as '… something produced or accomplished by effort, exertion, or exercise of skill … something produced by the exercise of creative talent or expenditure of creative effort …' He said that this word satisfies those conditions. It does not matter how much work went into it, subject, perhaps, to the principle *de minimis lex non curat*; it does not matter how poor the quality of the work is; if it was the result, or the product, of creative effort, the exercise of some skill and effort, it is a work, and if it is a work which is written down and consists of letters, it is a literary work. If you take the phrase 'original literary work' to pieces, this word 'Exxon' is original for the reason that I have given, it is literary and it is a work. Why, then, is it not an 'original literary work'?

… I would have thought, unaided or unhampered by authority, that unless there is something in the context of the Act which forbids it, a literary work would be something which was intended to afford either information and instruction, or pleasure in the form of literary enjoyment, whatever those last six words may add to the word 'pleasure.' Mr Price has not convinced me that this word 'Exxon' was intended to do, or does do, either of those things; nor has he convinced me that it is not of the essence of a literary work that it should do one of those things. Nor has he convinced me that there is anything in the Act, or in what Peterson J said about the words in the earlier Act, or in any authority, or in principle, which compels me to give a different construction from [the judgment of Davey LJ in *Hollinrake v Truswell* [1894] 3 Ch 420, extracted in Chapter 2] to the words 'literary work.' As I have already said, I agree with the way in which Graham J put the matter; I am not sure whether this can be said to be a 'work' at all, I am clearly of the opinion that it cannot be said to be a 'literary work.' I therefore agree with Graham J and I would dismiss this appeal.

Oliver LJ (at 144–145): I entirely agree. Section 2 of the Act of 1956 provides that copyright should subsist in every 'original literary work,' and in essence Mr Price's submissions were very simple. First, he said that the name 'Exxon' is undoubtedly original; it had not been thought of before or, so far as is known, used before; it is an artificial word, which does not appear in any known language. It is, he said, literary; it is composed of letters and it is written, typed or printed. It is a 'work' because work or effort went into its invention, and its selection as a suitable name for the plaintiff group which had no meaning, offensive or otherwise, in any other language. But 'original literary work' as used in the statute is a composite expression, and for my part I do not think that the right way to apply a composite expression is, or at any rate is necessarily, to ascertain whether a particular subject matter falls within the meaning of each of the constituent parts, and then to say that the whole expression is merely the sum total of the constituent parts. In my judgment it is not necessary, in construing a statutory expression, to take leave of one's common sense, and the result to which Mr Price sought to drive us is one which, to my mind, involves doing just that …

[Sir David Cairnes agreed with both of these judgments.]

CASE EXTRACT: CURRENT LAW

Fairfax Media Publications Pty Ltd v Reed International Books Australia Pty Ltd

[2010] FCA 984; (2010) 189 FCR 109
Federal Court of Australia

[Reed provided customers with daily abstracts of articles from newspapers and magazines including the *Australian Financial Review* (*AFR*), published by Fairfax. Each abstract included the headline of the article, the by-line of the journalist who wrote the article and a short summary written by an employee of Reed. Abstracts of 40–60 per cent of articles in each edition of the *AFR* were included (in a different order from the newspaper). Reed did not reproduce advertisements, photographs or quotes from the articles. Fairfax alleged infringement of its copyright in a series of differently pleaded literary works. Since Reed reproduced the *AFR* headlines verbatim, Fairfax's key claim was that each headline was itself a literary work. A set of sample headlines was used for the purposes of discussion, from two editions, listed in the table below (at [12] of the judgment]):

EDITION/PAGE/HEADLINE	
27 June 2007	
p 1	Investors warned on super changes
p 3	Returns after tax will be simply super
p 3	Employer lobby faces an uphill battle to fund ads
p 9	Blackout probe sheds little light
p 7 (special report)	Laser a ray of hope for eye problems
1 November 2007	
p 1	Fund managers reject Telstra chief's $11m pay deal
p 1	Health gaffes put coalition on back foot
p 12	Gunning for the vote in Bennelong
p 13	Uncertainty forces PM to rethink Victorian strategy
p 27	October a brilliant stage in dollar's tour de force

Bennett J accepted that headlines summarise and highlight important aspects of articles, attract attention, state facts or are intended to entertain or provoke, and can have an element of surprise, erudition, humour or charm. Feature headline writing may require skill and experience. Evidence indicated that on a difficult story and where time permits, it sometimes can take half an hour to find the right headline that is 'original and appealing'. Sub-editors discuss headlines with colleagues, and, during proofing, the chief sub-editor pays particular attention to the tone and quality of the headlines.]

Bennett J:
ARE HEADLINES LITERARY WORKS IN WHICH COPYRIGHT CAN SUBSIST?
30. ... [T]here has been general but not universal judicial acceptance that a literary work is one that gives 'information, instruction or pleasure in the form of literary enjoyment' (referring to the definition

of 'literary work' in *Hollinrake v Truswell* [1894] 3 Ch 420 at 427–428 per Davey LJ) and that it is not a question of literary merit. There is also acceptance generally that there must be a degree of originality: some labour, skill, judgment or ingenuity involved in the expression of the idea. An assessment of that originality involves knowledge of the author and an understanding or appreciation of what went into the claimed work. That may be apparent on the face of the work, such as a newly authored novel. It may require an understanding of the skill and labour involved, such as in the case of a compilation. It may, more usually, require some appreciation of both to varying degrees ... [T]he question is not the novelty or the worth of the thought which a person injects into their work, but whether the expression is original. As Dixon J said in *Victoria Park Racing & Recreation Grounds Co Ltd v Taylor* (1937) 58 CLR 479 at 511, '[t]he work need show no literary or other skill or judgment. But it must originate with the author and be more than a copy of other material'. As Isaacs J pointed out in *Sands & McDougall Pty Ltd v Robinson* (1917) 23 CLR 49 at 55, 'author' and 'original work' have always been correlative (as confirmed in *IceTV* [*Pty Ltd v Nine Network Australia Pty Ltd* [2009] HCA 14; (2009) 239 CLR 458] at [34]). However, his Honour also said at 53 that as 'author' connotes some amount of originality, the express use of the word 'original' in the Act must carry some additional meaning, which his Honour described as 'inventive originality' and said that a suggestion that it was sufficient for a person to be an author 'would be revolutionary'. For copyright to subsist in a work, one or more authors must have expended sufficient effort of a literary nature directed at the form of expression of the work (*IceTV* at [42] and [99]). The form of expression of the work must be the result of particular mental effort or exertion by the author(s) and cannot be essentially dictated by the nature of the information.

31. That is not to say that a copyright work must necessarily be 'inventive' but it must involve more than mere authorship. This is consistent with the opinion expressed by Isaacs J in *Sands*. This may be another way of saying that it must be not only original in the sense of authorship, but also a work. As French CJ, Crennan and Kiefel JJ said in *IceTV* at [16]–[28] in explaining the idea/expression dichotomy:

- Copyright is given in respect of the particular form of expression in which an author conveys ideas or information to the world (at [26]).
- Copyright does not protect facts or information. To do so would impede the reading public's access to and use of facts and information. It protects the particular form of expression of the information: the words, figures and symbols in which the pieces of information are expressed and the selection and arrangement of that information (at [28]).
- Copyright is not given to reward work distinct from the production of a particular form of expression (at [28]).

...

36. Reed contends that headlines are analogous to a title of a book or other work and relies on the fact that titles, slogans and other short phrases have been consistently refused separate protection under Australian and English copyright law. In *IceTV*, French CJ, Crennan and Kiefel JJ acknowledged that generally speaking, no copyright could be claimed in a programme title alone ... Reed concedes that there has been not been complete uniformity in reasoning in previous cases and texts and submits that the correct view is the *de minimis* principle: that titles and the like are simply too insubstantial and too short to qualify for copyright protection as literary works ...

37. Reed acknowledges that courts have recognised the possibility of copyright protection for short forms of literary expression in exceptional cases but relies on the fact that no modern Australian or

English cases involving titles, slogans or other short phrases have been brought within this preserve. It points out that a typical newspaper headline is far less substantial, in quantitative terms, than the example of the 'whole page of title' referred to in *Dick v Yates* (1881) 18 Ch D 76 at 89.

38. In other cases, the basis for denying protection appears to have been a perceived lack of originality (for example, in *Sullivan v FNH Investments Pty Ltd* (2003) 57 IPR 63 at [112]–[114]). Fairfax contends that this basis does not apply to the ten selected headlines because they are clearly 'original' in the relevant sense ... Fairfax accepts that copyright protection has been denied to works such as titles and single words but submits that past cases do not dictate the same result for the ten selected headlines in the present case.

39. The authors of Laddie H, Prescott P, Vitoria M et al, *The Modern Law of Copyright and Designs* (3rd ed, Butterworths, 2000) commented at [3.62] that most cases in which a work was considered too slight a matter to deserve copyright protection were cases concerning titles of publications and advertising slogans. This is so even where it is apparent that skill and labour had gone into the creation of the word (eg 'Exxon') or title (eg 'Where there's a Will there's a Way'). Interestingly, the authors acknowledge that Courts may now be more ready to afford copyright protection to advertising copy to recognise that such material may require creative activity of a high order (at [3.62] at footnote 10 and see *Budget Eyewear Australia Pty Ltd v Specsavers Pty Ltd* (2010) 86 IPR 479). However, they observe that the Courts may in fact be denying protection on the ground that some advertising slogans and titles are too short to be a literary work at all, regardless of any skill or labour. [K Garnett, G Davies, G Harbottle, *Copinger and Skone James on Copyright* (15th ed, Sweet & Maxwell, 2005)] also refers to the reluctance of English courts to confer copyright protection on titles of newspapers, magazines, books and the like (at [3-16]). Examples of refusal extend to the clever use of words to convey more than a simple description of the subject matter. The authors note that the courts have, however, been careful not to rule out the possibility for such protection in appropriate circumstances, although also noting that no such decision has ever been made.

40. In my view, the headline of each article functions as the title of the article. ...

41. It may be a clever title. That is not sufficient (cf 'Opportunity Knocks' for a game show; 'The Man who Broke the Bank at Monte Carlo' for a song; 'Splendid Misery' for a novel). It may be an indication of the content of the article and that is not sufficient (cf 'The Lawyer's Diary' for a diary). (See generally *Copinger* at [3-16] and Laddie et al at [3.62].) It may be a grouping of words that convey, in themselves, the subject matter such that the expression was inseparable from the idea conveyed [citing *Victoria v Pacific Technologies (Australia) Pty Ltd (No 2)* (2009) 177 FCR 61]. In each case it was determined that the contended work did not justify claims of copyright protection, although the reasoning was not identical ...

42. The headlines in the *AFR* range from the more prosaic: 'Investors warned on super changes' and 'Builders report fall in house sales' to ones that employ what might be thought of as a more interesting and clever use of words, such as 'Blackout probe sheds little light' and 'Returns after tax will be simply super'. While the use of devices such as puns and double entendres may be clever, evoke admiration and attract attention, the reasons for the denial of copyright protection to 'works' that are simply too slight have long been invoked and have formed the basis for much judicial precedent. In some cases the headline represents no more than the fact or idea conveyed.

43. In *Exxon Corporation v Exxon Insurance Consultants International Ltd* [1982] Ch 119, protection for an invented word ('Exxon') was denied on the basis that, while the word was original and was

created after considerable research and labour, it was not a 'literary' work because it was not intended to afford information and instruction or pleasure in the form of literary enjoyment (referring to the definition of 'literary work' in *Hollinrake*). A headline may come within the well-used criteria for a literary work as set out in *Hollinrake* but those criteria do not afford an exhaustive definition. They may well be necessary but they are not sufficient. Such criteria may well describe a literary work but the mere fact that a word or sequence of words provides information or pleasure is not necessarily sufficient to constitute a literary work for the purposes of the Act.

44. Headlines generally are, like titles, simply too insubstantial and too short to qualify for copyright protection as literary works. The function of the headline is as a title to the article as well as a brief statement of its subject, in a compressed form comparable in length to a book title or the like. It is, generally, too trivial to be a literary work, much as a logo was held to be too trivial to be an artistic work (*Cortis Exhaust Systems Pty Ltd v Kitten Software Pty Ltd* (2001) ATPR 41-837 at [33] per Tamberlin J), even if skill and labour has been expended on creation (*Exxon*).

45. Copyright can only subsist in a 'work'. Originality does not require novelty, inventiveness or creativity, whether of thought or expression, or any form of literary merit. Any words written by an author, original in that sense and not copied, could be said to satisfy the 'literary' part of a literary work for which copyright is claimed. Those words could well convey information and instruction (such as 'go outside, the sun is shining') or pleasure (such as 'you look beautiful'). However, not every piece of printing or writing which conveys information will be subject to copyright (*IceTV* at [45]). To obtain copyright protection under the Act, there must be a literary work. I appreciate that this has been the subject of much judicial consideration but I find it helpful to resort to dictionary definitions of 'work'. The Macquarie Dictionary relevantly defines 'work' as 'that on which exertion or labour is expended; the product of exertion, labour, or activity: a work of art, literary or musical works'. There may well be writings of original words or phrases that simply do not reach the level of constituting a 'work', regardless of literary merit. This is not just because they are short, as a deal of skill and effort can go into producing, for example, a line of exquisite poetry. It is because, on its face and in the absence of evidence justifying its description as a literary 'work', the writing does not, qualitatively or quantitatively, justify that description. A headline is, generally, no more than a combination of common English words (*Dick v Yates* at 88 per Jessel MR). It is 'does not involve literary composition, and is not sufficiently substantial to justify a claim to protection' (*Francis Day* [& *Hunter Ltd v Twentieth Century Fox Corp Ltd* [1940] AC 112] at 122–123); it does not, in the words of Jacobson J in *Sullivan* at [112], have 'the requisite degree of judgment, effort and skill to make it an original literary work in which copyright may subsist' for the purposes of the Act.

46. It may be that evidence directed to a particular headline, or a title of so extensive and of such a significant character, could be sufficient to warrant a finding of copyright protection (*Francis Day* at 123; see also *Milwell v Olympic Amusements Pty Ltd* (1999) 85 FCR 436 at [29]) but that is not the case here ...

47. The majority of the headlines in the sample editions are short factual statements of the subject of the article. The addition of a pun does not, of itself, in the absence of evidence, convert such statements into literary works ...

48. The headline and by-line is, as Reed says, meta-information about the work, not part of the work, the work being the article. The need to identify a work by its name is a reason for the exclusion of

titles from copyright protection in the public interest. A proper citation of a newspaper article requires not only reference to the name of the newspaper but also reproduction of the headline. This was a matter of common ground between the witnesses. If titles were subject to copyright protection, conventional bibliographic references to an article would infringe. Such considerations may well be a reason for the fact that headlines and 'short phrases' are excluded from copyright in the United States.

49. At *IceTV* at [161], Gummow, Hayne and Heydon JJ criticised the Full Court in *Nine Network Australia Pty Ltd v IceTV Pty Ltd* (2008) 168 FCR 14 [for] tipping the balance too far against the interest of viewers in digital free to air television in the dissemination by means of new technology of programme listings in favour of the interest in the protection of Nine against perceived competition by IceTV. Their Honours noted at [163] a submission that no litigation alleging breach of confidence would have succeeded to protect Nine after the information reached the public domain and that the copyright litigation was an attempt to control the further dissemination of the information. This was discussed in the context of broadcasting information but it does raise a matter of possibly more general application. In my view, to afford published headlines, as a class, copyright protection as literary works would tip the balance too far against the interest of the public in the freedom to refer or be referred to articles by their headlines.

50. This does not exclude the possibility of establishing a basis for copyright protection of an individual headline but Fairfax has failed to prove that the ten selected headlines amount to literary works in which copyright can subsist.

CURRENT LAW

Although Bennett J referred to both UK and Australian precedent denying protection to titles and headlines, the position appears to have changed in the UK in light of the European Court of Justice decision in Case C-5/08, *Infopaq International A/S v Danske Dagblades Forening* [2009] ECR I-6569. As mentioned in Chapter 3, the Court suggested that 11-word extracts from newspaper articles were potentially capable of expressing the 'author's own intellectual creation' and hence protected (see [38]). In a subsequent UK decision, *The Newspaper Licensing Agency Ltd v Meltwater Holding BV* [2010] EWHC 3099 (Ch); [2011] RPC 7, Proudman J held that 'headlines are capable of being literary works, whether independently or as part of the articles to which they relate' (at [71]).[2]

Bennett J's assertion that headlines, while literary, may not be 'works' raises an interesting question as to what other 'literary' items (or other items in words or writing) may not be 'works'. Although an improvised speech (if recorded) would seem likely to be a 'work', it is perhaps less clear whether words uttered by a celebrity during a television or newspaper interview would be.

COMPILATIONS

Section 10(1) of the *Copyright Act* extends the concept of literary work to tables and compilations, expressed in words, figures or symbols. This covers a wide gamut of objects: electronic databases,

---

2   Proudman J's decision on this point was upheld by the Court of Appeal ([2011] EWCA Civ 890; [2012] RPC 1) and this issue was not appealed when the case went to the UK Supreme Court (*Public Relations Consultants Association Ltd v The Newspaper Licensing Agency Ltd* [2013] UKSC 18; [2013] RPC 19).

catalogues, lists of football fixtures, television broadcasting schedules,[3] safety data sheets,[4] tables of figures,[5] encyclopaedias and anthologies of poems (as a compilation separate from copyright in each underlying poem). Especially since the High Court decision in *IceTV Pty Ltd v Nine Network Australia Pty Ltd* [2009] HCA 14; (2009) 239 CLR 458 and the Full Federal Court decision in *Telstra Corporation Ltd v Phone Directories Co Pty Ltd* [2010] FCAFC 149; (2010) 194 FCR 142 (both extracted in Chapter 3), cases involving copyright in compilations raise several difficult questions even at the stage of considering subsistence.

A first is what, exactly, is the work in which copyright subsists, and when was it first reduced to material form? This was a difficult issue in *IceTV*. In that case, the Nine Network sought to claim copyright in its weekly television program schedules. In fact, Nine pleaded three different versions of the weekly schedules:

1   the schedules consisting only of the details of the dates, titles, and intended starting and finishing times for the transmission of the television programs (without episode titles);

2   the schedules consisting of time and title information, including episode titles, together with additional information such as episode numbers, whether the show was a repeat, format (widescreen or high definition) and classification (PG, M, MA 15+, etc.);

3   the schedules including all the information in 1 and 2 above, together with short descriptive synopses of the programs.

These different pleaded versions included or excluded certain columns in the Excel spreadsheet document called the Weekly Schedule.[6] But as late as the second day of the hearing in the High Court appeal, the Nine Network was (also) arguing that the relevant copyright work might be the underlying internal database from which the Weekly Schedules were generated. This was rejected by the High Court: Nine's internal database included a range of pieces of information not included in the Weekly Schedule, and other documents which differed substantially from the Weekly Schedule were also produced from the Nine Database. Although the Nine Database might well have been a compilation, it was a different compilation from the Weekly Schedule alleged to have been infringed.

Another example where identification of the exact compilation was controversial is the interlocutory decision in *Sports Data Pty Ltd v Prozone Sports Data Pty Ltd* [2014] FCA 595; (2014) 107 IPR 1. Sports Data had collected detailed official statistics on Rugby League games for the NRL and had created a large relational database made up of 50 interrelated and interconnected tables of sports statistics and information. Their complaint, in essence, was that Prozone, having taken over statistics collection for the NRL, had copied some of Sports Data's categorisation of events for data collection. One issue was how the relevant copyright compilation was to be identified. As Wigney J noted:

> 83. ... it is necessary to describe a difficulty arising from the way Sports Data has identified its copyright work. As explained earlier, Sports Data identifies the copyright work as being

3   *IceTV Pty Ltd v Nine Network Australia Pty Ltd* [2009] HCA 14; (2009) 239 CLR 458.
4   *Acohs Pty Ltd v Ucorp Pty Ltd* [2012] FCAFC 16; (2012) 201 FCR 173.
5   *Milwell Pty Ltd v Olympic Amusements Pty Ltd* [1999] FCA 63; (1999) 85 FCR 436.
6   For a discussion of how courts determine the boundaries of the copyright-protected work, see B Sherman, 'What Is a Copyright Work?' (2011) 12 *Theoretical Inquiries in Law* 99.

essentially four of 50 tables within which data on the entire NRLHistory database is stored. In fact, Sports Data's case essentially relies almost entirely on one field or column in one (or perhaps two) of the tables which contain event descriptions. This raises the question whether it is legitimate or permissible to describe a copyright work as, essentially, a small extract from a much larger work. That is particularly so given the fact that issues of 'substantial' reproduction are involved. Can a person alleging copyright infringement effectively skirt around the 'substantiality' element by confining the relevant works to a small part of a much larger whole?

84. This is a difficult question. Ultimately, given the conclusions I have reached in relation to other issues, it is not necessary to answer this definitively. It is an issue that may have to be addressed at the final hearing. It may require further evidence. Suffice it to say at this stage that I have difficulty in seeing how it is legitimate to identify or define a relevant copyright work in this way.

A second set of difficult questions for compilations arises around originality: whether there is original expression in the final compilation, and whether (as seen in Chapter 3) there are human authors who contribute intellectual effort *directed to the creation of that expression*. This involves a detailed inquiry into the process of production of the compilation in which copyright is claimed, and results can vary significantly depending on exactly how a compilation has been created and which parts of its production have been automated. In this regard it is instructive to compare a series of recent Full Federal Court decisions concerning compilations:

- *Telstra Corporation Ltd v Phone Directories Co Pty Ltd* [2010] FCAFC 149; (2010) 194 FCR 142 (extracted in Chapter 3), where the considerable work by Telstra employees in gathering, and checking information was insufficiently directed to the expression embodied in the final telephone directories: the expression—the layout and arrangement of the information—was automated. Note, however, comments by the judges that the automated processes, if carried out by a human being, would be sufficient for subsistence.
- *Acohs Pty Ltd v Ucorp Pty Ltd* [2012] FCAFC 16; (2012) 201 FCR 173, which concerned Acohs' electronic Material Safety Data Sheets (MSDSs) (information sheets provided with hazardous substances and dangerous goods): MSDSs were generated from an underlying database, using a template written by employee programmers and information written by Acohs employees into the database or transcribed by employees from other sources (such as manufacturers' information sheets). The Full Federal Court held that the programmers' creation of the templates was separate from the creation of the MSDSs; Acohs only held copyright in MSDSs including information authored by employees.
- *Tonnex International Pty Ltd v Dynamic Supplies Pty Ltd* [2012] FCAFC 162; (2012) 99 IPR 31, which concerned Dynamic's electronic 'compatibility chart' that matched printer cartridges with compatible printers: the chart drew on information held in an internal company database. The Court distinguished between the skill, judgment and labour required to create the *database* and the skill, judgment and labour exercised by a particular individual employee in selecting material from the database and arranging it so as to be most useful to customers visiting the website and searching for appropriate cartridges for particular printers. Copyright subsisted in the compatibility chart as a compilation.

SUI GENERIS DATABASE RIGHT

Given the difficulties in applying copyright principles to electronic databases, some Australian judges (including Gummow, Hayne and Heydon JJ in *IceTV* at [139]) have queried whether the legislature should consider introducing a *sui generis* IP right tailored to databases. The EU created a *sui generis* right of this kind: *Directive 96/9/EC of the European Parliament and of the Council of 11 March 1996 on the legal protection of databases* (OJ L77/20). Under this Directive, compilations of data may be protected in two ways. First, *copyright* will subsist in databases 'which, by reason of the selection or arrangements of their contents, constitute the author's own intellectual creation'. Intellectual effort and skill in *creating* data are not relevant to copyright subsistence: only originality in selection and arrangement of data will count: Case C-604/10, *Football Dataco Ltd v Yahoo! UK Ltd* [2012] 2 CMLR 24. The second way is through the *sui generis* database right, the scope of which is described in the extract below.

CASE EXTRACT: COMPARATIVE LAW

Case C-444/02, Fixtures Marketing Ltd v Organismos Prognostikon Agonon Podosfairou (OPAP)

[2004] ECR I-10549
Court of Justice of the European Communities (Grand Chamber)

[The reference for a preliminary ruling arose in proceedings brought by Fixtures, a company retained by the organisers of English and Scottish league football to handle the exploitation of the football fixture lists outside the UK. Fixtures sued OPAP, which was using information from the fixture lists for the purpose of organising betting on games.]

LEGAL BACKGROUND

3. The directive, according to Article 1(1) thereof, concerns the legal protection of databases in any form. A database is defined, in Article 1(2) of the directive, as 'a collection of independent works, data or other materials arranged in a systematic or methodical way and individually accessible by electronic or other means'.

...

5. Article 7 of the directive provides for a sui generis right in the following terms:

Object of protection

1   Member States shall provide for a right for the maker of a database which shows that there has been qualitatively and/or quantitatively a substantial investment in either the obtaining, verification or presentation of the contents to prevent extraction and/or re-utilisation of the whole or of a substantial part, evaluated qualitatively and/or quantitatively, of the contents of that database.

2   For the purposes of this chapter:

(a)   'extraction' shall mean the permanent or temporary transfer of all or a substantial part of the contents of a database to another medium by any means or in any form;

(b)   're-utilisation' shall mean any form of making available to the public all or a substantial part of the contents of a database by the distribution of copies, by renting, by on-line or

COMPARATIVE LAW

COMPARATIVE LAW

other forms of transmission. The first sale of a copy of a database within the Community by the rightholder or with his consent shall exhaust the right to control resale of that copy within the Community.

Public lending is not an act of extraction or re-utilisation.

3   The right referred to in paragraph 1 may be transferred, assigned or granted under contractual licence.

4   The right provided for in paragraph 1 shall apply irrespective of the eligibility of that database for protection by copyright or by other rights. Moreover, it shall apply irrespective of eligibility of the contents of that database for protection by copyright or by other rights. Protection of databases under the right provided for in paragraph 1 shall be without prejudice to rights existing in respect of their content.

5   The repeated and systematic extraction and/or re-utilisation of insubstantial parts of the contents of the database implying acts which conflict with a normal exploitation of that database or which unreasonably prejudice the legitimate interests of the maker of the database shall not be permitted.

6. The directive was implemented in Greek law by Law No 2819/2000 (FEK A' 84/15–3–2000).

...

18. The referring court asks, first, in its first two questions, what the term database as defined in Article 1(2) of the directive covers and whether football fixture lists fall within that definition.

19. A database in the terms of the directive is defined in Article 1(2) as 'a collection of independent works, data or other materials arranged in a systematic or methodical way and individually accessible by electronic or other means'...

...

29. ... [C]lassification as a database is dependent, first of all, on the existence of a collection of 'independent' materials, that is to say, materials which are separable from one another without their informative, literary, artistic, musical or other value being affected. On that basis, a recording of an audiovisual, cinematographic, literary or musical work as such does not fall within the scope of the directive, according to the 17th recital of the preamble to the directive.

30. Classification of a collection as a database then requires that the independent materials making up that collection be systematically or methodically arranged and individually accessible in one way or another. While it is not necessary for the systematic or methodical arrangement to be physically apparent, according to the 21st recital, that condition implies that the collection should be contained in a fixed base, of some sort, and include technical means such as electronic, electromagnetic or electro-optical processes, in the terms of the 13th recital of the preamble to the directive, or other means, such as an index, a table of contents, or a particular plan or method of classification, to allow the retrieval of any independent material contained within it.

31. That second condition makes it possible to distinguish a database within the meaning of the directive, characterised by a means of retrieving each of its constituent materials, from a collection of materials providing information without any means of processing the individual materials which make it up.

32. It follows from the above analysis that the term database as defined in Article 1(2) of the directive refers to any collection of works, data or other materials, separable from one another without the value of their contents being affected, including a method or system of some sort for the retrieval of each of its constituent materials.

[The Court concluded that the fixture lists met this definition and then continued:]

38. Article 7(1) of the directive reserves the protection of the sui generis right to databases which meet a specific criterion, namely to those which show that there has been qualitatively and/or quantitatively a substantial investment in the obtaining, verification or presentation of their contents.

39. Under the 9th, 10th and 12th recitals of the preamble to the directive, its purpose, as OPAP and the Greek Government point out, is to promote and protect investment in data 'storage' and 'processing' systems which contribute to the development of an information market against a background of exponential growth in the amount of information generated and processed annually in all sectors of activity. It follows that the expression 'investment in … the obtaining, verification or presentation of the contents' of a database must be understood, generally, to refer to investment in the creation of that database as such.

40. Against that background, the expression 'investment in … the obtaining … of the contents' of a database must, as OPAP and the Belgian, Austrian and Portuguese Governments point out, be understood to refer to the resources used to seek out existing independent materials and collect them in the database, and not to the resources used for the creation as such of independent materials. The purpose of the protection by the sui generis right provided for by the directive is to promote the establishment of storage and processing systems for existing information and not the creation of materials capable of being collected subsequently in a database.

43. The expression 'investment in … the … verification … of the contents' of a database must be understood to refer to the resources used, with a view to ensuring the reliability of the information contained in that database, to monitor the accuracy of the materials collected when the database was created and during its operation. The expression 'investment in … the … presentation of the contents' of the database concerns, for its part, the resources used for the purpose of giving the database its function of processing information, that is to say those used for the systematic or methodical arrangement of the materials contained in that database and the organisation of their individual accessibility.

44. Investment in the creation of a database may consist in the deployment of human, financial or technical resources but it must be substantial in quantitative or qualitative terms. The quantitative assessment refers to quantifiable resources and the qualitative assessment to efforts which cannot be quantified, such as intellectual effort or energy, according to the 7th, 39th and 40th recitals of the preamble to the directive.

45. In that light, the fact that the creation of a database is linked to the exercise of a principal activity in which the person creating the database is also the creator of the materials contained in the database does not, as such, preclude that person from claiming the protection of the sui generis right, provided that he establishes that the obtaining of those materials, their verification or their presentation, in the sense described in paragraphs 40 to 43 of this judgment, required substantial investment in quantitative or qualitative terms, which was independent of the resources used to create those materials.

46. In those circumstances, although the search for data and the verification of their accuracy at the time a database is created do not require the maker of that database to use particular resources because the data are those he created and are available to him, the fact remains that the collection of those data, their systematic or methodical arrangement in the database, the organisation of their individual accessibility and the verification of their accuracy throughout the operation of the database

may require substantial investment in quantitative and/or qualitative terms within the meaning of Article 7(1) of the directive.

47. In the case in the main proceedings, the resources deployed for the purpose of determining, in the course of arranging the football league fixtures, the dates and times of and home and away teams playing in the various matches represent, as OPAP and the Belgian, Austrian and Portuguese Governments submit, an investment in the creation of the fixture list. Such an investment, which relates to the organisation as such of the leagues is linked to the creation of the data contained in the database at issue, in other words those relating to each match in the various leagues. It cannot, therefore, be taken into account under Article 7(1) of the directive.

48. Accordingly, it must be ascertained, leaving aside the investment referred to in the previous paragraph, whether the obtaining, verification or presentation of the contents of a list of football fixtures constitutes a substantial investment in qualitative or quantitative terms.

49. Finding and collecting the data which make up a football fixture list do not require any particular effort on the part of the professional leagues. Those activities are indivisibly linked to the creation of those data, in which the leagues participate directly as those responsible for the organisation of football league fixtures. Obtaining the contents of a football fixture list thus does not require any investment independent of that required for the creation of the data contained in that list.

50. The professional football leagues do not need to put any particular effort into monitoring the accuracy of the data on league matches when the list is made up because those leagues are directly involved in the creation of those data. The verification of the accuracy of the contents of fixture lists during the season simply involves, according to the observations made by Fixtures, adapting certain data in those lists to take account of any postponement of a match or fixture date decided on by or in collaboration with the leagues. Such verification cannot be regarded as requiring substantial investment.

51. The presentation of a football fixture list, too, is closely linked to the creation as such of the data which make up the list. It cannot therefore be considered to require investment independent of the investment in the creation of its constituent data.

52. It follows that neither the obtaining, nor the verification nor yet the presentation of the contents of a football fixture list attests to substantial investment which could justify protection by the sui generis right provided for by Article 7 of the directive.

COMPUTER PROGRAMS

Section 10(1) of the *Copyright Act* defines 'literary work' to include 'a computer program or compilation of computer programs', and further provides:

> *computer program* means a set of statements or instructions to be used directly or indirectly in a computer in order to bring about a certain result.

The reference to 'a certain result' highlights that computer programs are designed to make computers work, and thus protecting them poses a challenge to the fundamental principle, discussed in Chapter 2, that copyright does not protect systems or processes. This was perhaps even more explicit in the 1984–2001 definition of 'computer program', which described computer programs as 'intended ... to cause a device having digital information processing capabilities to perform a particular function'. The three extracts that follow illustrate how the courts have sought to accommodate this different subject matter while maintaining copyright principles.

PRECEDENT

CASE EXTRACT : PRECEDENT

Autodesk Inc v Dyason [No 2]

(1993) 176 CLR 300
High Court of Australia

[Autodesk owned copyright in a computer program known as AutoCAD, which as an anti-piracy measure required use of a hardware device attached to the computer (a 'dongle') in order to run. The software would 'interrogate' (send messages to) the device and continue to run only if an appropriate response was received. Dyason made a rival device which would generate the same response, enabling software use without the dongle, including use of infringing copies. The trial judge had held that since Dyason's device performed the same function as Autodesk's device, there was copyright infringement. The High Court rejected this reasoning in *Autodesk Inc v Dyason* (1992) 173 CLR 330. The respondents then sought to argue that they had not been afforded the opportunity of being heard on particular issues that the High Court had found to be decisive. In this second decision, Mason CJ usefully summarises the effect of the earlier ruling:]

Mason CJ (at 303–304): The decision in *Autodesk* confirmed two fundamental principles. First, the definition of a 'computer program' by reference to 'an expression ... of a set of instructions' should be understood as conferring protection upon the set of instructions itself—which must be identified with some precision—but as doing so in a way which is adapted to the nature of copyright. Thus, the protection of computer programs is to conform to the dominant principle of copyright law that protection is given not for ideas, but only for the form of expression. However, as the judgment of Mason CJ, Brennan and Deane JJ makes clear, this distinction must not be applied too strictly. A distinction needs to be drawn between the relevant set of instructions and the form of storage or representation of the instructions, so that a person who reproduces a set of instructions in a different form—such as by turning source code into object code—does not escape infringement. The object of protection is the computer program, not just the particular form of storage or representation chosen by the author.

The second fundamental proposition confirmed in *Autodesk* derives from the first. Functionality is not the proper object of copyright protection. As Dawson J stated in *Autodesk*, the purpose or function of a utilitarian work is its idea, while the method of arriving at that purpose or function is the expression of the idea.

CURRENT LAW

CASE EXTRACT : CURRENT LAW

Data Access Corporation v Powerflex Services Pty Ltd

[1999] HCA 49; (1999) 202 CLR 1
High Court of Australia

[Data Access owned copyright in Dataflex, a system of computer programs for developing customised databases. Dataflex used the 'Dataflex language', an application development language, which included 254 'Reserved Words', some of which were unique to Dataflex, others of which were ordinary English words or readily understood (e.g. DIRECTORY, SAVE, PAGEBREAK). Underlying each Reserved Word was a set of instructions, in source code (i.e. human-readable computer programming text) that would cause the computer to execute some function or set of functions (once translated into machine-readable language known as object code). Powerflex created a rival system for developing customised databases (PFXplus). The system was designed to be compatible with the Dataflex language and file structure, so that people familiar with Dataflex could use the product. PFXplus used Reserved Words from the Dataflex system, but the source code in which the underlying instructions in the PFXpus system was written was quite different from the source code in which the Dataflex system was written. Data Access claimed (*inter alia*) that each of the Reserved Words was a 'computer program' within the (then) s 10(1) definition, and that the collocation of the Reserved Words was a computer program.]

Gleeson CJ, McHugh, Gummow and Hayne JJ (some footnotes omitted): 19. The definition of 'computer program' requires that each Reserved Word be: (i) 'an expression,' (ii) 'in any language, code or notation,' (iii) 'of a set of instructions (whether with or without related information)' (iv) 'intended, either directly or after either or both of the following: (a) conversion to another language, code or notation; (b) reproduction in a different material form; to cause' (v) 'a device having digital information processing capabilities to perform a particular function.'

20. Each of the first four of these elements qualifies what follows and the scope of the definition is marked out by the requirement of an intention that the device be caused 'to perform a particular function'. In form, the definition of a computer program seems to have more in common with the subject matter of a patent than a copyright. Inventions when formulated as a manner of new manufacture traditionally fell within the province of patent law, with the scope of the monopoly protection being fixed by the terms of a public document, the patent specification. In Australia claims to computer programs which are novel, not obvious and otherwise satisfy the *Patents Act 1990* (Cth) and which have the effect of controlling computers to operate in a particular way, have been held to be proper subject matter for letters patent, as 'achieving an end result which is an artificially created state of affairs of utility in the field of economic endeavour', within the meaning of *National Research Development Corporation v Commissioner of Patents* [(1959) 102 CLR 252 at 275–277].

21. The [1984] amendment of the definition of 'literary work' in s 10(1) of the Act to include as item (b) 'a computer program or compilation of computer programs' obviously marked a significant departure from what previously had been the understanding of what was required for subsistence of copyright in an original literary work. It is true that copyright may subsist in a literary work which is related to the exercise of mechanical functions. A set of written instructions for the assembly and operation of a domestic appliance is an example. However, it is not to the point in copyright law that, if followed, the instructions do not cause the appliance to function. The protection of the function performed by the appliance will be for the patent law, including the law as to inutility. This is what was indicated by Bradley J in a passage in *Baker v Selden* [101 US 99 at 102 (1879)] which was repeated by Brennan J in *Computer Edge* [*Pty Ltd v Apple Computer Inc* (1986) 161 CLR 171 at 208–209]. Bradley J said that

no one would contend that the exclusive right to the manner of manufacture described in a treatise would be given by the subsistence of copyright in that work, and continued:

> The copyright of the book, if not pirated from other works, would be valid without regard to the novelty, or want of novelty, of its subject-matter ... To give to the author of the book an exclusive property in the art described therein, when no examination of its novelty has ever been officially made, would be a surprise and a fraud upon the public. That is the province of letters-patent, not of copyright.

22. Further, the requirement in copyright law that a work be 'original' is to be distinguished from the requirements that an alleged invention be novel and that it not be obvious. The question for copyright law is whether 'the work emanates from the person claiming to be its author, in the sense that he has originated it or brought it into existence and has not copied it from another'. If so, the work does not lack originality because of the anterior independent work of another, although, in such circumstances, an invention might lack novelty.

23. Finally, to say that the copyright law does not protect function and extends only to the expression of systems or methods does not deny that a work may serve utilitarian rather than aesthetic ends. A map and a recipe book are obvious examples.

24. There is, with respect, some oversimplification of these principles in the following statement by Dawson J in *Autodesk Inc v Dyason* ('*Autodesk No 1*'):

> [W]hen the expression of an idea is inseparable from its function, it forms part of the idea and is not entitled to the protection of copyright.

25. The 1984 amendment departed from traditional principles by identifying for copyright purposes a species of literary work, the very subsistence of which requires an expression of a set of instructions intended to cause a device to perform a particular function. The difficulties which arise from accommodating computer technology protection to principles of copyright law have been remarked upon but the Act now expressly requires such an accommodation.

26. ... The first issue in the appeal turns solely on the application of the definition of 'computer program' in s 10(1) of the Act.

27. The appellant submits that each Reserved Word meets each component of the definition of 'computer program'. The appellant contends:

(i) A Reserved Word itself is identified as being the relevant 'expression' for the purposes of the definition. The term 'expression' is used in the definition to preserve the distinction between the set of instructions and the manner in which the set is expressed in a particular programming language. The choice of expressions for words and commands in a language is determined by the author of the language.

(ii) Each Reserved Word is in a code or notation, the relevant code or notation being the Dataflex language.

(iii) Each Reserved Word expresses a set of instructions, that set being either the underlying set of instructions in source code, or the meaning and syntax of the word or command in question.

(iv) and (v) Each Reserved Word is in a high level language, and each is intended, after conversion into a lower level language by a compiler and runtime program, to cause a computer (which is a device having digital information processing capabilities) to perform a particular function.

CURRENT LAW

28. In our opinion, none of the Reserved Words satisfies the statutory definition. Each Reserved Word is undoubtedly in 'code or notation'—the Dataflex language. It follows that whether a Reserved Word is a 'computer program' within the meaning of the definition depends on whether it is an 'expression ... of a set of instructions ... intended ... to cause a device having digital information processing capabilities to perform a particular function'. However, each of the Reserved Words is a single word; none is a set of instructions in the Dataflex language. Further, none of the Reserved Words intends to express, directly or indirectly, an algorithmic or logical relationship between the function desired to be performed and the physical capabilities of the 'device having digital information processing capabilities' ...

53. The meaning of the phrase 'expression ... of a set of instructions' was referred to in the Explanatory Memorandum to the Copyright Amendment Bill 1984:

> The phrase 'expression ... of a set of instructions' is intended to make clear that it is not an abstract idea, algorithm or mathematical principle which is protected but rather a particular expression of that abstraction. The word 'set' indicates that the instructions are related to one another rather than being a mere collection.

54. It is the particular selection, ordering, combination and arrangement of instructions within a computer program which provide its expression. A computer program in a particular language may be relatively inefficient because it uses many instructions to achieve the function that a single instruction could achieve. A computer program in a particular language may also operate relatively inefficiently because of the way it is structured, in terms of the ordering of the instructions and the sequence in which they are executed. Considerations of efficiency are largely a function of the particular language which is used. It is the skill of the programmer in a particular language which determines the expression of the program in that language.

55. The Explanatory Memorandum states that it is a 'particular expression' of an abstract idea which is protected. As a particular expression is a function of the language of the expression, whether a word or words is or are a relevant expression of a set of instructions needs to be asked separately for each language in which there is purportedly a set of instructions.

56. For an item to be a computer program, it must not only be an 'expression ... of a set of instructions', but the expression of that set of instructions must also be designed to achieve a particular purpose. That is to say, it must be 'intended ... to cause a device having digital information processing capabilities to perform a particular function'. The emphasis on a singular function in the phrase 'a particular function' indicates that it is necessary to identify precisely the relevant function.

...

58. It is the ability to express in a computer language an algorithmic or logical relationship between an identifiable function which is desired to be performed and the physical capabilities of the computer, which is the true skill of the programmer. This remains true even if the programmer is working via the medium of a high level language and is unaware of the physical capabilities of the computer. It is the expression of this skill which is intended to be protected by the Act.

...

61. In our opinion, whether what is claimed to be a 'computer program' is an 'expression ... of a set of instructions ... intended ... to cause a device having digital information processing capabilities to perform a particular function' must be answered separately for each language in which the item in question is said to be a computer program.

CURRENT LAW

62. Moreover, something is not a 'computer program' within the meaning of the definition in s 10(1) unless it intends to express, either directly or indirectly, an algorithmic or logical relationship between the function desired to be performed and the physical capabilities of the 'device having digital information processing capabilities'. Thus, in the sense employed by the definition, a program in object code causes a device to perform a particular function 'directly' when executed. A program in source code does so 'after ... conversion to another language, code or notation'.

...

64. Once these principles are applied to each Reserved Word in the Dataflex language, it is clear that they are not 'computer programs'. Each Reserved Word comprises but a single instruction in that language. Each Reserved Word, considered alone, is not a 'set of instructions' in that language. It is not a 'computer program' expressed in the Dataflex language ...

In the result, Powerflex was held to have infringed copyright, not in the computer programs making up the Dataflex system but in a single compilation, the 'Huffman Compression Table', which Powerflex had to copy in its entirety in order to interoperate with databases produced in Dataflex. The *Copyright Act* was subsequently amended to allow reproduction of a computer program and/or associated documents in order to make interoperable programs.

Many computer programs are large and complex, and a question raised in recent cases is whether subparts of such a program are themselves computer programs. The High Court in *Data Access* suggested that a subpart which is 'functionally separate' could be an independent literary work (at [102]). This was considered further in the following case.

CURRENT LAW

CASE EXTRACT: CURRENT LAW

Dais Studio Pty Ltd v Bullet Creative Pty Ltd

[2007] FCA 2054; (2007) 165 FCR 92
Federal Court of Australia

[Dais Studio owned copyright in a content management system (CMS) known as 'WebStable' for managing the content on, and appearance of, websites. In total the system comprised over 220 000 lines of human-readable source code. Dais claimed that a former employee had copied two files, the 'table file' and the 'editor file', from within the WebStable CMS. These files worked in conjunction with other parts of WebStable and other software (such as the user's browser software) to enable companies to make modifications to the appearance of the website. The two files comprised less than 1 per cent of the WebStable code (and there was insufficient evidence to establish whether this was a substantial part of WebStable), so a key question in determining infringement was whether each file was itself a computer program.]

Jessup J: 27. In part, [the respondent's] submissions emphasise the smallness of the results arguably brought about by the table file and the editor file. I do not consider that such is a proper basis upon which to disqualify the files from satisfying the requirements of the definition of 'computer program'. In part, however, the submissions make a point of more substance, namely, that the definition requires that the instructions or statements to which it refers actually bring about the result in question, by their own doings and unaided as it were. The submissions point out that, as client-side functional files, the table file and the editor file play only a role, and a relatively minor role, in bringing a result about. The submissions call for a consideration of the current statutory definition of 'computer program'.

...

31. ... [T]he terms of the definition of 'computer program' have changed since [*Data Access v Powerflex*] was decided. The previous definition was concerned with a function, and required that the set of instructions be intended to cause the device to perform the function. The present definition requires that the set of instructions be used, directly or indirectly, to bring about a certain result. As a matter of ordinary language, a thing might be used to bring about a certain result notwithstanding that it is but a component in a collection or sequence of things which together bring about the result. It may be accurately said that a brake pedal is used to arrest the progress of a car, notwithstanding that the pedal alone would be incapable of achieving that result. It may also be accurately said that soap powder is used to clean the family wash, notwithstanding that the desired result could not be brought about by the application of dry powder alone.

...

34. If [the individual files are not themselves 'computer programs' within the definition in s 10], it must be because the requirement of use to bring about a certain result is limiting with respect to what may constitute the 'set' of statements or instructions. In other words, it must be because, as a matter of construction, the set will always be defined by its ability to bring about the result, such that, if some other statement, instruction or the like is also required, the statements or instructions putatively making up the original set could not be regarded as a 'set' in the statutory sense.

...

36. As the explanatory memorandum for the 1984 amendment stated, the word 'set' indicated 'that the instructions are related to one another rather than being a mere collection'. It is, therefore, the fact of interrelation, rather than the ability, unaided, to bring about the result, that should be treated as giving a practical connotation to the concept of a 'set' in any particular case. What should be the nature of the relationship? Clearly, the use to which the statements or instructions are put. If the statements or instructions are co-operatively used to bring about a certain result, that should be regarded as sufficient to satisfy the definition. That they require also the participation of other components of software, be they statements, instructions or otherwise, should not, in my view, be regarded as disqualifying.

...

39. The definition requires me to accept as a computer program any set of statements or instructions which is used to bring about a certain result. I consider that the instructions in the table file and the editor file were a set within the terms of the definition. Those files were discrete manageable entities. Either could be downloaded and used as such. Either could be included in, or excluded from, a CMS, depending on the developer's requirements. Each added functionality, in the sense that results were made possible by its inclusion. Each file (or either file as the occasion required) was sent as an entity to the user's computer to function co-operatively with the browser's software. The instructions on each file were related by function, by location and by utilisation. On any view, those instructions constituted a set. Further, the results for the bringing about of which the files were used were recognisable and definable. In the case of the table file, for instance, one result might be the highlighting of a line entry in a table. Another result might be the re-ordering of the lines in the table. For each result to be brought about required the participation of HTML software on the browser; but it required also the participation of the relevant instructions in the table file. That is to say, in the words of the definition, the bringing about of

the result in question required the use of those instructions. And the same conclusion could be drawn, *mutatis mutandis*, in the case of the instructions in the editor file.

40. For the sake of completeness, I mention here that [the two computer programming experts who gave evidence] expressed the opinion that neither the table file nor the editor file was a computer program. The question for the court, however, is not whether either file was a computer program as understood by professionals in the field; it is whether either file satisfied the statutory definition.

COMPUTER INTERFACES

One issue that has been discussed in the context of computer programs is the extent to which interfaces—such as graphical user interfaces or the 'look and feel' of a computer program—are protected by copyright. The next extract addresses this issue.

CASE EXTRACT: CURRENT LAW

StatusCard Australia Pty Ltd v Rotondo

[2008] QSC 181; [2009] 1 Qd R 559
Supreme Court of Queensland

[The plaintiff sold computer programs to people who bet on horse and greyhound racing. The programs were designed to enhance betting by organising and presenting betting information from the Totalisator Agency Board agencies (TABs), telecast as a subscription service (BettorData) by the Seven Network. The plaintiff's program was designed to highlight data about 'late bets' presumed to be lodged by insiders with better information about the likely chances of the various horses or greyhounds. Subscribers to the BettorData telecast, and the plaintiff's program, could follow the lead of the insiders and place bets where the 'smart money' had gone. The defendant wrote his own program to perform similar functions to the plaintiff's program. Chesterman J noted (at [61]) substantial similarities between the visual displays of the plaintiff's and defendant's programs: the colours chosen for the three TABs were identical, the same colour was chosen to identify the TAB of the state in which the race was being conducted, the time intervals less than five minutes from the designated start of a race were displayed in red numerals showing the time to the race in seconds. Further, the same colours were used to indicate horses on which the odds were shortening and the degree to which the odds were changing.]

Chesterman J: 85. There is a degree of difficulty and, indeed, artificiality in this part of the plaintiff's case. The difficulty arises from the fact that the functionality of a computer program, its behaviour, is not the subject of copyright protection. See eg *Autodesk Inc v Dyason [No 2]* (1993) 176 CLR 300 at 304. The artificiality comes from the fact that though basing its case upon the infringement of what is said to be a literary or artistic work, the depiction on the screen, the plaintiff is in fact attempting to restrain the first defendant from producing or selling his computer programs which perform the same functions as the plaintiff's. The plaintiff seeks to achieve that end by restraining the reproduction of images, which are an essential product of the functions of the program, but are said to be original works protected by s 31 of the Act.

86. The case has considerable similarity to *Navitaire Inc v easyJet Airline Co Ltd* [2006] RPC 3. It was described by Jacob LJ in *Nova Productions Ltd v Mazooma Games Ltd* [2007] EWCA Civ 219 at para 46:

> The facts ... were ... easyJet wanted to substitute its existing airline booking program with another because it had fallen out with Navitaire, the owner of the copyright in the existing program. It commissioned the second defendant to produce a substitute which would look and feel like its predecessor. So far as possible users were not to notice any difference when they used the new program. Without in any way using or even having access to the source code of Navitaire, this was achieved.

Nevertheless the plaintiff, Navitaire, lost its action. Pumfrey J said [2006] RPC 160–1:

> ... The question with which I am confronted ... is peculiar ... to computer programs. The reason it is a new problem is that two completely different computer programs can produce an identical result: not a result identical at some level of abstraction but identical at any level of abstraction. This is so even if the author of one has no access at all to the other but only to its results. The analogy with a plot is for this reason a poor one ... A computer program ... does not have a plot, merely a series of pre-defined operations intended to achieve the desired result in response to the request of the customer.

and at 162:

> What is left when the interface aspects of the case are disregarded is the business function of carrying out the transaction and creating the record, because none of the code was read or copied by the defendants. It is right that those responsible for devising OpenRes envisaged this as the end result for their program: but that is not relevant skill and labour.

87. The first defendant did not copy the plaintiff's computer program. Using a different program it managed to replicate many of the functions of the plaintiff's program and the manner in which the plaintiff's program displayed information. The plaintiff accepts that there is no copyright in the functionality, or the 'look and feel' of a computer program, and the concession is rightly made. In a useful discussion by Professor Ricketson, *The Law of Intellectual Property: Copyright, Designs & Confidential Information* para 9.255, the author points out that the protection afforded by copyright attaches to a computer program, the code, but not to the non-literal, behavioural, aspects of the program. The manner in which it functions, the results it produces, are not, or at least not generally, the subject of copyright. The author also notes that the decision of the High Court in *Data Access* is 'unsympathetic' to 'the protection of user interface aspects of a program'...

  ...

89. There is, I think, a real question whether something as evanescent as a computer screen display can be a work for the purposes of the Act. The topic is complicated and its resolution in a particular case will probably depend upon more detailed evidence as to the nature, origin and storage of the information which is transformed into the form of a screen display, than was adduced in this case. I note the subject was discussed in the report of the Copyright Law Review Committee in its report on computer software protection [*Computer Software Protection* (1995)]. The relevant paragraphs of the report are 9.43 to 9.48 ...

90. In para 9.44 the committee noted:

> Screen displays may be generated either by retrieving data stored in some form of machine memory or generated during a computer program ... Which of ... these two categories a particular screen display falls into will depend on the nature of what is being displayed, and in some cases, the nature of the program being used. Screen displays generated by a computer program can be characterised as part of the program's behaviour. The question which arises in this context is whether this particular form of program behaviour should be protected. The issues concerning the protection of these types of screen displays are different to those that apply where the screen display is generated by the retrieval of a work that is stored in computer memory. In respect of such displays the issue of protection is relatively straightforward. Where copyright subsists in the work that is being displayed, the unauthorised copying of the screen display of the work will infringe copyright in the work.

> ...

94. It is important, I think, that the information displayed on the screen is constantly changing and is not the product of the plaintiff's work. What the plaintiff's program does is display the telecast BettorData in a comprehensible form. The data comes, moment by moment, from the TABs via Seven Network. The relevant information changes as bets are placed, dividend pools increase and betting patterns emerge. This is the function of the program: displaying the BettorData for the assistance of punters.

95. The plaintiff's 'work', however categorised, is not the information, or BettorData, which appears on the screen display, but the framework in which it is displayed and organised. That is to say the 'work' consists of the lines, columns and colours which serve to confine the various categories of information. The colours readily identify the TABs and allow one to be selected by a function of the program.

96. When one looks at the screen display one has to imagine it as blank save for the vertical lines which demarcate the columns, the two horizontal lines which form the column headings, and the coloured background for the TAB columns ...

97. Section 10 of the Act provides that a literary work includes a written table or compilation. The plaintiff submits that the screen display is a compilation of the information contained in it. It relies, for authority, on *Mirror Newspapers Ltd v Queensland Newspapers Pty Ltd* [1982] Qd R 305. In that case the plaintiff newspaper successfully claimed copyright in a series of bingo cards it published each week. Connolly J described them (308):

> What is expressed in writing here is a sequence of numbers of a chosen length, from the series 1 to 100, capable of being applied to cards already in the hands of the players so as to result in the progressive cancellation of those cards. Not only the identity of the numbers but their sequence are essential features of the list ...

His Honour relied upon the judgment of Petersen J in *University of London Press Ltd v University Tutorial Press Ltd* [1916] 2 Ch 601 at 608:

> ... Many things which had no pretensions to literary style acquired copyright; for example, a list of registered bills of sale, a list of foxhounds and hunting days, and trade catalogues; ... the words 'literary work' cover work which is expressed in print or writing, irrespective of the question whether the quality or style is high. The word 'literary' seems to be used in a sense somewhat

similar to the use of the word 'literature' in political or electioneering literature and refers to written or printed matter.

His Honour referred also to the judgment of Street CJ in eq in *Real Estate Institute of NSW v Wood* (1923) 23 SR (NSW) 349 at 352 in which the Chief Judge posed the question:

> Whether the work in question, … a compilation, supplied intelligible information and whether mental effort and industry were required for its preparation.

98. In my opinion the framework, including column headings, devised by the plaintiff for the display of the BettorData is neither a table nor a compilation. It does not contain intelligible information. It has no content. It is no more than a series of rectangles, or 'boxes', some coloured, in which the BettorData can be displayed for ease of comprehension.

DRAMATIC WORKS

Section 10(1) of the *Copyright Act* provides:

> *dramatic work* includes:
>
> (a) a choreographic show or other dumb show; and
> (b) a scenario or script for a cinematograph film;
>
> but does not include a cinematograph film as distinct from the scenario or script for a cinematograph film.

The concept of a dramatic work readily covers written plays and screenplays (e.g. for films, television programs, or television or radio advertisements); as the definition indicates, it also includes choreography (provided it has been recorded in some material form: see Chapter 3). It does not, however, include films, which are separately protected under Part IV (unlike the situation in the UK: see *Norowzian v Arks Ltd (No 2)* [2000] FSR 363).

Australian courts have rejected some creative attempts to extend this category. In *Aristocrat Leisure Industries Pty Ltd v Pacific Gaming Pty Ltd* [2000] FCA 1273; (2000) 105 FCR 153, Tamberlin J rejected an argument that the specification for an electronic pokie (gambling) machine describing its display, its rules, the symbols and their order on the games reels and the prizes payable for different winning combinations was a dramatic work, holding:

> 61. While it is not necessary to the concept of 'dramatic work' to have something in the nature of a play by Shakespeare or Molière, there is a minimum requirement of some type of *performance*. This performance need not in my view be that of human beings. For example a script of an animated cartoon, such as 'South Park' or 'The Simpsons', may well be a dramatic work because it calls for performance by characters.
>
> 62. In the present case, while it is possible that the video races, taken in isolation, could be described as cinematograph films the specifications for the Aristocrat Games lack the element of *performance* by characters, and are insufficiently predetermined, to amount to 'dramatic works'. There is no apparent plot, nor is there any choreography, script, characterisation or interaction between characters and there is a strong element of unpredictability and randomness. None of these elements are essential or individually determine the question

but, weighing them cumulatively, I am led to the conclusion that the specifications do not give rise to any dramatic work.

In *Nine Network Australia Pty Ltd v Australian Broadcasting Corporation* [1999] FCA 1864; (1999) 48 IPR 333, Hill J, in an interlocutory decision, characterised an argument that the New Year's Eve fireworks display on Sydney Harbour was a dramatic work as 'not strong'. Although there was a script, which sequentially detailed the particular fireworks, in the order in which they were to be ignited and in conjunction with the accompanying music, Hill J doubted that such a display fell within the ordinary meaning of 'dramatic work', and queried whether there would be differences between the schedule and the actual event.

More difficult issues arise in relation to television 'formats', such as the formats for well-known reality television shows, which are often franchised internationally. When it comes to a television format, there is a real question whether there is any 'work' sufficiently definite to be the subject of copyright, or whether protection is really being sought for an idea rather than expression.

CASE EXTRACT: PRECEDENT

Green v Broadcasting Corporation of New Zealand

[1989] RPC 700
Privy Council (New Zealand)

[The appellant was a celebrity who had devised and compered an English television talent show entitled 'Opportunity Knocks'. The respondent, BCNZ, broadcast a similar television show under the same title in New Zealand. Green sued unsuccessfully for copyright infringement. After failing in the New Zealand Court of Appeal, he appealed to the Privy Council.]

Lord Bridge of Harwich (at 701–702): The copyright alleged to have been infringed was claimed to subsist in the 'scripts and dramatic format' of 'Opportunity Knocks' as broadcast in England. The appellant's primary difficulty arises from the circumstances that no script was ever produced in evidence. [The trial judge,] Ongley J concluded that:—

> There was really no evidence that any part of the show was reduced to a written text which could properly be called a script …

He added later:—

> No writing has been produced in evidence in this action in which, in my view, copyright could subsist.

The Court of Appeal differed from the trial judge to the extent that they accepted that the evidence established the existence of scripts. But the evidence as to the nature of the scripts and what their text contained was exiguous in the extreme. It is to be found in two short passages from the evidence given by the appellant himself. He said in the course of examination-in-chief:—

> In the year 1956, I wrote the scripts of Opportunity Knocks shows, such as they were, because we would have what we would call the introductions, our stock phrases like 'For So-and-So, Opportunity Knocks', phrases such as 'This is your show, folks, and I do mean you.' The other part

of the writing dealt with interviews with the people and one could not really call it writing because you were really only finding out what the artists wanted to talk about.

He said in cross-examination:—

The script of Opportunity Knocks has continuously been the same for the catch phrases, the interviews each week with the artists has differed, the script for the past 17 years and long before 1975 contained particularly the end of the show beginning with the words 'make your mind up time' using the clapometer and bringing back the five people.

On the basis of this evidence Somers J concluded that:—

... the scripts as they are inferred to be from the description given in evidence did not themselves do more than express a general idea or concept for a talent quest and hence were not the subject of copyright.

In the absence of precise evidence as to what the scripts contained, their Lordships are quite unable to dissent from this view.

The alternative formulation of the appellant's claim relies upon the 'dramatic format' of 'Opportunity Knocks', by which their Lordships understand is meant those characteristic features of the show which were repeated in each performance. These features were, in addition to the title, the use of the catch phrases 'for [name of competitor] opportunity knocks,' 'this is your show folks, and I do mean you,' and 'make up your mind time,' the use of a device called a 'clapometer' to measure audience reaction to competitors' performances and the use of sponsors to introduce competitors. It was this formulation which found favour with Gallen J.

It is stretching the original use of the word 'format' a long way to use it metaphorically to describe the features of a television series such as a talent, quiz or game show which is presented in a particular way, with repeated but unconnected use of set phrases and with the aid of particular accessories. Alternative terms suggested in the course of argument were 'structure' or 'package'. This difficulty in finding an appropriate term to describe the nature of the 'work' in which the copyright subsists reflects the difficulty of the concept that a number of allegedly distinctive features of a television series can be isolated from the changing material presented in each separate performance (the acts of the performers in the talent show, the questions and answers in the quiz show etc.) and identified as an 'original dramatic work'. No case was cited to their Lordships in which copyright of the kind claimed had been established.

The protection which copyright gives creates a monopoly and 'there must be certainty in the subject matter of such monopoly in order to avoid injustice to the rest of the world:' *Tate v Fulbrook* [1908] 1 KB 821, per Farwell J at p 832. The subject matter of the copyright claimed for the 'dramatic format' of 'Opportunity Knocks' is conspicuously lacking in certainty. Moreover, it seems to their Lordships that a dramatic work must have sufficient unity to be capable of performance and that the features claimed as constituting the 'format' of a television show, being unrelated to each other except as accessories to be used in the presentation of some other dramatic or musical performance, lack that essential characteristic.

For these reasons their Lordships will humbly advise Her Majesty that the appeal should be dismissed.

CASE EXTRACT: CURRENT LAW

Nine Films & Television Pty Ltd v Ninox Television Ltd

[2005] FCA 1404; (2005) 67 IPR 46
Federal Court of Australia

['Dream Home' was a very successful New Zealand reality television program, produced by television production company Ninox. In 1999 a director of Ninox met with an Australian production company to grant rights for the exploitation of 'Dream Home' in Australia. 'Australian Dream Home' was made, and was broadcast by Nine in Australia in 2000. In 2002, two employees from Nine came up with the concept of 'The Block', two seasons of which were produced in-house and broadcast by Nine in Australia in 2003–04. Ninox alleged that in producing 'The Block', Nine reproduced 'the "Dream Home" format' (at [31]), being a dramatic work. Nine denied there was 'any substantial similarity between "The Block" and the original copyright work embodied in "Dream Home" and its format' (at [34]), contending that there were many distinguishing features between the two shows, especially in the 'degree and form of the dramas and tensions which develop in "The Block"' (at [35]). Nine did not contest subsistence of copyright, with the result that the issues were fought in terms of whether there was a substantial reproduction. Nevertheless, the case is worth reading for its discussion of what exactly is protected by copyright in this context.]

Tamberlin J: 28. The 'Dream Home' format, as particularised by Ninox in its Cross-Claim, is said to comprise the following elements:

Events and Characters
Sponsor friendly
2 couples
Selection by public application
Attempt to out-renovate each other
Strict budget to work to
One room completed per episode
Time frames strictly enforced
Completely renovate and decorate
2 old relocatable houses
Houses same size
House same value
Helped by team of experts
Houses auctioned in finale
Winner keeps house
Second place winner keeps $20,000
Emotional elements
Pressure dealings with mess, budgets, builders
Impact on relationships
Tears, tantrums, trying to finish on time
Human drama, anger, sadness, joy, betrayal, triumph, despair

Builders do structural work when contestants at work during week

Couples work on decorating outside business hours

...

PRINCIPLES

36. To determine whether there has been an infringement of copyright by reproduction of a substantial part of the 'Dream Home' format and production, it is necessary to consider the whole context in which the claimed similarities and differences arise and in which the characters and plot develop. Television series often depend for their audience on the gradual development of character and plot over time, so that the audience becomes involved in the personalities, places, information and plot. To look at one or more episodes in isolation may result in a failure to appreciate the significance of individual scenes or events. Thus, a program may appear attractive to a devoted watcher, whereas a person who simply watches one episode may speculate as to the strange tastes of the dedicated aficionado who has traced the development of character and plot. Therefore, in determining whether copyright has been infringed, it is necessary to consider the whole of the series and the importance of the relevant parts in that context. In this case, I have subjected myself to viewing and hearing substantially all of the various productions tendered in evidence and I have weighed the similarities and differences between the programs in the light of each of the series as a whole.

[Tamberlin J quoted from *Green v Broadcasting Corporation of New Zealand*, extracted above, and continued:]

45. Another helpful case is *Zeccola v Universal City Studios Inc* (1982) 46 ALR 189. In that case, an application was made for interlocutory relief in respect of allegations of infringement by the appellants' film, *Great White*, of the respondent's copyright in a novel, screenplay and film, each entitled *Jaws*. The appellants' film was made by Italian filmmakers in 1980 under the name *La Ultimo Squalo* (*The Last Shark*). The respondent's film is the well-known film directed by Steven Spielberg, an American producer and director. After noting the submission of counsel for the appellants that *Jaws* and *Great White* are genre films based upon the idea of a savage monster menacing a community and a killer shark terrorising human beings, and the submission that neither film was entitled to protection because there was no copyright in a general idea, Lockhart and Fitzgerald JJ, in a joint judgment, said at 192:

> In general, there is no copyright in the central idea or theme of a story or play, however original it may be; copyright subsists in the combination of situations, events and scenes which constitute the particular working out or expression of the idea or theme. If these are totally different the taking of the idea or theme does not constitute an infringement of copyright.
>
> Of necessity certain events, incidents or characters are found in many books and plays. Originality, when dealing with incidents and characters familiar in life or fiction, lies in the association, grouping and arrangement of those incidents and characters in such a manner that presents a new concept or a novel arrangement of those events and characters. We accept that where a story is written based on various incidents which, in themselves, are commonplace, a claim for copyright must be confined closely to the story which has been composed by the author. Another author who materially varies the incidents and characters and materially changes the story is not an infringer of the copyright. If a literary or dramatic work is not wholly original

there is no copyright in the unoriginal part so as to prevent its use. Additional factors may fall for consideration where the alleged infringement is by cinematograph film.

46. At 193, their Honours observed that the primary Judge had correctly recognised that the two questions involved in the resolution of the major issue were: first, the degree of objective similarity between the appellants' film and the respondent's novel and screenplay; and, secondly, whether copying was established. The latter question involves a consideration of the inspiration for, and derivation of, the format and production of the alleged infringing film or dramatic work.

47. In *Tate v Fulbrook* [1908] 1 KB 821, Vaughan Williams LJ, emphasising contextual considerations, said at 829–830:

> I think that one ought to take the words of the first piece as presented to the public plus all their dramatic surroundings, and compare them with the words of the other piece, which is said to be a piracy, *not taking the latter words by themselves only, but with the stage situations and scenic effects by which they were accompanied, and to ask oneself, taking the whole of each piece together, whether there is such a similarity between the plaintiff's play as a whole and the defendant's play as a whole that the latter is an infringement* of the proprietary right of representation vested in the plaintiff ... my view of the true construction of the Act is that the subject matter, the right of the author ... which is intended to be thereby protected, is something which is capable of being printed and published. (Emphasis added)

48. In resolving the issue of copyright infringement in the present case, it is also important to take into account that copyright in a written story gives protection not simply to the words used but can take into account the expression of themes and ideas embedded in the production if they are sufficiently substantial. Copyright is directed to protect the work and skill embodied in the *expression* of an idea. As Laddie J points in *Autospin (Oil Seals) Ltd v Beehive Spinning (a firm)* [1995] RPC 683 at 697:

> ... this may well include the combination of the main themes, incidents and characters in the story. It may be said, therefore, that copyright protects that combination. Both the 1956 and 1988 Acts require the relevant skill and effort to be fixed in some material form. Frequently this takes the form of words on a page. But it is not the form of fixation which is protected, it is the relevant skill and effort involved in creating the literary work.

...

REPRODUCTION OF SUBSTANTIAL PART

71. Ninox's primary submission on this question is that, with the exception of the requirement that the contestants should live on the premises throughout the renovations, the dramatic format of 'The Block' involves a reproduction of the structure of 'Dream Home'. It is said that Barbour wanted to create a television series that had all of the essential features of 'Dream Home', namely, its focus on home renovation, episodic progression and the competitive elements resulting in a life-altering outcome for one of the couples. It is said that Barbour and Cress adopted the time and budgetary constraints in the concept for 'The Block' and also the idea of a program that had significant opportunities for sponsor involvement in the content of the program.

72. Ninox says that the '"Dream Home" Bible', as developed by the Australian and New Zealand productions of 'Dream Home', involves a strict and significant order of events. This order of events involves the introduction of the particular contestants in the 'set up' phase and the identification of the

rules that will constrain them in the renovation task undertaken. It also involves a series of individual programs to be screened over the life of the series in which the task of renovation of the entire residence is shown progressively room by room and area by area. It is said that both programs involve the audience following and comparing the efforts of the contestants and the outcome that they achieve at each stage. At each stage, and in each episode, the dramatic tension caused by the time and budgetary restrictions on the contestants is an important theme. There is said to be a constant and continuous demonstration of the fact that the couples are amateurs undertaking a task, albeit with some assistance from time to time by professionals, constrained by their own lack of training and the tightness of their budgets. The program involves observation of the strain and tiredness engendered by the imperatives of the contest, resulting in the problems and outbursts that occur from time to time. It is said that the program follows the progress of the contestants towards a final outcome dictated at the end of the series where a winner emerges as a consequence of the quality of the efforts employed in the task of renovation.

73. Ninox also says that it is significant that the events and dialogue are, to a large extent, unscripted and unanticipated by the maker of each series. This arises from the fact that the contestants are placed in situations where dramatic aspects emerge and are captured by the television producer. There are opportunities for editing so as to emphasise dramatic moments, with the exception of the final live episode. The final episodes of both 'The Block' and 'Dream Home' are live to air and this is said to dictate an important part of the structure of the series.

74. In my view, simply by reason of the fact that there are large elements of unscripted dialogue and interaction within the overall framework of the programs, there cannot be any substantial reproduction …

…

93. From my examination of all the episodes of both programs, I am not persuaded that there is any substantial reproduction or similarity at a generic level, taking into account the images, sounds, moods, themes, and emphases in the two programs and the context in which they are produced.

MUSICAL WORKS

The *Copyright Act* provides no statutory definition of 'musical work'. Mummery LJ offered the following useful discussion of the term in *Sawkins v Hyperion Records Ltd* [2005] EWCA Civ 565; [2005] RPC 32:

53. In the absence of a special statutory definition of music, ordinary usage assists: as indicated in the dictionaries, the essence of music is combining sounds for listening to. Music is not the same as mere noise. The sound of music is intended to produce effects of some kind on the listener's emotions and intellect. The sounds may be produced by an organised performance on instruments played from a musical score, though that is not essential for the existence of the music or of copyright in it. Music must be distinguished from the fact and form of its fixation as a record of a musical composition. The score is the traditional and convenient form of fixation of the music and conforms to the requirement that a copyright work must be recorded in some material form. But the fixation in the written score or on a record is not in itself the music in which copyright subsists. There is no reason why, for example,

a recording of a person's spontaneous singing, whistling or humming or of improvisations of sounds by a group of people with or without musical instruments should not be regarded as 'music' for copyright purposes.

...

55. In principle, there is no reason for regarding the actual notes of music as the *only* matter covered by musical copyright, any more than, in the case of a dramatic work, only the words to be spoken by the actors are covered by dramatic copyright. Added stage directions may affect the performance of the play on the stage or on the screen and have an impact on the performance seen by the audience. Stage directions are as much part of a dramatic work as plot, character and dialogue.

56. It is wrong in principle to single out the notes as uniquely significant for copyright purposes and to proceed to deny copyright to the other elements that make some contribution to the sound of the music when performed, such as performing indications, tempo and performance practice indicators, if they are the product of a person's effort, skill and time, bearing in mind, of course, the 'relatively modest' level (see Laddie, Prescott & Vitoria on *The Modern Law of Copyright and Designs* 3rd ed para 3.58) of the threshold for a work to qualify for protection.

Although the boundaries of a musical work are usually self-evident, arguments have occasionally been raised that try to dissect the musical work into a series of distinct works, as seen in the two extracts below.

CASE EXTRACT: CURRENT LAW

CBS Records Australia Ltd v Gross

(1989) 15 IPR 385
Federal Court of Australia

[Collette, an aspiring singer/songwriter, invited a songwriter, Guy Gross, to collaborate in writing the vocal lines and music of new songs, which they did. An employee of CBS advised Collette to record a cover version of an existing song, and suggested 'Ring My Bell', recorded in the 1970s by American singer Anita Ward. Collette and Guy recorded some of the songs they had written and a cover version of 'Ring My Bell' (this version was known as the 'Trackdown version' after the name of the recording studio). Collette sang the vocal lines while Guy produced the instrumental parts using a synthesiser. The resulting demo tape was passed on to CBS, which offered Collette a contract to record a version of 'Ring My Bell'. CBS did their own arrangement of the song. The CBS recording was a hit in Australia. Guy alleged that he owned copyright in the 'Trackdown version' and that the CBS version infringed his copyright. Much of the argument in the case concerned whether the Trackdown version was an original work—that is, whether the differences from the Ward version were sufficient to confer originality—but there were also some comments on what constituted the relevant musical work, and whether the version was divisible.]

CURRENT LAW

Davies J (at 392–398): As to whether any copyright subsists in the Trackdown version is a point of difficulty. For copyright in an arrangement to subsist, the differences from the work arranged must be such that a new original work can be identified. Differences resulting from mere interpretation, particularly differences brought about by an arrangement of a work to suit the qualities of a particular singer's voice, do not result in the creation of an original work. Particularly is this so in the area of popular music where the latitude given to a performer may be much greater than that in classical works, where the notes, phrasing, emphasis and the like tend to be specified in great detail. Creational composition is required to bring into being an original work ...

My impression is that the Trackdown version, if considered in its entirety, is the product of sufficient original skill and creative labour to sustain copyright. It is not just a copy of the Ward version. Independent judgment was applied to its creation. Original composition was required for the development of the instrumental backing so as to reflect principal elements of the Ward version yet to match the backing with Collette's style of singing. Were the Trackdown version to be faithfully copied or imitated by other performers, I would find it difficult to say that an original work was not infringed.

Guy claims to be the owner of the copyright in the Trackdown version. However, he did not work alone on its development. Collette and Guy collaborated together. It was Tony Briggs who suggested the use of a male singer for a part of the song and who introduced that singer. Kirke Godfrey, a sound engineer at the Trackdown studios, made many suggestions and was responsible for the final 'mix' of the many individual tracks which had been recorded. Thus, at most, Guy was a joint proprietor of the copyright in the Trackdown version ...

Mr DK Catterns, counsel for CBS, submitted that, if there were copyright in the Trackdown version, copyright in the instrumental backing resided in Guy and copyright in the vocal part resided in Collette. But the work ought not to be divided in this way. The work was a song having vocal lines and an instrumental backing. There were not two pieces of music. The vocal and instrumental parts were elements which combined together to form a single work. Whether there may be separate copyright in each map of a street directory, as discussed by Hill J in *Universal Press Pty Ltd v Provest Ltd & Brothers Publishing Pty Ltd* (1989) 14 IPR 623; 87 ALR 497 or in each chapter of a novel, as mentioned in *University of New South Wales v Moorhouse* (1975) 133 CLR 1; 6 ALR 193, the present is not such a case ...

I am satisfied that CBS did not infringe the copyright. The alleged copying does not reside in the instrumental backing of the CBS version. CBS developed its own instrumental backing and did not copy the Trackdown version. Any similarity between the instrumental parts comes simply from the fact that they were developed at about the same time for the same vocalist and for the same type of audience ...

Collette and Guy had copyright in material on the demonstration tape. Had CBS chosen to copy that material, Collette and Guy would have received royalties. But CBS chose not to do so. CBS simply adopted the idea that Collette should do a version of 'Ring My Bell', which was in any event the idea of Briggs. There was nothing unjust in what occurred, no reason why Guy should be remunerated by Collette for his work and no reason why Collette should not retain any benefit she may receive from CBS.

CASE EXTRACT: COMPARATIVE LAW

Coffey v Warner/Chappell Music Ltd

[2005] EWHC 449 (Ch); [2005] FSR 34
High Court of England and Wales, Chancery Division

[Ms Coffey, the author of a song called 'Forever After', claimed that the song co-written by Madonna and Patrick Leonard entitled 'Nothing Really Matters' infringed her copyright.]

Blackburne J: … 4. The claim as now formulated is that the recording of 'Forever After' '*includes* an original musical work *comprising* the combination of vocal expression, pitch contour and syncopation of or around the words "does it really matter" (emphasis added). She refers to this as 'the Work'. She pleads that the words 'does it really matter' are repeated throughout the song and comprise its lyrical hook. She claims that copyright subsists in the Work (as so defined) and that she owns the copyright …

5. Amended further information given … describes the features of 'Forever After' which are alleged to form the Work as the combination of those three features and makes clear that no others were relied on. The further information also explains what is to be understood by those three features. By 'voice expression' is meant, in effect, 'timbre' (illustrated by a comparison between the 'gravelly' vocal expression of one well-known performer and the 'twangy' vocal expression of another). By 'pitch contour' is meant 'the general shape of the pitches to which the words "does it really matter" [in "Forever After"] are sung' rather than, as I understood it, the notes themselves. By 'syncopation of or around the words "does it really matter"' is meant the 'unnatural metrical stress' given to the syllables of those four words 'in terms of their placement within the two bars [in which they are sung] and the unusual rhythmic and durational stress in terms of their elongated durations'.

6. Insofar as I have been able to follow precisely what is intended by those three features, they appear, at any rate in large part, to appertain to interpretation or performance characteristics by the performer, which is not the legitimate subject of copyright protection in the case of a musical work, rather than to composition, which is. Thus it is pleaded (in relation to 'pitch contour') that each sung version of the contour is subject to improvisation by the singer.

7. Be that as it may, the defendants, who appear by Mr Thomas Moody-Stuart, contend that the copyright work relied upon by the claimant which she alleges the defendants to have infringed cannot constitute a musical work in which copyright can exist in that it comprises no more than features of, or extractions from, what properly and objectively is to be regarded as the relevant work. They contend therefore that the claim should not be allowed to proceed any further. This is only one of the defences which the defendants have pleaded. (Another is that, in any event, no copying occurred.)

8. Mr Moody-Stuart submits that copyright subsists in a work in its entirety, not in parts of or extracts from the work. If a part of a work is copied, copyright in the work in its entirety may be infringed if the part copied constitutes a substantial part, qualitatively or quantitatively, of the work as a whole. It is not open, he says, to a claimant to pick and choose the elements of a work upon which he relies in order to make the question of whether a substantial part has been copied more likely to be answered in his favour.

9. I agree. The first step in a copyright action, as Laddie J pointed out in *IPC Media Ltd v Highbury-Leisure Publishing Ltd* [2004] EWHC 2985 (Ch) at [8], is for the claimant to identify what work or works

he relies on. The need, as Laddie J observed in that case, is '... to be alert to the possibility of being misled by what may be called similarity by excision ... In copyright cases, chipping away and ignoring all the bits which are undoubtedly not copies may result in the creation of an illusion of copying in what is left'. He warned against losing sight of the differences between the claimant's work and the alleged infringement and emphasised that the differences are important in deciding whether copying has taken place.

10. What the copyright work is in any given case is not governed by what the claimant alleging copyright infringement chooses to say that it is. Rather, it is a matter for objective determination by the court. (See, to this effect in relation to legislation which is not relevantly different from the *Copyright, Designs and Patents Act 1988*, the remarks of Drummond J in *Coogi Australia Pty Ltd v Hysport International Pty Ltd* (1998) 41 IPR 593 at 609.) The consequence of confining too narrowly the subject matter of the claimant's claim may be not only to deprive a defendant of what may be a good defence that what he took did not involve the taking of a substantial part of the true copyright work but also to create what in *IPC Media* Laddie J described (at [23]) as 'a legal millefeuilles with layers of different artistic copyrights' ...

11. It is clear that cherry-picking those features of 'Forever After' to identify as the material copyright work matters where arguably 'Nothing Really Matters' is the same is precisely what the claimant appears to have done. It is to be noted that the three features which alone, she says, constitute the musical work in which copyright is claimed do not extend to the surrounding melody, *i.e.* the notes themselves, their duration and rhythm, or to the rhythm of the particular phrase in which the three identified features are said to be found.

12. While I accept the submission of Mr Piers Acland, appearing for the claimant, that, as a general proposition, circumstances may exist which justify regarding a constituent part of a larger entity as in itself a copyright work, that can only be (as Drummond J in *Coogi v Hysport* at 610 pointed out) where the part in question can fairly be regarded as so separable from the material with which it is collocated as itself to constitute a copyright work. In the current case, it is obvious—indeed Mr Acland felt unable to advance any serious argument to the contrary—that identifying a separate copyright work in this way is simply not possible. The three somewhat elusive features identified by the claimant as her musical work cannot by any stretch of the imagination be said to be sufficiently separable from the remainder of the song as themselves to constitute a musical work.

ARTISTIC WORKS

Section 10(1) of the *Copyright Act* provides:

> *artistic work* means:
>
> (a) a painting, sculpture, drawing, engraving or photograph, whether the work is of artistic quality or not;
> (b) a building or a model of a building, whether the building or model is of artistic quality or not; or
> (c) a work of artistic craftsmanship whether or not mentioned in paragraph (a) or (b);
>
> but does not include a circuit layout within the meaning of the *Circuit Layouts Act 1989*.

Unlike most of the subject matter definitions in the *Copyright Act*, this definition is exhaustive: a work must fit within one of these categories to be recognised as an artistic work. Having said this, as the extracts below indicate, these categories can sometimes be read quite expansively.

PAINTINGS, DRAWINGS AND PHOTOGRAPHS

The interpretation section of the *Copyright Act* provides no statutory definition of 'painting'. For consideration, see *Merchandising Corporation of America v Harpbond Ltd* [1983] FSR 32. 'Photograph' is defined in s 10(1) of the *Copyright Act* to mean 'a product of photography or of a process similar to photography, other than an article or thing in which visual images forming part of a cinematograph film have been embodied, and includes a product of xerography'. Section 10(1) also provides that 'drawing' 'includes a diagram, map, chart or plan'.

CASE EXTRACT: CURRENT LAW

Elwood Clothing Pty Ltd v Cotton On Clothing Pty Ltd

[2008] FCAFC 197; (2008) 172 FCR 580
Federal Court of Australia, Full Court

[Copyright was claimed in the T-shirt design depicted below.]

ELWOOD 'NEWDEAL' T-SHIRT

Lindgren, Goldberg and Bennett JJ:

(1) WHAT WERE THE DESIGNS AND WERE THEY ORIGINAL ARTISTIC WORKS?

44. By its notice of contention, Cotton On argues that the Designs were 'original literary works' rather than 'original artistic works'.

45. … [F]or the purposes of this case the definition of 'artistic work' in s 10(1) has the effect that an artistic work *is* a drawing …

CURRENT LAW

46. We agree with Cotton On that the definition of 'literary work' suggests:

> that literary works typically will be expressed in some form of notation or code (as in the case of computer programs) and that the information contained within them will be comprehended by a human addressee through the process of reading.

47. In relation to the concept of a 'drawing', Heerey J, in *Woodtree* [*Pty Ltd v Zheng* [2007] FCA 1922; (2007) 164 FCR 369] (at [25]), quoted from Ricketson S, *The Law of Intellectual Property, Copyright, Designs and Confidential Information* at para 7.365:

> Essentially, a drawing is a two-dimensional work in which shapes and images are depicted by lines, often without colouring.

Of this description of a drawing, his Honour stated (at [26] and [27]):

> I would agree that this is the ordinary meaning of the term 'drawing'. The *Macquarie Dictionary* gives us several definitions of the noun 'drawing':
>
> ...
>
> 2.   representation by lines; delineation of form without reference to colour.
> 3.   a sketch, plan, or design, esp one made with pen, pencil, or crayon.
>
> In the context of the visual arts, the traditional distinction has been between paintings, which are coloured, and drawings, which are monotone, usually, but not always, black upon white. The statutory definition, particularly by its inclusion of maps, makes it clear that for the purposes of the Act something may be a drawing notwithstanding that it is coloured. However, the essence of a drawing remains the concept of a representation of some object by a pictorial line.

48. It is true that in many of the cases, drawings have been of things that already existed or were to be brought into existence: see, for example, *Dorling v Honnor Marine Ltd* [1965] Ch 1 (drawings of parts of a boat); *L B (Plastics) Ltd v Swish Products Ltd* [1979] RPC 551 (drawings of plastic drawers); *S W Hart & Co Pty Ltd v Edwards Hot Water Systems* (1985) 159 CLR 466 (drawings of parts of a solar energy hot water system); *Interlego AG v Croner Trading Pty Ltd* (1992) 39 FCR 348 (drawings of toy bricks).

49. In our view, however, a drawing does not necessarily represent something that exists or is to exist in the real world. There can be a drawing in the form of a pattern, using shapes, colours and other elements in order to give pleasure, or simply (as here) to attract attention and to convey a visual impression—a certain 'look and feel'. It is not inconsistent with Heerey J's understanding of the meaning of a 'drawing' expressed in *Woodtree* to suggest that the object represented by the pictorial line may be a shape, form or pattern that is not a recognisable image, and may be in an abstract style.

50. We would adopt the following extract from [12] of the primary Judge's reasons:

> [There is] a body of case law, which establishes that (1) whether a work will be recognized as an artistic work such as a drawing is highly fact-specific, such that no bright-line rule can be drawn; and (2) the important principle in deciding whether the work is a 'drawing' is whether the work at issue can be said to have a visual rather than 'semiotic' function: *Miller & Lang Ltd v Polak* [1908] 1 Ch 433 (concluding that decorative wording and designs on Christmas cards were drawings for the purpose of the *Fine Arts Copyright Act 1862* (UK); *Roland Corporation & Anor v Lorenzo & Sons Pty Ltd* (1991) 33 FCR 111 (holding that two logos consisting of a single

letter each, 'R' and 'B,' designed in a certain way were eligible for copyright protection as they were drawn with care and to obtain an effect); *Anacon Corporation Ltd v Environmental Research Technology* [1994] FSR 659, at 662 (suggesting that a circuit diagram depicting how components were to be connected together could be an artistic work because it is 'a thing to be looked at in some manner or other [and] is to be looked at in itself'); *Lott v JBW & Friends Pty Ltd* (2000) 76 SASR 105 (finding that a 'graphic bar' consisting of four words in a woodcut design or font that was selected from a computer program was a drawing within the meaning of the Act because it was not so simple that the time and effort in designing the graphic design could be ignored); *Australian Chinese Newspapers Pty Ltd v Melbourne Chinese Press Ltd* (2003) 58 IPR 1 at [107] (holding that a calligraphic rendering of a Chinese character used in a newspaper masthead was capable of constituting a 'painting' under the Act because Chinese calligraphy is a visual art and played 'an important cultural and aesthetic role in Chinese life of ancient origin'); *Woodtree Pty Ltd v Zheng* (2007) 74 IPR 484 (holding that a layout for a box label comprising a photograph and several short lines of explanatory text and numbers was not capable of constituting an artistic work).

51. As noted at [38] above, the boundary of the NewDeal design is a notional circumferential boundary enclosing all of the symbols, numbers, words and images (and the space between them), that appeared on the front and back of the NewDeal T-shirt.

52. It is not clear what meaning the words and numbers were intended to convey. What was the intended meaning, for example, of 'Durable By Design', 'Raging Bulls' and '9' and '6'?

53. Words conveying a semiotic meaning can form part of a drawing. In *Millar & Lang Ltd v Polak* [1908] 1 Ch 433, the works held to be drawings included more meaningful words such as 'Greetings', 'Friends ever', 'Good luck', 'Lest we forget' and 'For old times sake' in a distinctive form within an ornamental oval or circular scroll. Similarly, in *Lott v JBW & Friends Pty Ltd* (2000) 76 SASR 105, Mullighan J held that a graphic bar with the words 'Opera in the Outback' was a drawing. His Honour said (at [14]):

> The graphic designer had to create a design and make choices about the layout, font, colour and dimensions of each part of the design. Having perused the graphic bar, I do not regard it as so simple as to deny copyright. As was the case in *Roland Corporation*, the graphic bar was designed and drawn with care to obtain effect. The selection of the font from a computer program is no less creative than manual drawing …

54. In *Roland Corporation v Lorenzo & Sons Pty Ltd* (1991) 33 FCR 111, Pincus J held to be drawings certain stylised representations of the letters 'R' and 'B'. In *Woodtree* at [29], Heerey J thought it clear that a letter or letters of the alphabet can provide the subject matter of a drawing, and referred to the illuminated manuscripts of medieval works such as the Book of Kells. His Honour held that text itself did not constitute a drawing (at [28]).

55. In the present case, two views call for consideration. One view is that the text (words and numbers) is so insubstantial as not to constitute a literary work and forms part of a single artistic work. The alternative view is that both an artistic work and a literary work are present in the Designs, the artistic work comprising the arrangement, layout and pattern, and the literary work consisting of the words and numbers, but considered without regard to their layout, arrangement and pattern.

CURRENT LAW

56. It has been recognised in two 'circuit diagram' cases that the one work can comprise both an artistic work and a literary work: *Anacon Corporation Ltd v Environmental Research Technology Ltd* [1994] FSR 659 per Jacob J at 663 and *Audrey Max Sandman v Panasonic UK Ltd* [1998] FSR 651 per Pumfrey J at 657–658; but contrast *Electronic Techniques (Anglia) Ltd v Critchley Components Ltd* [1997] FSR 401 per Laddie J at 413–414.

57. We prefer the view that in the present case there is a single artistic work of which the words and numbers, including their size, font, placement and spatial relationships with other elements, form a part. Such semiotic meaning as the words and numbers convey (they do convey such meaning to some extent, being well recognised symbols that 'stand for' something else) is so insubstantial and vague that they do not constitute literary works.

58. Like the primary Judge, we do not think it an adequate account of the Designs to say that they are meant to be read. The expressions 'Durable By Design' and 'Raging Bulls' and the numerals '9' and '6' are meant to be read but that for which they stand is elusive and unimportant. Their importance is in the support they give to the 'look and feel'.

59. Dr Ricketson submitted that the 'verbal messages' include references to the Chicago Bulls basketball team and the film *Raging Bull*. These references, it was argued, 'are intended to evoke a team concept that males are particularly desirous to have'. The latter statement may be true; however this significance attaches to the words and numbers only when they are considered as part of the NewDeal design as a whole. What meaning would they convey, it may be asked rhetorically, taken out of that context? To the extent that the words and numbers evoke a 'team concept', they do so because they are elements in a layout which itself has the look and feel of college-style sporting team wear.

60. To the extent that the words and numbers convey some semiotic meaning, it is trifling when compared with, to use her Honour's words, 'the selection and arrangement of the various elements (text, colour, font, shape, and so on)' (at [16]). The drawing, so constituted, makes a visual impression notwithstanding the presence of the words and numbers. Alternatively, the text may be appreciated visually. In *Millar & Lang Ltd v Polak* [1908] 1 Ch 433 and *Roland Corporation v Lorenzo & Sons Pty Ltd* (1991) 33 FCR 111, the literary elements were treated in such a way as to provide a visual effect which transcended the letters and figures involved.

61. There is a strong artistic element in the NewDeal design. We refer, on the front of the shirt, to the size, style and separation of the digits '9' and '6' on the respective shoulders, the ellipse formed by the 'ELWOOD', the 'Raging Bulls' that surrounds the cursive 'Durable By Design' and the bull's head trademark; on the back of the shirt to the ellipse formed by the cursive 'Raging Bulls' at the top and the two lines 'Durable By Design' and 'Elwood Denims' at the bottom enclosing very large digits '9' and '6', and the small bull's head trademark; and to the overall 'V' shape on the front and the less pronounced 'V' shape on the back.

62. In our respectful opinion, the work on the NewDeal T-shirt, front and back, is an artistic work. The artistic quality of the work consists of the layout, balancing, form, font, positioning, shaping and interrelationship of the various elements. Any meaning conveyed by the numerals and text is so obscure, subjective to the reader and subservient to the artistic aspect that the numerals and text do not amount to a literary work.

SCULPTURES AND ENGRAVINGS

Three-dimensional objects may be analysed as 'sculptures' or 'engravings', which are defined as follows in s 10(1) of the *Copyright Act*:

> *engraving* includes an etching, lithograph, product of photogravure, woodcut, print or similar work, not being a photograph.
>
> ...
>
> *sculpture* includes a cast or model made for purposes of sculpture.

Courts have encountered some difficulties drawing a distinction between three-dimensional products with some visual appeal and 'sculptures' within the ordinary meaning of that term. Recall too that under the general definition of 'artistic work' in s 10, sculptures and engravings are protected 'whether the work is of artistic quality or not'. This has emboldened some claimants to argue that machine parts or mundane three-dimensional items were sculptures.

CURRENT LAW

CASE EXTRACT: CURRENT LAW

Greenfield Products Pty Ltd v Rover Scott Bonnar Ltd

(1990) 17 IPR 417
Federal Court of Australia

Pincus J (at 419–428): The applicant and the respondent are competing manufacturers of ride-on mowers for use in parks and gardens. The applicant's substantial case is that it designed a new kind of drive mechanism for its mowers; the respondent later used the same basic design, having carefully inspected the applicant's. The suit seeks an injunction to restrain further breaches of copyright, damages for infringement of copyright, an account of profits and other relief. ...There being no doubt that the respondent imitated the applicant's design to a considerable extent, taking advantage of the applicant's inventiveness and its development of that design over some years, some might have thought that the law would give the applicant some right of redress. The most obvious basis of a suit of that kind is the patent law, but the applicant had no patent for its invention (assuming it to be patentable) so the applicant has sued, as I have said, for breach of copyright, saying that the respondent copied its design.

COPYRIGHT IN THREE-DIMENSIONAL OBJECTS

...

It was argued on behalf of the applicant that copyright can subsist in the moulds and machine parts because they are 'engravings' and that the drive mechanism is an 'artistic work', being made up of its components which are themselves sculptures and therefore artistic works.

It is convenient to take the latter point first. Although the definition of 'sculpture' is not exhaustive, insofar as the word remains undefined it must be given its ordinary meaning, in accordance with orthodox principles of construction. It is for that reason that I rejected evidence proffered on behalf of the respondent to prove what 'sculpture' means in certain circles. The word 'sculpture' is, at least in this context, not a technical term so as to make evidence admissible on the issue of statutory construction.

It appears to me clear that neither the moulds nor the drive mechanism, nor the parts of the latter, are sculptures in the ordinary sense. It is true, as was pointed out in the course of argument, that some modern sculptures consist of or include parts of machines, but that does not warrant the conclusion that all machines and parts thereof are properly called sculptures, and similar reasoning applies to moulds. I respectfully agree with the conclusion arrived at in the New Zealand Court of Appeal, in *Lincoln Industries Ltd v Wham-O Manufacturing Co* (1984) 3 IPR 115 at 131 that frisbees are not sculptures under the *Copyright Act 1962* (NZ); that conclusion is consistent with mine.

I therefore reject the submission that there can be copyright in the drive mechanism. I do so with more confidence having regard to the concept of infringement by copying objects made from a copyright drawing; the development of that doctrine would have been unnecessary if machinery were itself the subject of copyright.

A submission which is not quite so easily disposed of is that the moulds are 'engravings' under the Act; this has some support from the *Lincoln Industries* case just referred to and from the reasons of the Court of Appeal of Hong Kong in *Interlego AG v Tyco Industries Inc* [1987] FSR 409 at 421 and 453. In the former case, there was evidence that the frisbee moulds were made by use of a tool, cutting metal blanks on a lathe. The Court remarked:

> We see no reason why the process involved in the production of the die or mould, particularly the creation of the cuts to produce the ribs or rings should not be regarded as the act of engraving within the provisions of s 2(1)(a) of the Act, and the mould or die so created an 'engraving' just as a 'print' is an engraving in terms of the extended definition in s 2 of the Act. (p 127)

The definition of 'engraving' in issue there differed slightly from that with which I am concerned, but the difference is not of present significance.

I do not well understand why the Court thought that working at a lathe cutting into a rotating piece of metal with a tool is the work of engraving. One can use a tool fixed in a lathe to inscribe a pattern onto the surface of metal or other materials, but even that would not, perhaps, ordinarily be called engraving. It is true that dictionary definitions of engraving refer to cutting, but it is not all cutting which is engraving; for example, to cut a piece of steel rod into lengths is not to engrave it. Nor, in my opinion, is the process of cutting metal from a block spinning on a lathe a process of engraving the block, in the ordinary sense of the word. The term does not cover shaping a piece of metal or wood on a lathe, but has to do with marking, cutting or working the surface—typically, a flat surface—of an object. The *Second Edition of the Oxford English Dictionary* cites usages of the word 'engrave' which appear to support the New Zealand decision. For example, a translation of the *Metamorphoses* has: 'The fatall steele ... he waues Deepe in his guts, and wounds on wounds ingraues.' But that was published in 1626 and no modern similar example is given. More generally, the text under 'engrave' supports the view that in current usage the physical meaning is confined to cutting, marking or otherwise working a surface. The same may be said of the dictionary's treatment of 'engraving', except that 'engraving' can mean the product as well as the process.

I note that the Court of Appeal went on to say (p 129) that each frisbee made from a mould is an 'image produced from an engraved plate' and therefore a 'print'. I was urged by Mr Hanger QC to adopt what he described as the 'flexible approach' evinced in this decision, particularly as it has at least the tentative approval of the Hong Kong Court of Appeal in the *Interlego* case.

No consideration of policy, or other orthodox approach, could justify straining the English language so far as to call the moulds engravings. Despite the respect which one must have for any decision of the New Zealand Court of Appeal, I find myself unable to follow the approach in the *Lincoln Industries* case. In particular, I cannot, with respect, agree with the view that a frisbee is an image or that it is a print. Similarly, in my opinion, the moulds from which these machine parts are made are not engravings. It is unnecessary to consider the question whether 'engraving' in the Act includes such objects as were dealt with in *James Arnold and Co Ltd v Miafern Ltd* [1980] RPC 397.

I should add that I am by no means convinced that the New Zealand decision, even if correct, produces success for the applicant on this point; as was pointed out on behalf of the respondent, the basis of that decision appears to have been that operations which involve cutting to create a shape are properly called engraving. But here there was no evidence that the moulds were produced by any sort of cutting.

The applicant also contended that the machine parts are themselves 'engravings'. Counsel did not shrink from the proposition that a machined steel shaft, however enormous, is an 'engraving'. That seems to me preposterous.

I therefore arrive at the conclusion that the applicant's claim to copyright in the moulds and machine parts is ill-founded and cannot succeed, because they cannot be the subject of copyright.

CASE EXTRACT: COMPARATIVE LAW

Lucasfilm Ltd v Ainsworth

[2009] EWCA Civ 1328; [2010] Ch 503
Court of Appeal of England and Wales

[The case concerned stormtrooper helmets from the first *Star Wars* film (*Episode IV: A New Hope*). Mr Ainsworth had been commissioned to produce the plastic helmets to be used as costumes. He had been supplied with drawings and a clay model of a stormtrooper helmet. Much later, he started using his original tools to produce replica helmets which he sold online, including to purchasers in the USA. Lucasfilm, the production company behind the *Star Wars* films, successfully sued for copyright infringement in the USA and then sought to sue for copyright infringement in the UK and to enforce the US judgment against Mr Ainsworth in the UK. A question in the case was whether the helmet was a 'sculpture' and hence an artistic work under the UK legislation.]

Jacob LJ (for the Court): 46. Although [the Act] defines an artistic work, there is no definition of sculpture beyond the direction that it includes a cast or model made for the purposes of sculpture. The closest one ever gets to a more comprehensive definition is in the *Sculpture Copyright Act* of 1814 which specified in some detail the type of sculptures or models which qualified for protection. Although there is no definition of sculpture as such even in that statute, it is clear from the words used that the Act was concerned with sculpture in its traditional and conventional sense of a work of art. That much is apparent both from the terms of the preamble to the Act and from the description of the types of work included.

47. Notions of what constitutes a work of sculpture have expanded over the years. In *Wham-O v Lincoln Industries* [1985] RPC 127 Davison CJ quoted the *Encyclopaedia Britannica:*

> In the *New Encyclopaedia Britannica,* vol 16, p 421 there appears an article on 'Art of sculpture'. The following passages are of some interest:
>
>> Sculpture is not a fixed term that applies to a permanently circumscribed category of objects or sets of activities. It is, rather, the name of an art that grows and changes and is continually extending the range of its activities and evolving new kinds of objects. The scope of the term is much wider in the second half of the 20th century than it was only two or three decades ago, and in the present fluid state of the visual arts, nobody can predict what its future extensions are likely to be.
>>
>> Certain features, which in previous centuries were considered essential to the art of sculpture, are not present in a great deal of modern sculpture and can no longer form part of its definition. One of the most important of these is representation. Before the 20th century, sculpture was considered a representational art; but its scope has now been extended to include non-representational forms. It has long been accepted that the forms of such functional three-dimensional objects as furniture, props and buildings may be expressive and beautiful without being in any way representational, but it is only in the 20th century that non-functional, non-representational, three-dimensional works of art have been produced.
>>
>> ...
>>
>> 20th century sculpture is not confined to the two traditional forming processes of carving and modelling or to such traditional natural materials as stone, metal, wood, ivory, bone and clay. Because present-day sculptors use any materials and methods of manufacture that will serve their purposes, the art of sculpture can no longer be identified with any special materials or techniques. Through all of these changes there is probably only one thing that has remained constant in the art of sculpture, and it is this that emerges as the central and abiding concern of sculptors: The art of sculpture is the branch of the visual arts that is especially concerned with the creation of expressive form in three dimensions.
>
> Likewise the dictionary definitions of 'sculpture' recognise that taste has changed. In the *Shorter Oxford English Dictionary* it is described as:
>
>> Originally the process or art of carving or engraving a hard material so as to produce designs or figures in relief, or in intaglio, or in the round. In modern use, that branch of fine art which is concerned with producing figures in the round or in relief, either by carving, by fashioning some plastic substance, or by making a mould for casting in metal.

48. The recognition of abstract shapes as works of art was established early in the twentieth century if not before ... Today no-one would dispute that abstract sculpture is a branch of the fine arts.

49. But the word sculpture can also be used to describe the process by which an object is created. Most usually this will consist of moulding or carving the relevant material into the desired shape or, in the case of a metal cast sculpture, of creating the necessary cast or mould.

50. The latter process is not, of course, confined to works of art. Casting or moulding is an industrial process commonly used where the end product is made of plastic or metal of some kind. It is used

in the production of millions of ordinary household objects, none of which would usually be described as sculptures. A motor-car is but one obvious example. Some would have qualified for protection as registered designs so as to be excluded under s 22(1) of the 1911 Act. But would they have qualified as 'sculpture'?

51. The judge gave a clear no to this question. His view was that the stormtrooper helmet, although created by a process of moulding, was primarily utilitarian in function:

> 121. First, the original Stormtrooper helmet. This has, as its genesis, the McQuarrie paintings. The purpose of the helmet was that it was to be worn as an item of costume in a film, to identify a character, but in addition to portray something about that character—its allegiance, force, menace, purpose and, to some extent, probably its anonymity. It was a mixture of costume and prop. But its primary function is utilitarian. While it was intended to express something, that was for utilitarian purposes. While it has an interest as an object, and while it was intended to express an idea, it was not conceived, or created, with the intention that it should do so other than as part of character portrayal in the film. That, in my view, does not give it the necessary quality of artistic creation inherent in the test suggested by Laddie J. Not everything which has design appeal is necessarily a sculpture. I think that the ordinary perception of what is a sculpture would be over-stretched by including this helmet within it, and when rationalised the reasons are those just given. It is not that it lacks artistic merit; it lacks artistic purpose. I therefore find that the Stormtrooper helmet is not a sculpture.
>
> 122. The same reasoning applies to the armour, and to the other helmets. They all shared the same sort of original purpose.

52. He took the same view about the toy stormtroopers:

> 123. Next, it is necessary to consider the toy Stormtroopers, and other characters, which are taken as being reproductions of the armour and helmets for the purposes of section 52. These are, as already described, articulated models which are sold as toys and which are intended for the purposes of play. Play is their primary, if not sole, purpose. While their appearance is obviously highly important (if they did not look like the original, the child would not be so interested) they are not made for the purposes of their visual appearance as such. While there is no accounting for taste, it is highly unlikely that they would be placed on display and periodically admired as such. The child is intended to use them in a (literally) hands-on way, in a form of delegated role play, and that is doubtless how they are actually used. That means, in my view, they are not sculptures. They can be distinguished from the model in *Britain v Hank Bros & Co* (1902) 86 LT 764 which apparently had a significant element of being admirable for its own visual sake. That does not apply to the Stormtrooper, whose only real purpose is play. In reaching this conclusion I am not saying that the *Britain* model is better at what it portrays than the Stormtrooper model. That would be to make judgments about artistic quality, which the statute understandably forbids. It is making a judgment about whether there is anything in the model which has an artistic essence, in the sense identified above. I conclude that there is not.

53. In order to reject their classification as sculpture the judge concentrated on purpose. Purely functional items (even though well designed and visually attractive) did not, in his view, qualify as sculptures because they were not created primarily for the purpose of their visual appeal. Essentially functional objects should look to protection for their visual merits as registered designs.

54. In putting forward this test the judge was expressly conscious of the need not to make value judgments about the artistic quality of the designs involved. The definition of 'artistic work' in the Copyright Acts makes that impermissible. But, after a review of the authorities, he set out a list of guidelines which he considered could be derived from the cases. We set it out verbatim:

> 118. From those authorities, and those approaches, a number of guidance factors can be extracted. I call them guidance rather than points of principle, because that gives them the right emphasis. The judges deciding the cases have not sought to lay down hard and fast rules in an area where subjective considerations are likely to intrude, and I will not attempt to do so either. However, I do think the following points emerge from the cases or from the concepts involved:
>
> (i)   Some regard has to be had to the normal use of the word.
>
> (ii)   Nevertheless, the concept can be applicable to things going beyond what one would normally expect to be art in the sense of the sort of things that one would expect to find in art galleries.
>
> (iii) It is inappropriate to stray too far from what would normally be regarded as sculpture.
>
> (iv)   No judgment is to be made about artistic worth.
>
> (v)   Not every three dimensional representation of a concept can be regarded as a sculpture. Otherwise every three dimensional construction or fabrication would be a sculpture, and that cannot be right.
>
> (vi)   It is of the essence of a sculpture that it should have, as part of its purpose, a visual appeal in the sense that it might be enjoyed for that purpose alone, whether or not it might have another purpose as well. The purpose is that of the creator. This reflects the reference to 'artist's hand' in the judgment of Laddie J in *Metix (UK) Ltd v GH Maughan (Plastics) Ltd* [1997] FSR 718, with which I respectfully agree. An artist (in the realm of the visual arts) creates something because it has visual appeal which he wishes to be enjoyed as such. He may fail, but that does not matter (no judgments are to be made about artistic merit). It is the underlying purpose that is important. I think that this encapsulates the ideas set out in the reference works referred to in *Wham-O* [1985] RPC 127 and set out above (and in particular the *Encyclopaedia Britannica*).
>
> (vii) The fact that the object has some other use does not necessarily disqualify it from being a sculpture, but it still has to have the intrinsic quality of being intended to be enjoyed as a visual thing. Thus the model soldier in *Britain* might be played with, but it still, apparently, had strong purely visual appeal which might be enjoyed as such. Similarly, the Critters in *Wildash v Klein* (2004) 61 IPR 324 had other functions, but they still had strong purely visual appeal. It explains why the Frisbee itself should be excluded from the category, along with the moulds in *Metix* and *J & S Davis (Holdings) Ltd v Wright Health Group Ltd* [1988] RPC 403. It would also exclude the wooden model in *Wham-O* and the plaster casts in *Breville Europe plc v Thorn EMI Domestic Appliances Ltd* [1995] FSR 77, and I would respectfully disagree with the conclusions reached by the judges in those cases that those things were sculptures. Those decisions, in my view, would not accord with the ordinary view of what a sculpture is, and if one asks why then I think that the answer is that the products fail this requirement and the preceding one—there is no intention that the object itself should have visual appeal for its own sake, and every intention that it be purely functional.
>
> (viii) I support this analysis with an example. A pile of bricks, temporarily on display at the Tate Modern for two weeks, is plainly capable of being a sculpture. The identical pile of bricks

dumped at the end of my driveway for two weeks preparatory to a building project is equally plainly not. One asks why there is that difference, and the answer lies, in my view, in having regard to its purpose. One is created by the hand of an artist, for artistic purposes, and the other is created by a builder, for building purposes. I appreciate that this example might be criticised for building in assumptions relating to what it seeks to demonstrate, and then extracting, or justifying, a test from that, but in the heavily subjective realms of definition in the artistic field one has to start somewhere.

(ix) The process of fabrication is relevant but not determinative. I do not see why a purely functional item, not intended to be at all decorative, should be treated as a sculpture simply because it is (for example) carved out of wood or stone.

...

70. ... Most of the cases proceed on the footing that one should not stray too far from the ordinary meaning of the word but there is considerable disagreement as to what that is. One of the difficulties is that the word can be used to describe both the physical process of moulding or carving necessary to create the finished object and that object itself. Copyright has, of course, to exist in the product of one's skill and labour. Not in the skill and labour itself. In looking therefore at the finished article, it seems to us wrong to interpret the use of the word sculpture in the 1911 Act (and therefore in succeeding Copyright Acts) divorced from the earlier legislative history. The 1814 Act was clearly concerned to identify sculpture as an artistic work. Its transposition into a wider category of 'artistic work' under the 1911 Act does not mean that one can ignore that context. Although some of the items included in the list such as a map or diagram may have a high level of functionality that should not be used as a guide to the interpretation of every item which the statutory definition contains. Sculpture, like painting (however good or bad it may be), does connote the work of the artist's hand and the visual purpose attributed to it by the judge in this case. Put simply, it has, broadly speaking, to be a work at least intended to be a work of art.

71. We therefore accept points (i)–(vi) on the judge's list. Mr Bloch criticises the reference in point (v) to the three dimensional representation of a concept on the largely metaphysical basis that all things in the world are representations of a concept. But that seems to be an issue about terminology. What the judge was referring to is clearly set out in the second sentence of that paragraph. Mr Bloch declined to accept that the well-designed saucepan or car would not be a sculpture but we think that this merely serves to confirm the correctness of the point made by the judge.

72. In point (vii) Mann J deals with questions of the object's utility. This is in many ways the most important and difficult issue because it highlights the existence of a grey area in which, even on the approach outlined in points (i)–(vi), there may be difficulties in drawing the line between sculpture and an object which, though well designed, does not qualify as such. Mr Bloch submits that the creation of these difficulties is due to the judge's concentration on the artistic or visual purpose of the work without which possibly fine distinctions would not have to be made. But, unless one is prepared to accept that almost any moulded version of a functional object is to be included in the definition, a line has to be drawn somewhere and some form of differentiation made.

73. One can think up any number of marginal examples to test where the boundary lies. Mr Bloch posed the example of a statue of a saint created as an object of veneration for use in a church. Its religious purpose or function would not alter its status as a sculpture. The same goes for props. A sculpture made for use in a play or film does not, he submits, make it any more utilitarian than the

statue of the saint and, again, should not affect its status as a sculpture for the purpose of inclusion in the definition of artistic work.

74. None of this is necessarily controversial but we are not convinced that these examples really help. A plaster statue of a saint can, in artistic terms, be very good or very bad. There are many examples of both. But most people would, we think, accept that both kinds were sculptures notwithstanding their religious purpose. Similarly, a well-designed stage prop may be highly artistic and one knows of stage sets for opera and ballet designed by a number of artists of great note. Again their status as an artistic work would not be negated by the use to which their designs were intended to be put.

75. The issue in this case and the judge's approach to it does not turn on the purpose for which it is actually used but on the purposive nature of the object: what the judge described as its 'intrinsic quality of being intended to be enjoyed as a visual thing'. As we read his judgment, the purpose of the object is simply one of the relevant guides to whether it qualifies as a sculpture. A precise definition of that term is not possible which is why the judge has outlined a number of considerations which should act as signposts to the right answer. One can demonstrate this by an example. Most people would not regard a real soldier's helmet as a sculpture. Although made of pressed metal from a mould, its essential functionality as such is to take it outside any reasonable use of that term. A medieval suit of armour, however highly decorated, is no different. Although now of largely historical interest, it was made for a practical purpose which, again, characterises it as an object of utility rather than an artistic work. This view of these objects would not change if they were used as props for a play or film. Their use in that context would not alter their nature or their description.

76. But if the soldier's helmet appears on a bronze statue of a soldier as part of an artistic representation of the man and his kit no-one would, we think, dispute that it formed part of a sculpture. It has no practical utility. It cannot be used as a helmet and, to that extent, it is not one.

77. The result of this analysis is that it is not possible or wise to attempt to devise a comprehensive or exclusive definition of 'sculpture' sufficient to determine the issue in any given case. Although this may be close to adopting the elephant test of knowing one when you see it, it is almost inevitable in this field. We therefore consider that the judge was right to adopt the multi-factorial approach which he did.

Jacob LJ concluded that the trial judge was correct to hold that the helmet (and other pleaded items, including some toy stormtroopers) were largely functional and hence not sculptures. Lucasfilm appealed to the Supreme Court. In *Lucasfilm Ltd v Ainsworth* [2011] UKSC 39; [2012] 1 AC 208 the Supreme Court agreed that the utilitarian function of the helmet 'in the sense that it was an element in the process of production of the film' (at [43]) meant that it was not a sculpture. Of the trial judge's multifactorial approach to determining whether something is sculpture, Lords Walker and Collins (with whom Lord Phillips and Baroness Hale agreed) commented:

47. We would uphold the judgments below very largely for the reasons that they give. But (at the risk of appearing humourless) we are not enthusiastic about the 'elephant test' in para 77 of the Court of Appeal's judgment ('knowing one when you see it'). Any zoologist has no difficulty in recognising an elephant on sight, and most could no doubt also give a clear and accurate description of its essential identifying features. By contrast a judge, even one very experienced in intellectual property matters, does not have some special power of divination which leads instantly to an infallible conclusion, and no judge would claim to have such a power. The judge reads and hears the evidence (often including expert evidence), reads and listens to the advocates' submissions, and takes what the Court of Appeal rightly

called a multi-factorial approach. Moreover the judge has to give reasons to explain his or her conclusions.

48. There is one other matter to which the Court of Appeal attached no weight, but which seems to us to support the judge's conclusion. It is a general point as to the policy considerations underlying Parliament's development of the law in order to protect the designers and makers of three-dimensional artefacts from unfair competition. After reviewing the legislative history the Court of Appeal took the view (para 40) that there was no assistance to be obtained from the relationship between copyright and registered design right. We respectfully disagree, especially if the relatively new unregistered design right is also taken into account. It is possible to recognise an emerging legislative purpose (though the process has been slow and laborious) of protecting three-dimensional objects in a graduated way, quite unlike the protection afforded by the indiscriminate protection of literary copyright. Different periods of protection are accorded to different classes of work. Artistic works of art (sculpture and works of artistic craftsmanship) have the fullest protection; then come works with 'eye appeal' (*AMP Inc v Utilux Pty Ltd* [1971] FSR 572); and under Part III of the 1988 Act a modest level of protection has been extended to purely functional objects (the exhaust system of a motor car being the familiar example). Although the periods of protection accorded to the less privileged types have been progressively extended, copyright protection has always been much more generous. There are good policy reasons for the differences in the periods of protection, and the court should not, in our view, encourage the boundaries of full copyright protection to creep outwards.

The Australian equivalents to the copyright/design overlap provisions mentioned by the House of Lords are discussed in Chapter 8 (p 361). Note that the fact that an item has some function does not necessarily prevent it from being a sculpture. The Australian case of *Wildash v Klein* [2004] NTSC 17; (2004) 61 IPR 324 concerned three-dimensional depictions of animals made out of wire, some of which incorporated a candle holder. The Supreme Court of the Northern Territory held that they were nevertheless sculptures.

BUILDINGS

Copyright was extended to works of architecture in the 1911 Act (UK) and 1912 Act (Australia). The definition of artistic works includes 'a building or a model of a building, whether the building or model is of artistic quality or not': a work need not be a work of fine architecture to be protected by copyright. Note also that 'building' is defined in s 10(1) of the *Copyright Act* to include 'a structure of any kind'.

CURRENT LAW

CASE EXTRACT: CURRENT LAW

Darwin Fibreglass Pty Ltd v Kruhse Enterprises Pty Ltd

(1998) 41 IPR 649
Supreme Court of the Northern Territory

[The plaintiff claimed that the defendant had breached the plaintiff's copyright in (1) a 'plug', being the model from which was created a mould for the manufacture of pre-cast fibreglass swimming pools, (2) the mould so created, and (3) a pool derived therefrom.]

CURRENT LAW

Mildren J (at 652–657): Copyright can exist in a building in addition to that subsisting in any plan or drawing of the building. These are two independent copyrights, and the subsistence of one is not dependent upon the subsistence of the other: *Meikle v Maufe* [1941] 3 All ER 144. In this case it is not asserted that there are any plans or drawings of the plug, mould or swimming pool.

... As to what is a 'building', s 10 provides that 'building includes a structure of any kind'. 'Structure' is not defined. It is plain that the ordinary meaning of the word 'building' includes structures, but not all structures (in the ordinary meaning of that word) are buildings. The addition of the words 'includes a structure of any kind' in the definition of 'building' was clearly intended to broaden the concept of what is a building, to include structures which would not ordinarily be buildings; the words are not mere surplusage: cf *R v Rose* [1965] QWN 35 at 43 per Gibbs J. *Copinger and Skone James on Copyright*, 13th ed (1991) Sweet & Maxwell, London at 31 observes (in reference to a similar definition in the *Copyright, Designs and Patents Act 1988* (UK)):

> A work of architecture is defined by the 1988 Act as being a building or a model for a building, and 'building' is defined by such Act as including any fixed structure, and a part of a building or fixed structure. Apart from this statutory definition, no general definition of 'building' can be given, although it has been said that, prima facie, a 'building' means 'a block of brick or stone work covered in by a roof'. The term must be construed reasonably, having regard to the object of the statute. Upon this principle, it is thought that the building or structure must be of such a character as is usually erected upon, or constructed under, the ground and that in each case it involves something of substance, with an element of permanence. If a building or structure has these characteristics, then it will be entitled to protection, not only as a whole, but in individual architectural features, including internal features of design. On this basis a chimney-piece might, it is thought, be entitled to copyright. It has been held that a garden, consisting of a layout including steps, walls, ponds and other structures in stone, was capable of protection as 'a structure'.

However, the *Copyright, Designs and Patents Act* [*1988* (UK)] definition of 'building' includes only 'fixed' structures, and to this extent is narrower than the Australian definition. In Australia, a half-tennis court was held by Dunn J to be a 'building', but there is no discussion in the case of the relevant criteria: *Half Court Tennis Pty Ltd v Seymour* (1980) 53 FLR 240 at 247–248.

Dictionary definitions suggest that a structure is 'something built or constructed; a building, bridge, dam, framework etc' (*Macquarie Dictionary*, 3rd ed, Delbridge et al, The Macquarie Library); 'a thing which is built or constructed; a building, and edifice. More widely any framework or fabric of assembled material parts': *New Shorter Oxford English Dictionary* (1993) Lesley Brow, Clarendon Press, Oxford.

I consider that, in interpreting what is meant by the word 'structure', the correct approach is to have regard to the object and purposes of the Act as a whole, the context within the Act in which it is used, and the history of the legislation. Buildings and models of buildings were first given protection as 'architectural works of art' in the *Copyright Act 1905* (Cth). Under that Act, some artistic quality was required, but this is no longer a requirement because, under the Berne Convention, it is a requirement that all works of architecture be protected: see Ricketson, *The Law of Intellectual Property* (1984) Law Book Co, Sydney at 124. Nevertheless even before 1968, the courts interpreted the necessary 'artistic character and design' requirement 'in a fairly liberal way': Ricketson. As previously stated, copyright exists not only in the plans of a building, but separately and independently in the building itself (as well as in models thereof).

... In the context of the *Copyright Act*, there is no requirement that the building or structure be occupied for human habitation, or that it is even occupied by living species at all, as it obviously includes bridges and dams, which are not inhabited. At least some structures designed for the keeping of animals, produce, plants or fish such as stables, silos, greenhouses or fish ponds would be included. Thus, there is no necessity for a structure to have steps, doors, a roof, or windows. In the case of dams, or large storage tanks, these could well be structures even though they are designed to store water or fuel. I think that the word 'structure' implies something which is of some substance, and is usually erected upon or constructed upon or in the ground with an element of permanence, although it need not be a fixture, so that prima facie, a prefabricated building which is designed to be removed may be a structure, and may still remain a structure even though it is in the process of being removed or is left temporarily unattached to the soil. I do not see why buildings, and therefore structures, need be built from concrete or stone; surely the form of building material used is not important, so long as the building or structure is a thing of some permanence. It flows from this that it is not necessary that the building or structure be built up from the ground in situ. Modern materials and methods of construction include buildings which are prefabricated off-site; nevertheless I do not see why such buildings are not 'buildings' in the ordinary sense of the word, if the intention is that the building when delivered on-site will become permanently, or relatively permanently, fixed to the ground. I do not accept Mr Houghton QC's submission that the Act contemplates only structures which are built from architectural plans or drawings, although it is clear that the Act does contemplate that buildings or structures may be built from such plans or drawings: see s 73(2) and s 217 ...

In my opinion having regard to the evident policy of the *Copyright Act* to which I have referred, all that can safely be said is that there is no single test for what is or is not a 'building' although there are a number of factors which are relevant including size, the evident proposed use of the object to an independent observer, whether or not the object is evidently fixed to or under the ground, or whether it is evidently intended to be portable, and the degree of permanence in location which it apparently has including the likely life-span of the object.

In my opinion neither the plug nor the mould is a 'building'. Although large objects, there is little else to commend them as structures. The 'plug' is designed to be destroyed in the process of making the mould. Neither it nor the mould is intended to be placed on or in the ground with any degree of permanency. On the other hand the plaintiff's swimming pools are not complete until placed into the hole in the ground, compacted into position with sand, and fixed to underground pipes which are in turn fixed to the filtration system and pumps. The photographs show that these pools are large objects—certainly as large as some small buildings. There is no evidence of this, but I think I can take judicial knowledge of the fact that fibreglass has a relatively long life. It is commonly used to build large boats as well as inground swimming pools and although it may require more maintenance than stone or concrete it was not suggested that fibreglass was not an enduring material if properly maintained. In my opinion, such a swimming pool is a structure, notwithstanding that it is largely manufactured off-site, and it is capable of being removed. In my opinion the evident intention is that it is intended to be relatively permanently located in the same position for many years, and it is sufficiently large to be substantial enough to be described as a structure. The decision in *Tefex Pty Ltd v Bowler* [(1981) 40 ALR 326] is distinguishable because the owner of the design in that case did not install the pools, but sold them in kit form without ancillary equipment. In any event, Rath J did not find that the pools in question were not buildings.

CURRENT LAW

If such a pool is a building, this leaves open the possibility that the plug and the mould are 'models of a building'. There is no definition in the Act of what is a 'model of a building' and counsel were unable to refer me to any authorities on the topic …

I think the word 'model' has two relevant primary meanings. First, it obviously includes a representation of some structure already built or to be built showing its proportions, shape, design and the arrangement of its parts. In this sense, the model is demonstrative only of what is made or intended to be made. Secondly, it may include a three-dimensional image which is a copy of an object or which is to be copied to make the actual object itself, and so would include a mould. The question is whether in the expression 'model of a building' the word is used only in the first sense or in both senses.

Looked at broadly, the object of copyright is to protect original forms in which ideas are expressed, but not the ideas themselves. Consequently, s 31(1) confers the exclusive right in the owner of the copyright to reproduce the work in a 'material form', which, as previously noted, includes 'any form … of storage from which the work; or a substantial part of the work can be reproduced'. It seems obvious that the plug and the mould stores the form or a substantial part of the form of the pool in a three dimensional way, from which it would be relatively easy to copy the form of the ideas therein expressed. With the advance of new technologies, it is now possible, as this case demonstrates, for quite large structures to be built from a mould, and it is not difficult to see how the form of an idea could be copied therefrom. The same applies to models of buildings in the first sense discussed above. Models, even small ones, store the forms of the structures they are intended to represent. Looked at in this broad way, I consider that it would enhance the objects of the Act to include a mould of a substantial portion of the work within the meaning of 'model of a building'.

It therefore follows that if the plug is protected, so is the mould, as only the owner of the copyright in the plug can reproduce it in a material form, and in my opinion it does not matter that the mould is a reverse image of the plug.

As to the argument that the pool and the mould are mere copies of the plug, and therefore lack originality, this was referred to by French J in *Kevlacat [Pty Ltd] v Trailcraft [Marine Pty Ltd* (1987) 79 ALR 534] (at 543), with reference to a number of authorities there cited, where his Honour observed (in relation to a prototype and mould produced from sketches) that in that event the relevant copyright existed in the sketches. However, the position with buildings is quite different from other works, in that copyright exists independently in both the plans and the building: see *Meikle v Maufe* (at 147–148). Likewise, I see no logical reason why there cannot be copyright in a model of a building, as well as in the building itself. In *Meikle v Maufe*, Uthwatt J said (at 147):

> It was contended on behalf of the defendants that there could not be a separate copyright in a building as distinct from a copyright in the plans on which the building was based, and that, if there were a separate copyright in the building, the copyright was in the builder. In the present case, neither of these contentions is material, except in so far as the correctness of either of them may affect the quantum of damages. Upon the first contention, it is argued that the originality lies in the plan, and that, therefore, there can be none in the building which reproduces the plans. Upon the second contention, it is said that, wherever originality may lie, the author, for copyright purposes, is the builder who has built the building, and not the architect responsible for the plans. In my opinion, neither contention is well-founded. As regards these contentions, an architectural plan finds its meaning and purpose in the use to which it is put. The point of the architect's activities is not the making of plans as such, but the embodiment in the building of artistic and

CURRENT LAW

other ideas which he has in mind and which are contained in his plan. The plan is a means to an end, and not an end in itself. To deny originality to the artistic design embodied in a building by attributing originality only to the plans which led to the building would be to give reality to the shadow and refuse it to the substance.

Similarly, the purpose of the plug is to make the mould, from which the pool is largely constructed, and is but a means to an end, and to deny originality to the pool as a structure by attributing originality only to the plug which led to it would 'give reality to the shadow and refuse it to the substance'. In any event, even if copyright existed only in the plug, it is no answer, in my opinion, that a copy taken from the pool did not infringe the copyright in the plug, as only the owner of the copyright in the plug is entitled to reproduce it in a material form.

[His Honour concluded that the pool was protected as a 'building' and the plug and mould were 'models of buildings', and therefore all 'artistic works'.]

WORKS OF ARTISTIC CRAFTSMANSHIP

The *Copyright Act* provides no definition of 'work of artistic craftsmanship'. Works of artistic craftsmanship are the only form of 'artistic work' where some kind of artistic quality is required. Examples of the kinds of craftsmanship this provision is intended to protect are given in the extract below. Craftsmanship does not require *hand* craft: *Coogi Australia Pty Ltd v Hysport International Pty Ltd* (1998) 86 FCR 154.

What fits within the category of work of artistic craftsmanship is important, because works of artistic craftsmanship are an important carve-out from the 'copyright/design overlap provisions' (*Copyright Act*, ss 74–77A). These provisions, which are discussed in Chapter 8, deny copyright protection to artistic works in certain circumstances where the work has been industrially manufactured. Plaintiffs are often therefore very keen to make the case that their work is a work of artistic craftsmanship.

CURRENT LAW

CASE EXTRACT: CURRENT LAW

Burge v Swarbrick

[2007] HCA 17; (2007) 232 CLR 336
High Court of Australia

[John Swarbrick was a naval architect. Through his company Swarbrick Yachts International Pty Ltd he manufactured a racing yacht marketed as the 'JS 9000'. At the time of litigation, 32 JS 9000 yachts had been constructed. Twenty had been delivered to customers at prices ranging from $A50 000 to $A65 000. The JS 9000 was marketed to highlight its simplicity, economical building costs, ease of sailing with a small crew, speed, and easy transportation. Swarbrick also gave evidence that he had intended to design a yacht of 'great aesthetic appeal'. Although boats, including yachts, are eligible for registered design protection, Swarbrick did not register a design. Burge et al acquired some deck

CURRENT LAW

and hull mouldings (in disputed circumstances) and were building a JS 9000 yacht when Swarbrick commenced proceedings for copyright infringement and obtained an injunction. The alleged works of artistic craftsmanship were the 'Plug', a hand-crafted, full-scale model of the hull and deck of the yacht (subsequently destroyed), and the hull and deck mouldings.]

Gleeson CJ, Gummow, Kirby, Heydon and Crennan JJ (some footnotes omitted): 12. Mr Swarbrick does not rely upon any design registration; it is the absence of any utilisation of the protection offered by registration under the *Designs Act* that is critical for this appeal. Rather, as noted above, Mr Swarbrick founds his claim for intellectual property protection upon the *Copyright Act* and its provisions respecting that species of original 'artistic work' which comprises 'a work of artistic craftsmanship'. In the absence of a design registration, s 77 of the *Copyright Act* permits reliance by Mr Swarbrick only on those copyrights he may have in works of 'artistic craftsmanship'. The ultimate issue is whether the JS 9000 embodies 'a work of artistic craftsmanship' in the statutory sense. If so, Mr Swarbrick may pursue his claim of copyright infringement and the absence of a design registration is no answer to his action for copyright infringement ...

...

ARTISTIC WORKS AND THE PLACE OF WORKS OF 'ARTISTIC CRAFTSMANSHIP'

49. This appeal immediately concerns the expression in par (c) of the definition of 'artistic work' in s 10 of the *Copyright Act* 'a work of artistic craftsmanship to which neither [par (a) nor par (b)] applies'. Paragraph (c) of the definition in s 3(1) of the 1956 UK Act is in terms essentially indistinguishable from s 10 of the *Copyright Act*. The 1956 UK Act was enacted after the treatment of 'artistic work' by the Gregory Committee. In Australia, the Spicer Committee (§72) had recommended a definition of 'artistic work' which was in conformity with that in the 1956 UK Act. The *Report of the Gregory Committee* stated (§260):

> It is clear that some protection of this kind is required to cover works of art other than such things as works of painting, drawing and sculpture, which are mentioned by name. We are here concerned not with articles manufactured under conditions of ordinary industrial production (artistically meritorious as many of these are) which can secure their own appropriate protection under [the *Registered Designs Act* 1949 (UK)], but with the works of craftsmen working in many media (silversmiths, potters, woodworkers, hand-embroiderers and many others) in circumstances for which that Act does not provide appropriate protection. We do not think it will be questioned that original works of the kind we have in mind are fully entitled to protection and but for [the 1911 Act] this would be lacking. We believe that copyright provides the proper basis for protecting these works and to ensure this protection we believe that it is necessary to retain the term 'works of artistic craftsmanship' in the Act.

The Gregory Committee went on to eschew any attempt at a further definition of the term 'works of artistic craftsmanship'. However, its reference to the inadequate protection given by the designs law to the work of craftsmen working in many media anticipated the statement by Drummond J in *Coogi* [*Australia Pty Ltd v Hysport International Pty Ltd* (1998) 86 FCR 154 at 168] ... emphasising, for the purposes of [the Act excluding works of artistic craftsmanship from the copyright/design overlap provisions], the desirability of encouraging 'real artistic effort' in the field of industrial design.

THE SIGNIFICANCE OF THE 1989 ACT

50. In its form after the changes made by the [*Copyright Amendment Act 1989* (Cth)], the *Copyright Act* employed the expression 'a work of artistic craftsmanship', both as a criterion to mark out the nature, duration and ownership of copyright in artistic works (Pt III, Div 1, ss 31–35) and to differentiate the protection given where artistic works were applied as industrial designs without a design registration (Pt III, Div 8, ss 74–77A) … [T]he phrase 'a work of artistic craftsmanship' was introduced by the 1989 Act into the 'overlap' provisions of Pt III, Div 8 of the Copyright Act upon a particular legislative view of the purpose it would serve. That view, as Drummond J indicated in *Coogi* [(1998) 86 FCR 154 at 168], was the encouragement of 'real artistic effort' in industrial design.

51. Several consequences for this appeal follow from this state of affairs. First, as the facts of this case demonstrate, encouragement of 'real artistic effort' to industrial design may be constrained by the nature of the functional purposes to be served by the object to which industrial design is applied and by the marketing imperatives for mass production. The evidence of the marketing of the JS 9000 class of racing yacht … is illustrative of these constraints. It is these constraints which make it difficult to support the Plug as 'a work of artistic craftsmanship'.

52. Secondly, the need after the 1989 Act to read consistently throughout the *Copyright Act* the phrase 'a work of artistic craftsmanship' entails caution, lest too little weight be given to the need for a real or substantial artistic element in what is posited for any purpose of the *Copyright Act* as 'a work of artistic craftsmanship'.

53. Thirdly, the 1989 Act places some check upon entire acceptance of what had been said earlier with respect to the 1956 UK Act in the most significant judicial treatment of the scope and purpose of the special treatment given the phrase 'a work of artistic craftsmanship'. This was the speech of Lord Simon of Glaisdale in *George Hensher Ltd v Restawile Upholstery (Lancs) Ltd* [[1976] AC 64]. We now turn to what was said by Lord Simon.

HENSHER

54. The plaintiff in *Hensher*, successfully before Graham J but unsuccessfully in the Court of Appeal and in the House of Lords, asserted infringement of copyright in artistic works, being the chairs which were components of a suite of furniture marketed as the *Bronx*. The artistic copyright relied upon was that in respect of works of 'artistic craftsmanship' as provided in the 1956 UK Act. There were no design registrations relied upon and the issue was a threshold one of whether, in any event, copyright subsisted in respect of any original artistic work.

55. Several points should be made respecting the *Hensher* litigation. First, the consideration in various of the speeches in the House of Lords of the purpose and scope of the term 'artistic craftsmanship' was skewed by a concession. The concession was that there was no dispute that the prototype from which the *Bronx* suite was constructed in 1966 and mass produced was 'a work of craftsmanship'; the only issue being whether the 'craftsmanship' involved was 'artistic'.

56. Secondly, the concession notwithstanding, Lord Simon went on to construe as a whole the phrase 'a work of artistic craftsmanship' as it appeared in s 3(1)(c) of the 1956 UK Act. He noted that the concession that the *Bronx* prototype was a work of craftsmanship had tended to distort the argument and that 'works of artistic craftsmanship' was a composite phrase to be construed as a whole. That approach by Lord Simon should, subject to what has been said above respecting the

significance of the 1989 Act, be adopted in dealing with the present appeal. In Australia, thus, there will be no occasion to attempt from all five speeches in *Hensher* a distillation of what can be regarded as the *ratio decidendi*.

57. Thirdly, Lord Simon noted that there was no relevant distinction between the phrase used in the 1956 UK Act and that found in the 1911 Act. His Lordship went on, in a manner now regarded in this Court as involving orthodox principles of interpretation, to consider what he called the social and legal backgrounds to the 1911 Act, saying [at 89]:

> When this is undertaken it will be found that [the social and legal backgrounds] chime together remarkably, leaving no doubt as to what sort of work it was that Parliament was extending copyright protection to in 1911.

58. Fourthly, after referring to the activities of Ruskin and Morris and the foundation of the Arts and Crafts Exhibition Society and the Central School of Arts and Crafts, and other events in the period 1862 to 1910, Lord Simon continued [at 90]:

> These are no more than a handful of key events; but they put beyond doubt what it was that prompted Parliament in 1911 to give copyright protection to 'works of artistic craftsmanship'— namely, the Arts and Crafts movement with its emphasis on the applied or decorative arts.

In that regard, the biographer of William Morris writes [MacCarthy, *William Morris: A Life for Our Time*, (1994) at 590]:

> In a totally convincing way he showed the wrong-headedness in separating off the design process from making: one was a necessary stage towards the other; the designer and maker could be one and the same person, the person who came to be defined as artist-craftsman. Another false perception he attacked was that the fine artist had no role in industrial production. Morris had designed for many factories and workshops, on varying scales and in different materials, and had proved this to be patently untrue.

59. There are further points respecting statutory construction to be made here. First, the statutory expression is 'artistic craftsmanship', not 'artistic handicraft', notwithstanding that the aesthetic of the Arts and Crafts movement may have been that of the living artisan in his workshop. Lord Simon noted that some leaders of the Arts and Crafts movement recognised that they would have to come to terms with the machine, and referred to a lecture by Frank Lloyd Wright, 'The Art and Craft of the Machine'. Lord Simon concluded [at 91]:

> The Central School of Arts and Crafts, though foremost a school of handicrafts, had as a declared aim to encourage 'the industrial application of decorative design.' So, although 'works of artistic craftsmanship' cannot be adequately construed without bearing in mind the aims and achievements of the Arts and Crafts movement, 'craftsmanship' in the statutory phrase cannot be limited to handicraft; nor is the word 'artistic' incompatible with machine production: see *Britain v Hanks Brothers and Co* [(1902) 86 LT 765] .

60. Secondly, coming to terms with machine production involves acceptance that a prototype such as the Plug may qualify as 'a work of artistic craftsmanship' even though it was to serve the purpose of reproduction and then be discarded. Doubts upon the matter expressed by several of the Law Lords in *Hensher* were somewhat misplaced. ...

61. Thirdly, whilst not denying an enduring distinction between fine arts and useful or applied arts, in dealing with artistic craftsmanship there is no antithesis between utility and beauty, between function and art. In that regard, Lord Simon said in *Hensher* [at 91]:

> A work of craftsmanship, even though it cannot be confined to handicraft, at least presupposes special training, skill and knowledge for its production … 'Craftsmanship', particularly when considered in its historical context, implies a manifestation of pride in sound workmanship—a rejection of the shoddy, the meretricious, the facile.

Lord Simon further said [at 93]:

> Even more important, the whole antithesis between utility and beauty, between function and art, is a false one—especially in the context of the Arts and Crafts movement. 'I never begin to be satisfied,' said Philip Webb, one of the founders, 'until my work looks commonplace.' Lethaby's object, declared towards the end, was 'to create an efficiency style.' Artistic form should, they all held, be an emanation of regard for materials on the one hand and for function on the other.

62. Finally, it may be noted that the course of the statutory and case law in the United States respecting works of artistic craftsmanship requires separate identification of pictorial, graphic or sculptural features from utilitarian aspects of the article concerned; the former features must be capable of 'existing independently' of utilitarian aspects. However, given what has just been said, such an approach should not be adopted in construing the Australian legislation. This is derived from the 1911 Act, which must be understood in the light of what was said in *Hensher* respecting the Arts and Crafts movement and because the language of the 1911 Act is apt to carry forward the objects of that movement.

WAS THE PLUG 'A WORK OF ARTISTIC CRAFTSMANSHIP'?—THE EVIDENCE

63. The answer to the question whether the Plug is a 'work of artistic craftsmanship' cannot be controlled by evidence from Mr Swarbrick of his aspirations or intentions when designing and constructing the Plug. His evidence was admissible. But the operation of the statute does not turn upon the presence or absence of evidence of that nature from the author of the work in question. The matter, like many other issues calling for care and discrimination, is one for objective determination by the court, assisted by admissible evidence and not unduly weighed down by the supposed terrors for judicial assessment of matters involving aesthetics.

64. The statute does not give to the opinion of the person who claims to be the author of 'a work of artistic craftsmanship' the determination of whether that result was obtained; still less, whether it was obtained because he or she intended that result. Given the long period of copyright protection, the author, at the stage when there is litigation, may be unavailable. Indeed, as Pape J noted in *Cuisenaire* [*v Reed* [1963] VR 719 at 730], the author may be dead. Again, intentions may fail to be realised. Further, just as few alleged inventors are heard to deny the presence of an inventive step on their part, so, it may be expected, will few alleged authors of works of artistic craftsmanship be heard readily to admit the absence of any necessary aesthetic element in their endeavours.

65. This is not to deny the admissibility of such evidence, nor to disparage the good character of such witnesses, and certainly not that of Mr Swarbrick; it is to reaffirm the well-recognised dangers of

CURRENT LAW

hindsight which are present in various fields of intellectual property law, as in many other disputes that come to litigation.

66. The various aspects of the definition of 'a work of artistic craftsmanship' which are discussed above with reference to *Hensher* have particular significance here. The primary judge considered 'craftsmanship' and 'aesthetic appeal' as distinct and consecutive questions, before going on and 'considering both aspects together'. This was an error in the construction and application of the *Copyright Act* and requires re-examination of what transpired at the trial …

[The Court summarised the evidence in the case: from Mr Swarbrick on the one hand that he had intended to create, and had created, a yacht of 'great aesthetic appeal', and evidence on the other hand that the design brief for the yacht, and promotional material, emphasised the speed, maneuverability, and transportability of the yacht.]

73. Taken as a whole and considered objectively, the evidence, at best, shows that matters of visual and aesthetic appeal were but one of a range of considerations in the design of the Plug. Matters of visual and aesthetic appeal necessarily were subordinated to achievement of the purely functional aspects required for a successfully marketed 'sports boat' and thus for the commercial objective in view.

CONCLUSIONS RESPECTING THE PLUG

74. This state of the evidence must strongly influence the answer to the question whether the Plug was 'a work of artistic craftsmanship', within the meaning of the *Copyright Act* and allowing for the 'overlap' provision made by the 1989 Act.

75. With wallpaper, a tapestry, stained glass window, piece of jewellery or Tiffany artefact, there is considerable freedom of design choice relatively unconstrained by the function or utility of the article so produced. But, as the evidence disclosed, that was not the case with the design constraints upon a class of yacht such as the JS 9000.

76. The general considerations in play in deciding whether the Plug was 'a work of artistic craftsmanship' appear from a discussion by Professor Denicola in his influential article, 'Applied Art and Industrial Design: A Suggested Approach to Copyright in Useful Articles' [(1982–83) 67 *Minnesota Law Review* 707]. The writer referred to the statement by Frank Lloyd Wright in 1894 challenging designers to use the machine to best advantage rather than to produce 'with murderous ubiquity forms born of other times'; Professor Denicola continued [at 739]:

> The dominant feature of modern industrial design is the merger of aesthetic and utilitarian concerns. It is the influence of nonaesthetic factors, the nexus between what the product must do and how it must look, that distinguishes true industrial design from other artistic endeavors. The industrial designer as engineer—a perspective no less valid than industrial designer as artist—is subject to the functional constraints inherent in each undertaking.

77. During his cross-examination, Mr Swarbrick agreed that yacht design was a very specialised branch of naval architecture and that a naval architect was 'basically an engineer'. Mr Hood referred to a number of works on the practice of naval architecture and the design of yachts. He described as the main and essential requirements of yacht design the application of mathematical and engineering principles together with the relevant principles of physics.

78. In cross-examination, Mr Hood was taken to a number of books written by yacht designers and agreed that there was a substantial body of opinion that yacht design is an art or involves creative ability and artistic ability. Some of these authors Mr Hood did not hold in high regard because he saw them as influenced by a poetic view of a vocation that was basically concerned with engineering. Naval architects who held themselves out as accepting design briefs to produce beautiful vessels for the rich and famous were regarded by Mr Hood as 'stylists'. If a client told Mr Hood that he wanted a beautiful boat, Mr Hood would be unable to proceed further with the brief without going into matters of purpose and function, of what must be always a significant piece of engineering.

79. This evidence adds force to the further statement by Professor Denicola in his article [at 739]:

> The designer cannot follow wherever aesthetic interests might lead. Utilitarian concerns influence,
> and at times dictate, available choices. Indeed, aesthetic success is often measured in terms of
> the harmony achieved between competing interests.

80. After referring to what he describes as 'utilitarian considerations', including ease of operation, maintenance and cost of manufacture, Professor Denicola concludes that the cumulative influence of such matters 'can render the designer's task quite unlike that confronting the painter or sculptor'. That was true of the design of the Plug for the JS 9000.

81. In *Hensher* [at 94], Lord Simon asked whether the work in question was 'the work of one who was in this respect an artist-craftsman?' He referred to 'aim and impact' [at 94]. The works of a cobbler or dental mechanic, and a wheelwright were not works of artistic craftsmanship [at 91]. At the other extreme, the work of the maker of hand-painted tiles would be so regarded. Lord Simon went on [at 91–92]:

> In between lie a host of crafts some of whose practitioners can claim artistic craftsmanship,
> some not—or whose practitioners sometimes exercise artistic craftsmanship, sometimes not.
> In the former class, for example, are glaziers. The ordinary glazier is a craftsman, but he could
> not properly claim that his craftsmanship is artistic in the common acceptation. But the maker
> of stained glass windows could properly make such a claim; and, indeed, the revival of stained
> glass work was one of the high achievements of the Arts and Crafts movement. In the latter class
> is the blacksmith—a craftsman in all his business, and exercising artistic craftsmanship perhaps
> in making wrought-iron gates, but certainly not in shoeing a horse or repairing a ploughshare.
> In these intermediate—or rather, straddling—classes come, too, the woodworkers, ranging
> from carpenters to cabinet-makers: some of their work would be generally accepted as artistic
> craftsmanship, most not. Similarly, printers, bookbinders, cutlers, needleworkers, weavers—and
> many others. In this straddling class also fall, in my judgment, the makers of furniture. Some of
> their products would be, I think, almost universally accepted as 'works of artistic craftsmanship';
> but it would be a misuse of language to describe the bulk of their products as such.

82. The thread running through this discussion is the significance of functional constraints, extreme for a dental mechanic, less so for a glazier or blacksmith, and depending upon the nature of the particular design brief. A horseshoe is one task; the Tijou gates, screens and grilles wrought for St Paul's Cathedral, Hampton Court and Chatsworth by the French Huguenot ironmaster were in a very different category.

CURRENT LAW

83. It may be impossible, and certainly would be unwise, to attempt any exhaustive and fully predictive identification of what can and cannot amount to 'a work of artistic craftsmanship' within the meaning of the *Copyright Act* as it stood after the 1989 Act. However, determining whether a work is 'a work of artistic craftsmanship' does not turn on assessing the beauty or aesthetic appeal of work or on assessing any harmony between its visual appeal and its utility. The determination turns on assessing the extent to which the particular work's artistic expression, in its form, is unconstrained by functional considerations. To decide the appeal it is sufficient to indicate the following.

84. The more substantial the requirements in a design brief to satisfy utilitarian considerations of the kind indicated with the design of the JS 9000, the less the scope for that encouragement of real or substantial artistic effort. It is that encouragement which underpins the favourable treatment by the 1989 Act of certain artistic works which are applied as industrial designs but without design registration. Questions of fact and degree inevitably arise.

85. In the present case, notwithstanding what Mr Swarbrick later said on the matter after litigation was on foot, the earlier statements in the promotional material and in the business plan, with the evidence of Mr Hood, should have led the primary judge to conclude that the Plug was not 'a work of artistic craftsmanship' because the work of Mr Swarbrick in designing it was not that of an artist-craftsman.

Note: Arguments that the hull and deck mouldings were independently 'works of artistic craftsmanship' and that the plug, hull and deck mouldings were 'sculptures' also failed.

PART IV OF THE *COPYRIGHT ACT*: COPYRIGHT IN SUBJECT MATTER OTHER THAN WORKS

Part IV of the *Copyright Act* introduced new categories of subject matter, which were designed to protect investment in some of the new technologies of distribution that had been developed since the early twentieth century—sound recordings, films, and sound and television broadcasts—as well as publishers' investment in publishing new editions of works. These 'subject matter other than works' often provide a mechanism for delivery or distribution of works, although they need not do so: a sound recording, for example, is protected regardless of whether it incorporates a literary or musical work. Copyright in Part IV subject matter is additional to, and separate from, copyright in any underlying Part III works, as set out in s 113 of the Act:

(1) ... where copyright subsists in any subject-matter by virtue of this Part, nothing in this Part shall be taken to affect the operation of Part III in relation to any literary, dramatic, musical or artistic work from which that subject-matter is wholly or partly derived, and any copyright subsisting by virtue of this Part is in addition to, and independent of, any copyright subsisting by virtue of Part III.

(2) The subsistence of copyright under any provision of this Part does not affect the operation of any other provision of this Part under which copyright can subsist.

The distinction between Part III and Part IV in the *Copyright Act* largely mirrors a distinction in the international conventions between 'authors' rights' (*droit d'auteur*; sometimes referred to simply as 'copyright') and 'neighbouring rights' (*droits voisins*; also referred to as entrepreneurial works) (see Chapter 2). Note, however, that the distinction is not identically drawn: in the Australian Act, 'cinematograph films' are treated as Part IV subject matter, whereas internationally 'cinematographic works' are included in the *Berne Convention for the Protection of Literary and Artistic Works* (1886) as works of authorship.

The *Copyright Act* treats Part IV subject matter quite differently from works. First, as noted in Chapter 3, originality is not a precondition for protection: no human author is required. Second, in general, the rights granted to owners of copyright in Part IV subject matter are more restricted than the rights granted in works. Third as also noted in Chapter 3, copyright in subject matter other than works endures for a fixed term following publication (or broadcast), rather than for a term following death of the creator. Fourth, the rights granted in Part IV subject matter are rights in the *sounds and images embodied* in the film, recording, broadcast or published edition. Unlike works, which can be 'non-literally' infringed, infringement of subject matter other than works requires a taking of the exact subject matter which is protected. Although strictly an infringement question, understanding this principle is relevant to understanding the subject matter of copyright under Part IV. The principle is illustrated in the case extracted below. But first it is important to note the statutory definition of 'sound recording', the first of the subject matters other than works considered here.

SOUND RECORDINGS

Section 10(1) of the *Copyright Act* provides the following definitions:

> *sound recording* means the aggregate of the sounds embodied in a record.
>
> ...
>
> *record* includes a disc, tape, paper, electronic file or other device in which sounds are embodied.

Section 23(2) provides:

> A reference in this Act to a record of a work or other subject-matter shall, unless the contrary intention appears, be read as a reference to a record by means of which the work or other subject-matter can be performed.

See also s 24, which provides a meaning for the concept of 'embodied':

> For the purposes of this Act, sounds or visual images shall be taken to have been embodied in an article or thing if the article or thing has been so treated in relation to those sounds or visual images that those sounds or visual images are capable, with or without the aid of some other device, of being reproduced from the article or thing.

These definitions are clearly intended to be technology-neutral: a sound recording could be made on a vinyl record, a tape, onto a CD, onto the hard drive of a digital recorder or computer, or any other form, provided that the sounds can be reproduced from the thing or article.

CASE EXTRACT: CURRENT LAW

CBS Records Australia Ltd v Telmak Teleproducts (Aust) Pty Ltd

(1987) 17 FCR 48
Federal Court of Australia

[The case concerned 'sound-alike' recordings of hit songs previously recorded by famous bands. Sound-alike recordings were made by hiring performers to create a new recording that sounded as much as possible like the original. Sound-alike recordings were, naturally enough, cheaper than the originals.]

Bowen CJ (at 49–50): The dispute between the parties concerned a compilation produced by Telmak entitled 'Chart Sounds 16 Hit Songs#1' in the form of a record and a cassette. One of several matters dealt with upon that interlocutory application was a claim for an injunction based upon the proposition that the sound recording 'Chart Sounds 16 Hit Songs#1' infringed copyright in various sound recordings in which one or other of the CBS companies, who were applicants, had copyright. One of the issues between the parties was whether a 'sound alike' (that is, a later sound recording by other performers which is an imitation of the original) was within the description of a copy of a sound recording which is referred to in s 10(3)(c) of the *Copyright Act 1968* (Cth) ...

Counsel for CBS referred me to a considerable amount of historical material in support of the proposition that the *Copyright Act 1968* treated sound recordings in the same way as musical works ...

The provisions dealing with sound recordings in the *Copyright Act 1968* are specific provisions which have to be interpreted having regard to the words used and the context in which they appear. I am not persuaded by the historical material placed before the Court that this necessarily involves applying to those statutory provisions an interpretation which equates the protection afforded sound recordings with the protection afforded musical works. There are sufficient problems in the wording used in relation to sound recordings without introducing the additional complexity of trying to make these provisions accord with notions applicable to the copyright afforded to musical works.

Section 101(1) of the *Copyright Act 1968* provides that Pt IV copyright is infringed by a person who (not being the owner or licensed by the owner of the copyright) does or authorises the doing of any act comprised in the copyright. Section 89(1) provides that copyright subsists in a sound recording. Section 85(a) provides that copyright in relation to a sound recording is the exclusive right to make a copy of the sound recording. Section 10(3)(c) provides that a reference to a copy of a sound recording shall be read as a reference to a record embodying a sound recording or a substantial part of a sound recording being a record derived directly or indirectly from a record produced upon the making of a sound recording. This is the critical provision, interpretation of which is in issue in the present case. Section 10(1) defines 'record' as a disc, tape, paper or other device in which sounds are embodied and further provides that 'sound recording' means the aggregate of the sounds embodied in a record. It was these words which led me to the provisional view on the interlocutory proceeding that a sound alike was not a copy in which the aggregate of the sounds embodied in the original record was contained. The word 'embody' is defined in the *Macquarie Dictionary*, p 587 as: '2. to give a concrete form to ...; 3. to collect into or include in a body; organise; incorporate' and is defined in the *Shorter Oxford English*

Dictionary (3rd Ed), p 644 as: '2. To give a material or concrete character or form to … 3. To unite into one body; to incorporate …'

It appears to me that the language of s 10(3)(c) of the *Copyright Act 1968* when it refers to 'a record embodying a sound recording or a substantial part of a sound recording' is referring to an actual embodiment of the very sounds on the original record however they may be copied.

CINEMATOGRAPH FILMS

Section 10(1) of the *Copyright Act* provides the following definitions:

> *cinematograph film* means the aggregate of the visual images embodied in an article or thing so as to be capable by the use of that article or thing:
>
> (a) of being shown as a moving picture; or
> (b) of being embodied in another article or thing by the use of which it can be so shown;
>
> and includes the aggregate of the sounds embodied in a sound-track associated with such visual images.
>
> …
>
> *sound-track*, in relation to visual images forming part of a cinematograph film, means:
>
> (a) the part of any article or thing, being an article or thing in which those visual images are embodied, in which sounds are embodied; or
> (b) a disc, tape or other device in which sounds are embodied and which is made available by the maker of the film for use in conjunction with the article or thing in which those visual images are embodied.

The definitions for 'record' and 'embodied' were quoted in the previous section and also apply in relation to films.

'Cinematograph film' as defined above clearly includes feature films, television programs, videos on YouTube and filmed advertisements. But just how far the concept extends was explored in the case extracted below, which also deals with the concept of 'embodiment' in s 24 of the Act.

CASE EXTRACT: CURRENT LAW

Galaxy Electronics Pty Ltd v Sega Enterprises Ltd

(1997) 75 FCR 8
Federal Court of Australia, Full Court

Wilcox J (at 10–20): These two appeals raise an important question of copyright law: whether computer-generated moving images fall within the statutory definition of 'cinematograph film'. If this question is answered affirmatively, the images are subject to copyright protection under Part IV of the *Copyright Act* 1968 ('the Act'). That Part relates to 'copyright in subject-matter other than works', including cinematograph films. If it is answered negatively, the images will usually be devoid of copyright protection …

THE GAMES

The respondents, Sega Enterprises Pty Ltd ('Sega') and Avel Pty Ltd ('Avel'), are respectively the manufacturer and exclusive Australian licensee of two video games, 'Virtua Cop' and 'Daytona USA Twin'. The appellant, Galaxy Electronic Pty Ltd ('Galaxy'), imported into Australia machines containing copies of the computer program that generated the visual images and sounds constituting the game 'Virtua Cop' and displayed them for sale or hire at its premises. The appellant, Gottlieb Electronics Pty Ltd ('Gottlieb'), did the same things in relation to 'Daytona USA Twin'. Both appellants concede that, if the video games are a 'cinematograph film', their actions constitute an infringement of the respondents' rights; but they say the games are not cinematograph films.

It is not necessary to describe both games in detail. They are similar in nature. The description given by the learned trial judge, Burchett J, was not challenged. I gratefully adopt it.

> There are two video games with which the cases are concerned, one entitled 'Virtua Cop' and the other 'Daytona USA'. Each presents on the video screen a series of images resembling, more or less, a traditional movie film. In the case of 'Virtua Cop', an extremely simple but violent tale is told of assaults by police upon a criminal organisation. In the case of 'Daytona USA', what is involved is car racing. The parties were agreed that it is sufficient to concentrate upon 'Virtua Cop', since the two video games are constructed upon the same principle. In 'Virtua Cop', the protagonists are two police officers (with whom the players of the game identify) whose investigations are resisted, first, at a cargo wharf, next, at a construction site, and finally at their antagonists' evil headquarters. To begin with, there is a brief introduction, followed by the main part of the game in which the player must keep shooting quickly and accurately, with a make-believe weapon or 'input' device, at the correct villainous targets, so that the various assaults will progress according to the script. At the end, there is a triumphant finale, when the police congratulate each other and the dastards are led away in handcuffed defeat. Only the successful player will reach this denouement, and only the very skilled can possibly do so without numerous setbacks along the way, caused by misdirected responses, or failures to respond, to the actions depicted on the screen. For example, if the player's shot misses a criminal, the player may himself be shot by the criminal; and if this happens a predetermined number of times, the assault fails, and the game ends. Also, each time a criminal is merely winged, he may react differently, depending on where he has been hit. Thus, except for the opening and closing sequences, the events represented on the screen will show differences from screening to screening, except where the player's responses are all correct.
>
> What this means, it will be appreciated, is that the apparatus is designed to screen the simple story only when the correct responses to a series of cues are fed into it by the player; and when incorrect responses are given, a number of variations will result.

Burchett J detailed the way 'Virtua Cop' was created. He said:

> Graphic designers developed the scenes, and representations of the characters. In doing so, they made drawings and models, and decided, for instance, how a particular character would walk. Sets were made up. A 'test version' was prepared on a computer and copied onto a video tape. Further detailed sketches of scenes to be depicted on the screen were prepared by hand. These sketches were used as the basis for the preparation of the computer programme, according to which particular scenes were ultimately enabled to be depicted on the screen. The programme itself was extremely sophisticated. It calculated the three-dimensional position of each part of

each object and character at each stage of all movements. An example of the sophistication involved is the windscreen of a car, which is shown three-dimensionally, with a superimposed two-dimensional image of a reflection of the sky appearing on it.

Sound effects, music, and very simple dialogue were also required. Over eighty sound effects were selected from a sound library or created, and then manipulated, for inclusion in the programme. Dialogue was recorded, and that recording was also manipulated and included in the programme. Music was added after composition on a synthesiser.

When all the work had been completed and was brought together, it was represented by a highly specialized piece of computer equipment, suitable, and suitable only, for bringing Virtua Cop to the screen. Although, as I have said, sketches, models and video tape were used in the course of the creation of the programme, in the finished product, the screen images were not represented by anything comparable to the tiny translucent images which characterize the original technology of cinematograph film. A closer analogy could be drawn to video tape, containing magnetic fields that may be transformed into visual images upon a screen. But the respondents argue that even this analogy misses the mark. According to their contention, Virtua Cop is not represented in any form until it is born on the screen out of the union between the player's input and the computer programme that calculates the three-dimensional reference points, not images, by reference to which the images themselves are made to appear on the screen. The respondents say that the visual images were not stored in any manner; mathematical co-ordinates of models of objects, together with animation and texture mapping data, were stored in digital form, and are used by the controlling programme to create images on the screen. In doing so, the respondents say, the 'microcomputer controls the sequence of visual displays and aural effects in response to a player's actions and this generates a different game play for each player within the overall limitations of objects and scenes available to be generated by the controlling program'. Thus, they contend, 'the visual imagery ... is an artefact of real-time computer graphics in that the images on the screen are synthesised on the fly by the controlling program'. On this basis, their argument asserts it is 'not correct to say that the 2-dimensional screen images themselves are stored in the computer like some form of 'digital movie' and simply played back during the game. ...

THE TRIAL JUDGE'S REASONING

At the beginning of his reasoning, Burchett J made an important observation:

> ... there is a significant concession involved in the proposition that the influence of the player's actions is confined within 'the overall limitations of objects and scenes available to be generated by the controlling program'. What this must mean is that stored within the computer is the capacity to produce, and the limitation to producing only, the co-ordinates and other effects necessary to constitute upon the screen a particular limited number of variants upon the basic theme. Of course, if a player, to use the technical jargon, responds at all times with the correct 'inputs', only the one version of the story will appear upon the screen.

His Honour then set out the definition of 'cinematograph film' in s 10 of the Act and its amplification in s 24 ... Section 24 reads:

> For the purposes of this Act, sounds or visual images shall be taken to have been embodied in an article or thing if the article or thing has been so treated in relation to those sounds or visual images that those sounds or visual images are capable, with or without the aid of some other device, of being reproduced from the article or thing.

CURRENT LAW

Burchett J commented:

> The expert evidence adduced by the respondents appeared to seize upon the expression 'the visual images embodied in an article or thing'. Plainly enough, what is seen by the viewer is shown as a moving picture; but the point made was 'that there does not exist inside the computer anywhere a 2-dimensional image [of what appears on the screen]. That 2-dimensional image is simply computed from looking at all the three-dimensional vertices of the polygon model [this is a reference to the way in which the computer apprehends objects] and doing what is a clever arithmetic on it'. The validity of this argument must depend on how the word 'embodied' is understood. This word, as is made clear by *The New Shorter Oxford English Dictionary* (1993), generally refers to the giving of 'a material or discernible form to (an abstract principle, concept, etc.).

His Honour called in aid the Lord Chancellor's song in *Iolanthe*, saying it indicated the 'precise sense' conveyed by 'embodied':

> The Law is the true embodiment
> Of everything that's excellent.
> It has no kind of fault or flaw,
>   And I, my Lords, embody the Law.

He also referred to the words of a real Lord Chancellor, Lord Cranworth, in *Jefferys v Boosey* (1854) 4 HLC 815; 10 ER 681:

> So long as a literary work remains unpublished at all, it has no existence, except in the mind of its author, or in the papers in which he, for his own convenience, may have embodied it.

The trial judge said:

> When Lord Cranworth used the word 'embodied' in that way, I think he was speaking of an author giving his creation a form in which it could be held for continued existence and use. In my opinion, that is the essence of the meaning also intended to be conveyed by the *Report on Computer Software Protection* (1995) of the Copyright Law Review Committee, chaired by Sheppard J, at para.10.142, where the Committee referred to the importation of an integrated circuit in order 'to import a copyright work embodied in that integrated circuit' (Burchett J's emphasis).

Burchett J rejected the notion that an embodiment of a visual image required something in the nature of a frame, as on a reel of film, of which the image is a reflection. He cited a number of judicial decisions favouring a liberal construction of copyright legislation. He said the legislative history shows Parliament intended to take a broad view in relation to copyright in a film, 'and not to tie the copyright to any particular technology'. He cited the United Kingdom's *Gregory Report* (1952) and the Second Reading Speech for the *Australian Copyright Bill*, both of which refer to the technical interchangeability of cinematograph film and video tape. Burchett J commented that, against this background:

> ... it seems to me that the definition of 'cinematograph film', expressed as it is in terms of the result achieved rather than of the means employed, points very strongly to an intention to cover new technologies which do actually achieve the same result. This view is, of course, strengthened by the terms of s 24. That section was plainly inserted to ensure that the word 'embodied' did not receive a narrow construction. It applies quite literally in the present case. With the aid

of 'some other device', namely, the input device utilised by the player of the video game, the apparatus is capable of reproducing quite precisely the aggregate of the visual images created by Sega Enterprises Ltd so that they are shown as a moving picture. To demonstrate this, it is sufficient, of course, to refer to the visual images created to be shown upon the reception by the apparatus of the 'correct' inputs. In any case, as I have already pointed out, the variations are within predetermined limits ...

After referring to other matters, Burchett J noted the applicants' alternative argument that the subject machines constituted a 'sound recording'. He pointed out that, if the computer-generated images constituted a 'cinematograph film', this argument must fail; s 23(1) of the *Copyright Act 1968* provides that 'sounds embodied in a sound track associated with visual images forming part of cinematograph film shall be deemed not to be a sound recording.' ...

CONCLUSIONS

... I agree with Burchett J that it would be wrong to interpret narrowly the definition of 'cinematograph film' in s 10 and s 24. These provisions were intended to cover new technologies, the emphasis being on the end product—motion pictures—rather than the means adopted to create those pictures. Nonetheless, the definition will apply to any particular new technology only if that technology satisfies the words of the definition, liberally read.

... The definition of 'cinematograph film' refers to 'the aggregate of the visual images embodied in an article or thing ...'. Section 24 sets out circumstances under which 'visual images shall be taken to have been embodied in an article or thing'. I also agree that the word 'embodied' refers to the giving of a material or discernible form to an abstract principle or concept. The Lord Chancellor's *Iolanthe* song neatly illustrates this meaning. According to his Lordship, the abstract concept of excellence achieves material manifestation in the Law; and the Law, in turn, is manifested in his noble person.

It seems inherent in both the dictionary definition and the *Iolanthe* illustration that the abstraction must pre-exist the material manifestation. Counsel for the appellants argue that the images visible to players of the games do not exist before the moment of visibility; accordingly, it cannot be said that they represent an embodiment of pre-existing images. Counsel make the point that computer-generated images are fundamentally different to film or video images; in the latter case the images are fixed on celluloid or videotape before the moment of projection and viewing.

This analysis is superficially attractive; but, I think, unsound. The visual images depicted in these video games did exist before the game was played. They existed in the minds of their creators and the drawings and models they made. The images were embodied in the computer program built into the video game machine so as to be capable, by the use of that program, of being shown as a moving picture. It does not matter that they were embodied in a different form; that is, three-dimension vertices of the polygon model, rather than a two-dimensional image. The statutory definition says nothing about the form of embodiment. Nor does it matter that the images seen by players are created by computer calculations only immediately before their appearance on the screen of the video game machine. Although that means, in a sense, that they are new, they are exact recreations of images previously devised by the graphic designers. Similarly, of course, it is unimportant that the images could not be seen on the screen as a moving picture until generated by the computer, any more than it matters that a length of video tape is incapable of being seen as a moving picture until passed through a video player ...

Upon analysis, the present case seems to fall directly within the terms of the s 10 definition of 'cinematograph film', without the necessity of resorting to s 24. However, that section puts the matter beyond doubt. The visual images that constitute the moving picture are taken to have been 'embodied' in the computer program because the computer program was so treated in relation to those images as to be capable of reproducing them.

Counsel for the appellants argue it is not enough that a particular article was capable of producing particular sounds or visual images. If capability is the test, they say, every piano would have to be held a 'sound recording' of Beethoven's 'Moonlight Sonata'. Every piano is capable of producing the notes that constitute that work. Counsel have in mind that the term 'sound recording' is defined by s 10 as meaning 'the aggregate of the sounds embodied in a record' and a 'record' includes any 'device in which sounds are embodied'.

I accept capability is not enough. It is important to note the requirement of s 24 that the article or thing 'has been so treated in relation to those sounds or visual images' that they are capable of being reproduced from the article or thing. There must have been a treatment of the article or thing that is related to specific sounds or visual images. This can be said of a computer program, not of a piano. It is necessary to include a keyboard in a piano, if it is to be capable of reproducing the notes that constitute the 'Moonlight Sonata'. But the inclusion of a keyboard is not something done 'in relation to' those particular sounds; it is done in relation to piano music generally.

I think Burchett J was correct in holding that the aggregate of the visual images generated by the playing of each of the two subject video games constituted a 'cinematograph film' within the meaning of s 10 of the *Copyright Act.*

A further provision of note is s 23(1), which provides:

> For the purposes of this Act, sounds embodied in a sound-track associated with visual images forming part of cinematograph film shall be deemed not to be a sound recording.

As quoted above, 'sound-track' here has the technical meaning of 'the part of any article or thing, being an article or thing in which [the visual images being the film] are embodied, in which sounds are embodied': that is, it is all the sounds that are part of the film (not a recording collecting the music associated with a film and sold separately). This provision is intended to deny separate protection as a sound recording for the sounds embodied in a sound-track which is part of a film. What happens, however, when a pre-existing sound recording (like a recording of a popular song) is incorporated into the sound-track of a film? As the High Court decision in *Phonographic Performance Company of Australia Ltd v Federation of Australian Commercial Television Stations* (1998) 195 CLR 158 makes clear, a sound recording so incorporated retains its identity as a sound recording: therefore, the broadcast of the cinematograph film will involve broadcast of that pre-existing sound recording (and will require a licence from the owners of copyright in the film and in the sound recording).

SOUND AND TELEVISION BROADCASTS

Section 10(1) of the *Copyright Act* sets out the following definitions:

> *broadcast* means a communication to the public delivered by a broadcasting service within the meaning of the *Broadcasting Services Act 1992.*

Note: A broadcasting service does not include the following:

(a) a service (including a teletext service) that provides only data or only text (with or without associated images); or

(b) a service that makes programs available on demand on a point-to-point basis, including a dial-up service.

...

sound broadcast means sounds broadcast otherwise than as part of a television broadcast.

...

television broadcast means visual images broadcast by way of television, together with any sounds broadcast for reception along with those images.

See also s 25(4), which provides:

(a) a reference to a cinematograph film of a television broadcast shall be read as including a reference to a cinematograph film, or a photograph, of any of the visual images comprised in the broadcast; and

(b) a reference to a copy of a cinematograph film of a television broadcast shall be read as including a reference to a copy of a cinematograph film, or a reproduction of a photograph, of any of those images.

Consistent with the approach in the rest of Part IV of the *Copyright Act*, broadcast copyright is separate from and cumulative with copyright in content that is broadcast. That is, there is likely to be separate copyright in the programs that are broadcast over television (both as cinematograph films, and in the underlying content such as scripts (dramatic works)), or in the content broadcast over radio (both as sound recordings, and in the content of those recordings (such as musical works)). Broadcasts are very different from other subject matters protected by copyright. Despite the difficulties sometimes encountered in determining the boundaries of the protected subject matter, other copyright subject matters generally can be conceived as intangible 'things' with a static identity and a definite beginning, middle and end. By contrast, a broadcast is an ephemeral, continuous stream of sounds and/or images delivered by broadcasters over the air or down wires. This difference is illustrated in the decision of Bennett J in *Seven Network Ltd v Commissioner of Taxation* [2014] FCA 1411. In that case, Channel Seven paid the International Olympic Committee (IOC) for access to multiple feeds, or data streams, from host broadcaster cameras placed at Games venues, as part of the arrangements for broadcasting the Olympic Games. Channel Seven used these data streams as input for its Games broadcast. Tax payable on the agreement depended on whether payment for this access was a copyright royalty. The Commissioner of Taxation argument was that the IOC's data streams were 'cinematograph films'. Bennett J disagreed: as an ephemeral medium of communication, the data streams did not 'embody' visual images so could not be films. In other words, the IOC data streams could only potentially be broadcasts (but clearly did not satisfy the other elements of the Australian statutory definition of 'broadcast').

If broadcast is ephemeral, how do you define, or plead, 'the broadcast'? This question arose squarely in *Network Ten Pty Ltd v TCN Channel Nine Pty Ltd* [2004] HCA 14; (2004) 218 CLR 273, extracted below. The differing views of the justices depend chiefly on whether they focused on the literal terms of the legislation (as Hely J did in his judgment in the Full Federal Court) or on an extrapolation of the intended object of protection from legislative history (as the majority did in their judgment in the High Court). Note, however, that even the dissenting justices in the High Court (Kirby and Callinan JJ) also drew on the goals of copyright to justify their interpretations.

CASE EXTRACT: CURRENT LAW

Network Ten Pty Ltd v TCN Channel Nine Pty Ltd

[2004] HCA 14; (2004) 218 CLR 273
High Court of Australia

[The litigation concerned alleged infringement by Ten of Nine's broadcast copyright (i.e. *not* the copyright in the underlying television programs as films). Ten broadcast a weekly television program called *The Panel*, which took the form of a humorous panel discussion of news, celebrities and things that had happened on television. *The Panel* had used short extracts from programs broadcast by Nine, ranging from news broadcasts to award ceremonies, daytime television shows (such as *The Today Show* and *Midday*) and serials (such as *Days of Our Lives*).

It was necessary to work out whether the short extracts constituted a 'substantial part' of Nine's broadcasts. Hely J in the Full Federal Court (with whom Sundberg and Finkelstein JJ agreed on this point) focused on the statutory provisions: the s 10(1) definition of 'television broadcast', s 87 (defining the rights in broadcasts to include the right 'to make a cinematograph film of the broadcast') and s 25(4) (which defines a 'cinematograph film of a broadcast' to include 'a cinematograph film, or a photograph, of any of the visual images comprised in the broadcast'). Hely J ruled that copyright subsisted in any broadcast of 'visual images and accompanying sounds': that is, mere seconds, or even fractions of a second, of a broadcast.]

McHugh ACJ, Gummow and Hayne JJ (some footnotes omitted): 8. … The gist of Ten's complaint is that the term 'a television broadcast' as it appears in the Act was misread by the Full Court, with the result that the content of that expression is so reduced that questions of substantiality have no practical operation and the ambit of the copyright monopoly is expanded beyond the interests the legislation seeks to protect.

9. Ten's submissions should be accepted and the appeal allowed.

STATUTORY INTERPRETATION

10. The submissions for Nine initially eschewed any detailed consideration of the anterior legal and historical context in the United Kingdom; this was despite the significance of the British legislation which then followed, upon the later Australian legislation. Nine also stressed the significance of what were said to be the plain words of the provisions of the Act immediately in issue and sought to discount any reaction to the decision of the Full Court which emphasised that the construction favoured by the Full Court appeared to be at odds with the overall scheme of the Act.

[McHugh ACJ et al quoted principles of statutory construction, noting that it is acceptable to read the plain words of legislation 'in the light of the mischief which the statute was designed to overcome and of the objects of the legislation', then continued:]

12. The context in which the broadcasting right was introduced, including well-established principles of copyright law, the inconvenience and improbability of the result obtained in the Full Court, and a close consideration of the text of various provisions of the Act relating to the broadcasting right, combine to constrain the construction given to the Act by the Full Court and to indicate that the appeal to this Court should be allowed.

13. Reference first will be made to two well-established principles, those concerned with the significance of copying, and with the taking of a substantial part of the protected material. Attention then will be given to the legislative context in which the broadcasting right first appeared, and thereafter to the particular issues of statutory construction involved in the appeal.

COPYRIGHT AND COPYING

14. Counsel for Nine invoked a well-known statement made in *University of London Press Ltd v University Tutorial Press Ltd* [[1916] 2 Ch 601 at 610]. This was a case of infringement of copyright in an original literary work and Peterson J applied 'the rough practical test that what is worth copying is prima facie worth protecting'. But later authorities correctly emphasise that, whilst copying is an essential element in infringement to provide a causal connection between the plaintiff's intellectual property and the alleged infringement, it does not follow that any copying will infringe. The point was stressed by Laddie J when he said [in *Autospin (Oil Seals) Ltd v Beehive Spinning* [1995] RPC 683 at 700]:

> Furthermore many copyright cases involve defendants who have blatantly stolen the result of the plaintiff's labours. This has led courts, sometimes with almost evangelical fervour, to apply the commandment 'thou shalt not steal'. If that has necessitated pushing the boundaries of copyright protection further out, then that has been done. This has resulted in a body of case law on copyright which, in some of its further reaches, would come as a surprise to the draughtsmen of the legislation to which it is supposed to give effect.

15. Professor Waddams, speaking of the use of terms such as 'piracy', 'robbery' and 'theft' to stigmatise the conduct of alleged infringers of intellectual property rights, describes 'the choice of rhetoric' as 'significant, showing the persuasive power of proprietary concepts' [*Dimensions of Private Law: Categories and concepts in Anglo-American legal reasoning*, Cambridge University Press, Cambridge, 2003, pp 175–6]. He also remarks:

> Against the merits of enlarging the property rights of one person or class of persons must always be set the loss of freedom of action that such enlargement inevitably causes to others.

16. In another English decision, Jacob J [in *Ibcos Computers Ltd v Barclays Mercantile Highland Finance Ltd* [1994] FSR 275 at 289] identified Peterson J's aphorism in *University of London Press* as an indication of the dangers in departing too far from the text and structure of the legislation; his Lordship said that the aphorism 'proves too much' because if 'taken literally [it] would mean that all a plaintiff ever had to do was to prove copying' so that 'appropriate subject matter for copyright and a taking of a substantial part would all be proved in one go'.

17. In Australia, the dangers in the use of the remarks in *University of London Press* were explained by Sackville J in *Nationwide News Pty Ltd v Copyright Agency Ltd* [(1996) 65 FCR 399 at 417–18] as follows:

> [T]he test has a certain 'bootstraps' quality about it. The issue of substantiality, in relation to a literary work, arises only where the work has been reproduced or published, at least in part.

If applied literally, the test would mean that all cases of copying would be characterised as reproducing a substantial part of the work. It is therefore unlikely to be of great assistance in determining whether a particular reproduction involves a substantial part of a work or subject matter of copyright.

'SUBSTANTIAL PART'

18. All the species of copyright enjoy a protection which is not limited to infringement by the taking of the whole of the protected subject-matter. The taking of something less will do. That lesser degree of exploitation is identified in s 14(1) by the phrase 'a substantial part' ...

19. The effect of the interpretation given by the Full Court to the term 'television broadcast' and related expressions in the Act is to go beyond s 14(1) and provide that, with respect to any given period of broadcasting, however brief, the copyright owner has the exclusive right to re-broadcast *any* of the images and accompanying sounds broadcast ...

21. The scheme of the 1911 Act, as with the UK Act and the Australian legislation which succeeded it, keeps separate the concepts of substantial part and fair dealing. Accordingly:

> ... acts done in relation to insubstantial parts do not constitute an infringement of copyright and the defences of fair dealing only come into operation in relation to substantial parts or more ...
> [S Ricketson, *The Law of Intellectual Property*, Law Book Co, Sydney, 1984, §10.3.]

It would be quite wrong to approach an infringement claim on the footing that the question of the taking of a substantial part may be by-passed by going directly to the fair dealing defences.

THE LEGISLATIVE CONTEXT

...

23. The [1968] Act was preceded by the Report ('the Spicer Report') delivered in 1959 of the Committee appointed by the Attorney-General of the Commonwealth to consider what alterations were desirable in the copyright law of the Commonwealth ('the Spicer Committee'). The Spicer Report had said it was significant that neither the Brussels Convention nor the Universal Copyright Convention recognised a copyright in sound broadcasts or television broadcasts (par 285). In the end, the Spicer Report concluded (pars 288, 289) that protection for broadcasters could properly be included in the copyright law with an adaptation of the provision then recently made by s 14 of the UK Act.

24. The introduction by s 14 of the UK Act of the new species of copyright protection followed Recommendation 31 in the *Report of the Copyright Committee* ('the Gregory Report') which had been presented in 1952. Recommendation 31 had been:

> That a broadcasting authority should have the right to prevent the copying of its programmes either by re-broadcasting, or by the making of records for sale and subsequent performance. (Paragraph 117)

Paragraphs 116 and 117 of the Gregory Report state the policy and objectives which were subsequently to find expression in the provisions of the Australian legislation upon which this appeal turns. Accordingly, pars 116 and 117 should be set out in full:

> 116. We now turn to the question whether a new right should be given to the broadcasting organisations in their own programme, additional to any copyright there may be in the individual

items which go to make up those programmes, and we deal at this stage solely with a right to prevent other persons from copying the programme either by way of again broadcasting a programme (in the event of there being more than one broadcasting authority in the future) or by way of recording such programmes for subsequent performance in some other way.

117. On the question of copyright in the ordinary sense, the *position of* the [British Broadcasting Corporation ('*the BBC*')], as we see it, *is not, in principle, very different from that of a gramophone company or a film company. It assembles its own programmes and transmits them at considerable cost and skill. When using copyright material it pays the copyright owner, and it seems to us nothing more than natural justice that it should be given the power to control any subsequent copying of these programmes by any means.* It has been represented to us that the absence of such a right has already caused considerable embarrassment to the BBC. Apparently, indifferent reproductions both of sound and television programmes have been made, and sold to the public, to the detriment alike of the [BBC] and of those taking part. We consider that a right should be given to the BBC or any other broadcasting organisation to prevent this happening again. Any right so conferred would be additional to the right of the author or composer to prevent mechanical recording where copyright material is broadcast. It would also extend to prevent the mechanical recording of a broadcast of material which is either non-copyright, or of a nature in which a right to prevent recording may not, under the present law, subsist at all, eg news, talks, music-hall 'gags'. (emphasis added)

25. In Australia, the Spicer Committee stressed the significance of the new head of copyright protection, saying (par 282):

> The conception of copyright which has hitherto been accepted is one which extends protection against copying and performing in public any work insofar as it is reduced to a permanent form. Copyright has not been extended to confer such protection in relation to a mere spectacle or performance which is transitory of its very nature.

In *Victoria Park Racing and Recreation Grounds Co Ltd v Taylor* [(1937) 58 CLR 479], the High Court had rejected the submission that by the expenditure of money the plaintiff had created a spectacle at its racecourse so that it had 'a quasi-property in the spectacle which the law would protect' [at 496] by enjoining the broadcast of a race-meeting there. The issue before the Spicer Committee was a different one, namely the protection of broadcasts themselves.

26. The Spicer Committee added (para 284):

> It is true that in many cases the broadcast will be recorded on tape or film, in which case the record or film will enjoy its own copyright protection, but the copyright here being considered is one which attaches to the broadcast itself.

27. In the second reading speech on the Bill for the Act, the Attorney-General, Mr NH Bowen QC, said that the matters of records and broadcasts were dealt with in the UK Act and that it was appropriate to deal with them in the Bill. He also referred to the provisions of the Rome Convention which had postdated the UK Act but to which Australia was yet to accede. The Rome Convention also provided for the grant of 'neighbouring rights' to various persons including broadcasters. Article 13 of the Rome Convention provided that '[b]roadcasting organisations [were to] enjoy the right to authorise or prohibit', among other things, 'the rebroadcasting of their broadcasts', 'the fixation of their broadcasts' and 'the reproduction ... of fixations, made without their consent, of their broadcasts'.

CURRENT LAW

28. Conti J [the trial judge] noted that the Gregory Report had spoken of the right to prevent the copying of the 'programmes' of broadcasting authorities, and the broadcasting systems established by the 1942 Act spoke of the provision of 'programmes' broadcast or televised from transmitting stations, and the Spicer Report spoke both of the protection of 'broadcasts' and (in par 286) of 'the programme received'. The Rome Convention, like the Act, used the term 'broadcast'. There was no significant step taken with this shift in language. At this time, the use of 'broadcast' as a noun indicated [*Webster's New International Dictionary*, 2nd ed 1958, vol 1, 339]:

  a Broadcasting as a medium of transmission.
  b The material, music, or pictures broadcast; also, a single program of such material.

29. The policy and objective in the recommendations of both Committees was to protect the cost to, and the skill of, broadcasters in producing and transmitting their programmes, in addition to what copyrights may have subsisted in underlying works used in those programmes. There is no indication, as Nine would have it, that, with respect to television broadcasting, the interest for which legislative protection was to be provided was that in each and every image discernible by the viewer of such programmes, so as to place broadcasters in a position of advantage over that of other stakeholders in copyright law, such as the owners of cinematograph films or the owners of the copyrights in underlying original works.

THE TELEVISION BROADCASTING RIGHT

30. ... Of Pt IV copyrights, it is accurately observed:

> In general, these subject matters receive a lower level of protection than works, with shorter terms and more restricted exclusive rights.

As indicated above, this case concerns copyright in television broadcasts.

  ...

THE MEDIUM OF COMMUNICATION

38. Where the 'subject-matter' of copyright protection is of an incorporeal and transient nature, such as that involved in the technology of broadcasting, it is to be expected that the legislative identification of the monopoly (eg, by s 87) and its infringement (eg, by s 101) of necessity will involve reference to that technology. But that does not mean that the phrase 'a television broadcast' comprehends no more than any use, however fleeting, of a medium of communication. Rather, as the Gregory Report indicated, protection was given to that which had the attribute of commercial significance to the broadcaster, identified by the use of the term 'a broadcast' in its sense of 'a programme'. In the same way, the words, figures and symbols which constitute a 'literary work', such as a novel, are protected not for their intrinsic character as the means of communication to readers but because of what, taken together, they convey to the comprehension of the reader.

39. In fixing upon that which was capable of perception as a separate image upon a television screen and what were said to be accompanying sounds as the subject-matter comprehended by the phrase 'a television broadcast', the Full Court appears to have fixed upon the medium of transmission, not the message conveyed by its use.

40. Because the medium is ephemeral, it is necessary to capture what a television broadcaster transmits if any practical use is to be made of the signal that is broadcast. For many purposes,

it is necessary not only to capture the signal, but also to translate it so that the images and sounds which the signal conveys can be seen and heard. The most common method of doing that is, of course, the television set, but other devices, such as various forms of video recorder, may be used. According to the device that is used, what is captured and translated may be only so much of a signal broadcast as has previously been, or can at the time of transmission of the signal be, translated into a single image or moment of sound. But in the ordinary course, what is captured and translated can, and will, be a faithful reproduction of all, or substantially all, that the broadcaster's signal permits.

41. Section 87 of the Act, in pars (a) and (b), identifies the nature of copyright in a television broadcast by reference to two methods by which what is transmitted can be captured and recorded in permanent or semi-permanent form. One method (s 87(a)) is to take a still visual image of what otherwise appears on a television set as part of a continuous visual transmission. In that context it may be sensible to speak of a single visual image that is broadcast. However, it by no means follows that it is sensible to confine the understanding of 'a television broadcast' by basing the meaning that is given to the expression upon the capacity to capture and record singular visual images. Especially is that so when it makes little sense to speak of a single 'moment' of sound accompanying that image. The instantaneous fixing of single visual images is familiar, but the instantaneous fixing of single sounds is not. When it is further observed that s 87(c), with its reference to re-broadcasting, at least encompasses the capture and simultaneous retransmission of a television broadcaster's signal, it is apparent that to understand 'a television broadcast' as a singular and very small portion of the signal which a broadcaster transmits virtually continuously, and a person receiving is intended to receive continuously, is to give the expression a very artificial meaning. Yet that is what the Full Court did.

[Their Honours considered the interpretation of Hely J, described in the facts above, then continued:]

47. As already emphasised in these reasons, the requirement that an infringer who takes less than the whole of the protected subject-matter must take at least a substantial part thereof plays a well-established and central part in copyright law. Questions of quality (which could include the potency of particular images or sounds, or both, in a broadcast) as well as quantity arise both in respect of Pt IV copyrights and those copyrights in original works to which Pt III applies.

48. The outcome of the decision of the Full Court now under appeal is that the interests of broadcasters are placed by the Act in a privileged position above that of the owners of copyright in the literary, dramatic, musical and artistic works which may have been utilised in providing the subject of the images and sounds broadcast. This is because the diminished requirements in respect of infringement of television broadcasts for the taking of a substantial part of the subject-matter facilitate the proof of infringement there while leaving the owners of copyrights under Pt III with a heavier burden. Ten points to this apparent incongruity as favouring a construction of the Act contrary to that adopted by the Full Court.

...

WHAT IS 'A TELEVISION BROADCAST'?

67. The definition given in s 10 is 'television broadcast', which is drawn in terms of the technology of broadcasting which is to be utilised. But the phrase in the exclusive right provisions of s 87 (as also in ss 91, 95, 99 and 101(4)) is '*a* television broadcast' (emphasis added).

68. In the present case, Hely J focused attention not upon the statutory phrase 'a television broadcast', but upon the use of technical language in the definition of 'television broadcast'. His Honour concluded:

> Here the interest protected by the copyright is the visual images broadcast by way of television and any accompanying sounds. It is the actual images and sounds broadcast which constitute the interest protected. The interest protected is not defined in terms of some larger 'whole' of which the visual images and sounds broadcast are but a part. The ephemeral nature of a broadcast, and the fact that copyright protection is conferred by reference to a broadcaster's output, rather than by reference to the originality of what is broadcast, may also help to explain why the interest protected is defined in this way.

69. That identification of the interest sought to be protected by the broadcast copyright should not be accepted.

70. The interest sought to be protected by the conferral of the television broadcast copyright was identified by the Spicer Committee with reference to the experience of the BBC and the Independent Television Authority. The latter was established by the *Television Act 1954* (UK) and charged by s 3 to 'broadcast … programmes' of a certain standard. This interest was identified as that in the cost and skill in assembling or preparing and transmitting programmes to the public. That activity of public broadcasting occurred in exercise of statutory authority which required the transmission of programmes of a certain standard or quality identified by their content. The Spicer Committee decided against leaving it to broadcasters to record or film their broadcasts and so depend upon the protection given to sound recordings and cinematograph films (par 287).

71. Further reference should be made to s 91. This limits the identity of those in whom there may subsist copyright in television broadcasts and sound broadcasts … The result is to render the subsistence of copyright dependent upon the making of 'a television broadcast' by the Australian Broadcasting Corporation ('the Corporation'), the Special Broadcasting Service Corporation ('the SBS') and those such as Nine and Ten holding the requisite licences or permits under the *Broadcasting Act*. What then is contemplated is the exercise by those identified broadcasters of the performance of their statutory powers or duties under their constituent legislation or the exercise of the authority given by their licences under the *Broadcasting [Services] Act*.

[Their Honours noted that the *Broadcasting Services Act 1992* (Cth), *Australian Broadcasting Corporation Act 1983* (Cth) and *Special Broadcasting Service Act 1991* (Cth) all refer to the service of the various broadcasters as being a service of 'providing programs', then continued:]

75. There can be no absolute precision as to what in any of an infinite possibility of circumstances will constitute 'a television broadcast'. However, the programmes which Nine identified in pars 5.1–5.11 of its pleading as the Nine Programs, and which are listed with their dates of broadcast in the reasons of Conti J, answer that description. These broadcasts were put out to the public, the object of the activity of broadcasting, as discrete periods of broadcasting identified and promoted by a title, such as *The Today Show*, *Nightline*, *Wide World of Sports*, and the like, which would attract the attention of the public.

76. However, Conti J was, with respect, correct in adding, with reference to *Copinger and Skone James on Copyright*, that:

> Television advertisements should be treated as discrete television broadcasts, particularly since
> 'A television or cinema commercial is typically the product of the creative and administrative

> work of many separate individuals' ... I would reject Ten's submission that because advertising is the 'life blood' of commercial television broadcasting, it is 'impossible for [Nine] to avoid the conclusion that these advertisements are part of that program'.

His Honour added:

> Moreover, where a given program divides into segments, it may be legitimate in the facts of a given case to use a segment of a program for measurement of the television broadcast, rather than the whole of the program.

77. We would reserve consideration of that proposition for a particular case where the point arises. However, the circumstance that a prime time news broadcast includes various segments, items or 'stories' does not necessarily render each of these 'a television broadcast' in which copyright subsists under s 91 of the Act.

Kirby J (dissenting):

PURPOSIVE CONSTRUCTION WITHIN TEXTUAL LIMITS

...

87. I accept wholeheartedly that the contemporary approach of this Court to the interpretation of contested statutory language is the purposive approach. However, adopting that approach does not justify judicial neglect of the language of the statute, whether in preference for historical or other materials, perceived legal policy or any other reason. A purposive construction is supported by s 15AA of the *Acts Interpretation Act 1901* (Cth). But that section also does not permit a court to ignore the words of the Act. Ultimately, in every case, statutory construction is a text-based activity. It cannot be otherwise.

88. In the present case, in the terms of the Act, I find it impossible to construe 'a television broadcast' as mentioned in ss 25 and 87 of the Act to exclude those 'visual images broadcast by way of television, together with any sounds broadcast for reception along with those images' of the kind described in the evidence, being the segments from the respondents' earlier television broadcasts recorded by the appellant and rebroadcast as part of its own programme, The Panel. Similarly, I find it impossible to read the plain language of s 101(1) and (4) of the Act somehow to confine the meaning of 'a television broadcast', so that it does not include segments of the type recorded and then rebroadcast by the appellant.

89. If one is truly looking for the 'purpose' of the Act, that purpose must be found not in some *a priori* view about the merits, or desirability, of the copyright in their television broadcasts which the respondents assert. Ultimately, that purpose must be found in the command of the Parliament, expressed in the Act. Moreover, because, following detailed official inquiries and the development of an international Convention, the Act afforded new and larger copyright entitlements in Australia, it would be contrary to basic principle and the ordinary canons of statutory construction to restrict those entitlements in a way that conflicted with the language of the Act or that unduly narrowed its operation. Normally, an amendment of an Act to provide new rights of such a kind will be given a beneficial construction so as to ensure that the purpose of the legislature is truly attained. I accept that in the context of the law of copyright, indeed intellectual property law generally, other considerations compete

with the protection of private rights. But in the end, it is the statutory text, not generalities or judicial policy judgments, that governs the task in hand and is determinative.

CRITICISMS OF THE AMBIT OF COPYRIGHT PROTECTION

90. I reach my conclusion without quite the same enthusiasm as Callinan J appears to feel for it. The opinion of the Full Court has been described as 'highly literal'. Perhaps it is; but the language of the Act leaves no scope for another approach. The most telling criticism voiced of the Full Court's interpretation is that it makes television broadcast copyright 'an extraordinarily strong right, easily the strongest of all copyrights in Australia, able to be infringed by taking less than a substantial part of the broadcast' [Handler, '*The Panel* Case and Television Broadcast Copyright' (2003) 25 *Sydney Law Review* 391 at 395]. This, it is said, is counterintuitive given the ephemeral nature of television broadcasts and the original reasons for granting copyright in them.

91. If I were free of the constraints of the language of the Act, I would be happy to agree in the conclusion reached in this court by McHugh ACJ, Gummow and Hayne JJ, whilst feeling anxiety about the lack of precision as to what, in any of an infinite range of circumstances, will constitute 'a television broadcast' on that view ...

93. ... The Act contemplated a form of copyright apt to the particular technology involved in television broadcasting. It therefore provided that copyright would attach to 'the visual images comprised in the broadcast'. Those who conceive the parliament as confining the scope of the new copyright protection for television broadcasts to entire programmes (or defined and undefined sections and segments of a continuous day's broadcasting) must not watch much television. It is the very power of particular, and often quite limited (even fragmentary) portions of 'visual images' on television that makes it such a potent and commercially valuable means of expressing thoughts and ideas: noble and banal, serious and humorous, uplifting and discouraging.

94. Everyone knows that still images or very brief segments in television broadcasts can constitute commercially valuable commodities, standing alone. The acquisition by a broadcaster of comparatively short filmed sequences will sometimes represent very important and commercially valuable rights that exist without the need of a surrounding context, let alone an extended programme or particular segment of a day's broadcast. The parties to the present appeal were in commercial competition with each other. That fact is itself also a consideration that generally favours the claim of a copyright owner.

...

98. ... [T]he parliament did not envisage the striking of a balance between public and private interests in the Act by the adoption of an unspecified and ultimately undefinable notion of 'a television broadcast' in the sense of a 'unit of programming'. The Act does not refer to that notion of a 'programme' or unit thereof. It might have done so. But it did not. Instead, the Act provides for copyright to attach to 'a television broadcast' that necessarily contains, of its nature, parts of such a programme, including therefore long as well as very short extracts. To strike an acceptable balance between public and private interests, the parliament looked elsewhere. By s 14(1) it provided, in effect, for a permissible degree of exploitation by introducing the notion that the proscribed act must be in relation to 'a substantial part' of the work or subject matter. And if that barrier is passed the defence of fair dealing may be invoked, precisely as the appellant claimed in this case.

...

Callinan J (dissenting): 142. The Act falls to be read … against the background of these indisputable facts. The parties compete with each other. The production of any programme, indeed each and every frame and segment of it, comes at a cost. It is produced in order to make money by inducing advertisers to pay to have their activities advertised in association with its broadcast one or more times. Further value may arise from the isolation, reproduction and broadcasting of an image or images, with or without sound, from it, and the licensing of it or an isolated image or images from it, whether by and in a photograph, a film or a video film. What is clear in this case is that value did lie in the copying, reproduction and rebroadcasting of segments, albeit generally fairly brief segments, of the respondents' programmes. That value had two aspects: it enabled the appellant to gain revenue from advertising associated with *The Panel*; and it relieved the appellant of the cost of buying or producing other matter to occupy the time taken by the rebroadcasting, during *The Panel*, of the copied and reproduced segments. The intention of Pt IV Div 2 of the Act was, as the Attorney-General said, broadly not only to place television footage on at least the same basis as other original work, particularly moving films, protected by the Act, but as appears from the language used in it, with necessary adaptations to suit the medium and the means available to competitors to exploit it, and in consequence to create new rights. Why should, it is reasonable to ask, the appellant, save to the extent that it deals fairly with any of the respondents' valuable broadcasted matter, get it and rebroadcast it for its own commercial benefit, for nothing? The question in this case is whether the Act prevents it from doing that.

143. The use by the appellant of excerpts from the respondents' broadcasts was blatant. And although blatant appropriation of the kind which has occurred here might not be such as to warrant an evangelical fervor in responding to it, in the nakedly commercial context of television broadcasting in Australia, the test of 'what is worth copying is prima facie worth protecting' posed by Peterson J in *University of London Press Ltd v University Tutorial Press Ltd* [[1916] 2 Ch 601 at 610] has much to commend it, and provides at least a reasonable starting point. After all, in recognising the validity of the respondents' copyright in excerpts from their programmes, the court would not be denying access to the general public of the golden words of a new Shakespeare. This is a case of blatant commercial exploitation, neither more nor less …

155. Nothing turns, in my opinion, upon any perceived differences between the quality or nature of the copyright afforded by the Act to television broadcasts and other copyright holders. It was and was intended to be a new and unique right. The medium is very different from others. To exploit it, different and perhaps more expansive infrastructures, fees, techniques and resources are required. The industry is, and has always been in this country, a highly competitive, and, as this case shows, a highly commercialised one. There may have been good reason for the legislature to single it out for special treatment. It is for the court to give effect to the language of the Act and not to speculate about that.

PUBLISHED EDITIONS

There is no definition of 'published edition' in the *Copyright Act*. Published edition copyright protects typographical layout, with the intention of preventing competitors from simply copying a particular edition (e.g. of copyright literary works, or public domain works such as the plays of Shakespeare or the writings of Jane Austen). Published edition copyright is very limited: the only right granted in published editions is the 'exclusive right to make a facsimile copy of the edition' (s 8) and, as we saw in Chapter 3, the right endures for only 25 years after the end of the calendar year in which the edition was first published (s 96).

CASE EXTRACT: CURRENT LAW

Nationwide News Pty Ltd v Copyright Agency Ltd

(1996) 65 FCR 399
Federal Court of Australia, Full Court

[The case concerned copying by educational institutions of individual articles from newspapers and magazines. One issue was whether, in copying individual articles, the educational institutions were exercising exclusive rights in the published edition (as opposed to the underlying literary works being the articles).]

Sackville J (at 416–418): The phrase 'published edition' is not defined in the Act. It will be necessary to say something more about the concept. However, it was common ground between the parties that an example of published edition copyright would be a new edition of an out-of-copyright work, such as a collection of Shakespeare's plays. The publisher of the edition has the exclusive right to make a reproduction of the edition, even though neither the publisher nor any other person has copyright in the works contained in the edition ...

The general principle of copyright law is that copyright does not extend to ideas, but only to the expression of those ideas. But in the case of a published edition copyright, what is protected is not a particular collocation of words or musical notes, or a photographic representation. Published edition copyright protects the presentation embodied in the edition. This form of copyright, as the legislative history shows, protects such matters as typographical layout. However, it also protects other aspects of presentation, such as juxtaposition of text and photographs and use of headlines. In the present case, a considerable volume of evidence was adduced on the importance of layout and presentation to magazines and newspapers. In modern times, the work of typesetters is shared among subeditors, layout artists or designers and production editors. It is clear that layout is often extremely important in attracting readers to read a particular story or magazine. It is also clear that the choice of layout, type-size, headings and colour is a skilled operation.

Published edition copyright thus protects the product of skill, labour and judgment in presenting material in an edition. Of course, copyright in a published work can be held by one person and the published edition copyright in relation to the same publication can be held by another person. A single act of copying can therefore infringe both copyright in the work and the published edition copyright. But it is not necessarily the case that an infringement of copyright in a work will constitute an infringement of published edition copyright, since the interests protected by each form of copyright are different.

In relation to a published edition, the quality of what is taken must be assessed by reference to the interest protected by the copyright. That interest, as has been seen, is in protecting the presentation and layout of the edition, as distinct from the particular words or images published in the edition ...

[Sackville J found that the material copied by the educational institutions represented only a relatively small proportion of the totality of each of the published editions, and that the evidence did not suggest that the object of copying either article was to take advantage of the typography, layout or presentation of the newspapers: the copying was for the purpose of distributing the content of the articles, presumably to students. Nor was there a significant interference with the interest protected by published edition copyright: it was not a situation, for example, where a competing publisher had utilised a distinctive feature of the copyright holder's layout or presentation for the purposes of a rival magazine or newspaper. There was no infringement of the published edition copyright.]

DENIAL OF COPYRIGHT PROTECTION?

Copyright exists in infringing works and it is no defence to infringement to argue that the plaintiff is liable to another party for the plaintiff's alleged copying.[7] However, historically it was argued that copyright may be denied in certain content on public policy grounds. The decision below casts doubt on the ongoing relevance of this law.

CASE EXTRACT: CURRENT LAW

Venus Adult Shops Pty Ltd v Fraserside Holdings Ltd

[2006] FCAFC 188; (2006) 157 FCR 442
Federal Court of Australia, Full Court

[The case concerned alleged infringement of copyright in adult (pornographic) films.]

Finkelstein J: 130. The *Copyright Act 1968* (Cth) does not expressly deny copyright to a work that is pornographic. Nevertheless, there is longstanding authority for the view that works that are blasphemous, seditious, libellous or obscene cannot be copyright. The doctrine can be traced back to *Burnett v Chetwood* (1720) 2 Mer 441; 35 ER 1008 and to observations made by Eyre CJ in *Dr Priestley's Case*, which is not reported but noted in *Southey v Sherwood* (1817) 2 Mer 435 at 437; 35 ER 1006 at 1007.

. . .

136. The true basis for denying protection to obscene works is not clear. One possibility is that there can be no copyright in an obscene work. Another is that there is copyright but the court will not lend its assistance to the owner because of the nature of the work, that is the court will not interfere on public policy grounds. This latter approach is well and good in a case where the court is being asked to grant discretionary relief, for example, an injunction or an account of profits. It is an oft stated principle that when a plaintiff seeks equitable relief he must have clean hands.

137. It seems to me that the only sound basis for the rule, if there be any rule, which is a basis that finds some support in the cases, is that when the plaintiff cannot turn his work to profit (as would be the situation if its publication were illegal), the plaintiff has not suffered any compensable loss. That would be an answer to a claim in law, but not when the plaintiff is seeking equitable relief. Then the doctrine of clean hands would apply. On the other hand, if the plaintiff is able to profit from his work (that is when dealings in it are not unlawful) what then? It seems to me there is no basis for denying him the usual relief whether it be in law or in equity.

---

7   See *A-One Accessory Imports Pty Ltd v Off Road Imports Ltd* (1996) 65 FCR 478.

138. The position has not been clarified by any of the recent English cases. In *Glyn v Weston Feature Film Co* [1916] 1 Ch 261 Younger J refused protection to a novel which advocated free love and justified adultery. It is not clear whether he founded his decision in the absence of copyright or whether he simply refused to allow copyright to be enforced on the basis that the novel was 'of a tendency so grossly immoral'. There are passages in his judgment which support each position. In *British Oxygen Co Ltd v Liquid Air Ltd* [1925] Ch 383 Romer J granted an injunction to prevent rival manufacturers publishing a letter written by the plaintiff manufacturer to a trade customer. In the reasons of his decision he had to consider whether the writing and sending of the letter (albeit a fairly rude letter) offering the plaintiff's goods at a low price 'was an act contrary to public policy, as being in restraint of trade' and therefore disentitled the plaintiff's to copyright protection: *British Oxygen* at 392. First, he found (at 391) that the plaintiff had copyright in the letter. He then held that the plaintiff should be entitled to protection because sending the letter was not unlawful or contrary to public policy. In the process he referred to *Glyn v Weston*. Lord Keith also referred to *Glyn v Weston* in his speech in the Spycatcher Case, *Attorney-General v Guardian Newspapers Ltd No 2* [1990] 1 AC 109 at 262. He said that 'the Courts of [England would not] enforce a claim by them to the copyright in a work the publication of which they had brought about contrary to the public interest'. Accordingly, 'Mr Wright [the author] was powerless to prevent anyone who chooses to do so from publishing [his work] in whole or in part in this country, or to obtain any other remedy against them'. Again it is not clear whether Lord Keith was of opinion that there was no copyright in the work or whether it was copyright, but the court would not protect it.

139. Finally, so far as the English cases are concerned, in *Hyde Park Residence Ltd v Yelland* [2001] Ch 143, Aldous LJ suggested that the rule could be justified on the basis that courts have an inherent jurisdiction to refuse to allow their processes to be used in certain circumstances. He noted (at 160), that 'the courts will not give effect to contracts which are, for example, illegal, immoral or prejudicial to family life because they offend against the policy of the law'. He then referred to s 171(3) of the *Copyright*[*, Designs and Patents*] *Act 1988* (UK) which provides that: 'Nothing in this Part affects any rule of law preventing or restricting the enforcement of copyright, on grounds of public policy or otherwise.' He said this made it clear that the jurisdiction to decline hearing a case could be exercised in a copyright case. The Australian Copyright Act, however, has no equivalent provision.

140. Where does this leave us? For my own part, I do not accept that there is no copyright in a pornographic work. There is no such exception in the Copyright Act. In my opinion the court does not have power to create the exception. I am prepared to assume, in conformity with the early cases, that, in some circumstances, public policy may require a court to deny to a pornographer the relief that Parliament has provided to all copyright owners, but then only when the relief is discretionary. Even so, prima facie at least, the owner is entitled to discretionary relief, for example, an injunction to restrain the unauthorised publication of his work. The pornographic nature of the work will be of relevance in a claim for damages only when it is illegal to sell the work. If an author cannot sell his work he cannot suffer damage.

141. I take this approach because, to my mind, there are insurmountable difficulties standing in the way of denying copyright or copyright protection to works that may be regarded as obscene or pornographic. For one thing there is no satisfactory definition of what is obscene or pornographic. The inquiry will inevitably involve both moral and political considerations. The inquiry will be complicated

because the question will often depend upon the audience which the publication is likely to reach. If Parliament requires such an issue to be considered by a judge then, of course, the judge must consider it. But, in truth, a judge is not well suited to the task and, as often as not, will reach the wrong result.

142. Here I have in mind that in Australia there have been many ill-considered decisions about which works are obscene. The list of obscene works includes (in no particular order): Lawrence's *Lady Chatterley's Lover*, Joyce's *Ulysses*, Nabakov's *Lolita*, Huxley's *Brave New World*, Balzac's *Droll Stories*, Reed's *Ten Days that Shook the World*, Stead's *Letty Fox: Her Luck* and *A Little Tea, a Little Chat*, Winsor's *Forever Amber* and Roth's *Portnoy's Complaint*. Inevitably a list of non-copyright works will, at some point, contain more great literary works.

143. True it is that the decisions to judge these works as obscene may be explained by the fact that the standard as to whether a work is obscene varies from time to time. But that merely identifies another problem. How will one know when a work is or is not protected. Ought we have a rule which in its operation denies copyright protection on one day but permits it the next? What, in any event, is the jurisprudential foundation for a rule that gives this kind of ambulatory effect to a copyright statute? A rule that is required to work in this way is, in my view, too arbitrary for it to be adopted.

[French and Kiefel JJ drew similar conclusions in their joint judgment.]

5

OWNERSHIP AND EXPLOITATION
OF COPYRIGHT

INTRODUCTION

Previous chapters have addressed the subsistence of copyright: we turn now to the question of who owns it. In dealing with issues of ownership and exploitation of copyright, it is common to slip into the mistake of referring to the copyright associated with a single cultural product as if it entailed one block of rights, owned by an author/artist. However, as is apparent from the previous discussions on authorship and subsistence, a single product may involve several separate underlying copyrights. So, for example, behind a hip hop song heard on the radio may be a literary work (lyrics); a musical work (original song); subsidiary musical works (any music samples); the sound recording (the digital recording of the song played); and rights to other sound recordings (from which the samples were taken), as well as separate rights in the broadcast. Each of these rights may originally have been owned by different parties and subsequently assigned to still further parties. From conception to commercial production there may also be many versions of works, each potentially giving rise to different, but still multiple, claims of authorship. Consequently, administration of ownership of copyright and the process of assignment or obtaining licences can be very complex. It is necessary to identify all the potential owners of all the various rights in order to effectively exploit copyright or avoid infringement.

OWNERSHIP OF COPYRIGHT

GENERAL PRINCIPLES

Ownership of Part III works is dealt with primarily in s 35 of the *Copyright Act 1968* (Cth). The most basic rule of ownership is that authors are the first owners of copyright in the works they create: s 35(2). This is subject to a number of qualifications, two of which are especially important. First, employers own works created by employee authors in the course of their employment: s 35(6) (discussed in more detail under 'Employee and contractor works' below, p 170). Second, the Act establishes default rules: parties are free to make their own arrangements through contract: s 35(1) and (3). Parties may assign ownership or partial ownership of existing copyright works: s 196; they may also assign *future* copyright so that the moment a work comes into existence it belongs to the assignee, not the author: s 197. Other parts of s 35 create special rules for some commissioned works, and works created by employee journalists.

As ownership depends on the author of a work, it is first necessary to identify exactly who *is,* or who *are,* the authors of a work. The concept of 'authorship' was discussed in Chapter 3. In many cases identifying the author or authors will be a simple exercise. In some cases—such as those involving computer-generated works—this may raise questions of human involvement and hence copyright subsistence. In other cases, however, there may be more than one potential author of a ork, and there may be a contest as to who will be considered an author, or whether the work is one of joint authorship.

WORKS OF JOINT AUTHORSHIP

A 'work of joint authorship' is defined in s 10(1) of the *Copyright Act* as follows:

> *work of joint authorship* means a work that has been produced by the collaboration of two or more authors and in which the contribution of each author is not separate from the contribution of the other author or the contributions of the other authors.

Sections 78–83 adjust the allocation of rights in copyright to take joint authorship into account. Under s 78, references throughout the Act to 'the author' are read as references to all of the authors of the work.[1] This means that each individual joint author holds exclusive rights in the work, and thus permission is required from each joint author to exploit copyright. Section 80 addresses the duration of copyright in works of joint authorship: the term is calculated from the end of the year in which the last joint author dies.

Subject to contractual arrangements to the contrary, joint authors take an undivided and equal share of ownership of the copyright in a work as tenants in common: *Prior v Sheldon* [2000] FCA 438; (2000) 48 IPR 301. Disputes are not uncommon because, although questions of ownership can be dealt with in advance by agreement, it often does not occur to creators collaborating on a project to think about who should be entitled to shares in the copyright until they are very far along the road to commercial success. Valuable commercial opportunities for exploitation are often identified by parties long after the first making of the work. Commercial success can put considerable pressure on historically harmonious and productive relationships if there are inequities in royalty distributions among collaborators because not all are accorded the status of author. Late claims of joint authorship are often made by writers, musicians and directors (but more rarely by actors and other performers). In circumstances where the personal relations between collaborators have broken down, the courts must retrospectively determine who contributed what efforts to which works in order to determine ownership or co-ownership of the rights.

The definition in s 10(1) requires *collaboration* between the joint authors, and requires that the contributions are *not separate*. Further, each alleged joint author must be an 'author'; that is, they must have made a *sufficient* contribution—*Godfrey v Lees* [1995] EMLR 307 at 325; *Hadley v Kemp* [1999] EMLR 589 at 643—and also the *right kind* of contribution, being an author's contribution. This means that a joint author must contribute expression, and not mere ideas. This further means that they must be closely involved in the final expression in the product, although it does not necessarily mean that a person must 'put pen to paper': *Cala Homes (South) Ltd v Alfred McAlpine*

---

[1]   Subject to s 79, which ensures that only *one* joint author need be a qualified person for copyright to subsist (s 32), and that identification of one joint author brings an otherwise anonymous or pseudonymous work under the usual rules of duration of copyright (s 34(2)).

Homes East Ltd [1995] FSR 818. A case where the 'right contribution' could not be identified is *Fylde Microsystems Ltd v Key Radio Systems Ltd* [1998] FSR 449, which concerned ownership of copyright in software written by employees of Fylde Microsystems. Key Radio Systems argued unsuccessfully that its employees were joint authors because of the skill, time and effort they put into testing the software. Laddie J accepted that Key Radio Systems' employees' contributions were extensive and technically sophisticated, and had required considerable time and effort; but he held that they were not contributions to the 'authoring' of the software.

There is considerable flexibility in determining the necessary extent and precise form of the contribution required. Note too that in the process of working through these disputes, distinctions are commonly made between authorship and (mere) interpretation. This hierarchy of creative value betrays copyright's literary bias. Ownership is formally determined by an inquiry into the personal contribution to 'the expression', not necessarily entailing consideration of the creative or market value of the particular contribution of a party to a work. While some efforts may be noted as significant, they still may not be 'the right kind of contribution'. The issue has been addressed in a number of UK cases involving the composition of pop songs, including *Hadley v Kemp* [1999] EMLR 589; *Beckingham v Hodgens* [2003] EWCA Civ 143; [2003] EMLR 18 and *Fisher v Brooker* [2006] EWHC 3239 (Ch); [2007] FSR 12. This legal reality can impact harshly on those with little legal or business experience.

The decision of the High Court in *IceTV Pty Ltd v Nine Network Australia Pty Ltd* [2009] HCA 14; (2009) 239 CLR 458 has also had an impact on the determination and importance of joint authorship in Australian copyright law. As discussed in Chapter 3, *IceTV* makes it imperative to identify authors (or at least acts of authorship) in a work, and provides a standard (of 'intellectual effort' or 'sufficient effort of a literary kind') for establishing authorship. It also focuses attention on expression embodied in the particular material form of the work in which copyright is claimed, and serves to exclude some preparatory work from consideration. This can make it more difficult to prove the element of *collaboration* required for joint authorship, as can be seen in the next two extracts below, in particular the second one: *Acohs Pty Ltd v Ucorp Pty Ltd* [2012] FCAFC 16; (2012) 201 FCR 173.

CASE EXTRACT: CURRENT LAW

Fairfax Media Publications Pty Ltd v Reed International Books Australia Pty Ltd

[2010] FCA 984; (2010) 189 FCR 109
Federal Court of Australia

[The facts of this case are summarised in Chapter 4, above p 81. One issue in the case was whether the following were works of joint authorship: (a) individual newspaper articles together with the headlines written by sub-editors, and (b) the compilation of articles embodied in an edition of a newspaper.]

Bennett J: 91. Fairfax submits that although the journalist identified in the by-line of an article plainly has an important role in researching, originating and the first writing of the story, the evidence shows that the ultimate literary product results from the collaboration of journalists and subeditors in a way that cannot be disentangled. It points to evidence that the articles and the headlines as they exist in their final, published form are the results of the joint efforts of both the authors identified in the by-line and the editorial staff who write the headlines and edit the text of the article in the subediting process, sometimes making substantial alterations to the stories. It points, for example, to the evidence of Mr Bailey that:

- The person laying out the page fits the article onto the page and gives instructions to the subeditor about whether there should be a quote, a picture and etc.
- Subeditors read the article for accuracy and for sense, fit it onto the page, write the headlines and write the quotes. If the story is too long for the allocated space, the subeditor would edit the story to keep the essence of the story but 'lose the words which won't fit'.

92. Fairfax contends that the articles and their headlines satisfy the requirement for joint authorship in that they are produced by the collaboration of two or more authors and the contribution of each author is not separate from the contribution of the other author or authors. It submits that there is no identifiable part of any article/headline combination which is attributable solely to the efforts of any one of the persons involved. Although each headline is generally worked on and finalised by one or more of the editorial staff, it often derives in one way or another from the content of the body of the article which is supplied by the author(s) named in the by-line, who may also provide the original suggestion as to the headline. Equally, Fairfax says, the content of the body of the article may be influenced by the headline in as much as the subeditor who writes the headline may also be involved in making significant edits to the body of the article. Fairfax points to the evidence of the creation of the Telstra headline ['Fund managers reject Telstra chief's $11m pay deal'] as an example of the interaction between story and headline.

93. Fairfax's proposition is to the effect that:

(a) a journalist writes the article;
(b) a subeditor edits the article;
(c) that makes the journalist and subeditor joint authors;
(d) the subeditor writes the headline, which is often derived from the article;
(e) therefore, the article/headline combination is a discrete work, with the editor and journalist as joint authors.

94. It has long been stated that a work of joint authorship is one produced by the collaboration of two or more authors in which the contribution of each author is not distinct from that of the other or others. The contributions must not have been distinct ([K Garnett, G Davies and G Harbottle, *Copinger and Skone James on Copyright*, 15th ed, Sweet & Maxwell, London, 2005] at [5-163]); each contributor must contribute a significant part of the skill and labour protected by the copyright (Laddie H, Prescott P, Vitoria M et al, *The Modern Law of Copyright and Designs* (3rd ed, Butterworths, 2000) at [4.71]). Straightforward editing of articles for the purpose of inclusion on a page, which may or may or not involve substantial changes to the article, is not sufficient to attract joint authorship for copyright purposes.

95. The evidence suggests that article writing is a process distinct from headline writing. Even if the subeditors and the journalists collaborate on producing an edition of the *AFR*, the evidence is that the writing of headlines is a separate task performed by subeditors and the person who writes the article is generally not the person who writes the headline. An article with its headline is not a work of joint authorship because the contribution of each author is separate from the contributions of

the other author. If the headlines were works, they would be works by the subeditors who are not the authors of the associated articles.

96. The fact that subeditors edit articles as well as write headlines does not establish that the contribution of journalist and subeditor are inseparable or overcome the conclusion that the writing of the headline is a separate exercise from the writing of the article. The presence of the by-line, citing the author of the article and not the subeditor, argues against the submission that the articles are works of joint authorship.

97. The assertion of joint authorship in the article/headline combination is inconsistent with Fairfax's case on the existence of copyright in the headlines alone and Fairfax has not established that articles and their headlines are together a discrete single work. The evidence does not establish that the articles and their headlines were written by the same person or that they were works of joint authorship. Fairfax has not adduced evidence of the process of creation of the ten selected articles and headlines to demonstrate that there was the requisite inability to separate the individual contributions, such as evidence of the extent of rewriting of articles and evidence that the same person wrote a headline and rewrote the associated article. The general evidence of Mr Bailey set out in [91] above suggests that subeditors edit in the traditional sense, in a manner insufficient to make them joint authors. The evidence demonstrates that a headline could be written by a number of people in the editorial and subeditorial hierarchy such that the same subeditor may not, in all cases, rewrite a story and write the headline.

...

101. The evidence does not establish joint authorship of the ten selected article/headline combinations within the meaning of s 10(1) of the Act, as Fairfax's evidence makes it clear that the writing of articles and the writing of headlines are separate and distinct tasks with different authors. Accordingly, the article/headline combination is not a discrete work in which copyright can subsist.

CASE EXTRACT: CURRENT LAW

Acohs Pty Ltd v Ucorp Pty Ltd

[2012] FCAFC 16; (2012) 201 FCR 173
Federal Court of Australia, Full Court

[Acohs and Ucorp produced and supplied electronic material safety data sheets (MSDSs), which were required by legislation to accompany the supply of certain hazardous substances and goods. Acohs generated its MSDSs through its Infosafe system. This comprised a database of information (Central Database, or CDB) on hazardous substances and goods, and a computer program which was written by a consultant and two employees of Acohs in the late 1990s. When a customer requested the MSDS relating to a particular hazardous substance or good, the computer program would call up the necessary information from the database and assemble it for presentation on the customer's screen. Acohs alleged that Ucorp had copied Acohs' MSDSs when constructing its own competing service. Acohs claimed copyright in the final MSDS generated by the computer program, comprising the written information from the database and the source code generated by the computer program which determined how the MSDS would appear on the customer's computer. Some of the Acohs MSDSs had been written by Acohs employees from scratch; for others, the information had been transcribed from existing materials into the database, and Acohs' contribution lay only in its presentation and arrangement. Acohs contended that the authors of each MSDS were the computer programmers who wrote the routines to generate the source code for presentation, *and* the employees who wrote, or transcribed, the information into the database.

Note the interaction in this case between questions of identification of the work, originality, and the requirements of joint authorship.]

Jacobson, Nicholas and Yates JJ: 40. [The trial judge concluded that] the source code for each identified MSDS was not a work of joint authorship. After noting ([*Acohs Pty Ltd v Ucorp Pty Ltd* [2010] FCA 577; (2010) 86 IPR 492] at [55]) that the definition of 'work of joint authorship' in s 10 of the *Copyright Act 1968* (Cth) (the *Copyright Act*) required the work to have been produced by the collaboration of two or more authors, the primary judge held (at [57]) that it would be quite artificial to say that the programmers, and the 'authors' and 'transcribers' who entered data into the CDB, collaborated with each other in writing the relevant source code. His Honour (at [57]) said:

> The programmers wrote the program which caused the Infosafe system to operate as it did: to generate source code in response to defined inputs by those using the system. They also wrote so much of the source code as caused particular layouts, and appearance attributes, to appear on the user's screen. However, the essence of their contribution was not the writing of the source code for a particular MSDS. Having written the program by reference to which source code would, under certain conditions, be generated, they had no further contribution (other than to amend the Visual Basic program from time to time). In no realistic sense did the programmers collaborate with every author and transcriber whose efforts directly led to the creation or transcription of an MSDS.

41. In relation to MSDSs that involved contributions by the appellant's customers, the primary judge (at [62]) identified a further difficulty with the appellant's case. Even if the programmers and the external 'authors' could be considered to be, jointly, the authors of the source code for a particular MSDS, the appellant, not being the employer of all such 'authors', could not rely on s 35(6) of the *Copyright Act* to claim ownership of any corresponding copyright. It is implicit in the primary judge's finding in this regard that no evidence of any assignment of copyright by external 'authors' was adduced.

42. The primary judge concluded (at [60]) as follows:

> Since the source code the subject of para 8(a) of Acohs' pleading was not the work of any one human author, and was not a work of joint authorship, that code cannot be regarded as an original literary work within the meaning of the *Copyright Act*.

...

67. ... [T]he primary judge noted but rejected (at [71]–[72]) the appellant's submission that copyright subsisted in the transcribed MSDSs simply because of their layout, presentation and appearance. In this connection it is critical to note that the appellant, by its pleading and in its submissions to the primary judge, specifically disavowed the layout, presentation and appearance of an MSDS as a separate copyright work. It submitted, however, that it owned copyright in each identified MSDS because its employees authored the layout, presentation and appearance of the MSDS.

CURRENT LAW

68. In this connection the primary judge reasoned that transcribers could not be originators of the layout, presentation and appearance of the MSDSs because they had no control over such matters in respect of the MSDSs they transcribed. Furthermore, the primary judge reasoned that the appellant was not assisted by introducing, as it sought to do, the contributions of Mr Cowie and the programmers. The primary judge (at [72]) said:

> Given that each MSDS was now alleged to be an original work (ie as contrasted with the original formulation of Acohs' pleading, in which only the layout, presentation and appearance was alleged to be such a work), it was necessary for Acohs to bring in the transcribers with Messrs Cowie, Lau etc, and to contend that the finished product was work of joint authorship. There are, however, two reasons why this submission should not be accepted. The first is that it would be quite artificial to regard Mr Cowie and the programmers as authors of any one MSDS. That they devised, wrote and later amended the computer program which gave Infosafe MSDSs their particular appearance, as distinct from making any contribution to their content, does not make them authors in the copyright sense. Neither does it give originality to a work which, because it was necessarily copied from something else, would not otherwise be original. The present case is, in relevant respects, quite different from *Ladbroke (Football) Ltd v William Hill (Football) Ltd* [1964] 1 WLR 273; [1964] 1 All ER 465, on which Acohs relied, and from *Lamb v Evans* [1893] 1 Ch 218, referred to in *Ladbroke*. The second reason is that, for the reasons given at paras 52–57 above, Mr Cowie and the programmers could not be regarded as joint authors together with the transcribers. On no fair usage of the language could they be regarded as having collaborated to produce the works constituted by the MSDSs.

...

70. The single ground of appeal on which the appellant proceeded in this regard was expressed as follows:

> His Honour erred in holding at [72] that Mr Cowie and/or the computer programmers who wrote the HTML routines were not authors of the MSDS in the copyright sense.

71. The appellant submitted that layout, presentation and appearance may be the subject of copyright protection: *Ladbroke*; *Kalamazoo (Aust) Pty Ltd v Compact Business Systems Pty Ltd* (1985) 5 IPR 213; [*Telstra Corporation Ltd v*] *Phone Directories* [*Co Pty Ltd* [2010] FCAFC 149; (2010) 194 FCR 142] at [102]. Here the appellant submitted that the layout, presentation and appearance of an Infosafe MSDS is determined by templates. The appellant pointed to the primary judge's findings, and the underlying evidence, that Mr Cowie gave instructions as to the basic layout, presentation and appearance that he wanted for the MSDSs, which were actioned by the programmers writing the code in the Infosafe program that would achieve that outcome.

72. The appellant submitted that the primary judge mischaracterised the evidence in relation to authorship by failing to recognise that part of the original form of expression of the Infosafe MSDSs was their layout, presentation and appearance, and that the primary judge had an unduly narrow appreciation of the appellant's copyright claim in this regard.

73. In our view this ground of appeal cannot be sustained.

74. When considering this ground of appeal it is of central importance, once again, to correctly identify the copyright works in suit.

75. During the course of the trial the appellant abandoned its case that copyright subsisted in the layout, presentation and appearance of each MSDS 'rendered' by the Infosafe system, that is, that copyright subsisted in the templates themselves ...

76. In its seventh further amended statement of claim the appellant plainly identified the case it ultimately pursued as one in which copyright subsisted in each identified MSDS which had a layout, presentation and appearance in accordance with one or other identified templates. It is at this point, however, that the appellant's case at trial, which it repeated on appeal, appears to have adopted a chameleon-like quality. While apparently continuing to eschew a case that the layout, presentation and appearance of each identified MSDS constituted a separate copyright work, and while apparently affirming its case that copyright subsisted in each of the identified MSDSs, the appellant sought to argue that copyright subsisted in an MSDS 'because its employees authored the layout, presentation and appearance of the MSDSs' and that that was an 'original contribution' to each MSDS ... In putting its case in this way, the appellant appears, once again, to have confused certain elements of the identified MSDSs with the MSDSs themselves.

77. It is trite that the postulated copyright work, as a whole, must be considered in order to see whether it is protected by copyright. When dealing with the question of the subsistence of copyright in the identified MSDSs that had come into existence by way of transcription, the primary judge correctly recognised that his attention must be directed to each MSDS, considered as a whole. Of course, when each Infosafe MSDS is considered in that way, its content cannot be ignored. It is this content which gives each MSDS its essential character as a particular MSDS dealing with a particular hazardous substance.

78. In this connection it is to be noted that, when advancing its case in relation to MSDSs created by Acohs-authors, the appellant submitted that the Acohs-authors were those individuals who brought together the information about the substance supplied by the MIS [(manufacturer, importer or supplier)], including the appropriate risk phrases as available in the Infosafe system or as devised by that author, as well as the pre-determined visual and organisational elements of the MSDS as governed by the Infosafe software. In short, the appellant's own submissions at trial in relation to those MSDSs recognised that the copyright work must be considered as a whole and that the focus of attention was the intellectual effort of the Acohs-authors. The primary judge (at [65]) recorded those submissions and (at [69]) accepted that the Acohs-author of an Infosafe MSDS should be regarded as the copyright-author of that work. His Honour's reason for so finding was as follows:

> Even in a case in which every verbal and numerical element of an MSDS created by an author was to be found in the CDB, the author was still required to select from the menu of sub-headings those that would be used and those that would be irrelevant (and thus would not be used). The electronic documentary entity which he or she thereby brought into existence was not merely the result of copying from something else.

79. This passage of the primary judge's reasons must also be considered in light of the passage in [70] ... In that passage the primary judge compared the work of the Acohs-transcribers, noting that those persons did not select the appropriate subheadings or the order in which they should be arranged; nor did they select the appropriate risk phrases and the like.

80. On appeal there was no challenge by the parties to the correctness of the primary judge's finding in relation to the work of the Acohs-authors ... Importantly for present purposes, it is implicit in his Honour's finding that authorship, for copyright purposes, in each MSDS resided in the Acohs-authors,

not those writing the computer programs in the Infosafe system that were used by the Acohs-authors to create a particular MSDS.

...

84. The primary judge properly and carefully distinguished between the question of authorship of each alleged copyright work (that is, each identified Infosafe MSDS) and the separate (and relevantly hypothetical) question of the authorship of the antecedent and underlying works to which Mr Cowie and the programmers were said to have contributed. The primary judge correctly recognised that Mr Cowie and the programmers were not authors of each MSDS created by the Acohs-transcribers simply because they wrote and amended computer programs in the Infosafe system that were used by the Acohs-transcribers, at the time when those transcribers came to do their work in creating, by transcription, each MSDS.

85. The primary judge also correctly recognised that, whatever originality might have been involved in the activities undertaken by Mr Cowie and the programmers in writing the underlying computer programs in the Infosafe system, those activities were separate and distinct from the activities involved in creating each MSDS, including those created by way of transcription. This is why the primary judge stated (at [72]) that the activities of Mr Cowie and the programmers could not confer originality on the MSDSs created by transcription.

86. The primary judge also correctly realised that by advancing the activities of Mr Cowie and the programmers as relevant to the question of copyright subsistence in the MSDSs themselves, the appellant could not avoid the consequence that it was propounding a case that each identified MSDS was a work of joint authorship. For the reasons he gave at [52]–[57] in relation to the similar question arising with respect to copyright subsistence in the HTML source code for each identified MSDS, the primary judge correctly found that it could not be said that Mr Cowie and the programmers collaborated with each Acohs-transcriber to subsequently create each relevant MSDS.

87. The appellant has not demonstrated that the primary judge erred in rejecting the case that copyright subsisted in the identified MSDSs that had come into existence by way of transcription or that had been 'authored' by the appellant's customers.

[The Court concluded that copyright subsisted in the Acohs-authored MSDSs. The authors of these works were the Acohs employees who gathered the information and wrote the text; the computer programmers were not joint authors. Copyright did not subsist in MSDSs in which information had merely been transcribed by Acohs employees.]

CURRENT LAW

CASE EXTRACT: COMPARATIVE LAW

Brighton v Jones

[2004] EWHC 1157 (Ch); [2005] FSR 16
High Court of England and Wales, Chancery Division

[The case involved a play, *Stones In His Pockets*. The plaintiff, Brighton, was a stage, television and radio director. The defendant, Jones, was an actor and a highly regarded author of plays. Both parties had, with others, founded a theatre production company, Dubbeljoint. Brighton was appointed to the Board as Artistic Director. The concept for *Stones In His Pockets* was collectively developed by the

COMPARATIVE LAW

theatre management, including Brighton, and the actors. Jones was then contracted by the company to write the script. Concerned about production schedules and delays, Brighton drafted pages of opening scenes and notes about characters and themes. Jones wrote the full draft of the play and was noted on the script as sole author. Rehearsals with Jones as director led to subsequent changes to the script. The play opened in August 1996. Jones was again noted as sole author, including on promotional material. The play met with reasonable success. In 1999 there was a revised script and production, with Jones' husband as director. This proved to be a huge success. Brighton claimed joint authorship of the 1996 version of the play.]

Park J: 37. A general point is that Miss Brighton and Miss Jones had worked together on rehearsals often in the past. There had always been a lot of discussion and interchange of opinions during the rehearsals of a new play, both between the two of them and with the actors. They regarded those processes as important and valuable. Miss Jones fully expected that, as rehearsals progressed, she would make changes to her original script, and that frequently these would flow from something raised by the director (whether Miss Brighton or another director) or by the actors. Thus on all plays if there was something in the original script written by Miss Jones which the director was not happy with, the director would say so, Miss Jones would listen, and she was entirely willing to consider making changes.

38. Turning more specifically to the rehearsals of *Stones in His Pockets*, there is something of an issue of how complete the script provided by Miss Jones was when the rehearsals first began. Miss Brighton believes now that the first act had been written, but that the second act had hardly been started, if at all. However, my view is that the first act had been written, and, although the second act had not been completed, most of it had already been written. There were still a few concluding episodes or scenes in the second act to be written, but I do not think that they were going to take Miss Jones very long, or that they did take her very long. She was staying in a rented house with her husband, Mr McElhinney, and their two young children, and she was acting in a play which was being presented at a Dublin theatre. Mr McElhinney commented that the circumstances were not at all suitable for her to be writing a lot of script for *Stones In His Pockets*, and he had no recollection of her doing so.

39. I specifically find that, when any day's rehearsal began, the actors and the director already had the script for the part of the play concerned. I do not think that there were any occasions when Miss Jones had not got the script prepared so that the actors, guided by Miss Brighton, had to begin by improvising dialogue which Miss Jones had not yet managed to write.

40. I do think that on occasions some improvisation occurred in the course of the rehearsals, but in my view it arose in either or both of two different ways. Sometimes if the actors and Miss Brighton felt that a passage of Miss Jones' original script was not working well, they would try something else. Miss Jones was unlikely to be there at that precise time to provide different dialogue for them, so they would devise something themselves. Alternatively or additionally there were occasions when it appeared to them—perhaps to Miss Brighton more than to either actor in this respect—that the action in Miss Jones' script had moved a little uncomfortably from one episode to another, and that it would be useful to have another episode inserted between the two. If that happened they would discuss the sort of episode to insert, and then try it out in rehearsal, using dialogue which they devised themselves on the spot. It is hard to say whether such dialogue was devised by Miss Brighton or by the actors or by a joint discussion of the three of them. I think that the last of those possibilities is the more likely.

41. When towards the end of each day Miss Jones came into the rehearsal room, there was a discussion of what had happened earlier in the day, and I do not doubt that it quite often led to changes being made to the part of the script to which that day's rehearsals had related. If Miss Brighton and the actors had worked out some possible changes to Miss Jones' dialogue, or if they had devised an additional episode to be inserted at some point, they used to demonstrate it to her. Her evidence was that, if she was content with the change, she would accept the principle of it. If she was not content with it, she would not accept it.

42. When she did agree that a change should be made she did not simply accept the particular dialogue which Miss Brighton and the actors had improvised earlier in the day. She chose the words herself. The script was saved on her laptop, which was in the rehearsal room. Mr Cranney [the stage manager] recalled that, when Miss Jones rewrote a piece of dialogue or wrote some new dialogue, she devised the words and he usually typed them into the laptop there and then …

43. … Miss Brighton was not entitled to give instructions to Miss Jones about what Miss Jones should write, and either she did not do so, or, if she attempted to do so, Miss Jones made up her own mind about what she was prepared and what she was not prepared to write by way of changes to her original script. Under the contract which she had with Dubbeljoint she had the ultimate say about the contents of her script, and I am satisfied that she did not allow her contractual position to be overborne by Miss Brighton, powerful though Miss Brighton's personality was. Mr Hill [one of the actors] was very clear on these aspects. In evidence he said that questions put to him in cross-examination made Miss Jones sound like a stenographer, but that in fact she would say in relation to the changes whether she liked them or not. He agreed that, if she accepted a change that was proposed to her, she would incorporate it into the script, adding: 'In her own way, yes' …

…

55. It must be remembered that … the burden of proof rests on Miss Brighton. The person described on the script of the play as the author was Miss Jones alone. She was also billed as the sole author in publicity material and in programmes. It never occurred to Miss Brighton to say that she ought to be regarded as a joint author until she commenced this case. None of that is conclusive against her, but it does at the least raise a substantial evidential hurdle for her to overcome.

56. I agree that, on all versions of what happened in the rehearsals, changes were made to Miss Jones' original script, and that the changes resulted from the experience of the rehearsals and the discussions in the rehearsals. I agree that Miss Brighton was involved in the rehearsals throughout, and I would accept (though the point was not specifically covered) that she probably knew about all the changes before they were made and had played a part in what had led to each of them. However, there are still several reasons why, in my opinion, she was not a joint author.

i)   In terms of the dialogue of the final play, I believe that 100% of the words spoken (or as near to 100% as makes no difference) were actually composed by Miss Jones. Miss Brighton no doubt identified passages and places where some rewriting was desirable, but it was Miss Jones who (if she agreed that there should be some rewriting at those points) actually chose the words which the actors were to use. There is a sentence in Miss Brighton's witness statement which reads: 'In respect of each Act, I was heavily responsible for the actual form of expression of the dialogue on paper.' That appears to be saying that Miss Brighton was responsible not just for determining where some rewriting was to take place, but also for determining what the precise new words were to be. All of the other evidence is contrary to that, and I do not accept it.

ii)   The point made in (i) above concerns the actual words used, and it is not in itself decisive. Copyright can subsist in a story or a plot, so that if what happened in rehearsals was that Miss Brighton determined what the plot of the play was to be (or Miss Brighton and Miss Jones determined in collaboration what it was to be), and then Miss Jones actually wrote the words to give effect to the plot, I can see that Miss Brighton might have been a joint author. But in my opinion that was not how it was. I believe that the script which Miss Jones provided in advance of the rehearsals, plus the fairly small part which she had not written before the rehearsals began but did write before the rehearsals got round to that part, contained a complete plot for the play. It was a dramatic work, and at that stage the copyright in it was solely owned by Miss Jones. ... I am sure that there were some changes to the plot before the final form of the 1996 script was reached, and I accept that Miss Brighton made her own input into what those changes were; but I do not believe that the changes were nearly significant enough to mean that a different dramatic work, of which Miss Brighton and Miss Jones were joint authors, had been created.

iii) Just focusing on the changes, Miss Brighton had played a part in what led up to them, but in my view, on the general thrust of the evidence and bearing in mind the burden of proof, she has not established that the contributions which she made were contributions to the creation of the dramatic work rather than contributions to the interpretation and theatrical presentation of the dramatic work. In the expression used in the *Fylde Microsystems case* ... they were not 'the right sort of contributions'.

iv)   It cannot be said that, whenever Miss Brighton wanted a change to be made to the script, Miss Jones simply and unquestioningly made it. I accept that she expected to have suggestions for changes made to her, that she was fully prepared to consider them, that she probably expected that she would agree to many of them, and that she did agree to many of them. But it is clear from the evidence which I summarised earlier that she would not make changes to the script if she did not agree to them. The decision whether to make a change or not was hers, and that was not just a theoretical position: it was also the reality of what actually happened.

v)   It is in any case unrealistic to distinguish, so far as the present issue is concerned, between what Miss Brighton did in the rehearsals and what the two actors did. The actors do not claim to have become joint authors simply by doing well one of the things which led to them being engaged: working on the rehearsals of a newly commissioned play which had not yet been performed, and by doing so assisting in making the script better than it had been before the rehearsals. It seems to me that Miss Brighton is in essentially the same position. Miss Jones presented her with a play upon which, during the rehearsals, she was expected to exercise her director's skills, together with Mr Murphy and Mr Hill exercising their actors' skills, in order to get it ready to be performed before live audiences. The actors did not become joint authors by reason of what they did, and I do not think that Miss Brighton became a joint author by reason of what she did either.

EMPLOYEE AND CONTRACTOR WORKS

Copyright in a literary, dramatic, artistic or musical work made by an employee usually vests in the employer, unless there is an agreement to the contrary or other provisions apply (see 'Commissioned works' and 'Journalists' copyright' below, p 174). As a result of s 35(6) copyright belongs to the employer where an employee or apprentice produces a work, pursuant to the terms of employment, under a contract of service or apprenticeship. This is justifiable on a range of grounds: since the employer pays the employee's salary, the employer is in fact the one 'investing' in creation (and the actual author has already been compensated for their work). Further, the concentration of ownership that results is more economically efficient: it reduces transaction costs and contributes to certainty by allowing the rights to be owned by as few parties as possible. Copyright in a work created by an independent contractor working pursuant to a contract for services, however, is not affected by s 35(6) and is retained by the author.

It is not uncommon for workplace relationships to be poorly defined, especially in the fields of the arts and technology, where there has never been much involvement of unions nor public sector organisation forcing a clear definition of standard conditions and related benchmarks. Even in other fields of employment, increasing flexibility in work arrangements has led to great diversity in workplace conditions and management practices, particularly for more highly skilled workers. Casual employment and short-term contracts linked to particular projects are common, and when a continual stream of work is available, a person can be in continuous employment for extended periods, and practically indistinguishable from permanent employees. The indeterminate nature of these employment relationships makes it difficult to decide whether the worker was, or is, an independent contractor working under a contract for services, or an employee under a contract of service.

In *Beloff v Pressdram Ltd* [1973] 1 All ER 241, Nina Beloff, a political correspondent for the *Observer* newspaper, had no written contract of employment. A dispute arose over ownership of copyright in a memorandum she had authored, which was subsequently incorporated without permission into an article in a new rival publication, *Private Eye*. Was the newspaper or the journalist entitled to sue for infringement? It was agreed that the work was produced pursuant to Beloff's employment, but Beloff argued that she was employed under a contract for services and had retained copyright. In reviewing the historical distinction between a contract of service and a contract for services, Ungoed-Thomas J (at 247–248) noted its class origins:

> [T]here appears to have been a tendency in the past towards considering, and therefore describing, contracts of service in terms of occupations of a lowly character—not surprisingly, because it was in such occupations that contracts of service were most apt to occur ... contracts of service of a lowly nature have been associated with each other, as contrasted with contracts for professional or similarly skilled services. So counsel's original submission for the plaintiff was that 'a contract of service means a contract for domestic, manual or clerical service whose execution is superintended by some higher official or employee'.

His Honour rejected this position, which centred on 'control' as determinative of a contract of service. He found that despite a high degree of independence in the workplace, Beloff was employed under a contract of service.[2]

This situation was discussed in the Australian context below, in relation to a claim that a young, skilled computer programmer retained copyright in his programs and libraries used to create new computer programs for his employer.

---

2   For a discussion of the case and why it was run the way it was, see J Bellido, 'The Failure of a Copyright Action: Confidence in the Papers of Nora Beloff' (2013) 18 *Media and Arts Law Review* 249.

CASE EXTRACT: CURRENT LAW

Redrock Holdings Pty Ltd v Hinkley

[2001] VSC 91; (2001) 50 IPR 565
Supreme Court of Victoria

Harper J: 20. Mr Hinkley submits that he was employed under a contract for services rather than under a contract of service. He relies on the so-called 'control test', saying that he was given little, if any, direction or control by Redrock and cites passages from the judgment of Evershed MR in *Stevenson Jordan & Harrison Ltd v MacDonald & Evans* [[1952] 1 TLR 101]. However, legal authority to control, while remaining relevant and indeed often decisive, is no longer the sole determining factor when assessing whether a person is employed under a contract of service, in particular where that person exercises a high degree of professional skill and expertise in the performance of his or her duties. So, in *Beloff v Pressdam Ltd* [[1973] 1 All ER 241] Ungoed-Thomas J cited with approval a number of passages to this effect and then said at 250:

> It thus appears, and rightly in my respectful view, that, the greater the skill required for an employee's work, the less significant is control in determining whether the employee is under a contract of service. Control is just one of many factors whose influence varies according to circumstances. In such highly skilled work as that of the plaintiff it seems of no substantial significance. The test which emerges from the authorities seems to me, as Denning LJ said, whether on the one hand the employee is employed as part of the business and his work is an integral part of the business, or whether his work is not integrated into the business but is only accessory to it, or, as Cooke J expressed it, the work is done by him in business on his own account.

In this case, there is no doubt that Mr Hinkley as a software programmer exercised a high degree of professional skill and expertise in the performance of his duties for Redrock. Moreover, as a skilled Macintosh technician employed to fill a gap in Redrock's technical staff, it could be expected that even as an employee he would be given a great deal of latitude. I therefore conclude that the evidence about control does not in the circumstances of this case establish that Mr Hinkley was employed under a contract for services.

21. In his judgment in *Stevenson Jordan & Harrison Ltd v MacDonald & Evans* [at 111] Lord Denning expressed reservations about the control test, and instead enunciated the famous passage which was to become the 'integration test':

> As [Evershed MR] has said it is almost impossible to give a precise definition of the distinction [between a contract of service and a contract for services]. It is often quite easy to recognise a contract of service when you see it, but very difficult to say wherein the difference lies. A ship's master, a chauffeur, and a reporter on the staff of a newspaper are all employed under a contract of service; but a ship's pilot, a taxi-man, and a newspaper contributor are employed under a contract for services. One feature which seems to me to run through the instances is that, under a contract of service, a man is employed as part of the business and his work, although done for the business, is not integrated into it but is only accessory to it.

22. The 'integration' or 'organisation' test has not been embraced by the High Court of Australia. However, it may be helpful in an appropriate case as one indicator of the totality of the relationship

between the parties, all aspects of which must be considered: *Stevens v Brodribb Sawmilling Co Pty Ltd* [(1986) 160 CLR 16 at 27 per Mason J and at 36–7 per Wilson and Dawson JJ]. In doing so, I find that Mr Hinkley's work as a software programmer was integrated into the business of Redrock. Mr Hamilton gave evidence in his witness statement that in the first 4 years of its business Redrock's emphasis was in developing the intellectual property in its products and that, after its staff, those products were the most significant asset of the company. Mr Hinkley's work as a programmer was therefore central to developing the business of Redrock.

23. There is other evidence which satisfies me that Mr Hinkley was employed under a contract of service. He was on a fixed salary, from which group tax was deducted. He signed an Australian Taxation Office Employee Declaration on 3 November 1995. He was entitled to annual leave, to sick leave and to long service leave. Superannuation contributions were made by Redrock on his behalf. Redrock provided Mr Hinkley with necessary equipment and with programs such as CodeWarrior all specially purchased to assist him in writing software for the company, together with access to the internet to download manuals, information or software as needed. Indeed, in his written submissions Mr Hinkley states on the issue of the use of an external hard disk owned by him that it would be 'unbelievable to suggest that I was expected to use my equipment for Redrock's work'. All the indicia put forward in the evidence are consistent with the conclusion that Adam Hinkley became an employee of Redrock in or about November 1995.

In addition to the requirement that there be a contract of service, for the employer to own copyright the work must also be produced pursuant to the terms of employment: s 35(6). This issue also arose in *Redrock Holdings*. In the software he developed for Redrock, Mr Hinkley had used and further developed software tools which he also used in his own separate software projects. The Court found that the tools had been developed during office hours and for his employer's projects, and in their final developed form at the time his employment ended belonged to Redrock: at [64]. The Court also noted that if he intended to use and incorporate his own copyright software into his employer's projects it was incumbent on Mr Hinkley to bring this to Redrock's attention: at [26].

The scope of employment also arose in *Insight SRP IP Holdings Pty Ltd v Australian Council for Educational Research Ltd* [2013] FCAFC 62; (2013) 101 IPR 484. In that case, a Dr Hart had been employed by Victorian Department of Education to evaluate a program designed to deal with problems of teacher stress. Based on his contemporaneous PhD studies, Dr Hart concluded that the Department's existing survey tools and methodology were inappropriate, and developed a new survey, identified as the School Organisational Health Questionnaire (SOHQ). The trial judge's conclusion (affirmed on appeal) was that although the survey was developed during office hours, and although the terms of Dr Hart's employment were sufficiently general that they *could* include the making of the SOHQ, the SOHQ was not in fact made pursuant to Dr Hart's terms of employment. He was not required to produce it; rather, the arrangement was that he could prepare it for his own purposes, albeit, the department could use it. This conclusion was bolstered by the fact that the Department had acted over many years on the basis that Dr Hart and the applicants were the owners of the copyright in the SOHQ.

COMMISSIONED WORKS

There is no general provision in s 35 of the *Copyright Act* to confer ownership of commissioned works on the commissioning party, although, as discussed further below (see 'Implied licences', p 190), a party who commissions a work will usually be able to argue they have at least an implied licence to use the work for the purposes envisaged when the work was commissioned. As discussed further below (p 175), the situation is different for subject matter other than works.

Section 35(5) deals with commissioned artworks where there is no agreement as to copyright ownership. The current provision, in effect since 30 June 1998, is limited to particular artistic subject matter: private and domestic photographs, portraiture in the form of paintings or drawings, or engravings. Today, s 35(5) protects the privacy of the commissioner, who retains control over public and commercial use of commissioned images of a private and domestic nature. It also protects the commercial interest of the photographer or artist, because the commissioner may be restrained from using the images for purposes other than those originally agreed with the photographer or artist. In this manner, the provision can be interpreted as sensitive to preserving the price charged for the original service agreed to, with subsequent additional uses leading to negotiation of an additional fee for the photographer or painter. Note that while s 35(5) may give the commissioner ownership of copyright, this does not affect the moral rights of the author (see Chapter 7).

JOURNALISTS' COPYRIGHT

Section 35(4) provides some journalists with certain special rights regarding ownership of their work. This provision reflects industry conventions and re-negotiations of past practice. Section 35(4) only applies to newspaper, magazine or periodical employee journalists and apprentices. In a case that pre-dates digital publishing and subsequent revisions of the Act, the meaning of the words 'newspaper', 'magazine' and 'periodical' in s 35(4) was interpreted according to popular usage (*De Garis v Neville Jeffress Pidler Pty Ltd* (1990) 37 FCR 99 at 115). Employee journalists working outside newspaper, magazine and periodical contexts (such as journalists working for television, radio or online formats, and those working for cable services such as AAP) are in the same position as all other employee authors, unless there is an agreement to the contrary.

Section 35(4) was changed in 1998 following the introduction of digital services, reducing the rights retained by newspaper and magazine journalists. For works created before 30 July 1998 the employer only owns the newspaper and magazine publication rights, while the newspaper journalist retains copyright for all other purposes (e.g. online reproduction, republication in a book, educational copying and reproduction by a clipping service). For works created on or after 30 July 1998, the journalist owns only the copyright for the photocopying of the work directly from a hardcopy original or for reproduction for inclusion in a book. The employer owns the copyright for all other purposes, including online and magazine publishing, digital copying and facsimile transmission.

Section 35(4) is subject to contract, and freelance relationships are also common in the industry. In accordance with the general rules relating to commissioned work discussed above, freelance journalists are the default owners of copyright, but ownership is usually determined in accordance with written agreements.

SUBJECT MATTER OTHER THAN WORKS: OWNERSHIP AND JOINT OWNERSHIP

Rules relating to ownership of copyright in subject matter other than works (under Part IV) are set out in the *Copyright Act*, ss 97–100. The general default rules are:

- Sound recordings (other than of live performances) are owned by the maker of the sound recording (s 97(2)), defined in s 22(3) as the person who owned the record at the time when the first record embodying the recording was produced.
- Cinematograph films are owned by the maker (s 98(2)), defined in s 22(4)(b) as 'the person by whom the arrangements necessary for the making of the film were undertaken'.
- Television and sound broadcasts are owned by the maker of the broadcast (s 99), defined in s 22(5) as the person who provided the broadcasting service by which the broadcast was delivered.
- Published editions are owned by the publisher (s 100).

A maker, unlike an author, need not be a human being, meaning that the first owner under these provisions could be a record company or film production company. These rules generally seek to ensure that the person or corporation who made the necessary financial investment to produce the subject matter is rewarded with ownership (e.g. with film, this is commonly the producer, not the director). Furthering this same goal, commissioned films and sound recordings belong to the commissioner, in the absence of any agreement to the contrary: ss 97(3), 98(3).

Twice in the past decade, the Australian government has introduced new ownership rules for Part IV subject matters in order to recognise new right holders. The *Copyright Amendment (Film Directors' Rights) Act 2005* amended the *Copyright Act* to give film directors a share of the copyright in the films that they direct. The Act provides for non-employee directors of non-commissioned films to share, as copyright owners, in remuneration payable by pay TV services for the re-transmission of films included in free-to-air broadcasts under Part VC of the Act: s 98(4)–(6).

Performers are also a relatively recent addition to the copyright-owning fraternity. Where a sound recording is made of a live performance (defined in s 22(7)), special ownership rules apply. These were introduced with effect from 1 January 2005 as a consequence of the *Australia–US Free Trade Agreement* (2004), in which Australia committed to becoming a signatory to the *WIPO Performances and Phonograms Treaty* (1996), requiring Australia to provide economic rights to performers in recordings of their performances. Essentially, these amendments added a new definition of maker in s 22 for sound recordings of live performances. For these recordings, *both* the person owning the record, *and* the performer(s) are deemed to be makers of the sound recording: ss 97, 22(3A). For recordings made after 1 January 2005, these various makers now own copyright in the sound recording as tenants in common in equal shares: s 97(2)–(2A) (subject to the usual rules regarding employees, and subject to contract: s 22(3B)–(3C)). Special transitional provisions apply in relation to sound recordings of live performances made prior to 1 January 2005, which, before that date, were owned by the producer alone (ss 100AA–100AH).

As with works, which may have joint authors, it is possible to have more than one owner of Part IV subject matter. The case extracted below explores the possibility that a film may have more than one maker.

CASE EXTRACT: CURRENT LAW

Seven Network (Operations) Ltd v TCN Channel Nine Pty Ltd

[2005] FCAFC 144; (2005) 146 FCR 183
Federal Court of Australia, Full Court

[Mr Murray, the organiser of a charity for troubled youth known as Camp Dare, entered an oral agreement with Channel Seven, under which the television station's camera operator and sound recordist would accompany Mr Murray and a group of schoolboys on a trek organised by Mr Murray on the Kokoda Track to produce footage (known as the 'Camera Tapes film') for Seven's 'Today Tonight' program. It was agreed that Seven could use the raw footage for the 'Today Tonight' story, and that after the airing of the program Seven would give the raw footage to Mr Murray. Mr Murray subsequently sought to make a documentary using the tape footage in development with Channel Nine. Seven sought an injunction to restrain Nine from using the footage. The Court needed to determine who owned the copyright in the Camera Tapes film.]

Lindgren J: 14. Seven submits that while Mr Murray made the arrangements for the trip, Seven alone made the arrangements for the production of the Camera Tapes film.

15. I disagree. In my opinion, both Seven and Mr Murray made the arrangements necessary for the production of the first copy of the Camera Tapes. I respectfully adopt [the trial judge's] description of the arrangement as a 'joint venture'. The idea for the trek *and for the filming of it* was Mr Murray's. He arranged for the selection of the school boys to go on it and for the consent of their parents. Accordingly, he arranged for the subject matter of the film: ten troubled and troublesome schoolboys walking the Kokoda Track. He arranged for the funding of the return airfares, two nights' hotel accommodation in Port Moresby, insurance, and the supply of shoes, socks, sporting undergarments, backpacks, one-man tents, sleeping bags and food and drink, not only for them and the Camp Dare personnel, but also for Messrs Shannon and Lynch.

16. Seven's contribution was:

(a)   remunerating the freelance camera operator, Mr Shannon, who was already providing his services to Seven (Seven paid Mr Shannon's tax invoices for his services totalling $6435);

(b)   remunerating the freelance sound recordist, Mr Lynch, who was also already providing his services to Seven (Seven paid Mr Lynch's tax invoice of $3850);

(c)   supplying, through Mr Simond, a 'script', in the sense of a list of the kinds of matters to be filmed, prepared by Mr Simond and given by him to Mr Shannon for use by him and Mr Lynch on the trip;

(d)   providing one Sony camera;

(e)   paying for the hire from Mr Shannon of a second Sony camera (Seven paid his invoice for $550);

(f)   supplying the blank Sony Mini DV tapes which were, in due course, recycled;

(g)   hiring the sound recording equipment for use by Mr Lynch from the Audio Sound Centre at Artarmon;

(h)   supplying the batteries for the cameras and for the sound recording equipment;

(i)   supplying the blank DV Pro tapes;

(j)   through Mr Shannon and Mr Lynch, deciding upon scenes and sequences to be filmed but with suggestions from Mr Murray and others.

CURRENT LAW

17. The evidence was that the cost of Seven's contribution was of the order of $10 000. The 'cost' of Mr Murray's contribution is difficult to identify. In one sense, he contributed nothing more than his own time. However, he obtained substantial cash and kind from others. Mr Murray estimated the total value at $150 000. The value of the cash, goods and services which Mr Murray obtained far exceeded the cost of Seven's contribution.

18. No doubt a person's contribution may be too distant from the production of the first copy of a cinematograph film, for that person to be regarded as a 'maker' of it, but that is not so in the present case. Mr Murray arranged for the trip and came to an arrangement with Seven for the filming of it. Without Mr Murray, there would have been no expedition, and, without his invitation to Seven, there would have been no filming of it by Messrs Shannon and Lynch, and therefore no Camera Tapes film. It is not as though Mr Murray was proposing only the trip, and Seven suggested the filming of it. The filming of it was Mr Murray's idea from the outset. Indeed, he had made or set in train arrangements for another camera operator (once, Honie Rowley and later Paul Croll) which, in the event, were not implemented.

19. As was no doubt to be expected, in the course of the trek, various individuals made suggestions as to what should be filmed. For example, Mr Murray suggested a shot which included boys in the background, praying, with a view to showing that their Islamic faith was respected and that Camp Dare's work was applicable to those of all faiths, nationalities and races. Of course, Mr Shannon, as the camera operator, had the ultimate say as to precisely what filming took place, but this does not signify that Seven alone was the maker of the film.

...

21. In my opinion, Mr Murray and Seven owned the copyright in the Camera Tapes film as tenants in common. We are not required to determine in what shares. The primary Judge said (at [59]) that '[c]opyright in the Camera Tapes was jointly held between DARE and Seven'. I have little doubt that his Honour was not intending to distinguish between 'joint' and 'in common' co-ownership. The word 'joint' is often used, even by the most highly respected of writers, in a broad sense to refer simply to co-ownership; cf *Copinger and Skone James on Copyright* (13th ed), ch 7; *Prior v Sheldon* [2000] FCA 438; (2000) 48 IPR 301 at [79].

22. Unless Seven assigned its interest in the copyright to Mr Murray, or the respondents enjoy the benefit of a licence, binding on Seven, to do what they propose, they threaten to infringe the copyright in the Camera Tapes film, and Seven is entitled to an injunction.

CROWN COPYRIGHT

The ownership rules in ss 35 and 97–100 are all subject to the operation of Part VII of the Act. This Part sets out special rules whereby the Crown (i.e. the Commonwealth[3] or a state) will own copyright in works and other subject matter. Under s 176(2) works created by, or under the direction or control of, the Commonwealth or a state will, as a default rule, be owned by the Commonwealth or the state (see also s 178(2) for sound recordings and films). Under s 177, the Commonwealth or a

---

3   Section 10(1) defines 'the Commonwealth' to include the administration of a territory.

state is the owner of copyright in work first published in Australia if first published by, or under the direction or control of, the Commonwealth or the state.

The concept of 'control' in the Crown copyright provisions was considered in *Copyright Agency Ltd v New South Wales* [2007] FCAFC 80; (2007) 159 FCR 213. The case concerned copyright in survey plans prepared by surveyor members of the Copyright Agency Ltd, and submitted under state legislation to the registrar-general as a necessary step in registration of property interests in land, and also retained as part of the land titles register. Survey plans were required to comply with detailed requirements set by New South Wales law and regulation, compliance with which was checked by government employees. Surveyors were commissioned (and paid) by clients to produce survey plans suitable for submission. A dispute arose over whether the New South Wales government was required to pay copyright licensing fees for use, reproduction and communication of the plans. New South Wales argued that it owned copyright, since the detailed regulatory requirements meant that the plans were produced 'under the control' of the state. This argument was rejected by the Full Federal Court. Emmett J (Lindgren J agreeing) gave the following explanation of the phrase:

> 125. ... [W]hen the provisions refer to a work being made under the direction or control of the Crown, in contrast to being made by the Crown, the provisions must involve the concept of the Crown bringing about the making of the work. It does not extend to the Crown laying down how a work is to be made, if a citizen chooses to make a work, without having any obligation to do so.
>
> 126. The question is whether the Crown is in a position to determine whether or not a work will be made, rather than simply determining that, if it is to be made at all, it will be made in a particular way or in accordance with particular specifications. The phrase 'under the direction or control' does not include a factual situation where the Crown is able, de facto, to exercise direction or control because an approval or licence that is sought would not be forthcoming unless the Crown's requirements for such approval or licence are satisfied. The phrase may not extend much, if at all, beyond commission, employment and analogous situations. It may merely concentrate ownership in the Crown to avoid the need to identify particular authors, employees or contracting parties.
>
> 127. The parliament did not intend that the Crown would gain copyright, or share in copyright, simply as a side effect of a person obtaining a statutory or other regulatory approval or licence from the Crown. The parliament is hardly likely to have intended that copyright would be lost merely by reason of satisfying a requirement or prerequisite for the grant by the Crown of an approval or a licence for something. The provisions in question were not intended to have the consequence that, where an approval or licence by the Crown was required in respect of a work, copyright would vest in the Crown as a side wind of the work complying with the requirements for such approval or licence: see *Land Transport Safety Authority of New Zealand v Glogau* [1999] 1 NZLR 261 at 272–3.

The existence of copyright in government materials is at odds with the position in some other countries, such as the USA, where such information would automatically be in the public domain. Crown copyright is hard to justify on an incentive rationale, but there may be other arguments for its existence, including that copyright enables the Crown to ensure the accuracy and integrity of certain works when published for public use and access. In 2005 the (now disbanded) Copyright Law Review Committee recommended that the special Crown subsistence and ownership provisions should be repealed.[4] The Committee also recommended that for certain materials, where the public interest in making information accessible to the public carries more weight than any justification for government control, such as legislation and parliamentary materials, copyright should be abolished. Australian governments have instead increased their use of open licensing (i.e. licensing that grants broad general permission for reproduction and communication) or regulatory waiver of copyright.[5]

EXPLOITATION OF COPYRIGHT

Copyright is personal property: it can be transmitted by assignment, will and operation of law: s 196(1). 'Future' copyright can also be assigned: copyright vests in the assignee when the work comes into existence: s 197. Assignments must be in writing (s 196(3)), although informal assignments may be given effect in equity: *Acorn Computers Ltd v MCS Microcomputer Systems Pty Ltd* (1984) 6 FCR 277.

Assignment of copyright can be partial: an owner of copyright can assign, or license, the right to publish a book to A, the right to make a film adaptation to B, and could even assign the rights as they pertain to different geographic areas to different people (e.g. assigning the right to publish the work in Victoria to one company, and the right to publish in Tasmania to another company). This is recognised by s 196(2), which provides:

> (2) An assignment of copyright may be limited in any way, including any one or more of the following ways:
>
>   (a) so as to apply to one or more of the classes of acts that, by virtue of this Act, the owner of the copyright has the exclusive right to do (including a class of acts that is not separately specified in this Act as being comprised in the copyright but falls within a class of acts that is so specified);
>
>   (b) so as to apply to a place in or part of Australia;
>
>   (c) so as to apply to part of the period for which the copyright is to subsist.

The freedom to divide up rights is limited only by the imagination and industry practice: a person could assign 'book rights' and 'magazine rights' to different people—even though both involve the same exclusive right of reproduction found in the *Copyright Act*. This facilitates a precise demarcation of rights, granting owners a significant level of autonomy in creating income streams and markets. Where partial assignment has occurred, s 30 provides:

> In the case of a copyright of which (whether as a result of a partial assignment or otherwise) different persons are the owners in respect of its application to:
>
> (a) the doing of different acts or classes of acts; or
>
> (b) the doing of one or more acts or classes of acts in different countries or at different times;
>
> the owner of the copyright, for any purpose of this Act, shall be deemed to be the person who is the owner of the copyright in respect of its application to the doing of the particular

---

4   Copyright Law Review Committee, *Crown Copyright* (2005).
5   For the use of Crown copyright to restrain publication of potentially politically sensitive or embarrassing information, see *Commonwealth v John Fairfax & Sons Ltd* (1980) 147 CLR 39 and B Toohey and M Wilkinson, 'The Timor Papers (1987)' in J Pilger, ed, *Tell Me No Lies: Investigative Journalism and its Triumphs*, Jonathan Cape, London, 2004.

act or class of acts, or to the doing of the particular act or class of acts in the particular country or at the particular time, as the case may be, that is relevant to that purpose, and a reference in this Act to the prospective owner of a future copyright of which different persons are the prospective owners has a corresponding meaning.

If an assignment of copyright has been made, the assignee can exercise and enforce all the economic rights of the copyright owner (assignor). Section 30 means that in the case of partial assignment, it will be necessary to identify the correct owner.

Copyright can also be licensed. A licence is a simple permission to do what would otherwise infringe copyright. A licence may be non-exclusive (meaning that the copyright owner retains the right to exercise the rights and may permit others to exercise the rights) or exclusive (meaning that the licensee has the sole right to exercise the rights to the exclusion of the copyright owner and any other person). Licences need not be in writing, except in the case of an exclusive licensee seeking to take advantage of the privileged position of an exclusive licensee to enforce copyright: see ss 117–125. A licence granted by a copyright owner will bind the grantor and the grantor's successors in title: s 196(4); see also *Concrete Pty Ltd v Parramatta Design & Developments Pty Ltd* [2006] HCA 55; (2006) 229 CLR 577 below, p 190. There is no limit to the number of non-exclusive licences that may be created.

While case law is predominantly concerned with the exercise of private exclusive rights, the last two decades have seen a rise in use of a range of free, open-source, educational and creative commons licences. These licences are standard-form agreements that reflect the author's willingness to 'unlock IP' and encourage public access to works, sometimes subject to conditions. What the licensee obtains is a non-exclusive right to use the work subject to the particular conditions of the licence (e.g. not to be used for a commercial purpose or without attribution of the source). There are now trade marks associated with some of these forms of open-access licensing to assist in educating the community in identifying such works and signal the politics of more open copyright arrangements.

ASSIGNMENT OR LICENCE?

Although s 196 requires that assignments of copyright be in writing, no particular form of words is required. The question whether there has been an assignment is one of construction of the particular instrument in light the surrounding circumstances: *Wilson v Weiss Art Pty Ltd* (1995) 31 IPR 423. Because of the way commercial opportunities develop, it can be difficult to determine precisely what the parties have agreed concerning copyright. Likewise it can be hard to discern from the facts whether what was intended was an assignment of copyright or a licence.

CURRENT LAW

CASE EXTRACT: CURRENT LAW

Larrikin Music Publishing Pty Ltd v EMI Songs Australia Pty Ltd

[2009] FCA 799; (2009) 179 FCR 169
Federal Court of Australia

[Marion Sinclair wrote the children's song 'Kookaburra Sits in the Old Gum Tree' and submitted it to the Girl Guides Association of Victoria as part of a competition. Larrikin claimed copyright in the work, based on an assignment from the executor of Ms Sinclair's estate, the Public Trustee, and another possible

CURRENT LAW

copyright owner (the Libraries Board of South Australia). EMI argued these purported assignments were ineffective owing to a prior assignment by Ms Sinclair to the Girl Guides Association and that accordingly Larrikin's action for copyright infringement against EMI should fail.]

Jacobson J:

THE VICTORIAN GIRL GUIDES COMPETITION

39. On, or shortly after 20 April 1934, the Victorian Girl Guides published a circular which was headed 'Guide Village'.

40. The circular commenced by stating that the Guide Village was a 'big effort' of all members of the Victorian Girl Guides to raise money for a proposed Guide Camp House, and that 'everything possible will be for sale'.

41. The circular stated that it was not a competition between Districts, but was:

... a great combined effort of everyone working together for the good of the whole.

42. The circular went on to announce certain competitions as follows:

The following Competitions will be held in connection with the Guide Village.
1   A Singing Round with Music.
2   A short Story (not more than 2500 words).
3   A Poem.
4   A design suitable for a Xmas Card.

43. The circular stated the following rules of entry:

RULES for ENTRY.
(a)   The entrance fee for each entry in any of the Competitions to be 6d.
(b)   A prize of 10/6 to be given to the winner of each section.
(c)   The Competitions to be open to all enrolled members of the Guide Association in Australia.
(d)   All matter entered to become the property of the Guide Association.
(e)   The decision of the Judges to be final.
(f)   All entries to be accompanied by the entrance fee of 6d. also name and address of entrants.
(g)   All entries to be in by July 31st.

44. On 2 July 1934, the Victorian Girl Guides' journal, known as 'Matilda', was published. It is not clear how regularly the publication was produced but the July 1934 edition was Vol 11 No 1.

45. The July 1934 edition of 'Matilda' recorded on p 5, under the heading 'Guide Village News', further details of the competition referred to in the April circular.

46. It enquired whether members had started working on the competitions and listed the four competitions stated in the circular, including the singing round with music.

47. It also listed the seven rules for entry in exactly the same terms as stated in the circular, including the rule that provided for all 'matter' entered in the competition to become the property of the Victorian Girl Guides.

48. The News item on p 5 of the July edition of 'Matilda' went on to say:

Now do let us have hundreds of entries, there is plenty of talent in the Guide Movement. Think of the PRIZE that you might win and also that every entry helps to swell the Fund for our Guide Camp House.

49. Also on p 5 of the July edition of 'Matilda', in the column directly opposite the details of the competition, was a short news piece under the heading 'Honours for the Chief Guide'. The news piece recorded details of the appointment of Lady Chauvel as the State Commissioner for the Victorian Girl Guides in a letter to 'Matilda' from Ms Sinclair. The piece concluded:

> On behalf of the Guiders of Victoria,
>
> Yours, etc,
>
> MARION SINCLAIR

...

THE CONTEMPORANEOUS CORRESPONDENCE

50. On 2 October 1934, the Victorian Girl Guides wrote to Ms Sinclair as follows:

> Dear Marion,
>
> I should have written to you weeks ago to express to you the thanks of Lady Chauvel and the Executive Committee for the gift of your three Rounds to the Association. We now have to thank you further for having these Rounds printed, and for your donation of the proceeds to the Guide House Fund. We do think it is ever so good of you to have made such a delightful contribution.

...

52. The three rounds referred to in the letter were included in a publication, the cover of which bore the heading 'Girl Guides' Association, Victoria, 1934'. The cover was described as 'Three Rounds by Marion Sinclair'. It stated 'Proceeds for Guide House Fund'.

53. The three rounds in the publication included a manuscript of the words and music of 'Kookaburra'. Although it is not entirely clear from the evidence, it seems likely that this was in the same form as the manuscript which was submitted for entry in the competition.

...

55. It seems clear from the letter of 2 October 1934 that Ms Sinclair paid for the printing and publication of the three rounds, that the publication was made available for sale by Ms Sinclair and that she donated the proceeds of sale to the Victorian Girl Guides' House Fund.

56. It is evident from two further letters to Ms Sinclair, written in 1935, that she continued to donate the proceeds of sale of the publication of the three rounds to the Victorian Girl Guides.

57. The first letter from the Victorian Girl Guides to Ms Sinclair was dated 22 February 1935. It was described, in the mode of that era, as a 'wee note' and was as follows:

> Dear Marion,
>
> Just a wee note to thank you from Lady Chauvel for what the enclosed receipt represents, she has asked me to say again how grateful the Committee are to you for your gesture, and how glad everyone is that Guides have a chance of purchasing your delightful songs.

[At [59]–[75] Jacobson J reviewed subsequent correspondence in which Ms Sinclair was asked for, and gave, permission to reproduce the song, as well as a subsequent assignment by her of all performing rights in her compositions to the Australasian Performing Right Association (APRA), prompted by a letter from the ABC warning her that 'Kookaburra' was being reproduced without authorisation, depriving her of royalties. There was a 1983 letter in which Ms Sinclair asserted that the words and music were copyright and that this should be acknowledged by the words 'by permission, M Sinclair'.]

ISSUE 1—WAS THERE AN 'ASSIGNMENT' IN WRITING TO THE VICTORIAN GIRL GUIDES

108. The first issue turns upon whether the rules of the Victorian Girl Guides' 1934 competition formed a part of a contract between that body and Ms Sinclair so as to satisfy the statutory requirement of writing.

109. Ordinarily, it would be thought that an entrant in a competition, particularly the winning entrant, would be bound by the rules of the competition. However, in the present case, there is a dearth of evidence about the circumstances in which Ms Sinclair entered 'Kookaburra' in the competition.

110. The documentary evidence shows that Ms Sinclair was a strong supporter of the Victorian Girl Guides movement and there are a number of competing inferences that are open as to how she came to enter 'Kookaburra' in the competition.

111. The essence of the argument of the composers and EMI was that Ms Sinclair was aware of the rules and accepted them by conduct in submitting the manuscript of 'Kookaburra' as her entry.

112. Rule (f) of the rules of entry stated that entries would be accompanied by a fee, and the name and address of entrants were to be submitted.

113. Mr Catterns QC, who appeared for the composers and EMI, submitted that, although rule (f) does not say so expressly, it contemplated the existence of a written entry form. However, he conceded that no such entry forms had been located.

114. Mr Catterns asked me to infer that such a form must have existed, or at very least, that Ms Sinclair read the circular of 20 April 1934, or the statement of the rules set out in the July edition of 'Matilda', before she submitted her entry.

115. The difficulty with this submission is that it depends upon speculation and conjecture rather than upon proved circumstances which raise a hypothesis that is more probable than not.

116. The distinction between inference and conjecture is aptly summed up in the observations by the learned author of *Cross on Evidence*, 7th Australian ed, LexisNexis Butterworths, New South Wales, 2004, JD Heydon and R Cross at [9055]. It is there pointed out that where satisfaction of the civil standard depends upon inference, there must be something more than mere conjecture, guesswork or surmise.

117. The test is that there must be shown to be more than 'conflicting inferences of equal degrees of probability so that the choice between them is a mere matter of conjecture': see *Nominal Defendant v Owens* (1978) 22 ALR 128 at 132, and the authorities there referred to.

118. Here, in the absence of an entry form or any evidence that Ms Sinclair had knowledge of the terms of the competition on submitting her entry, it is equally probable that Ms Sinclair learned of the existence of the competition without seeing the circular or the rules. She had an active interest in the Victorian Girl Guides' movement and it is equally probable that she learned of the competition through her association with the movement.

119. It is also equally probable that there were no formal documents constituting entry forms and that entries were submitted informally, by lodgement of the composition, the entry fee, and details of the entrant's name and address, if not already known to the Victorian Girl Guides.

120. No inference may be drawn from the proximity of Ms Sinclair's contribution in the July edition of 'Matilda' to the statement of the rules which appeared under the item 'Guide Village News'.

121. All that can be safely inferred from Ms Sinclair's piece in the July edition is that she contributed it. To suggest that she must have read the rules on the other side of the page is no more than conjecture. Indeed, what would be required to be established is that she read those rules before submitting her entry. This is mere speculation.

122. No support can be gained from the well-known 'ticket cases' in the law of contract. Those cases establish that where an exemption clause is contained in a ticket, and the other party is not actually aware of the terms of the clause when the contract was made, the party seeking to rely on it cannot do so unless, at the time when the contract was made, reasonable notice was given to the other party: see GC Cheshire, CHS Fifoot, N Seddon and MP Ellinghaus, *Cheshire and Fifoot's Law of Contract*, 9th Australian ed, LexisNexis Butterworths, New South Wales, 2008, at [10.28] and [10.70]; *Oceanic Sun Line Special Shipping Co Inc v Fay* (1988) 165 CLR 197 at 228–9.

123. This principle has no application here, because as the authors of Cheshire and Fifoot observe at [10.71], it is necessary to determine with some precision at what point the contract was made. That cannot be done in the present case.

124. What the composers and EMI would need to establish is that Ms Sinclair submitted her entry after the publication of the circular or after the July edition of 'Matilda' and that each of those publications constituted reasonable notice.

125. Having regard to Ms Sinclair's close connection with the Victorian Girl Guides, it is mere conjecture to say that this is what happened. It is equally probable that she heard of the competition by word of mouth and submitted her entry before the publication of those documents.

126. Accordingly, it has not been established on the evidence that Ms Sinclair entered into a contract in writing on the terms contained in the circular, or, at least, that the contract included the term which provided for all 'matter' to be the property of the Victorian Girl Guides. It follows that there was no assignment in writing to satisfy the requirements of s 5(2) of the British *Copyright Act*.

ISSUE 2—WAS THE ASSIGNMENT 'SIGNED'?

127. In view of the conclusion I have reached on the first issue, it is unnecessary to decide whether the 'assignment' was in writing. Nevertheless, I will deal briefly with this issue.

128. As I have said, Mr Catterns submitted that the requirement of writing was satisfied by Ms Sinclair's signature and initials on the manuscripts which were apparently submitted to the Victorian Girl Guides.

129. This submission depends upon the proposition that the signature and the initials were placed there for two purposes, the first being to identify the work, the second to effect an assignment.

130. It is plain in my view that the signature and the initials constituted identification of the work as one that had been composed and written by Ms Sinclair.

131. There is simply no evidentiary basis for the proposition that the signature and the initials were placed on the manuscripts to serve any other purpose. In particular, there is no basis for suggesting that they were intended to perform the work of assigning the copyright to the Victorian Girl Guides.

ISSUE 3—INTENTION TO ASSIGN

132. The letter to Ms Sinclair from the Victorian Girl Guides of 2 October 1934 makes it plain that Ms Sinclair paid for the printing and publication of the three rounds, including 'Kookaburra'.

133. The two other rounds were not entered in the competition but Ms Sinclair donated the proceeds of sale of all three rounds to the Victorian Girl Guides.

134. In my view, it is clear from this that Ms Sinclair acted upon the footing that she owned the copyright in all three rounds and that she made a gift of the proceeds of the sales, arranged by her, to the Victorian Girl Guides.

135. The Victorian Girl Guides acknowledged this by thanking Ms Sinclair for her 'gift' of the three rounds and her donation of the proceeds of sale.

136. The letter is not a legal document and should not be construed as such. The reference to the 'gift' was to the gift of the proceeds of sale of publication of the works, carried out by Ms Sinclair as copyright owner.

137. The 'wee note' of 22 February 1935 is to the same effect …

138. I reject the submission made by Mr Catterns that it is to be inferred from the circumstances in which the competition took place that the Victorian Girl Guides would sell the winning round to raise money for the Fund.

139. This is because the Guide Village News in the July 1934 edition of 'Matilda' asks members to 'let us have hundreds of entries' and 'every entry helps to swell the Fund'.

140. Thus, what was intended was that hundreds of 6 pence entry fees would be paid which would raise money for the Fund, even after allowing for the payment of the 10/6 prize to the winning entry.

141. There is nothing in this to suggest that the Victorian Girl Guides intended also to sell the winning entry, as copyright owner. Ms Sinclair's actions in printing the manuscript at her own expense and the correspondence to which I have referred are inconsistent with this.

142. I am therefore satisfied that Ms Sinclair and the Victorian Girl Guides did not intend that Ms Sinclair would assign the copyright in 'Kookaburra', as the winning entry, to the Victorian Girl Guides.

143. I do not think that any real assistance is obtained from a consideration of the subsequent correspondence.

   …

ISSUE 4—CONSTRUCTION OF THE RULE (D) OF THE COMPETITION

153. In my view, the words 'all matter entered [in the competition] to become the property' of the Victorian Girl Guides are not apt to effect an assignment of the copyright in the work. There are four reasons for this.

154. First, there is a well-known distinction in the law of copyright between the incorporeal right to the intellectual property, and the right to the physical property in a work: *Interstate Parcel Express Co Pty Ltd v Time-Life International (Netherlands) BV* (1977) 138 CLR 534 at 550 …

155. It seems to me that the word 'matter' is more apt to describe the physical property consisting of the manuscripts rather than the copyright in the works.

156. Second, there are good practical reasons why the Victorian Girl Guides might have wanted to retain the material object of the works, rather than become a bailee. The works would be likely to have been needed for archiving purposes and the persons conducting the competition would hardly have been likely to want the responsibility of returning the physical manuscripts to the entrants.

157. Third, if Mr Catterns' submissions were correct, the assignment would apply equally to all entrants in the competition. Thus, the winning and the losing entrants would all have been taken to have assigned their copyright to the Victorian Girl Guides. This does not seem likely.

158. Fourth, the surrounding circumstances indicate that the purpose of the competition was to raise funds through the entry fees, rather than to swell the Fund by the sale of the winning entry.

159. It is true, as the respondents submitted, that the authorities establish that no particular form of words is necessary to effect an assignment of copyright: see *Murray v King* (1984) 4 FCR 1 at 7 and 13 ...

160. However, in my view, this does not overcome the objections that I have listed above. This is because in order for the authorities such as *Murray* to apply, there must be some intention to assign copyright. As I have indicated above, in my view, it cannot be inferred on the evidence that either Ms Sinclair or the Victorian Girl Guides had the intention to effect an assignment of copyright.

161. In any event, I do not consider that the words in question in the present case are sufficient to disclose, on an objective consideration, an intention to effect an assignment of copyright.

CASE EXTRACT: CURRENT LAW

Seven Network (Operations) Ltd v TCN Channel Nine Pty Ltd

[2005] FCAFC 144; (2005) 146 FCR 183
Federal Court of Australia, Full Court

[The facts of this case are set out above, p 176. Having found that Seven and Murray were co-owners of copyright in the Camera Tapes film, the next issue for the Court was whether Seven had assigned its share of copyright to Murray.]

Lindgren J:

WAS THERE A CONTRACT FOR A FUTURE ASSIGNMENT OR FOR THE GRANT OF A LICENCE?

33. As at 11 February 2004, Seven owned the blank Camera Tapes [ie, the film stock], while it and Mr Murray were to own, as tenants-in-common, the copyright in the cinematograph film yet to be embodied in them. Because Seven had physical possession of the Camera Tapes, Mr Murray would be able to exploit the copyright only by getting access to them. Because of co-ownership of the copyright, each of Mr Murray and Seven would need the other's consent in order to do any of the acts, the exclusive right to do which constituted that copyright.

34. What were those exclusive rights? Section 86 of the Act provides:

> For the purposes of this Act, unless the contrary intention appears, copyright, in relation to a cinematograph film, is the exclusive right to do all or any of the following acts:
> (a) to make a copy of the film;
> (b) to cause the film, in so far as it consists of visual images, to be seen in public, or, in so far as it consists of sounds, to be heard in public;
> (c) to communicate the film to the public.

At the meeting, the parties did not speak in terms of any of these classes of act or refer to 'copyright' at all.

35. For whatever agreement Seven made at the meeting, Mr Murray furnished consideration: he agreed to permit Seven's Mr Shannon and Mr Lynch to go on the trip and to record the moving images and accompanying sounds, to bear the cost of their fares, accommodation and other expenses, and to allow Seven first use of the raw footage for the purpose of the making of a story and the broadcasting of it on 'Today Tonight'.

36. Was the consideration furnished by Mr Murray furnished for a promise by Seven to him to assign to him Seven's interest in the copyright in the cinematograph film to be made, or was it furnished for the grant of a licence by Seven? The answer to this question is not obvious. As McCardie J observed in *Messager v British Broadcasting Co* [1927] 2 KB 543 at 550, whether an assignment or licence is created often gives rise to difficulty, and (at 551):

> Intention must be the ultimate test for deciding whether an agreement be an assignment or a licence, and intention is to be gathered from the document itself and the surrounding circumstances.

37. The primary Judge was persuaded to find a promise to assign. In support he referred to the facts that Seven and Mr Murray were to be co-owners of the copyright; that Seven had no continuing use for the Camera Tapes after the broadcasting of the story on 'Today Tonight'; and that through Mr Simond, Seven handed over to Mr Murray the Camera Tapes, which were the only embodiment of the subject matter of the copyright.

38. To my mind, the handing over of the Camera Tapes carries little weight: since they were the only embodiment of the Camera Tapes film and Seven had no further use for them, it was inevitable that they would be delivered to Mr Murray in order that he be able to do any act at all comprised in the copyright, no matter how minor. For example, if Seven had consented to Mr Murray's copying a substantial part of the Camera Tapes film for the purpose of screening it for his family, the Camera Tapes would have had to be handed over (cf the delivery of the electro blocks of illustrative drawings in *Cooper v Stephens* [1895] 1 Ch 567 and *W Marshall & Co Ltd v AH Bull Ltd* (1901) 85 LT 77). In any event, Mr Murray agreed in cross-examination that the basis on which he was handed the Camera Tapes at Soldiers Beach was the basis, whatever it was, that had been agreed at the meeting on 11 February 2004. The property in them passed from Seven to Mr Murray upon delivery; but in implementation of the contract of 11 February 2004.

WHAT WAS SAID AT THE MEETING ON 11 FEBRUARY 2004?

39. It is necessary to consider closely what was said at the meeting relevant to what was to happen to the Camera Tapes after Seven's story had gone to air, against the background facts known to both parties. Although affidavits by all who attended the meeting were read, the material relating to the actual conversation at the meeting was not read, the evidence in that respect being given orally.

40. It seems to me that the possible analyses with respect to which the conversation at the meeting is to be considered are:

(1) that Seven contracted to assign its interest in the copyright to Mr Murray, and
   (a) Mr Murray promised that the acts comprised in the copyright would not be done except for promotional purposes; or
   (b) Mr Murray made no such contractual promise.

(2) that Seven granted Mr Murray a non-assignable licence to do the acts comprised in the copyright:

    (a) for promotional purposes only; or

    (b) for any purpose; and

(3) that Seven granted Mr Murray an assignable licence to do the acts comprised in the copyright:

    (a) for promotional purposes only; or

    (b) for any purpose.

[The trial judge's] conclusion was (1)(b). Of course, at the time of the conversation, the subject matter of the copyright had not come into existence. We are concerned with 'an agreement made in relation to a future copyright'; cf s 197 of the Act.

41. A careful reading of the transcript bears out his Honour's observation that the recollections of those who were present at the meeting have been affected by the conflict which subsequently arose and by their allegiances. His Honour was not satisfied either that Mr McPherson expressly imposed a limitation as to the use of the Camera Tapes by Camp Dare, or, on the other hand, that the request included such words as 'as we see fit' or 'at our discretion'. There is no challenge to his Honour's findings in either respect.

42. Nor is there a challenge to his Honour's finding that Mr Murray gave as the reason for the request, that he wanted the Camera Tapes for Camp Dare promotional purposes. It was inevitable that his reason for the request be given, although it might have been given with different degrees of detail and elaboration. Mr Murray said that both he and Mr Watt said that the tapes were required in order to promote Camp Dare. Mr Murray said that he added 'you know, DVDs ...'. Mr Watt denied referring to promotional purposes.

43. His Honour found that Mr Watt 'referred to rights as well as the physical tapes'. No doubt his Honour had in mind Mr Watt's testimony that he said 'Camp Dare would like the rights to the tape and the footage after [you] have used it on "Today Tonight"'. Mr Simond denied that anything was said on the topic of 'ownership of rights in the footage' and Mr McPherson's testimony was to the same effect. His Honour may be taken to have preferred the evidence of Mr Watt on this question.

CONCLUSIONS AS TO THE EFFECT OF THE CONVERSATION AT THE MEETING

44. The finding that Mr McPherson's response to the request was unequivocal does not necessarily mean that a 'promotional purpose' limitation was not part of the bargain reached. If it was, however, it was because of a limitation in the terms of the request to which Mr McPherson was responding.

45. It seems to me that the critical question is how Mr Murray's initial request is properly to be understood, in the light of all relevant surrounding circumstances. Mr Murray said 'I want their [Mr Shannon's and Mr Lynch's] footage because, you know, we want to be able to [do] promotional stuff for Camp Dare and, you know, DVDs ...', to which Mr McPherson replied 'Well, I can't see a problem with that'. It is possible to regard Mr Murray's statement of his reason as a gratuitous truthful statement of his intention at the time, but it is also possible to regard it as an integral part of the request.

46. After considerable fluctuation in my view, I have concluded, for the reasons which appear below, that the latter view is the correct one. The sense of the exchange is captured, in my opinion,

if we imagine Mr McPherson emphasising the word 'that'—'well I can't see a problem with that'. Mr McPherson's positive response incorporated the notion 'promotional stuff for Camp Dare, you know, DVDs'.

...

63. Mr Murray's request of Mr McPherson should be understood in the sense that he, Mr Murray, wanted the Camera Tapes for Camp Dare promotional purposes only. There is no good reason to regard Seven as having agreed to anything more than what Mr Murray requested, and to have granted to Mr Murray anything more than a non-assignable licence for those purposes.

64. An assignment of Seven's share in the copyright would result in Mr Murray being able to assign the copyright to any third party who would be at liberty to do the acts in the copyright for any purpose, for example, the copying of parts and using them to make a television advertisement for communication to the public.

65. Nor is there reason to regard the agreement as one for the grant of an assignable licence. It was probably inevitable that Mr Murray personally be the licensee, once it is accepted that the licence was one only for the promotion of Camp Dare. Moreover, '[a] licence is, prima facie, personal to the licensee': *Dorling v Honnor Marine Ltd* [1964] Ch 560 at 568.

66. This does not mean that Mr Murray could not exercise the licence through the engagement of others. Clearly, the parties contemplated that at least he would be entitled to have others produce 'DVDs' out of the Camera Tapes film. Perhaps too, if Mr Murray had engaged Look to produce a one-hour film to promote the work of Camp Dare for screening by him or on his behalf, in schools or public venues or before service organisations or prospective sponsors, this would have fallen within the notion of 'promotional purposes'.

67. We are not required to attempt to define the outer boundaries of Mr Murray's licence. It was not a licence for 'unrestricted use' as was pleaded in para 96(b) of the respondents' further amended defence ... According to the Licence Agreement between Look and Nine of late December 2004, Look produced a film described as:

> one commercial hour formatted with 5 breaks (6 segments) including all opening and closing titles and all play-ons and play-offs.

Look warranted to Nine that it owned the 'complete entire unfettered and exclusive rights in [the 'DAREing the Kokoda' film]'. Mr Murray was not a party.

68. In my opinion, this was not Mr Murray exercising his non-assignable licence to use the Camera Tapes for 'promotional purposes, you know, DVDs', notwithstanding some references in the Look Documentary to Camp Dare.

CONCLUSION

69. Seven agreed, for valuable consideration, that Mr Murray was to have a non-assignable licence to do the acts comprised in the copyright for the promotion of Camp Dare.

70. The proposed communication by Nine to the public of the documentary 'DAREing the Kokoda', lies outside that licence, and would, for lack of a licence binding on Seven, infringe the copyright in the Camera Tapes film.

IMPLIED LICENCES

A licence may be express, as considered in the extract above, or may be implied from the circumstances in which an owner deals with a work, according to ordinary principles relating to implied terms in contract law. The basic rule here is that a licence will be implied where—and to the extent that—business efficacy requires such a licence. One example is where work is commissioned for a particular purpose, in which case the copyright owner grants an implied licence to use the work or other subject matter as it was contemplated between the parties that it would be used at the time of the engagement. Importantly, the willingness of a court to create an ad hoc exception to copyright by means of recognising an implied licence will be highly sensitive to the availability of other exceptions in the copyright regime itself: see for example *Copyright Agency Ltd v New South Wales* [2008] HCA 35; (2008) 233 CLR 279. Certain contexts have given rise to the courts developing rebuttable presumptions of 'implied licences' in copyright: in particular, the commissioning of an architect to produce plans for a building will, in general, carry with it an implied licence to build the planned building.

CURRENT LAW

CASE EXTRACT: CURRENT LAW

Concrete Pty Ltd v Parramatta Design & Developments Pty Ltd

[2006] HCA 55; (2006) 229 CLR 577
High Court of Australia

[Two companies formed a joint venture and purchased a site for development. A director and shareholder of one of the companies in the joint venture was also sole director and shareholder of the architectural firm engaged to prepare architectural drawings for a development application. There was no professional fee tendered for this work. The relationship between the joint venturers soured and the site (now with building approval) was sold. The architect sought to restrain use of the plans by the purchaser, relying upon his ownership of copyright in the artistic works.]

Kirby and Crennan JJ (some footnotes omitted):

APPLICABLE LAW REGARDING ARCHITECTURAL PLANS AND DRAWINGS

...

59. The principles established by a series of cases concerning implied licences to use architectural drawings and plans were not in contest. Problems have frequently arisen in circumstances where the commissioner of architectural drawings and plans, a property owner (or a successor in title), wishes to assert an implied licence to use them in the absence of any express permission to do so. A non-exclusive licence to use architectural plans and drawings may be oral or implied by conduct, or may be implied, by law, to a particular class of contracts, reflecting a concern that otherwise rights conferred under such contracts may be undermined, or may be implied, more narrowly, as necessary to give business efficacy to a specific agreement between the parties. A term which might ordinarily be implied, by law, to a particular class of contracts may be excluded by express provision or if it is inconsistent with the terms of the contract. In some instances more than one of the bases for implication may apply....

61. By reference to the reasons of Jacobs J in *Beck v Montana Constructions Pty Ltd* [[1964–5] NSWR 229]] and the reasoning of the English Court of Appeal in *Blair v Osborne & Tomkins* [[1971] 2 QB 78], the parties agreed that where an architect is engaged to prepare plans and drawings which are the subject of copyright, and is paid a professional fee to do so, if the fee would normally be taken to cover the use of the plans and drawings for the purpose of constructing a building in substantial accordance with them, the commissioner of the plans and drawings (or a successor in title) will have an implied licence to use the plans and drawings for that purpose.

62. It has been recognised, at least since *Blair v Osborne*, that the preparation of plans and drawings as part of an application for a development consent by a local council is part of a progressive process governed by legislation. If a development application is successful it will form the basis of more detailed plans and drawings leading to final plans and drawings in accordance with which a building, as approved, will be built [[1971] 2 QB 78 at 87 per Widgery LJ].

...

IMPLIED LICENCE

69. ...The respondents sought to distinguish *Beck v Montana* and *Blair v Osborne* in two ways. First, they submitted that no fee was paid for the drawings in this case. Secondly, they submitted that the purchaser bought the land with notice of the architect's claim to copyright.

...

71. In *Beck v Montana*, a firm of architects contracted under a then standard form contract to produce plans for a block of units on particular land. When the owners sold the land they gave the purchaser the plans, and the purchaser decided to build in accordance with the plans but not to retain the architect. The rationale for finding an implied licence in favour of the purchaser to use the plans was explained by Jacobs J as follows [at 235]:

> [T]he engagement for reward of a person to produce material of a nature which is capable of being the subject of copyright implies a permission, or consent, or licence in the person giving the engagement to use the material in the manner and for the purpose in which and for which it was contemplated between the parties that it would be used at the time of the engagement.

There was no reference in *Beck v Montana* to any development consent or planning permission.

72. In *Blair v Osborne* an architect was retained by land owners to prepare drawings for the purpose of obtaining a planning permission and his clients subsequently sold the land with the benefit of the planning permission and gave the purchaser the architect's drawings. Before approving *Beck v Montana* in *Blair v Osborne*, Lord Denning MR (with whom Widgery and Megaw LJJ agreed) said [at 85]:

> ... when the owner of a building plot employs an architect to prepare plans for a house on that site, the architect impliedly promises that, in return for his fee, he will give a licence to the owner to use the plans for the building on that site. The copyright remains in the architect, so that he can stop anyone else copying his plans, or making a house from them; but he cannot stop the owner who employed him, from doing work on that very site in accordance with the plans. If the owner employs a builder or another architect, the implied licence extends so as to enable them to make copies of the plans and to use them for that very building on that site: but for no other purpose. If the owner should sell the site, the implied licence extends so as to avail the purchaser also.

73. The position may be otherwise if the architect has charged a nominal fee only to prepare drawings for the limited purpose of obtaining a planning permission. *Beck v Montana* and *Blair v Osborne* have been followed or recognised on many occasions in Australia and elsewhere. In those two cases and in *Stovin-Bradford v Volpoint Properties Ltd* [[1971] Ch 1007] the architects were utilising standard contract conditions and scales of professional fees determined by their professional institutes and the rationale for implying a consent or licence in all of them depended on the architect's reward or fee ...

...

82. Here the architectural plans and drawings were contemplated to be used by the owners to develop the site from the stage of obtaining development consent, through to achieving profits from the sale of any development built in accordance with that development consent. Those purposes must encompass and include a sale of the land with the benefit of the development consent, by the owners, after the development consent has been obtained and before completion of the development.

...

84. The principle which applies to these facts is this: in the absence of an agreement to the contrary, an express contract or an express reservation of copyright, an owner (or a co-owner) of land who is an architect, who himself prepares plans or drawings, free of charge, for himself (or for himself and other co-owners) impliedly consents to himself as owner (or co-owner) using the plans and drawings for the purposes for which they have been prepared. The 'reward' to the architect in such circumstances is not the 'fee' which accompanies an orthodox retainer between an architect and client. The reward is so much of the net profits expected to eventually flow at the conclusion of the joint venture in respect of which he is both 'architect to the joint venture' and a 'joint venturer', which are referrable to the fact that the joint venture partners did not have to incur a disbursement for architect's fees. The fact that an architect might be prepared to share that part of the net profit with his co-venturers does not detract from the foregoing analysis. For this reason, the argument that there is no consideration in these circumstances must be rejected. It follows that such circumstances are distinguishable from those cases in which there is a bare licence, revocable at will.

RESTRICTIONS ON FREEDOM OF CONTRACT: UNFAIR BARGAINS

Some copyright assignments and exclusive licences have been later challenged and set aside for reasons of unfairness, especially related to negotiation practices in the recording industry. There is no special copyright law in this regard: agreements may be set aside under equity and contract law principles. Agreements that bind the artist to the music publisher or recording company for a considerable time, with no potential for re-negotiation and little prospect of significant financial return, and establish a set of obligations and benefits that appear to be very one-sided, are inherently suspect. Usually in such cases there was unequal bargaining power between the parties and the inexperienced artist had no independent legal advice. It is the combination of factors and the individual circumstances that create an unenforceable unfair agreement: see *Schroeder Music Publishing Co Ltd v Macaulay* [1974] 1 WLR 1308; *Zang Tumb Tuum v Holly Johnson* [1993] EMLR 61; *Silvertone v Mountfield* [1993] EMLR 152. There are also cases where assignments have been challenged due to 'undue influence' on inexperienced artists: see *O'Sullivan v Management Agency & Music Ltd* [1985] QB 428; *Elton John v James* [1991] FSR 397. It is much harder for successful artists, with more experience and access to legal and accounting expertise, to argue contract 'slavery', especially where there had been opportunities for renegotiation: see *Panayiotou v Sony Music Entertainment (UK) Ltd* [1994] EMLR 229.

COLLECTIVE ADMINISTRATION OF COPYRIGHT

Collective administration is a system whereby specific copyright rights enjoyed by one or more categories of authors are administered for the benefit of those authors by an association known as a collecting society. Collecting societies safeguard their members' professional interests, but are also empowered to stand in their shoes in order to authorise (license) certain uses of their works. Their essential characteristic is the ability to negotiate and act without individual consultation with the author/owner; this may involve the copyright owner assigning the right in question to the society, or the role of the collecting society may arise from statutory licences established in legislation. The effect is that exclusive rights are pooled so as to create a repertoire of works which can be made available to potential users. The collecting societies negotiate with copyright users, either as associations of users or on an individual basis.

From its origin in the Stationers' Company Charter of 1557, copyright has been linked to the collective administration of rights. Collecting societies reduce the 'transaction costs' that would otherwise exist in ascertaining and negotiating copyright licences. A collecting society is useful to users because it provides a focal point through which they can locate and transact with owners. This is particularly important where a user wishes to utilise a large number of works that are protected by copyright, so that transacting on an individual basis would be time-consuming and costly: for example a radio station wanting to play music, or a university wanting to copy materials for course packs. Moreover, where the society grants a user a blanket licence this has the advantage of giving the user flexibility: for example a club or radio station need not determine in advance the works it is going to play. For the copyright owner, collective administration relieves them of part of the burden of policing and enforcing rights. It also confers on copyright owners bargaining power they would not possess as individuals. Competition concerns have long been raised regarding collecting societies' activities, but their benefits for both users and owners have been seen as outweighing these concerns.[6]

Collective management significantly changes the nature of copyright. The individual copyright owner loses the right to control how their copyright material will be used, and the fees charged. The copyright material may be used in contexts that the individual musician or author may not like. Collective administration also usually uses a 'sampling system' to calculate royalties, so a copyright owner may not receive payment even though their work is used, because the work was not exploited within the sampling period or by the sampled users. Each copyright loses its individuality, and the 'property form' is replaced by a 'liability form': the collecting societies turn an author's property into a right to receive payments, and a user's licence fee into a levy placed upon their activities.

Part VI of the *Copyright Act*, together with the *Copyright Regulations 1969* (Cth), provide for regulatory oversight over collective licensing. Sections 154–159 of the Act create a regime whereby a licence scheme may be referred to the Copyright Tribunal. 'Licence scheme' is defined under s 136

---

6   See M Kretschmer, 'The Failure of Property Rules in Collective Administration: Rethinking Copyright Societies as Regulatory Instruments' [2002] *European Intellectual Property Review* 126; Intellectual Property and Competition Review Committee, *Review of Intellectual Property Legislation under the Competition Principles Agreement* (2000).

as licensing in relation to the public performance right or broadcasting. The Act stipulates that on reviewing a licence scheme, the Copyright Tribunal may make an order 'either confirming or varying the scheme, as the Tribunal considers reasonable in the circumstances'. However, the law only regulates the licence fees paid by the users to the collecting society, not the amounts paid by the collecting society to the copyright owners, or the collecting society's administration costs. Such matters may be raised under a Code of Practice administered by the collecting societies themselves and periodically reviewed by an independent Code Reviewer.

The major not-for-profit Australian collecting societies that license or administer rights on behalf of their members and distribute royalties to them (some under 'statutory licences') are listed in Table 5.1.

TABLE 5.1 MAJOR NOT-FOR-PROFIT COLLECTING SOCIETIES OPERATING IN AUSTRALIA

SOCIETY	RIGHTS LICENSED	BENEFICIARIES	EXAMPLE OF USE OF THE LICENCE
APRA (Australasian Performing Right Association)	Public performance; communication to the public	Owners of musical, literary and dramatic works (mostly composers and writers of lyrics)	Music played in live venues, shops, radio, television, online, etc., including music for download (e.g. iTunes, ringtones)
PPCA (Phonographic Performance Company of Australia)	As above	Owners of sound recordings and performers	As above
AMCOS (Australian Mechanical Copyright Owners Society)	Mechanical rights (the right to make the recording/ copies)	Owners of musical and literary works (lyrics) (music publishers)	Cover versions of existing recordings; photocopying of sheet music
CAL (Copyright Agency Ltd)	Reproduction and communication of literary and some artistic works	Authors, journalists, publishers	Educational copying and communication of printed works; library copying and news clipping services; government copying and communications; CAL also manages resale royalties
VISCOPY	Reproduction of artistic works	Visual artists, including painters, designers, craft workers	Use in books, websites, greeting cards, posters, magazines and television, as well as educational and government copying (managed by CAL).
Screenrights (formerly AVCS)	Statutory licences under Parts VA and VC	Owners of broadcasts, and sound recordings, films, works included in broadcasts	Educational copying of film and television; re-transmission of free-to-air broadcasts (including directors' rights)

— 6 —

INFRINGEMENT OF COPYRIGHT

INTRODUCTION

In this chapter we consider copyright infringement. We start by considering elements necessary for proving direct infringement, namely: copying (derivation or causal connection); objective similarity to the copyright work; and the requirement that the whole or a substantial part of the copyright work has been used or reproduced. We move on to discuss in more detail the exclusive rights of the copyright owner. The chapter then addresses other kinds of infringement: liability for authorising the infringing acts of others, and indirect infringement through, for example, sale or importation of infringing copies. We briefly mention the criminal offences in the *Copyright Act 1968* (Cth), before concluding with a discussion of the defences that may be raised in response to an allegation of infringement.

DIRECT INFRINGEMENT: GENERAL PRINCIPLES

In order to succeed in an allegation of direct infringement, a claimant (generally the copyright owner) will need to establish the subject matter in which copyright subsists (discussed in Chapters 3 and 4) and their ownership of (or exclusive licence to) that subject matter (Chapter 5).

Next, the copyright owner will need to prove a sufficient 'relationship' between the defendant's alleged infringing work or act and the copyright owner's work or other subject matter. In establishing the necessary link, the Full Federal Court has stated that in an action for infringement of a Part III work, once the copyright owner has identified the work in suit, the copyright owner must also:[1]

1 identify in the alleged infringement the part taken (i.e. derived or copied) from the work in suit, which involves both:
   a establishing that the alleged infringement is *derived from, or causally connected to* the copyright work; and
   b showing that the alleged infringement is *objectively similar* to the copyright work; and
2 prove that the part taken constitutes a *substantial part* of the work in suit.

The analysis of these three matters—causal connection, objective similarity, and substantial part—is not as distinct as this list suggests: the facts on which their determination depends are closely interrelated. For example, causal connection may be proved by relying on the objective similarity

---

1   *Elwood Clothing Pty Ltd v Cotton On Clothing Pty Ltd* [2008] FCAFC 197; (2008) 172 FCR 580 at [41]. For a more elaborated, but similar list of issues in the UK, see *Baigent v Random House Group Ltd* [2007] EWCA Civ 247; [2007] FSR 24 at [124] (Mummery LJ).

between the alleged infringing work and the work it is said to have copied. In practice also, determining whether an alleged infringing work is objectively similar to a copyright work, and whether a substantial part of the copyright work has been copied, tend to involve overlapping issues and are not always clearly distinguished in judicial reasoning. Thus although this text treats these three issues under separate headings immediately below, it should be borne in mind that analysis will not always be so neat.

Note also that the Federal Court authorities that endorse the above approach to analysing direct infringement relate to artistic works protected under Part III of the *Copyright Act*.[2] The approach is necessarily somewhat different for Part IV subject matter (sound recordings, cinematograph films, broadcasts and published editions). As noted in Chapter 4, Part IV subject matters can only be 'literally' or 'mechanically' infringed; that is, through the taking of the actual visual images or sounds from the copyright-protected material. Once the actual images or sounds from Part IV subject matter have been identified in the alleged infringement, it must follow that causal connection and objective similarity are established. The next two headings, therefore, focus on works protected under Part III. It will still be necessary to address the second issue; that is, to establish the copying of a substantial part, as discussed below (see 'Subject matter other than works' below, p 214).

Causal connection, objective similarity and substantial part are the subject of detailed discussion below. But first, other matters relevant to the determination of infringement should be mentioned. Assuming that the copyright owner successfully establishes copyright subsistence, ownership, and a sufficient relationship between copyright content and alleged infringement, two key matters remain to be assessed in determining liability for direct infringement. First, the copyright owner will need to establish that the defendant has done an act falling within the exclusive rights of the copyright owner, without the licence of the copyright owner: ss 36(1), 101(1). The copyright owner has a bundle of exclusive rights, as set out in ss 31, 85–88; what acts fall within these rights is discussed in detail below ('The exclusive rights of the copyright owner', p 218). Second, a defendant may avoid liability if they can establish an exception to infringement (see 'Exceptions to infringement' below, p 261). Note that direct infringement requires no proof of intention or knowledge (although 'innocent' infringers can avoid damages: s 115(3); see Chapter 19). Although there was some suggestion in one judgment in *IceTV Pty Ltd v Nine Network Australia Pty Ltd* [2009] HCA 14; (2009) 239 CLR 458 that 'animus furandi' or the 'intent to steal' might be relevant, subsequent Full Federal Court authority states that this is not an element of infringement.[3]

CAUSAL CONNECTION

As noted above, the first matter to be proved in establishing the necessary relationship or link between a copyright work and an alleged infringement is *derivation*. There must be a causal connection between the plaintiff's and the defendant's works. Independent creation of a similar work is not infringement. If A and B both separately derive their work from a third source, C, then B will not have infringed A's copyright: see for example *Creation Records Ltd v News Group Newspapers*

---

2   *Elwood Clothing Pty Ltd v Cotton On Clothing Pty Ltd* [2008] FCAFC 197; (2008) 172 FCR 580; *Metricon Homes Pty Ltd v Barrett Property Group Pty Ltd* [2008] FCAFC 46; (2008) 248 ALR 364 at [23].

3   *EMI Songs Australia Pty Ltd v Larrikin Music Publishing Pty Ltd* [2011] FCAFC 47; (2011) 191 FCR 444 at [95]–[96] (Emmett J), [221] (Jagot J).

Ltd (1997) 39 IPR 1, in which both the plaintiff's copyright photograph and the defendant's alleged infringing photograph showed the same underlying scene, but had been taken independently by two different photographers.

Proving infringement involves more than simply alleging copying. However, the plaintiff often has no firm knowledge of the circumstances that led to the defendant producing a similar work; thus all the plaintiff can prove is: (1) the two works are substantially similar; and (2) the likelihood is that the defendant was aware of the plaintiff's work and had access to it. In *Francis Day & Hunter Ltd v Bron* [1963] Ch 587 it was suggested that evidence of a probable causal connection indirectly through evidence of similarity and access creates a rebuttable presumption of copying, notwithstanding that Lord Diplock also called this approach to proving causation 'unsophisticated' (at 626).

The defendant may rebut a presumption of copying with reference to evidence of independent creation (e.g. by showing development of the work through a series of sketches or drafts), lack of familiarity with the plaintiff's work, and/or familiarity with works other than the plaintiff's that may otherwise explain the alleged similarity.

A person may copy without even being aware of it, but intention is not an element of copyright infringement, thus such lack of awareness is no bar to liability. As there is no need to prove intention to copy, the UK and Australian courts have not been inclined to entertain broader discussions as to the significance of 'unconscious copying', though it is acknowledged that it does occur (see the '*George Harrison* case': *Bright Tunes Music Corp v Harrisongs Music, Ltd*, 420 F Supp 177 (1976) (extracted below); *ABKCO Music, Inc v Harrisongs Music*, 508 F Supp 798 (1981); 722 F 2d 988 (1983); also *Gondos v Hardy* (1982) 38 OR (2d) 555).

The psychological possibility of unconscious copying places defendants in an extremely difficult position, and creates potential unfairness for a defendant who is genuinely unaware of cultural references unwittingly made.

CASE EXTRACT: COMPARATIVE LAW

Bright Tunes Music Corp v Harrisongs Music, Ltd

420 F Supp 177 (1976)
US District Court, Southern District of New York

[It was claimed that George Harrison's song 'My Sweet Lord', released in 1970, infringed copyright in an earlier, successful song 'He's So Fine', composed by Ronald Mack and recorded by The Chiffons. 'He's So Fine' had been number one on the US charts for five weeks in 1963 and had also reached number 12 on the UK charts. Harrison gave evidence about the composition of 'My Sweet Lord', key elements of which he had come up with while '"vamping" some guitar chords, fitting on to the chords he was playing the words, "Hallelujah" and "Hare Krishna" in various ways'. The song was further developed in studio sessions involving Harrison and his group of musicians, including Billy Preston, an African-American gospel singer.]

Owen DJ (at 180–181) (footnotes omitted): Seeking the wellsprings of musical composition— why a composer chooses the succession of notes and the harmonies he does—whether it be

George Harrison or Richard Wagner—is a fascinating inquiry. It is apparent from the extensive colloquy between the Court and Harrison covering forty pages in the transcript that neither Harrison nor Preston were conscious of the fact that they were utilizing the He's So Fine theme. However, they in fact were, for it is perfectly obvious to the listener that in musical terms, the two songs are virtually identical except for one phrase.

What happened? I conclude that the composer, in seeking musical materials to clothe his thoughts, was working with various possibilities. As he tried this possibility and that, there came to the surface of his mind a particular combination that pleased him as being one he felt would be appealing to a prospective listener; in other words, that this combination of sounds would work. Why? Because his subconscious knew it already had worked in a song his conscious mind did not remember. Having arrived at this pleasing combination of sounds, the recording was made, the lead sheet prepared for copyright and the song became an enormous success. Did Harrison deliberately use the music of He's So Fine? I do not believe he did so deliberately. Nevertheless, it is clear that My Sweet Lord is the very same song as He's So Fine with different words, and Harrison had access to He's So Fine. This is, under the law, infringement of copyright, and is no less so even though subconsciously accomplished.

Infringement may be found to have occurred notwithstanding intervening links in the chain of causation: a person can infringe copyright in a sketch for a sculpture, for example, even they have only had access to the final sculpture. An extreme example of indirect copying is *Plix Products Ltd v Frank M Winstone (Merchants) Ltd* (1984) 3 IPR 390, extracted below. Note that under Australian law the copyright/design overlap provisions (ss 74–77A) now operate to prevent reliance on the copyright in drawings of utilitarian objects (such as packaging trays) once the design of the object has been industrially applied (see further Chapter 8).

CASE EXTRACT: PRECEDENT

Plix Products Ltd v Frank M Winstone (Merchants) Ltd

(1984) 3 IPR 390
High Court of New Zealand

[The plaintiff designed plastic pocket packs for kiwifruit. The New Zealand Kiwifruit Authority adopted specifications drawn from them as the industry standard for export of fruit. The defendant engaged designers who produced a competing range of trays without seeing the Plix packs and with no more information than they could gather from the packaging instructions, the Authority's specifications, and the weighing and measuring of a quantity of ungraded kiwifruit. The plaintiff argued that in so doing, the defendant had indirectly copied copyright in the original drawings as conveyed through visual description.]

Prichard J (at 415–418): The essence of copyright infringement is copying. There has to be at the very least a causal connection between the copyright work and the infringing work …

PRECEDENT

The proposition that indirect copying of an artistic work can be perpetrated through the medium of a written verbal description of the copyright material introduces the concept of copying via a medium (written words) which is wholly different in kind from either the copyright material or the alleged infringing material. The translation from two dimensional drawings into three dimensional copies and from a literary work into a dramatic work is provided for by the Act. But the translation of words into a material object (and vice versa) is not an infringement. A recipe for a rice pudding might be susceptible of literary copyright. But no one would suggest that to make a rice pudding by following a recipe would infringe the literary copyright in the recipe. Conversely, and by the same token, a written verbal description of an artistic work, however precise and explicit, is not an infringement of any copyright subsisting in that work. That, of course, is because the two media are so completely different that one can never, in a real sense, be a medium in which it is possible to reproduce the other—just as a painting cannot be played on a gramophone record.

But the question to be addressed in this case is not whether the making of an object according to a written description can be an infringement of literary copyright in that description, (it cannot); but whether the use of written description of copyright material as an intermediary in the process of copying an artistic work can ever constitute a sufficient link in the chain of causation to identify one product as having been copied from the other. An original work can be reproduced by process of making a copy of a reproduction of that work. It is readily comprehensible that copyright law should equate that process with actually copying the original work. But a written description of an artistic work is not a reproduction of the work, nor can the making of a physical object in accordance with the written description be equated with copying the written description. In *Purefoy Engineering Co Ltd v Sykes Boxall & Co Ltd* (1955) 72 RPC 88, the Master of the Rolls said: 'What we will call the intermediate stage or subject-matter copied by the alleged infringer must in some real and intelligible sense, in our judgment, be a "copy" or representation of the original work'. Sir Raymond Evershed was not concerned with a case like the present, where the intermediate step is said to be a verbal description of the copyright material: but I think the same principle should apply. Can it then be said that an alleged infringer, who succeeds in reproducing an original artistic work only by following a written description, has copied the original work? He has never seen it: he has never seen a copy of it. There is something to be said for the argument that, whatever this process may be called, it is not—in the ordinary literal sense of the word—'copying' ...

It is obvious that a sufficiently precise verbal description of the copyright material can fulfil the same function as a physical copy of the artistic work in providing a means by which the copyist can appropriate the substantial features of the copyright material. Although there is little by way of precedent to support the proposition that reproduction of an original work by following a written description is equivalent, in copyright law, to copying the original work, it seems to me that it has a foundation in logic.

Subject to the existence of the criteria to which I am about to refer, I would hold it to be the law that indirect copying can be perpetrated through the medium of a verbal description of the copyright work ...

Where copying via a verbal description is alleged in relation to copyright in drawings of industrial designs or in other utilitarian objects, I think the enquiry must be whether the description said to have been used by the alleged copyist conveys the form (shape or pattern) of those parts of the design

PRECEDENT

which are the copyright material alleged to have been 'copied' or whether the description conveys only the basic idea of the drawing or artefact. It is not enough to rely on an unqualified assertion that the verbal description is a 'link in the chain of causation'. This is a metaphorical expression which may be apt when the intermediate material is a physical copy of the form of the copyright material. But when related to a verbal description, I think expressions of this sort need to be handled with care. Whenever an alleged copyist uses a verbal description of the copyright material as a source of inspiration then obviously, it can be said that the description is a link (however nebulous) between what the alleged copyist makes and the copyright material—and this is so irrespective of whether the 'link' is to the form or shape of the original work or whether it is only to the basic idea of the original work. A designer who knows his subject and who is given the idea, or general concept, of a copyright product (and no more) may well be able, by drawing on his own skill and independent knowledge, to design a product which may, or may not, reproduce the form of copyright work. I would regard this as independent work—not copying …

Only when the form of the copyright material is perceptible from the description can it be said 'in a real and intelligible sense' to convey to the reader the form or shape of the copyright material and thus take the place of a physical copy of the original work as the intermediate stage in the process of copying that form or shape.

OBJECTIVE SIMILARITY

The second issue relevant to establishing the necessary relationship between a copyright work and an alleged infringement is similarity. Similarity of an alleged infringing work to the copyright work is not always in issue. Sometimes, however, an alleged infringer will dispute whether their work is sufficiently similar to the copyright work to be considered a copy at all. An example of such a case is extracted below.

CURRENT LAW

CASE EXTRACT: CURRENT LAW

EMI Songs Australia Pty Ltd v Larrikin Music Publishing Pty Ltd

[2011] FCAFC 47; (2011) 191 FCR 444
Federal Court of Australia, Full Court

[This case concerned the alleged infringement of copyright in the Australian children's song 'Kookaburra Sits in the Old Gum Tree' through a tune embodied in a flute riff in a popular Australian rock song from the early 1980s, 'Down Under', performed by the group Men At Work. The composers of 'Down Under' were Colin Hay and Ronald Strykert, and the flautist was Greg Ham. The original 'Kookaburra' song (transcribed into D major from its original F major) is set out in Example A below. The flute riff appearing in 'Down Under' (which is in B minor), is shown below (the flute riff is in bar four of Example D and in bars two and four of Example E).

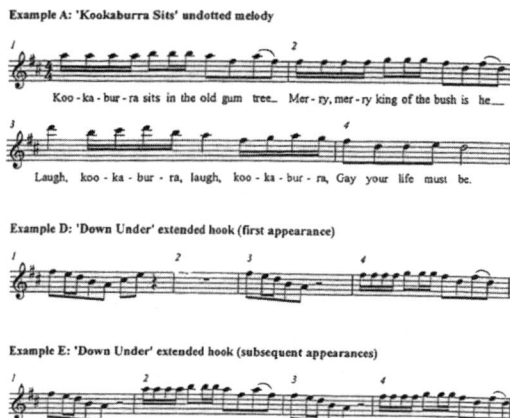

Example A: 'Kookaburra Sits' undotted melody

Koo - ka - bur - ra sits in the old gum tree_ Mer - ry, mer - ry king of the bush is he_

Laugh, koo - ka - bur - ra, laugh, koo - ka - bur - ra, Gay your life must be.

Example D: 'Down Under' extended hook (first appearance)

Example E: 'Down Under' extended hook (subsequent appearances)

Both works were recognised iconic Australian songs. Despite this, the alleged infringement was identified only in 2007. This delay in identification raised an interesting question as to whether there could be sufficient similarity. Both at trial and on appeal there was an extended discussion of how similarity is assessed, including how expert evidence is relevant, and what the test of similarity should be in the case of music. Expert evidence was given by two composers, Dr Ford and Mr Armiger. Note that in the judgment of Jagot J, similarity and substantial part are dealt with together. In arguing that a 'substantial part' had not been reproduced, EMI submitted that 'If elements of the second work are such as to obscure (as in this case) any similarity between it and the copyright work, there can be no substantial reproduction'. Only elements of the judgment going specifically to the assessment of similarity, however, are extracted here.]

Jagot J: 138. At [157]–[208] the trial judge dealt with the issue of objective similarity. At [157]–[158] the trial judge said:

> 157. In my opinion, there is a sufficient degree of objective similarity between the bars of Kookaburra which are seen and heard in Down Under to amount to a reproduction of a part of Miss Sinclair's round. The question of whether it is a reproduction of a substantial part of that work is a different question which I will address later.
>
> 158. The view which I have reached as to reproduction of a part of Kookaburra follows from my aural comparison of the musical elements, as well as my visual comparison of the notated songs, with particular assistance from the evidence of the experts.

...

140. At [160]–[162] the trial judge summarised his reasoning process as follows:

> 160. The relevant musical elements that I have considered are melody, key, tempo, harmony and structure.
>
> 161. But perhaps the clearest illustration of the objective similarity is to be found in Mr Hay's frank admission of a causal connection between the two melodies and the fact that he sang the relevant bars of Kookaburra when performing Down Under at a number of concerts over a period of time from about 2002.
>
> 162. The failure to call Mr Ham and the admissions which were tendered from his affidavit reinforce the conclusion I have reached.

141. The trial judge then dealt with each of the identified musical elements.

142. As to *melody*, the trial judge identified (at [163]) the 'relevant comparison' as between:

- the melody of the flute riff when it plays the fourth bar of Dr Ford's Example D, and the second bar of Kookaburra; and
- the melody of the flute riff when it plays the second and fourth bars of Dr Ford's Example E, and the first and second bars of Kookaburra.

143. The trial judge said (at [164]):

> With the assistance of Dr Ford and Mr Armiger's evidence, as well as that of Mr Hay, I was able to detect a sufficient degree of objective similarity between the melody to meet the test stated in the authorities.

144. The trial judge referred to Dr Ford's description of these two melodies (as defined in [163]) as 'exact', 'identical' and 'too long ... to be coincidental' (at [165]–[166]) and to Mr Armiger's evidence that the two were 'shared phrases' (at [167]), and described Mr Hay's evidence as putting the question of objective similarity between the two 'beyond any real doubt' (at [168]). Mr Hay accepted that the fourth bar of Down Under is a 'direct reference to Kookaburra' and that 'the fourth bar of [Dr Ford's] Example D and the second and fourth bars of Example E are "unmistakably" the melody of Kookaburra': at [168]. The trial judge also said (at [169]):

> This is graphically illustrated by the fact that Mr Hay has on occasions sung the words of Kookaburra where the flute riff would ordinarily be played in Down Under.

145. The trial judge accepted (at [171]) that he may have become 'sensitised to the similarity between the melodies so as to be able to hear the objective similarity between them' but did not consider that this 'overcomes the force of the expert evidence and the conclusion which seems to follow almost inevitably from the frank admissions made by Mr Hay'. The trial judge continued (at [172]):

> In any event, the test is that of the ordinary reasonably experienced listener and the comparison is not concerned with deceptive similarity as in a passing-off action: *Francis Day & Hunter* at 610, 623–624; [*Designers Guild Ltd v] Russell Williams [(Textiles) Ltd* [2000] 1 WLR 2416] at 2425.

146. The trial judge recognised that 'the shared phrases in the melodies occupy a different space in the full sentence of the melody of Down Under than that which they occupy in Kookaburra' but considered that an issue of musical structure: at [173].

147. As to *key*, the trial judge acknowledged Kookaburra was notated in F major and 'the quotation from Kookaburra in Down Under in D major, although it is set against a background of B minor', but accepted Dr Ford's evidence that 'ultimately nothing turns on this' (at [176]) because the precise key or pitch is not relevant to an appreciation or recognition of a tune and Mr Armiger agreed that 'choice of key was insignificant, as it is the relative pitches within the song which allow the listener to identify the song': at [176]–[177]. Further, the trial judge accepted Dr Ford's evidence that, apart from pitch, the two melodies 'not merely resemble each other, they are note-for-note the same': at [178].

148. As to *tempo and rhythm*, the trial judge identified the dispute between the parties (Dr Ford's evidence to the effect that the tempo of the two was 'more or less' the same and Mr Armiger's that

'Kookaburra has a folk-style, four-four or two-four square rhythm, the accompaniment to Down Under is in more of a reggae style, which places a different emphasis on a different beat'): at [179]–[182]. The trial judge concluded that nothing turned on the issue of rhythm as 'it is possible to do a song in lots of different ways' and the tempo of the melodies is more or less the same: at [184]–[185]. Further, that the slur on 'tree-ee' and 'he-ee' is 'a distinctive element of the melody and rhythm of Kookaburra which is replicated in Down Under': at [186]).

149. As to *harmony*, the trial judge noted that Mr Armiger's evidence relating to the different keys concerned the underlying harmony of the flute riff in Down Under: at [188]. The trial judge found, however, that 'the difference in harmony does not make the phrases from Kookaburra unrecognisable' but, as Dr Ford said, was 'a bit like shining a different light on it': at [189]. In this context the trial judge referred to *D'Almaine* [*v Boosey* (1835) 1 Y & C Ex 288] (at 302) to the effect that 'the mere adaptation of an air by transferring it from one instrument to another does not alter the original subject' (at [189]) and *Grignon v Roussel* (1991) 38 CPR (3d) 4 in which it was held that there was 'sufficient objective similarity in melodic, harmonic and rhythmic terms, notwithstanding minor differences resulting from arrangement or substitution of chords' (at [191]).

150. As to *context and structure*, the trial judge described the different structural context of the flute riff in Down Under compared to Kookaburra as at 'the heart of the respondents' answer to the claim of reproduction': at [192]. The trial judge noted Larrikin's acceptance that the 1981 recording of Down Under is a much more layered song than Ms Sinclair's round and continued (at [195]):

> But the question of structure is not concerned with the structure of the entirety of the 3 minute recording. Rather, it turns solely upon the structure of the flute riff and the separation and punctuation of the bars of Kookaburra by Men at Work's distinctive sound in what Dr Ford called 'the basic hook'.

151. The trial judge concluded (at [196]) that:

> In my opinion, this question is resolved by Dr Ford's evidence that the separation of the notes does not make them different, but means that we hear them differently.

152. In reaching this conclusion the trial judge had regard to Mr Armiger's evidence about the separation of the phrases from Kookaburra in the flute riff of Down Under and their different musical function and context creating an 'integrated musical statement'. The trial judge also noted Mr Armiger's agreement that the notes from Kookaburra play 'an important, indeed essential function' in the flute riff of Down Under: at [197]–[198]. For these reasons the trial judge did not consider the separation of the Kookaburra phrases in the Down Under flute riff to be material: at [199]. Although it was said in *D'Almaine v Boosey* that 'if one does not take the bars of a composition sequentially, but breaks them up by the 'intersection of others' it may not be an infringement', the trial judge described this as a question of fact in respect of which he was 'satisfied that the melody is the same and the separation or punctuation does not overcome the conclusion of reproduction': at [200]–[201].

153. The trial judge repeated the respondents' rhetorical question (at [202]) 'if both Kookaburra and Down Under are such icons, and the similarities so strong, why did it take so long for anyone to recognise the connection'. In considering this fact the trial judge referred to the evidence that the

connection was exposed in the television program *Spicks and Specks* (a television show on the ABC) in 2007. This evidence was described by the trial judge as follows (at [204]–[205]):

> 204. The question which was asked was '… name the Australian nursery rhyme that this riff has been based on'. A part of Down Under, including Dr Ford's Example E, was then played. The panel did not answer immediately and the excerpt from Down Under was played again. The host then said 'this bit especially' and one of the panel members made the link.
>
> 205. Once the first panel member gave the correct answer, the others recognised the connection.

154. The trial judge acknowledged that the panel members 'are not the ordinary reasonably experienced listener and that even they had difficulty in recognising the connection between the songs' but concluded this was not 'sufficient to overcome the conclusion that the relevant degree of objective similarity is made out': at [206]. In a passage emphasised by the EMI parties and Mr Hay in this appeal the trial judge then said (at [207]–[208]):

> 207. What Spicks and Specks does show is that there are difficulties in the recognition of the work, but a sensitised listener can detect the aural resemblance between the bars of Kookaburra and the flute riff of Down Under.
>
> 208. For reasons which I have already given, this is sufficient to satisfy the test of objective similarity.

…

175. In oral submissions the EMI parties and Mr Hay listed six matters said to deprive the two bars of Kookaburra taken in Down Under of essential characteristics that resided in Kookaburra and five matters in Down Under said to change the character of how the notes are heard.

176. The six matters are that in Down Under:—(i) there is no use of any lyrics, (ii) there is no use of a round, (iii) there is no context of a nursery rhyme or folk melody, (iv) two of the four bars of Kookaburra are not used at all, (v) to the extent that any bar is referenced, it is robbed of its relationship to the surrounding bars, and (vi) the two bars that do appear do so as 'fragments' of a melody difficult to detect: [*Larrikin Music Publishing Pty Ltd v EMI Songs Australia Pty Ltd (No 2)* [2010] FCA 698; (2010) 188 FCR 321] at [138]. The EMI parties and Mr Hay subsequently accepted that the relevant copyright was Kookaburra as a musical work so the first point was immaterial. However, in so doing they said that it must also follow that Dr Ford's evidence about the first two bars of Kookaburra being its 'signature' (and related evidence) could not have been material to the trial judge's findings because their signature status depended on the lyrics.

177. The five matters said to change the character of how the notes are heard are that:—(i) within the flute riff itself, the two bars referring to Kookaburra are incorporated within a new, larger integrated musical statement, (ii) there is a change in harmony and the bars in question are heard in a minor key, (iii) the flute riff is but one of a number of ornaments, and no part of Kookaburra is incorporated into a central verse of chorus of Down Under, (iv) the flute riff co-operates with other features of Down Under, including lyrics and title, to achieve a rock anthem celebrating aspects of Australia, and (v) the reggae rhythm infuses the whole of Down Under.

…

180. [The trial judge is alleged to have erred in] in failing to give weight to the aural perception of the two works. If this had been done, the EMI parties and Mr Hay submitted, the reason the similarity went

unnoticed in two iconic Australian songs for 20 years would have been apparent to the trial judge—an aural assessment discloses the differences between the two works such that only a sensitised listener assisted by expert evidence and with repeated listening, not an ordinary reasonable listener, can detect the similarity. This 'sensitised listener', submitted the EMI parties and Mr Hay, involved the wrong test. The relevant listener is the ordinary, reasonably experienced listener uninstructed by experts such as Dr Ford, Mr Armiger and Mr Hay.

...

197. The discussion of the relevant authorities ... shows that the trial judge's approach of dealing with objective similarity and substantiality sequentially was orthodox and did not involve any impermissible fragmentation of the relevant inquiry. A fair reading of his reasons [at [2010] FCA 29; (2010) 263 ALR 155] does not support a conclusion that he determined the case merely by an impermissible 'note for note comparison': *Austin v Columbia Graphophone Co Ltd* [1923] Mac CC 398 at 415 (*Austin*). That is not to say, however, that the notes are irrelevant. As stated in *Austin* at 409, 'music must be treated by the ear as well as by the eye'. In *Francis Day* Wilberforce J at first instance, whose approach was said by the EMI parties and Mr Hay to disclose the error in that of the trial judge, considered the same range of matters as the trial judge in the present case including the notes.

198. The trial judge considered 'aural comparison of the musical elements, as well as my visual comparison of the notated songs' (at [158]), as well as melody, key, tempo, harmony and structure. It is true that the trial judge defined the relevant melodies (at [163]) as involving a comparison between, first, the flute riff in Down Under when it plays the fourth bar of Dr Ford's Example D, and the second bar of Kookaburra and, second, the flute riff in Down Under when it plays the second and fourth bars of Dr Ford's Example E, and the first and second bars of Kookaburra. This involved the trial judge in doing nothing more than implementing the first two steps of what was described as the correct approach in *Metricon Homes* [*Pty Ltd v Barrett Property Group Pty Ltd* [2008] FCAFC 46; (2008) 248 ALR 364] at [23] and *Elwood Clothing* [*Pty Ltd v Cotton On Clothing Pty Ltd* [2008] FCAFC 197; (2008) 172 FCR 580] at [41] by:

(1) identifying the work in suit in which copyright subsists (that is, Kookaburra);
(2) identifying in the alleged infringing work (that is, Down Under) the part taken (that is derived or copied) from the work in suit (that is, the flute riff in Down Under when it plays the fourth bar of Dr Ford's Example D and the second and fourth bars of Dr Ford's Example E); and
(3) determining whether the part taken constitutes a substantial part of the work in suit (that is, by reference to the importance of the part taken to Kookaburra, not to Down Under).

199. It is not the case that, by this definition of the relevant melody, the trial judge failed to consider the other factors which he identified as relevant including the aural perception, key, tempo, harmony and structure of the part taken from Kookaburra as it appears in Down Under. The trial judge also considered the facts that Down Under was in a different key, had a somewhat different rhythm, and involved a different harmonic shape due to the difference in key, and that the part taken from Kookaburra as it appears in the flute riff in Down Under involves a different structure in which bars of Kookaburra are separated and punctuated by Men at Work's distinctive sound and the basic hook of Down Under. As the trial judge correctly said (at [195]), the question of structure is not concerned with the entirety of the 3-minute recording of Down Under. It is concerned with the flute riff in which the parts taken from Kookaburra appear. For the trial judge to have done otherwise and adopted the approach of the EMI parties and Mr Hay of determining objective similarity by reference to the whole of Down Under, would have involved a departure from established principle.

...

202. For the purpose of determining objective similarity the trial judge was assisted by experts for both sides. In addition to their contention that the trial judge had become a sensitised listener and incorrectly applied his sensitised ear to the task overly assisted by expert evidence, the EMI parties and Mr Hay suggested that there was some error in such expert evidence being available at all. To the extent that this was suggested, it should be rejected. The use of expert evidence to assist in resolving the issue of objective similarity is orthodox. For example, evidence for the same purpose was admitted in *Austin*; *D'Almaine v Boosey*; [*Francis Day & Hunter Ltd v Bron* [1963] Ch 587]; [*G Ricordi & Co (London) Ltd v Clayton & Waller Ltd* [1928–35] MacG Cop Cas 154], and *CBS Records Australia Ltd v Gross* (1989) 15 IPR 385. More to the point, the EMI parties and Mr Hay relied on the expert evidence of Mr Armiger addressing the same issue. No error can be sustained merely because the trial judge used the expert evidence the parties chose to make available to him. The error, if there be one, is confined to the contention that the trial judge applied the wrong test to the task—namely, that of a sensitised listener overly assisted by expert evidence rather than the ordinary reasonable listener ...

...

208. The phrase 'ordinary reasonably experienced listener' was used in *Francis Day* at 596 in a conclusion that the degree of similarity was sufficient for such a listener to think that one might have come from the other. In *G Ricordi & Co*, to which the EMI parties and Mr Hay also referred in this context, there was evidence from one expert that the resemblance of the part alleged to have been taken from the copyright work was very strong while another expert said the resemblance was of the very slightest character. The present case, it must be recalled, is different. All of the expert witnesses recognised that the flute riff in Down Under directly and unmistakably quoted, borrowed or took two bars from Kookaburra. This is consistent with the fact that once the panel members of *Spicks and Specks* had been directed to the relevant part of the flute riff all ultimately said that they could recognise the bars taken from Kookaburra. However, as the trial judge recognised, the panel members are musical experts and not the ordinary reasonably experienced listener: at [206].

209. It is clear from the trial judge's reasons that he was aware of the approach of the ordinary reasonably experienced listener to objective similarity. He referred to that phrase as the relevant test at [172] and [206]. At [172] the trial judge in fact said:

> In any event, the test is that of the ordinary reasonably experienced listener and the comparison is not concerned with deceptive similarity as in a passing-off action: *Francis Day & Hunter* at 610, 623-624; *Russell William Textiles* at 2425.

210. Having correctly identified the relevant test, the question is whether, in referring to the 'sensitised listener' and making the use of the expert evidence as he did, the trial judge in fact failed to apply the test he had identified. To answer this question the passages from the reasons on which the EMI parties and Mr Hay relied must be considered in context.

211. At [171] the trial judge accepted that there was force in the submission that he had become sensitised to the similarities between the melodies so as to be able to hear objective similarity between them. The trial judge said he did not think this overcame the force of the expert evidence and the conclusion which seems to follow inevitably from the frank admissions by Mr Hay ...

212. At [207], after referring to the test of the ordinary reasonably experienced listener at [206], the trial judge said that *Spicks and Specks* showed that 'there are difficulties in the recognition of the

work, but a sensitised listener can detect the aural resemblance between the bars of Kookaburra and the flute riff of Down Under'.

213. It is apparent from [171] that the trial judge could hear the objective similarity between Kookaburra and part of the flute riff in Down Under. By 'sensitised listener' the trial judge could not have meant expert listener. It is clear from the context that he meant an ordinary reasonably experienced listener who had heard the relevant parts of the works more than once and, perhaps, repeatedly. As Larrikin submitted, however, the task the trial judge was addressing was objective similarity. There is no principle that the ordinary reasonably experienced listener may not hear a work or part of it more than once. Nor do the cases suggest that the trial judge was not entitled to have regard to the expert evidence when determining objective similarity. Moreover, and as noted, all of the expert evidence was to the same effect at least in so far as it established that the flute riff in Down Under directly borrowed bars from Kookaburra. The fact that Mr Armiger described these borrowings as 'shared phrases' confirms the taking of bars from Kookaburra.

. . .

218. Analysed in this way it is apparent that none of these aspects of the challenge to the trial judge's decision can be sustained as an error of principle. The trial judge could detect the similarity between the two pieces. He identified and applied the test of the ordinary reasonably experienced listener to objective similarity. He accepted that he may have become a sensitised listener. He made use of the expert evidence to support the finding of objective similarity. In all these respects the trial judge's reasoning was orthodox.

[Nicholas J agreed with her Honour's reasons. Emmett J was critical of aspects of the trial judge's approach but also concluded, on the basis of his Honour's own consideration of the similarities and differences between the works, that there was a 'reasonably ready aural perception' of similarity. Emmett J also agreed that 'it is not erroneous to direct oneself to the relevant parts of the works, to listen to the works a number of times, and to accept the assistance of the views of experts, in determining the question of objective similarity': at [86]; His Honour also indicated some 'disquiet' about the conclusion in the circumstances (at [98]), openly questioning whether the result indicated that copyright provided rights that were too extensive in the particular case: at [100].]

SUBSTANTIAL PART

Copyright may be infringed by a defendant who copies the whole of a copyright work (Part III) or a subject matter other than a work (Part IV). But, in accordance with s 14(1), copyright may also be infringed by a person who uses a 'substantial part' of the copyright-protected material.

COPYRIGHT WORKS

Certain general principles for determining whether the defendant has copied, or taken, a substantial part of a copyright work are well-established. The assessment is a one of degree, turning more on questions of the quality of what has been copied rather than quantity. The significance of what has been copied is assessed by reference to the *copied* work, not the infringing work: *Designers Guild Ltd v Russell Williams (Textiles) Ltd* [2000] 1 WLR 2416 (HL); *EMI Songs Australia Pty Ltd v Larrikin Music Publishing Pty Ltd* [2011] FCAFC 47; (2011) 191 FCR 444 (extracted above).

In assessing the quality of what has been copied, courts will look at whether the defendant's work makes substantial use of those features of the copyright owner's work which constitute it as an original copyright work; that is, courts look at the originality of the part that has been copied: *Data Access Corporation v Powerflex Services Pty Ltd* [1999] HCA 49; (1999) 202 CLR 1 at [83]–[84]; *IceTV Pty Ltd v Nine Network Australia Pty Ltd* [2009] HCA 14; (2009) 239 CLR 458 at [155].

Despite agreement on these general principles, determining whether a substantial part has been taken is not straightforward. In literary and cultural theory and in IP law there are ongoing debates about the degree to which all Western creativity is appropriative in nature.[4] Within 'genres' of work there may be certain conventions or expected features, and drawing a line between what is original and what is not, and what is permissible and impermissible, can be difficult in this context.

Protection extends beyond the precise expression embodied in a work. As such, notwithstanding judicial reliance on an idea/expression dichotomy to demarcate what is able to be used without permission/what is protected, taking ideas can still give rise to infringement. This creates confusion. It becomes very hard to determine the line between permitted referencing of general ideas or themes shared among all works of a particular genre, and acts of piracy of more specific expression of ideas.

In the *Jaws* case (*Zeccola v Universal City Studios Inc* (1982) 46 ALR 189, extracted below) it was argued that Enzo Castellari's film *The Last Shark* infringed copyright in the original novel, *Jaws* (a literary work), and in the screenplay (a dramatic work) of Steven Spielberg's movie *Jaws*. This case, and the following comparative extract concerning the book *The Da Vinci Code* (*Baigent v Random House Group Ltd* [2007] EWCA Civ 247; [2007] FSR 24), both raise interesting questions about the utility of the idea/expression distinction in copyright and notions of 'genre', 'central theme' and 'idea'. Are these useful legal and extra-legal concepts, or are they merely tools that legitimate more intuitive feelings for justice as applied in any given fact scenario?

CASE EXTRACT: CURRENT LAW

Zeccola v Universal City Studios Inc (the '*Jaws* case')

(1982) 46 ALR 189
Federal Court of Australia, Full Court

[The case concerned copyright in the very successful and arguably groundbreaking film *Jaws* and the underlying novel and screenplay. The alleged infringing product was an Italian film, known as either *La Ultima Squalo* (*The Last Shark*) or *Great White*. This case was an appeal from a decision of the Victorian Supreme Court granting an interlocutory injunction to prevent distribution of the Italian film.]

Lockhart and Fitzgerald JJ (at 191–195): It was submitted by counsel for the appellants that the primary judge committed a fundamental error in his approach to the question whether the appellants had infringed the copyright of the respondent in the film 'Jaws'. It was submitted that copyright in a film

---

4   See for example R Coombe, *The Cultural Life of Intellectual Properties,* Duke University Press, Durham, NC, 1998; L Lessig, *Free Culture: How Big Media Uses Technology and the Law to Lock Down Culture and Control Creativity,* Penguin Press, New York, NY, 2004.

CURRENT LAW

subsists only in those parts of the film capable of being the subject-matter of copyright, that is, having the requisite character of originality, and that it is necessary to excise other parts from the whole. It was said that it is only the residue that can be the subject of copyright and thereby be protected from infringement.

Counsel for the appellants submitted that both films, 'Jaws' and 'Great White' are genre films based upon the idea of a savage monster menacing a community. Each is a film about a killer shark terrorizing human beings and it was said that neither film was entitled to protection as there is no copyright in that general idea.

The difficulties involved in severing films into parts which are capable of characterization as original works and other parts that are not is obvious. Indeed, it is the subject of only limited exploration by the laws of this country and the United Kingdom. We were referred to certain decisions of United States courts where this question has been considered from time-to-time and we have found those cases helpful in resolving the questions before us. In general, there is no copyright in the central idea or theme of a story or play, however original it may be; copyright subsists in the combination of situations, events and scenes which constitute the particular working out or expression of the idea or theme. If these are totally different the taking of the idea or theme does not constitute an infringement of copyright.

Of necessity certain events, incidents or characters are found in many books and plays. Originality, when dealing with incidents and characters familiar in life or fiction, lies in the association, grouping and arrangement of those incidents and characters in such a manner that presents a new concept or a novel arrangement of those events and characters. We accept that where a story is written based on various incidents which, in themselves, are commonplace, a claim for copyright must be confined closely to the story which has been composed by the author. Another author who materially varies the incidents and characters and materially changes the story is not an infringer of the copyright. If a literary or dramatic work is not wholly original there is no copyright in the unoriginal part so as to prevent its use. Additional factors may fall for consideration where the alleged infringement is by cinematograph film.

The primary judge closely analysed the two films 'Jaws' and 'Great White'. Notwithstanding that the subject-matter of the film 'Jaws' was not particularly striking his Honour held the view, in essence, that the combination of the principal situations, singular events and basic characters was sufficient to constitute an original work that was susceptible of protection under the law of copyright in this country. In our opinion his Honour's finding has not been shown to be in error. It must be remembered that all his Honour did was make his findings on the basis that a prima facie case was established. He did not make any final or definitive finding on this, or indeed any other question.

CASE EXTRACT: COMPARATIVE LAW

Baigent v Random House Group Ltd

[2007] EWCA Civ 247; [2007] FSR 24
Court of Appeal of England and Wales

COMPARATIVE LAW

[Two of the authors of a purportedly non-fiction book *The Holy Blood and The Holy Grail* (HBHG) claimed that Dan Brown's mystery-thriller novel *The Da Vinci Code* (DVC) was derived from their original research and historical conjecture. HBHG advanced the thesis that: (1) Jesus Christ was of royal blood with a legitimate claim to the throne of Palestine; (2) Mary Magdalene was married to Jesus Christ;

(3) they had offspring; (4) after the crucifixion, Mary Magdalene and at least one child found refuge in southern France; and (5) the bloodline (sangreal, or Holy Grail) of Jesus was preserved and perpetuated, and eventually in the fifth century became allied with the royal line of the Franks, engendering the Merovingian dynasty, descendants of whom were protected by the Knights Templar.

The substantial part alleged to have been taken was claimed to be the 'Central Theme' of HBHG comprising 15 elements (a list of individual assertions of actual or virtual history contained in HBHG). The trial judge found that there were 11 similarities or common elements between the works; however, the Central Theme was not to be found 'expressed as such' in HBHG, and that even if it were there, it was no more than 'an expression of a number of facts and ideas at a very general level'. The authors appealed.]

Mummery LJ: 146. It is not … sufficient for the alleged infringing work simply to replicate or use items of information, facts, ideas, theories, arguments, themes and so on derived from the original copyright work.

…

153. I appreciate that the Central Theme and its elements particularised … are important to the Claimants. They are by-products of their years of research, discussion and speculation. Viewed objectively, however, in the context of the necessary and sufficient conditions for infringement, they are not 'a substantial part' of HBHG. They are not substantial *in the copyright sense*, any more than a fact or theory that took a lifetime to establish, or a discovery that cost a fortune to make.

154. The position is that the individual elements of the Central Theme Points distilled from HBHG … are not of a sufficiently developed character to constitute a substantial part of HBHG. In the words of the judge they are 'too generalised' to be a substantial part of HBHG. They are an assortment of items of historical fact and information, virtual history, events, incidents, theories, arguments and propositions. They do not contain detailed similarities of language or 'architectural' similarities in the detailed treatment or development of the collection or arrangement of incidents, situations, characters and narrative, such as is normally found in cases of infringement of literary or dramatic copyright. The 11 aspects of the Central Theme in DVC are differently expressed, collected, selected, arranged and narrated.

155. Of course, it takes time, effort and skill to conduct historical research, to collect materials for a book, to decide what facts are established by the evidence and to formulate arguments, theories, hypotheses, propositions and conclusions. It does not, however, follow, as suggested in the Claimants' submissions, that the use of items of information, fact and so on derived from the assembled material is, in itself, 'a substantial part' of HBHG simply because it has taken time skill and effort to carry out the necessary research.

156. The literary copyright exists in HBHG by reason of the skill and labour expended by the Claimants in the original composition and production of it and the original manner or form of expression of the results of their research. Original expression includes not only the language in which the work is composed but also the original selection, arrangement and compilation of the raw research material. It does not, however, extend to clothing information, facts, ideas, theories and themes with exclusive property rights, so as to enable the Claimants to monopolise historical research or knowledge and prevent the legitimate use of historical and biographical material, theories propounded, general arguments deployed, or general hypotheses suggested (whether they are sound or not) or general themes written about.

COMPARATIVE LAW

157. The reported cases in which infringement claims have succeeded in relation to historical works or semi-historical works do not assist the Claimants' case. They are decisions by experienced Chancery judges at first instance correctly applying well established general principles to the particular facts of the case. For example in *Ravenscroft v Herbert* [1980] RPC 193 Brightman J found that there was copying of a substantial part of a work of non-fiction (*The Spear of Destiny*) in the form of a novel. To an appreciable extent they were competing works. The Defendant's novel was alleged to contain as many as 50 instances of deliberate language copying, as well as copying of the same historical characters, historical incidents and interpretation of the significance of historical events.

158. *Harman Pictures NV v Osborne* [1967] 2 All ER 324, [1967] 1 WLR 723 is another well known example of a case in which the author of a historical work (*The Reason Why*) obtained an interlocutory injunction in a copyright claim against the writer of a film script, which had much in common with the original copyright work in its selection of incidents and quotations supplemented by some alterations and additions attributed to other sources. Goff J found 'many similarities of detail' in John Osborne's film script (p 735) and he was impressed by 'the marked similarity of the choice of incidents ... and by the juxtaposition of ideas' for which there was a lack of explanation on the Defendant's side.

159. In my judgment, the judge rightly held that the Claimants have not established that a substantial part of HBHG has been copied, either as to the original composition and expression of the work or as to the particular collection, selection and arrangement of material and its treatment in HBHG.

[Both Lloyd and Rix LJJ agred that the appeal should be dismissed.]

As noted above, a key consideration in determining the quality of what has been copied is the originality of what the defendant has copied. As we saw in Chapter 3, the concept of originality in copyright has undergone an intense period of development since the decision of the High Court in *IceTV Pty Ltd v Nine Network Australia Pty Ltd* [2009] HCA 14; (2009) 239 CLR 458. In that case, the High Court emphasised that the originality of a work arises from the author's intellectual effort or intellectual contribution, directed to the expression in the copyright-protected work. This has implications for determining what will constitute a substantial part of a compilation, as the application of this reasoning to the facts in *IceTV* itself shows.

CASE EXTRACT: CURRENT LAW

CURRENT LAW

IceTV Pty Ltd v Nine Network Australia Pty Ltd

[2009] HCA 14; (2009) 239 CLR 458
High Court of Australia

[The facts of the case are set out in Chapter 2, p 41. The Full Federal Court had held that that the pieces of information copied by IceTV constituted a substantial part of Nine's Weekly Schedule. In quantitative terms, numerous discrete pieces of information were copied: *Nine Network Australia Pty v*

IceTV Pty Ltd [2008] FCAFC 71; (2008) 168 FCR 14 at [113]. But the key consideration was the quality of the parts copied, as to which the Full Federal Court had held, at [111]–[115]:

> 111. Ice, to the extent it reproduced time and title information from the Weekly Schedules, appropriated the skill and labour used by Nine to create the Weekly Schedules. … [T]he skill and labour in selecting and arranging programming should not be regarded as separate and discrete from the extremely modest skill and labour involved in setting down on paper the programs already selected and presenting them in the form of the Weekly Schedules. The skill and labour expended by Nine were part of a single process leading to the creation of the copyright work as the written record of Nine's programming decisions and the associated program information. …
>
> …
>
> 115. When the quality of the material taken by Ice is considered, the substantiality of the part taken becomes even clearer. Ice took … precisely the pieces of information that reflected the exercise of skill and labour by Nine in determining the program for a particular day or other period … Ice's use of material derived from the time and title information … appropriated the most creative elements of the skill and labour utilised by Nine in creating the Weekly Schedules.]

French CJ, Crennan and Kiefel JJ (some footnotes omitted): 41. The Weekly Schedule (and the Nine Database) as a whole involves orderly arrangement of its various elements and the evidence showed choices were made about what programmes were included or excluded. As a whole, it is an original (ie not copied) collocation of both information and creative material.

42. However, the expression of the time and title information, in respect of each programme, is not a form of expression which requires particular mental effort or exertion. The way in which the information can be conveyed is very limited. Expressing a title of a programme to be broadcast merely requires knowledge of the title, generally bestowed by the producer of the programme rather than by a broadcaster of it. Expressing the time at which a programme is broadcast, for public consumption, can only practically be done in words or figures relating to a 12 or 24-hour time cycle for a day. The authors of the Weekly Schedule (or the Nine Database) had little, if any, choice in the particular form of expression adopted, as that expression was essentially dictated by the nature of the information. That expression lacks the requisite originality (in the sense explained) for the part to constitute a substantial part.

43. Counsel for Nine sought to place importance upon the reproduction not only of time and title information in respect of each programme, but also of the chronological arrangement of the time and title information for various programmes. Whether a selection or arrangement of elements constitutes a substantial part of a work depends on the degree of originality of that selection or arrangement. In this case, a chronological arrangement of times at which programmes will be broadcast is obvious and prosaic, and plainly lacks the requisite originality.

44. These considerations lead to the conclusion that the part of the Weekly Schedule (or the Nine Database) alleged to have been reproduced was not a substantial part. Something must be said, then, of the relevance of 'skill and labour' to this question and how it may lead to error.

…

49. In the context of infringement, in particular the determination of whether a part reproduced is a 'substantial part', a matter often referred to is whether there has been an 'appropriation' of the author's skill and labour. As already noted, both the primary judge and the Full Court adopted that approach in

CURRENT LAW

this case. However, it is always necessary to focus on the nature of the skill and labour, and in particular to ask whether it is directed to the originality of the particular form of expression.

...

52. Rewarding skill and labour in respect of compilations without any real consideration of the productive effort directed to coming up with a particular form of expression of information can lead to error. The error is of a kind which might enable copyright law to be employed to achieve anti-competitive behaviour of a sort not contemplated by the balance struck in the Act between the rights of authors and the entitlements of the reading public. The Act mandates an inquiry into the substantiality of the part of the work which is reproduced. A critical question is the degree of originality of the particular form of expression of the part. Consideration of the skill and labour expended by the author of a work may assist in addressing that question: that the creation of a work required skill and labour may indicate that the particular form of expression adopted was highly original. However, focussing on the 'appropriation' of the author's skill and labour must not be allowed to distract from the inquiry mandated by the Act. To put aside the particular form of expression can cause difficulties, as evidenced by *Desktop Marketing*.

53. It is not seriously in dispute that skill and labour was expended on producing the Weekly Schedules (and the Nine Database). The evidence disclosed considerable skill and labour involved in programming decisions. There was a contest about whether it mattered if some of the skill and labour expended was directed to business considerations. Plainly, the skill and labour was highly relevant to matters such as advertising revenue. It is not difficult to understand that questions of the timing of particular broadcasts are crucial for advertising revenues. The fact that business considerations inform the decision to adopt a particular form of expression will not necessarily detract from the originality of that form of expression.

54. However, the critical question is whether skill and labour was directed to the particular form of expression of the time and title information, including its chronological arrangement. The skill and labour devoted by Nine's employees to programming decisions was not directed to the originality of the particular form of expression of the time and title information. The level of skill and labour required to express the time and title information was minimal. That is not surprising, given that, as explained above, the particular form of expression of the time and title information is essentially dictated by the nature of that information.

...

56. Any reproduction of the time and title information in the IceGuide was not a reproduction of a substantial part of any of the Weekly Schedules (or the Nine Database).

Another kind of case where courts must assess whether a substantial part has been taken by reference to the idea/expression dichotomy, and consider arguments about which features are 'commonplace', relates to project home architecture. These homes are commonly distinguished by reference to general design concepts. It is often argued that similarities in the expression of the particular design concepts are the result of external demands and factors including block sizes, economic efficiencies in service provision, and planning laws and related regulations. Defendants also rely on the idea/expression dichotomy: see for example *Metricon Homes Pty Ltd v Barrett Property Group Pty Ltd* [2008] FCAFC 46; (2008) 248 ALR 364. Nevertheless, unless the defendant provides convincing evidence of independent creation, such as through a series of sketches showing internal development of their plan, the fact of similarities often leads to findings of infringement. For a successful defence, see *Inform Designs and Construction Pty Ltd v Boutique Homes Melbourne Pty Ltd* [2008] FCA 912; (2008) 77 IPR 523.

SUBJECT MATTER OTHER THAN WORKS

Australian courts considering infringement of Part III works have emphasised that in determining the quality of a part copied for the purposes of assessing whether it constitutes a 'substantial part' of a copyright work, the critical consideration is the originality of the part copied. This raises an interesting question as to how Part IV subject matter should be treated, since originality is not a precondition of protection: should quantity be dominant in consideration of infringement for Part IV, or should some analogous principle to originality be developed? The High Court in *Network Ten Pty Ltd v TCN Channel Nine Pty Ltd* [2004] HCA 14; (2004) 218 CLR 273 stated, in *obiter dicta*, that quality as well as quantity should be considered. As to how 'quality' should be assessed, Gummow ACJ, McHugh and Hayne JJ at [47] stated only that quality 'could include the potency of particular images or sounds, or both, in a broadcast'. The case was then remitted to the Full Federal Court to determine whether Ten had taken a substantial part of each of Nine's 'broadcast programs'. Both the High Court's *obiter dicta*, and the application of the 'substantial part' test for Part IV subject matter in the extract from *TCN Channel Nine Pty Ltd v Network Ten Pty Ltd (No 2)* [2005] FCAFC 53; (2005) 145 FCR 35 below, sit uneasily with the otherwise technologically specific and restricted approach to Part IV subject matter. Note also that aspects of the Full Federal Court's reasoning may need to be qualified in light of the High Court decision in *IceTV Pty Ltd v Nine Network Australia Pty Ltd* [2009] HCA 14; (2009) 239 CLR 458 particularly Gummow J et al's comments at [131] that the Act does not recognise a general doctrine of misappropriation and at [155]–[156] and [159]–[161] on the problems with looking to the 'interest' protected in the grant of copyright in undertaking the substantial part enquiry.

CURRENT LAW

CASE EXTRACT: CURRENT LAW

TCN Channel Nine Pty Ltd v Network Ten Pty Ltd (No 2)

[2005] FCAFC 53; (2005) 145 FCR 35
Federal Court of Australia, Full Court

[The facts are outlined in the extract from the High Court's decision in *Network Ten Pty Ltd v TCN Channel Nine Pty Ltd* [2004] HCA 14; (2004) 218 CLR 273 set out in Chapter 4, p 145. The High Court determined that the interest to be protected in a broadcast is the cost and skill in assembling or preparing and transmitting the program to the public. Determination of whether each of the segments from *The Panel* was a substantial part of the source television broadcast was remitted to the Full Federal Court.]

Hely J:

SUBSTANTIALITY

46. The term 'substantial' is imprecise and ambiguous. It takes its meaning from the context. Ten submits that in the present context, 'substantial' is a reference to taking 'the substance of' the source television broadcast. That submission pays insufficient regard to the statutory language, which is expressed in

terms of 'a substantial part' of a television broadcast, which is a different thing. There may be many parts of a television broadcast which qualify as a substantial part of that broadcast.

47. Both parties accepted that in determining whether a substantial part of a copyright work or other subject matter is taken, the relevant comparison is between the part taken and the copyright work or subject matter: see *Autodesk Inc v Dyson (No 2)* (1993) 176 CLR 300 ('*Autodesk (No 2)*') at 305. The issue is not the importance of the part taken to the defendant's product: *Designers Guild Ltd v Russell Williams (Textiles) Ltd* [2001] 1 All ER 700 at 709 …

…

49. The High Court has also confirmed that an approach to the assessment of substantiality in the case of Part IV subject matter involves taking into account questions of quality (which could include the potency of particular images or sounds, or both, in a broadcast) as well as the quantity of the material taken: *Network Ten Pty Ltd v TCN Channel Nine Pty Ltd* [[2004] HCA 14; (2004) 218 CLR 273] at [47] (McHugh ACJ, Gummow and Hayne JJ). A small portion in quantitative terms may constitute a substantial part having regard to its materiality in relation to the work as a whole: [2004] HCA 14 at [100] (Kirby J) …

…

51. Whether the part taken is a substantial part of the source broadcast thus involves an assessment of the importance of the part taken to the source broadcast. In some cases the issue has been expressed in terms of whether what is taken is an 'essential' or 'material' part of the total work: *Autodesk (No 2)* at 305; *Nationwide News Pty Ltd v Copyright Agency Ltd* (1996) 65 FCR 399 ('*Nationwide News*') at 418. In other cases the issue has been expressed in terms of whether the part taken is recognisable as part of the original work (see *Hawkes & Son (London) Ltd v Paramount Film Services Ltd* [1934] Ch 593 at 604), or distinctive of it (see *Nationwide News* at 420). In *The Modern Law of Copyright* (H Laddie, P Prescott et al, 3rd ed, Butterworths, London, 2000 at [7.59]) the matter is put in the context of substantial part and films, as follows:

> … The Act does not attempt to define what it means by a 'substantial part', so Parliament must be taken to have left it to the courts to apply a commonsense value judgment, having regard to the facts of each individual case. An approach which is frequently useful for the traditional subjects of copyright law (ie original literary, dramatic, musical and artistic works) is to enquire whether the aspect of the work which has been taken required a substantial amount of skill and labour for its origination. It is submitted that this approach is not satisfactory in the case of films. Films can be made which are copyright even though no skill and labour at all were expended in their making: they do not have to be 'original'. *Nor would it be correct to approach the question on the basis of some crude mathematical apportionment: the Act says 'a substantial part' not 'a substantial percentage'. It is suggested that a better approach is to enquire whether the taking amounts to something real and consequential, as opposed to that which is trifling or insignificant.* (emphasis added)

…

53. Broadcast copyright protects the sounds and images embodied in a television broadcast or programme. It protects the cost to, and the skill of, broadcasters in transmitting their programmes: [2004] HCA 14 at [29]. There is no requirement for originality in the case of Part IV copyright, a fact which leads Ten to submit that it is wrong to look to the originality of content as a touchstone for assessing substantiality in relation to Part IV subject matter. Nine's focus on whether the Panel

Segments were 'distinctive' of, or were 'recognisable' as having come from Nine's broadcasts is, in Ten's submission, to do just that.

54. In the case of Part IV copyright, 'originality' is not a touchstone for the assessment of substantiality as originality forms no part of the identification of the interest protected by the copyright. For that reason, the notion that reproduction of non-original matter will not ordinarily involve a reproduction of a substantial part of a copyright work can have no application in the case of Part IV copyright. Nonetheless, the High Court's observation that the element of 'quality' bears on the substantiality question, and may involve consideration of the 'potency of particular images or sounds, or both', invites an assessment of the relative significance in terms of story, impact and theme conveyed by the taken sounds and images relative to the source broadcast as a whole. Whether the part taken represents one of the highlights of the source broadcast has a bearing on that assessment as does whether the Panel Segments were 'distinctive of' or were 'recognisable' as having come from Nine's broadcast. Ten's submission to the contrary should be rejected ...

...

59. In the present case, Ten submitted that the evaluation of what constitutes a material part of a television broadcast is a classic jury question. One takes into account all the circumstances. Accepting that to be so, the fact that the Panel Segments were used by Ten for the purpose of satire or light entertainment strikes me, with respect, as throwing little, if any, light on whether the parts taken were a substantial part of the source broadcasts.

60. No doubt Ten used the Panel [S]egments because it considered that the Panel Segments would contribute to Ten's programme, even though the contribution made to that programme may be quite different from the contribution made by the Panel Segments to the source broadcast. But that says little, if anything, about whether those segments are a material part of the source broadcast.

...

Finkelstein J: 11. There will be cases where a visual or oral comparison will not enable the tribunal to decide whether the part taken is indeed substantial. This is especially so when the amount copied is small. There will be an infringement if the defendant has reproduced something that is of aesthetic significance. Sometimes, however, '[w]hen it comes down to a question of quantity [the answer] must be very vague': *Bramwell v Halcomb* (1836) 40 ER 1110 at 1110–1111 per Lord Cottenham LC. In a doubtful case other factors must be considered ...

...

15. The effect of the authorities seems to be this. The test of substantiality—that is the notion of quality—is not confined to an examination of the intrinsic elements of the plaintiff's work. The test of substantiality may involve a broader enquiry, an enquiry which encompasses the context of the taking. The key ideas here are first that copyright is granted to protect the owner's financial interest in his property. The second idea links financial harm to the rationale of unfair use or the injurious appropriation of the plaintiff's skill and labour. The level of financial harm may indicate that the use of that labour is unfair. In *Blackie & Sons Ltd v The Lothian Book Publishing Co Pty Ltd* (1921) 29 CLR 396 Starke J (at 402–403) said that the question was '[whether] the defendant, to use the words of the statute, reproduced a substantial part of the plaintiff's book ... or ... has an unfair or undue use been made of the work protected by copyright?' One of the factors upon which Starke J relied to conclude

(at 403) that the defendant '[appropriated] a substantial and valuable portion' of the plaintiff's work was that the defendant's books were intended to be, and were, in direct competition with the plaintiff's. The third idea draws on the paradigm of piracy. The 'clear case' of copyright infringement is where the defendant sells a cheaper version of the plaintiff's work, causing the plaintiff financial harm. The fourth idea is the concept of 'value', which denotes more fully than the word 'quality' a financial dimension as well as the notion of originality or artistic merit.

16. Evidence of the harm caused by the defendant's conduct is potentially relevant in a number of ways. First, and most importantly, it might indicate that the financial interest protected by copyright has been interfered with. Its absence might indicate the contrary. Second, it may indicate that the extent of the taking has been unfair, for example when it causes the plaintiff injury by reducing his profits. Third, it may be evidence of a straightforward piracy, being an intentional 'stealing' for profit of the author's skill or labour. Last, it might highlight that the part taken is important, vital or material in the sense that the part gives the work its financial value. As Lord Herschell LC said in *Leslie v J Young & Sons* [1894] AC 335 at 342: '[i]t may be the very thing that the presence or absence of which would most largely promote or retard the sale of the work.'

...

20. A number of things must be borne in mind when applying the traditional test to broadcast copyright. The first is that the exclusive right of the owner of a television broadcast is, broadly speaking, to make a cinematograph film of the broadcast, to re-broadcast it or to communicate (that is make available online or to electronically transmit) the broadcast to the public otherwise than by broadcasting it: see *Copyright Act*, s 87 and the definition of 'communicate' in s 10. Thus there will only be an infringement if the actual broadcast or a substantial part of the broadcast is faithfully copied or rebroadcast. It will not suffice to show that the defendant has broadcast a colourable copy of the plaintiff's work as it would in the case of, say, artistic copyright. The second thing to be borne in mind is that 'the quality of what is taken must be assessed by reference to the interest protected by the copyright': *Nationwide News Pty Ltd v Copyright Agency Ltd* (1996) 65 FCR 399, 418 per Sackville J. The High Court (at [70]) identified this interest as 'the cost and skill in assembling or preparing and transmitting programmes to the public'. The interest covers the different kinds of programmes that are broadcast. They range from live broadcasts (such as news and sports programmes) to programmes recorded in the studio and the transmission of cinematographic film, such as a motion pictures or a television series ...

[His Honour discussed the test applied at first instance.]

27. It is now clear that the starting point for any enquiry into substantiality is not, as the judge would have it, 'primarily quantitative'. Nor is the principal enquiry whether harm has been caused to the plaintiff's commercial interests. The first thing that must be done is to look at the part taken, compare it with the copyright work and ask whether it is possible to conclude from that comparison whether that part is a 'substantial part' of the plaintiff's programme. The question will often boil down to one of the following (dependent on the type of programme): Does what has been taken amount to 'essentially the heart' of the copyrighted work?: *New Era Publications International v Carol Publishing Group* 904 F 2d 152, 158 (2d Cir, 1987). Is what has been taken 'the essential part of the copyright work?': *Cable/Home Communications Corporation v Network Productions, Inc* 902 F 2d 829, 844

(11th Cir, 1990). Is what has been taken 'at least an important ingredient' of the copyright work?: *Salinger v Random House* 881 F 2d 90, 99 (2d Cir, 1987). Have the best scenes been taken from the programme?: *Hi-Tech Video Productions Inc v Capitol Cities/ABC* 804 F Supp 950, 956 (WD Mich, 1992). Are the excerpts 'highlights' from the programme?: *New Boston Television Inc v Entertainment Sports Programming Network Inc* 215 USPQ 755, 757 (D Mass, 1981). Are the excerpts central to the programme in which it appeared?: *Roy Expert Company Establishment of Vaduz Liechtenstein, Black Inc v Columbia Broadcasting System Inc* 503 F Supp 1137, 1145 (2d Cir, 1980). Does the portion used 'constitute the 'heart'—the most valuable and pertinent portion—of the copyright material?': *Los Angeles News Service v CBS Broadcasting Inc* 305 F 3d 924, 940 (9th Cir, 2002).

28. If what has been taken does not meet any of those descriptions that will often be the end of the enquiry. There will, however, be borderline cases where an enquiry based on a visual comparison will not yield a result. Take as an example a programme that has no 'core' or 'heart'. Here I have in mind two cinematograph films by the 1960s icon Andy Warhol. The films are 'Sleep' and 'Empire', films that few people have seen. 'Sleep' has been described as 'one of the most famous of unseen films': F Camper, 'The Lover's Gaze', *Chicago Reader Movie Review*, section 1, 28 April, 2000. It is a six-hour (some say longer) film taken by a stationary 16 mm camera of a man sleeping. The reviewer Jonas Mekas writing in the *Village Voice* (September, 1963) queried whether the film was: 'An exercise in hypnosis? Test of patience? A Zen joke?' 'Empire' is a single shot from late dusk to early morning of the Empire State Building taken from the 44th floor of the Time-Life Building. Mr Koch described 'Empire' as 'the most profoundly mute motion picture ever filmed': S Koch, Stargazer: *Andy Warhol's World and His Films* (2nd ed, M Boyars, New York, 1985) at 60. The film has no plot and only two things happen. The sun moves through the sky and, at dusk, floodlights are turned on to illuminate the upper floors of the Empire State Building. If part of 'Sleep' or 'Empire' is taken, no amount of visual comparison would enable a tribunal to determine whether that part is a substantial part of the film. It would be necessary to consider factors such as the plaintiff's financial interest as well as the defendant's purpose to resolve the issue.

THE EXCLUSIVE RIGHTS OF THE COPYRIGHT OWNER
EXCLUSIVE RIGHTS IN WORKS

Copyright provides for specific exclusive rights. The rights that attach to works are set out in s 31(1). Owners of copyright in literary, dramatic and musical works are granted the following exclusive rights under s 31(1)(a):

- to reproduce the work in material form;
- to publish the work;
- to perform the work in public;
- to communicate the work to the public; and
- to make an adaptation of the work, and to do any of the above acts in relation to an adaptation.

They are also granted certain specific rights to make commercial rental arrangements for the work: s 31(1)(c)–(d).

The rights of owners of copyright in artistic works are set out in s 31(1)(b): they do not include an exclusive right to perform (or more relevantly, display) an artistic work in public, nor an adaptation or rental right.

The next several sections focus on the exclusive rights in relation to works under Part III of the Act. The rights in subject matter other than works are contained in ss 85–88. These Pt IV rights differ from the Part III rights, and are discussed separately afterwards.

Particular acts of the defendant may infringe one right or multiple rights, depending upon the facts. Note that the focus is on the *acts*: copyright infringement is a matter of strict liability requiring no proof of intention or knowledge.

REPRODUCE THE WORK IN MATERIAL FORM

The oldest and still a core right of copyright is the right to reproduce the work in material form, set out in s 31(1)(a)(i) and (b)(i). This covers obvious acts—such as photocopying a book or sheet music, making copies of sound recordings which involves reproduction of embodied musical works, printing copies of a script, etc.—but it extends well beyond such acts. Section 21(3) of the *Copyright Act*, for example, provides that an artistic work can be reproduced transdimensionally; that is, a three-dimensional sculpture can reproduce a sketch, and vice versa. Further, s 21(1) states that:

> a literary, dramatic or musical work shall be deemed to have been reproduced in a material form if a sound recording or cinematograph film is made of the work, and any record embodying such a recording and any copy of such a film shall be deemed to be a reproduction of the work.

Thus for example every copy of a film is also likely to embody reproductions of underlying literary, dramatic and, if there is a sound track, musical works. The terms 'record' and 'copy' (in relation to a film) used in s 21(1) are both broadly defined in s 10(1) so as to cover existing and future items in which copyright works can be embodied, whether physical discs or portable digital memory such as USB keys, or the digital memory of a computer or server.

Digital copies in computer memory are comprehensively covered. As discussed in Chapter 3, s 10(1) of the Act defines 'material form' expansively, to include both long-term and temporary reproductions in digital memory:

> *material form*, in relation to a work ... includes any form (whether visible or not) of storage of the work ... (whether or not the work ... can be reproduced).

Prior to the *US Free Trade Agreement Implementation Act 2004* (Cth), the definition of 'material form' required that a work be able to be reproduced from storage. This was interpreted in *Australian Video Retailers Association Ltd v Warner Home Video Pty Ltd* [2001] FCA 1719; (2001) 114 FCR 324. In that case Emmett J found that when a DVD was played, computer programs were copied from the DVD into the temporary memory of the DVD player or computer. These computer programs, however, were not shown on screen. Nor could they be extracted, or reproduced, from the memory of the DVD player or computer without specialised equipment. Thus the computer programs had been reproduced, but not *in material form* as defined by the Act at that time. The *Australia–US Free Trade Agreement* (AUSFTA) (2004) required that Australia confer an exclusive right to control 'all reproductions, in any manner or form, permanent or temporary (including temporary storage in material form)' (Art 17.4.1). The Australian government took the view that Australian law did not comply with this requirement, and inserted the present definition of material form, clearly overturning *Warner*. The result is a very expansive definition of material form covering any and all digital copies.

Crucially, and as we have already seen in the extracts from the *Jaws* case (above, p 208) and *Baigent v Random House Group Ltd* [2007] EWCA Civ 247; [2007] FSR 24 (above, p 209), reproduction does not require direct 'identity' between works: it includes both literal and non-literal copies.

PUBLISH THE WORK

Owners of copyright in works have the exclusive right to publish the work: s 31(1)(a)(ii) and (b)(ii). As discussed in Chapter 2, the concept of 'publication' is important in determining the subsistence and duration of copyright, and s 29 provides a deeming provision for determining when a work has been published for those purposes. An important question considered in *Avel Pty Ltd v Multicoin Amusements Pty Ltd* (1990) 171 CLR 88 (extracted below) was whether s 29 was also relevant to interpreting the right to publish the work in s 31.

CURRENT LAW

CASE EXTRACT: CURRENT LAW

Avel Pty Ltd v Multicoin Amusements Pty Ltd

(1990) 171 CLR 88
High Court of Australia

[Avel had been appointed exclusive distributor of pinball machines produced by a US manufacturer. Multicoin ordered a consignment of secondhand pinball machines. The case is complicated, but relevantly for present purposes Avel claimed that importation of secondhand machines would involve exercise of the exclusive right to publish artistic works (in the form of the various decorations on the pinball machines), an argument that depended on the Court accepting that every sale of a pinball machine was an exercise of the right to publish.]

Mason CJ, Deane and Gaudron JJ (at 93): The provision of s 29(1)(a) defining when a work 'shall be deemed *to have been published*' (emphasis added) for the purposes of the Act does not operate as a definition of what is encompassed by the words 'to publish' for the purposes of s 31(1). The words 'to publish' in s 31(1) should be read as meaning to make public that which has not previously been made public in the copyright territory. We are, of course, conscious of the fact that there is an element of artificiality involved in a literalistic confinement of s 29(1)(a) to defining when a work 'has been published' (eg for the purposes of determining the subsistence of copyright: see s 32) as distinct from what constitutes the act of publishing (eg for infringement purposes: see s 31). That confinement of s 29(1)(a) is, however, dictated by the content of other provisions of the Act (see, in particular, ss 36, 37 and 38), by general concepts of copyright law and by considerations of policy (cf *Infabrics Ltd v Jaytex Ltd* [1982] AC 1 at 15–17, 22–5; Lahore, *Copyright Law*, pp 3563–4; but note Ricketson, *The Law of Intellectual Property*, 1984, pp 221–2).

Dawson J (at 101–103): The meaning of the word 'publish' in the *Copyright Act* is far from clear. It is not defined, although s 29 in part provides:

(1) Subject to this section, for the purposes of this Act:

    (a) a literary, dramatic, musical or artistic work, or an edition of such a work, shall be deemed to have been published if, but only if, reproductions of the work or edition have been supplied (whether by sale or otherwise) to the public.

Avel relies upon s 29(1)(a) and says that within the meaning of the Act, and in particular s 31, 'publish' amounts to the same thing as 'supply to the public'. ...

However, s 29(1)(a) is not a definition. By deeming a work to have been published if, but only if, reproductions have been supplied to the public, the provision may afford assistance in determining whether or not publication has taken place at a particular point in time. For example, the provision may be of assistance in determining when a work was published for the purpose of determining the subsistence of copyright or calculating the duration of copyright in the work: see ss 32(2), 33. But to treat s 29(1)(a) as supplying the meaning of the word 'publish' throughout the Act would be to produce a result that was obviously not intended ...

If 'to publish' means, as it would if s 29(1)(a) were to be regarded as a definition, 'to supply to the public', every act of supply (including sale) of a work in which copyright subsists, without the consent of the owner of the copyright, would, without any knowledge on the part of the supplier, constitute an infringement of copyright under s 36. The purchaser of an article subject to copyright would be severely curtailed in any subsequent dealings with the article if each dealing constituted a publication: see *Interstate Parcel Express Co Pty Ltd v Time-Life International (Nederlands) BV* (1977) 138 CLR 534 at 553. Moreover, ss 37 and 38—the sections dealing with indirect infringement—would have little or no work to do, because the acts which they contemplate by and large involve the supply of the article in question to the public. Thus a person otherwise falling within the terms of s 37 or s 38 would be deprived of the defence of lack of knowledge because his act would also constitute direct infringement under s 36, for which no knowledge is required.

PERFORM THE WORK IN PUBLIC

Owners of copyright in literary, dramatic and musical works (but not artistic works) have the exclusive right to perform the work in public: s 31(1)(a)(iii). 'Performance' is defined in s 27(1) to include 'any mode of visual or aural presentation, whether the presentation is by the use of reception equipment, by exhibition of a cinematograph film, by the use of a record or by any other means': thus playing a radio in public will involve performance of any musical works. Subsections 27(2) and (3) draw a distinction between communications (considered next below) and performances. Where visual images or sounds are displayed or emitted by reception equipment (e.g. by turning on a radio), it is the person operating the equipment (i.e. the person turning on the radio), not the broadcaster, who exercises the right to perform the work in public.

Only performances *in public* fall within the exclusive right: performances in private do not require permission of the copyright owner. The Act also provides that certain kinds of performances will not require a licence: including reciting an extract of reasonable length from a published literary or dramatic work (s 45), performances at premises where persons reside or sleep (s 46) and performances in class at educational institutions (s 28). How the line is drawn between public and private performances is the subject of consideration in the next two case extracts.

CASE EXTRACT: CURRENT LAW

Australasian Performing Right Association Ltd v Tolbush Pty Ltd

[1986] 2 Qd R 146
Supreme Court of Queensland

[The defendants played radios and tapes in the sales premises of 'Super Cheap Car Accessories & Spare Parts' to demonstrate their sound equipment. The plaintiff, the Australasian Performing Right Association (APRA), held the performing rights for musical works heard played on the premises. When requested by the plaintiff, the defendants failed to acquire a licence for the public performance of such works.]

de Jersey J (at 149--150): The defendant's major submission was that by having its radio sets, on display for sale in its shops, play songs copyright in which vested in the plaintiff, the first defendant could not be said to 'perform' the songs (in public). To perform the works in public would amount to infringement of copyright: cf s 31(1)(a)(iii). Counsel for the defendants did not argue that those shops were not public places. The evidence was that the public had free access to them, and that some members of the public (although few) were within them at the times of the alleged offences. I have little hesitation concluding, as a matter of fact, that any performance has taken place 'in public'. In my view, the character of the audience is the decisive factor. Consistently with the decision in *Performing Right Society Ltd v Harlequin Record Shops Ltd* [1979] 1 WLR 851, 'a performance given to an audience consisting of the persons present in a shop which the public at large were permitted, indeed encouraged, to enter without payment or invitation with a view to increasing the shop owner's profit, could only be described as a performance in public' (cf *Copinger and Skone James on Copyright*, 12th ed, Sweet & Maxwell, para 573).

The term 'perform' is not comprehensively defined in the Act. Section 27(1) does, however, say that a reference to performance should be read as including a reference to 'any mode of ... aural presentation, whether the presentation is by the operation of wireless telegraphy apparatus ... or by any other means'. Now read literally, that would of course be amply wide to include what has occurred here. The decision of the Court of Appeal in *Performing Right Society Ltd v Hammond's Bradford Brewery Co* [1934] 1 Ch 121 is strong authority—if authority be needed—that there has here been a performance within s 27(1), taken alone, in that the first defendant has utilized a 'mode of ... aural presentation'.

CASE EXTRACT: CURRENT LAW

Australasian Performing Right Association Ltd v
Commonwealth Bank of Australia

(1992) 40 FCR 59
Federal Court of Australia

[APRA owned the performing right in a musical work which had been incorporated into an instructional video. The Commonwealth Bank played the video to 11 employees at one of its premises, outside operating hours and so at a time when members of the public could not enter the premises.]

Gummow J (at 74–75): The phrase in s 31(1)(a)(iii) of the 1968 Act is 'to perform the work in public' not before 'members of the public' or 'a public audience' or 'the general public'. Running through the authorities I have discussed is the notion that for the purposes of this performing right a performance will be 'in public' if it is not 'in private', and the perception of an antithesis between performances which are in public and those which are 'domestic' or 'private' in character. In determining whether a performance answers the latter description, the nature of the audience is important. In coming together to form the audience for the performance were the persons concerned bound together by a domestic or private tie or by an aspect of their public life? Their 'public life' would include their presence at their place of employment for the supply of a performance to assist the commercial purposes of their employer.

Looked at in that way, the reasoning in the authorities supports the proposition ... that if a performance occurs as an adjunct to a commercial activity the performance is likely to be regarded as public, indeed, ... 'almost certainly so'. When the facts of the present case are then considered against this background, the answer appears.

The judgments to which I have referred do not purport to expound the meaning of the statutory phrase by which the performing right is conferred, with a precision sufficient to point clearly to a result once the facts have been found in any given case. What the courts have been endeavouring to do is to give the statutory grant a reasonable construction in favour of the grantee, given the general considerations underpinning copyright law ...

In the present case, the audience was confined to membership of a class which excluded customers of the respondent and the general public, the numbers present were quite small in one sense, and no fee was paid by the audience. Nor, on the evidence, was the use of the musical work in the video of such a character as to diminish its interest to the audience (and value to the applicant) in the same sense as discussed in [*Harms (Incorporated) Ltd v Martans Club Ltd* [1927] 1 Ch 526] at 530, 538. There the work was from a musical play which had been produced in the United States but not in England and the activities of the defendant were apt to speed up the process whereby the freshness of the work would wear off and its value to the copyright owner would be diminished. ...

However, these matters, taken together, or in combination, are not decisive of the question of whether the performance in this case was in public, in the statutory sense. The occasion of the performance was the imparting of information by the employer to its employees and the musical work was used to facilitate that process. The audience was brought together by the commercial purposes of the respondent and their public lives as employees. These are the most significant facts which, consistently with the pre-1968 case law, support the characterisation of the performance of the work as one 'in public' within the meaning of s 31(1)(a)(iii) of the 1968 Act.

COMMUNICATE THE WORK TO THE PUBLIC

This right, found in s 31(1)(a)(iv) (literary, dramatic and musical works) and s 31(1)(b)(iii) (artistic works) was a key element of the *WIPO Copyright Treaty* (1996), which was designed to update copyright law in light of digital technology and the rise of the internet. In Australia it was introduced by the *Copyright Amendment (Digital Agenda) Act 2000* (Cth). It is a broad, technology-neutral right, and replaced two rights: the broadcast right (that had only applied to wireless broadcasts of works) and the right to transmit to subscribers of a diffusion service (that had applied to cable transmissions of works). 'Communicate' is defined in s 10(1):

> *communicate* means make available online or electronically transmit (whether over a path, or a combination of paths, provided by a material substance or otherwise) a work or other subject-matter, including a performance or live performance within the meaning of this Act.

Thus the new right encompasses both making available copyright material online and the transmission of such material, regardless of the combination of transmission paths and mechanisms utilised (e.g. copper wire, optic fibre and microwaves). As noted above, subss 27(2) and (3) draw a distinction between performance and communication, such that causing visual images to be seen or sounds to be heard in public by the operation of reception equipment (e.g. a radio or television) is a performance, while transmission of the images or sounds *to* the reception equipment (e.g. by broadcasting) is not a performance, but could be a communication.[5]

Only communications *to the public* fall within the copyright owner's exclusive rights. This phrase is defined in s 10(1) to mean 'to the public within or outside Australia', thus ensuring that communications originating in Australia but intended to be received only outside Australia involve an exercise of the exclusive right. The concept of 'the public' has developed through case law, including the performance cases extracted above.

An important decision relating to communication is the High Court decision in *Telstra Corporation Ltd v Australasian Performing Right Association Ltd* (1997) 191 CLR 140, below. Although the case was brought under the pre-2000 law, the Court's analysis of which transmissions were broadcast to the public remains relevant to the communication right.

CASE EXTRACT: PRECEDENT

Telstra Corporation Ltd v Australasian Performing Right Association Ltd

(1997) 191 CLR 140
High Court of Australia

[Telstra provided a 'music on hold' service: companies would subscribe so that their customers would hear music when placed on hold on their home (landline) telephones or on mobile telephones. One issue was whether, when music was transmitted by wireless means (in the then terminology of the Act, 'broadcast') to a customer using a mobile telephone, was this a transmission *to the public* within the scope of the broadcast right? The trial judge held that it was a private communication, on the basis that it was received by a single person, and the privacy of mobile telephone communications was protected by laws prohibiting interception.]

5　Compare the situation in the EU, where the Court of Justice has held that where the operator of a pub displays content to customers via a television screen and speakers, that operator is exercising the right of communication to the public: Joined Cases C-403/08 and C-429/08, *Football Association Premier League Ltd v QC Leisure and Karen Murphy v Media Protection Services Ltd* [2011] ECR I-9083 at [196].

PRECEDENT

Dawson and Gaudron JJ (at 154–157) (some footnotes omitted): The concept of the copyright owner's public was developed in a series of cases which, however, were concerned with the distinction between a performance in public and a private or domestic performance. Section 31(1)(a)(iii) speaks of the right to perform a work 'in public', but the definition of 'broadcast', with which we are concerned, speaks of transmission 'to the public'. If anything, the use of the words 'to the public' conveys a broader concept than the use of the words 'in public' since it makes clear that the place where the relevant communication occurs is irrelevant. That is to say, there can be a communication to individual members of the public in a private or domestic setting which is nevertheless a communication to the public. A broadcast by a radio station is just such a communication.

A performance or broadcast to the world at large is obviously a performance or broadcast to the public. But the situation becomes a little more difficult in the case of a performance or broadcast to a limited class of persons. In that context, in considering what constitutes a performance in public, the cases recognise that the relationship of the audience to the owner of the copyright is significant in reaching a conclusion. It is from this that the notion of the copyright owner's public developed. In *Duck v Bates* [(1884) 13 QBD 843 at 847] Brett MR said:

> the representation must be other than domestic and private. There must be present a sufficient part of the public who would go also to a performance licensed by the author as a commercial transaction; otherwise the place where the drama is represented will not be a 'place of dramatic entertainment' within the meaning of the statute.

In *Harms (Inc) Ltd and Chappell & Co v Martans Club Ltd* [[1927] 1 Ch 526 at 532] Lord Hanworth MR said:

> In dealing with the tests which have been applied in the cases, it appears to me that one must apply one's mind to see whether there has been any injury to the author. Did what took place interfere with his proprietary rights? As to that, profit is a very important element.

The idea of the copyright owner's public first explicitly emerged in *Jennings v Stephens* [[1936] Ch 469 at 485] where Greene LJ said:

> The question may therefore be usefully approached by inquiring whether or not the act complained of as an infringement would, if done by the owner of the copyright himself, have been an exercise by him of the statutory right conferred upon him. In other words, the expression 'in public' must be considered in relation to the owner of the copyright. If the audience considered in relation to the owner of the copyright may properly be described as the owner's 'public' or part of his 'public', then in performing the work before that audience he would in my opinion be exercising the statutory right conferred upon him; and any one who without his consent performed the work before that audience would be infringing his copyright.

The view expressed by Greene LJ in *Jennings v Stephens* was repeated by him in *Ernest Turner Electrical Instruments Ltd v Performing Right Society Ltd* [[1943] Ch 167 at 171, 172–3] and was adopted by Luxmoore and Goddard LJJ, the latter adding that the relevant question is: 'Is the audience one which the owner of the copyright could fairly consider a part of his public?' [at 175–6] In *Performing Right Society Ltd v Harlequin Record Shops Ltd* [[1979] 1 WLR 851 at 857] Browne-Wilkinson J also adopted the view of Greene LJ, saying that it is important to see whether the performance is given to an audience for performances to which the composer would expect to receive a fee, this being what he understood Greene LJ to have meant by the copyright owner's public.

In this country, the concept of the copyright owner's public was adopted in *APRA v Canterbury-Bankstown League Club Ltd* [[1964–5] NSWR 138] and *Rank Film Production Ltd v Colin S Dodds* [[1983] 2 NSWLR 553]. In the latter case the playing of films transmitted by a video cassette recorder to television sets in motel rooms was held to be 'in public'. Rath J observed at 559]:

> In the present case the motel guest in his room may easily be envisaged as part of the copyright owner's public. It is not the restricted size of the audience, or the privacy of the surroundings, that is decisive on the issue; the critical matter is the presentation of the movie by the occupier of the motel to his guest in that capacity.

The distinction between what is 'in public' and what is 'in private' is of little assistance in determining what is meant by transmission 'to the public'. The transmission may be to individuals in private circumstances but nevertheless be to the public. Moreover, the fact that at any one time the number of persons to whom the transmission is made may be small does not mean that the transmission is not to the public. Nor does it matter that those persons in a position to receive the transmission form only a part of the public, though it is no doubt necessary that the facility be available to those members of the public who choose to avail themselves of it. In *Rank Film Production Ltd v Colin S Dodds* the number of guests playing films in their rooms may not have been large, but the motel was open to the paying public. Similarly, those members of the public who choose to call a relevant number on their mobile telephone may be relatively small, but the facility is available to members of the public generally.

What is important is the nature of the audience constituted by those who receive music on hold. Lying behind the concept of the copyright owner's public is recognition of the fact that where a work is performed in a commercial setting, the occasion is unlikely to be private or domestic and the audience is more appropriately to be seen as a section of the public. It is in a commercial setting that an unauthorised performance will ordinarily be to the financial disadvantage of the owner's copyright in a work because it is in such a setting that the owner is entitled to expect payment for the work's authorised performance. In this case it is not so much the preparedness of the audience of music on hold to pay to hear the works were it not for their unauthorised performance that is significant. That simple analysis belongs to an age where communications were less technologically advanced and business and marketing techniques were less developed. Rather, it is the preparedness of those who wish the music on hold to be played to bear the cost of the arrangement which provides the key, for it reveals the commercial character of the broadcast and the commercial deprivation suffered by the copyright owner. Callers on hold constitute the copyright owner's public, not because they themselves would be prepared to pay to hear the music, but because others are prepared to bear the cost of them having that facility. For the performance of the music to that audience the copyright owner would expect to receive payment, even if not from the members of the audience. For these reasons, we conclude that when the works were transmitted to persons using mobile telephones when placed on hold, in each of the three situations revealed by the evidence, they were broadcast within the meaning of s 31(1)(a)(iv).

[McHugh J and Toohey J both concurred; Kirby J reached a similar conclusion for similar reasons.]

Many different entities will be involved in the uploading, transmission and downloading of material online, including the originator of a communication, internet service providers, and intermediaries such as online hosts, as well as the final recipient. Given the breadth of the definition of 'communicate', it was important for the legislation to make clear which of these many parties would be exercising the exclusive right. Section 22(6) states that 'a communication other than a broadcast is taken to have been made by the person responsible for determining the content of the communication'. Section 22(6A) clarifies that merely gaining access to online material, or receiving a transmission, does not make a person responsible for determining the content of the communication.

CASE EXTRACT: CURRENT LAW

Universal Music Australia Pty Ltd v Cooper

[2005] FCA 972; (2005) 150 FCR 1
Federal Court of Australia

[Mr Cooper created and operated a website known as MP3s4Free, which aggregated hyperlinks to MP3 music files available online. The site was configured so that users of the site could submit links which were posted automatically. Many links pointed to MP3 music files which infringed copyright owned by or exclusively licensed to Universal Music or the other applicants. Cooper's site was investigated by Mr Beckett and Mr Speck for Music Industry Piracy Investigations (MIPI), an enforcement body for the music industry. The chief case of the applicants was that Cooper authorised infringement by users and third party sites. The trial judge decided that Cooper had authorised infringement; this decision was appealed to the Full Federal Court. However, at first instance the applicants also argued that Cooper directly exercised the communication right. The trial judge's decision on this aspect of the case was not appealed, and is extracted here.]

Tamberlin J: 59. The applicants point to both of the limbs of the definition of 'communicate', namely, 'make available online' and 'electronically transmit the subject matter'.

60. It is further submitted by the applicants that the sound recordings have been made available by Cooper through the displaying of hyperlinks on the website, which, when activated by a user clicking an electronic mouse, produce the result that there is an automatic direct downloading of the sound recording to the user's computer from the remote computer of a third party on which the recording is stored. The evidence indicates that for present purposes there are no sound recordings located on the Cooper website. Therefore, there is not, and cannot, be any downloading or transmission of the recordings from the Cooper website.

61. The applicants point out that there is no statutory definition of the expression 'make available online'. They say that in the absence of such a definition, the words should be given their ordinary and natural meaning. The applicants refer to the discrete individual definitions of the words 'make', 'available' and 'online' in the *Macquarie Dictionary* to support their submission that Cooper, via his website, has made available the recordings to the public. I do not consider that such a literal analytical

approach, namely, a word-by-word dissection of the dictionary meaning of the expression 'make available online', is appropriate in this case. As Learned Hand J said in *Helvering v Gregory* (1934) 69 F 2d 809 at 810–11:

> ... the meaning of a sentence may be more than that of separate words, as a melody is more than the notes, and no degree of particularity can ever obviate recourse to the setting in which all appear, and which all collectively create.

62. The applicants also refer to extrinsic material, including a July 1997 discussion paper entitled *Copyright Reform in the Digital Agenda*, in support of their submission that Cooper has made the sound recordings available online. However, the references relied on by the applicants, in particular, the references at paras 1.12 and 4.14 to the legislature's intention that the 'making available' aspect of the communication right would cover 'interactive on-demand on-line' services and transmissions, do not advance their case. The three examples referred to by the applicants of situations in which it was envisaged by the legislature that the communication right would, or may be, infringed, namely, the uploading of a copy of a copyright work or other subject matter onto a publicly accessible internet site, the uploading of copyright material onto a server which is connected to the internet and the act of connecting a file server with a copyright work or other subject matter already on it to a public accessible network such as the internet, are of no assistance in the present case.

63. I am not satisfied that the Cooper website has 'made available' the music sound recordings within the meaning of that expression. It is the remote websites which make available the sound recordings and from which the digital music files are downloaded as a result of a request transmitted to the remote website.

64. As discussed above, the evidence indicates that no music sound recordings are actually stored on the Cooper website. The music sound recordings have initially been made available to the public by being placed on the remote websites. The evidence given by Mr Beckett was to the effect that the digital music files to which links were provided on the Cooper website were also available to users through the internet generally. That is, internet users can access the music sound recordings via an alternative route by directly accessing the remote websites, either by typing that website's URL address into the address bar on the user's internet browser or by using a search engine such as Google or Yahoo, rather than by visiting the Cooper website ...

65. The Cooper website contains hyperlinks to thousands of sound recordings which are located on remote websites and are downloaded directly from those websites to the computer of the internet user. When a visitor to the Cooper website clicked on a link on the website to an MP3 file hosted on another server, this caused the user's browser to send a 'GET' request to that server, resulting in the MP3 file being transmitted directly across the internet from the host server to the user's computer. The MP3 file does not pass through or via or across the Cooper website. The Cooper website facilitates the easier location and selection of digital music files and specification to the remote website, from which the user can then download the files by clicking on the hyperlink on the Cooper website. However, the downloaded subject matter is not transmitted or made available from the Cooper website and nor does the downloading take place through the Cooper website. While the request that triggers the downloading is made from the Cooper website, it is the remote website which makes the music file available and not the Cooper website.

CURRENT LAW

66. The applicants also submitted that Cooper, by establishing and operating the website, has 'electronically transmitted' the sound recordings. I am of the view that Cooper cannot be said to have transmitted the sound recordings. In my view, the actual transmission of the music sound recording begins with the commencement of the downloading of the recording from the remote website on which the recording is located to the end user. I accept that the electronic transmission of the sound recording to a user who triggers the hyperlink on the Cooper website is a communication to a member of the public from the remote website, however, it is not a transmission from the Cooper website.

67. Accordingly, for these reasons, I do not consider that Cooper has 'communicated' the sound recording to the public. That is, Cooper has not made the sound recording available to the public or electronically transmitted it to the public.

68. I do consider, however, that the remote websites have made available online and electronically transmitted the music sound recordings to the public.

THE COMMUNICATION RIGHT—PERSON RESPONSIBLE FOR THE COMMUNICATION

69. Section 22(6) was introduced by the *Copyright Amendment (Digital Agenda) Act 2000* (Cth) (the 2000 amendment) and is in the following terms:

> For the purposes of this Act, a communication other than a broadcast is taken to have been made by the person responsible for determining the content of the communication.

70. The November 1999 advisory report on the Copyright Amendment (Digital Agenda) Bill 1999 at para 6.13 states that this section was specifically intended to address 'the issue arising from the music on hold case', namely, *Telstra Corporation Ltd v Australasian Performing Right Association Ltd* (1997) 191 CLR 140. That is, the section was intended to protect ISPs, carriers and carriage service providers from liability for direct infringement of the communication right where they were not responsible for determining the content of the infringing material: see *Digital Agenda Copyright Amendments: Exposure Draft and Commentary* (February 1999), para 116; *Copyright Reform and the Digital Agenda, Discussion Paper* (July 1997), para 4.72; Revised Explanatory Memorandum to the Copyright Amendment (Digital Agenda) Bill 2000, para 41.

71. There is no statutory definition of the expression 'person responsible for determining the content'. Counsel for the applicants again resorts to the *Macquarie Dictionary*, which defines 'responsible for' to mean 'chargeable with being the author, cause or occasion of'. The word 'determine' is defined to mean 'to decide upon.' As discussed above, the approach of the applicants suffers from the difficulty that it is too literal and analytical and does not pay sufficient attention, in my view, to the collocation of the expressions used, as distinct from the individual words.

72. The applicants say that the focus of attention of s 22(6) of the Act is not on the person carrying out the technical processes involved in the communication but rather on the person bearing the responsibility for the content of the communication. They note, however, that the criteria for the court to take into account in determining responsibility for a communication are not set out in the Act.

73. The applicants point out that statements in the extrinsic materials which they rely upon, namely, the Revised Explanatory Memorandum to the Copyright Amendment (Digital Agenda) Bill 2000 (Cth) and the *Digital Agenda Copyright Amendments: Exposure Draft and Commentary* (February 1999), generally speak of 'the person' or 'a person' who is responsible for determining the content of a communication. They note that there is no specific discussion in the extrinsic material of a situation in which two or

more persons jointly determine the content of a communication. However, I accept the applicants' submission that there is no logical reason why more than one person could not be responsible for a communication and that it is open to read the reference to 'the person' in s 22(6) in the plural where the context indicates.

74. On the natural and ordinary meaning of the words used in s 22(6), in the context of the present dispute, I do not think it can be said that a person who is the proprietor, manager or operator of a website which provides hyperlinks to other websites on which the sound recordings are hosted *determines* the content of the communication. It is artificial in the extreme to suggest that the person or body who facilitates access from the website to a remote site and provides a trigger which enables sound recordings to be downloaded from that remote site is responsible for the content of the communication from the remote website. The fact is that, on the evidence, Cooper does not 'determine', 'formulate' or 'create' the content of the remote website from which the communication takes place.

75. The applicants point to Cooper's ability to control the links on his website, to determine precisely what files would be made available by means of the links created on his website and the manner in which the files were made available to internet users as indicative of his responsibility for determining the content of the communication. However, a power to remove a hyperlink to a remote website from the Cooper website is not a power or responsibility for determining the content of that remote website and the content of the communication to the internet user. The capacity to prevent hyperlinks from being added to the website and therefore to prevent internet users from accessing sound recordings via the Cooper website, is not the same as the ability to determine the content of a communication from a remote website. In cross-examination, Mr Speck agreed that Cooper had no control over whether a music file remained available on a remote website. Mr Speck said that should a remote website become unavailable, a visitor to the Cooper website would be unable to access the music files listed on the Cooper website as being available from the hosting website and would receive an error message whenever he or she attempted to visit that site and recover files from it.

76. It is the entitlement and role of the designer, operator and owner of a remote website to determine what is placed on that website and therefore what is the 'content' of that website. If the content includes infringing copyright material, then the responsibility for that lies with the person or persons who place that material on the remote website and thereby make it available for transmission to the public. This is consistent with the 'Digital Agenda Copyright Amendments: Exposure Draft and Commentary' (February 1999).

The right of communication to the public in the *WIPO Copyright Treaty* has been implemented and interpreted quite differently in other jurisdictions, and has been the subject of considerable controversy in recent years. In the USA, the right to communicate to the public was enacted by amending the right to perform works publicly. There have been ongoing disputes over the scope of this right, especially in the context of one-to-one communications: see for example *American Broadcasting Companies, Inc v Aereo, Inc*, 134 S Ct 2498 (2014), in which Aereo installed thousands of television antennae in order to transmit television programs to individual customers using a unique transmission from an individual antennae and dedicated copy for each customer. The US Supreme Court held that this constituted a public performance under US law.[6]

---

6   For a discussion, see R Giblin and J Ginsburg, 'We (Still) Need to Talk About Aereo: New Controversies and Unresolved Questions After the Supreme Court's Decision' (2015) 38 *Columbia Journal of Law and the Arts* (forthcoming).

Member states of the European Union are required under Art 3 of *Directive 2001/29/EC of the European Parliament and of the Council of 22 May 2001 on the Harmonisation of Certain Aspects of Copyright and Related Rights in the Information Society* to provide owners of copyright with a right 'to authorise or prohibit any communication to the public of their works, by wire or wireless means, including the making available to the public of their works in such a way that members of the public may access them from a place and at a time individually chosen by them'. The Court of Justice of the EU has held that communication *to the public* must be to 'fairly large number' of potential listeners or viewers—playing sound recordings in a dentist's waiting room did not involve a communication to the public: Case C-135/10, *Società Consortile Fonografici (SCF) v Del Corso* [2012] ECDR 16; screening football matches to customers in the pub was however a communication to the public: Joined Cases C-403/08 and C-429/08, *Football Association Premier League Ltd v QC Leisure and Karen Murphy v Media Protection Services Ltd* [2011] ECR I-9083 (note that in Australia this would be considered a performance rather than a communication: s 27(1)). In the case extracted below, the Court of Justice of the EU considered the status of a website which, like Cooper's website in *Universal Music v Cooper* (extracted above), aggregated links to material available from third party websites online.

CASE EXTRACT: COMPARATIVE LAW

Case C-466/12, Svensson, Sjögren, Sahlman, Gadd v Retriever Sverige AB

[2014] ECDR 9
Court of Justice of the European Union (Fourth Chamber)

[Svensson and others were journalists who wrote articles which were published in a newspaper and made freely available on the newspaper's website. Retriever Sverige operated a website which provided clients with links to articles published on other websites. No articles were hosted on Retriever Sverige's website. Svensson argued that Retriever Sverige was communicating the articles to the public within the meaning of Art 3(1) of *Directive 2001/29 on the Harmonisation of Copyright in the Information Society*. The Swedish Court referred to the Court of Justice of the EU questions relating to whether conduct like that engaged in by Retriever Sverige amounted to a communication to the public.]

The Court: 14. By its first three questions, which it is appropriate to examine together, the referring court asks, in essence, whether art 3(1) of Directive 2001/29 must be interpreted as meaning that the provision, on a website, of clickable links to protected works available on another website constitutes an act of communication to the public as referred to in that provision, where, on that other site, the works concerned are freely accessible.

15. In this connection, it follows from art 3(1) of Directive 2001/29 that every act of communication of a work to the public has to be authorised by the copyright holder.

16. It is thus apparent from that provision that the concept of communication to the public includes two cumulative criteria, namely, an 'act of communication' of a work and the communication of that work to a 'public' (see, to that effect, *ITV Broadcasting Ltd v TVCatchup Ltd* (C-607/11) [2013] ECDR 9 at [21] and [31]).

COMPARATIVE LAW

17. As regards the first of those criteria, that is, the existence of an 'act of communication', this must be construed broadly (see, to that effect, *Football Association Premier League Ltd v QC Leisure* (C-403/08) [[2011] ECR I-9083] at [193]), in order to ensure, in accordance with, inter alia, recitals 4 and 9 in the preamble to Directive 2001/29, a high level of protection for copyright holders.

18. In the circumstances of this case, it must be observed that the provision, on a website, of clickable links to protected works published without any access restrictions on another site, affords users of the first site direct access to those works.

19. As is apparent from art 3(1) of Directive 2001/29, for there to be an 'act of communication', it is sufficient, in particular, that a work is made available to a public in such a way that the persons forming that public may access it, irrespective of whether they avail themselves of that opportunity (see, by analogy, *Sociedad General de Autores y Editores de España (SGAE) v Rafael Hoteles SL* (C-306/05) [2007] ECDR 2 at [43]).

20. It follows that, in circumstances such as those in the case in the main proceedings, the provision of clickable links to protected works must be considered to be 'making available' and, therefore, an 'act of communication', within the meaning of that provision.

21. So far as concerns the second of the abovementioned criteria, that is, that the protected work must in fact be communicated to a 'public', it follows from art 3(1) of Directive 2001/29 that, by the term 'public', that provision refers to an indeterminate number of potential recipients and implies, moreover, a fairly large number of persons (*SGAE* [2007] ECDR 2 at [37] and [38], and *ITV* [2013] ECDR 9 at [32]).

22. An act of communication such as that made by the manager of a website by means of clickable links is aimed at all potential users of the site managed by that person, that is to say, an indeterminate and fairly large number of recipients.

23. In those circumstances, it must be held that the manager is making a communication to a public.

24. Nonetheless, according to settled case law, in order to be covered by the concept of 'communication to the public', within the meaning of art 3(1) of Directive 2001/29 , a communication, such as that at issue in the main proceedings, concerning the same works as those covered by the initial communication and made, as in the case of the initial communication, on the internet, and therefore by the same technical means, must also be directed at a new public, that is to say, at a public that was not taken into account by the copyright holders when they authorised the initial communication to the public (see, by analogy, *SGAE* [2007] ECDR 2 at [40] and [42]; order of 18 March 2010 in *Organismos Sillogikis Diacheirisis Dimiourgon Theatrikon kai Optikoakoustikon Ergon v Divani Akropolis Anonimi Xenodocheiaki kai Touristiki Etairei Akropolis Anonimi Xenodocheiaki kai Touristiki Etaireai* (C-136/09) (unreported) at [38]; and *ITV* [2013] ECDR 9 at [39]).

25. In the circumstances of this case, it must be observed that making available the works concerned by means of a clickable link, such as that in the main proceedings, does not lead to the works in question being communicated to a new public.

26. The public targeted by the initial communication consisted of all potential visitors to the site concerned, since, given that access to the works on that site was not subject to any restrictive measures, all internet users could therefore have free access to them.

27. In those circumstances, it must be held that, where all the users of another site to whom the works at issue have been communicated by means of a clickable link could access those works directly on the site on which they were initially communicated, without the involvement of the manager of that other site, the users of the site managed by the latter must be deemed to be potential recipients of the initial communication and, therefore, as being part of the public taken into account by the copyright holders when they authorised the initial communication.

28. Therefore, since there is no new public, the authorisation of the copyright holders is not required for a communication to the public such as that in the main proceedings.

29. Such a finding cannot be called in question were the referring court to find, although this is not clear from the documents before the Court, that when internet users click on the link at issue, the work appears in such a way as to give the impression that it is appearing on the site on which that link is found, whereas in fact that work comes from another site.

30. That additional circumstance in no way alters the conclusion that the provision on a site of a clickable link to a protected work published and freely accessible on another site has the effect of making that work available to users of the first site and that it therefore constitutes a communication to the public. However, since there is no new public, the authorisation of the copyright holders is in any event not required for such a communication to the public.

31. On the other hand, where a clickable link makes it possible for users of the site on which that link appears to circumvent restrictions put in place by the site on which the protected work appears in order to restrict public access to that work to the latter site's subscribers only, and the link accordingly constitutes an intervention without which those users would not be able to access the works transmitted, all those users must be deemed to be a new public, which was not taken into account by the copyright holders when they authorised the initial communication, and accordingly the holders' authorisation is required for such a communication to the public. This is the case, in particular, where the work is no longer available to the public on the site on which it was initially communicated or where it is henceforth available on that site only to a restricted public, while being accessible on another Internet site without the copyright holders' authorisation.

32. In those circumstances, the answer to the first three questions referred is that art 3(1) of Directive 2001/29 must be interpreted as meaning that the provision on a website of clickable links to works freely available on another website does not constitute an act of communication to the public, as referred to in that provision.

MAKE AN ADAPTATION OF THE WORK

Owners of copyright in literary, dramatic and musical works have an exclusive right to make an adaptation of the work: s 31(1)(a))(vi). They also have the right to do, in relation to an adaptation of a work, any of the acts specified in s 31(1)(a)(i)–(iv) (i.e. to reproduce the work in material form, publish it, perform it or communicate it to the public): s 31(1)(a)(vii). 'Adaptation' is exhaustively defined in s 10(1), to mean:

- for literary and dramatic works: to adapt a non-dramatic literary work to dramatic form, and vice versa; to translate the literary work; or to produce a version in which a story or action is conveyed solely or principally by means of pictures; and
- for musical works: to arrange or transcribe the musical work.

An adaptation can attract its own copyright protection if it meets the requirement of originality (see Chapter 3). Note that in relation to dramatisation of works there is some overlap between infringement of the reproduction right and the adaptation right. The *Jaws* case (extracted above, p 208) was argued in terms of infringement of the reproduction right, with no real discussion of the right of adaptation.

For computer programs, the s 10(1) definition of 'adaptation' also provides that an adaptation means:

> (ba) in relation to a literary work being a computer program—a version of the work (whether or not in the language, code or notation in which the work was originally expressed) not being a reproduction of the work.

CASE EXTRACT: CURRENT LAW

Coogi Australia Pty Ltd v Hysport International Pty Ltd

(1998) 86 FCR 154
Federal Court of Australia

[Coogi designed and manufactured sculptural machine knitted fabrics embodying the 'XYZ design'. Hysport produced a similar looking sculptural fabric. The first run of the Coogi product was protected as a 'work of artistic craftsmanship', however infringement of artistic copyright was not established. Coogi also claimed infringement of the reproduction and adaptation right in the XYZ design computer program (a literary work). The Coogi program was written in Sintral language. Hysport's computer program was in a 'Shimatronic' language created by Shima Seiki, a Japanese knitting machine manufacturer whose machines were used by Hysport. Hysport argued that there was no objective similarity between the code of the two computer programs. Was the Hypsort program, nonetheless, an unauthorised adaptation; that is, a 'translation' or 'version' of the Coogi XYZ program?]

Drummond J (at 184–189): Despite the criticisms that have been made of the accuracy of the proposition, it is settled law in Australia that copyright protects not the underlying idea, but only the form of expression of the idea: see *Autodesk* [*Inc v Dyason (No 1)* (1992) 173 CLR 330] at CLR 344–5 and *Powerflex Services* [*Pty Ltd v Data Access Corp* (1997) 37 IPR 436] (at 450). It is also the law in Australia that merely because one program performs the same function as another, that is insufficient to make the one an infringement of copyright in the other: *Autodesk (No 1)* (at CLR 344); *Autodesk* [*v Dyason*] [*No 2*] [(1993) 176 CLR 300] (at CLR 304) and *Powerflex Services* (at 455). Consistently with this, a computer program can only be an 'adaptation' of another when it is 'a version of the work', that is, a version of the particular form of expression of that other in which alone copyright can subsist, and not merely an expression of the idea or function of that other program.

In *Powerflex Services*, the Full [Federal] Court placed a precise and limiting gloss on the statutory definition, holding (at 454) that, while the word 'version' in the statutory definition of 'adaptation' is used in its ordinary English sense, the legislature intended that it should bear one particular meaning of those which it has in ordinary speech, viz, a translation; at 457 it repeated that 'the word "adaptation", as used in s 10, means "translation"'. In ordinary usage, the term 'version' is applicable to a wider range of renderings of the original literary work than is the term 'translation': a version can apply to as literal as possible a rendering of the original in another language, as well as to a work in the same or another language that is only recognisable as related to the original because that is the identifiable source of the theme of the version. The term 'translation' has a much narrower reach. In ordinary speech, Piave's libretto in Italian for Verdi's opera 'Macbeth' could fairly be called a version of Shakespeare's play; it could not, however, be properly described as a translation of the English original. The Full Court supported its conclusion that 'adaptation' means 'translation' with references to various paragraphs of the explanatory memorandum in respect of the amending Act of 1984 which introduced para (ba) into the definition of 'adaptation' into the *Copyright Act* including:

> 11. Copyright in literary works includes exclusive rights to reproduce or adapt such works and computer programs will be treated as literary works. However, the present definition of adaptation in relation to literary works only includes translation, conversion between dramatic and non-dramatic forms, and conversion to a pictorial form.
>
> 12. Of these, only translation is likely to be relevant to adaptation of programs and there are legal doubts as to whether this refers only to translations between human languages.
>
> 13. The new definition is intended to cover translation either way between the various so-called 'high level programming languages' in which the programs may be written by humans (often called 'source code') and languages, codes or notations which actually control computer operations (often called 'machine code' or 'object code'). Thus 'adaptation' is intended, for example, to cover the compilation of fortran program to produce machine code which will directly control the operation of a computer. Languages etc of intermediate level would also be covered.

The court also referred to para 14 of the explanatory memorandum which states that the legislative intent was to include within the concept of a 'version' of a computer program that which results from a process such as compilation followed by decompilation, that is, by translation from a higher to a lower level of computer language and by translation the other way, even though 'the differences may be so substantial that one cannot speak of a reproduction although the final product is clearly derived from the original'.

... Translation, as that term is ordinarily used, connotes more than conveying in a different language the same ideas expressed in another language. It describes a closer connection between the original and the translated text than that. I do not think an activity could be described in ordinary speech as a translation unless it involves the expenditure of effort on the original words or text to render them into words or text in a different language that conveys with precision the same meaning as that conveyed by the original. A person can probably be said to make a translation, in the ordinary meaning of that term, indirectly, for example, by translating into English from a French rendering of the original German text. But there can be no translation without the expenditure of effort, directly or indirectly, on the original text. Further, translation into a second language of instructions for achieving a result expressed in another language involves more than describing in the second language some method for achieving that same result. To be a translation, as that term is ordinarily used, of the original instructions, the new text would have to describe the particular sequence of steps for achieving the results that are expressed in the original text. Assume A writes in German a set of instructions for the making of a device, for example, a clock, and that someone uses those instructions to make a clock. B does not make a translation of A's original instructions by taking the clock, breaking it down into its parts and then writing his own set of instructions in English for reproducing the clock. The reason is that he has not produced his manual of instructions in English by working directly or indirectly (via a translation of the original in a third language) from the original text in German.

It is, I think, in this narrow sense which the word 'translation' has in ordinary speech that the Full Court in *Powerflex Services* considered that the definition of 'adaptation' applicable to computer programs should be understood. One computer program will therefore be an unauthorised 'adaptation' of another, first, only if the whole or a substantial part of the particular form of expression of the program in which copyright is claimed appears in the allegedly infringing program in a different computer language, either at the same language level or at a different language level and, secondly, only if the allegedly infringing program has been produced by direct or indirect use, in the sense described, of the copyright program. It is a meaning of 'adaptation' that is supported by paras 13 and 14 of the explanatory memorandum and one which preserves, so far as concerns copyright in computer programs, the function/expression dichotomy that is currently entrenched in Australian copyright law.

The correctness of the proposition central to the respondents' case that Hysport's programs could only be infringements of Coogi's program if there was objective similarity between them can now be considered. That question will necessarily have to be determined when the allegation is that one program is an unauthorised reproduction of the other: *Computer Edge Pty Ltd v Apple Computer Inc* (1986) 161 CLR 171 at 186. But in view of the definition of 'adaptation' in the Copyright Act, a reproduction of a computer program and an adaptation (that is, a translation) of such a program are mutually exclusive concepts. A translation of a literary work into a different language from the original will necessarily be in a form of expression different from the original. The making of a translation also necessarily involves the expenditure of original skill and effort by the translator: the making of a translation involves much more than the mere taking of the original author's own skill and effort. It was this consideration, coupled with the perceived need to respect the idea/expression dichotomy, that led courts, until the matter was dealt with by legislation, to hold that a translation of an original literary work into another language did not infringe copyright in the original: see, for example, the discussion in the old American case of *Stowe v Thomas* (1853) 23 F Cas 201. It is clear from paras 13 and 14 of the explanatory memorandum in respect of the amending Act of 1984 and from the Full Court decision in *Powerflex Services*, that para (ba) of the definition of the expression 'adaptation' in s 10 of the Act was intended to cover computer programs derived from the original program, but expressed in quite different forms from the original, that is, even though there is no objective similarity between the forms in which they are expressed. It is therefore difficult to see how, as the respondents suggest and the applicants accept, there can be any room for a requirement, where the allegation is that one computer program infringes copyright in another because it is an adaptation, that is, a translation, of that other, that there be objective similarity between the two forms of expression, if the first is to be an infringement of copyright in the second.

I consider that a computer program will be an infringing 'adaptation', that is, translation, of an original program only if the court can be convinced that, although the two programs are quite different so far as their forms of expression are concerned, use has been made of the original not just to identify the idea of the original or the function it performs, but as an aid to devising the descriptions of the activities (and any accompanying data) which together comprise the allegedly infringing program. Unless the expression 'objective similarity' as used in copyright infringement law is to be given a new, highly artificial and technical meaning, instead of the ordinary usage meaning it has hitherto had, so that

CURRENT LAW

it will import into infringement law tests like that adopted in the American case, *Computer Associates International Inc v Altai Inc* (1992) 23 IPR 385 and favoured by the Copyright Law Review Committee Report [*Computer Software Protection*] (Canberra, 1995) para 9.27, it cannot sensibly be employed, in my opinion, in order to determine whether one program is an unauthorised adaptation of another.

In my opinion, the F823 program is not an adaptation, in the sense of a translation, of the particular form of expression of instructions that constitutes the Coogi XYZ program … It is, in my opinion, a misuse of language to say that, by examining a Coogi XYZ garment to identify how the fabric was produced and by then writing a program of its own to cause its computerised knitting machine to perform the sequence of steps necessary to produce a like fabric, Shima Seiki made an adaptation, that is, a translation of the particular form of expression constituting the Coogi XYZ program, which alone can be the subject matter of Coogi's program copyright. All it seems to me that Shima did, and all it could do without access to an XYZ program, was reproduce, in the program which it wrote in its own Shimatronic language, the same function that Coogi's XYZ program written in Sintral language performed, viz, the function of causing an appropriately computerised knitting machine to produce fabric of one particular design. Copyright in a computer program protects that skill and effort of the author that is expended in devising only the form in which the program is expressed. I am not prepared to find that Shima in producing its F823 program took any of that skill or effort. Hysport's programs derived from the Shima F823 program cannot therefore be infringements of the Coogi program.

I would therefore dismiss Coogi's claim against all respondents for this reason.

ENTER A COMMERCIAL RENTAL ARRANGEMENT

Owners of copyright in literary, dramatic and musical works have the exclusive right:

- for literary works (other than computer programs), dramatic and musical works: to enter into a commercial rental arrangement in respect of the work reproduced in a sound recording (s 31(1)(c)); and
- for computer programs: to enter into a commercial rental arrangement in respect of the program (s 31(1)(d)), provided that the computer program is the essential object of the rental (s 31(5)).

The rental right is intended to prevent people from avoiding the need to purchase computer programs or sound recordings by renting a copy and then making their own copy for longer term use. The right as it relates to computer programs is not intended to cover situations where the computer program is embodied in some machine or device (e.g. a hire car with embedded software): s 31(3). The meaning of *commercial* rental arrangement is further elaborated in s 30A. In many countries the rental right also extends to films: see the *Agreement on Trade-Related Aspects of Intellectual Property Rights* (the 'TRIPS Agreement') (1994), Art 11.

EXCLUSIVE RIGHTS IN SUBJECT MATTER OTHER THAN WORKS

The exclusive rights held by owners of Part IV subject matter differ from the rights in Part III works in two key ways. First, owners of Part IV subject matter receive a more limited set of rights that varies: it is important to refer to the relevant provision to determine exactly what rights are conferred in each subject matter: ss 85–88. The rights that attach to Part IV subject matters are summarised in Table 6.1.

TABLE 6.1 RIGHTS ATTACHING TO PART IV SUBJECT MATTERS

SOUND RECORDINGS	CINEMATOGRAPH FILMS	BROADCASTS	PUBLISHED EDITIONS
To make a copy: s 85(1)(a)	To make a copy: s 86(a)	To make a film of a television broadcast, or a copy of such a film: s 87(a) To make a sound recording of a television or a sound broadcast: s 87(b)	To make a facsimile copy of the edition: s 88
To cause the recording to be heard in public: s 85(1)(b)	To cause the film, in so far as it consists of visual images, to be seen in public, or, in so far as it consists of sounds, to be heard in public: s 86(b)		
To communicate the recording to the public: s 85(1)(c)	To communicate the film to the public: s 86(c)	To rebroadcast the broadcast or communicate it to the public otherwise than by broadcasting: s 87(c)	
To enter a commercial arrangement in respect of the recording: s 85(1)(d)			

Note that there is no equivalent of certain rights conferred in respect of works under Part III: for example there is no right to publish or make an adaptation of Part IV subject matter.

Second, as Table 6.1 illustrates, certain exclusive rights are expressed differently. Rather than a right to 'reproduce' a work in material form, there is an exclusive right to 'make a copy' of the film or sound recording. 'Copy' in relation to cinematograph films is defined in s 10(1) to mean 'any article or thing in which the visual images or sounds comprising the film are embodied'. In relation to broadcasts, a reference to a film of a television broadcast is read as including a reference to a photograph of any of the visual images comprised in the broadcast: s 25(4).

The different language used to express rights in Part IV subject matter has the effect, noted in Chapter 4, of confining the right to 'literal' infringements only. The actual subject matter protected must be copied, or seen or heard in public—recreating the subject matter by, for example, making a very similar film or a 'sound-alike' sound recording will not infringe: see *CBS Records Australia Ltd v Telmak Teleproducts (Aust) Pty Ltd* (1987) 17 FCR 48 (extracted in Chapter 4); also *Telmak Teleproducts (Aust) Pty Ltd v Bond International Pty Ltd* (1985) 66 ALR 118.

WHO IS RESPONSIBLE FOR DOING THE ACT?

It is important to identify the person or persons who are doing the act falling within the exclusive rights of the copyright owner. Persons who do not *directly* infringe, but who facilitate direct infringement, may be liable for authorising infringement (considered under the next heading). But particularly as technologies arise in which people may use equipment or services supplied by others to copy or transmit content, the question arises: who is the direct infringer? In considering the communication right, above p 227, we noted s 22(6) which states that 'a communication other than a broadcast is taken to have been made by the person responsible for determining the content of the communication'. Questions about who is the person doing the act within the exclusive right have also arisen in relation to the 'reproduction' and 'making a copy' rights. Who makes the reproduction or copy in circumstances where a company sets up a system to automatically copy works or other subject matter on request by a customer? This question arose in the case extracted below.

CASE EXTRACT: CURRENT LAW

National Rugby League Investments Pty Ltd v Singtel Optus Pty Ltd

[2012] FCAFC 59; (2012) 201 FCR 147
Federal Court of Australia, Full Court

[Optus developed a system called 'TV Now', which allowed Optus' mobile phone customers to record and access free-to-air broadcast television on their computers and mobile devices. Customers downloaded an app onto their phone or computer, which allowed them to view an electronic program guide (EPG), choose their desired programs and press a 'record button'. Optus set up television antennae to capture the free-to-air broadcast signal. If any customer requested a program, four copies (in different formats, for different devices) for that individual customer would be made on Optus' servers. When the customer later pressed a 'play' button on their device, the relevant copy would be used to stream the program to that device. Only the customer could access their particular recorded copies. On some devices, customers were able to stream programs 'near live'; that is, from the recorded copy a few seconds after the program started.

The National Rugby League (NRL), which had granted Telstra Corporation Ltd an exclusive licence to communicate rugby league matches to the public, by internet and to mobile devices, alleged that Optus was infringing copyright by making copies of its broadcasts and later communicating those broadcasts. Optus argued that it was *the customer* who exercised any exclusive rights. This was important because customers had the benefit of an exception to allow copying television broadcasts to watch later (s 111). The trial judge held that the customer made the copies; NRL appealed.]

Finn, Emmett and Bennett JJ: 49. The question to be answered is easily stated: 'Who "does" the act of copying?': *Copinger and Skone James on Copyright*, 7–21 (16th ed, 2011). Its answering is the less easy because of the sophistication of the automated technologies used and the electronic communications made. Yet a legal person has to be identified who or which does that act. Considering the matter from the standpoint of s 101 of the Act, this identification requires an analysis both of who does what, when and where and of how the TV Now system itself functions. The rival contenders are Optus, the subscriber, or Optus and the subscriber jointly. Each can be advanced with varying plausibility in the circumstances as the person(s) who does the act of copying.

50. The first matter to be noted is Optus' TV Now Service itself. Optus designed it; gave it its functionality; owned the intellectual property in it ...; and marketed the service it provided to its customers. The system itself was configured so as to be able to receive, copy, store and permit the

viewing of on compatible mobile and PC devices, the free-to-air broadcasts of the 15 TV channels in each of the five mainland state capitals. And it was fully automated. Its function in short was to receive, copy, store and stream to a subscriber's device, programmes required by a subscriber to the TV Now service.

51. ... [T]erms of the Optus-subscriber relationship were contractual in character. It again is unnecessary to consider here how these terms fitted into the larger contractual web between Optus and its customers. The terms and conditions to which the subscriber was required to agree personalised what the service offers to a subscriber: it 'allows you to record and store television shows. *You* can then access those recordings for a limited period'; it 'is for *your* individual and personal use': italics in original. There is obvious licence and colloquialism in the language so used. The subscriber does not 'store' television shows. Optus stores copies. To say that the subscriber 'records' such shows and that Optus TV Now is for the subscriber's 'use', are familiar and unexceptionable uses of language, but they by no means ordain the character of what a subscriber does (for example 'records') and of the subscriber's relationship to the system itself (for example a 'user' of it).

52. Before turning to how the act of copying fits within the Optus-subscriber relationship, one additional matter requires notice. Optus at all times retained possession, ownership and control of the physical copies made on the hard disc of its NAS computer until they were deleted by Optus after the expiry of 30 days from recording or by the subscriber before then. Viewing of the programmes copied was achieved by way of streaming the appropriate compatible version of playback data to the user's device. No data, no copies of the programme, were thereby stored in that device in any permanent form in that process.

53. There are four possible characterisations of the maker of the copies in this matter: (i) they were made by Optus but as agent for the subscriber; (ii) they were made by the subscriber as a principal using a facility made available by Optus pursuant to its contract with the subscriber; (iii) they were made by Optus as a principal using its own technology but subject to its contractual obligation to store and to allow subscriber viewing of the recordings so made at the time(s) of his or her choosing; or (iv) they were made jointly by Optus and the subscriber both of whom, consistent with their contract, acted in concert with one another pursuant to a common design to have a broadcast copied on Optus' technology and made available to be viewed by the subscriber.

(I) AGENCY

54. This possibility can be dismissed shortly. It seems only to have been raised by Optus in its appeal submissions and then only faintly. That the relationship of the subscriber and Optus in relation to the making of copies could be that of principal and agent, has no resonance at all either in the TV Now terms and conditions or, more generally, in the customer-service provider relationship of the parties. ...

(II) THE SUBSCRIBER AS PRINCIPAL

55. This is in essence what the primary judge has held and underpins Optus' submission. Put shortly, it is that Optus makes available to a subscriber a facility (a service) which enables the subscriber as and when he or she is so minded to use that facility to record broadcasts and later to view them. The copies that are made are the result of the subscriber's use of the facility though the actual making of them requires Optus' technology to function as it was designed to.

CURRENT LAW

56. Underpinning this is a particular conception of what 'make' means—a conception which robs the entirely automated copying process of any significance beyond that of being the vehicle which does the making of copies. As the primary judge put it, 'make' means 'to create' by selecting what is to be recorded and by initiating a process utilising technology or equipment that records the broadcast: [*Singtel Optus Pty Ltd v National Rugby League Investments Pty Ltd (No 2)* [2012] FCA 34; (2012) 199 FCR 300] at [64]. Or, as Optus put it in submissions, it means 'to cause, induce, or compel': the subscriber was the 'causative agency' in the making of copies.

57. There are two additional matters relied upon in support of the contention that the subscriber is the maker. The *first* relates to the technology itself. It is that it is analogous, as his Honour suggested, to devices which can be used to make a copy of copyright material but which when so used by a third party do not result in the person who made, sold or hired out the device in question or in whose possession or control the device remains, being held to be the 'maker' of that copy. His Honour instanced the photocopier provided by the university to student copiers in [*University of New South Wales v Moorhouse* (1975) 133 CLR 1], having earlier observed that the 'service that TV Now offers the user is substantively no different from a VCR or DVR': reasons [63]. The *second* matter, which flows from the facts that the subscriber both selects the programme to be copied and initiates the process of copying, is that the subscriber's is the last 'volitional act' in the sequence of acts leading to a copy being made and, for that reason, is significant in determining the identity of the maker—the more so as a s 101 infringement requires a 'person' to do or authorise the doing of, any 'act' comprised in the copyright.

58. We consider that there are several reasons for rejecting the proposition that the subscriber was the maker for s 101, hence s 111, purposes. *First*, the meaning given 'make' is, in our view, a contrived one. When s 86(a) refers to making a 'copy' of a film, when s 87(a) refers to making a cinematograph film of a television broadcast or a copy of the film, when s 87(b) refers to making a sound recording or a copy of such, they each are referring to so acting as to embody images and sound in an 'article or thing' (see the s 10 definitions of 'cinematograph film' and 'copy') or a 'record'. In our view 'make', as it appears in ss 86(a) and 87(a) and (b), is a fundamental concept underpinning the Act and the essence of it is the idea of making (that is creating or producing) a physical thing (that is the embodiment of the copyright subject matter). We agree with the AFL's submission to this effect. The OED definition with its emphasis on producing a 'material thing' is an apt one for the purposes of ss 86(a) and 87(a) and (b)—and hence for ss 101(1) and 111 of the Act. In saying this we do not discountenance the need for there to be a causative agency if a copy of a particular thing is to be made. The issue is not simply how something is made. It is by whom is it made. This, as will be seen, is of some importance when we come to consider whether copies were made by Optus and the subscriber jointly.

59. The *second* reason for rejecting the proposition that the subscriber alone is the maker relates to how the system itself works. This is better discussed when considering whether Optus itself is the maker. We merely note here that a subscriber's clicking on a button labelled 'record' may trigger a sequence of actions which result in copies of a selected programme being made, but it does not necessarily follow that the subscriber alone makes that copy.

60. *Third*, analogies are not necessarily helpful in this setting because they both divert attention from what the TV Now system has been designed to do and pre-suppose what is the function (albeit automated) it performs in the ongoing Optus–subscriber relationship. To anticipate matters, we consider

that the system itself has been designed in a way that makes Optus the 'main performer of the act of [copying]' (to adopt the language used in a recent Japanese decision involving a service relevantly similar to the present, which has been supplied to the court in translation): see *Rokuraku II*, First Petty Bench of the Supreme Court, Japan, 20 January 2011.

61. *Fourth*, there is some division between federal courts in the United States as how properly to differentiate between 'direct' and 'contributory' liability for copyright infringement where automated technologies are employed to make copies of copyright material: contrast for example *Cartoon Network LP, LLLP* [*v CSC Holdings Inc* 536 F 3d 121 (2d Cir, 2008)] and *Wolk v Kodak Imaging Network Inc* 2012 WL 11270 at 17–18 (SDNY) with *Arista Records LLC v Myxer Inc* 2011 US Dist Lexis 109668 (CD Cal) at 12–13. In distinguishing the two forms of liability—a distinction which is of no concern to this court in these appeals—the 'volitional conduct' concept (and as well, the analogies with photocopier use by third parties and use of VCRs and DVRs) have been deployed.

62. So, in *Cartoon Network* (at 131–2) the United States Court of Appeals, Second Circuit, commented:

> [V]olitional conduct is an important element of direct liability … In determining who actually 'makes' a copy, a significant difference exists between making a request to a human employee, who then volitionally operates the copying system to make the copy, and issuing a command directly to a system, which automatically obeys commands and engages in no volitional conduct … Here, by selling access to a system that automatically produces copies on command, Cablevision more closely resembles a store proprietor who charges customers to use a photocopier on his premises, and it seems incorrect to say, without more, that such a proprietor 'makes' any copies when his machines are actually operated by his customers.

63. Whatever utility the volitional conduct concept has in distinguishing the two forms of infringement (given the need to do so in US jurisprudence), its adoption in this country would, in our view, require a gloss to be put on the word 'make' in ss 86(a) and 87(a) and (b) of the Act. The need for so doing is not apparent to us, the more so because we have our own legislative and common law devices for imposing liability on third persons who are implicated or join in the infringing acts of another as, for example, by authorising the doing of such acts: see *Copyright Act*, s 101(1) and (1A) or by acting in concert with another to infringe copyright in pursuit of a common design: see for example *Aristocrat Technologies Australia Pty Ltd v Global Gaming Supplies Pty Ltd* [[2009] FCA 1495; (2009) 84 IPR 222] at [620]–[624]; and see below *(iv) Optus and the subscriber jointly?*

64. It equally is not apparent to us why a person who designs and operates a wholly automated copying system ought as of course not be treated as a 'maker' of an infringing copy where the system itself is configured designedly so as to respond to a third party command to make that copy: see generally the criticism of *Cartoon Network* in [J] Ginsburg ['Recent Developments in US Copyright Law—Part II, Caselaw: Exclusive Rights on the Ebb?' (2008) *Columbia Public Law & Legal Theory Working Papers*, Paper 08158], at 15–18.

65. Although we have concluded that the subscriber cannot properly be said to be the maker of the copies in this matter, we return below to the question whether the subscriber can none the less be said to have acted jointly with Optus in making the copies.

CURRENT LAW

(III) OPTUS AS THE MAKER

66. It is the case that no copies will be made of a programme unless the subscriber selects that programme to be recorded and communicates his or her confirmation of that selection to Optus, albeit by an electronic communication to its MACF servers. In at least this 'but for' sense, the actions of the subscriber are causative of a recording later being made. Optus places emphasis on the necessity for that action of the subscriber, as well as the action of Optus, in setting up the system, in causing that recording to be made and, subsequently, causing the recording to be communicated to the subscriber. An Optus employee cannot press the record button. However, once that communication is made, the automated processes described by his Honour come into play—the server enters or creates a schedule ID in respect of the programme selected and the user's unique identifying number in the user database; the recording controllers poll that database once a minute inquiring whether any users have scheduled the recording of any programme due to be broadcast at the time of polling; when the poll so identifies that the user's selection is due to be broadcast, the MACF server informs the recording controllers which then cause four recordings to be made on the NAS hard disk—that is the timing of the recording coincides with Optus' recording controller causing the recording to be made, rather than when the subscriber communicates its selection to Optus.

67. Accepting as we do the appropriateness of the OED definition for the purposes of ss 86, 87 and 101, we consider that Optus' role in the making of a copy—that is in capturing the broadcast and then in embodying its images and sounds in the hard disk—is so pervasive that, even though entirely automated, it cannot be disregarded when the 'person' who does the act of copying is to be identified. The system performs the very functions for which it was created by Optus. Even if one were to require volitional conduct proximate to the copying, Optus' creating and keeping in constant readiness the TV Now system would satisfy that requirement. It should also be emphasised that the recording is made by reason of Optus' system remaining 'up' and available to implement the subscriber's request at the time when its recording controllers poll the user database and receive a response indicating that a recording has been requested. What Optus actually does has:

> a nexus sufficiently close and causal to the illegal copying that one could conclude that the machine owner ... trespassed on the exclusive domain of the copyright owners: *CoStar Group Inc v LoopNet Inc* 373 F3d 544 at 550 (4th Cir 2004).

We would note this was quoted in *Cartoon Network* at 130.

68. Put shortly Optus is not merely making available its system to another who uses it to copy a broadcast: compare *CoStar Group Inc* at 550. Rather it captures, copies, stores and makes available for reward, a programme for later viewing by another: compare *New York Times Co Inc v Tasini* (2001) 533 US 483 at 504; and see Ginsburg at 15–16.

69. The real issue in consequence is whether Optus alone does the act of copying or whether Optus and the subscriber are jointly and severally responsible for that act.

(IV) OPTUS AND THE SUBSCRIBER JOINTLY?

70. The appellants' preferred characterisation of the Optus-subscriber relationship was that it was one in which Optus undertook to provide recordings of such free-to-air television programmes as the subscriber required to be recorded from time to time, the programmes after recording to be available to be viewed at the time or times of the subscriber's choosing on any one of four types of Optus

compatible mobile phone or PC. It was, in short, a service for which Optus solicited subscribers and in which it was obliged to provide recordings for viewing of programmes the subscriber required to be recorded.

71. As the recording could only occur as and when the broadcast occurred of the programme sought but that programme itself had to be notified to Optus in advance, Optus established the wholly automated system, described above, which it so configured that the required recording did occur. If that part of the system embodied the steps taken by Optus to ensure that the required programme was recorded at the right time for the subscriber who required it, then the selection and notified confirmation by the subscriber of the programme required to be recorded could be said to be merely the necessary precondition to be satisfied to activate Optus' obligation to perform its service. If this be correct, then Optus can properly be identified as the maker of the copies of the recording. As the AFL has put it, Optus' data centre carries out the user's instruction to record a programme; it records that programme. In other words, if analogies are helpful in this particular setting (which we doubt), Optus is to be analogised with a commercial photocopier which copies copyright material provided to it for copying by it.

72. We would add that the circumstance of Optus making four copies to accommodate the four types of compatible playing devices on which a programme could be viewed lends support to this particular 'service provision' conclusion. The parties ordinarily would not have agreed which device would be used to provide the viewing platform. Optus of necessity thus had to make four copies if it were to be able to discharge its obligation to provide the service required in all cases. It is difficult to characterise the subscriber, in using the service, as in all cases making four copies of the programme selected, some at least of which copies are likely to be of no use at all to him or her, in circumstances where the subscriber is probably unaware of the making of the four copies.

73. To view the matter in contractual terms, the terms and conditions of the service are quite unyielding of any clear indication as to what actually is the true character of the parties' relationship ...

74. However, the contractual allocation of functions and responsibilities in making a copy of copyright material may, but does not necessarily, identify the person (or persons) who 'make(s)' the copy for copyright infringement purposes. The making of the copy may be the product of the concerted action of both parties to the contract such that they together are the 'makers' of the copy.

75. So one comes back to the question of construction raised by the word 'make' and its application in the present setting. As we have indicated, Optus not only has solicited subscriber utilisation of its service, it has also designed and maintained a sophisticated system which can effectuate the making of recordings wanted for viewing by subscribers. For s 101 purposes, it manifestly is involved directly in doing the act of copying. It counts as a maker of copies for the subscriber. Does the subscriber as well?

76. If one focused not only upon the automated service which is held out as able to produce, and which actually produces, the copies but also on the causative agency that is responsible for the copies being made at all, the need for a more complex characterisation is suggested. The subscriber, by selecting the programme to be copied and by confirming that it is to be copied, can properly be said to be the person who instigates the copying. Yet it is Optus which effects it. Without the concerted actions of both there would be no copy made of a football match for the subscriber. Without the subscriber's involvement, nothing would be created; without Optus' involvement nothing would be copied. They have needed to act in concert to produce—they each have contributed to—a commonly desired outcome.

CURRENT LAW

The subscriber's contributing acts were envisaged by the contractual terms and conditions. How they were to be done were indicated by the prompts given on the Optus TV Now TV guide page. The common design—the production of the selected programme for transmission to the subscriber—informed the solicitation and the taking of a subscription by the subscriber; it was immanent in the service to be provided.

77. In consequence, they could both properly be said to be jointly and severally responsible for the act of making the copies.

Special leave to appeal the Full Federal Court decision was refused by the High Court: *Singtel Optus Pty Ltd v Australian Rugby Football League Ltd* [2012] HCATrans 214.

LIABILITY FOR AUTHORISING INFRINGEMENT
GENERAL PRINCIPLES

Sections 36 and 101 provide that a person can be liable for authorising direct infringement committed by third parties. The meaning of 'authorisation' in this context extends beyond agent–principal relationships. Determining whether a person has authorised infringement is a complex, and highly fact-sensitive inquiry;[7] the concept has been fleshed out by courts over the course of more than a century, with judges articulating a range of factors relevant in determining whether a party's conduct amounts to authorisation. It has been applied in situations where a person has purported to grant permission to a third party to do an act which would infringe copyright: *Falcon v Famous Players Film Co* [1926] 2 KB 474; *EMI Songs Australia Pty Ltd v Larrikin Music Publishing Pty Ltd* [2011] FCAFC 47; (2011) 191 FCR 444; or where a person controls premises where infringing performances occur: *APRA v Jain* (1990) 26 FCR 53. It has also been applied in situations in which a person has enabled infringement by supplying equipment or facilities, provided that other conditions, such as knowledge and the ability to prevent the infringement, are present. There is no authorisation liability unless direct infringement is proved to have occurred: *WEA International Inc v Hanimex Corporation Ltd* (1987) 17 FCR 274.

The *Copyright Amendment (Digital Agenda) Act 2000* (Cth) introduced ss 36(1A) and 101(1A), setting out certain factors that courts must take into account in determining whether a person has authorised infringement:

   (a) the extent (if any) of the person's power to prevent the doing of the act concerned;

   (b) the nature of any relationship existing between the person and the person who did the act concerned;

   (c) whether the person took any reasonable steps to prevent or avoid the doing of the act, including whether the person complied with any relevant industry codes of practice.

This amendment was intended partially to codify authorisation without displacing development of the concept by the courts. The statutory factors must be taken into account, but the court is not obliged to give any particular weight to any one factor; nor is it confined to these factors.

---

7   *Roadshow Films Pty Ltd v iiNet Ltd* [2012] HCA 16; (2012) 248 CLR 42 at [5] and [63] (French CJ, Crennan and Kiefel JJ); *University of New South Wales v Moorhouse* (1975) 133 CLR 1 at 12 (Gibbs J); *Performing Right Society Ltd v Ciryl Theatrical Syndicate Ltd* [1924] 1 KB 1 at 9 (Bankes LJ); *Adelaide Corporation v Australasian Performing Right Association Ltd* (1928) 40 CLR 481 at 504 (Gavan Duffy and Starke JJ).

One benefit of authorisation liability is that it can enable more effective enforcement of copyright. The transaction costs incurred in pursuing a large number of individual infringers, especially for relatively minor infringements, can be prohibitive. Authorisation liability allows owners to target intermediaries who, by providing copying equipment or access to other means of infringement, in some way facilitate individual infringing acts.

Authorisation is not the only basis for liability for third parties who do not themselves directly infringe copyright. A person can also be liable as a 'joint tortfeasor' with a primary infringer in circumstances where they are engaged in a common design aimed at infringement: *WEA International Inc v Hanimex Corporation Ltd* (1987) 17 FCR 274.

PRECEDENT

CASE EXTRACT: PRECEDENT

University of New South Wales v Moorhouse

(1975) 133 CLR 1
High Court of Australia

[This was a test case organised by the Australian Copyright Council in which it was argued that, by providing photocopiers in the library and placing no restrictions on their use, and taking no steps to supervise their use, the University was authorising infringements committed by library users.[8]]

Gibbs J (at 12–13): The word 'authorize', in legislation of similar intendment to s 36 of the Act, has been held judicially to have its dictionary meaning of 'sanction, approve, countenance': *Falcon v Famous Players Film Co* [1926] 2 KB 474, at p 491; *Adelaide Corporation v Australasian Performing Right Association Ltd* (1928) 40 CLR 481, at pp 489, 497. It can also mean 'permit', and in *Adelaide Corporation v Australasian Performing Right Association Ltd* 'authorize' and 'permit' appear to have been treated as synonymous. A person cannot be said to authorize an infringement of copyright unless he has some power to prevent it: *Adelaide Corporation v Australasian Performing Right Association Ltd.* [at pp 497–498, 503]. Express or formal permission or sanction, or active conduct indicating approval, is not essential to constitute an authorization; 'Inactivity or 'indifference, exhibited by acts of commission or omission, may reach a degree from which an authorization or permission may be inferred': *Adelaide Corporation v Australasian Performing Right Association Ltd* [at p 504]. However, the word 'authorize' connotes a mental element and it could not be inferred that a person had, by mere inactivity, authorized something to be done if he neither knew nor had reason to suspect that the act might be done. Knox CJ and Isaacs J referred to this mental element in their dissenting judgments in *Adelaide Corporation v Australasian Performing Right Association Ltd.* Knox CJ, [at p 487] held that indifference or omission is 'permission' where the party charged (amongst other things) 'knows or has reason to anticipate or suspect that the particular act is to be or is likely to be done'. Isaacs J. apparently considered that it is enough if the person sought to be made liable 'knows or has reason to know or believe' that the particular act of infringement 'will or may' be done [at pp 490–491]. This latter statement may be too widely expressed: cf. *Sweet v Parsley* [1970] AC 132, at p 165. It seems to me to follow from these statements of principle that a person who has under his control the means by

---

8   For an interesting background to the case, see S Ricketson and D Catterns, 'Of Vice-Chancellors and Authors: *UNSW v Moorhouse*' in A Kenyon, M Richardson and S Ricketson, eds, *Landmarks in Australian Intellectual Property Law*, Cambridge University Press, Melbourne, 2009.

which an infringement of copyright may be committed—such as a photocopying machine—and who makes it available to other persons, knowing, or having reason to suspect, that it is likely to be used for the purpose of committing an infringement, and omitting to take reasonable steps to limit its use to legitimate purposes, would authorize any infringement that resulted from its use. Cases such as *Mellor v Australian Broadcasting Commission* [1940] AC 491 and *Winstone v Wurlitzer Automatic Phonograph Co of Australia Pty Ltd* [1946] VLR 338 are consistent with this view. Although in some of the authorities it is said that the person who authorizes an infringement must have knowledge or reason to suspect that the particular act of infringement is likely to be done, it is clearly sufficient if there is knowledge or reason to suspect that any one of a number of particular acts is likely to be done, as for example, where the proprietor of a shop installs a gramophone and supplies a number of records any one of which may be played on it: *Winstone v Wurlitzer Automatic Phonograph Co of Australia Pty Ltd*.

Jacobs J (with whom McTiernan ACJ agreed) (at 20–21): It is established that the word ['authorize'] is not limited to the authorizing of an agent by a principal. Where there is such an authority the act of the agent is the act of the principal and thus the principal himself may be said to do the act comprised in the copyright. But authorization is wider than authority. It has, in relation to a similar use in previous copyright legislation, been given the meaning, taken from the Oxford Dictionary, of 'sanction, approve, countenance'. See *Falcon v Famous Players Film Co* which was approved in *Adelaide Corporation v Australasian Performing Right Association Ltd*. I have no doubt that the word is used in the same sense in s 36(1). It is a wide meaning which in cases of permission or invitation is apt to apply both where an express permission or invitation is extended to do the act comprised in the copyright and where such a permission or invitation may be implied. Where a general permission or invitation may be implied it is clearly unnecessary that the authorizing party have knowledge that a particular act comprised in the copyright will be done.

The acts and omissions of the alleged authorizing party must be looked at in the circumstances in which the act comprised in the copyright is done. The circumstances will include the likelihood that such an act will be done. '… [t]he Court may infer an authorization or permission from acts which fall short of being direct and positive; … indifference, exhibited by acts of commission or omission, may reach a degree from which authorization or permission may be inferred. It is a question of fact in each case what is the true inference to be drawn from the conduct of the person who is said to have authorized …' (per Bankes LJ in *Performing Right Society Ltd v Ciryl Theatrical Syndicate Ltd* [1924] 1 KB 1 at p 9).

[Both Gibbs J and Jacobs J held that the university was liable for authorising infringement.]

Following the decision in *Moorhouse*, the *Copyright Act* was amended to ensure that libraries would not be liable for authorising infringing copies made by patrons, provided that the library displays a prescribed notice near the machines: ss 39A, 104B and *Copyright Regulations 1969* (Cth), reg 4B, 17A and Sch 3.

PERFORMANCES

Another common scenario involving potential authorisation liability arises where a person provides premises in which an infringing performance occurs. Section 39 of the *Copyright Act* provides that a person who permits a place of public entertainment to be used for an infringing performance of a work is liable for infringement, unless they establish that (1) they were not aware and had no reasonable grounds for suspecting the performance would be infringing; or (2) they gave permission to use the premises gratuitously or for a nominal fee. Cases can also be pleaded and argued under general authorisation liability under s 36(1A), such as the case extracted below. This case is also interesting for its discussion of the relevance of contractual provisions which attempt to shift responsibility for infringements.

CASE EXTRACT: CURRENT LAW

Australasian Performing Right Association Ltd v Metro on George Pty Ltd

[2004] FCA 1123; (2004) 64 IPR 57
Federal Court of Australia

[APRA grants a range of licences for performances of musical works with respect to the whole of its (extensive) repertoire on a 'blanket' basis. Metro held regular live performances of music and had a venue licence for a number of years. In 2002 Metro elected not to renew its licence and instead sought to rely on contractual clauses that shifted responsibility for copyright licensing onto the venue hirer or performer.]

Bennett J: 39. In detailed correspondence between the parties, the respondents assert:

- Metro does not arrange or provide performances or entertainment by 'live artist performers' or by recorded means. It simply hires out its theatre to third parties so that those third parties can then promote or arrange live artists or dance parties. Metro does not retain any 'gross sums paid for admission' to Metro on George. If the theatre has not been hired out to a third party, it does not open for business.
- Metro does not exercise any artistic judgment in the decision to hire the venue to potential bands and has no control over what performances will be given at any event.
- Metro does not authorise or permit the performance of any copyright material at Metro on George.
- Licence fees paid to APRA from 1 August 1994 to 30 June 1998 were incorrectly paid, as no venue licence was required ...

...

APPROVAL, SANCTIONING OR COUNTENANCING

42. The Metro contract states that Metro does not authorise or permit any particular performance, whether containing copyright material or otherwise and that the hirer warrants that it will ensure that all performances comply with the Act and the licence requirements of APRA.

43. The inclusion of these clauses in the Metro contract is said by Metro to bring it within s 36(1A) (c) of the Act, being a reasonable step to prevent or avoid the doing of the act, being the act comprised in the copyright.

44. The inclusion of the warranty in the Metro contract was a reasonable step to take which, if implemented by the hirer, would have prevented an unlicensed performance. However, s 36(1A)(c) does not address steps to prevent or avoid infringement generally, rather it addresses steps to prevent or

CURRENT LAW

avoid the doing of the act itself, that is the act comprised in the copyright in a work. Metro did not take steps to prevent or avoid the performances.

45. Further, the inclusion of the warranty in the Metro contract was not, in the majority of cases, implemented. It did not result in the hirer obtaining an APRA licence, although some hirers did. APRA informed Metro that unlicensed performances had taken place and there is no evidence that Metro took any action. Metro did not take steps to inquire whether a licence had been obtained or to ensure that it had. From the evidence, it is apparent that Metro took the view that it need do nothing further. While the warranty under the Metro contract amounted to more than a warning, to the extent that it notified the hirers of their obligations it was, in the circumstances, insufficient to exonerate Metro.

46. [Counsel for Metro] Mr Bannon submits that authorisation or permission requires knowledge or suspicion of particular acts of infringement and questions whether that was present here. In my view, the authorities and, in particular, *Moorhouse* (at CLR 13) support [counsel for APRA] Mr Catterns' submission that the absence of prior notice as to which particular works would be performed does not assist Metro. There can be no dispute that Metro, after the May letter at the least, had reason to suspect that works in APRA's repertoire would be performed, even if there was no knowledge of a particular work.

47. Metro asserts that, in the absence of the identification of a particular act or acts on the part of Metro, finding Metro liable for authorising infringement would require expansion of accepted principle. This submission is not borne out by examination of the relevant authorities. In [*Australasian Performing Right Association v*] *Jain* [(1990) 26 FCR 53] the court considered authorisation in the sense of 'countenance': at FCR 61 ... It was held that a studied and deliberate course of action ignoring APRA's rights and allowing a situation to develop and to continue in which the alleged infringer must have known that it was likely that APRA's music would be played without any licence, where it was within power to control what was occurring, was sufficient to amount to authorisation of infringement.

48. Metro has not established that it was not aware or had no reasonable grounds for suspecting that performances would be an infringement of copyright. It was made clear in the letter from BHF [solicitors Banki, Haddock & Fiora] of 15 July 2002, that APRA's contention was that unlicensed performances were taking place at Metro and that they constituted, in APRA's view, infringements of copyright. At least from this time, Metro was on notice that, despite the clause in the Metro contract, hirers of the venue were not taking APRA licences and that the clause was being ignored ... I am satisfied that, prior to the July letter, Metro was either aware of or was indifferent to the occurrence of unlicensed performances at Metro on George. The failure to make an inquiry of the hirer, in the face of APRA's assertions, can at best be described as a wilful disregard of whether the performance of works which it knew or ought reasonably to have known would include works within APRA's copyright were performed with APRA's authorisation or not. As was said by Kiefel J in *Golden Editions Pty Ltd v Polygram Pty Ltd* (1996) 61 FCR 479 at 487–8 ... 'a deliberate choice not to inquire, in such circumstances, may enable a further finding, since it may suggest a mind in which real suspicion resided' and a failure to put such a question operated 'to his peril'. It is inconsistent with the application of s 39(2) of the Act ...

...

83. Metro cannot, after the notification letter of 15 July 2002, avail itself of the defence afforded by s 39(2) ...

INTERNET INTERMEDIARIES AND INTERNET SERVICE PROVIDERS (ISPS)

Authorisation liability has been used by copyright owners in an attempt to address mass infringement online, with cases brought against a series of website and peer-to-peer software providers: see for example *A&M Records Inc v Napster Inc*, 239 F 3d 1004 (9th Cir 2001) (an early peer-to-peer filesharing system); *Universal Music Australia Pty Ltd v Sharman License Holdings Ltd* [2005] FCA 1242; (2005) 65 IPR 289 (providers of Kazaa peer-to-peer software); *Metro-Goldwyn-Mayer Studios Inc v Grokster Ltd*, 545 US 913 (2005) (providers of Grokster peer-to-peer software); *Cooper v Universal Music Australia Pty Ltd* [2006] FCAFC 187; (2006) 156 FCR 380 (the MP3s4free website). Some peer-to-peer providers have developed commercial models that capitalise on the legal difficulties of pursuing infringers in an online environment.[9] This activity is a major affront to owners as well as to the authority of the law.

To some degree the authorisation provisions direct the energies of third parties to assist with enforcement of copyright. However, this increases costs and complicates their relations with customers, so third parties are often reluctant to investigate and pursue alleged infringers on behalf of copyright owners. One particularly contentious debate internationally and in Australia has been over the extent to which ISPs should be required to take steps to reduce peer-to-peer filesharing by customers using their services: whether by passing on warnings or taking stronger action such as reduction, suspension or termination of service.

The Australian provisions relating to the liability of ISPs for copyright infringement are complex as a result of piecemeal amendment over time. Although general principles of authorisation liability apply, a number of specific provisions also address liability online. First, the *Copyright Amendment (Digital Agenda) Act 2000* (Cth) introduced ss 39B and 112E, the former of which provides:

> A person (including a carrier or carriage service provider) who provides facilities for making, or facilitating the making of, a communication is not taken to have authorised any infringement of copyright in a work merely because another person uses the facilities so provided to do something the right to do which is included in the copyright.

Section 112E is in identical terms, except that it refers to 'an audio-visual item' rather than 'a work'. Both 'carrier' and 'carriage service provider' are defined in the *Telecommunications Act 1997* (Cth): broadly, they refer to a set of telecommunications providers, including ISPs, operating under that Act; they do not include other online service providers such as website hosts, search engines, universities or schools, or other institutions providing internet service and hosting to staff and students. In addition, in 2004, as a requirement of AUSFTA, Australia also introduced 'safe harbours' in Part V Div 2AA of the *Copyright Act*. The safe harbours are discussed in Chapter 19. Broadly, a carriage service provider, which carries out certain online activities set out in ss 116AC–116AF (transmitting communications, caching, hosting and providing information location tools), and which complies with certain conditions (set out in s 116AH), is protected from any monetary liability for both direct and authorisation liability, although it can be subject to certain kinds of injunctions (s 116AG). For ISPs providing internet access to customers and transmitting the communications of third parties in an unmodified way, the conditions are limited: they must comply with any industry code in force (at the time of writing no such codes exist) and they must 'adopt and reasonably implement a policy that provides for the termination, in appropriate circumstances, of the accounts of repeat infringers'. The liability of ISPs for infringement by their customers under

---

9   R Giblin, *Code Wars: 10 Years of P2P Litigation*, Edward Elgar, Cheltenham, 2011.

current law was considered in *Roadshow Films Pty Ltd v iiNet Ltd* [2012] HCA 16; (2012) 248 CLR 42, extracted below.

Some jurisdictions have sought to involve ISPs in copyright enforcement through specific legislation implementing a system of 'graduated response': involving initial warnings to infringing customers followed by escalating measures against users who continue to infringe.[10] In other countries, like the USA, similar systems have been instituted through private agreements between some copyright owners and ISPs. In July 2014, the Australian Attorney-General's Department and Department of Communications issued an *Online Copyright Infringement Discussion Paper* which proposed a series of measures, including amending ss 36(1A) and 101(1A) to expand authorisation liability to provide incentives for ISPs to respond to customers' infringement, as well as a new power in the court to issue injunctions to require ISPs to block access to websites that have the dominant purpose of infringing copyright. In December 2014, the government indicated that it would not be making any changes to the law of authorisation, but rather would require ISPs and copyright owners to negotiate a code of practice incorporating mechanisms for passing notices on infringing users, as well as a process for facilitated discovery to allow right holders to take direct infringement against a user after an agreed number of notices. The government also indicated that it would amend the *Copyright Act*, to enable rights holders to apply for a court order requiring ISPs to block access to an overseas website providing access to infringing content. Website blocking injunctions are available in the UK under s 97A of the *Copyright, Designs and Patents Act 1988* (UK) and have been granted in a series of UK High Court decisions including *Twentieth Century Fox Film Corporation and others v Newzbin Ltd* [2010] EWHC 608 (Ch); [2010] FSR 21; *Twentieth Century Fox Film Corp v British Telecommunications plc* [2011] EWHC 1981 (Ch); [2012] 1 All ER 806; and *EMI Records Ltd v British Sky Broadcasting Ltd* [2013] EWHC 379 (Ch); [2013] FSR 31.

CASE EXTRACT: CURRENT LAW

Roadshow Films Pty Ltd v iiNet Ltd

[2012] HCA 16; (2012) 248 CLR 42
High Court of Australia

[The appellants were 34 film and television production companies that owned, or had exclusive licences to, copyright in popular movies and television series. The litigation was coordinated by the Australian Federation Against Copyright Theft (AFACT). The respondent, iiNet, was one of Australia's largest ISPs providing internet access to the general public. Some of iiNet's customers were using the BitTorrent protocol to download and 'share' the appellants' films. Software using BitTorrent (known as the BitTorrent 'client') allowed an individual user to download (and simultaneously upload) bits of a digital file from many different users also interested in the same file (the 'swarm'). At the time of the case, an individual would obtain a .torrent file for the desired movie or television program from a website (such as The Pirate Bay). The .torrent file contained information about the relevant file and where to find the 'tracker'—the computer program on a server that monitored the relevant swarm and which could provide the client with the IP addresses of people sharing the file at that time. Armed with

---

10 For example, in France (*Loi 2009-1311 du 28 Octobre 2009 relative à la Protection Pénale de la Propriété Littéraire et Artistique sur Internet*, Arts 6 and 7, 251 Journal Officiel de la République Française, 29 October 2009, 18290) and New Zealand (*Copyright (Infringing File Sharing) Amendment Act 2011* (NZ)).

this information the client could start downloading bits of the file from swarm members (and uploading to other members).

AFACT hired a company, DtecNet, which used modified software to connect with swarms sharing the appellants' films and television programs, download bits only from iiNet subscribers, and log information about the pieces downloaded. AFACT then sent weekly notices of infringement to iiNet including this information, sufficient to identify subscriber accounts involved. The notices did not, however, contain any explanation of how the data was generated: DtecNet's methods were only fully revealed to iiNet during proceedings.

AFACT's notices demanded that iiNet prevent the accounts from being used to infringe copyright, and 'take any other action available under iiNet's Customer Relationship Agreement (CRA) which was appropriate having regard to their conduct'. The CRA gave iiNet the right to terminate service for illegal conduct. iiNet took the view that it had no obligation to act. The appellants commenced proceedings alleging that iiNet's failure to act constituted authorisation of copyright infringement. This claim failed at both first instance and on appeal to the Full Federal Court; an appeal was brought to the High Court.]

French CJ, Crennan and Kiefel JJ (some footnotes omitted): 5. The key question in the appeal, whether iiNet authorised its customers' infringing acts, 'depends upon all the facts of the case' [*University of New South Wales v Moorhouse* (1975) 133 CLR 1 at 12 per Gibbs J]. The facts and circumstances on which the appellants rely to support their contention that iiNet authorised its customers' infringing acts include the following:

- the provision by iiNet to its customers (and to other users of those customers' accounts) of access to the internet, which can be used generally and, in particular, to access the BitTorrent system;
- the infringement of the copyright in the appellants' films by customers of iiNet who have made the films available online in whole or in part using the BitTorrent system;
- the knowledge by iiNet of specific infringements, as drawn to its attention by notices from the Australian Federation Against Copyright Theft (AFACT), representing the appellants;
- the technical and contractual power of iiNet to terminate the provision of its services to customers infringing copyright; and
- the failure by iiNet to take reasonable steps to warn identified infringing customers to cease their infringements and, if appropriate, to terminate the provision of its services to them.

For the reasons that follow, in our opinion, the conduct of iiNet did not constitute authorisation of its customers' infringing acts.

. . .

63. The appeal can be determined by asking interrelated questions informed by s 101(1A). Did iiNet have a power to prevent the primary infringements and, if so, what was the extent of that power (s 101(1A)(a))? Did reasonable steps to prevent those infringements (after receipt of the AFACT notices) include warnings and subsequent suspension or termination of the accounts of all customers identified as infringing the appellants' copyrights (s 101(1A)(c)), if such customers failed to cease communicating infringing material using the BitTorrent system? How does the relationship between iiNet and its customers (s 101(1A)(b)) bear on each of those questions? It will be observed that these are largely questions of fact and the ultimate question of whether iiNet authorised the infringements will be an inference to be drawn from those facts.

64. Before turning to those questions, some general observations as to matters of fact need to be reiterated. Access to the internet can be used for diverse purposes, including viewing websites,

CURRENT LAW

downloading or streaming non-infringing content, sending and receiving emails, social networking, accessing online media and games, and making voice over IP telephone calls. The BitTorrent system is also capable of being used for non-infringing purposes.

IINET'S POWER TO PREVENT PRIMARY INFRINGEMENTS
TECHNICAL POWER

65. It is important to note that iiNet has no involvement with any part of the BitTorrent system and therefore has no power to control or alter any aspect of the BitTorrent system, including the BitTorrent client. Further, iiNet is not a host of infringing material, or of websites which make available .torrent files relating to infringing material. iiNet does not assist its customers to locate BitTorrent clients or .torrent files by any indexing service or database entries. It cannot monitor the steps taken by users of its internet services under the BitTorrent system, it cannot directly prevent users of its internet services from downloading a BitTorrent client or .torrent files, and it cannot identify specific films to which users of its internet services seek access. Once infringing material is stored on a customer's computer iiNet cannot take down or remove that material, and cannot filter or block the communication of that material over its internet service. Nor has iiNet any power to prevent its customers from using other internet services—and, as noted earlier, several users of an internet service may share an IP address. While the relationship between iiNet and its customers involves the provision of technology, iiNet had no direct technical power at its disposal to prevent a customer from using the BitTorrent system to download the appellants' films on that customer's computer with the result that the appellants' films were made available online in breach of s 86(c).

CONTRACTUAL POWER

66. Under the CRA, iiNet contracted to give its customers access to the internet (which carried with it power to use the internet for infringing or non-infringing purposes) on the basis (set out in cl 4.2(a) and (e) of the CRA) that iiNet was not thereby purporting to grant to the customer any right to use the internet to infringe another person's rights, or for illegal purposes.

67. Because the CRA, in its terms, indicated iiNet's express, formal and positive disapproval of using access to the internet for infringing or illegal purposes, the appellants were driven to rely on the notion that iiNet's inactivity (after receipt of the AFACT notices) amounted at least to 'countenancing' acts of primary infringement.

68. 'Countenance' is a long-established English word which, unsurprisingly, has numerous forms and a number of meanings which encompass expressing support, including moral support or encouragement. In both the United Kingdom and Canada, it has been observed that some of the meanings of 'countenance' are not co-extensive with 'authorise' [*Amstrad Consumer Electronics plc v British Phonographic Industry Ltd* [1986] FSR 159 at 207 per Lawton LJ, approved in *CBS Songs Ltd v Amstrad Consumer Electronics plc* [1988] AC 1013 at 1055; per Lord Templeman. See also *CCH Canadian Ltd v Law Society of Upper Canada* [2004] 1 SCR 339 at [38]]. Such meanings are remote from the reality of authorisation which the statute contemplates. The argument highlights the danger in placing reliance on one of the synonyms for 'authorise' to be found in a dictionary. While resort to such meanings may have been necessary in the past, attention is now directed in the first place to s 101(1A). That provision is intended to inform the drawing of an inference of authorisation by reference to the facts and circumstances there identified, and recourse must be had to it. That is an express requirement.

CURRENT LAW

69. Even it if were possible to be satisfied that iiNet's inactivity after receipt of the AFACT notices, and its subsequent media releases, 'supported' or 'encouraged' its customers to continue to make certain films available online, s 101(1A) (construed with both ss 22(6) and 112E) makes it plain that that would not be enough to make iiNet a secondary infringer. An alleged authoriser must have a power to prevent the primary infringements [*WEA International Inc v Hanimex Corporation Ltd* (1987) 17 FCR 274 at 286–8]. *Australasian Performing Right Association Ltd v Jain* [(1990) 26 FCR 53], *Australian Tape Manufacturers Association Ltd v Commonwealth* [(1993) 176 CLR 480], *Universal Music Australia Pty Ltd v Sharman License Holdings Ltd* [(2005) 220 ALR 1] and *Cooper v Universal Music Australia Pty Ltd* [(2006) 156 FCR 380] all confirm that there must be such a power to prevent. So much had been recognised earlier, in any event, in *Adelaide Corporation [v Australasian Performing Right Association Ltd* (1928) 40 CLR 481 at 498-9] and [*University of New South Wales v*] *Moorhouse* [(1975) 133 CLR 1 at 12].

70. As explained, the extent of iiNet's power was limited. It had no direct power to prevent the primary infringements and could only ensure that result indirectly by terminating the contractual relationship it had with its customers.

REASONABLE STEPS

71. The nature of the internet, the BitTorrent system, and the absence of any industry code of practice adhered to by all ISPs are all factors which are relevant to the statutory task of assessing whether iiNet took reasonable steps to prevent or avoid the primary infringements, given its indirect power to do so.

72. Conventionally, the efficacy of warnings to infringers from owners (or licensees) of copyright derives from, and is reinforced by, the potential for successful injunctive proceedings, including interim relief, coupled with an award of damages or an account of profits, and an order for costs against a proven infringer. Whether a non-responsive infringer is continuing to infringe after receipt of a warning notice from a copyright owner may often be checked with relative ease if infringing material is in the public market place.

73. Termination of an iiNet account with a customer who has infringed will assuredly prevent the continuation of a specific act of communicating a film online using a particular .torrent file on a particular computer. Regrettably, however, on receiving a threat of such termination, it is possible for a customer to engage another ISP for access to the internet on that computer or access the internet on another computer using a different ISP. While any new infringement would be just as serious as the specific primary infringements about which the appellants complain, this circumstance shows the limitations on iiNet's power to command a response from its customers, or to prevent continuing infringements by them.

74. Whatever responses iiNet received to warnings, iiNet would be obliged to update the investigative exercise underlying the AFACT notices either itself or by reference to subsequent AFACT notices (allowing an appropriate interval for compliance with a request to cease infringement) before proceeding further.

75. Updating the investigative exercise in the AFACT notices would require iiNet to understand and apply DtecNet's methodology—which, among other things, involved a permission to DtecNet from AFACT to use the BitTorrent system to download the appellants' films. Before the filing of experts' reports in the proceedings, the information in the AFACT notices did not approximate the evidence which would be expected to be filed in civil proceedings in which interlocutory relief was sought by a copyright owner in respect of an allegation of copyright infringement. Also, any wrongful termination of

CURRENT LAW

a customer's account could expose iiNet to risk of liability. These considerations highlight the danger to an ISP, which is neither a copyright owner nor a licensee, which terminates (or threatens to terminate) a customer's internet service in the absence of any industry protocol binding on all ISPs, or any, even interim, curial assessment of relevant matters.

76. iiNet's inactivity after receipt of the AFACT notices was described by the appellants as demonstrating a sufficient degree of indifference to their rights to give rise to authorisation. However, the evidence showed that the inactivity was not the indifference of a company unconcerned with infringements of the appellants' rights. Rather, the true inference to be drawn is that iiNet was unwilling to act because of its assessment of the risks of taking steps based only on the information in the AFACT notices. Moreover, iiNet's customers could not possibly infer from iiNet's inactivity (if they knew about it), and the subsequent media releases (if they saw them), that iiNet was in a position to grant those customers rights to make the appellants' films available online.

CONCLUSIONS

77. The appellants' submission, that iiNet should be taken to have authorised the infringements unless it took measures with respect to its customers, assumes obligations on the part of an ISP which the *Copyright Act* does not impose. A consideration of the factors listed in s 101(1A) does not permit a conclusion that iiNet is to be held liable as having authorised the infringements.

78. The extent of iiNet's power was limited to an indirect power to prevent a customer's primary infringement of the appellants' films by terminating the contractual relationship between them. The information contained in the AFACT notices, as and when they were served, did not provide iiNet with a reasonable basis for sending warning notices to individual customers containing threats to suspend or terminate those customers' accounts. For these reasons, iiNet's inactivity after receipt of the AFACT notices did not give rise to an inference of authorisation (by 'countenancing' or otherwise) of any act of primary infringement by its customers.

79. This final conclusion shows that the concept and the principles of the statutory tort of authorisation of copyright infringement are not readily suited to enforcing the rights of copyright owners in respect of widespread infringements occasioned by peer-to-peer file sharing, as occurs with the BitTorrent system. The difficulties of enforcement which such infringements pose for copyright owners have been addressed elsewhere, in constitutional settings different from our own, by specially targeted legislative schemes, some of which incorporate cooperative industry protocols, some of which require judicial involvement in the termination of internet accounts, and some of which provide for the sharing of enforcement costs between ISPs and copyright owners.

Gummow and Hayne JJ: 117. As was emphasised in *Stevens v Kabushiki Kaisha Sony Computer Entertainment* [(2005) 224 CLR 193 at [54]], given the complexity of the characteristics of modern copyright law it perhaps is inevitable that the legislation will give rise to difficult questions of construction. After a century, the selection of the term 'authorise' to identify the activity constituting secondary infringement continues to give rise to difficulty. But the difficulties, which reflect both technological developments and changes in business methods, are unlikely to be resolved merely by recourse to a dictionary.

. . .

120. The history of the Act since 1968 shows that the parliament is more responsive to pressures for change to accommodate new circumstances than in the past. Those pressures are best resolved

by legislative processes rather than by any extreme exercise in statutory interpretation by judicial decisions.

...

125. Like Gibbs J [in *Moorhouse* at 12], Jacobs J accepted as applicable to the current Australian legislation the meaning 'sanction, approve, countenance' given to 'authorise' as it appeared in s 1(2) of the Imperial Act in *Evans v E Hulton & Co Ltd* [[1923–28] MacG Cop Cas 51] by Tomlin J and then in *Falcon v Famous Players Film Co* [[1926] 2 KB 474] by Bankes LJ. Two points should be made respecting that expression. The first is that it would be wrong to take from it one element, such as 'countenance', and by fixing upon the broadest dictionary meaning of that word to seek to expand the core notion of 'authorise'. The second point is that, given the generality of that expression, there is force in the following statement by Herring CJ in *Winstone v Wurlitzer Automatic Phonograph Co of Australia Pty Ltd* [[1946] VLR 338 at 345]:

> As the acts that may be complained of as infringements of copyright are multifarious, so, too, the conduct that may justify an inference of authorisation may take on an infinite variety of differing forms. In these circumstances any attempt to prescribe beforehand ready-made tests for determining on which side of the line a particular case will fall, would seem doomed to failure.

...

128. In *Moorhouse*, Jacobs J adopted a passage in the judgment of Bankes LJ in [*Performing Right Society Ltd v Ciryl Theatrical Syndicate Ltd* [1924] 1 KB 1]. This was to the effect that indifference, exhibited by acts of commission or omission, 'may reach a degree' from which there may be inferred authorisation. It is upon this notion of indifference to the requisite degree on the part of iiNet that the appellants rely for the proposition that iiNet sanctioned, in the sense of countenanced, the scheduled infringements. The contrast between the notion of indifference, and the requirement by the United States Supreme Court in [*Metro-Goldwyn-Mayer Studios Inc v Grokster Ltd* 545 US 913 (2005) at 930] of intentional inducement or encouragement of 'contributory infringement', will be apparent.

129. The appellants rely upon the notion of 'countenancing' to encompass acts or omissions which are less precise or explicit than those involved in 'sanctioning' or 'approving'. But in considering *Moorhouse*, and the adoption by Jacobs J of the statement by Bankes LJ in *Ciryl*, it should be emphasised that the university controlled access not only to the coin or token operated photocopying machines in a room close to the library but also to the book copied by Mr Paul Brennan and the premises containing the library and the machines.

130. The relief granted by this court in *Moorhouse* was limited to a declaration that the university on a particular date had authorised the doing by Mr Brennan of the act of reproducing a particular literary work in a material form and thereby had infringed the copyright in that work of the respondents [*Moorhouse* at 25]. In *Australian Tape Manufacturers Association Ltd v Commonwealth* [(1993) 176 CLR 480 at 498] Mason CJ, Brennan, Deane and Gaudron JJ described as critical to the decision in *Moorhouse* the power of the university to control what was done by way of copying; the university not only had failed to take steps to prevent infringement but had provided potential infringers with both copyright material and the use of its machines by which copies of the copyright material could be made.

Their Honours referred in that regard to a passage in the reasons of Jacobs J, and distinguished the case before them as follows [at 498]:

> manufacture and sale of articles such as blank tapes or video recorders, which have lawful uses, do not constitute authorization of infringement of copyright, even if the manufacturer or vendor knows that there is a likelihood that the articles will be used for an infringing purpose such as home taping of sound recordings, so long as the manufacturer or vendor has no control over the purchaser's use of the article.

. . .

135. Section 101(1A) is so drawn as to take an act of primary infringement and ask whether or not a person has authorised that act of primary infringement. In answering that question there will be 'matters' that must be taken into account. These include, but are not confined to, the matters identified in paras (a), (b) and (c). Was there any relationship that existed between the primary infringer and the (alleged) secondary infringer? If so, what was its nature (par (b))? Did the secondary infringer have power to prevent the primary infringement; if so, what was the extent of that power (para (a))? Other than the exercise of that power, did the secondary infringer take any reasonable steps to prevent the primary infringement, or to avoid the commission of that infringement (para (c))?

136. In answering these questions an ISP is not to be taken to have authorised primary infringement of a cinematograph film 'merely because' it has provided facilities for making it available online to a user who is the primary infringer: s 112E.

137. As indicated earlier in these reasons, the power of iiNet as an ISP with respect to the use of facilities provided to subscribers was limited by the nature of their commercial relationship; iiNet could not control the choice of its subscribers and other users to utilise the BitTorrent software, nor could iiNet modify the BitTorrent software or take down the appellants' films which were made available online.

138. At all material times iiNet had many thousands of account holders. Was it a reasonable step to require of iiNet that it monitor continually the activities of IP addresses to provide precise details of primary infringements that had been committed, and then take further steps to forestall further infringements? Warnings might or might not have that effect. Evidence was lacking of likely behaviour in that respect by users of ISP facilities. Further, with respect to the AFACT notices, was it reasonable to expect iiNet to issue warnings or to suspend or terminate the contracts of customers when AFACT had not fully disclosed the methods used to obtain the information in the AFACT notices? Those methods were disclosed only by the provision of expert evidence during the preparation of the case for trial.

139. In truth, the only indisputably practical course of action would be an exercise of contractual power to switch off and terminate further activity on suspect accounts. But this would not merely avoid further infringement; it would deny to the iiNet customers non-infringing uses of the iiNet facilities. And, in any event, in the absence of an effective protocol binding ISPs (and there is no such protocol) the iiNet subscribers whose agreements were cancelled by iiNet would be free to take their business to another ISP.

. . .

142. The 'key facts' as to the 'indifference' of iiNet upon which the appellants relied in this court were four in number. They were: (i) the provision by iiNet of the internet connections, a necessary but insufficient step for the acts of primary infringement; (ii) the technical ability of iiNet to control the use of its service and its contractual ability to issue warnings and suspend or terminate accounts; (iii) the

evidence provided by the AFACT notices given before and after suit; and (iv) the absence of action by iiNet in response to the AFACT notices.

143. These matters, taken together, do not establish a case of authorisation of those primary infringements which are the scheduled infringements in respect of the authorisation of which the appellants seek relief in this court. The progression urged by the appellants from the evidence, to 'indifference', to 'countenancing', and so to 'authorisation', is too long a march.

144. The facts of this case are well removed from those which in *Moorhouse* led Jacobs J to adopt what had been said on the subject of indifference by Bankes LJ in *Ciryl*. The rhetorical question with reference to what had been said by Bankes LJ, which Whitford J posed in *CBS Inc v Ames Records & Tapes Ltd* [[1982] Ch 91 at 112], may be asked here:

> Is this again a case of the indifference of somebody who did not consider it his business to interfere, who had no desire to see another person's copyright infringed, but whose view was that copyright and infringement were matters in this case not for him, but for the owners of the copyright? It must be recalled that the most important matter to bear in mind is the circumstances established in evidence in each case.

...

146. The present case is not one where the conduct of the respondent's business was such that the primary infringements utilising BitTorrent were 'bound' to happen in the sense apparent in *Evans v E Hulton & Co Ltd* [at 60], and discussed earlier in these reasons. Further, iiNet only in an attenuated sense had power to 'control' the primary infringements utilising BitTorrent. It was not unreasonable for iiNet to take the view that it need not act upon the incomplete allegations of primary infringements in the AFACT notices without further investigation which it should not be required itself to undertake, at its peril of committing secondary infringement.

Both judgments also considered the exception in s 112E for persons providing facilities for communications, holding that the exception was redundant, enacted, perhaps, out of an 'abundance of caution' (Gummow and Hayne JJ at [113]). French CJ, Crennan and Kiefel JJ stated at [26]:

> The 2000 amendments predated the release of the BitTorrent system. Their evident purpose was to respond to new communications technology by attempting to strike a balance between conflicting policy considerations. Access to internet technology is fostered by ss 22(6), 22(6A), 112E and 39B, and the 'safe harbour' provisions, ss 116AA to 116AJ; the rights of copyright owners are enhanced by relevant amendments to ss 10, 31, 85, 86 and 87; the statutory clarification of the concept of authorisation in s 101(1A) is balanced against ss 22(6) and 112E. All three of those last-mentioned provisions can apply to a third party intermediary between copyright owners and copyright infringers (such as an ISP) although, as noted correctly by the primary judge (Cowdroy J), s 112E appears to provide protection where none is required [*Roadshow Films (No 3)* at [574]. See also M Ficsor, 'Copyright for the Digital Era: The WIPO "Internet" Treaties' (1997) 21 *Columbia-VLA Journal of Law & Arts* 197, p 214.]

The High Court did not address the application of the safe harbours in Part V Div 2AA and the point was not pressed by iiNet on appeal. At first instance, the trial judge held that iiNet would have been entitled to rely on the safe harbours: *Roadshow Films Pty Ltd v iiNet Ltd (No 3)* [2010] FCA 24; (2010) 83 IPR 430 at [634]. The Full Federal Court unanimously overturned the trial judge's conclusions on this point (while finding iiNet was not liable for authorising infringement on the facts). The issue was whether iiNet had, and had reasonably implemented, a policy for the termination of repeat infringers as required by s 116AH. iiNet argued that its policy was to terminate the accounts of repeat infringers in three circumstances: (1) when ordered to do so by a court; (2) when a customer admitted to infringing copyright; or (3) when a customer was found by a court or other authority to have infringed. There was a debate in the case over whether iiNet had in fact adopted such a policy, but the Full Federal Court held that this policy, even if adopted, would not have been sufficient. The policy was insufficiently specific in failing to identify who would be treated as a 'repeat infringer' and the circumstances in which service would be terminated: *Roadshow Films Pty Ltd v iiNet Ltd* [2010] FCAFC 23; (2011) 194 FCR 285 at [520] (Jagot J) and [805] (Nicholas J). A majority also held that the policy failed to provide for termination in some circumstances where it would be appropriate: in the majority's view, iiNet's policy ought to have provided for termination of a customer's account where iiNet was aware of knowing, repeated infringements on a commercial scale using that customers' account: at [264] (Emmett J) and [806] (Nicholas J). The Full Federal Court decision suggests that, unlike US courts under equivalent provisions,[11] Australian courts may be willing to judge the substantive merits of policies adopted by ISPs under the safe harbours.

INDIRECT INFRINGEMENT

Indirect infringement relates to certain conduct specifically prescribed by the Act that either facilitates direct infringement or involves dealing with infringing copies of works. The *Copyright Act* provisions include:

* providing a place of public entertainment to be used for infringing performances (s 39: 'Infringement by permitting place of public entertainment to be used for performance of work', as mentioned above);
* unauthorised importation of works (ss 37, 102: 'Infringement by importation for sale or hire'); and
* commercial dealings with infringing works (ss 38, 103: 'Infringement by sale and other dealings').

Under ss 37 and 38 the onus of proving the absence of the licence of the owner of the copyright lies on the party who asserts infringement. The reason why that is so is that the absence of such licence constitutes an element of the wrong of infringement under those sections: see *Avel Pty Ltd v Multicoin Amusements Pty Ltd* (1990) 171 CLR 88.

Liability under ss 37–39 also requires that the defendant had actual or constructive knowledge that the copy, or performance, was an infringement of copyright. In *Pioneer Electronics Australia Pty Ltd v Lee* [2000] FCA 1926; (2000) 108 FCR 216 Sundberg J noted at [34] that this was not a 'reasonable man' test, but 'a court is entitled to infer knowledge on the part of a particular person on the assumption that such a person has the ordinary understanding expected of persons in his line of business'. He went on to add:

> a court is entitled to approach the matter in two stages; where opportunities for knowledge
> on the part of the particular person are proved and there is nothing to indicate that there are

---

11 *Corbis Corp v Amazon.com, Inc*, 351 F Supp 2d 1090 (WD Wash 2004); *UMG Recordings, Inc v Veoh Networks, Inc*, 665 F Supp 2d 1099 (CD Cal 2009).

obstacles to the particular person acquiring the relevant knowledge, there is some evidence from which the court can conclude that such a person has the knowledge. However, this conclusion may be easily overturned by a denial on his part of the knowledge which the court accepts, or by a demonstration that he is properly excused from giving evidence of his actual knowledge.

IMPORTATION AND PARALLEL IMPORTATION

The effect of ss 37 and 38 is to deem importers to have been makers of the infringing article in Australia (see *Polo/Lauren Company LP v Ziliani Holdings Pty Ltd* [2008] FCAFC 195; (2008) 173 FCR 266); that is, importation of an article is prohibited if it would be infringement had the importer made the article in Australia. This gives copyright owners the right to prevent importation of works into Australia, including legitimate product, made with the permission of the copyright owner overseas but then imported into Australia without the permission of the local copyright owner. This enables owners to divide the world into separate markets in which they hold a monopoly, which raises free trade and competition concerns.[12] Several government inquiries have suggested that parallel importation restrictions lead to upward pressure on prices paid by Australian consumers, along with poor distribution and market inefficiencies, including most recently the *Inquiry into IT Pricing* (2013) conducted by the House of Representatives Standing Committee on Infrastructure and Communications.[13]

There has been a gradual winding back of parallel importation restrictions. At the time of writing copyright owners' rights to prevent importation are restricted in the following cases:

- *Books:* To qualify for protection, the Australian territorial rights holder must release the book in Australia within 30 days of it being published elsewhere in the world, and must maintain capacity to resupply it within 90 days. This does not affect the right of consumers to purchase books directly from overseas booksellers, and booksellers can import to fill a customer order: ss 44A, 112A.
- *Electronic versions of books, periodicals and printed music:* There are no restrictions on legitimate goods: ss 44F, 112DA.
- *Computer Games:* There are no restrictions on legitimate goods: s 44E.
- *Sound recordings:* There are no restrictions on legitimate goods where it can be shown that it is sourced from a country that is party to the *Berne Convention for the Protection of Literary and Artistic Works* (1886) or the TRIPS Agreement: ss 44D, 112D, 10AA.
- *Artistic works and literary works:* Copyright in product labels (an accessory to an article) cannot be used to prevent importation of legitimate goods (e.g. relying on copyright in the label to prevent importation of that product that would otherwise have unrestricted entry): ss 44B, 44C; see *Polo/Lauren Co LP v Ziliani Holdings Pty Ltd* [2008] FCAFC 195; (2008) 173 FCR 266.

---

12 See J Nielsen, 'Competition Law and Intellectual Property: Establishing a Coherent Approach' in K Bowrey, M Handler and D Nicol, eds, *Emerging Challenges in Intellectual Property*, Oxford University Press, Melbourne, 2011.

13 See also *Universal Music Australia Pty Ltd v Australian Competition & Consumer Commission* [2003] FCAFC 193; (2003) 131 FCR 529; Intellectual Property and Competition Review Committee, *Review of Intellectual Property Legislation under the Competition Principles Agreement* (2000); Productivity Commission, *Restriction on the Parallel Importation of Books: Research Report* (2009).

CRIMINAL OFFENCES

Criminal offences were part of the first federal copyright law (*Copyright Act 1905* (Cth)), and it has long been thought that some criminal offences are necessary in particular in order to ensure that enforcement is possible in the case of 'an offender who is a man of little means'.[14] The *Copyright Amendment Act 2006* (Cth) transformed the criminal provisions, introducing a tiered regime of offences including indictable, summary and strict liability offences. There are criminal offence provisions relating to making, selling, offering, exhibiting and importing infringing copies; and distributing and possessing infringing copies; as well as making or possessing devices for the making of infringing copies: see ss 132AD–132AM.

Not every infringement of copyright is criminal; in general, criminal liability will arise in relation to infringing acts done (or infringing copies possessed) for commercial purposes, or significant infringements on a commercial scale that cause substantial prejudice to the copyright owner (s 132AC).

Indictable, summary and strict liability offences are differentiated via the fault elements that attach to elements of the offence. In order to understand the fault elements it is necessary to read the criminal provisions in conjunction with the provisions of the Australian Criminal Code (*Criminal Code Act 1995* (Cth)). Indictable offences carry a penalty of 550 penalty units and/or five years' imprisonment, while summary offences carry 120 penalty units and/or two years' imprisonment. The Explanatory Memorandum notes that the inherent seriousness of the offences justifies the higher than usual maximum penalty for the summary offences. Strict liability offences carry a penalty of 60 penalty units. Infringing copies and devices and equipment used or intended to be used for making infringing copies can be seized and destroyed: *Copyright Act*, s 133.

The 2006 Act introduced the legislative framework for infringement notices which would allow law enforcement officers to issue on-the-spot fines for copyright infringement; however, no regulations have been issued to bring such a system into effect.[15]

EXCEPTIONS TO INFRINGEMENT

INTRODUCTION

Even if a defendant does an act falling within the exclusive rights of the copyright owner, they may avoid liability if an exception applies. The *Copyright Act* contains a large number of exceptions dotted throughout the Act. The most general are the 'fair dealing' exceptions, which allow the exercise of any of the exclusive rights, without permission or payment, in relation to any kind of copyright subject matter, provided it is for certain defined statutory purposes, is fair and (in some cases) provides for sufficient acknowledgment. In addition to fair dealing, the Act also includes:

- exceptions to allow uses of specific kinds of subject matter—these exceptions adjust the 'one size fits all' copyright rules according to the different nature, or role, of certain subject matters; they include provisions on artistic works (Part III Div 7, ss 65–73) and computer programs (Part III Div 4A, ss 44AB–44H);

---

14 Copyright Law Review Committee (the 'Spicer Committee'), *Report of the Committee appointed by the Attorney-General of the Commonwealth to Consider what Alterations are Desirable in the Copyright Law of the Commonwealth* (1959) at [330].

15 For discussion, see K Weatherall, 'Of Copyright Bureaucracies and Incoherence: Stepping Back from Australia's Recent Copyright Reforms' (2007) 31 *Melbourne University Law Review* 967.

- exceptions for certain institutions which provide some kind of public service or public benefit, warranting qualifications on copyright owners' exclusive rights, such as libraries and archives (ss 48–53; 110A, 110B, 110BA, 112AA), educational institutions (ss 28, 44) and broadcasters (ss 45, 47, 70, 107, 47A, 65, 67); and
- exceptions for private and domestic use of some content, which allow people to make limited copies of works legitimately acquired, for example to move them onto different devices (ss 43C, 47J, 109A, 110AA, 111).

These examples overlap, and this is not a comprehensive list of copyright exceptions. The overlap between copyright and designs is another important set of exceptions, dealt with in Chapter 8. Although it has in the past been suggested that there might be a general, unlegislated 'public interest' exception to copyright, as applies in the UK,[16] Australian courts have not been inclined to entertain arguments beyond the provisions of the *Copyright Act*.[17] It is possible that the constitutional implied freedom of political communication might, in very specific circumstances, prevail over copyright law, but this is untested.[18]

There are also remunerated exceptions. These allow certain uses by certain kinds of people and institutions, without permission, but subject to a requirement to pay the copyright owners equitable remuneration, at a rate either agreed between the parties or determined by the Copyright Tribunal. Most of the remunerated exceptions are administered by collecting societies (discussed in Chapter 5). The justification for most remunerated exceptions lies in the need to correct a market failure. In most of these cases the use is desirable, but there are a large number of copyright owners, and/or a large number of users, meaning that the transaction costs of obtaining voluntary licences are very high. An exception ensures the use can occur, while the requirement of remuneration ensures that incentives for creation are maintained.

The remunerated exceptions allow:

- educational institutions to make copies and communications of some copyright material for educational purposes (Parts VA and VB);
- persons with a disability, or institutions that assist persons with a disability, to make accessible copies (ss 135ZN–135ZT);
- government copying and communication (ss 183 and 183A);
- published sound recordings to be heard in public, which means that restaurants, bars and night clubs can play commercial sound recordings (s 108);
- the broadcasting of published sound recordings (s 109);
- cover versions of published musical works (ss 54–64); and
- the re-transmission of free-to-air television (e.g. by subscription television providers) (Part VC).

The details of the remunerated exceptions are beyond the scope of this text.

In 2013 the Australian Law Reform Commission (ALRC) produced Report No 122, *Copyright and the Digital Economy*. The ALRC was tasked with considering (at p 7):

---

16   *Lion Laboratories v Evans* [1985] QB 526; *Ashdown v Telegraph Group Ltd* [2001] EWCA Civ 1142; [2002] Ch 149.

17   *Collier Constructions Pty Ltd v Foskett Pty Ltd* (1990) 97 ALR 460.

18   For discussion, see R Burrell and J Stellios, 'Copyright and Freedom of Political Communication in Australia' in J Griffiths and U Suthersanen, eds, *Copyright and Freedom of Expression: Comparative and International Analyses*, Oxford University Press, Oxford, 2005.

whether existing exceptions are appropriate and whether further exceptions should recognise fair use of copyright material; allow transformative, innovative and collaborative use of copyright materials to create and deliver new products and services of public benefit; and allow appropriate access, use, interaction and production of copyright material online for social, private or domestic purposes.

The ALRC made a number of recommendations which are discussed at the end of this chapter (see p 295 below).

FAIR DEALING

Fair dealing is one of the ways in which copyright provides for a balance between the needs of owners and users. This end is achieved through reference to specific nominated exceptions to infringement. Fair dealing is permitted for purposes of:

- research or study (ss 40, 103C);
- criticism or review (ss 41, 103A);
- parody or satire (ss 41A; 103AA);
- reporting news (ss 42, 103B); and
- professional advice (s 43(2); the equivalent provision in Pt IV, s 104 is not subject to a 'fairness' test).

The Australian approach to interpretation of these 'user rights'[19] is rather technical and categorical. Courts have tended to focus closely on whether use is for one of the prescribed purposes, with less attention paid to fairness.[20] There is little foundational discussion as to the broad purpose or social objectives served by these exceptions.[21]

Given courts' reluctance in copyright to arbitrate on matters of aesthetics and to promote particular cultural values, it is not surprising that fair dealing causes confusion. Providing legal advice as to when a fair dealing exception applies can be difficult. While it is relatively easy to explain the general compass of the exceptions, the way particular scenarios will be interpreted is less clear.

FAIRNESS

The factors relevant to fairness have been developed mostly through case law; only one pair of statutory provisions, ss 40(2) and 103C(2) (research or study), actually lists statutory fairness factors, these being:

- the purpose and character of the dealing;
- the nature of the (copyright-protected) material;
- the possibility of obtaining the copyright material within a reasonable time at an ordinary commercial price;

---

19   For a characterisation of exceptions as 'user rights', see R Burrell and A Coleman, *Copyright Exceptions: The Digital Impact*, Cambridge University Press, Cambridge, 2005, p 279; *CCH Canadian Ltd v Law Society of Upper Canada* [2004] SCC 13; [2004] 1 SCR 339 at [40].

20   M Handler and D Rolph, '"A Real Pea Souper": *The Panel Case* and the Development of the Fair Dealing Defences to Copyright Infringement in Australia' (2003) 27 *Melbourne University Law Review* 381.

21   See D Lindsay, 'Copyright and Freedom of Expression' in K Bowrey, M Handler and D Nicol, eds, *Emerging Challenges in Intellectual Property*, Oxford University Press, Melbourne, 2011.

- the effect of the dealing upon the potential market for, or value of, the copyright material; and
- the amount and substantiality of the part used by the defendant.

Similar considerations are taken into account by the courts under the other fair dealing exceptions. In addition, the courts consider whether the defendant genuinely holds the permitted purpose, whether the copyright-protected material was published, and the means by which the defendant obtained the copyright material.

Whether the parties are commercial rivals is important. Fairness was, for example, rejected in *De Garis v Neville Jeffress Pidler Pty Ltd* (1990) 37 FCR 99 where the defendant had 'taken the whole of [the plaintiff's] work and supplied it to its customers for its own reward in the course of a trading activity'. No particular factor is determinative however: fair dealing cases are highly fact-specific.

CASE EXTRACT: PRECEDENT

Hubbard v Vosper

[1972] 2 QB 84
Court of Appeal of England and Wales

[The defendants were Vosper, the author of a critical book on Scientology, and his publisher. Vosper was a former member of the Church of Scientology and used substantial extracts from books and other material written by L Ron Hubbard, the founder of Scientology. Some of the material upon which the book drew was considered confidential by the Church, and provided only to highly ranked members.]

Lord Denning MR (at 93–95): Mr Pain for Mr Hubbard says that what Mr Vosper has done is to take important parts of Mr Hubbard's book and explain them and amplify them. That, he says, is not fair dealing. Mr Caplan for Mr Vosper says that Mr Vosper has, indeed, taken important parts of Mr Hubbard's book, but he has done it so as to expose them to the public, and to criticise them and to condemn them. That, he says, is fair dealing.

It is impossible to define what is 'fair dealing'. It must be a question of degree. You must consider first the number and extent of the quotations and extracts. Are they altogether too many and too long to be fair? Then you must consider the use made of them. If they are used as a basis for comment, criticism or review, that may be fair dealing. If they are used to convey the same information as the author, for a rival purpose, that may be unfair. Next, you must consider the proportions. To take long extracts and attach short comments may be unfair. But, short extracts and long comments may be fair. Other considerations may come to mind also. But, after all is said and done, it must be a matter of impression. As with fair comment in the law of libel, so with fair dealing in the law of copyright. The tribunal of fact must decide. In the present case, there is material on which the tribunal of fact could find this to be fair dealing.

Mr Pain took, however, another point. He said that the defence of 'fair dealing' only avails a defendant when he is criticising or reviewing the plaintiff's literary work. It does not avail a defendant, said Mr Pain, when he is criticising or reviewing the doctrine or philosophy underlying the plaintiff's work. In support of this proposition, Mr Pain relied on the words of Romer J in *British Oxygen Co Ltd v Liquid Air Ltd* [1925] Ch 383, 393: 'I am inclined to agree with Mr Upjohn that, in this proviso [as to

PRECEDENT

"fair dealing"], the word "criticism" means a criticism of the work as such.' But, when you refer back to Mr Upjohn's arguments, you will see that all he means is that the criticism must be a criticism of the plaintiff's work, and not of the plaintiff's conduct.

I do not think that this proviso is confined as narrowly as Mr Pain submits. A literary work consists, not only of the literary style, but also of the thoughts underlying it, as expressed in the words. Under the defence of 'fair dealing' both can be criticised. Mr Vosper is entitled to criticise not only the literary style, but also the doctrine or philosophy of Mr Hubbard as expounded in the books.

Mr Pain took yet another point. This was on the bulletins and letters. These, he said, were not published to the world at large, but only to a limited number of people and, in particular, to those who took classes in Scientology. He said that, whilst it might be 'fair dealing' to criticise the books, it was not 'fair dealing' to take extracts from these bulletins and letters and criticise them. He quoted again the words of Romer J in *British Oxygen Co Ltd v Liquid Air Ltd* [1925] Ch 383, 393:

> ... it would be manifestly unfair that an unpublished literary work should, without the consent of the author, be the subject of public criticism, review or newspaper summary. Any such dealing with an unpublished literary work would not, therefore, in my opinion, be a 'fair dealing' with the work.

I am afraid I cannot go all the way with those words of Romer J. Although a literary work may not be published to the world at large, it may, however, be circulated to such a wide circle that it is 'fair dealing' to criticise it publicly in a newspaper, or elsewhere. This happens sometimes when a company sends a circular to the whole body of shareholders. It may be of such general interest that it is quite legitimate for a newspaper to make quotations from it, and to criticise them—or review them—without thereby being guilty of infringing copyright. The newspaper must, of course, be careful not to fall foul of the law of libel. So also here, these bulletins and letters may have been so widely circulated that it was perfectly 'fair dealing' for Mr Vosper to take extracts from them and criticise them in his book.

Although the point did not hold in *Hubbard v Vosper*, dealings with unpublished works are often considered unfair. The logic of this is explained in the case below (see also *Salinger v Random House*, 811 F 2d 90 (2d Cir, 1987)).

CASE EXTRACT: PRECEDENT

PRECEDENT

Commonwealth v John Fairfax & Sons Ltd

(1980) 147 CLR 39
High Court of Australia

[This was an interlocutory decision on an application to extend an ex parte injunction to restrain publication of a book, *Documents on Australian Defence and Foreign Policy 1968–1975*, and associated extracts in the defendant newspaper. The book contained unpublished government 'memoranda, assessments, briefings and cables' relating to topics such as: the East Timor crisis; the re-negotiations of the agreements covering US military bases in Australia; the presence of the Soviet Navy in the Indian

[Ocean; Australia's support for the Shah of Iran and predictions for the future of his regime; the structure of the US and UK intelligence services; and the Australia, New Zealand, United States Security (ANZUS) Treaty. The 437-page book consisted of nine pages of biographical notes, and 50 pages of background observations and comments by the authors. The rest reproduced government documents verbatim. The application for the extension of the injunction was based on copyright infringement, breach of confidence and offences under the *Crimes Act 1914* (Cth). The non-copyright claims were rejected.]

Mason J (at 54–58) (some footnotes omitted): The plaintiff is the owner of the copyright in those documents which have been brought into existence by the relevant departments and by public servants. Publication of the three instalments by the defendants will infringe the plaintiff's copyright unless the defendants can establish defences under ss 41 and 42 of the *Copyright Act 1968* (Cth), as amended, or the so-called common law defence of 'public interest'.

To bring themselves within s 41 the defendants must show that what they proposed to publish is 'a fair dealing' with the plaintiff's documents 'for the purpose of criticism or review' and that 'a sufficient acknowledgment of the work' was made. It has been suggested that s 41 does not provide a defence in the case of unpublished literary works, as distinct from unpublished dramatic or musical work, on the ground that criticism or review of an unpublished literary work could never amount to 'a fair dealing' (*Copinger and Skone James on Copyright* 11th ed, para 463). This suggestion is based on the remarks of Romer J in *British Oxygen Co Ltd v Liquid Air Ltd* [1925] Ch 383 at 393, where his Lordship said that it would be unfair that an unpublished literary work should, without the consent of the author, be the subject of public criticism or review.

In *Hubbard v Vosper* [1972] 2 QB 84; [1972] 1 All ER 1023, Lord Denning MR qualified these remarks by observing that a literary work not published to the world at large might be circulated to such a wide circle, eg a circular sent by a company to its shareholders, as to make it 'a fair dealing' to criticize or review it ([1972] 2 QB 84 at 94–5). With this qualification I agree.

To my mind the absence of consent, express or implied, or such circulation by the author of an unpublished literary work as to justify criticism or review is ordinarily at least an important factor in deciding whether there has been 'a fair dealing' under s 41.

There has been no such consent or conduct on the part of the plaintiff here. As I have said, the defendants knew on the Friday evening that the plaintiff objected to any publication at all and knew, or ought to have known, that the documents had been 'leaked' without the plaintiff's authority. There is a difficulty in saying that a publication of leaked documents, which could not without the leak have been published at all, is 'a fair dealing' with unpublished works in the circumstances to which I have referred (see *Beloff v Pressdram Ltd* [1973] 1 All ER 241 at 264).

However, there is another possible approach to the concept of 'fair dealing' as applied to copyright in government documents, an approach which was not spelled out in argument by the defendants. It is to say that a dealing with unpublished works which would be unfair as against an author who is a private individual may nevertheless be considered fair as against a government merely because that dealing promotes public knowledge and public discussion of government action. This would be to adopt a new approach to the construction of ss 41 and 42 and it would not be appropriate for me on an interlocutory application to proceed on the footing that it is a construction that will ultimately prevail. Situations such as the present case would scarcely have been within the contemplation of the draftsman when the two sections and their ancestors were introduced.

PRECEDENT

There is another obstacle in the way of a s 41 defence. The presentation to readers which the newspapers planned to publish was a presentation of hitherto unpublished documents from the secret files of the government. The attraction offered to the reader was that, by courtesy of the newspapers, he was able to read for the first time documents which were so important that the government had maintained a secrecy blackout on them. The accompanying comment, which was significant only in the case of the first instalment, appears to have been designed to place the documents in their appropriate setting, to enable them to be understood and to highlight the more dramatic features. To speak of the publication of the three instalments as having been undertaken for the purpose of criticism or review is to add a new dimension to criticism and review. If there was criticism or review of the documents by the newspapers it was merely a veneer, setting off what is essentially a publication of the plaintiff's documents. The defendants did not propose to make any reference at all to the questions raised in the Introduction to the book ...

Similar problems surround the defendants' endeavour to mount a defence under s 42. The defendants seek to show that there has been 'a fair dealing' with a literary work 'for the purpose of, or ... associated with, the reporting of news in a newspaper ... and a sufficient acknowledgment of the work is made'. The arguments advanced scarcely went beyond a bold assertion, and an equally stern denial, that what the defendants proposed to publish was 'for the purpose of ... the reporting of news'.

I am inclined to allow that 'news', despite its context of 'the reporting of news' 'in a newspaper, magazine or similar periodical' is not restricted to 'current events'. Even so, the concept of 'a fair dealing' with a literary work in the circumstances mentioned in s 42(1)(a) again presents a difficulty for the defendants. As things presently stand, it will not be easy for the defendants to bring their use of the plaintiff's documents, particularly in the two unpublished instalments, within the subsection. I refer to the East Timor cables and the 'profiles' ...

It is not to the point that the plaintiff does not ordinarily exploit for commercial advantage its copyright in documents. The fact that the plaintiff does not choose to take full advantage of its legal rights does not give the defendants a title to infringe them. The real point is that the plaintiff's ownership of copyright entitles it to prevent others from copying its documents, whether it proposes to publish them or not. The essence of copyright in an unpublished work is that it enables the owner to prevent others from publishing that work. Damages will rarely be an adequate remedy for infringement of that right.

Another factor that may be relevant in assessing fairness is industry practice or industry convention. However, as noted by Allsop J, 'what commercial participants in any given industry think is fair is unlikely to be necessarily determinative of the issue ... what is fair dealing in news reporting is a question of judgment and impression which takes into account the public interest inherent in s 103B as a law of the parliament': *Telstra Corporation Pty Ltd v Premier Media Group* [2007] FCA 568; (2007) 72 IPR 89 at [48]; see also *TCN Channel Nine v Network Ten* [2001] FCA 841, where Conti J held at [27]:

> There does not exist in Australia, at least among the major television broadcasters, such as those the subject of the present proceedings, any established trade practice or custom constituting a mutually implied licence to the effect that a television broadcaster is entitled to make a video tape of a programme, or an excerpt of a programme, previously broadcast by another television broadcaster.

FAIR DEALING FOR SPECIFIC PURPOSES
Research or study

Sections 40 and 103C allow fair dealings with works and audio-visual items, respectively, for the purpose of 'research or study'. These provisions are the most detailed fair dealing exceptions. First, as noted above (pp 262–263), they provide a list of matters relevant in assessing fairness: ss 40(2) and 103C(2). Second, s 40 creates a category of 'deemed' fair dealings, in cases where a person reproduces no more than a 'reasonable portion' of a published edition of a literary, dramatic or musical work (not including a computer program) or a published literary or dramatic work in electronic form (not including a computer program or electronic compilation). 'Reasonable portion' is defined as 10 per cent of the pages of a published edition of more than 10 pages, or a single chapter, or 10 per cent of the words or a single chapter of a published electronic literary or dramatic work. Copying more than a reasonable portion may still be fair, but requires assessment under the factors in s 40(2) (note that there is no equivalent deeming provision in s 103C).

The existence of the statutory licence in Parts VA and VB makes it harder for schools and universities to argue that copying by teachers for their students is a fair dealing under ss 40 or 103C; as McLelland J noted in *Copyright Agency Ltd v Haines* [1982] 1 NSWLR 182 at 190 (considering the relationship between s 40 and the then equivalent to Part VB, s 53B):

> One matter to which regard must be had in determining whether a copying constitutes a 'fair dealing' is 'the effect of the dealing upon the ... value of, the work. ...' (s 40(2)(d)), and it might be argued that the 'value' of a work is significantly dependent upon the existence of provisions of the law including s 53B which enable the owners of copyright to obtain remuneration in respect of the doing by others of acts comprised in the copyright, including the making of copies of the work or a substantial part thereof. But independently of any such argument based on para (d) of s 40(2), the availability to schools of the right to make copies under s 53B upon compliance with conditions designed to provide 'equitable remuneration' to the owners of copyright, must necessarily have an influence upon what amount and type of copying done in a school could properly be regarded as 'fair dealing' under s 40. It is not possible for a court in the abstract to lay down specific rules that are not found in the Act. The legislation is deliberately vague, no doubt because it was thought that by reason of its potential application to an infinite variety of particular circumstances, flexibility was preferable to certainty.

While it may well have been that in some circumstances copying which might have been carried out under s 53B would have constituted a 'fair dealing for the purpose of research or study' under s 40, much copying which could have been carried out under s 53B would not have constituted 'fair dealing' under s 40. The meaning of 'research or study' was considered in *De Garis v Neville Jeffress Pidler Pty Ltd* (1990) 37 FCR 99, extracted first below. A recent Canadian case, *Alberta (Minister of Education) v Canadian Copyright Licensing Agency (Access Copyright)* [2012] SCC 37; [2012] 2 SCR 354, extracted second below, provides a contrasting interpretation. It is also interesting to note that in 2014 the UK, which has a similar fair dealing exception to ss 40/103C, introduced an additional exception (s 29A of the *Copyright, Designs and Patents Act 1988* (UK)) aimed at allowing non-commercial data and text mining (i.e. computational analysis of databases of works in electronic form looking for patterns).

CASE EXTRACT: PRECEDENT

De Garis v Neville Jeffress Pidler Pty Ltd

(1990) 37 FCR 99
Federal Court of Australia

[Neville Jeffress Pidler ('Jeffress') conducted a press-clipping service, providing copies of newspaper articles to subscribers on a commercial basis. De Garis was an author of one of the articles reproduced and supplied. It was argued that the reproductions constituted fair dealing for purpose of (1) research or study; (2) criticism and review; or (3) reporting the news.]

Beaumont J (at 105–106): Can it be said that the Jeffress' dealing with the work (assuming, for the moment, without deciding, that the dealing is 'fair') is done by Jeffress 'for the purpose of research' within the meaning of s 40(1)?

... According to the *Macquarie Dictionary*, 'research' may be defined as: '1. diligent and systematic enquiry or investigation into a subject in order to discover facts or principles: *research in nuclear physics* ...'

In my view, 'research' in s 40 is intended to have this dictionary meaning.

In my opinion, Jeffress' dealing with the work is not something done for the purpose of research. Although the retrieval of the material may be a complicated exercise, it does not follow that the purpose of Jeffress is research. Its purpose, which is purely commercial, is to supply a photocopy of material already published in return for a fee. This is an activity engaged in by Jeffress in the ordinary course of trade, which, in my view, is in the nature of an information audit and should be distinguished from research activity of the kind contemplated by s 40: see *Re Attorney-General of British Columbia and Messier* (1984) 8 DLR (4th) 306.

There is another reason why s 40 cannot apply here. The relevant purpose required by s 40(1) is that of Jeffress, not that of its customer. That is to say, even if a customer were engaged in research, this would not assist Jeffress. In *Sillitoe v McGraw-Hill Book Co (UK) Ltd* [1983] FSR 545, Judge Mervyn Davies said at 558: 'The onus of showing that an exception applies is on the defendants. Mr Jeffs contended that s 6(1) is widely drawn and not limited to the actual student, so that if a dealing is fair and for the purposes of private study the sub-section applies whether the private study in mind is one's own or that of somebody else. Here, he said, the dealing was for the purpose of private study by the examinees who would acquire the notes. I do not accept that argument. To my mind s 6(1) authorises what would otherwise be an infringement if one is engaged in private study or research. The authors of the Notes, when writing the Notes and thus 'dealing' with the original work, were not engaged in private study or research. To my mind *University of London Press Ltd v University Tutorial Press Ltd* [1916] 2 Ch 601 at 613, affords some support for this view.'

In the *University of London case*, above, Peterson J said at 613: 'The defendants on these facts contend that their publication of the three papers set by Professor Lodge and Mr Jackson is a fair dealing with them for the purposes of private study within s 2, sub-s (1), of the Act of 1911, and is therefore not an infringement of copyright. It could not be contended that the mere republication of a copyright work was a 'fair dealing' because it was intended for purposes of private study; nor, if an author produced a book of questions for the use of students, could another person with impunity republish the book with the answers to the questions. Neither case would, in my judgment, come within the description of 'fair dealing'. In the present case the paper on more advanced mathematics has been taken without any attempt at providing solutions for the questions, and the only way in which the defendants have dealt with this paper is by appropriating it, except that there are 11 lines of criticism of it, dividing the questions into easy, troublesome, and difficult questions.'

It follows, in my view, that the activities of Jeffress cannot be characterised as 'research' for the purposes of s 40.

IS THE DEALING DONE FOR THE PURPOSE OF 'STUDY'?

The *Macquarie Dictionary* definitions of the noun 'study' include the following: '1. application of the mind to the acquisition of knowledge, as by reading, investigation or reflection. 2. the cultivation of a particular branch of learning, science, or art: *The study of law*. 3. a particular course of effort to acquire knowledge: '... 5. a thorough examination and analysis of a particular subject ...'

In my view, 'study', where used in s 40 is intended to have this dictionary meaning. In *Messier's case*, above, the question for determination before the court was whether a 'nursing audit committee' was relevantly a 'research group' for the purposes of the *Evidence Act*, RSBC 1979. If it was, then a report of the committee would attract an evidentiary privilege under the legislation. After citing the dictionary definition of 'research', 'study', 'inquiry' and 'investigation', MacKinnon J pointed out the dichotomy between the process of gathering facts, on the one hand, and conducting a course of study or research, on the other.

Again, even if 'study' were the purpose for which a subscriber retained the services of Jeffress, it cannot be said that 'study' was the purpose of Jeffress.

It follows, in my view, that s 40 has no application in the present case.

CASE EXTRACT: COMPARATIVE LAW

Alberta (Minister of Education) v Canadian Copyright Licensing Agency (Access Copyright)

[2012] SCC 37, [2012] 2 SCR 354
Supreme Court of Canada

[Access Copyright is the Canadian equivalent to the Copyright Agency Ltd: it represents authors and publishers of literary and artistic works in printed materials, offers licences for copying, and collects and distributes royalties to members. The dispute related to the appropriate rate at which schools should pay for copying. One issue in dispute was whether copies were fair dealing for the purposes of 'private research or study' under s 29 of the Canadian *Copyright Act* (RSC, 1985, C-42), when made at a teacher's initiative from textbooks, and distributed to students as a complement to the main textbook with instructions to students to read the excerpts. The decision below drew a distinction between copies made by teachers at the request of students (fair dealing) and those made by teachers for students (not fair dealing).]

Abella J (for the majority) (some footnotes omitted): 22. ... [F]air dealing is a 'user's right', and the relevant perspective when considering whether the dealing is for an allowable purpose under the first

COMPARATIVE LAW

stage of [*CCH Canadian Ltd v Law Society of Upper Canada* [2004] SCC 13; [2004] 1 SCR 339] is that of the user (*CCH*, at paras 48 and 64). This does not mean, however, that the copier's purpose is irrelevant at the fairness stage. If, as in the 'course pack' cases, the copier hides behind the shield of the user's allowable purpose in order to engage in a separate purpose that tends to make the dealing unfair, that separate purpose will also be relevant to the fairness analysis.

23. In the case before us, however, there is no such separate purpose on the part of the teacher. Teachers have no ulterior motive when providing copies to students. Nor can teachers be characterized as having the completely separate purpose of 'instruction'; they are there to facilitate the students' research and private study. It seems to me to be axiomatic that most students lack the expertise to find or request the materials required for their own research and private study, and rely on the guidance of their teachers. They study what they are told to study, and the teacher's purpose in providing copies is to enable the students to have the material they need for the purpose of studying. The teacher/copier therefore shares a symbiotic purpose with the student/user who is engaging in research or private study. Instruction and research/private study are, in the school context, tautological.

...

25. ... [P]hotocopies made by a teacher and provided to primary and secondary school students are an essential element in the research and private study undertaken by those students. The fact that some copies were provided on request and others were not, did not change the significance of those copies for students engaged in research and private study.

26. Nor, with respect, do I accept the statement made by the Board and endorsed by the Federal Court of Appeal, relying on *University of London Press* [v *University Tutorial Press Ltd* [1916] 2 Ch 601], that the photocopies made by teachers were made for an unfair purpose—'*non*-private study'—since they were used by students as a group in class, and not 'privately'. As discussed above, the holding was simply that the publisher could not hide behind the students' research or private study purposes to disguise a separate unfair purpose—in that case, a commercial one. The court did *not* hold that students in a classroom setting could never be said to be engaged in '*private* study'.

27. With respect, the word 'private' in 'private study' should not be understood as requiring users to view copyrighted works in splendid isolation. Studying and learning are essentially personal endeavours, whether they are engaged in with others or in solitude. By focusing on the geography of classroom instruction rather than on the *concept* of studying, the Board again artificially separated the teachers' instruction from the students' studying.

[The Supreme Court majority also found that the Board's assessment of 'fairness' was incorrect, and remitted the matter for reconsideration.]

Note that Canada's copyright law now includes an exception for fair dealing for the purposes of 'education': *Copyright Act* (RSC, 1985, c. C-42) s 29. On the same day that the decision in *Access Copyright* was handed down, the Canadian Supreme Court also handed down *Society of Composers, Authors and Music Publishers of Canada v Bell Canada* [2012] SCC 36; [2012] 2 SCR 326. In the latter case, the Court held that excerpts of musical works provided online for customers to 'preview' music prior to purchase constituted fair dealing for the purposes of 'research'. Research, the Court held, was not limited to research for the purposes of creation, but also included consumer research.

Criticism or review

Section 41 allows fair dealing with a work for the purpose of 'criticism or review, whether of that work or another work'; while s 103A permits fair dealing with an audio-visual item for the purpose of 'criticism or review, whether of the first-mentioned audio-visual item, another audio-visual item or a work'. In both cases, sufficient acknowledgment of the work/audio-visual item must be made. 'Sufficient acknowledgment' is defined in s 10(1) to mean 'an acknowledgment identifying the work by its title or other description and, unless the work is anonymous or pseudonymous or the author has previously agreed or directed that an acknowledgment of his or her name is not to be made, also identifying the author' (note that the definition does not cover sufficient acknowledgment of subject matter other than a work).

In reading these excerpts it is interesting also to note that Art 10(1) of the Berne Convention recognises an exception for the potentially broader 'quotations from a work which has already been lawfully made available to the public, provided that their making is compatible with fair practice, and their extent does not exceed that justified by the purpose'. In 2014 the UK amended its exception for fair dealing for the purpose of criticism or review to include quotation as a permissible purpose: *Copyright, Designs and Patents Act 1988* (UK), s 30(1ZA).

CASE EXTRACT: PRECEDENT

De Garis v Neville Jeffress Pidler Pty Ltd

(1990) 37 FCR 99
Federal Court of Australia

Beaumont J (at 106–107): The origins of this defence were explained by Lord Hatherley in *Chatterton v Cave* (1878) 3 App Cas 483 at 492: 'Books are published with an expectation, if not a desire, that they will be criticised in reviews, and if deemed valuable that parts of them will be used as affording illustrations by way of quotation, or the like—and if the quantity taken be neither substantial nor material, if, as it has been expressed by some judges, "a fair use" only be made on the publication, no wrong is done and no action can be brought.'

On the other hand, a work cannot be published under the pretence of quotation: see *Mawman v Tegg* (1826) 2 Russ 385; *Commonwealth v John Fairfax & Sons Ltd* (1980) 147 CLR 39 at 54–7; 32 ALR 485; *Commonwealth v Walsh* (1980) 147 CLR 61 at 63; 32 ALR 500; Lahore, *Copyright Law*, p 7562.

The *Macquarie Dictionary* definition of 'criticism' includes the following: '1. the act or art of analysing and judging the quality of a literary or artistic work, etc: *literary criticism*. 2. the act of passing judgment as to the merits of something … 4. a critical comment, article or essay; a critique.'

In my opinion, 'criticism' in the context of s 41 is used in these senses. It has been held that criticism of any kind, and not only literary criticism, is within the provision: see *Sillitoe's case,* above, at 559.

The *Macquarie* definition of 'review' includes the following: '1. a critical article or report, as in a periodical, on some literary work, commonly some work of recent appearance; a critique …'

PRECEDENT

In my opinion, 'review' is used in s 41 in this sense.

It would seem that the word 'review' in the sense in which it is to be understood in s 41 is cognate with the word 'criticism'. It may be said that one is the process and the other is the result of the critical application of mental faculties. The extent of Jeffress' input, there being no material or evidence (apart from the order form) to support a contrary inference, appears to be limited only. The process involves scanning media for particular subjects according to the requests of subscribers. It does not appear to extend to the passing of a judgment as to the merit of the articles identified. Once an article is located which falls within the description of the nominated subject matter, the quality of that article is immaterial for the purposes of the exercise. The task undertaken is one of *location* rather than evaluation. This is the concern of the subscriber and will depend upon his or her particular purpose for subscribing.

In my view, the activities of, and service provided, by Jeffress cannot be characterised as either 'criticism' or 'review' for the purposes of s 41.

CASE EXTRACT: COMPARATIVE LAW

COMPARATIVE LAW

Pro Sieben Media AG v Carlton UK Television Ltd

[1999] FSR 610
Court of Appeal of England and Wales

[A German television company claimed that the defendants had infringed its copyright by using a 30-second extract from a broadcast. The program was about Mandy Allwood, a British woman who was pregnant with eight live embryos as a result of fertility treatment, and included an interview with, and other film of, Allwood and her partner. Allwood, through a public relations agent, had given the exclusive right to broadcast the interview with Allwood in Germany. The defendants' program was critical of chequebook journalism. The judge decided that the defendants had failed to discharge the onus of proving that the extract had been included in their program for the purpose of criticism or review and found that the use made of the extract was not fair in all the circumstances. The defendants appealed.]

Robert Walker LJ (at 619–621): If the fair dealing is for the purpose of criticism that criticism may be strongly expressed and unbalanced without forfeiting the fair dealing defence; an author's remedy for malicious and unjustified criticism lies (if it lies anywhere) in the law of defamation, not copyright. The position was summarised by Henry LJ in *Time Warner Entertainments v Channel Four Television* [1994] EMLR 1, 14, in rejecting the submission that unrepresentative excerpts should lose the benefit of the fair dealing defence,

> As Lord Atkin said in a different context 'The path of criticism is a public way: The wrongheaded are permitted to err therein …' *(Ambard v A-G for Trinidad and Tobago* [1936] AC 322 at 335). 'Fair dealing' in its statutory context refers to the true purpose (that is, the good faith, the intention and the genuineness) of the critical work—is the programme incorporating the infringing material a genuine piece of criticism or review, or is it something else, such as an attempt to dress up the infringement of another's copyright in the guise of criticism, and so profit unfairly from another's work? As Lord Denning said in *Hubbard v Vosper* ([1972] 2 QB 84 at 93): 'It is not fair dealing for a rival in the trade to take copyright material and use it for his own benefit.

COMPARATIVE LAW

... It is not necessary for the Court to put itself in the shoes of the infringer of the copyright in order to decide whether the offending piece was published 'for the purposes of criticism or review'. This court should not in my view give any encouragement to the notion that all that is required is for the user to have the sincere belief, however misguided, that he or she is criticising a work or reporting current affairs. To do so would provide an undesirable incentive for journalists, for whom facts should be sacred, to give implausible evidence as to their intentions. The point is illustrated by two cases to which the court was referred, *Hindley v Higgins and News Group Newspapers* (23 August 1983, CA) and *Associated Newspapers v News Group Newspapers* [1986] RPC 515.

...

'Criticism or review' and 'reporting current events' are expressions of wide and indefinite scope. Any attempt to plot their precise boundaries is doomed to failure. They are expressions which should be interpreted liberally, but I derive little assistance from comparisons with other expressions such as 'current affairs' or 'news' (the latter word being used in the Australian statute considered in *De Garis v Neville Jeffress Pidler* (1990) 18 IPR 292). However it can be said that the nearer that any particular derivative use of copyright material comes to the boundaries, unplotted though they are, the less likely it is to make good the fair dealing defence.

CURRENT LAW

CASE EXTRACT: CURRENT LAW

TCN Channel Nine Pty Ltd v Network Ten Pty Ltd

[2002] FCAFC 146; (2002) 118 FCR 417
Federal Court of Australia, Full Court

[The High Court's decision in this case was extracted in Chapter 4, where the facts are set out on p 145. A separate issue was whether Network Ten's use of the excerpts from Channel Nine's broadcasts, if prima facie infringing, constituted fair dealing either for the purpose of criticism or review (s 103A) or the reporting of news (s 103B). The case illustrates both the highly fact-specific nature of fair dealing analysis, and the fact that different judges can apply these exceptions to the same conduct in very different ways. At trial, infringement was argued in relation to 20 excerpts, 19 of which Network Ten claimed were fair dealings. The trial judge concluded in obiter that 12 excerpts were fair dealing. Some of the trial judge's conclusions were not appealed, but the findings on 10 excerpts were appealed to the Full Federal Court. The members of the Full Federal Court reached different conclusions on three of these excerpts.

Extracted below are some comments from Hely and Finkelstein JJ on their general approach to the fair dealing defences in this case, and discussion from all three judges of two of the 10 excerpts, on which the Full Federal Court was split: 'Simply the Best' and 'Midday (PM Singing)'. These two excerpts were discussed by Conti J at first instance (*TCN Channel Nine Pty Ltd v Network Ten Pty Ltd* [2001] FCA 108; (2001) 108 FCR 235 at [72]) as follows:

'Simply the Best'

Ten raises the defence of fair dealing for purposes of criticism and review in relation to this re-broadcast. No issue is raised by Nine as to sufficient acknowledgment. Ten frames its contention as follows:

The underlying artistic work was a design for the set which was criticised. The underlying method of scoring which was the outcome of a literary work, being a treatment for the program, was criticised. It is not necessary to criticise the audio-visual item, being the program Simply The Best, itself, although that was also undertaken.

The essence or substance of The Panel's commentary upon the footage here re-broadcast was mainly a discussion of what had occurred on the Nine 'Simply The Best' program, and an answering of the questions of those members of The Panel who had watched it or who had not understood it. There was, however, a somewhat oblique reference to 'the set' in the following terms:

> ... this is the program on Channel Nine last night with Ray Martin? The voting one?
>
> Yes
>
> I think he should have come out dressed in a toga.
>
> The set was a little ...
>
> Perplexing.
>
> It was sort of like the seats were 'Who Wants To Be A Millionaire' meets the desks of 'The Footy Show' meets an inner-city brothel. It was just ... what I imagine an inner-city brothel would look like is what I mean ...
>
> Yeah, isn't that ... they've recycled a few sets there.
>
> Oh dame [sic] it ... he didn't keep going because he actually said the joke 'How about the set eh?' Funny thing happened on the way to the forum.

However, the paucity of evidence as to what was in substance the criticism of the so-called 'set' has not left a viable basis for comprehending, much less resolving, what was the true nature of the alleged criticism, and what was the purported basis therefore.

There is insufficient evidence upon which I could have made a finding in favour of Ten, pursuant to s 103A, and had it been necessary so to do, I would have rejected Ten's defence of criticism and review.

'Midday'

Ten contends that its re-broadcast constituted fair dealing for the purpose of criticism or review of the 'Midday' program, and of the role of the presenter Ms Kennerley in that program, and Ten relied on the principle in [Hubbard v Vosper [1972] 2 QB 84] at 94, to the effect that criticism or review may extend to ideas underlining the subject matter of copyright ... I extract below the following on-screen remarks of various members of The Panel, in order to illustrate the major thrust of The Panel's comments of relevance:

> ... did anyone see when Kerri-Anne got the Prime Minister John Howard to sing Happy Birthday to Don Bradman?
>
> That will get him back in.
>
> Its [sic] not right to mock someone's stature but he really looks like he should have a hand up his a ... moving his mouth when he sits on that little stool.
>
> ...
>
> Well I reckon if he didn't sing it, she would have put her hand up his a ...

Kerri-Anne will not take no for an answer.

She is essentially a Labor voter cause she got Costello to do the macarena ... and made him look like an idiot and now she's done it with John Howard.

It is interesting with Midday because it was funny at the Logies this year (be)cause she was hot favourite for the Gold Logie. And I remember a conversation. I'll never forget this. A Nine executive coming up to me and saying 'Hey does Kerri-Anne win?' And I said 'Oh no, she doesn't actually'. He goes 'Thank God'. And I was like 'Why's that?' And he goes 'Mate, she would be unbearable'.

Leave Kerri-Anne alone. She does a good job I reckon.

She resurrected it.

You think about that though, what is it five hours.

Five days a week.

She is an ideal Midday host. It is interesting when Derryn Hinch was hosting it, the rating(s) aren't much better with Kerri-Anne, yet Derryn was looked upon as a Midday failure.

A total failure.

Whereas Kerri-Anne like on Monday, she was beaten by Judge Judy in Adelaide and Perth.

I have encountered difficulty in deciding whether the purpose of Ten in re-broadcasting the subject material was that of criticism and review, despite the somewhat disparaging remarks made concerning Ms Kennerley and the 'Midday' program which she had been hosting for some time. Ten has submitted that the purpose of the criticism or review related to both the program and Ms Kennerley's role in it, but I think that the submission is not sufficiently supported by what I have extracted above. I would conclude that the purpose of Nine's dealing with the subject footage of 'Midday' was to satirise aspects of Ms Kennerley's performance as presenter of 'Midday', and certain supposed personality traits and political allegiances. I do not think that on balance, and as an issue of fact and degree, it can rightly be postulated that The Panel here engaged in criticism or review of 'Midday', and that such was its purpose. If it had become necessary to determine Ten's reliance upon s 103A in relation to what would have otherwise constituted breach of copyright constituted by this re-broadcast, I would have rejected such basis of defence.]

Hely J: 96. At first instance both parties professed reliance on the decision of the United Kingdom Court of Appeal in *Pro Sieben Media AG v Carlton UK Television Ltd* [1999] FSR 610. The court there held that the test of whether an extract from a copyright work had been used for one of the purposes laid down in the corresponding provisions of the *Copyright, Designs and Patents Act 1988* (UK) is an objective one:

The words 'in the context of' or 'as part of an exercise in' could be substituted for 'for the purpose of' without any significant alteration of meaning. [at 614]

97. That decision was followed by the UK Court of Appeal in the subsequent case of *Hyde Park Residence Ltd v Yelland* [2001] Ch 143. In that case, whether a work was used 'for the purpose of

reporting current events' was a matter to be ascertained by a reading of the relevant parts of the work in question. However, both cases make it clear that the intentions and motives of the user of the copyright material are highly relevant in relation to the issue of fair dealing.

98. After reviewing the authorities, and the submissions of the parties, the primary judge summarised the principles emerging from the authorities involving fair dealing defences as follows:

(i)   Fair dealing involves questions of degree and impression; it is to be judged by the criterion of a fair minded and honest person, and is an abstract concept;

(ii) Fairness is to be judged objectively in relation to the relevant purpose, that is to say, the purpose of criticism or review or the purpose of reporting news; in short, it must be fair and genuine for the relevant purpose, because fair dealing truth of purpose [sic];

(iii) Criticism and review are words of wide and indefinite scope which should be interpreted liberally; nevertheless criticism and review involve the passing of judgment. Criticism and review may be strongly expressed;

(iv) Criticism and review must be genuine and not a pretence for some other form of purpose, but if genuine, need not necessarily be balanced;

(v)   An oblique or hidden motive may disqualify reliance upon criticism and review, particularly where the copyright infringer is a trade rival who uses the copyright subject matter for its own benefit, particularly in a dissembling way; 'the path of criticism is a public way';

(vi) Criticism and review extends to thoughts underlying the expression of the copyright works or subject matter;

(vii) 'News' is not restricted to current events; and

(viii) 'News' may involve the use of humour though the distinction between news and entertainment may be difficult to determine in particular situations.

99. Nine submitted on the hearing of the appeal that the criticism or review must be of the work itself, but this may include the doctrine or philosophy underlying the work. However, s 103A expressly provides that the criticism or review may relate to 'the first-mentioned audio-visual item, another audio-visual item or a work'.

100. Nine's written submissions on the appeal also challenged principle (ii) in the summary of the trial judge quoted above. It was submitted that the requisite purpose must be that of the respondent rather than some third party, and there was no evidence before the trial judge that Ten itself (as distinct from Working Dog Pty Ltd and its Executive Producer, Mr Hirsh) had a relevant purpose of criticism or review or of news reporting. Contrary to the position which it had adopted at first instance, Nine's submission then proceed[ed] upon the basis that it was incumbent upon Ten to call evidence as to the actual purposes, intentions and motives of those who produced the programmes.

101. Ten engaged Working Dog Pty Ltd ('Working Dog') ... to produce for it a television programme which would, amongst other things, involve criticism and review and the reporting of news events. The purpose of Working Dog in the production of these programmes was the purpose of Ten. Consistently with the decisions of the UK Court of Appeal earlier referred to, the 'purpose' referred to in s 103A and s 103B is to be ascertained objectively, and it was neither necessary nor appropriate for officers of Ten or of Working Dog to give evidence that they had a sincere belief that he or she was criticising a work or an audio-visual item or reporting news.

102. Nine also submits that to the extent that it is discernible, Ten's purpose in re-broadcasting the Nine material was to entertain, provide programme content and achieve ratings. This purpose is the same purpose that Nine, its trade rival, had in broadcasting the material originally. It does not ground a fair dealing defence.

103. Ten accepted the proposition that if it had used the Panel Segments as a 'potted' substitute for entertainment, so that a television viewer could obtain ready and easy access to the same in a shorter time, such kind of activity on its part would constitute an unfair dealing. Ten denied that it had used any of the Panel Segments in that way, and the primary judge found that its denial was justified.

104. Ten's purpose in broadcasting its programme 'The Panel' may have been, as Nine asserts, to entertain and to achieve ratings. If it does so by means of a programme involving or including criticism, review or reporting of news in which there is fair dealing with material in which copyright would otherwise subsist, then Ten is not disentitled from relying on the s 103A and s 103B defences by reason only of the commercial nature of its activities. Criticism may involve an element of humour, or 'poking fun at' the object of the criticism. The fact that news coverage is interesting or even to some people entertaining, does not negate the fact that it could be news: *Nine Network Australia Pty Ltd v Australian Broadcasting Corporation* (1999) 48 IPR 333 at 340 pars [34]–[37]. News may be reported with humour and still fall within the ambit of s 103B.

. . .

107. In *Pro Sieben Media* the UK Court of Appeal said that a trial judge's conclusions on fair dealing should not be disturbed unless 'they proceeded from some error of principle or are clearly unsustainable'. That view was endorsed by Conti J, sitting as a member of a Full Federal Court, in *Aldi Stores Ltd Partnership v Frito-Lay Trading Co GmbH* (2001) 54 IPR 344 at [198]. The position that an appellate court will not interfere with a finding of the primary judge in an area such as the present, unless it is 'clearly unsustainable', may be a slight overstatement of the Australian approach: *Australian Capital Territory v Badcock* (2000) 169 ALR 585 at [37], [48] and [51].

. . .

2 MIDDAY

111. At 72(ii), the primary judge found that:

> … the purpose of Nine's dealing with the subject footage of 'Midday' was to satirise aspects of Ms Kennerley's performance as presenter of 'Midday', and certain supposed personality traits and political allegiances. I do not think that on balance, and as an issue of fact and degree, it can rightly be postulated that The Panel here engaged in criticism or review of 'Midday', and that such was its purpose.

112. In context, the issue is whether the purpose for which the Panel Segment was shown was criticism or review of the broadcast of which the Panel Segment formed part, or criticism or review of some other broadcast of the Midday programme. An appraisal of Ms Kennerley's role as the presenter of the Midday show could amount to criticism or review of the television broadcast constituted by the 'Midday' programme, but there was no real connection between the Panel Segment and such discussion as there was of Ms Kennerley's role. The Panel Segment was shown for its own sake, either

as something worth seeing again, or for the benefit of those who had missed it when it was originally broadcast by Nine. I agree with the primary judge's conclusions.

113. The primary judge also rejected Ten's claimed entitlement to a defence under s 103B(1)(b) on the purported basis that the prime minister's singing of 'Happy Birthday' to Sir Donald Bradman was 'newsworthy'. It may be accepted that unusual or incongruous moments in the life of a world leader may be 'news', and elsewhere in his reasons, the primary judge accepted that 'news' for the purposes of s 103B(1) was not restricted to current events. But a contention that The Panel was reporting an item of news, namely that the prime minister had sung Happy Birthday to Sir Donald Bradman on the Midday show some 14 days earlier, and that the Panel Segment was shown for the purpose of or in association with the reporting of that news is, to my mind, an exaggeration or distortion of the facts. The Panel Segment was simply shown for its entertainment value. No error has been shown in the primary judge's conclusion in this respect.

...

6 SIMPLY THE BEST

119. The primary judge held that the s 103A defence of criticism or review was not made out. He did so on the basis of a 'paucity of evidence' which left no 'viable basis for comprehending, much less resolving, what was the true nature of the alleged criticism, and what was the purported basis therefore'.

120. Ten contends that the comments by the Panel members clearly reveal the purpose of criticism or review in relation to the set (and underlying artistic work) used in Nine's programmes; and that once this is accepted, there is no need to inquire further as to the nature or basis for the criticisms made.

121. Criticism or review may be unbalanced or strongly expressed and nevertheless fall within s 103A. Nonetheless, it has to be recognisable as criticism or review. As I read his Honour's decision the defence failed because the so-called criticism or review in relation to the set was not recognisable as such. I agree with his Honour's conclusions in this regard ...

Finkelstein J: 17. On the question of fair dealing, I agree in the reasons of Hely J except with regard to three broadcasts. To understand our differences, I need to say something about the program on which they were broadcast. The program is styled The Panel. The Panel is a late night television program, screened weekly on Channel Ten. The regular members of the Panel are Tom Gleisner, Rob Sitch, Kate Langbroek, Glenn Robbins (some viewers refer to him as 'Uncle Arthur') and Santo Cilauro. They are well known personalities. The program's production company, Working Dog Pty Ltd, has also produced The Castle and The Dish, two highly successful comedy feature films. The Panel adopts an unusual format. Members of the Panel (not always all of them) sit around an oval desk, often with one or more invited guests, and discuss in a humorous way a variety of topics including, but not limited to, current affairs, sport, the arts and other items which they think are of interest. Although there is some serious discussion, the items are usually presented in an entertaining manner. The Channel Ten website invites people to '[t]une into The Panel for an irreverent look at the week's events, featuring news, views and reviews.' The discussion is, or at least appears to be, largely unscripted, though the choice of topics must have been settled in advance. The show is punctuated by pre-recorded excerpts of other television programs. While there appears to be no evidence on this point, a casual observer of the show might conclude that Channel Nine programs are a favourite target.

18. Let me now deal with the broadcasts where I am in disagreement with Hely J.

...

MIDDAY

21. The Midday Show, as its title indicates, is a show Channel Nine formerly broadcast at midday each day. It had a studio audience and was, or purported to be, a live to air program catering for people who happen to be at home at that time of day. The presenter, Ms Kerri-Anne Kennerley, is a well-known television presenter. A feature of the Midday Show was that it dealt with topical events and often had invited guests. During the program in question, the prime minister was an invited guest and was interviewed by Ms Kennerley. She asked the prime minister to sing happy birthday for Sir Donald Bradman, Australia's greatest cricketer.

22. The Panel replayed the prime minister singing. Members of the Panel then made humorous, but disparaging, comments about the manner in which the prime minister performed. It was suggested that Ms Kennerley must be a Labor supporter because during a previous show she had also made the treasurer 'look like an idiot'. Fair dealing is made out in two respects. First the Panel is undertaking a review of sorts of the Midday Show. Indeed, after the excerpt was shown, there was a general discussion about Ms Kennerley's talents as the program's host. Second, and more obviously, an incident where the prime minister of a country has behaved in a way which some might call 'silly' is certainly newsworthy. It is not only the political activities of a person such as a prime minister that make the news. His or her perceived indiscretions or other unusual actions warrant reporting. In a sense, all behaviour of a prime minister can be regarded as 'political' because it may affect voters' perceptions and is newsworthy for that reason.

SIMPLY THE BEST

23. Simply the Best was a evening television program hosted by Ray Martin, who is yet another well-known personality. The precise nature of the program is not apparent, but it seems that minor celebrities were invited to appear before a live audience. During the course of the show, the audience was asked to cast a vote on which is the 'best' of a variety of things. In this particular program The Panel broadcast a segment showing Mr Martin walking on to the studio set and another segment where the audience was asked to vote on how much they liked 'Bandstand' and 'Countdown', each of which was a television program in which rock 'n roll music was performed.

24. The Panel introduced the first excerpt by commenting on the studio set. Tom said that it was a cross between that used on the television programs 'Who Wants to be a Millionaire' and 'The Footy Show', and 'an inner city brothel'. While the excerpt was being played, Tom commented '[t]hey've recycled a few sets there'. Clearly this was criticism about the production side of the program. The second excerpt was introduced by Kate with the comment that it was not possible to understand the basis on which the audience was being asked to vote. It was said that the voting had no context.

CURRENT LAW

Immediately after the excerpt was broadcast, other members of the Panel said, in effect, that one could not tell what the voting was about. Various possibilities were discussed. From the segment of the show that I was able to see, the criticism, for that is what it was, about the show's format appears to be justified. The defence of fair dealing under s 103A is made out.

Sundberg J: 2. Except as to *Simply the Best* (the Ray Martin rebroadcast) I agree with Hely J's conclusions on the fair dealing defences. I deal specifically with the three broadcasts upon which Hely J and Finkelstein J differ. They are sufficiently described in their Honours' judgments, and I do not need to repeat that exercise. My approach has been to uphold the primary judge's decision on the availability of the defences in relation to a broadcast unless convinced it is wrong. Fair dealing involves questions of degree and impression, on which different minds can reasonably come to different conclusions.

...

SIMPLY THE BEST—RAY MARTIN REBROADCAST

4. On each of my viewings of this broadcast I had the clear impression that what was involved was criticism of the set and of the fact that it was not possible to determine the basis on which the audience was being asked to vote. I am satisfied that the primary judge's decision that the s 103A defence was not made out because of the paucity of evidence which left no 'viable basis for comprehending, much less resolving, what was the true nature of the alleged criticism and what was the purported basis therefor' was wrong.

MIDDAY—JOHN HOWARD SINGING REBROADCAST

5. On each occasion on which I viewed the broadcast my impression was that The Panel was not engaged in criticism or review of the *Midday* presenter (s 103A), and that showing the Prime Minister singing Happy Birthday to Sir Donald Bradman was not for the purpose of reporting news (s 103B(1)(b)) but for its entertainment value. That was the primary judge's view ...

Parody or satire

Sections 41A and 103AA allow fair dealing 'for the purposes of parody or satire'. These provisions were introduced by the *Copyright Amendment Act 2006* (Cth), following concerns that, following AUSFTA, Australian copyright law was more restrictive for users than US copyright law.

There is no statutory definition of either parody or satire. In his Second Reading Speech the Attorney-General suggested that the new exception was to protect free speech for cartoonists and comics. At the time of the new exception the Attorney-General's Department 'New Copyright Law Fact Sheet' advised:

> Satire often involves attacking an idea or attitude, an institution or a social practice, through irony, derision, or wit. Parody often involves the imitation of the characteristic style of an author or a work for comic effect or ridicule.

In line with the other categories, dictionary definitions of parody and satire may be influential in interpreting the breadth of the provision.[22] The US approach to the issue of parody may also be instructive.

Parody and satire will not always be considered fair dealing or fair use: although the defendants were successful in establishing that fair use was strongly arguable in *Campbell v Acuff-Rose Music, Inc*, 510 US 569 (1994) (below), this contrasts, for example, with *Dr Seuss Enterprises, LP v Penguin Books USA, Inc*, 109 F 3d 1394 (9th Cir 1997), in which the defendant had written a book in the style of Dr Seuss' 'The Cat in the Hat' about a celebrity murder trial. The defendant's claim of fair use was unsuccessful.[23] It is also important to remember that the Australian exception covers both parody *and* satire, whereas some US cases have suggested that satire is less likely to be fair use than parody; but note the footnotes to *Campbell v Acuff-Rose Music, Inc*, 510 US 569 (1994), extracted below, and for a successful claim of fair use for satire, see *Blanch v Koons*, 467 F 3d 244 (2d Cir, 2006).

In Australia, it needs to be noted that in addition to infringement actions, artists may also have recourse to moral rights actions to protect their right to attribution and integrity (see Chapter 7).

The UK introduced its own parody exception in 2014; however that provision takes its text from the EU's *Directive 2001/29 on the Harmonisation of Copyright in the Information Society*, in allowing for fair dealing 'for the purposes of caricature, parody or pastiche: *Copyright, Designs and Patents Act 1988* (UK), s 30A.

CASE EXTRACT: COMPARATIVE LAW

Campbell v Acuff-Rose Music, Inc

510 US 569 (1994)
Supreme Court of the United States

[Acuff-Rose held copyright in the Roy Orbison and William Dees song 'Oh, Pretty Woman'. Campbell, part of a rap group known as 2 Live Crew, wrote a new version of the song, with very different lyrics, set out in the table below (from the Appendices to the judgment at 594–596), which 2 Live Crew recorded in their own rap style. 2 Live Crew's manager informed Acuff-Rose that 2 Live Crew had written a parody of 'Oh, Pretty Woman,' that they would afford all credit for ownership and authorship, and that they were willing to pay a fee. Although Acuff-Rose refused permission, 2 Live Crew released the song anyway. Some time later, Acuff-Rose sued for copyright infringement. The trial court gave summary judgment in favour of 2 Live Crew; the Court of Appeals for the 6th Circuit reversed this finding, on the basis that the commercial nature of the parody weighed against fair use and 2 Live Crew had taken too much from the original. Note that two important footnotes to the Supreme Court judgment are included at the end of the extract.]

---

22 J Milner Davis et al, 'Defining Parody and Satire: Australian Copyright Law and its New Exception: Part 2—Advancing Ordinary Definitions' (2008) 13 *Media and Arts Law Review* 273.

23 See also *Rogers v Koons*, 960 F 2d 301 (2d Cir, 1992); *United Features Syndicate, Inc v Koons*, 817 F Supp 370 (SDNY 1993).

COMPARATIVE LAW

'OH, PRETTY WOMAN' BY ROY ORBISON AND WILLIAM DEES	'PRETTY WOMAN' AS RECORDED BY 2 LIVE CREW
Pretty Woman, walking down the street,	Pretty woman walkin' down the street
Pretty Woman, the kind I like to meet,	Pretty woman girl you look so sweet
Pretty Woman, I don't believe you, you're not the truth,	Pretty woman you bring me down to that knee
No one could look as good as you	Pretty woman you make me wanna beg please
Mercy	Oh, pretty woman
Pretty Woman, won't you pardon me,	Big hairy woman you need to shave that stuff
Pretty Woman, I couldn't help but see,	Big hairy woman you know I bet it's tough
Pretty Woman, that you look lovely as can be	Big hairy woman all that hair it ain't legit
Are you lonely just like me?	'Cause you look like 'Cousin It'
Pretty Woman, stop a while,	Big hairy woman
Pretty Woman, talk a while,	Bald headed woman girl your hair won't grow
Pretty Woman give your smile to me	Bald headed woman you got a teeny weeny afro
Pretty Woman, yeah, yeah, yeah	Bald headed woman you know your hair could look nice
Pretty Woman, look my way,	Bald headed woman first you got to roll it with rice
Pretty Woman, say you'll stay with me	Bald headed woman here, let me get this hunk of biz
'Cause I need you, I'll treat you right	for ya
Come to me baby, Be mine tonight	Ya know what I'm saying you look better than rice a roni
Pretty Woman, don't walk on by,	Oh bald headed woman
Pretty Woman, don't make me cry,	Big hairy woman come on in
Pretty Woman, don't walk away,	And don't forget your bald headed friend
Hey, OK.	Hey pretty woman let the boys
If that's the way it must be, OK.	Jump in
I guess I'll go on home, it's late	Two timin' woman girl you know you ain't right
There'll be tomorrow night, but wait!	Two timin' woman you's out with my boy last night
What do I see	Two timin' woman that takes a load off my mind
Is she walking back to me?	Two timin' woman now I know the baby ain't mine
Yeah, she's walking back to me!	Oh, two timin' woman
Oh, Pretty Woman.	Oh pretty woman

Souter J (delivering the opinion of the Court) (at 574–594) (some footnotes and references omitted):

II

It is uncontested here that 2 Live Crew's song would be an infringement of Acuff-Rose's rights in 'Oh, Pretty Woman,' under the *Copyright Act of 1976*, 17 USC §106 (1988 ed and Supp IV), but for a finding of fair use through parody. From the infancy of copyright protection, some opportunity for fair use of copyrighted materials has been thought necessary to fulfill copyright's very purpose, '[t]o promote the Progress of Science and useful Arts …' US Const, Art I, §8, cl 8. For as Justice Story explained, '[i]n truth, in literature, in science and in art, there are, and can be, few, if any, things, which in an abstract sense, are strictly new and original throughout. Every book in literature, science and art, borrows, and must necessarily borrow, and use much which was well known and used before.' *Emerson v Davies*, 8 F Cas 615, 619 (No 4,436) (CCD Mass 1845) …

In *Folsom v Marsh*, 9 F Cas 342 (CCD Mass 1841), Justice Story distilled the essence of law and methodology from the earlier cases: 'look to the nature and objects of the selections made, the quantity and value of the materials used, and the degree in which the use may prejudice the sale, or diminish the profits, or supersede the objects, of the original work.' *Id* at 348. Thus expressed, fair use remained exclusively judge-made doctrine until the passage of the 1976 *Copyright Act*, in which Justice Story's summary is discernible:

§107 Limitations on exclusive rights: Fair use

Notwithstanding the provisions of sections 106 and 106A, the fair use of a copyrighted work, including such use by reproduction in copies or phonorecords or by any other means specified by that section, for purposes such as criticism, comment, news reporting, teaching (including multiple copies for classroom use), scholarship, or research, is not an infringement of copyright. In determining whether the use made of a work in any particular case is a fair use the factors to be considered shall include—

(1) the purpose and character of the use, including whether such use is of a commercial nature or is for nonprofit educational purposes;

(2) the nature of the copyrighted work;

(3) the amount and substantiality of the portion used in relation to the copyrighted work as a whole; and

(4) the effect of the use upon the potential market for or value of the copyrighted work.

The fact that a work is unpublished shall not itself bar a finding of fair use if such finding is made upon consideration of all the above factors. 17 USC §107 (1988 ed and Supp IV).

... The fair use doctrine thus 'permits [and requires] courts to avoid rigid application of the copyright statute when, on occasion, it would stifle the very creativity which that law is designed to foster.' *Stewart v Abend*, 495 US 207, 236 (1990) (internal quotation marks and citation omitted).

The task is not to be simplified with bright-line rules, for the statute, like the doctrine it recognizes, calls for case-by-case analysis ... The text employs the terms 'including' and 'such as' in the preamble paragraph to indicate the 'illustrative and not limitative' function of the examples given ... which thus provide only general guidance about the sorts of copying that courts and Congress most commonly had found to be fair uses. Nor may the four statutory factors be treated in isolation, one from another. All are to be explored, and the results weighed together, in light of the purposes of copyright ...

A

The first factor in a fair use enquiry is 'the purpose and character of the use, including whether such use is of a commercial nature or is for nonprofit educational purposes.' §107(1). This factor draws on Justice Story's formulation, 'the nature and objects of the selections made' *Folsom v Marsh*, 348. The enquiry here may be guided by the examples given in the preamble to §107, looking to whether the use is for criticism, or comment, or news reporting, and the like, see §107. The central purpose of this investigation is to see, in Justice Story's words, whether the new work merely 'supersede[s] the objects' of the original creation ... ('supplanting' the original), or instead adds something new, with a further purpose or different character, altering the first with new expression, meaning, or message; it asks, in other words, whether and to what extent the new work is 'transformative.' Leval, ['Toward a Fair Use Standard', 103 *Harvard Law Review* 1105 (1990),] 1111. Although such transformative use is not absolutely necessary for a finding of fair use ... the goal of copyright, to promote science and the arts, is generally furthered by the creation of transformative works. Such works thus lie at the heart of the fair use doctrine's guarantee of breathing space within the confines of copyright ... and the more transformative the new work, the less will be the significance of other factors, like commercialism, that may weigh against a finding of fair use.

... [P]arody has an obvious claim to transformative value, as Acuff-Rose itself does not deny. Like less ostensibly humorous forms of criticism, it can provide social benefit, by shedding light on an earlier work, and, in the process, creating a new one ...

COMPARATIVE LAW

The germ of parody lies in the definition of the Greek *parodeia*, ... as 'a song sung alongside another.' ... Modern dictionaries accordingly describe a parody as a 'literary or artistic work that imitates the characteristic style of an author or a work for comic effect or ridicule,' [*American Heritage Dictionary* 1317 (3d ed 1992)] or as a 'composition in prose or verse in which the characteristic turns of thought and phrase in an author or class of authors are imitated in such a way as to make them appear ridiculous.' [11 *Oxford English Dictionary* 247 (2d ed 1989).] For the purposes of copyright law, the nub of the definitions, and the heart of any parodist's claim to quote from existing material, is the use of some elements of a prior author's composition to create a new one that, at least in part, comments on that author's works ... If, on the contrary, the commentary has no critical bearing on the substance or style of the original composition, which the alleged infringer merely uses to get attention or to avoid the drudgery in working up something fresh, the claim to fairness in borrowing from another's work diminishes accordingly (if it does not vanish), and other factors, like the extent of its commerciality, loom larger.[14] Parody needs to mimic an original to make its point, and so has some claim to use the creation of its victim's (or collective victims') imagination, whereas satire can stand on its own two feet and so requires justification for the very act of borrowing.[15]

The fact that parody can claim legitimacy for some appropriation does not, of course, tell either parodist or judge much about where to draw the line. Like a book review quoting the copyrighted material criticized, parody may or may not be fair use, and petitioners' suggestion that any parodic use is presumptively fair has no more justification in law or fact than the equally hopeful claim that any use for news reporting should be presumed fair ... The Act has no hint of an evidentiary preference for parodists over their victims, and no workable presumption for parody could take account of the fact that parody often shades into satire when society is lampooned through its creative artifacts, or that a work may contain both parodic and nonparodic elements. Accordingly, parody, like any other use, has to work its way through the relevant factors, and be judged case by case, in light of the ends of the copyright law.

Here, the District Court held, and the Court of Appeals assumed, that 2 Live Crew's 'Pretty Woman' contains parody, commenting on and criticizing the original work, whatever it may have to say about society at large. As the District Court remarked, the words of 2 Live Crew's song copy the original's first line, but then 'quickly degenerat[e] into a play on words, substituting predictable lyrics with shocking ones ... [that] derisively demonstrat[e] how bland and banal the Orbison song seems to them.' 754 F Supp at 1155 (footnote omitted). Judge Nelson, dissenting below, came to the same conclusion, that the 2 Live Crew song 'was clearly intended to ridicule the white-bread original' and 'reminds us that sexual congress with nameless streetwalkers is not necessarily the stuff of romance and is not necessarily without its consequences. The singers (there are several) have the same thing on their minds as did the lonely man with the nasal voice, but here there is no hint of wine and roses.' 972 F 2d at 1442. Although the majority below had difficulty discerning any criticism of the original in 2 Live Crew's song, it assumed for purposes of its opinion that there was some ...

We have less difficulty in finding that critical element in 2 Live Crew's song than the Court of Appeals did, although having found it we will not take the further step of evaluating its quality. The threshold question when fair use is raised in defense of parody is whether a parodic character may reasonably be perceived. Whether, going beyond that, parody is in good taste or bad does not and should not matter to fair use. As Justice Holmes explained, '[i]t would be a dangerous undertaking for persons trained only to the law to constitute themselves final judges of the worth of [a work], outside of the narrowest and most obvious limits. At the one extreme some works of genius would be sure to miss appreciation. Their very novelty would make them repulsive until the public had learned the new language in which their author spoke.' *Bleistein v Donaldson Lithographing Co* 188 US 239 (1903) ...

While we might not assign a high rank to the parodic element here, we think it fair to say that 2 Live Crew's song reasonably could be perceived as commenting on the original or criticizing it, to some degree. 2 Live Crew juxtaposes the romantic musings of a man whose fantasy comes true, with degrading taunts, a bawdy demand for sex, and a sigh of relief from paternal responsibility. The later words can be taken as a comment on the naiveté of the original of an earlier day, as a rejection of its sentiment that ignores the ugliness of street life and the debasement that it signifies. It is this joinder of reference and ridicule that marks off the author's choice of parody from the other types of comment and criticism that traditionally have had a claim to fair use protection as transformative works.

The Court of Appeals, however, immediately cut short the enquiry into 2 Live Crew's fair use claim by confining its treatment of the first factor essentially to one relevant fact, the commercial nature of the use ... In giving virtually dispositive weight to the commercial nature of the parody, the Court of Appeals erred.

The language of the statute makes clear that the commercial or nonprofit educational purpose of a work is only one element of the first factor enquiry into its purpose and character. Section 107(1) uses the term 'including' to begin the dependent clause referring to commercial use, and the main clause speaks of a broader investigation into 'purpose and character.' As we explained in *Harper & Row* [*Publishers, Inc v Nation Enterprises* 471 US 539 (1985)], Congress resisted attempts to narrow the ambit of this traditional enquiry by adopting categories of presumptively fair use, and it urged courts to preserve the breadth of their traditionally ample view of the universe of relevant evidence. 471 US at 561. Accordingly, the mere fact that a use is educational and not for profit does not insulate it from a finding of infringement, any more than the commercial character of a use bars a finding of fairness. If, indeed, commerciality carried presumptive force against a finding of fairness, the presumption would swallow nearly all of the illustrative uses listed in the preamble paragraph of §107, including news reporting, comment, criticism, teaching, scholarship, and research, since these activities 'are generally conducted for profit in this country.' ... Congress could not have intended such a rule, which certainly is not inferable from the common-law cases, arising as they did from the world of letters in which Samuel Johnson could pronounce that '[n]o man but a blockhead ever wrote, except for money.' 3 *Boswell's Life of Johnson* 19 (G Hill ed 1934).

...

B

The second statutory factor, 'the nature of the copyrighted work,' §107(2), draws on Justice Story's expression, the 'value of the materials used.' *Folsom v Marsh* 9 F Cas at 348. This factor calls for recognition that some works are closer to the core of intended copyright protection than others, with the consequence that fair use is more difficult to establish when the former works are copied ... We agree with both the District Court and the Court of Appeals that the Orbison original's creative expression for public dissemination falls within the core of the copyright's protective purposes ... This fact, however, is not much help in this case, or ever likely to help much in separating the fair use sheep from the infringing goats in a parody case, since parodies almost invariably copy publicly known, expressive works.

C

The third factor asks whether 'the amount and substantiality of the portion used in relation to the copyrighted work as a whole,' §107(3) … are reasonable in relation to the purpose of the copying. Here, attention turns to the persuasiveness of a parodist's justification for the particular copying done, and the enquiry will harken back to the first of the statutory factors, for, as in prior cases, we recognize that the extent of permissible copying varies with the purpose and character of the use …

Parody presents a difficult case. Parody's humor, or in any event its comment, necessarily springs from recognizable allusion to its object through distorted imitation. Its art lies in the tension between a known original and its parodic twin. When parody takes aim at a particular original work, the parody must be able to 'conjure up' at least enough of that original to make the object of its critical wit recognizable … What makes for this recognition is quotation of the original's most distinctive or memorable features, which the parodist can be sure the audience will know. Once enough has been taken to assure identification, how much more is reasonable will depend, say, on the extent to which the song's overriding purpose and character is to parody the original or, in contrast, the likelihood that the parody may serve as a market substitute for the original. But using some characteristic features cannot be avoided.

We think the Court of Appeals was insufficiently appreciative of parody's need for the recognizable sight or sound when it ruled 2 Live Crew's use unreasonable as a matter of law. It is true, of course, that 2 Live Crew copied the characteristic opening bass riff (or musical phrase) of the original, and true that the words of the first line copy the Orbison lyrics. But if quotation of the opening riff and the first line may be said to go to the 'heart' of the original, the heart is also what most readily conjures up the song for parody, and it is the heart at which parody takes aim. Copying does not become excessive in relation to parodic purpose merely because the portion taken was the original's heart. If 2 Live Crew had copied a significantly less memorable part of the original, it is difficult to see how its parodic character would have come through …

This is not, of course, to say that anyone who calls himself a parodist can skim the cream and get away scot free. In parody, as in news reporting, … context is everything, and the question of fairness asks what else the parodist did besides go to the heart of the original. It is significant that 2 Live Crew not only copied the first line of the original, but thereafter departed markedly from the Orbison lyrics for its own ends. 2 Live Crew not only copied the bass riff and repeated it, but also produced otherwise distinctive sounds, interposing 'scraper' noise, overlaying the music with solos in different keys, and altering the drum beat. This is not a case, then, where 'a substantial portion' of the parody itself is composed of a 'verbatim' copying of the original. It is not, that is, a case where the parody is so insubstantial, as compared to the copying, that the third factor must be resolved as a matter of law against the parodists.

Suffice it to say here that, as to the lyrics, we think the Court of Appeals correctly suggested that 'no more was taken than necessary,'… but just for that reason, we fail to see how the copying can be excessive in relation to its parodic purpose, even if the portion taken is the original's 'heart.' As to the music, we express no opinion whether repetition of the bass riff is excessive copying, and we remand to permit evaluation of the amount taken, in light of the song's parodic purpose and character, its transformative elements, and considerations of the potential for market substitution sketched more fully below.

COMPARATIVE LAW

D

The fourth fair use factor is 'the effect of the use upon the potential market for or value of the copyrighted work.' §107(4). It requires courts to consider not only the extent of market harm caused by the particular actions of the alleged infringer, but also 'whether unrestricted and widespread conduct of the sort engaged in by the defendant ... would result in a substantially adverse impact on the potential market' for the original. M Nimmer and D Nimmer, *Nimmer on Copyright: a treatise on the law of literary, musical and artistic property, and the protection of ideas,* New York: M Bender, 1978–, §13.05[A] [4], p 13-102.61. ... The enquiry 'must take account not only of harm to the original but also of harm to the market for derivative works.' *Harper & Row*, 471 US at 568.

Since fair use is an affirmative defense, its proponent would have difficulty carrying the burden of demonstrating fair use without favorable evidence about relevant markets. In moving for summary judgment, 2 Live Crew left themselves at just such a disadvantage when they failed to address the effect on the market for rap derivatives, and confined themselves to uncontroverted submissions that there was no likely effect on the market for the original. They did not, however, thereby subject themselves to the evidentiary presumption applied by the Court of Appeals. In assessing the likelihood of significant market harm, the Court of Appeals quoted from language in *Sony* [*Corp of America v Universal City Studios, Inc* 464 US 417 (1984)] that '[i]f the intended use is for commercial gain, that likelihood may be presumed. But if it is for a noncommercial purpose, the likelihood must be demonstrated.' ...

No 'presumption' or inference of market harm that might find support in *Sony* is applicable to a case involving something beyond mere duplication for commercial purposes. *Sony*'s discussion of a presumption contrasts a context of verbatim copying of the original in its entirety for commercial purposes, with the noncommercial context of *Sony* itself (home copying of television programming). In the former circumstances, what *Sony* said simply makes common sense: when a commercial use amounts to mere duplication of the entirety of an original, it clearly 'supersede[s] the objects,' ... of the original and serves as a market replacement for it, making it likely that cognizable market harm to the original will occur. *Sony* 464 US at 451. But when, on the contrary, the second use is transformative, market substitution is at least less certain, and market harm may not be so readily inferred. Indeed, as to parody pure and simple, it is more likely that the new work will not affect the market for the original in a way cognizable under this factor, that is, by acting as a substitute for it ... This is so because the parody and the original usually serve different market functions ...

We do not, of course, suggest that a parody may not harm the market at all, but when a lethal parody, like a scathing theater review, kills demand for the original, it does not produce a harm cognizable under the *Copyright Act*. Because 'parody may quite legitimately aim at garroting the original, destroying it commercially as well as artistically,' B Kaplan, *An Unhurried View of Copyright* (1967), 69, the role of the courts is to distinguish between '[b]iting criticism [that merely] suppresses demand [and] copyright infringement[, which] usurps it.' *Fisher v Dees* 794 F 2d [432 (9th Cir 1986)] at 438.

... [Parody has] a more complex character, with effects not only in the arena of criticism but also in protectible markets for derivative works, too. In that sort of case, the law looks beyond the criticism to the other elements of the work, as it does here. 2 Live Crew's song comprises not only parody but also rap music, and the derivative market for rap music is a proper focus of enquiry ... Evidence of substantial harm to it would weigh against a finding of fair use, because the licensing of derivatives is an important economic incentive to the creation of originals ... Of course, the only harm to derivatives

COMPARATIVE LAW

that need concern us, as discussed above, is the harm of market substitution. The fact that a parody may impair the market for derivative uses by the very effectiveness of its critical commentary is no more relevant under copyright than the like threat to the original market.

Although 2 Live Crew submitted uncontroverted affidavits on the question of market harm to the original, neither they, nor Acuff-Rose, introduced evidence or affidavits addressing the likely effect of 2 Live Crew's parodic rap song on the market for a nonparody, rap version of 'Oh, Pretty Woman.' And while Acuff-Rose would have us find evidence of a rap market in the very facts that 2 Live Crew recorded a rap parody of 'Oh, Pretty Woman' and another rap group sought a license to record a rap derivative, there was no evidence that a potential rap market was harmed in any way by 2 Live Crew's parody, rap version. ... it is impossible to deal with the fourth factor except by recognizing that a silent record on an important factor bearing on fair use disentitled the proponent of the defense, 2 Live Crew, to summary judgment. The evidentiary hole will doubtless be plugged on remand.

III

It was error for the Court of Appeals to conclude that the commercial nature of 2 Live Crew's parody of 'Oh, Pretty Woman' rendered it presumptively unfair. No such evidentiary presumption is available to address either the first factor, the character and purpose of the use, or the fourth, market harm, in determining whether a transformative use, such as parody, is a fair one. The court also erred in holding that 2 Live Crew had necessarily copied excessively from the Orbison original, considering the parodic purpose of the use. We therefore reverse the judgment of the Court of Appeals and remand the case for further proceedings consistent with this opinion.

---

14   A parody that more loosely targets an original than the parody presented here may still be sufficiently aimed at an original work to come within our analysis of parody. If a parody whose wide dissemination in the market runs the risk of serving as a substitute for the original or licensed derivatives ... it is more incumbent on one claiming fair use to establish the extent of transformation and the parody's critical relationship to the original. By contrast, when there is little or no risk of market substitution, whether because of the large extent of transformation of the earlier work, the new work's minimal distribution in the market, the small extent to which it borrows from an original, or other factors, taking parodic aim at an original is a less critical factor in the analysis, and looser forms of parody may be found to be fair use, as may satire with lesser justification for the borrowing than would otherwise be required.

15   Satire has been defined as a work 'in which prevalent follies or vices are assailed with ridicule,' 14 Oxford English Dictionary, at 500, or are 'attacked through irony, derision, or wit,' American Heritage Dictionary, at 1604.

Reporting news

Sections 42 and 103B allow fair dealing for the purpose of 'reporting news'. Section 42 provides that a fair dealing with a work does not constitute infringement if:

(a) it is for the purpose of, or is associated with, the reporting of news in a newspaper, magazine or similar periodical and a sufficient acknowledgment of the work is made; or

(b) it is for the purpose of, or is associated with, the reporting of news by means of a communication or in a cinematograph film.

Section 103B(1) is in similar terms, in relation to audio-visual items or works included within audio-visual items. In addition, s 42(2) provides that the 'playing of a musical work in the course of reporting news by means of a communication or in a cinematograph film is not a fair dealing with the work for the purposes of this section if the playing of the work does not form part of the news being reported'.

Cases already extracted above are relevant to this exception: note in particular the extracts from *Commonwealth v John Fairfax & Sons Ltd* (p 265) and *TCN Channel Nine Pty Ltd v Network Ten Pty Ltd* (p 274). The latter case also included an interesting analysis by Hely J, with which the other members of the Full Federal Court agreed, concerning an excerpt from a broadcast of the Allan Border Medal dinner. The Network Ten program *The Panel* had shown the moment when cricketer Glenn McGrath was named winner of the Allan Border Medal. When rising to accept the award, McGrath failed to notice Prime Minister John Howard attempting to congratulate him. *The Panel* had slowed down the clip to highlight this moment of 'embarrassment'. Network Ten argued that this was fair dealing for reporting news, which the trial judge accepted, but which Hely J rejected (at [122]):

> [W]as it news that Glenn McGrath did not notice the prime minister's attempt to congratulate him at the dinner? There is no suggestion that Mr McGrath deliberately ignored the prime minister, or that on the actual night anyone thought that the prime minister had been publicly embarrassed. The only public embarrassment was created by The Panel's publicising of a background and unnoticed incident. It was done by showing the footage in slow motion (unlike the original). Section 103B proceeds upon the basis that the news exists independently of the Panel Segment, and the defence is attracted if the Panel Segment is broadcast for the purpose of or in association with the reporting of that news. Yet here, if there is any news, it arises by reason of the slowing down of the footage so as to display a hitherto unnoticed incident which, had it been noticed, might have been a source of embarrassment for the prime minister. I agree with Nine's submission that it is not a fair dealing for the purpose of reporting news to use footage in a particular way so as to create the appearance of a public embarrassment and then to assert that the rebroadcast of the footage was merely the report of a public embarrassment.

CASE EXTRACT: PRECEDENT

De Garis v Neville Jeffress Pidler Pty Ltd

(1990) 37 FCR 99
Federal Court of Australia

[The facts of the case are set out above, p 272.]

Beaumont J (at 107–109): By s 42(1), a fair dealing with a literary work does not constitute an infringement of copyright if it is for the purpose of, or associated with, the reporting of news in a newspaper, magazine or similar periodical and a sufficient acknowledgment of the work is made.

It may be accepted that the 'reporting of news' in this context can go beyond a report of events which are current. In *John Fairfax*, above, Mason J said of s 42(1) (CLR at 56; ALR at 496): 'I am inclined to allow that 'news', despite its context of 'the reporting of news' 'in a newspaper, magazine or similar periodical' is not restricted to 'current events'.'

In *Hawkes & Son (London) Ltd v Paramount Film Service Ltd* [1934] Ch 593, the owners of the copyright in the musical march 'Colonel Bogey' sued for infringement. The defendants exhibited a 'news reel' film recording a motion picture of the scene at the public opening of a new school, together with the accompanying sounds, including the playing by a band of part of 'Colonel Bogey'. It was held that there had been an actionable infringement; and that the playing of 'Colonel Bogey' was not a 'newspaper summary' within the meaning of the English legislation, as it then stood: see *Copinger and Skone James*, 12th ed, p 207, para 515. Romer LJ said at 609:

> Then it is said by the defendants that they are protected by the first proviso to s 2, sub-s (1), of the Act, which enacts that amongst the acts which shall not constitute an infringement of copyright are: 'Any fair dealing with any work for the purposes of private study, research, criticism, review, or newspaper summary.' Mr Macgillivray has asked us to hold that a cinematograph screen when displaying items of news is a newspaper within the meaning of that proviso. I see obvious difficulties in so holding. But let me assume it is a newspaper. Even then, what the defendants have done cannot be described as a fair dealing with any work for the purposes either of criticism, review, or newspaper summary. Test it in this way. The item of news with which we are dealing is the item of news that on a certain day the Prince of Wales reviewed the boys of the Naval School in question, and that they marched past him to the tune of 'Colonel Bogey'. Of course, any newspaper is entitled to say that, and that would be a summary of an item of news. The paper would also, of course, be entitled to publish a photograph of the boys marching past the Prince of Wales. But what they would not be entitled to do would be to say: 'For the benefit of those who were not able to be present, we publish the principal 28 bars of the 'Colonel Bogey' march.' That is just what the defendants have done. They have, for the benefit of those who were not present, photographed the boys marching past the Prince of Wales; and have also provided, for the people who would see that, a representation of the 'Colonel Bogey' march.

   ...

As has been said, in order to justify its conduct under s 42(1), Jeffress must first establish that its activity was carried out for the purpose of, or is associated with, 'the reporting of news'.

The *Macquarie* definition of 'news' includes: '1. a report of any recent event, situation etc. 2. the report of events published in a newspaper, journal, radio, television, or any other medium. 3. information, events, etc, considered as suitable for reporting: *it's very interesting, but it's not news.* 4. information not previously known: *that's news to me ...*'

In my opinion, the reference to the 'reporting of news' in s 42(1) is intended to comprehend these matters, subject to the possible extension mentioned by Mason J in *John Fairfax*, supra. It follows, in my view, that the reproduction by Jeffress of the review written by Mr de Garis was not done for the purpose of the reporting of news. Nor, in my opinion, was the conduct of Jeffress 'associated' with such a purpose. The work of which Mr de Garis was the author was itself a literary review. Its reproduction by Jeffress had nothing to do with the reporting of news within the meaning of s 42(1).

Further, the defence provided by s 42(1) is only available where the reporting is in a newspaper, magazine or similar periodical. In considering Mr Moore's claim, I deal later with the meaning of the term 'newspaper' where used in s 35(4). In my view, that reasoning is applicable here also, with the consequence that, in my opinion, the reproduction by Jeffress cannot be said to be reporting in a newspaper, magazine or similar periodical.

Professional advice and judicial proceedings

Section 43(2) allows fair dealings with Part III works by legal practitioners, and patent and trade mark attorneys, for the purposes of giving professional advice. Interestingly, the equivalent provision in Part IV is broader, allowing use for the purpose of both seeking and giving advice without any requirement of fairness: s 104(b). Both Part III works and Part IV subject matter can be used for the purpose of a judicial proceeding or report of a judicial proceeding without any need to prove fairness: ss 43(1), 104(a). Thus inclusion of images or text in the report of a judgment will not infringe copyright.

PERSONAL USE: FORMAT, SPACE AND TIME SHIFTING

Personal copying exceptions to infringement were introduced into Australian law in 2006. The exceptions are very technical, and subject to stringent conditions. In all cases, only personal copying from legitimate (non-infringing) source copies falls within the exceptions, and no circumvention of technical protections is allowed.

The *format shifting exceptions* allow single copies to be made of: (1) literary works contained in books, newspapers or periodical publications (s 43C); (2) photographs (s 47J); and (3) films (s 110AA). The right only covers analogue-to-digital copying or vice versa (not digital-to-digital). Copies cannot be sold, hired, performed in public or broadcast, but can be lent to family or household members. In 2008 the Attorney-General conducted a review into the format shifting exception to consider in particular the issue of copying of DVDs; however no changes to ss 47J and 110AA were recommended.

The *space shifting exception* (s 109A) allows individuals to make copies of a legitimate sound recording for use on a device owned by the individual that plays sound recordings (e.g. an MP3 player, mobile phone or personal computer). Unlike the format shifting exception, under the space shifting exception the copy can be in the same format as the original, and serial copying (from CD, to laptop, to MP3 player or mobile phone) is allowed. This right specifically excludes shifting recordings of radio broadcasts such as podcasts and webcasts onto a playing device, although this may be permitted under licence.

Under the *time shifting exception* (s 111), copying of radio or television broadcasts for accessing at a later time is permitted, but this must be for private and domestic use by an individual. Copies cannot be sold, hired, performed in public or broadcast, but can be lent to family or household members. There is no time limit attached to the copy, nor any requirement to destroy the copy after viewing. The time shifting exception was considered in the case extracted below, which addressed whether the exception allowed for recording of television 'in the cloud' (i.e. by online providers), as well as at home, on dedicated devices.

CURRENT LAW

CASE EXTRACT: CURRENT LAW

National Rugby League Investments Pty Ltd v Singtel Optus Pty Ltd

[2012] FCAFC 59; (2012) 201 FCR 147
Federal Court of Australia, Full Court

[The facts of this case are extracted at p 239 above. One aspect of Optus' argument was that copies made for the purposes of its TV Now service were made entirely for the private and domestic use of its customers and hence covered by the exception in s 111. The issue was whether Optus was entitled to rely on s 111, or whether only the consumer making copies for their own private and domestic use could benefit from the exception. Section 111(1) and (2) provides that:

(1)   This section applies if a person makes a cinematograph film or sound recording of a broadcast solely for private and domestic use by watching or listening to the material broadcast at a time more convenient than the time when the broadcast is made.

(2)   The making of the film or recording does not infringe copyright in the broadcast or in any work or other subject-matter included in the broadcast.]

Finn, Emmett and Bennett JJ: 82. … [I]t was implicit in the terms of s 111 in its original draft form that, to attract the exception, the copy had to be made in domestic premises and the specified private and domestic purpose had to be that of the maker. As the matching explanatory memorandum made plain, the then provision would 'allow individuals in their homes to copy a broadcast for personal use to enable it to be viewed or listened to at a more convenient time'. The two subsequent amendments which directly affected s 111 and its interpretation were, first, the inclusion of a definition in s 10 of 'private and domestic use' which allowed such use to be 'on *or off* domestic premises' (emphasis added); and the requirement that copying itself be 'in domestic premises' was removed.

83. There is one fundamental issue of construction which follows from the pre-enactment amendments made to s 111. The amendments ensured there was no prescribed *place of making or of viewing* a copy made solely for private and domestic etc purposes. But does the provision on its proper construction none the less prescribe a person (or class of persons) who can be the maker or viewer of the recording made?

84. One can put to one side any question relating to who are viewers whose watching is mandated by the section. That is not in issue here. We would note, though, that it seems to be accepted for present purposes that viewing by, say, close family members of the copy-maker could fall within the description 'private and domestic'.

85. In its original form the proposed s 111 addressed private copying by individuals in their own homes using personal recording devices. We emphasise that for this reason. Optus has sought to draw comfort from an observation in the explanatory memorandum for the original form of s 111 which said:

This [proposal] benefits domestic consumers who would be assured that time-shifting and format-shifting do not infringe copyright. *This option also provides legal certainty for industries that provide* products and *services that assist consumers carry out these copying activities.* It will also facilitate the growth of digital television and radio services. (emphasis added.)

86. The emphasised passage, it is said, reveals that Parliament was alive to the possibility that these activities would be 'outsourced' by consumers to business to conduct them, for them, without destroying the required purpose.

87. … Having regard to the terms of the original proposed s 111 and to its concern with private copying by individuals in their homes, the 'certainty' being referred to in the above quoted passages was to industries that provided products and services to assist them so to carry out such copying. Further in the immediately following paragraph of that explanatory memorandum it was observed:

This [proposal] impacts on the owners of the copyright in television program content. However, *in simply recognising present practices*, market impact is likely to be negligible. (emphasis added.)

This is hardly likely to have been said if outsourcing to commercial providers was in contemplation.

88. The changes made by the two pre-enactment amendments removed the requirements that the copies be made and watched in domestic premises. There is nothing to suggest that they in any way affected the clear premise of both the originally proposed ss 111 and 111 as enacted. They both were concerned with private copying done by individuals for the prescribed purpose. If the language of the section is said to raise any doubt about this, the explanation given in the Further Supplementary Explanatory Memorandum (dealing with the amendment eliminating the *place of making* requirement) dispels that doubt:

> This amendment provides greater flexibility in the conditions that apply to 'time-shift' recording. The development of digital technologies is likely to result in increasing use of personal consumer devices and other means which enable individuals to record television and radio broadcasts on or off domestic premises. *The revised wording of s 111 enables an individual to record broadcasts, as well as view and listen to the recording, outside their homes as well as inside for private and domestic use.* (emphasis added.)

89. There is nothing in the language, or the provenance, of s 111 to suggest that it was intended to cover commercial copying on behalf of individuals. Moreover, the natural meaning of the section is that the person who makes the copy is the person whose purpose is to use it as prescribed by s 111(1). Optus may well be said to have copied programmes so that others can use the recorded programme for the purpose envisaged by s 111. Optus, though, makes no use itself of the copies as it frankly concedes. It merely stores them for 30 days. And its purpose in providing its service—and, hence in making copies of programmes for subscribers—is to derive such market advantage in the digital TV industry as its commercial exploitation can provide. Optus cannot invoke the s 111 exception.

...

96. We are conscious that the construction which we are satisfied the language of s 111 requires is one that is capable of excluding, and does in fact in this instance exclude, a later technological development in copying. However, no principle of technological neutrality can overcome what is the clear and limited legislative purpose of s 111. It is not for this court to redraft this provision to secure an assumed legislative desire for such neutrality: *R v L* (1994) 49 FCR 534 at 538 ...

TECHNICAL COPIES MADE IN THE COURSE OF USE AND COMMUNICATION

Many temporary or incidental reproductions of copyright material are made in the course of the technical process of using, making available and transmitting copyright material on computers and the internet. Many of these copies will be 'temporary', in the sense that, for example, running software from a DVD may involve creating copies of the software in the temporary memory of a computer, which are soon deleted or overwritten. To avoid granting copyright owners rights to control each and every use of digital works, and hindering digital infrastructure, Australian law recognises a series of exceptions for these 'technical' copies, covering:

- temporary copies of copyright subject matter made 'as part of the technical process of making or receiving a communication' (ss 43A, 111A); and
- temporary copies of copyright subject matter 'incidentally made as a necessary part of a technical process of using a copy of the work' (ss 43B, 111B).

Also relevant here is s 47B, which allows reproductions 'incidentally and automatically made as part of the technical process of running a copy of the program for the purposes for which the program was designed'. Note, however, that there are qualifications on these exceptions: ss 43A(2), 43B(2) and (3), 47B(2), 111A(2), 111B(2) and (3); in particular, if the source work is infringing, or the communication is infringing, the exceptions do not apply.

REFORM PROPOSALS

Australia's specific copyright exceptions have been criticised as lacking flexibility. The difference between Australian 'fair dealing' and US 'fair use' is often commented upon. US jurisprudence on fair use, which draws upon the US Constitution and free speech ideals, allows for greater debate about the nature, character, purpose and commercial merits of the defendant's use. By comparison, the Australian approach to exceptions is much more restrictive. To be a 'fair dealing' the use has to meet a benchmark requirement of 'fairness' *and* fall within one of the possible categories of exception (e.g. the use must be for the purpose of a 'criticism', a 'review', or for 'reporting the news'). Other exceptions have not accommodated new technologies, as illustrated in *NRL v Singtel Optus*, extracted above. This has led to Australian law being criticised as out of touch and difficult to explain to the public.

In light of these concerns, the ALRC was tasked in 2012 with reviewing 'whether existing exceptions are appropriate and whether further exceptions should recognise fair use of copyright material; allow transformative, innovative and collaborative use of copyright materials to create and deliver new products and services of public benefit; and allow appropriate access, use, interaction and production of copyright material online for social, private or domestic purposes'. In 2013 the ALRC produced Report No 122, *Copyright and the Digital Economy*; the report was published in February 2014.

The ALRC concluded that Australian copyright law was insufficiently flexible in its approach to exceptions. It argued that Australian law does not permit activities of social and economic value, and, by focusing on specific exceptions and conditions, does not allow the right questions to be asked; namely, whether a given use is beneficial and, conversely, whether it impacts unjustifiably or unfairly on copyright owners' interests. The key recommendation of the ALRC was that Australia should repeal many of its existing specific exceptions and instead introduce an open-ended exception.

The key recommendations of the ALRC were as follows:

> **Recommendation 4–1** The *Copyright Act 1968* (Cth) should provide an exception for fair use.

> **Recommendation 5–1** The fair use exception should contain:
> (a) an express statement that a fair use of copyright material does not infringe copyright;
> (b) a non-exhaustive list of the factors to be considered in determining whether the use is a fair use ('the fairness factors'); and
> (c) a non-exhaustive list of illustrative uses or purposes that may qualify as fair use ('the illustrative purposes').

Recommendation 5–2 The non-exhaustive list of fairness factors should be:

(a) the purpose and character of the use;

(b) the nature of the copyright material;

(c) the amount and substantiality of the part used; and

(d) the effect of the use upon the potential market for, or value of, the copyright material.

Recommendation 5–3 The non-exhaustive list of illustrative purposes should include the following:

(a) research or study;

(b) criticism or review;

(c) parody or satire;

(d) reporting news;

(e) professional advice;

(f) quotation;

(g) non-commercial private use;

(h) incidental or technical use;

(i) library or archive use;

(j) education; and

(k) access for people with disability.

According to the ALRC, a key benefit of a fair use exception is that it would allow the interests—particularly the market or economic interests—of the copyright owner to be taken into account. The ALRC acknowledged concerns that fair use would create too much uncertainty, but responded that reference to overseas cases, as well as the fact that fair use builds on existing Australian law relating to fair dealing, would allay that concern; together with the fact that parties can negotiate their own codes of practice. The ALRC also noted that current Australian law is not certain in its application. As a second-best option, the ALRC recommended a series of fair dealing exceptions covering the illustrative purposes identified in recommendation 5–3.

The ALRC also made recommendations relating to the relationship between exceptions and contract. The question is whether copyright owners and users should be able, by contract, to override copyright exceptions, including exceptions that protect freedom of expression, such as the fair dealing exceptions. The concern is that if 'contracting out' is allowed, copyright owners will (or already do) make this part of their standard form agreements. In an earlier report, *Copyright and Contract* (2002), the Copyright Law Review Committee had recommended that contractual provisions abrogating some exceptions should be void. The ALRC concluded that contracting out puts at risk the public benefit that copyright exceptions are intended to provide and, therefore, that some express limitations should be considered. It would not be sensible to adopt a blanket rule against contracting out of fair use, but if fair dealing exceptions were retained (and expanded as recommended) they should be protected from contractual abrogation, as should the library and archive provisions.

At the time of writing, the government has not responded to the ALRC report.

INTERNATIONAL RULES RELATING TO EXCEPTIONS: THE THREE-STEP TEST

Australia's ability to reform copyright law is subject to its international obligations. Article 9(2) of the Berne Convention, as developed in Art 13 of the TRIPS Agreement, provides for a 'three-step test' as follows:

> Members shall confine limitations or exceptions to exclusive rights to certain special cases which do not conflict with a normal exploitation of the work and do not unreasonably prejudice the legitimate interests of the right holder.

A similar provision exists in Art 10 of the *WIPO Copyright Treaty* and other recent multilateral, regional and bilateral agreements, including, for example, Art 17.4.10 of AUSFTA.

The three-step test in copyright as implemented in the TRIPS Agreement was the subject of one dispute (extracted below) arbitrated through the World Trade Organization's (WTO's) Dispute Settlement Understanding: a challenge brought by the European Communities against provisions of the US *Copyright Act* 1976.

CASE EXTRACT: COMPARATIVE LAW

US—Section 110(5) of the US Copyright Act

Report of the Panel, 15 June 2000, WT/DS160/R
WTO Dispute Settlement Panel

[The European Communities brought a challenge under Art 13 of the TRIPS Agreement in relation to two provisions of the US *Copyright Act*, contained in §110(5), which created exceptions to §106, the public performance right. The 'homestyle exception' allowed a person to do acts which in Australian law would be public performances—that is, turning on apparatus to perform dramatic works (such as operas or musicals) 'on a single receiving apparatus of a kind commonly used in private homes', provided that there was no direct charge for the performance and it was not further transmitted to the public. Thus people and businesses playing dramatic works via a radio or television would not be required to pay licence fees. The 'business exemption' allowed restaurants, bars under a certain size, or using equipment up to a certain size/number, to perform non-dramatic musical works, provided that they were playing public broadcasts which had been licensed by the copyright owner.]

The Panel (some footnotes omitted):

CERTAIN SPECIAL CASES

6.107. We start our analysis of the first condition of Article 13 by referring to the ordinary meaning of the terms in their context and in the light of its object and purpose. It appears that the notions of 'exceptions' and 'limitations' in the introductory words of Article 13 overlap in part in the sense that an 'exception' refers to a derogation from an exclusive right provided under national legislation in some respect, while a 'limitation' refers to a reduction of such right to a certain extent.

6.108. The ordinary meaning of 'certain' is 'known and particularized, but not explicitly identified', 'determined, fixed, not variable; definitive, precise, exact'. In other words, this term means that, under the first condition, an exception or limitation in national legislation must be clearly defined. However, there is no need to identify explicitly each and every possible situation to which the exception could apply, provided that the scope of the exception is known and particularized. This guarantees a sufficient degree of legal certainty.

6.109. We also have to give full effect to the ordinary meaning of the second word of the first condition. The term 'special' connotes 'having an individual or limited application or purpose', 'containing details; precise, specific', 'exceptional in quality or degree; unusual; out of the ordinary' or 'distinctive in some way'. This term means that more is needed than a clear definition in order to meet the standard of the first condition. In addition, an exception or limitation must be limited in its field of application or exceptional in its scope. In other words, an exception or limitation should be narrow in a quantitative as well as a qualitative sense. This suggests a narrow scope as well as an exceptional or distinctive objective. To put this aspect of the first condition into the context of the second condition ('no conflict with a normal exploitation'), an exception or limitation should be the opposite of a non-special, i.e., a normal case.

6.110. The ordinary meaning of the term 'case' refers to an 'occurrence', 'circumstance' or 'event' or 'fact'. For example, in the context of the dispute at hand, the 'case' could be described in terms of beneficiaries of the exceptions, equipment used, types of works or by other factors.

6.111. As regards the parties' arguments on whether the public policy purpose of an exception is relevant, we believe that the term 'certain special cases' should not lightly be equated with 'special purpose'. It is difficult to reconcile the wording of Article 13 with the proposition that an exception or limitation must be justified in terms of a legitimate public policy purpose in order to fulfill the first condition of the Article.

6.112. In our view, the first condition of Article 13 requires that a limitation or exception in national legislation should be clearly defined and should be narrow in its scope and reach. On the other hand, a limitation or exception may be compatible with the first condition even if it pursues a special purpose whose underlying legitimacy in a normative sense cannot be discerned. The wording of Article 13's first condition does not imply passing a judgment on the legitimacy of the exceptions in dispute. However, public policy purposes stated by law-makers when enacting a limitation or exception may be useful from a factual perspective for making inferences about the scope of a limitation or exception or the clarity of its definition.

[The Panel concluded that the business exemption was not confined to a certain special case: it covered a substantial majority of eating and drinking establishments and close to half of all retail establishments. On the other hand the homestyle exception covered a small set of establishments, a limited kind of equipment and a limited set of works: it was therefore confined to a certain special case.]

NOT CONFLICT WITH A NORMAL EXPLOITATION OF THE WORK

. . .

6.165. The ordinary meaning of the term 'exploit' connotes 'making use of' or 'utilising for one's own ends'. We believe that 'exploitation' of musical works thus refers to the activity by which copyright owners employ the exclusive rights conferred on them to extract economic value from their rights to those works.

. . .

6.183. We believe that an exception or limitation to an exclusive right in domestic legislation rises to the level of a conflict with a normal exploitation of the work (ie, the copyright or rather the whole bundle of exclusive rights conferred by the ownership of copyright), if uses, that in principle are covered by that right but exempted under the exception or limitation, enter into economic competition with the

COMPARATIVE LAW

ways that right holders normally extract economic value from that right to the work (ie, the copyright) and thereby deprive them of significant or tangible commercial gains ...

...

6.186. ... [I]n respect of the exclusive rights related to musical works, we consider that normal exploitation of such works is not only affected by those who actually use them without an authorization by the right holders due to an exception or limitation, but also by those who may be induced by it to do so at any time without having to obtain a licence from the right holders or the CMOs representing them. Thus we need to take into account those whose use of musical works is free as a result of the exemptions, and also those who may choose to start using broadcast music once its use becomes free of charge.

6.187. We base our appraisal of the actual and potential effects on the commercial and technological conditions that prevail in the market currently or in the near future. What is a normal exploitation in the market-place may evolve as a result of technological developments or changing consumer preferences. Thus, while we do not wish to speculate on future developments, we need to consider the actual and potential effects of the exemptions in question in the current market and technological environment.

6.188. We do acknowledge that the extent or exercise or non-exercise of exclusive rights by right holders at a given point in time is of great relevance for assessing what is the normal exploitation with respect to a particular exclusive right in a particular market. However, in certain circumstances, current licensing practices may not provide a sufficient guideline for assessing the potential impact of an exception or limitation on normal exploitation.

[The Panel decided that the business exemption did conflict with a normal exploitation of the works: it covered a large number of restaurants and bars and deprived right holders of a significant potential source of revenue. The homestyle exception did not conflict with a normal exploitation.]

NOT UNREASONABLY PREJUDICE THE LEGITIMATE INTERESTS OF THE RIGHT HOLDER

6.222. We note that the analysis of the third condition of Article 13 of the TRIPS Agreement implies several steps. First, one has to define what are the 'interests' of right holders at stake and which attributes make them 'legitimate'. Then, it is necessary to develop an interpretation of the term 'prejudice' and what amount of it reaches a level that should be considered 'unreasonable'.

6.223. The ordinary meaning of the term 'interests' may encompass a legal right or title to a property or to use or benefit of a property (including intellectual property). It may also refer to a concern about a potential detriment or advantage, and more generally to something that is of some importance to a natural or legal person. Accordingly, the notion of 'interests' is not necessarily limited to actual or potential economic advantage or detriment.

6.224. The term 'legitimate' has the meanings of

(a) conformable to, sanctions or authorized by, law or principle; lawful; justifiable; proper;
(b) normal, regular, conformable to a recognized standard type.

Thus, the term relates to lawfulness from a legal positivist perspective, but it has also the connotation of legitimacy from a more normative perspective, in the context of calling for the protection of interests that are justifiable in the light of the objectives that underlie the protection of exclusive rights.

...

6.226. Given that the parties do not question the 'legitimacy' of the interest of right holders to exercise their rights for economic gain, the crucial question becomes which degree or level of 'prejudice' may be considered as 'unreasonable' ...

6.227. In our view, one—albeit incomplete and thus conservative—way of looking at legitimate interests is the economic value of the exclusive rights conferred by copyright on their holders. It is possible to estimate in economic terms the value of exercising, eg, by licensing, such rights. That is not to say that legitimate interests are necessarily limited to this economic value.

...

6.229. The crucial question is which degree or level of 'prejudice' may be considered as 'unreasonable', given that, under the third condition, a certain amount of 'prejudice' has to be presumed justified as 'not unreasonable'. In our view, prejudice to the legitimate interests of right holders reaches an unreasonable level if an exception or limitation causes or has the potential to cause an unreasonable loss of income to the copyright owner.

[The Panel concluded that the business exemption unreasonably prejudiced the interests of the right holders. By contrast, the homestyle exception did not cause unreasonable prejudice.]

It has sometimes been argued that the three-step test, as interpreted in this decision, prevents the adoption of a flexible exception in copyright law. However, it is notable that the fair use exception in the USA has never been challenged for inconsistency with the three-step test. In *Copyright and the Digital Economy*, the ALRC considered this issue at length and concluded that its proposal for adoption of a fair use exception was consistent with Australia's international obligations.[24]

Interestingly, Australia already has a flexible exception which incorporates the three-step test. Section 200AB, introduced in 2006, allows use made by or on behalf of:

- the body administering a library or archives, for the purpose of maintaining or operating the library or archives (s 200AB(2));
- a body administering an educational institution, for the purpose of giving educational instruction (s 200AB(3)); or
- a person with a disability that causes difficulty in reading, viewing or hearing copyright content, or someone else, for the purpose of the person obtaining a reproduction or copy of the work or other subject matter in another form, or with a feature, that reduces the difficulty (s 200AB(4)).

In addition to falling within one of these categories, use under s 200AB must also:

- not be made partly for the purpose of obtaining a commercial advantage or profit (s 200AB(2) (c), (3)(c), (4)(c));
- not be covered by some other exception or statutory licence (s 200AB(6)); and
- comply with the three-step test; that is, the circumstances must amount to a special case, must not conflict with normal exploitation of the copyright content, and must not unreasonably prejudice the legitimate interests of the owner of copyright (s 200AB(1)).

Although s 200AB is flexible (in that it can, for example, apply to new uses arising from new technology), the ALRC received evidence that it is unwieldy and that the intended beneficiaries found the use of the three-step test language confusing.[25]

---

24   ALRC, Report No 122, *Copyright and the Digital Economy* (2013) at [4.164].
25   ALRC, Report No 122, *Copyright and the Digital Economy* (2013) at [12.24].

— 7 —

OTHER RIGHTS OF CREATORS AND OWNERS

INTRODUCTION

Previous chapters have focused on copyright's economic rights: the exclusive rights granted to authors and producers, and their assignees, to exploit their creations in certain ways. In this chapter we shift focus to certain other kinds of rights, concerned, for the most part, with promoting more personal and cultural interests of creators. Thus this chapter deals with authors' moral rights, which protect the personal connection between authors and their work through rights of attribution and rights to protect the integrity of the work by shielding it from derogatory treatment. It then discusses performers' rights to prevent unauthorised recording of their performances and distribution of unauthorised recordings (bootlegging). It also deals with artists' resale royalty rights, which grant visual artists a right to payment of a percentage of the sale price when their original, physical artworks are onsold; and the particular relationship between Anglo-Australian copyright law and Indigenous creativity and cultural practices. Finally it deals with rights against circumvention of technologies used to protect copyright material, and another *sui generis* system, circuit layout protection. The rights dealt with in this chapter are diverse and not united by any particular theme. With the exception of circuit layout rights, they are, for the most part, non-proprietary: they create personal rights of action rather than property rights.

AUTHORS' MORAL RIGHTS

SOURCES AND BASIC FEATURES

Australian copyright law has a strong economic bias: legal provisions and reform discussions are more often focused on facilitating a market for creative products than engaging with artists' or creators' interests. This is reflected in our common law history, the fact that all copyright's economic rights are proprietary and fully transferable, and the failure to adopt any particular philosophical underpinning to copyright.

The economic bias of Anglo-Australian law is somewhat at odds with approaches and philosophies of some other countries. Historically, civil law countries such as France and Germany had a stronger author-centric focus, recognising both economic and moral rights of authors.[1] These *droit d'auteur*

---

1   J Ginsburg, 'A Tale of Two Copyrights: Literary Property in Revolutionary France and America' in B Sherman and A Strowel, eds, *Of Authors and Origins*, Oxford University Press, Oxford, 1994; E Adeney, *The Moral Rights of Authors and Performers*, Oxford University Press, Oxford, 2006.

systems have long recognised that authors have certain personal rights in their creations, which we know as moral rights. In the negotiations that led to the *Berne Convention for the Protection of Literary and Artistic Works* (1886) a compromise was reached between the differing philosophical approaches, where it was agreed that the Berne Convention would require (only) limited moral rights: a right of attribution and a right of integrity for authors. This is reflected in Art *6bis*(1) of the Berne Convention:

> Moral Rights
> (1) Independently of the author's economic rights, and even after the transfer of the said rights, the author shall have the right to claim authorship of the work and to object to any distortion, mutilation or other modification of, or other derogatory action in relation to, the said work, which would be prejudicial to his honor or reputation.

Article 15(1) of the *International Covenant on Economic, Social and Cultural Rights* (1966) also recognises the right 'to benefit from the protection of the *moral* and material interests resulting from any scientific, literary or artistic production of which he is the author' (emphasis added). Article 27(2) of the *Universal Declaration of Human Rights* (1948) is to similar effect.

Anglo-Australian systems have been slow to accept moral rights as part of copyright law. The *Agreement on Trade-Related Aspects of Intellectual Property Rights* (the 'TRIPS Agreement') (1994) imports the substantive provisions of the Berne Convention in copyright but specifically excludes Art *6bis*. For most of the twentieth century Australia argued that passing off, defamation and a right against false attribution in the *Copyright Act 1968* (Cth) sufficed to fulfil the Berne requirements. However this view was disputed during the Copyright Law Review Committee consideration of moral rights in 1988.[2]

Moral rights for authors were finally introduced by the *Copyright Amendment (Moral Rights) Act 2000* (Cth) which inserted a new Part IX into the *Copyright Act*.[3] The rights granted in Part IX include a right of attribution of authorship, a right to prevent false attribution of authorship and a right of integrity of authorship. The provisions of Part IX are complex and repetitive. It is necessary to pay close attention to:

- the special definitions in s 189, which give certain terms a specific meaning only applicable in considering Part IX; and
- slight variations in drafting which may indicate a legislative intention to give different moral rights in relation to different subject matters. Films and performers (discussed further below: see 'Moral rights of performership', p 318) receive differential treatment, out of a concern to ensure that the introduction of moral rights did not disturb existing industry arrangements.[4] The provisions on films reflect industry negotiations prior to the enactment of Part IX.

Only individuals—human beings, not companies—can have moral rights: s 190. If there is more than one author, each author may separately assert moral rights: s 195AZI.

---

2   Copyright Law Review Committee, *Report on Moral Rights* (1988). Note however that the USA still adheres to this approach, and has only limited moral rights for visual artists only.

3   The previous Part IX provided for a very limited moral right against false attribution.

4   For example, moral rights of attribution and integrity only attach to films made after the moral rights came into effect: ss 195AZM–195AZO; for other subject matter, the moral rights attach to subject matter created before 2000 although they only apply in the case of acts done after the amendments came into force: ss 195AZM–195AZO.

Employees have moral rights in works created in the course of employment; however, these rights are limited in two important ways. First, employers are entitled to seek general consents from their employees, in advance (e.g. in the employment contract) which will enable employers to do things (such as fail to give attribution) that would otherwise breach moral rights. Second, the fact that a work is created in the course of employment is also relevant in determining whether an otherwise infringing act was 'reasonable' and therefore falls within an exception to infringement.

Moral rights attach to original literary, dramatic, musical and artistic works, and to cinematograph films. 'Work' is defined, for the purposes of Part IX only, to include films: s 189. The 'author' of a film is also defined, for Part IX purposes only, to mean the director, producer and screenwriter. If there is more than one person in any of these categories, it is the principal director, producer or screenwriter who holds moral rights: s 191 (although the Act envisages there may be more than one principal: ss 195AZJ–195AZL).

The recognition of moral rights in films departs from the general structure of the *Copyright Act*, which treats films as 'productions' rather than original works. It is, however, consistent with the Berne Convention and with approaches in some other countries which treat films as original works of authorship. There was a push in the early 2000s for more extensive recognition of film directors as authors in Australia. However, it was largely unsuccessful. As noted in Chapter 5, directors will often not hold economic rights in their films, and reforms to s 98 introduced by the *Copyright Amendment (Film Directors' Rights) Act 2005* (Cth) only afforded certain directors a limited economic right to a share in the royalties generated when films broadcast over free-to-air television are re-transmitted.

Moral rights continue for the duration of the copyright (except for the right of integrity in films, which expires with the death of the author): s 195AM.

Moral rights are personal rights, and cannot be assigned or transmitted by will or any other devolution by operation of law: s 195AN(3). They remain with the author even after economic rights in copyright have been assigned. After the author's death, moral rights are exercised by an appointed legal representative: s 195AN(1) and (2). In the case of films and other works as included in films, the authors may enter into a written co-authorship agreement by which each of them agrees not to exercise his or her right of integrity of authorship except jointly with the other author(s): s 195AN(4). Note that while moral rights cannot be assigned, it is possible for authors to consent in advance to acts that would otherwise breach moral rights (ss 195AW–195AWA), and it would not be uncommon for such consents to be secured as part of an agreement assigning economic rights in copyright material: see further below, p 315.

Further moral rights exist in some countries but are not part of the international legal framework or Australian law. These include (1) the right to *divulge or disclose*, which is intended to enable an author to be the person who can determine if and when a work is to be divulged to the public; and (2) the right to *withdraw, repent or retract*, which is intended to enable an author to withdraw a work from the public if the author wishes to do so. The French Intellectual Property Code, for example, includes both these moral rights.

MORAL RIGHTS OF ATTRIBUTION AND TO PREVENT FALSE ATTRIBUTION

The right of attribution of authorship is the right to be acknowledged as the author of a work. Specifically, the right of attribution (s 193(2)) requires identification of the author when an 'attributable act' is done, by any reasonable means including any reasonable way that the author has made known they wish to be identified: s 195. Identification must be clear and reasonably prominent: ss 195AA, 195AB. 'Attributable acts' include the exercise of exclusive rights (such as reproduction and communication), and, in the case of artistic works, exhibiting the work to the public: s 194. A person infringes an author's right of attribution if the person does, or authorises the doing of, an attributable act without appropriately identifying the author: s 195AO.

Authors also have a right not to have authorship of their work falsely attributed to someone else: (s 195AC(2)). Note that the right lies with the (true) author. The *Copyright Act* does not provide a cause of action for the person to whom authorship has been falsely attributed: compare this to the UK where the right is framed as the right of a person 'not to have a literary, dramatic, musical or artistic work falsely attributed to him as author': *Copyright, Designs and Patents Act 1988* (UK), s 84. The framing of the right in Australia means there is overlap between the right of attribution and the right against false attribution, as illustrated in *Meskenas v ACP Publishing Pty Ltd* [2006] FMCA 1136; (2006) 70 IPR 172, extracted below.

The Act identifies certain 'acts of false attribution', which include attaching someone else's name to a work in such a way as to imply, falsely, that they are the author of the work, and knowingly dealing with reproductions that have a false attribution attached: ss 195AD–195AF. It is also an act of false attribution to deal with a work that has been altered by someone other than the author as if it were the unaltered work of the author: ss 195AG–195AH (unless the effect of the alteration is insubstantial). In the case of multiple authors, false attribution as to *one* author infringes the right of *all* authors: if a work by A and B is falsely attributed to A and C, the right against false attribution of *both* A *and* B has been breached: ss 195AZI–195AZL. A person infringes an author's right against false attribution if the person does an above-mentioned act of false attribution in respect of the work: s 195AP.

As noted below there is no infringement of the right of attribution if it was reasonable in all the circumstances not to identify the author: s 195AR. Section 195AR(2) identifies a series of factors relevant to the assessment of reasonableness, including the purpose, manner and context of the use, whether the work was made in the course of employment, any relevant industry practice, and any difficulty or expense that would be involved in identifying the author. There is no equivalent defence to infringement of the right against false attribution.

There has been very little moral rights litigation in Australia. *Meskenas*, extracted below, is one of the few cases decided under the provisions. It discusses the rights, the reasonableness defence and the difficulties in calculating damages for moral rights breaches.

CASE EXTRACT: CURRENT LAW

Meskenas v ACP Publishing Pty Ltd

[2006] FMCA 1136; (2006) 70 IPR 172
Federal Magistrates Court of Australia[5]

[Meskenas' portrait of Dr Victor Chang was hung in the reception area of the Victor Chang Cardiac Research Institute, St Vincent's Hospital. A photograph of Princess Mary of Denmark was taken standing next to the portrait and published in *Woman's Day*. The magazine wrongly attributed the

---

5   The Federal Magistrates Court of Australia has since been renamed the Federal Circuit Court of Australia.

CURRENT LAW

painting to another painter, Jiawei Shen. Mr Meskenas claimed that when he saw this attribution to Mr Shen he was distressed: he was concerned that a portrait that had particular emotional importance to him was wrongly attributed to another portrait painter whom he considered a rival. The magazine was notified of the error but no apology or correction was published notwithstanding a meeting, over 90 follow-up phone calls and repeated promises by magazine employees. An apology was finally published 16 months after the mistake and shortly before the case commenced; the apology further upset Mr Meskenas as it was accompanied by an image of the portrait in reverse. The Federal Magistrate found that the publication of the photograph constituted an infringement of copyright, and considered the additional issue of moral rights.]

Raphael FM:

THE APPLICANT'S MORAL RIGHTS

16. The publication of the portrait gives rise to a requirement for an attribution of authorship under s 194(2)(d). It is clear from the photograph that the portrait itself is of significant importance and is not just incidental to the composition of the photograph. I infer from the fact that an attribution was made, albeit the wrong one, that the respondent accepted it was bound by s 194(2)(d).

17. The respondent raises two arguments to resist a finding that it has infringed the applicant's moral rights, in particular the rights not to have the authorship falsely attributed and the right of attribution. As I understand its argument in respect of the alleged infringement of the right of attribution it says that the making of a wrong attribution has the effect that the author of the work is not identified and thus it can seek to utilise the defence found at s 195AR.

18. The right of attribution expressed in s 193 is a positive right and prima facie was breached by the publication. The publication did not identify Vladas Meskenas as the author. In looking at the matters to be taken into account in deciding whether or not it was reasonable not to identify Mr Meskenas in s 195AR(2), I cannot see there is anything in the nature of the work which would prevent him from being properly identified. As I understand the evidence the portrait was signed. There was no evidence provided to me by the respondents to indicate that there was anything difficult arising out of the purpose for which the work was used in identifying him nor in respect of the manner or context in which it was used. The identification of another artist would seem to indicate that the magazine had no trouble about making an identification, albeit a wrong one. There was no evidence about any practice in the industry which was relevant, nor was there any evidence of a voluntary code or difficulty or expense as a result of identifying the author. I would not be inclined to hold that it was reasonable in all the circumstances not to identify the author.

19. The second argument put by the respondent is that there is a requirement for some form of intent in order to have infringed the author's right not to have the work falsely attributed. This raises the issue of the meaning of the word 'falsely' in the context of the *Copyright Act*.

20. Whether 'false' in the moral rights provisions of the *Copyright Act* means 'purposely wrong' or simply 'incorrect' is ultimately a question of statutory construction given there is no accepted definition of 'false' ...

[The Federal Magistrate considered authorities on the interpretation of 'false' and whether it means 'objectively incorrect' or includes an element of intention.]

31. I am satisfied that unless it could be suggested that there were some quasi-penal ramifications to a finding of infringement of moral rights the word 'falsely' used in the context of s 194 does not require an intention and will bear the meaning of objectively incorrect.

...

34. A general consideration of the provisions of s 195AZA(1) leads one to the view that the purpose of them is restitutional. This subsection can be contrasted with s 115(4) [the additional damages provision in the *Copyright Act*], that might well be construed as providing for a pecuniary penalty for an infringing act. I am of the view that the respondent cannot escape liability for its actions in infringing the moral right of the applicant not to falsely attribute the authorship of the painting on the [basis that the error was not intentional].

...

INFRINGEMENT OF MORAL RIGHTS

39. Although I think the applicant has a remedy for the infringement of his right of attribution and of his right not to have authorship falsely attributed, I do not believe damages should be awarded separately under these heads. I have not been assisted in coming to a decision as to how much I should award by way of damages by other Australian authorities, for none have been revealed in the research undertaken by counsel or by myself. [*Laddie, Prescott and Victoria: The Modern Law of Copyright and Designs*, 3rd ed, 2000] at [39.59] deals with the matter in this way:

> In an action for infringement of the right to be identified as author of a work or director of a film or the right to object to derogatory treatment, in addition to any specific pecuniary loss which could be proved, it is likely that the damages would be assessed on the basis of the damage to the goodwill and reputation enjoyed by the author or director, this type of damage being regarded as an economic loss. [It is] also likely that, where appropriate, an author or director may also claim compensation for injured feelings ...

In a case of false attribution of authorship, there is little guidance as to the principles on which damages are assessed. It has been held that where a claimant is a professional author, particularly one with a significant reputation, a false attribution is calculated to place his reputation and goodwill at risk of substantial damage and that damage may be presumed. In *Moore v News of the World* [1972] 1 QB 441 at 450 it was held that the plaintiff was entitled to something for the annoyance and irritation of having somebody taking the liberty of passing off the newspaper article as hers and that £100 was not an excessive sum and in *Noah v Shuba* [1991] FSR 14, where a statement endorsing certain after-care procedures was falsely attributed to a medical man, £250 was awarded.

40. Lahore, [*Copyright and Designs*, LexisNexis, Sydney, 2004], draws attention to subs (4) and (5) of s 195AZA of the *Copyright Act* and notes at [48,210] that:

> Damages recovered in other proceedings arising out of the same operation or transaction must also be taken into account in assessing damages for infringement of moral rights.

But there is otherwise no commentary upon the quantum of damage. In my view the primary damages for the infringement of moral rights in this case should reflect those which I would have awarded if I had believed that there was an infringement of the applicant's copyright. I say this because there has been no commercial dealing with the right. There were no copies of the painting produced for sale, the portrait serves only as an important reference point and reason for the photograph of the Princess Mary. I took these matters into account when considering damages should be nominal. In other words, I would award the sum of $1100 for the wrongful attribution which includes the 'non-attribution' and the distress which it caused to the applicant. Although the applicant is not required to adduce evidence of actual harm to his reputation only that the false attribution was of such a character that it 'might' affect his reputation: *Clark v Associated Newspapers Ltd* [1998] 1 All ER 959, and *Carlton Illustrations & Anor v Coleman & Company Ltd* [1910] 1 KB 771 at 780. I have to admit to some doubt as to whether the reputation of such a distinguished portrait artist would be so adversely affected by the respondent's activity that it should sound in substantial damages. Certainly the portrait was an important one, and to be identified as its author would enhance the applicant's reputation. But the evidence is that his reputation has already been made by virtue of his previous commissions and his previous success in being hung at the Archibald Prize. I none the less take the question of reputation into account when making my assessment. But I have also had regard to Mr Evatt's submission that any damage would have been alleviated by an early retraction.

41. I also believe that the applicant would be entitled to aggravated damages arising out of the conduct of the respondent following the time when the infringement of his moral rights was made known. The effects of the consistent failure to provide the applicant with the apology and retraction that he had requested and the reversal of the image of the portrait when that retraction was finally produced should not go unremedied. Lahore et al at [36,255] states (albeit in relation to breach of copyright) that:

> There would therefore appear to be no reason for not awarding exemplary damages which are punitive in nature and also aggravated compensatory damages for the plaintiff's suffering from injured feelings, distress and strain.

I cannot see why the sum which I would have awarded in respect of these damages under s 115(4) of the *Copyright Act* should be any different where aggravated damages are justifiable in respect of an infringement of moral rights and I would therefore award the sum of $8000. I should make it clear this award relates to the conduct of the respondent and the additional hurt caused by that conduct to the applicant following his advice to it that his copyright/moral right had been infringed. It is therefore additional to the lesser sum awarded in respect of the original infringement. It is not also to be considered a species of exemplary or punitive damages.

MORAL RIGHT OF INTEGRITY

The right of integrity of authorship is a right not to have a work subjected to derogatory treatment: s 195AI(2). 'Derogatory treatment' means:

- the doing, in relation to the work, of anything that results in a material distortion of, the mutilation of, or a material alteration to, the work that is prejudicial to the author's honour or reputation; or
- the doing of anything else in relation to the work that is prejudicial to the author's honour or reputation (ss 195AK (a) and (c) (artistic works), 195AJ (other works) and 195AL (films)).

For artistic works, 'derogatory treatment' also includes 'an exhibition in public of the work that is prejudicial to the author's honour or reputation because of the manner or place in which the exhibition occurs': s 195AK (b).

There is no infringement if the treatment to which the work was subjected was reasonable in all the circumstances: s 195AS. Section 195AS(2) lists factors relevant to the consideration of reasonableness, including the purpose, manner and context of the use, whether the work was made in the course of employment, and any relevant industry practice. For films, s 195AS(3) adds as a factor 'whether the primary purpose for which the film was made was for exhibition at cinemas, for broadcasting by television or for some other use'.

An interesting issue arises as to how courts are to judge whether a given treatment is 'prejudicial to the author's honour or reputation'. The question is the extent to which the author's (subjective) sense of outrage is relevant or decisive, or whether the determination is an objective one, concerned with what is generally said or believed about a person. There is no Australian case on point. Adeney points out that the inclusion of 'honour', if interpreted consistently with the civil law or Roman concept of *dignitas*, requires consideration of the author's subjective response.[6] Adeney also notes, however, that the provision was never intended 'to allow authorial hypersensitivity to dictate the outcome of a case'.[7]

This question arose squarely in a decision of the Ontario High Court of Justice, *Snow v Eaton Centre Ltd* (1982) 70 CPR (2d) 105. The case concerned a sculpture produced by an internationally renowned artist, known as 'Flight Stop', comprising 60 flying geese and hung in the atrium of a large shopping centre in Ontario. At Christmas, the operators of the centre, without the artist's knowledge, placed ribbons around the geese's necks. O'Brien J noted:

> 5. ... I believe the words 'prejudicial to his honour or reputation' in s 12(7) involve a certain subjective element or judgment on the part of the author so long as it is reasonably arrived at.
>
> 6. The plaintiff is adamant in his belief that his naturalistic composition has been made to look ridiculous by the addition of ribbons and suggests it is not unlike dangling earrings from the Venus de Milo. While the matter is not undisputed, the plaintiff's opinion is shared by a number of other well respected artists and people knowledgeable in his field.
>
> ...
>
> 8. I am satisfied the ribbons do distort or modify the plaintiff's work and the plaintiff's concern this will be prejudicial to his honour or reputation is reasonable under the circumstances.

As Adeney notes, this approach combined both subjective and objective elements.[8] Adeney further notes that the framework of the Australian legislation may allow for a combination of subjective and objective elements:

> [W]e see nothing in either legislation or case law [in Australia] suggesting that the author's subjective response might be given free rein. Nevertheless, there is also nothing in the Act to prevent subjective response being taken into account by a tribunal. In Australia a certain

---

6   E Adeney, 'The Moral Right of Integrity: The Past and Future of "Honour"' [2005] *Intellectual Property Quarterly* 111, 125–126 (collecting other commentary).

7   Ibid, 126.

8   Ibid, 128.

treatment of the work must be established that is 'prejudicial to the author's honour or reputation' [ss 195AI–195AL]. The word 'prejudicial', suggesting propensity to harm, does not appear to demand evidence of actual or quantifiable damage, the establishment of which would require the most extreme form of objectivity. The author could therefore be the prime witness in the case for prejudice to honour, able to give evidence as to how demeaned or diminished he or she feels by the treatment of the work. The subjectivity of this evidence, however, would be counterbalanced by the objectivity of the defence of reasonableness [s 195AS]. If, given the nature of the work, or the manner or context in which it is used, or other factors, the act of the defendant is reasonable, then there will be no infringement. This allows more dispassionate community judgments to come into play.[9]

CASE EXTRACT: CURRENT LAW

Perez v Fernandez

[2012] FMCA 2; (2012) 206 FLR 1
Federal Magistrates Court of Australia

[Mr Perez, known professionally as 'Pitbull' and 'Mr 305', was an international recording artist who held (with two companies) copyright in a sound recording and musical work titled *Bon, Bon*. Mr Fernandez, also known as 'DJ Suave', was a Perth-based DJ. Mr Fernandez obtained a recording known as an 'Audio Drop' in which Mr Perez spoke the words to the effect of 'This is Mr 305 and I am putting it down with DJ Suave'. The Audio Drop was provided to Mr Fernandez for the purposes of promoting an Australian tour by Mr Perez which Mr Fernandez was organising. The tour fell through (leading to separate proceedings). Mr Fernandez combined a recording of *Bon, Bon* with the Audio Drop. Mr Fernandez streamed the mixed version on his website, and played it in nightclubs.]

Driver FM (some footnotes omitted): 81. ... The moral rights protections in Part IX of the *Copyright Act* were introduced by the *Copyright Amendment (Moral Rights) Act 2000* (Cth). They have independent existence from the bundle of 'economic' rights protected by copyright, are inalienable to the author, and give protection to the investment of the author's personality in his or her creation. Moral rights draw their jurisprudential force from civil law traditions and a number of international copyright and human rights conventions to which Australia is a party. Further, in his Second Reading Speech introducing the relevant amendments to the *Copyright Act*, the then Attorney-General said:

> But this bill is not just about fulfilling international obligations. More importantly, it is about acknowledging the great importance of respect for the integrity of creative endeavour. At its most basic, this bill is a recognition of the importance to Australian culture of literary, artistic, musical and dramatic works and of those who create them.

82. Although Australia and other common law jurisdictions were slow to recognise moral rights, Part IX of the *Copyright Act* now gives full force to Australia's international obligations in this respect. In 2011, an expert group of copyright academics convened by the Australian Copyright Council recognised

---

9   Ibid, 129.

moral rights protection as one of the four fundamental principles of Australian copyright law [Copyright Council Expert Group, *Directions in Copyright Reforms in Australia*, Copyright Symposium 2011].

...

84. Here, the act in question undertaken by Mr Fernandez consisted of the deletion of a prominent part of *Bon, Bon* (the Spanish words *je, je, je, je, je, mira que tu estas rica*) and its replacement with words performed by Mr Perez in an entirely different context ('Mr 305 and I am putting it right down with DJ Suave'—intended to promote the failed tour). This made it appear that Mr Fernandez was a subject of the song. This alteration was carried out skilfully (presumably drawing on Mr Fernandez's DJ skills), and exploited the fact that Mr Fernandez already had in his possession the Audio Drop provided to him by Mr Perez. This created the impression that the author had authored the altered content himself and included it in the song. The reference to Mr Perez's alter ego 'Mr 305' particularly attracts the listener's attention. The change made to the song by Mr Fernandez must be regarded as a 'distortion' or 'alteration' (if not a 'mutilation') of the work, which is material, thereby satisfying that element of s 195AJ.

85. The fact that Mr Fernandez's treatment of *Bon, Bon* was 'prejudicial to the author's honour or reputation' (the second element which must be satisfied to engage s 195AJ) is evident in two ways.

86. First, given that the work had only recently been released in the United States, and not in Australia at the time of the infringement (Mr Fernandez obtained it from a friend in Chile), there will have been a class of listeners, who upon listening to *Bon, Bon* for the first time through the Suave Website, will have presumed that the altered section formed part of the authentic, original work. In other words, they would have presumed that Mr Fernandez was indeed a subject of the song, and that Mr Perez had written and performed it about him.

87. I accept the affidavit evidence provided by Ms Martinez that, associations between artists and DJs in the hip-hop/rap genre are highly significant. Artists go to great lengths to choose whom they associate with, and these associations form a central part of their reputation. In those circumstances, I accept that the fact that the reference to Mr Fernandez in the altered version of the song had not been authorised by the author should be regarded as prejudicial to him *per se*. Were it to be suggested otherwise, Ms Martinez's affidavit establishes to my satisfaction that the association with Mr Fernandez is one which Mr Perez himself strongly considered to be prejudicial to his reputation, and which caused him anger and distress.

88. Secondly, there will have been an alternative class of listeners who were more intimately aware of both Mr Perez's music and Mr Fernandez. This class is likely to have been alert to Mr Fernandez's ruse. Persons in this class are also likely to have been aware of the circumstances of the failed Australian tour, and the fact that Mr Fernandez is suing Mr Perez in the NSW Supreme Court in relation to it. These are matters which Mr Fernandez has sought to publicise for himself. Listeners in this class will know the significance of Mr Perez's associations as an artist, and will understand the alterations to the song made by Mr Fernandez to be mocking Mr Perez's reputation.

89. The defence of reasonableness is not available to Mr Fernandez to excuse his conduct. In fact, an examination of the matters to be taken into account by the Court when deciding whether this defence is available, as set out in s 195AS of the *Copyright Act*, only serves to emphasise the harm caused by Mr Fernandez. In particular:

a)   the nature of the work, which is one existing in a genre in which associations between artists is of considerable significance;

b) the purpose for which the work was used, which in this case was to either promote Mr Fernandez for his own benefit, or to mock Mr Perez as an act of retribution;

c) the manner and context, which in this case includes the fact that the work was streamed from Mr Fernandez's own website, and the existing relationship between the parties.

...

91. In *Meskenas v ACP Publishing Pty Ltd* [[2006] FMCA 1136; (2006) 70 IPR 172], when considering the approach to be taken to awarding damages, the Court took account of the academic commentary on moral rights, which notes among other things, that an author may also claim for injured feelings arising from the infringement. In this case, the Martinez affidavit establishes to my satisfaction that such harm was suffered by Mr Perez. He is entitled to be compensated for it.

92. In *Meskenas*, the Court ultimately took the view that the compensation awarded for moral rights infringement should reflect that which it would have awarded for copyright infringement. The applicants submit that this approach would not be apposite here. In this case there are two distinct groups of applicants involved: Mr Perez sues on the basis of his moral rights; the second and third applicants sue on the basis of their copyright. Were the conflation of copyright and moral right damages in *Meskenas* to be applied here without appreciation of the underlying factual differences it would leave one class of applicant uncompensated at the expense of the other. Here, the copyright and moral rights causes of action should sound in separate and cumulative heads of damage, in relation to compensatory damages for copyright infringement and breach of moral rights. However, as I have already found above, the considerations relevant to an award of additional damages are those bearing on the award of damages for breach of moral rights, as matters bearing on the interests of Mr Perez.

93. In *Meskenas* the Court also noted the availability of aggravated damages for moral rights infringement, which were awarded in that case on the basis of the respondent's conduct following the time when the infringement of the moral rights was made known. Mr Fernandez here has allegedly similarly aggravated the harm caused by his conduct after the infringement was made known to him, as has been set out above.

94. Mr Fernandez continues to deny that his conduct has resulted in any harm or embarrassment. His affidavit evidence continues to maintain that he is entitled to do as he pleases with the Audio Drop. I do not accept that Mr Fernandez has displayed contrition. The conduct following the infringement further aggravated the harm caused, for which, Mr Perez is also entitled to be compensated. However, Mr Fernandez is entitled to the benefit of his acknowledgment of his infringements (however belatedly).

95. An action for infringement of moral rights is actionable as a breach of statutory duty without proof of damage. What is required for a breach of the author's right of integrity (provided for in s 195AI) is the subjection of the work to 'derogatory treatment', which means the doing of anything in relation to a work that results in a material distortion of, the mutilation of, or a material alteration to the work (or anything else) that is prejudicial to the author's honour or reputation. A person infringes the author's right of integrity if he or she so subjects the work to derogatory treatment.

96. In other words, all that is required is proof that Mr Fernandez's act in respect of the *Bon, Bon Song* was prejudicial to Mr Perez's honour or reputation, not that Mr Perez suffered damage. This approach has also been taken under the equivalent UK legislation [*Clark v Associated Newspapers* [1998] 1 All ER 959].

97. The *Copyright Act* does not require that Mr Perez's reputation has been prejudiced. All that is required is that the respondent's act in relation to the work 'is prejudicial'. That statutory language is

derived from Article 6*bis* of the Berne Convention, which requires Australia to afford authors the right to object to derogatory treatment 'which *would be prejudicial* to their honour or reputation' (emphasis added).

98. As is evident from the Martinez affidavit, issues concerning the reputation and honour of an artist in the rap/hip-hop genre in which Mr Perez creates are highly attuned:

a) an artist's honour and reputation depends on whom he or she associates with, and is a driver of artistic (and with it commercial) success. The artist goes to great lengths to control whom he or she associates with;

b) given that evidence, the distortion of Mr Perez's work, such as to create a false association, should be regarded as prejudicial to his honour and reputation as an artist *per se*;

c) that it is in fact prejudicial is made clear by the circumstances of Mr Perez's relationship with Mr Fernandez; it is not necessary for the applicants to lead evidence from members of the public as to the way the work would be received;

d) that the treatment of the work was prejudicial may be presumed.

99. In *Meskenas* the Court awarded damages of $9100 for breach of ss 195AO and 195AP of the *Copyright Act*, for breach of the author's right of attribution, in circumstances where Raphael FM held that he would have awarded the same amount for copyright infringement (for both compensatory and additional damages).

100. However, the basis for compensation is not the same. Section 195AZA(1) provides that the remedies for moral rights infringement include 'damages for loss resulting from the infringement'. Moral rights are not proprietary rights (a matter which is evident by the absence in the statute of any provision allowing assignment). Moral rights attach to the personality of the author. They may be compared, for instance, with the reputational interests protected by an action in defamation.

101. It is relevant to consider that prior to the introduction of Part IX one of the ways that Australia sought to comply with its Berne obligations with respect to the right of integrity, was pursuant to the law of defamation. There are clear parallels between the two laws (noting that defamation protects reputation, whereas moral rights protect both 'honour and reputation').

102. This means that the loss which is compensable includes not only pecuniary loss, but also damage to goodwill and reputation enjoyed by the author [*Laddie, Prescott and Vitoria: The Modern Law of Copyright and Designs* (2011) at [13.57]].

103. In awarding damages for moral rights infringement on this basis the Court should have regard to the matters described above, with respect to extent and value of Mr Perez's reputation as an artist, and the harm caused by Mr Fernandez's conduct. This includes the fact that the distortion of the work and the false association created by it occurred at a time when the song was newly released, the artistic significance which associations have within the genre in which Mr Perez creates, the fact that the distorted work was performed in nightclubs which reach the target audience for Mr Perez, and that the distorted work was communicated on the internet where its audience was potentially unlimited.

104. In addition, damages awarded under s 195AZA(1) may further provide compensation for injured feelings, and vindication of the artist, by way of an award of aggravated damages. A parallel here may be drawn with an award of damages under this limb in the law of defamation. An award of aggravated damages may also take account of the respondent's conduct in the litigation. This would also accord with the approach taken in the law of defamation, where it has been held that conduct by

CURRENT LAW

counsel during the trial may also justify the award of aggravated damages through increasing the hurt done to the plaintiff.

...

106. Here, it is submitted that the Court should have regard to the need to provide compensation to Mr Perez for the distress caused to Mr Perez as an artist both at the time of the infringement, the conduct of Mr Fernandez since that time, including the ongoing campaign which is said to be being waged by Mr Fernandez, and the need to provide vindication to Mr Perez as an artist. In doing so, the Court may have regard for the range of damages it would award under s 115(4) for infringement of the copyright.

107. The applicants seek $35 000 for the harm to Mr Perez's reputation and $50 000 aggravated damages for distress to Mr Perez. That claim considerably overstates the applicants' case, trespasses into matters more appropriate to be dealt with in the NSW Supreme Court proceedings, and gives no acknowledgment of Mr Fernandez's concessions, undertakings and apology. I do not accept that Mr Perez's reputation has suffered any lasting damage. His moral rights were infringed in circumstances which caused him distress, and which were serious, but Mr Fernandez ultimately saw the error of his ways and appropriately gave undertakings and an apology, however grudgingly. In all the circumstances, I have decided that an appropriate award of damages for the infringement of Mr Perez's moral rights is $10 000.

CASE EXTRACT: COMPARATIVE LAW

COMPARATIVE LAW

Confetti Records v Warner Music UK Ltd

[2003] EWHC 1274 (Ch); [2003] EMLR 35
High Court of England and Wales, Chancery Division

[Mr Alcee, who was connected to a loose association of artists, the Ant'ill Mob, composed the track 'Burnin' and sold it to Confetti Records, a small label specialising in UK Garage or Speed Garage music, run by Mr Pascal and Ms Joachim. The original version consisted of an insistent instrumental beat accompanied by the vocal repetition of the word 'burning' or variants of it. A mix was produced where 'Burnin' was used as a backing track to a rap performed by the Heartless Crewe (DJ Fonti, and MCs Mighty Mo and Bushkin) and another MC called Elephant Man. It was alleged that this rap recording involved derogatory treatment.]

Lewison J: 150. It is clear that in art 6*bis* the author can only object to distortion, mutilation or modification of his work if it is prejudicial to his honour or reputation. ...

151. The nub of the original complaint, principally advanced by Mr Pascal, is that the words of the rap (or at least that part contributed by Elephant Man) contained references to violence and drugs. This led to the faintly surreal experience of three gentlemen in horsehair wigs examining the meaning of such phrases as 'mish mish man' and 'shizzle (or sizzle) my nizzle.'

152. The 'author' in the present case is the Third Claimant, Mr Alcee. The assignment of his copyright to the First and/or Second Claimants does not affect his authorship. The First and Second Claimants are not entitled to complain of prejudice to their honour or reputation. Thus the evidence that

I heard about the kinds of songs produced by Confetti, and in particular about the meaning of the lyrics of 'Champion Puffa', is, to my mind, irrelevant.

153. When played at normal speed the words of the rap overlying 'Burnin' are very hard to decipher, and indeed the parties disagreed on what the words were. Even when played at half speed there were disagreements about the lyrics. The very fact that the words are hard to decipher itself militates against the conclusion that the treatment was 'derogatory' in the statutory sense.

154. Mr Pascal did not himself claim to know what street meanings were to be attributed to the disputed phrases, but said that he had been told what they were by an unnamed informant conversant with the use of drugs. Mr Howe [counsel for the defendant] submitted, correctly in my opinion, that the meaning of words in a foreign language could only be explained by experts. He also submitted, again correctly in my opinion, that the words of the rap, although in a form of English, were for practical purposes a foreign language. Thus he submitted that Mr Pascal's evidence, not being the evidence of an expert, was inadmissible. I think that he is right, although the occasions on which an expert drug dealer might be called to give evidence in the Chancery Division are likely to be rare.

155. But even if I pay regard to Mr Pascal's evidence on this topic, I do not find that the meaning of the disputed words has been proved. Mr Pascal's evidence was hearsay, and the source of his information was not identified. Mr Hunter, one of the MCs with The Heartless Crew, (professionally known as MC Bushkin) had not heard of the meanings that Mr Pascal attributed to the disputed phrases. Nor had Mr Thomas [an artists and repertoire employee of the defendant]. A search on the Internet discovered the Urban Dictionary which gave some definitions of 'shizzle my nizzle' (and variants) none of which referred to drugs. Some definitions carried sexual connotations. The most popular definitions were definitions of the phrase 'fo' shizzle my nizzle' and indicated that it meant 'for sure'. There were no entries for 'sizzle my nizzle' or for 'mish mish man', and Mr Hunter said that Elephant Man (the MC who uttered the disputed phrases) often made up words for their rhyming effect.

156. To be fair, Mr Shipley [counsel for the claimants] did not press this complaint in his closing submissions. Instead he sought to advance a new case. First he said that the treatment was derogatory because all coherence of the original work has been lost as a result of the superimposition of the rap. Second he said, whatever a 'mish mish man' was, the words of the rap 'string dem up one by one' was an invitation to lynching. It is by no means clear that the words on the rap are in fact 'string dem up'. Moreover, I am not at all sure that the meaning Mr Shipley attributes to the phrase 'string dem up' is the only possible meaning. A proponent of capital punishment who says that murderers should be 'strung up' would usually be taken to advocate the return of a hangman, rather than lynching.

157. However, it seems to me that the fundamental weakness in this part of the case is that I have no evidence about Mr Alcee's honour or reputation. I have no evidence of any prejudice to either of them. Mr Alcee himself made no complaint about the treatment of 'Burnin' in his witness statement. Mr Shipley invites me to infer prejudice. Where the author himself makes no complaint, I do not consider that I should infer prejudice on his behalf.

158. I do not infer any prejudice from the fact that The Heartless Crew rode the rhythm right through the track. If I am to draw any inference, the inference I would draw, having listened to the original mix of 'Burnin', is that it was designed to be the background track to a rap. Indeed the proposed mix for the single of 'Burnin' by the Ant'ill Mob (called the vocal mix) was itself a rap which rode the rhythm throughout the track.

159. There was a suggestion that Mr Alcee is the only permanent member of the Ant'ill Mob. He did not say this in his own witness statement, and Mr Pascal said in his witness statement that the Ant'ill

Mob 'do not have identifiable members in the traditional sense of a group.' He also said that when they perform Confetti hire session musicians to form the group.

160. If, however, Mr Alcee is a member (or perhaps the only member) of the Ant'ill Mob, then the way in which they are presented may impinge on his own honour and reputation. It is clear to me, despite Mr Pascal's protestations to the contrary, that the Ant'ill Mob were costumed to look like 1930s gangsters. As it was put in a newspaper article in February 2002, the release of 'Burnin' was twinned 'with a video showing the Mob in true 1930s gangster style'. My own viewing of the video confirmed this impression. I do not therefore infer any prejudice from the invitation to 'string up' 'mish mish men', even if it bears the meaning that Mr Shipley attributes to it.

INFRINGEMENT AND DEFENCES

Moral rights can be infringed by directly doing an act that infringes or by authorising another person to do such an act: ss 195AO–195AQ, s 195AVA. The Act also prohibits knowing importation for sale of articles that infringe moral rights: s 195AU; and knowing dealings with such articles: s 195AV. Only acts occurring in Australia infringe moral rights: s 195AX. Moral rights in respect of a work apply in relation to a whole or a substantial part of the work: for example reproduction and mutilation of only part of a work could therefore infringe the right of integrity: s 195AZH.

There are two key defences to moral rights infringement. The first, mentioned above, is that the defendant's acts were reasonable in all the circumstances. This is a defence to infringements of the right of attribution (s 195AR) and the right of integrity (s 195AS). Architecture and public sculpture pose considerable difficulties for moral rights as artistic objectives may become compromised for a range of reasons, such as budget or engineering constraints or the need to renovate a building. Accordingly, specific acts will not constitute an infringement of the author's right of integrity in relation to buildings and moveable artworks: s 195AT.

The second significant 'defence' is that the author's consent has been obtained. At the time of the passage of the moral rights legislation there was a controversial suggestion of 'waiver' provisions. Media owners argued that the moral right of integrity would lead to significant disruption and undermine investment. A compromise was negotiated, allowing for the author or performers to consent to certain acts or omissions (ss 195AW (films and works included in films), 195AWA (other works)). For films and works included in films, a general consent is allowed (covering all or any acts or omissions occurring before or after the consent is given): s 195AW. Employees may similarly give general consents: ss 195AW(4), 195AWA(4). In all other cases, consent is valid only if it relates to specified acts or omissions, in relation to specified works: s 195AWA(3). Duress or the making of misleading statements are reasons for invalidating consent: s 195AWB. There is no case law on any of these provisions. In the case of films and works included in films, joint authors may enter into a written co-authorship agreement in which they agree to exercise their right of integrity only jointly with the other author(s): s 195AN.

There are no exceptions in the moral rights provisions equivalent to exceptions to economic rights, such as fair dealing, although the defence of reasonableness may cover at least some situations where an act would be fair dealing. One interesting question is whether a parody involving significant copying could ever be excused as a fair dealing (under ss 41A/103AA) but still breach the moral right of integrity. When introducing the parody fair dealing exception in 2006, the government chose not to proscribe any particular relationship with moral rights. It is likely that

COMPARATIVE LAW

parodies would be excusable under the reasonableness defences, but a separate analysis, focusing on the different interests involved, would be necessary.[10]

Remedies for breach of the moral rights provisions are set out in s 195AZA, and include the usual remedies (injunctions, damages) but also some remedies more tailored to the nature of moral rights: an order that the defendant make a public apology (s 195AZA(1)(d)) and an order that any false attribution or derogatory treatment be reversed (s 195AZA(1)(e)). Section 195AZA(2) sets out factors the court is to consider in granting remedies, including whether the defendant was aware (or ought reasonably to have been aware) of the author's moral rights, any mitigating action a defendant has already taken, and the expense of any reversal of the breach.

PERFORMERS' PROTECTION

Historically, copyright treated performers, no matter how creative and innovative, as of lesser importance than authors. Performers were disadvantaged by a (dubious) characterisation as mere 'interpreters' or 'translators' of an underlying literary, dramatic or musical vision created by others.[11] Widespread access to recording equipment in the late twentieth century made performers particularly vulnerable. If they had no ownership in an underlying work, and no copyright in their performances, the party who had recorded their act would have an exclusive right to that recording.

In 1961 the *Rome Convention for the Protection of Performers, Producers of Phonograms and Broadcasting Organizations* awarded performers certain 'anti-bootlegging' rights: in essence, rights against unauthorised recording and communication of performances (considered further below). The *WIPO Performances and Phonograms Treaty* (1996) (WPPT) expanded the international legal framework, by requiring that performers be granted both moral rights, and exclusive economic rights in their recorded performances. Unlike the Rome Convention, however, which grants anti-bootlegging rights to *all* performers, the WPPT only relates to live performances and performances which are recorded in *sound recordings*. Performances recorded in audio-visual form (i.e. film) are not covered, owing to disagreements between the various countries with significant film industries around transferability of rights. In 2012 the World Intellectual Property Organization (WIPO) concluded the *Beijing Treaty on Audiovisual Performances*, which would similarly extend both moral and economic rights to performers recorded in audio-visual form. At the time of writing Australia is not a signatory to the Beijing Treaty and the Treaty is not yet in force.

Australia has enacted performers' protection in a piecemeal way. The first anti-bootlegging rights were enacted in 1989 in Part XIA of the *Copyright Act*, and the Rome Convention came into force in Australia in 1992. As a result of signing the *Australia–US Free Trade Agreement* (2004) Australia committed to joining the WPPT. The WPPT came into force in Australia on 26 July 2007. The *US Free Trade Agreement Implementation Act 2004* (Cth) contained extensive provisions on performers' economic rights and performers' moral rights.[12] Australia's provisions implementing the

---

10   See M Sainsbury, 'Parody, Satire, Honour and Reputation: The Interplay between Economic and Moral Rights' (2007) 18 *Australian Intellectual Property Journal* 149.

11   See *Hadley v Kemp* [1999] EMLR 589.

12   See K Weatherall, 'On the Insanely Complicated New Regime for Performers' Rights in Australia, and How Australian Performers Got Ripped Off' in F Macmillan and K Bowrey, eds, *New Directions in Copyright Law, Vol 3*, Edward Elgar, Cheltenham, 2006; A Taubman, '"Nobility of Interpretation": Equity, Retrospectivity and Collectivity in Implementing New Norms For Performers' Rights' (2005) 12 *Journal of Intellectual Property Law* 351.

WPPT are confined in scope the same way that the Treaty is confined: to certain rights in relation to live performances, and rights relating to live performances recorded in sound recordings, but not films. The 2004 implementation of the WPPT also made amendments to the anti-bootlegging provisions (Part XIA), in particular narrowing some of the exceptions, because the Australian government took the view that the exceptions allowed under the WPPT were narrower than those allowed under the Rome Convention. Again, those amendments *only* apply to live performances and performances recorded in sound recordings, so the broader Rome Convention exceptions still apply for performances recorded in film. Owing to this piecemeal reform, and the attempt to confine performers' rights to those required by treaty, performers' rights are legislatively complex. The table below helps to give some structure to thinking about the rights of performers.

TABLE 7.1 PERFORMERS' RIGHTS: SOURCES AND SCOPE

	PERFORMERS' ECONOMIC RIGHTS IN SOUND RECORDINGS	PERFORMERS' MORAL RIGHTS	PERFORMERS' NON-ECONOMIC (ANTI-BOOTLEGGING) RIGHTS
Key provisions	*Copyright Act*, ss 22, 85, 89, 93, 97	*Copyright Act*, Part IX	*Copyright Act*, Part XIA
Definition of performer	Live performers who contribute sound to a sound recording (including a conductor): s 22(7)	Each performer who contributes sounds to a 'performance' as defined in Part XIA: s 189	Live performers of performances (as defined in s 248A), whether contributing sounds or not (term undefined in Act)
Rights granted	Performer(s) is/are 'maker(s)' of the sound recording and therefore hold a half-share of copyright in the sound recording of the live performance: s 22(3A), 97(2A) Exclusive rights in s 85 comprise the rights to make a copy, cause the recording to be heard in public, communicate the recording to the public and enter into commercial rental arrangements Rights apply to recordings regardless of whether consent was given to the making of the recording	• Right of attribution: s 195ABA • Right against false attribution: s 195AHA • Right of integrity of performership: s 195ALA Rights apply to recordings regardless of whether consent was given to the making of the recording	Right to bring an action for 'unauthorised use of a performance': s 248J Unauthorised use (s 248G) consists of: • Making an unauthorised film or sound recording of a performance • An unauthorised communication of a performance (e.g. a broadcast) • Communicating an unauthorised film or sound recording of a performance • Certain knowing dealings with unauthorised recordings Note that once consent has been given for the performance to be recorded, Part XIA is not relevant
Duration	70 years from first publication: s 93	Right of attribution and right against false attribution endure for 70 years from first publication: s 195ANA(1)–(2) Right of integrity continues until performer dies: s 195ANA(3)	Generally: 20 years following the performance: s 248CA(1) Extended to 50 years from the performance for certain acts in relation to sound recordings of live performances: s 248CA(3) and (4)
Nature of right	Fully assignable property right	Personal non-assignable cause of action	Personal non-assignable cause of action: s 248N

ANTI-BOOTLEGGING RIGHTS (PART XIA PERFORMERS' RIGHTS)

Part XIA of the *Copyright Act* prohibits bootlegging; that is, unauthorised communications, and unauthorised sound or film recordings of, live performances. Both *direct* recordings and communications (i.e. by a person present at the live performance) and *indirect* acts (e.g. unauthorised recording from a broadcast performance) are prohibited. Once a performer has given their consent to a recording or communication, the Part XIA rights are no longer relevant: subsequent uses of a recording made with consent are not captured, even if not specifically consented to. That is, Part XIA rights are not exclusive rights in recordings.

The structure of Part XIA is unusual. The prohibited actions are characterised as 'unauthorised use of a performance' and defined in s 248G. Rather than create free-standing exceptions to this prohibition, the Act defines certain recordings and uses as 'exempt': these are found in the definitions section of Part XIA (s 248A). Fair dealings are exempt, as are some film recordings made for private and domestic purposes, scientific research and educational use. As noted above, recordings which are 'exempt' vary as between sound recordings and films owing to the different international legal framework for sound versus audio-visual recordings of performances.

MORAL RIGHTS OF PERFORMERSHIP

The WPPT obliges member states to provide moral rights protection for performers. The WPPT, and amendments to Part IX of the *Copyright Act* giving such rights to performers, came into force in Australia in July 2007. These are characterised as moral rights of 'performership', which appears to be a peculiarly Australian expression: the WPPT, and legislation overseas such as the UK Act, simply refer to performers' moral rights in their performances.

Like authors, performers (defined in s 189 and 191B) are granted:

- a right of attribution of performership: s 195ABA;
- a right not to have performership falsely attributed: s 195AHA; and
- a right of integrity of performership: s 195ALA.

Performers' moral rights apply both in the context of live performances fixed in sound recordings, and the live performances themselves: thus a performer has a right to be attributed appropriately at, and to object to derogatory treatment of, *the performance* as well as thereafter on sound recordings.

These rights have the same labyrinthine structure as the authors' moral rights provisions: in most cases there are performers' moral rights provisions that simply shadow the authors' provisions. Performers have moral rights over the same kinds of acts; have the same defences of reasonableness (ss 195AXD–195AXE) and consent (s 195AXJ); and have the same remedies (s 195AZGC). The performers' moral rights provisions adopt the limited model of authors' moral rights in films: the right of integrity lasts only until the death of the performer (s 195ANA); general consents to breaches can be given in advance (s 195AXJ); and the rights only apply to live performances occurring, and sound recordings of live performances which occurred, after the provisions came into force in 2007: s 195AZR.

An interesting limitation on performers' moral right of integrity is that it is concerned only with acts that are prejudicial to the performer's *reputation* (s 195ALB): there is no reference to the performer's *honour*. This reflects a similar omission of performers' honour in the WPPT. This raises an interesting question as to whether the mix of objective and subjective concerns in the right of integrity (discussed above) falls out differently for performers' moral rights.

RESALE ROYALTY RIGHTS OF VISUAL ARTISTS

Whereas writers and composers can continue to profit from copyright over a long time frame through royalties and sales of copies, visual artists earn income mainly from the sale of their original artworks. Artistic reputation and the value of past works may rise over the course of a career, but the artist historically has received no financial benefit from the sale of artworks sold on the secondary art market. The incongruity of record prices being reached for Australian artwork sold at auction, and the poverty of artists, especially in the Indigenous art sector, has created discomfort.

Whether Australia should have a 'resale royalty' scheme, and who is likely to benefit from it, has been much debated.[13] Article 14*ter* of the Berne Convention provides for a resale right for artists: i.e. an inalienable right to an interest in any sale of the work subsequent to the first transfer by the artist.[14] This is not an obligatory provision, but more than 50 countries do have a resale royalty scheme, including the UK following the *Directive 2001/84/EC of the European Parliament and of the Council of 27 September 2001 on the resale right for the benefit of the author of an original work of art*.

In 2009 a resale royalty scheme was introduced in Australia through the *Resale Royalty for Visual Artists Act 2009* (Cth), which came into effect on 9 June 2010. It provides that a royalty is payable to the artist on the sale of an original 'work of visual art' after that date (ss 6, 8). If the artwork was in existence on that date, the royalty is only payable on the second sale after that date (s 11). 'Work of visual art' is defined to include artists' books, batiks, carvings, ceramics, collages, digital artworks, drawings, engravings, fine art jewellery, glassware, installations, lithographs, multimedia artworks, paintings, photographs, pictures, prints, sculptures, tapestries, video artworks and weavings (s 7). A flat royalty of 5 per cent of the sale price (s 18) applies to the 'commercial resale' of visual art to sales involving art market professionals, public institutions or organisations (s 8). There is no cap on the maximum royalty that may be earned on an individual resale, but there is a minimum threshold sale price of $1000 (s 10). The royalty applies for the duration of copyright (s 32). The Copyright Agency has been given responsibility for administration of the scheme. While the Act applies only to works sold in Australia, works by Australian artists sold overseas may now also be eligible for royalty payments under reciprocal arrangements provided under international copyright law. At the time of writing, the resale royalty scheme is under review by the Commonwealth Ministry for the Arts.

TRADITIONAL CULTURAL EXPRESSIONS

There has been significant policy analysis of Indigenous IP in Australia and internationally. Major Australian reports include: *Report of the Working Party on the Protection of Aboriginal Folklore* (1981);[15] *Stopping the Rip Offs* (1994);[16] and *Our Culture, Our Future* (1998).[17] National interest has been matched by significant discussion of the subject in international fora. The United Nations (UN),[18] the United Nations Educational, Scientific and Cultural Organization (UNESCO) and

---

13 House of Representatives, *Inquiry into Resale Royalty Right for Visual Artists Bill 2008* (2009)
14 Article 14*ter* also provides a resale right to authors in their original manuscripts. Australia has not implemented this right.
15 Department of Home Affairs and the Environment, *Report of the Working Party on the Protection of Aboriginal Folklore* (1981).
16 Attorney-General's Department, *Stopping the Rip Offs: Intellectual Property Protection for Indigenous Arts and Cultural Expression* (1994).
17 T Janke, *Our Culture, Our Future* (1998) (prepared for the Australian Institute of Aboriginal and Torres Strait Islander Studies and the Aboriginal and Torres Strait Islander Commission).
18 See E Daes, *The Final Report on the Protection of the Heritage of Indigenous Peoples*, United Nations' Sub-Commission on the Prevention of Discrimination and Protection of Minorities (1993).

WIPO[19] all recognise the need to protect traditional cultural expressions. There is an ongoing debate in Australia and internationally about whether *sui generis* rights should be developed to better protect indigenous IP.[20]

A large number of Australian cultural and educational institutions and media organisations have developed protocols to acknowledge Indigenous perspectives on the appropriate use of Indigenous knowledge.[21] While nominally voluntary, where adherence to protocol is tied to access to funding they have significant potential to influence cultural practice.

Cultural expressions created by Indigenous artists can of course be protected by copyright subject to fulfilment of all of the requirements for subsistence. One issue however in reconciling Australian copyright law with Indigenous cultural expressions has been the mismatch in conceptions of ownership and control. The Western cultural bias towards private, exclusive rights over the recognition of communal rights has been acknowledged in a number of cases.[22] In *Bulun Bulun v R & T Textiles Pty Ltd* (1998) 86 FCR 244, extracted below, von Doussa J rejected a claim of communal 'joint authorship' as the community had not made the 'right kind of contribution' to the painting in question. However, in support of the efforts made in the case by the Aboriginal claimants and their lawyers to have communal title in traditional ritual knowledge—in particular in artwork—recognised and protected by the Australian legal system, he acknowledged a role for equity to intervene to protect communal property interests in traditional knowledge in certain circumstances.

CASE EXTRACT: CURRENT LAW

Bulun Bulun v R & T Textiles Pty Ltd

(1998) 86 FCR 244
Federal Court of Australia

[Mr Bulun Bulun and Mr Milpurrurru were leading Aboriginal artists and senior members of the traditional Aboriginal owners of Ganalbingu country, in Arnhem Land in the Northern Territory. Mr Bulun Bulun painted an artistic work 'Magpie Geese and Water Lilies at the Waterhole', drawing on a corpus of ritual knowledge of the Ganalbingu people. Members of the Ganalbingu had obligations under customary law to create artworks associated with the ownership of and obligations to the land. Mr Bulun Bulun

---

19 UNESCO/WIPO *Model Provisions for the Protection of Expressions of Folklore from Illicit Exploitation and Other Prejudicial Actions* (1999); *WIPO Report on Fact Finding Missions on Intellectual Property and Traditional Knowledge (1998–1999)* (2001); Intergovernmental Committee of Intellectual Property and Genetic Resources, Traditional Knowledge and Folklore, *Preliminary Systematic Analysis of National Experiences with the Legal Protection of Expressions of Folklore* (2002).

20 Senate Standing Committee on Environment, Communications, Information Technology and the Arts, *Indigenous Art—Securing the Future Australia's Indigenous Visual Arts and Craft Sector* (2007).

21 See T Janke and R Quiggin, *Background Paper 12: Indigenous Cultural and Intellectual Property and Customary Law,* Law Reform Commission of WA, 2005.

22 *Yumbulul v Reserve Bank of Australia* (1991) 21 IPR 481; *Milpurrurru v Indofurn Pty Ltd* (1994) 30 IPR 209. See K Bowrey, 'Indigenous Culture, Knowledge and Intellectual Property: The Need for a New Category of Rights?' in K Bowrey, M Handler and D Nicol, *Emerging Challenges in Intellectual Property*, Oxford University Press, Melbourne, 2011.

painted the work with the permission of senior members of the Ganalbingu people. The respondent imported fabric printed with an infringing copy of the artistic work. Mr Bulun Bulun sued for copyright infringement. The respondent admitted his claim and submitted to consent orders. Mr Milpurrurru also brought an action as representative of the Ganalbingu people, whom Mr Milpurrurru claimed were the equitable owners of the copyright in the artistic work, as an incident of Ganalbingu customary law. Evidence on customary rules was also given by Mr Ashley, another Ganalbingu artist holding a position as Mr Bulun Bulun's Djungaye (a community member with customary obligations to maintain the integrity of the land and associated ritual knowledge). Mr Milpurrurru's claim proceeded to judgment. Counsel for the Minister for Aboriginal and Torres Strait Islander Affairs intervened with leave of the court so that claims regarding Indigenous ownership of cultural heritage and its relationship to copyright could be fully considered.]

Von Doussa J (at 257–265): These proceedings represent another step by Aboriginal people to have communal title in their traditional ritual knowledge, and in particular in their artwork, recognised and protected by the Australian legal system. The inadequacies of statutory remedies under the *Copyright Act* as a means of protecting communal ownership have been noted in earlier decisions of this court: see *Yumbulul v Reserve Bank of Australia* (1991) 21 IPR 481 at 490 and *Milpurrurru v Indofurn Pty Ltd* (1994) 54 FCR 240 at 247 …

In 1788 there may have been scope for the continued operation of a system of indigenous collective ownership in artistic works … If the common law had not been amended in the meantime by statute, an interesting question would arise as to whether Aboriginal laws and customs could be incorporated into the common law. However, the common law has since been subsumed by statute. The common law right until first publication was abolished when the law of copyright was codified by the *Copyright Act* of 1911 in the United Kingdom. That Act, subject to some modifications, became the law in Australia by s 8 of the *Copyright Act 1912* (Cth). Copyright is now entirely a creature of statute: McKeough and Stewart, *Intellectual Property in Australia* 1991 at para 504, *Copinger and Skone James on Copyright*, 13th edn para 3. The exclusive domain of the *Copyright Act 1968* in Australia is expressed in s 8 (subject only to the qualification in s 8A) namely that 'copyright does not subsist otherwise than by virtue of this Act'.

Section 35(2) of the *Copyright Act 1968* provides that the author of an artistic work is the owner of the copyright which subsists by virtue of the Act. That provision effectively precludes any notion of group ownership in an artistic work, unless the artistic work is a 'work of joint [authorship]' within the meaning of s 10(1) of the Act … In this case no evidence was led to suggest that anyone other than Mr Bulun Bulun was the creative author of the artistic work. A person who supplies an artistic idea to an artist who then executes the work is not, on that ground alone, a joint author with the artist: *Kenrick & Co v Lawrence & Co* (1890) 25 QBD 99. Joint authorship envisages the contribution of skill and labour to the production of the work itself: *Fylde Microsystems Ltd v Kay Radio Systems Ltd* (1998) 39 IPR 481 at 486.

In *Coe v Commonwealth* (1993) 118 ALR 193 at 200 Mason CJ rejected the proposition that Aboriginal people are entitled to rights and interests other than those created or recognised by the laws of the Commonwealth, its States and the common law. See also *Walker v New South Wales* [(1994) 182 CLR 45] (at 45–50) and Kirby J in *Wik Peoples v Queensland* [(1996) 187 CLR 1] (at 214). To conclude that the Ganalbingu people were communal owners of the copyright in the existing work would ignore the provisions of s 8 of the *Copyright Act,* and involve the creation of rights in indigenous peoples which are not otherwise recognised by the legal system of Australia.

DO THE CIRCUMSTANCES IN WHICH THE ARTISTIC WORK WAS CREATED GIVE RISE TO EQUITABLE INTERESTS IN THE GANALBINGU PEOPLE?

The statement of claim alleges 'on the reduction to material form of a part of the ritual knowledge of the Ganalbingu people associated with Djulibinyamurr by the creation of the artistic work, [Mr Bulun Bulun] held the copyright subsisting in the artistic work as a fiduciary and/or alternatively on trust, for the second applicant and the people he represents'. The foundation for this contention is expanded in written submissions made on Mr Milpurrurru's behalf. It is contended that these rights arise because Mr Milpurrurru and those he represents have the power under customary law to regulate and control the production and reproduction of the corpus of ritual knowledge. It is contended that the customs and traditions regulating this use of the corpus of ritual knowledge places Mr Bulun Bulun as the author of the artistic work in the position of a fiduciary, and, moreover, make Mr Bulun Bulun a trustee for the artwork, either pursuant to some form of express trust, or pursuant to a constructive trust in favour of the Ganalbingu people. The right to control the production and reproduction of the corpus of ritual knowledge relating to Djulibinyamurr is said to arise by virtue of the strong ties which continue to exist between the Ganalbingu people and their land.

WAS THERE AN EXPRESS TRUST?

The possibility that an express trust was created in respect of the artistic work or the copyright subsisting in it was not at the forefront of the applicants' submissions. In my opinion that possibility can be dismissed on the evidence in this case. The existence of an express trust depends on the intention of the creator ...

In the present case it is suggested that it should be inferred that by creating the artistic work with the permission of those of the Ganalbingu people who had the right to control the corpus of ritual knowledge associated with Djulibinyamurr Mr Bulun Bulun intended to hold the copyright subsisting in the artistic work for the benefit of the Ganalbingu people.

The artwork, when completed, was sold by Mr Bulun Bulun to the Maningrida Arts and Crafts Centre. It is not suggested that he did not receive and retain the sale price for his own use. Moreover, the evidence indicates that on many occasions paintings which incorporate to a greater or lesser degree parts of the ritual knowledge of the Ganalbingu people are produced by Ganalbingu artists for commercial sale for the benefit of the artist concerned.

On the evidence there is no suggestion that ownership and use of the artistic work itself should be treated separately from ownership in the copyright to the artistic work. The evidence was directed to uses made of the artwork itself that were permissible or impermissible under Ganalbingu law and customs. Notions of copyright ownership have not developed under Ganalbingu law. If it were possible to infer an express trust, on the evidence the subject matter of the trust would be the artistic work itself and all the rights that attach to its creation under the Australian legal system.

There is no usual or customary practice whereby artworks are held in trust for the Ganalbingu people. In the present case neither Mr Bulun Bulun's Djungaye or Mr Milpurrurru suggest that the commercial sale of the artwork by Mr Bulun Bulun was contrary to customary law, or to the terms of the permission which was given to him to produce the artwork. In these circumstances, the fact of the sale and the retention of the proceeds for his own use is inconsistent with there being an intention on the part of Mr Bulun Bulun to create an express trust. Further, the fact that the artwork was sold commercially, and has been the subject of reproduction, with the apparent permission of those who

CURRENT LAW

control its reproduction, in 'Arts of the Dreaming—Australian Living Heritage' forecloses any possibility of arguing that the imagery in the artwork is of such a secret or sacred nature that it could be inferred that the artist must have had the intention in accordance with customary law to hold the artwork for the benefit of the Ganalbingu people …

DID MR BULUN BULUN HOLD THE COPYRIGHT AS A FIDUCIARY?

In *Breen v Williams* (1995) 186 CLR 71 at 82, Brennan CJ identified two sources of fiduciary duties, the first being the circumstances in which a relationship of agency can be said to exist, and the other is founded in a relationship of ascendancy or influence by one party over another, or dependence or trust on the part of that other. The applicants' counsel did not seek to characterise the fiduciary relationship for which he contends as derived from either source in particular. The existence of a fiduciary relationship is said to arise out of the nature of ownership of artistic works amongst the Ganalbingu people.

… [T]he fiduciary concept has developed incrementally throughout the case law which itself provides guidance as to the traditional parameters of the concept. The essential characteristics of fiduciary relationships were referred to by Mason J in *Hospital Products* [*Ltd v United States Surgical Corporation* (1984) 156 CLR 41] at 96–97:

> The critical feature of [fiduciary] relationships is that the fiduciary undertakes or agrees to act for or on behalf of or in the interests of another person in the exercise of a power or discretion which will affect the interests of that other person in a legal or practical sense. The relationship between the parties is therefore one which gives the fiduciary a special opportunity to exercise the power or discretion to the detriment of that other person who is accordingly vulnerable to abuse by the fiduciary of his position … It is partly because the fiduciary's exercise of the power or discretion can adversely affect the interests of the person to whom the duty is owed and because the latter is at the mercy of the former that the fiduciary comes under a duty to exercise his power or discretion in the interests of the person to whom it is owed.

In *Mabo* [*v Queensland [No 2]* (1992) 175 CLR 1], Toohey J said at 200:

> Underlying such relationships is the scope for one party to exercise a discretion which is capable of affecting the legal position of the other. One party has a special opportunity to abuse the interests of the other. The discretion will be an incident of the first party's office or position.

In *Wik Peoples v State of Queensland* (1996) 187 CLR 1 at 95 Brennan CJ said with respect to the asserted existence of a fiduciary duty owed by the Crown to the indigenous inhabitants of the leased areas under consideration:

> It is necessary to identify some action or function the doing or performance of which attracts the supposed fiduciary duty to be observed (*Breen v Williams* (1996) 186 CLR 71 at 82). The doing of the action or the performance of the function must be capable of affecting the interests of the beneficiary and the fiduciary must have so acted that it is reasonable for the beneficiary to believe and expect that the fiduciary will act in the interests of the beneficiary (or, in the case of a partnership or joint venture, in the common interest of the beneficiary and fiduciary) to the exclusion of the interest of any other person or the separate interest of the beneficiary.' (some footnotes omitted) …

The relationship between Mr Bulun Bulun as the author and legal title holder of the artistic work and the Ganalbingu people is unique. The 'transaction' between them out of which fiduciary relationship is said to arise is the use with permission by Mr Bulun Bulun of ritual knowledge of the Ganalbingu people, and the embodiment of that knowledge within the artistic work. That use has been permitted in accordance with the law and customs of the Ganalbingu people.

The grant of permission by the Djungayi and other appropriate representatives of the Ganalbingu people for the creation of the artistic work is predicated on the trust and confidence which those granting permission have in the artist. The evidence indicates that if those who must give permission do not have trust and confidence in someone seeking permission, permission will not be granted.

The law and customs of the Ganalbingu people require that the use of the ritual knowledge and the artistic work be in accordance with the requirements of law and custom, and that the author of the artistic work do whatever is necessary to prevent any misuse. The artist is required to act in relation to the artwork in the interests of the Ganalbingu people to preserve the integrity of their culture, and ritual knowledge.

This is not to say that the artist must act entirely in the interests of the Ganalbingu people. The evidence shows that an artist is entitled to consider and pursue his own interests, for example by selling the artwork, but the artist is not permitted to shed the overriding obligation to act to preserve the integrity of the Ganalbingu culture where action for that purpose is required.

In my opinion, the nature of the relationship between Mr Bulun Bulun and the Ganalbingu people was a fiduciary one which gives rise to fiduciary obligations owed by Mr Bulun Bulun.

The conclusion that in all the circumstances Mr Bulun Bulun owes fiduciary obligations to the Ganalbingu people does not treat the law and custom of the Ganalbingu people as part of the Australian legal system. Rather, it treats the law and custom of the Ganalbingu people as part of the factual matrix which characterises the relationship as one of mutual trust and confidence. It is that relationship which the Australian legal system recognises as giving rise to the fiduciary relationship, and to the obligations which arise out of it ...

THE FIDUCIARY OBLIGATION

Central to the fiduciary concept is the protection of interests that can be regarded as worthy of judicial protection: J Glover, *Commercial Equity—Fiduciary Relationships* (1995) para 3.4. The evidence is all one way. The ritual knowledge relating to Djulibinyamurr embodied within the artistic work is of great importance to members of the Ganalbingu people. I have no hesitation in holding that the interest of Ganalbingu people in the protection of that ritual knowledge from exploitation which is contrary to their law and custom is deserving of the protection of the Australian legal system.

Under the *Copyright Act*, the owner of the copyright has the exclusive right to reproduce the work in a material form, and to publish the work. The copyright owner is entitled to enforce copyright against the world at large. In the event of infringement, the copyright owner is entitled to sue and to obtain remedies of the kind actually obtained by Mr Bulun Bulun in this case.

Having regard to the evidence of the law and customs of the Ganalbingu people under which Mr Bulun Bulun was permitted to create the artistic work, I consider that equity imposes on him obligations as a fiduciary not to exploit the artistic work in a way that is contrary to the laws and custom of the Ganalbingu people, and, in the event of infringement by a third party, to take reasonable and appropriate action to restrain and remedy infringement of the copyright in the artistic work.

Whilst the nature of the relationship between Mr Bulun Bulun and the Ganalbingu people is such that Mr Bulun Bulun falls under fiduciary obligations to protect the ritual knowledge which he has been permitted to use, the existence of those obligations does not, without more, vest an equitable interest in the ownership of the copyright in the Ganalbingu people. Their primary right, in the event of a breach of obligation by the fiduciary is a right in personam to bring action against the fiduciary to enforce the obligation.

In the present case Mr Bulun Bulun has successfully taken action against the respondent to obtain remedies in respect of the infringement. There is no suggestion by Mr Milpurrurru and those whom he seeks to represent that Mr Bulun Bulun should have done anything more. In these circumstances there is no occasion for the intervention of equity to provide any additional remedy to the beneficiaries of the fiduciary relationship.

However, had the position been otherwise equitable remedies could have been available. The extent of those remedies would depend on all the circumstances, and in an extreme case could involve the intervention of equity to impose a constructive trust on the legal owner of the copyright in the artistic work in favour of the beneficiaries. Equity will not automatically impose a constructive trust merely upon the identification of a fiduciary obligation. Equity will impose a constructive trust on property held by a fiduciary where it is necessary to do so to achieve a just remedy and to prevent the beneficiary from retaining an unconscionable benefit: *Muschinski v Dodds* (1985) 160 CLR 385 at 619–620 and *Baumgartner v Baumgartner* (1987) 164 CLR 137 at 148. By way of example, had Mr Bulun Bulun merely failed to take action to enforce his copyright, an adequate remedy might be extended in equity to the beneficiaries by allowing them to bring action in their own names against the infringer and the copyright owner, claiming against the former, in the first instance, interlocutory relief to restrain the infringement, and against the latter orders necessary to ensure that the copyright owner enforces the copyright. Probably there would be no occasion for equity in these circumstances to impose a constructive trust.

On the other hand, were Mr Bulun Bulun to deny the existence of fiduciary obligations and the interests of the parties asserting them, and refuse to protect the copyright from infringement, then the occasion might exist for equity to impose a remedial constructive trust upon the copyright owner to strengthen the standing of the beneficiaries to bring proceedings to enforce the copyright. This may be necessary if the copyright owner cannot be identified or found and the beneficiaries are unable to join the legal owner of the copyright: see *Performing Rights Society Ltd v London Theatre of Varieties* [1924] AC 1 at 18.

It is well recognised that interlocutory injunctive relief can be claimed by a party having an equitable interest in copyright: Laddie, Prescott and Vitoria, *The Modern Law of Copyright* (2nd ed 1995) at par 11.79–11.81, although as a matter of practice injunctive relief will not be granted without the legal owner of copyright being joined: *Performing Rights Society Ltd v London Theatre of Varieties* at 19–20, 29, *Acorn Computers Ltd v MCS Microcomputer Systems Pty Ltd* (1984) 57 ALR 389 at 394. For an example of proceedings brought to establish the existence of an equitable interest in copyright based

CURRENT LAW

on a constructive trust imposed in consequence of a breach of fiduciary duty see *Missinglink Software v Magee* [1989] 1 FSR 361 at 367.

I do not consider Mr Milpurrurru and those he seeks to represent have established an equitable interest in the copyright in the artistic work. In my opinion they have established that fiduciary obligations are owed to them by Mr Bulun Bulun, but as Mr Bulun Bulun has taken appropriate action to enforce the copyright, he has fulfilled those obligations and there is no occasion to grant any additional remedy in favour of the Ganalbingu people. However, in other circumstances if the copyright owner of an artistic work which embodies ritual knowledge of an Aboriginal clan is being used inappropriately, and the copyright owner fails or refuses to take appropriate action to enforce the copyright, the Australian legal system will permit remedial action through the courts by the clan.

ANTI-CIRCUMVENTION RULES

Another personal, non-assignable cause of action related to copyright arises under Australia's 'anti-circumvention' rules, found in Part V Div 2AA of the *Copyright Act*. With the rise of digital technologies (which allow perfect replication of content) and digital networks (which enable global instantaneous distribution of digital content), copyright owners became concerned about their ability to enforce copyright. A hope in the 1990s was that the 'answer to the machine was in the machine'; that is, that technical means would be developed to enable copyright owners to exert fine-grained control over use of their works. Encryption, access controls such as paywalls and passwords, and software systems that limit the number of copies a user may make or the number of machines on which a work may be viewed are all examples of the use of technological measures to control copyright content.

Technological measures are, however, often 'hacked' or broken. Policymakers were concerned therefore that in the absence of laws against circumvention, either copyright owners would have disincentives against making work available digitally, or there would be a wasteful 'arms race' between copyright owners and people determined to 'crack' such measures. Articles 11 and 12 of the *WIPO Copyright Treaty* (1996) (and equivalent provisions in the WPPT) respond to this concern by requiring contracting parties to 'provide adequate legal protection and effective legal remedies against the circumvention' of such technologies. It is not clear that technological protections have in fact played as significant a role in the digital environment as was envisaged in the mid-1990s: many copyright owners continue to disseminate content without encryption or other technical measures. Nevertheless, anti-circumvention rules remain part of the legal framework for copyright enforcement in the digital environment.

New provisions came into force in Australia as part of the *Copyright Amendment (Digital Agenda) Act 2000* (Cth). These reforms created new prohibitions separate from the exclusive rights of copyright owners: a person can breach the anti-circumvention provisions by doing one of the prescribed acts, *regardless* of whether copyright infringement results. Indeed, it is possible that any copyright owner or exclusive licensee who uses a particular technological measure could take action against a person providing the tools for circumventing the measure, regardless of whether their particular work, or film, was a target of any hacking efforts.[23]

---

23 This results from the broad drafting of the provisions which state that a copyright owner whose work is protected by a technological measure can take action against a person who circulates a circumvention device for that technological measure: see, for example, s 116AO.

AUSTRALIA'S FIRST ANTI-CIRCUMVENTION LAWS AND *STEVENS V SONY* (2005)

The *Digital Agenda* reforms instituted a unique Australian version of anti-circumvention laws, with three key features. First, out of a concern for privacy and to avoid enacting provisions that would be hard to enforce, there was no prohibition on the act of circumventing technological protection measures (TPMs): the prohibitions focused on people providing circumvention devices or services. Second, the law created a regime whereby a 'qualified person' wishing to make use of certain copyright exceptions was entitled to get access to circumvention devices or services on making a declaration stating (among other things) that that device or service would only be used for a permitted purpose. Third, the definition of TPM confined protection to technological measures that *prevented or inhibited infringement* of copyright.

This last feature was the subject of litigation in *Stevens v Kabushiki Kaisha Sony Computer Entertainment* (2005) 224 CLR 193. This litigation made it clear that not all technologies adopted by owners were TPMs under Australian law.

The case concerned the Sony PlayStation, which controlled the copying of games distributed on CD-ROMs by including on legitimate CD-ROMs an 'access code' (a string of encrypted sectors of data) which could not be copied by most commercial machines. When a CD-ROM embodying a game was inserted in the console, a Boot ROM chip in the PlayStation console would read the string of encrypted data—and the console would not work if the access code was incorrect or absent. PlayStations were sold in many parts of the world and the format of the consoles and the CD-ROMs varied. Different access codes were used in different geographical regions. Thus legitimate games sourced from other regions, and unauthorised copies of games, could not be played on an Australian console. Mr Stevens sold unauthorised copies of PlayStation games and sold and installed 'mod chips' into PlayStation consoles that provided the required access code to unlock games. The issue for the High Court was whether the technology used by Sony was a TPM under s 116A of the Act as it then stood. Gleeson CJ, Gummow, Hayne and Heydon JJ at [38] accepted the interpretation of the trial judge, Sackville J, [*Kabushiki Kaisha Sony Computer Entertainment v Stevens* [2002] FCA 906; (2002) 200 ALR 55 at 81] that:

> a 'technological protection measure', as defined, must be a device or product which utilises technological means to deny a person access to a copyright work [or other subject matter], or which limits a person's capacity to make copies of a work [or other subject matter] to which access has been gained, and thereby 'physically' prevents or inhibits the person from undertaking acts which, if carried out, would or might infringe copyright in the work [or other subject matter].

The Sony access code was not a TPM because the measure taken did not prevent or inhibit the making of an infringing copy of the work. A strict interpretation of the wording of the legislation was considered by the High Court to be essential, as the limitation in the definition of a protected TPM was a consequence of legislative choice, reflecting a compromise between owner and user interests: at [34]. As Gleeson CJ et al noted at [47], another consideration in favour of a narrow interpretation was that:

> [I]n construing a definition which focuses on a device designed to prevent or inhibit the infringement of copyright, it is important to avoid an overbroad construction which would

extend the copyright monopoly rather than match it. A defect in the [broader construction urged by Sony] is that its effect is to extend the copyright monopoly by including within the definition not only technological protection measures which stop the infringement of copyright, but also devices which prevent the carrying out of conduct which does not infringe copyright and is not otherwise unlawful. One example of that conduct is playing in Australia a program lawfully acquired in the United States.

THE *AUSTRALIA–US FREE TRADE AGREEMENT* AND POST-2006 LAWS

The *Australia–US Free Trade Agreement* (AUSFTA) (2004) contains highly prescriptive provisions on anti-circumvention law in Art 17.4.7, modelled on the US *Digital Millennium Copyright Act 1998*. Australia's new anti-circumvention regime was enacted via the *Copyright Amendment Act 2006* (Cth) and is contained in Part V Div 2A. The drafting of these provisions was 'a difficult endeavour, particularly given the conflicting demands of the executive, the Federal Parliament, and the High Court of Australia'[24] (and, one might add, the USA). The new laws grant broader rights of control to copyright owners and narrowly confine the circumstances in which 'hacking' TPMs is allowed.

Part V Div 2A now covers a broader set of technologies. There are now two categories of TPM (defined in s 10(1) of the *Copyright Act*). The first is 'a device, product, technology or component ... [which,] in the normal course of its operation, prevents, inhibits or restricts the doing of an act comprised in the copyright'. The second is an 'access control technological protection measure' (ACTPM) (also defined in s 10(1)), which is a measure used:

- 'by, with the permission of, or on behalf of the [copyright] owner';
- 'in connection with the exercise of the copyright'; and which
- 'in the normal course of its operation, controls access to the work or other subject–matter'.

This broader definition seems to capture the access code/reader technology which arose in the *Stevens v Sony* case, although it does raise interesting legal questions in relation to newer technologies, such as those used to 'geoblock' websites (i.e. limit access to websites to users in certain countries only).[25] There are two specific exclusions from the definition of TPM: (1) geographic market segmentation technologies controlling playback, such as region coding (meaning the Sony technology might still be excluded); and (2) certain technologies used to control aftermarket competition (such as measures that prevent 'unauthorised' printer cartridges).[26]

Three prohibitions are set out in Part V Div 2A: (1) circumventing ACTPMs (s 116AN); (2) manufacturing, providing, communicating (etc.) a circumvention device (s 116AO) for any TPM; and (3) providing a circumvention service (s 116AP) for any TPM. Exceptions to these prohibitions are confined by AUSFTA, Art 17.4.7(e) and (f). Australia is not entitled to introduce new exceptions to the trafficking prohibitions (ss 116AO–116AP) (AUSFTA, Art 17.4.7(f)). Australia may create new exceptions to the prohibition on circumventing access controls (s 116AN) where an

---

24 M Neilsen and R Bell, 'Copyright Amendment Bill 2006', *Bills Digest No 51*, APH 2006–07, p 30.
25 This issue is discussed in the final report of the House of Representatives Standing Committee on Infrastructure and Communications, *Inquiry into IT Pricing* (2013).
26 The background to these exclusions, and the AUSFTA anti-circumvention regime, can be found in the final report of the House of Representatives Standing Committee on Legal and Constitutional Affairs, *Inquiry into Technological Protection Measures (TPM) Exceptions* (2006).

actual or likely adverse impact on those non-infringing uses is credibly demonstrated in a legislative or administrative review or proceeding (AUSFTA, Art 17.4.7(e)(viii)). Exceptions are introduced via regulation if the Minister (i.e. the Attorney-General) receives submissions demonstrating such an adverse impact (s 249(2)–(9); *Copyright Regulations 1969* (Cth), reg 20Z and sch 10A). In response to criticism that this creates exceptions for individuals but no exception for their supplier, the government stated that:

> This is not a drafting error. It is an intentional limitation on the availability of circumvention devices under the liability scheme. The Government notes that individuals and organisations will be able to take advantage of the exceptions granted under the AUSFTA by using existing devices in their possession, making their own devices or importing devices. The legislation implementing the AUSFTA will give effect to its terms in accordance with relevant principles of international law.[27]

CIRCUIT LAYOUT PROTECTION

Circuit layout protection is a *sui generis* scheme, based on copyright principles, which protects the design of integrated circuit chips in computers, mobile phones, heart pacemakers and related chip-based technologies. It came about as result of lobbying by chip makers such as Intel, which led to the introduction of semiconductor chip protection emerging in the USA in 1984, the *Washington Treaty on Intellectual Property in Respect of Integrated Circuits* (1989) and Arts 3–8 of the TRIPS Agreement (1994).[28]

The *Circuit Layouts Act 1989* (Cth) came into force on 1 October 1990.[29] The domestic rationale for protection was discussed in *Avel Pty Ltd v Wells* (1992) 36 FCR 340 at 344:

> The Attorney-General noted that the Australian computer chip industry was small but nevertheless important and growing. Australian computer chips were used in a number of items including bionic ears, heart pacemakers and the conversion of sunlight to power. Australian specialised computer chips had found valuable overseas markets. On the other hand, Australia imported most of its chips, either inside consumer products or for installation in products actually made in Australia.
>
> The different commercial interests of Australia are reflected in the two strands of thought which run through the legislation. The first gives what the Attorney-General (Hansard at 2399) referred to as 'sui generis, copyright-style, protection' ...
>
> As the Attorney-General observed in the Second Reading Speech, a consequence of reforms both to the copyright law and to the design law, following the Designs Law Review Committee Report of 1973, was that neither copyright law nor design law provided suitable protection to designers of computer chips. There was therefore a need to separately address the question of appropriate protection.

---

27 *Government Response to the House of Representatives Standing Committee on Legal and Constitutional Affairs Report 'Review of Technological Protection Measures Exceptions'* (2006).

28 For an international comparative analysis, see I Chiu and W Shen, 'A Sui Generis Intellectual Property Right for Layout Designs on Printed Circuit Boards? An Analysis of Current Intellectual Property Laws and Proposal for Reform' [2006] *European Intellectual Property Review* 38.

29 For discussion relating to the constitutionality of the *sui generis* legislation, see *Nintendo Co Ltd v Centronics Systems Pty Ltd* (1994) 181 CLR 134; *Grain Pool of Western Australia v Commonwealth* (2000) 202 CLR 479.

KEY PROVISIONS

- The object of protection is a 'circuit layout', which s 5 defines as 'a representation, fixed in any material form, of the three-dimensional location of the active and passive elements and interconnections making up an integrated circuit'. Material form includes any form of storage (whether visible or not) from which the layout, or a substantial part of it, can be reproduced. Both the layout and the integrated circuit that embodies the layout are protected.
- 'Eligible layouts' (ELs) must either be made by an eligible person (Australian citizen, resident, body corporate, or citizens or corporation of an eligible country) or be commercially exploited for the first time in Australia or in an eligible country.
- There is a requirement of originality (s 11), which is not met if there was no creative contribution by the maker or if the design was commonplace at the time it was made.
- The person who makes an eligible layout is the first owner of any rights in that layout (s 16(1)). However, where a person makes a layout under the terms of his or her employment, the employer will be the owner of any EL rights (s 16(2)).
- There is no registration requirement.
- Protection lasts for 10 years from the day on which the layout was made if it is not commercially exploited. If a layout is commercially exploited within 10 years of being made, then it is protected for a further 10 years from the year in which the layout was first commercially exploited with a maximum of 20 years' protection.

The exclusive rights of the owner (s 17) are:

    (a) to copy the layout, directly or indirectly, in a material form;

    (b) to make an integrated circuit in accordance with the layout ... [i.e. a three-dimensional copy of the layout]; and

    (c) to exploit the layout commercially in Australia.

Commercial exploitation may occur by importation, sale, hire or distribution of a layout or an integrated circuit made according to the layout (s 8). This includes the case where an integrated circuit is contained within a computer, for example.

Section 19 provides that infringement occurs if another person copies, or authorises the copying of, the layout or the integrated circuit without the licence or permission of the owner. There are exceptions to infringement for private use (s 21); copying for research or teaching purposes (s 22); research evaluation and analysis (s 23); or uses of layouts for Commonwealth defence or security (s 25).

Difficult issues arise when a company deals with chips or machines that incorporate chips which embody protected circuit layouts. A person will infringe if they commercially exploit a layout knowing that they did not have licence to do so (or if they ought reasonably to have known): s 19(3). But innocent infringement is a defence: s 20. The policy behind these provisions is explained in the extract from *Nintendo Co Ltd v Centronics Systems Pty Ltd* (1994) 181 CLR 134, below. In addition, s 24 allows importation of legitimate copies of circuit layouts and integrated circuits embodying such layouts, as well as further exploitation/sale of legitimately acquired copies of the layouts and chips.[30]

---

30   For a discussion, see *Avel Pty Ltd v Wells* (1992) 36 FCR 340 at 345–346.

PRECEDENT

CASE EXTRACT: PRECEDENT

Nintendo Co Ltd v Centronics Systems Pty Ltd

(1994) 181 CLR 134
High Court of Australia

[Nintendo claimed infringement of its rights under the *Circuit Layouts Act 1989* (Cth) in an original circuit layout (the 'Nintendo layout'). The Nintendo layout was a plan showing the location of the components of a complex electronic circuit which, incorporated in a Read Only Memory (ROM) chip, was used in video game machines manufactured and marketed by Nintendo. Centronics sold video game machines in Australia known as Spica Entertainment Units; the units included a chip which the trial judge found embodied the whole or a substantial part of Nintendo's layout. The units were imported before the 1989 Act, but sold after it came into force.]

Mason CJ, Brennan, Deane, Toohey, Gaudron and McHugh JJ (at 148–154) (some footnotes omitted):

SECTION 19(3) OF THE ACT

As has been seen, Nintendo's claim of infringement of its [Eligible Layout (EL)] rights is based upon s 19(3) of the [*Circuit Layouts Act 1989* (Cth)] which provides that the EL right referred to in para (c) of s 17 in a protected eligible layout is infringed by unauthorised commercial exploitation of the layout by a person who 'knows or ought reasonably to know, that he or she is not licensed by the owner of that right to do so'. It is common ground that Nintendo bore the onus of establishing that Centronics knew or ought reasonably to have known that it was 'not licensed by the owner of [the EL] right'. Centronics has submitted, at all stages of the proceedings, that Nintendo failed to discharge that onus …

As a matter of mere language, the requirement that an alleged infringer 'knows or ought reasonably to know, that he or she is not licensed by the owner of [the relevant EL] right' is ambiguous … If the words are understood in that more general and innominate sense (the non-specific construction), the requirement of actual or constructive knowledge on the part of the alleged infringer that he or she is not licensed by 'the owner'—whoever that may be—involves, in a case where X is ultimately identified as the owner, more than actual or constructive knowledge of the mere fact that he or she is not licensed by X. The requirement will not be satisfied unless, at the time of the relevant act of commercial exploitation of the layout, the alleged infringer knows or ought reasonably to know that he or she is not licensed by any person satisfying the description of 'the owner of [the relevant EL] right'. That being so, actual or constructive knowledge that he or she is not licensed by X would satisfy the requirement only if it were accompanied by actual or constructive knowledge that X is in fact the owner of that EL right. For the reasons which follow, the non-specific construction is the preferable one.

Section 19(3)'s requirement of actual or constructive knowledge is confined to those cases where the alleged infringement of an EL right in an eligible layout is 'secondary' or 'indirect' in the sense that it does not involve the copying of the layout itself or the making of an integrated circuit in accordance with the layout. Cases involving 'primary' or 'direct' infringement, either by a copying of the layout or by a making of an integrated circuit in accordance with the layout, fall within either s 19(1) or s 19(2). The effect of those subsections is that there is infringement of the relevant EL right if the copying or making was without the licence of the owner of that right regardless of whether there was any actual or constructive knowledge of the lack of such a licence. The legislative policy underlying s 19(1) and s 19(2) would seem to be the understandable one that a person who, for other than a permitted purpose, copies a circuit layout made by another or makes an integrated circuit in accordance with such a layout should be required to take whatever steps are necessary to identify, and obtain a licence from, the owner of relevant EL rights in the layout.

Not surprisingly, the legislative policy to be discerned in s 19(3) with respect to cases involving commercial dealing with an existing original or copy layout or an existing integrated circuit is somewhat different. Under the Act, ownership of the EL rights in an eligible layout is acquired by the maker without any need to observe the requirements of a registration process. A person who deals commercially with an original layout which he or she has acquired in good faith from another may neither know nor have the means of ascertaining that the person from whom he or she acquired it did not have the EL rights in it. A fortiori, a person who deals commercially with an existing copy of a protected layout or an existing integrated circuit made in accordance with the layout may do so in circumstances where he or she neither knows nor has the means of ascertaining that the original layout either exists or is protected by the Act. Generally speaking, the Commonwealth intellectual property legislation in force at the time when the Act was enacted specified some significant requirement of actual or constructive knowledge as a condition of either infringement or liability in cases of alleged infringement by mere commercial dealing. Clearly enough, it was the legislative intent that s 19(3)'s requirement of actual or constructive knowledge should provide a significant degree of protection of the alleged infringer in such cases. The specific designation construction of the requirement would go a long way towards defeating that legislative intent and rendering the protection of the requirement illusory. Thus, its effect would be that, provided the alleged infringer knew or ought reasonably to have known that he or she was not licensed by X, the requirement of actual or constructive knowledge would afford no protection at all if X happened to be the owner of the EL right to exploit the relevant layout commercially in Australia notwithstanding that the alleged infringer by commercial dealing neither knew nor could reasonably be expected to have known that there was any connection at all between X and the layout.

Moreover, the specific designation construction of the requirement would give it a somewhat arbitrary and irrational character. The mere fact that an alleged infringer knows or ought reasonably to know that he or she is not licensed by a particular named person is likely to be of little or no relevance to questions either of fault or of meaningful knowledge or notice unless the alleged infringer also knows or ought reasonably to know that that particular person is the owner of the EL right to exploit the particular layout commercially in Australia. Much to be preferred is the wider and non-specific construction of the words 'the owner" which has the result that the requirement is one of actual or constructive knowledge by an alleged infringer that he or she is unauthorised to exploit the protected layout commercially in Australia in the sense that he or she has actual or constructive knowledge of the existence of the layout and of EL rights in it and of the fact that he or she is not licensed by the owner of those rights, whoever that may be.

It follows that s 19(3)'s requirement of actual or constructive knowledge was not satisfied in the present case by the mere fact that, (as was conceded) Centronics knew, at the time of the acts of alleged infringement, that it was not licensed by Nintendo to exploit the Nintendo layout commercially in Australia. It was necessary that it also be established that Centronics also knew or ought reasonably to have known, at that time, that the Nintendo layout existed and that Nintendo was the owner of the exclusive EL rights in it. The learned trial judge's findings … disclose that his Honour was satisfied that Centronics did, in fact, have such constructive knowledge. …

SECTION 20 OF THE ACT

Section 20 of the Act excludes what is described as 'Innocent commercial exploitation' from conduct which might otherwise constitute infringement of EL rights. In its present form (the current s 20), the section is expressly confined to the commercial exploitation of an integrated circuit made in accordance with an eligible layout in which EL rights subsist. It reads:

(1) The EL rights in an eligible layout are not infringed by a person who commercially exploits, or authorises the commercial exploitation of, an unauthorised integrated circuit in Australia, being a circuit made in accordance with the layout, if, at the time when the person acquired the circuit, the person did not know, and could not reasonably be expected to have known, that the circuit was unauthorised.

(2) Where a person referred to in subsection (1) becomes aware, or could reasonably be expected to have become aware, that the integrated circuit is unauthorised, that subsection ceases to apply to any subsequent commercial exploitation of the circuit, unless the person pays to the owner or exclusive licensee of the EL rights in the layout such equitable remuneration as is agreed, or as is determined by a method agreed, between the person and the owner or exclusive licensee or, in default of agreement, as is determined by the Federal Court of Australia on application made by either of them.

(3) In this section:

'unauthorized', in relation to an integrated circuit made in accordance with an eligible layout, means made without the licence of the owner of the EL rights in the layout.

The legislative policy underlying the current s 20 of the Act is not difficult to discern. It was to make special provision for circumstances in which it would be unjust to impose liability for infringement on a person who innocently acquires and subsequently deals with an unauthorised integrated circuit. One can readily envisage circumstances in which an ordinary person who innocently acquires, and subsequently commercially deals with, an item of electronic equipment would have no means of knowing or ascertaining that some concealed integrated circuit in the article was an unauthorised copy of an eligible circuit layout in which EL rights subsist. An innocent retail purchaser of one of the Spica Entertainment Units involved in the present case who resold the unit a few days before the institution of the present proceedings would provide an obvious example. Even if such a purchaser had dismantled the unit and managed to identify the ROM chip incorporating the Spica integrated circuit, careful examination of the chip with the strongest of magnifying glasses would have disclosed nothing which suggested that the integrated circuit was made in accordance with the Nintendo layout. In that regard, it is relevant to note that the possible need to make special provision to cover the case of innocent commercial dealing with an unauthorised integrated circuit was recognised by Art 6(4) of the [*Washington Treaty on Intellectual Property in Respect of Integrated Circuits*] which, after referring to an earlier paragraph of the Treaty (Art 6(1)(a)(ii) relating to commercial dealing), provided:

PRECEDENT

no Contracting Party shall be obliged to consider unlawful the performance of any of the acts referred to in that paragraph in respect of an integrated circuit incorporating an unlawfully reproduced layout-design (topography) where the person performing or ordering such acts did not know and had no reasonable ground to know, when acquiring the said integrated circuit, that it incorporates an unlawfully reproduced layout-design (topography).

[Although Centronics fell within s 20(1), on the facts it could not rely on a differently drafted s 20 from that quoted above, which was in force at the time.]

There has been very limited litigation involving the *Circuit Layouts Act* and little academic commentary. Chip production is dominated by two companies, Intel (frequently found in computers and servers) and ARM (which dominates the production of chips used in mobile devices). While the protection awarded in the 1980s in the US and 1990s globally may have been of significance in building Intel market leadership, many other factors are at play in technological and market development today. In the *Review of Intellectual Property Legislation under the Competition Principles Agreement* (2000), the Ergas Committee noted (at pp 200–201):

> Like other intellectual property rights, the *Circuit Layouts Act* is designed primarily to correct market failure by preventing unfair copying and free riding by those who have not contributed to the original investment in the creation of the circuit layout. The Committee was not presented with any evidence to suggest that the *Circuit Layouts Act* restricts competition, above and beyond those restrictions inherent in providing an intellectual property right ... However, the Committee questions the value of, and the need for, sui generis laws such as the *Circuit Layouts Act*. By their nature, such laws are highly specialised, technology specific and narrowly defined. Their ability to keep pace with technological changes is limited.

— 8 —

REGISTERED DESIGNS

INTRODUCTION

In this chapter we turn to consider the legal regulation of designs. This involves a consideration of the registration system under the *Designs Act 2003* (Cth), and the intersection between design law and copyright law.

HISTORY, JUSTIFICATIONS AND CONTEXT

The visual appearance of products has long been recognised to be fundamental to their appeal and marketability. Design laws are intended to provide incentives for, and reward the effort involved in, the development of new designs for products by affording designers exclusive rights to deal with the products embodying their designs, and to prevent others from dealing with products of a similar appearance. It is important to note that the legal regulation of designs touches on only one aspect of design. Whereas successful design will seek to reconcile the demands of a wide range of considerations—including ease of operation, value for money, ergonomics, safety and durability, as well as aesthetic considerations—this branch of the law is only interested in protecting the visual appearance of things: features of shape, or patterns, or ornamentation. As Kitto J said in *Re Wolanski's Registered Design* (1953) 88 CLR 278 at 280: 'what the proprietor of a design gets ... is a monopoly for one thing only, and that is "one particular individual and specific appearance"'.

It can immediately be seen that design law has a much more limited scope than copyright law, which protects more types of creative content, as well as a variety of mechanical forms of reproduction and distribution of such content. Further, while the design of articles will often combine functional and aesthetic considerations, the protection of function tends to fall under the rubric of patent law or the laws protecting confidential information. Given the breadth of both copyright and patent law, design laws only have a relatively small sphere of operation.

One reason why designs have a somewhat awkward place within the IP regime is that design laws took their modern form much earlier than either copyright or patent laws. The *Designs Registration Act 1839* (UK), followed by the *Ornamental Designs Act 1842* (UK) and the *Utility Designs Act 1843* (UK), set up registration systems for designs, and gave protection to the shape and configuration of any articles of manufacture, for up to three years. These Acts became the model for later UK designs legislation, on which Australian law came to be based. At the time of their introduction, these Acts provided protection that was further advanced than that available under other systems of law protecting industrial or creative property.[1] However, as the form and substance of patent and copyright law became more settled in the latter half of the nineteenth century, design law came to take on a much more limited role. For example, drawings came to be protected as copyright subject matter in the latter part of the nineteenth century, while under the *Copyright Act 1911* (UK):

- 'works of artistic craftsmanship' became recognised as a protectable category of work;
- the reproduction of two-dimensional artistic works (like drawings) was specifically stated to cover the making of three-dimensional representations of those works; and
- the term of protection for many artistic works was extended to the life of the author plus 50 years.

Thus as a modern patent and copyright law became more fixed, and more generous, this tended to marginalise the role of design protection. The expansion of copyright law in particular raised questions about the relationship or overlap between copyright and design protection for industrially produced goods. This relationship has undergone a number of refinements over the last century but, as we will see at the end of this chapter (see 'The overlap with copyright protection' below, p 361), it remains one of the more vexed areas in IP law.

In Australia, the *Designs Act 1906* (Cth) regulated designs for close to a century. Based on nineteenth-century UK legislation, this Act set up a registration scheme for 'new or original' designs, which encompassed features of shape, pattern, configuration or ornamentation applied to an article. This regime was criticised as failing to provide useful legal protection. It was thought to be too easy to obtain design registration and that design rights were too difficult to enforce. Accordingly, after a number of inquiries—most notably the Australian Law Reform Commission's (ALRC's) Report No 74, *Designs* (1995)—the *Designs Act 2003* (Cth) and the *Designs (Consequential Amendments) Act 2003* (Cth) were passed. Both came into force on 17 June 2004. The *Designs Act 2003* substantially changed design law in Australia, in particular the registration process, the scope of the infringement action and the term of protection. The goal was to 'provide a simple, cost-effective designs system that provides Australian designers with more effective rights'.[2] The *Designs (Consequential Amendments) Act 2003* made important changes to the *Copyright Act 1968* (Cth) in relation to the relationship between copyright and design protection. In addition, the *Designs Regulations 2004* (Cth) set up detailed requirements relating to the design registration process.

In 2012–15 the Advisory Council on Intellectual Property (ACIP) reviewed the *Designs Act*. An Options Paper was published in late 2014.[3] ACIP noted that the Australian designs system gives designers more limited rights than are available in other jurisdictions. ACIP also asked (at pp 60–61):

> whether the policies reflected in the 2003 Act—in essence, continuing a fairly narrowly tailored designs system based entirely on registration and embodying the full logic of a registration system (with registration before publication a requirement) still make sense. Some overseas jurisdictions have moved beyond the logic of design registration to embrace, for example, unregistered anti-copying rights in designs, or full copyright protection for all artistic works regardless of 'industrial application'. Other jurisdictions do seem to provide

---

1   See generally B Sherman and L Bently, *The Making of Modern Intellectual Property Law*, Cambridge University Press, Cambridge, 1999, ch 4.
2   Explanatory Memorandum to the Designs Bill 2002 (Cth), p 2.
3   ACIP, *Review of the Designs System: Options Paper* (2014).

registered design rights that are broader than the rights available in Australia ... Feedback to this review suggests that the current Australian system is expensive for what it offers, and is, as a result, neglected by designers who find it doesn't offer the rights they need. The question is whether the Australian designs system is so parochial, and so restrictive, that we are failing to encourage innovative design.

ACIP noted that it had not received evidence sufficient to support significant change, such as the introduction of a right to prevent the copying of unregistered designs as found in Europe, but suggested that, in the longer term, the role of designs protection is under challenge. ACIP's final report is due in the first half of 2015.

Although the 1906 Act has been repealed, it is still important to designs registered under that Act. Section 151(2) of the 2003 Act provides that such 'old Act' designs are taken to be registered under the 2003 Act. However, s 151(3) states that the 1906 Act continues to apply for the purposes of determining the validity of the registration of such designs. Further, while s 156(2) provides that actions for infringement of such 'old Act' designs can be brought under the 2003 Act, s 156(3) states that the 1906 Act still applies when determining whether such designs have been infringed. This means that, in practice, certain provisions of the 1906 Act will remain relevant until the last of the designs registered under the 1906 Act expires, potentially in 2020: see s 152 of the 2003 Act. In this chapter, however, we focus only on designs registered under the 2003 Act.

As a final introductory point, the influence of international treaties on design law is limited compared with other types of IP. The *Paris Convention on the Protection of Industrial Property* (1883), to which Australia is a signatory, requires parties to protect 'industrial designs' (Art 5*quinquies*) and to ensure that a person who files for registration of a design in one member state is given a right of priority—that is, the ability to apply for registration of the same design in another member state within six months, which will then to be assessed on the basis of the filing date of the earlier application (Art 4). The *Agreement on Trade-Related Aspects of Intellectual Property Rights* (the 'TRIPS Agreement') (1994) also obliges World Trade Organization (WTO) members to protect 'industrial designs' that are 'new or original' (Art 25.1) and to ensure that owners are afforded rights to prevent others making articles embodying the protected design, subject only to limited exceptions (Art 26). In addition, the *Hague Agreement Concerning the International Registration of Industrial Designs* (administered by the World Intellectual Property Organization (WIPO)) streamlines the procedures for obtaining protection for the same design (designated as the 'international design') in multiple member states. Australia is not a member of the Hague Agreement but has agreed to 'make its best efforts to comply with' the Geneva Act of the Hague Agreement (1999)[4] (*Australia–US Free Trade Agreement* (AUSFTA) (2004), Art 17.1.5). At the time of writing, an advanced text for a Draft Designs Law Treaty was also under negotiation in WIPO, focusing on harmonising domestic design registration procedures.

---

4   The Hague Agreement is the subject of four major 'versions' or Acts: the original Hague Agreement of 1925 (no longer in force), the London Act of 1934, the Hague Act of 1960 and the Geneva Act of 1999. States may be parties to one or more of these Acts: for relations between the different Acts, see Art 31 of the Geneva Act (1999); Art 31 of the Hague Act. Applications under the 1934 Act were frozen on 1 January 2010; thus the primary Acts in force are the 1960 and 1999 Acts.

THE REGISTRATION PROCESS

Unlike copyright, design protection does not arise as soon as a product with a particular appearance has been created or designed. Rather, protection only arises following a process of registration. That is, parties seeking protection in Australia must apply to a government agency—the Designs Office, which is a division of IP Australia—in compliance with certain provisions of the *Designs Act* and the *Designs Regulations* in order to obtain registration of their designs.

Chapter 3 of the *Designs Act* covers applications for registration. Section 21 provides:

(1) A person may file an application (a design application) in respect of a design.

(2) A design application must comply with:

(a) any requirements prescribed by the regulations in relation to representations of designs disclosed in the application; and

(b) any other requirements prescribed by the regulations.

These are the minimum filing requirements.

...

(4) A design application must specify the entitled person or persons in relation to the designs disclosed in the design application.

The persons entitled to register a design (broadly, the designer, their employer or other person claiming through the designer) are discussed below (see 'Ownership and duration', p 354). Regulation 3.01 of the *Designs Regulations* also provides that the application must contain information that identifies the applicant and allows the applicant to be contacted, as well as a representation of the design, which can be a drawing, photograph or specimen (*Designs Act*, s 5). A statement of 'newness and distinctiveness' may also be provided to the Registrar of Designs at the timing of filing (s 69). If the design application meets the 'minimum filing requirements' in s 21, then the Registrar will notify the applicant of this and will give the application a filing date. This date will, in most cases, be the priority date of the application (the main exception being if the application was based on an earlier 'Convention application', i.e. an application made in a country which is a signatory to the Paris Convention or the TRIPS Agreement, and hence entitled to an earlier priority date as mentioned above: s 27).

Under the 1906 Act, applications for design protection were formally examined in the Designs Office for compliance with the requirements for registrability of a design prior to registration. Under the 2003 Act, the applicant only needs to request registration of the design(s) disclosed in the design application, following which the Registrar undertakes a formalities check (see ss 39–40 and reg 4.04). If the application complies with the formalities requirements, and does not contain a design excluded by s 43 (see below), the Registrar must register the design. At this point, certain particulars are entered in the Designs Register (see s 111), and the Registrar will issue a certificate of registration to the applicant, who now becomes the 'registered owner' of the design.[5]

---

5   Alternatively, the applicant can request that its design be published but not registered, in which case the Registrar will check that certain filing requirements have been met (s 57 and reg 4.15), following which the design is published in the *Australian Official Journal of Designs*. Publication might be a useful alternative for applicants in a fast-moving industry who merely want to ensure that competitors do not attempt to gain exclusivity over similar designs. However, mere publication through the Designs Office has been rarely used since 2003, and there is nothing to stop a person from publishing elsewhere, for example online, to frustrate others' attempts to secure monopolies.

A design that has only been registered, however, is of limited practical value, as infringement proceedings cannot be commenced until the design has been examined (s 73(3)). Chapter 5 of the Act deals with formal examination, which now takes place only after registration and on the request of any person (the registered owner, or a third party) or a court (s 63). If the Registrar receives such a request, under s 65(1) he or she must consider whether the registration should be revoked on any of the following grounds, set out in s 65(2):

- that the design is not a registrable design—this requires an assessment of s 15; and
- any other ground prescribed by the regulations—reg 5.02 provides that a prescribed ground is that, under s 43, the design should not have been registered.

Sections 15 and 43 are discussed below (see 'The requirement of newness and distinctiveness', p 342, and 'Excluded designs', p 354).

If the design is held to be valid after examination, the Registrar must issue a certificate of examination under s 67: such a design is referred to as a 'certified design' and is enforceable. If the design is not valid, the Registrar must revoke the registration under s 68.

In addition to their right to request examination of a registered, but unexamined design mentioned above, a third party may also apply to have a design revoked in a number of circumstances. First, a person can apply to the Registrar under s 52 to have a registered design revoked, either because:

- a person (or persons) was an 'entitled person' (see s 13) at the time the design was first registered, and one or more of the original registered owners of the design was not an entitled person at that time; or
- each original registered owner of the design was an entitled person at the time of registration, but another person (or persons) was also entitled at that time.

Second, under s 93, a person may apply to a prescribed court (most commonly the Federal Court) for an order that a certified (i.e. examined) design be revoked, on one or more of the following five grounds in s 93(3):

(a) that the design is not a registrable design; or

(b) that one or more of the original registered owners was not an entitled person in relation to the design when the design was first registered; or

(c) that each of the original registered owners was an entitled person in relation to the design when the design was first registered, but another person or persons were entitled persons in relation to the design at that time; or

(d) that the registration of the design was obtained by fraud, false suggestion or misrepresentation; or

(e) that the design is a corresponding design to an artistic work, and copyright in the artistic work has ceased.

WHAT IS A REGISTRABLE DESIGN?
THE DEFINITION OF 'DESIGN'

Design laws have always attempted to draw a distinction between an 'article' or 'product' on the one hand and the particular visual features of that article or product on the other, for the purpose of giving legal protection in respect of the latter only. This practice is continued in the *Designs Act*, s 5 of which provides that:

> *design*, in relation to a product, means the overall appearance of the product resulting from one or more visual features of the product.

Two of the elements of this definition are further defined. Section 6 defines 'product' as follows:

> (1) For the purposes of this Act, a thing that is manufactured or hand made is a product (but see subsections (2), (3) and (4)).
>
> (2) A component part of a complex product may be a product for the purposes of this Act, if it is made separately from the product.
>
> (3) A thing that has one or more indefinite dimensions is only a product for the purposes of this Act if any one or more of the following applies to the thing:
>
>   (a) a cross-section taken across any indefinite dimension is fixed or varies according to a regular pattern;
>
>   (b) all the dimensions remain in proportion;
>
>   (c) the cross-sectional shape remains the same throughout, whether or not the dimensions of that shape vary according to a ratio or series of ratios;
>
>   (d) it has a pattern or ornamentation that repeats itself.
>
> (4) A kit which, when assembled, is a particular product is taken to be that product.

The term 'visual feature' is defined in s 7:

> (1) *visual feature*, in relation to a product, includes the shape, configuration, pattern and ornamentation of the product.
>
> (2) A visual feature may, but need not, serve a functional purpose.
>
> (3) The following are not visual features of a product:
>
>   (a) the feel of the product;
>
>   (b) the materials used in the product;
>
>   (c) in the case of a product that has one or more indefinite dimensions:
>
>   (i) the indefinite dimension; and
>
>   (ii) if the product also has a pattern that repeats itself—more than one repeat of the pattern.

Six points should be made about the definition of design. First, it contemplates the existence of a three-dimensional manufactured or hand-made 'thing' (see s 6(1)) that has a particular appearance. This thing can have a number of indefinite dimensions (such as a piece of industrial piping that is cut to size), provided that s 6(3) is satisfied. But the requirement of a three-dimensional thing in which the design is embodied excludes from protection certain features that might in common parlance be thought of as 'designed', as can be seen from the Microsoft decision, extracted below.

Similar reasoning would arguably apply to other digital entities, such as graphical user interfaces (GUIs) or screen icons for apps. Australian Designs Office practice which requires that visual features be visible in the product's rest state (i.e. when it is turned off) also makes it difficult to register such items.[6] ACIP's 2014 Options Paper notes that Australian practice on such 'virtual designs' differs from international practice: many countries accept such designs.[7]

---

6   IP Australia, *Designs Examiners Manual of Practice and Procedure*, [D04.3.2].

7   ACIP, *Review of the Designs System: Options Paper* (2014), p 50. For a discussion of the position in the USA, see J du Mont and M Janis, 'Virtual Designs' (2013) 17 *Stanford Technology Law Review* 107.

CURRENT LAW

CASE STUDY: CURRENT LAW

Microsoft Corporation

[2008] ADO 2
Australian Designs Office

D Herald (Delegate of the Deputy Registrar of Designs): 1. On 11 Nov 2005 the applicant filed a design application for 'Type Font', requesting registration. The representation sets out the design using the following characters:

A B C D E F G H I J K L M N O P Q R S T U V W X Y Z
a b c d e f g h i j k l m n o p q r s t u v w x y z
1 2 3 4 5 6 7 8 9 0
. : ! ? , ; ( ) < > @ # $ ^ & % * ' " + - = [ ] { } \ /

with the design being associated with the particular appearance of the characters.

...

14. The present design is for a font. It is not a hammer for a typewriter; it is not a type element for use in type-setting with metal blocks; it is not a rubber stamp. It is the shape of characters that might be applied to any of these things—as well as any other medium—be that paper, computer screen, light projection etc. Indeed, in the computer environment a type font exists as a binary file (in the Windows® environment, usually as a .TTF or .FON file), with that file being used to control how information is presented on computer output—whatever that output might be (monitor, printer, etc). I do not think that the present design shows a product bearing visual features. Rather, the representations show a collection of visual features intended to be applied to unspecified products in unspecified arrangements.

...

16. In my view, the present design does not disclose a product bearing visual features. It only discloses visual features.

The second point that should be made about the definition of design is that it refers to the 'overall appearance of the product', with the exception of component parts of complex products (but only if separately made). This contrasts with provisions in Europe, the UK and the USA which allow the registration of designs for parts of products.[8] Registration of partial product designs will tend to lead to broader rights over very different-looking products. It is possible in Australia to highlight parts of a design using a statement of newness and distinctiveness (see further below), which allows a court to pay particular regard to those parts if reproduced in a defendant's product (s 19(2)(b)). This is not, however, equivalent to registration of a partial design, as the court must still have regard to the overall appearance of the whole product.[9]

---

8   *Directive 98/71/EC of the European Parliament and of the Council of 13th October 1998 on the Legal Protection of Designs*, Art 1(1); *Council Regulation (EC) No 6/2002 of 12th December 2001 on Community Designs*, Art 3(a); *Registered Designs Act 1949* (UK), s 1(2)). In the USA, see *Ex parte Cady*, 1916 CD 62, 232 OG 621, and Chapter 1500, Section 1502 of the *Manual of Patent Examining Procedure*.

9   ACIP, *Review of the Designs System: Options Paper* (2014), pp 47–48.

A third point about the definition is that once the three-dimensional 'product' is identified, then the visual features can themselves be three-dimensional (such as the shape of a lamp), or two-dimensional (such as a pattern to be screen-printed on a T-shirt), or a combination of the two (such as a dress design). The distinction between two- and three-dimensional features becomes particularly important when considering the overlap between copyright and design protection, which we discuss at the end of the chapter (p 361).

Fourth, the definition of 'visual features' is non-exhaustive. This means that features such as the look of a surface or the colour of a product could well be part of its design. The practical effect of this is that an applicant's design rights might be limited if the applicant files the representation of its design in colour, as distinct from in black and white.[10]

Fifth, s 7(2) makes clear that a visual feature can serve a functional purpose: this differs from the position in, for example, Europe, where certain functional features cannot be registered.[11] However, an Australian registered design does not prevent another party from copying the functions of a product unless the visual appearance is also copied.

Sixth, the definition of 'design' under the former (1906) Act referred to features 'that, in the finished article, can be judged by the eye'. In light of this, courts sometimes asked in respect of three-dimensional designs whether the alleged design had sufficient individuality or specificity of appearance to distinguish it from 'mere shapes' or 'general shapes'. This involved tribunals at times having to draw tenuous distinctions between the 'fundamental form' of articles and the particular shapes of such articles. We would suggest that the different language and structure of the 2003 Act means that courts are no longer required to attempt to draw these sorts of distinctions. If it is thought that the appearance of the product is indistinguishable from that of similar products, this should go only to the questions of 'newness' and 'distinctiveness', discussed immediately below.

THE REQUIREMENT OF NEWNESS AND DISTINCTIVENESS

Section 15 is the key provision that sets out the requirements for a design to be registrable. A design that fails to meet these requirements is liable to be revoked: ss 65, 93. Section 15(1) provides:

> A design is a registrable design if the design is new and distinctive when compared with the prior art base for the design as it existed before the priority date of the design.

These are stricter criteria than in the 1906 Act (under which a design merely had to be 'new or original').

Newness and distinctiveness are both assessed in light of the 'prior art base' as it existed before the priority date, which s 15(2) indicates consists of:

(a) designs publicly used in Australia; and
(b) designs published in a document within or outside Australia; and
(c) designs in relation to which each of the following criteria is satisfied:

---

10   See *Review 2 Pty Ltd v Redberry Enterprise Pty Ltd* [2008] FCA 1588; (2008) 173 FCR 450.
11   Compare Art 7(1) of the EU *Directive 98/71/EC of the European Parliament and of the Council of 13 October 1998 on the Legal Protection of Designs*, which precludes registration of features 'solely dictated by its technical function'. See similarly, for European Community designs, *Council Regulation (EC) No 6/2002 of 12th December 2001 on Community Designs*, Art 8(1).

(i) the design is disclosed in a design application;

(ii) the design has an earlier priority date than the designated design;

(iii) the first time documents disclosing the design are made available for public inspection under section 60 is on or after the priority date of the designated design.

Under s 16(1), a design will be 'new' unless it is 'identical to a design that forms part of the prior art base'. Under s 16(2), a design will be 'distinctive' unless it is 'substantially similar in overall impression to a design that forms part of the prior art base', a phrase that is interpreted in light of s 19, which provides:

(1) If a person is required by this Act to decide whether a design is substantially similar in overall impression to another design, the person making the decision is to give more weight to similarities between the designs than to differences between them.

(2) The person must also:

(a) have regard to the state of development of the prior art base for the design; and

(b) if the design application in which the design was disclosed included a statement (a *statement of newness and distinctiveness*) identifying particular visual features of the design as new and distinctive:

(i) have particular regard to those features; and

(ii) if those features relate to only part of the design—have particular regard to that part of the design, but in the context of the design as a whole; and

(c) if only part of the design is substantially similar to another design, have regard to the amount, quality and importance of that part in the context of the design as a whole; and

(d) have regard to the freedom of the creator of the design to innovate.

(3) If the design application in which the design was disclosed did not include a statement of newness and distinctiveness in respect of particular visual features of the design, the person must have regard to the appearance of the design as a whole.

(4) In applying subsections (1), (2) and (3), the person must apply the standard of a person who is familiar with the product to which the design relates, or products similar to the product to which the design relates (the *standard of the informed user*).

Section 19 was intended to effect significant change in Australian designs law. Section 19(1) in particular was intended to depart from practice under the 1906 Act, where small differences from the prior art would be sufficient to enable registration of a design (making design registrations easy to obtain), but where small changes would also avoid infringement (making designs hard to enforce). Section 19 is used both in assessing distinctiveness for validity and in determining infringement—a defendant's product will infringe where it is substantially similar in overall impression to the registered design: s 71.

Other notable features of s 19 are:

• the relevance of the statement of newness and distinctiveness (SoND), which is a short statement by an applicant pointing out those features which make the design distinctive; if a SoND is included in the registration, the examiner or court should 'have particular regard' to the highlighted features while considering the design as a whole (s 19(2));

• the reference to the 'freedom of the creator of the design to innovate': s 19(3);

- the perspective from which distinctiveness is judged: that is, the standard of the 'informed user' in s 19(4).

The meaning of these provisions, and how tribunals will go about assessing the 'distinctiveness' of designs under ss 15, 16 and 19, are considered in the following extracts.

CASE STUDY: CURRENT LAW

LED Technologies Pty Ltd v Elecspess Pty Ltd

[2008] FCA 1941; (2008) 80 IPR 85
Federal Court of Australia

[LED Tech was the registered owner of a number of designs for light emitting diode (LED) lamps. Each of its designs had the following statement of newness and distinctiveness: 'Separate clip in lenses. Base to take a variety of 2, 3 or 4 combination lenses for stop, tail, indicator, reverse LED lenses, no visible screws.' LED Tech brought infringement proceedings against Elecspess, the maker of the 'Condor' LED lamp, and Elecspess cross-claimed for revocation of the registrations on the basis that the designs were not registrable under s 15(1) because they lacked distinctiveness.]

Gordon J: 53. As a result of difficulties in interpretation and application, the Australian Law Reform Commission ('ALRC') recommended that the 'innovation threshold' in s 17(1) of the 1906 Designs Act be replaced by the two-step 'new and distinctive' test now found in the 2003 Designs Act: Report No 74, *Designs* (1995) (the 'ALRC Report'). The ALRC addressed the issue in the following terms:

> **5.8. Meaning of distinctive**. Distinctiveness is a term used by the courts to express the quality that a design must have to differentiate it sufficiently from previously published or used designs. For example the courts have said
>
> > for a design to be protected there must be a special or distinctive appearance, something in the design which captures and appeals to the eye. To have that effect, the design must be noticeable and have some perceptible appearance of an individual character: [*Dart Industries Inc v Decor Corporation Pty Ltd* (1989) AIPC [¶]90-569, 38,975. In another case, relating to furniture design, it was said that design in such a field is a subtle thing and, provided it is distinctive to the trained eye, I think that registration should not be denied in view of the element of subtlety which is involved in the combination of old features in a particular way and the manner in which they are combined: *D Sebel & Co Ltd v National Art Metal Co Pty Ltd* (1965) 10 FLR 224, 227; approved in *Australian Building Industries Pty Ltd v Woodman McDonald (Glass) Pty Ltd* [1986] AIPC [¶]90-302.]
>
> > Other cases have spoken of 'the overall distinctive appearance of the registered design' [*Firmagroup Australia Pty Ltd v Byrne & Davidson Doors (Vic) Pty Ltd* (1987) AIPC [¶]90-410]] the ridging or grooving of a design being 'sufficiently bold and distinctive in its appeal to the eye', [*Aluminum Specialities Pty Ltd v Ibis Building Products Pty Ltd* (1982) 42 ALR 127, 133] a shape or configuration that is 'distinctly different' from that in

respect of which a design is registered [*Turbo Tek Enterprises Inc v Sperling Enterprises Pty Ltd* [(1989) AIPC [¶90-616]] and a design that must be 'distinct and must present an appearance that strikes the eye as being different' [*Fisher LJ & Co Ltd v Fabtile Industries Pty Ltd* (1979) 49 AOJP 3611] ...

5.9. Grounds for adopting the new test. The [ALRC] favours the two tiered approach and the distinctiveness test for several reasons.

- The distinctiveness test is a design approach. It recognises the importance of design in product differentiation. It is consistent with the way in which designers work.
- It will discourage the tendency to focus narrowly on 'one individual specific appearance' and to count up the differences between designs.
- It incorporates in a single concept many of the qualities sought in other unsatisfactory expressions such as 'judged by the eye', 'eye appeal', 'immaterial detail', 'trade variants', and 'obvious adaptation'.
- It is a more focussed test for assessing the degree to which a design is an advance on the prior art.
- It allows a different prior art base to be defined for novelty as against distinctiveness. This is useful because the aim with the novelty test is to exclude identical designs but the aim with the distinctiveness test is to recognise innovation.
- It directly addresses the need for greater differentiation between designs, both for registration and infringement purposes, that was evidenced by submissions, consultations and the [ALRC's] survey of design users.

54. The ALRC Report formed the basis of the 2003 *Designs Act*: Explanatory Memorandum to the Designs Bill 2002 (Cth) at 1. Under the 2003 *Designs Act*, a design is distinctive 'unless it is substantially similar in overall impression to *a* design that forms part of the prior art base for the design' as it existed before the priority date of each Design: s 16(2) (emphasis added). As noted earlier, that test has an important temporal aspect: anything which occurs after the priority date (the filing date of the application for registration) is irrelevant: s 16(3).

55. Secondly, contrary to the Respondents' submissions, distinctiveness is to be assessed not by comparing the design in question to the prior art base as a whole but by comparing it individually to each relevant piece of prior art: s 15(1) read with ss 16(1) and (2) ... As a result, a design that combines various features, each of which can be found in the prior art base when considered as a whole but not in any one particular piece of prior art, is capable of being distinctive: *Review 2 Pty Ltd v Redberry Enterprise Pty Ltd* [2008] FCA 1588 at [60]; *Karen Millen Ltd v Dunnes Stores Ltd* [2008] ECDR 11 at [82]–[84] (stating that the registered design must be assessed with regard to particular prior designs rather than a hypothetical amalgam of a number of prior designs). See also *Lockwood Security Products Pty Ltd v Doric Products Pty Ltd* (2007) 235 CLR 173 (upholding the validity in the patent context of a combination of features known collectively in the prior art).

56. Thirdly, the judgment is an objective one. In assessing substantial similarity in overall impression, the standard to be applied is that of the informed user—namely, the court standing in the shoes of a notional person who is familiar with the product to which the design relates, or products similar to the product to which the design relates: s 19(4); *Review 2 Pty Ltd v Redberry Enterprise Pty Ltd* [2008]

FCA 1588; see also *Dart Industries Inc v Decor Corporation Pty Ltd* (1989) 15 IPR 403, 408–409. That informed user, in assessing substantial similarity in overall impression:

1   gives more weight to similarities between the designs than to differences between them: s 19(1);
2   considers the state of development of the prior art base for the design: s 19(2)(a);
3   considers the particular visual features of the design described in the statement of newness and distinctiveness in the context in which they appear: s 19(2)(b) and (c);
4   if only part of the design is substantially similar to another design, considers the amount, quality and importance of that part in the context of the design as a whole: s 19(2)(c); and
5   considers the freedom of the creator of the design to innovate: s 19(2)(d).

. . .

58. The 'informed user' concept has also been considered by the courts in the United Kingdom. In *Woodhouse UK plc v Architectural Lighting Systems* [2006] RPC 1 at [59], Judge Fysh QC of the Patents County Court defined an informed user in the following terms:

> First, this notional person must obviously be a user of articles of the sort which is subject of the registered design—and I would think, a regular user at that. He could thus be a consumer or buyer or be otherwise familiar with the subject matter say, through use at work. The quality smacks of practical considerations. In my view the informed user is first, a person to whom the design is directed. Evidently he is not a manufacturer of the articles and both counsel roundly rejected the candidature of 'the man in the street'. 'Informed' to my mind adds a notion of familiarity with the relevant rather more than what one might expect of the average consumer; it imports the notion of 'what's about in the market?' and 'what has been about in the recent past?' I do not think it requires an archival mind (or eye) or more than an average memory but it does I think demand some awareness of product trend and availability and some knowledge of basic technical considerations (if any). In connection with the latter, one must not forget that we are in the territory of designs and thus what matters most is the appearance of things; as Mr Davis reminded me, these are not petty patents. Therefore, focus on eye appeal seems more pertinent than familiarity with the underlying operational or manufacturing technology (if any). I feel uncomfortable with analogy to the 'man skilled in the art' whose 'nerd-like' (and other) attributes seem too technical: *Technip France SA's Patent* [2004] EWCA Civ 381; [2004] RPC 46 at [6]–[12] (CA).

. . .

59. Although it would be dangerous to attempt some comprehensive statement of principles that might be applied to the concept, it is apparent that an informed user:

1   is reasonably informed; not an expert but more informed than an average consumer;
2   is an objective standard. However, expert evidence may still be adduced in court to assist the Court in applying the informed user concept;
3   focuses on visual features and is not concerned with internal features or features that are not visible to the naked eye.

60. In the present case, the Respondents accept that each Design is new when compared to the prior art base as it existed before the priority date of each Design. The question which then arises is whether each Design is distinctive. In order to answer that question, two sub-questions arise for consideration. What was the prior art base before the priority date of each Design? What are the visual features of each Design?

...

62. Before turning to consider the prior art base, at this point in the argument it is important to remember that the Respondents accept that the following distinctions existed between the prior art base (which, incorrectly, they would have considered as a whole) and the Designs:

1   the absence of visible screws;
2   the different visual features of the rear or base views of the Designs;
3   the 'cut-out' or 'recess' at the end of a lamp; and
4   the sloping, rounded mounting bracket surrounding the lenses.

63. The question is whether an informed user—a person familiar with the product to which the design relates, or products similar to the product to which the design relates, and having regard to those matters listed in [56] above—would consider a Design with the distinct features listed in [62] as substantially similar in overall impression to a design that forms part of the prior art base for the design? In my view, such a person would not consider either Design to be substantially similar in overall impression to a design that forms part of the prior art base for the design.

64. If one looks at the designs which comprise the prior art base, one can identify designs and products, including LED Tech's single-lens lamp, with some of the features found in each of the Designs—a lens separate from the base and from each other, a low profile with an open base and no visible screws. However, none of those designs include all or most of the features listed in [62] above, being features described in the statement of newness and distinctiveness for each of the Designs ... For example, if one looks at LED Tech's single-lens lamp, it is apparent that, apart from the absence of visible screws, the product contains none of the other features.

65. If one turns to consider the state of development of the prior art base, each of the Designs and the features described in the statement of newness and distinctiveness was a distinct advance over the prior art base in the sense that it combined various existing features in a way that had not been done before. On application to register each Design, the advances recorded in those Designs over the prior art base were substantial. And, as was acknowledged by Mr Garrard [an expert called by the alleged infringers], each of the features listed in [62] was quite arbitrary from a design point of view. That is to say, the features were the product of conscious design choice rather than compelled by industry-wide standards or technological constraints. Contrary to the Respondents' contentions, the visual features chosen by Mr Ottobre [a director of LED Tech] were not 'so little different from the designs available in the prior art base' as to be substantially similar in overall impression. Visually the product was different—it was modern and streamlined with curved edges. No product in the prior art base incorporated all (or most) of the features listed in [62] in one product. In those circumstances, I do not consider that a person familiar with the product to which the design relates, or products similar to the product to which the design relates, would consider either Design as substantially similar in overall impression to any of the designs that form part of the prior art base.

66. In considering the prior art base and the issue of whether each Design is substantially similar in overall impression to any of the designs that form part of the prior art base, the Respondents submitted that it was necessary to consider a product comprising several of LED Tech's single-lens lamps set side by side. Although at least one witness, Mr Carpenter, gave evidence that he had seen LED's single lenses installed side by side on vehicles, it was by no means clear when he saw such a configuration or what the precise configuration as to number and composition looked like. That lack of detail is probably

CURRENT LAW

fatal to the contention that each Design is substantially similar in overall impression to an arrangement of LED Tech's single-lens lamps side by side.

67. Furthermore, even if I were to assume, hypothetically, that a person had physically abutted two or three of LED Tech's single-lens lamps side by side before the priority date of each Design and that such a creation constituted a design publicly used in Australia within the meaning of s 15(2) so as to make it a part of the prior art base, I do not consider that a person familiar with the product to which the design relates, or products similar to the product to which the design relates, would consider each Design to be substantially similar in overall impression to such a configuration. Instead of one continuous base along the long axis, there would be two or three bases with no flat strip or landing between each lens. And the sides of each base would not comprise a sloping, rounded mounting bracket surrounding a lens but would have vertical or straight sidewalls surrounding each lens. The underside of the bases would be different in shape, with mounting holes in different positions. For those reasons as well, the cross-claimants' contention of substantial similarity is rejected.

Gordon J's decision that LED Tech's designs were registrable was upheld by the Full Federal Court: *Keller v LED Technologies Pty Ltd* [2010] FCAFC 55; (2010) 185 FCR 449. It is clear, from the Full Federal Court's decision and subsequent authority,[12] that distinctiveness requires a 'design by design' comparison. The Full Court also rejected the appellant's argument that Gordon J had failed to place any or sufficient weight on LED Tech's statement of newness and distinctiveness (see Emmett J at [55] and Besanko J at [249]).

Gordon J's discussion of the 'standard of the informed user' (s 19(4)) is consistent with that of Kenny J in *Review Australia Pty Ltd v New Cover Group Pty Ltd* ('*Review Australia*') [2008] FCA 1589; (2008) 79 IPR 236 at [29]–[30] and *Review 2 Pty Ltd v Redberry Enterprise Pty Ltd* ('*Review 2*') [2008] FCA 1588; (2008) 173 FCR 450 at [26]–[27]. In both cases Kenny J held that the 'informed user' would include a 'user of ladies' garments, which would include a potential purchaser, either in retail sales (such as a buyer for a fashion store) or at the ultimate consumer level [but not a] designer or manufacturer of ladies' garments'. This approach was queried by Yates J in *Multisteps Pty Ltd v Source & Sell Pty Ltd* [2013] FCA 743; (2013) 214 FCR 323, extracted below.

CURRENT LAW

CASE STUDY: CURRENT LAW

Multisteps Pty Ltd v Source & Sell Pty Ltd

[2013] FCA 743; (2013) 214 FCR 323
Federal Court of Australia

[Multisteps owned six certified designs in respect of the clear plastic containers used for the transport and retail of strawberries, cherry tomatoes, kumatoes and similar. It sued Source & Sell for infringement. The Court was required to assess whether the defendant's containers were 'substantially similar in overall impression' to the registered designs under s 19.]

Yates J: 63. Uninstructed by the decisions of this court ... I would not, myself, have considered that a person's status as a user had a direct role in applying the standard defined in s 19(4) of the *Designs*

Act. In cases decided under legislation reflecting the provisions of the Designs Directive—in particular, the UK *Designs Act*—the emphasis on the notional person being a user of the articles in respect of which the design is registered can be explained by the fact that the informed user is the touchstone specifically provided by that legislation. The position is not quite the same under the *Designs Act*. Section 19(4) explicitly states that the standard is that of a person who is familiar with the product to which the design relates, or products similar to the product to which the design relates. Section 19(4) uses the expression 'the standard of the informed user', but merely as a tag. In my respectful view, it is not a statement of the content of the test. The expression 'the standard of the informed user' is defined by the preceding words of the provision. So viewed, the expression cannot colour the meaning of the express words of the test.

64. The Australian Law Reform Commission Report No 74, *Designs* (Sydney, 1995) (the ALRC Report)—to which the *Designs Act* responds—adopted, as its recommended standard, the idea of the informed user. It seems that, in doing so, it was inspired by European developments in relation to the protection of Community designs. However, in adopting this idea, the Australian Law Reform Commission (the Commission) was not dogmatic about the status of the notional person as a user of products. ...

65. Paragraph 5.17 of the ALRC Report is illuminating:

> *Informed user.* The Commission recommends that the novelty and distinctiveness of designs should be assessed from the perspective of the 'informed user'. The concept of the informed user is flexible enough to incorporate where relevant the views of consumers, experts, specialists and skilled tradespersons. At the same time it does not, and should not, require that the expert or consumer be the test in all cases. The informed user would be defined as a person who is reasonably familiar with the nature, appearance and use of products of the relevant kind ...

66. The test in s 19(4) of the *Designs Act* reflects this more general approach. Apart from the tag 'the informed user', the standard prescribed by s 19(4) appears to be indifferent as to how and in what circumstances familiarity is acquired. In my respectful view, the standard does not proceed on the requirement that the notional person be a user of the products in question—although, obviously, familiarity can be gained through use. Similarly, it does not proceed on the distinctions that the United Kingdom and European cases draw about who can and who cannot be a user.

67. Importantly, however, s 19(4) does not impose a standard higher than familiarity. The standard fixes the appropriate level of generality (or particularity) at which a design is to be assessed ... This may be a reason for saying that the notional person is not a design expert, lest it be thought that a standard of design evaluation more rigorous or exacting than familiarity is involved. However, in my view, it is not a reason for excluding, necessarily, a design expert from being a person having the required familiarity.

68. In the present case, the standard of the informed user is the standard of a person who is familiar with produce or similar containers. So much is clear from an application of the text of s 19(4) of the *Designs Act*. No greater elaboration is required.

69. The applicant submits that, relevantly, '[t]he informed user is a purchaser or seller of fresh produce punnets who considers the needs of the packer and the eye appeal of the filled container to the consumer'. The respondent submits that the informed user is a 'fruit packer' who uses the plastic containers in question for that purpose.

70. In my view, the class of persons whose attributes might be taken as representing the standard of the informed user is not as confined as the applicant or the respondent would have it. The text of s 19(4) does not require that confinement. The standard of the informed user in the present case might well be represented by a person who acquires produce containers for the purpose of using them, or having them used, in packing operations to produce packaged products. The standard of the informed user might be represented by the person who is the producer of the packaged product (relevantly, on the evidence in the present case, the producer of packaged fruit such as small tomatoes) or by a person engaged in packing operations on behalf of such a producer. The standard of the informed user might also be represented by a sophisticated purchaser at wholesale of the packaged product who has particular requirements in relation to, for example, the storage, transport, and display of the packaged product in such containers. There may be others whose perceptions could be taken as representing the standard of the informed user. However, in all cases, the necessary and only qualification is that the person be familiar with produce or similar containers. No matter how such a person might come to be appropriately qualified, he or she will have an awareness and appreciation of the visual features of a produce container that serve its functional as well as its aesthetic purposes.

71. I do not regard the perceptions of the general body of consumers who purchase packaged products at retail to be indicative of the standard of the informed user in the present case. It is entirely possible, of course, that some consumers, for whatever reason, might have a particular interest in produce containers and, because of particular circumstances, possess the requisite familiarity to meet the standard under s 19(4). However, as a matter of general approach, I would regard this to be the exception rather than the rule. Neither the applicant nor the respondent advanced a case that the general impressions of retail consumers, as such, set the proper standard by which the relevant designs were to be evaluated and compared in the present case.

The meaning and role of the designer's 'freedom to innovate' in s 19(2)(d) has been considered in *Review 2* [2008] FCA 1588; (2008) 173 FCR 450 and *Review Australia* [2008] FCA 1589; (2008) 79 IPR 236. In both cases, Review owned a design for a sleeveless, cross-over dress. Review alleged infringement against two parties that had made similar dresses. The defendants' challenge to the validity of the registered design in both cases failed, for the reasons set out at [59] of *Review 2*:

[T]aking into account the freedom of the designer to innovate, the informed user would be aware that there is limited freedom to design a cross-over or wrap dress ... and that, for the most part, what gives the Review Design its different overall impression from the prior art, from the perspective of the informed user, is the shape and configuration of the skirt, combined with differences in pattern ... [T]here were numerous designs for V-necked fixed-wrap or cross-over dresses in the prior art, both with and without sleeves, but none was substantially similar in overall impression to the Review Design, when judged by reference to the informed user. Thus, for example, the design embodied in [one garment] depicted a figure-hugging cross-over bodice and V-neck, with a fitted waist and black tie, but it also depicted a hip-hugging straight skirt, and a bold pattern of large white hibiscus flowers and leaves on a black background. Having regard to the factors to which s 19(2) and (3) direct attention, the informed user would not consider the Review Design to be substantially similar to it in overall impression. The Review Design might also be thought reminiscent of the design embodied in [another garment], which disclosed a cross-over bodice and ruffled hem. Notwithstanding these similarities, differences in the shoulder straps and the overall 'look' of the design, including the skirt, combined with differences in pattern (including colour), would lead an informed user to conclude that this design and the Review Design were also essentially different in overall impression. This latter conclusion flows in part from an application of s 19(2)(c), which in each instance requires the Court to consider the amount, quality and importance of the part that is substantially similar in the context of the design as a whole.

In *Multisteps* (extracted above) Yates J considered freedom to innovate in relation to produce containers as used for small fruit such as strawberries and cherry tomatoes (at [80]–[85]). Yates J accepted that the designer's freedom to innovate was limited by the functional need for certain features, including 'a "boxish" shape; a hinged lid; holes for ventilation; small protruding feet on the lower surface of the base; and ribbing at the corners or ribbed pillars, for strength or decoration, with otherwise clear surfaces or panels between the corners or pillars' (at [85]). Possession of these features did not make the infringing designs 'substantially similar in overall impression'.

Newness and distinctiveness are assessed against the 'prior art base'. A case in which this issue was contentious is extracted below.

CASE STUDY: CURRENT LAW

World of Technologies (Aust) Pty Ltd v Tempo (Aust) Pty Ltd

[2007] FCA 114; (2007) 71 IPR 307
Federal Court of Australia

[Both the applicant and respondent were Australian importers of vacuum cleaners. The applicant was first to import a particular model MC-801 vacuum cleaner from a Chinese manufacturer called Suzhou Fak, and had secured the design registration in respect of the vacuum cleaner pursuant to a 'design registration authorisation' provided by Suzhou Fak. Although the applicant believed that it was the exclusive Australian distributor for the vacuum cleaner, Suzhou Fak had also supplied the same cleaner to the respondent knowing that it would be sold in Australia. When the applicant sued the respondent for infringement, the respondent sought revocation of the design under s 93(3)(a) on the basis that it was not a registrable design under s 15.]

Jessup J: 60. The respondent relies first upon the publication, at the Canton Fair in April 2005, of a brochure depicting the appearance of the MC-801 vacuum cleaner, for the purposes of s 15(2)(b) of the *Designs Act*. The original of that brochure is before the court. I have compared the brochure with the design as registered. It is common ground that the vacuum cleaner shown in each document is one and the same product. The copy of the registered design which is before the court is a photocopy. The representations of the vacuum cleaner in it are less distinct than the corresponding printed colour photographs appearing on the Suzhou Fak brochure of April 2005. Further, in the design as registered the product is shown in side view (both sides), in bottom view, in top view, in back view, in front view, in back perspective view and in front perspective view. As represented on the brochure, the product is shown only in front perspective view. For that reason, I am unable to conclude that the design is identical to that shown in the brochure. Accordingly, I do not hold that the design is not new for the purposes of s 16(1) of the *Designs Act*.

61. However, I consider that the design as applied for and subsequently registered is substantially similar in overall impression to the design disclosed in the Suzhou Fak brochure of April 2005. Although shown on the brochure in front perspective view only, the impression obtained from that angle permits the viewer to make a reasonable assessment not only of the side, but also of the front, of the vacuum cleaner. Assuming, as I do, that the product is symmetrical, I take it that the other front perspective view would convey the same impression. Further, the item is displayed on the brochure in such a way as to permit the viewer to gain a reasonably good impression of the appearance of the product from the top. The only faces of the product which it is impossible to perceive from the brochure are those of the rear and of the underside. Notwithstanding these omissions, I consider that the vacuum cleaner is sufficiently represented on the Suzhou Fak brochure to give a good impression of the appearance of the design of the product as a whole, as required by s 19(3) of the *Designs Act*. Taking that approach, I find that the design for which the applicant applied for, and subsequently secured, registration is substantially similar in overall impression to that which appeared on the printed brochure for the MC-801 vacuum cleaner distributed at the Canton Fair in April 2005. The latter was a design published in a document outside Australia and was, accordingly, part of the prior art base for the purposes of registrability ...

...

65. The respondent relies also on a 'jpeg' file sent by the applicant to an advertising company on 31 May 2005. The file contained the artwork for the packaging in which the MC-801 was to be sold by Godfreys—as the 'Genius 2200 bagless' vacuum cleaner. The file, as represented in an exhibit tendered in court, shows the vacuum cleaner very clearly in front perspective view. Save for the colour and the attachment of a hose, it justifies the same conclusion as that which I reached above with respect to the Suzhou Fak brochure distributed at the Canton Fair in April 2005. I consider that, by the sending of this file to the advertising company, the applicant published the design in a document within Australia for the purposes of s 15(2)(b) of the *Designs Act*. The registered design is, I consider, substantially similar in overall impression, having regard to the appearance of the design as a whole, to that published on 31 May 2005 when the applicant sent the artwork to the advertising company ...

...

67. The respondent relies also upon the receipt of samples of the MC-801 vacuum cleaner by Godfreys in March 2004, and upon the subsequent examination and testing of those samples for the purpose of determining their commercial suitability. I take it that the respondent proposes that this constituted the 'public use' of the design in Australia for the purposes of s 15(2)(a) of the *Designs Act*. I was not addressed on what constituted 'public use' in this context, and I am not disposed to hold that the sending of samples for these purposes to Godfreys constituted such use. Furthermore, no example of the samples was put in evidence. Although it is implicit in the respondent's case that I should regard it as self-evident that these samples were at least substantially similar in overall impression to the design that was later sought to be registered, the respondent made no attempt to make good that proposition by putting the actual item upon which it relied before the court. In the circumstances, I make no finding that these samples constituted part of the prior art for the purposes of s 15(2)(a) of the *Designs Act*.

68. The respondent relied also upon the fact that a sample of the MC-801 vacuum cleaner had been sent to the Queensland Department of Industrial Relations, for the purposes of obtaining a certificate of approval for an electrical article under the *Electrical Safety Act*. The certificate was issued in May 2005, and Mr Jabbour said that the process of approval would have taken about ten weeks. The respondent's point is that the provision of a sample of the product constituted a public use of the design in Australia for the purposes of s 15(2)(a) of the *Designs Act*. As with the dispatch of samples to Godfreys, I am not persuaded that the provision of a single sample to a government department for the purposes of electrical safety certification constituted public use in the relevant sense. I would not, in the circumstances, hold that such a dispatch was part of the prior art base apropos the applicant's application for registration of the relevant design.

The findings in *World of Technologies* that the design was published in the Suzhou Fak brochure in China and that this put the design into the prior art base, and that the sending of samples to a government department for certification was not 'public use', are both unproblematic. Similarly, the finding that the sending of samples to a retailer was not a public use is sustainable on the facts, although a demonstration of a prototype product embodying the design to potential retailers (who were not placed under confidentiality obligations) was considered to be a public use under the 1906 Act.[13] However, the idea that the sending of a jpeg file as an email attachment could constitute the 'publishing' of a design in a document is more controversial, as such an interpretation is broader than how 'publication' is understood in copyright law: compare *Copyright Act 1968* (Cth), s 29.

Two further points about the operation of the newness and distinctiveness tests are worth noting.

First, use or publication of the applicant's own design before the priority date can fall within the prior art base: i.e. an applicant can undermine its own application through precipitous use. To mitigate the harshness of this outcome, s 17(1) provides that any pre-priority date publication or use of the design either:

- with the consent of the registered owner or predecessor in title in certain prescribed circumstances (namely, at certain international exhibitions: reg 2.01(1)), or
- without the consent of the registered owner but by a person who derived or obtained the design from the registered owner of the design or predecessor in title,

is to be disregarded in assessing newness and distinctiveness, but only if the application for registration is made within six months of that first publication or use (see also reg 2.01(3)).

Registration systems in some other countries provide a 'grace period': a set time (e.g. six months), prior to the priority date, during which disclosure of a design by or derived from the applicant will not prevent the design being new and distinctive. This is primarily intended to protect designers who inadvertently publish before registration and/or do not understand the need to apply for protection before publication. A grace period does not change the priority date: third party activities can still defeat registration. The 2014 ACIP Options Paper notes that as well as existing in Australia's patent law (see Chapter 11), grace periods are common internationally and could be introduced in Australia.

---

13   See *Safe Sport Australia Pty Ltd v Puma Australia Pty Ltd* (1985) 5 IPR 120.

Second, under s 18 certain designs consisting of features of shape or configuration which, when embodied in a product, result in a reproduction of an artistic work (for the purposes of copyright law), are not to be treated as other than new or distinctive by reason only of any use previously made of the artistic work, with certain exceptions for 'industrially applied' designs: s 18. The scope of s 18 will become clearer when we come to consider the provisions of the *Copyright Act* dealing with overlapping copyright and design protection (see below, p 361).

EXCLUDED DESIGNS

Section 43(1) requires that the Registrar refuse to register certain designs. These include designs those that would contravene s 18 of the *Olympic Insignia Protection Act 1987* (Cth) (e.g. because they contain a design of the Olympic symbol), or designs that either are, or are part of, an integrated circuit. The Registrar must also refuse to register certain prescribed designs, which are set out in reg 4.06 to include medals; designs containing the Arms, flags, seals or emblems of the Commonwealth, a state or a territory; and scandalous designs.

OWNERSHIP AND DURATION

Section 14(1) of the 2003 Act provides that the registered owner of a registered design at a particular time is:

(a) the person who, at that time, is entered in the Register as the registered owner of the design; or

(b) if, at that time, there are 2 or more such persons—each of them.

However, this does not mean that the position of the registered owner is inviolable. This is because s 13 sets out five categories of people who are *entitled* to be registered as the owner of a design:

(a) the person who created the design (*the designer*);

(b) if the designer created the design in the course of employment, or under a contract, with another person—the other person, unless the designer and the other person have agreed to the contrary;

(c) a person who derives title to the design from a person mentioned in paragraph (a) or (b), or by devolution by will or by operation of law;

(d) a person who would, on registration of the design, be entitled to have the exclusive rights in the design assigned to the person;

(e) the legal personal representative of a deceased person mentioned in paragraph (a), (b), (c) or (d).

The registration of a design can be revoked if the original registered owner was not an entitled person (see ss 52 and 93(3)(b)), as demonstrated in the following case.[14]

---

14   Note that since the *Intellectual Property Laws Amendment (Raising the Bar) Act 2012* (Cth), lack of entitlement no longer necessarily leads to revocation of a patent: see *Patents Act 1990* (Cth), s 138(4). ACIP's Options Paper proposes that the position under the *Designs Act* should be amended to match the *Patents Act*: ACIP, *Review of the Designs System: Options Paper* (2014), p 60.

CASE STUDY: CURRENT LAW

World of Technologies (Aust) Pty Ltd v Tempo (Aust) Pty Ltd

[2007] FCA 114; (2007) 71 IPR 307
Federal Court of Australia

[The facts of the case are set out above, p 351.]

Jessup J: 70. The respondent also submits that the applicant was not an 'entitled person' when the design was first registered, and that the design should be revoked on that ground also ... The respondent's point is that the applicant did not come within any of the categories of person entitled to be registered as the owner of the design under s 13(1) of the *Designs Act* ... It is clear from the evidence that neither the applicant nor any person employed by, or contracted to, the applicant was the actual designer. That leaves, effectively, two possibilities under s 13(1) of the *Designs Act*: is the applicant a person who derived title to the design from the original designer, or from someone who employed, or contracted with, that designer, within the meaning of par (c); and was the applicant a person who would, on registration of the design, be entitled to have the exclusive rights in the design assigned to it, within the meaning of par (d)?

71. The respondent placed into evidence, but otherwise did not explain the significance of, a printed document on the letterhead of Suzhou Fak dated 8 June 2005. That document was headed 'MC-801 inventor certification'. The text of the document was as follows:

> We would like to certify that the inventor of the MC-801 bagless vacuum cleaner is Mr Ding Wei
> Ming of our company.

The document had Mr Ding's name printed at the base, but it was not signed. It seems, however, to be common ground that the original designer of the MC-801 was a person in the employ of Suzhou Fak. That being so, Suzhou Fak would have been entitled to apply for registration under s 13(1)(b) of the *Designs Act*.

72. Did the applicant derive title to the design from Suzhou Fak? The only evidence which would, even arguably, sustain an affirmative answer to that question is the 'design registration authorisation' sent by Suzhou Fak to the applicant on about 30 May 2005 ... That certificate authorised the applicant to 'proceed' the registration of the MC-801 design, but made it clear that ownership of the design was to remain the property of Suzhou Fak. Whatever else may be said about that document, in my opinion it does not constitute any basis from which the applicant might have derived title to the design within the meaning of s 13(1)(c) of the *Designs Act*. At most, the document constitutes an authority to the applicant to register the design in the name of Suzhou Fak.

73. As to par (d) of s 13(1) of the *Designs Act*, had the design been registered in the name of the true owner (the designer or Suzhou Fak), I can see no basis upon which the applicant would have been entitled to insist upon an assignment of those design rights to itself. There was certainly no contractual or like obligation imposed upon the designer or Suzhou Fak to make any such assignment.

74. In the circumstances, had it not been for my decision to revoke the design under par (a) of s 93(3) of the *Designs Act*, I would also have held the ground of revocation with which par (b) is concerned to have been made out, namely, that the original registered owner was not an entitled person in relation to the design when the design was first registered.

Turning to the issue of duration, under the 1906 Act the registration of a design lasted for an initial period of one year from the date of registration, but could be renewed for a further three five-year periods to last for a maximum of 16 years. Under the 2003 Act, the registration of a design:

- lasts for five years from the filing date of the design application (s 46(1)(a)); and
- can be renewed for a further period of five years (ss 46(1)(b), 47).

The 10-year maximum term is the minimum required by the TRIPS Agreement (Art 26.3), although if Australia accedes to the *Geneva Act of the Hague Agreement Concerning the International Registration of Industrial Designs 1999*, as Art 17.1.5 of AUSFTA suggests, it will need to provide at least international registrations with a 15-year term of protection (Art 17).

The reduction in the overall term of protection in the 2003 Act was not recommended by the ALRC. The ALRC did acknowledge, however, that no particular rationale put forward justified any particular term of protection (something that could well be said about IP rights more generally). In the Explanatory Memorandum to the Designs Bill 2002 (Cth), it was stated at [16] that:

> it would not be in Australia's interest to provide a period of registration in excess of its international obligations as Australia is a net importer of intellectual property.

This can perhaps be contrasted with the subsequent extension of the term of copyright under the *US Free Trade Agreement Implementation Act 2004* (Cth) (discussed in Chapter 3).

EXCLUSIVE RIGHTS AND INFRINGEMENT

Section 10(1) of the *Designs Act* provides that the registered owner has a number of exclusive rights during the term of registration, namely:

(a) to make or offer to make a product, in relation to which the design is registered, which embodies the design; and

(b) to import such a product into Australia for sale, or for use for the purposes of any trade or business; and

(c) to sell, hire or otherwise dispose of, or offer to sell, hire or otherwise dispose of, such a product; and

(d) to use such a product in any way for the purposes of any trade or business; and

(e) to keep such a product for the purpose of doing any of the things mentioned in paragraph (c) or (d); and

(f) to authorise another person to do any of the things mentioned in paragraph (a), (b), (c), (d) or (e).

These rights relate to doing certain acts with a *product* embodying the registered design. Like copyright, these rights are personal property and are capable of assignment and of devolution by will or by operation of law: s 10(2).

Section 71(1), which closely reflects s 10(1), provides that a person infringes an examined registered design if he or she, without the licence or authority of the registered owner of the design:

(a) makes or offers to make a product, in relation to which the design is registered, which embodies a design that is identical to, or substantially similar in overall impression to, the registered design; or

(b) imports such a product into Australia for sale, or for use for the purposes of any trade or business; or

(c) sells, hires or otherwise disposes of, or offers to sell, hire or otherwise dispose of, such a product; or

(d) uses such a product in any way for the purposes of any trade or business; or

(e) keeps such a product for the purpose of doing any of the things mentioned in paragraph (c) or (d).

Three points should be noted about infringement of registered designs. First, infringement only occurs where a person makes a product *in relation to which the design is registered*. Thus if a design is registered in relation to cars, it would not be an infringement to make a toy car in the same shape. This contrasts with the European approach, for example, where enforcement is not limited to particular classes of products.[15] Second, as the rights only apply to dealings with *products*, circulation of design drawings is not a direct infringement of the *Designs Act* (although copyright law may apply). Third, unlike s 10, s 71 does not refer to authorising acts falling within the exclusive rights. It is clear that a person may be liable for design infringement as a joint tortfeasor, if they intend and procure that infringement occur or share a common design that infringement should occur: *Keller v LED Technologies Pty Ltd* [2010] FCAFC 449; (2010) 185 FCR 449. It is less clear that the broader forms of authorisation liability analogous to those available under copyright law (see Chapter 6) are available to enforce registered design rights. ACIP's 2014 Options Paper notes that this may complicate attempts to enforce registered designs against, for example, websites that distribute infringing design documents such as might be used in a 3D printer.[16]

Under the 1906 Act courts would look to whether there was an 'obvious' or 'fraudulent' imitation,[17] and often very minor variations to the registered design would avoid infringement. One of the aims of the 2003 Act was to liberalise the test for infringement; the approach under the Act is illustrated in the extract below.

CASE STUDY: CURRENT LAW

LED Technologies Pty Ltd v Elecspess Pty Ltd

[2008] FCA 1941; (2008) 80 IPR 85
Federal Court of Australia

[The facts of the case are set out above, p 344.]

Gordon J: 70. The 2003 *Designs Act* was drafted so that the test of whether an allegedly infringing product is substantially similar in overall impression to the registered design is the same test applied to determine whether a design was distinctive for registration purposes: ALRC Report pars 5.22–5.23. As the ALRC said, '[T]he infringement and distinctiveness tests should be the same so that an infringing

---

15 *Directive 98/71/EC of the European Parliament and of the Council of 13 October 1998 on the Legal Protection of Designs*, Art 12(1); see also in relation to European Community designs: *Council Regulation (EC) No 6/2002 of 12 December 2001 on Community Designs*, Art 19(1).

16 ACIP, *Review of the Designs System: Options Paper* (2014), pp 56–58.

17 See for example *Polyaire Pty Ltd v K-Aire Pty Ltd* [2005] HCA 32; (2005) 221 CLR 287.

design is not a distinctive design and vice versa': para 5.22. Adopting the same test for distinctiveness and infringement broadens the scope of protection. The extent of difference required to make a design distinctive will depend on the state of development of the relevant prior art base. A more developed prior art base will mean that smaller differences will be sufficient to result in a finding that there is no substantial similarity: para 5.23 ...

...

72. As s 71 of the 2003 *Designs Act* (read with s 19) makes clear, the court assesses whether the allegedly infringing design is substantially similar in overall impression to the registered design by comparing the allegedly infringing product to the registered design in the context of the whole appearance of the designs: see also ALRC Report para 6.25. The whole appearance is relevant as the context for the design even though, strictly, the design is only the distinctive visual features of the product. Greater weight is given to distinctive features than to other parts of the design, although still in the context of the whole of the appearance. The same principles of assessment apply where the distinctive features relate only to part of the design: ss 19(2)(b)(ii) and (c). Moreover, in determining whether a design is infringed the Court must give more weight to similarities between the designs than to differences between them: s 19(1).

73. This legislative approach to the question of infringement ensures that courts assess infringement in the context of the whole appearance of competing designs rather than focusing on the differences between them. In addition, the scheme of the 2003 *Designs Act* requires the Court looking through the eyes of an informed user to consider:

1   the state of development of the relevant prior art base. As stated earlier, one measure is whether the difference in distinctiveness between the Design and any previously known design is greater than the difference between the Design and the allegedly infringing design: s 19(2)(a);
2   the new and distinctive features of the design: s 19(2)(b)(i);
3   where only part of a design is substantially similar to another design, the amount, quality and importance of that part in the context of the design as a whole: s 19(2)(c);
4   the freedom of the creator of the design to innovate. In other words, the nature and use of a product, or part of it, is a factor in defining the scope of the designer's freedom to choose shape and materials: s 19(2)(d).

74. There is little doubt that first impressions are important when comparing a registered design with an allegedly infringing product in the manner prescribed by the 2003 *Designs Act*: ALRC Report para 5.15. In the United Kingdom, in applying an 'overall impression' test, the approach is to hold a product embodying the registered design (provided that the Court is satisfied that it is a true embodiment of the registered design) and the alleged infringing product in hand and undertake a reasonably careful comparison between the two: *Proctor & Gamble Co* [v *Reckitt Benckiser (UK) Ltd* (2007)] 73 IPR 605 at [12]. See also *J Choo (Jersey) Ltd v Towerstone Ltd* [2008] FSR 19 at [6] (citing *Proctor & Gamble* for the proposition that court may have regard to a physical embodiment of the registered design in making the comparison to the allegedly infringing product); but see *Rolawn Lawn Ltd v Turfmech Machinery Ltd* [2008] EWHC 989 (Pat); [2008] RPC 27 at [124] (stating that the exercise involves comparing the registered design to a photograph of the allegedly infringing product rather than the product itself).

75. With respect, I disagree with the proposition that as a general matter a court should start out by comparing product with product rather than registered design with product. First and most importantly,

such an approach is inconsistent with the statutory language. Section 71(1)(a) directs the court to perform the substantial similarity analysis by comparing a product (the allegedly infringing item) to the registered design. Secondly, Jacob LJ's approach is inconsistent with that taken by Kenny J in *Review 2 Pty Ltd v Redberry Enterprise Pty Ltd* [2008] FCA 1588; (2008) 173 FCR 450 at [28], [35]. Significantly, the expert evidence in *Review* was challenged on the basis that the witness had improperly compared product with product (and had even tried the products on): see [33]. Although Kenny J ultimately allowed the evidence, her Honour nevertheless proceeded on the basis that the comparison for the court was between registered design and product and the expert evidence in question had to be taken subject to the complaints made by the other side: see [34]–[36].

76. I am of a similar view. While there may be circumstances in which it is appropriate (or at least not wholly inappropriate) for an expert witness giving evidence as an informed user to have regard to a product embodying the registered design in providing an opinion on the substantial similarity question, the task for the court itself as laid down by the statute remains to compare the registered design to the allegedly infringing product. Moreover, even if I were not inclined to the view of Kenny J, I could not, in light of the statutory language, consider her Honour's approach plainly wrong, and thus I would follow it in preference to Jacob LJ's approach in any event.

77. I therefore conclude that infringement is determined by comparing the allegedly infringing product against the registered design, not by comparing a product embodying the registered design against the infringing product: s 71. Thus the fact that the actual LED light is similar to the Condor TL light is not relevant. Moreover, infringement is determined by comparing only the visible features of the design to the infringing product: ss 7 and 19. Thus the fact that the products have different materials in the lens or have different voltages is also irrelevant.

78. If a visual comparison is made of the top view of a Condor product ... against the registered design ... the Condor product is 'substantially similar in overall impression' to the Designs: s 71(1)(a) ... There is a continuous base. There is a flat strip or landing between each lens. The sides of the base of both the Designs and the Condor product comprise a sloping, rounded mounting bracket surrounding the lenses.

79. It is true that the Condor Products contain visible screws while the statement of newness and distinctiveness accompanying the Designs emphasises the 'no visible screws' feature of the Designs. However, although the Condor product contains two screws in each flat strip or landing between each lens, it is not a feature which in my view substantially distinguishes the Condor product from the registered Design. The presence of the screws does not create a different 'visual appeal'. The screws are the same colour as the flat strip or landing between each lens and sit low in the socket. They are not 'visual' screws as one would describe the screws in some of [the] prior art ... where the screws are chrome in colour and protruding.

80. ... Upon a visual comparison of the rear view of the same Condor product against ... the Design, the Condor product is 'substantially similar in overall impression' to the Designs. Again, there is one base with rounded corners. There is an opening for each lens of similar shapes with the shapes in the same configuration. There is the same number of mounting holes for the screws and the holes are in the same position.

[Gordon J held the registered designs to have been infringed. On appeal, the Full Court agreed with this finding.]

The registered owner's fortunes were more mixed in *Review 2* [2008] FCA 1588; (2008) 173 FCR 450 and *Review Australia* [2008] FCA 1589; (2008) 79 IPR 236. In *Review Australia*, the registered design for a cross-over dress and the defendant's design were found to be substantially similar in overall impression, differing only as to pattern and colour; contrast, in *Review 2* by contrast, Kenny J held that despite the similarities between the registered design and the defendant's dresses, the differences in terms of the pattern and ornamentation and the shape and configuration of the skirt were such that the defendant's dress conveyed a different overall impression, such that the defendant had not infringed (see quote above, discussing the designer's freedom to innovate: p 350).[18]

DEFENCES

A defendant in infringement proceedings can counterclaim for revocation under s 93: see s 74. But the only specific defence in the 2003 Act is the 'repair' defence (s 72), which is concerned with spare parts.

The 1906 Act allowed the registration and enforcement of designs in relation to spare parts without restriction. Under the 2003 Act, registration is still allowed. The definition of a 'product', in relation to which a design may be registered under 2003 Act, includes a component part of a complex product if it is made separately from the product: s 6(2). There is no exclusion in the 2003 Act for the registration of functional designs, unlike in some jurisdictions;[19] nor, in contrast to some jurisdictions, is there any limitation on registration of designs for spare parts.[20]

Recognition of exclusive rights in the shape, configuration or appearance of spare parts that are sold separately can raise competition concerns, especially where a product involves a significant investment, such as a car or a piece of mining equipment. A monopoly supplier of spare parts for expensive items might be able to charge very high prices. However, as the ALRC recognised, at least in theory, the price and availability of spare parts may be part of a package which can be considered at the time of an original purchase, especially by large or well-informed purchasers such as fleet purchasers (in the case of cars) or mining companies (in the case of mining equipment). Nor is it always true that purchasers have limited market power: insurers, for example, involved in car repair, have more market power than the average consumer. There are numerous other factors relevant to competition, including the integration of sales and servicing.

---

18 For an exploration of the tensions in the fashion industry which calls into question the idea that design rights are necessarily needed to promote the development of new, visually appealing products, see K Raustiala and C Sprigman, 'The Piracy Paradox: Innovation and Intellectual Property in Fashion Design' (2006) 92 *Virginia Law Review* 1687.

19 Compare Art 7(1) of the EU *Directive 98/71/EC of the European Parliament and of the Council of 13 October 1998 on the Legal Protection of Designs*, which provides that a design right 'shall not subsist in features of appearance of a product which are solely dictated by its technical function'. See similarly, for European Community designs, *Council Regulation (EC) No 6/2002 of 12th December 2001 on Community Designs*, Art 8(1).

20 Compare Art 7(2) of the EU *Directive 98/71/EC of the European Parliament and of the Council of 13 October 1998 on the legal protection of designs*, which provides that '[a design] shall not subsist in features of appearance of a product which must necessarily be reproduced in their exact form and dimensions in order to permit the product in which the design is incorporated or to which it is applied to be mechanically connected to or placed in, around or against another product so that either product may perform its function'. See similarly, for European Community designs, *Council Regulation (EC) No 6/2002 of 12th December 2001 on Community Designs*, Art 8(2).

The ALRC's response was to propose a two-part process to address competition concerns in relation to spare parts at the point of examination. Under the ALRC's proposal, the Registrar would identify whether a design was a potentially anti-competitive design, and the Australian Competition and Consumer Commission (at the time, the Trade Practices Commission) would assess whether the granting of a design right would, or would be likely to, have the effect of substantially lessening competition in a market (Recommendation 165).

These recommendations were not adopted; instead Parliament enacted a new defence to infringement in s 72(1) of the 2003 Act:

> a person does not infringe a registered design if:
>
> (a) the person uses, or authorises another person to use, a product:
>   (i) in relation to which the design is registered; and
>   (ii) which embodies a design that is identical to, or substantially similar in overall impression to, the registered design; and
> (b) the product is a component part of a complex product; and
> (c) the use or authorisation is for the purpose of the repair of the complex product so as to restore its overall appearance in whole or part.

Section 72(3)–(5) set out further detail as to the meaning of 'repair', and when the repair is taken to restore the overall appearance of a complex product.

In its *Review of the 'Spare Parts' Provision in the Designs Act 2003* (2005), IP Australia considered that it was too early to assess the impact of s 72 on industry and consumers, and that there was no case for revisiting the policy balance that the government had attempted to draw in enacting a spare parts exception. The ACIP Options Paper noted competing submissions from the car industry on the repair defence, but did not propose any change to the current provision.[21]

THE OVERLAP WITH COPYRIGHT PROTECTION

The final issue that needs to be considered in this chapter is the intersection between copyright and design law. The *Copyright Act 1968* (Cth) protects original artistic works, defined to include drawings, sculptures, buildings or models of buildings and 'works of artistic craftsmanship' (s 10(1)). It also provides that making a version of an artistic work in another dimension constitutes a reproduction of the work (s 21(3)). What this means is that if a party can:

- show that a product embodying its design can be classified as a sculpture, building or work of artistic craftsmanship, or
- point to a drawing of that product containing the design features,

then provided that copyright subsists in the sculpture, building, work of artistic craftsmanship or drawing as an artistic work, a third party that makes a product embodying a similar design will, prima facie, infringe copyright. Relying on copyright protection is likely to be very attractive to designers: copyright arises without the need for registration, foreign works are routinely protected in Australia, and copyright in artistic works lasts for the life of the author plus 70 years. Thus copyright could usurp the role of designs law. A key concern is that allowing extensive and lengthy copyright

---

21 ACIP, *Review of the Designs System: Options Paper* (2014), pp 35–37.

protection for designs or design drawings might inhibit innovation by restricting the public domain of useful designs.

Opinions divide on how the overlap between design law and copyright should be addressed. Some countries have been prepared to allow dual protection for items of 'industrial art', notably France which long ago abandoned the attempt to draw distinctions between the applied and fine arts. Others have sought to reconcile the two systems by limiting copyright in industrial products to a term equivalent to that available under designs law.[22] Others historically attempted to develop exceptions to copyright infringement or otherwise exclude or limit copyright protection for industrial products and force designers into using registered designs.

Australia takes the last of these approaches, through three complex statutory exceptions to copyright infringement set out in ss 74–77A of the *Copyright Act*, as amended. The exceptions to copyright infringement apply in relation to 'corresponding designs'. Under s 74(1) of the *Copyright Act*:

> *corresponding design* in relation to an artistic work, means visual features of shape or configuration which, when embodied in a product, result in a reproduction of that work, whether or not the visual features constitute a design that is capable of being registered under the *Designs Act 2003*.

'Embodied in', in relation to a product, 'includes woven into, impressed on or worked into the product' (s 74(2)). We will return to these s 74 definitions shortly.

The first exception to copyright infringement is contained in s 75, which for relevant purposes provides that:

> where copyright subsists in an artistic work ... and a corresponding design is or has been registered under the *Designs Act 1906* or the *Designs Act 2003* ... it is not an infringement of that copyright to reproduce the work by embodying that, or any other, corresponding design in a product.

In other words, where a design consisting of features of shape or configuration (but not pattern or ornamentation) of a product *has been registered*, and:

- a drawing of that product embodying those features has been reproduced in three dimensions by a third party making that product, or
- the product is a sculpture, building, model of a building or a work of artistic craftsmanship, and has been reproduced by a third party in three dimensions,

then those acts of reproduction will not infringe copyright in the artistic work in question. The owner of the registered design will, of course, be able to take action under the *Designs Act* for infringement of the design. However, once the design registration expires, the owner's rights under the *Copyright Act* do not revive.

The second exception to copyright infringement is contained in s 77, which applies as follows:

> (1) This section applies where:
>   (a) copyright subsists in an artistic work (other than a building or a model of a building, or a work of artistic craftsmanship) ... ;

---

22 For example New Zealand: see *Copyright Act 1994* (NZ), s 75.

> (b) a corresponding design is or has been applied industrially, whether in Australia or elsewhere ... by or with the licence of the owner of the copyright in the place of industrial application; and
>
> (c) at any time on or after [17 June 2004], products to which the corresponding design has been so applied (the products made to the corresponding design) are sold, let for hire or offered or exposed for sale or hire, whether in Australia or elsewhere; and
>
> (d) at that time, the corresponding design is not registrable under the *Designs Act 2003* or has not been registered under that Act or under the *Designs Act 1906*.
>
> (1A) This section also applies if:
>
> (a) a complete [patent] specification that discloses a product made to the corresponding design; or
>
> (b) a representation of a product made to the corresponding design and included in a design application;
>
> is published in Australia, whether or not paragraphs (1)(b) and (c) are satisfied in relation to the corresponding design.

If these conditions are satisfied, then under s 77(2):

> It is not an infringement of the copyright in the artistic work to reproduce the work, on or after the day on which:
>
> (a) products made to the corresponding design are first sold, let for hire or offered or exposed for sale or hire; or
>
> (b) a complete [patent] specification that discloses a product made to the corresponding design is first published in Australia; or
>
> (c) a representation of a product made to the corresponding design and included in a design application is first published in Australia;
>
> by embodying that, or any other, corresponding design in a product.

The broad effect of s 77(2) is that a party that makes enough products to qualify as industrial application, and sells or offers those products in Australia, but which has not registered a design, will be unable to use copyright law to prevent the reproduction in three dimensions of artistic works such as drawings or sculptures that embody that design. A relatively straightforward recent example of the operation of s 77 is *Muscat v Le* [2003] FCA 1540; (2003) 60 IPR 276. In that case the applicant owned copyright in drawings and patterns of designs for trousers, which were used to make a large number of trousers that were sold in Australia. The applicant had not registered its designs. The respondent used the applicant's trousers to make its own trousers, which involved the three-dimensional reproduction of the applicant's drawings and patterns. These reproductions did not infringe copyright in the drawings by virtue of s 77.

The third exception to copyright infringement is contained in s 77A:

> (1) It is not an infringement of copyright in an artistic work to reproduce the artistic work, or communicate that reproduction, if:
>
> (a) the reproduction is derived from a three-dimensional product that embodies a corresponding design in relation to the artistic work; and

(b) the reproduction is in the course of, or incidental to:

  (i) making a product (*the non-infringing product*), if the making of the product did not, or would not, infringe the copyright in the artistic work because of the operation of [ss 75 or 77]; or

  (ii) selling or letting for hire the non-infringing product, or offering or exposing the non-infringing product for sale or hire.

(2) It is not an infringement of copyright in an artistic work to make a cast or mould embodying a corresponding design in relation to the artistic work, if:

  (a) the cast or mould is for the purpose of making products; and

  (b) the making of the products would not infringe copyright because of the operation of [ss 75 or 77].

As an example of how s 77A will operate, in *Muscat v Le* (which was decided before the enactment of s 77A) the respondent, in the course of making its trousers, had also made drawings of the applicant's trousers and made its own patterns based on the applicant's trousers. This conduct also constituted reproduction of the applicant's drawings and patterns. However, given the respondent's reproductions were derived from the applicant's trousers (i.e. from the three-dimensional product embodying the applicant's corresponding design), and that they were made in the course of the respondent making its own trousers (this being a non-infringing act under s 77), these reproductions would now be non-infringing under s 77A. Section 77A also ensures that a respondent in a case like *Muscat v Le* would be able to make and communicate photographs of its product for marketing purposes.

Three aspects of the copyright/design overlap provisions in ss 74–77A require further elaboration:

- what constitutes a 'corresponding design';
- s 77 and the exclusion of 'works of artistic craftsmanship'; and
- the meaning of 'applied industrially'.

WHAT CONSTITUTES A 'CORRESPONDING DESIGN'?

Sections 75, 77 and 77A only apply if a corresponding design to the artistic work has been registered or applied industrially. As noted above, s 74 defines a design as 'corresponding' to a particular artistic work if it consists of 'visual features of shape or configuration which, when embodied in a product, result in a reproduction of that [artistic] work'. It is important to note that this definition is limited to features of '*shape and configuration*', even though it is also possible to register features of pattern or ornamentation under the *Designs Act*. Copyright and design protection, in other words, can coexist for two-dimensional patterns or images. This is because the overlap provisions of the *Copyright Act* are not intended to apply to the exploitation of an artistic work in two-dimensional form, for example, printed on T-shirts or plates. This seems to be because an artistic work applied as a two-dimensional decorative design 'retain[s] its essential character as an artistic work'.[23] As mentioned above, this thinking is carried through by s 18 of the 2003 Act, which ensures that prior use of an artistic work protected by copyright (other than by selling three-dimensional products) will not

---

23 J Luck, 'Section 18 of the *Designs Act 2003*: The Neglected Copyright/Design Overlap Provisions' (2013) 23 *Australian Intellectual Property Journal* 68 at 80.

prevent a corresponding design from being new and distinctive. Applying the statutory language and distinguishing between two- and three-dimensional features is complex, however, as shown in the following extract.

CASE STUDY: CURRENT LAW

Seafolly Pty Ltd v Fewstone Pty Ltd

[2014] FCA 321; (2014) 106 IPR 85
Federal Court of Australia

[Both Seafolly and Fewstone (trading as City Beach) designed, manufactured and sold swimwear and beachwear. Seafolly brought proceedings against Fewstone alleging infringement of copyright in two two-dimensional prints on swimwear, and a third design known as 'Senorita'. 'Senorita' consisted of diagonal criss-crossing stitching over the top of smocking (gathered material).]

Dodds-Streeton J: 443. In *Polo/Lauren* [*Co LP v Ziliani Holdings Pty Ltd* [2008] FCAFC 195; (2008) 173 FCR 266], the Full Court gave detailed consideration to the definition of 'corresponding design' under s 74(1) and (2) of the *Copyright Act*. In *Polo/Lauren*, the applicant, Polo/Lauren Co LP (Polo), was the owner of the copyright in the artistic work. The work represented a polo player swinging a mallet while astride a cantering pony. It was depicted in the logo affixed to the applicant's garments and was made up of 784 stitches. The respondents, Ziliani Holdings Pty Ltd and its principal, Mr Ziliani (Ziliani), without the applicant's permission imported into Australia for sale and subsequently sold genuine Polo garments bearing Polo's logo.

444. ... Polo alleged that Ziliani had infringed its copyright by knowingly importing into Australia a copyright work without its permission under ss 37 and 38 of the *Copyright Act* ... Ziliani relied upon the defence in s 77 of the *Copyright Act*, submitting that the logo was a 'corresponding design' within the meaning of the *Copyright Act* that was not registrable and had been applied industrially to products that had been sold.

...

446. ... [I]n contrast to the trial judge, [the Full Court] concluded, in obiter, that the s 77 defence would not have been established: at [36], [57].

447. Rares J [at trial] reasoned that the defence under s 77 would have been established because the 784 stitches used to embroider the logo onto the garments created 'an area of relief between the ordinary surface of the garment and the subtle, but none the less noticeable, rising of the surface of the garment in the places where the stitching, or embroidery, has been applied': [*Polo/Lauren Co LP v Ziliani Holdings Pty Ltd* [2008] FCA 49; (2008) 75 IPR 143] at [78]. His Honour stated at [81]:

> Embroidery, of its nature, affects the shape of the fabric on to which the stitching is applied ...
> it is immediately apparent that the polo player logo is embroidered, not printed, and that the
> fabric surrounding the embroidery is subtly, but noticeably, differently woven to the distinct area
> embroidered.

448. Rares J concluded that the embroidered polo player logo fell within the definition of a 'corresponding design' because it had 'visual features of shape or configuration being the distinctive alternation of the fabric created by the embroidery of the logo using at least 784 stitches': at [84].

449. In contrast, the Full Court concluded that the logo was not a 'corresponding design' because it was 'not embodied in the garments in the requisite sense': at [57].

450. Ziliani submitted that the logo was sufficiently three dimensional due to the embroidery made up of 784 stitches which protruded, albeit slightly, from the surface of the garments. Ziliani also submitted that the words of s 74(2) illustrated that 'embodiment' could include a design which was 'woven into, impressed on or worked into the product': at [46].

451. The Full Court rejected those submissions. Black CJ, Jacobson and Perram JJ accepted that, as Polo argued, 'the language of s 74 has a statutory history which reveals that the expression "visual features of shape or configuration" refers to a situation in which a three dimensional design is embodied in an article': at [46]. It concluded that the definition of 'corresponding design' was intended to apply to circumstances where an artistic work is embodied in three dimensions: at [54]. By that, the Full Court maintained the traditional position, where a design applied as the shape of a product was excluded from copyright protection, but a design exploited in basically two dimensional form continued to receive protection as an artistic work.

452. Their Honours observed that (subject to one qualification) at [48]:

> ... it is clear that the amendments to s 74 introduced by the *Designs (Consequential Amendments) Act 2003* (Cth) were not intended to change the understanding that copyright protection was not available for three dimensional renditions of designs but was available when a design was exploited in two dimensions.

453. The Full Court noted that the words of the previous provision (which excluded 'a design consisting solely of features of two dimensional pattern or ornament applicable to surface of an article') were 'drawn from designs law and connoted a two dimensional concept', whereas the concept of 'shape or configuration' was used to refer to 'the embodiment of a design in three dimensions': at [49].

454. Their Honours considered the Australian Law Reform Commission's review of the designs legislation in its Report No 74, *Designs*, the explanatory memorandum to the Designs (Consequential Amendments) Bill 2003 (Cth), the Senate's Economic Legislation Committee's report into the provisions of the Designs Bill 2002 (Cth) and the Designs (Consequential Amendments) Bill 2002 (Cth) (the immediate predecessor to the bill just under consideration). They concluded that 'the definition of "corresponding design" was intended to cover a situation where an artistic work is embodied in three dimensions': at [50]–[54].

455. Their Honours concluded that the insertion of wording contained in s 74(2) was not intended to remove the traditional requirement that the article 'embody' the design. They stated at [55]:

> Ziliani relies upon the words 'woven into', 'impressed on' or 'worked into the product' to show that something may be sufficiently three dimensional merely by being woven into another thing. Those words in s 74(2) were added by the *Designs (Consequential Amendments) Act*. Paragraphs 14 and 15 of the Explanatory Memorandum show that a debate as to whether objects such as carpets and bas-relief, whose qualities as a design might arguably be seen as either two or three dimensional, was to be resolved by requiring those objects to be protected under the designs legislation. We do not think that it was intended thereby to remove the requirement that the article 'embody' the design. This is so both because there is the absence of an indication of an intention on the part of Parliament that that notion was to be removed and because the language of

ss 74–77 exhibits textual examples which show that the relationship between the corresponding design and the article is one of embodiment rather than application. Section 74(1) uses the word 'embody' as does s 77(2) …

456. Their Honours considered that, in context, 'embody' meant to 'give a material or discernible form to an abstract principle or concept', rather than to 'include as a constituent element': at [56]. They stated at [55]–[56]:

> The word 'embody' is defined in the *Shorter Oxford Dictionary on Historical Principles* (6th ed, Oxford University Press, 2007) to mean:
>
> > 1. Provide (a spirit) with a bodily form. 2. Unite into one body or mass; incorporate in a larger whole. Include as a constituent part. 3. Give a material or corporeal character to (what is spiritual). 4. *Give a material or discernible form to (an abstract principle, concept, etc.)*; express (such a principle etc.) in such a form. Of a material or actual thing or person: be an embodiment of (an abstract concept, quality, etc.) 5. Form (people) into a body, esp. for military purposes. Form or join a (military) body. 6. Coalesce, form a homogeneous mass. [Emphasis added.]
>
> While it is possible that the word 'embody' can mean, effectively, 'include as a constituent element', we do not think, given the background to the provisions, that that is what it means in ss 74 to 77. Rather, in the cases with which ss 74 to 77 are concerned, it means 'give a material or discernible form to an abstract principle or concept'—the relevant abstract principle or concept is the design itself. Once that is accepted as the meaning of 'embody' in ss 4 to 77 there is no warrant for giving it the additional meaning 'include as a constituent element'—such a reading would be inconsistent with the language and history of the provisions.

…

458. On one view, the Full Court did not indicate whether it viewed the logo as three dimensional or not, but 'did not consider it self-evident that the Logo was three-dimensional despite the noticeable protrusion of the Logo from the fabric of the garments': Luck ['Section 18 of the *Designs Act 2003*: The neglected copyright/design overlap provisions' (2013) 23 *Australian Intellectual Property Journal* 68] at 82. There are indications, however, that the Full Court rejected Ziliani's argument on that question as, having referred to it in [46], the Full Court stated at [48] that Ziliani's submissions should be rejected.

459. In my opinion, as Luck stated, the Full Court's decision in *Polo/Lauren* indicates that features of shape and configuration can only be embodied in a product by making the product in that shape or configuration. In Luck's view, the decision also suggests that the product must acquire its shape or configuration during the making and not by a subsequent 'add-on': Luck at 84.

460. Luck stated that, '[f]eatures of the shape or configuration of whole three-dimensional products will qualify as corresponding designs' while 'features of pattern or ornamentation applied to the surface of products by a printing type process will not qualify …': Luck at 84.

461. Luck argued that the Full Court's decision limits the loss of copyright protection more than the language of the relevant provisions requires and may create potential difficulties if it is not self-evident how a product acquired its shape and configuration: Luck at 83.

462. In her article 'Too many stitches in time? The Polo Lauren case, non-infringing accessories and the copyright/design overlap defence' (2009) 20 *Australian Intellectual Property Journal* 39

(McCutcheon), Jani McCutcheon concluded that *Polo/Lauren* imposes two conditions for reliance upon the defence in s 77 of the *Copyright Act*: at 45. First, the reproduction must embody the artistic work, which 'cannot be merely a constituent element of another article'. Second, the reproduction must be three dimensional (although three-dimensionality is not of itself sufficient to satisfy s 77).

463. McCutcheon concluded that, on the Full Court's interpretation of s 77, if the artistic work effectively becomes the product (such as where pump drawings become the pump) it would fall within the scope of a corresponding design, but artistic works that cannot be converted to a product, or must necessarily be manufactured as a constituent element of another product, would appear to be excluded: McCutcheon at 46.

464. The Full Court in *Polo/Lauren* appeared to accept that designs forming part of articles such as carpets, knits, weaves, tapestries and bas-relief could be embodied in such articles by being woven into, impressed on or worked to the product and could thus amount to corresponding designs. The Full Court referred to the explanatory memorandum to the Designs (Consequential Amendments) Bill 2003 (Cth) which indicated that the words in s 74(2) were introduced to clarify the status of such borderline cases. Ms McCutcheon stated at 48:

> The strong similarity between embroidery and in particular tapestry would suggest that embroidery is three-dimensional, and provided the embroidery is 'non-constituent', s 77 will provide a defence unless such items are works of artistic craftsmanship (which may often be the case).

465. McCutcheon nevertheless noted that such articles are 'whole article' embodiments of the artistic work and s 77 may not apply where the artistic work is only reproduced in a portion of, for example, a carpet, as s 77 was never intended to apply to the three dimensional embodiment of an artistic work in a part of a product. McCutcheon concluded that consistently with the Full Court's decision, the reproduction of an artistic work in only a part of the product, albeit a carpet or bas-relief, would fall into the same category as the logo in *Polo/Lauren* and would be treated as a constituent part of the product: McCutcheon at 47.

CONSIDERATION

466. In my opinion, consistently with Full Court's reasoning in *Polo/Lauren*, the Senorita diamond pattern embroidery design is not embodied in the Senorita garments.

467. The Full Court's reasoning is not consistently explicit, but must be inferred, in some instances, from the materials it cites or extracts.

468. Further, the Full Court's final comment (at [58]), viewed in isolation, and at face value, could suggest it would have found that the artwork on the logo in *Polo/Lauren* was relevantly embodied in the shirt if the logo had been applied or incorporated into the shirt in such a way that it did not exist in its own right and could not survive removal from the garment.

469. The Full Court in *Polo/Lauren* indicated at [58], that had the logo not been conceptually distinct from the garment, Polo would probably have failed on the corresponding design issue, because if the logo and the garment were conceptually indistinguishable, the garment would have embodied the label. The Full Court then remarked that another way of putting it was that neither party could have succeeded simultaneously on both defences [that is, on both the overlap provisions and s 44C of the *Copyright Act*], because the garments could not logically, at the one time, embody the logo and be distinct from it: at [58].

470. The observation at [58], taken literally, could indicate 'embodiment' will occur if a logo is woven into the fabric of an article in such a way as to become indistinguishable. Nevertheless, that conclusion would not be consistent with the requirements for embodiment that emerge from the Full Court's reasons as a whole. The reasons in substance indicate that it is the features of shape or configuration of an artwork (not a label on which the artwork is reproduced) that must be relevantly embodied in a product, which will occur when the product (in the present case, a garment) is made in the shape or configuration of the artwork.

471. Unless that requirement is satisfied, the defence based on a corresponding design will not be made out even if the design is placed on or in the article in a three dimensional way, as embodiment and three dimensionality are both necessary conditions.

472. In the present case, in my opinion, features of shape or configuration of the Senorita diamond pattern artwork are not embodied in the Senorita garments in the requisite sense.

473. It is true that, in contrast to the logo in *Polo/Lauren* itself, the reproduction of the Senorita artwork sewn on to the relevant garment may not retain a separate existence, as probably, it could not survive removal and is not conceptually distinct from the garment. Accordingly, if the Full Court's observations in [58] represent the correct and comprehensive test, the Senorita artwork could be embodied within the meaning of s 74(1). As stated above, however, the comment at [58] does not comprehensively reflect the reasoning of the Full Court's judgment.

474. In so far as the definition of a corresponding design may require the product to acquire its shape or configuration during the making and not as an 'add on' (see Luck at 83), in this case, the evidence did not establish whether the shirring and smocking were accomplished simultaneously.

475. The evidence established that shirring and smocking are two distinct processes that can be carried out separately. Although Mr Brough [design expert for Fewstone] stated that the terms 'smocking' and 'shirring' are sometimes used interchangeably and sometimes designate distinct concepts, according to the predominant usage, as in this case, shirring refers to the gathering of the fabric, while, as Mr McLaurin [another expert witness with experience in industrial sewing machines] stated, smocking refers to a decorative pattern that is placed on top of the fabric, whether it is shirred or flat. It is clear that a garment can be shirred but not smocked, or alternatively, smocked but not shirred.

476. Further, fabric can be shirred and smocked simultaneously using one machine or, alternatively, may be first shirred after which the smocking is 'placed on' or 'on top of' the shirred fabric. Mr Brough's evidence indicated that there were various methods of shirring/smocking. In one method, the shirring or gathering is accomplished first, and a pattern is then placed on top of it, according to which the decorative embroidery is applied.

477. In this case, the evidence did not establish by precisely what process the Senorita garments [of Seafolly] and the Richelle garments [the Fewstone garments alleged to infringe the Senorita artwork] were shirred and smocked …

478. If it be relevant, in my opinion, the shirring of the garments created their three dimensional gathered structure while the smocking was a separate process by which a part only of the surface of the garments (albeit not flat) was embroidered (or decorated) with an artistic design. (This is so whether the processes in practice occurred concurrently (which cannot be confidently determined) and notwithstanding that the smocking was closely affixed.) Moreover, even if the shirring of the fabric and the sewing on of the smocking were achieved by simultaneous processes, it would not follow that the

garment, as the product, acquired features of shape or configuration of the Senorita artwork during its making.

479. The explanatory memorandum accompanying the Designs (Consequential Amendments) Bill 2003 (Cth) recognised that there were certain articles (such as texture designs, bas-relief, embroidery, weaves and knits) where a design would not be strictly applied to the article's surface, but instead would form part of the article. The addition of the words in s 74(2) was intended to clarify that, in relation to such 'intermediate' articles (whose design qualities, as the Full Court stated (at [55]), might arguably be seen as either two or three dimensional) the definition of a corresponding design could be satisfied and accordingly, the articles could obtain protection under the designs, rather than the copyright, regime.

480. Following the insertion of the words 'woven into', 'impressed on' or 'worked into' in s 74(2), it seems clear that features of shape or configuration of an artwork can be embodied in an article which is itself a piece of embroidery, a carpet, bas-relief or similar, by being woven or worked in. This was the qualification to the maintenance of the tradition position to which the Full Court referred at [48]. The amendment to s 74(2) did not, however, apply to the circumstances of *Polo/Lauren* itself as the relevant product was a garment rather than a carpet, bas-relief or embroidery (although the design was applied or attached by means of embroidery or 'weaving in').

481. In the light of the Full Court's emphasis that the position was otherwise unchanged, it would seem that it rejected Rares J's analysis not simply or principally because the logo remained conceptually distinct from the garment, but because the garment was not made in the shape or configuration of the artistic work, irrespective of whether it was three dimensional.

482. In the present case, the smocking has stronger claims to being conceptually indistinguishable from the garment than the logo in *Polo/Lauren*, as it may not exist independently. It is, however, similar to the logo in *Polo/Lauren* in that it occupies only a part of the garment, which is not itself made in the shape or configuration of the artwork.

483. Accordingly, I do not consider that the features of shape or configuration of the Senorita artwork are embodied in the garment in the sense endorsed by the Full Court in *Polo/Lauren*. Rather, they are included as a constituent element. The Senorita artwork is thus not a corresponding design within the definition in s 74(1).

484. While the failure to satisfy the requirement of embodiment makes it unnecessary to consider the further requirement of three dimensionality, in my opinion the latter was not satisfied either.

485. The Full Court in *Polo/Lauren* stated that it was unnecessary to resolve whether the logo was three dimensional or not, but at an earlier point it appeared to reject Ziliani's argument to that effect. The logo in *Polo/Lauren* was composed of hundreds of stitches and visibly, although slightly, protruded from the flat surface of the garment's fabric.

486. In the present case, the surface of the garment onto which the smocking is sewn is not flat because the fabric is shirred. Any protrusion of the smocking from the surface is minimal and probably significantly less than that in *Polo/Lauren* itself, which on a fair reading of its judgment, the Full Court nevertheless thought insufficient.

487. Accordingly, the Senorita artwork is not a corresponding design and City Beach has not established a defence to infringement under s 77 of the *Copyright Act*.

SECTION 77 AND THE EXCLUSION OF 'WORKS OF ARTISTIC CRAFTSMANSHIP'

It must be remembered that the s 77(2) defence only applies where copyright subsists in an artistic work *other than a building or a model of a building, or a work of artistic craftsmanship* (s 77(1)(a)). In other words, a party that fails to register a design corresponding to a work of artistic craftsmanship (such as the design of a piece of jewellery or wrought iron) under the *Designs Act* can still prevent third parties from copying the work of artistic craftsmanship under the *Copyright Act*. Note that for the purposes of s 77, 'building or a model of a building' does *not* include portable buildings, demountables, or pre-constructed swimming pools (s 77(5)), thus overcoming the effects of *Darwin Fibreglass Pty Ltd v Kruhse Enterprises Pty Ltd* (1998) 41 IPR 649 (discussed in Chapter 4). The thinking behind the s 77(1)(a) exclusion—which was introduced in 1989—and its impact on how the concept of 'work of artistic craftsmanship' should be interpreted, has been discussed by the High Court.

CASE STUDY: CURRENT LAW

Burge v Swarbrick

[2007] HCA 17; (2007) 232 CLR 336
High Court of Australia

Gleeson CJ, Gummow, Kirby, Heydon and Crennan JJ (some footnotes omitted): 42. …. The reason for this special provision was stated tersely in the Explanatory Memorandum [to the Copyright Amendment Bill 1988 (Cth)] to be that 'these articles are more appropriately protected under [the *Copyright Act*] whether industrially applied or not' … The effect of that special provision is that buildings or models of buildings or works of artistic craftsmanship retained copyright protection, but only if they were not registered as designs. This is not, speaking strictly, overlapping or dual protection.

43. Subsequently, in his reasons in *Coogi Australia Pty Ltd v Hysport International Pty Ltd* [(1998) 86 FCR 154 at 168], Drummond J observed of what was said in the Explanatory Memorandum:

> What may justify the special status conferred on works of artistic craftsmanship by ss 74–77 is recognition that the real artistic quality that is an essential feature of such works and the desirability of encouraging real artistic effort directed to industrial design is sufficient to warrant the greater protection and the accompanying stifling effect on manufacturing development that long copyright gives, in contrast to relatively short design-protection. …

…

50. In its form after the changes made by the 1989 Act, the *Copyright Act* employed the expression 'a work of artistic craftsmanship', both as a criterion to mark out the nature, duration and ownership of copyright in artistic works (Pt III, Div 1, ss 31–35) and to differentiate the protection given where artistic works were applied as industrial designs without a design registration (Pt III, Div 8, ss 74–77A). The statute in this amended form is to be considered with respect to subsequent events as a coherent

whole. The phrase 'a work of artistic craftsmanship' should be read consistently. There has been debate as to the extent to which a statute in its unamended form may be construed with respect to past events by reference to amendments ... But however that may be, the phrase 'a work of artistic craftsmanship' was introduced by the 1989 Act into the 'overlap' provisions of Pt III, Div 8 of the *Copyright Act* upon a particular legislative view of the purpose it would serve. That view, as Drummond J indicated in *Coogi*, was the encouragement of 'real artistic effort' in industrial design.

See also the extract from *Burge v Swarbrick* set out in Chapter 4 (p 128) as to why the 'Plug' (a hand-crafted, full-scale model of the hull and deck of a yacht) was not a 'work of artistic craftsmanship'.

MEANING OF 'APPLIED INDUSTRIALLY'

For s 77(2) to apply the corresponding design must have been 'applied industrially': s 77(1)(b). Regulation 17 of the *Copyright Regulations 1969* relevantly provides:

  (1) For the purposes of section 77 of the Act, a design is taken to be applied industrially if it is applied:
    (a) to more than 50 articles; or
    (b) to one or more articles (other than hand-made articles) manufactured in lengths or pieces.
  (2) For the purposes of paragraph (1) (a), any 2 or more articles:
    (a) that are of the same general character; and
    (b) that are intended for use together; and
    (c) to which the same design, or substantially the same design, is applied;
  are taken to constitute a single article.
  (3) For the purposes of this regulation, a design is taken to be applied to an article if:
    (a) the design is applied to the article by a process (whether a process of printing, embossing or otherwise); or
    (b) the design is reproduced on or in the article in the course of the production of the article.

The requirement of 'industrial application' is further discussion in the final extract below.

CASE STUDY: CURRENT LAW

Gold Peg International Pty Ltd v Kovan Engineering (Aust) Pty Ltd

[2005] FCA 1521; (2005) 225 ALR 57
Federal Court of Australia

[One issue in this case was whether Gold Peg's copyright in certain drawings of parts of cookers known as 'bottom elbows' and 'rotors' was infringed by Kovan's making of those parts and drawings of those parts. Gold Peg had applied the corresponding design of the rotor five times, and the corresponding design of the bottom elbow 26 times, and had sold at least one of the rotors and bottom elbows. The designs had not been registered.]

Crennan J:

APPLICABLE PRINCIPLES

210. While reg 17 stipulates that a design is taken to have been applied industrially where it is applied to 50 or more articles, this is not an exhaustive definition. In an interlocutory matter where only three prototypes of the plaintiff's helmets had been made, King J in *Safe Sport Australia Pty Ltd v Puma Australia Pty Ltd* (1985) 4 IPR 120 at 126 noted:

> ... there is nothing incongruous in leaving it to be decided as a question of fact whether there is industrial application of a design in a case where less than fifty applications of the design as taken place.

211. This approach is also apparent in *Kevlacat Pty Ltd v Trailcraft Marine Pty Ltd* (1987) 11 IPR 77 per French J ('*Kevlacat*') and in *Press-Form* [*Pty Ltd v Henderson's Ltd* (1993) 40 FCR 274] where Gummow J stated at 281:

> There may be designs applicable to articles of such a substantial or complex nature that whilst it is unlikely that more than 50 articles will ever be made by the owner of the design registration, in ordinary parlance the design will have been applied industrially by manufacture of something less than 50 articles. If the design is subsequently registered by the industrialist and the legislation and reg. 17 has the meaning contended for by the respondents, the design will not have been applied industrially before registration. This means that the design will not be treated as invalid by reason of the previous exploitation, albeit that exploitation maximised the use to which the owner of the design wished to put it.

Clearly the type of article being manufactured is a critical matter.

212. In *Press-Form*, Gummow J noted at 285 that 'industry' may be described as 'a trade or other form or branch of productive labour, and something as 'industrialised' when devoted or directed to such an activity'. He explained at 282:

> What reg 17 does do is to supply a fairly plain measure by which there may be drawn the line beyond which there is industrialisation of a design.

213. In *Shacklady v Atkins* (1994) 30 IPR 387 at 393, Davies J cited Gummow J in *Press-Form* and held:

> In my opinion, the regular application of the design in the construction of yachts is an application of an industrial nature being the repetitive application of a design in the manufacture or construction of goods for sale.

214. It was contended on behalf of Gold Peg that the definition of 'industrial application' denotes a 'system' and 'repetition', citing French J in *Kevlacat*. In exploring the concept of such a 'process' his Honour noted at 90:

> Whatever the outer limits of the word 'process' may be, it is, in my opinion, quite wide enough to encompass the systematic use of a mould to reproduce a series of like articles.

215. Counsel for the applicant has sought to draw a distinction between the 'process' described in *Kevlacat* and the 'process' used by the first respondent in manufacturing the rotors and the bottom elbows. In particular, it is the applicant's case that although each of the rotors and bottom elbows manufactured by the first respondent were based on the [applicant's] Drawings, each was tailored to the particular customer's requirements.

216. Counsel for the respondents also sought to enlarge the applicant's interpretation of his Honour French J's decision in *Kevlacat*. It was submitted on behalf of the respondents that although his Honour 'did conclude that an element of a 'system' seems central to both 'industry' and 'process' ... his Honour did not conclude that that 'system' must be mechanical, or must not involve care or skill, or any human involvement'.

217. Accordingly, it is the respondents' submission that the fact that some human involvement and care and skill was required to tailor each of the rotors or bottom elbows for each ... Cooker that does not mean that those parts were not created by a 'process' for the purposes of determining whether the drawings of those parts have been industrially applied.

218. As the abovementioned authorities, particularly *Safesport*, *Kevlacat* and *Press-Form* make clear, the statutory concept of 'industrial application' has always involved the notion that products, which incorporate the 'corresponding design' have been made pursuant to a manufacturing process for the systematic production of articles ... 'Systematic' suggests questions of degree are relevant ... Stripped to essentials, the applicant's argument is that 'industrial application' requires systematic manufacture and repetition and cannot be determined merely by considering whether an item is produced as an item of commerce. The respondents' argument, stripped to essentials, is that if an item is produced for commercial purposes, even production limited to 5 instances (or 26) which incorporates a corresponding design (whether the item is finalised by hand or not) the corresponding design has been 'industrially applied.'

219. Neither party mentioned the fact that all of the customers were subject to confidentiality agreements in respect of each of their custom-built products ... The insistence on systematic production or repetition or process, under the previous regime, was partly explicable by the fact that it was theoretically possible to produce a limited number of items in circumstances, which did not destroy a design's novelty prior to an application for registration. A copyright owner did not lose protection until a certain threshold had been crossed. It is conceivable, even if unlikely, that a copyright owner could reproduce a small number of items for commercial purposes (whether prototypes or not) but maintain confidentiality and secrecy to avoid such publication as would be sufficient to destroy novelty. This explains, at least in part, the reiterated requirement in the authorities that 'industrial application' must be 'systematic', a requirement which may seem obscure given the terms of s 77(1)(d), but it is a requirement which still has relevance because the regulations have not changed and also because the phrase 'applied industrially' used in s 77(1)(b) is a term about which considerable case law has been established.

FINDINGS
BOTTOM ELBOW

220. The evidence which was not contradicted was that a wooden/epoxy pattern was used [by the applicant] each time a bottom elbow was made. Then a wax die was prepared and destroyed once each

bottom elbow was manufactured. Then each bottom elbow needed to be hand milled for precision. Having regard to their simple nature, their manner of manufacture as described in the evidence, and their incorporation into all 26 of the DSI Cookers made ... for the applicant, I am satisfied that the production of the elbows in question involves systematic manufacture which therefore falls within the statutory concept of an industrial application of the relevant design. To the extent that s 77(2) applies the respondents can also invoke successfully the provisions of s 77A in respect of those drawings.

ROTOR

221. The evidence of manufacture of the five rotors in question which was uncontradicted showed the rotors were a more complex component than the bottom elbows. At least 12 different versions of rotors were used in the abovementioned 26 custom-built cookers. While some parts of the rotor could be made in advance the final construction of the rotor as depicted in the drawings was a painstaking and skilful task. This was not an industrial manufacturing process involving system and repetition. Having regard to the complex nature of the rotors and their manner of manufacture as described in the evidence I am not satisfied, on the civil standard of proof, that the production of the rotors in question, involved systematic manufacture and therefore I find their production falls outside the statutory concept of an industrial application of a corresponding design. Section 77A will not avail the respondents in respect of these drawings.

— 9 —

PATENT LAW: JUSTIFICATION, HISTORY AND CONTEXT

INTRODUCTION

Patents are generally described as the oldest and strongest form of IP protection. They were first given statutory recognition in England in the *Statute of Monopolies 1623* (21 Jac 1, c 3). The patent system in Australia is governed by the *Patents Act 1990* (Cth) and administered by IP Australia through its Patent Office.

Patents provide temporary monopoly rights. Once a patent has been granted, the owner of the patent (the patentee) is entitled to exclude all others from making, using, selling or otherwise dealing with the invention as claimed for a limited period (usually 20 years), subject to certain limitations. In s 13 of the *Patents Act* this is referred to as giving the patentee the right to 'exploit' the invention (see also the definition of 'exploit' in the dictionary in Sch 1 of the Act). Once the patent period has expired, the invention becomes available for public use without restriction by the patentee.

Inventions are protected by patents in Australia only if they are granted by the Patent Office at IP Australia, and a patent must be renewed on an annual basis. A patent application will generally be drafted by the inventor or by a skilled draftsperson known as a patent attorney. Lawyers are not permitted to draft patent applications. The patent application must be filed with the Patent Office and examined to confirm that it fulfils all of the essential requirements prescribed in the *Patents Act*. The first threshold that must be overcome is that there must be appropriate subject matter for patenting (discussed in Chapter 10). Modern technologies—particularly biotechnology and information technology—are pushing against the traditional boundaries of patentable subject matter. If there is patentable subject matter, two further sets of requirements must be satisfied: the patentability requirements, which serve the purpose of ensuring that patents are only granted for true inventions; and the disclosure and claiming requirements, which serve the purpose of informing the public about the nature of the invention and delimiting the boundaries of the patent claim. The validity of a patent can be challenged throughout its entire life. The criteria for satisfying the patentability requirements are considered in Chapter 11 and the disclosure and claiming requirements are discussed in Chapter 12. Chapter 13 reviews the law relating to patent ownership and patent rights, and the legal limitations on those rights.

This chapter provides background information on the justification for the patent system and its history, together with a brief account of the framework of the modern patent system in Australia. It concludes with a short discussion of other patent-like IP rights.

JUSTIFICATION FOR THE PATENT SYSTEM

The present patent system is justified on the basis that the grant of patents encourages innovation, which is beneficial to the Australian economy. For example, a report commissioned by the Senate Standing Committee on Science and the Environment, *Industrial Research and Development in Australia* (1979), stated at p 129:

> the primary function of patent legislation should be to serve as an instrument of national economic policy aimed at the stimulation of Indigenous industrial innovation not as a means for giving effect to the 'natural right' of the inventor.

This has not always been accepted as the only rationale for the existence of the patent system. For example, Fritz Machlup and Edith Penrose, in 'The Patent Controversy in the 19th Century' (1950) 10 *Journal of Economic History* 1 at 10 identified four distinct theses as providing possible justifications for the nineteenth-century patent system, which can be conveniently summarised as:

- the natural law thesis: that people have a natural right to property in their own ideas;
- the reward-by-monopoly thesis: that there should be some reward to the inventor for his or her efforts in producing a useful invention, and the greater the usefulness, the greater should be the reward;
- the monopoly-profit-incentive thesis: that, assuming that innovation and economic growth are desirable, there should be some incentive to encourage inventive activity, which further assumes that inventive activity is causally linked to economic growth; and
- the exchange-for-secrets thesis: that the patent is a bargain between the inventor, who gains a temporary monopoly, and the public, who gain by disclosure of the invention.

There are also a large number of more recent commentaries that identify and analyse a range of economic rationales for current patent systems.[1] The monopoly-profit-incentive thesis is widely accepted as the primary justification for the modern patent system. This thesis makes two important assumptions: that technological innovation leads to greater economic welfare, and that patenting encourages innovation. Both of these are contestable.

In 1984 a report was published by the Australian Industrial Property Advisory Committee (IPAC), *Patents, Innovation and Competition in Australia* (1984), the aim of which was to suggest ways in which the patent system might better enhance Australia's long-term economic development through innovation. The outcome of this report was the *Patents Act 1990* (Cth). The report recognised that the patent system is most clearly justified when social benefits outweigh social costs. Social benefits include:

- incentives for innovation; and
- disclosure of inventions.

Social costs include:

- direct costs of running the patent system; and
- indirect costs to society of the grant of monopoly rights.

---

1   See particularly R Mazzolini and R Nelson, 'Economic Theories and the Benefits and Costs of Patents' (1998) 32 *Journal of Economic Issues* 1031.

As part of its inquiry, IPAC commissioned an empirical study of the costs and benefits of the patent system in Australia, which was reported in T Mandeville et al, *Economic Effects of the Australian Patent System* (1982). The Mandeville Report found that there was no convincing evidence that the patent system does in fact encourage innovation and that there was no clear benefit to the public from disclosure of inventions. The study estimated that the direct costs of administering the system were approximately $17 million in 1979–80. Social costs were said to be too difficult to quantify with any accuracy, although probably the greatest cost was identified as restrictive terms and conditions in licensing agreements.

The Mandeville Report suggests that the benefit-to-cost ratio in Australia is negative, or at the very best in balance. Despite this, there was not a hint in the subsequent IPAC Report that the patent system should be abolished. The words of Fritz Machlup in *An Economic Review of the Patent System* (1958)[2] at p 80 are salutary:

> If we did not have a patent system, it would be irresponsible, on the basis of our present knowledge of its economic consequences, to recommend instituting one. But since we have had a patent system for a long time, it would be irresponsible, on the basis of our present knowledge, to recommend abolishing it.

In terms of international commercial and political relations, the costs to Australia of abolition of the patent system would be significant. The primary recommendation of the IPAC Report was that Australia should continue to operate a patent system but that there was no justification for increasing its reach. The role of patent law in this area is to provide a balance: patentees and their assignees and licensees need sufficient protection so that innovation is encouraged, but if there is too much protection other innovation could be stifled. The public benefit may be distorted if patentees are overly rewarded with too great a monopoly for their innovation, or if there is insufficient disclosure of the invention leading to uncertainty as to its true nature and its best method of performance. Both could discourage or restrict innovation by others. Problems may also arise if patentees are inadequately rewarded for their innovation. This can happen if the patent monopoly is unduly restrictive, or if the validity of the patent is uncertain. In such situations, patentees might be discouraged from making optimal use of a patent monopoly, and both patentees and others may be discouraged from further innovation. Hence, patent law should set proper and certain boundaries on what is and is not patentable, and ensure that patents are only granted for inventions that meet the patentability and disclosure and claiming requirements. These considerations need to be borne in mind when considering the operation of patent law, as discussed in the next four chapters.

HISTORY OF THE PATENT SYSTEM
OF KINGS AND KNAVES: PLAYING CARDS AND OTHER MONOPOLIES

Various accounts exist of the early history of the patent grant and its incorporation into the common law system. In this section, a brief summary will be provided of early patent history, with reference to some of the leading commentaries, to provide the context to our analysis of current patent law in the following chapters.

---

2   Study No. 15, Subcommitttee on Patents, Trademarks, and Copyrights, Committee on the Judiciary, 85th Cong., 2d Sess, US Senate.

In the sixteenth century, early feudal practice was incorporated into the common law, which was subsequently incorporated into legislation in the seventeenth century. Current Australian legislation still refers to that seventeenth-century legislation in s 18(1) of the *Patents Act*, para (a) of which requires that a patentable invention must be a 'manner of manufacture within the meaning of section 6 of the Statute of Monopolies'. This requirement is discussed in detail in Chapter 10.

JUSTINE PILA, 'THE COMMON LAW INVENTION IN ITS ORIGINAL FORM'

[2001] *Intellectual Property Quarterly* 209 at 211–213 (footnotes omitted)

[In this article Justine Pila traces the development of patentability at common law up to the enactment of the *Statute of Monopolies 1623*. She argues that the objective underlying the formulation of these common law principles was the stimulation of local economy in order to encourage the creation of new industries and the greater exploitation of existing native resources. As noted above, this remains the primary objective of the patent system.]

The practice of granting patents in England originated with the feudal custom of conferring privileges on the early merchant and craft guilds in order to reserve to them exclusive control over the manufacture of goods and the provision of services. The guilds were essentially group monopolies controlled by the Crown, and dominated all aspects of domestic English trade throughout the twelfth and thirteenth centuries.

By the fourteenth century, however, England's economy was lagging behind that of Europe and its industry fast outgrowing the jurisdiction and capacity of the guilds. There was thus increasing recognition of the need for some form of special stimulus to encourage the creation of new native industries and the greater exploitation of existing native resources. There were two ways this could be done: first, through the importation of knowledge of successful industries from abroad; and secondly, through local innovation. Initially importation was the favored mode, presumably on the ground that an industry that had succeeded abroad was likely to succeed locally, and in 1326 Edward II formulated a policy of encouraging skilled foreign workmen to settle and introduce their trades within England. Under that policy, 'letters of protection' were offered to such workmen promising exemption from the strict guild rules and other forms of royal patronage, in exchange for an undertaking to work their trades within the realm and to teach their crafts to local apprentices. The first grant of letters of protection under this policy was made in 1331 to wool weaver John Kempe of Flanders.

The early letters of protection offered by Edward II and his successors generally used expedients other than monopolies to encourage the introduction of new industries into England. The grant of monopolies to encourage industry did, however, become usual at around the same time in the city-states of Italy. Thus in 1421 the Italian engineer and architect Filippo Brunelleschi was granted the exclusive right for three years to manufacture and use a device of his own conception for transporting heavy loads on the Arno and other rivers. The first general patent statute was enacted in Venice in 1474.

Knowledge of the Italian custom spread throughout England during the sixteenth century … That custom received a formal basis in 1561 when Elizabeth I, three years after ascending to the throne, committed to a new policy of granting monopolies in respect of new trades and devices in the hope of finally making the realm industrially and economically self-sufficient.

While originally designed to encourage the setting up of new industries, it appears that the monopoly system began to be abused from the late sixteenth century onwards, particularly during the reign of Queen Elizabeth I. Many monopolies were granted even though the subject matter already existed at the time of grant, such as monopolies for the production and sale of vinegar and starch. At the same time, the Queen rejected a large number of petitions for real inventions. There are various detailed accounts of the early history of patent development and abuse.[3]

Abuse of the monopoly system reached its zenith with the grant of a monopoly for importing, manufacturing and selling playing cards. Notwithstanding the monopoly grant, many traders continued to engage in card manufacturing and selling activity. In 1602, Edward Darcy, groomsman to Queen Elizabeth and the owner of the patent at that time, brought an infringement action against a London trader, Thomas Allen. The case of *Darcy v Allen* became known as the *Case of Monopolies*. Although there was no formal judicial opinion in the case, reports by Edward Coke ((1603) 11 Co Rep 84b; 77 ER 1260) and others provide a detailed account of the submissions made by the parties and the decision that the patent was void for restraint of trade. Documentation associated with the *Case of Monopolies* is helpfully compiled and summarised in J Corre, 'The Argument, Decision and Reports of *Darcy v Allen*' (1996) 45 *Emory Law Journal* 1261.

In 1603 James I acceded to the English throne. Notwithstanding the outcome in *Darcy v Allen*, he continued to grant 'odious' monopolies. By 1621, public anger and complaints about monopolies were widespread, and the House of Commons decided to introduce a Bill giving a statutory power to declare monopolies illegal. The *Statute of Monopolies 1623* declared all monopolies void, aside from the exception contained in s 6, which stated:

> Provided also that any declaration before mentioned shall not extend to any letters patent and grants of privilege for the term of fourteen years or under, thereafter to be made, of the sole working or making of any manner of new manufactures within this Realm, to the true and first inventor and inventors of such manufactures which others at the time of making such letters patent and grants shall not use so as also they be not contrary to the law or mischievous to the state, by raising prices of commodities at home, or hurt of trade, or generally inconvenient.

THE UNHAPPY LOT OF THE PATENTEE

The enactment of the *Statute of Monopolies* set the scene for the development of the modern patent system in common law countries. However, many of the criticisms raised in relation to the modern system were already emerging in the seventeenth and eighteenth centuries. Despite the fact that the grant of a patent was a simple process of registration at the time, with no examination of its validity, formalities were complex and litigation was convoluted, requiring recourse both to the common law courts and equity courts. A detailed account of these difficulties can be found in C MacLeod's *Inventing the Industrial Revolution: The English Patent System 1660–1800*.[4] The inefficiencies of the system led Charles Dickens and others to rail against it. Dickens' fictional short story, 'A Poor Man's Tale of a Patent', exemplifies some of these problems.

---

3   See particularly E Hulme, 'The History of the Patent System Under the Prerogative and at Common Law' (1896) 12 *Law Quarterly Review* 141, continued at (1900) 16 *Law Quarterly Review* 44.

4   Cambridge University Press, Cambridge, 1988, chs 3 and 4.

CHARLES DICKENS, 'A POOR MAN'S TALE OF A PATENT'

(1850) *Household Words* II(70), extracted in D Vaver, ed, *Intellectual Property Rights: Critical Concepts in Law*, Routledge, London, 2006, p 37

I have been twenty year, off and on, completing an Invention and perfecting it. I perfected of it, last Christmas Eve at ten o'clock at night. Me and my wife stood and let some tears fall over the Model, when it was done and I brought her in to take a look at it.

...

William Butcher and me had a long talk, Christmas Day, respecting of the Model. William is very sensible. But sometimes cranky. William said, 'What will you do with it, John?' I said, 'Patent it.' William said, 'How patent it, John?' I said, 'By taking out a Patent.' William then delivered that the law of Patent was a cruel wrong. William said, 'John, if you make your invention public, before you get a Patent, any one may rob you of the fruits of your hard work. You are put in a cleft stick, John. Either you must drive a bargain very much against yourself, by getting a party to come forward beforehand with the great expenses of the Patent; or, you must be put about, from post to pillar, among so many parties, trying to make a better bargain for yourself, and showing your invention, that your invention will be took from you over your head.' I said, 'William Butcher, are you cranky? You are sometimes cranky.' William said, 'No, John, I tell you the truth;' which he then delivered more at length. I said to W. B. I would Patent the invention myself.

...

Thomas Joy delivered (from a book he had) that the first step to be took, in Patenting the invention, was to prepare a petition unto Queen Victoria. William Butcher had delivered similar, and drawn it up. Note. William is a ready writer. A declaration before a Master in Chancery was to be added to it. That, we likewise drew up. After a deal of trouble I found out a Master, in Southampton Buildings, Chancery Lane, nigh Temple Bar, where I made the declaration, and paid eighteen-pence. I was told to take the declaration and petition to the Home Office, in Whitehall, where I left it to be signed by the Home Secretary (after I had found the office out), and where I paid two pound, two, and sixpence. In six days he signed it, and I was told to take it to the Attorney-General's chambers, and leave it there for a report. I did so, and paid four pound, four. Note. Nobody all through, ever thankful for their money, but all uncivil.

My lodging at Thomas Joy's was now hired for another week, whereof five days were gone. The Attorney-General made what they called a Report-of-course (my invention being, as William Butcher had delivered before starting, unopposed), and I was sent back with it to the Home Office. They made a Copy of it, which was called a Warrant. For this warrant, I paid seven pound, thirteen, and six. It was sent to the Queen, to sign. The Queen sent it back, signed. The Home Secretary signed it again. The gentleman throwed it at me when I called, and said, 'Now take it to the Patent Office in Lincoln's Inn.' I was then in my third week at Thomas Joy's living very sparing, on account of fees. I found myself losing heart.

At the Patent Office in Lincoln's Inn, they made 'a draft of the Queen's bill,' of my invention, and a 'docket of the bill.' I paid five pound, ten, and six, for this. They 'engrossed two copies of the bill; one for the Signet Office, and one for the Privy-Seal Office.' I paid one pound, seven, and six, for this. Stamp duty over and above, three pound. The Engrossing Clerk of the same office engrossed the Queen's bill for signature. I paid him one pound, one. Stamp-duty, again, one pound, ten. I was next to take the Queen's bill to the Attorney-General again, and get it signed again. I took it, and paid five pound more. I fetched it away, and took it to the Home Secretary again. He sent it to the Queen again. She signed it again. I paid seven pound, thirteen, and six, more, for this. I had been over a month at Thomas Joy's. I was quite wore out, patience and pocket.

Thomas Joy delivered all this, as it went on, to William Butcher. William Butcher delivered it again to three Birmingham Parlours, from which it got to all the other Parlours, and was took, as I have been told since, right through all the shops in the North of England. Note. William Butcher delivered, at his Parlour, in a speech, that it was a Patent way of making Chartists.

But I hadn't nigh done yet. The Queen's bill was to be took to the Signet Office in Somerset House, Strand—where the stamp shop is. The Clerk of the Signet made 'a Signet bill for the Lord Keeper of the Privy Seal.' I paid him four pound, seven. The Clerk of the Lord Keeper of the Privy Seal made 'a Privy-Seal bill for the Lord Chancellor.' I paid him, four pound, two. The Privy-Seal bill was handed over to the Clerk of the Patents, who engrossed the aforesaid. I paid him five pound, seventeen, and eight; at the same time, I paid Stamp-duty for the Patent, in one lump, thirty pound. I next paid for 'boxes for the Patent,' nine and sixpence. Note. Thomas Joy would have made the same at a profit for eighteen-pence. I next paid 'fees to the Deputy, the Lord Chancellor's Purse-bearer,' two pound, two. I next paid 'fees to the Clerk of the Hanapar,' seven pound, thirteen. I next paid 'fees to the Deputy Clerk of the Hanaper,' ten shillings. I next paid, to the Lord Chancellor again, one pound, eleven, and six. Last of all, I paid 'fees to the Deputy Sealer, and Deputy Chaff-wax,' ten shillings and sixpence. I had lodged at Thomas Joy's over six weeks, and the unopposed Patent for my invention, for England only, had cost me ninety-six pound, seven, and eightpence. If I had taken it out for the United Kingdom, it would have cost me more than three hundred pound.

. . .

Thereby I say nothing of my being tired of my life, while I was Patenting my invention. But I put this: Is it reasonable to make a man feel as if, in inventing an ingenious improvement meant to do good, he had done something wrong? How else can a man feel, when he is met by such difficulties at every turn? All inventors taking out a Patent MUST feel so. And look at the expense. How hard on me, and how hard on the country if there's any merit in me (and my invention is took up now, I am thankful to say, and doing well), to put me to all that expense before I can move a finger! Make the addition yourself, and it'll come to ninety-six pound, seven, and eightpence. No more, and no less . . .

THE SCOURGES OF MODERN PATENT LAW: EPIDEMICS, GOLD RUSHES, THICKETS AND TROLLS

In the modern era of patenting, patentees continue to rail about the cost of patenting and delays in examination and grant. But 'odious' monopolies also continue to dominate the patent landscape.

Concerns about enforcement of patent rights for pharmaceuticals feature prominently in international human rights discourse because of the severe health problems, accentuated by lack of access to available treatments, in developing and least-developed countries. Even in the international trade arena, these problems have not been ignored. At the end of the twentieth century, debate about access to medicines for the treatment of AIDS and other global epidemics reached crisis point, and the WTO was forced to confront this issue. Members of the WTO entered into discussions at a Ministerial Conference in Doha on 9–14 November 2001, as a result of which the Doha Declaration on the TRIPS Agreement and Public Health (the 'Doha Declaration') was promulgated (as noted in Chapter 1, the *Agreement on Trade-related Aspects of Intellectual Property Rights* ('the TRIPS Agreement') (1994) is the most influential international instrument on IP). Paragraphs 1 and 3 of the Doha Declaration succinctly state the problem:

1   We recognize the gravity of the public health problems afflicting many developing and least-developed countries, especially those resulting from HIV/AIDS, tuberculosis, malaria and other epidemics.

...

3   We recognize that intellectual property protection is important for the development of new medicines. We also recognize the concerns about its effects on prices.

Quite how well the TRIPS Agreement and the Doha Declaration resolve these issues is a matter of ongoing controversy. This matter is discussed further in Chapter 13.

Patenting of genetic inventions is also a matter of heated debate and policy discussion. Patent applications claiming gene sequences and other genetic technologies continue to be filed in ever-increasing numbers, creating a veritable 'gold rush' of patent claims. A 2005 study by Kyle Jensen and Fiona Murray suggested that nearly 20 per cent of all human genes have been claimed in patents granted in the USA.[5] Patenting of software and business methods raises similar concerns. New concepts such as 'patent thickets' and 'patent trolls' have entered the patent language (see the extract below).

DONALD CHISUM, 'REFORMING PATENT LAW REFORM'

(2005) 4 *John Marshall Review of Intellectual Property Law* 336 at 339–340 (footnotes omitted)

In assessing [the need for patent law reform] I start with a very general description of what is alleged to be 'wrong' with the patent system. If it ain't broke don't fix it. How is the patent system deemed to be broken by proponents of reform?

A first and perhaps primary complaint is that there is a continuing surge in the volume of patent applications and patents that is overwhelming the system. The statistics are indeed scary. The United States Patent and Trademark Office (USPTO) has hundreds of thousands of pending, not yet examined applications. In addition to the volume, the applications deal with a wide range of subject matter, ranging from the cutting edge in technological complexity—for example, nanotechnology—to the mundane. In the latter category are a regular flow of what may be regarded as 'silly' patents which are a bit embarrassing to those who regard the patent system as indeed serious and important. The most recent one getting publicity is US Pat No 6,004,596. Claim 1 describes a 'sealed and crustless sandwich' comprising, inter alia, a certain 'crimped edge' between 'a first bread layer' and a 'second

---

5   K Jensen and F Murray, 'Intellectual Property Landscape of the Human Genome' (2005) 310 *Science* 239.

bread layer' and 'at least one filling of an edible food.' Dependent claims 4, 5 and 6 limit the claim to three fillings. Dependent claim 7 limits the claim to the first and third fillings of 'peanut butter' and a second filling 'of a jelly'. So, a patent claiming a peanut butter and jelly sandwich—of, presumably, an improved sort. How could the USPTO issue such a thing—with so much 'prior art' out there.

It is charged that the USPTO does not—and perhaps cannot—completely examine all these applications. If it cannot handle a peanut butter sandwich, what can we expect with nanotechnology, etc. The result, it is charged, is that a lot of 'weak' patents issue—patents that can be attacked only with difficulty and great expense in the United States district courts.

Related to this concern about general volume and quality is the alleged existence of 'patent thickets'. A thicket exists when there are numerous patents held by different entities, each of which may be technologically and legally distinct, but all of which overlap to cover actual commercial products. So, a company desiring legitimately to launch a product cannot do so without getting multiple licenses, which may be difficult because of unreasonable independent demands—or because it is too difficult to determine which of the patent 'thorns' in the thicket endanger the product.

And then there are the patent 'trolls'. I looked up the traditional, dictionary meaning of 'troll' but did not find it helpful. Roughly, those expressing concern about 'trolls' seem to mean individuals, small companies, or investment groups who obtain, by issue or by purchase, patents but who do not actually produce anything under the patent or even enter into prospective, cooperative licensing arrangements. Instead, a troll hides under bridges, metaphorically speaking, waiting for companies to produce and market products, that is, to approach and cross the bridge. The ugly, evil troll then leaps up and demands a huge toll, that is, a licensing fee settling actual or threatened patent litigation, litigation that could result in an injunction halting the product line. ... A troll is particularly irritating to a company that not only has a successful product but also a strong patent portfolio covering its product. Faced with a competitor, the company could assert its own patent portfolio and reach a reasonable cross-licensing arrangement. But a troll does not need a license and therefore is uninterested in cross-licensing.

Screeds have been written about the need for reform of the modern patent system. In Australia alone there have been at least 10 separate law reform inquiries in the past 15 years. The Advisory Council on Intellectual Property (ACIP) is regularly given references by the federal government to inquire into the need for law reform. Relevant ACIP inquiries include:

- *Report on the Review of Enforcement of Industrial Property Rights* (1999);
- *Report on Consideration of a Position on the Patenting of Business Methods* (2003);
- *Report on Consideration of Excluding Plant and Animal Material from the Innovation Patent* (2004);
- *Report on Consideration of Crown Use Provisions for Patents and Designs* (2005);
- *Report on the Review of Patents and Experimental Use* (2005);
- *Report on Review of Post-grant Enforcement Strategies* (2010);
- *Report on Review of Patentable Subject Matter* (2011); and
- *Report on Review of the Innovation Patent System* (2014).

Other significant inquiries this century include:

- Intellectual Property and Competition Review Committee, *Review of Intellectual Property Legislation under the Competition Principles Agreement* (2000);
- Australian Law Reform Commission, Report No 99, *Genes and Ingenuity: Gene Patenting and Human Health* (2004);
- Senate Community Affairs Committee, *Report on Gene Patents* (2010);
- Senate Legal and Constitutional Affairs Legislation Committee, *Report on the Patent Amendment (Human Genes and Biological Materials) Bill 2010* (2011); and
- Productivity Commission, *Compulsory Licensing of Patents* (2013).

Until recently the reports from these inquiries have tended to sit on bookshelves gathering dust. However, there have been some significant reforms of patent law—both in the USA and in Australia—in the past few years. In the USA, the *Leahy-Smith America Invents Act 2011* included a range of reforms, the most notable of which was a change to the rule relating to priority between competing patent applications from 'first to invent' to 'first to file'. This brings the US rule in line with those of most other jurisdictions, including Australia. There is ongoing discussion in the USA about the need for further patent law reform specifically to deal with the 'troll problem'.

Substantial changes were made to Australian patent law in 2012 as a result of the *Intellectual Property Laws Amendment (Raising the Bar) Act 2012* (Cth) (the '*Raising the Bar Act*'), affecting patentability criteria (Chapter 11), disclosure and claiming requirements (Chapter 12) and legal limitations on patent rights (Chapter 13). More recently, the Australian parliament passed the *Intellectual Property Laws Amendment Act 2015* (Cth), which will create a new regime to promote access to medicines in developing countries (see Chapter 13).

CONTEXT: THE FRAMEWORK OF THE AUSTRALIAN PATENT SYSTEM

Before commencing our detailed analysis of patent law in the next four chapters, it is necessary to be aware of some key basics.

SOURCES OF PATENT LAW

As noted earlier in this chapter, patent law is governed by the *Patents Act*. In 1903 the first *Patents Act* entered into force in Australia and was not superseded until 1952. Both Acts were generally based on existing UK legislation at the time. The *Patents Act 1952* was replaced by the current Act, which gave effect to recommendations of the 1984 IPAC Report,[6] mentioned earlier in this chapter. As a result, the legislation was extensively redrafted and rearranged using 'plain English', although the core concepts remained unchanged. In fact, the language used is far from plain, as will be seen as we progress.

The *Patents Act 1990* and the case law interpreting and applying it are the main sources of patent law that are relevant for present purposes. However, it is also necessary to be familiar with the language of certain key provisions of the 1952 Act. The reason for this is that although some of

---

6   *Patents, Innovation and Competition in Australia.*

the most authoritative judicial decisions were made under that Act, a number of significant changes were made to the patentability requirements in the new Act, and even the slightest of difference in wording of the legislative provisions must be taken into account when applying past precedents.

There is also a large body of regulations that govern patents, particularly the *Patents Regulations 1991* (Cth). These regulations deal mainly with prescribed times, prescribed fees and other prescribed matters. Practice notes are put out by the Patent Office whenever there is a change or clarification in the law by the courts. The Patent Office also has a *Manual of Practice and Procedures* to guide its patent examiners. This is available online on the IP Australia website.

There have been several amendments to the *Patents Act* since it entered into force in 1991. In particular, there were major amendments in 2000 pursuant to the *Patents Amendment (Innovation Patents) Act 2000* (Cth) (introducing an innovation patent system) and in 2001 pursuant to the *Patents Amendment Act 2001* (Cth) (amending the novelty and inventive step requirements). It is important to be aware of these and other amendments, particularly the most recent amendments introduced through the *Raising the Bar Act* mentioned above. Case law has to be read in the context of the legislation that was operational at the time the cause of action arose. Where the validity of a patent is in issue, the relevant time is the 'priority date' of the patent, discussed further below under 'The Australian patent system: The application process'.

Although the patent systems of Australia, the UK, the USA and other common law countries all had common origins, a period of divergence has led to considerable variation in the legislative requirements for patenting between countries and in the interpretation of those requirements by the courts. In the UK, for example, reference to the *Statute of Monopolies* was removed from the *Patents Act 1977* (UK) in order to achieve harmonisation with the *European Patent Convention* (1973). Despite ongoing calls for greater harmonisation globally, the legislative provisions and their interpretation continue to differ. Any such differences have to be taken into account in considering case law from jurisdictions outside Australia.

A number of international treaties and conventions have been agreed upon to facilitate the process of lodgment of patent applications in multiple countries and to attempt to create greater harmonisation in patent law between countries.

- *Paris Convention for the Protection of Industrial Property* (1883), revised in Stockholm (1967)— The main aims of the Paris Convention are to ensure first the equal treatment of foreign and national applications for patents, and second that the first applicant in one country has priority over other applicants for the same invention in different countries.
- *Patent Cooperation Treaty* (PCT) (1970)—The PCT gives a single international application for a patent the same effect as if applications had been filed separately in each of the countries in which patent protection is requested. The application is then processed separately in each country.
- *Budapest Treaty on the International Recognition of the Deposit of Microorganisms for the Purpose of Patent Procedure* (1977)—The Budapest Treaty requires that microorganisms are deposited in prescribed depositary institutions on or before the date of filing of the patent application. Section 6 of the *Patents Act* sets out the Australian deposit requirements. Provided these are complied with, the invention will be taken to comply with other requirements in the legislation to describe fully the invention.

- TRIPS Agreement (1994)—The TRIPS Agreement prescribes certain minimum requirements that must be included in patent legislation in all countries that are members of the WTO. The core requirement is found in Art 27(1):

  > patents shall be available for any inventions, whether products or processes, in all fields of technology, provided that they are new, involve an inventive step [synonymous with the term 'non-obvious'] and are capable of industrial application [synonymous with the term 'useful'] ...

  Australian patent obligations under the TRIPS Agreement were implemented through the *Patents (World Trade Organization Amendments) Act 1994* (Cth). The main change was to extend the life of patents from 16 years to 20 years.

- *Australia–US Free Trade Agreement* (AUSFTA) (2004)—The amendments to the *Patents Act* resulting from the entry into force of AUSFTA were minor in nature: see Sch 8 of the *US Free Trade Agreement Implementation Act 2004* (Cth). The AUSFTA provisions relating to patent law largely reflected Australian law at the time of the Agreement. Despite this, the Agreement does have important consequences for domestic patent law in that it means that amendments to the law cannot conflict with those provisions. Although Australia has since entered into a number of other bilateral free trade agreements, it is AUSFTA that has had the most profound effect on domestic IP law.

  As noted in Chapters 1 and 2 of this book, Australia is also a party to the *Trans-Pacific Partnership Agreement* (TPP) negotiations. The aim of the TPP is to facilitate free trade in the Asia–Pacific region. An overview of TPP negotiations is provided on the website of the Department of Foreign Affairs and Trade at www.dfat.gov.au/fta/tpp. IP is one of the issues listed as being covered by the TPP.

THE AUSTRALIAN PATENT SYSTEM: THE APPLICATION PROCESS

The *Patents Act* and associated regulations establish the parameters within which the Australian patent system functions. Any person can apply for either a standard or an innovation patent for a patentable invention. Section 67 provides that the term of a standard patent is 20 years, which is not normally extendable.

However, a specific provision allows for an extension of the term for a pharmaceutical patent because of the long time it takes for new pharmaceuticals to gain regulatory approval. Following enactment of the *Intellectual Property Laws Amendment Act 1998* (Cth) the term for pharmaceutical patents can be extended for up to a further five years subject to certain conditions, as provided in ss 70–79A of the *Patents Act*. A major review of pharmaceutical patents was undertaken in 2013, which included an analysis of the history, purpose, cost and scope of the extension of term provisions.[7]

The innovation patent was introduced in 2000. Prior to this, a petty patent system was available to protect small-scale innovations with short commercial life (some of the case law discussed in the following chapters relates to petty patents). Petty patents were granted for 12 months, extendable for another six years. Innovation patents are available for up to eight years. The aim of the innovation patent is to meet the needs of small and medium Australian businesses, which tend to focus on

---

7   A Harris, N Gruen and D Nicol (Review Panel), *Pharmaceutical Patents Review Final Report* (2013).

minor and incremental innovations. The patenting requirements for innovation patent applications are less onerous than for standard patents, with a lower inventive threshold. Innovation patents are relatively inexpensive, quick and easy to obtain. Essentially all that is required for registration is compliance with formalities. The complex and expensive examination process does not need to be undertaken unless there is a need to enforce the patent or unless its validity is challenged.

The chapters that follow focus primarily on the requirements for a standard patent. Flow charts available from IP Australia's website set out the typical steps involved in obtaining a standard patent.

A person may make either a provisional application or a complete application, as provided in s 29. Provisional applications need only set out the invention in broad terms. Section 38 provides that the applicant can then make one or more complete applications associated with the provisional application at any time within the prescribed period of 12 months. Provisional applications are useful because they allow the inventor to file an application before all the work on the invention has been done, but also to secure as the priority date of the invention the date on which the provisional application is lodged. This is very important strategically. Priority dates are of vital importance to patentees, as these are the dates on which the newness and inventiveness of the invention are assessed, based on a comparison with the 'prior art'. The prior art includes all prior public disclosures, whether oral, written or by use. Prior art is discussed more fully in Chapter 11.

Applications for patents made under the Paris Convention and the PCT can also affect the priority date of Australian patents (ss 29A, 29B). A person who has filed an application in another country that is a party to the Paris Convention may also seek protection in Australia by way of a Convention application (s 29B). The Convention application must be lodged within 12 months of the foreign application. The priority date for the Australian patent is then taken to be the date of the foreign application. A PCT application is somewhat different from a Convention application, in that only one application is filed. The priority date is the date on which that application is filed. The applicant nominates the countries in which the application is to be considered. Generally applicants will nominate a number of countries in which patents are to be filed. Australian applicants will, as a matter of course, tend to nominate the largest markets for Australian products: the USA, European countries and Japan, as well as other countries. The difficulty with this is that filing fees have to be paid in each country. The PCT system allows for deferral of filing fees for 18 months after the initial processing fee has been paid. Nevertheless, costs are high. It is generally estimated that the cost of a patent registered in the USA, Germany and Japan, including filing and renewal fees and patent attorney fees, is more than $100 000 over the life of a patent. In contrast, costs will be in the tens of thousands if the patent is restricted to Australia.[8] The highest renewal fees are in the last five years of the patent's 20-year life. It is also necessary to budget for infringement proceedings and challenges to the validity of the patent.

The first stage after application is publication, which occurs at 18 months. The next stage is examination. This has to be requested by the applicant. The Patent Office does not automatically examine every patent application. In fact, many applications lapse before they are examined.

---

8   IP Australia provides a summary of patent fees at www.ipaustralia.gov.au/get-the-right-ip/patents/time-and-costs/fees.

The examination requirements are provided in s 45 of the *Patents Act* (as amended by the *Raising the Bar Act*):

(1) Subject to subsection (1A), if an applicant asks for an examination of a patent request and complete specification relating to an application for a standard patent, the Commissioner must examine the request and specification and report on:

(a) whether the specification complies with subsections 40(2) to (4); and

(b) whether, to the best of his or her knowledge, the invention, so far as claimed, satisfies the criteria mentioned in paragraphs 18(1)(a), (b) and (c); and

(c) whether the invention is a patentable invention under subsection 18(2); and

(d) such other matters (if any) as are prescribed.

(1A) If a PCT application has been made and the prescribed requirements have not been met, the Commissioner may decline to examine the request and specification under subsection (1) until the requirements have been met.

(2) The examination must be carried out in accordance with the regulations.

Section 45(1) makes it clear that s 40 and s 18(1) are the two key provisions in the legislation for determining whether or not a patent should be granted.

Section 40 (as amended by the *Raising the Bar Act*) provides:

(1) A provisional specification must disclose the invention in a manner which is clear enough and complete enough for the invention to be performed by a person skilled in the relevant art.

(2) A complete specification must:

(a) disclose the invention in a manner which is clear enough and complete enough for the invention to be performed by a person skilled in the relevant art; and

(aa) disclose the best method known to the applicant of performing the invention; and

(b) where it relates to an application for a standard patent—end with a claim or claims defining the invention; and

(c) where it relates to an application for an innovation patent—end with at least one and no more than 5 claims defining the invention.

(3) The claim or claims must be clear and succinct and supported by matter disclosed in the specification.

(3A) The claim or claims must not rely on references to descriptions or drawings unless absolutely necessary to define the invention.

(4) The claim or claims must relate to one invention only.

Section 18(1) provides:

(1) Subject to subsection (2), an invention is a patentable invention for the purposes of a standard patent if the invention, so far as claimed in any claim:

(a) is a manner of manufacture within the meaning of section 6 of the Statute of Monopolies; and

(b) when compared with the prior art base as it existed before the priority date of that claim:

(i) is novel; and

(ii) involves an inventive step; and

(c) is useful; and

(d) was not secretly used in the patent area before the priority date of that claim by, or on behalf of, or with the authority of, the patentee or nominated person or the patentee's or nominated person's predecessor in title to the invention.

The s 18 requirements are discussed in Chapters 10 and 11 and the s 40 requirements are considered in Chapter 12.

Prior to examination, the invention has to be classified according to the area of technology to which it relates in accordance with the International Patent Classification. A search list is then prepared of all the relevant prior art against which the patent requirements are assessed. Following examination, the examiner prepares a report. If the report is adverse to the applicant, certain amendments are allowed to be made. This process of filing and amending the application is referred to as 'prosecuting' the patent. When the examiner makes a favourable report, the patent is accepted and that acceptance is advertised in the *Official Journal of Patents*. Any person then has three months to lodge a formal opposition to the patent. If there is no opposition, or if opposition proceedings are unsuccessful, the patent is granted.

Section 59 of the *Patents Act* provides grounds for opposition:

> The Minister or any other person may, in accordance with the regulations, oppose the grant of a standard patent on one or more of the following grounds, but on no other ground:
>
> (a) that the nominated person is either:
>   (i) not entitled to a grant of a patent for the invention; or
>   (ii) entitled to a grant of a patent for the invention but only in conjunction with some other person;
> (b) that the invention is not a patentable invention;
> (c) that the specification filed in respect of the complete application does not comply with subsection 40(2) or (3).

As with examination, the patentability (s 18) and disclosure and claiming (s 40) requirements are critical in opposition proceedings. Oppositions are heard by the Commissioner of Patents, or his or her delegate, but may be appealed to the Federal Court and, with leave, on to the Full Court of the Federal Court and High Court.

Validity of the patent is not guaranteed by the Patent Office, but may be challenged post-grant in revocation proceedings, the grounds for which are provided in s 138:

> (1) Subject to subsection (1A), the Minister or any other person may apply to a prescribed court for an order revoking a patent.
> (1A) A person cannot apply for an order in respect of an innovation patent unless the patent has been certified.
> (2) At the hearing of the application, the respondent is entitled to begin and give evidence in support of the patent and, if the applicant gives evidence disputing the validity of the patent, the respondent is entitled to reply.
> (3) After hearing the application, the court may, by order, revoke the patent, either wholly or so far as it relates to a claim, on one or more of the following grounds, but on no other ground:
>   (a) that the patentee is not entitled to the patent;
>   (b) that the invention is not a patentable invention;

(d) that the patent was obtained by fraud, false suggestion or misrepresentation;

(e) that an amendment of the patent request or the complete specification was made or obtained by fraud, false suggestion or misrepresentation;

(f) that the specification does not comply with subsection 40(2) or (3).

(4) A court must not make an order under subsection (3) on the ground that the patentee is not entitled to the patent unless the court is satisfied that, in all the circumstances, it is just and equitable to do so.

Revocation proceedings are instituted in the Federal Court. It is often the case that proceedings for revocation will be made as a counterclaim to infringement proceedings instituted by the patentee. The Act also provides for an appeal to the Federal Court against decisions of the Commissioner relating to examination (s 51), as well as pre-grant revocation of acceptance by the Commissioner (s 50A) and pre- and post-grant re-examination by the Commissioner (s 77).

OTHER PATENT-LIKE IP RIGHTS

Before canvassing patent law in more depth, some mention should be made of the protection afforded to new varieties of plants through plant breeder's rights (PBRs), which are given statutory recognition in the *Plant Breeder's Rights Act 1994* (Cth) (the '*PBR Act*'). The case of *Grain Pool of Western Australia v Commonwealth* [2000] HCA 14; (2000) 202 CLR 429, extracted in Chapter 1, recognises the constitutional validity of this legislation under the IP head of power in s 51(xviii) of the Constitution.

The Australian PBRs regime shares many of the same features as the patents regime. The regime is administered by IP Australia. Registration is required for the grant of PBRs, which provides the owner with a personal property right for a 20-year period. In addition to provisions relating to applications for and grant of PBRs, the legislation also provides for revocation and enforcement proceedings. Furthermore, the legislation establishes a Registrar of Plant Breeder's Rights and a Plant Breeder's Rights Advisory Committee.

Section 11 of the *PBR Act* provides the owner of the PBRs with exclusive rights to produce or reproduce, condition, offer for sale, sell, import and export the propagating material of the plant variety protected by the PBR and to stock the material for those purposes. These rights are subject to other provisions in the legislation. Important exemptions are provided in s 16, which allows use of the variety privately and for non-commercial purposes, for experimental purposes, and for breeding other plant varieties; and s 17, which allows farmers to save seed from one season to the next, provided that there has been no declaration that prevents the saving of seed from that particular crop.

The requirements for registration are prescribed in s 43 of the *PBR Act*, the most important provisions of which are extracted below:

(1) For the purposes of this Act, a plant variety in which an application for PBR is made is registrable if:

(a) the variety has a breeder; and

(b) the variety is distinct; and

(c) the variety is uniform; and

(d) the variety is stable; and

(e) the variety has not been exploited or has been only recently exploited.

(2) For the purposes of this section, a plant variety is distinct if it is clearly distinguishable from any other variety whose existence is a matter of common knowledge.

(3) For the purposes of this section, a plant variety is uniform if, subject to the variation that may be expected from the particular features of its propagation, it is uniform in its relevant characteristics on propagation.

(4) For the purposes of this section, a plant variety is stable if its relevant characteristics remain unchanged after repeated propagation.

(5) For the purposes of this section, a plant variety is taken not to have been exploited if, at the date of lodging the application for PBR in the variety, plant material of the variety has not been sold to another person by, or with the consent of, the breeder.

(6) For the purposes of this section, a plant variety is taken to have been only recently exploited if, at the date of lodging the application for PBR in the variety, plant material of the variety has not been sold to another person by, or with the consent of, the breeder, either:

    (a) in Australia—more than one year before that date; or

    (b) in the territory of another contracting party:

        (i) in the case of trees or vines—more than 6 years before that date; or

        (ii) in any other case—more than 4 years before that date.

Note: For the definition of **sell** see subsection 3(1).

    ...

(10) In this section:

    ...

plant material, in relation to a plant variety, means one or more of the following:

    (a) propagating material of the plant variety;

    (b) harvested material of the plant variety;

    (c) products obtained from harvested material of the plant variety.

The following cases provide some guidance in interpretation of the legislation: *Sun World Inc v Registrar, Plant Variety Rights* (1997) 75 FCR 528; *Sun World International Inc v Registrar, Plant Breeder's Rights* (1998) 87 FCR 405; *Cultivaust Pty Ltd v Grain Pool Pty Ltd* [2005] FCAFC 223; (2005) 147 FCR 265; *Fleming's Nurseries Pty Ltd v Siciliano* [2006] FCA 757; (2006) 68 IPR 545 (interlocutory decision of Mansfield J; it should be noted that consent orders were subsequently made in *Fleming's Nurseries Pty Ltd v Hannaford* [2009] FCA 884); and *Elders Rural Services Australia Ltd v Registrar of Plant Breeder's Rights* [2012] FCAFC 14; (2012) 199 FCR 520.[9]

---

9   See further J Sanderson, 'Intellectual Property and Plants: Constitutive, Contingent and Complex' in K Bowrey, M Handler and D Nicol, eds, *Emerging Challenges in Intellectual Property*, Oxford University Press, Melbourne, 2011.

—10—

THE SUBJECT MATTER OF PATENTABLE INVENTIONS: MANNER OF MANUFACTURE

INTRODUCTION

This chapter considers the threshold subject matter requirement for patenting. In Australian law, this requirement is found in s 18(1)(a) of the *Patents Act 1990* (Cth), which still retains the original language from the *Statute of Monopolies 1623* (21 Jac 1, c 3) of 'manner of manufacture'. This threshold requirement for patentable subject matter is also reflected in the opening phrase of Art 27 of the *Agreement on Trade-Related Aspects of Intellectual Property Rights* (the 'TRIPS Agreement') (1994), that patents must be made available for 'any inventions'.

It is only when there is appropriate subject matter that the technical patent criteria of novelty, inventive step (non-obviousness) and industrial applicability (utility) need to be assessed. In practice, however, the subject matter requirement and the technical patent requirements are generally considered together by patent offices and courts at examination and re-examination, and in opposition and revocation proceedings.

Certain types of subject matter will always fall foul of this threshold requirement. As noted in the US Supreme Court's decision in *Diamond v Diehr*, 450 US 175 (1981) at 185, the laws of nature, physical phenomena and abstract ideas are not patentable subject matter. Although subject matter of this nature is considered unpatentable across jurisdictions, the legislative tools for distinguishing between patentable subject matter and these categories of unpatentable subject matter vary, and some jurisdictions have added further categories of unpatentable subject matter.

The language of 'manner of manufacture' is not used in the USA, but the approach is similar to that in Australia, in that it is left to the patent offices and courts to determine both which categories of subject matter are unpatentable and whether particular applications for patents fall within these categories. The subject matter requirement in the USA is found in 35 USC §101, which provides:

> Whoever invents or discovers any new and useful process, machine, manufacture, or composition of matter, or any new and useful improvement thereof, may obtain a patent thereof, subject to the conditions and requirements of this title.

In contrast, the approach of signatory countries to the European Patent Convention (EPC) is to provide a discrete list of unpatentable subject matter. The EPC provides, in Art 52 (as amended in 2000):

> (1) European patents shall be granted for any inventions, in all fields of technology, provided that they are new, involve an inventive step and are susceptible of industrial application.

(2) The following in particular shall not be regarded as inventions within the meaning of paragraph 1:
    (a) discoveries, scientific theories and mathematical methods;
    (b) aesthetic creations;
    (c) schemes, rules and methods for performing mental acts, playing games or doing business, and programs for computers;
    (d) presentations of information.
(3) Paragraph 2 shall exclude the patentability of the subject-matter or activities referred to therein only to the extent to which a European patent application or European patent relates to such subject-matter or activities as such.

In determining the patentability of subject matter that includes any item from the list of unpatentable subject matter in Art 52(2), much turns on the words 'as such' in Art 52(3). These words have been extensively litigated in the UK and other European jurisdictions that are signatories to the EPC. As a consequence of these provisions, it would appear that in general European patent offices and courts have only a limited interpretive role in determining whether particular applications for patents satisfy the threshold subject matter requirement.

Additional categories of subject matter are excluded in Art 53 of the EPC (as amended in 2000) on grounds other than failure to satisfy the threshold patentability requirement. This provision states that European patents shall not be granted in respect of:

(a) inventions the commercial exploitation of which would be contrary to 'ordre public' or morality; such exploitation shall not be deemed to be so contrary merely because it is prohibited by law or regulation in some or all of the Contracting States;
(b) plant or animal varieties or essentially biological processes for the production of plants or animals; this provision shall not apply to microbiological processes or the products thereof;
(c) methods for treatment of the human or animal body by surgery or therapy and diagnostic methods practised on the human or animal body; this provision shall not apply to products, in particular substances or compositions, for use in any of these methods.

These exclusions are permitted in Art 27(2) and (3) of the TRIPS Agreement, but they are not mandatory.

In Australia there is only one express exclusion, found in s 18(2) of the *Patents Act*:

(2) Human beings, and the biological processes for their generation, are not patentable inventions.

Section 50 of the *Patents Act* further provides the Commissioner of Patents with the limited discretion to exclude certain subject matter:

(1) The Commissioner may refuse to accept a patent request and specification, or to grant a patent:
    (a) for an invention the use of which would be contrary to law; or
    (b) on the ground that the specification claims as an invention:
        (i) a substance which is capable of being used as food or medicine (whether for human beings or animals and whether for internal or external use) and is a mere mixture of known ingredients; or
        (ii) a process producing such a substance by mere admixture.

(2) The Commissioner may refuse to accept a specification containing a claim that includes the name of a person as the name, or part of the name, of the invention so far as claimed in that claim.

Section 18(3) and (4) of the *Patents Act* excludes plants and animals, and biological processes for the generation of plants and animals (but not microbiological processes) from being the subject of innovation patents. Although exclusion of plants and animals is permissible under the TRIPS Agreement, Australia and the USA agreed not to make this exclusion in the *Australia–US Free Trade Agreement* (AUSFTA) (2004). Because the reference to 'patents' in AUSFTA only extends to standard patents, and because the exclusion in s 18(3) and (4) is limited to innovation patents, s 18 (3) and (4) do not fall foul of this requirement.

The Australian Industrial Property Advisory Committee (IPAC), in its report into patent law reform, *Patents, Innovation and Competition in Australia* (1984), urged that the manner of manufacture test should be retained in its existing form in what was to become the *Patents Act* rather than replacing it with a more explicit statement of what is patentable. The Committee argued that the manner of manufacture test has exhibited the capacity to respond to technological innovations through an extensive body of case law. The government endorsed this recommendation, stating in the Explanatory Memorandum to the Patents Bill 1989 that this test was preferred over a more inflexible codified definition.

The Advisory Council on Intellectual Property (ACIP) undertook a review of the patentable subject matter requirement in 2008–10. In its final report, *Patentable Subject Matter* (2010), ACIP recommended that the test for patentable subject matter should be redefined using clear and contemporary language and embodying the principles of inherent patentability developed in the case law. To date, no legislative action has been taken by the government in response to this recommendation.

This chapter considers the interpretation of the manner of manufacture test by the Australian courts, with particular focus on the test's responsiveness to new technological developments. Although the patentable subject matter requirement has been interpreted as setting a low threshold to patenting in the recent past, it is very much a live issue at present, particularly in the areas of information technology and biotechnology. The chapter compares the developing body of Australian jurisprudence with the approaches in the USA and Europe. A number of the recent Australian decisions provide summaries of the key points from the decisions in other jurisdictions. In light of this, longer extracts from the Australian decisions are provided in this chapter rather than shorter extracts from the foreign cases themselves. This assists in comparing and contrasting the differences in approaches between jurisdictions.

THE SUBJECT MATTER REQUIREMENT
AUSTRALIA: MANNER OF MANUFACTURE

Following enactment of the *Statute of Monopolies 1623*, numerous attempts were made in the early English cases to define the term 'manufacture'—the tendency being to give it a flexible and expansive meaning, including both products of manufacture and processes of manufacture. In *Boulton v Bull* (1795) 126 ER 651, for example, Eyre CJ included in the concept 'any new results of principles carried into practice' and also 'new processes in any art producing effects useful to the public'.

In the nineteenth and early twentieth centuries, various attempts were made to narrow the scope of manner of manufacture for processes by introducing the requirement of a 'vendible product' arising out of the process of manufacture. In *Re GEC's Application* [1942] RPC 1, Morton J, while denying that he was laying down a hard-and-fast rule, proposed at 4 that:

> a method or process is a manner of manufacture if it (a) results in the production of some vendible product or (b) improves or restores to its former condition a vendible product or (c) has the effect of preserving from deterioration some vendible product to which it is applied.

The Morton 'rule', as it became known, was adopted in a number of subsequent cases. It proved to be a major obstacle to patenting in some circumstances where a previously described product was given a new, previously unknown or unthought-of application, because of the difficulty in demonstrating that a vendible product had been produced.

PRECEDENT

CASE EXTRACT: PRECEDENT

National Research Development Corporation v Commissioner of Patents ('NRDC')

(1959) 102 CLR 252
High Court of Australia

[The *NRDC* case gave the High Court the opportunity to consider whether the requirement for a 'vendible product' should be a component of the manner of manufacture test in Australia. It was an appeal from a decision of the Deputy Commissioner of Patents under the *Patents Act 1952* (Cth) to refuse certain claims in an application for a patent relating to the eradication of weeds from crop areas by the application of known chemicals with new properties using new processes, on the basis that the manner of manufacture test was not fulfilled. The High Court first discussed the requirements for patenting subject matter that is a new use of a known product, distinguishing between:

- analogous new uses that are unpatentable because they are nothing but a claim for a new use of an old substance;
- new uses that take advantage of a hitherto unknown or unsuspected property of the product, which may be patentable even though the method of use is neither novel nor inventive; and
- new and inventive methods of using the product, which may also be patentable.]

Dixon CJ, Kitto and Windeyer JJ (at 262–277): The principles which govern the power to refuse a patent have been discussed recently in the case of *Commissioner of Patents v Microcell Ltd* (1959) 102 CLR 232. It is shown in that case that in the portion of the definition of invention which includes in the meaning of the word an alleged invention, the word 'alleged' goes only to the epithet 'new' in the expression 'a manner of new manufacture', and that accordingly the Commissioner may properly reject a claim for a process which is not within the concept of a 'manufacture'. But the case cited shows also that even if the process is within the concept the Commissioner is not bound to accept the allegation of the applicant that it is new, if it is apparent on the face of the specification, when properly construed, that the allegation is unfounded: see also *Re Johnson's Patent* (1937) 55 RPC 4, at p 19. It is therefore open to the Commissioner in a proper case to direct the deletion of a claim for a process which may be seen from the specification, considered as a whole, to be 'outside the whole scope of what is known as invention' because, in the words of Lord Buckmaster, when Solicitor-General, in *Re BA's Application* (1915) 32 RPC 348 it is 'nothing but a claim for a new use of an old substance', at p 349.

But, as the *Microcell Case* (1959) 102 CLR 232 emphasizes, it must always be remembered how much is wrapped up in the 'nothing but'. Lord Buckmaster did not use the words without explanation:— ' … when once a substance is known,' he said, 'its methods of production ascertained, its characteristics and its constituents well defined, you cannot patent the use of that for a purpose which was hitherto unknown' (1915) 32 RPC, at p 349. And why? Because in the postulated state of knowledge the new purpose is no more than analogous to the purposes for which the utility of the substance is already known, and therefore your suggestion of the new purpose lacks the quality of inventiveness: see per Bowen LJ in *Elias v Grovesend Tinplate Co* (1890) 7 RPC 455, at p 468. Unless invention is found in some new method of using the material or some new adaptation of it so as to serve the new purpose, no valid patent can be granted: see *Moser v Marsden* (1893) 10 RPC 350, at p 358; *Pirrie v York Street Flax Spinning Co Ltd* (1894) 11 RPC 429, at p 452. If, however, the new use that is proposed consists in taking advantage of a hitherto unknown or unsuspected property of the material, the situation is not that to which Lord Buckmaster's language refers. In that case there may be invention in the suggestion that the substance may be used to serve the new purpose; and then, provided that a practical method of so using it is disclosed and that the process comes within the concept of patent law ultimately traceable to the use in the *Statute of Monopolies* of the words 'manner of manufacture,' all the elements of a patentable invention are present: see the *Microcell Case* (1959) 102 CLR, at pp 248, 249. It is not necessary that in addition the proposed method should itself be novel or involve any inventive step: *Hickton's Patent Syndicate v Patents and Machine Improvements Co Ltd* (1909) 26 RPC 339.

This, we consider, differs not at all from the view which Lindley LJ expressed in the passage in his judgment in the case of *Lane Fox v Kensington and Knightsbridge Electric Lighting Co* [1892] 3 Ch 424, at pp 428, 429; (1892) 9 RPC 413, at p 416 which is often cited and was referred to more than once in the argument of the present case, namely that a man who discovers that a known machine (his Lordship might equally have said a known substance) can produce effects which no one before him knew could be produced by it has made a discovery, but has not made a patentable invention unless he so uses his knowledge and ingenuity as to produce either a new and useful thing or result, or a new and useful method of producing an old thing or result. His Lordship went on to say that the discovery how to use a known thing for a new purpose will be a patentable invention if there is novelty in the mode of using it as distinguished from novelty of purpose, or if any new modification of the thing or any new appliance is necessary for using it for its new purpose, and if such mode of user, or modification, or appliance involves any appreciable merit. But the whole passage is directed to the case of a thing which is known—not only the existence of which is known as a scientific fact, but the characteristics and properties of which are understood, so that the 'appreciable merit' (1892) 3 Ch, at p 429; (1892) 9 RPC, at p 416 which is requisite for a patentable invention must be found, if it is to be found at all, exclusively in something which the alleged invention has superadded to the existing knowledge concerning the thing. There is nothing in the judgment of Lindley LJ to justify a denial that, in respect of a process for achieving a useful result by the employment of a substance to produce effects which

PRECEDENT

PRECEDENT

antecedently it was not understood to be capable of producing, the inventiveness which is essential for a valid grant of a patent may be found in the step which consists of suggesting the use of the thing for the new purpose, notwithstanding that there is no novelty or 'appreciable merit' in any suggested mode of using the thing, or any modification of the thing or of an appliance necessary for using it for the new purpose. It is not decisive—it is not even helpful—to point out in such a case that beyond discovery of a scientific fact nothing has been added except the suggestion that nature, in its newly ascertained aspect, be allowed to work in its own way. Arguments of this kind may be answered as Frankfurter J answered them in *Funk Bros Seed Co v Kalo Inoculant Co* (1948) 333 US 127 (92 Law Ed 588). 'It only confuses the issue,' the learned Justice said, 'to introduce such terms as "the work of nature" and the "laws of nature". For these are vague and malleable terms infected with too much ambiguity and equivocation. Everything that happens may be deemed "the work of nature", and any patentable composite exemplifies in its properties "the laws of nature". Arguments drawn from such terms for ascertaining patentability could fairly be employed to challenge almost any patent' (1948) 333 US, at pp 134, 135 (92 Law Ed, at p 591). The truth is that the distinction between discovery and invention is not precise enough to be other than misleading in this area of discussion. There may indeed be a discovery without invention—either because the discovery is of some piece of abstract information without any suggestion of a practical application of it to a useful end, or because its application lies outside the realm of 'manufacture'. But where a person finds out that a useful result may be produced by doing something which has not been done by that procedure before, his claim for a patent is not validly answered by telling him that although there was ingenuity in his discovery that the materials used in the process would produce the useful result no ingenuity was involved in showing how the discovery, once it had been made, might be applied. The fallacy lies in dividing up the process that he puts forward as his invention. It is the whole process that must be considered; and he need not show more than one inventive step in the advance which he has made beyond the prior limits of the relevant art. This is perhaps nowhere more clearly put than it was by Fletcher Moulton LJ in *Hickton's Patent Syndicate v Patents and Machine Improvements Co Ltd* (1909) 26 RPC 339 when he said of Watt's invention for the condensation of steam, out of which the steam engine grew: 'Now can it be suggested that it required any invention whatever to carry out that idea when once you had got it? It could be done in a thousand ways and by any competent engineer, but the invention was in the idea, and when he had once got that idea, the carrying out of it was perfectly easy. To say that the conception may be meritorious and may involve invention and may be new and original, and simply because when you have once got the idea it is easy to carry it out, that that deprives it of the title of being a new invention according to our patent law, is, I think, an extremely dangerous principle and justified neither by reason nor authority' (1909) 26 RPC, at pp 347–348.

No one reading the specification in the present case can fail to see that what it claims is a new process for ridding crop areas of certain kinds of weeds, not by applying chemicals the properties of which were formerly well understood so that the idea of using them for this purpose involved no inventive step, but by applying chemicals which formerly were supposed not to be useful for this kind of purpose at all. There is a clear assertion of a discovery that a useful result can be attained by doing something which the applicant's research has shown for the first time to be capable of producing that result. This is not a claim which can be put aside as a claim for a new use of an old substance, true though it be that the chemicals themselves were known to science before the applicant's investigations began ...

PRECEDENT

[The Court then turned its attention to the nature of the manner of manufacture test, particularly focusing on the 'vendible product' requirement.]

The central question in the case remains. It is whether the process that is claimed falls within the category of inventions to which, by definition, the application of the *Patents Act* is confined. The definition, it will be remembered, is exclusive: invention means any manner of new manufacture the subject of letters patent and grant of privilege within s 6 of the *Statute of Monopolies*. The Commissioner, adopting certain judicial pronouncements to which reference will be made, emphasizes the word 'manufacture' and contends for an interpretation of it which, though not narrow, is restricted to vendible products and processes for their production, and excludes all agricultural and horticultural processes. On the grounds both of the suggested restriction and of the suggested exclusion he denies that a process for killing weeds can be within the relevant concept of invention. The appellant, on the other hand, urges upon us a wider view: that there is a 'manufacture' such as might properly have been the subject of letters patent and grant of privilege under s 6 of the *Statute of Monopolies* whenever a process produces, either immediately or ultimately, a useful physical result in relation to a material or tangible entity.

... The inquiry which the definition [in s 6 of the *Statute of Monopolies*] demands is an inquiry into the scope of the permissible subject matter of letters patent and grants of privilege protected by the section. It is an inquiry not into the meaning of a word so much as into the breadth of the concept which the law has developed by its consideration of the text and purpose of the *Statute of Monopolies* ... The word 'manufacture' finds a place in the present Act, not as a word intended to reduce a question of patentability to a question of verbal interpretation, but simply as the general title found in the *Statute of Monopolies* for the whole category under which all grants of patents which may be made in accordance with the developed principles of patent law are to be subsumed. It is therefore a mistake, and a mistake likely to lead to an incorrect conclusion, to treat the question whether a given process or product is within the definition as if that question could be restated in the form: 'Is this a manner (or kind) of manufacture?' It is a mistake which tends to limit one's thinking by reference to the idea of making tangible goods by hand or by machine, because 'manufacture' as a word of everyday speech generally conveys that idea. The right question is: 'Is this a proper subject of letters patent according to the principles which have been developed for the application of s 6 of the *Statute of Monopolies*?'

...

[The Court then went on to consider the case law relating to the vendible product requirement.]

Notwithstanding the tendency of these decisions, the view which we think is correct in the present case is that the method the subject of the relevant claims has as its end result an artificial effect falling squarely within the true concept of what must be produced by a process if it is to be held patentable. This view is, we think, required by a sound understanding of the lines along which patent law has developed and necessarily must develop in a modern society. The effect produced by the appellant's method exhibits the two essential qualities upon which 'product' and 'vendible' seem designed to insist. It is a 'product' because it consists in an artificially created state of affairs, discernible by observing over a period the growth of weeds and crops respectively on sown land on which the method has been put into practice. And the significance of the product is economic; for it provides a remarkable advantage, indeed to the lay mind a sensational advantage, for one of the most elemental activities by which man has served his material needs, the cultivation of the soil for the production of its fruits. Recognition that the relevance of the process is to this economic activity old as it is, need not be inhibited by any fear

PRECEDENT

of inconsistency with the claim to novelty which the specification plainly makes. The method cannot be classed as a variant of ancient procedures. It is additional to the cultivation. It achieves a separate result, and the result possesses its own economic utility consisting in an important improvement in the conditions in which the crop is to grow, whereby it is afforded a better opportunity to flourish and yield a good harvest.

The decision in *NRDC* was described by Barwick CJ in *Joos v Commissioner of Patents* (1972) 126 CLR 611 as a watershed, and it has had important consequences, not just in Australia but also in other jurisdictions. Its ongoing relevance in interpreting s 18(1)(a) of the *Patents Act* has been strongly endorsed in cases such as *Anaesthetic Supplies Pty Ltd v Rescare Ltd* (1994) 50 FCR 1 and *CCOM Pty Ltd v Jiejing Pty Ltd* (1994) 51 FCR 260. It was also accepted as the appropriate test in New Zealand in *Swift & Co's Application* [1960] NZLR 775 and *Wellcome Foundation Ltd v Commissioner of Patents* [1979] 2 NZLR 591 and was accepted in the UK prior to the enactment of the *Patents Act 1977*, for example, in *Swift & Co's Application* [1962] RPC 37.

CURRENT LAW

CASE EXTRACT: CURRENT LAW

Research Affiliates LLC v Commissioner of Patents

[2014] FCAFC 150
Federal Court of Australia, Full Court

[This case related to two patents assigned to Research Affiliates, both of which were rejected by the Commissioner of Patents. The subject matter of the patents is outlined in a later extract from this case (see below, p 409). Here, the Full Court provided an overview of recent case law considering the *NRDC* case.]

Kenny, Bennett and Nicholas JJ: 6. Section 18(1)(a) of the Act provides that an invention is a patentable invention if, so far as claimed in any claim, it is a manner of manufacture within the meaning of s 6 of the *Statute of Monopolies 1623* (Imp) (*Statute of Monopolies*). '*Invention*' is defined in Sch 1 to the Act as 'any manner of new manufacture the subject of letters patent and grant of privilege within s 6 of the *Statute of Monopolies*, and includes an alleged invention'. Section 6 of the *Statute of Monopolies* relevantly provides that what is patentable is ' ... any manner of new Manufactures'. While this may be seen to make the definition of 'invention' as simply a repetition of the reference to a 'manner of new manufacture', the reference to s 6 of the Statute of Monopolies incorporates the jurisprudence that has developed as to that concept.

7. This was most helpfully crystallised in what Crennan and Kiefel JJ in *Apotex Pty Ltd v Sanofi-Aventis Australia Pty Ltd* (2013) 103 IPR 217; [2013] HCA 50 (*Apotex*) at [216] called '*the celebrated case*' of *National Research Development Corporation v Commissioner of Patents* (1959) 102 CLR 252 (*NRDC*).

8. At the outset, it is worth repeating the following principles established by *NRDC*, as approved and applied in *Apotex*, *Grant v Commissioner of Patents* (2006) 154 FCR 62 (*Grant*) and *D'Arcy v Myriad Genetics Inc* [2014] FCAFC 115 (*Myriad*). *Grant* also concerned the patentability of a business scheme.

CURRENT LAW

- The right question is: 'Is this a proper subject of letters patent according to the principles which have been developed for the application of s 6 of the *Statute of Monopolies*?' (at 269).
- There is a 'manufacture' such as might properly have been the subject of letters patent and grant of privilege under s 6 of the *Statute of Monopolies* whenever a process produces, either immediately or ultimately, a useful physical result in relation to a material or tangible entity (at 268, 276).
- The method the subject of the relevant claim must have as its end result an artificial effect falling squarely within the true concept of what must be produced by a process if it is to be held to be patentable (at 277).
- There may be a discovery without invention, either because the discovery is some piece of abstract information without any suggestion of a practical application of it to a useful end, or because its application lies outside the realm of 'manufacture' (at 264).
- To fall within the limits of patentability, the process must be one that offers some advantage which is material in the sense that the process belongs to a useful art as distinct from a fine art and that its value to the country is in the field of economic endeavour (at 275).

9. There is no issue in this case that the claimed invention has economic significance.

10. As was said by the High Court in *Advanced Building Systems Pty Ltd v Ramset Fasteners (Aust) Pty Ltd* (1998) 194 CLR 171 at [34], in order for a discovery to be elevated to a patentable invention there needs to be a practical means of carrying out the idea so as to add to the sum of human art. Similarly, Lord Hoffmann in *Kirin-Amgen Inc v Hoechst Marion Roussel Ltd* [2005] 1 All ER 667 at [76] (citing *Genentech Inc's Patent* [1987] RPC 553 at 566), said that '[i]t is trite law that you cannot patent a discovery, but if on the basis of that discovery you can tell people how it may be usefully employed, then a patentable invention may result'. A manufacture is not limited, for example, by reference to the idea of making tangible goods by hand or by machine (*NRDC* at 269). As the Full Court said in *Grant* at [38]–[39], there is unpredictability in the advances of human ingenuity and what may be, or may be described as, science or technology, but on the other hand, the mere taking of sequential steps may represent a collocation of integers rather than a new combination. Methods may involve ingenuity and imagination and may produce new kinds of transactions which 'could well warrant the description of discoveries. But they are not inventions' (at [34]).

11. However, is the fact that a claimed method to a new kind of transaction requires the use of a computer for implementation sufficient to bring it within the realm of patentability?

12. In *Apotex*, the High Court endorsed the approach taken in *NRDC*. Chief Justice French noted at [10] that the objectives of s 6 were: 'the encouragement of industry, employment and growth rather than justice to the 'inventor' for his intellectual percipience' (citing Cornish, Llewelyn and Aplin, *Intellectual Property: Patents, Copyright, Trade Marks and Allied Rights* (8th ed, 2013) at 123). His Honour adopted the reasoning in *NRDC* that 'manner of manufacture' as applied to a method or process was not constrained by requiring the method or process to be linked to a narrowly defined understanding of a 'vendible product' and that a widening conception of the notion of 'manufacture' had characterised the growth of patent law. Justices Crennan and Kiefel observed that judicial determinations were preferable to specific legislative exclusions from patentability which, as noted by the Industrial Property Advisory Committee in its report on the *Patents Act 1952* (Cth) dated 29 August 1984, 'would be likely to prove a very slow, blunt and inefficient instrument for influencing the economic direction of particular industries or fields of technological development in Australia'.

THE USA: PROCESS, MACHINE, MANUFACTURE OR COMPOSITION OF MATTER

CASE EXTRACT: COMPARATIVE LAW

Diamond v Chakrabarty

447 US 303 (1980)
Supreme Court of the United States

[Like *NRDC*, *Chakrabarty* is often described as a watershed. In 1972 Ananda Chakrabarty filed patent claims for a human-made, modified bacterium that was capable of breaking down multiple components of crude oil. The invention involved the transfer into Pseudomonas bacteria of four different plasmids capable of degrading four different components of oil. The patent application included a number of claims including a claim to the bacterium itself. This claim was rejected by the patent examiner on two bases:

1   that microorganisms are products of nature;
2   that as living things they are not patentable subject matter.

The majority judgment of the Supreme Court was handed down by Burger CJ, with four other judges. The minority in this case comprised four judges. As such, there was a slim 5:4 majority. Yet *Chakrabarty* remains one of the most influential decisions in terms of patentability of life forms, both in the USA and in other jurisdictions.

In construing 35 USC §101, Burger CJ first looked to the wording of the section and concluded at 308 that '[i]n choosing such expansive terms as "manufacture" and "composition of matter", modified by the comprehensive "any", Congress plainly contemplated that the patent laws would be given wide scope.' His Honour then considered other factors which provided assistance in the exercise of construing the legislation.]

Burger CJ (delivering the judgment of the majority) (at 308–310): The relevant legislative history also supports a broad construction. The *Patent Act* of 1793, authored by Thomas Jefferson, defined statutory subject matter as 'any new and useful art, machine, manufacture, or composition of matter, or any new or useful improvement [thereof].' ... The Act embodied Jefferson's philosophy that 'ingenuity should receive a liberal encouragement.' ... Subsequent patent statutes in 1836, 1870 and 1874 employed this same broad language. In 1952, when the patent laws were recodified, Congress replaced the word 'art' with 'process,' but otherwise left Jefferson's language intact. The Committee Reports accompanying the 1952 Act inform us that Congress intended statutory subject matter to 'include anything under the sun that is made by man.' ...

This is not to suggest that 101 has no limits or that it embraces every discovery. The laws of nature, physical phenomena, and abstract ideas have been held not patentable ... Thus, a new mineral discovered in the earth or a new plant found in the wild is not patentable subject matter. Likewise, Einstein could not patent his celebrated law that $E=mc^2$; nor could Newton have patented the law of gravity. Such discoveries are 'manifestations of ... nature, free to all men and reserved exclusively to none.' *Funk Brothers Seed Co v Kalo Inoculant Co*, 333 US 127, 130 (1948), at 130.

Judged in this light, respondent's micro-organism plainly qualifies as patentable subject matter. His claim is not to a hitherto unknown natural phenomenon, but to a nonnaturally occurring manufacture or composition of matter—a product of human ingenuity 'having a distinctive name, character [and] ... use.' *Hartranft v Wiegmann*, 121 US 609, 615 (1887). The point is underscored dramatically by comparison of the invention here with that in *Funk*. There, the patentee had discovered that there existed in nature certain species of root-nodule bacteria which did not exert a mutually inhibitive effect on each other. He used that discovery to produce a mixed culture capable of inoculating the seeds of leguminous plants ...

Here, by contrast, the patentee has produced a new bacterium with markedly different characteristics from any found in nature and one having the potential for significant utility. His discovery is not nature's handiwork, but his own; accordingly it is patentable subject matter under 101.

THE EPC: SUBJECT MATTER NOT REGARDED AS INVENTIONS

As the EPC (and equivalent national legislation) has an exclusive list of unpatentable subject matter, the subject matter inquiry is focused more on what is unpatentable rather than what is patentable.

CASE EXTRACT: COMPARATIVE LAW

Aerotel Ltd v Telco Holdings Ltd; Macrossan's Application

[2006] EWCA Civ 1371; [2007] RPC 7
Court of Appeal of England and Wales

[This decision involved two appeals relating to the patentable subject matter provisions in Art 52 of the EPC. The 'Aerotel appeal' involved a counterclaim for revocation brought by Telco in response to an action for infringement brought by Aerotel. The patent in issue claimed a method of making telephone calls and a system for facilitating telephone calls. The 'Macrossan appeal', on the other hand was an appeal by Macrossan from a decision by the UK Patent Office that the subject matter of his patent application was unpatentable. The Macrossan patent application claimed an automated method of acquiring the documents necessary to incorporate a company.

The subject matter in both appeals related to computer programs and business methods, which are discussed later in this chapter (see 'Computer programs and computer-implemented methods of doing business' below, p 406). The focus in this extract is on the approach to interpretation of Art 52 of the EPC taken by the Court.]

Jacob LJ (for the Court): 8. The provisions about what are not to be 'regarded as inventions' are not easy. Over the years there has been and continues to be much debate about them and about decisions on them given by national courts and the Boards of Appeal of the EPO ... There has also been much political debate too: some urging removal or reduction of the categories, others their retention or enlargement. With the political debate we have no concern—it is our job to interpret them as they stand.

9. As the decisions show this is not an easy task. There are several reasons for this:

i)   In the first place there is no evident underlying purpose lying behind the provisions as a group—a purpose to guide the construction. The categories are there, but there is nothing to tell you one way or the other whether they should be read widely or narrowly.

ii)   One cannot form an overall approach to the categories. They form a disparate group—no common, overarching concept, for example, links rules for playing games with computer programs or either of these with methods for doing business or aesthetic creations.

iii) Some categories are given protection by other intellectual property laws. Most importantly, of course, aesthetic creations and computer programs have protection under the law of copyright. So the legislator may well have formed the view that additional protection by way of patentability was unnecessary or less appropriate.

iv)   Further, some categories are so abstract that they are unnecessary or meaningless. For instance a scientific theory as such is excluded. But how could a scientific theory ever be the subject of a patent claim in the first place? Einstein's special theory of relativity was new and non-obvious but it was inherently incapable of being patented. A patent after all is to a legal monopoly over some commercial activity carried out by human beings such as making or dealing in goods or carrying out a process. A scientific theory is not activity at all. It simply is not the sort of thing which could be made the subject of a legal monopoly.

Nor can the presence of the exclusion be explained on the narrower basis that it was intended to exclude woolly and general claims such as 'Any application of $E=mc^2$'. For such a claim would be bad for the more conventional reason that it does not disclose the invention 'in a manner sufficiently clear and complete for it to be carried out by a person skilled in the art' (Arts 83 and 100(b));

v)   There is or may be overlap between some of the exclusions themselves and between them the overall requirement that an invention be 'susceptible of industrial application.' The overall requirement is, perhaps surprisingly, hardly ever mentioned in the debate about the categories of 'non-invention' (no-one relied upon it before us) but it is clearly a factor lying behind some of the debate.

[Jacob LJ then concluded that the *travaux preparatoire* to the EPC provided little guidance as to how to approach the task of interpreting Art 52. He also considered the extent to which *Chakrabarty* and other US case law and other considerations assisted with the task of interpretation.]

15. The 'exceptions' referred to in the US cases, e.g. laws of nature, have some equivalents in Art 52(2). But that is really, as we have pointed out, because they are by their very nature incapable of being the subject of a legal monopoly. The fact that there are some parallels between what is declared by the judges to be unpatentable in the US and what is declared by Art 52(2) to be an excluded category of invention is no guide as to the interpretation of Art 52.

OTHER CONSIDERATIONS

16. Before moving on we would add three things. First there has been some political pressure on Europe to remove or reduce the categories of non-inventions ...

17. Secondly there is pressure from would-be patentees on patent offices. People are applying for what are, or arguably are, business method and computer program patents in significant numbers. This is evidenced, for example, by the fact that whereas a few years ago the Comptroller only had one or two hearings a year concerned with these topics, he now has about four a week—a number are awaiting on the outcome of these appeals.

...

19. Thirdly it by no means follows that because of pressure from applicants, the grant of patents for excluded categories should be allowed or that the excluded categories (particularly business methods and computer programs) should be construed narrowly. Just as with arms, merely because people want them is not sufficient reason for giving them.

20. Fourthly despite the fact that such patents have been granted for some time in the US, it is far from certain that they have been what Sellars and Yeatman would have called a 'Good Thing.' The patent system is there to provide a research and investment incentive but it has a price. That price (what economists call 'transaction costs') is paid in a host of ways: the costs of patenting, the impediment to competition, the compliance cost of ensuring non-infringement, the cost of uncertainty, litigation costs and so on. There is, so far as we know, no really hard empirical data showing that the liberalisation of what is patentable in the USA has resulted in a *greater* rate of innovation or investment in the excluded categories. Innovation in computer programs, for instance, proceeded at an immense speed for years before anyone thought of granting patents for them as such. There is evidence, in the shape of the mass of US litigation about the excluded categories, that they have produced much uncertainty. If the encouragement of patenting and of patent litigation as industries in themselves were a purpose of the patent system, then the case for construing the categories narrowly (and indeed for removing them) is made out. But not otherwise.

21. In our opinion, therefore, the court must approach the categories without bias in favour of or against exclusion. All that is clear is that there was a positive intention and policy to exclude the categories concerned from being regarded as patentable inventions. We must simply try to make sense of them using the language of the Convention.

SUBJECT MATTER AT THE BORDERLINE OF PATENTABILITY

In new areas of technology, such as information technology and biotechnology, the line between patentable and unpatentable subject matter has become decidedly blurred. The subject matters of patent claims in these areas are closely linked with the traditional categories of unpatentable subject matter. Courts and patent offices have had to decide whether there has been sufficient input of human ingenuity to bring them under the umbrella of patentable subject matter.

As noted by the High Court in *NRDC* at 264: 'There may indeed be a discovery without invention—either because the discovery is of some piece of abstract information without any suggestion of a practical application of it to a useful end, or because its application lies outside the realm of "manufacture".' Prior to *NRDC* there was some authority for the proposition that agricultural and horticultural processes fell within the traditional boundaries of unpatentable subject matter. The High Court's findings on this matter—set out in the second extract from this case, below—are instructive in determining how the courts should approach the issue in other areas of technology where the claimed invention is grounded in subject matter that has been traditionally considered as unpatentable.

CASE EXTRACT: PRECEDENT

National Research Development Corporation v Commissioner of Patents ('NRDC')

(1959) 102 CLR 252
High Court of Australia

[The Commissioner of Patents argued that even if the manner of manufacture test was satisfied, the invention in this case should be excluded because it was an agricultural or horticultural process. At 279 the Court emphatically rejected any notion that agricultural and horticultural processes per se are unpatentable. Rather, the focus must always be on whether the claimed invention satisfies the manner of manufacture requirement.]

Dixon CJ, Kitto and Windeyer JJ (at 278–279): [I]n the *Standard Oil Development Co's Case* (1951) 68 RPC 114, where a patent was sought for a selective herbicidal process, it emerged from the examiner's report that an 'established Office practice' had grown up of denying that any agricultural or horticultural process could be a 'manner of manufacture'. Upon this, Lloyd-Jacob J made no comment, and the office view has since been adhered to: *Re Dow Chemical Co's Application* [1956] RPC 247; *Re Canterbury Agricultural College's Application* [1958] RPC 85. The proposition seems an example of a generalization not supported by the reasons leading to the conclusions in the particular instances from which the generalization is drawn. If it means that there is some consideration wrapped up in the label 'agricultural or horticultural' which necessarily takes a process outside the area of patentability even though it is a novel process and of sufficient inventiveness, the consideration is not easy to identify. There seems to be here a classic illustration of thinking in terms of the everyday concept of manufacture instead of following the lines along which, over a long period, the courts have given effect to the real purpose and operation of s 6 of the *Statute of Monopolies* ...

We are here concerned with a process producing its effect by means of a chemical reaction, and the ultimate weed-free, or comparatively weed-free condition of the crop-bearing land is properly described as produced by the process. The fact that the relevance of the process is to agricultural or horticultural enterprises does not in itself supply or suggest any consideration not already covered which should weigh against the conclusion that the process is a patentable invention.

COMPUTER PROGRAMS AND COMPUTER-IMPLEMENTED METHODS OF DOING BUSINESS

There has, in the past, been reluctance to accept computer programs as manners of manufacture because they could be regarded as merely reciting mathematical algorithms, which are abstract ideas.[1] Burchett J of the Federal Court considered the patentability of computer programs in *International Business Machines Corporation v Commissioner of Patents* (1991) 33 FCR 218. The patent application stated that '[t]he present invention relates to computer graphics and more specifically to a method and apparatus for generating curves in computer graphics displays'. Burchett J applied the broad

---

1   See A Christie and S Syme 'Patents for Algorithms in Australia' (1998) 20 *Sydney Law Review* 517.

principle in *NRDC*, concluding at 224 that: 'it is ... by the production of some useful effect that patent law has distinguished, so far as it has distinguished, between the discovery of a principle of science and the making of an invention.'

The Full Court of the Federal Court was given the opportunity to revisit this issue in the case extracted below.

CASE EXTRACT: PRECEDENT

CCOM Pty Ltd v Jiejing Pty Ltd

(1994) 51 FCR 260
Federal Court of Australia, Full Court

[The patent at issue in this case claimed a computer-processing apparatus for assembling text in Chinese characters. At first instance Cooper J held that the claim was not a manner of manufacture. His decision was overturned on appeal. The invention was an important development in information technology, involving the use of a word processor to assemble text in Chinese characters. Prior to this, each of the 6000 characters of Chinese language had to be assembled separately using a large number of keystrokes, or a digital pad had to be attached to the computer.]

Spender, Gummow and Heerey JJ (at 292–295): What then of patent law in Australia? Professor Lahore pointed out [in 'Computers and the Law: The Protection of Intellectual Property' (1978) 9 *Federal Law Review* 15] (at 22–23):

> Some matter has never been considered to constitute a patentable invention. This matter includes a method of calculation or a process of mathematical operations, (including ways of solving mathematical problems), business, commercial and financial schemes, schemes of operation, and printed sheets, cards, tickets or the like which are mere records of intelligence.

A distinction also has been drawn between the discovery of laws or principles of nature and the application thereof to produce a particular practical and useful result. A reason why the former has not been treated as a proper subject of patent according to the principles developed pursuant to the Statute of 1623 was considered as long ago as 1852 in Carpmael, 'The Law of Patents for Inventions' 5th ed, 42–43:

> Let it not however be supposed that the minds of the individuals making such discoveries of principles are underrated, on the contrary, the highest respect is due to both, but it will be evident that their discoveries are not of that kind which should secure to them the right of toll on all future practical applications of such principles; such a course would lead to endless difficulties, and tend to prevent those rapid strides to improvements by which the existence of the present law has been marked.

...

Once full weight is given to the reasoning in the *NRDC Case* and to other decisions, including those of the Patents Appeal Tribunal in England before the commencement of the 1977 Act, it follows that the

PRECEDENT

Petty Patent should not have been held invalid on the footing that the claim was not for a manner of manufacture within the meaning of para 18(1)(a) of the 1990 Act.

The *NRDC Case* (102 CLR at 275–277) requires a mode or manner of achieving an end result which is an artificially created state of affairs of utility in the field of economic endeavour. In the present case, a relevant field of economic endeavour is the use of word processing to assemble text in Chinese language characters. The end result achieved is the retrieval of graphic representations of desired characters, for assembly of text. The mode or manner of obtaining this, which provides particular utility in achieving the end result, is the storage of data as to Chinese characters analysed by stroke-type categories, for search including 'flagging' (and 'unflagging') and selection by reference thereto.

Traditionally, business methods were also considered unpatentable because they were thought of as ideas or schemes, as indicated in the quote from James Lahore extracted in *CCOM*, above. However, the US case of *State Street Bank & Trust Co v Signature Financial Group Inc*, 149 F 3d 1368 (1998) forced a reassessment of the scope of this limitation on patenting. Signature Financial held a patent for a 'hub and spoke' system for pooling assets of mutual funds (spokes) in an investment portfolio (the hub). State Street demanded a licence from Signature Financial to use the hub and spoke system. Signature Financial refused, and State Street filed for invalidity on the basis that what was claimed was not patentable subject matter. The Federal Circuit Court of Appeals held that the system was patentable on the basis that the transformation of data by a machine through a series of mathematical calculations was a practical application of a mathematical algorithm and produced a 'useful, concrete and tangible result' (in that case, the machine produced a final share price). Following *State Street* and other judicial decisions, large numbers of patents claiming business methods were granted in the USA and a new category was added to the US patent classification. Many thousands of applications have been filed since then. Business method patents typically include such subject matter as methods of trading, transacting, financing, resource management, advertising, marketing and customer service. They tend to be directed towards the way business information is obtained and used, rather than towards development of new technologies. However, the US Supreme Court decision in *Bilski v Kappos*, 561 US 593 (2010) caused a re-evaluation of the role of the patentable subject matter requirement in determining the patentability of business methods. Although the Supreme Court in *Bilski* did not specifically overrule *State Street*, it clearly rejected any notion that a 'useful, concrete and tangible result' is *the* test for patentable subject matter in the USA. More recently, the US Supreme Court was given the opportunity to revisit the patentability of business methods in *Alice Corporation Pty Ltd v CLS Bank International*, 134 S Ct 2347 (2014). Key aspects of these decisions, together with relevant UK and European jurisprudence, were summarised by the Full Court of the Federal Court in its recent decision in *Research Affiliates LLC v Commissioner of Patents* [2014] FCAFC 150, extracted below.

In Australia, the Federal Court has also been given a number of opportunities to consider the patentability of business methods. In *Welcome Real-Time SA v Catuity Inc* [2001] FCA 445; (2001) 113 FCR 110, Heerey J considered whether smart card technology was patentable subject matter, guided by the US decision in *State Street*. The Full Federal Court explored the patentability of business methods more fully in *Grant v Commissioner of Patents* [2006] FCAFC 120; (2006)

154 FCR 62. In 2013, two more cases relating to computer-implemented business methods came before the Federal Court, with differing results. Both cases were appeals from decisions of the Commissioner of Patents not to grant the patents in issue. In the first of these, *Research Affiliates LLC v Commissioner of Patents* [2013] FCA 71; (2013) 300 ALR 724, Emmett J rejected the appeal. That decision was subsequently appealed to the Full Court of the Federal Court, which handed down its decision on 10 November 2014 (extracted below), affirming the first instance decision. In the second case, *RPL Central Pty Ltd v Commissioner of Patents* [2013] FCA 871, Middleton J upheld the appeal. The Full Court in *Research Affiliates* discussed the key points of the *RPL Central* decision, and the rationale for the different outcomes. Although the Commissioner of Patents filed an appeal against the first instance decision in *RPL Central* with the Full Court, the hearing was postponed, pending the outcome of the *Research Affiliates* appeal. At the time of writing, it is not yet clear whether *RPL Central* will proceed to a hearing by the Full Court.

CASE EXTRACT: CURRENT LAW

Research Affiliates LLC v Commissioner of Patents

[2014] FCAFC 150
Federal Court of Australia, Full Court

[Research Affiliates claimed a software application for constructing security portfolios. The essence of the claimed invention was a method of passive investing using indexes that include non-financial and non-market capitalisation metrics, thereby better reflecting the economic scale or long-term growth potential of the individual securities than systems that rely solely on market-based weightings. The Court considered in some detail the relevant law in other jurisdictions prior to reaching its decision on whether the manner of manufacture requirement was satisfied.]

Kenny, Bennett and Nicholas JJ:

THE POSITION IN OTHER JURISDICTIONS

15. A consideration of the way in which some other courts and tribunals have dealt with the question is helpful, although the differences between the legislative contexts governing their decisions and our own governing law must be borne in mind.

EUROPE AND THE UNITED KINGDOM (UK)

16. In the UK, in *International Business Machines Corporation's Application* [1980] FSR 564 *(IBM 1)*, Graham and Whitford JJ found a claim directed to a data handling system suitable for establishing prices to commodities such as shares, based on buy and sell orders, patentable. Their Honours' reasoning was based on the fact that a computer was programmed in a particular way, such that the computer operated in accordance with the method. The method was embodied in the program and in the apparatus in physical form, on the basis of which Graham and Whitford JJ concluded that the claims should be allowed to proceed.

17. There has been some apparent divergence of approach between the UK Courts and the Board of Appeal and the Enlarged Board of Appeal of the European Patent Office (together, the Board) as to

the analysis of patentability of computer-implemented methods, although in each case the basis of the analysis is Art 52 of the European Patent Convention (EPC). Some of the difficulties have been outlined by the UK Court of Appeal in *Symbian Ltd v Comptroller General of Patents* [2009] RPC 1 (*Symbian*). In discussing various decisions of the Board, and bearing in mind the specific statutory context in which the Board and the English courts operate, the different explanations of what can be patentable are, to say the least, confusing.

18. The context is that Art 52 of the EPC and the corresponding UK statutory provision exclude from patentability, relevantly:

a)   discoveries, scientific theories and mathematical methods;
b)   aesthetic creations;
c)   schemes, rules and methods for performing mental acts, playing games or doing business, and programs for computers;
d)   presentations of information.

19. Article 52 is expressed subject to the proviso that the statute prevents such things from being treated as an invention for the purpose of the convention 'only to the extent to which a [patent] or [application for a patent] relates to such subject-matter or activities as such'. The corresponding UK provision contains a similar proviso.

20. This has given rise to numerous discussions as to what is more than a computer program '*as such*' and as to the 'technical effect' or 'technical contribution' of the claimed invention.

21. The approach in some of the decisions of the Board has been summarised by Kitchin J (as he then was) in *Astron Clinica Ltd v Comptroller General of Patents, Designs and Trade Marks* [2008] 2 All ER 742 at 753 as being that 'any program on a carrier has a technical character and so escapes the prohibition in art 52'. The Board in its decision of *FUJITSU/File search method and apparatus, and index file creation method and device* T1351/04, 18 April 2007 effectively adopted its own position rather than that of the UK courts and made, in what was described in *Symbian* at [45], as 'the bald statement':

> The claimed method requires the use of a computer. It is therefore technical in character and constitutes an invention within the meaning of Art 52.

22. The UK Court of Appeal has rejected this approach as being inconsistent with previous Board decisions and with earlier decisions of the Court of Appeal (*Symbian* at [46]).

23. In our opinion, it is more helpful to consider the analysis of the issue in the UK decisions which, with respect, provide a consistent approach. Despite being in the context of the statutory exclusion of computer programs 'as such', the UK decisions are of assistance in understanding the distinction to be drawn in the Australian context between an unpatentable business method and a claimed invention which may be patentable if the invention results in an 'artificial effect', within the understanding of that concept as explained in *NRDC*.

24. The approach of the UK courts can be understood by a consideration of the decisions of the UK Court of Appeal in *Aerotel Ltd v Telco Holdings Ltd; Re Macrossan's Application* [2007] 1 All ER 225 (*Aerotel*), *Symbian* and *HTC Europe Co Ltd v Apple Inc* [2013] RPC 30 (*HTC*).

AEROTEL

...

26. It is not necessary to go into the detail of Jacob LJ's description of the bases for conflicting decisions of the Board and the UK courts, or the different approaches which have been adopted in order

to ascertain patentability under Art 52. Suffice to say that it has not been easy for the UK courts or the Board to determine whether or not a claim is to a computer program 'as such' and thereby excluded from patentability, or whether the invention makes 'a technical contribution to the known art'.

27. Lord Justice Jacob also said that, as a matter of logic (at [32]):

> Patents are essentially about information as to what to make or do. If all the patentee has taught new is something about an excluded category, then it makes sense for the exclusion to apply. If he has taught more, then it does not.

28. In discussing this issue, his Lordship expressed the view that claims to a computer program loaded onto a known form of medium, or a claim to a particular system of conducting business over the internet using standard hardware, are examples of what is excluded by Art 52. This is in contrast to a hard drive loaded with such program where the hard drive specified was itself new and inventive. In the latter case, it would not be the program which caused the claim to escape Art 52 but the newness of the kind of hard drive on which the music was loaded.

29. *Aerotel* sets out an approach, in four steps:

1. properly construe the claim;
2. identify the actual contribution;
3. ask whether it falls solely within the excluded subject matter; and
4. check whether the actual or alleged contribution is actually technical in nature.

30. The second step requires the court to consider what the inventor 'has really added to human knowledge', looking at substance and not form. According to the third step, if the contribution identified consisted of excluded subject matter as such, it would be excluded and it would be unnecessary to progress to the fourth step.

31. One of the patents in *Aerotel* related to an automated method of acquiring the documents necessary to incorporate a company, and involved a user sitting at a computer and communicating with a remote server, answering questions. As explained in [63], it was not suggested that what was invented was a new kind of hardware. Rather:

> What [the inventor] has thought of is an interactive system which will do the job which otherwise would have been done by a solicitor or company formation agent. Questions are asked, the answers incorporated in the draft, and depending on some particular answers, further questions are asked and the answers incorporated. That is his contribution.

32. At [68]–[73], Jacob LJ said that whether as an abstract or generalised activity or specific activity, if the claim is to a method of doing business as such, it is excluded. His Honour rejected the analogy of '*a tool*' used in business, such as a telephone, saying that the method was for the very business itself, 'the business of advising upon and creating appropriate company formation documents'. Apart from the mere fact of running a computer program, there was nothing technical about the contribution where it amounted to a computer program which could be used to carry out the method where the hardware used was standard and not part of the contribution.

  ...

SYMBIAN

37. The Court of Appeal in *Symbian* endorsed the approach previously taken in *Aerotel* when applying the principle to a UK patent application entitled 'Mapping dynamic link libraries in a computer device',

which concerned a method of accessing data in a dynamic link library in a computing device. Lord Justice Jacob (with whom Kay and Neuberger LJJ agreed) said at [48] that '[t]he mere fact that what is sought to be registered is a computer program is plainly not determinative'. The question, his Lordship said, was whether it revealed a 'technical' contribution to the state of the art (as is reflected in the fourth step in *Aerotel*).

38. Recognising that the boundary line between what is and what is not a technical contribution is imprecise, Jacob LJ commented that there are difficulties in formulating a precise test for deciding whether a computer program is excluded from patentability.

39. In *Symbian*, the Court held that the claimed invention was not a method of doing business, or a mathematical method, or a method for performing mental acts, and so did make a technical contribution. The Court considered that as a result of the invention, not only would the computer containing the instructions in question be a better computer, but also that the instructions solved a 'technical' problem lying within the computer itself (at [53]–[54]). Further, the invention would have an effect within the computer as programmed with the relevant instructions; the beneficial consequence of those instructions would also feed into cameras and other devices and products. The invention resulted in improved speed and reliable functioning of the computer, such that: '[a]s a matter of such reality there is more than just a 'better program', there is a faster and more reliable computer' (at [55]–[56]). The Court highlighted that more is needed than a code as embodied on a physical medium which causes the computer to operate in accordance with that code.

HTC

40. The UK Court of Appeal gave further consideration to the patentability in this field of endeavour in *HTC*. This involved consideration of *Aerotel* and *Symbian*. Lord Justice Kitchin noted that the Board had considered *Aerotel* in *Duns Licensing Associates* [2007] EPOR 38 (*Duns*) and had been critical of it, describing it as 'not consistent with a good-faith interpretation' of the EPC; in fact, 'irreconcilable' with it.

41. On the *Aerotel* approach, a claimed invention whose only contribution is not technical or lies in an excluded field falls to be rejected under Art 52. On the *Duns* approach, the invention falls to be rejected under Art 56 because such a contribution must be cut out of the assessment of inventive step. Lord Justice Kitchin observed that, whichever route is taken when assessing whether computer programs were excluded from patentability, 'one ought to end up at the same destination' (at [41]). He said that the approach was to consider whether the invention made a technical contribution to the known art, with the rider that novel or inventive purely excluded subject matter did not count as a technical contribution, and to follow the structured approach adopted in *Aerotel*.

42. Lord Justice Kitchin summarised the test in principle, from *Aerotel*, *Symbian* and *Duns*, as whether the contribution can or cannot be characterised as technical (at [45]–[49]).

- It is not possible to define a clear rule to determine whether or not a program is excluded.
- The fact that improvements are made to the software rather than hardware forming part of the computer does not make a difference. The analysis is one of substance, not form.
- The exclusions operate cumulatively. For example, a program relating to a new way of calculating a square root with the aid of a computer and stored on a ROM (such as in *Gale's Application* [1991] RPC 305) is still a computer program (excluded matter) incorporating a mathematical method (also an excluded matter).

- It is helpful to ask what the invention contributes to the art as a matter of practical reality over and above the fact that it relates to a program for a computer. If the only contribution lies in excluded subject matter then it is not patentable.
- It is also helpful to consider whether the invention may be regarded as solving a problem which is essentially technical and whether that problem lies inside or outside the computer. An invention that solves a technical problem within the computer will have a relevant technical effect. An invention which solves a technical problem outside the computer will also have a relevant technical effect, for example by controlling an improved technical process.

43. The Court endorsed (at [50]–[51]) the 'useful signposts' approach derived by Lewison J (as he then was) from *Aerotel* and *Symbian* in *AT&T Knowledge Ventures LP v Comptroller General of Patents* [2009] EWHC 343 (Pat), as set out below.

- The claimed technical effect has a technical effect on a process which is carried on outside the computer.
- The claimed technical effect operates at the level of the architecture of the computer, that is to say whether the effect is produced irrespective of the data being processed or the applications being run.
- The claimed technical effect results in the computer being made to operate in a new way.
- There is an increase in the speed or reliability of the computer. This signpost was revisited by Lewison LJ in his judgment in *HTC*, such that the question ought be phrased in a less restrictive way, to be whether a program makes a computer a better computer in the sense of running more efficiently and effectively as a computer.
- The perceived problem is overcome by the claimed invention as opposed to it being merely circumvented.

44. Lord Justice Lewison, in *HTC*, pointed out that, because the interaction between hardware and software in a computer is inherently technical in the ordinary sense of the word, this is not enough for software to qualify as making a 'technical contribution'.

45. These analyses as to the necessary 'technical contribution' are pertinent to a consideration of a necessary 'technical effect'.

THE UNITED STATES
BILSKI V KAPPOS 130 S CT 3218 (2010) (BILSKI)

In *Bilski*, the United States Supreme Court considered patentability in the context of three specific exceptions to the otherwise broad patent eligibility principles in §101 of 35 US Code (US Patent Act), namely, 'laws of nature, physical phenomena and abstract ideas'.

46. Justice Kennedy, with whom the other judges either agreed or concurred, said that a categorical rule denying patent protection for inventions in areas not contemplated by Congress would frustrate the purposes of the US Patent Act (relying on *Diamond v Chakrabarty*, 447 US 303, 315 (1980)). Their Honours also recognised that questions of patent eligibility under §101 of the US Patent Act are only the threshold test for patent protection, and that requirements for novelty, non-obviousness and compliance with other matters (such as those set out in Australia in s 40 of the Act) provide a further balance between the protection of inventors and impeding progress by granting patents that are not justified. Justice Stevens with whom Ginsburg, Breyer and Sotomayor JJ joined, pointed out (at 3232) that '[f]or

centuries, it was considered well established that a series of steps for conducting business was not, in itself, patentable'. However, Kennedy J said that it is not clear how far a prohibition on business method patents would reach.

47. The invention there under consideration explained how buyers and sellers of commodities in the energy market could protect or hedge against the risk of price changes. The claim was not to a computer-implemented method. That is, that the invention was not implemented on a specific apparatus. The Supreme Court held that this reduced the concept of hedging to a mathematical formula, which was an abstract idea and thus not a patentable process.

48. Justice Kennedy emphasised (at 3227) that there was nothing in the US Patent Act that confined a process, such that it required that it be tied to a machine or to transform an article (referred to as the 'machine-or-transformation test'), although it may be a useful investigative tool for determining whether a claimed invention is a patent-eligible process. It was not the sole criterion for determining patent eligibility.

49. Recognising that in the current 'Information Age' it is necessary to set a bar at a height that enables the Court to balance creative endeavour and dynamic change with the special problems raised by some business method patents, such as vagueness and suspect validity, Kennedy J suggested (at 3229) that the unpatentability of abstract ideas could prove a useful tool in searching for a limiting principle. His Honour endorsed what had been said in *Parker v Flook*, 437 US 584 (1978), which rejected the notion 'that post-solution activity, no matter how conventional or obvious in itself, can transform an unpatentable principle into a patentable process'. That is, the prohibition against patenting abstract ideas cannot be circumvented by attempting to limit the use to, for example, a particular technological environment, or by adding 'insignificant post-solution activity' (*Diamond v Diehr*, 450 US 175, 191–192 (1981)).

50. Interestingly Stevens J, in considering English law and the *Statute of Monopolies* (at 3240), observed that there is no basis in the *Statute of Monopolies* or in pre-1790 English precedent to infer that business methods could qualify for a patent. This was despite the fact that during the 17th and 18th centuries, as his Honour said at 3241–3242:

> … Great Britain saw innovations in business organization, business models, management techniques, and novel solutions to the challenges of operating global firms in which the board of managers could be reached only by a long sea voyage. Few if any of these methods of conducting business were patented.

ALICE CORPORATION PTY LTD V CLS BANK INTERNATIONAL 134 S CT 2347 (2014) (*ALICE CORPORATION*)

51. In *Alice Corporation*, the patents at issue disclosed a computer-implemented scheme for mitigating 'settlement risk', that is the risk that only one party to a financial transaction will meet its financial obligations. The question for the Supreme Court was whether the claims were patent eligible under §101 of the US Patent Act, or were drawn to 'a patent-ineligible abstract idea'. The Court (Thomas J, with Sotomayor J filing a concurring opinion in which Ginsberg and Breyer JJ joined) held that the claims were to an abstract idea of intermediated settlement and that merely requiring generic computer implementation failed to transform that abstract idea into a patent eligible invention. This had also been the conclusion of the United States Courts of Appeals for the Federal Circuit (*CLS Bank International v Alice Corporation Pty Ltd*, 717 F 3d 1269 (2013)).

52. As summarised by Thomas J (at 2353), the patents claimed:

1. a method for exchanging financial obligations;
2. a computer system configured to carry out the method;
3. a computer readable medium containing program code for performing the method of exchanging obligations.

53. All of the claims were implemented using a computer; the system and media claims expressly recited a computer and the method claims required a computer.

54. In the specification, the invention was said to 'enable the management of risk relating to specified, yet unknown, future events' and that the 'invention relates to methods and apparatus, including electrical computers and data processing systems applied to financial matters and risk management'. The Court recorded that the claims were designed to facilitate the exchange of financial obligations between two parties using a computer system as a third party intermediary. The intermediary created 'shadow' credit and debit records that mirrored the balances in the parties' real world accounts at 'exchange institutions' eg banks. The intermediary updated the shadow records in real time as transactions were entered, allowing only those transactions for which the parties' shadow records indicated sufficient resources to satisfy their mutual obligations. All of the claims were implemented using a computer and some claims expressly recited a computer.

55. That is, the claimed method required the use of a computer to create electronic records, track multiple transactions, and issue simultaneous instructions. In that sense 'the computer [was] itself the intermediary' leading the Court to conclude that 'in light of the foregoing, the relevant question is whether the claims here do more than simply instruct the practitioner to implement the abstract idea of intermediated settlement on a generic computer. They do not.'

56. The plurality in the Federal Circuit followed the Supreme Court decision in *Mayo Collaborative Services v Prometheus Laboratories Inc*, 132 S Ct 1289 (2012) first to identify the abstract idea represented in the claim and then to determine whether the balance of the claim adds 'significantly more [than a patent upon the ineligible concept]'. The plurality concluded that the use of a computer to maintain, adjust and reconcile shadow accounts added nothing to the substance of the abstract idea of reducing settlement risk by effecting trades through a third party intermediary. Certain of the judges in the Federal Circuit issued a dissenting opinion, which said that the system claims were patentable because they were 'detailed, specific claims to a system of particular hardware programmed to perform particular functions [and t]he computer in the system claims [was] the entire detailed 'solution' without which it would have been impossible to achieve the invention's purpose' (at 1320).

57. Justice Thomas characterised the claims as being drawn to the concept of intermediate settlement, 'a fundamental economic practice long prevalent in our system of commerce' which, like the hedging in *Bilski*, was an abstract idea. Justice Sotomayor reiterated Stevens J's observation in *Bilski* that there was no suggestion in the early English cases that processes for organising human activity were patentable.

58. The Court concluded that the method claims merely required generic computer implementation and were insufficient to 'transform' the abstract idea into a patentable application and that the transformation has to be more than stating the abstract idea while adding the words 'applied'. The computer implementation did not supply the necessary inventive concept where the process could be carried out in existing computers long in use. Simply implementing a mathematical principle on

a physical machine was not, their Honours said, a patentable application of that mathematical principle sufficient to confer patentability, where the computer implementation is purely conventional. The prohibition against patenting abstract ideas cannot be circumvented by attempting to limit the use of the idea to a particular technological environment or by adding the words 'apply it with a computer'. The result would be different, as it was in *Diehr*, where an existing technological process was improved. However, where the claims did not contain any 'express language to define the computer's participation' (717 F 3d at 1286 per Lourie J) and the claims did not purport to include the functioning of the computer, they amounted to an instruction to apply the abstract idea of intermediated settlement using some unspecified generic computer.

RELEVANCE OF DECISIONS IN OTHER JURISDICTIONS

59. While decisions in other jurisdictions are not binding, it is noteworthy that the Australian approach to patentability in respect of inventions such as those considered here, is consistent with that taken in the United States and the UK to the extent discussed above. Such an outcome cannot guide the application of Australian patent law but, as explained by the High Court in *Aktiebolaget Hassle v Alphapharm Pty Ltd* (2002) 212 CLR 411 and *Apotex* [*Pty Ltd v Sanofi–Aventis Australia Pty Ltd* [2013] HCA 50], it is interesting to observe and, if the reasoning is apposite, it should be considered. As already indicated, the decisions in other jurisdictions cannot assist us where they are inconsistent with the Act and the authorities binding on us, as illustrated in [*D'Arcy v*] *Myriad* [*Genetics Inc* [2014] FCAFC 115] (see, for example, [131], [207]).

   . . .

AUSTRALIAN AUTHORITY ON CLAIMS TO COMPUTER-IMPLEMENTED METHODS

89. In *CCOM* [*Pty Ltd v Jiejing Pty Ltd* (1994) 51 FCR 260], the Full Court concluded that the use of word processing to assemble text in Chinese language characters was patentable. In *Welcome Real-Time SA v Catuity Inc* (2001) 113 FCR 110 (*Catuity*), Heerey J concluded that the necessary 'physically observable effect' was sufficiently found in the writing of new information to a file and the printing of a coupon concerning the operation of smart cards in connection with traders' loyalty programs.

   90. In *Grant* [*v Commissioner of Patents* (2006) 154 FCR 62], the Full Court considered relevant authorities, to that time. It endorsed (at [14]) the principle that business, commercial and financial schemes as such have never been considered patentable. The Full Court, after consideration of the then state of authority, drew a distinction between an unpatentable idea or scheme and a method that results in a new machine or process or gives an old machine a new or improved result. Put another way, it was a distinction between mere intellectual information and a method that affected the operation of an apparatus in a physical form.

   91. The Full Court adopted the reasoning in *NRDC*, including noting the following.

- The ability to adapt the notion of patentability to new scientific discoveries and technologies should not be fettered by contrived constraints and must be able to adapt to accommodate new inventions (at [8]).
- A process, to fall within s 6 of the *Statute of Monopolies*, must belong to a 'useful art as distinct from a fine art' and must have an 'industrial or commercial or trading character' (at [12] citing *NRDC* at 275).
- A product, in relation to a process, is 'only something in which the new and useful effect may be observed'; that '"something" need not be a "thing" in the sense of an article; it may be any physical

phenomenon in which the effect, be it creation or merely alteration, may be observed' (at [12] citing *NRDC* at 276).

- The effect of a method is a product if it consists of 'an artificially created state of affairs' (at [12] citing *NRDC* at 277).

92. Their Honours turned to some of the authorities concerning methods utilising computers, including UK authority in *Burroughs* [*Corporation (Perkin's) Application* [1974] RPC 147] and *IBM 1* to conclude that the distinction drawn was between mere intellectual information and a method that affected the operation of an apparatus in a physical form and that '[w]hen the method is practiced in a way that is embodied in a physical form it is a manner of manufacture' (at [18]).

93. Although much of the United States authority there cited has been superseded, the conclusion drawn in *Grant* at [23] stands, that the same tests apply for patents for business methods as for any other claimed invention and that the distinction is between the employment of an abstract idea or law of nature and the idea or law itself. There is a distinction between a technological innovation which is patentable and a business innovation which is not (at [24] citing *Catuity*). The Full Court's description in *Grant* at [29] of what may be patentable is helpful: '[a] product of a method is something in which a new and useful effect may be observed. For claimed computer programs, the courts looked to the application of the program to produce a practical and useful result, so that more than "intellectual information" was involved'.

94. When the authorities in Australia prior to and including *Grant* are considered, a consistent approach emerges as to the relevance of:

- a distinction between a claim to a business scheme and claims to methods which in practice result in a new machine or process or an old machine giving a new and improved result—that is, a distinction between mere intellectual information and a method that affects the operation of an apparatus in a physical form (*Grant* at [18]);
- the fact that the claimed steps are foreign to the normal use of computers, such as the production of an improved curve image ([*International Business Machines Corporation v Commissioner of Patents* (1991) 33 FCR 218] (*IBM 2*) at 225–226);
- the particular mode or manner of achieving an end result which is an artificially created state of affairs, such as the storage of data as to Chinese characters and retrieval of graphic representations to enable word processing (*CCOM* at 295);
- whether part of the invention is an inventive method which includes the application and operation in a physical device (*Grant* at [30]);
- the distinction drawn in *Catuity*, as explained in *Grant* (at [24]), between 'a technological innovation which is patentable and a business innovation which is not'. In *Catuity*, Heerey J did not accept that a physically observable effect was necessarily required (at [128]) but the Full Court in *Grant* expressed the opinion that a physical effect in the sense of a concrete effect or phenomenon, or manifestation or transformation is required (at [32]).
- the fact that a physical effect is required does not make it sufficient to confer patentability;
- the fact that a method may be called a business method does not prevent it being properly the subject of letters patent (*Grant* at [26] citing *Catuity* at [125]–[126]);
- the fact that for claimed computer programs, the courts look to the application of the program to produce a practical and useful result, so that more than 'intellectual information' is involved (*Grant*

at [29]). A method that is in the nature of directions for use does not constitute an invention or a manner of manufacture in the absence of some previously unrecognised property of an aspect of the method (*Grant* at [29]).

95. Since the first instance decision in the present case, Middleton J has had cause to consider patentability in *RPL Central Pty Ltd v Commissioner of Patents* [2013] FCA 871 (*RPL Central*) which concerned an invention entitled 'Method and System for Automated Collection of Evidence of Skills and Knowledge'. It related to the assessment of the competency or qualifications of individuals with respect to recognised standards, or Recognition of Prior Learning (RPL). In very summary form, the invention was said to enable the automation of the process of converting extensive criteria into a more convenient single entry 'question and answer' format.

96. At [40], Middleton J observed that while the invention was primarily concerned with the gathering of information relevant to the assessment of an individual's competency relative to a recognised qualification standard, an objective of the invention was to facilitate improvements in the overall RPL process, by means of a use of, and configuration of, the assessment server. As set out at [44], the invention enabled the automated generation of a wizard or similar user interface to perform the administrative work necessary to gather evidence from a prospective candidate, with a particular focus on 'online' implementation of such functions as the assessment of the competencies of individuals, the issue of qualifications, and the recommendation of suitable pathways based on an individual's competencies.

97. Justice Middleton recognised the fact that methods of calculations and theoretical schemes were not patentable (at [61]) and the distinction between mathematical formulae and a formula applied to achieve an end, such as the production of an improved curve image by a computer (*IBM 2*) and using a particular method of characterisation of character stokes, applied to an apparatus in such a way that the operation of a keyboard would enable the selection (through a computer) of the appropriate Chinese characters required for word processing in that language (*CCOM*).

98. Justice Middleton summarised the invention in *RPL Central* at [139] as one that enabled the retrieval of relevant data from a remotely located server via the internet and the generation of questions for, and presentation of questions to, the user based on this data. The effect of the process was experienced by the individual user on a computer. The user's responses were transferred to the assessment server. Importantly, 'the involvement of the computer in the invention is described in these claims in such a manner that it is inextricably linked with the invention itself'. In [172], his Honour said that the specification and the claims provided significant information about the invention which was to be implemented by means of the computer and that the computer was 'integral' to the invention there claimed. His Honour distinguished it from the primary judgment in the present case on that basis.

99. As we read his Honour's reasons, he aligned the invention with a new use of a computer as in *IBM 2* and *CCOM*, in contrast to mere implementation of the invention by a computer.

100. Relevantly to this appeal, Middleton J looked to whether the 'product' itself gave rise to an artificially created state of affairs (at [133]). Insofar as there was computer implementation, his Honour recognised (at [135]) the distinction between a mere 'modern and efficient tool by which to perform the method of the claimed invention (being a method of performing an aspect of a business)' which could be performed without use of a computer and would not be patentable, and an invention where 'the method was "tied to a machine"' and which would be patentable, such as in *IBM 2*, *CCOM* and *Catuity*. Justice Middleton held that the invention fell into the latter category, distinguishing it from the method

in *Grant* which 'truly' was, as there described, 'a mere scheme, an abstract idea, mere intellectual information' with no relevant physical effect whatsoever.

CONSIDERATION

101. Turning to the present appeal, the relevant inquiry is not into the form of the words to determine whether what is claimed is properly the subject of a patent. If a process is to be patentable, it must offer some advantage which is material, in the sense that the process belongs to a useful art. The characterisation of patentability by reference only to the description in *NRDC* of a product which consists of an artificially created state of affairs of economic significance was part of the High Court's reasoning but did not represent a sufficient or exhaustive statement of the circumstances in which a claimed invention is patentable.

102. Research Affiliates submits that the inexorable conclusion is that the present claim is to a patentable invention. It points to the steps of transformation of data occurring in the computer at each stage of the process, of accessing data, processing data, accessing the weighting function and applying the weighting function, culminating in the creation of an index. We do not agree. Rather, the inexorable conclusion applying the principles of patentability, is that the present claim is not to a patentable method.

103. As Thomas J said in *Alice Corporation*, there is a distinction, between mere implementation of an abstract idea in a computer and implementation of an abstract idea in a computer that creates an improvement in the computer. There is also a distinction between, on the one hand, a method involving components of a computer or machine and an application of an inventive method where part of the invention is the application and operation of the method in a physical device *and*, on the other, an abstract, intangible situation which is a mere scheme, an abstract idea and mere intellectual information.

104. A useful description of the distinction to be drawn was set out by Lourie J in *Bancorp Services LLC v Sun Life Assurance Co of Canada (US)* 687 F 3d 1266 (2012), 1277, 1278 (citations omitted):

> Modern computer technology offers immense capabilities and a broad range of utilities, much of which embodies significant advances that reside firmly in the category of patent-eligible subject matter. At its most basic, however, a 'computer' is 'an automatic electronic device for performing mathematical or logical operations'. As the Supreme Court has explained, '[a] digital computer ... operates on data expressed in digits, solving a problem by doing arithmetic as a person would do it by head and hand'. Indeed, prior to the information age, a 'computer was not a machine at all; rather, it was a job title: "a person employed to make calculations"'. Those meanings conveniently illustrate the interchangeability of certain mental processes and basic digital computation, and help explain why the use of a computer in an otherwise patent-ineligible process for no more than its most basic function—making calculations or computations—fails to circumvent the prohibition against patenting abstract ideas and mental processes. As we have explained, '[s]imply adding a "computer aided" limitation to a claim covering an abstract concept, without more, is insufficient to render the claim patent eligible'.
>
> *To salvage an otherwise patent-ineligible process, ... a computer must be integral to the claimed invention, facilitating the process in a way that a person making calculations or computations could not.*

(emphasis added)

105. The use of a computer necessarily involves the writing of information into the computer's memory. This means that there are a number of 'physical effects' in the sense of transformed data and memory storage during the claimed process. The claimed index in this case is data that exist in computer-readable form. The question is whether this is sufficient to make the claimed method properly the subject of letters patent. Research Affiliates contends that the information, once entered into or produced by means of the computer, becomes 'an artificially created state of affairs' which is of economic significance. It submits that the primary Judge erred in importing 'extraneous requirements' on computer implemented schemes that 'have no basis in the Australian authorities' which required there to be 'a specific effect being generated by the computer' (at [70]) or that the invention must 'improve the operation of or effect of the use of the computer' (at [70]). Research Affiliates challenges the primary Judge's description of the claimed invention as one which, absent computer implementation, could be simply written on paper (at [67]). It says that the fact of computer implementation simply cannot be ignored or dismissed as a modern equivalent of writing down on a piece of paper, thus ignoring the artificially created state of affairs. This, it submits, ignores an essential integer of the claim.

106. The determination whether the claimed invention is truly 'an artificially created state of affairs' in satisfaction of *NRDC* is made not by some mechanistic application of the criterion of artificiality or physical effect, but by an understanding of the claimed invention itself. The invention is to be understood as a matter of substance and not merely as a matter of form.

107. It is apparent from the description in the specification that the computer is simply the means whereby the analyst accesses data to generate an index. The work in generating the index and weighting is described in terms of the work of the analyst rather than as some technical generation by the computer. Indeed, while the specification states that the invention may be used for investment management or investment portfolio benchmarking, the exemplary embodiment makes it clear that it may be, but is not necessarily, implemented on a computer.

108. The computer that may be utilised is described in general terms, without an indication that any unusual technical effect is utilised. Although the specification states that '[t]hese computer program products may provide software to computer systems' and that '[t]he invention may be directed to such computer program products', little further specificity is provided.

109. The accepted evidence is that the result of implementation in a computer, and using computerised databases, will be a set of data relating to securities and other assets, stored in electronic form in the computer's RAM, which will initially comprise electrical signals in the computer's RAM. The required processing must be expressed as a series of algorithms in a programming language. Those algorithms can be incorporated into a computer program to implement the index generation method. The evidence also explains how one of the inventors made changes to a pre-written computer program, which caused the program to gather and process data and perform data manipulations and calculations to generate four 'fundamental' metrics. The inventor also outlined the steps of selecting and weighting the securities forming part of the index, which involved writing algorithms or 'macros' to further manipulate and refine the data. The end result of the entire process is an Excel file which identifies the top securities within the index (say, 200 top securities of the 250 securities in the index), which are then reweighted by dividing the fundamental score for each security by the sum of the fundamental scores of those top securities. This file is the index.

110. From the evidence, it cannot be said, as it was in *IBM 2* at 225–6, that the claimed method and the use of the algorithms involved steps which are foreign to the normal use of computers. In *CCOM*, the Full Court (at 291) warned against bringing into the determination of 'manner of manufacture' considerations of whether what was claimed involved anything new and unconventional in computer use and repeated the test in *NRDC* (at 276–277), that in so far as 'manufacture' suggests a 'vendible product', this is to be understood as covering every end produced or artificially created state of affairs which is of utility in practical affairs and whose significance thus is economic. Their Honours also drew upon the reasoning of Graham and Whitford JJ in *IBM 1*, where software had been designed to calculate automatically the selling price of stock or shares by comparing a set of buying and selling orders. The scheme was not itself novel and a standard computer could be programmed to perform it. The method was held to involve the operation or control of a computer, such that it was programmed in a particular way to operate in accordance with the inventor's method. The method was involved in the program and in the apparatus in physical form and was patentable. In *CCOM*, the field of economic endeavour was the use of word processing to assemble text in Chinese language characters. The end result achieved was the retrieval of graphic representations of desired characters, for assembly of text. The mode or manner of obtaining this was the storage of data as to Chinese characters analysed by stroke-type categories.

111. With great respect to the primary Judge, we do not see that the question of patentability can be answered by the observation that the method is simply the writing down of the information—a modern equivalent of writing the schemes on a piece of paper. This ignores the utilisation of the power of a computer to generate information. It would also render unpatentable many methods that are inventive uses of a computer that utilise previously unknown abilities of software and hardware.

112. However, as well as this analogy drawn upon by the primary Judge, his Honour drew a distinction between 'mere' use of a computer and a method involving a specific effect being generated by the computer or an improvement in the operation of, or effect of the use of, the computer (at [70]).

113. The effect of Research Affiliates' submissions is that the mere implementation of any abstract idea or scheme in a well-known machine is sufficient to render that unpatentable subject matter patentable because it gives rise to an 'artificial effect'. This approach is inconsistent with *NRDC* and is one of form not substance.

114. The invention set out in the specification is directed to the index itself. The method of the invention is not one that has any artificial or patentable effect other than the implementation of a scheme, which happens to use a computer to effect that implementation. There is no technical contribution to the invention or artificial effect of the invention by reason of the intervention of the inventors. To take the words of *NRDC* at 268, the process does not produce 'either immediately or ultimately, a useful physical result in relation to a material or tangible entity.' The claimed method, the result of the ingenuity of the inventors, does not *produce* such a result; the ingenuity is in the scheme. Again, drawing from *NRDC* at 270, there is a useful result of the claimed process but there is no physical thing 'brought into existence or so affected as the better to serve man's purposes'. There is no 'physical phenomenon in which the effect, be it creation or merely alteration, may be observed' (*NRDC* at 276).

115. The High Court (in *NRDC* at 277) spoke in terms of a separate result achieved by the claimed method that has its own economic utility consisting in the improvement. By this reasoning, the High

Court directed attention to the subject matter to which the claimed method was directed, which needed to exhibit the required characteristics of a manner of manufacture to be patentable. Here, that subject matter is truly the scheme, the idea, the index. As set out in the specification it may be, and in the claimed method it is, implemented in a computer, but the ingenuity of the inventors, the end result of which is the invention, is directed to the idea, which is not patentable. That method does not have an artificial effect falling squarely within the true concept of what must be produced by a process if it is to be held patentable (*NRDC* at 277).

116. The approach to be taken to deciding whether a claimed method or product is properly the subject of letters patent must be flexible and must allow for new technologies presently unknown. The principles should be applied irrespective of the area of human endeavour and invention under consideration. However, that is not to say that any and every claimed method or process is properly the subject of a patent. Examples of exceptions have been identified, such as abstract ideas and mere schemes. There is no formula to be mechanically applied. It is a question of understanding what has been the work of, the output of, and the result of, human ingenuity, and to apply the principles that have been developed and explained so well in *NRDC*.

117. In the context of the claim, the significance lies in the content of the data rather than any specific effect generated by the computer. The computer-implementation is an essential integer of the claimed process. That is, of course, important. It is of particular importance in the assessment of, for example, novelty and infringement. However, in examining whether a claimed invention is properly the subject of letters patent, it is necessary to look not only at the integers of that claimed invention but also at the substance of that invention.

118. The claimed method in this case clearly involves what may well be an inventive idea, but it is an abstract idea. The specification makes it apparent that any inventive step arises in the creation of the index as information and as a scheme. There is no suggestion in the specification or the claims that any part of the inventive step lies in the computer implementation. Rather, it is apparent that the scheme is merely implemented in a computer and a standard computer at that. It is no part of the claimed method that there is an improvement in what might broadly be called 'computer technology'.

119. The claims are not to a patentable invention within s 18(1)(a) of the Act.

120. Based on the reasoning in the cases discussed above, they would not be found to claim patentable subject matter in the UK or the United States either.

METHODS EMBODYING LAWS OF NATURE

There is an emerging body of case law in the USA which indicates that the courts will not accept the patent eligibility of methods that amount to patenting of a law of nature. To be patent eligible, another inventive concept would have to be added, to avoid pre-empting all further uses of the law of nature.[2] The US Supreme Court explored this issue in the case extracted below.

Australian courts have not yet had the opportunity to consider whether the same principles would apply in relation to methods embodying laws of nature.

---

2   See K Strandburg, 'Much Ado about Preemption' (2012) 50 *Houston Law Review* 563.

COMPARATIVE LAW

CASE EXTRACT: COMPARATIVE LAW

Mayo Collaborative Services v Prometheus Laboratories, Inc

132 S Ct 1289 (2012)
Supreme Court of the United States

[The patent in this matter claimed a method of comparing and analysing rates of drug metabolism in the human body with reference data.]

Breyer J (delivering the opinion of the Court) (at 1293–1297): 'Phenomena of nature, though just discovered, mental processes, and abstract intellectual concepts are not patentable, as they are the basic tools of scientific and technological work.' *Gottschalk v Benson*, 409 US 63, 67 (1972). And monopolization of those tools through the grant of a patent might tend to impede innovation more than it would tend to promote it.

The Court has recognized, however, that too broad an interpretation of this exclusionary principle could eviscerate patent law. For all inventions at some level embody, use, reflect, rest upon, or apply laws of nature, natural phenomena, or abstract ideas. Thus, in *Diamond v Diehr*, 450 US 175, 187 (1981) the Court pointed out that 'a process is not unpatentable simply because it contains a law of nature or a mathematical algorithm.' ... (quoting *Parker v Flook*, 437 US 584, 590 (1978)). It added that 'an *application* of a law of nature or mathematical formula to a known structure or process may well be deserving of patent protection.' *Diehr*, *supra*, at 187. And it emphasized Justice Stone's similar observation in *Mackay Radio & Telegraph Co v Radio Corp of America*, 306 US 86 (1939):

> While a scientific truth, or the mathematical expression of it, is not a patentable invention, a novel
> and useful structure created with the aid of knowledge of scientific truth may be. 450 US, at 188
> (quoting Mackay Radio, supra, at 94)

See also *Funk Brothers* [*Seed Co v Kalo Inoculant Co*, 333 US 127 (1948)], at 130 ('If there is to be invention from [a discovery of a law of nature], it must come from the application of the law of nature to a new and useful end').

Still, as the Court has also made clear, to transform an unpatentable law of nature into a patent-eligible *application* of such a law, one must do more than simply state the law of nature while adding the words 'apply it.' See, eg, *Benson*, *supra*, at 71–72.

The case before us lies at the intersection of these basic principles. It concerns patent claims covering processes that help doctors who use thiopurine drugs to treat patients with autoimmune diseases determine whether a given dosage level is too low or too high. The claims purport to apply natural laws describing the relationships between the concentration in the blood of certain thiopurine metabolites and the likelihood that the drug dosage will be ineffective or induce harmful side-effects. We must determine whether the claimed processes have transformed these unpatentable natural laws into patent eligible applications of those laws. We conclude that they have not done so and that therefore the processes are not patentable.

COMPARATIVE LAW

Our conclusion rests upon an examination of the particular claims before us in light of the Court's precedents. Those cases warn us against interpreting patent statutes in ways that make patent eligibility 'depend simply on the draftsman's art' without reference to the 'principles underlying the prohibition against patents for [natural laws].' *Flook, supra*, at 593. They warn us against upholding patents that claim processes that too broadly preempt the use of a natural law ... *Benson, supra*, at 71–72. And they insist that a process that focuses upon the use of a natural law also contain other elements or a combination of elements, sometimes referred to as an 'inventive concept,' sufficient to ensure that the patent in practice amounts to significantly more than a patent upon the natural law itself. *Flook, supra*, at 594; see also *Bilski* [*v Kappos*, 561 US 593, 610–611 (2010)] ('[T]he prohibition against patenting abstract ideas 'cannot be circumvented by attempting to limit the use of the formula to a particular technological environment' or adding 'insignificant post solution activity' (quoting *Diehr, supra*, at 191–192)).

We find that the process claims at issue here do not satisfy these conditions. In particular, the steps in the claimed processes (apart from the natural laws themselves) involve well-understood, routine, conventional activity previously engaged in by researchers in the field. At the same time, upholding the patents would risk disproportionately tying up the use of the underlying natural laws, inhibiting their use in making further discoveries.

...

Prometheus' patents set forth laws of nature—namely, relationships between concentrations of certain metabolites in the blood and the likelihood that a dosage of a thiopurine drug will prove ineffective or cause harm. Claim 1, for example, states that *if* the levels of 6–TG in the blood (of a patient who has taken a dose of a thiopurine drug) exceed about 400 pmol per 8×10^8 red blood cells, *then* the administered dose is likely to produce toxic side effects. While it takes a human action (the administration of a thiopurine drug) to trigger a manifestation of this relation in a particular person, the relation itself exists in principle apart from any human action. The relation is a consequence of the ways in which thiopurine compounds are metabolized by the body—entirely natural processes. And so a patent that simply describes that relation sets forth a natural law. The question before us is whether the claims do significantly more than simply describe these natural relations. To put the matter more precisely, do the patent claims add *enough* to their statements of the correlations to allow the processes they describe to qualify as patent-eligible processes that *apply* natural laws? We believe that the answer to this question is no.

...

If a law of nature is not patentable, then neither is a process reciting a law of nature, unless that process has additional features that provide practical assurance that the process is more than a drafting effort designed to monopolize the law of nature itself. A patent, for example, could not simply recite a law of nature and then add the instruction 'apply the law.' Einstein, we assume, could not have patented his famous law by claiming a process consisting of simply telling linear accelerator operators to refer to the law to determine how much energy an amount of mass has produced (or vice versa). Nor could Archimedes have secured a patent for his famous principle of flotation by claiming a process consisting of simply telling boat builders to refer to that principle in order to determine whether an object will float.

DISCOVERIES AND PRODUCTS OF NATURE

Traditionally, mere discoveries were considered unpatentable because of the requirement that knowledge and ingenuity be used to produce a new and useful thing.[3] Discoveries are neither new nor useful, first, because they are already in existence, and second, because they do not have the requisite industrial applicability. In *NRDC* the difficulty in distinguishing between discoveries and inventions was recognised by the High Court. They insisted that the whole process must be looked at and that it was enough to show that there was one inventive step beyond the prior art (at 264). Even though discoveries are not patentable, patents can be claimed for methods embracing discoveries, or for products of discoveries, provided they fulfil the other patenting requirements.

Products of nature fall within the concept of discovery: they are already in existence and generally do not have the requisite industrial applicability. In *Chakrabarty* Burger CJ held that Chakrabarty's modified microorganism plainly qualified for patenting on the basis that he had 'produced a new bacterium with markedly different characteristics from any found in nature and one having the potential for significant utility. His discovery is not nature's handiwork but his own, accordingly it is patentable subject matter under §101'. His Honour held that the true distinction is between products of nature and human-made inventions, not between living and inanimate things, and that there was nothing in the language or history of any of the Acts to suggest that living things are not included in §101.

Chakrabarty paved the way for patenting of other inventions in the field of biotechnology. It would seem that until recently the US Patent and Trademarks Office only required that biological material is isolated or purified and that it offered some material advantage in utility over the naturally occurring material to bring it under the umbrella of patentable subject matter.

In Australia, even prior to *Chakrabarty*, in *Rank Hovis McDougall Ltd's Application* (1976) 46 AOJP 3915 the Assistant Commissioner of Patents granted a patent for a new strain of microorganism that could be used in a process for the production of an edible protein. The process itself was also patentable, but a patent was refused for the original microorganism because it was held to be naturally occurring. An official notice from the Patent Office confirmed this decision in 1980. The Patent Office has continued with the practice of granting patents for processes involving naturally occurring living organisms. It has also accepted patent applications for living organisms themselves, provided that they are not naturally occurring, and for isolated components of living organisms, including genes, proteins and cells. Despite the controversial nature of such patents, it was not until recently that the Australian courts had the opportunity to consider the applicability of the *NRDC* test in relation to subject matter of this nature. US courts have had more opportunity to consider relevant subject matter and have, as a consequence, developed a 'product of nature' doctrine. Yet the US courts also had to wait until 2010 before they had the opportunity to rule on whether gene sequences isolated from the natural world were patentable subject matter. Interestingly, the same subject matter was considered in both jurisdictions: gene sequences linked with hereditary forms of breast and ovarian cancer. However, the outcomes were different, with patent eligibility of the subject matter being upheld in Australia and denied in part in the USA. The decision of the Full Court of the Federal Court of Australia in *D'Arcy v Myriad Genetics Inc* [2014] FCAFC 115; (2014) 107 IPR 478, extracted below, which involved American and Australian applicants, provides an account of the US litigation, as well as the Australian position.

---

3   Lindley LJ in *Lane Fox v Kensington and Knightsbridge Electric Lighting Co* [1892] 3 Ch 424 at 428–429.

CASE EXTRACT: CURRENT LAW

D'Arcy v Myriad Genetics Inc

[2014] FCAFC 115; (2014) 107 IPR 478
Federal Court of Australia, Full Court

[The sole ground of appeal raised by the applicants in this case was that the isolated nucleic acid sequences claimed in Myriad Genetics' Australian patent (also referred to as nucleotide sequences, DNA sequences or gene sequences) were not patentable subject matter under Australian law. The sequences related to the 'BRCA1' gene, mutations in which have been linked to breast and ovarian cancer. The equivalent US litigation, considered in detail below by the Full Federal Court, concerned Myriad's US patents over the same 'BRCA1' gene sequences, as well as over 'BRCA2' gene sequences (it also involved a separate question of whether the methods of using the sequences for diagnostic purposes were patentable: the Federal Circuit Court of Appeals held that they were not, and this was not appealed to the Supreme Court).]

Allsop CJ, Dowsett, Kenny, Bennett and Middleton JJ: 9. What are the principles and considerations relevant to the applicability of s 6 of the *Statute of Monopolies* that inform the answer to the question whether the claims here are patentable? These are discussed more fully below, but the following are worthy of emphasis at the outset.

10. First, the boundaries of the conception of patentability are not dictated only by deductive logic from the linguistic premises formulated in the scientific knowledge of a particular age; rather, the boundaries must be such as to be apt to encompass the development of science and technology, and human ingenuity. This explains the broadening concept of patentability since the first quarter of the 17th century.

11. Secondly, human intervention that creates an artificial state of affairs that has some discernible effect is essential.

12. Thirdly, whilst notions of utility, ingenuity and invention have their place after one concludes that the claim is within the field of s 6, such notions also inform the context of analysis of patentability by assisting in describing the claims to processes or products that are claimed new results of principles carried into practice through human intervention and that create some claimed useful result by involving an artificial state of affairs.

13. Fourthly, expressions such as 'the work of nature' or 'the laws of nature' are not found in the statute; nor are they useful tools of analysis.

14. Fifthly, the distinction between discovery of a scientific principle or fact and a deployment of such to a useful end by a procedure is real.

15. These important informing principles and considerations assist in the conclusion that, for the reasons set out below, the relevant claims as analysed below are patentable as within the meaning and boundaries of s 6 of the *Statute of Monopolies*.

. . .

LEGAL PRINCIPLES

...

ASSOCIATION FOR MOLECULAR PATHOLOGY V MYRIAD GENETICS INC [*133 S CT 2107* (2013)]

130. Justice Thomas delivered the opinion of the US Supreme Court. The Court characterised Myriad's work. Myriad had identified the exact location of the BRCA1 and BRCA2 genes, allowing Myriad to determine their typical nucleotide sequence. That information in turn enabled Myriad to develop medical tests useful for detecting mutations in the genes and thereby assessing whether the patient has an increased risk of cancer.

131. The Court held that a naturally occurring DNA segment is a product of nature and not patent eligible merely because it has been isolated, because DNA's information sequences and the processes that create mRNA, amino acids and proteins occur naturally within cells. cDNA [that is, 'complementary DNA', or a laboratory-created DNA sequence] was held to be patent eligible because it is not naturally occurring.

...

134. The approach of the Supreme Court was set out as follows ...:

> Myriad's patents would, if valid, give it the exclusive right to isolate an individual's BRCA1 and BRCA2 genes (or any strand of 15 or more nucleotides within the genes) by breaking the covalent bonds that connect the DNA to the rest of the individual's genome.

135. The reasoning of the Court, in summary, can be set out as follows:

- Laws of nature, natural phenomena and abstract ideas are not patentable, as an implicit exception to patentability.
- Products of nature are not created and manifestations of nature are free to all men and are reserved exclusively to none ([*Diamond v*] *Chakrabarty* [447 US 303 (1980)]). However, the rule against patents on naturally occurring things is not without limits. All inventions, at some level, use or apply laws of nature.
- Patent protection strikes a delicate balance between creating incentives and impeding the flow of information that might permit or spur invention. This 'well established stand' must be used to determine the patentability of the Myriad claims.
- The Myriad claims fall 'squarely' within the law of nature exception. Myriad found the location of the BRCA1 and BRCA2 genes, but that discovery by itself does not lend to the BRCA genes new compositions of matter within §101 of the US Act.
- Myriad did not create or alter any of the genetic information encoded in BRCA1 and BRCA2 or the location and order of the nucleotides. It 'found' an important and useful gene.
- Separating the gene from its surrounding genetic material is not an act of invention.
- Myriad's extensive research efforts cannot be imported into a patentability inquiry.
- The claims focus on the genetic information. They are not saved by the fact of isolation and the severing of chemical bonds, because Myriad's claims are not expressed in terms of chemical composition nor do they rely in any way on chemical changes that result from the isolation.
- The practice of the American Patent and Trade Mark Office is not relevant because it was not endorsed by Congress. Indeed, the US Government argued that isolated DNA was not patent eligible.

CURRENT LAW

136. The Court recognised that the creation of a cDNA sequence from [messenger RNA] results in an exon-only molecule that is not naturally occurring. While it was argued that the nucleotide sequence of cDNA is dictated by nature, the Court said that mankind unquestionably created something new when cDNA was made. It was not thereby a product of nature and, accordingly, was held to be patent eligible. The exception was very short series of DNA that may have no intervening introns to remove when creating cDNA, where that short strand of cDNA may be indistinguishable from natural DNA.

137. The Court was careful to note that the patent claims were not to an innovative method of manipulating genes, that the processes used by Myriad to isolate DNA were well understood by geneticists at the time and that the case did not involve patents of new applications of knowledge about the BRCA1 and BRCA2 genes. The underlying conclusion was that 'genes and the information they encode are not patent eligible under §101 simply because they have been isolated from the surrounding genetic material'.

...

ASSOCIATION FOR MOLECULAR PATHOLOGY V UNITED STATES PATENT AND TRADEMARK OFFICE AND MYRIAD GENETICS, INC, 689 F 3D 1303 (2012)

139. It is worth also examining some of the reasoning in the Court of Appeals for the Federal Circuit, in particular because it contains a more detailed analysis of the underlying chemistry, which is not in dispute in this proceeding. The arguments before the Federal Circuit were similar to those presently advanced.

140. The question was, similarly, the extent to which isolated nucleic acid, whether limited to cDNA or not, falls within the patentability exception for products of nature.

141. In coming to the conclusion that isolated DNAs, including cDNAs, are patent eligible subject matter under §101, Lourie J cited the US Supreme Court decisions in *Chakrabarty* and *Funk Brothers* [*Seed Co v Kalo Inoculant Co*, 333 US 127 (1948)].

142. His Honour decided that the relevant question was whether a change in the claimed composition's identity compared to what exists in nature is such that when combined or altered in a manner not found in nature, the two compositions have similar characteristics or whether human intervention has given the composition 'markedly different or distinctive characteristics'. This has some similarity to the reasoning in *NRDC*.

143. As his Honour observed, some derision had been directed to his reliance on the fact of the breaking of chemical bonds to conclude that the isolated nucleic acid is in fact a different compound. That, as we read his Honour's reasons, does them injustice. The subject matter of the claims is a chemical compound, not pure information content. It cannot be inappropriate to view it as such. Judge Lourie said (at 1329) that a covalent bond is the defining boundary between one molecule and another, but that was not the sole basis for his Honour's reasoning. His Honour's conclusion was that, chemically, the isolated DNA molecule is a distinct chemical entity. It is not a purified form of a natural material. The claimed isolated DNA molecule does not exist as in nature. The point, as his Honour says at 1328, is that the claim is to a composition 'having a distinctive chemical structure and identity' from that of a native element, molecule or structure such that it has a markedly different chemical nature from the native DNA. In describing a distinction between an isolated gene and a leaf snapped from a tree, Lourie J incorporated matters that are reflected in *NRDC*, namely that isolated genes provide useful diagnostic tools and medicines—and so are within the concept of economic significance considered important by the High Court.

144. In dealing with the submission that the claims were to mere reflections of a law of nature, Lourie J said that they are not so any more than any product of man reflects and is consistent with the law of nature: 'everything and everyone comes from nature, following its laws', whereas these claims are to 'the products of man'. These words bear resemblance to the High Court's reasoning in *NRDC*.

145. Judge Moore was also alive, with respect, to the distinction between claims to subject matter that had previously existed in nature exactly as claimed, and the present case. Apart from citing *Funk Brothers* and *Chakrabarty*, her Honour referred to *Parke-Davis & Co v HK Mulford Co*, 189 F 95, 103 (SDNY 1911) where purified adrenaline was considered patentable subject matter because it was 'for every practical purpose a new thing commercially and therapeutically'. Similarly, in *Merck & Co v Olin Mathieson Chemical Corp*, 253 F 2d 156 (1958), the Fourth Circuit found purified vitamin B12 to be patentable, because it had 'such advantageous characteristics as to replace [the naturally occurring] liver products. What was produced was, in no sense, an old product'; this was in contrast to 'mere' purification, where the purified subject matter was of a naturally occurring element with inherent physical properties unchanged upon purification. Judge Moore applied *Funk Brothers* and *Chakrabarty* and said that she found 'no reason to deviate from this longstanding flexible approach in this case'.

...

150. Judge Bryson, in dissent, concluded that 'Myriad is claiming the genes themselves'. His Honour looked to what he regarded as the only material change made to those genes, which he said was necessarily incidental to the extraction of the genes from the environment in which they are found in nature. He concluded that this meant that the isolated genes were not materially different than the native genes and drew on the metaphors of a 'new mineral discovered in the earth', 'a new plant found in the wild' compared to a baseball bat that is 'extracted' or 'isolated' from an ash tree, necessarily changing the nature, form and use of the ash tree and thus results in a man-made manufacture, with a function entirely different from that of the raw material from which it was obtained and not a naturally occurring product.

151. The breaking of the chemical bonds was, in his Honour's view, simply necessary to uphold the gene in its place in the body while the genetic coding sequence remained the same. The isolation process was, he said, 'according to nature's predefined boundaries; i.e., at points that preserve the ability of the gene to express the protein for which it is coded' (at 1352). That is, his Honour held that they were not 'the products of invention'. In that regard, he likened the new uses to which an isolated nucleic acid sequence could be put to extracting minerals or taking plant cuttings from wild plants.

...

AUSTRALIAN LEGISLATIVE AND PUBLIC HISTORY

156. The primary judge looked at the legislative history of the Act to determine whether the conclusion to which he had come might for some reason be seen to be inconsistent with Parliament's intentions.

157. His Honour turned to the decision in the Australian Patent Office in *Kirin-Amgen Inc v Board of Regents of University of Washington* (1995) 33 IPR 557, where the Deputy Commissioner of Patents observed that an objection of manner of manufacture might arise if the claims to a purified and isolated gene DNA sequence were directed to a mere chemical curiosity 'but that is plainly not the case with this invention'. That decision was appealed to the Federal Court and then to the Full Court. No concern as to the patentability of the claimed DNA sequence was expressed and the question of manner of manufacture did not arise.

158. The Australian Law Reform Commission (ALRC) later published a report into gene patenting. The report stated that 'there are attractive arguments for the view that such materials [isolated and purified biological materials] should not have been treated as patentable subject matter ... however, the time for taking this approach ... has long since passed' ([6.51–6.52]). Even so, the ALRC did consider whether a new approach to the patentability of genetic materials was warranted (as at 2004). It concluded that it was not ([6.53]). It is worth setting out the reasons for that conclusion (as did the primary judge at [116]):

> Nonetheless, the ALRC considers that a new approach to the patentability of genetic materials is not warranted at this stage in the development of the patent system, for the following reasons:
>
> • It would represent a significant and undesirable departure from accepted international practice with respect to genetic inventions, and may adversely affect investment in the Australian biotechnology industry.
>
> • It may fail to deliver the anticipated benefits because many pure and isolated genetic sequences do not exist in exactly the same form in nature—for example, patented sequences may not contain the introns that are found in the naturally occurring material.
>
> • Claims to genetic materials in their natural form (that is, in situ) do not constitute patentable subject matter.
>
> • Arguments that genetic materials are not patentable inventions do not always take adequate account of the fact that—in addition to the threshold requirement of 'patentable subject matter'—a number of statutory requirements must be satisfied for patent protection to be obtained. In particular, patent protection cannot be conferred over genetic materials unless a use for such materials has been identified and fully disclosed.
>
> • It would be difficult, on any rational basis, to confine reform to genetic materials and technologies, yet the extension of the reform to other fields—where the patenting of pure and isolated chemicals that occur in nature is uncontroversial—may have unknown consequences.

159. Subsequently, in late 2010, a Private Members' Bill (the Bill) was introduced into the Australian Senate which, if passed, would have excluded patents for 'biological materials including their components and derivatives, whether isolated or purified or not and however made, which are identical or substantially identical to such materials as they exist in nature'. The term 'biological materials' was defined to include DNA and RNA. The Legal and Constitutional Affairs Legislation Committee to which the Bill was referred for inquiry recommended by majority that the Senate not pass the Bill, which eventually lapsed.

160. The Australian Government's response to the Bill and the ALRC report specifically accepted the ALRC recommendation that the Act not be amended to exclude genetic materials and technologies from patentable subject matter. It did make a number of recommendations, including stricter tests in relation to other patentability requirements and, importantly in the consideration of the balance between incentives and the flow of information (taken into account by the US Supreme Court), the introduction of a new 'experimental use' defence. The recommendations resulted in the *Intellectual Property Laws Amendment (Raising The Bar) Act 2012* (Cth).

161. While these legislative matters do not affect what constitutes patentable subject matter under the rubric of 'manner of manufacture', Parliament has considered, and has specifically declined, to exclude purified and isolated gene sequences from the scope of patentable subject matter.

...

CONCLUSION

204. This case is not about the wisdom of the patent system. It is about the application of Australian patent law, as set out in the Act and as developed by the courts since the *Statute of Monopolies*.

205. It is not about whether, for policy or moral or social reasons, patents for gene sequences should be excluded from patentability. That has been considered by the ALRC and by Parliament and has not occurred. It is not a matter for the court, but for Parliament to decide. Parliament has considered the question of the patentability of gene sequences and has chosen not to exclude them but to make amendments to the Act to address, in part, the balance between the benefits of the patent system and the incentive thereby created, and the restriction on, for example, subsequent research.

206. This case is about whether, under Australian law and the concept of patentable invention as discussed by the courts, in particular by the High Court in *NRDC*, the challenged claims of the patent are to patentable inventions, that is, whether they are properly the subject of letters patent. *NRDC* is not to be applied in a narrow sense. The principles of patentability as there discussed are principles which are apposite to the present case and with which, with respect, we fully agree. Questions of novelty and inventive step do not arise. Novelty has not been challenged and it is not in dispute that an inventive step was involved in the invention as claimed in the challenged claims.

207. In Australia, there is no statutory or jurisprudential limitation of patentability to exclude 'products of nature'. To the contrary, the High Court has specifically rejected such an approach. A mere discovery is not patentable and an idea is not patentable, but a 'manner of manufacture', as that term has been developed, is.

208. In *NRDC*, the High Court upheld a patent for a herbicide, rejecting the argument that the claim was to a 'mere' new use of a known material. For the High Court, what was required was 'an inquiry not into the meaning of a word so much as into the breadth of the concept which the law has developed by its consideration of the text and purpose of the *Statute of Monopolies*'. The Court held that it is sufficient for a product to result in 'an artificially created state of affairs', leading to 'an economically useful result'.

209. This was consistent with the High Court's reasoning three months earlier in *Commissioner of Patents v Microcell Ltd* (1959) 102 CLR 232, where their Honours held that emphasis must be put on the phrase 'nothing but' in Lord Buckmaster's seminal caution of the patent ineligibility of 'nothing but a claim for a new use of an old substance' (at [8]).

210. The appeal centres on claim 1 of the patent; that is, to 'an isolated nucleic acid coding for a mutant or polymorphic BRCA1 polypeptide, said nucleic acid containing in comparison to the BRCA1 polypeptide encoding sequence set forth in SEQ.ID No:1 one or more mutations or polymorphisms selected from the mutations set forth in Tables 12, 12A and 14 and the polymorphisms set forth in Tables 18 and 19'. There are a number of features of the subject matter of the claims:

- It is to a compound; a nucleic acid. It is not a claim to information.
- It is to the isolated nucleic acid; i.e. a nucleic acid taken out of the genome and removed from the cell. Isolated nucleic acid cannot be the subject of cellular processes like transcription and translation as can its naturally occurring counterpart; it has been removed from the cellular environment and thus from natural cellular processes (e.g. intron removal, dependent upon the spliceosome). It can only be transcribed and translated by artificial intervention. In the absence of transcription and translation, or following their malfunction, mutations may arise, resulting in disease or an increased risk thereof.

- It contains the code for a particular polypeptide; a mutant or polymorphic protein.
- It contains a sequence identified by comparison with tables created following extensive epidemiological research which describes the location of the mutations or polymorphisms as they exist in DNA. The DNA was constructed and these locations identified by the work of the inventors.
- The nucleic acids have admitted valuable economic use.

211. In the decision of the US Court of Appeals for the Federal Circuit, Bryson J (dissenting) drew on a metaphor, likening an isolated nucleic acid and a branch being snapped off a tree. That is inapposite. The branch has not changed—it is simply divorced from the tree, whereas the chemical and physical makeup of the isolated nucleic acid renders it not only artificial but also different from its natural counterpart.

212. The claim is wider than for a 'mere discovery'. The 'magic microscope' theory relied upon by the parties in the Federal Circuit is that if an imaginary microscope could focus in on the claimed nucleic acid as it exists in the human body, the claim covers ineligible subject matter. This metaphor does not assist. What is being claimed is not the nucleic acid as it exists in the human body, but the nucleic acid as isolated from the cell. The claimed product is not the same as the naturally occurring product. There are structural differences but, more importantly, there are functional differences because of isolation. As Lourie J explains, 'the ability to visualise a DNA molecule through a microscope, or by any other means, when it is bonded to other genetic material [and in a particular regulatory environment] is worlds apart from processing an isolated DNA molecule that is in hand and useable'.

213. To this extent we differ, with respect, to the primary judge. In our view the products the subject of claim 1 are different to the gene comprising the nucleic acid sequence as it exists in nature. It follows that the notice of contention based on this ground succeeds.

214. The isolation of the nucleic acid also leads to an economically useful result—in this case, the treatment of breast and ovarian cancers. This is surely what was contemplated by a manner of new manufacture in the *Statute of Monopolies*. As Moore J explained in the Federal Circuit, 'it is not the chemical change alone, but that change combined with the different and beneficial utility which leads me to conclude that small isolated DNA fragments are patentable subject matter'.

215. The US Supreme Court rejected the claim over isolated nucleic acids for much the same reasons as those pressed by the appellant in this case. It is difficult to reconcile that Court's endorsement of the reasoning in *Chakrabarty*, with its rejection of isolated nucleic acid as eligible for patentability. With respect, the Supreme Court's emphasis on the similarity of '*the location and order of the nucleotides*' existing within the nucleic acid in nature before Myriad found them is misplaced. It is the chemical changes in the isolated nucleic acid which are of critical importance, as this is what distinguishes the product as artificial and economically useful.

216. The fact that, hypothetically, if the isolated DNA sequence were replaced into the cell it would express the same proteins is irrelevant. Following *Chakrabarty* and *NRDC*, the isolated nucleic acid has 'markedly different characteristics from any found in nature'; Myriad did not merely 'separate that gene from its surrounding genetic material'. It should make no difference that in *Chakrabarty* there was an 'addition' (of the plasmids) to the natural product (the bacterium); this is not the appropriate test. Myriad's claim, properly considered is not, as the US Supreme Court considered, concerned 'primarily with the information contained in the genetic sequence [rather than] with the specific chemical composition of a particular molecule'.

CURRENT LAW

217. The reasoning of Lourie and Moore JJ of the Federal Circuit is persuasive. It accords with the High Court's reasoning in *NRDC* and *Microcell*. The US Supreme Court accepted that cDNA is patentable. It rejected the isolated nucleic acid of claim 1 because it accepted wrongly, with respect, that the isolated nucleic acid is a 'product of nature'. In any event, that exclusion is not in accordance with the principles of patent law in Australia and has been specifically rejected as a reason for exclusion in *NRDC*.

218. The isolated nucleic acid, including cDNA, has resulted in an artificially created state of affairs for economic benefit. The claimed product is properly the subject of letters patent. The claim is to an invention within the meaning of s 18(1) of the Act.

219. The appeal should be dismissed.

The High Court granted special leave to appeal the decision of the Full Court of the Federal Court on 13 February 2015: *D'Arcy v Myriad Genetics Inc* [2015] HCATrans 12.

METHODS OF TREATMENT

The issue of whether or not methods of treatment are patentable subject matter is generally considered separately from the discussion of other subject matter that lies on the borderline between being patentable or unpatentable. The distinction between methods of treatment and other unpatentable subject matter is highlighted in the separation between the list of unpatentable subject matter in Art 52(2) of the EPC and the treatment exclusion in Art 53(c). The TRIPS Agreement also allows methods of treatment as a distinct ground of exclusion in Art 27(3). Relevant methods of treatment include surgical, pharmaceutical, diagnostic and therapeutic methods practised on the body (but not *in vitro*) and other non-therapeutic methods of treatment and they apply to both humans and other animals.

Prior to TRIPS, methods of treating the human and animal body had already been held to be unpatentable in a number of jurisdictions. The exclusion was first pronounced by Lord Buckmaster in *C & W's Application* (1914) 31 RPC 235. His Lordship stated that the refusal of the Patent Office to patent an invention for the removal of lead from human bodies because it related simply to human bodies was sound. The justification for this conclusion was that such treatment had no reference to any form of manufacture or trade and therefore was not a manner of manufacture. That is, it did not satisfy the subject matter requirement.

In much later cases the UK position changed. The courts accepted that the rationale for the exclusion in *C & W's Application* was no longer tenable after *NRDC* and like UK cases; that is, the courts accepted that methods of treatment satisfied the manner of manufacture requirement. However, it was concluded in a series of UK decisions that the exclusion of methods of treatment could be justified on the basis of ethics, and because the exclusion was well established in the case law, any change should come from the legislature.[4] Notwithstanding, the exclusion was read strictly so that only the medical treatment of ailments was excluded, and not, for example, contraception.

The situation was much less clear in Australia until recently. In fact, there seemed to be some reluctance in the courts to wrestle with the preliminary issue of whether or not this subject matter should be excluded, before embarking on the even more difficult issue of teasing out the underlying rationale for such exclusion.

---

4 See the discussion of these cases in J Pila, 'Methods of Medical Treatment within Australian and United Kingdom Patents Law' (2001) 24 *University of New South Wales Law Journal* 420.

The Federal Court was given the opportunity to explore the patentability of methods of treatment in two cases in the 1990s. In the Full Court decision in *Anaesthetic Supplies Pty Ltd v Rescare Ltd* (1994) 50 FCR 1 the patent in issue claimed a method of preventing snoring. However, the patent was held to be invalid on other grounds, and as such there was some debate about its precedential value in later cases. In *Rescare Ltd v Anaesthetic Supplies Pty Ltd* (1993) 25 IPR 119, at first instance Gummow J had held that methods of treatment were patentable. This reasoning was upheld by the majority on appeal, with Lockhart J stating at 19: 'I see no reason in principle why a method of treatment of the human body is any less a manner of manufacture than a method of ridding crops of weeds'.

In later litigation, the Federal Court examined the patentability of a method of administering the anti-cancer drug, taxol. At first instance, in *Bristol-Myers Squibb Co v FH Faulding & Co Ltd* (1998) 41 IPR 467, Heerey J concluded that he was not bound by *Rescare* and decided that methods of treatment were not patentable on ethical grounds. In the appeal decision, *Bristol-Myers Squibb Co v FH Faulding & Co Ltd* [2000] FCA 316; (2000) 97 FCR 524, the Full Court unanimously held that methods of treatment are patentable. Black CJ and Lehane J discussed their findings under the heading 'Manner of manufacture: "generally inconvenient"?', but did not fully canvass the distinction between a per se exclusion and one based on ethics. Finkelstein J, on the other hand, drew a clear distinction between the two rationales for exclusion. His consideration of ethical grounds for the exclusion of methods of treatment is extracted in the next section: see 'Morality, public interest and general inconvenience' below, p 439. The High Court was given the opportunity to reflect on the applicability of a per se methods of treatment exclusion more recently in *Apotex v Sanofi-Aventis* [2013] HCA 50; (2013) 103 IPR 217, extracted below.

CASE EXTRACT: CURRENT LAW

Apotex Pty Ltd v Sanofi-Aventis Australia Pty Ltd

[2013] HCA 50; (2013) 103 IPR 217
High Court of Australia

[This case related to a method of using a known drug, Leflunomide, for a new purpose, the treatment of skin disorders. The Court was given the opportunity to consider whether there should be a broad exclusion of all types of methods of medical treatment or whether all or some types of methods should be considered patentable subject matter. Four separate judgments were delivered. Given that the joint judgment of Crennan and Kiefel JJ was largely adopted by Gageler J, their judgment is relied on here. As with the other recent subject matter decisions, their Honours helpfully provided a summary of relevant law in other jurisdictions. Here, as elsewhere in this chapter, the position in the UK, Europe and the USA is the focus of attention.]

Crennan and Kiefel JJ (some footnotes omitted): 220. The question posed by Apotex's claim for revocation of the Patent is whether, assuming all other requirements for patentability are met, a method of medical treatment of the human body can be a patentable invention. That question has not been decided by this Court. There being no express exclusion of such methods in the 1990 Act, the question of the construction of s 18(1)(a) is to be decided by reference to the principles developed for the application of s 6 of the *Statute of Monopolies* [*NRDC Case* (1959) 102 CLR 252 at 269].

221. Whether a method of medical treatment of the human body is a proper subject matter for a grant of monopoly under a patent system has been considered by tribunals and courts in a number of major jurisdictions, some with patent legislation which similarly defines invention by reference to the expression 'manner of manufacture' in s 6 of the *Statute of Monopolies* (as in the United Kingdom, until 1977, and New Zealand), and some with patent legislation which defines invention otherwise (as in the United States of America and Canada).

222. To speak of 'methods of medical treatment of the human body' is to employ an expression of sufficient generality to encompass both drug therapies capable of industrial application and the know-how involved in a medical practitioner's diagnosis and methods of treatment (including surgery) of patients.' Distinguishing the two types of activity has proved problematic in many jurisdictions [Moufang, 'Methods of Medical Treatment Under Patent Law' (1993) 24 *International Review of Industrial Property and Copyright Law* 18; Dworkin, 'Patents Relating to Methods of Medical Treatment', in Hansen (ed), *International Intellectual Property Law & Policy* (2001), vol 6, Ch 12; Pila, 'Methods of Medical Treatment within Australian and United Kingdom Patents Law' (2001) 24 *University of New South Wales Law Journal* 420; Visser, 'The Exclusion of Medical Methods', in Kur, Luginbühl and Waage (eds), *Patent Law on the Move* (2005) 469].

223. Irrespective of the differences in national patent legislation, a clear, perhaps insoluble, conflict has emerged between two relevant competing considerations. The first consideration is the undesirability of having a patent system intruding on the freedom of a medical practitioner to treat a patient, without being restrained by the need to consider whether a patent licence is necessary. The conflicting consideration is the desirability of having a logical patent system which encourages research and invention in relation to drug therapies, not only by granting monopolies for novel medicines (and for that matter novel medical implements), but also by not excluding from patentability hitherto unknown therapeutic uses of known compounds, where novelty requirements can most directly be satisfied by a claim to a method or process, which is in effect a claim limited to the hitherto unknown therapeutic use. Professor Cornish and his co-authors have remarked [Cornish, Llewelyn and Aplin, *Intellectual Property: Patents, Copyright, Trade Marks and Allied Rights*, 7th ed (2010) at 238 [5-65]]:

> In the second half of the twentieth century, patent law in every industrial state had to develop in ways which mediated this conflict.

...

EUROPE

...

245. In conformity with Art 27(1) of the TRIPs Agreement, Art 52(1) of the EPC provides that 'patents shall be granted for any inventions, in all fields of technology, provided that they are new, involve an inventive step and are susceptible of industrial application.' Article 53, headed 'Exceptions to patentability', provides for heterogeneous exceptions to that general approach to patentability [*Aerotel Ltd v Telco Holdings Ltd; Macrossan's Patent Application* [2007] RPC 117 at 155].

246. Relevantly, an exception for methods of treatment of the human body is set out in Art 53(c):

> European patents shall not be granted in respect of ...
>
> (c) methods for treatment of the human or animal body by surgery or therapy and diagnostic methods practised on the human or animal body; this provision shall not apply to products, in particular substances or compositions, for use in any of these methods.'

247. Article 54(4) ameliorates the effect of that exception: a substance or compound is deemed novel in respect of a new therapeutic use [Article 54(4) does not exclude from patentability 'any substance or composition, comprised in the state of the art, for use in [an excepted method], provided that its use for any such method is not comprised in the state of the art.']. That such use of a (known) substance or compound is not denied novelty is squarely within the general principle established in the *NRDC Case*, that the discovery of a new use of a known substance which has both an artificial effect and economic utility can be a 'manner of manufacture', and therefore a patentable invention.

248. Claims for a second (or subsequent) hitherto unknown therapeutic use of a known compound were not expressly permitted under the original (1973) EPC but came to be allowed in a decision of the Enlarged Board of Appeal of the European Patent Office ('EPO') in *Eisai/Second medical indication* [[1979–1985] EPOR B241 ('*Eisai*')] approving 'Swiss type' claims. A 'Swiss type' claim is generally in the form of a claim to 'the use of [known] compound X in the manufacture of a medicament for a specified (and new) therapeutic use' [*Bristol-Myers Squibb Co v Baker Norton Pharmaceuticals Inc* [1999] RPC 253 at 271 [44]], the Swiss Federal Intellectual Property Office having first instituted a practice of allowing such claims in 1984.

249. The essential purpose of a 'Swiss type' claim was described by Jacob J in *Bristol-Myers Squibb Co v Baker Norton Pharmaceuticals Inc* [[1999] RPC 253 at 271 [44]]:

> By taking the [Swiss] form ... the claim is trying to steer clear of two obstacles to patentability, namely the requirement of novelty and the ban on methods of treatment of the human body by therapy.

250. Of the sophistry involved, Jacob J said [at 274 [51]]:

> [I]f one accepts that a patent monopoly is a fair price to pay for the extra research incentive, then there is no reason to suppose that that would not apply also to methods of treatment. It is noteworthy that in the US any such exception has gone, and yet no-one, so far as I know, suggests that its removal has caused any trouble.

Inevitably, the monopoly granted in respect of such claims is limited given that the substance has prior therapeutic uses.

...

254. The current position in Europe is set out in the EPO Guidelines for Examination 2012 ... As a result of the amendments to the EPC in 2000, claims for second (or subsequent) hitherto unknown uses of known substances or compounds may be drafted more simply and directly than 'Swiss type' claims (now not permitted) as 'substance X for use in the treatment of disease Y'.

UNITED KINGDOM

255. Since the passage of the *Patents Act 1977* (UK), law and practice in the United Kingdom have followed that in Europe.

...

260. The decision in *Eisai* was followed by the English Court of Appeal in *Actavis UK Ltd v Merck & Co Inc* [[2009] 1 WLR 1186 at 1193–1196 [18]–[31]; cf *Bristol-Myers Squibb Co v Baker Norton Pharmaceuticals Inc* [2001] RPC 1]. The Court of Appeal confirmed that '[n]ovelty of purpose for use can confer novelty even if the substance is old and unpatentable as such' [[2009] 1 WLR 1186 at 1193 [18]]. The Court of Appeal also said that the difficulties concerning infringement with such

'purpose' claims, referred to by Lord Hoffmann in the *Merrell Dow Case* [[1996] RPC 76], were ameliorated in the pharmaceutical industry by the strict regulation of the manufacture and sale of pharmaceutical products.

...

UNITED STATES OF AMERICA

...

270. It appears that significant numbers of patents have been granted in the United States in respect of methods of medical treatment of the human body (including surgery). Sanofi was able to point to an example where a method of treatment claim was in similar form to claim 1 of the Patent [*Merck & Co Inc v Teva Pharmaceuticals USA Inc*, 395 F 3d 1364 (2005)].

271. However, after an eye surgeon sued other surgeons for patent infringement in respect of a new technique for cataract surgery [*Pallin v Singer*, 36 USPQ 2d 1050 (1995)], the *Patents Act 1952* was amended by the inclusion of §287(c), the effect of which is to permit the patenting of surgical methods to continue but to bar actions for patent infringement against medical practitioners (and 'related health care entit[ies]') for 'the performance of a medical or surgical procedure on a body'.

...

CAN METHODS OF MEDICAL TREATMENT OF THE HUMAN BODY BE PATENTABLE INVENTIONS?

276. Claim 1, for a method of preventing or treating psoriasis, claims a hitherto unknown therapeutic use of a pharmaceutical substance which was first disclosed, together with prior therapeutic uses, in Patent 341 (now expired).

277. Apotex's submissions, derived from *obiter dicta* in the *NRDC Case*, that the subject matter of claim 1 is 'essentially non-economic' must be rejected.

278. First, in the context of patent law, the expression 'essentially non-economic' takes its meaning from the long-understood requirement that the subject matter of a patent (whether a product, or a method or process) must have some useful application, that is, must be capable of being practically applied in commerce or industry. A requirement that an invention have 'economic utility' raises the same considerations as the requirement in the *Patents Act 1977* (UK) and the EPC that an invention must be susceptible or capable of industrial application. So much is apparent from the definition of 'exploit' in the 1990 Act, referring to products and to methods or processes, and the case law developed and applied for a very long time in respect of the requirement of utility [See generally *Eli Lilly and Co v Human Genome Sciences Inc* [2008] RPC 733], now found in ss 18(1)(c) and 18(1A)(c).

279. Secondly, the 1990 Act contains no specific exclusion from patentability of methods of medical treatment of the human body, nor can any be implied. Section 133, which provides for compulsory licensing, is in general terms and covers both patented articles and patented methods or processes. Section 70, providing for extensions of term in respect of pharmaceutical substances that are defined in terms of effects on the human body, infers that patents which claim a method of treatment of the human body can be granted, but not extended. Section 119A [which creates an exemption from infringement for acts done for purposes connected with obtaining the inclusion of pharmaceuticals on the Australian Register of Therapeutic Goods] defines a 'pharmaceutical patent' to include method patents for using or administering a pharmaceutical substance.

280. Parliament accepted the IPAC's recommendation that the 1990 Act should not include a codification of requirements for patentability. Section 119A, described above, was introduced in 2006. It can be noted that Parliament has amended the 1990 Act 24 times since its enactment, including 20 times since the TRIPs Agreement entered into force on 1 January 1995. Relevantly, amendments to the 1990 Act following the TRIPs Agreement did not enact Art 27(3) into Australian domestic law. That Article gives contracting States the option to exclude methods of medical treatment of the human body from patent protection. However, to construe s 18(1)(a) of the 1990 Act as excluding methods of medical treatment of the human body would be to introduce a lack of harmony between Australia and its major trading partners, where none exists at present.

281. Thirdly, as noted by the primary judge in *Rescare Ltd v Anaesthetic Supplies Pty Ltd*, there is no normative distinction to be drawn from the provisions of the 1990 Act between methods of treatment of the human body which are cosmetic and those which are medical [(1992) 111 ALR 205 at 239].

282. Fourthly, and critically, the subject matter of a claim for a new product suitable for therapeutic use, claimed alone (a product claim) or coupled with method claims (combined product/method claims) [as in claims 1 and 4 of Patent 341], and the subject matter of a claim for a hitherto unknown method of treatment using a (known) product having prior therapeutic uses (a method claim) [as in claim 1 of the Patent], cannot be distinguished in terms of economics or ethics. In each case the subject matter in respect of which a monopoly is sought effects an artificially created improvement in human health, having economic utility. It could not be said that a product claim which includes a therapeutic use has an economic utility which a method or process claim for a therapeutic use does not have. It could not be contended that a patient free of psoriasis is of less value as a subject matter of inventive endeavour than a crop free of weeds. Patent monopolies are as much an appropriate reward for research into hitherto unknown therapeutic uses of (known) compounds, which uses benefit mankind, as they are for research directed to novel substances or compounds for therapeutic use in humans. It is not possible to erect a distinction between such research based on public policy considerations.

283. Fifthly, leaving aside, for the moment, the relevant *obiter dicta* in the *NRDC Case*, a method claim in respect of a hitherto unknown therapeutic use of a (known) substance or compound satisfies the general principle laid down in the *NRDC Case*. Such a method belongs to a useful art, effects an artificially created improvement in something, and can have economic utility. The economic utility of novel products and novel methods and processes in the pharmaceutical industry is underscored by s 119A of the 1990 Act and by their strict regulation in the *Therapeutic Goods Act 1989* (Cth) ('the TGA').

284. Sixthly, while not determinative of the construction issue, the practice of the Australian Patent Office, following *Joos [v Commissioner of Patents* (1972) 126 CLR 611], is consonant with Art 27(1) of the TRIPs Agreement.

285. Seventhly, the *obiter dicta* in the *NRDC Case*, upon which Apotex relied, conveys some hesitation about 'putting aside' methods of treatment of the human body [*NRDC Case* (1959) 102 CLR 252 at 270]. That hesitation arose in circumstances where this Court was not called upon to decide whether the position under the 1952 Act, in relation to methods of medical treatment of humans, differed from the position in the United Kingdom under the *Patents Act 1949* (UK) and case law in the United Kingdom following *Re C & W's Application* [(1914) 31 RPC 235]. In other respects, the decision in the *NRDC Case* diverged from the case law in the United Kingdom, not only in respect of a 'vendible product' requirement for a patentable process, but also in respect of the eligibility of agricultural products for patenting. The *obiter dicta* plainly refers to medical treatments, which are readily distinguishable from therapeutic uses of pharmaceutical substances as defined in the 1990 Act.

CONCLUSION ON PATENTABILITY

286. Assuming that all other requirements for patentability are met, a method (or process) for medical treatment of the human body which is capable of satisfying the *NRDC Case* test, namely that it is a contribution to a useful art having economic utility, can be a manner of manufacture and hence a patentable invention within the meaning of s 18(1)(a) of the 1990 Act.

287. There is, however, a distinction which can be acknowledged between a method of medical treatment which involves a hitherto unknown therapeutic use of a pharmaceutical (having prior therapeutic uses) and the activities or procedures of doctors (and other medical staff) when physically treating patients. Although it is unnecessary to decide the point, or to seek to characterise such activities or procedures exhaustively, speaking generally they are, in the language of the *NRDC Case*, 'essentially non-economic' and, in the language of the EPC and the *Patents Act 1977* (UK), they are not 'susceptible' or 'capable' of industrial application. To the extent that such activities or procedures involve 'a method or a process', they are unlikely to be able to satisfy the *NRDC Case* test for the patentability of processes because they are not capable of being practically applied in commerce or industry, a necessary prerequisite of a 'manner of manufacture'.

288. Apotex's claim for revocation of the Patent, on the ground that claim 1 does not disclose a patentable invention, cannot succeed and should stand dismissed.

MORALITY, PUBLIC INTEREST AND GENERAL INCONVENIENCE

Article 27(3) of the TRIPS Agreement allows for a limited exclusion where the publication or exploitation of an invention would be contrary to *ordre public* or morality, and Art 53(a) of the EPC expressly provides for such exclusion. There is no specific mention of such matters in the Australian legislation, but arguably this exclusion could be read into s 6 of the *Statute of Monopolies 1623*, which does not allow letters patents for manners of new manufacture that are:

- contrary to law;
- mischievous to the state by raising prices or harming trade; or
- generally inconvenient.

These provisions are often referred to as 'provisos'. It was accepted by the Full Court in *Rescare* that the *Patents Act* imports the whole of s 6 through s 18(1) and the definition of invention in Sch 1.

The 'general inconvenience' proviso has been used a number of times in Australia to deny patent claims for particular uses of or actions on subject matter to which the public expect to have free access, including purchased computers (*Telefon A/B LM Ericssons Application* [1975] FSR 49), lunch boxes (*Clayton Furniture Ltd's Application* [1965] AOJP 2303) and picture frames (*Boccari's Application* [1967] AOJP 1380). It is a matter of ongoing debate whether patent claims may also be denied using the general inconvenience proviso for ethical or public interest reasons, for example where there would be life-threatening consequences of allowing a patent for a method of medical treatment. Note that in challenging the patentability of methods of medical treatment in *Apotex v Sanofi-Aventis* (extracted above), Apotex placed no reliance on any exclusion of 'generally inconvenient' subject matter.

There have been a number of decisions by the European Patent Office Opposition Division, Technical Board of Appeal and Enlarged Board of Appeal interpreting the *ordre public* and morality provision in Art 53(a) of the EPC, mostly in the context of biotechnology inventions. *Plant Genetic Systems* T356/93 (1995) OJEPO 545 (below, p 443) provides some broad guidance on the applicability of this provision.

CASE EXTRACT: PRECEDENT

Joos v Commissioner of Patents

(1972) 126 CLR 611
High Court of Australia

[This case involved an application for patent for an invention entitled 'Process for improving strength and elasticity of keratinous material'. The process involved treatment of material such as hair and nails with a mixture of thiourea and formaldehyde to improve elasticity. The application was refused on the basis that it involved a process for treatment of a part of the living human body. The applicant appealed to the High Court. Accepting that the application satisfied the *NRDC* test, Barwick went on to consider whether there were other grounds for refusal. His judgment suggests that the general inconvenience proviso could play a role in excluding methods of treatment on ethical grounds.]

Barwick CJ (at 618–623): It seems to me, therefore, that I may begin my consideration of the question in this appeal, namely, whether it is obvious that a grant could not be made on this application, at the point which is reached by the Court's decision in the *NRDC Case* (1959) 102 CLR 252. Having regard to what that case decides, the only matter for consideration in this appeal is whether a process, otherwise appropriate for the grant of a monopoly under the Statute, must be held not to be a proper subject for a grant simply because it is a process for 'treatment' of a part of the human body. For the purpose of deciding this question it may be granted that a process for the treatment of the human body as a means of curing or preventing a disease, correcting a malfunction or removing or ameliorating an incapacity is not a proper subject matter for the grant of a monopoly under the Act. It is not essential to the decision of this matter to controvert that proposition or to discover and express its basis in law. But I think it significant that the concession is limited to the medical treatment of disease, malfunction or incapacity. Important in that connexion is the consideration that the concept of treatment, where medical treatment is spoken of, is not satisfied, in my opinion, by any application of a substance to the human body or part of it. Those who apply chemical preparations to the skin to prevent sunburn in climates which enjoy sunshine and moderate air temperatures can scarcely be regarded either as, in a relevant sense, treating their bodies or as undergoing treatment. On the other hand, the application to the skin of an ointment designed and effective to remove keratoses from the skin would be an instance of medical treatment. To be treatment, in the relevant sense, it seems to me that the purpose of the application to the body whether of a substance or a process must be the arrest or cure of a disease or diseased condition or the correction of some malfunction or the amelioration of some incapacity or disability. With that sense of 'treatment', I see no difficulty in conceding, for the purpose of the decision of this case, that a process for the medical treatment of a part of the human body is not a proper subject of letters patent.

...

In my opinion, if it be accepted that process claims for medical treatment of human disease, malfunction, disability or incapacity of the human body or of any part of it cannot satisfy the requirements of an invention under the Act, the class of such claims should be narrowly defined. I can find no warrant in public policy or in the decided cases for including in that class processes and methods for improving, or at any rate for changing, the appearance of the human body or of parts of it. Such cosmetics processes and methods are, in my opinion, not of a like kind with medical prophylactic or therapeutic processes or methods.

There may, of course, be many borderline instances of processes for use upon the human body or parts of it in respect of which a decision as to whether the process constitutes medical treatment or not may prove difficult. But I do not have here such a borderline case. The process with which I am presently concerned is clearly not a method of treatment of a disease, malfunction, disability or incapacity of the human body or of any part of it. In fact, it does not purport to deal with living tissue of the body; ... As I have mentioned earlier, I am not concerned in this case to discover and express a basis for excepting such a class of process claims. If I had to do so, as at present advised, I would place the exception, if it is to be maintained, on public policy as being, in the language of the *Statute of Monopolies*, 'generally inconvenient', not limiting what may fall within those words to things of a like kind to those described by the preceding words. Thus, after due consideration, I have reached the conclusion that it cannot properly be said that the appellant's application cannot be granted simply because its claims are for a process for application to the human body. They are not, in my opinion, claims for a manner or method of medical treatment of the human body within the narrow exception to patentability to which I have referred.

CASE EXTRACT: CURRENT LAW

Bristol-Myers Squibb Co v FH Faulding & Co Ltd

[2000] FCA 316; (2000) 97 FCR 524

Federal Court of Australia, Full Court

[As noted earlier in this chapter (see above, p 434), this case considers the patentability of a method of administering the anti-cancer drug, taxol. Black CJ and Lehane J agreed with Finkelstein J that the method was not patentable, but it was only Finklestein J who considered in detail whether the general inconvenience proviso should be applied to exclude methods of medical treatment.]

Finkelstein J: 131. I can now consider the second, and that which appears to me to be the critical, question on this aspect of the case, namely whether a medical or surgical process should be excluded from patentable subject matter because it falls within the proviso to s 6. Such a process is not of course contrary to law or mischievous to the State by raising the price of commodities. However, to grant a patent for such a process may be 'generally inconvenient', that is to say, it may be contrary to public policy and be excluded for that reason. It is to this issue I now turn.

132. There now appears to be general consensus that medical and surgical products are appropriate subject matter for patents. The [TRIPS Agreement], Article 27 provides, in part, that 'patents shall be available for any inventions, whether products or processes, in all fields of technology, provided they are new, [are non-obvious] and are capable of an industrial application' subject to the proviso that member States may exclude from patentability 'diagnostic, therapeutic and surgical methods for the treatment of humans or animals'. This is so notwithstanding the fact that many patients (perhaps millions around the world) are denied access to new pharmaceuticals, because of the price charged by the monopolist or its

licensee. No doubt it is the ever-increasing cost of developing new and more effective pharmaceuticals and surgical products that underlies the support for medical and surgical product patents. That is to say, the investment needed for the research and the development of these products justifies patent protection. The support may also be explained, in part at least, by the fact that it is usually a commercial organisation rather than a physician that is the inventor of pharmaceuticals and surgical products.

133. The opponents to the grant of a monopoly in respect of medical and surgical processes raise objections that can be put into two broad groups: (i) the adverse effects on the provision of medical care; and (ii) the adverse effects on medical progress and education. In addition there is the related 'ethical' question whether a medical practitioner (medical and surgical processes are usually invented by a medical practitioner) should be entitled to patent her invention consistent with her obligation to provide medical services to humanity.

134. Perhaps the most powerful argument against patenting is the idea that a patient may be denied medical treatment that she needs. It is certainly the most emotive of the arguments. It presumes that a medical practitioner may be unable to obtain the right to use a particular process, or may not be able to do so within due time, and therefore will be unwilling to undertake the process on her patients for fear of legal action.

135. It is also said that the traditional commitment of medical practitioners to develop, share and disseminate new knowledge will be repressed. That is to say, the medical practitioner who is seeking to discover a new medical or surgical process will deliberately withhold new medical knowledge from her colleagues so as to protect her discovery and enhance her ability to obtain patent protection for financial reward. Another aspect of this argument is the potential conflict of interest which could arise when a medical practitioner has an economic interest in a patent: a conflict that might result in the practitioner not acting in the best interests of her patient. A further aspect of this argument is the suggestion that the existence of a patent is a disincentive to further invention.

136. On the other side of the debate is the underlying objective of patents, namely the promotion of science and the advancement of the arts for the general welfare of the State. As a general principle there can be no doubt that patent protection is desirable to encourage new medicines and surgical methods. It is an inescapable fact that inducement is necessary to encourage the great expense that is now required to evaluate and investigate the utility of many new medical processes and surgical methods.

...

140. How is a court able to resolve these competing contentions? None of them are supported by evidence. Some may not even be capable of proof. Even if evidence was called to make good the unsubstantiated assertions, on what basis is the court to decide how the public interest will best be served? In *Diamond v Chakrabarty*, 447 US 303 (1980) the Supreme Court of the United States was asked to rule on whether a live human-made micro-organism is patentable subject matter. The argument against patentability raised the spectre of a serious threat to the human race posed by genetic research. The Supreme Court said, in relation to the dangers of allowing the patent (at 318):

> [W]e are without competence to entertain these arguments—either to brush them aside as fantasies generated by fear of the unknown, or to act on them. The choice we are urged to make is a matter of high policy for resolution within the legislative process after the kind of investigation, examination, and study that legislative bodies can provide and courts cannot. That process involves the balancing of competing values and interests, which in our democratic system

CURRENT LAW

is the business of elected representatives. Whatever their validity, the contentions now pressed on us should be addressed to the political branches of the Government, the Congress and the Executive, and not to the courts.

141. I do not believe that in a controversial issue such as is raised by the present argument, I would be abandoning my responsibility as a judge to follow this approach and to hold that if public policy demands that a medical or surgical process should be excluded from patentability, then that is a matter that should be resolved by the Parliament.

142. It is likely that few of the arguments admit of a definitive answer. The area of controversy is great. Public interest groups, medical and professional associations, medical scientists and the pharmaceutical industry, among others, would need to be approached and their views ascertained before a court could ever hope to arrive at a reasoned conclusion, if it could ever do so. Indeed a court might well be asked to take account of ethical and moral considerations to arrive at a decision. This is not the function of a court on an issue such as this. In my opinion, medical treatment and surgical process are patentable under the legislation and, if public policy requires a different result, it is for the Parliament to amend the 1990 Act.

COMPARATIVE LAW

CASE EXTRACT: COMPARATIVE LAW

Plant Genetic Systems

T356/93 (1995) OJEPO 545

European Patent Office, Technical Board of Appeal

[The patent in issue in this matter claimed processes and plants involving genetic modification for the production of an enzyme capable of neutralising or inactivating a herbicide. Issues relating to the *ordre public*/morality exclusion in Art 53(a) and the plant and animal exclusion in Art 53(b) were considered by the Technical Board of Appeal. Although the matter was heard subsequently by the Enlarged Board of Appeal, this was only on the Art 53(b) ground. The extract that follows focuses on the interpretation of the Art 53(a) ground.]

The Board: 5. It is generally accepted that the concept of '*ordre public*' covers the protection of public security and the physical integrity of individuals as part of society. This concept encompasses also the protection of the environment. Accordingly, under Article 53(a) EPC, inventions the exploitation of which is likely to breach public peace or social order (for example, through acts of terrorism) or seriously prejudice the environment are to be excluded from patentability as being contrary to 'ordre public'.

6. The concept of *morality* is related to the belief that some behaviour is right and acceptable whereas other behaviour is wrong, this belief being founded on the totality of the accepted norms which are deeply rooted in a particular culture. For the purposes of the EPC, the culture in question is the culture inherent in European society and civilisation. Accordingly, under Article 53(a) EPC, inventions the exploitation of which is *not* in conformity with the conventionally-accepted standards of conduct pertaining to this culture be excluded from patentability as being contrary to morality.

...

COMPARATIVE LAW

8. From the historical documentation relating to the EPC it appears that the view according to which 'the concept of patentability in the European patent law must be as wide as possible' predominated … Accordingly, the exceptions to patentability have been narrowly construed, in particular in respect of animal and plant varieties … In the Board's view, this approach applies equally in respect of the provisions in Article 53(a) EPC.

[In its consideration of the applicability of the 'contrary to morality' prohibition in Article 53(a) of the EPC to plant biotechnology, the Board saw little difference between plant biotechnology and traditional selective breeding practices (at [17]). In considering the 'contrary to *ordre public*' prohibition, which includes bars to patentability where the exploitation of an invention is likely to seriously prejudice the environment, the Board agreed with the Appellants' submission that 'patent offices are placed at the crossroads between science and public policy, but concluded that 'the assessment of hazards stemming from the exploitation of a given technology is one of the important duties of … regulatory authorities and bodies' (at [18]). As such, the prohibition will only apply if the threat to the environment is sufficiently substantiated by such bodies. The possibility of undesirable environmental outcomes was not sufficient to motivate the Board to revoke the patent.]

THRESHOLD REQUIREMENTS FOR NEWNESS AND INVENTIVENESS

In addition to the requirement for patentable subject matter, it could also be argued that an invention has to display some threshold of newness and inventiveness, even before the technical patent criteria are assessed. If this were the case, then admissions about relevant prior art in the patent specification itself could be used to invalidate a patent without the necessity of fully reviewing the prior art. This threshold requirement has been considered by the Australian High Court in a series of cases. It now seems clear that in Australia, as in other jurisdictions, it is not appropriate for patent examiners and judges to engage in preliminary judgments about newness and inventiveness of alleged inventions before the prior art is properly marshalled and examined.

PRECEDENT

CASE EXTRACT: PRECEDENT

NV Philips Gloeilampenfabrieken v Mirabella International Pty Ltd

(1995) 183 CLR 655

High Court of Australia

[In this matter, the Federal Court heard infringement and revocation proceedings on a patent granted to Philips under the 1952 Act for the manufacture of compact fluorescent lamps. The general conclusion of all the justices in relation to the call for revocation was that the claim was for nothing more than a *new use of an old substance.* There was nothing inventive per se about the new use. As such, it is difficult to see how Philips could have satisfied the inventive step test.

Difficulties arose for Mirabella because the inventive step ground was conceded at trial and the invention was found to satisfy the novelty requirement. Because the novelty and inventive step grounds were not available, that appeared to leave manner of manufacture as the only possible ground for revocation. The Philips invention did not fail on this basis. Yet on its face what was claimed was not a new invention. The question for the High Court, then, was whether there was any requirement to demonstrate newness or inventiveness, outside of the novelty and inventive step requirements.]

Brennan, Deane and Toohey JJ (at 663–664): The primary focus of inquiry should, as we have indicated, be upon the opening words ('… a patentable invention is an invention that …') of that sub-section which impose a threshold requirement which must be satisfied before one reaches that contained in the body of par (a) (This approach to the construction of s 18(1) was raised in the course of argument in this Court and adopted by Mirabella as a subsidiary argument).

The effect of those opening words of s 18(1) is that the primary or threshold requirement of a 'patentable invention' is that it be an 'invention'. Read in the context of s 18(1) as a whole and the definition of 'invention' in the Dictionary in Schedule 1, that clearly means 'an alleged invention'(see the final words of the definition), that is to say, an 'alleged' 'manner of new manufacture the subject of letters patent and grant of privilege within section 6 of the *Statute of Monopolies*'(see the first part of the definition). In the light of what has been said above about what is involved in an alleged manner of new manufacture, that threshold requirement of 'an alleged invention' will, notwithstanding an assertion of 'newness', remain unsatisfied if it is apparent on the face of the relevant specification that the subject matter of the claim is, by reason of absence of the necessary quality of inventiveness, not a manner of new manufacture for the purposes of the *Statute of Monopolies*. That does not mean that the threshold requirement of 'an alleged invention' corresponds with or renders otiose the more specific requirements of novelty and inventive step (when compared with the prior art base) contained in s 18(1)(b). It simply means that, if it is apparent on the face of the specification that the quality of inventiveness necessary for there to be a proper subject of letters patent under the *Statute of Monopolies* is absent, one need go no further …

PRECEDENT

CASE EXTRACT: CURRENT LAW

Lockwood Security Products Pty Ltd v Doric Products Pty Ltd (No 2) ('Lockwood No 2')

[2007] HCA 21; (2007) 235 CLR 173

High Court of Australia

[This case, '*Lockwood No 2*', will be discussed in more detail in the next chapter for what it says about the inventive step requirement in Australia. The earlier High Court decision in this action, *Lockwood Security Products Pty Ltd v Doric Products Pty Ltd* [2004] HCA 58; (2004) 217 CLR 274 ('*Lockwood No 1*') will be discussed in Chapter 12 in relation to the 'fair basis' disclosure requirement. In passing in *Lockwood No 2*, the High Court made an important statement about the ongoing relevance of the *Philips v Mirabella* threshold test.

In this case, Doric attempted to argue that admissions about the prior art made by Lockwood in the specification were fatal to the validity of the patent.]

CURRENT LAW

Gummow, Hayne, Callinan, Heydon and Crennan JJ (some footnotes omitted): 105. Admissions may be made in a specification, particularly about prior art and common general knowledge. This is consistent with conventional methods of drafting patent specifications intended and recognised as a way of clearly articulating the advance over prior art made by the invention. Such an approach also facilitates an understanding of the relevant inventive step, irrespective of whether the inventive step is identified with any precision in the specification, a task which may be difficult [*British United Shoe Machinery Co Ltd v A Fussell & Sons Ltd* (1908) 25 RPC 631 at 650]. While not every invention constitutes a solution to a problem, it is commonplace so to describe an invention where it is appropriate to do so ... Admissions in a specification about any problem said to be overcome by an invention are made from the vantage point of knowing the solution. When used as evidence, they would always need to be weighed with evidence, if it exists, from persons skilled in the relevant art of their perception of any problem at the time before the priority date, before their exposure to any solution contained in the invention.

106. In *Chapman and Cook and Lectro Linx Ltd v Deltavis Ltd* [(1930) 47 RPC 163 ('*Chapman*')], Clauson J remarked [at 173]:

> [I]f a Patentee, though entirely erroneously, does state by way of what I may call recital in his Specification that a particular form of thing is common and then by some oversight or some mistake claims a monopoly in that particular form of thing he will have, so to speak, recited himself out of Court and I venture to doubt whether he could possibly maintain any claim to a monopoly in a thing which he has recognised to be something which existed.

Chapman may be understood as a case which exemplifies a specification showing 'on its face' that an invention did not involve an inventive step. The expression derives from *Commissioner of Patents v Microcell Ltd* [(1959) 102 CLR 232 ('*Microcell*')], which stands for a narrow proposition that a Commissioner of Patents, or his or her delegate, may refuse an application for patent protection where a specification 'on its face' shows the invention claimed is not a manner of new manufacture. This may arise, for example, from admissions concerning novelty. The decision in *Microcell* has not always been properly understood; it does not involve a separate ground of invalidity or a discrete 'threshold' test [*NV Philips Gloeilampenfabrieken v Mirabella International Pty Ltd* (1995) 183 CLR 655 at 664].

—11—

THE PATENT CRITERIA

INTRODUCTION

This chapter examines the criteria for satisfying the patentability requirements. The relevant provisions in international and domestic law were set out in Chapter 9. To reiterate, Art 27(1) of the *Agreement on Trade-Related Aspects of Intellectual Property Rights* (the 'TRIPS Agreement') (1994) requires that patents must be granted for inventions that are new, involve an inventive step (sometimes referred to as non-obviousness) and are capable of industrial application (sometimes referred to as usefulness).

Section 18(1) of the *Patents Act 1990* (Cth) (as amended by the *Intellectual Property Laws Amendment (Raising the Bar) Act 2012* (Cth) (the '*Raising the Bar Act*')) prescribes the patentability requirements in Australian law for standard patents. Chapter 10 considered the requirement that there must be an invention that is capable of being patented, otherwise known as the subject matter requirement (or manner of manufacture, in Australian law) as provided in s 18(1)(a). Section 18(1)(b) prescribes the novelty and inventive step requirements. There is also a usefulness requirement in s 18(1)(c). As will be explained below, prior to entry into force of the *Raising the Bar Act*, the usefulness ground in Australia simply required that the invention did what it was claimed to do. Following entry into force of the *Raising the Bar Act* on 15 April 2013, Australia now has a much more explicit usefulness requirement. Section 18(1)(d) imposes an additional patentability criterion, that the invention has not been 'secretly used'.

The patent requirements for an innovation patent are prescribed in s 18(1A) of the *Patents Act*. Essentially they are the same as for a standard patent, except that an 'innovative step' is required, which is a lesser requirement than an inventive step.

Sections 7 and 7A of the *Patents Act* and some of the definitions in Sch 1 provide the framework within which novelty, inventive step, innovative step and usefulness are assessed. Section 7 provides:

Novelty

(1) For the purposes of this Act, an invention is to be taken to be novel when compared with the prior art base unless it is not novel in the light of any one of the following kinds of information, each of which must be considered separately:

   (a) prior art information (other than that mentioned in paragraph (c)) made publicly available in a single document or through doing a single act;

(b) prior art information (other than that mentioned in paragraph (c)) made publicly available in 2 or more related documents, or through doing 2 or more related acts, if the relationship between the documents or acts is such that a person skilled in the relevant art would treat them as a single source of that information;

(c) prior art information contained in a single specification of the kind mentioned in subparagraph (b)(ii) of the definition of prior art base in Schedule 1.

Inventive step

(2) For the purposes of this Act, an invention is to be taken to involve an inventive step when compared with the prior art base unless the invention would have been obvious to a person skilled in the relevant art in the light of the common general knowledge as it existed (whether in or out of the patent area)[1] before the priority date of the relevant claim, whether that knowledge is considered separately or together with the information mentioned in subsection (3).

(3) The information for the purposes of subsection (2) is:

(a) any single piece of prior art information; or

(b) a combination of any 2 or more pieces of prior art information that the skilled person mentioned in subsection (2) could, before the priority date of the relevant claim, be reasonably expected to have combined.[2]

Innovative step

(4) For the purposes of this Act, an invention is to be taken to involve an innovative step when compared with the prior art base unless the invention would, to a person skilled in the relevant art, in the light of the common general knowledge as it existed (whether in or out of the patent area)[3] before the priority date of the relevant claim, only vary from the kinds of information set out in subsection (5) in ways that make no substantial contribution to the working of the invention.

(5) For the purposes of subsection (4), the information is of the following kinds:

(a) prior art information made publicly available in a single document or through doing a single act;

(b) prior art information made publicly available in 2 or more related documents, or through doing 2 or more related acts, if the relationship between the documents or acts is such that a person skilled in the relevant art would treat them as a single source of that information.

(6) For the purposes of subsection (4), each kind of information set out in subsection (5) must be considered separately.

---

1   Prior to entry into force of the *Raising the Bar Act* on 15 April 2013, the common general knowledge was determined only within the patent area.

2   Prior to entry into force of the *Raising the Bar Act*, subsection (3) specified that the information was required to be 'information that the skilled person mentioned in subsection (2) could, before the priority date of the relevant claim, be reasonably expected to have ascertained, understood, regarded as relevant and, in the case of information mentioned in paragraph (b), combined as mentioned in that paragraph'.

3   Prior to entry into force of the *Raising the Bar Act*, the common general knowledge was determined only within the patent area.

The definition of 'prior art base' is provided in Sch 1:

(a) in relation to deciding whether an invention does or does not involve an inventive step or an innovative step:
  (i) information in a document that is publicly available, whether in or out of the patent area; and
  (ii) information made publicly available through doing an act, whether in or out of the patent area.
(b) in relation to deciding whether an invention is or is not novel:
  (i) information of a kind mentioned in paragraph (a); and
  (ii) information contained in a published specification filed in respect of a complete application where:
    (A) if the information is, or were to be, the subject of a claim of the specification, the claim has, or would have, a priority date earlier than that of the claim under consideration; and
    (B) the specification was published after the priority date of the claim under consideration; and
    (C) the information was contained in the specification on its filing date and when it was published.

The definition of 'prior art information' is also provided in Sch 1:

(a) for the purposes of subsection 7(1)—information that is part of the prior art base in relation to deciding whether an invention is or is not novel; and
(b) for the purposes of subsection 7(3)—information that is part of the prior art base in relation to deciding whether an invention does or does not involve an inventive step; and
(c) for the purposes of subsection 7(5)—information that is part of the prior art base in relation to deciding whether an invention does or does not involve an innovative step.

Section 7A provides a new meaning of usefulness:

(1) For the purposes of this Act, an invention is taken not to be useful unless a specific, substantial and credible use for the invention (so far as claimed) is disclosed in the complete specification.
(2) The disclosure in the complete specification must be sufficient for that specific, substantial and credible use to be appreciated by a person skilled in the relevant art.
(3) Subsection (1) does not otherwise affect the meaning of the word *useful* in this Act.

NOVELTY

Perhaps novelty is the most self-evident requirement for patenting: logically, an invention must be something that is new. Over time, novelty has become very much a technical term of art in this area of the law. Novelty is lost when the invention has already been disclosed to the public in writing, or orally, or by prior use. In essence, in assessing novelty, an examiner or court is looking for something already disclosed that *matches* the invention described in the patent application. Lack of novelty is also often referred to as anticipation and enabling disclosure.

The key points about the novelty requirement may conveniently be summarised as follows:

- Novelty is measured against the prior art base at the priority date as understood by a person skilled in the art. According to Lord Westbury in *Hill v Evans* (1862) 4 De G F & J 288; (1862) 31 LJ Ch 457 at 463, the prior art:

  > must be such that a person of ordinary knowledge of the subject would at once perceive, understand, and be able practically to apply the discovery without the necessity of making further experiments and gaining further information before the invention can be made useful.

- The prior art base includes all publicly available information from anywhere in the world, whether disclosed in writing or by acts, in accordance with the definitions in Sch 1. Prior to entry into force of the *Patents Amendment Act 2001* (Cth), prior art information under the *Patents Act* included (1) documents from anywhere in the world; and (2) acts done in Australia, extending out to the continental shelf through the definition of 'patent area' in Sch 1. Under the *Patents Act 1952* (Cth) the standard was documents available in Australia and acts done in Australia. The *Raising the Bar Act* has not effected any changes to the novelty requirement.

- Certain disclosures are not considered to be part of the prior art base, as provided in s 24(1)(a) of the *Patents Act* and regs 2.2 and 2.3 of the *Patents Regulations 1991*. The relevant disclosures must be made by the patentee or their nominee, or with their consent, within a prescribed period, which, depending on the circumstances, varies from six months to 18 months. In summary, relevant circumstances include:
  - publication or use of the invention within 12 months prior to the filing of a complete application, under the so-called 'grace period' provision;[4] the grace period is intended mostly to protect applicants from the impact of inadvertent disclosure; it should be noted that although both Australia and the USA have a grace period, many other countries, including signatories to the European Patent Convention, do not; hence, despite the grace period, applicants for patents should take care not to disclose their inventions prior to filing applications because this could compromise the novelty of their inventions in some jurisdictions;
  - showing or using the invention at a recognised exhibition;
  - publication of the invention during a recognised exhibition at which the invention was shown or used;
  - publication of the invention in a paper written by the inventor and read before a learned society or published with the inventor's consent by or on behalf of a learned society;
  - working the invention in public within the period of 12 months before the priority date of a claim for the invention for the purposes of reasonable trial, but only if, because of the nature of the invention, it is reasonably necessary for the working to be in public; or
  - disclosure to the Commonwealth or a state or territory or to a person authorised by the Commonwealth or a state or territory to investigate the invention, together with anything done for the purpose of an investigation.

---

4   IP Australia provides further information on the operation of the grace period at www.ipaustralia.gov.au/get-the-right-ip/patents/time-and-costs/grace-periods.

Section 24(1)(b) adds further that information disclosed without the consent of the patentee or their nominee during the prescribed period is also to be disregarded.

- The test for novelty is the 'reverse infringement test', as articulated by Aickin J in *Meyers Taylor Pty Ltd v Vicarr Industries Ltd* (1977) 137 CLR 228 at 235:

  > The basic test for anticipation or want of novelty is the same as that for infringement and generally one can properly ask oneself whether the alleged anticipation would, if the patent were valid, constitute an infringement.

- To anticipate an invention, disclosure must generally occur in one piece of prior art (one document or one act). Piecing together items of information from the prior art in an attempt to assert lack of novelty ('mosaicing') is not allowed. According to Aickin J in *Minnesota Mining and Manufacturing Co v Beiersdorf (Australia) Ltd* (1980) 144 CLR 253 at 293, making a mosaic entails 'the picking out of individual items of information from prior publications or prior objects and assembling them together so as to give them an appearance of unity and then alleging such a mosaic reveals the very thing claimed.' His Honour went on to say at 293: 'That is an understandable, though not permissible, process'.

- It is permissible to use two or more pieces of prior art information if they are sufficiently cross-referenced. According to Gummow J in *Nicaro Holdings Pty Ltd v Martin Engineering Co* (1990) 91 ALR 513 at 538: 'What degree of lack of connection between two or more documents will make them "independent" and so forbid the making of a mosaic to destroy novelty, will be very much a question in the particular case'.

- To destroy novelty, information in the prior art must disclose all of the key features or 'essential integers' of the invention.

- If the only difference from the prior art is in inessential integers, the invention will lack novelty because it is a mere 'mechanical equivalent' to the prior art. The language of 'workshop improvement' is sometimes used instead of 'mechanical equivalent'. However, caution is required in making this assessment to avoid introducing inventive step considerations into the novelty requirement. As Gummow J held in *Nicaro* at 532:

  > Where, in a case such as the present, the question is whether one or more integers of a claimed combination is not disclosed in an alleged anticipation, and it is said that what is disclosed does sufficiently reveal that integer within the principles of *Hill v Evans*, it will not be helpful to ask whether variations between the anticipation and the claimed combination answer the description 'workshop improvement'. Perhaps recognising this, in reply counsel for the appellants put his case simply on the alternative basis that the differences represented no more than the substitutions of mechanical equivalents, thereby bringing his case back to the legal mainstream.

NOVELTY PRECEDENTS, CURRENT LAW AND COMPARATIVE LAW

As illustrated above, important pronouncements were made about the novelty test in Australia by Aickin J of the High Court of Australia in *Meyers Taylor* and *Minnesota Mining and Manufacturing v Beiersdorf* and by Gummow J in the decision of the Full Court of the Federal Court of Australia in *Nicaro*. The decision of the Full Court of the Federal Court in *RD Werner & Co Inc v Bailey*

Aluminium Products Pty Ltd (1989) 25 FCR 565 is also influential with regard to the interpretation of the test for novelty in Australia, as are two UK cases: *Hill v Evans* and *General Tire & Rubber Co v Firestone Tyre & Rubber Co Ltd* [1972] RPC 457. However, UK case law has become less relevant in the Australian context since 1977, with the entry into force of the *Patents Act 1977* (UK) which is based on the European Patent Convention and tied to its interpretive principles.

In a decision of the Full Court of the Federal Court in *H Lundbeck A/S v Alphapharm Pty Ltd* [2009] FCAFC 70; (2009) 177 FCR 151 Bennett J provided a helpful overview of the current law on novelty and the role of these and other cases in shaping the law. Rather than providing further short extracts of each of these cases, a longer extract of the relevant parts of Bennett J's decision is provided below to put the case law into its modern context. Bennett J's judgment also illustrates the distinctions between modern Australian law and modern UK law with regard to the novelty requirement. Under Australian law the issues of whether the invention has been disclosed in the prior art and whether it has been disclosed to the public are considered together. In the UK, in contrast, the issues of disclosure in the prior art and making available to the public are considered separately under the banners of 'disclosure' and 'enablement', as illustrated in the judgment of Lord Hoffmann in the House of Lords case of *Synthon BV v Smithkline Beecham plc* [2006] RPC 10, referred to below in Bennett J's judgment.

CURRENT LAW

CASE EXTRACT: CURRENT LAW

H Lundbeck A/S v Alphapharm Pty Ltd

[2009] FCAFC 70; (2009) 177 FCR 151
Federal Court of Australia, Full Court

[In this case, the dispute involved a pharmaceutical patent granted to Lundbeck, with the title: '(+)-Enantiomer of Citalopram and process for the preparation thereof.' Pharmaceutical patents of this nature are becoming increasingly common. Essentially, they extend the life of existing patents by claiming new attributes, a process sometimes referred to as 'evergreening'. Questions of novelty and inventive step inevitably arise in such circumstances.

In this instance, Lundbeck had already been granted another patent for Citalopram, a pharmaceutical for the treatment of depression. Citalopram is a molecule that can exist in two forms called enantiomers, each of which is the mirror image of the other. Citalopram is a racemic mixture, or racemate, comprising the two enantiomers in equal parts. As the title for the patent in issue illustrates, it claimed the (+)-enantiomer also known as Escitalopram. The patent disclosed that Escitalopram is therapeutically far more active than Citalopram. Among other matters, the issue for the Full Court was whether claims 1–5 of the patent were invalid for lack of novelty. Emmett and Bennett JJ gave separate judgments. Middleton J was in agreement with Bennett J.

Although the Court found in favour of Lundbeck on the novelty and inventive step grounds in this case, Alphapharm was successful in its application to remove Lundbeck's extension of patent term beyond the usual 20-year period. This extension had been granted by the Commissioner of Patents in 2004 pursuant to ss 70 and 71 of the *Patents Act*. The Full Court held that the extension had been improperly granted. Lundbeck appealed this aspect of the Full Court decision to the High Court, but special leave to hear that appeal was refused in *Alphapharm Pty Ltd v H Lundbeck A/S* [2009] HCATrans 324. Subsequently, Lundbeck successfully applied to the Commissioner of Patents for a shorter extension of term, and this decision of the Commissioner was upheld in *Alphapharm Pty Ltd v H Lundbeck A/S* [2014] FCA 1185.]

Bennett J:

GENERAL PROPOSITIONS

173. The following general propositions emerge from the authorities:

- An invention is a piece of information (*Merrell Dow Pharmaceuticals Inc v HN Norton & Co Ltd* (1995) 33 IPR 1 at 8). It follows that a disclosure is the communication of information.
- Commonly the only question may be whether the prior publication describes the claimed invention with sufficient clarity (*Bristol-Myers Squibb Co v FH Faulding & Co Ltd* (2000) 97 FCR 524 at [67]).
- The disclosure is assessed by reference to the skilled addressee, a person of ordinary skill in the art.
- The question is whether the prior publication is sufficient to make the claimed invention apparent to the skilled addressee (*Nicaro Holdings Pty Ltd v Martin Engineering Co* (1990) 91 ALR 513 at 529).
- A prior publication does not invalidate a patent unless it supplies sufficient information to enable a person of ordinary skill to produce the product subsequently claimed (*Acme Bedstead Co Ltd v Newlands Brothers Ltd* (1937) 58 CLR 689 at 707). A specification is not to be read as in a vacuum but by the reader having at least the common knowledge of the art (*Acme Bedstead* at 701; *Nicaro* at 530).
- The requirement is that a person of ordinary knowledge of the relevant subject would be able practically to apply the prior published discovery without the necessity of making further experiments (*Hill v Evans* (1862) 1A IPR 1 at 6–7).
- The further experiments do not include those that formed part of standard procedure or common general knowledge. They are experiments with a view to discovering something not disclosed ([*C Van der Lely NV v Bamfords Ltd* (1962) 1A IPR 86] at 90).
- The further experiments do not mean ordinary methods of trial and error (*Van der Lely* at 90).
- If the alleged anticipation is to a process that produces the claimed product, it is not an anticipation if the process would not necessarily achieve the result claimed for it (*Olin Corporation v Super Cartridge Co Pty Ltd* (1977) 180 CLR 236 at 260–261).
- Something less than a full description of the invention allegedly anticipated may be sufficient to invalidate it for want of novelty (*Nicaro* at 529).
- Something less than a full description of an effective means by which the combination claimed in a patent may be produced may be sufficient to a reader having common general knowledge in the art (*Nicaro* at 531).
- A direction, recommendation or suggestion may be implicit in what is described (*Bristol-Myers* at [67]).
- A disclosure that describes an effective means by which a claimed invention may be produced falls short of anticipation if it requires the exercise of inventive ingenuity or the taking of any inventive step (*Nicaro* at 531).

Where the prior disclosure is to a broad chemical claim encompassing many compounds, there may not be anticipation in the absence of the skilled addressee understanding or perceiving a specific compound in the disclosure (*Imperial Chemicals Industries Pty Ltd v Commissioner of Patents* (2005) 213 ALR 399 at [64]–[65]). That is, there is no actual description of the particular compound to the skilled addressee; there is no relevant disclosure. There may be a distinction, albeit fine, between a 'fleeting' or 'paper' disclosure or the 'intellectual content' of a disclosure on the one hand and a 'disclosure for novelty purposes' or 'enabling disclosure' on the other (*Imperial Chemicals* at [68]; *University of Georgia Research Foundation v Biochem Pharma Inc* (2000) 51 IPR 222, a decision of Dr Barker of the Patent Office described by Crennan J in *Imperial Chemicals* as a 'sound account of the relevant distinctions between a "paper disclosure" and an "enabling disclosure" in the field of chemistry' (at 412)). It depends on what the skilled reader would understand …

174. A reading of *Hill v Evans*, the acknowledged foundation of the law of novelty, is worthwhile. Lord Westbury made a number of points in the context of his opinion as to whether there was matter in a prior specification which rendered the subsequent invention a matter of public knowledge and therefore a matter of public property anterior to the granting of the patent. The expression is often quoted that the antecedent statement 'must be such that a person of ordinary knowledge of the subject would at once perceive, understand, and be able practically to apply the discovery without the necessity of making further experiments and gaining further information before the invention can be made useful' (*Hill v Evans* at 6). However, his Lordship continued to explain what that means in a context where a prior publication does or does not actually disclose the subsequent invention. He said that the information as to the alleged invention given by the prior publication must, for the purposes of practical utility, be equal to that given by the subsequent patent. It is apparent that in *Hill v Evans*, the disclosures in the prior publications were not of the integers of the subsequently claimed invention. His Lordship did not say that the invention had to have been previously made but that it had to have been previously made known.

175. Interestingly, in the context of a discussion as to whether further information is required over a prior application for it to be novelty defeating, the example that Lord Westbury gave was the difference between the ore and the refined and pure metal which is extracted from it. His Lordship also observed that in such cases it is not true to say that knowledge and the means of obtaining knowledge are the same. It was in that context that he said (at 7) '[t]o carry me to the place at which I wish to arrive is very different from merely putting me on the road that leads to it', which undoubtedly formed the basis for the frequently cited comment in *General Tire* as to the planting of a flag.

176. 'Upon principle', Lord Westbury concluded that the prior knowledge of an invention to avoid a patent must be knowledge equal to that required to be given by the patent.

177. Lord Westbury endorsed the conclusions in *Househill Co v Neilson* 1 Webst Pat Ca 718. In that case, Lord Lyndhurst held that where a prior publication included a distinct and clear description of a machine, there was anticipation if the description corresponded with that in the patent, even though the machine as described in the prior publication had never been worked. In *Hill v Evans*, there was information missing in the prior publications and there was no anticipation.

CONCLUSION ON ANTICIPATION AND 'ENABLING DISCLOSURE'

178. Care must be taken to distinguish between the tests for novelty and want of inventive step, in particular when looking to see what the prior art 'teaches'. The concept of novelty in Australia involves

a comparison between the invention as claimed in the claims of the patent and prior art information. Often, this must be determined by looking to prior publications which are to be read by the skilled addressee to determine what they disclose. Generally speaking, the consideration of what a prior publication 'teaches', especially when one talks of 'teaching away' from the claimed invention, tends to be relevant to questions of obviousness and inventive step.

179. As Lord Hoffmann said in *Merrell Dow* at 8, an invention is a piece of information and making matter available to the public therefore requires the communication of information. Whether or not such information has been communicated depends on the subject matter of the claim and the extent of the prior disclosure to the skilled addressee.

180. Where the prior publication discloses exactly what is claimed, there is anticipation. This can be objectively determined and, apart from an understanding of terms of art, the evidence of the skilled addressee is not likely to be of much further assistance. However, this does not always occur and many of the authorities contain discussions of the extent to which a disclosure less than the entirety of the claim constitutes an anticipation of a product or a process to deprive the claimed invention of novelty.

181. If the prior art discloses some but not all integers of a claimed patent to a product, such as a combination, there is anticipation if the skilled addressee would add the missing information as a matter of course and without the application of inventive ingenuity or undue experimentation (*Nicaro* at 530–531).

182. It may be that the prior disclosure is of a method that produces the claimed product. If that method leads inexorably to the product, there is anticipation (*General Tire [& Rubber Co v Firestone Tyre and Rubber Co Ltd* (1971) 1A IPR 121] at 138). If it may or may not result in the claimed product, there is no anticipation.

183. It is these last two examples that, in Australia, could be said to be within a shorthand description of 'enabling disclosure'. That is, the disclosure is not complete but it is sufficient to enable the skilled addressee, in the ordinary course and without invention, to add what is missing in the prior publication to obtain the claimed invention. The term 'enabling disclosure' may also be apposite to disclosure to the skilled addressee of an asserted prior use: whether what the skilled addressee observes on inspection is sufficient to enable him or her to comprehend the complete invention (eg *Insta Image Pty Ltd v KD Kanopy Australasia Pty Ltd* (2008) 78 IPR 20; *Jupiters Ltd v Neurizon Pty Ltd* (2005) 222 ALR 155), that is, whether it is sufficient to amount to a disclosure of the invention.

184. It is necessary to be careful in applying more recent United Kingdom decisions. In *Nicaro*, Gummow J noted at 529 that there had been some 'drift in the authorities as to the degree of rigour with which the alleged anticipation is to be tested'. Further, there are differences between the test for novelty in the 1977 Act (UK) and the 1990 Act and the 1952 Act. While care must be taken in a reading of post-1977 United Kingdom decisions, a discussion of the earlier authorities is enlightening. An understanding that the earlier authorities drew a distinction between a prior disclosure of the invention itself and a prior disclosure of a means of obtaining the invention, or of some but not all of the integers of the claimed invention, was restated by Lord Hoffmann in [*Synthon BV v] Smithkline Beecham plc* [[2006] RPC 10] commencing at [22]. Under the heading 'Disclosure', after reciting the tests in *Hill v Evans* and *General Tire*, Lord Hoffmann said (at [22]):

> If I may summarise the effect of these two well-known statements, the matter relied upon as prior art must disclose subject matter which, if performed, would necessarily result in an infringement

of the patent. That may be because the prior art discloses the same invention. *In that case there will be no question that performance of the earlier invention would infringe and usually it will be apparent to someone who is aware of both the prior art and the patent that it will do so ...* [W]henever subject matter described in the prior disclosure is capable of being performed and is such that, if performed, it must result in the patent being infringed, the disclosure condition is satisfied. The flag has been planted, even though the author or maker of the prior art was not aware that he was doing so. (Emphasis added)

185. As to a description of a means of obtaining the claimed product, his Lordship said at [23] that it was not sufficient if infringement were a possible or even a likely consequence of performing the invention disclosed by the prior disclosure. It must be necessarily entailed. It is not sufficient even if it may be obvious to perform the prior disclosure in a way that would lead to the subsequently claimed invention. Again, his Lordship, emphasised that the prior disclosure must be construed as it would have been understood by the skilled person.

186. 'Enablement' was dealt with by Lord Hoffmann under a separate heading and as a separate requirement, under United Kingdom law, for anticipation. In the United Kingdom, there is a requirement for novelty under s 2 of the 1977 Act (UK) that an invention does not form part of the state of the art but also that the invention has been made 'available to the public'. The test of enablement of a prior disclosure for the purposes of anticipation as discussed by Lord Hoffmann was the same as the test of enablement of the patent for the purposes of sufficiency. Lord Hoffmann emphasised at [28] that the concepts of disclosure and enablement are distinct concepts each of which has to be satisfied under United Kingdom law and each of which has its own rules.

187. Lord Hoffmann accepted that, even under the UK test, the same disclosure may satisfy the requirements of disclosure and enablement. His Lordship said (at [29]):

Indeed, when the prior art is a product, the product itself, though dumb, may be enabling if it is 'available to the public' and a person skilled in the art can discover its composition or internal structure and reproduce it without undue burden.

188. This is consistent with *Nicaro*.

189. For the purposes of disclosure, the prior art must disclose an invention which, if performed, would necessarily infringe the patent. Once the very subject matter of the invention has been disclosed, the person skilled in the art is assumed to be willing to make trial and error experiments to get it to work. For the purposes of disclosure, the disclosure is either of an invention which, if performed, would infringe the patent, or it is not. When Lord Hoffmann went on to say that, for the purposes of enablement, the question is no longer what the skilled person would think the disclosure meant but whether he was able to work the invention which the court has held it to disclose, his Lordship was talking of what, in Australia, is covered by *sufficiency* of disclosure or description.

190. It follows that, where the prior publication is of the subsequently claimed invention, that is sufficient. Where the prior disclosure falls short of a complete disclosure, the question of the sufficiency of that disclosure arises. It is there that consideration must be given to the quality of a disclosure to the skilled addressee armed with common general knowledge. It is in that context that, in a limited fashion, questions of 'enablement' can be said to arise. The use of that expression tends to cause confusion between anticipation and sufficiency. Rather, the Court, armed with the evidence of the skilled

addressee as to terms of art and the nature and extent of the disclosure in the prior art document, must determine whether the prior disclosure is sufficient to enable the skilled addressee to perceive, understand and, where appropriate, apply the prior disclosure necessarily to obtain the invention.

191. Where the prior disclosure is of large numbers of compounds by reference to a chemical formula, evidence will establish whether or not such a form of disclosure in the context of the examples and the discussion in the specification is disclosure of any particular subsequently claimed compound. I agree with Dr Barker in *University of Georgia* that a disclosure of a racemate does not necessarily amount to a disclosure of the individual enantiomers. It depends upon the disclosure in the context of the prior art document.

192. The primary judge said that enabling disclosure in the context of a product claim means simply that the earlier disclosure must point unmistakably to the (+)-enantiomer of citalopram as distinct from the racemate. That is consistent with authority. When his Honour added 'as a drug desirable to obtain', I take that to mean that one takes into account the context of a specification to ascertain whether the earlier disclosure is a disclosure of the (+)-enantiomer where it is not specifically referred to.

THE ALLEGED ANTICIPATIONS
THE PRIOR CITALOPRAM PATENT FOR THE RACEMATE

193. The prior citalopram patent described the racemate. It did not describe the pure or isolated (+)-enantiomer. There is no anticipation unless the disclosure of the racemate was, to the skilled addressee, a disclosure of the (+)-enantiomer. As the primary judge pointed out at [171], the skilled but non-inventive addressee would have understood that (+/–)-citalopram consisted of the (+)-enantiomer and the (–)-enantiomer and would have been able to identify the formulae for the S and R enantiomers but would not have known in the absence of experimentation which was the (+)-enantiomer and which the (–)-enantiomer. As his Honour said, these facts would not point specifically to the independent existence of the enantiomers. They did not disclose an invention which, if performed, would necessarily infringe the Patent.

194. It is the case that the skilled addressee knew that the racemate could be resolved into the enantiomers but there was nothing to tell him or her to do so. Further, the prior citalopram patent was silent as to the means of obtaining the enantiomers and there were different methods available to try to do so. There were no clear and unmistakable directions to obtain the enantiomers. Some of the available methodology may have been successful, other methods may not.

195. The prior citalopram patent does not render claim 1 of the Patent not novel. It follows that it does not render claims 2, 3, 4 and 5 not novel.

[Her Honour then considered whether a second alleged anticipation, an article entitled 'The Stereoselectivity of Serotonin Uptake in Brain Tissue and Blood Platelets: The Topography of the Serotonin Uptake Area' by Donald F Smith ('the Smith article'), destroyed novelty.]

209. The Smith article does not describe the (+)-enantiomer. It does not disclose whether the R- or the S-enantiomer is the (+)-enantiomer. It does not give directions to obtain the (+)-enantiomer. The skilled addressee wishing to obtain an enantiomer of citalopram would, as the primary judge observed at [168], have to conduct further experiments, conduct research and gain further information to hit upon the present invention. Such experimentation and the steps that it would entail were not inevitable.

210. The Smith article does not contain information equivalent to the disclosure of the (+)-enantiomer of claim 1. It does not anticipate claim 1 of the Patent.

211. The primary judge was not in error in concluding that the attack on the Patent on the ground that the invention lacked novelty fails.

NOVELTY AND COMBINATION PATENTS

Combination patents raise particular issues with regard to the novelty requirement, because novelty resides in the combination of integers rather than each integer of itself. Therefore, to destroy novelty, all of the essential integers of the combination must be described in a single piece of prior art information or two or more cross-referenced pieces of prior art. A claim for a combination patent is a claim which 'combines a number of elements which interact with each other to produce a new result or product' (per Aickin J in *Minnesota Mining and Manufacturing v Beiersdorf* (1980) 144 CLR at 266). Bennett J again has provided a useful summary of the key issues relating to the determination of the novelty requirements for combination patents in the extract below.

CASE EXTRACT: CURRENT LAW

SNF (Australia) Pty Ltd v Ciba Specialty Chemicals Water Treatments Ltd

[2012] FCAFC 95; (2012) 204 FCR 325
Federal Court of Australia, Full Court

[Proceedings in this case involved a series of innovation patents owned by Ciba. SNF sought orders for revocation of the patents and relief under s 128 of the *Patents Act* in respect of alleged unjustified threats of infringement. Ciba cross-claimed for infringement. The Court at first instance held that the patents were valid. Issues on appeal related to construction of the patent claims, novelty, innovative step and sufficiency. It was agreed between the parties that differences between the patents were immaterial and that one, referred to as Patent 944, would serve as an 'exemplar'. Various documents and acts were relied on by SNF in arguing that there was lack of novelty. Bennett J's analysis of one particular prior art patent, Slatter 3 is extracted below. Finn J agreed with Bennett J, and although Dowsett J handed down a separate judgment, the Court was unanimous that the appeal should be dismissed. The patents related to the treatment of waste mineral slurries at mining sites, specifically improvements to 'the rigidification of the material while retaining the fluidity of the material during transfer'. Much attention in the early part of Bennett J's judgment was focused on the meaning of rigidification. With regard to the novelty requirement, attention was particularly focused on integer (e) in claim 1: an aqueous solution of a water-soluble polymer having an intrinsic viscosity of at least 5 dl/g (measured in 1M NaCl at 25° C). Special leave to appeal to the High Court was refused in *SNF (Australia) Pty Ltd v CIBA Specialty Chemicals Water Treatment Ltd* [2013] HCATrans 54.]

Bennett J:

315. This is not a case where Slatter 3 is said to contain clear and unmistakable directions to carry out the claimed process. There is no relevant signpost on the road to the patentee's invention. The key question, in determining whether Slatter 3 discloses the combination of the claims of Patent 944,

is whether Slatter 3 discloses the combination of integer (e) with the other integers of the claimed process. It is not sufficient if, in the context of Slatter 3, the disclosure is of integer (e) alone.

316. The references within Slatter 3 to the use of pre-formed solutions of water-soluble polymers are limited. The disclosure is in terms of alternative treatments but does not descend into the detail of those alternative treatments. In context, Slatter 3 clearly refers to a process resulting in rigidification. However the following is not clear:

- whether the process using the water-soluble polymers is a process for improving rigidification where it is stated that an advantage of the addition in powder form is that the viscosity does not increase or diminish as rapidly as the solution based addition;
- whether the use of water-soluble polymers results in a process which retains the fluidity of the material during transfer;
- whether the waste material is transferred as a fluid to the deposition area and only then allowed to stand and rigidify; and
- whether the water-soluble polymer is combined with the material during transfer.

317. I accept that integer (e) is, of itself and in isolation, disclosed. However, it is not disclosed as part of a process which includes the remaining integers of the claimed process, nor is there a 'teaching', in the sense of a recommendation, a direction or a signpost that discloses or results in those other integers being present. To the contrary, the warning in Slatter 3 that viscosity may increase or diminish rapidly with a solution based addition argues against its use with the material such that the requisite fluidity is maintained.

318. Consideration of the reasoning of Black CJ and Lehane J in *Bristol-Myers [Squibb Co v FH Faulding & Co Ltd* (2000) 97 FCR 524] at [71]–[72] does not affect the proper conclusions to be drawn from Slatter 3. Their Honours were there considering a disclosure of an administration schedule that proved to be feasible in respect of a particular drug. In context, the question of whether the particular publication anticipated the claimed invention involved a consideration of whether or not the prior publication gave a direction or made a recommendation or suggestion that, if the skilled reader followed it, would result in the claimed invention, either expressly or implicitly (at [67]). Their Honours noted the acceptance by counsel in that case that mere speculation as to whether a method subsequently claimed would work would not of itself destroy novelty and said at [68] that 'the question is still, what does the prior publication teach?'.

319. In my view, their Honours were not there referring to what a prior publication discloses where all integers are said to be disclosed. The word 'teach' in that context was an examination of something less than an actual disclosure of all integers, as discussed in *General Tire [& Rubber Co v Firestone Tyre & Rubber Co Ltd* (1971) 1A IPR 121], *Nicaro [Holdings Pty Ltd v Martin Engineering Co* (1990) 91 ALR 513] and [H] *Lundbeck [A/S v Alphapharm Pty Ltd* (2009) 177 FCR 151]. There may be a direction capable of being carried out in a manner which would infringe the patentee's claim; there may be a disclosure to the skilled addressee of a 'missing integer' within the context of the prior publication. Their Honours said at [72] that 'there can be no serious doubt that the abstract teaches the shorter infusion period'. As I understand what was meant, this was an acceptance that the abstract did disclose the shorter infusion period to the skilled reader.

320. The Full Court in *Merck & Co Inc v Arrow Pharmaceuticals Ltd* (2006) 154 FCR 31 reached a similar conclusion as to the analysis in *Bristol-Myers*. Their Honours pointed out at [110] that the use of the word 'teach' was in the sense of 'direct, recommend or suggest'. The Court also pointed out

that a characterisation of an alleged anticipation as a suggestion is not necessarily fatal to a novelty argument but emphasised that the question was whether or not there was disclosure. That is, as stated in *Hill v Evans*:

> The invention must be shewn to have been before made known. Whatever, therefore, is essential to the invention *must be read out of the prior application*.

321. *Lundbeck* contains other observations relevant to the novelty issues in this appeal (at [169]–[188]):

- If the prior publication contains a definite statement of facts and material from which the ordinary skilled addressee would clearly infer the existence of the integers of the claim, this is sufficient for an anticipation.
- The question is whether the prior publication is sufficient to make the claimed invention apparent to the skilled addressee.
- A prior publication does not invalidate a patent unless it supplies sufficient information to enable a person of ordinary skill, having at least the common general knowledge of the art, to produce the product subsequently claimed.
- Prior knowledge of an invention must be knowledge equal to that required to be given by the patent if it is to invalidate it.
- If prior information discloses some but not all of the integers of a claimed patent, there is anticipation if the skilled addressee would add the missing information as a matter of course and without the application of inventive ingenuity. The skilled addressee must be able to add what is missing in the prior information to obtain the claimed invention. Where there is an asserted prior use, what the skilled addressee observes on inspection must be sufficient to enable him or her to comprehend the complete invention. That is, it must be sufficient to amount to a disclosure to the skilled addressee of the claimed invention. The prior art must disclose subject matter which, if performed, would necessarily result in infringement of the claims of the patent.

322. SNF does not, in the appeal, rely upon the 'teaching' of Slatter 3. It relies upon actual disclosure despite the absence of explicit disclosure of the other integers of the claim and process of Patent 944. However, as stated in *General Tire*, to anticipate the patentee's claim the prior publication must then contain clear and unmistakable directions to do what the patentee claims to have invented. Slatter 3 does not direct the use of an aqueous solution of water-soluble polymers as a process for improved rigidification.

323. SNF submits that anticipation should be tested by asking whether the skilled addressee who applied the teaching that polymers could be of an aqueous solution would inevitably have infringed the claims of the patent. It submits that the answer must be 'yes', as all other integers of claim 1, including rigidification as defined by Dr Farrow, would clearly be present. However, there is no direction in Slatter 3 to use polymers in an aqueous solution and no evidence that the skilled reader would read Slatter 3 as recommending or disclosing that such a course would produce a process of improving rigidification. To the contrary, as the primary judge concluded at [96], based on Dr Farrow's analysis and Professor Slatter's concession, Slatter 3 recommends against the addition of polymer in aqueous solution.

324. Slatter 3 cannot be said to provide sufficient disclosure to constitute an anticipation of the process of claim 1 of Patent 944.

INVENTIVE STEP

It is not enough for an invention to be novel. There must also be some inventive ingenuity, some difficulty overcome, some barrier crossed. In the terms of the statute, the invention must 'involve an inventive step': s 18(1)(b)(ii) of the *Patents Act*. This element can also be expressed in terms of the need for the invention to be non-obvious. In Australia, the test for inventive step has been broken up into three considerations:

- Who is the hypothetical person skilled in the relevant art?
- What was the state of their knowledge before the priority date of the invention?
- In the light of these considerations, was the invention obvious?

Other key points about the inventive step requirement can conveniently be summarised as follows:

- In the fields of 'scientific inventions, intricate mechanical arrangements, chemical processes, electrical and electronic devices and so forth', 'the persons skilled in the art are not just skilled artisans. They are often trained engineers and scientists, who are well versed in the periodical literature of their subjects' (Windeyer J in *Sunbeam Corporation v Morphy-Richards (Aust) Pty Ltd* (1994) 180 CLR 98 at 112). Furthermore, '[i]f the art is one having a highly developed technology, the notional skilled reader to whom the document is addressed may not be a single person but a team' (*Minnesota Mining & Manufacturing Co v Tyco Electronics Pty Ltd* [2002] FCAFC 315; (2002) 56 IPR 248 at [40]).

- In assessing the state of knowledge of the hypothetical skilled person under current Australian law, s 7(2) and (3) provides that this includes the common general knowledge together with any single piece of prior art information or a combination of any two or more pieces of prior art information that the skilled person mentioned in subsection (2) could, before the priority date of the relevant claim, be reasonably expected to have combined.

- The material that can be considered in determining the existence of an inventive step has broadened over time. It is necessary to be aware of the requirements for determining the state of knowledge of the hypothetical skilled addressee at particular points in time because they significantly influence judicial determinations as to presence or absence of inventive step.

- Under the *Patents Act 1952* (Cth) only the common general knowledge could be considered in determining whether or not there was an inventive step, as illustrated by the decision of Aickin J in *Minnesota Mining and Manufacturing v Beiersdorf* (1980) 144 CLR 253. In explaining the notion of common general knowledge, Aickin J noted at 293 that it 'involves the use of that which is known or used by those in the relevant trade. It forms the background knowledge and experience which is available to all in the trade'. In that case, Aickin J held that in the particular trade of hospital products, patent specifications were not part of the common general knowledge. But in other trades, patent specifications have been considered by the courts to be part of the common general knowledge.

- When the 1990 Act was first introduced, it was permissible to include single pieces of prior art information or two or more sufficiently cross-referenced pieces of prior art information, in addition to the common general knowledge, but only to the extent that the skilled person *could reasonably be expected to have ascertained, understood and regarded them as relevant to work in the patent area.*

- Entry into force of the *Patents Amendment Act 2001* (Cth) extended the field to remove the limitation that the work had to be done in the patent area.
- The *Raising the Bar Act* amendments further extended the field by removing the requirement that the prior art information is of the nature that the skilled person ought reasonably be expected to have ascertained, understood and regarded as relevant.
- The question of whether or not an invention is obvious is objective and is a question of fact to be determined on the evidence admitted. In one of his other major patent cases, Aickin J in *Meyers Taylor v Vicarr Industries* (1977) 137 CLR 228 at 249 referred to a 'scintilla of inventiveness' being enough for an invention to be non-obvious. It is irrelevant that the idea is simple, or that once the idea is conceived it is simple to put it into effect. A number of tests have been suggested in the cases, which are discussed further later in this chapter (see 'The test for obviousness' below, p 468). The burden of proof is on the person challenging the validity of the patent.
- Secondary evidence of failure of attempts to solve a well-known problem may be used to impute non-obviousness, by indicating a 'long-felt want'. Commercial success, of itself, can never be determinative of non-obviousness, but is a material consideration. Evidence of the patentee's experiments may also suggest either that the experiments were part of the inventive step, or that they were routine trial and error.
- Hindsight and ex post facto analysis of the steps taken to create the invention are matters of concern, particularly in relation to combination patents, as noted by Aickin J in the extract from *Minnesota Mining and Manufacturing v Beiersdorf* provided below.

THE STATE OF KNOWLEDGE OF THE HYPOTHETICAL SKILLED PERSON

As with novelty, a number of the judgments of Aickin J during his short tenure as a justice of the Australian High Court make important contributions to the developing body of jurisprudence on inventive step. Aickin J's decision in *Minnesota Mining and Manufacturing v Beiersdorf* (extracted below) provides definitive guidance on the notion of the common general knowledge. *Meyers Taylor v Vicarr Industries* and *Wellcome Foundation Ltd v VR Laboratories (Aust) Pty Ltd* (1981) 148 CLR 262 are other important judgments by Aickin J on inventive step.

PRECEDENT

CASE EXTRACT: PRECEDENT

Minnesota Mining and Manufacturing v Beiersdorf (Australia) Ltd

(1980) 144 CLR 253
High Court of Australia

[In this case, the patent in issue claimed a new type of breathable, porous, pressure-sensitive adhesive surgical tape. It was recognised as being a combination of known integers. Aickin J gave the leading judgment, with the agreement of the other members of the Court.]

Aickin J (at 287–295): The *Patents Act 1952–1973* ('the *Patents Act 1952*') s 100 (1) sets out the grounds upon which a patent may be revoked of which grounds (e) and (g) are material. They are as follows:

(e) that the invention, so far as claimed in any claim, was obvious and did not involve an inventive step, having regard to what was known or used in Australia on or before the priority date of that claim

(g) that the invention, so far as claimed in any claim, was not novel in Australia on the priority date of that claim.

In *HPM Industries Pty Ltd v Gerard Industries Ltd* (1957) 98 CLR 424 ('the *HPM Case*') Williams J, sitting as a single justice, held that in s 100(1)(e) the words 'known or used' embraced more than the common general knowledge of a skilled worker in the relevant field at the priority date. He said (1957) 98 CLR, at p 437:

> Paragraph (g) appears to accept the law relating to want of novelty as it existed at the date of the *Patents Act*. But par (e) appears to have widened the law relating to want of subject matter. It requires the Court to have regard to what is known or used in Australia before the priority date of the claim, and the words 'known or used' appear to embrace more than what had become commonly known or used or in other words more than the common general knowledge of a skilled craftsman in the particular art on that day ...

[Aickin J then reviewed the legislation, law reform inquiries and relevant case law in the UK and Australia.]

I am satisfied that we should not regard the observations of Williams J in the *HPM Case* as correctly stating the law in Australia. It is not a matter of overruling the decision because, as I have said, it was based upon a different ground. The dicta however should not be followed.

Williams J did not deal expressly with the question whether in the case of an allegation of obviousness it is possible to 'make a mosaic' out of existing publications not forming part of common general knowledge but it is nonetheless clear that he regarded such a course as open in view of the contrasting statement quoted above on novelty. The notion of common general knowledge itself involves the use of that which is known or used by those in the relevant trade. It forms the background knowledge and experience which is available to all in the trade in considering the making of new products, or the making of improvements in old, and it must be treated as being used by an individual as a general body of knowledge. I do not with respect think that it is correct to describe that process as the making of a mosaic although it has often been so described, a usage which however may be misleading. The process of applying such common general knowledge to the solution of a problem is not a process of picking out individual pieces of information and combining them, including inferences from known facts and known principles, as well as the application of such principles. The making of a mosaic prohibited in the case of an allegation of want of novelty is the picking out of individual items of information from prior publications or prior objects and assembling them together so as to give them an appearance of unity and then alleging that such mosaic reveals the very thing claimed. That is an understandable, though not a permissible, process.

In the case of alleged lack of an inventive step the question of making a mosaic must operate (if at all) in a very different matter. An allegation of want of inventive step is not made out by saying you may take one or two, or twenty-one or twenty-two, prior publications and then select from them appropriate extracts or pieces of information, which will add up to the invention claimed and so demonstrate that it was obvious. So to proceed is to mistake the nature of an invention and the nature of the objection of obviousness. The question is, is the invention itself obvious, not whether a diligent searcher might find pieces from which there might have been selected the elements which make up the patent. If this were not so, there could never be a valid patent for a new combination of old integers. The proper question is not whether it would have been obvious to the hypothetical addressee who was presented with an ex post facto selection of prior specifications that elements from them could be combined to produce a new product or process. It is rather whether it would have been obvious to a non-inventive skilled worker in the field to select from a possibly very large range of publications the particular combination subsequently chosen by the opponent in the glare of hindsight and also whether it would have been obvious to that worker to select the particular combination of integers from those selected publications. In the case of a combination patent the invention will lie in the selection of integers, a process which will necessarily involve rejection of other possible integers. The prior existence of publications revealing those integers, as separate items, and other possible integers does not of itself make an alleged invention obvious. It is the selection of the integers out of, perhaps many possibilities, which must be shown to be obvious.

It is in relation to this process that the misuse of hindsight is most common. When once an idea or an object or a process or a combination, admittedly novel, has been published, it is very easy to say after perhaps months of search and study in the Patent Office and the public libraries that the integers into which the patent might be dissected could be found scattered amongst the prior documents by a person who already knew the solution to the problem and therefore knew what to look for and what to discard. But that process does not demonstrate lack of an inventive step. The opening of a safe is easy when the combination has been already provided.

It is pointless to say, as some witnesses did in the present case that given the description in the claims in the patent they could with the aid of some prior specifications have produced the end product. This is an extreme example of the ex post facto dissection of an invention which has been vigorously criticized in many courts.

It is worth quoting yet again the words of Fletcher-Moulton LJ in *British Westinghouse Electric and Manufacturing Co Ltd v Braulik* (1910) 27 RPC 209, at p 230 where he said:

> I confess that I view with suspicion arguments to the effect that a new combination, bringing with it new and important consequences in the shape of practical machines, is not an invention, because, when it has once been established, it is easy to show how it might be arrived at by starting from something known, and taking a series of apparently easy steps. This ex post facto analysis of invention is unfair to the inventors, and in my opinion it is not countenanced by English Patent Law.

Similar statements may be found in many cases; see, eg, per Latham CJ in *Palmer v Dunlop Perdriau Rubber Co Ltd* (1937) 59 CLR 30, at pp 60–61.

It may be observed that in the cases where obviousness is in issue very often the larger the number of prior publications which are relied upon as together establishing absence of an inventive step, the more likely it is that the alleged invention was not obvious for the wider one has to look to find all the integers the less likely it is that it would have been obvious to put them together in the particular manner in which the inventor did.

It may be noted that even in England where the process of making a mosaic out of prior publications is regarded as permissible under the *Patents Act 1949* it is still necessary that the mosaic must be one which 'can be put together by an unimaginative man with no inventive capacity'—see per Lord Reid in *Technograph Printed Circuits Ltd v Mills and Rockley (Electronics) Ltd* [1972] RPC 346, at p 355.

There may be some fields of endeavour in which those who work therein study and make themselves familiar with all patent specifications as they become available for inspection in one or in many countries so that what was contained therein becomes common general knowledge in that particular trade or field of manufacture in the country in question. Examples are provided by *Vidal Dyes Syndicate Ltd v Levinstein Ltd* (1912) 29 RPC 245, at pp 279–280 and *British Celanese Ltd v Courtaulds Ltd* (1933) 50 RPC 259, at p 280. Indeed in the present case it appears that the first appellant in its establishment in the United States at one time had employees who did just this in the field of adhesives. But this is not so in all fields or in all countries. There was no evidence in the present case that those working in Australia in the field of adhesives or of surgical tapes followed such a practice or that any of the specifications relied upon was part of the common general knowledge of those working in these fields in Australia.

The respondent relied upon a number of prior specifications which had been available in Australia for public inspection before the priority date as providing a basis for the argument that the invention claimed was obvious. For the reasons which I have set out above I do not regard such specifications as capable of sustaining that argument without evidence that they were part of common general knowledge at that time. There was no such evidence and accordingly it is not necessary for me to examine those specifications.

Following Aickin J's decision in *Minnesota Mining and Manufacturing v Beiersdorf*, prior art information was only considered to be relevant to the inventive step inquiry under the *Patents Act 1952* if it was part of the common general knowledge. The content of the common general knowledge varies depending on the nature of the industry.

As a result of the legislative changes in 1990 and again in 2001 and 2012, the hypothetical skilled person in the field has become increasingly more like the diligent searcher mentioned by Aickin J in *Minnesota Mining and Manufacturing v Beiersdorf* at 293. There has not yet been the opportunity for judicial scrutiny of the 2012 *Raising the Bar Act* amendments. There have been some opportunities for judicial consideration of the requirement introduced by the *Patents Act* as enacted in 1990, that the prior art information must have been reasonably expected to have been ascertained, understood and regarded as relevant by the skilled person. The High Court provided guidance on the application of s 7(3) in the case extracted below. In reading this case, it is important to recognise that it does not reflect current legislative provisions. Nevertheless, there is a good reason for including this extract: there will be cases coming before the courts for many years to come in which the relevant law is that which applied prior to entry into force of the *Raising the Bar Act* amendments, at the priority date of the patent in issue.

CASE EXTRACT: PRECEDENT

Lockwood Security Products Pty Ltd v Doric Products Pty Ltd (No 2) ('Lockwood No 2')

[2007] HCA 21; (2007) 235 CLR 173
High Court of Australia

[This case, 'Lockwood No 2', has already been mentioned briefly in Chapter 10 in relation to the issue of lack of inventiveness on the face of the specification. The earlier High Court decision in *Lockwood Security Products Pty Ltd v Doric Products Pty Ltd* [2004] HCA 58; (2004) 217 CLR 274 ('*Lockwood No 1*') is discussed in Chapter 12 in relation to the 'fair basis' disclosure requirement. This extract from *Lockwood No 2* addresses the inventive step requirement. The subject matter of the case was a patent for a deadlock for doors. The alleged inventive step was the addition of an actuator, which allowed the internal side of the deadlock to be unlocked from the outside. The case was decided under the *Patents Act* as it stood prior to the 2001 and 2012 amendments.]

Gummow, Hayne, Callinan, Heydon and Crennan JJ (some footnotes omitted): 126. What is obvious under Australian law is to be determined by the combined operation of ss 7(2), 7(3), 18(1)(b)(ii) and Sched 1 to the Act. These provisions are all directed to determining whether an invention 'is to be taken to involve an inventive step when compared with the prior art base' (s 7(2)). Schedule 1 defines 'prior art base' and s 7(3) contains the statutory test for enlarging the prior art base beyond common general knowledge.

127. As stated above, by enlarging the prior art base through including relevant prior disclosures beyond those disclosures proven to be part of the common general knowledge, these provisions raise the threshold for inventiveness. However, the idea remains that the prior disclosures to be taken into account, even as enlarged by s 7(3), are being considered for a particular purpose. That purpose is the purpose of looking forward from the prior art base to see what a person skilled in the relevant art is likely to have done when faced with a similar problem which the patentee claims to have solved with the invention.

...

THE APPLICATION OF S 7(3)

148. It is not to be doubted that ss 7(2), 7(3) and 18(1) read together provide that each claim needs to be examined independently of the other claims when considering whether an alleged invention involves an inventive step. It is also axiomatic that an alleged invention in a combination of integers which constitutes a solution to a particular problem must necessarily involve rejecting other combinations of other integers as a solution to that particular problem.

149. The exercise, of which s 7(3) is an integral part, is the exercise of determining whether 'an invention' (s 7(2)) as disclosed 'in any claim' (s 18(1)) 'involve[s] an inventive step when compared with the prior art base' (s 7(2)). The 'prior art base' for s 7(2) is enlarged by s 7(3), so as to go beyond common general knowledge and to bring into consideration 'prior art information' which 'could ... be reasonably expected to have [been] ascertained, understood and regarded as relevant to work in the relevant art' (s 7(3)) by 'a person skilled in the relevant art' (s 7(2)). This brings to mind Lord Reid's

reference to a 'diligent searcher' in *Technograph Printed Circuits Ltd v Mills & Rockley (Electronics) Ltd* [[1972] RPC 346 at 355] and suggests a person skilled in the relevant art familiar with some, but not necessarily every piece of, publicly available information in the relevant art beyond common general knowledge.

CONSTRUCTION OF SS 7(2) AND 7(3)

150. The proper construction of ss 7(2) and 7(3) has been considered in *Firebelt Pty Ltd v Brambles Australia Ltd* [(2002) 188 ALR 280 at 287–289] ('*Firebelt*'). In recognising that s 7(3) relaxes the previous rule under the 1952 Act which forbade the use of prior disclosures not proved to be part of the common general knowledge at the priority date, this Court approved a statement by Burchett J in the Federal Court [in *Tidy Tea Ltd v Unilever Australia Ltd* (1995) 32 IPR 405 at 414] where he noted that s 7(3) in its pre-2001 version is limited:

> by the words 'being information that the skilled person … could, before the priority date of the relevant claim, be reasonably expected to have ascertained, understood and regarded as relevant to work in the relevant art in the patent area'. And if a prior [disclosure] passes those tests, it must still be able to be said that, if that [disclosure] had been considered by the hypothetical skilled person together with the common general knowledge at the relevant time, 'the invention would have been obvious'.

151. That passage, noting the words of limitation in s 7(3), reflects the two statutory tests which have already been mentioned: the s 7(2) test of whether an invention is obvious when compared with the prior art base, and the s 7(3) test of whether information is to be included in the prior art base, each test to be determined objectively by the standard of 'a person skilled in the relevant art'.

152. Given the history, context, purpose and specific words of limitation in s 7(3), all of which were addressed by this Court in *Firebelt* [at 289], the phrase 'relevant to work in the relevant art' should not be construed as meaning relevant to any work in the relevant art, including work irrelevant to the particular problem or long-felt want or need, in respect of which the invention constitutes an advance in the art. The phrase can only be construed as being directed to prior disclosures, that is publicly available information (not part of common general knowledge) which a person skilled in the relevant art could be expected to have regarded as relevant to solving a particular problem or meeting a long-felt want or need as the patentee claims to have done. Otherwise the words of limitation in the last 40 words of s 7(3) would have no role to play. Any piece of public information in the relevant art would be included, as is the case with the much broader and quite different formulation in the cognate provisions in the United Kingdom, which do not depend on the standard of a skilled person's opinion of the relevance of the information.

153. The question of what a person skilled in the relevant art would regard as relevant, when faced with the same problem as the patentee, is to be determined on the evidence. The starting point is the subject matter of the invention to be considered together with evidence in respect of prior art, common general knowledge, the way in which the invention is an advance in the art, and any related matters. It should be mentioned that the starting point is not necessarily the inventive step as claimed, or even agreed between parties, because the evidence, particularly in respect of a combination of integers, may support a different inventive step.

THE TEST FOR OBVIOUSNESS

The test for obviousness establishes patent law's 'innovation threshold' by dictating how great an advance on the prior art is required for an invention to have an inventive step as required by s 18(1)(b)(ii). As with novelty, recent judicial decisions on the test for obviousness provide comprehensive reviews of the Australian and UK precedents and illustrate how they are to be applied under modern Australian law. Also as with novelty, these cases illustrate that the interpretation of Australian patent law by the courts is moving away from the interpretation of like provisions in UK law, which must operate within the confines of the European Patent Convention.

PRECEDENT

CASE EXTRACT: PRECEDENT

Aktiebolaget Hässle v Alphapharm Pty Ltd

[2002] HCA 59; (2002) 212 CLR 411
High Court of Australia

[Like *Lundbeck,* extracted earlier in this chapter, *Alphapharm* involved an 'evergreening'-type patent— in this case a new preparation of delivery of the anti-ulcer drug omeprazole. Omeprazole is a chemical that is rapidly degraded in an acidic environment, like that encountered in the human stomach. The delivery mechanism described in the patent provides sub-coating and outer coating layers to protect the omeprazole 'core material' during its passage through the stomach. Alphapharm applied to the Therapeutic Goods Administration to import generic omeprazole. Proceeding were instituted in the Federal Court to restrain apprehended infringement by Aktiebolaget Hässle and an Australian subsidiary of the multinational Astra pharmaceutical group (it should be noted that the High Court referred to the appellants collectively as 'Astra' throughout its judgment). Alphapharm cross-claimed, seeking revocation of the patent. Although a number of grounds were raised at first instance, the only issue before the High Court was that of inventive step. The relevant law was the *Patents Act 1952* (Cth).]

Gleeson CJ, Gaudron, Gummow and Hayne JJ (some footnotes omitted):

OBVIOUSNESS OR LACK OF INVENTIVE STEP

19. The use of terms such as 'obviousness', and lack or absence of 'ingenuity', 'subject-matter' and 'inventive step', to distinguish a ground of revocation from that involved with 'lack of novelty', 'prior publication', 'anticipation' and 'prior use', has a fairly lengthy and evolving history in the decisions on patent law before the embodiment of the distinction in modern legislation. Paragraph (e) of s 100(1) of the 1952 Act, like par (f) of s 32(1) of the *Patents Act* 1949 (UK) ('the 1949 UK Act'), uses the expression 'was [or 'is'] obvious and did [or 'does'] not involve an [or 'any'] inventive step having regard to what was known or used ... before the priority date of that claim'.

20. On the other hand, in the United States, when a requirement for inventive quality was first embodied in statutory form by §103 of the 1952 *Patents Act* ('the 1952 US Act'), this was done under a heading 'Non-obvious Subject Matter' and with a text which did not refer to absence of 'inventive step'. Section 103 asks whether 'the differences between the subject matter sought to be patented

and the prior art are such that the subject matter as a whole would have been obvious at the time the invention was made to a person having ordinary skill in the art to which said subject matter pertains'. However, with respect to the juxtaposition of the phrases 'was obvious' and 'did not involve an inventive step', in the United Kingdom and Australia it has been accepted, as it was put in *Beecham Group Ltd's (Amoxycillin) Application* [[1980] RPC 261 at 290], '[o]bviousness and inventiveness are antitheses. What is obvious cannot be inventive, and what is inventive cannot be obvious.' In the present case, the Full Court made a statement to the same effect and this is accepted by both parties in this Court.

HINDSIGHT AND COMBINATIONS

21. The defendant to an infringement action who cross-claims for revocation on the ground of obviousness bears the onus of establishing that case. This obliges the defendant to lead evidence looking back to the priority date, sometimes, as here, many years before trial. In those circumstances, the warnings in the authorities against the misuse of hindsight are not to be repeated as but prefatory averments and statements of trite law. The danger of such misuse will be particularly acute where what is claimed is a new and inventive combination for the interaction of integers, some or all of which are known. It is worth repeating what was said by Lord Diplock in *Technograph Printed Circuits Ltd v Mills & Rockley (Electronics) Ltd* [[1972] RPC 346 at 362]:

> Once an invention has been made it is generally possible to postulate a combination of steps by which the inventor might have arrived at the invention that he claims in his specification if he started from something that was already known. But it is only because the invention has been made and has proved successful that it is possible to postulate from what starting point and by what particular combination of steps the inventor could have arrived at his invention. It may be that taken in isolation none of the steps which it is now possible to postulate, if taken in isolation, appears to call for any inventive ingenuity. It is improbable that this reconstruction *a posteriori* represents the mental process by which the inventor in fact arrived at his invention, but, even if it were, inventive ingenuity lay in perceiving that the final result which it was the object of the inventor to achieve was attainable from the particular starting point and in his selection of the particular combination of steps which would lead to that result.

...

THE LAW RESPECTING OBVIOUSNESS

33. The starting point is the statement by Hoffmann LJ in *Société Technique de Pulverisation Step v Emson Europe Ltd* [[1993] RPC 513 at 519]:

> The words 'obvious' and 'inventive step' involve questions of fact and degree which must be answered in accordance with the general policy of the *Patents Act* to reward and encourage inventors without inhibiting improvements of existing technology by others.

34. In *General Tire & Rubber Co v Firestone Tyre and Rubber Co Ltd* [[1972] RPC 457], the English Court of Appeal, with reference to the ground in par (f) of s 32(1) of the 1949 UK Act, said [at 497]:

> 'Obvious' is, after all, a much-used word and it does not seem to [us] that there is any need to go beyond the primary dictionary meaning of 'very plain'.

PRECEDENT

These words do not aid Alphapharm; to the contrary, Alphapharm relies upon the Full Court judgment which employed such terms as 'worthwhile to try', a phrase not readily understood as synonymous with 'obvious'.

35. More recently [in *Chiron Corporation v Murex Diagnostics Ltd* [1996] RPC 535 at 557], Aldous J said that obvious is an 'ordinary English word' which in patent law does not have 'any technical meaning'.

36. However, those statements in the English cases should be treated with caution. The term 'obvious' first appeared in the United States, United Kingdom and Australian legislation after detailed judicial exegesis over many years. Further, 'obvious' does not stand by itself in the statute to specify a ground of revocation; the reader is required to 'have regard' to what was 'known or used' on or before a particular date, and to a particular geographical area. The notions of meaning and construction are interdependent and the meaning of 'obvious' in par (e) of s 100(1) must be affected by the other words and syntax of the whole of s 100(1)(e). Finally, the statute does not identify the characteristics of the persons with the knowledge or use in question, thus making further judicial exegesis inevitable for the operation of the provision.

37. It is at this stage that further and for this appeal acute difficulties commence. They may be introduced by observations by Diplock LJ in a passage frequently cited in the English authorities. In *Johns-Manville Corporation's Patent* [[1967] RPC 479 at 493–494], Diplock LJ remarked:

> I have endeavoured to refrain from coining a definition of 'obviousness' which counsel may be tempted to cite in subsequent cases relating to different types of claims. Patent law can too easily be bedevilled by linguistics, and the citation of a plethora of cases about other inventions of different kinds. The correctness of a decision upon an issue of obviousness does not depend upon whether or not the decider has paraphrased the words of the Act in some particular verbal formula. *I doubt whether there is any verbal formula which is appropriate to all classes of claims.*' (emphasis added)

38. This last point is borne out by a consideration of the judgment of Aickin J in *Wellcome Foundation Ltd v VR Laboratories (Aust) Pty Ltd* [(1981) 148 CLR 262]. In the course of that judgment, his Honour emphasised (i) inventions may be the result not only of long experiments and profound research but also of chance, sudden lucky thought or mere accidental discovery; (ii) not all inventions are to be classified as successful solutions to a problem which had presented a 'long-felt want'; (iii) to the contrary, inventions which are an advance of contemporary expectations and thus reveal an 'unfelt want' may well involve an inventive step; and (iv) in cases falling within (iii), experiments and research would throw no light on the quality of what was claimed as an inventive step.

39. Proposition (i) certainly also represented the law under the 1949 UK Act. In *Dow Corning Corporation's Application* [[1969] RPC 544 at 560], Graham J said:

> An inventor may well arrive at his invention by a flash of genius which causes him no difficulty or concentrated thought at all, but the invention may still be a most brilliant one which would never have occurred to the notional skilled man in the art at all or only after prolonged investigation and the concentrated exercise of his, perhaps lesser, inventive faculty. In such a case, though it is in a sense obvious to the inventor, nevertheless the invention is undoubtedly worthy of patent protection.

40. However, propositions (ii), (iii) and (iv) may not represent the effect of the current English case law. Certainly they deny the general application of the proposition expressed by Lord Hoffmann in *Biogen Inc v Medeva plc* [[1997] RPC 1]. This was:

PRECEDENT

> A proper statement of the inventive concept needs to include some express or implied reference to the problem which it required invention to overcome

Biogen was the first case in which the House of Lords considered obviousness under the *Patents Act 1977* (UK) ('the 1977 UK Act'). What was said may reflect the 'problem and solution' approach which is apparently mandated by the European Patent Convention which requires European patent applications to disclose the claimed invention 'in such terms that the technical problem (even if not expressly stated as such) and its solution can be understood'. It will be necessary to return to the significance of the 1977 UK Act. However, earlier, in *Amoxycillin*, decided under the 1949 UK Act, Buckley LJ had spoken of the solution of 'some recognised problem' and the meeting of 'some recognised need'.

...

'MATTER OF ROUTINE'

50. In *Wellcome Foundation*, Aickin J referred to the taking of a series of routine steps and the making of a series of routine experiments and continued [at 286]:

> The test is whether the hypothetical addressee faced with the same problem *would have taken as a matter of routine whatever steps* might have led from the prior art to the invention, whether they be the steps of the inventor or not. (emphasis added)

Lehane J, in critical passages in his reasoning, referred to and applied what he understood to follow from this passage. Was that understanding correct? Alphapharm submits that his Honour was correct, and Astra the opposite. Both sides accept that *Wellcome Foundation* is binding; they differ as to its meaning.

51. What Aickin J had in mind as 'routine' appears from an earlier passage in his judgment in which he was discussing the question whether evidence of the steps taken by the patentee was relevant and therefore admissible in a revocation action. His Honour said [at 280–281]:

> Evidence of what he did by way of experiment may be another matter. It might show that the experiments devised for the purpose were part of an inventive step. Alternatively it might show that the experiments were of *a routine character* which the uninventive worker in the field *would try as a matter of course*. The latter could be relevant though not decisive in every case. It may be that the perception of the true nature of the problem was the inventive step which, once taken, revealed that straightforward experiments will provide the solution. It will always be necessary to distinguish between experiments leading to an invention and subsequent experiments for checking and testing the product or process the subject of the invention. The latter would not be material to obviousness but might be material to the question of utility. (emphasis added)

52. There are distinct strands of thought in this passage which may now be considered in terms applicable to the issues in this litigation. First, the working trials of which Dr Cederberg gave evidence may be (it is not necessary to determine the point) an example of the 'subsequent experiments for checking and testing', to which Aickin J referred at the end of the above passage. Secondly, the invention claimed in the Patent lay not in perceiving 'the true nature of the problem' to which 'straightforward experiments' then would provide the solution; the invention was in the interaction between the integers of the compound, to answer the known problem. Thirdly, in a case such as the present, the relevant

question was that posed in the first part of the passage. Were the experiments 'part of' that inventive step claimed in the Patent or were they 'of a routine character' to be tried 'as a matter of course'? If the latter be attributable to the hypothetical addressee of the Patent, such a finding would support a holding of obviousness.

53. That way of approaching the matter has an affinity with the reformulation of the 'Cripps question' by Graham J in *Olin Mathieson Chemical Corporation v Biorex Laboratories Ltd* [[1970] RPC 157]. This Court had been referred to *Olin* in the argument in *Wellcome Foundation*. Graham J had posed the question [at 187–188]:

> *Would* the notional research group at the relevant date, in all the circumstances, which include a knowledge of all the relevant prior art and of the facts of the nature and success of chlorpromazine, *directly be led as a matter of course to try* the $-CF_3$ substitution in the '2' position in place of the $-C1$ atom in chlorpromazine or in any other body which, apart from the $-CF_3$ substitution, has the other characteristics of the formula of claim 1, *in the expectation that it might well* produce a useful alternative to or better drug than chlorpromazine or a body useful for any other purpose?' (emphasis added)

That approach should be accepted.

...

'OBVIOUS' OR 'WORTHWHILE' TO TRY

...

73. In the United States, any criterion which adopts a notion of 'obvious to try' has been rejected in a long series of decisions upon §103 of the 1952 US Act. The judgment in a number of these was given by Judge Rich, first as a member of the United States Court of Customs and Patent Appeals and latterly as a member of the United States Court of Appeals, Federal Circuit. In 1966, in *Application of Tomlinson* [363 F 2d 928 at 931], his Honour wrote:

> Slight reflection suggests, we think, that there is usually an element of 'obviousness to try' in any research endeavor, that it is not undertaken with complete blindness but rather with some semblance of a chance of success, and that patentability determinations based on that as the test would not only be contrary to statute but result in a marked deterioration of the entire patent system as an incentive to invest in those efforts and attempts which go by the name of 'research.'

74. Later, in *In re O'Farrell* [853 F 2d 894 at 903 (1988)], a case concerned with an invention using genetic engineering, Judge Rich observed:

> [F]or many inventions that seem quite obvious, there is no absolute predictability of success until the invention is reduced to practice. There is always at least a possibility of unexpected results, that would then provide an objective basis for showing that the invention, although apparently obvious, was in law nonobvious.

75. Earlier, in *In re Farbenindustrie AG's Patents* [(1930) 47 RPC 289], Maugham J had dealt with an application to revoke three 'selection patents' relating to the manufacture of dyestuffs. The grounds advanced included lack of subject-matter, as it was then identified. His Lordship said [at 321–322]:

> In a sense it is still true to say that there is no prevision in chemistry. Any one of the millions of dyestuffs in question might be found to possess some unexpected and distinctive properties,

either of colour or fastness, or to have some other incidental advantage. There is no short cut to knowledge of this kind. A laborious and systematic investigation of a long series of combinations becomes necessary; and it is the fact that of recent years certain industrial organisations with enormous financial resources have established laboratories where numbers of chemists of high scientific attainments devote their lives to a systematic examination on scientific principles of a vast number of chemical substances.

76. In *In re O'Farrell* [at 903], Judge Rich also said:

The admonition that 'obvious to try' is not the standard under §103 has been directed mainly at two kinds of error. In some cases, what would have been 'obvious to try' would have been to vary all parameters or try each of numerous possible choices until one possibly arrived at a successful result, where the prior art gave either no indication of which parameters were critical or no direction as to which of many possible choices is likely to be successful. ... In others, what was 'obvious to try' was to explore a new technology or general approach that seemed to be a promising field of experimentation, where the prior art gave only general guidance as to the particular form of the claimed invention or how to achieve it.

The reasoning in these and other United States authorities should be accepted in preference to the path apparently taken in the English decisions, particularly after the 1977 UK Act, upon which Alphapharm relied. The United States decisions reflect an approach to the subject closer to that adopted in *Minnesota Mining* and *Wellcome Foundation*.

Although the decision in *Alphapharm* referred to a number of US cases with approval, the US position has since become rather more closely aligned with that in Europe following the Supreme Court decision in *KSR International Co v Teleflex, Inc*, 550 US 398 (2007), extracted below.

CASE EXTRACT: COMPARATIVE LAW

KSR International Co v Teleflex, Inc

550 US 398 (2007)
Supreme Court of the United States

[The patent in issue in this case was owned by Teleflex and claimed a mechanism for combining an electronic sensor with an adjustable car pedal so that the pedal's position could be transmitted to a computer that controlled the throttle in the vehicle's engine. Teleflex alleged infringement by KSR and KSR counterclaimed invalidity. The issue of obviousness went to the Supreme Court after the Court of Appeals held that the invention was non-obvious. Two other patents were included in the prior art, one of which, the 'Asano patent', is referred to in the following extract.]

Kennedy J (delivering the opinion of the Court) (at 405–422): In *Graham v John Deere Co of Kansas City*, 383 US 1 (1966), the Court set out a framework for applying the statutory language of §103, language itself based on the logic of the earlier decision in *Hotchkiss v Greenwood*, 11 How 248 (1851), and its progeny. See 383 US, at 15–17. The analysis is objective:

> Under §103, the scope and content of the prior art are to be determined; differences between the prior art and the claims at issue are to be ascertained; and the level of ordinary skill in the pertinent art resolved. Against this background the obviousness or nonobviousness of the subject matter is determined. Such secondary considerations as commercial success, long felt but unsolved needs, failure of others, etc., might be utilized to give light to the circumstances surrounding the origin of the subject matter sought to be patented. Id, at 17–18.

While the sequence of these questions might be reordered in any particular case, the factors continue to define the inquiry that controls. If a court, or patent examiner, conducts this analysis and concludes the claimed subject matter was obvious, the claim is invalid under §103.

Seeking to resolve the question of obviousness with more uniformity and consistency, the Court of Appeals for the Federal Circuit has employed an approach referred to by the parties as the 'teaching, suggestion, or motivation' test (TSM test), under which a patent claim is only proved obvious if 'some motivation or suggestion to combine the prior art teachings' can be found in the prior art, the nature of the problem, or the knowledge of a person having ordinary skill in the art. See, eg, *Al-Site Corp v VSI Int'l, Inc,* 174 F 3d 1308, 1323–1324 (CA Fed, 1999). KSR challenges that test, or at least its application in this case.

[The details of the invention and the prior art and the procedural history were then discussed. At 415, Kennedy J rejected the Court of Appeals' reasoning as too rigid, taking into account the expansive and flexible approach of the Supreme Court to the question of obviousness. Kennedy J continued with the criticism of the Court of Appeals' decision at 419.]

The flaws in the analysis of the Court of Appeals relate for the most part to the court's narrow conception of the obviousness inquiry reflected in its application of the TSM test. In determining whether the subject matter of a patent claim is obvious, neither the particular motivation nor the avowed purpose of the patentee controls. What matters is the objective reach of the claim. If the claim extends to what is obvious, it is invalid under §103. One of the ways in which a patent's subject matter can be proved obvious is by noting that there existed at the time of invention a known problem for which there was an obvious solution encompassed by the patent's claims.

The first error of the Court of Appeals in this case was to foreclose this reasoning by holding that courts and patent examiners should look only to the problem the patentee was trying to solve. 119 Fed Appx, at 288. The Court of Appeals failed to recognize that the problem motivating the patentee may be only one of many addressed by the patent's subject matter. The question is not whether the combination was obvious to the patentee but whether the combination was obvious to a person with ordinary skill in the art. Under the correct analysis, any need or problem known in the field of endeavor at the time of invention and addressed by the patent can provide a reason for combining the elements in the manner claimed.

The second error of the Court of Appeals lay in its assumption that a person of ordinary skill attempting to solve a problem will be led only to those elements of prior art designed to solve the same problem. Ibid. The primary purpose of Asano was solving the constant ratio problem; so, the court concluded, an inventor considering how to put a sensor on an adjustable pedal would have no reason

COMPARATIVE LAW

to consider putting it on the Asano pedal. Ibid. Common sense teaches, however, that familiar items may have obvious uses beyond their primary purposes, and in many cases a person of ordinary skill will be able to fit the teachings of multiple patents together like pieces of a puzzle. Regardless of Asano's primary purpose, the design provided an obvious example of an adjustable pedal with a fixed pivot point; and the prior art was replete with patents indicating that a fixed pivot point was an ideal mount for a sensor. The idea that a designer hoping to make an adjustable electronic pedal would ignore Asano because Asano was designed to solve the constant ratio problem makes little sense. A person of ordinary skill is also a person of ordinary creativity, not an automaton.

The same constricted analysis led the Court of Appeals to conclude, in error, that a patent claim cannot be proved obvious merely by showing that the combination of elements was 'obvious to try.' Id, at 289 (internal quotation marks omitted). When there is a design need or market pressure to solve a problem and there are a finite number of identified, predictable solutions, a person of ordinary skill has good reason to pursue the known options within his or her technical grasp. If this leads to the anticipated success, it is likely the product not of innovation but of ordinary skill and common sense. In that instance the fact that a combination was obvious to try might show that it was obvious under §103.

The Court of Appeals, finally, drew the wrong conclusion from the risk of courts and patent examiners falling prey to hindsight bias. A factfinder should be aware, of course, of the distortion caused by hindsight bias and must be cautious of arguments reliant upon ex post reasoning. See *Graham*, 383 US, at 36 (warning against a 'temptation to read into the prior art the teachings of the invention in issue' and instructing courts to 'guard against slipping into the use of hindsight" (quoting *Monroe Auto Equipment Co v Heckethorn Mfg & Supply Co*, 332 F 2d 406, 412 (CA6 1964))). Rigid preventative rules that deny factfinders recourse to common sense, however, are neither necessary under our case law nor consistent with it.

We note the Court of Appeals has since elaborated a broader conception of the TSM test than was applied in the instant matter. See, eg, *DyStar Textilfarben GmbH & Co Deutschland KG v CH Patrick Co*, 464 F 3d 1356, 1367 (2006) ('Our suggestion test is in actuality quite flexible and not only permits, but requires, consideration of common knowledge and common sense'); *Alza Corp v Mylan Labs, Inc*, 464 F 3d 1286, 1291 (2006) ('There is flexibility in our obviousness jurisprudence because a motivation may be found implicitly in the prior art. We do not have a rigid test that requires an actual teaching to combine …'). Those decisions, of course, are not now before us and do not correct the errors of law made by the Court of Appeals in this case … What we hold is that the fundamental misunderstandings identified above led the Court of Appeals in this case to apply a test inconsistent with our patent law decisions.

The High Court of Australia in both *Alphapharm* and *Lockwood No 2* rejected the 'problem and solution' and 'obvious to try' approaches from UK and European law in determining whether or not the invention is obvious. In light of the decision of the US Supreme Court in *KSR*, one question for the Australian courts is whether they, too, should revisit the 'obvious to try' test. The Full Court of the Federal Court was provided with the opportunity to consider this and other tests for obviousness in the case extracted below.

CASE EXTRACT: CURRENT LAW

Generic Health Pty Ltd v Bayer Pharma Aktiengesellschaft

[2014] FCAFC 73; (2014) 106 IPR 381
Federal Court of Australia, Full Court

[The respondents in this case were two Bayer companies (the 'Bayer parties'). The patent in issue related to a combination of formulas for use as an oral contraceptive. One of the difficulties faced by formulators was to find an appropriate mechanism to deliver the combination by oral means to the ovaries (referred to as 'bioavailability'). The Bayer parties sued for infringement. Generic Health and others (the 'GH parties') cross-claimed for revocation of the patent on the grounds of lack of inventive step, lack of novelty and lack of fair basis. The novelty ground was abandoned by the GH parties during the course of proceedings. At first instance, Jagot J held that the patent was valid and infringed. The appeal decision considers both inventive step and fair basis. The focus of inquiry for the inventive step ground was what would be obvious to a 'hypothetical formulator'.]

Besanko, Middleton and Nicholas JJ: 24. The primary judge said that the two issues of principle to which the dispute gave rise were both 'founded' on the reasoning of the High Court in *Aktiebolaget Hässle v Alphapharm Pty Ltd* (2002) 212 CLR 411 ('*Alphapharm*'). The first issue of principle was whether the expectation of the hypothetical formulator was a necessary part of the resolution of the issue of obviousness. The Bayer parties submitted that it was, whereas the GH parties submitted that it was not. The GH parties submitted that the only question was whether the hypothetical addressee of the Patent, faced with the same problem, would have taken, as a matter of routine, whatever steps might have led from the prior art to the invention. The primary judge considered the reasoning of the High Court in *Alphapharm* and of this Court in *Pfizer Overseas Pharmaceuticals v Eli Lilly and Co* (2005) 225 ALR 416 ('*Pfizer*') and concluded that, in determining the question of obviousness, it was necessary to consider the expectation of the hypothetical skilled addressee of the Patent.

25. The second issue of principle was whether the expectation of the hypothetical formulator (assuming it to be relevant) must be an expectation of the production of the invention or an expectation relating to 'some other useful result' (*Alphapharm Pty Ltd v H Lundbeck A/S* (2008) 76 IPR 618, at [180]), and if so, what is meant by the words 'some other useful result'. The primary judge rejected the suggestion that 'some other useful result' could be the obtaining of information to ascertain whether there was any bioavailability problem with an immediate release formulation of DRSP. The primary judge rejected the GH parties' contention, and held that 'some other useful result' in the context of obviousness must be understood as the claimed invention or at least something very like the claimed invention.

. . .

LACK OF INVENTIVE STEP/OBVIOUSNESS

64. The GH parties submit that the primary judge erred in her application of the relevant principles, that she erred in various ways in relation to the eight matters which she identified, that she misunderstood Krause I and Krause III [prior art patents], and that she made a number of associated factual errors.

65. The thrust of the first challenge is not just in the application of the relevant principles, but also in the identification of the principles to be applied in a case such as the present. The GH parties submitted that the primary judge erred in concluding that it is an element of the test of obviousness that the party alleging the lack of an inventive step show that the experiment or test which would have led to the invention was undertaken with an expectation of success. The primary judge held by reference to *Alphapharm* that the expectation of the hypothetical formulator is a necessary part of the resolution of the issue of obviousness and the expectation is that the experiment might well produce the invention. Nowhere did she suggest that the expectation need be any higher than that.

66. The GH parties did not argue that there were not passages in *Alphapharm* that supported the primary judge's approach. Their argument was that *Alphapharm* did not lay down a test of universal application. It did not lay down a test to be applied in all cases and, in particular, in a case such as this where the choices are both limited and simple. There were two choices, being a preformulation study and an enteric coating on the one hand, *or* a preformulation study and a limited or pilot bioavailability test or study on the other. Both these choices involve (it was submitted) relatively simple exercises and, in fact, they could be carried out at the same time. The GH parties submit that in such a case the reformulated Cripps question [referred to above in the *Alphapharm* extract, p 468] is not the appropriate test. When addressing the expert evidence, the GH parties identified the test the primary judge ought to have applied in a variety of ways, including whether a person skilled in the art would be led to try an immediate release formulation in a pilot bioavailability study, whether it was obvious to do a routine test on an immediate release formulation to see whether it did absorb before degradation, whether the idea of an immediate release formulation and of a pilot bioavailability study was beyond the skill of the calling or represented some barrier crossed and, finally, whether an immediate release formulation lies in the way.

. . .

68. In support of their contention that in a case such as the present the reformulated Cripps question was not the appropriate test, the GH parties relied on the following matters. First, they submitted that the plurality in *Alphapharm* approved Diplock LJ's statement in *Johns-Manville Corporation's Patent* [1967] RPC 479, at 493–494, that it is doubtful whether there is a verbal formula appropriate to determine obviousness in all classes of claim (*Alphapharm* at 428, [37]). Secondly, they pointed out that the facts in *Alphapharm*, unlike the facts in this case, involved a course of action which was complex and detailed, as well as laborious, with a good deal of trial and error, with dead ends and the retracing of steps (*Alphapharm* at 436, [58]). Thirdly, they pointed out that, although the fact that the 'worthwhile to try' or 'obvious to try' tests were rejected by the plurality in *Alphapharm* by reference to United States authorities such as *In re O'Farrell* (1988) 853 F 2d 849, that rejection must be considered in light of more recent United States authority. They referred to *KSR International Co v Teleflex Inc* (2007) 75 IPR 434 [extracted above] ...

69. Fourthly, they submitted that the plurality in *Alphapharm* did not qualify the test of steps of a routine character to be tried as a matter of course and said no more than that the test had an affinity to the reformulated Cripps question. Fifthly, they pointed out that, in *Olin Mathieson Chemical Corporation v Biorex Laboratories Ltd* [1970] RPC 157 itself, Graham J did not suggest that the

reformulated Cripps question was the sole test or sole determination of the question of obviousness. His Lordship said (at 188):

> I do not think it matters very much whether the question is put in the form I have suggested or in the Cripps form as long as one has clearly in mind what is meant by the word 'obvious', which the Cripps question does not define. Sir Lionel rightly pointed out, however, that in fact the Cripps question does not seem to have been applied in the judgments in the *Sharpe & Dohme* case, and that its application and form must depend on the form of the claim. Here, for example, claim 1 makes no reference to therapeutic qualities and covers any body within the formula whatever its use may be. It would not, therefore, be right to include a limitation to therapeutic qualities in the question, at any rate then applied to claim 1. Though the Cripps question has been approved from time to time, some of the difficulties which occur in framing it are pointed out in Mr Blanco White's book, *Patents for Inventions* at page 127.
>
> In this case, in my judgment, provided one is quite clear as to the sense of the word 'obvious', one arrives at the same result whether the appropriate question is put in the Cripps form or in the form which I have formulated. I prefer the latter because it incorporates in effect a definition of 'obvious' and makes it clear that there is no limitation in the claim to therapeutic qualities. The word 'obvious', as Sir Lionel agreed, and as its derivation implies, means something which lies in the way, and in the context of the Act is used in its normal sense of something which is plain or open to the eye or mind, something which is perfectly evident to the person thinking on the subject.

70. Finally, the GH parties submitted that, in the later case of *Lockwood Security Products Pty Ltd v Doric Products Pty Ltd [No 2]* (2007) 235 CLR 173, at 195–196, [52], the High Court did not suggest that the obviousness question was always to be determined by reference to the reformulated Cripps question. Their Honours referred to 'some difficulty overcome, some barrier crossed' (*RD Werner & Co Inc v Bailey Aluminium Products Pty Ltd* (1989) 25 FCR 565, at 574 per Lockhart J) or 'beyond the skill of the calling' (*Graham v John Deere Co of Kansas City* (1966) 383 US 1, at 15; *Leonardis v Sartas No 1 Pty Ltd* (1996) 67 FCR 126, at 146).

71. We do not think that the plurality in *Alphapharm* were saying that the reformulated Cripps question was the test to be applied in every case. Rather, it is a formulation of the test which will be of assistance in cases, particularly those of a similar nature to *Alphapharm*. The plurality did not reject as an alternative expression of the test the question whether the experiments were of a routine character to be tried as a matter of course (*The Wellcome Foundation Ltd v VR Laboratories (Aust) Pty Ltd* (1981) 148 CLR 262, at 280-281, 286, per Aickin J). We do not think there is a divide here in terms of whether an expectation of success is relevant between a test which refers to routine steps to be tried as a matter of course and the reformulated Cripps question. It is difficult to think of a case where an expectation that an experiment might well succeed is not implicit in the characterisation of steps as routine and to be tried as a matter of course. On the other hand, we think a test formulated in terms of worthwhile to try was firmly rejected by the High Court in *Alphapharm* (see also *Pfizer*, at 476, [287], per French and Lindgren JJ). The fact (if it be the fact) that the position in the United States may have shifted does not affect the binding nature of what the plurality said in *Alphapharm*.

72. In any event, the difficulty the GH parties face with their submission is in showing that, even if accepted, it makes any difference. The primary judge said that strictly it was not necessary to address

CURRENT LAW

the issues of principle because of her factual findings. One of the findings she made was that a hypothetical skilled addressee would not have carried out the type of bioavailability study described by Dr Rowe and Dr Walters as a matter of routine and thereby be led, as a matter of course, to the invention. Furthermore, even when her Honour did consider the matter having regard to an expectation of success, she found that there would be an expectation in the hypothetical formulator of failure, in that failure was very likely.

The High Court refused special leave to appeal in *Generic Health Pty Ltd v Bayer Pharma Aktiengesellschaft* [2014] HCATrans 261. Crennan J concluded that:

> These applications for special leave concern questions mainly in respect of the statutory test for obviousness under the *Patents Act 1990* (Cth). Both the primary judge and the Full Court of the Federal Court of Australia rejected the applicants' argument that the respondents' patent for an oral contraceptive should be revoked for lack of inventive step and lack of fair basis. The concurrent findings of material facts, which were made by the primary judge and the Full Court, make this an inappropriate vehicle to reconsider settled principles in relation to obviousness.

INNOVATIVE STEP

Section 7(4)–(6) of the *Patents Act* imposes a lower threshold for the innovation step. Section 7(4) requires that the innovation must differ from the prior art base, in the light of the common general knowledge, in ways that make some sort of substantial contribution to the working of the invention.

CASE EXTRACT: CURRENT LAW

CURRENT LAW

Dura-Post (Aust) Pty Ltd v Delnorth Pty Ltd

[2009] FCAFC 81; (2009) 177 FCR 239
Federal Court of Australia, Full Court

[The invention in this case related to roadside posts for supporting signage or delineating paths, roadways or boundaries. Issues of manner of manufacture, novelty and innovative step were raised. The Court took the opportunity to discuss the introduction of the innovation patent system before considering the grounds for invalidity. In considering innovative step, the Court focused attention on whether the test was anything more than a modified novelty test as expounded by Dixon J in *Griffin v Isaacs* (1938) 1B IPR 619; 12 ALJ 169.]

Kenny, Stone and Perram JJ: 78. The 1995 ACIP report … recommended that the test for innovation patents should be a modified form of the novelty test in *Griffin v Isaacs* (1938) 1B IPR 619; 12 ALJ 169. This was apparently accepted in the Government Response, although with some changes in language.

It suffices to refer to the primary judge's helpful discussion of *Griffin v Isaacs*: see *Delnorth* [2008] FCA 1225 at [57]–[59] and to draw attention to Dixon J's observation (at 624) that:

> Where variations from a device previously published consist in matters which make no substantial contribution to the working of the thing … and the merit if any of the two things, considered as inventions, is the same, it is, I think, impossible to treat the differences as giving novelty.

Plainly enough, the legislature drew on the language of Dixon J in framing the test of 'no substantial contribution to the working of the invention' in s 7(4). The Revised Explanatory Memorandum does not lead to a different conclusion. In referring to the working of the 'thing', Dixon J had in mind the waistband on a pair of trousers that was the subject of the applicant's patent application. The drafter of s 7(4) has picked up Dixon J's language and substituted for the word 'thing', the word 'invention'—the latter covering not only a claimed device but also a claimed process.

79. The adoption of a modified novelty test deriving from *Griffin v Isaacs* (1938) 1B IPR 619; 12 ALJ 169 emphasises that s 7(4) requires a narrow comparison between the invention as claimed and the relevant prior disclosure, having regard to the fact that the threshold for an innovation patent is intended to be lower than for a standard patent … In substance, s 7(4) deems an invention as claimed to involve an innovative step unless the invention does not differ from the relevant prior disclosure in a way that makes a substantial contribution to the working of the invention as claimed—in the sense of the device or process the subject of each claim. This is a factual inquiry. The assessment is, of course, from the perspective of a person skilled in the art, having regard to the relevant common general knowledge.

The Advisory Council on Intellectual Property (ACIP) in its *Final Report on the Review of the Innovation Patent System* (2014) noted that the innovative step requirement was seen as being too easy to meet and not justifying an eight-year monopoly. ACIP recommended raising the level of the innovative step. According to ACIP's preferred formulation, in order to be innovative an invention would need to be non-obvious by reference to common general knowledge (within or outside Australia). This would be a lower threshold than is applied to standard patents, where the invention must be non-obvious by reference to common general knowledge *and* any piece of prior art.

USEFULNESS

Old UK case law indicates that all that was required of the usefulness requirement was that 'the invention does what it was intended by the patentee to do, and the end in itself is useful'.[5] The position in the UK has since changed, with closer alignment with the European Patent Convention and the enactment of the *Patents Act 1977* (UK). The UK legislation now has a requirement that the invention is capable of industrial application: s 1(1)(c) of the *Patents Act 1977*. In Australia, in *Rescare Ltd v Anaesthetic Supplies Pty Ltd* (1993) 25 IPR 119, Gummow J affirmed at 142–143 that the test for usefulness continued to be aligned with the test in the old UK case law. The question to ask is whether the invention attains the result promised.

---

5   *Fawcett v Homan* (1896) 13 RPC 398 at 405.

Although the first-instance decision in *Rescare* was appealed to the Full Court of the Federal Court, the appeal was on different grounds and the first-instance decision therefore continues to be a helpful pronouncement on the law of usefulness, bearing in mind the new meaning provided in s 7A of the *Patents Act*, introduced pursuant to the *Raising the Bar Act* amendments (discussed further later in this chapter: see below, p 483).

CASE EXTRACT: PRECEDENT

Rescare Ltd v Anaesthetic Supplies Pty Ltd

(1993) 25 IPR 119
Federal Court of Australia

[This case involved a patent claiming a device for the treatment of snoring sickness, or sleep apnoea. Rescare instituted infringement proceedings and Anaesthetic Supplies counterclaimed for invalidity on a range of grounds, including lack of usefulness.]

Gummow J: I have referred already to the concept embodied in s 40 [of the 1952 Act] of insufficiency. The distinction between insufficiency and ambiguity on the one hand, and inutility on the other, is said to be that insufficiency occurs when the apparatus cannot be made, and inutility occurs when the apparatus can be made but, when made, does not work. However, as has been pointed out, the distinction is often less clear in practice ... The result in this case is that there has been some overlapping in the submissions on these topics.

It is also important to bear in mind two related propositions. The first is that a claim may have utility even though the promised advantage is not achieved in all cases and the second is that there may be infringement of an apparatus claim if the machine can be used in a manner which infringes even though it can also be used in a manner which does not infringe: *Martin Engineering Co v Nicaro Holdings Pty Ltd* (1991) AIPC 90-799 at 37,582–583, per Burchett J.

Section 100(1) provides that a standard patent may be revoked either wholly or insofar as it relates to any claim of the complete specification on the ground that:—

(h) that the invention, so far as claimed in any claim of the complete specification ... is not useful;

The ground of inutility is not concerned with the question of whether, in the present case, the apparatus to be used by following the directions in the Patent would not be commercially viable; rather, the question is whether the invention as claimed does not attain the result promised for it by the patentee: *Decor Corporation Pty Ltd v Dart Industries Inc* [(1989) AIPC 90-549] at 38,829 per Lockhart J. A distinction is to be drawn between cases where the invention claimed is not useful unless an additional integer or integers be added (such claims being invalid) and those cases where qualifications and expedients necessary to make work the article which has been claimed can be, and on a proper construction of the claim are, left to the skilled reader to supply for himself; *Welch Perrin and Co Pty Ltd v Worrel* [(1961) 106 CLR 588] at 601 ...

Thus, in the present case, whilst claim 1 and some of the dependent claims do not claim an apparatus including a blower (an absence relied upon by the respondent) this does not mean that there is a lack of utility. The need for a particular air source would be apparent to the skilled addressee. If it be necessary, resort to the body of the specification shows that the air supply in a preferred form consists of a high volume air pump and one particular proprietary product is described as having been found to be ideal …

The respondent also complains that claim 1 does not specify the appropriate weight, size or degree of comfort in the apparatus nor the appropriate means by which the nose piece is to be sealingly attached to the face of the patient in an airtight manner. However, it must [be] borne in mind that it is not the task of the claims to teach the application of the invention; the task of the claims is to define the invention and mark out the area of the monopoly. Claims should not be construed in a way which the skilled addressee would appreciate would lead to unworkability. The Court should be reluctant to place a construction upon a claim so as to include embodiments which to the qualified reader would appear useless. A different result may obtain where the terms of a claim positively point to some useless construction, as in *Cincinnati Grinders (Inc) v BSA Tools Ltd* (1931) 48 RPC 33 at 73. Claim 1 and the dependent apparatus claims are not within this category.

The respondent also submits that claim 1 is bad for inutility because in 'normal patients' the necessary seal will not be effected and air would leak out of the mouth. I referred to this point earlier in dealing with infringement. The conclusion there reached [was] that the apparatus is for use upon patients suffering from conditions which are characterised by occlusion of the upper air passage and which respond to the administration of CPAP [continuous positive airway pressure]. This indicates what is promised in the body of the complete specification. One looks at the claim to see whether there is a failure to fulfil that promise. It is not necessary to show utility that the promise be fulfilled in every case. On the evidence, the claimed invention plainly is of considerable practical utility in the treatment of substantial numbers of persons who are 'patients' within the meaning of claim 1.

There was said also to be ambiguity, associated with inutility, in the use of the term 'nasal passages' in claim 1. In the body of the complete specification the phrase is used 'occlusion of the upper air passage'. If the phrase be ambiguous, then it is to be read as identifying the upper air passages spoken of in the body of the specification.

However, the respondent submitted that claim 1 is bad for inutility and, that, in any event, the respondent's apparatus do not infringe because in claim 1 the 'nasal passages' do not extend any further down than the soft palate and therefore, because in ma[n]y cases of patients with OSA the obstruction occurs at least in major part lower down than the soft palate, the pressure which is sufficient to keep the nasal passages open may not be sufficient to clear the obstruction further down the throat.

[His Honour then proceeded to review the expert evidence before reaching his conclusion on this point.]

I accept that the need for a low dynamic resistance is made apparent to the skilled addressee by claim 1 by the specification of air pressure being maintained at the aperture at slightly greater than atmospheric pressure throughout the breathing cycle. There is no lack of sufficiency and no ambiguity or inutility in this respect in claim 1. The same conclusion applies to the remaining apparatus claims.

In the USA, the utility requirement focuses much more on the practical utility of the invention. In the 1990s, as a result of a flood of applications claiming gene sequences, the US Patent and

Trademark Office (USPTO) began to re-evaluate the utility requirement in that jurisdiction. The USPTO revised its guidelines on the utility requirement in 2001. The revised guidelines require the disclosure of specific, substantial and credible utility. The interpretation of the specific, substantial and credible utility requirement was examined in the US Court of Appeals in *In re Fisher*, 421 F 3d 1365 (Fed Cir, 2005), extracted below. This terminology has now been adopted in Australia in the new s 7A of the *Patents Act*.

CASE EXTRACT: COMPARATIVE LAW

In re Fisher

421 F 3d 1365 (Fed Cir, 2005)
United States Court of Appeals, Federal Circuit

[This case considered a patent claiming five partial gene sequences (known as expressed sequence tags or ESTs) isolated from maize leaves. The patent claimed various different uses of the ESTs, including as molecular markers for mapping the entire maize genome.]

Michel CJ (delivering the judgment of the majority) (at 1370–1371): The government agrees with Fisher that the utility threshold is not high, but disagrees with Fisher's allegation that the Board applied a heightened utility standard. The government contends that a patent applicant need disclose only a single specific and substantial utility pursuant to *Brenner* [*v Manson*, 383 US 519 (1966)], the very standard articulated in the PTO's 'Utility Examination Guidelines' ('Utility Guidelines') and followed here when examining the '643 application. It argues that Fisher failed to meet that standard because Fisher's alleged uses are so general as to be meaningless. What is more, the government asserts that the same generic uses could apply not only to the five claimed ESTs but also to any EST derived from any organism. It thus argues that the seven utilities alleged by Fisher are merely starting points for further research, not the end point of any research effort. It further disputes the importance of the commercial success of ESTs in the marketplace, pointing out that Fisher's evidence involved only databases, clone sets, and microarrays, not the five claimed ESTs. Therefore, the government contends that we should affirm the Board's decision.

Several academic institutions and biotechnology and pharmaceutical companies write as amici curiae in support of the government. Like the government, they assert that Fisher's claimed uses are nothing more than a 'laundry list' of research plans, each general and speculative, none providing a specific and substantial benefit in currently available form. The amici also advocate that the claimed ESTs are the objects of further research aimed at identifying what genes of unknown function are expressed during anthesis and what proteins of unknown function are encoded for by those genes. Until the corresponding genes and proteins have a known function, the amici argue, the claimed ESTs lack utility under §101 and are not patentable.

We agree with both the government and the amici that none of Fisher's seven asserted uses meets the utility requirement of §101. Section 101 provides: 'Whoever invents ... any new and *useful* ... composition of matter ... may obtain a patent therefor ...' (Emphasis added). In *Brenner*, the Supreme Court explained what is required to establish the usefulness of a new invention, noting at the outset that 'a simple, everyday word ['useful,' as found in §101] can be pregnant with ambiguity when applied to the facts of life.' 383 US at 529. Contrary to Fisher's argument that §101 only requires an invention that is not 'frivolous, injurious to the well-being, good policy, or good morals of society,' the Supreme Court appeared to reject Justice Story's de minimis view of utility … The Supreme Court observed that Justice Story's definition 'sheds little light on our subject,' on the one hand framing the relevant inquiry as 'whether the invention in question is 'frivolous and insignificant'' if narrowly read, while on the other hand 'allowing the patenting of any invention not positively harmful to society' if more broadly read. *Id* at 533. In its place, the Supreme Court announced a more rigorous test, stating:

> The basic *quid pro quo* contemplated by the Constitution and the Congress for granting a patent monopoly is the benefit derived by the public from an invention with *substantial utility*. Unless and until a process is refined and developed to this point—where *specific benefit exists in currently available form*—there is insufficient justification for permitting an applicant to engross what may prove to be a broad field.

Brenner, 383 US at 534–535 (emphases added).

Following *Brenner*, our predecessor court, the Court of Customs and Patent Appeals, and this court have required a claimed invention to have a specific and substantial utility to satisfy §101. See, eg, *Fujikawa v Wattanasin*, 93 F 3d 1559, 1563 (Fed Cir, 1996) ('Consequently, it is well established that a patent may not be granted to an invention unless substantial or practical utility for the invention has been discovered and disclosed.').

The Supreme Court has not defined what the terms 'specific' and 'substantial' mean per se. Nevertheless, together with the Court of Customs and Patent Appeals, we have offered guidance as to the uses which would meet the utility standard of §101. From this, we can discern the kind of disclosure an application must contain to establish a specific and substantial utility for the claimed invention.

Courts have used the labels 'practical utility' and 'real world' utility interchangeably in determining whether an invention offers a 'substantial' utility. Indeed, the Court of Customs and Patent Appeals stated that "[p]ractical utility" is a shorthand way of attributing "real-world" value to claimed subject matter. In other words, one skilled in the art can use a claimed discovery in a manner which provides some *immediate benefit to the public*.' *Nelson*, 626 F 2d at 856 (emphasis added). It thus is clear that an application must show that an invention is useful to the public as disclosed in its current form, not that it may prove useful at some future date after further research. Simply put, to satisfy the 'substantial' utility requirement, an asserted use must show that that claimed invention has a significant and presently available benefit to the public.

Turning to the 'specific' utility requirement, an application must disclose a use which is not so vague as to be meaningless. Indeed, one of our predecessor courts has observed 'that the nebulous expressions "biological activity" or "biological properties" appearing in the specification convey no more explicit indication of the usefulness of the compounds and how to use them than did the equally obscure expression "useful for technical and pharmaceutical purposes" unsuccessfully relied upon by the appellant in *In re Diedrich*.' *In re Kirk*, 376 F 2d 936, 941 (CCPA, 1967). Thus, in addition to providing a 'substantial' utility, an asserted use must also show that that claimed invention can be used to provide a well-defined and particular benefit to the public.

The Explanatory Memorandum to the Intellectual Property Laws Amendment (Raising the Bar) Bill 2011 makes it clear that the intention of inserting s 7A into the *Patents Act* was to incorporate US notions of 'specific, substantial and credible utility'. However, it is not intended to replace existing common law interpretations of the usefulness requirement.

EXPLANATORY MEMORANDUM, INTELLECTUAL PROPERTY LAWS AMENDMENT (RAISING THE BAR) BILL 2011

(at 43–45) [Sch 1, item 6 of the Bill] amends the definition of 'useful' to require that the specification discloses a 'specific, substantial and credible' use for the claimed invention.

Usefulness in paragraph 18(1)(c) of the *Patents Act* is a key criterion for patentability. Patents should not be granted for inventions that are not useful: that have no practical application or do not work. Broadly speaking the claimed invention must actually achieve what is promised by the patentee.[49] This does not mean that an invention must equate to a commercial product in order to be useful, rather it must achieve the use promised by the patentee in the specification.

Two reviews have recommended clarifying the meaning of 'usefulness' to accord more closely with the meaning of 'useful' in US patent law. The Intellectual Property Competition Review Committee (IPCRC) Report[50] recommended ensuring in examination practice that the use described in the specification is specific, substantial and credible to a person skilled in the art. The Australian Law Reform Commission (ALRC)[51] went further and recommended amending the *Patents Act* to provide that an invention will satisfy the requirement of 'usefulness' only if the patent application discloses a specific, substantial and credible use. These amendments are intended to implement the ALRC recommendation.

The specific, substantial and credible use test is not intended to displace the existing Australian case law on usefulness. An invention must have both a specific, substantial and credible use that is disclosed in the patent specification and meet the requirements of the existing case law (broadly that the invention must achieve the promised benefit).

There is also concern that in some fields the uses claimed are often speculative and that the current provision does not effectively prevent the claiming of such speculative inventions.[52]

The item bolsters the existing requirement that the claimed invention be useful with the requirement that the invention has a specific, substantial and credible use. The intent is that specific, substantial and credible be given the same meaning as is currently given by the US courts and the United States Patent and Trade Mark Office (USPTO).

Currently, the US courts interpret the terms as follows:

- 'specific' means a use specific to the subject matter claimed and can 'provide a well-defined and particular benefit to the public.'[53]
- 'substantial' means the claimed invention does not require further research to identify or reasonably confirm a 'real world use'. 'An application must show that an invention is useful to the public as disclosed in its current form, not that it prove useful at some future date after further research'.[54]
- an asserted use will be 'credible' 'unless there is evidence that the invention is inoperative (ie does not operate to produce the results claimed by the patent application) or there is reason to doubt the objective truth of the statements in the specification.'[55]

The relevant principles are set out in more detail by the USPTO.[56]

The amendment will strengthen the test for usefulness and prevent the speculative claiming of inventions that would require further experimental effort before they could be put into practice.

The specific, substantial and credible use must be disclosed in the specification. This could be an explicit disclosure. Alternatively, it need not be explicit if the skilled person could appreciate the use, with their background knowledge in the art and without undue burden. If however, further invention would be required to ascertain the use, then the specification would not meet the requirement. This ensures that the public is given sufficient information in the specification to understand how the invention is useful and how to put that use into practice.

49   *Rescare Ltd v Anaesthetic Supplies Pty Ltd* (1992) 111 ALR 205 at 231; *Rehm Pty Limited v Webster's Security Systems (International) Pty Ltd* (1981) 81 ALR 79 at 96; *Welcome Real-Time SA v Catuity Inc* (2001) 113 FCR 110 at 144; *Fawcett v Homan* (1896) 13 RPC 398 at 405; and *Lane Fox v Kensington & Knightsbridge Electric Lighting Co Ltd* (1892) 9 RPC 411 at 417.
50   IPCRC, *Review of Intellectual Property Legislation under the Competition Principles Agreement*, September 2000 (the 'Ergas Report').
51   ALRC, *Review of Gene Patenting and Human Health, Genes and Ingenuity: Gene Patenting and Human Health*, 2004.
52   ALRC, *Review of Gene Patenting and Human Health, Genes and Ingenuity: Gene Patenting and Human Health*, 2004 at 6.100.
53   *In re Fisher*, 421 F 3d 1365, 1371 … (Fed Cir 2005).
54   *In re Fisher*, 421 F 3d at 1371 …
55   *In re Marzocchi*, 439 F2d 220, 223, 169 USPQ 367, 369 (CCPA 1971).
56   See sections 2107 – 2107.03 of the Manual of Patent Examining Procedure (http://www.uspto.gov/web/offices/

SECRET USE

Public use of an invention before the priority date of a patent will invalidate the patent for lack of novelty. Although 'closet use' will not ground an attack on the basis of lack of novelty, in some circumstances secret use of the invention before the priority date will also threaten the validity of the patent through s 18(1)(d). Challenges can be made to patent validity on the secret use ground in opposition proceedings under s 59(b) and revocation proceedings through s 138(3)(b).

Invalidity for secret use is justified on the basis that the inventor must make a commercial decision between protection through the patent system or through trade secrecy, and should not have the benefit of both. In addition, allowing commercial use prior to the patent's priority date would allow a person to extend the patent monopoly for longer than the fixed monopoly term of 20 years.

Section 9 sets out the types of secret use that do not threaten validity through the secret use provision in s 18(1)(d). These include: use by the patentee or with his or her authority within a 12 month grace period, for reasonable trial or experiment, in the course of confidential disclosure or for any purpose other than the purpose of trade or commerce; or use by or on behalf of the Commonwealth, a state or a territory where the patentee has disclosed the invention to the Commonwealth, state or territory.

CASE EXTRACT: PRECEDENT

Azuko Pty Ltd v Old Digger Pty Ltd

[2001] FCA 1079; (2001) 52 IPR 75
Federal Court of Australia, Full Court

[This case considered a patent for a percussive hammer drill with a collar for collecting rock samples in the mining industry. Infringement and revocation proceedings had been instituted. Both the novelty and secret use grounds were raised. Trials of the hammer drill had been carried out in late 1989 and early 1990, some of which were undertaken by a potential customer, Gaden. A provisional application was filed on 19 April 1990, and by that time 15–20 hammers had been manufactured. Although none had been sold, Gaden had placed an order for five or six. These facts raised questions of reasonable trial and experimentation, and purposes other than trade and commerce. Beaumont and Gyles JJ gave majority judgments, but only Gyles J addressed the secret use issue. His Honour concluded that none of the protections afforded by s 9 of the *Patents Act* applied in the circumstances.]

Gyles J:

4   WHETHER INVENTION SECRETLY USED

...

120. Counsel for the respondent argued that there was no 'use' within s 18(1)(d) because there was no 'taint of commerciality'. Mr Giehl's making and keeping the hammers for later use or sale 'stopped well short of a relevant commercial dealing and there (was) no evidence that his conduct resulted in the reaping of a commercial benefit'.

121. It may be that 'commerciality' is relevant to the question whether a particular activity involves using an invention: see *Re Wheatley's Application* (1984) 2 IPR 450 at 451, discussed infra. However, in the Act this aspect may shade into s 9(c) which excludes what would otherwise be prior secret use where there is use of the invention by the patentee 'for any purpose other than the purpose of trade or commerce' ... Counsel for the respondent did not rely on s 9(c), and understandably so. Plainly Mr Giehl had a purpose of trade or commerce. This is probably sufficient in itself to answer the commerciality point, but I shall return to this aspect.

[His Honour then turned to consideration of the relevant authorities.]

144. Before leaving this issue, the facts of the present case should be recalled. This was not, as the respondent submitted, 'bare manufacture'. Mr Giehl, before the priority date, manufactured fifteen or twenty hammers. It was his intention to sell them, doubtless at a profit. Some of those hammers were destined to fill Mr Gaden's order for five or six. There is no evidence that any of the hammers had been appropriated to Mr Gaden so that property passed to him: *Sale of Goods Act 1895* (SA) s 18 rule 5(1). However, there may well have been a binding contract constituted by Mr Gaden's order and Mr Giehl accepting that order by his conduct in manufacturing hammers: *Cheshire and Fifoot Law of Contract* (7th Australian ed) 95, *Chitty on Contracts* (28th ed) 101. Had the market for hammers collapsed and Mr Gaden refused to take delivery, Mr Giehl may well have had an action in damages. Whether this be so or not, the present case is a far cry from *Morgan v Seaward* (1837) 2 M&W 544, 150 ER 874. When one asks why Mr Giehl made these fifteen or twenty hammers, the answer must be that he proposed to sell them, including some five or six to Mr Gaden to fill an order already received. This has a distinctly commercial look about it. No philanthropy or hobby was involved. Mr Giehl's activity was, in the words of counsel in *Beecham*, something done for gain or for industrial or commercial purposes. When one asks how he made the hammers, the answer must be that he employed and applied the idea embodied in the Giehl patent and the detailed specification contained therein.

145. Looked at another way, on the priority date Mr Giehl had fifteen or twenty hammers ready for sale and delivery (subject to Mr Gaden's right in relation to five or six of them). This was a new and inventive product. Mr Giehl could immediately go into the market with this new, and presumably

PRECEDENT

superior, product and thus obtain an immediate advantage over his competitors, who could not lawfully copy his product. How had he obtained this advantage? Because he had manufactured the hammers before the priority date employing the information of the Giehl patent.

146. In my opinion this was a use of the invention of the Giehl patent. The element of secrecy not being in dispute, the appellants established that the invention was secretly used before the priority date of the patent within the meaning of s 18(1)(d).

5 WHETHER REASONABLE TRIAL AND EXPERIMENT—S 9(A)

147. The evidence permitted of only one conclusion. Production of fifteen or twenty hammers in a condition ready for commercial sale, an order having been received for five or six, cannot be considered a matter of trial and experiment, let alone *only* trial and experiment. Having obtained a clear admission from Mr Giehl as to the manufacture and its purpose it was not for the cross-examiner to elicit evidence which might have taken Mr Giehl outside the section. The respondent's counsel could have raised such matters in re-examination. In any event, the manufacture of fifteen or twenty hammers in a condition ready for sale (or of 'commercial quality' as his Honour put it) indicates that trial and experiment had concluded in Darwin and commercial production commenced in Adelaide. As Mr Giehl accepted, the hammers were 'ready to work'.

148. There is a total lack of evidence from Mr Giehl as to what trials or experiments were carried out on the Adelaide hammers. The reasonable inference is that there were none. Even if he were making a limited number to see if production was commercially viable, I do not think that would be the kind of trial and experiment of which s 9(a) speaks. The provision is limited to trial or experiment to see how the product of an invention performs and whether any improvements are needed, as distinct from commercial or marketing assessments. But in any event Mr Giehl did not suggest his manufacture was for the limited purpose found by his Honour. The inference to be drawn is simply that Mr Giehl manufactured hammers because he proposed to sell them.

6 WHETHER IN THE COURSE OF CONFIDENTIAL DISCLOSURE—S 9(B)

149. While it was accepted Mr Giehl's employees would be under obligations of confidence, s 9(b) speaks of use of the invention 'solely in the course of a confidential disclosure'. This suggests some larger transaction, properly characterised as a confidential disclosure of the invention, in the course of which the invention is 'used'. An example would be a demonstration to a patent attorney or potential purchaser or investor. Here there was no such disclosure. The hammers were simply manufactured for the purpose of sale. Such disclosure of the invention as there may have been by Mr Giehl to his employees—and he gave no evidence as to this—was not a disclosure in the course of which the invention was used. It was the other way around. He disclosed the invention to them so they could manufacture a product of the invention and thus 'use' the invention. In any event, the use was not solely in the course of confidential disclosure—it was also for the purpose of sale.

—12—

DISCLOSURE AND CLAIMING
REQUIREMENTS

INTRODUCTION

Patents are not private contracts between individuals. They are social contracts, providing state-sanctioned monopolies. In return for the patent monopoly, the patentee has to disclose the invention fully, including the best method known to the inventor of performing it, and has to define the extent of the patent monopoly that is being sought through the patent claims. These disclosure and claiming requirements serve a number of purposes:

- they have a similar effect to a certificate of title over land, defining the boundaries of the property right so that others know when they are encroaching on it and when they are working outside it;
- they provide the necessary information to enable others to practise the invention once the patent expires, so that the monopoly does not extend beyond the period of the patent grant; and
- they provide the necessary information to enable others to test the invention to see if it does what it claims to do and if what is being claimed is justified given what has actually been invented.

This information is provided in the patent specification, which has two components: the body and the claims. The body of the specification describes the invention. The claims set out the boundaries of what is being claimed.

In this chapter, the law relating to the Australian disclosure and claiming requirements for complete specifications for standard patents is discussed (Chapter 9 explains the differences between complete and provisional applications, and standard and innovation patents). Section 40 of the *Patents Act 1990* (Cth) specifies these requirements. Complete specifications are required to provide detailed accounts of the prior art, the contribution made by the invention and the method of performing it. In general, a clear statement of the nature of the invention, known as the consistory clause, is included in the specification.

The specification requirements for provisional applications are less onerous than for complete applications. Prior to entry into force of the *Intellectual Property Laws Amendment (Raising the Bar) Act 2012* (Cth) (the '*Raising the Bar Act*'), provisional specifications needed only to describe the invention in general terms. Section 40(1) of the *Patents Act 1990* (Cth) now requires that a provisional specification must disclose the invention in a manner which is clear enough and complete enough for the invention to be performed by a person skilled in the relevant art.

The first part of this chapter outlines the legislative provisions for disclosure and claiming. Entry into force of the *Raising the Bar Act* in 2013 has resulted in significant amendment to the s 40 requirements. Because patents with priority dates before the entry into force of the *Raising the Bar Act* amendments are open to challenge for the entirety of their patent life, it is necessary to consider the s 40 provisions both pre- and post-*Raising the Bar Act*.

The next part of this chapter considers the rules for construing patent documents. It is necessary to construe the patent document to determine whether the claims are clear and succinct, as required under s 40(3) of the *Patents Act*. Beyond this, construction is also the first task for the courts and the Patent Office in any of the matters specified in s 40 of the *Patents Act*. It is also a necessary part of the process of determining infringement (discussed in Chapter 13) and satisfaction of the novelty and inventive step patent criteria under s 18(1) of the *Patents Act* (discussed in Chapter 11).

Following this analysis of the rules of construction, the requirements for disclosure and claiming are considered in more detail and key cases are extracted. Finally, the new grounds for disclosure and claiming post-*Raising the Bar Act* are considered using the Explanatory Memorandum to the Intellectual Property Laws Amendment (Raising the Bar) Bill 2011 and European case law to assist in their interpretation.

In reading this chapter, it is important to bear in mind that applicants for patents are faced with a trade off in deciding how much information to provide and what to claim. If they *disclose too little*, or *claim too much*, they risk invalidity on one or more of the s 40 grounds. But if they *claim too little* it will be easy for others to 'invent around' their claims without risk of infringement. In some areas of modern technology, particularly biotechnology, commentators have expressed concern that patent offices and courts are allowing patent applicants to claim too broadly.

LEGISLATIVE REQUIREMENTS FOR DISCLOSURE AND CLAIMING

Article 29.1 of the *Agreement on Trade-Related Aspects of Intellectual Property Rights* (the 'TRIPS Agreement') (1994), sets out the minimum disclosure requirements that must be included in domestic patent legislation:

> Members shall require that an applicant for a patent shall disclose the invention in a manner sufficiently clear and complete for the invention to be carried out by a person skilled in the art and may require the applicant to indicate the best mode for carrying out the invention known to the inventor at the filing date or, where priority is claimed, at the priority date of the application.

As noted above, in Australia the disclosure and claiming requirements are provided in s 40 of the *Patents Act*. The following table sets out the differing requirements, pre- and post- entry into force of the *Raising the Bar Act*.

SECTION 40, PRE-*RAISING THE BAR ACT* AMENDMENTS	SECTION 40, POST-*RAISING THE BAR ACT* AMENDMENTS
(1) A provisional specification must describe the invention.	(1) A provisional specification must disclose the invention in a manner which is clear enough and complete enough for the invention to be performed by a person skilled in the relevant art.
(2) A complete specification must: (a) describe the invention fully, including the best method known to the applicant of performing the invention; and (b) where it relates to an application for a standard patent—end with a claim or claims defining the invention; and (c) where it relates to an application for an innovation patent—end with at least one and no more than 5 claims defining the invention.	(2) A complete specification must: (a) disclose the invention in a manner which is clear enough and complete enough for the invention to be performed by a person skilled in the relevant art; and (aa) disclose the best method known to the applicant of performing the invention; and (b) where it relates to an application for a standard patent—end with a claim or claims defining the invention; and (c) where it relates to an application for an innovation patent—end with at least one and no more than 5 claims defining the invention.
(3) The claim or claims must be clear and succinct and fairly based on the matter described in the specification.	(3) The claim or claims must be clear and succinct and supported by matter disclosed in the specification. (3A) The claim or claims must not rely on references to descriptions or drawings unless absolutely necessary to define the invention.
(4) The claim or claims must relate to one invention only.	(4) The claim or claims must relate to one invention only.

The amended s 40(1) applies to provisional applications made on or after 15 April 2013. The amended s 40(2) and (3) and the new s 40(3A) apply, for the most part, to complete applications for standard and innovation patents made on or after 15 April 2013, and to applications for standard patents made before that date but where examination had not been requested by that date.

In summary, prior to the *Raising the Bar Act* amendments, s 40 provided one ground for invalidity based on insufficiency of disclosure: failure to fully describe the invention and the best method of performing it (former s 40(2)(a)). It also provided two grounds based on deficiencies in claiming: lack of clarity and succinctness; and lack of fair basing (both in the former s 40(3)).

The *Raising the Bar Act* amendments have changed the disclosure ground by adding a further nuance to the disclosure requirement (that the invention must now be disclosed 'in a manner which is clear enough and complete enough for the invention to be performed by a person skilled in the relevant art': new s 40(2)(a)). The best method of performance requirement remains unchanged, but is now contained in s 40(2)(aa). With regard to claiming, the *Raising the Bar Act* amendments have replaced the fair basing ground with a requirement that the claim or claims are 'supported' by the matter disclosed in the specification. The clarity and succinctness requirement remains unchanged (both grounds are contained in the new s 40(3)).

The purpose of the new provision in s 40(3A) is to deter 'omnibus' claims. This is a type of claim that references back the whole or part of the specification. As noted in item 43 of the Explanatory Memorandum to the Intellectual Property Laws Amendment (Raising the Bar) Bill 2011, this type of claiming can lead to 'a lack of clarity as to the exact scope of the monopoly. As far as possible, it is desirable that a claim should be free-standing, so that any person reading the claim will be able to ascertain the exact scope of the monopoly from the face of the claim.' The new subsection only allows omnibus claims when it is 'absolutely necessary'.

As a matter of procedure, patent examiners must be satisfied that the s 40 requirements are met at examination (s 45(1)(a)). Section 40 grounds can also be raised in opposition proceedings (s 59(c)) and revocation proceedings (s 138(3)(f)). The High Court decision in *Lockwood Security Products Pty Ltd v Doric Products Pty Ltd* [2004] HCA 58; (2004) 217 CLR 274 ('*Lockwood No 1*'), extracted below, makes it clear that each of the pre-*Raising the Bar Act* requirements in s 40 is a separate and distinct ground of invalidity and, moreover, that there is no overlap between the s 40 grounds and the s 18 grounds. It is unlikely that the courts would come to a different conclusion on this point post-*Raising the Bar Act*.

PRECEDENT

CASE EXTRACT: PRECEDENT

Lockwood Security Products Pty Ltd v Doric Products Pty Ltd ('*Lockwood No 1*')

[2004] HCA 58; (2004) 217 CLR 274
High Court of Australia

[The validity of the patent at issue in this case has been discussed already in Chapter 11. The case extracted in that chapter was the second High Court decision relating to this patent (*Lockwood Security Products Pty Ltd v Doric Products Pty Ltd (No 2)* [2007] HCA 21; (2007) 235 CLR 173) ('*Lockwood No 2*'). In this, the first High Court decision, the focus was solely on the ground of fair basing. A summary of the key facts relating to this litigation is provided with an extract from the case later in this chapter.]

Gleeson CJ, McHugh, Gummow, Hayne and Heydon JJ: 43. The language of the legislation suggests that it is wrong to employ reasoning relevant to one ground of invalidity in considering another.

44. *Section 18 compared with s 40.* Section 18 of the Act is in Ch 2, headed 'Patent rights, ownership and validity'. Section 18 sets out requirements which go to the nature and subject-matter of patents. In contrast, s 40 appears in Ch 3, which is headed 'From application to acceptance', and which deals with the filing, examination and acceptance of patent applications. Section 40 sets out requirements that are certainly important: in the specification, patentees give the public directions about how the advantages of the invention may be obtained after the patent expires, while in the claims, patentees warn their rivals what they must not do before the patent expires [*Rehm Pty Ltd v Websters Security Systems (International) Pty Ltd* (1988) 81 ALR 79 at 94–95 per Gummow J; *CCOM Pty Ltd v Jiejing Pty Ltd* (1994) 51 FCR 260 at 277 per Spender, Gummow and Heerey JJ]. The requirements of s 40, however, unlike those of s 18, say nothing about the nature or subject-matter of patents, and go more to the form that specifications must take. Both the differences in the requirements which ss 18 and 40 impose, and their respective locations in the Act, suggest that s 18 issues have no relevance to s 40. So far as s 18 refers to 'patentable inventions' and s 40 to 'inventions', that conclusion is also supported by the definition in Sched 1 of the Act of 'invention' as including an 'alleged invention'.

45. *Separation of matters going to and grounds of invalidity.* That conclusion is also supported by the fact that the s 45(1) matters which an applicant can ask the Commissioner to conduct an examination into, the s 59 grounds on which a patent application may be opposed and the s 138(3) grounds for revoking a patent are separately stated in the paragraphs of each section.

PRECEDENT

46. *The distinctness of the grounds of invalidity.* It is common in patent infringement litigation for invalidity to be alleged, and for more than one ground of invalidity to be relied on. Certain matters of fact and construction may be relevant to more than one issue. Thus common general knowledge is relevant not only to issues of construction by the skilled addressee, which underlie the infringement inquiry and interact with issues of validity [*Welch Perrin & Co Pty Ltd v Worrel* (1961) 106 CLR 588 at 610 per Dixon CJ, Kitto and Windeyer JJ], but also to obviousness [Section 7(2) of the Act and *Firebelt Pty Ltd v Brambles Australia Ltd* (2002) 76 ALJR 816 at 821–823 [31]–[36] per Gleeson CJ, McHugh, Gummow, Hayne and Callinan JJ]. Other factual matters may be relevant to more than one ground of invalidity [*Sunbeam Corporation v Morphy-Richards (Aust) Pty Ltd* (1961) 180 CLR 98 at 111–112 per Windeyer J]. The issues may 'intersect and overlap' [*Kimberly-Clark Australia Pty Ltd v Arico Trading International Pty Ltd* (2001) 207 CLR 1 at 19 [34]]. However, as Doric conceded in this Court, the grounds of invalidity themselves are, and must be kept, conceptually distinct. In particular, as Doric also conceded, a lack of fair basing is a distinct ground for revocation. Hence the 'inventiveness' or 'meritoriousness' of, or the technical contribution made by, the specification are issues to be examined if there is an objection under s 18(1)(b) of the Act for want of novelty or absence of an inventive step (ie obviousness). There is no reason to introduce them into the fair basing question.

...

49. *Section 40 grounds analysed.* The distinctness of the grounds of invalidity can also be illustrated by comparing the fair basing objection with those most closely connected with it, namely the failure to describe the invention fully, and the failure to claim clearly and succinctly. Section 59(c) of the Act creates as grounds for opposition, and s 138(3)(f) creates as grounds for invalidity, non-compliance with s 40(2) or (3). They are commonly called 's 40 points', and they do form a genus in that it is not necessary to look at common general knowledge at the priority date, except in construing the patent [*Welch Perrin & Co Pty Ltd v Worrel* (1961) 106 CLR 588 at 610 per Dixon CJ, Kitto and Windeyer JJ]. But the genus contains several distinct grounds. Section 40(2) deals with the 'complete specification', that is, with a document which concludes with the claims defining the invention (s 40(2)(b)), and in which the material preceding the claims is commonly called the 'body of the specification', or the 'specification' for short. In assessing whether a patent complies with the requirement of s 40(2)(a) that the complete specification must describe the invention fully, it is necessary to take into account the whole of the complete specification—both the body of the specification and the claims [*Kimberly-Clark Australia Pty Ltd v Arico Trading International Pty Ltd* (2001) 207 CLR 1 at 12–13 [14] and [16]]. On the other hand, when assessing whether there is fair basing within the meaning of s 40(3), it is necessary to split the patent into the claims and the body of the specification, in order to see whether the former are fairly based on the matter described in the latter [*Kimberly-Clark Australia Pty Ltd v Arico Trading International Pty Ltd* (2001) 207 CLR 1 at 12 [15]]. These statutorily compelled differences in the mode of analysis point against any overlap in the provisions when considered as grounds of opposition or invalidity.

RULES OF CONSTRUCTION

While ordinary rules of construction of contracts and other written documents are relevant, the fact that the patent specification is a public document defining a state-sanctioned monopoly means that particular rules of construction apply, more akin to the rules of statutory interpretation than to construction of contracts.

RULES FROM THE AUSTRALIAN CASES

CASE EXTRACT: PRECEDENT

Decor Corporation Pty Ltd v Dart Industries Inc

(1988) 13 IPR 385

Federal Court of Australia, Full Court

[The patent in issue in this matter was a closure mechanism for plastic food containers, owned by Dart. The key issue was use of the word 'biased' in one of the essential integers of the closure mechanism, as claimed in claim 1, extracted from para [17] of Sheppard J's judgment:

> A locally distortable closure member contractably and distensibly constructed and having an elastic memory such that it is adapted to hermetically seal an open-mouthed container, said closure member comprising:
>
> (1) a center main wall including a *biased* area radially emanating from a central portion thereof to a peripheral terminus, said center main wall being adapted for the application of pressure to the approximate center thereof in such manner that said *biased* area tends to collapse upon itself and substantially uniformly displace said peripheral terminus until said closure is easily positionable in an open-mouthed container; ... [emphasis added]

The primary issue was whether 'biased' in this context took its ordinary meaning of 'oblique' or whether it took the more limited meaning used throughout the body of the specification of 'corrugated, fluted or plaited' or 'conical, corrugated, fluted'. This went to the question of whether Decor had infringed Dart's patent, but the approach taken to construing the claims is also relevant to the application of the s 40 requirements.]

Sheppard J (at 400):

[After a detailed review of the case law, Sheppard J extracted the following principles.]

In summary, the relevant rules of construction which may be distilled from the authorities referred to are as follows:

1   The claims define the invention which is the subject of the patent. These must be construed according to their terms upon ordinary principles. Any purely verbal or grammatical question that can be answered according to ordinary rules for the construction of written documents is to be resolved accordingly.

2   It is not legitimate to confine the scope of the claims by reference to limitations which may be found in the body of the specification but are not expressly or by proper inference reproduced in the claims themselves. To put it another way, it is not legitimate to narrow or expand the boundaries of monopoly as fixed by the words of a claim by adding to those words glosses drawn from other parts of the specification.

3   Nevertheless, in approaching the task of construction, one must read the specification as a whole.

4   In some cases the meaning of the words used in the claims may be qualified or defined by what is said in the body of the specification.

5   If a claim be clear, it is not to be made obscure because obscurities can be found in particular sentences in other parts of the document. But if an expression is not clear or is ambiguous, it is

permissible to resort to the body of the specification to define or clarify the meaning of words used in the claim.

6   A patent specification should be given a purposive construction rather than a purely literal one.

7   In construing the specification, the Court is not construing a written instrument operating inter partes, but a public instrument which must define a monopoly in such a way that it is not reasonably capable of being misunderstood.

8   The body, apart from the preamble, is there to instruct those skilled in the art concerned in the carrying out of the invention; provided it is comprehensible to, and does not mislead, a skilled reader, the language used is seldom of importance.

9   Nevertheless, the claims, since they define the monopoly, will be scrutinized with as much care as is used in construing other documents defining a legal right.

10 If it is impossible to ascertain what the invention is from a fair reading of the specification as a whole, it will be invalid. But the specification must be construed in the light of the common knowledge in the art before the priority date.

CASE EXTRACT: CURRENT LAW

Kimberly-Clark Australia Pty Ltd v Multigate Medical Products Pty Ltd

[2011] FCAFC 86; (2011) 92 IPR 21
Federal Court of Australia, Full Court

[This case relates to a series of three patents referred to in the judgment as the 'grandparent patent', the 'parent patent' and the 'child patent'. The parent patent was a divisional of the grandparent patent and the child patent was a divisional of the parent. A divisional application can be used to divide a patent application into two or more separate applications, each of which retains the priority date of the original patent application provided that it complies with the statutory requirements. The patent provided a method for double-wrapping sterilised surgical instruments. The Kimberly-Clark group commenced proceedings for threatened infringement by Multigate, and Multigate cross-claimed for invalidity. At first instance both actions were dismissed. The construction issue related to the question of whether the claims were only infringed if two separate sheets of wrapping material were joined together, or whether the claims also encompassed a single sheet that was folded over to create inner and outer layers of sterilisation wrap.]

Greenwood and Nicholas JJ: 38. The principles relevant to the construction of the patent specification are well established and there was no dispute between the parties as to what they are. A helpful summary is found in the joint judgment in *Jupiters Ltd v Neurizon Pty Ltd* (2005) 222 ALR 155 where the Full Court (Hill, Finn and Gyles JJ) said at para [67]:

(i)   the proper construction of a specification is a matter of law: *Decor Corporation Pty Ltd v Dart Industries Inc* (1988) 13 IPR 385 at 400;

(ii) a patent specification should be given a purposive, not a purely literal, construction: *Flexible Steel Lacing Co v Beltreco Ltd* (2000) 49 IPR 331 at [81]; and it is not to be read in the abstract but is to be construed in the light of the common general knowledge and the art before the priority date: *Kimberly-Clark Australia Pty Ltd v Arico Trading International Pty Ltd* (2001) 207 CLR 1 at [24];

(iii) the words used in a specification are to be given the meaning which the normal person skilled in the art would attach to them, having regard to his or her own general knowledge and to what is disclosed in the body of the specification: *Decor Corporation Pty Ltd* at 391;

(iv) while the claims are to be construed in the context of the specification as a whole, it is not legitimate to narrow or expand the boundaries of monopoly as fixed by the words of a claim by adding to those words glosses drawn from other parts of the specification, although terms in the claim which are unclear may be defined by reference to the body of the specification: *Kimberly-Clark v Arico* at [15]; *Welch Perrin & Co Pty Ltd v Worrel* (1961) 106 CLR 588 at 610; *Interlego AG v Toltoys Pty Ltd* (1973) 130 CLR 461 at 478; the body of a specification cannot be used to change a clear claim for one subject matter into a claim for another and different subject matter: *Electric & Musical Industries Ltd v Lissen Ltd* (1938) 56 RPC 23 at 39;

(v) experts can give evidence on the meaning which those skilled in the art would give to technical or scientific terms and phrases and on unusual or special meanings to be given by skilled addressees to words which might otherwise bear their ordinary meaning: *Sartas No 1 Pty Ltd v Koukourou & Partners Pty Ltd* (1994) 30 IPR 479 at 485–486; the Court is to place itself in the position of some person acquainted with the surrounding circumstances as to the state of the art and manufacture at the time (*Kimberly-Clark v Arico* at [24]); and

(vi) it is for the Court, not for any witness however expert, to construe the specification; *Sartas No 1 Pty Ltd*, at 485–486.

39. A patent specification may incorporate a definition of a word or expression which subsequently appears in the claims. Leaving that possibility aside, ordinary words which are used in a patent claim should be given their ordinary meaning unless the skilled addressee would give them a different meaning. There are words used in patent claims that have no ordinary meaning apart from their technical or scientific meaning. There are also words used in patent claims that have a technical or scientific meaning as well as an ordinary meaning. In the latter situation the words may have been intended to be used in accordance with their technical or scientific meaning or in accordance with their ordinary meaning. Expert evidence may be received to assist in determining which of these meanings was intended.

40. Difficulties of construction may still arise even if it is apparent that the words of a claim were intended to be given their ordinary meaning. This is because the ordinary meaning of words may vary depending on the context in which they are used. Thus, it is necessary to read a patent specification as a whole even if there is no apparent ambiguity in the language of the claims.

41. There are two aspects to the principle which requires that a patent specification be given a purposive rather than a purely literal construction. The first concerns the well recognised need to read words in their proper context. The second is directly related to the nature and function of a patent specification. It is a document that is taken as intended to be read through the eyes of the skilled addressee who is equipped with the common general knowledge in the relevant art. The question is what, in an objective sense, such a person would understand the relevant words of the claim to mean. Ultimately, however, it is the claim that must be construed, and it is not permissible to vary or qualify the plain and unambiguous meaning of the claim by reference to the body of the specification: *Interlego AG v Toltoys Pty Ltd* (1973) 130 CLR 461 at 478.

42. A patent specification has a basic structure made up of different parts which have different functions. This is something to which regard must be had when construing a patent specification. In some respects the structure of patent specifications is dictated by the requirements of the *Patents Act 1990* (Cth) but in other respects it is simply the product of practices developed over time by those responsible for their drafting.

43. A complete specification must describe the invention fully, including the best method known to the patentee of performing the invention (s 40(2)). It must also end with a claim or claims defining the invention which must be clear and succinct and fairly based on the matter described in the specification (s 40(3)). And the claim or claims must relate to a single invention only (s 40(4)).

44. Since a patent specification must include a detailed description of the invention, and the best method known to the inventor of performing the invention, a patent specification will usually contain a detailed description of at least one embodiment of the invention. But provided a claim is fairly based upon matter disclosed in the specification, a claim may define the invention as having fewer integers than are present in an embodiment so described. Equally, the claim may define an invention as having more features than are present in any such embodiment. It is always open to the patentee to introduce such a limitation if he or she so chooses provided that the claim is fairly based on the matter disclosed in the specification. But if such a limitation has been introduced, it cannot be disregarded simply because the patentee could have framed a valid claim without it.

45. A patentee may have good reason for introducing a limitation into a claim. As Lord Hoffmann explained in *Kirin-Amgen Inc v Hoechst Marion Roussel Ltd* [2005] 1 All ER 667 at para [35], a seemingly inexplicable limitation may have been introduced to avoid arguments in relation to prior art. Lord Upjohn made the same point in *Rodi & Wienenberger AG v Henry Showell Ltd* [1969] RPC 367 at 392: '... some claims may on a superficial reading appear to be unnecessarily circumscribed, but those who have drafted them may have done so in the light of the prior art ...'. See also the judgment of Dixon J in *Walker v Alemite Corporation* (1933) 49 CLR 643 at 656 where his Honour quoted the following well known statement of Lord Parker in *Fellows v Thomas William Lench Ltd* (1917) 34 RPC 45 at 55 who said '[a] claiming clause operates as a disclaimer of what is not specifically claimed and for such disclaimer there may be reasons known to the inventor but not to the Court'.

46. Patent specifications often include a general description or summary of the invention which may include a consistory clause. A consistory clause is in the nature of a general description of an invention which is often expressed in terms which mirror the broadest of the claims: *Welch Perrin & Co Pty Ltd v Worrell* (1961) 106 CLR 588 at 612. Such clauses are not compulsory but are routinely included by those responsible for drafting patent specifications often with a view to providing fair basis for the broadest claim. Whether or not a consistory clause does so will depend upon whether there are other matters disclosed in the body of the specification which show that the invention is narrower than that described in the consistory clause: *Lockwood Security Products Pty Ltd v Doric Products Ltd* (2004) 217 CLR 274 at para [99].

47. The part of a patent specification which is put forward by the patentee as a general description or summary of the invention may have a significant role to play in the construction of a claim which is open to different interpretations. This is because the general description or summary of the invention will often describe the invention by reference to features that the skilled addressee would understand to be common to all possible embodiments of the invention.

CURRENT LAW

[Greenwood and Nicholas JJ proceeded to construe each of the patents in issue, drawing particular attention to language including 'inner wrap sheet', 'outer wrap sheet', 'bonding or joining two separate sheets of sterilization wrap', 'each of the individual sheets'. Their Honours were persuaded that the claims in each patent did not extend to single sheets folded over, irrespective of what might have been intended.]

88. We should add that Kimberly-Clark emphasised in its submissions that the fact that the inventions the subject of the patents in suit were directed to problems encountered by hospital staff when double wrapping articles for sterilization using two separate sheets of sterilization wrap did not mean that the claims might not be read as extending to the use of a single sheet of sterilization wrap which was folded over. That is certainly true. However, it is not the description of the problem so much as the language of the claims themselves that is most significant to our interpretation of them. In our view each of the relevant claims, read in the context of the specification in which it appears, is limited to arrangements involving the use of two sheets which have been joined together. Whether or not a valid claim that did not include such a limitation might have been included in any of the patents in suit is not a relevant consideration.

89. Similarly, whether or not any of the claims were intended by Kimberly-Clark to be interpreted as encompassing the use of a single sheet of sterilization wrap folded over to provide inner and outer layers is irrelevant to the question of construction which we have to decide. It is conceivable that the invention has been defined as it has to avoid any suggestion that hospital staff who may have used a single sheet which was folded over to double wrap surgical supplies might have anticipated one or more of the relevant claims. We raise this not because it is suggested that this was Kimberly-Clark's intention or that this actually occurred but to illustrate the point made by Lord Hoffmann in *Kirin-Amgen Inc v Hoechst Marion Roussel Ltd* [2005] 1 All ER 667 at para [35] and Lord Upjohn in *Rodi & Wienenberger AG v Henry Showell Ltd* [1969] RPC 367 at 392 to which we previously referred.

ADDITIONAL COMPLEXITIES IN EUROPE

The construction exercise is somewhat more complex in European jurisdictions, particularly the UK, because cases such as *Catnic Components Ltd v Hill & Smith Ltd* [1982] RPC 183 (HL) provide precedents on the rules of construction, but the European Patent Convention (EPC) also has its own rules of interpretation. Article 69(1) provides that:

> The extent of the protection conferred by a European patent or a European patent application shall be determined by the terms of the claims. Nevertheless, the description and drawings shall be used to interpret the claims.

Article 1 of the *Protocol on the Interpretation of Article 69 of the EPC*, adopted at the Munich Diplomatic Conference for the setting up of a European System for the Grant of Patents on 5 October 1973, provides guidance on how Art 69 should be interpreted:

> Article 69 should not be interpreted in the sense that the extent of the protection conferred by a European patent is to be understood as that defined by the strict, literal meaning of the wording used in the claims, the description and drawings being employed only for the

purpose of resolving an ambiguity found in the claims. Neither should it be interpreted in the sense that the claims serve only as a guideline and that the actual protection conferred may extend to what, from a consideration of the description and drawings by a person skilled in the art, the patentee has contemplated. On the contrary, it is to be interpreted as defining a position between these extremes which combines a fair protection for the patentee with a reasonable degree of certainty for third parties.

CASE EXTRACT: COMPARATIVE LAW

Kirin-Amgen Inc v Hoechst Marion Roussel Ltd

[2004] UKHL 46; [2005] 1 All ER 667
House of Lords

[This case illustrates the difficulties faced by UK courts in deciding what rules to apply in construing patent documents in the light of the Protocol and prior case law.]

Lord Hoffmann: 30. It seems to me clear that the Protocol, with its reference to 'resolving an ambiguity', was intended to reject these artificial English rules for the construction of patent claims. As it happens, though, by the time the Protocol was signed, the English courts had already begun to abandon them, not only for patent claims, but for commercial documents generally. The speeches of Lord Wilberforce in *Prenn v Simmonds* [1971] 1 WLR 1381 and *Reardon Smith Line Ltd v Yngvar Hansen-Tangen* [1976] 1 WLR 989 are milestones along this road. It came to be recognised that the author of a document such as a contract or patent specification is using language to make a communication for a practical purpose and that a rule of construction which gives his language a meaning different from the way it would have been understood by the people to whom it was actually addressed is liable to defeat his intentions. It is against that background that one must read the well known passage in the speech of Lord Diplock in *Catnic Components Ltd v Hill & Smith Ltd* [1982] RPC 183, 243 when he said that the new approach should also be applied to the construction of patent claims:

> A patent specification should be given a purposive construction rather than a purely literal one derived from applying to it the kind of meticulous verbal analysis in which lawyers are too often tempted by their training to indulge.

. . .

33. In the case of a patent specification, the notional addressee is the person skilled in the art. He (or, I say once and for all, she) comes to a reading of the specification with common general knowledge of the art. And he reads the specification on the assumption that its purpose is to both to describe and to demarcate an invention—a practical idea which the patentee has had for a new product or process—and not to be a textbook in mathematics or chemistry or a shopping list of chemicals or hardware. It is this insight which lies at the heart of 'purposive construction'. If Lord Diplock did not invent the expression, he certainly gave it wide currency in the law. But there is, I think, a tendency to regard it as a vague description of some kind of divination which mysteriously penetrates beneath

the language of the specification. Lord Diplock was in my opinion being much more specific and his intention was to point out that a person may be taken to mean something different when he uses words for one purpose from what he would be taken to mean if he was using them for another. The example in the *Catnic* case was the difference between what a person would reasonably be taken to mean by using the word 'vertical' in a mathematical theorem and by using it in a claimed definition of a lintel for use in the building trade. The only point on which I would question the otherwise admirable summary of the law on infringement in the judgment of Jacob LJ in *Rockwater Ltd v Technip France SA* (unreported) [2004] EWCA Civ 381, at paragraph 41, is when he says in sub-paragraph (e) that to be 'fair to the patentee' one must use 'the widest purpose consistent with his teaching'. This, as it seems to me, is to confuse the purpose of the utterance with what it would be understood to mean. The purpose of a patent specification, as I have said, is no more nor less than to communicate the idea of an invention. An appreciation of that purpose is part of the material which one uses to ascertain the meaning. But purpose and meaning are different. If, when speaking of the widest purpose, Jacob LJ meant the widest meaning, I would respectfully disagree. There is no presumption about the width of the claims. A patent may, for one reason or another, claim less than it teaches or enables.

34. 'Purposive construction' does not mean that one is extending or going beyond the definition of the technical matter for which the patentee seeks protection in the claims. The question is always what the person skilled in the art would have understood the patentee to be using the language of the claim to mean. And for this purpose, the language he has chosen is usually of critical importance. The conventions of word meaning and syntax enable us to express our meanings with great accuracy and subtlety and the skilled man will ordinarily assume that the patentee has chosen his language accordingly. As a number of judges have pointed out, the specification is a unilateral document in words of the patentee's own choosing. Furthermore, the words will usually have been chosen upon skilled advice. The specification is not a document inter rusticos for which broad allowances must be made. On the other hand, it must be recognised that the patentee is trying to describe something which, at any rate in his opinion, is new; which has not existed before and of which there may be no generally accepted definition. There will be occasions upon which it will be obvious to the skilled man that the patentee must in some respect have departed from conventional use of language or included in his description of the invention some element which he did not mean to be essential. But one would not expect that to happen very often.

. . .

45. In *Improver Corp v Remington Consumer Products Ltd* [1989] RPC 69 the Court of Appeal said that Lord Diplock's speech in *Catnic* advocated the same approach to construction as is required by the Protocol. (See also *Southco Inc v Dzus Fastener Europe Ltd* [1992] RPC 299.) But in *PLG Research Ltd v Ardon International Ltd* [1995] RPC 287, 309 Millett LJ said:

> Lord Diplock was expounding the common law approach to the construction of a patent. This has been replaced by the approach laid down by the Protocol. If the two approaches are the same, reference to Lord Diplock's formulation is unnecessary, while if they are different it is dangerous.

46. This echoes, perhaps consciously, the famous justification said to have been given by the Caliph Omar for burning the library of Alexandria: 'If these writings of the Greeks agree with the Book

of God, they are useless and need not be preserved: if they disagree, they are pernicious and ought to be destroyed'—a story which Gibbon dismissed as Christian propaganda. But I think that the Protocol can suffer no harm from a little explanation and I entirely agree with the masterly judgment of Aldous J in *Assidoman Multipack Ltd v The Mead Corporation* [1995] RPC 321, in which he explains why the *Catnic* approach accords with the Protocol.

47. The Protocol, as I have said, is a Protocol for the construction of article 69 and does not expressly lay down any principle for the construction of claims. It does say what principle should not be followed, namely the old English literalism, but otherwise it says only that one should not go outside the claims. It does however say that the object is to combine a fair protection for the patentee with a reasonable degree of certainty for third parties. How is this to be achieved? The claims must be construed in a way which attempts, so far as is possible in an imperfect world, not to disappoint the reasonable expectations of either side. What principle of interpretation would give fair protection to the patentee? Surely, a principle which would give him the full extent of the monopoly which the person skilled in the art would think he was intending to claim. And what principle would provide a reasonable degree of protection for third parties? Surely again, a principle which would not give the patentee more than the full extent of the monopoly which the person skilled in the art would think that he was intending to claim. Indeed, any other principle would also be unfair to the patentee, because it would unreasonably expose the patent to claims of invalidity on grounds of anticipation or insufficiency.

48. The *Catnic* principle of construction is therefore in my opinion precisely in accordance with the Protocol. It is intended to give the patentee the full extent, but not more than the full extent, of the monopoly which a reasonable person skilled in the art, reading the claims in context, would think he was intending to claim. Of course it is easy to say this and sometimes more difficult to apply it in practice, although the difficulty should not be exaggerated. The vast majority of patent specifications are perfectly clear about the extent of the monopoly they claim. Disputes over them never come to court. In borderline cases, however, it does happen that an interpretation which strikes one person as fair and reasonable will strike another as unfair to the patentee or unreasonable for third parties. That degree of uncertainty is inherent in any rule which involves the construction of any document. It afflicts the whole of the law of contract, to say nothing of legislation. In principle it is without remedy, although I shall consider in a moment whether uncertainty can be alleviated by guidelines or a 'structured' approach to construction.

THE DISCLOSURE REQUIREMENT

The disclosure requirement in the former s 40(2) provided simply that the specification must describe the invention fully, including the best method known to the applicant of performing the invention. The High Court was given the opportunity to consider this requirement in *Kimberly-Clark Pty Ltd v Arico Trading International Pty Ltd* [2001] HCA 8; (2001) 207 CLR 1, extracted first below, and the Federal Court gave detailed consideration to the best method requirement in *Apotex Pty Ltd v Les Laboratoires Servier* [2013] FCA 1426, in the second extract.

FULL DESCRIPTION

CASE EXTRACT: PRECEDENT

PRECEDENT

Kimberly-Clark Australia Pty Ltd v Arico Trading International Pty Ltd

[2001] HCA 8; (2001) 207 CLR 1
High Court of Australia

[The patent in issue in this case was described as follows: 'A unitary disposable diaper with elasticised legs is provided having a fluid pervious liner a fluid impervious backing with absorbent material positioned there between. A fecal containment flap is positioned along each side of the diaper and extends inward from the lateral edges.' The heart of the dispute in this case went to the nature of the flap material. In summary, the claims specified that there should be elasticised fluid pervious flaps, but the description of the invention stated only that: 'The flap material is *preferably* soft, conformable and vapor and/or fluid permeable.'

Kimberly-Clark brought infringement proceedings against Arico, and Arico counterclaimed revocation on various grounds, including failure to fully describe the invention in s 40(2)(a) and lack of fair basing in s 40(3). The only ground to go to the High Court was the alleged failure to fully describe the invention. As a first step in addressing this issue, the Court turned its attention to the construction of s 40, concluding that different considerations apply depending on whether the inquiry relates to fair basing in s 40(3) or failure to fully describe the invention in s 40(2)(a). For fair basing, the claims and description in the text of the specification must be kept distinct, but this case is authority for the proposition that for failure to fully describe the invention, it is permissible to construe the specification as a whole, including the claims.]

Gleeson CJ, McHugh, Gummow, Hayne and Callinan JJ (some footnotes omitted): 14. One matter of construction of s 40 of the 1990 Act should be noted immediately because it is significant for this appeal. The respondents submit, consistently with the approach taken by the majority in the Full Court, that, in deciding whether the invention is fully described, the claims cannot be looked at as part of the specification. That submission should be rejected. Section 40 distinguishes between the description and the definition of the invention. The complete specification must describe the invention and end with claims defining the invention. However, the claims are as much a part of the complete specification as the preceding matter, which usually is identified as the 'body' of the specification.

...

16. ... [W]here the issue concerns par (a) of s 40(2) ... [t]he question then is whether the invention has been fully described in the complete specification. The text speaks here of the complete specification, not any one part thereof. From the distinction drawn in s 40(2) between describing the invention in the complete specification and defining the invention in any claims with which the complete specification ends, it does not follow that the description is to be gleaned solely from one part (the body) and that it is forbidden to obtain any assistance by regard to the remainder (the claims) of the complete specification. Rather, the text indicates that the specification must be read as a whole and that reference to the claims may dispel ambiguity or uncertainty from the body of the specification concerning the description of the invention.

...

24. It is well settled that the complete specification is not to be read in the abstract; here it is to be construed in the light of the common general knowledge and the art before 2 July 1984, the priority date [*Samuel Taylor Pty Ltd v SA Brush Co Ltd* (1950) 83 CLR 617 at 624–625; *Welch Perrin & Co Pty Ltd v Worrel* (1961) 106 CLR 588 at 610; *Sunbeam Corporation v Morphy-Richards (Aust) Pty Ltd* (1961) 180 CLR 98 at 102; *Populin v HB Nominees Pty Ltd* (1982) 41 ALR 471 at 476]; the court is to place itself 'in the position of some person acquainted with the surrounding circumstances as to the state of [the] art and manufacture at the time' [*British Dynamite Co v Krebs* (1879) 13 RPC 190 at 192].

25. Section 25(2)(h) of the *Patents and Designs Act* 1907 (UK) ('the 1907 Act'), as amended by s 3 of the *Patents and Designs Act* 1932 (UK), made it a ground of revocation that the complete specification did not 'sufficiently and fairly describe and ascertain the nature of the invention and the manner in which the invention [was] to be performed'. The resemblance to s 40(2)(a) of the 1990 Act will be apparent. Speaking of the 1907 Act in *No-Fume Ltd v Frank Pitchford & Co Ltd* [(1935) 52 RPC 231 at 243], Romer LJ repeated par (h) of s 25(2) and continued:

> [I]n other words, [it is essential] that the patentee should disclose his invention sufficiently to enable those who are skilled in the relevant art to utilise the invention after the patentee's monopoly has come to an end. Such disclosure is, indeed, the consideration that the patentee gives for the grant to him of a monopoly during the period that the patent would run ...
>
> . It is not necessary that he should describe in his specification the manner in which the invention is to be performed, with that wealth of detail with which the specification of the manufacturer of something is usually put before the workman who is engaged to manufacture it.

The question is, will the disclosure enable the addressee of the specification to produce something within each claim without new inventions or additions or prolonged study of matters presenting initial difficulty? [Blanco White, *Patents for Inventions*, 5th ed (1983), §4-502.]

26. In the present case, [the trial judge] accepted the evidence of an employee of Kimberly-Clark responsible for product development of diapers, Mr Butler, that, at the priority date, the skilled addressee of the Patent would understand the disclosure therein 'to be directing him, as a practical matter, to make a disposable nappy falling within the terms of claims 1 and 2', and thereby as directing the adoption of 'fluid pervious flaps'.

27. However, in the Full Court, Wilcox and Branson JJ appear to have decided the appeal on the footing that 'the specification says nothing as to an essential integer of the claimed invention itself'. Their Honours referred to Mr Butler's evidence, in particular what appear to have been passages in his cross-examination designed to provide support for what in the event was the unsuccessful attack on the ground of obviousness. They concluded that 'read as a whole', his evidence did 'not provide a basis' for Burchett J's finding that a person skilled in the art at the priority date in 1984 would unhesitatingly have chosen liquid pervious flaps.

...

29. Section 116 of the 1990 Act authorises a court, in interpreting a complete specification as amended, to refer to the specification without amendment. In its original form accompanying the Convention application, the complete specification added the integer of fluid permeability of the flaps as claim 2, and as a narrowing of claim 1 as it then stood. Both claims were recast and this integer then appeared in both claim 1 and claim 2, which now were not interdependent. This may have been

PRECEDENT

prompted to meet an Examiner's objection of prior publication of claim 1 in its original form. But, with respect to the issue now arising under par (a) of s 40 (2), that history does not detract from the effect of Mr Butler's evidence that, at the priority date in 1984, a skilled addressee would have imposed such a limitation after reading the Patent.

THE REASONING OF THE FULL COURT MAJORITY

30. The majority in the Full Court also stated that the references in the body of the claims to 'fluid pervious flaps' did not assist 'in determining whether the complete specification describes the invention fully' because the expressions in the body of the specification 'vapour and/or fluid permeable' could not be regarded as 'relevantly doubtful in meaning'. Their Honours said [*Arico Trading International Pty Ltd v Kimberly-Clark Australia Pty Ltd* (1999) 46 IPR 1 at 3]:

> The expression cannot fairly be interpreted so as to call necessarily for a material which is fluid permeable. That is, on one available construction of the specification, it says nothing as to an essential feature of the claimed invention; on the other available construction, it is misleading as to that essential feature.

31. There are several deficiencies in this reasoning. The first concerns their Honours' use here of the term 'the specification' and is a matter which is dealt with above under the heading 'The construction of s 40'. There appears to be an assumption, contrary to the text of the 1990 Act and to the authorities, that the 'complete specification' spoken of in s 40(2)(a) is the body of the specification, exclusive of the claims, rather than the whole document. Secondly, whilst their Honours assert lack of relevant doubt in meaning, they posit two available constructions of the expression in question. They do not take the next step, indicated by, for example, statements by Dixon and McTiernan JJ in *Kauzal v Lee* (1936) 58 CLR 670 at 687, to ask whether that difficulty arising from the body of the specification was removed by references in claims 1 and 2 to 'fluid pervious flaps'. Thirdly, as also appears from the passage from the majority judgment set out earlier in these reasons under the heading 'The skilled addressee', in addition to discounting the expert evidence, the majority proceeded on the footing that they were to read the specification by asking what it instructed a reader ignorant of the prior art.

BEST METHOD

PRECEDENT

CASE EXTRACT: PRECEDENT

Apotex Pty Ltd v Les Laboratoires Servier

[2013] FCA 1426
Federal Court of Australia

[The patent in this matter was a new arginine salt of the drug perindopril, which is used to lower blood pressure in patients with high blood pressure (or hypertension). Apotex challenged the validity of the patent on a number of grounds, including failure to satisfy the best method requirement is s 40(2)(a) (pre-*Raising the Bar Act* amendments)].

Rares J: 164. The requirement imposed by s 40(2)(a), that a complete specification describe the best method known to the applicant for performing the invention, is a fundamental aspect governing the grant of a patent. It supplements the co-ordinate requirement in s 40(2)(a) that the complete specification also describe the invention fully. Relevantly, the obligation on the applicant is to describe the best method that the applicant knows. The applicant cannot leave to chance that a skilled addressee could readily ascertain that method, or some essential feature of that method by omitting from the complete specification a sufficient description of it. However, as French and Lindgren JJ said in *Pfizer Overseas Pharmaceuticals v Eli Lilly & Co* (2005) 68 IPR 1 at 77 [374], with Crennan J agreeing on this issue at 83 [408], the best known method need not be identified as such in the complete specification. Rather, the requirement in s 40(2)(a) is that that method be *disclosed* in the complete specification.

165. Thus, it does not matter that the applicant does not identify any particular method in the complete specification as the best method, and s 40(2)(a) will be satisfied so long as the best method known to the applicant is disclosed there. The requirements of disclosure in s 40(2)(a) is specifically linked to the performance of the invention: *Firebelt Pty Ltd v Brambles Australia Ltd* (2000) 51 IPR 531 at 544 [51]–[53] per Spender, Drummond and Mansfield JJ. They said (51 IPR at 544–545 [53]):

> The requirement of s 40(2) of the Act is that the patentee is required to give the best information in his power as to how to carry out the *invention*. **That requirement is ordinarily satisfied by including in the specification a detailed description of one or more preferred embodiments of the invention offered, with reference to drawings of specific mechanisms or structures or examples of specific process conditions or chemical formulations, depending on the field of the invention and the nature of the instruction to be conveyed.** It is necessary to have regard to what is *the invention* claimed in the petty patent. The invention here claimed is not a particular type of lid opening device operating at any particular time. It is only if it were such a claim that there might be a failure such as the primary judge found. (italic emphasis in original, bold emphasis added)

166. Thus, it is crucial, *first*, to identify the invention claimed in order to determine whether the complete specification discloses the best method of performing that invention [known] to the applicant. The purpose of this obligation of disclosure is to ensure that the patentee observes good faith in his, her or its application for the grant of the monopoly. It is also to protect the public against a patentee deliberately withholding from the public, in the complete specification, something novel and not previously published that the patentee knows or has found out gives the best results without giving to the public, as consideration for the grant of the monopoly, that knowledge of the best method of performing the invention: *Firebelt* 51 IPR at 544 [48], *Pfizer* 68 IPR at 77 [374]. In *Firebelt* 51 IPR at 544 [49]–[50] the Full Court identified how the requirement of disclosure of the best method should be understood by quoting with approval from a well-known text as follows:

> Blanco White in *Patents for Inventions*, 4th ed, Stevens, London, 1974 at para 4-502 notes:
>
> > To be proper and sufficient, the complete specification as a whole (that is, read together with the claims [*Evans v Hoskins and Sewell* (1907) 24 RPC 517 at 522 (CA)], and in the light of the drawings, if any [*Bloxam v Elsee* (1827) 1 C & P 558 at 564]) **must** in the first place *contain such instructions as will enable all* [*Knight v Argylls* (1913) 30 RPC 321 at 348 (CA)] those to *whom the specification is addressed to produce something within*

PRECEDENT

> each claim 'by following the directions of the specification, without any new inventions
> or additions of their own' [R v Arkwright (1785) 1 WPC 64 at 66; Otto v Linford (1882)
> 46 LT 35 at 41 (CA); No-Fume v Pitchford (1935) 52 RPC 231 at 243 (CA)] and without
> 'prolonged study of matters which present some initial difficulty' [Valensi v BRC [1972]
> FSR 273 at 311 (CA)].

Of the objection based on the provisions of the United Kingdom legislation, Blanco White says at
para 4-516:

> There would seem to be no obligation under this provision to include information not
> strictly relating to 'the invention', however necessary to anyone needing to work the
> invention.

The learned author continues:

> Thus it would seem unnecessary to disclose how starting materials for a process are to
> be obtained [American Cyanamid's (Dann) Patent [1971] RPC 425, ante, §4-507]; while
> it has been held that the patentee of a new article need not disclose the best method of
> making it, 'performing' here going only to the design of the article and not to techniques
> for manufacturing it [Illinois Tool Works v Autobars [1972] FSR 67 at 71–2. But cf ante,
> §4-502].' (emphasis added)

167. A complete specification must disclose each essential element or feature for performing the
invention, even if a skilled addressee would know or could readily ascertain that element: Norton and
Gregory Ltd v Jacobs (1937) 54 RPC 271 at 277 per Greene MR, Romer and Scott JJ; see too per
Clauson J (as the trial judge) at 54 RPC 58 at 74–75; Colgate-Palmolive Co v Cussons Pty Ltd (1993)
26 IPR 311 at 355 per Sheppard J. Importantly, the requirement in s 40(2)(a) is to describe every
essential element or feature for performing the invention, as opposed to what a skilled addressee
would know from the description actually given in the complete specification, about details such as
well-known analytical agents, commonly used methods, well-known terms of art or a description of
machinery in standard use: Expo-Net Danmark A/S v Buono-Net Australia Pty Ltd (No 2) [2011] FCA
710 at [14] per Bennett J.

168. The party seeking revocation must prove that the patentee knew of a better method than
was disclosed at the time of filing of the complete specification: Expo-Net [2011] FCA 710 at [15]. Her
Honour found useful the analysis of an analogue of s 40(2)(a) by Harms J, the Supreme Court of South
Africa, Transvaal Provincial Division in Enka BV v E I Du Pont de Nemours & Co 1987 BP 13 at 22–23
(Ackerman and Van Zyl JJ concurring). Bennett J summarised that analysis as follows at [16]:

> Justice Harms said that an applicant for revocation must show that:
>
> (a) the method which the patentee failed to disclose is a method of performing the invention;
> (b) the method is in fact a better method of performing the invention than the method disclosed
>   in the specification;
> (c) the method was known to the patentee at the time when the application for the patent was
>   lodged at the Patent Office;
> (d) the method is not disclosed in the specification; and
> (e) the patentee knew that the method was better than the method(s) described in the
>   specification.

169. The patentee's subjective state of mind must be proved by a person seeking revocation of a patent. That is because s 40(2)(a) prescribes that the best method that the specification must prescribe is 'known to the patentee'. The parties debated the significance of Graham J's decision in *Illinois Tool Works Inc v Autobarn Co* [1974] RPC 337 at 369 (also partly reported in [1972] FSR 67). However, that decision is of little assistance on the construction of s 40(2)(a) because Graham J did not discuss what was involved in the requirement to describe the best method.

170. The complete specification is not read in the abstract when considering whether it satisfies s 40(2)(a). It must be read from the vantage point of the skilled addressee, i.e. a person acquainted with the surrounding circumstances as to the state of the art and manufacture in light of the common general knowledge and the art immediately before the priority date: *Kimberly-Clark* [*Australia Pty Ltd v Arico Trading International Pty Ltd* (2001)] 207 CLR at 16 [24]. Gleeson CJ, McHugh, Gummow, Hayne and Callinan JJ formulated a test at [25] after citing with approval what Romer LJ had said in *No-Fume Ltd v Frank Pitchford & Co Ltd* (1935) 52 RPC 231 at 243 of a requirement that the complete specification 'sufficiently and fairly describe and ascertain the nature of the invention and the manner in which the invention [was] to be performed', namely:

> [I]n other words, [it is essential] that the patentee should disclose his invention sufficiently to enable those who are skilled in the relevant art to utilise the invention after the patentee's monopoly has come to an end. Such disclosure is, indeed, the consideration that the patentee gives for the grant to him of a monopoly during the period that the patent would run
>
> ...
>
> It is not necessary that he should describe in his specification the manner in which the invention is to be performed, with that wealth of detail with which the specification of the manufacturer of something is usually put before the workman who is engaged to manufacture it.

171. Immediately after setting out those remarks the High Court enunciated the test under s 40(2)(a) in *Kimberly-Clark* 207 CLR at 17 [25]:

> The question is, will the disclosure enable the addressee of the specification to produce something within each claim without new inventions or additions or prolonged study of matters presenting initial difficulty [Blanco White, *Patents for Inventions*, 5th ed (1983), §4-502]?

172. Disputed questions of fact in litigation must be decided on the evidence actually adduced at the hearing and not on speculation as to what other evidence might possibly have been led. Thus, the Court can draw more confidently an inference in favour of one party for which there is a basis in the evidence when a person, whose evidence presumably might put a true complexion on facts is, without a sufficient explanation, not called as a witness by the opponent: *Australian Securities and Investments Commission v Hellicar* (2012) 247 CLR 345 at 412–413 [165]–[167] per French CJ, Gummow, Hayne, Crennan, Kiefel and Bell JJ.

173. In essence the question is whether Servier's description in the complete specification of preparing perindopril arginine from L-arginine and perindopril according to a classical method of salification of organic chemistry (p 2 line 17, p 3 lines 22–23) satisfied the requirement in s 40(2)(a) to state the best method of performing the invention known to it. The invention was identified in the claims. The claims were for, among others, the arginine salt of perindopril and its hydrates, and pharmaceutical compositions comprising that salt and its hydrates, as active ingredient in combination with one or more pharmaceutically acceptable excipients (claims 1 and 2).

...

179. I am of opinion that the expert evidence revealed that the mere reference to utilising a classical method of salification was wholly inadequate to describe the best method, or any substantive content of any particular classical method that the patentee knew of performing the invention. The generalised and unspecific description of the method in the complete specification left too much to chance for a skilled addressee to select from in order to perform the invention. While the patentee need not disclose the best method of *making* an article provided that the complete specification describes its design, and hence performance, the patent for an article ordinarily will illustrate and provide detail of that design from which a skilled addressee will be able to deduce how to manufacture the invention: *Firebelt* 51 IPR at 544 [49]–[50]. The bare description 'a classical method of salification' does not allow the skilled addressee to follow a routine process of deduction from that description because it leaves open too many variables.

180. Servier's argument was that because the patentee disclosed in the complete specification a method of performing the invention and that method, by its generality, included both of the actual methods it used in 1986 and 1991, Apotex had the onus of proving that those methods were better than the general one. That argument was syllogistic. The mere fact that a complete specification described a method for performing the invention so that sufficient information was conveyed to a skilled addressee to enable him or her to work it, does not necessarily satisfy the patentee's additional obligation to describe the best method he, she or it knows. ...

181. The teaching in the patent of how to perform the invention was unlike that in cases involving articles such as *Firebelt* 51 IPR 531 and *Illinois Tool Works* [1974] RPC 337. In *Illinois Tool Works* [1974] RPC at 369 Graham J said:

> ... in the case of an article claim which is directed to the shape of that article, the method of performance means the production of an article in the shape described, irrespective of how it may in fact have been made.

182. The inventions claimed in the patent were, *first*, the arginine salt in all its forms and, *secondly*, that salt in pharmaceutical compositions. Thus, the inventions concerned not simply a new salt but also one that was useful in pharmaceutical compositions. The description in a patent of the shape of an article by reference to illustrations, such as the paper cup in *Illinois Tool Works* [1974] RPC 337, will expose to the skilled addressee what he or she can produce by working the invention. There, the machinery needed to manufacture the cup was not part of the invention. But here, the very general description of one method (classical) of salification that itself afforded many possible means of performance that could involve considerable trial and error is not the same as a description of the best method that Servier knew.

...

185. Servier had used a particular method or methods of classical salification and parameters that produced a guaranteed result. The complete specification described a broad and very general method of performing the invention that left to chance whether the skilled addressee would choose, from among the very large range of variables identified by the first joint expert report, *the* method (or one of the 1986 or 1991 methods) that the patentee knew actually worked to enable the API to be used in a tablet form. The variety of choice left open by the complete specification's generalised identification of '*a*', and not a particular, method of classical salification, coupled with the omission of the description

PRECEDENT

of *the* method that the patentee had used and which it knew worked, was analogous to Sir Winston Churchill's description in October 1939 of the future behaviour of the Soviet Union in World War II:

> I cannot forecast to you the action of Russia. It is a riddle, wrapped in a mystery, inside an enigma; but perhaps there is a key. That key is Russian national interest.

186. Here, the only key to the riddle of producing a salt in the complete specification is the reference to a classical salification. But, for the reasons given by the experts, the best solution to the riddle known to the patentee was wrapped in the mystery of choices of such salifications and the enigma of choices of parameters to apply. These vagaries occur in science before the accepted use of the chemist's or skilled addressee's 'dark art' in actually getting crystallisation to occur, which the patent need not describe.

187. By omitting a sufficient description of the or one successful method it had employed, the patentee failed to describe in the complete specification the best method known to it of performing the invention. Hence, the complete specification did not satisfy one of the essential requirements of s 40(2)(a).

The best method requirement remains unchanged following entry into force of the *Raising the Bar Act* amendments. As such, cases like *Apotex v Les Laboratoires Servier* and the other cases cited therein will continue to provide guidance on the interpretation of this requirement. In contrast, the amendments to the requirement to describe the invention fully are significant. *Kimberly-Clark v Arico* will continue to provide guidance on the aspects of the specification that can be consulted when considering satisfaction of this requirement, but is likely that the courts will look to the case law in jurisdictions with similar legislative requirements for assistance in interpreting the new wording (i.e. that the invention must be disclosed in a manner which is clear enough and complete enough for the invention to be performed by a person skilled in the relevant art). Later this chapter we consider the extent to which guidance may be found in UK jurisprudence, in particular (see p 519, below).

THE CLAIMING REQUIREMENTS: LACK OF FAIR BASING

The term 'fair basing' is of fairly recent origin in patent law, appearing for the first time in the *Patents Act 1949* (UK) and the *Patents Act 1952* (Cth), and subsequently reflected in s 40(3) of the *Patents Act 1990* as originally enacted. As noted earlier, the language of fair basing is no longer used in the UK and, following the *Raising the Bar Act* amendments, it has been replaced in s 40(3) of the *Patents Act* with the requirement that the claims be 'supported' by the matters disclosed in the specification. It is important to understand how fair basing was interpreted to understand what was contemplated with this change to s 40(3).

Early case law in the UK prior to the introduction of the fair basing requirement suggested that the relevant inquiry is into the width of the claims relative to the inventive idea. This was taken up in other cases as the relevant inquiry in relation to the fair basing requirement.

ORIGINS OF THE FAIR BASING REQUIREMENT

CASE EXTRACT: PRECEDENT

Mullard Radio Valve Co Ltd v Philco Radio and Television Corporation of Great Britain Ltd

(1936) 53 RPC 323
House of Lords

[This case was decided at a time when there was no equivalent to the disclosure and claiming requirements in modern Australian and UK patent law. Rather, novelty and inventive step were in issue.]

Lord Macmillan (at 347): But a claim may be for an article which is new, which is useful and which has subject-matter, yet it may be too wide a claim because it extends beyond the subject-matter of the invention. The consideration which the patentee gives to the public disclosing his inventive idea entitles him in return to protection for an article which embodies his inventive idea but not for an article which, while capable of being used to carry his inventive idea into effect, is described in terms which cover things quite unrelated to his inventive idea, and which do not embody it at all.

. . .

It is undoubtedly the case that a claim may be too wide, in the sense that it claims protection for that for which the patentee is not entitled to protection, or that it gives him a wider protection than his discovery entitles him to receive. In the present instance the Patentee has claimed a monopoly of all valves with a certain feature of construction although the merit of his invention does not lie in that feature but in the utilisation in a particular and limited way of a valve containing that feature of construction. In so doing he has in my opinion over-reached himself and his claim is wider than the law will support.

CASE EXTRACT: PRECEDENT

CCOM Pty Ltd v Jiejing Pty Ltd

(1994) 51 FCR 260
Federal Court of Australia, Full Court

[This case related to a computer program for writing Chinese characters. CCOM applied for petty patents relating to the claimed invention. Issues were raised with regard to the novelty of the invention, which made it crucial for CCOM to be able to rely on the earliest priority date possible. However, this in turn raised issues as to whether the petty patent in issue was fairly based on an earlier provisional application.

The Court provided a detailed account of the law relating to fair basing in their judgment, highlighting its two roles: first, that the complete specification is fairly based on the provisional specification and second, that the claims made at the end of the complete specification are fairly based on the disclosure made in the body of the specification. The Court did not accept that *Mullard Radio Valve* provided definitive guidance as to the interpretation of the Australian fair basing provision.]

Spender, Gummow and Heerey JJ (at 276–279): The term 'fairly based' was introduced into Australian patent law by ss 40 and 45 of the 1952 Act. It was used to describe the relationship between the claims defining the invention and the matter described in the complete specification (sub-s 40 (2)), and as a criterion for fixing the priority date of a claim of a complete specification fairly based on matter disclosed in the preceding provisional specification (sub-ss 45 (2) and (3)). Other uses of the term in the 1952 Act, as amended, (for example, with international applications) are detailed in *Rehm Pty Ltd v Websters Security Systems (International) Pty Ltd* (1988) 81 ALR 79 at 94. Sub-s 159(1) of the 1952 Act made it clear that disconformity on the ground that the invention claimed was wider than that of the specification was not of itself a ground of objection to grant or of invalidity; see *Coopers Animal Health Australia Ltd v Western Stock Distributors Pty Ltd* (1987) 15 FCR 382 at 388, per Fox J. This serves to emphasise the width and significance of the ground now covered by what in 1952 was the new concept of 'fair basing'.

As we have indicated, the phrase 'fairly based' is carried over into the 1990 Act. In particular, claims must be fairly based on matter described in the specification (sub-s 40 (3)), and the priority date of a claim may be determined as the date of making the 'relevant application' in which the matter was first disclosed, if the claim is fairly based on that matter (reg 3.12).

The term 'fair basing' had been introduced into British patent law by ss 4, 5 and 6 of the *Patents Act 1949* (UK), and served the same functions as it was to serve in the 1952 Act. However, 'fair basing' has disappeared from British patent law: *Asahi Kasei Kogyo KK's Application* [1991] RPC 485 at 510 (CA), 536–537, 546–547 (HL). Instead, sub-s 14 (5) of the *Patents Act 1977* (UK) ('the 1977 Act'), requires that claims 'be supported by the description' of the invention in the specification. Further, para 5(2)(a), which deals with priority dates, looks to the earliest relevant application which disclosed matter supporting the invention to which the application in suit relates. Subsection 130(7) states that these provisions were designed to give effect to the European Patent Convention of 1973.

The term 'fair basing' was introduced in Britain and Australia after the growth of a body of case law dealing with two related but distinct propositions. The first was that a claim should not be wider than warranted by the disclosure made in the body of the specification. The second was that the complete specification should conform to the provisional specification. These requirements had their source in the history of English patent law: *Tate v Haskins* (1935) 53 CLR 594 at 606.

. . .

Of course, in *Mullard* the House of Lords had been concerned to find a rationale for disconformity between the body and claims in a complete specification, in the absence of express statutory provision. The rationale was found in the concept of the disclosure as the consideration for the monopoly delimited by the claim. But, in applying *Mullard* to what since 1952 are express statutory provisions, some caution is needed lest the history swamp the new text. Hence the observation by Barwick CJ in *Olin [Corporation v Super Cartridge Co Pty Ltd* (1977) 51 ALJR 525] (at 527), which emphasises the importance of that text:

> The question whether the claim is fairly based is not to be resolved, in my opinion, by considering whether a monopoly in the product would be an undue reward for the disclosure. Rather, the question is a narrow one, namely whether the claim to the product being new, useful, and inventive, that is to say, the claim as expressed, travels beyond the matter disclosed in the specification.

MODERN INTERPRETATION OF THE FAIR BASING REQUIREMENT

CASE EXTRACT: PRECEDENT

Lockwood Security Products Pty Ltd v Doric Products Pty Ltd ('Lockwood No 1')

[2004] HCA 58; (2004) 217 CLR 274
High Court of Australia

[The patent in issue in this litigation related to deadlocks. Para 8 of the High Court's judgment encapsulates the problem to be overcome:

> The problem was that while it was possible for an occupant of the premises to enter by unlocking the door from the outside and then to close it, the internal handle or knob remained locked until the key was used to unlock it from the inside. If the occupant failed to do this on entry, dangerous circumstances could arise. For example, an occupant, encumbered by full shopping bags, who entered by using a key from the outside, left the key in the door or misplaced it and then discovered that the door had banged shut would find it impossible to leave through the door if a fire broke out inside, or if a child were seen entering a position of danger outside.

Integer (vi) of claim 1 in Lockwood's patent was an actuator which allowed the inside lock to be unlocked from the outside, solving the problem outlined above. Essentially, Lockwood claimed all means of achieving this end. The patent however only detailed one mechanism by which this could be achieved. Among a range of other grounds, Doric alleged lack of fair basing. The question before the Court on this point was whether Lockwood could rely on the definition of the invention in the consistory clause in the body of the specification, which stated, in a language corresponding with integer (vi) in claim 1: 'According to the present invention, a latch assembly of the foregoing kind (i.e. using integers (i)–(v)) is characterised in that it includes lock release means which is responsive to operation of the second actuator to render the locking means inactive.' Doric's argument was that the claims should be limited to the particular arrangement shown in the drawings and associated text in the body of the specification.

At first instance, the trial judge accepted Doric's argument on the fair basing issue and ordered that all but one of Lockwood's claims should be revoked for lack of fair basing. This was upheld on appeal to the Full Federal Court. The High Court did not accept the reasoning of either of the lower courts and, like the Full Federal Court in *CCOM*, rejected the argument that *Mullard Radio Valve* provided guidance in interpreting the Australian fair basing requirement.

Before assessing the merits of the submissions presented by Lockwood and Doric with regard to fair basing, the Court pointed to six difficulties that could be encountered by Lockwood (and other patentees) if the Court accepted Lockwood's submission that the fair basing requirement was satisfied simply because the invention as claimed was stated in the body of the specification in the consistory clause. Ultimately these difficulties were not faced by Lockwood, for reasons explained below.]

Gleeson CJ, McHugh, Gummow, Hayne and Heydon JJ (some footnotes omitted): 31. First, so broad a statement of the invention exposed it to attack on the ground that the complete specification

PRECEDENT

had not described it fully, contrary to s 40(2)(a) of the Act. A limited attack of that kind was made, but it was rejected by the trial judge. No broad attack based on the failure of the Patent to say how a suitable lock release means could be constructed was made: that was within the knowledge of a skilled addressee, and, as the trial judge said, any allegation of that kind would have contradicted Doric's case on obviousness.

32. Secondly, so broad a statement of an invention that was said to achieve a new result prima facie made the Patent vulnerable to attack on the ground that it was obvious in that it did not involve an inventive step, contrary to s 18(1)(b)(ii) of the Act. The trial judge found that while the problem was obvious, the solution was not, and thus he rejected that attack.

33. Thirdly, so broad a statement of achieving a new result prima facie made the Patent vulnerable to the contention that it was not novel, contrary to s 18(1)(b)(i) of the Act. The trial judge rejected this, save in relation to nine of the claims.

34. Fourthly, an invention so broadly expressed was liable to attack on the ground that the claims defining it were ambiguous and therefore not clear, contrary to s 40(3) of the Act. The trial judge rejected this attack as well.

35. Fifthly, while it might have been argued that the invention did not constitute a manner of manufacture, contrary to s 18(1)(a) of the Act, that objection was not taken.

36. Sixthly, the trial judge rejected a limited contention that the invention lacked utility.

[In construing section 40(3) the Court rejected the notion that inventive step or merit were relevant considerations.]

50. To some extent, various of the judgments below assume that the relevant test under s 40(3) requires a comparison between the claims and the 'inventive step' [*Lockwood Security Products Pty Ltd v Doric Products Pty Ltd* (2003) 56 IPR 479 at 496 [72]–[73] per Wilcox J, 503 [102] per Merkel J], or a comparison between the claims and the 'merit' of the invention [*Lockwood Security Products Pty Ltd v Doric Products Pty Ltd* (2003) 56 IPR 479 at 502 [100] per Merkel J], or a comparison between the claims and the 'technical contribution to the art' made by the patent [*Doric Products Pty Ltd v Lockwood Security Products Pty Ltd* (2001) 192 ALR 306 at 347–348 [235]–[236] per Hely J].

51. There are some key features of the legislation which suggest that these assumptions are wrong.

52. *The imprecision of 'inventive merit'.* This Court has recently warned against use of the expression 'inventive merit'. It was employed in the 19th century to express ideas now relevant to what is novel and to what is an inventive step (ss 18(1)(b)(i) and (ii) of the Act). 'The phrase invites error through imprecision of legal analysis.' [*Advanced Building Systems Pty Ltd v Ramset Fasteners (Aust) Pty Ltd* (1998) 194 CLR 171 at 188 [26] per Brennan CJ, Gaudron, McHugh and Gummow JJ].

53. *The language of s 40(3).* Further, conceptions like 'inventive step', 'merit' and 'technical contribution to the art' find no support in the statutory language of s 40(3). Section 40(1) speaks of a provisional specification describing 'the invention' and s 40(2)(a) speaks of a complete specification describing 'the invention fully'. Section 40(2)(b) speaks of the claims 'defining the invention'. Section 40(4) speaks of the claims relating 'to one invention only'. Although s 40(3) does not use the word 'invention', this context suggests, and the parties agreed, that the requirement in s 40(3) that the claims be fairly based on the matter described in the specification is a requirement that they be fairly based on the matter in it that discusses the 'invention' (an expression which includes the 'alleged

invention'). In s 40(1), 'invention' means 'the embodiment which is described, and around which the claims are drawn' [*AMP Inc v Utilux Pty Ltd* (1971) 45 ALJR 123 at 127 per McTiernan J; revd on other grounds: *Utilux Pty Ltd v AMP Inc* (1974) 48 ALJR 17; *Kimberly-Clark Australia Pty Ltd v Arico Trading International Pty Ltd* (2001) 207 CLR 1 at 14–15 [21] per Gleeson CJ, McHugh, Gummow, Hayne and Callinan JJ]. It has the same meaning in s 40(2) [*Kimberly-Clark* at 15 [21]]. So far as s 40(3) implicitly refers to an invention, it must bear the same meaning there. It does not mean the 'inventive step taken by the inventor' or the 'advance in the art made by the inventor' [*Kimberly-Clark* at 15 [21]]. Nor does it refer to inventive 'merit' or to any 'technical contribution to the art'.

54. Even if s 40(3) did not impliedly refer to an invention, the language points to a comparison between the claims and what is described in the specification only, and again it does not call for any inquiry into an 'inventive step', or inventive 'merit' or a 'technical contribution to the art' …

[The Court rejected Doric's other submissions: that old UK case law such as *Mullard Radio Valve*, extracted above, and the more recent UK case of *Biogen Inc v Medeva Plc* [1997] RPC 1 had any bearing on the interpretation of s 40(3); that fairness equates with reasonableness; that the consistory clause in this matter was not a true consistory clause; and that their argument was supported by authority.]

102. Although Doric did not explicitly request this Court to change settled principles in Australia respecting fair basing, it advanced arguments which could only be accepted if the law were changed. Thus its reliance on *Biogen Inc v Medeva plc* [1997] RPC 1 was an implicit invitation to adopt for s 40(3) the United Kingdom construction of a different provision.

103. Doric contended, in effect, that success for the Patentee would be in various ways objectively 'unfair', and hence that the claims were not 'fairly based'. But the kinds of unfairness it complained of, if remediable at all, had to be remedied under other heads of invalidity. If they could not be remedied under those heads, their 'unfairness' did not mean that the claims were not 'fairly based' on the matter described, and to hold otherwise would radically change the law. One source of these unfairnesses was said to be the fact that s 40(2)(a), on the construction given by this Court in *Kimberly-Clark*, is complied with if the complete specification enables the addressee to produce something within each claim without new inventions or additions or prolonged study of matters presenting initial difficulty [*Kimberly-Clark* at 17 [25]] but Doric, whilst willing to attempt to sap life from *Kimberly-Clark*, prudently eschewed any attack upon that binding authority.

104. For the above reasons the appeal must be allowed.

Although it is possible to point to cases subsequent to *Lockwood No 1* in which the courts held claims to be invalid for lack of fair basis (*Pfizer Overseas Pharmaceuticals v Eli Lilly and Co* [2005] FCAFC 224; (2005) 225 ALR 416 being a prominent example), for the most part, the fair basing requirement was seen as little more than a formality which failed to adequately protect the bargain between the disclosure of the invention and the patent monopoly, as claimed. Moreover, it was out of step with the disclosure and claiming requirements in other jurisdictions. It is hardly surprising, then, that reform of the s 40 provisions was a priority in the IP Australia Consultation Paper, *Getting the Balance Right: Towards a Stronger and More Efficient IP Rights System* (2009). As noted in the Executive Summary, p 3:

At present Australia's patentability standards are set at a level that is lower than the standards set in countries who are our major trading partners. Our standard for full description of inventions is lower than that elsewhere, as is our standard for inventive step. These differences potentially upset the balance between the patent system and competition. They allow the grant of broader patents in Australian than elsewhere, and they allow the grant of patents that may disclose less information about the inventions that they claim than is disclosed elsewhere. This reduces access to follow-on innovation for Australian innovators and the advantages that flow to Australian consumers from access to information about new technology and competition in the Australia marketplace.

THE NEW SUFFICIENCY AND SUPPORT REQUIREMENTS FOR DISCLOSURE AND CLAIMING

To date, there has not been the opportunity for the Australian courts to examine the new Australian provisions in s 40 of the *Patents Act* post-*Raising the Bar Act*. It is likely that the courts will look to other jurisdictions to assist in the interpretation of these new provisions.

EUROPEAN AND US LEGISLATIVE REQUIREMENTS

In the UK, the language of fair basing was dropped from the *Patents Act 1977* (UK) to give effect to Arts 83 and 84 of the EPC:

> Article 83:
>
> The European patent application must disclose the invention in a manner sufficiently clear and complete for it to be carried out by a person skilled in the art.
>
> Article 84:
>
> The claims shall define the matter for which protection is sought. They shall be clear and concise and be supported by the description.

These two requirements are commonly referred to as 'sufficiency' (Art 83) and 'support' (Art 84). These requirements are provided in s 14(3) and (4) of the *Patents Act 1977* (UK) respectively.

Similar requirements to the UK and EPC provisions are expressed in the US patent legislation in 35 USC §112:

> The specification shall contain a written description of the invention, and of the manner and process of making and using it, in such full, clear, concise, and exact terms as to enable any person skilled in the art to which it pertains, or with which it is most nearly connected, to make and use the same, and shall set forth the best mode contemplated by the inventor of carrying out his invention.
>
> The specification shall conclude with one or more claims particularly pointing out and distinctly claiming the subject matter which the applicant regards as his invention ...

As *University of Rochester v GD Searle & Co, Inc*, 358 F 3d 916 (2004), extracted below, illustrates, three grounds of invalidity can be drawn from §112.

COMPARATIVE LAW

CASE EXTRACT: COMPARATIVE LAW

University of Rochester v GD Searle & Co, Inc

358 F 3d 916 (2004)
United States Court of Appeals, Federal Circuit

[As with *Lockwood No 1* in Australia, this case clearly states that the requirements in 35 USC §112 are separate and that each is a ground for invalidity.]

Lourie J (at 921–922): Three separate requirements are contained in that provision [35 USC §112]: (1) '[t]he specification shall contain a written description of the invention'; (2) '[t]he specification shall contain a written description ... of the manner and process of making and using it [i.e., the invention] in such full, clear, concise, and exact terms as to enable any person skilled in the art to which it pertains, or with which it is most nearly connected, to make and use the same'; and (3) '[t]he specification ... shall set forth the best mode contemplated by the inventor of carrying out his invention.'

In common parlance, as well as in our and our predecessor court's case law, those three requirements are referred to as the 'written description requirement,' the 'enablement requirement,' and the 'best mode requirement,' respectively ... The United States Supreme Court also recently acknowledged written description as a statutory requirement distinct not only from the best mode requirement, but also from enablement. See *Festo Corp v Shoketsu Kinzoku Kogyo Kabushiki Co*, 535 US 722, 736, 122 S Ct 1831, 152 L Ed 2d 944 (2002) ('[A] number of statutory requirements must be satisfied before a patent can issue. The claimed subject matter must be useful, novel, and not obvious. 35 USC §§101–103 (1994 ed and Supp V). In addition, the patent application must *describe, enable, and set forth the best mode* of carrying out the invention. §112 (1994 ed). These latter requirements must be satisfied before issuance of the patent, for exclusive patent rights are given in exchange for disclosing the invention to the public.' (emphasis added)).

Although there is often significant overlap between the three requirements, they are nonetheless independent of each other. *In re Alton*, 76 F 3d 1168, 1172 (Fed Cir 1996). Thus, an invention may be described without an enabling disclosure of how to make and use it. A description of a chemical compound without a description of how to make and use it, unless within the skill of one of ordinary skill in the art, is an example. Moreover, an invention may be enabled even though it has not been described. See, eg, *In re DiLeone*, 58 CCPA 925, 436 F 2d 1404, 1405 (CCPA 1971) ('[I]t is possible for a specification to *enable* the practice of an invention as broadly as it is claimed, and still not describe that invention.'). Such can occur when enablement of a closely related invention A that is both described and enabled would similarly enable an invention B *if* B were described. A specification can likewise describe an invention without enabling the practice of the full breadth of its claims. Finally, still further disclosure might be necessary to satisfy the best mode requirement if otherwise only an inferior mode would be disclosed. *Spectra-Physics, Inc v Coherent, Inc,* 827 F 2d 1524, 1535 (Fed Cir, 1987).

The 'written description' requirement serves a teaching function, as a '*quid pro quo*' in which the public is given 'meaningful disclosure in exchange for being excluded from practicing the invention for a limited period of time.' *Enzo*, 323 F 3d at 970. Rochester argues, however, that this teaching, or 'public notice,' function, although 'virtually unchanged since the 1793 Patent Act,' in fact 'became redundant with the advent of claims in 1870.' We disagree. Statutory language does not become redundant unless repealed by Congress, in which case it no longer exists.

The later decision of the Federal Circuit Court of Appeals in *Ariad Pharmaceuticals, Inc v Eli Lilly and Co*, 598 F 3d 1336 (Fed Cir, 2010) affirmed that the three requirements are separate, and particularly that written description and enablement are independent statutory requirements.

INTERPRETATION OF THE NEW AUSTRALIAN REQUIREMENTS

GUIDANCE FROM THE EXPLANATORY MEMORANDUM

The Explanatory Memorandum to the Raising the Bar Bill 2011 confirms that it is appropriate to be guided by equivalent provisions in other jurisdictions, particularly those in the *Patents Act 1977* (UK) and the EPC.

EXPLANATORY MEMORANDUM, INTELLECTUAL PROPERTY LAWS AMENDMENT (RAISING THE BAR) BILL 2011

ITEM 8: REQUIREMENT TO DESCRIBE THE INVENTION FULLY
[S 40]

This item amends paragraph 40(2)(a) by imposing the requirement that a patent specification must disclose the invention in a manner which is clear enough and complete enough for the invention to be performed by a person skilled in the relevant art. This is intended to align the disclosure requirement with that applying in other jurisdictions with the effect that sufficient information must be provided to enable the whole width of the claimed invention to be performed by the skilled person without undue burden, or the need for further invention. This more clearly reflects a fundamental principle of the patent system: in exchange for the exclusive rights given to the patentee, the patentee must share with the public the information necessary to make and use the invention.

An application for a standard patent must be accompanied by a complete specification, which fully describes the invention for which patent protection is sought—s 40(2)(a). There are two aspects to this requirement [*Patent Gesellschaft AG v Saudi Livestock Transport and Trading Co* (1997) 37 IPR 523 at 530]:

- the specification must make the nature of the invention plain; and
- the specification must make it plain how to make or perform the invention. [Note that, although the patentee has a monopoly during the patent term, any person may use the invention afterwards: this person must be able to make the invention. Additionally, item 1, Schedule 2 is intended to clarify that other people may use the invention for certain research and regulatory approval purposes during the monopoly period: again, for this to be effective, these other people must be able to make or perform the invention.]

The person reading the specification is assumed to have reasonably competent knowledge of and skill in the relevant technical field [*Universal Oil Products v Monsanto* (1973) 46 ALJR 658].

Recent case law has clarified the extent of the current description requirement. It is met if the applicant discloses enough to enable the person reading the specification to produce something within each claim without new inventions or additions or prolonged study of matters presenting initial difficulty [*Kimberly-Clark Australia Pty Ltd v Arico Trading International Pty Ltd* (2001) 207 CLR 1 at 17; *Lockwood Security Products Pty Ltd v Doric Products Pty Ltd* (2004) 217 CLR 274 at 297; *Pfizer Overseas Pharmaceuticals v Eli Lilly and Co* (2005) 225 ALR 416; [2005] FCAFC 224 at [330]]. Despite the fact that multiple examples or embodiments of the invention may be claimed, enabling only one is sufficient. There are two problems with this:

• a patentee may gain protection over something which they have not sufficiently disclosed: the monopoly extends beyond the knowledge that the patentee has shared with the public; and

• other innovators do not have the information necessary to allow them to improve on embodiments that have not been disclosed: this hinders follow-on innovation and denies to the public the benefits of subsequent improvements on the invention.

An alternative to the existing Australian description requirement is the more stringent requirement that the skilled person reading the specification must be able to perform the invention across the whole width of the claims, not merely in relation to one among other embodiments within their scope. This requirement is consistent with the principle that the description accords with the scope of the monopoly granted.

The item is intended to modify the wording of paragraph 40(2)(a) of the Act so as to require enablement across the full width of the claims, while adopting language that is consistent with that used in other jurisdictions. The wording in the amendment is similar to s 14(3) of the UK patents legislation [*Patents Act 1977* (UK)], which has been interpreted as imposing this requirement [*Biogen Inc v Medeva plc* [1997] RPC 1; *Generics (UK) Limited v H Lundbeck A/S* [2008] EWCA Civ 311, [2008] RPC 19 at [27]]. The wording is also similar to art 83 of the European Patent Convention [*Convention on the Grant of European Patents* (European Patent Convention), opened for signature 5 October 1973, 1065 UNTS 199 (entered into force 7 October 1977)], which has been interpreted with similar effect [See European Patent Office (EPO), Board of Appeal decision T 409/91, OJ 1994, 653 …]. The intention is that paragraph 40(2)(a) be given, as close as is practicable, the same effect as the corresponding provisions of UK legislation and the European Patent Convention

A specification that provides a single example of the invention may satisfy the requirements, but only where the skilled person can extend the teaching of the specification to produce the invention across the full width of the claims, without undue burden, or the need for further invention.

However, it is expected to be more likely that, where the claims are broad, the specification will need to give a number of examples or describe alternative embodiments or variations extending over the full scope of the claims. This ensures that the monopoly extends only to that which could reasonably be said to be disclosed and no further.

If, on its face, the specification would appear to the skilled person to lack sufficient disclosure, the onus of establishing that the invention is described in enough detail lies with the applicant (see item 14).

The item also clarifies that the existing requirement for a complete specification to include the best method known to the applicant of performing the invention remains unchanged.

…

ITEM 9: FAIR BASIS
[S 40]

This item amends the Act to replace the 'fair basis' requirement with a 'support' requirement.

Subsection 40(3) of the *Patents Act* requires the claims of a complete specification to be, among other things, 'fairly based' on the matter described in the specification. The concept of 'fair basis' in Australian patent law is intended to achieve two results:

- ensuring consistency between the monopoly claimed in the patent and the description of the invention; and
- ensuring that the claims of a patent are entitled to the priority date which the patent applicant asserts.

A lengthy body of case law has developed interpreting the 'fair basis' requirement, culminating in the High Court decision *Lockwood Security Products Pty Ltd v Doric Products Pty Ltd* [(2004) 217 CLR 274] ...

Overseas law generally requires there to be a relationship between the claims and the description, and between the claims and any document from which priority is being claimed. This is expressed by the requirement that a claim be 'supported by' [European Patent Convention, Article 84; UK *Patents Act 1977*, paragraph 14 (5)(c)] or 'fully supported by' [Patent Cooperation Treaty, Article 6; draft Substantive Patent Law Treaty, May 2004, Article 10 (3)] the description. Broadly speaking, the terms 'support' and 'full support' pick up two concepts [*Guidelines for Examination in the European Patent Office*, European Patent Office, April 2009, at 6.1, accessed 6 November 2009]:

- there must be a basis in the description for each claim; and
- the scope of the claims must not be broader than is justified by the extent of the description, drawings and contribution to the art.

Despite the underlying concept and policy between fair basis and support being similar, the different terminology has produced different substantive law in different countries.

The difference in substantive law in different countries causes unnecessary complexity and uncertainty for applicants seeking protection in Australia and other jurisdictions ... [H]aving different standards in different countries imposes costs on global innovators, who must familiarise themselves with the varying requirements.

This item is intended to align the Australian requirement with overseas jurisdictions' requirements (such as the UK). Overseas case law and administrative decisions in respect of the 'support' requirement will be available to Australian courts and administrative decision-makers to assist in interpreting the new provision.

There must also be consistency, or basis, for each claim in the description.

GUIDANCE FROM EUROPEAN JURISPRUDENCE

Despite the clear message in the Explanatory Memorandum that UK and European case law can be relied on to provide guidance on the interpretation of the new s 40 provisions, there are differences in the legislative requirements between jurisdictions that need to be taken into account. As a consequence Australian courts may need to take a cautious approach as to the reliance they place on the interpretation of sufficiency and support provided in UK and European jurisprudence.

One particular curiosity about UK law is that s 72(1)(c) of the *Patents Act 1977* (UK) provides for revocation pursuant to the sufficiency ground; that is, where the specification of the patent does not disclose the invention clearly enough and completely enough for it to be performed by a person skilled in the art. However, there is no specific ground for revocation based on lack of support. This anomaly has led to a body of jurisprudence considering whether there is a single unified concept of 'enabling disclosure', embacing both sufficiency and support. Lord Walker succinctly summarised this body of case law at [17]–[20] of his judgment in *Generics (UK) Ltd v H Lundbeck A/S* [2009] UKHL 12; [2009] RPC 13, extracted below. Given that both the sufficiency and support grounds are available pursuant to s 138(3)(f) of the *Patents Act 1990*, the Australian courts may not find that this body of UK and European case law is particularly illuminating. There are other aspects of UK and European jurisprudence that may not particularly suit the Australian situation. In particular, the courts may not find the UK and European requirement that the patent monopoly corresponds to the 'technical contribution to the art' (a notion raised by Lord Hoffmann in *Biogen Inc v Medeva Plc* [1997] RPC 1), to be particularly persuasive. *Generics v Lundbeck* again provides a useful summary on the technical contribution component of the enabling disclosure requirement in UK and European law. One difficulty with this decision of the House of Lords, however, is that the three Law Lords who provided detailed reasons for their decision (Lords Walker, Mance and Neuberger) provided somewhat different views on the meaning of this requirement. This particular point is illustrated at [22]–[37] in Lord Walker's judgment, [47] in Lord Mance's judgment, and [83] and [95]–[101] in Lord Neuberger's judgment in the extract below.

In Australia, the High Court in *Lockwood No 1* specifically addressed this issue at [46], holding that:

> the 'inventiveness' or 'meritoriousness' of, or the technical contribution made by, the specification are issues to be examined if there is an objection under s 18(1)(b) of the Act for want of novelty or absence of an inventive step (ie obviousness). There is no reason to introduce them into the fair basing question.

Recognising that fair basing has been replaced by support, it is nevertheless difficult to see how this alone could persuade the Australian courts to introduce technical contribution considerations into their interpretation of the new s 40 grounds. On the other hand, the Explanatory Memorandum clearly suggests an intention that the requirement of consistency between claims and description (fair basing under s 40 pre-*Raising the Bar Act*) is *additional* to the requirement that the claims not be broader 'than is justified by the description, drawings *and contribution to the art*' (our emphasis). In this context it is not clear how 'contribution' is to be understood, unless by reference to the invention. The legislative history suggests an intention to narrow the scope of the monopoly patentees can obtain; how exactly this is understood or implemented by the Australian courts remains to be seen.

Another particular feature of UK and European jurisprudence that is linked with the technical contribution requirement is whether a distinction can be made between claims to products by process and products per se. Again, this was a matter dealt with at some length in *Generics v Lundbeck*, particularly at [22]–[25] in Lord Walker's judgment and [85]–[99] in Lord Neuberger's judgment.[1] A careful reading of these reasons and other UK case law suggests that the difference between Australian law pre-*Raising the Bar Act* may be less than might appear if one focuses only on *Biogen Inc v Medeva Plc*.

CASE EXTRACT: COMPARATIVE LAW

Generics (UK) Ltd v H Lundbeck A/S

[2009] UKHL 12; [2009] RPC 13
House of Lords

[This case concerned the same subject matter as in the Australian case of *H Lundbeck A/S v Alphapharm Pty Ltd* [2009] FCAFC 70; (2009) 177 FCR 151, discussed in Chapter 11 with regard to the Australian novelty requirement. As with the Australian case, it has had a convoluted litigation history. This decision of the House of Lords focused solely on the ground for revocation found in s 72(1)(c) of the *Patents Act 1977* (UK).]

Lord Walker: 17. Some judges have in the past been puzzled that section 72 of the *Patents Act 1977* (power to revoke patents on application) reproduces (in subsection (1)(c)) the substance and wording of the requirement in section 14(3) [sufficiency], but does not appear to reproduce section 14(5)(c) [support]. That puzzle was near the surface of the discussion, but was not in terms resolved, by this House in *Asahi Kasei Kogyo KK's Application* [1991] RPC 485 ('*Asahi*'). That appeal raised an issue on section 5(2)(a) of the *Patents Act 1977* (which also refers to an invention being 'supported'). Lord Oliver of Aylmerton, with the agreement of the rest of the House (and with Lord Jauncey of Tullichettle delivering a concurring opinion), seems to have treated the requirements of section 14(3) as necessarily including those of section 14(5)(c). Lord Oliver said at pp 535–6:

> The Act does not contain any definition of the word 'supported' but some assistance can be obtained from the provisions of section 14(5) which require the claim in an application to be 'supported' by the description. That must, I think, involve the conclusion that if that which is contained in the description of the specification does not enable the claim to be established, it cannot be said to 'support' it, for the Act can hardly have contemplated a complete application for a patent lacking some of the material necessary to sustain the claims made. Since, therefore, subsection (3) of section 14 requires in terms that the specification disclose the invention in a way which will enable it to be performed by a person skilled in the art (i.e. it must contain an 'enabling disclosure') it follows that a description in an earlier application which contains no enabling disclosure will not 'support' the invention so as to enable it, as an invention, to claim priority from the date of that application under section 5(2)(a).

---

1   A detailed review of these aspects of UK and European jurisprudence, and their consequences for Australia is provided by S Burley, 'Is *Lockwood v Doric* Really Dead, or Does It Just Look That Way?—A Review of the New Requirements for Textual Disclosure under the Australian Patents Act' (2014) 99 *IP Forum* 36.

COMPARATIVE LAW

18. That is how Lord Hoffmann (with the concurrence of the rest of the House) understood *Asahi* in *Biogen*. He stated (at p 47):

> The explanation of section 14(5)(c) in *Asahi* seems to me to provide an answer to a point which puzzled the Court of Appeal in *Genentech Inc's Patent* [1989] RPC 147. The Court noted that although section 14(5)(c) is a statutory requirement for a valid patent application, non-compliance is not a ground for revocation of a patent which has been granted. Section 72(1) states exhaustively the grounds upon which a patent may be revoked. These grounds do not, as such, include non-compliance with section 14(5). But the substantive effect of section 14(5)(c), namely that the description should, together with the rest of the specification, constitute an enabling disclosure, is given effect by section 72(1)(c). There is accordingly no gap or illogicality in the scheme of the Act.

Lord Mustill (at p 31) expressly concurred in this. In dividing his opinion into sections Lord Hoffmann distinguished between 'support for the claims' (section 12) and 'sufficiency' (section 14) but he applied the same reasoning to both.

19. There is therefore high authority that the requirements of section 14(3) and section 14(5)(c) are closely connected. The main difference between them is that section 14(3) relates to the specification as a whole, whereas section 14(5)(c) relates to the claims which define the monopoly sought by the inventor. I repeat in a fuller form the citation from para 3.3 of *Exxon/Fuel Oils* (T 409/91) [1994] OJEPO 653:

> Furthermore, Article 84 EPC also requires that the claims must be supported by the description, in other words it is the definition of the invention in the claims that needs support. In the Board's judgment, this requirement reflects the general legal principle that the extent of the patent monopoly, as defined by the claims, should correspond to the technical contribution to the art in order for it to be supported, or justified ...

20. Section 14(3) and (5)(c) operate together, as EPC Articles 83 and 84 operate together, to spell out the need for an 'enabling disclosure', which is central to the law of patents: see Lord Oliver in *Asahi* at pp 531–532, and Lord Hoffmann in *Biogen* [*Inc v Medeva Plc* 1997] RPC 1] at pp 46–51 and in *Kirin-Amgen Inc v Hoechst Marion Roussel Ltd* [2005] RPC 169 ('*Kirin-Amgen*') at paras 102–116. The disclosure must be such as to enable the invention to be performed (that is, to be carried out if it is a process, or to be made if it is a product) to the full extent of the claims. The question whether there is sufficient enabling disclosure often interacts with a question of construction as to the extent of the claims. For instance in *American Home Products Corp v Novartis Pharmaceuticals UK Ltd* [2001] RPC 159 ('*American Home Products*') the disclosure would have been insufficient if the claims had extended, not merely to rapamycin (a known antifungal antibiotic which proved effective as an immunosuppressant) but also to derivatives of rapamycin. The Court of Appeal held that the claims should be narrowly construed, and on that basis there was sufficient enabling disclosure.

...

PRODUCT CLAIMS

22. Judges have often observed that the wide abstract terms in which patent law is expressed must always be related to the facts of the particular case. That is especially true in relation to the sufficiency of a product claim, since the term 'product' covers such an extremely wide variety. A product may be as simple as a baby's disposable diaper (see *Mölnlycke AB v Procter & Gamble Ltd* [1992] FSR 549

COMPARATIVE LAW

('*Mölnlycke*') or a corkscrew (see *Hallen Co v Brabantia (UK) Ltd* [1991] RPC 195) or as complex as an 'heavier-than-air flying machine' referred to by Lord Hoffmann in *Biogen*, or a class of microscopic organisms, produced by recombinant DNA technology, such as was considered by this House in *Biogen* and *Kirin-Amgen*. Where the product is manufactured the specification is likely to include drawings as well as a verbal description, but the drawings are almost always described as an example (or embodiment). Otherwise (in the absence from United Kingdom patent law of a doctrine of equivalents— see *Kirin-Amgen* [2005] RPC 169, paras 36 ff) competitors would probably be able, by some small variation in design, to exploit the inventive concept without infringement. For similar reasons (especially in the field of chemical compounds) patent applications are likely to seek to obtain protection, not for a single compound, but for a class of compounds, and sometimes an almost unimaginably large class (see for instance *Pharmacia Corp v Merck & Co Inc* [2002] RPC 41, where claim 1 is set out, in an accessible form, in para 11; Arden LJ recorded, in para 150, that it comprised 'literally trillions' of formulae).

...

24. A 'product-by-process' claim is a claim to a product, but described in such a way as to define it by the process by which it is produced. Such claims are discouraged by the European Patent Office ('EPO'). They are permitted by the EPO only where there is a claim to a new substance whose difference from a known substance cannot be described in chemical or physical terms (see *Kirin-Amgen* [2005] RPC 169 at paras 88–91, and also at para 109; note that erythropoietin itself could not have been patented because it was a known substance occurring in nature). The expression 'product-by-process' was used in argument in *Biogen* (at p 27) and this submission was accepted, if not in those precise terms, by Lord Hoffmann in his opinion in the paragraph (at p 40) which is quoted in paragraph 26 below. Lord Hoffmann also used it, in relation to *Biogen*, in his judgment in the Court of Appeal (in para 33).

25. A single chemical compound is a product for the purposes of UK patent law (the restrictive provisions of section 38A of the *Patents Act* 1907, as amended in 1919, having disappeared from the *Patents Act* 1949). It is moreover a product of a special character, since it is a product which, simply as a chemical compound (as in claim 1 of the patent in suit), can have only one embodiment (though if it is used in a pharmaceutical preparation it can of course have numerous embodiments in terms of dosages and non-active ingredients, as in claims 3 and 5 of the patent in suit). Statements of general principle relating to inventions with many embodiments may be irrelevant to an invention which consists of a single chemical compound.

...

35. My noble and learned friends Lord Mance and Lord Neuberger of Abbotsbury (whose opinions I have had the advantage of reading in draft) both draw attention to the importance of UK patent law aligning itself, so far as possible, with the jurisprudence of the EPO (and especially decisions of its Enlarged Boards of Appeal). National courts may reach different conclusions as to the evaluation of the evidence in the light of the relevant principles, but the principles themselves should be the same, stemming as they do from the EPC. There is no decision of an Enlarged Board of Appeal directly in point on the subject of technical contribution. The most relevant decision of a Technical Board of Appeal is *Exxon*, decided in 1993.

...

37. The Board also stated (para 3.5):

> Although the requirements of Article 83 and Article 84 are directed to different parts of the patent application, since Article 83 relates to the disclosure of the invention, whilst Article 84 deals with the definition of the invention by the claims, the underlying purpose of the requirement of support by the description, insofar as its substantive aspect is concerned, and of the requirement of sufficient disclosure is the same, namely to ensure that the patent monopoly should be justified by the actual technical contribution to the art. Thus a claim may well be supported by the description in the sense that it corresponds to it, but still encompass subject-matter which is not sufficiently disclosed within the meaning of Article 83 EPC as it cannot be performed without undue burden, or vice versa.

38. These statements of principle appear to me to support the views that I have expressed. But for present purposes the most significant part of the decision in *Exxon* is in the later part of para 3.5:

> In the Board's judgment, this case differs from those where a class of chemical compounds is claimed and only one method of preparing them is necessary to enable a skilled person to carry out the invention, ie to prepare all compounds of the claimed class. Rather, the present case is comparable to cases where a group of chemical compounds is claimed, and not all of the claimed compounds can be prepared by the methods disclosed in the description or being part of the common general knowledge (see eg T 206/83, OJ EPO 1987, 5). In the latter case, it was not held sufficient for the purpose of Article 83 EPC to disclose a method of obtaining only some members of the claimed class of chemical compositions.

That statement could hardly be clearer. Claim 1 in the patent in suit is to a single chemical composition.

...

Lord Mance: 47. There are passages in Lord Hoffmann's speech in *Biogen Inc v Medeva plc* which can be read as supporting an approach tying the scope of any patent, whether to a product or to a process, to the inventive step or technical contribution involved in its creation, and as justifying this on utilitarian grounds. Thus Lord Hoffmann referred at p 49 to the Technical Board of Appeal in *Exxon/Fuel Oils* (T 409/91) [1994] OJEPO 653, para 3.3 as reasserting 'well-established principles for what amounts to sufficiency of disclosure', when it said that the requirement for the claims to be supported by the description (article 84 of the European Patent Convention, mirrored in s 14(5)(c) of the *Patents Act 1977*) 'reflects the general legal principle that the extent of the patent monopoly, as defined by the claims, should correspond to the technical contribution to the art in order for it to be supported, or justified'. Lord Hoffmann also said at p 52 in *Biogen Inc v Medeva plc* that Professor Murray 'showed by his invention' (the word being here used I think to mean inventive step) that 'it could be done', i.e. that 'known recombinant techniques could ... be used to make the antigens in a prokaryotic host cell' (see p 51 lines 46–47). He continued:

> Those who followed, even by different routes, could have greater confidence by reason of his success. I do not think this is enough to justify a monopoly of the whole field. I suppose it could be said that Samuel Morse had shown that electric telegraphy could be done. The Wright Brothers showed that heavier-than-air flight was possible, but that did not entitle them to a monopoly of heavier-than-air flying machines. ... The technical contribution made in such cases deserves to be recognised. But care is needed not to stifle further research and healthy competition by allowing

the first person who has found a way of achieving an obviously desirable goal to monopolise every other way of doing so. (See Merges and Nelson, 'On the Complex Economics of Patent Scope' (1990) 90 *Columbia Law Review* 839.)

. . .

Lord Neuberger: 83. It was also contended on behalf of the appellants that, if the Patent extended to escitalopram as a product, the respondents would be accorded a monopoly which exceeded their technical contribution to the art. Although it is an extra-statutory concept, I accept that, at least as a general rule, the monopoly to be granted to the patentee is to be assessed by reference to the 'technical contribution' made by the teaching of the patent. That is an approach regularly adopted by the Technical Board of Appeal of the European Patent Office ('the Board'): see, for example, T 409/91 *EXXON/Fuel Oils* [1994] OJEPO 653, para 3.3. However, to put it at its lowest, it can be said that the respondent's technical contribution in this case was to make available, for the first time, a product which had previously been unavailable, namely the isolated (+)-enantiomer of citalopram. On that basis, it would appear to follow that the respondent was entitled to claim the enantiomer.

. . .

85. It seems to me, however, that the application of that observation to this case could, to put it at its lowest, fairly be said to assist the respondent: given that the (+)-enantiomer claimed has been judged to be new, it should be patentable. However, that observation was concerned with the permissible breadth of a process claim, not with the circumstances in which it is permissible to make a product claim. Indeed, it is interesting to note that [the trial judge] Kitchin J's formulation of the principle he was applying at the end of [2007] RPC 32, para 265, and quoted at the end of para 78 above, seems also to be concerned with process claims, not product claims.

. . .

90. In the light of this discussion, it appears clear to me that, unless precluded by the reasoning in *Biogen* [1997] RPC 1, on which Kitchin J primarily relied in his decision and on which Mr Thorley primarily relies in his argument, the product claim in the present case is valid. I appreciate that this means that, by finding one method of making a product, a person can obtain a monopoly for that product. However, that applies to any product claim. Further, where (as here) the product is a known desideratum, it can be said (as Lord Walker pointed out) that the invention is all the more creditable, as it is likely that there has been more competition than where the product has not been thought of. The role of fortuity in patent law cannot be doubted: it is inevitable, as in almost any area of life. Luck as well as skill often determines, for instance, who is first to file, whether a better product or process is soon discovered, or whether an invention turns out to be valuable. Further, while the law must be principled, it must also be clear and consistent.

THE INSUFFICIENCY ARGUMENT BASED ON *BIOGEN* [1997] RPC 1

91. As I have mentioned, the principal plank in the appellants' argument is the opinion of Lord Hoffmann in *Biogen* [1997] RPC 1, no doubt for the reasons just discussed. Mr Thorley was able to point to a number of observations in that opinion which, at least if read on their own, might at first sight be said to support his contention that, given that the (+)-enantiomer was known to be a desirable goal, the only technical contribution of the Patent was the diol method of making the enantiomer, and accordingly it is that process, and not the enantiomer, which should have been claimed.

92. Of the seven passages in the speech of Lord Hoffmann Mr Thorley particularly relied on, I shall limit myself to three, although the observations which follow apply equally to the other passages. At [1997] RPC 1, 48, Lord Hoffmann said that 'if the claims include a number of discrete methods or products, the patentee must enable the invention to be performed in respect of each of them'. But in this case the claim is to a single product, and it is clear that the product is enabled by the disclosure in the Patent.

93. At [1997] RPC 1, 50, there is this: '[The issue] is not whether the claimed invention could deliver the goods, but whether the claims cover other ways in which they might be delivered: ways which owe nothing to the teaching of the patent or any principle which it disclosed'. This is perhaps the most important of the three passages for present purposes. The vital point is that Lord Hoffmann was not dealing with a simple product claim, as is involved in this Patent. As he explained at [1997] RPC 1, 40, the claim in that case was 'to a product, a molecule identified partly by the way in which it has been made …. and partly by what it does'. In that case, the patentee could claim neither the product (a DNA fragment of the so-called Dane particle), as it had already been made (see per Aldous J at first instance at [1995] RPC 25, 57), nor the process (recombinant DNA technology enabling expression in a cell), as it had already been invented (see at [1995] RPC 25, 58 and 65). Nor could he identify the product in any other way, as it had not been mapped or sequenced (see e.g. at [1995] RPC 25, 65).

94. Accordingly, the invention claimed in *Biogen* [1997] RPC 1 was, as it were, the notion of subjecting the product (the unsequenced DNA fragment from the Dane particle) to the process (recombinant DNA technology) in order for it to be expressed to produce HBV antigens. It was therefore at least as much as a process claim as a product claim. In those circumstances, one can well see why the claim was held to be insufficient. The patent disclosed one way in which the DNA fragments could produce HBV antigens, but the claim 'cover[ed] other ways in which they might be delivered, ways which owed nothing to the teaching of the patent or any principle which it disclosed' [1997] RPC 1, 50. Accordingly, the claim was very different from a simple product claim as in the present case. This analysis of the facts in *Biogen* [1997] RPC 1 also explains why Lord Hoffmann said at pp 51–52 that 'the excessive breadth' of the patent in that case was due 'to the fact that the same results could be produced by different means' from that disclosed by the patent.

95. Finally, at [1997] RPC 1, 54, Lord Hoffmann emphasised that 'the extent of the monopoly claimed [should not] exceed … the technical contribution to the art made by the invention as described in the specification'. As already explained, in the context of a simple product claim such as the present (especially where the claim is to a single chemical product), the technical contribution is (at least in the absence of special factors) the product itself. As I have suggested, the technical contribution can often be equated with non-obvious novelty—what is new to the art and not obvious is really another way of identifying the technical contribution.

96. The notion that Lord Hoffmann was not seeking to depart from the established approach of the Board is supported by the weight he placed on the reasoning in its decisions, especially *Genentech/ Polypeptide expression* [1989] OJEPO 275 and T409/91 *EXXON/Fuel Oils* to which I have referred— see at [1997] RPC 1, 48–53. The fact that he took a different view from the Board on the patent in suit does not detract from this point: he was considering an argument which had not been raised in the opposition proceedings—see section 12 of his judgment at [1997] RPC 1, 52–53. Indeed, at the

COMPARATIVE LAW

end of that section Lord Hoffmann was at pains to point out that there was no 'divergence between the jurisprudence of this court and that of the EPO'.

. . .

99. In my opinion, therefore, in agreement with the Court of Appeal, the opinion of Lord Hoffmann in *Biogen* [1997] RPC 1, though a tour de force as Lord Walker says, is of no assistance to the appellants in this case. It applied in the light of the very unusual nature of the claim in that case. Far from being a straightforward product claim (as in this case) or even a product-by-process claim (as discussed in *Kirin-Amgen* [2005] RPC 9, paras 86–91 and 101), the claim was to a product identified in part by how it was made and in part by what it did – almost a process-by-product-by-process claim.

. . .

101. It may be that this is in part attributable to the focussing by Lord Hoffmann in *Biogen* [1997] RPC 1, 42–46 on the 'inventive step' involved in the alleged invention in that case. There is a difference between the 'inventive step' or 'inventive concept', on the one hand, and the 'technical contribution to the art', on the other hand. I respectfully agree with the explanation of the difference between the two concepts given in paras 29 to 31 of Lord Walker's opinion. When considering the validity of a simple product claim (such as is under scrutiny on this appeal), it may be that concentrating on the identification of the inventive step rather than the technical contribution can lead to error. 'Inventive step' suggests how something has been done, and, in the case of a product claim at any rate, one is primarily concerned with what has been allegedly invented, not how it has been done. On the other hand where the claim is for a process or (as in *Biogen* [1997] RPC 1) includes a process, the issue of how the alleged invention has been achieved seems to be more in point.

—**13**—

PATENT OWNERSHIP, RIGHTS AND LIMITATIONS

INTRODUCTION

This chapter analyses the legal consequences of the patent grant: who owns it, what can they do with it, and how are they restricted in what they can do with it? The chapter proceeds on the assumption that a valid patent is in existence, recognising that patents are open to challenge throughout their entire life and that counterclaims for revocation frequently accompany infringement actions.

The chapter begins by reviewing the law relating to patent ownership. Section 15 of the *Patents Act 1990* (Cth) is the starting point for the consideration of patent ownership. It provides:

> (1) Subject to this Act, a patent for an invention may only be granted to a person who:
>   (a) is the inventor; or
>   (b) would, on the grant of a patent for the invention, be entitled to have the patent assigned to the person; or
>   (c) derives title to the invention from the inventor or a person mentioned in paragraph (b); or
>   (d) is the legal representative of a deceased person mentioned in paragraph (a), (b) or (c).
> (2) A patent may be granted to a person whether or not he or she is an Australian citizen.

The grant of a patent gives the patentee exclusive property rights during the term of the patent, as provided in s 13 of the *Patents Act*:

> (1) Subject to this Act, a patent gives the patentee the exclusive rights, during the term of the patent, to exploit the invention and to authorise another person to exploit the invention.
> (2) The exclusive rights are personal property and are capable of assignment and of devolution by law.
> (3) A patent has effect throughout the patent area.

The definition of 'exploit' in Sch 1 of the *Patents Act* is also relevant:

> in relation to an invention, [exploit] includes:
>
> (a) where the invention is a product—make, hire, sell or otherwise dispose of the product, offer to make, sell, hire or otherwise dispose of it, use or import it, or keep it for the purpose of doing any of those things; or

(b) where the invention is a method or process—use the method or process or do any act mentioned in paragraph (a) in respect of a product resulting from such use.

Although these rights are cast in positive terms in Australian patent legislation, they are not absolute. This chapter considers limitations on the rights of the patentee included in the *Patents Act*, including exemptions from infringement, compulsory licensing, and use by or with the authority of the various Australian governments (collectively, 'the Crown'). Uses of the rights granted under a patent are also subject to other legislation. For example, a pharmaceutical protected by an Australian patent can only be marketed once the requirements of the *Therapeutic Goods Act 1989* (Cth) have been satisfied.

In some patent instruments the patentee's rights are cast in a negative, rather than positive, light. These instruments provide that the patentee has the right to stop others from exploiting the invention (by instituting infringement proceedings) rather than the right to exploit it. Article 28 of the *Agreement on Trade-Related Aspects of Intellectual Property Rights* (the 'TRIPS Agreement') (1994) is drafted in this way:

1   A patent shall confer on its owner the following exclusive rights:
    (a)   where the subject matter of a patent is a product, to prevent third parties not having the owner's consent from the acts of: making, using, offering for sale, selling, or importing for these purposes that product;
    (b)   where the subject matter of a patent is a process, to prevent third parties not having the owner's consent from the act of using the process, and from the acts of: using, offering for sale, selling, or importing for these purposes at least the product obtained directly by that process.
2   Patent owners shall also have the right to assign, or transfer by succession, the patent and to conclude licensing contracts.

OWNERSHIP

It can be very difficult to sort out who has the right of ownership in patents. As indicated in s 15(1)(a) of the *Patents Act*, the inventor has the first right to the grant of a patent. It will often be the case that there will be more than one inventor. Section 16(1) provides for co-ownership, stating that unless there is agreement to the contrary, each co-owner is entitled to an equal undivided share of the patent and entitled to exercise the exclusive rights given by the patent for their own benefit without accounting to the others. However, each co-owner may not grant a licence under the patent, or assign an interest in it, without the consent of the others.

Unlike the *Copyright Act 1968* (Cth), there is no express provision in the *Patents Act* dealing with ownership in the employment context, although s 15(1)(b) and (c) might have a role to play. Arguably a term can be implied into the employment contract to the effect that patents and other IP rights arising from the course of employment are to be assigned to the employer. Terms of this nature may be implied by fact and law. Generally, however, it is prudent to include in the employment contract express terms providing for ownership of IP and rights to apportionment of royalties and licence fees. Some employers may require deeds of assignment to be made.

CASE EXTRACT: PRECEDENT

Spencer Industries Pty Ltd v Collins

[2003] FCA 542; (2003) 58 IPR 425
Federal Court of Australia

[This is an appeal from a decision of a delegate of the Commissioner of Patents, who decided that ownership of a petty patent vested solely in Collins and not in Spencer Industries, his employer. Spencer Industries argued that the invention was made by Collins during the course and scope of his employment.]

Branson J: 78. There is no written employment contract between Spencer Industries and Mr Collins which defines with precision the scope of Mr Collins' employment. I accept the submission of Spencer Industries that in this circumstance, in considering the scope of Mr Collins' employment, it is necessary to give consideration to the nature and seniority of the employee's position with Spencer Industries, the nature of his duties as Sales Manager and whether he received a specific directive relating to the invention.

79. In my view the evidence makes it plain that the position that Mr Collins held within Spencer Industries was principally a sales position. However, as might be expected in a relatively small, family owned, company he occasionally undertook tasks outside his area of principal responsibility. I find that it was in the nature of Mr Collins' employment that he could be given reasonable directions to perform duties outside of the area of sales that were within the area of his technical skills and that were not incompatible with his principal responsibility for sales.

80. More particularly, I find that it fell within the scope and course of Mr Collins' employment as Sales Manager for him to recommend expansion of the product range of Spencer Industries where his contact with purchasers and potential purchasers suggested that expansion would be in the interest of Spencer Industries. I further find that it fell within the scope and course of Mr Collins' employment as Sales Manager for him to use his technical skills to demonstrate the function and utility of the products that it was his responsibility to sell.

81. I find that Mr Collins in fact contributed to the invention of the air-cooled hub and the design of the tyre rasp spacer. These activities, I find, fell outside his ordinary duties as Sales Manager but within the residual area in which it was open to Spencer Industries to direct him, whether expressly or implicitly, to use his technical skills to undertake additional duties.

82. However, I reject the submission of the appellant that because Mr Collins had a duty as Sales Manager of Spencer Industries to advance the sales of Spencer Industries any invention made by him which was capable of advancing Spencer Industries' sales was an invention made by him within the course and scope of his employment. This submission is, in my view, unacceptably broad in ambit.

83. It was no part of Mr Collins' ongoing duties to invent products for Spencer Industries. Mr Pincott [who, until March 2002, controlled Spencer Industries], the evidence discloses, on more than one occasion reminded Mr Collins that his ongoing duties were exclusively sales related. Nor was the Invention the outcome of a direction given to Mr Collins within what I have described as the residual

PRECEDENT

area in which he could be directed to perform tasks other than sales tasks. Mr Collins was not directed by Mr Pincott, or anyone, to invent a new rasp blade or to undertake any inventive activities which resulted in the Invention. Mr Collins advised Mr Pincott of the Invention, which he had conceived and developed in his own time, only when the inventive steps concerning it had been completed. The Invention was not, in my view, the product of the work which Mr Collins was paid to do (*Sterling [Engineering] Co Ltd v Patchett* [[1955] AC 534] per Lord Reid at 547).

84. In arguing to the contrary of the above, the respondent placed weight on Mr Collins' seniority within Spencer Industries. As is mentioned above, Spencer Industries is a family owned company. The evidence satisfies me that at all relevant times actual authority within the company vested almost exclusively in Mr Pincott and members of his family ('the family'). Mr Collins did not in any way control the business of Spencer Industries. Nor was his relationship with Spencer Industries of the close and confidential character considered by Byrne J in *Worthington Pumping Engine Co v Moore* [(1902) 20 RPC 41] at 46. The fact that Mr Collins' salary exceeded that of the Managing Director and the General Manager, both members of the family, does not indicate to the contrary. It was for the family, and particularly I assume Mr Pincott, to determine how, when and in what form family members should reap the benefit of the company's success.

85. The respondent also placed weight on conduct of Mr Collins by which he appears to have acknowledged that Spencer Industries was entitled to the benefit of the Invention. The fact that Mr Collins envisaged, as I find that he did, that the Invention would be exploited by Spencer Industries does not establish that he undertook the invention within the course and scope of his employment by Spencer Industries. I am satisfied that Mr Collins had little understanding of intellectual property law while he was employed by Spencer Industries. I am also satisfied Mr Collins hoped that he and Spencer Industries would work together to exploit the Invention; that it would be added to the [Spencer] Industries range of products which he was responsible for selling. However, I am also satisfied that Mr Collins expected that Spencer Industries would appropriately reward him if the Invention proved a commercial success. It was when Mr Pincott made it quite clear to Mr Collins that [Spencer] Industries proposed to assume complete control of the benefit of the Invention without negotiating any financial reward for Mr Collins that Mr Collins unequivocally refused to sign the deed of assignment offered to him by Mr Pincott.

86. In my view, the decision of the Delegate that the Invention was made by Mr Collins outside the course of his duties as an employee of Spencer Industries should be upheld. Mr Collins has not assigned the benefit of the Invention to Spencer Industries. Spencer Industries would not, on the grant of a patent for the Invention, have been entitled to have the patent assigned to it within the meaning of s 15(1)(b) of the Act.

THE UNIVERSITY CONTEXT

In the public research sector, funding agencies in many jurisdictions have relinquished ownership rights to patents arising out of funded research. In the USA, for example, the *Bayh-Dole Act* (as incorporated into 35 USC §§200–212) vests ownership in universities rather than in the federal government, although the government does retain 'march-in' rights (providing it with the right to take over exploitation of the patented invention). In Australia the National Principles of Intellectual

Property Management for Publicly Funded Research were released by the Australian Research Council and adopted by the National Health and Medical Research Council in 2013, replacing an earlier set of principles. They also initially vest ownership in research institutions receiving and administering research funding.

Many universities and other research organisations have IP policies providing for ownership and royalty sharing. However, unless these have been properly promulgated they will not be binding on employees. Two cases illustrate the risks to universities if they do not address ownership of IP generated by academics during the course of employment and outside the employment context.

In *Victoria University of Technology v Wilson* [2004] VSC 33; (2004) 60 IPR 392, academics employed by the Victoria University of Technology had developed an electronic international trade exchange to facilitate transactions through a controlled electronic trading environment during the course of their employment at the university. They subsequently developed the technology in the private sphere and acquired a patent. The university alleged that it had a constructive trust in the patent. Nettle J held that the university's IP policy did not apply as it had not been properly promulgated. His Honour then considered the implication of terms in the employment contract, encapsulating the key legal issues at [104]:

> The law is well settled upon the position of an officer or employee who makes an invention affecting the business of his or her employer. It is an implied term of employment that any invention or discovery made in the course of the employment of the employee in doing that which he is engaged and instructed to do during the time of his employment, and during working hours, and using the materials of his employers, is the property of the employer and not of the employee. Having made a discovery or invention in course of such work, the employee becomes a trustee for the employer of that invention or discovery, and he is therefore as a trustee bound to give the benefit of any such discovery or invention to his employer. But the mere existence of the employer/employee relationship will not give the employer ownership of inventions made by the employee during the term of the relationship. And that is so even if the invention is germane to and useful for the employer's business, and even though the employee may have made use of the employer's time and resources in bringing the invention to completion. Certainly, all the circumstances must be considered in each case, but unless the contract of employment expressly so provides, or an invention is the product of work which the employee was paid to perform, it is unlikely that any invention made by the employee will be held to belong to the employer.

Nettle J did not accept that the academics in the circumstances of this case were 'retained to invent' (at [119]–[122]). However, in the circumstances his Honour did accept at [149] that there was breach of fiduciary obligations, in that the academics had taken advantage of an opportunity which they ought to have pursued (only) on behalf of the university.

The following case involved a more complex patent ownership dispute in the university context.

CASE EXTRACT: CURRENT LAW

University of Western Australia v Gray

[2009] FCAFC 116; (2009) 179 FCR 346
Federal Court of Australia, Full Court

[The dispute in this matter related to the ownership of patents for surgical methods. Dr Bruce Gray was appointed as Professor of Surgery at the University of Western Australia (UWA) in 1985. The dispute also involved Sirtex Medica Ltd, of which he was the director, and the Cancer Research Institute, an entity that was created to support his research. UWA alleged that Dr Gray breached his contract of employment and his fiduciary duty by failing to disclose patentable inventions to it. In the appeal decision of the Full Court, it was held that the sole question was whether there was an implication of a term by law that Dr Gray was under a 'duty to invent'.]

Lindgren, Finn and Bennett JJ: 181. Although UWA changed its stance on the implied term during the hearing before us, it finally accepted (Transcript 159) that it was required to establish that Dr Gray's employment contract was one of the class or type in which the employee invention term would be implied. To that end, and to put the matter shortly, UWA contended, first, that there was no relevant distinction between a university as an employer and any other employer; and, secondly, that Dr Gray's contractual duty to undertake research was, in the circumstances, sufficient to bring it within the class of contract attracting the implied term.

182. We disagree with both contentions. The first disregards the distinctiveness of universities (such as UWA); the second disregards both the distinctiveness of academic 'employment' in universities (such as UWA) and the terms and research circumstances of Dr Gray's own employment … There was in this sense a 'threshold question' …

183. First, there is the distinctiveness of UWA as a university. As we earlier indicated, UWA is a special purpose statutory corporation. It was created to serve the public purposes served by a 'university' (as the language of [the *University of Western Australia Act 1911* (WA)] makes plain: see the preamble to the Act and s 2). As such, UWA is, at least, an institution of higher education offering courses and providing research facilities in various disciplines and having amongst its acknowledged powers and privileges that of conferring degrees: … *UWA Act*, s 29.

184. We accept that UWA has not been immune from the forces, financial and otherwise, that are forcing changes in the character of the university sector in Australia. As French J noted [at first instance], UWA has engaged in commercial activities, as have done 'most, if not all, universities'. The evidence put on by UWA as to the range, character and significance of such activities of UWA was slight, though it hoped on the appeal that we would take judicial notice of these matters: cf *Evidence Act,* s 144(1) (Cth). What is notable for present purposes is that there is nothing in the evidence to suggest that those commercial activities have displaced, either totally or if in part to what extent, UWA's traditional public function as an institution of higher education in favour of the pursuit of commercial purposes (if it lawfully could do so under its Act). Its function, in other words, was not limited to that of engaging academic staff for its own commercial purposes. Accordingly, we agree with French J that on the evidence Dr Gray was not required to advance a commercial purpose of UWA when selecting the research he would undertake.

185. A further distinctive feature of many, but not all, universities (including UWA) is that their academic staff are part of the membership that constitutes the corporation and as such are bound by the statutes, regulations, etc of the university. Their membership is integral to their status and place in the university. To define the relationship of an academic staff member with a university simply in terms of a contract of employment is to ignore a distinctive dimension of that relationship.

186. Secondly, there is the distinctiveness of academic employment in a university. The two faceted character of an academic staff member's relationship with a university—ie as member and as employee—is 'not without significance' as French J observed ... It probably is the case—though it is not a matter we need explore—that some of the practices revealed in the evidence in this matter (not repudiated by UWA), and the underlying values which seem to inform them, are more likely to be referable to understandings that have been traditionally associated with membership. The seeming freedom to choose the subject or line of research and the manner of its pursuit and the freedom to decide when and how to publish the products of one's research to the extent that these subsist, sit uneasily with employment notions such as the implied duty of an employee to obey all lawful and reasonable instructions of the employer within the scope of the employee's employment, or to maintain the secrecy of confidential information generated in the course of employment. Yet they are apparent manifestations of the contested value of 'academic freedom': Cornish, 'Rights in University Innovations', (1992) 14(1) [*European Intellectual Property Review*], at 2–3.

...

193. This leads us to consider the circumstances of Dr Gray's employment and of the research environment in which he worked, upon which French J relied to negative the implication that UWA sought.

194. First, his Honour found that under his contract of employment Dr Gray had no duty to invent anything, though he had a duty to research and to stimulate research ... To put the matter as we earlier put it, he had not been engaged to use his inventive faculty in an agreed way or for an agreed purpose, for UWA's benefit. While his duty to research was in an applied science, it cannot for that reason be transformed into a duty to invent, notwithstanding that his actual research, in fact, carried the possibility of developing inventions capable of attracting patent protection.

195. We reject UWA's contention to the contrary and we agree with the primary Judge's reasons and conclusions. The insuperable difficulty in UWA's submissions is that Dr Gray's employment duties did not even require him to perform tasks from which inventions might result. The subject matter and the manner of discharge of his duty to research were in his discretion. He was not employed to invent. UWA put on extensive written submissions criticising French J's use of the formula 'duty to invent'. The shorthand expression is widely used in scholarly writing: see Dean, [*The Law of Trade Secrets and Personal Secrets* (2nd ed, 2002),] 238 ff; Monotti and Ricketson, *Universities and Intellectual Property: Ownership and Exploitation* (2003),] 6.56–6.67. As so used, and as used by French J, its meaning is self-evident and unobjectionable.

196. UWA has sought to circumvent his Honour's conclusion in the following way. Though Dr Gray was entitled to determine the subject and manner of his research, if what he chose to do required him to bring his inventive faculty to bear, then the doing of that research should, it is said, be regarded as that which he was engaged to do and for which he was paid. Any invention resulting from his so doing should, in consequence, attract the implied term.

197. Such a deemed, contingent duty to invent requires an untenable implication. It is not what Dr Gray's terms of employment required; there is no 'necessity' for it being implied by law into the employment contracts of university academic staff; and, importantly, it is inconsistent with the researcher's freedom to share and to publish research results.

198. Secondly, French J regarded the freedom to publish the results of research, including invention, notwithstanding that the publication might destroy patentability, as another circumstance telling against the implication. From what we have already said about the constraining character of the duty of confidence and of its underpinning of the implied term relating to employee inventions, the importance of this particular 'freedom' is self-evident. We earlier referred both to Dr Burton's evidence, accepted by his Honour, on the Gray group's 'strong commitment to the publication and dissemination of research results', and of Professor Barber's evidence of the 'kudos and reputation' that UWA desired 'from academic publication in the peer-reviewed literature'. While we do not suggest that Dr Gray and his researchers may not have controlled the time and manner of their publications, the evidence clearly suggests that Dr Gray enjoyed the freedom to publish that French J found. He was not constrained by a secrecy obligation.

199. As noted earlier in its submissions, UWA appears to have accepted that this was the case. In its oral submissions, it contended, seemingly for the first time, that a prohibition on publication arose only if and when 'an invention' had been developed and then only by virtue of reg 7 of the *Patents Regulations*. We have already indicated that those regulations were devoid of significance for the purposes of UWA's contract claim. In any event, reg 7 was not itself a free standing prohibition. It was a proscription that arose once a particular point in a regulatory régime was reached. In the circumstances of this matter that point was not, and could not have been, reached, because UWA had abandoned the Patents Regulations régime in favour of an 'alternative pathway': see 'The Patents Regulations' above.

200. Thirdly, French J considered that the extent to which Dr Gray and those working with him were expected to and did solicit funds for their research was another circumstance militating against the implication. We accept as a starting point that the solicitation of funds from public or private sources for the purposes of conducting research is not a phenomenon unique to universities. It is commonplace in the private sector: cf *Industry Research and Development Act 1986* (Cth). What was 'a striking feature of this case' … was the amount of time and effort devoted by Dr Gray and his researchers in applying for research grants, and the extent of their dependence on their success. UWA may have wished to foster, but seemingly could not fund, Dr Gray's research. To the extent that the *Sterling Engineering* principle [from *Sterling Engineering Co Ltd v Patchett* [1955] AC 534] has nascent in it the idea that the employer pays the researcher and, in significant degree, for the research itself, it can be said, without criticism of UWA that, if sustained, the suggested implied term would allow UWA to reap where various entities had sown. Importantly, it is implicit in what French J said that Dr Gray was raising the funds for *his* research, the metes and bounds of which *he* determined, though UWA received and managed the funds. Further, it also can probably be inferred that the grants were made to Dr Gray as an established researcher and not to UWA as such, although its involvement as institutional manager of the grant would also be taken into account by the funding body. So considered, the 'grant factor' can properly be said to be a consideration that further weakens UWA's claim to the benefits of any inventions so generated.

201. UWA seeks to counter this argument by saying that Dr Gray's post-contractual conduct cannot be used to negate an implication into a contract.

202. After referring to this factor and to the necessity, consistent with the kind of work Dr Gray was doing, to enter into collaborative arrangements, French J went on to use Dr Gray's experience to characterise 'the role of the researcher at UWA' in the area in which Dr Gray was working. His Honour described that as being 'required ... to act as entrepreneurs in securing the resources which would enable them to carry out their work' ... It was immediately following this that his Honour made the following important observation:

> The circumstances of his employment were a long way removed from the situations which gave rise to the common law implications discussed in the English cases.

In these circumstances we consider that the proper complexion to place upon what his Honour said is that he was describing the known context and shared expectations of the parties in relation to raising funds for research at the time of contracting, using what happened post-contract as the manifestation of what was anticipated. We would add that we were not taken to any evidence which suggested what contractual arrangements, if any, there were as to the raising of funds for research by UWA or by Dr Gray. If there was no such arrangement, we see nothing impermissible in French J having regard to Dr Gray's subsequent behaviour in fund raising to negative the suggested implication.

203. The fourth and final negativing circumstance adverted to by the primary Judge was the necessity, consistent with research of the kind he was doing, for Dr Gray to enter into collaborative arrangements with external organisations. The evidence was replete with instances of such collaborations and of information exchanges between Dr Gray and his researchers on the one hand and between them and researchers in other institutions on the other. Informative examples of both processes at work can be seen in the evolution of the research on the binding of Yttrium90 to microspheres ... and the use made in it of notes of Dr Self of St Vincent's Hospital written in 1984 ...

204. Implicit in his Honour's reliance upon the collaborations is the appreciation that the need for inter-institutional cooperation in the research being conducted tells against the exclusive appropriation of its product to one institution (ie UWA) via an implied term in the event that an invention is made. Further, and we consider importantly, the evidence on collaboration and information exchanges in Dr Gray's field of research suggests that some level of sharing of research results and know-how was a necessary and accepted practice in the particular research community so as to increase 'the stock of available knowledge': cf *Taylor v Taylor* (1910) 10 CLR 218 ... at 224.

205. As we earlier noted, the principles governing terms implied by law themselves raise a threshold question which French J correctly identified. The onus is on the proponent of the term to show that the contract is of a class, type or kind to which the legal implication applies ... Save in cases of first impression, the discharge of that onus will pose few problems. Thereafter the question becomes one as to whether the terms agreed by the parties to the contract are inconsistent with, or negate, the implied term. The opponent of the implication bears this onus. The present case is of the former variety.

INFRINGEMENT

Chapter 11 of the *Patents Act* has provisions relating to infringement and infringement proceedings, non-infringement declarations and unjustified threats of infringement proceedings. However, there is no definition of infringement in the Act.

DIRECT INFRINGEMENT

Infringement arises when the invention claimed in the patent is exploited by persons other than the patentee or persons authorised by the patentee. In determining whether or not a patent has been infringed the court does not compare the patented product or process with the alleged infringer's product or process. The comparison that the court makes is between the claims made in the patent as granted and the alleged infringer's product and process. The question asked is whether the alleged infringer's product or process falls within the boundaries of the patent claims. For infringement to occur, each essential integer of the claim must be taken by the alleged infringer and incorporated into his or her own product or process. A person will avoid infringement if he or she omits an essential integer or modifies it in a manner that has a material effect on the way the invention works. According to the High Court in *Populin v HB Nominees Pty Ltd* (1982) 41 ALR 471 at 475:

> The patentee must show that the defendant has taken each and every one of the essential integers of the patentee's claim. Therefore, if, on its true construction, the claim in a patent claims a particular combination of integers and the alleged infringer omits one of them he will escape liability.

However, an alleged infringer will not avoid infringement simply by modifying an essential integer in a manner so small as to be insignificant and in a way that adds nothing to the way that the invention works. Often all that the alleged infringer will have done is to create a simple variant to the invention—a minor change. In such circumstances, the rules that the courts apply in construing the patent claims become critical. The general rules of construction of patent documents were discussed in Chapter 12, where it was shown that the courts favour a purposive rather than a literal approach.

Where an alleged infringement involves a variant to the patented invention, the UK courts have adopted a simple three-step test, known as the '*Improver* questions', to determine whether or not there is, in fact, infringement.

CASE EXTRACT: COMPARATIVE LAW

COMPARATIVE LAW

Improver Corporation v Remington Consumer Products Ltd

[1990] FSR 181
HIgh Court of England and Wales, Chancery Division (Patents Court)

Hoffmann J (at 189): If the issue was whether a feature embodied in an alleged infringement which fell outside the primary, literal or acontextual meaning of a descriptive word or phrase in the claim ('a variant') was nevertheless within its language as properly interpreted, the court should ask itself the following three questions:

(1) Does the variant have a material effect upon the way the invention works? If yes, the variant is outside the claim. If no—

(2) Would this (i.e. that the variant had no material effect) have been obvious at the date of publication of the patent to a reader skilled in the art. If no, the variant is outside the claim. If yes—

(3) Would the reader skilled in the art nevertheless have understood from the language of the claim that the patentee intended that strict compliance with the primary meaning was an essential requirement of the invention. If yes, the variant is outside the claim.

On the other hand, a negative answer to the last question would lead to the conclusion that the patentee was intending the word or phrase to have not a literal but a figurative meaning (the figure being a form of synecdoche or metonymy) denoting a class of things which included the variant and the literal meaning, the latter being perhaps the most perfect, best-known or striking example of the class.

There has been some debate in the Australian case law on the extent to which the *Improver* questions should be applied where the alleged infringement is outside the literal scope of the claims, bearing in mind that the *Improver* questions were formulated in respect of the application of European Patent Convention rules of interpretation. The trend in recent Australian case law has been to adopt the *Improver* questions, as illustrated by the decision of Merkel J in the case extracted below.

CASE EXTRACT: CURRENT LAW

PhotoCure ASA v Queen's University at Kingston

[2005] FCA 344; (2005) 216 ALR 41
Federal Court of Australia

[In this case, DUSA Pharmaceuticals Inc was assigned ownership of an Australian patent with the title 'Method of Detection and Treatment of Malignant and Non-Malignant Lesions by Photochemotherapy' from Queen's University. PhotoCure filed a claim for revocation and a counterclaim was made for infringement. DUSA claimed that PhotoCure's product infringed its patent both textually and in substance. After reviewing the evidence (at [161]–[193]), Merkel J rejected DUSA's claim of textual infringement (at [194]). He then shifted his focus to infringement in substance.]

Merkel J: 196. DUSA submitted that the *Improver* questions do not precisely reflect the position under Australian law, and claimed that this is because they were articulated by Hoffmann J for the purpose of assisting UK courts in applying the Protocol on Interpretation of Article 69 of the *European Patent Convention*. According to DUSA, the Australian approach is 'related to' the UK approach, 'but is less formulaic'. Nonetheless, DUSA accepted that the *Improver* questions 'represent a consistent and developed approach to problems' such as those arising in the present case. However, DUSA submitted that the Court should have regard to the approach of the Australian courts, particularly in *Populin* [*v HB Nominees Pty Ltd* (1982) 41 ALR 471]; *Rehm* [*Pty Ltd v Websters Security Systems (International) Pty Ltd* (1988) 81 ALR 79]; *Commonwealth Industrial Gases Ltd v MWA Holdings Pty Ltd* (1970) 180 CLR 160 and *Minnesota Mining* [*and Manufacturing Co*] *v Beiersdorf* [*(Australia) Ltd* (1980) 144 CLR 253].

197. The authorities relied upon by DUSA predate the decision in *Improver* and, although relevant, are not determinative of whether Australian courts should follow that decision. Since *Improver* a number

of decisions of the Court have considered the question of 'infringement in substance' without reference to *Improver* or the *Improver* questions: see for example *Doric Products Pty Ltd v Lockwood Security Products Pty Ltd* (2001) 192 ALR 306; *Leonardis* [*v Sartas No 1 Pty Ltd* (1996) 67 FCR 126]; *Azuko* [*Pty Ltd v Old Digger Pty Ltd* (2001) 52 IPR 75] and most recently *Gambro* [*Pty Ltd v Fresenius Medical Care South East Asia Pty Ltd* (2004) 61 IPR 442]. However, in at least three instances the Court has applied *Improver*. In *Nesbit Evans Group Australia Pty Ltd v Impro Ltd* (1997) 39 IPR 56 the Full Court referred to the *Improver* questions as relevant, although there was no dispute in that case as to their applicability under Australian law: per Lindgren J (with whom Hill J agreed) at 80–81, and per Wilcox J at 58. The *Improver* questions were also applied by Finkelstein J in *Root Quality* [*Pty Ltd v Root Control Technologies Pty Ltd* (2000) 177 ALR 231] at [55] and [69]–[74], and more recently by Kiefel J in *Neurizon Pty Ltd v Jupiters* Ltd (2004) 62 IPR 569 at [139]. See also *Sydney Cellulose Pty Ltd v Ceil Comfort Home Insulation Pty Ltd* (2001) 53 IPR 359 ('*Sydney Cellulose*') at [43].

198. It is correct that in *Improver* the patent in suit was a European Patent to which the *Patents Act 1977* (UK) applied. Section 125 of that Act incorporates the content of Art 69 of the *European Patent Convention* and the *Protocol on the Interpretation of Article 69 of the European Patent Convention*. It is also correct that in *Wheatley* [*v Drillsafe Ltd* [2001] RPC 133] Aldous LJ wrote (at 142) that the *Improver* questions were 'better called the Protocol questions'. However, the approach of the Convention and Protocol to infringement is merely that 'the scope of the invention must be found in the language of the claims' (as paraphrased by Hoffmann J in *Improver* at 190) and has been held to be the same as the approach taken by Lord Diplock in *Catnic* [*Components Ltd v Hill & Smith Ltd* [1982] RPC 183]: see *Improver* at 190. In fact, Hoffmann J's explanation of the *Improver* questions itself makes it clear that he intended the questions to be a mere elaboration of the approach taken in *Catnic*. He refers to the questions as 'Lord Diplock's three questions' (at 190) and in explaining the source of the questions states (at 188–189):

> The proper approach to the interpretation of patents registered under the *Patents Act 1949* was explained by Lord Diplock in *Catnic Components Ltd v Hill & Smith Ltd*. The language should be given a 'purposive' and not necessarily a literal construction …

199. The source of the *Improver* questions can be found in the explanation given by Lord Diplock in *Catnic* at 242–243:

> My Lords, a patent specification is a unilateral statement by the patentee, in words of his own choosing, addressed to those likely to have a practical interest in the subject matter of his invention (i.e. 'skilled in the art'), by which he informs them what he claims to be the essential features of the new product or process for which the letters patent grant him a monopoly. It is those novel features only that he claims to be essential that constitute the so-called 'pith and marrow' of the claim. A patent specification should be given a purposive construction rather than a purely literal one derived from applying to it the kind of meticulous verbal analysis in which lawyers are too often tempted by their training to indulge. The question in each case is: whether persons with practical knowledge and experience of the kind of work in which the invention was intended to be used, would understand that strict compliance with a particular descriptive word or phrase appearing in a claim was intended by the patentee to be an essential requirement of the invention so that *any* variant would fall outside the monopoly claimed, even though it could have no material effect upon the way the invention worked.

The question, of course, does not arise where the variant would in fact have a material effect upon the way the invention worked. Nor does it arise unless at the date of publication of the specification it would have been obvious to the informed reader that this was so. Where it is not obvious, in the light of the then-existing knowledge, the reader is entitled to assume that the patentee thought at the time of the specification that he had good reason for limiting his monopoly so strictly and had intended to do so, even though subsequent work by him or others in the field of the invention might show the limitation to have been unnecessary. It is to be answered in the negative only when it would be apparent to any reader skilled in the art that a particular descriptive word or phrase used in a claim cannot have been intended by a patentee, who was also skilled in the art, to exclude minor variants which, to the knowledge of both him and the readers to whom the patent was addressed, could have no material effect upon the way in which the invention worked. [emphasis added]

200. In *Root Quality*, Finkelstein J viewed the approach taken in *Improver* as an elaboration of the 'purposive' approach enunciated in *Catnic*, as distinct from the 'pith and marrow' position which his Honour considered to be a different approach that had prevailed prior to *Catnic*. At 242 [44]–[45] Finkelstein J explained the current state of the law:

It seems that the following is the position that now pertains. Before *Catnic*, the subject matter of a patent was defined in accordance with the literal meaning of the claim. Nevertheless, if the substance (pith and marrow) or mechanical equivalent of the claim was taken, there would be an infringement. The rules were made necessary to render patents useful. The change brought about by *Catnic* was that a patent specification is to be given a purposive and not a literal construction. The question to be determined under this approach is whether the patentee intended strict compliance with an element of the invention to be an essential requirement of the invention. On this basis the former approach, that is, whether the 'pith and marrow' or substance of a claim has been taken, is no longer necessary.

In Australia the so-called 'purposive approach' to construction has been adopted (see *Populin v HB Nominees Pty Ltd* (1982) 41 ALR 471; *Nesbit Evans Group Australia Pty Ltd v Impro Ltd* (1997) 39 IPR 56) although some cases imply that the former approach can still have application: see *Populin* at 475–477; see also JW Dwyer and A Dufty (eds) *Lahore on Patents Trade Marks and Related Rights*, 1996 paras 18,135 and 18,140. On the other hand, when the *Improver* questions are posed and answered, it is difficult to see what can be achieved by recourse to the 'pith and marrow' approach.

201. The questions posed by Hoffmann J in *Improver* do not constitute a novel test of infringement, but rather are an application of the purposive approach adopted by Lord Diplock in *Catnic*, which is also reflected in the *European Patent Convention* and *Protocol*.

202. Whether or not the *Catnic* approach represents a divergence from the position that had been taken previously in Australia (as was the view of Finkelstein J in *Root Quality* at [44]; cf *Rehm* at 92; *Nicaro* [*Holdings Pty Ltd v Martin Engineering Co* (1990) 91 ALR 513] at 528–529 per Gummow J; *Minnesota Mining & Manufacturing Co v Tyco Electronics Pty* (2001) 53 IPR 32 at [127]; *Azuko* at 93 [20] and *Flexible Steel* [*Lacing Co v Beltreco Ltd* (2000) 49 IPR 331] at 349 [81]) it has clearly been cited with approval by Australian courts on a number of occasions: see, for example, *Populin* at 476–477; *Sydney Cellulose* at [43]; *Bartlem Pty Ltd v CMMC Pty Ltd* (2001) 53 IPR 124 at [70]; *Azuko*

at 92–93 [20]; *Great Western Corporation Pty Ltd v Grove Hill Pty Ltd* [2001] FCA 423 at [43]; *Flexible Steel* at 349 [81]; *Wimmera Industrial Minerals Pty Ltd v RGC Mineral Sands Ltd (No 3)* (1997) AIPC 91-366 at 39,787–39,788; *Innovative Agriculture* [*Products Pty Ltd v Cranshaw* (1996) 35 IPR 643] at 649; *Hutt v Enig Pty Ltd* (1998) 41 IPR 559 at 564; *Cenefill Pty Ltd v Australian Sheetpiling Pty Ltd* (1996) 35 IPR 64 at 67; *Winner v Morey Haigh & Associates (A'Asia) Pty Ltd* (1996) 33 IPR 215 at 220; and *Astra Lakemedel Aktiebolag v Commissioner of Patents* (1995) 56 FCR 208 at 214.

203. There is, therefore, nothing controversial about the *Improver* questions. The questions do not supplant the purposive approach that was explained in *Catnic*. Rather, they are an application of that approach to the claims in question in *Improver*.

204. The views expressed above as to the role of the *Improver* questions were recently re-affirmed by Lord Hoffmann (with whom the other members of the House of Lords agreed) in *Kirin-Amgen Inc v Hoechst Marion Roussel Ltd* [2005] 1 All ER 667 ('*Kirin-Amgen*'). Lord Hoffmann at [48] observed that the *Catnic* and *Protocol* principles of construction were identical in that each intends:

> ... to give the patentee the full extent, but not more than the full extent, of the monopoly which a reasonable person skilled in the art, reading the claims in context, would think he was intending to claim.

205. In explaining the role of the *Improver* questions (which his Lordship referred to as the Protocol questions) Lord Hoffmann stated at [52]:

> These questions, which the Court of Appeal in *Wheatley v Drillsafe Ltd* [2000] IP & T 1076 at 1084, [2001] RPC 133 at 142 dubbed 'the Protocol questions' have been used by English courts for the past 15 years as a framework for deciding whether equivalents fall within the scope of the claims. On the whole, the judges appear to have been comfortable with the results, although some of the cases have exposed the limitations of the method. When speaking of the '*Catnic* principle' it is important to distinguish between, on the one hand, the principle of purposive construction which I have said gives effect to the requirements of the Protocol, and on the other hand, the guidelines for applying that principle to equivalents, which are encapsulated in the Protocol questions. The former is the bedrock of patent construction, universally applicable. The latter are only guidelines, more useful in some cases than in others. I am bound to say that the cases show a tendency for counsel to treat the Protocol questions as legal rules rather than guides which will in appropriate cases help to decide what the skilled man would have understood the patentee to mean.

206. For the reasons stated by Lord Hoffmann, the submission of DUSA, that the *Improver* questions are not to be treated as formulaic or as rules of construction, correctly represents the legal position in the United Kingdom. There is no reason why it does not also correctly represent the legal position in Australia, where the purposive approach to the construction of contracts, statutes and patents, has also prevailed.

207. However, in a case such as the present the *Improver* questions are useful guidelines because they can be of assistance in determining whether a reasonable person skilled in the art, reading the claims in context, would think that the patentee was not intending to employ the primary meanings of the relevant phrases used in claims 1 and 9 but, rather, was intending that the meaning of those phrases would include the use of an equivalent ...

208. Accordingly, I propose to consider the *Improver* questions within the framework outlined by Lord Hoffmann in *Kirin-Amgen*.

[After considering the application of each of the three *Improver* questions to the facts in issue, his Honour concluded at [248] that DUSA did not make out its case for infringement.]

AUTHORISATION OF INFRINGEMENT

As is the case with other kinds of IP rights considered in this book, a person can also be directly liable for authorising infringement of a patent.

CURRENT LAW

CASE EXTRACT: CURRENT LAW

Inverness Medical Switzerland GmbH v MDS Diagnostics Pty Ltd

[2010] FCA 108; (2010) 85 IPR 525
Federal Court of Australia

[The patents in issue in this case related to pregnancy-testing devices. The authorisation issue arose in respect of the third respondent, Dr Appanna, who was the managing director of the first and second respondents.]

Bennett J: 194. It is an infringement of the patentee's exclusive rights not only to exploit an invention but also to authorise another person to exploit it (s 13 of the 1990 Act). The word 'authorise' in s 13 has the meaning in the comparable context of the *Copyright Act* (*Bristol-Myers Squibb Co v FH Faulding & Co Ltd* (2000) 97 FCR 524 at [97] per Black CJ and Lehane J; see also *Rescare* [*Ltd v Anaesthetic Supplies Pty Ltd* (1992) 25 IPR 119] at 155 per Gummow J). A person authorises an infringement if he or she 'sanctions, approves or countenances' the infringement (*University of New South Wales v Moorhouse* (1975) 133 CLR 1 at 12 per Gibbs J, at 20–21 per Jacobs J (McTiernan ACJ agreeing); *Cooper* [*v Universal Music Australia Pty Ltd* (2006) 156 FCR 380] at [137]–[140] per Kenny J (French J agreeing)). As Burchett J said in *Kimberly-Clark Australia Pty Ltd v Arico Trading International Pty Ltd* (1998) 42 IPR 111 at 129 (appeal allowed on validity, but not on infringement), s 13 at least embraces the case where a person 'made himself a party to the act of infringement' (*Walker v Alemite Corp* (1933) 49 CLR 643 at 658 per Dixon J).

195. MDS submits that the meaning of 'authorises' in s 101 of the *Copyright Act 1968* (Cth) (the *Copyright Act*) is irrelevant and not analogous to 'authorise' in s 13(1) of the 1990 Act. MDS says that as s 101 of the *Copyright Act* defines a species of infringement of authorising another to perform an infringing act, 'authorise' means 'sanction, approve, or countenance' because it is the infringer who is authorising another to perform the relevant acts although it has no legal right to do so. On the other hand, as the purpose of s 13(1) of the 1990 Act is to define the rights of the patentee, MDS contends that 'authorise' in that section means 'to give legal or formal warrant to (a person) to do something' (one of several definitions from the Oxford English Dictionary Online) as this is what only the patentee has the right to do.

196. In *Bristol-Myers Squibb Co v FH Faulding & Co Ltd* (1998) 41 IPR 467 at 488, Heerey J, at first instance, discussed the meaning of 'authorise' in s 13 of the 1990 Act. Justice Heerey considered that 'authorise' in s 13 does not have the same meaning as 'authorise' in the *Copyright Act* but rather has the meaning:

- 'To give authority or legal power to; empower (to do something)' from the *Macquarie Dictionary*; or
- 'To give legal or formal warrant to (a person) to do; to empower, permit authoritatively' from the *Shorter Oxford Dictionary*.

Although Black CJ and Lehane J expressly disagreed on this point on appeal at [97] in obiter, MDS relies on the reasoning of Heerey J.

197. The latter aspects of the definitions in the Macquarie and Shorter Oxford Dictionary of 'empower (to do something)' and 'empower, permit authoritatively' do not support MDS's submission that 'authorise' in s 13 is limited to the giving of legal authority. In any event, it is unlikely that s 13 can have that restricted meaning. The patentee has the right to exclude all others from authorising another to infringe the rights of the patentee. If authorisation required the legal right in the patent, then only the patentee has that right and there could be no infringement by authorisation by any person.

198. Interestingly, in *Bristol-Myers* Heerey J concluded, based on the definition he adopted, that mere supply of an infringing product with instructions for use did not constitute infringement but that the lease of a factory containing machinery the use of which infringed the patent did constitute infringement by authorisation. This does not support MDS. The acts of Dr Appanna relied on by Inverness go beyond mere provision of the opportunity to infringe and are analogous to the example that Heerey J gave of an act that did amount to infringement by authorisation. Dr Appanna's actions, in the context of his position with MDS, empowered the infringement.

199. MDS submits that the word 'authorise' in s 13(1) is not relevant to the alleged liability of a director for infringing acts by a company and is not a concept that defines any infringing act by a third party. MDS submits that the different contexts of s 13(1) of the 1990 Act and s 101 of the *Copyright Act* have not been argued before and so were not properly considered by Gummow J in *Rescare*, by Burchett J in *Kimberly-Clark* or by the Full Court in *Bristol-Myers*. I do not accept MDS' argument that the different statutory contexts justify different meanings for the word 'authorise' in patent and copyright law. As Inverness points out, the 1990 Act, unlike the *Copyright Act,* does not separately define the exclusive rights of the intellectual property owner and the acts which constitute infringement of those rights. Those acts which trespass on the patentee's exclusive rights under s 13 of the 1990 Act constitute infringement. Further, s 13(2) of the *Copyright Act* uses the word 'authorise' in a similar way to s 13 of the 1990 Act to describe the exclusive right of the copyright owner to authorise a person to do particular acts.

200. MDS contends that a director can never be held liable for patent infringement on the 'authorisation' ground because only the company can give the requisite warrant to invoke liability. It submits that a director cannot give such warrant to the company because of the distinction between the company as a separate, distinct entity and its directors who have an internal role in the management of the company.

201. Put together, MDS' submissions amount to saying that there can be no infringement by authorisation unless the authoriser is in such a position or such a relationship with the person being authorised that the authoriser has formal authority, in a technical sense, to authorise that person to do the infringing act. If that submission is that only the patentee has the right to authorise exploitation of a patent, it would follow that no person or company other than the patentee can grant the legal right to another to exploit the invention. This construction of 'authorise' does not accord, in my view, with s 13 or the scheme of the 1990 Act, including s 117, or the meaning of 'authorise'. To the extent that MDS is arguing that Dr Appanna could not have authorised MDS NZ or MDS Aus to infringe as he was a director without proper authority formally to authorise actions of the company, I reject such a submission. Section 13 does not carry that limitation.

202. I do not accept MDS' proposition that the position stated in each of *Rescare*, *Kimberly-Clark* and by the Full Court in *Bristol-Myers* should not be followed. I see no reason to construe 'authorise' in s 13 in the narrower way contended for by MDS. That is not to say that a director of a company, by reason only of that position, authorises any act of infringement by the company. It is still necessary to show actions that demonstrate that the person did sanction, approve or countenance the act of infringement.

203. There can be no dispute that Dr Appanna knew that the infringing act of the sale of the MDS devices would occur. He had the power to prevent those acts and some duty to interfere. Express or formal permission is not essential and inactivity or indifference may reach a degree from which authorisation or permission may be inferred (*Australasian Performing Right Association Ltd v Metro on George Pty Ltd* (2004) 61 IPR 575 at [19] per Bennett J). Dr Appanna authorised MDS to sell the infringing products. I am satisfied that he had the power to prevent the companies from committing the acts of exploitation (*Metro on George* at [18]). He arranged for the sourcing of the products and personally participated in the distribution of those products. Dr Appanna sanctioned, approved and countenanced the sale of products that infringed Inverness' exclusive right to exploit the invention of the first patent and the second patent.

CONTRIBUTORY INFRINGEMENT UNDER S 117

A distinction needs to be drawn between authorisation of infringement, which is contrary to the rights of the patentee in s 13 of the *Patents Act*, and contributory infringement under s 117(1), which states that if the use of a product by a person would infringe a patent, the supply of that product by one person to another is an infringement of the patent by the supplier unless the supplier is the patentee or licensee of the patent.

CASE EXTRACT: PRECEDENT

Northern Territory v Collins

[2008] HCA 49; (2008) 235 CLR 619
High Court of Australia

[The High Court was given the opportunity to consider the applicability of s 117(1) in this case. Mr and Mrs Collins owned a patent for methods of producing oil from certain species of trees. They alleged that the Northern Territory had 'supplied' to Australian Cypress Oil Co Pty Ltd (ACOC) certain timber from blue cypress trees, and that ACOC had used that timber to produce an oil called 'blue cypress oil' by means of a process claimed by the patent. The alleged supply was said to be found in statutory licences granted to ACOC to take timber from certain Crown lands in the Territory. The Court particularly focused on three issues: whether the supply of an input into a patented method or process engages s 117(1); the definition of 'supply' in Sch 1 (supply by way of sale, exchange, lease, hire or hire-purchase); and the role of s 117(2)(b), which clarifies that if the product is not a staple commercial product, then use of the product includes any use, if the supplier had reason to believe that the person would put it to that use.

Crennan J gave the leading judgment. Her Honour's judgment included a detailed account of the legislative history of s 117, at [100]–[116]. She then addressed each of the issues in turn, concluding that although supply of an input into a method or process was caught by s 117(1) and the Northern Territory was engaged in supply, it was supply of a staple commercial product which was protected by s117(2)(b).]

Crennan J (footnotes omitted): 131. Consideration of the entire definition of 'exploit' in respect of a method or process patent and of the whole of s 117 confirms that s 117 can be engaged in respect of a supply of a raw material for carrying out a patented method. That construction applies s 117 according to its terms and promotes the objectives of the legislation which can be gleaned from the secondary materials. Whether a particular use of an input into a method (or an input into a resulting product) 'would infringe' in terms of s 117 will turn on the claims.

132. In terms of the claims in this case, and the assumption made by the primary judge that ACOC infringed the patent, the alleged use which ACOC makes of the bark and wood of the trees (the 'supplied' product) is making, selling and offering for sale, the oil (the 'infringing' product) extracted from the supplied product by steam distillation (the patented method). Nothing more needs to be said in the context of determining separate issues other than that the Northern Territory fails in respect of its submission on the first question that s 117 has no application to the timber supplied to ACOC.

...

135. The licences to ACOC were undoubtedly in the form of statutory permissions to take timber, as contended by the Northern Territory. As the judgment of French J demonstrates, through the comprehensive consideration of numerous authorities, whether a contract to take timber is a sale of goods, or an interest in realty, depends on the context in which the characterisation is considered, then on a number of factors. Relevant statutory provisions affect the characterisation of an interest. Some simple distinctions which affected rights as between a life tenant and a remainderman are not without interest. A tree severed from the land was personalty, whereas a tree attached to the land was realty. Trees containing a useable quantity of wood were 'timber' trees, distinguishable from trees which do not bear timber. However, as part of a statutory regime concerning Crown land, the licences need to be characterised 'in the light of the relevant statutory provisions without attaching too much significance to similarities ... with the creation of particular interests by the common law owner of land'.

136. The licences, when considered in the light of the [relevant] provisions of the *Crown Lands Act* [(NT)] and the *Crown Lands Regulations*, grant to licensees a personal rather than a proprietary interest in the timber of the plantation.

137. It has already been explained that the intention of the Northern Territory when setting up the Howard Springs Plantation was cultivation of the trees for the production of commercial (ie saleable) timber. In the context of argument concerning the expression 'staple commercial product' the Northern Territory relies, correctly, on numerous commercial uses of the timber in question. The licences are a means of passing, to ACOC, for commercial exploitation by ACOC, quantities of timber from trees cultivated by the Northern Territory to produce timber. The fact that an *ad valorem* royalty is charged in respect of the timber taken only serves to emphasise the fact that the interest granted under the licences involved commercial terms. The licences constitute a 'supply' of raw materials for commercial use; this is a 'supply' for the purposes of s 117. Accordingly, the Northern Territory fails in respect of its submissions on the second question.

PRECEDENT

...

145. The phrase 'staple commercial product' means a product supplied commercially for various uses. This does not mandate an enquiry into whether there is 'an established wholesale or retail market' or into whether the product is 'generally available' even though evidence of such matters may well be sufficient to show that a product is a 'staple commercial product'. The relevant enquiry is into whether the supply of the product is commercial and whether the product has various uses. Leaving aside the supply to ACOC, the timber here was supplied on commercial terms to various licensees for a variety of non-infringing uses. Accordingly, the Northern Territory is protected by the limitation in s 117(2)(b).

Since the High Court decision in *Northern Territory v Collins* there has been further consideration of the applicability of the contributory infringement provisions in s 117 for supply of pharmaceutical products that have both patented and unpatented indications. The final report of a review of pharmaceutical patents undertaken in 2012–13 addressed this issue,[1] noting at p 138 that:

> Supplying a product for a non-patented indication is commonly referred to as a 'carve out'. The use of a carve out is currently sufficient to avoid liability for patent infringement in the EU and the US, but not yet in Australia. The result of a carve out is that a generic manufacturer can supply a drug for a treatment indication which is not covered by a patent, without being liable for the infringement of a patent covering another indication for the drug. [Footnotes omitted.]

The Review Panel recommended at p 140 that:

> Section 117 of the *Patents Act* should be amended to provide that the supply of a pharmaceutical product subject to a patent which is used for a non-patented indication will not amount to infringement where reasonable steps have been taken to ensure that the product will only be used in a non-infringing manner. The law should establish a presumption that 'reasonable steps' have been taken where the product has been labelled with indications which do not include any infringing indications.

There has also been some judicial activity relating to the applicability of s 117 in the context of pharmaceutical patents, including a High Court decision and a number of decisions of the Full Court of the Federal Court. In particular, the courts have focused on whether the 'staple commercial product' provision applies.[2] The case extracted below provides a useful overview of the key issues.

---

1   A Harris, N Gruen and D Nicol, Review Panel, *Pharmaceutical Patents Review Final Report* (2013).
2   See for example *Apotex Pty Ltd v Sanofi-Aventis Australia Pty Ltd* [2013] HCA 50; (2013) 304 ALR 1; *Generic Health Pty Ltd v Otsuka Pharmaceutical Co Ltd* [2013] FCAFC 17; (2013) 296 ALR 50; *Warner-Lambert Co LLC v Apotex Pty Ltd* [2014] FCAFC 59; (2014) 311 ALR 632; *AstraZeneca AB v Apotex Pty Ltd* [2014] FCAFC 99; (2014) 312 ALR 1.

CASE EXTRACT: CURRENT LAW

AstraZeneca AB v Apotex Pty Ltd

[2014] FCAFC 99; (2014) 312 ALR 1
Federal Court of Australia, Full Court

[The subject matter in issue was two patents relating to drugs for lowering cholesterol levels in humans. The key claims in the first patent, 051 (the 'low dose patent') referred to a method of using a low dose of the known anti-cholesterol drug rosuvastatin. The second patent, 842 (the 'cation patent'), claimed pharmaceutical compositions that included rosuvastatin as an active ingredient. A number of generic pharmaceutical companies (including Watson Pharma Pty Ltd) sought to market tablets of various sizes containing rosuvastatin. AstraZeneca brought an action for infringement and the generic parties cross-claimed revocation. At first instance the 051 patent and many of the claims of the 842 patent were revoked on various grounds. The primary judge also rejected an infringement action based on s 117(2)(b) and (c). AstraZeneca's appeal was heard by a five-judge Full Court.]

Besanko, Foster, Nicholas and Yates JJ: 424. At trial AstraZeneca relied upon s 117 of the Act to establish that the supply by the generic parties of 5 mg, 10 mg, 20 mg and 40 mg dosages of rosuvastatin would constitute an infringement of the claims of the 051 or low dose patent. On the assumption that those claims were valid, the primary judge found for AstraZeneca in relation to the 5 mg and 10 mg dosages, but not the 20 mg and 40 mg dosages.

425. The primary judge considered and rejected an argument raised by AstraZeneca based upon s 117(2)(a) of the Act. That aspect of her Honour's decision is not in issue in the appeals. What remains is a challenge to various findings made by the primary judge in relation to s 117(2)(b) and s 117(2)(c) of the Act. AstraZeneca has appealed against the primary judge's rejection of the infringement case under s 117(2)(b) and (c) based upon the supply of the 20 mg dosage but has not appealed against her Honour's rejection of the case based upon the supply of the 40 mg dosage.

426. As to s 117(2)(c), the primary judge rejected a submission by AstraZeneca founded upon the Watson product information document which included an express statement that '[t]he 10, 20 and 40 mg tablets can be divided into equal halves'. AstraZeneca contended this constituted an inducement to use their 20 mg and 40 mg products by splitting the tablets into two and four parts respectively so that they might then be taken as 10 mg dosages in a manner that would infringe one or more of the claims. The primary judge rejected this argument at [510] for the following reason:

> ... Despite the reference to the tablets being able to be divided in the Watson and Ascent product information, on the whole of the evidence, including the proposed communications with medical practitioners and pharmacists, it cannot be said that the generic parties will instruct or induce any person to split a 20 or 40 mg tablet into two or four.

427. We should say at once that, in our view, the Watson product information document provided a clear inducement to consumers of its 20 mg dosage product to engage in tablet splitting. Had we been of the opinion that the claims of the 051 or low dose patent were valid, we would have found Watson (but not the other respondents) liable for infringement under s 117(1) when read with s 117(2)(c) of the Act. We respectfully disagree with the primary judge in so far as she was of a different opinion.

428. The generic parties also submitted to the primary judge, and again on the appeals, that s 117(2)(b) could have no application in this case because rosuvastatin is a 'staple commercial product'. In support of this submission, they relied on the decision of the High Court in *Northern Territory of Australia v Collins* (2008) 235 CLR 619 ('*Collins*'). The primary judge recorded the generic parties' submission in these terms (at [502]):

> The generic parties contend that rosuvastatin is a staple commercial product. Rosuvastatin, on the evidence, is 'used to treat various different conditions or for other effects including (i) pleomorphic (anti-inflammatory) effects to reduce the incidence of plaque rupture and heart attacks; (ii) treatment of diabetes; (iii) treatment of stroke; (iv) treatment of chronic renal disease; and (v) coronary artery disease or peripheral vascular disease'. Further, the 'most common group of patients seen by Dr Wilson appear not to be hypercholesterolemia patients but those requiring secondary prevention such [as] patients with coronary artery disease or peripheral vascular disease and diabetes independent of their cholesterol level'. As rosuvastatin can be used in various non-infringing ways, it is a staple commercial product by analogy to the reasoning in *Northern Territory v Collins* [citation omitted].

Her Honour was not persuaded that rosuvastatin is a staple commercial product. She said (at [511]):

> Despite the fact that I accept that rosuvastatin has a number of medical uses, not just the treatment of hypercholesterolemia, I cannot accept that it should be characterised as a 'staple commercial product'. The difficulty I have arises from the word 'staple', which does indicate something more than merely a 'commercial product'. The reasoning in *Collins* does not lead me to the view that the fact that a product can be used in one or even a number of non-infringing ways is itself sufficient to make the product a staple commercial product. While 'staple' is not concerned with the economic significance of uses, it is concerned with the variety of uses. The variety of uses in this case is confined by the nature of the product to a limited class, being the treatment of diseases of a particular kind or class (albeit different diseases) in humans. Rosuvastatin, despite its usefulness for a variety of disease conditions, is not able to be compared to timber (as in *Collins*) or, for example, types of pharmaceutical products which might be useful for many human conditions. It is for these reasons I conclude that the rosuvastatin products proposed to be supplied by the generic parties are not staple commercial products.

429. In argument before us, the generic parties placed considerable reliance on the judgment of Crennan J in *Collins* at [145]. Her Honour said that the phrase 'staple commercial product' means 'a product supplied commercially for various uses.' Hayne J (at [41]) and Heydon J (at [57]) agreed. However, Crennan J's statement must be read in its proper context including the factual setting in which it came to be made. *Collins* involved the supply of a species of timber which Crennan J acknowledged at [143] to [144] constituted '[a] basic product commonly used for various purposes.'

430. Whether a product meets that description is a question of fact. Considerations relevant to the question whether a product is a staple commercial product include how widely the product is used and for what range of purposes. In a passage in Thorley S, Miller R, Burkill G, Birss C and Campbell D, *Terrell on the Law of Patents* (16th ed, Thomson Sweet & Maxwell, 2006) at [8-37] referred to in a footnote

CURRENT LAW

to Crennan J's judgment at [144] the learned authors, referring to the use of the expression 'staple commercial product' in s 60(3) of the *Patents Act 1977* (UK), state:

> The use of the word 'staple' is presumably a reference to raw materials or other basic products commonly available and with a multitude of possible applications, and the purpose of the subsection is to protect the supplier of such products even if he has knowledge that they are to be put to an infringing purpose. The scope of the words is far from clear and the dividing line between protecting the supplier of raw materials on the one hand and giving a fair monopoly to the patentee must be a question of fact in each case.

The authors of the IPAC report referred (at paragraph 14.2) to the undesirability of preventing a person from selling 'a staple commodity with a wide variety of possible uses' suggesting that they also considered that a staple commodity was one that had a wide range of uses.

431. We are not satisfied that rosuvastatin is a staple commercial product. The fact that it may be used for both infringing and non-infringing purposes is not conclusive. There are many products capable of being used for both infringing and non-infringing purposes that cannot be characterised as either raw materials or basic products commonly used for a variety of purposes. The uses to which rosuvastatin may be put appear to us to be limited to the prevention or treatment of cardiovascular disease and its associated risk factors (eg, high cholesterol). This is apparent from the evidence of Dr Wilson, a cardiologist called by AstraZeneca, who said that he does not prescribe rosuvastatin (or any other statin) for any indication other than cardiovascular disease or its associated risk factors. It is true that Dr Hay, a general practitioner called by AstraZeneca, gave evidence that he also prescribes rosuvastatin for the treatment of conditions such as cerebrovascular disease, chronic renal disease and diabetes. However, as we read his evidence, rosuvastatin is prescribed by Dr Hay in order to prevent or treat cardiovascular disease in situations where there is increased risk of it occurring due to the existence of these conditions.

432. Although the primary judge was not satisfied that rosuvastatin is a staple commercial product, AstraZeneca's argument based on s 117(2)(b) was rejected by her Honour on other grounds. Her Honour said (at [512]):

> I do not accept that s 117(1) and (2)(b) requires AZ to prove that any particular person will split a 20 mg tablet into two 10 mg doses. In the present case the evidence is sufficient to infer that whatever the instructions the generic parties give to medical practitioners and pharmacists there remains a risk that some people will obtain the 20 mg dose of the generic tablets for the purpose of dividing them into two 10 mg doses. Risk, however, is one thing. Proof on the balance of probabilities that any person 'would' infringe the 051 or low dose patent is another. Given the steps proposed by the generic parties to instruct medical practitioners and pharmacists not to endorse or encourage tablet splitting, it is a long stretch on the currently available evidence to conclude that any person would split the tablets into 10 mg doses and thereby infringe the patent. I accept that AZ has proved a real risk that it might occur, given the economic incentives. But in terms of proof that is insufficient.

433. Her Honour's rejection of the first of the arguments referred to in [512] of her reasons was challenged in the generic parties' notices of contention but the point was not developed in submissions. In any event, the primary judge was right to reject it. Section 117 owes its existence, in large part, to

the difficulties that patentees are likely to experience in enforcing their rights against consumers at the end of a supply chain who engage in infringing use of products supplied to them by others. The inability of the patentee to identify the particular person or persons who engage in such use is one of the very difficulties confronting patentees that s 117 was intended to ameliorate (see the IPAC report at paragraph 14.2). It is not necessary for a patentee to succeed under s 117 that he or she identify any particular person or persons who the supplier has reason to believe will use the product in question in an infringing manner.

434. The second argument relied upon by the generic parties in relation to s 117(2)(b), which was accepted by the primary judge, raises what is primarily a question of fact. In short, the primary judge was not satisfied, on the evidence, that any of the generic parties had reason to believe that consumers would engage in tablet splitting and use the generic parties' 20 mg or 40 mg products in a manner that would infringe the claims of the 051 or low dose patent.

435. So far as the economic incentive to engage in tablet splitting is concerned, the evidence showed that AstraZeneca's rosuvastatin product (whether it is in 5 mg, 10 mg or 20 mg dosages) comes in the same size pack and (at least for patients with PBS prescriptions) at the same price. This means that a patient who is directed by a doctor to take 10 mg dosages will have a financial incentive to purchase a pack of 20 mg tablets which he or she may then split into 10 mg dosages.

436. There was evidence from Mr Sanghvi, a pharmacist from Melbourne called by AstraZeneca, as to the widespread availability of 'tablet splitting' devices used by patients in relation to many different kinds of prescription medicines. There was also evidence from Dr Wilson who said he was aware that some of his patients split their statin tablets. He said that he regularly agrees to requests from patients to prescribe a higher dosage of statin to permit them to engage in tablet splitting in order to save money. Dr Hay also gave evidence to much the same effect, although he was more specific in his evidence as to his prescribing practices in such situations than was Dr Wilson. Dr Hay said that if he wanted to prescribe a 10 mg dose of rosuvastatin to a patient who wants to split tablets (to save money) he would always write '20 mg, take half a tablet' on the script.

437. Market research data relied upon by AstraZeneca indicated that only a small percentage (2.75%) of prescriptions written by medical practitioners directed patients to take half a 20 mg tablet. AstraZeneca submitted that there are likely to be more patients who engage in tablet splitting who do so in circumstances where there is no relevant direction on their prescription. However, this submission is not supported by the evidence. It seems doubtful that doctors would prescribe rosuvastatin in 20 mg tablets to a patient who was to be treated in 10 mg dosages without taking the same precautions taken by Dr Hay. One can see why a doctor would feel the need to guard against the patient taking more than the prescribed dosage by making it clear on the prescription that the patient was to take half a tablet in order to ensure the patient received the correct dosage.

438. On the primary judge's analysis of the evidence, AstraZeneca established that the generic parties were aware (or, objectively, should have been aware) that there was a risk that consumers would split the generic parties' 20 mg tablets in order to save money. However, her Honour stopped short of holding that they had reason to believe that consumers would engage in such a practice.

439. It is difficult to draw any precise conclusions as to how widespread the practice of 20 mg tablet splitting might become (at the time of trial the generic parties' products were not yet on sale) without knowing what developments might occur in the market place with respect to the pricing of

CURRENT LAW

both the generic parties' 20 mg products and AstraZeneca's 10 mg product. The more AstraZeneca's 10 mg product costs relative to the generic parties' 20 mg products, the more likely it is that consumers would buy and split the generic parties' 20 mg products. However, in our view, contrary to the finding of the primary judge, the evidence established that the generic parties had reason to believe that some consumers would put the generic parties' 20 mg products to an infringing use.

440. Section 117(2)(b) raises a special problem that was referred to by Hayne J in *Collins* (at [41] to [51]) in the context of his Honour's consideration of the meaning of the phrase 'staple commercial product'. His Honour drew attention to the potentially wide operation of s 117(1) when read with s 117(2)(b) in circumstances where the relevant product is one that may be used for both infringing and non-infringing uses. The facts of the present case highlight one aspect of the problem referred to by Hayne J.

441. It is important to note that the relief sought by AstraZeneca in respect of the 051 or low dose patent included a *quia timet* injunction that would have the effect of restraining the supply by the generic parties of their 20 mg rosuvastatin products to any person (in particular wholesalers and/or pharmacists) through whose hands such products may pass on their way to consumers including, but not limited to, the relatively small proportion of such consumers who the generic parties have reason to believe would engage in infringing use.

442. Section 117(2)(b) uses the expression 'the person' which is the same person referred to in the opening words of s 117(1), *viz* '[i]f the use of a product by *a person* would infringe a patent'. Section 117(1) when read with 117(2)(b) is therefore only engaged if the supplier has reason to believe that *the person* to whom the product is or may be supplied would put it to an infringing use. As we have said, it is not necessary for the patentee to identify any particular person or persons in order to successfully rely upon s 117(1) when read with s 117(2)(a), (b) or (c). But the application of s 117(1) when read with s 117(2)(b) may be particularly challenging for a patentee both in establishing an actual or threatened supply to which s 117(1) can apply and in fashioning appropriate injunctive relief in circumstances where there are many users of the product only some of whom are likely to put the product to an infringing use.

443. The first difficulty arises out of the fact that s 117(1) and s 117(2)(b) deem a supply of a product to be an infringement of a patent if, but only if, the supplier has reason to believe that *the person* to whom the product is or may be supplied will put it to an infringing use. It is not easy to apply s 117(1) and s 117(2)(b) literally in circumstances involving the supply of product in large quantities for use by a large number of consumers where the first supplier in the relevant supply chain has reason to believe that some, but not all, of the consumers to whom the product might ultimately be supplied will put it to an infringing use. If s 117(1) is engaged in such circumstances then some consideration of proportionality as between the extent of the infringing use that is forecast and the scope of any injunctive relief is warranted.

444. It may be undesirable to impose a blanket restraint upon a supplier who has reason to believe that only some consumers, perhaps a very small minority, may put the product that is or may be supplied to them to an infringing use. This is because the effect of such an injunction may be to deny a supplier access to a market, and consumers' access to a product, in circumstances where the supplier could have no reason to believe that the majority of consumers would put the product to an infringing use. It seems to us that, all other things being equal, the more difficult it is for the patentee

CURRENT LAW

to establish that there is a likelihood of widespread infringing use, the more difficult it should be for the patentee to obtain injunctive relief in the broad terms restraining *any* supply of the relevant product. In the present case, even if AstraZeneca established that the generic parties had reason to believe that some consumers would engage in infringing use, the likely scale of that activity, were it to occur, was not shown to be such as would justify the grant of the wide injunction that AstraZeneca sought. Given our conclusion in relation to the validity of claims of the 051 or low dose patent, it is not necessary for us to consider what other injunctive relief, if any, might have been appropriate in lieu of that sought by AstraZeneca.

EXEMPTIONS FROM INFRINGEMENT

Chapter 6 illustrates the wide-ranging exemptions from infringement in the *Copyright Act 1968* (Cth). No similarly wide set of exceptions exists for patents. Very few exemptions are recognised internationally, and currently the Australian *Patents Act* does not even include all of the internationally recognised exemptions.

Article 30 of the TRIPS Agreement allows the following exemptions (or exceptions, as they are referred to in this Article):

> Members may provide limited exceptions to the exclusive rights conferred by a patent, provided that such exceptions do not unreasonably conflict with a normal exploitation of the patent and do not unreasonably prejudice the legitimate interests of the patent owner, taking account of the legitimate interests of third parties.

Prior to entry into force of the *Intellectual Property Laws Amendment (Raising the Bar) Act 2012* (Cth) (the '*Raising the Bar Act*'), only three express exemptions were provided in the *Patents Act*:

- use in or on foreign vessels, aircraft or vehicles (s 118);
- prior use (s 119); and
- acts necessary for obtaining regulatory approval for pharmaceuticals (s 119A).

The *Raising the Bar Act* extended the regulatory approvals exemptions and introduced a new exemption for use of a patented invention for experimental purposes through ss 119B and 119C. The new exemption applies to acts done on or after 16 April 2012 in relation to patents granted before, on or after that date.

119B Infringement exemptions: acts for obtaining regulatory approval (non-pharmaceuticals)

(1) A person may, without infringing a patent, do an act that would infringe the patent apart from this subsection, if the act is done solely for:

  (a) purposes connected with obtaining an approval required by a law of the Commonwealth or of a State or Territory to exploit a product, method or process; or

  (b) purposes connected with obtaining a similar approval under a law of another country or region.

(2) This section does not apply in relation to a pharmaceutical patent within the meaning of subsection 119A(3).

119C Infringement exemptions: acts for experimental purposes

(1) A person may, without infringing a patent for an invention, do an act that would infringe the patent apart from this subsection, if the act is done for experimental purposes relating to the subject matter of the invention.

(2) For the purposes of this section, *experimental purposes* relating to the subject matter of the invention include, but are not limited to, the following:

  (a) determining the properties of the invention;

  (b) determining the scope of a claim relating to the invention;

  (c) improving or modifying the invention;

  (d) determining the validity of the patent or of a claim relating to the invention;

  (e) determining whether the patent for the invention would be, or has been, infringed by the doing of an act.

The Explanatory Memorandum to the Intellectual Property Laws Amendment (Raising the Bar) Bill 2011, both in its Regulation Impact Statement on pp 12–13 and in the discussion of items 1 and 2 of Sch 2 of the Bill on pp 69–72, explain the rationale for the introduction of these provisions.

EXPLANATORY MEMORANDUM, INTELLECTUAL PROPERTY LAWS AMENDMENT (RAISING THE BAR) BILL 2011

REGULATION IMPACT STATEMENT

The following Regulation Impact Statements apply only to the items in Schedule 2.

EXEMPTIONS TO PATENT INFRINGEMENT: EXPERIMENTAL USE

PROBLEM

Background

1. The last 20 years has seen a shift in the Australian economy from a reliance on traditional resource and agricultural industries, to industries such as banks, financial services, telecommunications and retailers which rely heavily on intellectual property.[1] Even in traditional industries, the intellectual property underpinning Australian innovation has substantially contributed to increases in productivity and efficiency. Australia now ranks amongst the top innovative economies in the world,[2] with the total value of Australia's intellectual property standing at about AU$30 billion.[3]

2. One of the keystones of an innovative economy is its intellectual property regime.[4] For a country such as Australia, which is a net importer of technology, a strong and well regulated IP regime encourages the flow of innovation, technology and knowledge into the country by giving importers confidence that their technology will be protected from copying. This gives Australians access to new technology and helps Australian businesses which rely on foreign technology to remain competitive. Intellectual property is also vital for companies to attract investment to fund research, generate returns

on investment and continue the cycle of innovation. These activities support economic growth and competitiveness.[4]

. . .

The problem

5. A second keystone of an innovative economy is a strong and active research community. The patent system supports research by encouraging investment in the research that underpins development of new technologies. However, this support is reduced where there is uncertainty about the overlap between patent rights and researchers' freedom to operate. Such uncertainty currently exists in Australia.

- It is widely assumed that a common law experimental use exemption exists alongside the patent system and it is likely that a court would find that, in some circumstances, use of a patented invention for experimental or research purposes would not constitute an infringement of a patent. However it is difficult to predict how broadly or narrowly an Australian court would interpret the scope of an experimental or research exception.[8]

- In countries where there is no statutory experimental use provision, courts have struggled to ascertain the scope of the exemption or have applied overly restrictive tests that are potentially detrimental to research. For example, a recent US case considered the existence and scope of the common law experimental use exemption in the United States.[5] Consistent with earlier court decisions this defence was interpreted narrowly, finding that it was dependent on the experiments involved being 'for amusement, to satisfy idle curiosity, or for strictly philosophical inquiry'.[6] There have been suggestions that this decision has adversely impacted on research organisations that previously thought they were subject to a broader experimental use exemption.[7]

- Whilst there is no strong empirical evidence of patents preventing follow-on innovation in Australia,[8] it has been cautioned that an absence of evidence in Australia is not an absence of a problem, and that 'it is risky to assume that the present lack of evidence is indicative of future trends'.[9] Anecdotal evidence from a survey of Australian researchers and research institutions[10] showed that there is considerable uncertainty among researchers in respect of where they have freedom to operate around patented technology. This study considered survey responses from 49 companies, 23 research institutions and 18 genetic testing laboratories. About 40 interviews were also held with respondents. The researchers concluded that a 'practice-based' research exemption had developed in Australia, under which companies were loathe to enforce their rights against researchers because it would have a negative effect on the company's image and because research institutions generally lack financial resources to make legal challenge worthwhile. However the study also cautioned that this attitude may not continue into the future.

6. The absence in Australia of both statute and case law provides researchers and business with little guidance as to whether or not experimental use of a patented invention constitutes an infringement. As a consequence the potential for litigation may deter businesses and researchers from researching in areas covered by patents. This could have significant impact on Australian business by inhibiting research, or driving it overseas to countries with more favourable experimental use provisions, leading to a loss of research investment in Australia.

. . .

1   Wilson T, 'Intellectual Property and the Australian Economy', Institute of Public Affairs, 2008, http://www.ipa.org.au/library/publication/1219635913_document_080612_-_paper_-_ip_and_the_australian_economy_in.pdf.
2   Gans J et al, 'Assessing Australia's Innovative Capacity: 2006 Update', Melbourne Business School and Intellectual Property Research Institute of Australia, 2006.
3   Department of Foreign Affairs and Trade, 'Intellectual Property and International Trade', viewed 25 September 2009 at http://www.dfat.gov.au/ip/.
4   Zink R, 'The role of IP in promoting economic growth through innovation', *Intellectual Asset Management*, pp 23-29, May/June 2009.
5   *Madey v Duke University* 307 F 3d 1351, 1362 (Fed Cir 2002).
6   *Roche Products Inc v Bolar Pharmaceutical Co, Inc*, 733 F 2d, 858, 863 (Fed Cir 1984).
7   See for example, Donaldson R, 'An update on the proposed experimental use exemption to patent infringement', *Australian Intellectual Property Law Bulletin*, 19(9), pp 147–148 (2007).
8   Advisory Council on Intellectual Property, *Patents and Experimental Use*, October 2005 at page 22.
9   McBratney A et al, 'Australia Experiments with Experimental Use', *Nature Biotechnology* p 22, 2004.
10 D Nicol and J Nielsen, 'Patents and Medical Biotechnology: An Empirical Analysis of Issues Facing the Australian Industry' (2003) Centre for Law and Genetics Occasional Paper No 6.

SCHEDULE 2—FREE ACCESS TO PATENTED INVENTIONS FOR REGULATORY APPROVALS AND RESEARCH

INTRODUCTION

This schedule contains two amendments that give researchers greater certainty about where they have freedom to operate around patented technology.

The first amendment expands the existing exemption from patent infringement for activities necessary to gain regulatory approval for pharmaceutical products to all technologies. The second amendment introduces an exemption from patent infringement for research and experimental activities.

ITEM 1: INFRINGEMENT EXEMPTIONS

ACTS FOR OBTAINING REGULATORY APPROVAL

[s 119B]

This item amends the *Patents Act* to introduce an exemption from patent infringement for activities undertaken for the purpose of obtaining information required for regulatory approval of a non-pharmaceutical product.

The patent system seeks to strike a balance between rewarding primary innovations and allowing subsequent competition. Twenty years is currently accepted by most countries as the appropriate maximum duration of patent protection for most technologies. After the expiry of a patent, any third party is able to market the previously patented product in competition with the former patent holder. These competing products are referred to as 'generic' products.

However, this balance can be upset where a generic manufacturer must seek regulatory approval before marketing their product. The approval process often involves making or using the patented invention, with the result that the generic manufacturer must wait until the term of the patent has ended before seeking regulatory approval in order to avoid infringing the patent. This has the effect of giving the patent owner a de facto extension of the patent term beyond the 20 years ostensibly given by the *Patents Act*.

The issue was first addressed in regards to pharmaceutical patents. The *Intellectual Property Laws Amendment Act 1998* introduced, and the *Intellectual Property Laws Amendment Act 2006* subsequently extended, an exemption from infringement for certain acts to gain regulatory approval in respect of pharmaceutical patents only. This permitted generic manufacturers to obtain regulatory approval during the term of the pharmaceutical patent so they could compete with the patentee as soon as the term expired.

However, pharmaceutical patents are not the only type of patentable product where pre-market regulatory approval is required. For example agricultural chemicals and certain medical devices require regulatory approval. There is no reason, in principle, why non-pharmaceutical technologies should be treated differently and why patentees in non-pharmaceutical technologies should be afforded a de facto extension of term.

Accordingly, this amendment seeks to extend the regulatory approval exemption to all technologies. The new exemption will apply to activities undertaken solely for purposes connected with obtaining regulatory approval of goods (other than the pharmaceutical goods covered by section 119A) under Australian law or under the law of a foreign country, or both.

The use of 'solely' ensures that a generic manufacturer may not use the exemption for purposes other than seeking regulatory approval. For example, they may not, in the process of seeking regulatory approval, stockpile the patented product for sale upon expiry of the patent, or manufacture the product for export to another country.

The amendments are not intended to limit the type of regulatory approval for which the exemption may be used, save for the requirement that it must be imposed by law (in Australia or another jurisdiction). The provision is intended to account for changes in existing regulatory requirements. It is also intended to cover regulatory requirements that do not exist now, but may be imposed in the future as new regulatory regimes are created.

The exemption is not intended to cover experimental uses of the patented invention. Rather, experimental uses are intended to be dealt with under the related amendment discussed below.

ACTS FOR EXPERIMENTAL PURPOSES

[s 119C]

This item amends the *Patents Act* to exempt experimental activities from patent infringement.

The patent system exists to encourage innovation and promote the dissemination of technical knowledge. It rewards the innovator who has invented a new and useful product with a time-limited exclusive right to exploit their invention. In exchange the inventor must disclose their invention to the public. In this way innovators gain a competitive advantage to commercialise their inventions, while the public and the research community gain access to information about new technology. Researchers can then study, test and improve on the new technology for the benefit of society as a whole.

However, the benefits of this system are diminished where there is uncertainty about the extent to which patent rights impinge on freedom to do research.

Uncertainty discourages researchers from working in areas where there are patents, and where they may be at risk of being sued for infringement. It also leads to researchers expending effort and expense on obtaining advice, where they have concerns about how their experiments intersect with the patent system. These inefficiencies detract from the system.

Concerns have been raised that the lack of a statutory exemption from infringement for research and experimental activities in Australia is causing uncertainty and disincentives in the research community, and for follow-on innovators. Although it is generally accepted that some form of implicit experimental use exemption exists, there has been no litigation of this under Australia's current patent legislation. As a consequence the existence and scope of any implicit exemption remains uncertain.

The issue of an experimental use exemption has previously been considered by both the Australian Law Reform Commission[4] (ALRC) and the Advisory Council on Intellectual Property[5] (ACIP). Both confirmed that the lack of a statutory exemption was creating uncertainty for the research community. Both recommended introduction of an explicit exemption.

The item implements these recommendations by introducing a statutory exemption from infringement for research and experimental activities.

It is intended that 'experimental' be given its ordinary English meaning. The exemption should apply to tests, trials and procedures that a researcher or follow-on innovator undertakes as part of discovering new information or testing a principle or supposition.

To provide certainty and clarity for researchers, an additional inclusive list of activities that are deemed to be experimental has been included. This list is not intended to be exhaustive and a court may find that other activities also fall within the meaning of 'experimental'.

The exemption is not intended to apply only to circumstances where activities are undertaken solely for experimental purposes. This would ignore the reality of the current research environment, where research is frequently undertaken for mixed purposes.

For example:

- a researcher may be contracted and paid to undertake experiments;
- research may be conducted with a view to ultimately commercialising the endproducts of the experimentation; and
- research may be undertaken with, and partially funded by, a commercial partner.

In each of these circumstances the exemption should apply as long as the specific acts are undertaken for the predominant purpose of gaining new knowledge, or testing a principle or supposition about the invention. Thus if an activity is conducted primarily for the purpose of improving a patented invention, the activity would still be exempt, even if the person also had in mind commercialising the improvement in the future.

However, the exemption is not intended to apply where the main purpose of the acts is to commercialise the invention, or to manufacture it for the purpose of sale or use for commercial purposes. Additionally, 'market research' on a patented invention (eg making and using the invention to test the likely commercial demand for a product) is not intended to be exempt. This too has a predominantly commercial purpose.

The amendment requires that the experiments be 'related to' the patented invention. This choice of words is intended to achieve two ends.

First, it is intended to cover circumstances where experiments inherently include the subject matter of a patent, perhaps as part of a larger or more complex experiment, but the researcher is unaware of the existence of the patent. This is consistent with the policy objective of freeing researchers to innovate. Researchers should not have to conduct extensive patent searches before starting every experiment.

Secondly, it is not intended to exempt the use of patented 'research tools' from infringement. A 'research tool' is something that is used to facilitate an experiment, rather than something that is the subject of the experiment. For example, a researcher testing the effect of a particular herbicide on different plants might use a patented wetting agent to facilitate uptake of the herbicide. Here use of the wetting agent should not be exempt from infringement. The agent is being used as a tool: the experiments do not relate to it.

Research tools are often used exclusively or primarily in research. If the experimental use exemption were to apply to such tools it would substantially diminish the economic incentive to develop better research tools.

The amendments explicitly preserve any implicit experimental use defence that may be found by a court. The addition of an explicit exemption is not intended to detract in any way from any existing protection that researchers may enjoy.

---

4   ALRC Report 99, Genes and Ingenuity: *Gene Patenting and Human Health* (the ALRC 99 Report), published June 2004, available through www.alrc.gov.au.
5   Advisory Council on Intellectual Property', November 2005, available through www.acip.gov.au.

LICENSING OF PATENT RIGHTS AND LIMITATIONS ON LICENCE CONDITIONS

Although patentees have exclusive rights to exploit their inventions, in many instances they will lack capacity to do so, particularly when it comes to the manufacture of patented products which are market-ready. It is likely that manufacture of commercial quantities will need to be contracted out. In some areas, product development will need to be handed over to other parties at a much earlier stage. This is particularly likely to be the case for university-owned inventions, because product development is well outside their core functions and they lack the skills and resources to carry it out. Decisions need to be made as to whether to assign ownership or license exploitation rights in such circumstances.

Many inventions have value as research tools rather than as end products in their own right. For inventions of this nature, more complex decisions have to be made about self-exploitation, assignment and licensing. In some instances, exclusive licensing may be the most appropriate way to exploit the invention, but in other instances non-exclusive licensing to multiple users may be more appropriate. 'Exclusive licensees' are given certain rights under the *Patent Act* (e.g., to bring infringement proceedings). Note that an 'exclusive licensee' must have been given the right to 'exploit' the invention in its entirety: if the patentee has reserved some of the rights of exploitation (e.g., if it has retained the right to make the patented product, while giving the licensee the exclusive right to sell the product), the licensee will not be exclusive (see *Bristol-Myers Squibb Co v Apotex Pty Ltd* [2015] FCAFC 2). Each licensing negotiation is likely to be different and raise its own distinctive issues.

Licensing of IP is generally governed by contract law principles rather than IP laws. The TRIPS Agreement has little to say about the terms and conditions of IP licences, aside from a general 'motherhood' statement in the objects clause in Art 7:

The protection and enforcement of intellectual property rights should contribute to the promotion of technological innovation and to the transfer and dissemination of technology, to the mutual advantage of producers and users of technological knowledge and in a manner conducive to social and economic welfare, and to a balance of rights and obligations.

Some limitations on licensing are imposed in domestic patent legislation. Section 144 of the *Patents Act* prohibits conditions in contracts that create tying arrangements in relation to patents. Examples of conditions that will be void include terms that the licensee must purchase other unpatented products from the licensor, or that royalty payments continue after the patent expires. However, according to s 144(3) and (4), the prohibition does not apply if, at the time the contract was entered into:

- the licensee had the option of engaging in the relevant dealings on reasonable terms without the prohibited condition; and
- the licensee has the opportunity to avoid the condition by giving reasonable notice.

Australian competition law also provides some limitations on licensing of patented inventions. Through s 51(1) of the *Competition and Consumer Act 2010* (Cth), anti-competitive conduct resulting from the exercise of IP rights granted under the *Patents Act* and other IP legislation is not exempt from trade practices law. However, s 51(3) goes on to provide an exemption from some of the provisions in Part IV of the Act for conditions in patent licences: 'to the extent that the condition relates to ... (iii) the invention to which the patent relates or articles made by use of the invention'.[3] This section has not received judicial scrutiny to date, and a series of law reform reports have recommended that s 51(3) should be repealed, including, most recently, the report by the Productivity Commission, *Compulsory Licensing of Patents* (2013), p 142, and the Competition Policy Review Panel's *Draft Report* (2014), p 87.

USES WITHOUT THE AUTHORISATION OF THE PATENTEE

In some limited circumstances, it is possible to exploit a patented invention without the consent of the patentee. Australian patent legislation has provisions allowing for compulsory licences and Crown use. A compulsory licence is a court or administrative order requiring the patentee to grant a licence to work the invention, in effect limiting the patentee's exclusive right to exploit the invention but ensuring that the patentee does receive remuneration for the use. Crown use is self-explanatory: use of the invention by the Crown for the purposes of the state.

The rationale for these provisions is that the purpose of the patent system is to encourage innovation because that is good for the economy. If a patent is granted and not exploited, there is no innovation and therefore no benefit from the patent grant. In such circumstances, it is recognised that others should be allowed to exploit the invention. The circumstances in which use without authorisation is allowed varies from country to country. In the USA the primary ground on which compulsory licences are issued is to remedy anti-competitive conduct. Many such licences have been issued under anti-trust decrees. In Australia, however, an anti-competitive ground has only recently

---

3   See further J Nielsen, 'Competition Law and Intellectual Property: Establishing a Coherent Approach' in K Bowrey, M Handler and D Nicol, eds, *Emerging Challenges in Intellectual Property*, Oxford University Press, Melbourne, 2011.

been added to the compulsory licensing provisions in the *Patents Act* (see 'Current Australian compulsory licensing provisions' below, p 562).

THE TRIPS PROVISIONS

Article 31 of the TRIPS Agreement allows for use without authorisation subject to certain limitations. As the provisions in Art 31 are quite complex, they are set out in full here:

> Where the law of a Member allows for other use of the subject matter of a patent without the authorization of the right holder, including use by the government or third parties authorized by the government, the following provisions shall be respected:
>
> (a) authorization of such use shall be considered on its individual merits;
>
> (b) such use may only be permitted if, prior to such use, the proposed user has made efforts to obtain authorization from the right holder on reasonable commercial terms and conditions and that such efforts have not been successful within a reasonable period of time. This requirement may be waived by a Member in the case of a national emergency or other circumstances of extreme urgency or in cases of public non-commercial use. In situations of national emergency or other circumstances of extreme urgency, the right holder shall, nevertheless, be notified as soon as reasonably practicable. In the case of public non-commercial use, where the government or contractor, without making a patent search, knows or has demonstrable grounds to know that a valid patent is or will be used by or for the government, the right holder shall be informed promptly;
>
> (c) the scope and duration of such use shall be limited to the purpose for which it was authorized, and in the case of semi-conductor technology shall only be for public non-commercial use or to remedy a practice determined after judicial or administrative process to be anti-competitive;
>
> (d) such use shall be non-exclusive;
>
> (e) such use shall be non-assignable, except with that part of the enterprise or goodwill which enjoys such use;
>
> (f) any such use shall be authorized predominantly for the supply of the domestic market of the Member authorizing such use;
>
> (g) authorization for such use shall be liable, subject to adequate protection of the legitimate interests of the persons so authorized, to be terminated if and when the circumstances which led to it cease to exist and are unlikely to recur. The competent authority shall have the authority to review, upon motivated request, the continued existence of these circumstances;
>
> (h) the right holder shall be paid adequate remuneration in the circumstances of each case, taking into account the economic value of the authorization;
>
> (i) the legal validity of any decision relating to the authorization of such use shall be subject to judicial review or other independent review by a distinct higher authority in that Member;
>
> (j) any decision relating to the remuneration provided in respect of such use shall be subject to judicial review or other independent review by a distinct higher authority in that Member;

(k) Members are not obliged to apply the conditions set forth in subparagraphs (b) and (f) where such use is permitted to remedy a practice determined after judicial or administrative process to be anti-competitive. The need to correct anti-competitive practices may be taken into account in determining the amount of remuneration in such cases. Competent authorities shall have the authority to refuse termination of authorization if and when the conditions which led to such authorization are likely to recur;

(l) where such use is authorized to permit the exploitation of a patent ('the second patent') which cannot be exploited without infringing another patent ('the first patent'), the following additional conditions shall apply:

(i) the invention claimed in the second patent shall involve an important technical advance of considerable economic significance in relation to the invention claimed in the first patent;

(ii) the owner of the first patent shall be entitled to a cross-licence on reasonable terms to use the invention claimed in the second patent; and

(iii) the use authorized in respect of the first patent shall be non-assignable except with the assignment of the second patent.

COMPULSORY LICENSING FOR ACCESS TO MEDICINES

The extreme public health crises facing the developing world were recognised at the World Trade Organization's (WTO's) Ministerial Conference in Doha on 4 November 2001. As a result a Declaration on the TRIPS Agreement and Public Health was agreed to by the parties. Prior to the Declaration the ambit of the provisions in Art 31 of the TRIPS Agreement had been unclear—particularly the extent to which the 'national emergency or other circumstances of extreme urgency' provision in Art 31(b) could be relied on to justify compulsory licensing of pharmaceuticals. The Declaration affirms that the TRIPS Agreement 'does not and should not prevent Members from taking measures to protect public health'. Importantly, it states, *inter alia*, in Art 5:

(b) Each Member has the right to grant compulsory licences and the freedom to determine the grounds upon which such licences are granted.

(c) Each Member has the right to determine what constitutes a national emergency or other circumstances of extreme urgency, it being understood that public health crises, including those relating to HIV/AIDS, tuberculosis, malaria and other epidemics, can represent a national emergency and other circumstances of extreme urgency.

One of the many remaining difficulties was that large numbers of countries lack the capacity to set up their own drug-manufacturing industries. A decision was reached by TRIPS Council members in August 2003 that compulsory licences would be allowed for manufacture in one country and import in another, subject to stringent limitations; and that the right to object based on the requirement that the licence is primarily for the domestic market would be waived, pending amendment of the TRIPS Agreement to reflect this.[4]

In 2005 a proposal was made to amend the TRIPS Agreement, by adding Art 31*bis* and a further Annex to the Agreement. The purpose of these amendments is to avoid the requirement in Art 31(f) that

---

4   The text of the decision is available at www.wto.org/english/tratop_e/trips_e/implem_para6_e.htm.

the use must be predominantly for the supply of the domestic market in circumstances where the use is for the supply of pharmaceuticals to least-developed countries and certain developed countries in national emergencies or other circumstances of extreme urgency. By September 2014, 53 members had formally accepted the amendment. Acceptances are needed from two-thirds of members for entry into force (requiring over 50 more acceptances). The deadline for acceptance has been extended to 31 December 2015.

The patent legislation in some countries has been amended to reflect the TRIPS provisions relating to the supply of pharmaceuticals in circumstances of national emergency or other circumstances of extreme urgency. Canada was the first WTO member to pass implementing legislation in May 2004: *An Act to amend the Patent Act and the Food and Drugs Act—The Jean Chrétien Pledge to Africa*. The Act, along with supporting regulations, established the legal framework for Canada's Access to Medicines Regime, which came into force on 14 May 2005.[5]

On 9 February 2015 the *Intellectual Property Laws Amendment Act 2015* (Cth) was passed by the federal parliament. Once the Act enters into force it will create a compulsory licensing regime to enable Australian pharmaceutical manufacturers to supply generic versions of patented medicine to developing countries. Together with other amendments, Clause 19 in Schedule 1 of the Act inserts s 136B into the *Patents Act*, which provides a simplified outline of the new regime:

> The Federal Court may make an order under this Part requiring the grant of a compulsory licence to exploit a patented pharmaceutical invention for manufacture and export to an eligible importing country.
>
> The court may order a compulsory licence to be granted if the proposed use of the pharmaceutical product is to address a public health issue in the eligible importing country:
>
> (a) in a national emergency (or other extremely urgent circumstances); or
> (b) by the public non-commercial use of the product.
>
> The order may be amended or revoked by another order of the court.
>
> The patentee must be paid an agreed amount of remuneration, or an amount of remuneration determined by the court.

CURRENT AUSTRALIAN COMPULSORY LICENSING PROVISIONS

The main ground for compulsory licensing under s 133 of the Australian *Patents Act* as enacted in 1990 was that the 'reasonable requirements of the public' had not been met by the patentee. Additionally, s 133 provided that a compulsory licence could be granted for a dependent patent where the new product involved an important technical advance of considerable economic significance on the other invention. The compulsory licensing provisions were amended in 2006, pursuant to the *Intellectual Property Laws Amendment Act 2006* (Cth), adding a further ground for anticompetitive conduct. Section 133 of the *Patents Act* now reads:

> (1) Subject to subsection (1A), a person may apply to the Federal Court, after the end of the prescribed period, for an order requiring the patentee to grant the applicant a licence to work the patented invention.
> (1A) A person cannot apply for an order in respect of an innovation patent unless the patent has been certified.

---

5   Information about the regime is available at www.camr-rcam.gc.ca/index_e.html.

(2) After hearing the application, the court may, subject to this section, make the order if satisfied that:

   (a) all the following conditions exist:

      (i) the applicant has tried for a reasonable period, but without success, to obtain from the patentee an authorisation to work the invention on reasonable terms and conditions;

      (ii) the reasonable requirements of the public with respect to the patented invention have not been satisfied;

      (iii) the patentee has given no satisfactory reason for failing to exploit the patent;
or

   (b) the patentee has contravened, or is contravening, Part IV of the *Trade Practices Act 1974* or an application law (as defined in section 150A of that Act) in connection with the patent.

(3) An order must direct that the licence:

   (a) is not to give the licensee, or a person authorised by the licensee, the exclusive right to work the patented invention; and

   (b) is to be assignable only in connection with an enterprise or goodwill in connection with which the licence is used;
and may direct that the licence is to be granted on any other terms specified in the order.

(3B) If the patented invention cannot be worked by the applicant without his or her infringing another patent:

   (a) the court is to make the order only if the court is further satisfied that the patented invention involves an important technical advance of considerable economic significance on the invention (other invention) to which the other patent relates; and

   (b) the court must further order that the patentee of the other invention:

      (i) must grant to the applicant a licence to work the other invention insofar as is necessary to work the patented invention; and

      (ii) is to be granted, if he or she so requires, a cross-licence on reasonable terms to work the patented invention; and

   (c) the court must direct that the licence granted by the patentee of the other invention may be assigned by the applicant:

      (i) only if he or she assigns the licence granted in respect of the patented invention; and

      (ii) only to the assignee of that licence.

(4) An order operates, without prejudice to any other method of enforcement, as if it were embodied in a deed granting a licence and executed by the patentee and all other necessary parties.

(5) The patentee is to be paid in respect of a licence granted to the applicant under an order:

   (a) such amount as is agreed between the patentee and the applicant; or

   (b) if paragraph (a) does not apply—such amount as is determined by the Federal Court to be just and reasonable having regard to the economic value of the licence and the desirability of discouraging contraventions of Part IV of the *Trade Practices Act 1974* or an application law (as defined in section 150A of that Act).

(6) The patentee or the Federal Court may revoke the licence if:

    (a) the patentee and the licensee are agreed, or the court on application made by either party finds, that the circumstances that justified the grant of the licence have ceased to exist and are unlikely to recur; and

    (b) the legitimate interests of the licensee are not likely to be adversely affected by the revocation.

Section 135 sets out the circumstances in which the reasonable requirements of the public are taken not to have been satisfied:

    (a) an existing trade or industry in Australia, or the establishment of a new trade or industry in Australia is unfairly prejudiced, or the demand in Australia for the patented product, or for a product resulting from the patented process, is not reasonably met, because of the patentee's failure:

        (i) to manufacture the patented product to an adequate extent, and supply it on reasonable terms; or

        (ii) to manufacture, to an adequate extent, a part of the patented product that is necessary for the efficient working of the product, and supply the part on reasonable terms; or

        (iii) to carry on the patented process to a reasonable extent; or

        (iv) to grant licences on reasonable terms; or

    (b) a trade or industry in Australia is unfairly prejudiced by the conditions attached by the patentee (whether before or after the commencing day) to the purchase, hire or use of the patented product, the use or working of the patented process; or

    (c) if the patented product is not being worked in Australia on a commercial scale, but is capable of being worked in Australia.

Very few applications have been made for compulsory licences. There has been no judicial interpretation of the compulsory licensing provisions in the current *Patents Act* and there is only one judicial decision examining the equivalent provisions in the *Patents Act 1952* (Cth) (extracted below).

CASE EXTRACT: PRECEDENT

Fastening Supplies Pty Ltd v Olin Mathieson Chemical Corp

(1969) 119 CLR 572
High Court of Australia

Menzies J (at 575–580): An examination of the circumstances set out in the lettered paragraphs of s 110 suggests that the objects of the compulsory licensing provisions of the Acts cover both (1) fostering Australian manufacturing industry to make the patented article or to use the patented process and (2) ensuring that the Australian demand for the patented article or articles made in accordance with the patented process should be reasonably met whether from local production or from imports. It could, therefore, be that the reasonable requirements of the public would not have been satisfied simply by the importation of enough patented articles to meet the Australian demand. See particularly s 110(1)

PRECEDENT

(c) and (d). The circumstance that to foster Australian manufacture is an object of the provisions as a whole might well dictate that in some circumstances a compulsory licence should be confined to the use of the invention for local manufacture and the sale of the products of such manufacture and should not afford the licensee the right to import and sell patented articles.

As to the construction of s 110(1)(a), I am of the opinion that the demand for the patented article has not been reasonably met if the Court should be satisfied that, because of its superiority over articles already on the market, potential purchasers would have bought it had it been available. A market for a less efficient article indicates, other things being equal, a market for a more efficient article.

There is one further matter of construction to be mentioned. Mr Searby argued that, in the exercise of its discretion under s 108(3), the Court should confine its attention to circumstances as they existed when the petition was lodged. I do not agree. Apart from the inherent unreasonableness of so doing, it appears to me that s 110(2) indicates quite clearly that the Court will have regard to circumstances as they may exist at the time of the actual hearing of the petition.

The petitioner here seeking a compulsory licence is a Victorian company. The patent in respect of which the application is made is No 215562, an invention patent with priority date 27th February 1957 ...

The Commissioner of Patents who, under s 108(2), has referred the petition to the Court, has appeared and been heard by counsel for my assistance.

The patent was sealed on 5th December 1958. The petition was lodged on 23rd December 1968, some ten years after the sealing of the patent.

The patent relates to a fastener driving tool in the form of a captive-bolt gun. The gun is loaded with a metal fastener and with a cartridge. It is fired by a trigger and the explosion of the cartridge actuates a driving ram which propels the fastener through a muzzle into the material to be fastened, against which, the muzzle bushing is pressed by the operator. The fastener penetrates the material to be fastened and the material to which it is to be fastened, e.g., steel to steel, or to masonry. Such fastener driving tools are widely used in industry, particularly the building industry. Despite some conflict in the evidence, I find that timber may be fastened to concrete by use of the tool. There are, of course, other uses. There is a substantial and constant demand for tools of this kind.

The patent is concerned with improvements to captive-bolt guns for use for the purposes mentioned and, in particular, to provide for the automatic return of the driving ram from its fired position to its firing position. This is described in detail in col. 13 of the complete specification. It is not, I think, necessary to go into further particulars about the invention. It is common ground between the parties that guns made in accordance with the invention are better guns than those of earlier types. There has at all times material been a potential market for guns made in accordance with the invention in Australia.

There is no doubt in my mind that when the petition was lodged in December 1968 it correctly alleged that the reasonable requirements of the public with respect to the patented article had not been satisfied. None had been available to the public despite a potential demand which became actual as soon as the articles made in accordance with the invention became available to the market.

...

The evidence establishes to my satisfaction that the manufacture, which has now been established in Australia by Ramset, is not merely a belated response to the petition for a compulsory licence.

[Menzies J was also not convinced that the petitioner had the necessary skills and resources to undertake manufacture and in all the circumstances refused the petition.]

Given the lack of case law considering the compulsory licensing provisions, it is difficult to identify the types of cases that might persuade the court to grant a compulsory licence. There may be some circumstances—for example when patent claims are made for new products to be used in the treatment of serious disease—in which delay in bringing the invention to the phase of commercial application is inexcusable in terms of the public interest. In such circumstances it is entirely appropriate for the courts to look favourably on applications for compulsory licences.

In 2013, the Productivity Commission undertook a major review of the Australian compulsory licensing provisions. To date there has been no response from the federal government. The following recommendations are pertinent.

PRODUCTIVITY COMMISSION, *COMPULSORY LICENSING OF PATENTS* (2013)

RECOMMENDATION 6.1

The Australian Government should seek to remove s 133(2)(b) from the *Patents Act 1990* (Cwlth), so that a compulsory licence order based on restrictive trade practices of the patent holder is only available under the *Competition and Consumer Act 2010* (Cwlth). The remedy provisions in the *Competition and Consumer Act* should be amended to explicitly recognise compulsory licence orders to exploit a patented invention as a remedy under the Act. The new remedy provision should specify that an order must:

- not give the licensee, or a person authorised by the licensee, the exclusive right to work the patented invention
- be assignable only in connection with an enterprise or goodwill in connection with which the licence is used.

The new provision should also contain a clause specifying the basis for determining remuneration, which is identical to the corresponding clause in the *Patents Act.*

...

RECOMMENDATION 6.2

The Australian Government should seek to amend the *Patents Act 1990* (Cwlth) to replace the 'reasonable requirements of the public' test for a compulsory licence with a new public interest test. The new test should specify that a compulsory licence to exploit the patented invention would be available if the following conditions are met:

- Australian demand for a product or service is not being met on reasonable terms, and access to the patented invention is essential for meeting this demand.
- The applicant has tried for a reasonable period, but without success, to obtain access from the patentee on reasonable terms and conditions.

- There is a substantial public interest in providing access to the applicant, having regard to:
  - benefits to the community from meeting the relevant unmet demand
  - commercial costs and benefits to the patent holder and licensee from granting access to the patented invention
  - other impacts on community wellbeing, including those resulting from greater competition and from the overall effect on innovation.

The new provisions should require the Federal Court to set the terms of the licence, including—where the parties cannot reach agreement—any remuneration, consistent with the public interest, having regard to the rights of:

- the patentee to obtain a return on investment commensurate with the regulatory and commercial risks involved
- the public to the efficient exploitation of the invention.

...

RECOMMENDATION 10.1

IP Australia and the Australian Competition and Consumer Commission (ACCC) should jointly develop a plain English guide on the compulsory licensing provisions. The guide should be available on both the IP Australia and ACCC websites.

THE AUSTRALIAN CROWN USE PROVISIONS

Chapter 17 of the *Patents Act* has a number of provisions relating to the Crown. Sections 162 and 163 are of relevance here.

162 Commonwealth and State authorities

A reference in this Chapter to the Commonwealth includes a reference to an authority of the Commonwealth and a reference to a State includes a reference to an authority of a State.

163 Exploitation of inventions by Crown

(1) Where, at any time after a patent application has been made, the invention concerned is exploited by the Commonwealth or a State (or by a person authorised in writing by the Commonwealth or a State) for the services of the Commonwealth or the State, the exploitation is not an infringement:
  (a) if the application is pending—of the nominated person's rights in the invention; or
  (b) if a patent has been granted for the invention—of the patent.

(2) A person may be authorised for the purposes of subsection (1):
  (a) before or after any act for which the authorisation is given has been done; and
  (b) before or after a patent has been granted for the invention; and
  (c) even if the person is directly or indirectly authorised by the nominated person or patentee to exploit the invention.

(3) Subject to section 168, an invention is taken for the purposes of this Part to be exploited for services of the Commonwealth or of a State if the exploitation of the invention is necessary for the proper provision of those services within Australia.

The courts have decided that these provisions cover such things as use by a state rail authority of an invention for the construction of rail carriages (*General Steel Industries Inc v Commissioner of Railways (NSW)* (1964) 112 CLR 125) and use by a local government authority of a meter relating to measurement of water supply (see *Stack v Brisbane City Council* (1995) 32 IPR 69, below).

CASE EXTRACT: PRECEDENT

Stack v Brisbane City Council

(1995) 32 IPR 69
Federal Court of Australia

Cooper J (at 80–84): The invention was exploited (in fact or on the assumption) by the BCC contracting to buy from the third respondent and the third respondent supplying water meters incorporating the invention to measure water supplied by the BCC to properties in the BCC territorial unit for the purpose of levying charges for supply on users based on levels of consumption. The water meters supplied by the third respondent are manufactured by the second respondent and sold or otherwise disposed of by the second respondent to the third respondent.

It is submitted for the applicants that the installation of water meters is a revenue-gathering function of the BCC and is not exploitation for the services of the State. Mr Crowe of counsel submitted that on the proper construction of s 163 the exploitation referred to must be exploitation for the State or the services of the State and not for, or for the services of, the 'authority of a State'. It is submitted that the benefit of the installation of water meters is enjoyed by the BCC and not by the State and therefore the exploitation is not 'for the services of the State' within Chapter 17.

In my view the question is initially one of statutory interpretation. By s 162, a reference in Chapter 17 of the Act to a State includes a reference to an authority of a State. Therefore, the real question here is whether the exploitation of the invention was for the services of an authority of a State, viz the BCC. The contention that ss 162 and 163 of the Act should be read such that 'authority of a State' is interposed in the phrase 'exploited by ... a State' but not in the phrase 'for the services of ... the State' which follows almost immediately after the former cannot be supported by any principle of law nor by logical argument. Furthermore, no assistance is to be gained for the applicants by the fact that the exploitation referred to in s 163 must be by 'a State' while the exploitation be for the services of 'the State'. The plain meaning of ss 162 and 163 is that the exploitation by a State (or an authority of a State) is not an infringement of a patent where the exploitation is for the services of the State (or authority of a State) which is exploiting the invention.

The focus of inquiry must then turn to the meaning of 'for the services of'.

[His Honour then considered the case law interpreting similar provisions in the *Patents Act 1952* (Cth) and UK patent law.]

PRECEDENT

In the instant case the water meters were, or are to be, supplied to the BCC to be attached to its pipework to measure the quantity of water supplied by it from the public supply to any landowner to whose land reticulated water is supplied. The water meter is not re-supplied to the land owner; it is not used in the relevant sense by the land owner. The water meter is an asset of the BCC which enables it to quantify the water actually supplied and to charge for it by reference to that quantity. The water meter becomes a component part of the apparatus by which water is supplied by the BCC for consumption in the territorial area of the BCC, such supply being a function of local government.

Conformably with the approach taken by Barwick CJ in *General Steel Industries Inc v Commissioner of Railways (NSW)* (1964) 112 CLR 125 the use of the water meters by the BCC as part of the supply by it of reticulated water in the Brisbane local authority area is the exploitation by the BCC as an authority of a State of the invention, the subject of Australian petty patent number 645740, for the services of it as such an authority. In consequence, s 163(1) of the Act operates to prevent the exploitation by the BCC of the invention constituting an infringement of the said petty patent.

There is some uncertainty about the full ambit of the Crown use provisions. The Productivity Commission considered these provisions in its 2013 report into compulsory licensing and made the following recommendations:

PRODUCTIVITY COMMISSION, *COMPULSORY LICENSING OF PATENTS* (2013)

RECOMMENDATION 7.1
The Australian Government should seek to amend s 163 of the *Patents Act 1990* (Cwlth) to make it clear that Crown use can be invoked for the provision of a service that the Australian, State and/or Territory Governments have the primary responsibility for providing or funding.

RECOMMENDATION 7.2
The Australian Government should seek to amend the *Patents Act 1990* (Cwlth) to require:

- the Crown to attempt to negotiate use of the patented invention prior to invoking Crown use
- the Crown to provide the patentee with a statement of reasons no less than 14 days before such use occurs
- Crown use to be approved by a Minister (the relevant Federal Minister or State Attorneys-General)
- that in instances of Crown use, the patentee is entitled to remuneration determined on the same basis as that for a compulsory licence.

The first two requirements should be able to be waived in emergencies. However, in all cases patentees should be provided with immediate notice that their patents have been used, and a statement of reasons as soon as practical thereafter.

—14—

TRADE SECRETS: PROTECTION OF CONFIDENTIAL INFORMATION

INTRODUCTION

Trade secrets are as important a component of a business's IP portfolio as patents, trade marks, industrial designs and copyrighted materials. Think, for a moment, of the economic value of the recipes for Coca-Cola and for KFC, both of which are classic examples of trade secrets. In this chapter the consequences of disclosure and threatened disclosure of trade secrets are discussed within the context of the equitable action for breach of confidence and the common law action for breach of contract. Particular attention is focused on the employer–employee relationship.

SOURCES OF LAW PROTECTING CONFIDENTIAL INFORMATION

The *Agreement on Trade-Related Aspects of Intellectual Property Rights* (the 'TRIPS Agreement') (1994) imposes obligations on World Trade Organization (WTO) member states to provide protection for undisclosed information, but these obligations are cast in very general terms. Article 39 provides in part that:

(1) In the course of ensuring effective protection against unfair competition as provided in Article 10*bis* of the Paris Convention (1967), Members shall protect undisclosed information in accordance with paragraph 2 …

(2) Natural and legal persons shall have the possibility of preventing information lawfully within their control from being disclosed to, acquired by, or used by others without their consent in a manner contrary to honest commercial practices* so long as such information:

   (a) is secret in the sense that it is not, as a body or in the precise configuration and assembly of its components, generally known among or readily accessible to persons within the circles that normally deal with the kind of information in question;

   (b) has commercial value because it is secret; and

   (c) has been subject to reasonable steps under the circumstances, by the person lawfully in control of the information, to keep it secret.

* For the purpose of this provision, 'a manner contrary to honest commercial practices' shall mean at least practices such as breach of contract, breach of confidence and inducement to breach, and includes the acquisition of undisclosed information by third parties who knew, or were grossly negligent in failing to know, that such practices were involved in the acquisition.

Trade secrets are recognised and protected under Australian law in a manner that is very different from other forms of IP. Patents, registered trade marks and designs all have to satisfy the registration requirements imposed through legislation before enforceable property rights are created and, although there is no registration requirement for copyright, enforceable property rights in copyright subject matter are also created by statute. There is, however, no 'trade secret' statute in Australian law, and trade secrets are not protected at law as a species of property. They are protected in equity, through an action for breach of confidence,[1] or by express or implied contractual terms.

As a general rule, express contractual provisions take priority. The extract below from *AG Australia Holdings Ltd v Burton* [2002] NSWSC 170; [2002] NSWLR 464 clearly illustrates that it will only be necessary to have recourse to implication of contractual terms or equity in the following circumstances:

- where there is no express contractual provision creating an obligation of confidentiality;
- where the alleged breach of confidence goes beyond the scope of the express contractual provision; or
- where the express provision is otherwise unenforceable.

However, the later case of *Optus Networks Pty Ltd v Telstra Corporation Ltd* [2010] FCAFC 21; (2010) 265 ALR 281 (also extracted below) makes it clear that a party alleging breach of confidence can, in some circumstances, rely on the equitable action even where an express contractual obligation of confidence is enforceable. Much will depend on whether the express terms of the contract exclude recourse to equity.

CASE EXTRACT: CURRENT LAW

AG Australia Holdings Ltd v Burton

[2002] NSWSC 170; (2002) 58 NSWLR 464
Supreme Court of New South Wales

[The plaintiff was formerly known as GIO. After suffering significant losses, shareholders brought a class action against GIO, based on a number of causes of action. Burton was an ex-employee of GIO and had entered into express confidentiality undertakings during the course of employment. The issue was whether the making of a witness statement to the solicitors representing the shareholders amounted to breach of these undertakings.]

Campbell J: 73. The law recognises three different ways in which an obligation of confidentiality might arise. The first is by express provision in a contract. The second is by an implied term in a contract. The third is as an obligation recognised in the exclusive jurisdiction of equity.

74. In any litigation which seeks to enforce an obligation of confidentiality, it is important to recognise which of these three types of obligation is alleged. The considerations which enter into the validity, and means of enforcement, of an obligation of confidentiality can differ, between these three types.

---

1   On the origins of the equitable action, and for the most comprehensive treatment of Anglo-Australian law, see T Aplin et al, *Gurry on Breach of Confidence: The Protection of Confidential Information*, 2nd ed, Oxford University Press, Oxford, 2012.

75. In the present case, the obligation which is sought to be enforced is, primarily, an express contractual obligation, namely that arising under the confidentiality undertaking which Mr Burton executed on 31 May 1999 ... It would only be to the extent that this express confidentiality agreement could not be enforced that GIO would need to fall back on an implied term in Mr Burton's contract of employment, or an equitable obligation of confidence.

CASE EXTRACT: CURRENT LAW

Optus Networks Pty Ltd v Telstra Corporation Ltd

[2010] FCAFC 21; (2010) 265 ALR 281
Federal Court of Australia, Full Court

[Optus and Telstra are both telecommunications carriers that share confidential telecommunications traffic information from time to time. In this case, Optus alleged that Telstra had misused this information, amounting to breach of the Access Agreement between the parties and the equitable duty of confidence, and unconscionable conduct. The Access Agreement specified the obligations relating to confidentiality in cl 15 and remedies available for breaches under the Agreement in cl 16. Optus wished to rely on equitable remedies, particularly an account of profits. Gordon J at first instance held that there was no reason for equity to intervene on the basis that the Access Agreement was exhaustive and comprehensive. The Full Court was asked to rule on whether equity will intervene when an action in contract is available.]

Finn, Sundberg and Jacobson JJ: 29. In our view the issue raised by the application for leave, and by the appeal if leave be granted, is whether by the Access Agreement the parties have excluded equitable obligations of confidence. It is true, as the primary judge said, that 'Confidential Information' is defined in an exhaustive fashion ... However, we do not see that as indicating an intention to exclude equitable obligations. All the parties have done by their definition is codify what is to be treated as confidential information for the purposes of their contract.

30. The primary judge described clause 15 as a regulation of the obligations of each party in relation to the confidential information of the other on a comprehensive basis. We do not agree that this admittedly detailed provision discloses an intention to exclude equitable obligations in relation to confidential information ...

[Their Honours then discussed the relevant provisions in the Agreement at some length before considering the relevant case law.]

35. Gordon J relied on *Deta Nominees Pty Ltd v Viscount Plastic Products Pty Ltd* [1979] VR 167 at 195 for the proposition that equity does not intervene where there is an adequate remedy at law. There Fullagar J, having found that certain confidential information was in the eyes of equity the plaintiff's property, who was entitled to restrain the defendants from using the information beyond certain limits, went on to say that because the plaintiff was entitled by reason of contract to perpetual injunctions restraining the defendants from manufacturing the goods to which the information related, equity would withhold any further relief for breaches of confidence because the remedies derived from contract were adequate. Those observations are not applicable to the present case because, at this stage, it is not

known whether damages will be an adequate remedy. Again, we refer to the contemplation in clause 15.6 that an account of profits is available under the agreement ...

36. In *Coles Supermarkets* [*Australia Pty Ltd v FKP Ltd* [2008] FCA 1915] at [64] Gordon J said that quite apart from authority, the conclusion that contractual and equitable obligations cannot co-exist would follow as a matter of logic and basic principles:

> If a party were allowed to elect whether to bring an action in equity for breach of confidence (which Coles does to get an account of FKP's profits on the Woolworth's deal, in the hopes that those profits are more than its damages), that would effectively eliminate the efficient breach theory of contract because whenever a defendant entered into inconsistent contracts the party whose contract ended up being not performed could then capture any extra profit made by the defendant by suing in equity instead of recovering his own losses at law.

37. After *Coles Supermarkets* was decided the High Court in *Tabcorp Holdings Ltd v Bowen Investments Pty Ltd* (2009) 236 CLR 272 at [13] made unfavourable observations about the doctrine of efficient breach. The whole Court said the efficient breach theory took no account of the existence of equitable remedies, such as specific performance and injunction, which ensure or encourage the performance of contracts rather than the payment of damages for breach. We need not pursue the efficient breach matter further, because, as we have said, the Access Agreement ... preserves equitable rights. We can discern no reason why parties cannot agree that one who claims that its confidential information has been misused can elect to sue either for damages for breach of contract under clause 15 or for an account of profits under clauses 15.6 and 20.22.

38. The notion that no equitable duty of confidence arises where there is a comparable contractual duty is opposed to much authority. Dr Dean says that 'Equitable protection ... may be used in preference to an existing contractual obligation or alongside a contractual obligation': Dean, *The Law of Trade Secrets and Personal Secrets* (2nd ed, 2002) at [2.55] where many examples in the case law are recorded. They include *Morison v Moat* (1851) 9 Hare 241, *Robb v Green* [1895] 2 QB 315, *Mense v Milenkovic* [1973] VR 784, *Attorney-General v Jonathan Cape Ltd* [1976] QB 752 and *Nicrotherm Electrical Co Ltd v Percy* (1957) 74 RPC 207. See also *Australian Medic-Care Co Ltd v Hamilton Pharmaceuticals Pty Ltd* (2009) 261 ALR 501 at [628]–[629] per Finn J and Gurry, *Breach of Confidence* (1984) pp 39–46.

THE DISTINCTION BETWEEN CONFIDENTIAL INFORMATION AND PROPERTY

CASE EXTRACT: CURRENT LAW

TS & B Retail Systems Pty Ltd v 3Fold Resources Pty Ltd (No 3)

[2007] FCA 151; (2007) 158 FCR 444
Federal Court of Australia

[Three employees of 3Fold Resources Pty Ltd allegedly used information acquired during the course of employment with another company, Trollope Silverwood and Beck Pty Ltd (TS&B). TS&B Retail (the applicant in this action) subsequently bought the assets of TS&B. One key issue for determination was whether the confidential information could be assigned from TS&B to TS&B Retail.]

Finkelstein J: 72. A rather more difficult question is whether, as TS&B Retail asserts, it took an assignment of TS&B's confidential information. According to the agreement there was an attempt to assign confidential information to TS&B Retail. The first letter records that 'all intellectual property and proprietary rights ... including ... drawings, trade secrets, technical data formulae ... databases, know-how ... and similar industrial or intellectual property rights' was the contract's subject matter.

73. In *Norman v Federal Commissioner of Taxation* (1963) 109 CLR 9, 26 Windeyer J said, and Dixon CJ (at 16) agreed that '[a]ssignment means the immediate transfer of an existing proprietary right, vested or contingent, from the assignor to the assignee. Anything that in the eye of law can be regarded as an existing subject of ownership, whether it be a chose in possession or a chose in action, can today be assigned, unless it be excepted from the general rule on some ground of public policy or by statute.' That is to say, the only thing capable of being assigned is property or a right in property.

74. Confidential information, however, is not property 'in any normal sense': *Boardman v Phipps* [1967] 2 AC 46, 128. Indeed it is not property at all. Confidential information is protected by equity by 'the notion of an obligation of conscience arising from the circumstances in or through which the information was communicated or obtained': *Moorgate Tobacco Co Ltd v Philip Morris Ltd (No 2)* (1984) 156 CLR 414, 438. A court of equity will protect information only if it is truly confidential and the confidence is worth preserving.

75. Although confidential information is not property and hence is not capable of being assigned, it now seems to be accepted that confidential information can be passed on by one person to another, and the person to whom it has been imparted can take action to protect the information. In *Mustad & Son v Dosen* [1964] 1 WLR 109 the liquidator of a company sold to the appellant the company's business including the benefit of trade secrets. One of the former employees took up employment with a competitor, with the intention of passing on trade secrets to his new employer. The appellants obtained an injunction to restrain the disclosure. In *Douglas v Hello! Ltd (No 3)* [2006] QB 125, 168 it was observed that the decision in *Mustad & Son* 'supports the proposition that a purchaser of confidential information can restrain disclosure of that information in breach of confidence, but again the picture is complicated by the fact that the benefit of [the employee's] contractual obligation not to disclose the information was purchased by Mustad.'

76. That may be a good explanation for the decision of the Law Lords but, even if the employment contract had not been assigned, in my opinion, consistent with principle, a 'purchaser' of the confidential information is entitled to the court's protection. In the Spycatcher case (*Attorney-General v Guardian Newspapers Ltd (No 2)* [1990] 1 AC 109, 281) Lord Goff said: 'a duty of confidence arises when confidential information comes to the knowledge of a person (the confidant) in circumstances where he has noticed ... that the information is confidential, with the effect that it would be just in all the circumstances that he should be precluded from disclosing the information to others.'

77. It follows, in my opinion, that TS&B Retail is entitled to whatever protection a court of equity will give in respect of the confidential information it obtained from the receivers ...

This view as to the non-proprietary nature of confidential information expressed by Finkelstein J was confirmed by the High Court in *Farah Constructions Pty Ltd v Say-Dee Pty Ltd* [2007] HCA 22; (2007) 230 CLR 89 at [118] (a case relating primarily to breach of fiduciary duty rather than breach of confidence).

THE RELATIONSHIP BETWEEN TRADE SECRETS AND OTHER FORMS OF IP

Trade secrecy provides an alternative form of protection to patents. Both prevent competitors from free-riding on commercially valuable subject matter created during the course of research and development. Patents provide enforceable monopoly rights for a limited period (usually 20 years) in return for disclosure of the subject matter being claimed in the patent. The value of trade secrets, on the other hand, is that because they have not been disclosed they cannot be used by competitors during the whole period that they remain secret.

Although patents provide monopoly rights, there are also some significant disadvantages in patenting subject matter created by a business, including that:

- the protection provided by patents is limited to subject matter that satisfies the stringent statutory tests for patentability;
- full public disclosure of the subject matter being claimed must be made, including disclosure of the best method of performing the invention;
- the patent monopoly is of limited duration, after which the subject matter can be freely used; and
- considerable time and expense are involved in obtaining and maintaining a patent.

There are, however, also significant disadvantages in relying on trade secrecy to prevent use of a business's valuable subject matter by a competitor, including that:

- once disclosed in public or to competitors, the value of the secret is lost;
- there are no monopoly rights—there is no prohibition on another person independently creating the same subject matter as the trade secret; and
- commercial exploitation of the trade secret may enable others to obtain the relevant information by reverse engineering.

The owner of secret subject matter must decide whether to opt for trade secrecy or patenting before the decision is made to commercially exploit the subject matter. Once a decision to patent is made and the application is filed, it becomes subject to the disclosure requirements in the *Patents Act 1990* (Cth) (see Chapter 12). On the one hand, if the decision to patent is made too late, some of the other essential requirements for patenting may not be capable of being fulfilled—particularly the requirement that the subject matter has not been secretly used prior to filing the patent application (s 18(1)(c) of the *Patents Act*: see Chapter 11). On the other hand, if the decision to patent is made without due regard to the limitations of the patentability or disclosure requirements, some or all of the subject matter may not be adequately protected from use by competitors (on this point, see the extract from *Maggbury Pty Ltd v Hafele Australia Pty Ltd* [2001] HCA 70; (2001) 210 CLR 181 provided later in this chapter). Despite patent disclosure requirements, it is often possible for companies to use a combination of patents (for technologies that must be made public or which can be readily reverse-engineered) and trade secrecy (for internal processes and/or internal know-how).

There is an overlap in the legal protection afforded to copyrighted subject matter and to trade secrets. As was seen in Chapter 2, copyright protects the expression of information in material form. Hence, if secret information is expressed in material form it may be protected both through copyright law and through equity or contract law, if it fulfils the requirements for being classified as confidential information. In some circumstances subject matter may qualify as confidential information even though it does not fulfil the requirements for copyright subsistence. The idea/expression dichotomy is a crucial aspect of copyright protection. Although equity will not intervene to protect bare ideas, the courts may be motivated to do so if the idea is sufficiently developed.

CASE EXTRACT: CURRENT LAW

Talbot v General Television Corp Pty Ltd

[1980] VR 224
Supreme Court of Victoria

[The plaintiff, Talbot, was a film producer who had developed a concept for a television series, which he called 'To Make a Million'. The series would present stories of successful millionaires to inspire viewers to make their own fortunes. He prepared a written submission and a pilot script for the program, which he provided to Channel 9, but after initial negotiations he received no response from them, despite various attempts to get back in touch. Later, Channel 9 commenced broadcast of a new segment on 'A Current Affair' in which millionaires were interviewed about their success. Talbot applied for an injunction to restrain further broadcasts.]

Harris J (at 231–232): The real problem, Mr Archibald [counsel for Talbot] said, was to decide whether the idea, or concept, had been sufficiently developed. Where it has been developed to the point of setting out a format in which it could be presented, so that it was apparent that the concept could be carried into effect, then, said Mr Archibald, it was something that is capable of being the subject of a confidence. Without deciding that it is always necessary for a plaintiff to go that far, I am satisfied that where a concept or idea has been developed to the stage where the plaintiff had developed his concept, it is capable of being the subject of a confidential communication. The plaintiff had developed his concept so that it would be seen to be a concept which had at least some attractiveness as a television programme and to be something which was capable of being realized as an actuality.

. . .

I am satisfied that what was called the 'commercial twist', or the particular slant, of the plaintiff's concept (or idea) does give it a quality which takes it out of the realm of public knowledge. It is clear enough that programmes about successful persons, in which such persons are asked questions about their success, have been known on television for some considerable time, but, in my opinion, there is a distinct difference between such programmes and a programme which has as its theme stories of the careers of some self-made millionaires, in which as an integral part of the programme the successful men give their recipes for success to the viewers.

ELEMENTS OF THE EQUITABLE ACTION FOR BREACH OF CONFIDENCE

Equity will restrain a person from making unauthorised use of information relating to private or secret matters when it is imparted on the express or implied understanding that the communication is for a restricted purpose.

CASE EXTRACT: PRECEDENT

Saltman Engineering Co Ltd v Campbell Engineering Co Ltd

(1948) 65 RPC 203
Court of Appeal of England and Wales

[Campbell Engineering had been requested by a third party to make leather punches for Saltman, and was given drawings for this specific purpose. Campbell proceeded to manufacture a large number of punches from the drawings for its own purposes. One problem for Saltman was that it was difficult to establish that a contractual relationship existed between the parties. Ultimately, the decision of the Court of Appeal focused on breach of confidence.]

Lord Greene MR (at 215): I think that I shall not be stating the principle wrongly, if I say this with regard to the use of confidential information. The information, to be confidential, must, I apprehend, apart from contract, have the necessary quality of confidence about it, namely, it must not be something which is public property and public knowledge. On the other hand, it is perfectly possible to have a confidential document, be it a formula, a plan, a sketch, or something of that kind, which is the result of work done by the maker on materials which may be available for the use of anybody; but what makes it confidential is the fact that the maker of the document has used his brain and thus produced a result which can only be produced by somebody who goes through the same process.

CASE EXTRACT: PRECEDENT

Coco v AN Clark (Engineers) Ltd

[1969] RPC 41
High Court of England and Wales, Chancery Division

[Lord Greene MR's statement as to the nature of confidential information in *Saltman* was followed in this case, where it was seen as the first of three elements required to be established for an equitable action for breach of confidence.]

Megarry J (at 47): First, the information itself, in the words of Lord Greene, MR in the *Saltman* case on page 215, must 'have the necessary quality of confidence about it.' Secondly, that information must have been imparted in circumstances importing an obligation of confidence. Thirdly, there must be an unauthorised use of that information ...

CASE EXTRACT: CURRENT LAW

Smith Kline & French Laboratories (Aust) Ltd v Secretary, Department of Community Services and Health

(1990) 22 FCR 73
Federal Court of Australia

[The facts of this case are provided in an extract of the appeal decision provided below (see 'Unauthorised use (outside the scope of disclosure)', p 591) in relation to the scope of the obligation of confidence. In this first-instance decision, Gummow J provided clear articulation of the elements that, in his Honour's view, must be satisfied to establish an action for breach of confidence in Australia.]

Gummow J (at 87): A general formulation apt for the present case of an equitable obligation of confidence has four elements: (i) the plaintiff must be able to identify with specificity, and not merely in global terms, that which is said to be the information in question, and must be able to show that (ii) the information has the necessary quality of confidentiality (and is not, for example, common or public knowledge), (iii) the information was received by the defendant in such circumstances as to import an obligation of confidence, and (iv) there is actual or threatened misuse of that information, without the consent of the plaintiff.

PROTECTABLE INFORMATION AND ESTABLISHING THE CONFIDENTIALITY OF THE INFORMATION

As stated by Lord Greene MR in *Saltman*, in order to be confidential, information must *not* be something which is in the public domain. If the information is a matter of public knowledge, equity will not enforce an obligation of confidence even if the confidant has agreed to be bound by it (but see the discussion later in this chapter of the 'The springboard doctrine', p 599). However, absolute secrecy is not required. For example, there may be circumstances where the information will retain its quality of confidence even though it has entered into the public domain transiently. Information can also retain its confidential quality even though it is known by a number of people (e.g. a distinct class, such as the employees of a business), although much will depend on the nature of the disclosure. See, for example, *Franchi v Franchi* [1967] RPC 149, where disclosure of information in a patent specification in Belgium was held to have put the information in the public domain in the UK, because British patent attorneys would have been in the habit of inspecting foreign specifications.

In addition to trade secrets (the primary focus of this chapter), the equitable action can be instituted in respect of private secrets—for example between husbands and wives and friends and acquaintances, and also to protect a person's identity. There is also a special category for government information.

IDENTIFICATION OF THE INFORMATION WITH SUFFICIENT SPECIFICITY

Although the requirement for specificity is not always articulated as a discrete element of the equitable action for breach of confidence, it is widely recognised that the information claimed to be confidential must be described with sufficient particularity for an action to succeed. In contract, too, a plaintiff alleging breach of an express or implied confidential information obligation will need to be able to identify clearly the information alleged to be confidential.

CASE EXTRACT: PRECEDENT

O'Brien v Komesaroff

(1982) 150 CLR 310
High Court of Australia

[The respondent, Komesaroff, who was the plaintiff in this action, was a solicitor. The appellant/defendant, O'Brien was an accountant and life insurance salesman. The breach of confidence action was based on alleged misuse of information provided by Komesaroff to O'Brien relating to tax minimisation schemes.]

Mason J (at 325–327): According to the written submissions now presented to us the confidential information relates to (1) discretionary trusts and private unit trusts; and (2) private unit trusts having an overseas trust in a 'tax haven' country as a beneficiary, being information which was valuable for tax avoidance or tax minimization purposes. The confidential information is then described as comprising information which is embodied: (1) in the unit trust deeds drafted by the respondent in Ex 'B20'; (2) in the respondent's draft memorandum and articles of association for a proprietary company; (3) in oral communications by the respondent to the appellant in 1973 and 1974 as to the effect and practical operation of discretionary trusts and of the unit trust scheme devised by the respondent; (4) in oral communications by the respondent to the appellant in November 1975 and 1976 ... and (5) in oral communications by the respondent to the appellant as to the legal and practical defects and legal inadequacies of a discretionary trust which had been adopted by lawyers and accountants in Australia and the United Kingdom as a means of reducing income tax and estate duty and the manner in which the 'unit trust' overcame these defects and inadequacies.

Plainly enough, in the light of the findings of the primary judge and the evidence, there is very little, if anything, in the documents mentioned in pars (1) and (2) above that can constitute confidential information. Generally speaking the contents of the unit trust deeds and the articles of association were matters of common knowledge. Information may be categorized as public knowledge though only notorious in a particular industry or profession: see Finn, *Fiduciary Obligations* (1977), p 146. Only those improvements evolved by the respondent could give rise to a claim for relief for breach of confidence. See generally *Saltman Engineering Co Ltd, Ferotec Ltd and Monarch Engineering Co (Mitcham) Ltd v Campbell Engineering Co Ltd* (1948) 65 RPC 203, at p 215; *Seager v Copydex Ltd* (1967) 1 WLR 923, at p 931; (1967) 2 All ER 415, at p 417; *Coco v AN Clark (Engineers) Ltd* [1969] RPC 41, at p 47. It is at this point that the respondent has consistently failed to identify the particular contents of the documents which he asserts constitute information the confidentiality of which he is entitled to protect. The consequence is that he has failed to formulate a basis on which the court could grant him relief on the assumption that some part or parts of the documents constitute confidential information.

It is a fundamental problem with the information which the respondent seeks to protect that it is information which, by way of advice to others, he regularly publishes to the world at large, albeit for a limited purpose. The nature of such information ill accords with the accepted conception of

PRECEDENT

confidentiality, which in substance involves the person seeking to protect the information largely keeping it to himself. See *Ansell Rubber Co Pty Ltd v Allied Rubber Industries Pty Ltd* (1967) VR 37, at p 49. In the result the respondent's relief in respect of the documents should be confined to infringement of copyright.

The information mentioned in pars (3) and (5) above falls into the same category. To simply say that the information is as to the effect and practical operation of discretionary trusts and private unit trust schemes does not identify the information and enable the Court to formulate an order. One needs to know not only what was the information conveyed but also what part of that information was not common knowledge.

The description of the information referred to in par (4) suffers from the same defect. It consists of (a) advice (unspecified) as to the effect of three sections of the *Income Tax Assessment Act* and the *Banking (Foreign Exchange) Regulations*; (b) the form of resolutions for the issue of, and investment in, special units; (c) the provisions of the trust deed; and (d) minutes and resolutions giving effect to the proposal.

PERSONAL INFORMATION

The leading authority on the protection of personal information is the UK case of *Margaret, Duchess of Argyll v Duke of Argyll* [1967] Ch 302. The case arose from intense media scrutiny relating to the divorce of the Duke and Duchess. The Duchess had released certain articles to the media relating to the Duke's personal conduct and financial affairs. In response the Duke threatened to communicate secrets of the Duchess relating to her private life, personal affairs and private conduct communicated to him in confidence during their marriage. The Duchess sought an interlocutory injunction to prevent the communication and publication of this information. Ungoed-Thomas J identified confidentiality as the very essence of the marital relationship. Even though the Duchess had published information relating to the Duke's personal and financial affairs, his Honour held that this was not of the same level of perfidy as the disclosures threatened by the Duke. On this basis, the Duchess was granted an injunction to restrain the publication of the information.

More recently there has been an expansion in the use of the equitable action for breach of confidence, particularly in the UK, as a means of indirectly protecting personal privacy. Lack of recognition of a common law tort of privacy by the courts in that jurisdiction has fuelled the drive to use breach of confidence for that purpose. Currently, it is not clear how the law will develop in Australia. The High Court case of *Victoria Park Racing and Recreation Grounds Co Ltd v Taylor* (1937) 58 CLR 479 was, for many years, seen as an insuperable obstacle in the development of a tort of privacy in this jurisdiction. However, in the later High Court case of *Australian Broadcasting Corporation v Lenah Game Meats Pty Ltd* [2001] HCA 63; (2001) 208 CLR 199 the Court intimated that *Victoria Park* imposed no such obstacle. Gleeson CJ at [39]–[42] appeared to prefer the use of breach of confidence rather than the development of a new tort of privacy, but the other justices provided less direction in this regard. There have been some lower court decisions on point since *Lenah Game Meats*, but no obvious pattern has yet emerged.

In 2014 the Australian Law Reform Commission (ALRC) completed a major review of privacy law in Australia, culminating in Report No 123, *Serious Invasions of Privacy in the Digital Era.*

The ALRC recommended a statutory cause of action under Commonwealth law for serious, intentional or reckless invasions of privacy. It also recommended that:

> [i]f a statutory cause of action for serious invasion of privacy is not enacted, appropriate federal, state, and territory legislation should be amended to provide that, in an action for breach of confidence that concerns a serious invasion of privacy by the misuse, publication or disclosure of private information, the court may award compensation for the plaintiff's emotional distress [Recommendation 13-1].

It is generally beyond the scope of IP law courses to discuss the case law and law reform developments relating to the protection of personal privacy in any detail.[2]

GOVERNMENT INFORMATION

A number of Australian court decisions have accepted that government secrets can be protected by equity. However, the courts have imposed an additional requirement for establishing breach of confidence in such circumstances: that the public interest in disclosure must not outweigh the public interest in keeping the information secret.

The leading decision is *Commonwealth v John Fairfax & Sons Ltd* (1980) 147 CLR 39 (extracted in the discussion of copyright exceptions in Chapter 6). This case concerned the publication of a book, *Documents on Australian Defence and Foreign Policy*, and excerpts in *The Age* and *The Sydney Morning Herald* newspapers. The Australian Government had obtained ex parte injunctions to suppress publication, and it made an interlocutory application to extend them. By that time there had already been some public disclosure of the contents of the book. Mason J was not prepared to extend the injunction on the grounds of breach of confidence, holding (at 52):

> It is unacceptable in our democratic society that there should be a restraint on the publication of information relating to government when the only vice of that information is that it enables the public to discuss, review and criticize government action.
>
> Accordingly, the court will determine the government's claim to confidentiality by reference to the public interest. Unless disclosure is likely to injure the public interest, it will not be protected.
>
> The court will not prevent the publication of information which merely throws light on the past workings of government, even if it be not public property, so long as it does not prejudice the community in other respects. Then disclosure will itself serve the public interest in keeping the community informed and in promoting discussion of public affairs. If, however, it appears that disclosure will be inimical to the public interest because national security, relations with foreign countries or the ordinary business of government will be prejudiced, disclosure will be restrained. There will be cases in which the conflicting considerations will be finely balanced, where it is difficult to decide whether the public's interest in knowing and in expressing its opinion, outweighs the need to protect confidentiality.

Disclosure of government information, especially information related to national security, is also governed by a range of specific pieces of legislation that will not be covered in this text. As with

---

2   For further information see D Rolph et al, *Media Law: Cases, Materials and Commentary*, 2nd ed, Oxford University Press, Melbourne, 2015.

personal privacy, it is generally beyond the scope of IP law courses to discuss the government confidence cases in detail.

TRADE SECRETS

There is no precise definition of the term 'trade secret,' although the case law does provide some guidance on the types of subject matter that are embraced by this term. The key requirement is that the subject matter has to have some commercial value, such that disclosure to a competitor would cause detriment to the owner of the subject matter.

CASE EXTRACT: PRECEDENT

Ansell Rubber Co Pty Ltd v Ansell Rubber Industries Pty Ltd

[1967] VR 37
Supreme Court of Victoria

[Both parties in this case were manufacturers of rubber goods. Two former employees of the plaintiff were employed by the defendant. The plaintiff alleged that the defendant used confidential information obtained by the employees during the course of employment with the plaintiff about the design, construction and operation of a machine for making rubber gloves. After reviewing the English case law on point, Gowans J discussed the notion of trade secrecy.]

Gowans J (at 49): There is very little in these English cases to enable one to identify a 'trade secret'. But some collation of the characteristics may be attempted, without trying to make it an exhaustive statement. Its subject-matter may not be a process in common use, or something which is public property and public knowledge, but if it is the result of work done by the maker upon materials which may be available for the use of anybody, so as to achieve a result which can only be produced by somebody who goes through the same process, it will be sufficient. All of its separate features may have been published, or capable of being ascertained by actual inspection by any member of the public, but it the whole result has not been achieved, and could not be achieved, except by someone going through the same kind of process as the owner, it will not fail to qualify by reason of the publication. It may derive from a maker in another country without losing its character if it is used, or entitled to be used, by the owner alone in the country in which the owner operates. There is no suggestion of the need for invention. Little can be gathered of the degree of secrecy required beyond what is implied in what is said. But it is a fair inference from what is said that the employer must have kept the matter to himself and from his competitors. The emphasis in the cases is on confidence.

ESTABLISHING CONFIDENTIAL CIRCUMSTANCES

The courts tend to use an objective test in determining whether confidential information has been imparted in circumstances creating an obligation of confidence.

RELEVANT CIRCUMSTANCES

PRECEDENT

CASE EXTRACT: PRECEDENT

Coco v AN Clark (Engineers) Ltd

[1969] RPC 41
High Court of England and Wales, Chancery Division

Megarry J (at 48): The second requirement is that the information must have been communicated in circumstances importing an obligation of confidence. However secret and confidential the information, there can be no binding obligation of confidence if the information is blurted out in public or is communicated in other circumstances which negative any duty of holding it confidential. From the authorities cited to me, I have not been able to derive any very precise idea of what test is to be applied in determining whether the circumstances import an obligation of confidence. In [*Margaret, Duchess of Argyll v Duke of Argyll* [1967] Ch 302] at page 330, Ungoed-Thomas J concluded his discussion of the circumstances in which the publication of marital communications should be restrained as being confidential by saying, 'If this was a well-developed jurisdiction doubtless there would be guides and tests to aid in exercising it.' In the absence of such guides or tests he then in effect concluded that part of the communications in question would on any reasonable test emerge as confidential. It may be that that hard-working creature, the reasonable man, may be pressed into service once more; for I do not see why he should not labour in equity as well as in law. It seems to me that if the circumstances are such that any reasonable man standing in the shoes of the recipient of the information would have realised that upon reasonable grounds the information was being given to him in confidence, then this should suffice to impose upon him the equitable obligation of confidence. In particular, where information of commercial or industrial value is given on a business-like basis and with some avowed common object in mind, such as a joint venture or the manufacture of articles by one party for the other, I would regard the recipient as carrying a heavy burden if he seeks to repel a contention that he was bound to an obligation of confidence: see the *Saltman* case at 216. On that footing, for reasons that will appear, I do not think I need to explore this head further. I merely add that I doubt whether equity would intervene unless the circumstances are of sufficient gravity; equity ought not to be invoked merely to protect trivial tittle-tattle, however confidential.

THE EMPLOYMENT AND POST-EMPLOYMENT CONTEXTS

Actions for breach of confidence often arise from the employment context, because it is inevitable that if a business possesses confidential information it will have to be disclosed to employees in order for them to do their jobs. Tensions arise when employment comes to an end: ex-employees will want to be able to continue to practise their trade, but ex-employers will want to retain their trade secrets as well as other commercially sensitive information, such as lists of suppliers and customers. As the UK Supreme Court noted in *Vestergaard Frandsen A/S v Bestnet Europe Ltd* [2013] UKSC 31; [2013] RPC 33 at [44]:

> Particularly in a modern economy, the law has to maintain a realistic and fair balance
> between (i) effectively protecting trade secrets (and other intellectual property rights) and

(ii) not unreasonably inhibiting competition in the market place. The importance to the economic prosperity of the country of research and development in the commercial world is self-evident, and the protection of intellectual property, including trade secrets, is one of the vital contributions of the law to that end. On the other hand, the law should not discourage former employees from benefitting society and advancing themselves by imposing unfair potential difficulties on their honest attempts to compete with their former employers.

In this context the courts generally draw a distinction between 'know-how' and confidential information. Know-how is a person's accumulated skill, knowledge and experience in a particular field. In distinguishing between know-how, trade secrets and other commercially sensitive information, the court balances two competing considerations:

1   Employees should not be restricted in using the skill, knowledge and experience acquired during the course of employment once they have left the service of their employer. The courts will not restrain a person from carrying out their occupation.
2   Trade secrets and other commercially sensitive information belonging to a business should not be misused.

In *Wright v Gasweld Pty Ltd* (1991) 22 NSWLR 317 Kirby P posited that, in the employment context, information generally falls into one of three categories:

1   information that, because of its triviality or public availability, cannot be regarded as confidential;
2   information that the employee must treat as confidential until the termination of his or her employment, but which, once learned, remains in the employee's head and becomes part of his or her skill and knowledge; and
3   specific trade secrets that cannot lawfully be used other than for the employer's benefit.

Businesses that possess trade secrets and other commercially sensitive information will usually include express confidentiality clauses in their employment contracts, which are enforceable during the course of employment. Depending on how they are drafted they may also extend beyond the term of employment, provided they do not amount to an unreasonable restraint of trade. Restraint of trade is most likely to arise when a former employer attempts to enforce a contractual obligation of confidence relating to Kirby P's second category of information. The courts have also implied a duty of good faith into the employment contract, which includes an obligation not to disclose confidential information falling within Kirby P's second and third categories.[3] Equitable protection also extends to the second and third categories, although in the second it is limited to the duration of the employment. There is some uncertainty in the case law as to how an obligation of confidence will be enforced post-employment, outside express contractual provisions, as discussed in the following case extract, which leans towards protection through equity rather than through an implied contractual provision.

---

3   On this point see, for example, *Robb v Green* [1895] 2 QB 315.

CASE EXTRACT: CURRENT LAW

Del Casale v Artedomus (Aust) Pty Ltd

[2007] NSWCA 172; (2007) 73 IPR 326
New South Wales Court of Appeal

[Artedomus was an importer of products for the building industry, including a popular type of modica stone from Italy called Isernia. Del Casale and the second appellant, Savini, were directors and employees of Artedomus whose employment was terminated. Both former employees formed a new company, and used their knowledge to find a supplier of Isernia for import and sale. Artedomus alleged that this amounted to a breach of confidence, which was accepted at first instance. On appeal, the distinction between confidential information and know-how was examined within the context of an employee's obligations during and after employment. Despite a relevant contractual provision, the Court considered the implied duty of good faith and the equitable obligation of confidence.]

Hodgson JA: 31. Although criteria for confidentiality were discussed in *Wright v Gasweld* (1991) 22 NSWLR 317, there is not in that case or in any of the cases to which we have been referred a clear elaboration of what would determine whether the confidentiality went beyond that which could be protected by agreement so as to be such as to continue to affect the employee after the employment had ended, without the need for an agreement. Another difficulty is that it is not entirely clear whether the implication of terms in the employment contract has any relevance to the issue; and it is not entirely clear whether equitable principles concerning confidential information apply in the case of employment in the same way as they apply in other areas where one party gives confidential information to another party, in circumstances of confidence, so as to give rise to an obligation of confidence that equity will enforce.

32. In the first place, it is clear that a contract of employment generally includes an implied term imposing a duty of good faith on the employee, and that this [in] turn carries with it an obligation on the employee not to divulge confidential information or to use it in a way that could be detrimental to the employer: *Robb v Green* [1895] 2 QB 315. The content of this duty will vary according to the position of the employee: generally, more senior employees, having access to more confidential information, will be subject to greater restraint than more junior employees.

33. If this obligation is breached during employment, for example by copying customer lists or even deliberately memorising them so that they can be used after the employment comes to an end, that breach of contract may justify the grant of relief when the employee seeks to use that information after the employment has come to an end. There is no suggestion in this case that the claimants obtained confidential information, during their employment, in breach of this implied term.

34. There is authority for the proposition that this implied term imposing a duty of good faith continues to operate after the employment comes to an end, albeit in a more restricted way: *Faccenda Chicken Ltd v Fowler* [1987] Ch 117 at 136. I am doubtful that this is so as a general rule, at least in so far as it suggests there may be a remedy in contract that goes beyond such remedy as may be available on the basis of general equitable principles of confidentiality. It is clear that there can be terms of an employment contract that continue to operate after the employment comes to an end; but generally that will be because they are express terms which so provide. Implied terms may also

operate in that way if the nature of the employment is such as to clearly require a term operating after the end of employment, as could be the case where a person is employed as an in-house professional adviser to whom confidential information is given for the purpose of obtaining professional advice, such as legal advice. Apart from such special cases, in my opinion the difficulty illustrated by the *Faccenda Chicken* case of determining the extent of any obligation of confidentiality, extending after the end of employment, counts against such obligation being implied, either as an incident of the relationship or a matter of business efficacy.

35. In my opinion, generally questions concerning an employee's obligation of confidentiality after employment has come to an end, in the absence of an express contract dealing with the matter, are best dealt with as part of the general law concerning confidentiality of information, both because it is very doubtful what, if any, term can be implied into a contract, and also because it is very unlikely that relief obtainable pursuant to any such implied term would go beyond relief obtainable on general equitable principles. There is the theoretical difference that damages may be obtainable for breach of contract; but this is unlikely to make the remedy available in contract more extensive than that based on general equitable principles, because it seems clear that compensation is available for breach of fiduciary duty (and thus probably is available for breach of a duty of confidentiality): *Nocton v Lord Ashburton* [1914] AC 932, *Beach Petroleum v Kennedy* (1999) 48 NSWLR 1, *Cassis v Kalfus (No 2)* [2004] NSWCA 315.

...

37. ... [I]n applying [the] general equitable principles to the particular case of post-employment use, by an ex-employee, of the confidential information of an employer obtained during employment, there are particular considerations which tend to qualify their operation. They are that very often an employee will necessarily through employment come to have knowledge which the employer would prefer not to have generally known, that often such knowledge will become part of the employee's know-how (which the employee should be able to use after employment ceases), that very often it is difficult or impossible to isolate from the employee's general know-how particular pieces of confidential information which the employee is not permitted to use while otherwise being free to use know-how generally, and that competition should not be prevented by preventing ex-employees using their know-how.

38. Considerations such as these have led to a distinction being drawn, in cases such as *Faccenda Chicken* and *Wright v Gasweld* (1991) 22 NSWLR 317, between two classes of confidential information, one of which an ex-employee cannot use (even in the absence of contractual restrictions), and the other of which an ex-employee can use, at least unless there is a valid contractual restraint. There is some variation in the naming of these two classes. For example, there is a question whether both are properly called trade secrets, with the latter being a particular class of trade secrets which is also given the appellation 'know-how'; or whether only the former class should be called trade secrets. In either event, the latter class is often called 'know-how'.

39. It is clear that information may be confidential, even if it is known to persons other than the person claiming confidentiality: it may be sufficient that the information is not freely available, particularly if it is not freely available to competitors of the employer. There is no challenge to what the primary judge said about this matter at pars [24]–[26] of his judgment, at [2006] NSWSC 146. There is no real dispute that the information identified by the primary judge is confidential in the sense of falling into one of these classes; and the substantial question is whether it falls into the former class or latter class.

40. In *Wright v Gasweld*, at 334, Kirby P listed some factors that helped in determining whether information may be considered confidential. That list has been expanded by R Dean, *The Law of Trade Secrets and Personal Secrets*, (2002) 2nd Ed, at 190 to include:

1. The extent to which the information is known outside the business.
2. The extent to which the trade secret was known by employees and others involved in the plaintiff's business.
3. The extent of measures taken to guard the secrecy of the information.
4. The value of the information to the plaintiffs and their competitors.
5. The amount of effort or money expended by the plaintiffs in developing the information.
6. The ease or difficulty with which the information could be properly acquired or duplicated by others.
7. Whether it was plainly made known to the employee that the material was [regarded] by the employer as confidential.
8. The fact that the usages and practices of the industry support the assertions of confidentiality.
9. The fact that the employee has been permitted to share the information only by reason of his or her seniority or high responsibility.
10. That the owner believes these things to be true and that belief is reasonable.
11. The greater the extent to which the 'confidential' material is habitually handled by an employee, the greater the obligation of the confidentiality imposed.
12. That the information can be readily identified.

41. In my opinion, the stronger these factors are in any particular case, the more likely it is that the particular information will be treated as a trade secret that the ex-employee is not entitled to use or divulge; but in my opinion, there is another factor or class of factors which is also extremely important to this question, namely the extent to which the particular information can be readily isolated from the employee's general know-how which the employee is entitled to use after the end of employment.

42. In cases where the confidential information is of the nature of a secret formula or process, involving a number of elements such that independent discovery by enquiry or experiment is unlikely to occur, that confidential information can quite readily be distinguished from an employee's general know-how. In those cases, the courts are ready to restrain use of that information by an ex-employee: see for example *Amber Size & Chemical Co Ltd v Menzel* [1913] 2 Ch 239.

43. However, where the confidential information is something that is ascertainable by enquiry or experiment, albeit perhaps substantial enquiry or experiment, and the know-how which the ex-employee is clearly entitled to use extends to knowledge of the *question* which the confidential information answers, it becomes artificial to treat the confidential information as severable and distinguishable from that know-how; and in that kind of case, courts have tended not to grant relief.

. . .

47. Before considering the circumstance of this case, I would note that this line of reasoning may justify a distinction being drawn in cases such as these between an ex-employee *using* this information as part of the know-how acquired from the employment, on the one hand, and *disclosing* it to other persons on the other hand. In *Worsley v Cooper* [[1939] 1 All ER 290] at 308–309, Morton J placed some reliance on the circumstance that the ex-employee in that case was merely using the information, not disclosing it; and he referred to statements to similar effect in the judgment of Joyce J in the Court

of Appeal in *Herbert Morris Ltd v Saxelby* [1915] 2 Ch 57 at 88 and Bennet J in *United Indigo Chemical Co Ltd v Robinson* (1939) 49 RPC 178 at 187. In my opinion, it may well be the case that equitable relief could be granted against an ex-employee *disclosing* confidential information in some cases where it would not be granted against the ex-employee *using* it.

48. Turning to the circumstances of this case, it seems to me very difficult to separate out, from the general know-how in relation to stone acquired by Mr Del Casale and Mr Savini, as a severable piece of confidential information, the information that Isernia is modica stone. Certainly, subject to any contract that may have existed, they were entitled to compete with Artedomus in the stone business after their employment had come to an end, and they were entitled to obtain stone for that purpose from any source. They were entitled to go to a trade fair, and to look for suppliers of stone at that fair, including suppliers of stone similar to Isernia. What restraint of use of this particular piece of confidential information would require is that in doing so, they somehow blot out their knowledge that Isernia was modica stone and undertake the attempt to find similar stone under those artificial circumstances.

49. The degree of confidentiality of the information in this case was quite high, having regard to the criteria mentioned above; but not it seems to me higher than that in *Wright v Gasweld*; and as I have explained, it does not seem to me that this information is information that can realistically be separated out from the general know-how in relation to the stone business acquired by Mr Del Casale and Mr Savini. It is to be remembered that they were not merely employees of Artedomus, but directors; but subject to the effect of s 183 of the Corporations Act, to which I will come, I do not think that makes any difference in principle to the considerations I have discussed: these considerations apply similarly to directors as to other very senior employees.

50. For those reasons, in my opinion the primary judge was in error in finding that the information was confidential to the extent that its use would be prohibited after cessation of the employment and/or directorship of Mr Del Casale and Mr Savini, in the absence of express contractual restraint.

INFORMATION IMPROPERLY OR SURREPTITIOUSLY OBTAINED

The courts have recognised that there will be some circumstances where an obligation of confidence should be imposed even where there is no communication between the parties importing an obligation of confidence. Essentially, the courts determine that the party allegedly in breach ought to have known that the information was confidential. The courts will consider the nature of the information (e.g. whether it is particularly sensitive or private) and the means by which the information was obtained (e.g. whether it was stolen or otherwise covertly obtained). As Lord Goff held in *Attorney-General v Guardian Newspapers Ltd (No 2)* [1990] 1 AC 109 at 281: '[A] duty of confidence arises when confidential information comes to the knowledge of a person (the confidant) in circumstances where he has notice ... that the information is confidential, with the effect that it would be just in all the circumstances that he should be precluded from disclosing the information to others' (cited with approval by Callinan J in *Australian Broadcasting Corporation v Lenah Game Meats Pty Ltd* [2001] HCA 63; (2001) 208 CLR 199 at [306]).

CASE EXTRACT: PRECEDENT

Franklin v Giddins

[1978] Qd R 72
Supreme Court of Queensland

[The plaintiffs had developed a new strain of nectarines that could be propagated by grafting from budwood. The defendants stole budwood from the plaintiffs and were convicted of theft. The plaintiffs also brought an action for breach of confidence.]

Dunn J (at 80–81): I have already expressed the opinion that, when the male defendant stole budwood from the plaintiffs' orchard, what he got was a trade secret. The secret was the technique of propagating Franklin Early White nectarines, using budwood from the plaintiffs' orchard. The technique of budding was no secret, but the budwood existed only in the plaintiffs' orchard, where the plaintiffs guarded it by exercising general surveillance over fruit-pickers and visitors, and by bruiting it abroad that it was theirs and theirs alone. The 'information' which the genetic structure of the wood represented was of substantial commercial value, much time and effort had been expended by the male plaintiff in evolving it and it could not be duplicated by anybody whatsoever.

It is true that the plaintiffs' orchard was not surrounded by an electric fence nor patrolled by guard-dogs, but I consider that the plaintiffs were entitled to rely on the fact that other people could normally be expected to respect their rights of property.

The factors which I have mentioned enable one, in my opinion, to identify the technique of propagating this variety as a trade secret ...

I hold that the male defendant has been guilty of infringement of the plaintiffs' rights since he stole and used the budwood; as for the female defendant, she has since at least the middle of last year known that the Franklin Early White nectarine trees in the orchard conducted by her husband and herself are the produce of a stolen trade secret, and—this being so—it is unconscionable for her to derive any benefit from the trees, and she too infringes the plaintiffs' rights.

The expansion of the doctrine of confidentiality to protect privacy mentioned earlier in this chapter has, to some extent, been driven by increasing recognition that where sensitive information is obtained by underhand means it would be unconscionable for the wrongdoer to profit from its use.

INNOCENT RECEIPT OF CONFIDENTIAL INFORMATION BY THIRD PARTIES

Consistent with the above, the case law also makes it clear that third parties can be bound by the equitable obligation of confidence, even when they innocently come into possession of confidential information. In doing so, the courts have rejected the analogy with the concept of '*bona fide* purchaser for value without notice'. As a consequence, trade secrecy will not create legal rights *in rem* but only *in personam*, and third parties will tend not to be bound by contractual obligations of confidence because of the doctrine of privity of contract.

CASE EXTRACT: PRECEDENT

Wheatley v Bell

[1982] 2 NSWLR 544
Supreme Court of New South Wales

[The defendant had set up a business allegedly in breach of an obligation of confidence to the plaintiff. Three third parties who asserted that they had no knowledge of the breach were also joined as defendants.]

Helsham CJ in Eq (at 549–550): I am satisfied that the analogy which has been drawn in some of the American cases and by some of the text writers, of the situation of innocent defendants to a *bona fide* purchaser for value without notice, is not the correct way of approaching the question of whether the injunction should go in the present circumstances or not. The defence of *bona fide* purchaser for value is an equitable defence directed towards the resolution of priorities in relation to property rights. It is an attempt to sort out amongst the claimants interested in property the order in which their various interests should prevail. But I believe that there are no property rights associated with the type of equity involved here; it is equity to restrain a person from acting in breach of confidence which is owed to another, arising from all the circumstances, and I believe that this is the way in which the authorities, to which I should pay a great regard, have treated the matter.

CASE EXTRACT: CURRENT LAW

Dart Industries Inc v David Bryar & Associates Pty Ltd

(1997) 38 IPR 389
Federal Court of Australia

[This was an application for interlocutory injunctions relating to drawings and designs for Tupperware containers. It was likely that there had been misuse of confidential information, but the respondents alleged that they were innocent third parties, unaware of the confidential nature of the information.]

Goldberg J (at 406): The present state of the evidence suggests that if there has been a copying or misuse of the applicants' plans and confidential information, such copying or misuse occurred initially at the hands of some party other than the respondents but that the respondents have become the recipients of that misused confidential information and those copied plans. In such circumstances a court will, in an appropriate case, grant an injunction against a person who has acquired information to which he is not entitled without any knowledge or notice of any breach of duty on the part of the person from whom he obtained the information: *Printers & Finishers Ltd v Holloway* [1965] 1 WLR 1, 7; *Butler v Board of Trade* (1971) Ch 680, 690; *Talbot v General Television Corporation Pty Ltd* [1980] VR 224; *Wheatley v Bell* [1982] 2 NSWLR 544; *English & American Insurance Co Ltd v Smith* [1988] FSR 232.

Mr Clarke [counsel for the respondents] accepted, as the cases establish, that the court has jurisdiction to enjoin a third party recipient of confidential information obtained by it innocently but submitted that that principle depends upon it being established that the initial wrongdoing which brought about the misuse of confidential information would be carried into effect by the third party's conduct. In my opinion such a situation will arise in the present case if the claims by the applicants are ultimately established. If either Superior Focus or Mah Sing [manufacturers of Tupperare moulds] has copied or used the applicants' confidential information or product drawings in having [the drawings alleged to be based on confidential information] prepared the end result of the respondents' conduct, if not restrained, will be to deliver to Superior Focus and Mah Sing moulds from which they can manufacture and sell plastic containers which will be produced by reference to, and by means of, the use of the applicants' confidential information and product drawings.

UNAUTHORISED USE (OUTSIDE THE SCOPE OF DISCLOSURE)

There will be breach of the obligation of confidence when the use of confidential information goes beyond what was contemplated by the parties when the information was disclosed. Essentially the courts will be required to determine what limitations were imposed by the confider on the confidant (or 'confidee' in the extract below) and whether the use made of the information goes beyond these limitations. There is no requirement that the unauthorised use be intentional: for example, in *Talbot v General Television Corp Pty Ltd* [1980] VR 224, the television network was held to have made unauthorised use of Talbot's confidential pitch for a television series, notwithstanding that the network executives with whom Talbot had met had lost their recollections of the meeting. A person who assists a recipient of confidential information in misusing that information can also be liable for breach of confidence, but such an accessory will normally have to know that the recipient was abusing that information. Thus, in the recent UK Supreme Court decision in *Vestergaard Frandsen A/S v Bestnet Europe Ltd* [2013] UKSC 31; [2013] RPC 33 an ex-employee of a company who received no confidential information in the course of her employment, who then set up business with another ex-employee who misused confidential information in the new business, was held not to be liable for breach of confidence given that she had no knowledge of her business partner's unauthorised use.

CASE EXTRACT: CURRENT LAW

Smith Kline & French Laboratories (Aust) Ltd v Secretary, Department of Community Services and Health

(1991) 28 FCR 291
Federal Court of Australia, Full Court

[This case relates to two appeals concerning the use by Commonwealth health authorities of confidential information supplied by Smith Kline and French (SKandF). SKandF argued that confidential information provided for the purpose of obtaining regulatory approval of the use of a pharmaceutical drug may only be used in considering SKandF's application, and may not be used when considering an application by [a third party relating to a generic version of the same drug following expiry of the patent on the original drug. SKandF could not claim that the information in the original *patent* was confidential owing to the patent disclosure requirements (see Chapter 12), but they sought protection for other information in the application for regulatory approval. The courts at first instance and on appeal accepted that some of the information submitted by SKandF was confidential. The issue was whether its use was limited in the way alleged.]

Sheppard, Wilcox and Pincus JJ (at 302–304): There is indeed some authority which, at least superficially, supports that view [that the use of the confidential information was limited solely to consideration of SKandF's application]. One learned commentator has remarked:

> The test which has found widespread acceptance is whether or not the information was disclosed for a limited purpose. If the information was disclosed for a limited purpose, the confidence crystallises around that limited purpose. The confidant will be bound by an obligation the content of which is not to use or disclose the information for any purpose other than the limited one for which the information was imparted—F Gurry in Finn, *Essays in Equity* (1985) at p 118.

In many circumstances, that suggested test will produce a proper result, but the circumstances in which confidential information is supplied may vary widely. To determine the existence of confidentiality and its scope, it may be relevant to consider whether the information was supplied gratuitously or for a consideration; whether there is any past practice of such a kind as to give rise to an understanding; how sensitive the information is; whether the confider has any interest in the purpose for which the information is to be used; whether the confider expressly warned the confidee against a particular disclosure or use of the information—and, no doubt, many other matters. Confidential information is commonly supplied without payment: for example, by a prospective employee (or his referee) to support an application for employment. The understanding ordinarily would be that the prospective employer would not disclose the information to any third party; but it would hardly be expected that its use would necessarily be confined to the employment application itself. If that application were successful, the employee would not act on the assumption that material in the relevant file would be destroyed. He would surely be inclined to assume that it might be resorted to later to assist the employer in making decisions relevant to the employee—for example, as to whether the employee (rather than another) should be promoted, or dismissed.

The test of confider's purpose will not ordinarily be appropriate where each party's interest is quite different, and known to be so. Here, the confider's purpose is simple and narrow, the confidee's much broader. SKandF had only the purpose of having its applications approved. A person supplying confidential information to the government for the purpose of obtaining a licence (or a permission or concession) would ordinarily assume that the government would not destroy the application file after the confider had attained his purpose. The confider would probably expect that the information would be kept against the day when it might be needed to serve the government's legitimate interests: for example, to provide a record in case the decision is challenged as improper; to enable statistical information to be collected; or, acting directly against the interests of the confider, to compare the information supplied with the confider's subsequent performance, in determining whether to cancel the licence. Gummow J referred to the reasons of McHugh JA (as his Honour then was) in *Attorney-General (UK) v Heinemann Publishers Australia Pty Ltd* (1987) 10 NSWLR 86 at 191; amongst other things, McHugh JA said:

> But the relationship between the modern State and its citizens is so different in kind from that which exists between private citizens that rules worked out to govern the contractual, property, commercial and private confidences of citizens are not fully applicable where the plaintiff is a government or one of its agencies. Private citizens are entitled to protect or further their own interests, no matter how selfish they are in doing so ... (b)ut governments acts (sic), or at all events are constitutionally required to act, in the public interest.

Megarry J has suggested a broad test to determine whether an obligation of confidence exists. In *Coco v AN Clark (Engineers) Ltd* [1969] RPC 41 [at 48], Megarry J said:

> It seems to me that if the circumstances are such that any reasonable man standing in the shoes of the recipient of the information would have realised that upon reasonable grounds the information was being given to him in confidence, then this should suffice to impose upon him the equitable obligation of confidence.

However, this test does not give guidance as to the scope of an obligation of confidentiality, where one exists. Sometimes the obligation imposes no restriction on use of the information, as long as the confidee does not reveal it to third parties. In other circumstances, the confidee may not be entitled to use it except for some limited purpose. In considering these problems, and indeed the whole question, it is necessary not to lose sight of the basis of the obligation to respect confidences:

> It lies in the notion of an obligation of conscience arising from the circumstances in or through which the information was communicated or obtained.

This is quoted from *Moorgate Tobacco Co Ltd v Phillip Morris Ltd (No 2)* (1984) 156 CLR 414 at 438 per Deane J, with whom the other members of the Court agreed. A similar broad view has been taken in the United States: *El Dupont de Nemours Powder Co v Masland* (1917) 244 US 102:

> Therefore the starting point for the present matter is not property or due process of law, but that the defendant stood in confidential relations with the plaintiffs, or one of them. These have given place to hostility, and the first thing to be made sure of is that the defendant shall not fraudulently abuse the trust reposed in him. It is the usual incident of confidential relations.

Similar expressions recur in other cases: *Seager v Copydex Ltd* [1967] RPC 349 at 368:

> The law on this subject ... depends on the broad principle of equity that he who has received information in confidence shall not take unfair advantage of it.

To avoid taking unfair advantage of information does not necessarily mean that the confidee must not use it except for the confider's limited purpose. Whether one adopts the 'reasonable man' test suggested by Megarry J or some other, there can be no breach of the equitable obligation unless the Court concludes that a confidence reposed has been abused, that unconscientious use has been made of the information.

Here, SKandF supplied, in pursuit of its commercial interests, a mass of information, part of which was confidential. It did not trouble to identify that part when furnishing the information. Nor did it, until very late in the piece, make the assertion that was so much pressed upon us in this Court, namely that the Department could not make purely internal use of the information other than for SKandF's purposes, not even when public health and safety made that necessary. In those circumstances, it appears to us that the primary Judge was correct in concluding as he did that no equitable obligation was breached, except as to the use of the sample for the government of Papua New Guinea.

THE PUBLIC INTEREST AND INIQUITY DEFENCES

In the discussion above, it was noted that government information is a special category. To establish the cause of action, the plaintiff must show not only that such publication would be a breach of confidence, but also that the public interest requires that the publication be restrained, and that there are no other contradictory or more compelling public interests justifying disclosure. Public interest is not a necessary requirement for establishing the cause of action for non-government information, but it may be a matter that can be raised in defence to justify the disclosure. The case law from the UK initially limited the defence to circumstances where there was disclosure of 'iniquity', in the form of a crime or fraud. The defence was subsequently expanded in the UK to include disclosure of misconduct that is of such a nature that it ought in the public interest to be disclosed (including breach of statutory duty: see *Initial Services v Putterill* [1968] 1 QB 396), as well as other disclosures that are necessary to protect the community from destruction, damage or harm.

The Australian position with regard to defences to actions for breach of confidence is much less clear. One line of cases supports a narrow iniquity defence and another favours a broader public interest defence.

CURRENT LAW

CASE EXTRACT: CURRENT LAW

AG Australia Holdings Ltd v Burton

[2002] NSWSC 170; (2002) 58 NSWLR 464
Supreme Court of New South Wales

[As set out in the first extract from this case (see above, p 571), the issue in this case was whether making a witness statement to the solicitors representing the shareholders amounted to breach of express contractual undertakings. As such, Campbell J did not need to consider whether or not the public interest defence applied, given that this defence, if it exists at all in Australia, only applies in relation to the equitable action for breach of confidence. Nevertheless, Campbell J provided a useful overview of the case law on the public interest defence.]

Campbell J: 177. The present status of a 'public interest' defence in Australia in an action for breach of confidence in equity's exclusive jurisdiction is not clear. Both before, and after, the decision of Gummow J in *Corrs Pavey* [*Whiting & Byrne v Collector of Customs* (1987) 14 FCR 434] there was some (though not universal) acceptance of the line of cases developed in England, in part on the basis of *Gartside v Outram* [(1856) 26 LJ Ch 113], whereby there was a 'public interest defence' to actions for breach of confidence in equity's exclusive jurisdiction. By a 'public interest defence' I mean a defence whereby it is the task of the individual trial judge to decide whether, in the circumstances of the individual case before him or her, the public interest is better served by enforcing, or not enforcing, an obligation of confidence. In *Commonwealth v John Fairfax & Sons Ltd* [(1980) 147 CLR 39] (at 56–57) Mason J (sitting as a single judge of the High Court) said, 'It has been accepted that the so called common law defence of public interest applies to disclosure of confidential information.' (This statement does not make clear whether it 'has been accepted' by courts, or by the parties in the instant case.) In *David Syme & Co Ltd v General Motors-Holden's Ltd* [1984] 2 NSWLR 294 Hutley A-P said, at 305–306:

> The case for the appellant was that there had to be a balancing between the interests of the respondent and the confidentiality of its material and the right of the public to know and the right of the press to assist the public to know and that on a proper weighting of these interests no injunctions should have been granted. I am unable to accept the basis of the appellant's case. This is not a case in which the right of confidentiality is destroyed by iniquity: see *Initial Services Ltd v Putterill* [1968] 1 QB 396. This is a case in which the technical information must be of high commercial value and is a trade secret upon the acquisition [of] which great sums of money have been, and may be expended. It is something in which a right of property is recognised: see *Scott v Scott* [1913] AC 417 at 443. This right of property is not to be taken away from its proprietor without good reason … if the correct way to approach the matter were to weigh the interest of the respondent in confidentiality of its technical and project information and the interest of the public to know, represented by the professional disseminator of information, namely, the newspaper, there could be only one answer: industrial progress is more worthy than satisfied curiosity. However, in my opinion, there is no question of weighing one against the other at all. The proprietary right in its confidential information of this kind is not to be weighed against other circumstances, except in cases where questions of iniquity are involved.

178. Samuels JA, at 309, rejected the notion of confidence as property, and agreed with the remark of Lord Denning MR in *Woodward v Hutchins* [1977] 1 WLR 760 at 764, that, 'In these cases of confidential information it is a question of balancing the public interest in maintaining the confidence against the public interest in knowing the truth.' Samuels JA went on (at 310) to say, 'It therefore seems to me, without finally determining the matter, that the parties before us were correct in perceiving their dispute to depend upon a balance of competing interests. I deal with the matter on that footing.'

179. Street CJ adopted the approach (at 297–298) of setting out the appellant's submission (which summarised circumstances which English cases had held to justify disclosure of confidential information in the public interests) [and] said (at 298):

> I do not, however, wish to be taken to accede either to the proposition that there is a common thread running through the categories put forward by the appellant or to that proposition that, if there be a common thread, it is crystallised in the formulation of principle put forward. No matter how benevolently one views the approach advocated by the appellant, the evidentiary material in the present case does not establish any error on the part of the learned judge of first instance involving this concept of public interest.

180. In *Westpac Banking Corporation v John Fairfax Group Pty Ltd* (1991) 19 IPR 513 at 525 Powell J said:

> I turn, then, to the question of the public interest, as I indicated in *Spycatcher* [*Attorney-General for the United Kingdom v Heinemann Publishers Australia Pty Ltd* (1987) 8 NSWLR 341] (NSWLR at 382), it seems to me that the law in this area has now progressed to the stage where the so called 'iniquity rule' has been subsumed in a more general rule, namely, that publication of otherwise confidential material might be permitted in cases in which there is shown to have been some impropriety which is of such a nature that it ought, in the public interest, be exposed. However, as I also sought to point out in *Spycatcher* (NSWLR at 380), a decision that, in a particular case, information might be allowed to be published, does not inevitably lead to publication to the community at large being permitted: cf and cp *Francome v Mirror Group Newspapers Ltd* [1984] 1 WLR 392; *Lion Laboratories Ltd v Evans* [1984] 3 WLR 539 (Powell J went on to say that the 'balancing' exercise could rarely be carried out satisfactorily at an interlocutory stage of proceedings.)

181. However, the view that there is no 'public interest defence' of the type I have described has also had its supporters.

182. In *Castrol Australia Pty Ltd v Emtech Associates Pty Ltd* (1980) 51 FLR 184 at 210–214, Rath J reviewed the development which had occurred in England of the 'no confidence as to disclosure of iniquity' dictum. He noted (at 212) that Viscount Finlay in *Weld-Blundell v Stephens* [1920] AC 956 at 965–966 said:

> It would be startling if it were the law that an agent who is negligent in the custody of a letter handed to him in confidence by his principal might plead in defence that the letter was libellous. There may, of course, be cases where some higher duty is involved. Danger to the State or public duty may supersede the duty of the agent to his principal.

Rath J (at 213) quoted from the judgment of Ungoed-Thomas J in *Beloff v Pressdram Ltd* [1973] 1 All ER 241 at 260, where Ungoed-Thomas J said:

> The defence of public interest clearly covers, and, in the authorities does not extend beyond, disclosure, which as Lord Denning MR emphasised must be disclosure justified in the public interest, of matters carried out or contemplated, in breach of the country's security, or in breach of law, including statutory duty, fraud, or otherwise destructive of the country or its people including matters medically dangerous to the public; and doubtless other misdeeds of similar gravity. Public interest, as a defence in law, operates to override the rights of the individual (including copyright) which would otherwise prevail and which the law is also concerned to protect. Such public interest, as now recognised by the law, does not extend beyond misdeeds of a serious nature and importance to the country and thus, in my view, clearly recognisable as such.

Rath J went on to say (at 213–214):

> This passage, in my respectful view, expresses no more than a reasonable elaboration of Viscount Finlay's 'higher duty' concept, and is an acceptable statement of the law as to the defence of public interest in an action for breach of contract ... what is particularly important in Ungoed-Thomas J's formulation of principle is his emphasis on the gravity of the conduct that may give rise to the defence. If there is to be a defence labelled public interest, some such confinement of its vague boundaries is in my view essential.

And then (at 215):

> In my opinion the court, in considering whether just cause for breaking confidence exists, must have regard to matters of a more weighty and precise kind than a public interest in the truth being told.

183. In *Smith Kline & French Laboratories (Aust) Ltd v Secretary, Department of Community Services and Health* (1990) 22 FCR 73 at 111, Gummow J said:

> Further, I would accept the submissions by counsel for the applicants in the SK&F proceedings that (i) an examination of the recent English decision shows that the so called 'public interest' defence is not so much a rule of law as an invitation to judicial idiosyncrasy by deciding each case on an ad hoc basis as to whether, on the facts overall, it is better to respect or to override the obligation of confidence; and (ii) equitable principles are best developed by reference to what conscionable behaviour demands of the defendant not by *'balancing'* and then overriding those demands by reference to matters of social or political opinion.

184. A similar conclusion concerning the operation of the 'public interest defence' was reached in *Bacich v Australian Broadcasting Corporation* (1992) 29 NSWLR 1 at 16 by Brownie J, who, referring to the decision of Rath J in *Castrol Australia Pty Ltd v Emtech Associates Pty Ltd* (1980) 51 FLR 184 at 210–216, said that Rath J:

> ... described the decision in *Woodward v Hutchins* [1977] 1 WLR 760; [1977] 2 All ER 751 as being 'the spring tide' (at 214; 56) of the notion, substantially developed through a series of decisions to which Lord Denning MR was a party, more or less equating the defence of iniquity to the balancing of competing public interests, a view which his Honour rejected, correctly in my respectful view.

See also *Sullivan v Sclanders* (2000) 77 SASR 419 at 427.

...

[Having concluded that uncertainty as to the existence of the public interest defence was irrelevant with regard to the matter in issue, Campbell J proceeded to discuss how iniquity, or what he referred to as the disclosure of 'wickedness' is dealt with differently, depending on the source of the obligation of confidence.]

193. Whether the obligation of confidentiality arises from express contract, implied contract, or in the exclusive jurisdiction will bear upon how legal principles deal with the fact that the subject matter of the confidence involves some form of wickedness ...

194. Concerning an obligation of confidence of that type [where equity recognises the obligation], the fact that the subject matter of the confidence is some form of wickedness can be relevant in two ways. The first concerns whether the obligation of confidence exists at all. Concerning some types of information, communicated in circumstances which might ordinarily give rise to an obligation of confidence, the recipient of the information is entitled to say, 'I am not, in conscience, obliged to keep quiet about conduct like that.' The second way in which the wickedness of the conduct might be relevant, in equity's exclusive jurisdiction, is if the person seeking to enforce an obligation of confidence has himself engaged in conduct which gives rise to an equitable defence of unclean hands (*Dewhirst v Edwards* [1983] 1 NSWLR 34 at 51; *FAI Insurances Ltd v Pioneer Concrete Services Ltd*

(1987) 15 NSWLR 552 at 561, *Attorney-General (UK) v Heinemann Publishers Australia Pty Ltd* (1987) 8 NSWLR 341 at 383–384; *Corrs Pavey Whiting & Byrne v Collector of Customs* (at 456–457).

195. If the obligation being sought to be enforced is said to be an implied term in a contract, the wickedness of the conduct sought to be kept confidential is relevant to whether the implication of confidentiality is made—*Gartside v Outram*; *Tournier v National Provincial and Union Bank of England* [1924] 1 KB 461; *Smorgon v Australia & New Zealand Banking Group Ltd* (1976) 134 CLR 475 at 486–490. In deciding what are the implied terms in a contract, the court uses well established tests for deciding whether the term is implied so as to give the contract business efficacy (*BP Refinery (Westernport) Pty Ltd v Shire of Hastings* (1977) 180 CLR 266 at 282–283; *Codelfa Construction Pty Ltd v State Rail Authority of NSW* (1982) 149 CLR 337 at 347), a term implied by law from the nature of the contract itself (*Liverpool City Council v Irwin* [1977] AC 239; *Byrne v Australian Airlines Ltd* (1995) 185 CLR 410 at 448–452 per McHugh J and Gummow J), or implied from custom (*Byrne v Australian Airlines Ltd* (at 440)), or is an implication contained in the express words of the contract (*Marcus Clarke (Vic) Ltd v Brown* (1928) 40 CLR 540 at 553–554). (This listing is substantially drawn from Heydon JA in *Brambles Holdings Ltd v Bathurst City Council* (2001) 53 NSWLR 153 at 164 [28].) Further, these rules of implication are ones which apply where there is a formal contract complete on its face. When there is no such formal contract, the court must first infer what the terms of the contract are before any question of implication arises (*Byrne v Australian Airlines Ltd* (at 422), per Brennan CJ, Dawson and Toohey JJ). As well, if an injunction is sought to enforce an obligation of confidentiality arising from an implied term in a contract, whether the person seeking the injunction had engaged in conduct which is iniquitous can be relevant to the equitable defence of unclean hands.

196. Where there is an express term in a contract, the contract will be enforced, unless there is some public policy which prevents it being enforced. For example, I would not doubt that there is a public policy which makes void an express contract to keep secret the committing of a widespread and serious fraud, and that a contract to keep quiet about such a fraud would be void regardless of whether the way the defendant was proposing to breach the contract was by bringing legal proceedings, or assisting other people to bring legal proceedings, to redress the consequences of the fraud. The scope, and limitations, of any such public policy which makes void or unenforceable an express contract to keep confidential some iniquitous subject matter are decided by engaging in the same sort of enquiry as I have earlier engaged in to decide whether GIO's contract with Mr Burton is void or unenforceable on the ground that it interferes with the administration of justice. As well, if an injunction is sought to enforce an express obligation of confidentiality, questions of whether the plaintiff has engaged in iniquitous conduct can be relevant to whether a defence of unclean hands is made out.

DURATION OF THE OBLIGATION

Equity and contract law only protect *confidential* information. Hence, once information enters the public domain, it might be expected that the protection afforded by equity and contract law will come to an end. However, two important issues have been raised in the cases. The first is whether a party in breach of an obligation of confidence is only restrained from using the confidential information while it retains its quality of confidence. Is that party at liberty to use the information once it enters the public domain? The courts have held that parties in breach of an equitable obligation of confidence should not be allowed to use the information as a 'springboard' to give them a competitive advantage. Courts will award an injunction to prohibit use of the information for the springboard period, which is the length of time that the party in breach is deemed to have a head start over competitors who obtain the information from the public domain. The second issue is whether anyone who agrees to a contractual obligation of confidence should be held to that promise after the information has entered the public domain. The question here is whether it would be contrary to public policy to enforce an obligation of this nature, on the ground of restraint of trade.

THE SPRINGBOARD DOCTRINE

CASE EXTRACT: PRECEDENT

Terrapin Ltd v Builders' Supply Co (Hayes) Ltd

[1967] RPC 375
High Court of England and Wales, Chancery Division

[The plaintiff disclosed to the defendant in confidence certain drawings, technical information and know-how needed to make a pre-fabricated building, as part of a contract between the parties. Four months after the contract between the parties expired, the defendant released a building that contained the features of the plaintiff's designs that had been disclosed to it. One issue was whether the fact that the plaintiff's own buildings had already been marketed by that stage meant that the information had lost its confidence, such that the defendant was discharged from its obligation of confidence.]

Roxburgh J (at 391–392): As I understand it, the essence of this branch of the law, whatever the origin of it may be, is that a person who has obtained information in confidence is not allowed to use it as a springboard for activities detrimental to the person who made the confidential communication, and springboard it remains even when all the features have been published or can be ascertained by actual inspection by any member of the public ... The dismantling of a unit might enable a person to proceed without plans or specifications, or other technical information, but not, I think, without some of the know-how and certainly not without taking the trouble to dismantle. I think it is broadly true to say that a member of the public to whom the confidential information had not been imparted would still have to prepare plans and specifications. He would probably have to construct a prototype, and he would certainly have to conduct tests. Therefore, the possessor of the confidential information still has a long start over any member of the public. ... It is, in my view, inherent in the principle upon which the *Saltman* case rests that the possessor of such information must be placed under a special disability in the field of competition in order to ensure that he does not get an unfair start

In *Vestergaard Frandsen A/S v Bestnet Europe Ltd* [2009] EWHC 1456 (Ch); [2010] FSR 2, Arnold J explained that *Terrapin* should be understood as a case involving information that 'retained a limited degree of confidentiality which could be expressed in terms of the time it would take to obtain it by reverse engineering' (at [46]). His Honour thought that where a defendant who had obtained such a springboard is continuing to misuse that information at the time of the hearing, an injunction can be granted, 'limited, however, to the time it would take someone starting from public domain sources to reverse engineer or compile the information] (at [80]).

CASE EXTRACT: CURRENT LAW

Titan Group Pty Ltd v Steriline Manufacturing Pty Ltd

(1991) 19 IPR 353

Federal Court of Australia

[The subject matter in this case was gym equipment. In essence Titan alleged that Steriline was engaged to manufacture hydraulically operated gym equipment that included a novel pressure release valve developed by an employee of Titan. However, Titan argued that Steriline misused Titan's confidential information and set up as a manufacturer and distributor of similar equipment in competition with Titan.]

O'Loughlin J (at 376–378): Subject to the application of the springboard principle, there can, of course, be no unauthorised use of confidential information, if at the time of the use, it had ceased to be confidential. Information that might properly be described as confidential when it was originally conveyed to a party may well lose that protective mantle of confidence if subsequently there is a public awareness of the information. The start (and finish) of the springboard can not be ascertained from the cases, except by analogy, for the determination of the duration of the springboard is 'a question of degree depending on the particular case': *Franchi v Franchi* [1967] RPC 149 at 153 per Cross J. But in every case, the period of the springboard will always be 'one of limited duration': *Harrison v Project and Design Co (Redcar) Ltd* [1978] FSR 81 at 87 per Graham J.

The following are three examples of assessments by Courts of springboard periods:

(a) *British Franco Electric Pty Ltd v Dowling Plastics Pty Ltd* [1981] 1 NSWLR 448: The first defendant, pursuant to a joint venture with the first plaintiff, was to manufacture and market twin-wheel furniture castors, the design of which had been registered by the first plaintiff. Twelve months after the agreement was terminated, the first defendant began manufacturing the castors for itself. Wooten J held that the wheels had been on the market and available to the public for some twelve months and thus the springboard commenced at the time the product was commercially available. His Honour said at 453 that if the defendants 'had a springboard, it would no longer have projected them ahead of competitors'.

(b) *Ackroyds (London) v Islington Plastics Ltd* [1962] RPC 97: Under contract, the defendants manufactured swizzle sticks for the plaintiffs, who supplied the defendants with a tool for the process of manufacture. The defendants then began to supply the swizzle sticks to the plaintiff's major customer, using the tool for the process. This conduct was alleged to be in breach of confidence. Havers J held at p 104, 'mere publication of an article by manufacturing it and placing it upon the market ... is not necessarily sufficient to make such information available to the public. The question in each case is: Is such information available to the public? It is not, in my view, if work would have to be done upon it to make it available'. It must be remembered that this case was decided prior to the enunciation of the springboard concept by Roxburgh J in the *Terrapin* case. However, it is useful as it reinforces the focus on the public. Thus, it must not be assumed that in every case lawful reverse engineering of a product, means, without more, that all relevant information is thereby available to the public. The extent to which the development difficulties that were overcome by Steriline would delay a member of the public in producing a commercially viable product must be considered. Unlike the assessment of Havers J, this does not delay the point at

CURRENT LAW

which the information is publicly available, but really goes to the length of the springboard period, ie the time it would take a member of the public to manufacture the item.

(c) *Deta Nominees Pty Ltd v Viscount Plastic Products Pty Ltd* [1979] VR 167: As to the duration of the springboard period, Fullagar J at 194–5 said:

> In my opinion the plaintiff is entitled to restrain the defendants from using the confidential information beyond certain limits. Prima facie the plaintiff is entitled to prevent the defendants from making or selling any injection-moulded, all plastic, one-piece, polypropylene furniture drawers, at least for a period of time found by adding together the following periods:
>
> 1. The time it will now reasonably take the plaintiff to get its plastic drawer on the market in substantial quantities.
> 2. The time it would thereafter reasonably take some uninformed competitor or designer (that is to say one without the current know-how of the defendants derived from their design work performed for the plaintiff and from their sales in breach of contract) to pull apart and analyse the drawer and ascertain its mode of construction and thereafter design and construct and get into production a tool for the manufacture of similar drawers.
>
> A not unfair estimate for the aggregate period would be something of the order of a year, having regard to the present evidence.

As Titan's products have been on the market for some time, the first period mentioned by Fullagar J is not relevant to the facts of this case. What is relevant here is the conduct of Titan in regard to its efforts to keep the information in question confidential (see for example *Amway Corp v Eurway International Ltd* [1974] RPC 82; *Ansell Rubber Co Pty Ltd v Allied Rubber Industries Pty Ltd* [1967] VR 37; *Mense v Milenkovic* [1973] VR 784; see also *British-Franco Electric Pty Ltd v Dowling Plastics Pty Ltd* supra at 450–1 per Wootten J). Thus in the case at bar, the actual period of time that it would have taken Steriline to develop the product for sale must be ignored; instead it is necessary to focus on the 'uninformed competitor' who, for example, purchased equipment from Titan after the equipment had entered the public domain.

[Taking into account the evidence presented in court, O'Loughlin J concluded that in the present circumstances the springboard period was 15 months. Given that it actually took Steriline around this time to enter the market, it was not appropriate to grant an injunction in all the circumstances.]

ONGOING CONTRACTUAL OBLIGATIONS WHERE THE INFORMATION HAS ENTERED THE PUBLIC DOMAIN, AND RESTRAINT OF TRADE

CASE EXTRACT: CURRENT LAW

Maggbury Pty Ltd v Hafele Australia Pty Ltd

[2001] HCA 70; (2001) 210 CLR 181
High Court of Australia

[Mr GW Allen, a director of Maggbury, was an inventor who had developed a new type of fold-away ironing board. Maggbury filed patent applications, and sought commercial partners, entering negotiations with Hafele, which included execution of confidentiality agreements. Ultimately the patents

CURRENT LAW

were not granted, negotiations between the parties broke down and Hafele started to distribute its own fold-away ironing boards. Maggbury sought to enforce the confidentiality agreements. The difficulty for Maggbury was that the subject matter of the confidentiality agreement had been publicly disclosed in the patent applications and at trade fairs. The issue before the Court was whether it would amount to a restraint of trade to hold Hafele to the contractual obligation of confidence after the information had lost the quality of confidence. The first confidentiality agreement included the following term in cl 11.1: 'It is a condition of this agreement that Hafele [Australia] will forever observe the obligations of confidence set out in this Agreement, unless released from such obligations in writing by the Inventor.']

Gleeson CJ, Gummow and Hayne JJ: 45. Ordinarily, the obligations relating to the use and disclosure of the Information would be construed as limited to subject-matter which retained the quality of confidentiality at the time of breach or threatened breach of those obligations ...

...

50. A construction of the restraints in the two agreements which gave them a limited temporal operation after public disclosure and after failure of the negotiations might be supported as the contractual imposition upon the Hafele companies of a 'head start' handicap. This would reflect the advantage to those companies, over the position of competitors who had not dealt with Maggbury, in having had access to the Information over a period preceding its public disclosure [cf *United States Surgical Corporation v Hospital Products International Pty Ltd* [1983] 2 NSWLR 157 at 228–233 (revd on other grounds (1984) 156 CLR 41]. Public disclosure occurred at the latest in February 1997. It may be accepted for present purposes that a contractual restraint of this nature upon the Hafele companies would not exceed the reasonable protection of the interests of Maggbury. It is unnecessary to determine the point. This is because what the appellants seek from this Court is the restoration of an absolute perpetual and unconditional injunction, granted as if the confidential quality of the information in question still persists.

51. What then is the effect, upon their proper construction, of the contractual restraints in question here? Three provisions are particularly in point. Clause 5.1 obliged the Hafele companies to 'treat' the Information as 'confidential'. The agreements contained no warranty by Maggbury that the Information had this character at the date of the agreements or that it would have that character when disclosed or supplied by Maggbury during the negotiations with respect to the Purpose. Clause 5.1 obliged the Hafele companies to deal with the Information when supplied or disclosed during the negotiations on the agreed footing that it had this confidential character. However, were it not for the provisions of cl 11.1, cl 5.1 might properly be construed as not obliging the disclosees to continue to accept that the Information had the confidential character after it had been disclosed publicly by Maggbury itself. The obligation to 'treat' the Information as 'confidential' answers the description in the first sentence of cl 11.1 as one of the 'obligations of confidence set out in this Agreement'. Clause 11.1 states it as a condition of the agreement that the Hafele companies 'forever' observe those obligations.

52. Further, cl 5.6 forbids the use without consent of the Information 'for any purpose' 'at any time' thereafter. Both cl 5.1 and cl 5.6 use 'Information' in the broader of the senses referred to earlier in these reasons. Thus they do not proceed on the footing that, for example, after the prototypes had been returned no further obligations subsist with respect to the information derived from inspection of the prototypes.

53. The terms of cll 5.1 and 5.6 as so construed would, on the findings of Byrne J [at first instance], found the injunctive relief, unlimited in time, respecting the wall-mounted Hafele model. It is not fairly open to avoid that result by construing these provisions as having as their subject-matter only information which at the time of the alleged breach of covenant retains a confidential character which it had when first disclosed by Maggbury. The emphatic temporal extensions applied to cl 5.1 by cl 11.1 and the terms of cl 5.6 are expressions of 'explicit' intent [*Picard v United Aircraft Corporation* 128 F 2d 632 at 637 (1942)] and are put in 'inescapable terms' [*Conmar Products Corporation v Universal Slide Fastener Co* 172 F 2d 150 at 156 (1949)]. Any implied term to other effect would contradict the express terms.

54. The question then arises as to whether these contractual terms are subjected to and survive the application of the restraint of trade doctrine. Undoubtedly the provisions impose restraints upon the activities of the Hafele companies, as is apparent from the terms of the injunction. They restrict the liberty of the Hafele companies in the future to conduct their operations and dealings with third parties in such manner as they think fit. The Hafele parties undoubtedly are in 'trade' and the activities restrained are part of that trade. Contrary to the submissions pressed for the appellants, the restraints which they seek to have enforced in this litigation are not of the same character as terms of licences to use intellectual property ... Whatever else may be said of the notion that confidential information is to be regarded as proprietary in nature, that analysis cannot be sustained where the information has become available from public sources as a result of disclosures by the party asserting that quality of confidence. Other intangible proprietary rights such as those conferred by the law of copyright are not involved. Allegations of the subsistence and the infringement of copyright were removed from the further amended statement of claim. The source of the rights which the appellants seek to enforce is found in contract. In particular in the contractual obligation imposed upon the Hafele companies to treat or deal with the Information as having the quality of confidence.

55. Why then does the common law doctrine respecting restraint of trade not apply? The appellants submit that the doctrine does not apply because the Hafele companies could carry on their trade without relying upon the particular disclosures by Maggbury by, for example, having recourse to the public domain and their own previously acquired skills and experience. But that circumstance does not demonstrate that the doctrine has no application ...

56. The fact that the restraint can be said to have freely been bargained for by the parties to the contract provides no sufficient reason for concluding that the doctrine should not apply. All contractual restraints can be said to be of that character.

57. The result is that the doctrine applied to the restraints we have identified and rendered them invalid, subject to their justification as reasonable in the interests of the public and the parties. The respondents correctly emphasise that such an enterprise was not undertaken at the trial. Further, it may be added that there would be substantial difficulty in doing so.

—15—

TRADE MARKS, PASSING OFF AND PROTECTING TRADE REPUTATION: HISTORY, JUSTIFICATIONS AND CONTEXT

INTRODUCTION

In this and the following three chapters we consider the legal protection afforded in Australia to traders in respect of the marks and other indicia they use to distinguish their goods or services from those of other traders. There are two main legal mechanisms by which Australian law provides such protection. The first, which we consider in detail in Chapter 16, is the tort of passing off, as supplemented by consumer protection legislation. In essence, these actions prohibit parties from engaging in misrepresentations, or misleading or deceptive conduct, by adopting other traders' distinctive signs or indicia. The second, which we consider in Chapters 17 and 18, is the system of registered trade mark protection under the *Trade Marks Act 1995* (Cth). This system provides an additional degree of protection for signs which, upon meeting certain criteria, can be registered as trade marks under that Act.

In this chapter we focus on the intertwined histories of the tort of passing off and registered trade marks in the UK and Australia, provide an overview of the current international and domestic laws, and consider the justifications for protecting trade marks and indicia (focusing on the relationship between these justifications and the scope of protection afforded to such indicia).

HISTORY OF PASSING OFF AND TRADE MARK PROTECTION
ORIGINS OF PASSING OFF

The tort of passing off has its origins in British law in the action on the case at common law for deceit. From the seventeenth century, the common law courts provided a remedy to a trader whose trade name or symbol had been adopted by another trader with the intention of inducing its customers to believe that its goods were in fact those of the first trader. The main rationale was that the second trader's actions were thought to constitute a fraud on the public. By the nineteenth century these had became known as cases of 'passing off', the essential element being a fraudulent misrepresentation by the defendant that its goods were those of the plaintiff.[1]

---

[1]   See for example *Perry v Truefitt* (1842) 49 ER 749.

By the early nineteenth century, actions could also be brought in the courts of Chancery, which were able to grant injunctions. Initially, Chancery courts only intervened in aid of a legal right—that is, the plaintiff had to show it had a right to bring an action at common law. The basis of the equitable action was that of fraudulent conduct by the defendant. However, in *Millington v Fox* (1838) 40 ER 956 the Lord Chancellor granted an injunction in a case involving a misrepresentation as to the origin of goods by the adoption of the plaintiff's mark in the absence of any fraud. Following this development, in a number of decisions in the 1860s and 70s the Chancery courts came to articulate a view that equity's intervention in cases of this type was based on the plaintiff's *property* rights in the 'mark' itself.[2]

MODERN FORM OF THE TORT OF PASSING OFF

The idea that the 'mark' itself could constitute a form of legal property proved to be important, but for different reasons, which we explore below, under 'Origins of registered trade mark law'. In the context of the passing off action the idea had relatively little impact. This was chiefly because by the late nineteenth and early twentieth centuries, the common law courts had arrived at the view that a different property interest was protected by the tort of passing off, and it was only at that time that the action came to take on its modern form. This development is described in the following extract.

CASE EXTRACT: PRECEDENT

Erven Warnink BV v J Townend & Sons (Hull) Ltd

[1979] AC 731
House of Lords

Lord Diplock (at 740–741): At the close of the century in *Reddaway v Banham* [1896] AC 199, it was said by Lord Herschell that what was protected by an action for passing off was not the proprietary right of the trader in the mark, name or get-up improperly used. Thus the door was opened to passing off actions in which the misrepresentation took some other form than the deceptive use of trade names, marks, letters or other indicia; but as none of their Lordships committed themselves to identifying the legal nature of the right that was protected by a passing off action it remained an action sui generis which lay for damage sustained or threatened in consequence of a misrepresentation of a particular kind.

Reddaway v Banham, like all previous passing off cases, was one in which Banham had passed off his goods as those of Reddaway, and the damage resulting from the misrepresentation took the form of the diversion of potential customers from Reddaway to Banham. Although it was a landmark case in deciding that the use by a trader of a term which accurately described the composition of his own goods might nevertheless amount to the tort of passing off if that term were understood in the market in which the goods were sold to denote the goods of a rival trader, *Reddaway v Banham* did not extend the nature of the particular kind of misrepresentation which gives rise to a right of action in passing off beyond

---

2   See for example *Edelsten v Edelsten* (1863) 46 ER 72 and *Leather Cloth Co v American Leather Cloth Co* (1865) 11 ER 1435.

PRECEDENT

what I have called the classic form of misrepresenting one's own goods as the goods of someone else nor did it provide any rational basis for an extension.

This was left to be provided by Lord Parker in *AG Spalding & Bros v AW Gamage Ltd* (1915) 84 LJ Ch 449, 450. In a speech which received the approval of the other members of this House, he identified the right the invasion of which is the subject of passing off actions as being the 'property in the business or goodwill likely to be injured by the misrepresentation.' The concept of goodwill is in law a broad one which is perhaps best expressed in words used by Lord Macnaghten in *Inland Revenue Commissioners v Muller & Co's Margarine Ltd* [1901] AC 217, 223–224: 'It is the benefit and advantage of the good name, reputation, and connection of a business. It is the attractive force which brings in custom.'

The goodwill of a manufacturer's business may well be injured by someone else who sells goods which are correctly described as being made by that manufacturer but being of an inferior class or quality are misrepresented as goods of his manufacture of a superior class or quality. This type of misrepresentation was held in *AG Spalding & Bros v AW Gamage Ltd*, 84 LJ Ch 449 to be actionable and the extension to the nature of the misrepresentation which gives rise to a right of action in passing off which this involved was regarded by Lord Parker as a natural corollary of recognising that what the law protects by a passing off action is a trader's property in his business or goodwill.

The significance of this decision in the law of passing off lies in its recognition that misrepresenting one's own goods as the goods of someone else was not a separate genus of actionable wrong but a particular species of wrong included in a wider genus of which a premonitory hint had been given by Lord Herschell in *Reddaway v Banham* [1896] AC 199, 211 when, in speaking of the deceptive use of a descriptive term, he said:

> I am unable to see why a man should be allowed in this way more than in any other to deceive purchasers into the belief that they are getting what they are not, and thus to filch the business of a rival.

Thus, in its modern form, the passing off action provides 'a remedy for the invasion of a right of property not in the mark, name or get-up improperly used, but in the business or goodwill likely to be injured by the misrepresentation made by passing off one person's goods as the goods of another' (Lord Diplock in *Star Industrial Co Ltd v Yap Kwee Kor* [1976] FSR 256 at 269). In addition, what constitutes a misrepresentation in passing off cases extends beyond the classic case of one trader using another trader's mark to pass off its goods as those of that trader. Rather, by the early twentieth century a broader notion of 'misrepresentation' had been established.

These notions of goodwill and misrepresentation, and how they have developed in Australia since the start of the twentieth century, will be explored in detail in the next chapter, which will also involve consideration of the impact of related Australian consumer protection legislation in the late twentieth century. It is worth noting at this stage that under Australian law, fraud still has a continuing role to play in the passing off action.

ORIGINS OF REGISTERED TRADE MARK LAW

At much the same time that the Chancery courts determined that the passing off action protected a form of property in the mark itself, the UK Parliament was taking steps to provide further protection for trade marks. In 1862 it passed the *Merchandise Marks Act*, which made it a criminal offence to misuse others' 'trade marks' with the intention to defraud. A trade mark here was broadly defined as 'any Name, Signature, Word, Letter, Device, Emblem, Figure, Sign, Seal, Stamp, Diagram, Label, Ticket or other Mark of any other Description lawfully used by any person to denote any chattel, to be the Manufacture, Workmanship, Production or Merchandise of such Person'. At the same time, and more significantly, Parliament was also considering adopting a system of registration of trade marks. The impetus for this reform came largely from developments abroad. France, which had had a trade mark registration scheme since 1803, passed a law in 1857 whose effect was that protection for foreign traders and their marks was only available in France if that foreign country agreed to provide reciprocal protection for French traders and their marks.[3] The UK entered into a number of bilateral treaties on trade mark law with France and other countries in the 1860s and 70s which, combined with domestic pressures for reform, led to the adoption of the *Trade Marks Registration Act 1875* (UK). That Act established a trade marks registry and allowed for a trade mark to be registered in relation to a specified class of goods and entered on a register of trade marks. The major restrictions on registration were that the mark:

- either had to be a 'special or distinctive word or words or combination of letters, words or figures or letters used as a trade mark' before 13 August 1875, or had to consist of certain 'essential particulars'; these were tightly defined: the mark could only consist of the name of an individual or firm 'printed, impressed, or woven in some particular and distinctive manner', a written signature of an individual or firm, or a 'distinctive device, mark, heading, label or ticket' (to which particulars might be added any letters, words, figures or combination thereof) (s 10);
- could not be identical with a mark already registered in respect of the same goods, or which so nearly resembled a mark already registered as to be likely to deceive (s 6); and
- could not consist of a 'scandalous design' or, by reason of it being calculated to deceive or otherwise, be disentitled to protection in a court of equity (s 6).

A person who successfully applied for registration of a mark became its 'proprietor', and registration was evidence of the proprietor's exclusive right to use the mark (s 3).

Thus, by the mid-1870s, trade marks had become widely accepted as a form of property. Lionel Bently makes a number of observations about this:

> [T]rade marks started to be treated as part of a law of 'industrial property', included in legislation relating also to patents and designs [i.e., the *Patents, Designs, and Trade Marks Act 1883*], and, before long, in the first significant multilateral international treaty, the Paris Convention. Moreover, perceived as 'property', trade marks were frequently compared and contrasted by commentators with analogous but distinct laws of patents and copyright. Courts too occasionally were prepared to reason from an understanding of trade marks as property when developing applicable rules, for example, on 'abandonment'. But while designation of trade marks as 'property' was important, no-one in the 1870s or 1880s would have inferred from this that trade-mark rights extended to the use of the protected sign on dissimilar goods.[4]

---

3   See generally P Duguid, 'French Connections: The International Propagation of Trademarks in the Nineteenth Century' (2008) 10 *Enterprise and Society* 3.

4   L Bently, 'From Communication to Thing: Historical Aspects of the Conceptualisation of Trade Marks as Property' in G Dinwoodie and M Janis, eds, *Trademark Law and Theory: A Handbook of Contemporary Research*, Edward Elgar, Cheltenham, 2008, p 6.

Two further observations can be made. First, registered trade marks did not have all the characteristics of other forms of property. Most notably, the 1875 Act contained an express restriction on trade marks being assigned separately from the goodwill of the business in respect of which the mark was used (s 2). This corresponded with the view at common law. Second, explicit recognition of rights in the mark itself as a form of property meant that the action for trade mark infringement differed from the passing off action. An action for infringement of a registered trade mark did not require the plaintiff to demonstrate any trading goodwill or reputation: mere proprietorship was sufficient. Further, a registered mark was infringed simply by its use in relation to the specified goods—there was no need to show that the defendant's use of the mark conveyed a misrepresentation. Having said that, the proprietor's rights were interpreted strictly: for example, in *Hargreaves v Freeman* (1891) 8 RPC 273 the owner of a mark registered in respect of 'tobacco' was refused an injunction to restrain the defendant's use of the mark on cigars.

The UK law of registered trade marks underwent a number of refinements, with further Acts in 1883 and 1905. Those Acts provided a model for the first Commonwealth statute: the *Trade Marks Act 1905* (Cth).[5]

The 1905 Australian Act, like its UK counterpart, contained a broader list of 'essential particulars' of which a registrable trade mark could consist. It included invented words and words having no direct reference to the character or quality of the applicant's goods (ss 16–17), and allowed other marks to be registered if they had become distinctive of the applicant's goods through the applicant's use of the mark (s 20). It was an infringement of a registered trade mark to use a mark 'substantially identical with the trade mark or so nearly resembling it as to be likely to deceive' (s 53), which did not turn on showing that an actual misrepresentation had taken place. Registration lasted for 14 years, but could be renewed (ss 48, 54). The Act also built on earlier UK legislation in setting out the bureaucratic requirements for registration, including as to the form of the application, its examination by the Registrar, and opposition proceedings.

Two later UK Acts followed. In Australia, the report of the Knowles Committee in 1938 led to some interim reform in 1948. Then, following the report of the Dean Committee in 1954, Parliament enacted the *Trade Marks Act 1955* (Cth), which remained in force until its repeal by the current 1995 Act. Before that repeal, Australian registered trade mark law had developed such that:

- both a 'mark' and a 'trade mark' had been defined (in terms not dissimilar to the definition in the *Merchandise Marks Act 1862* (UK));
- the Register had become divided into various Parts, in order to accommodate a category of marks that were merely capable of becoming distinctive, as well as new types of marks (defensive and certification marks);
- applicants could register marks in respect of services as well as goods;
- registration lasted seven years, but could be renewed;
- a registered mark could be removed on the basis of non-use; and
- the exploitation of registered marks had become more straightforward: marks could be assigned separately from the goodwill of the underlying business, and could also be licensed in limited circumstances.

---

5   For consideration of the pre-federation trade mark laws of the Australian colonies and how they were used, see A Scardamaglia, 'Opening up the Australian Archives on Colonial Trade Mark Registrations' (2013) 23 *AustralianIntellectual Property Journal* 222.

As discussed in Chapters 17 and 18, the *Trade Marks Act 1995* further liberalised what can be registered as a trade mark, what constitutes an infringement, and the assignment and licensing provisions.

Two final introductory points should be made. First, although the registered trade mark system was not simply a statutory re-enactment of the passing off action, there has always been a close and symbiotic relationship between the two. On its introduction, the registration system provided easier-to-enforce rights for many marks. In turn, the tort of passing off soon expanded to provide broader protection than that available under registered trade mark law—for example protecting signs that could not be registered as marks, or preventing use by defendants on non-competing goods. These developments in turn fed calls for further expansion of registered trade mark law. This feedback loop continued well into the twentieth century. Thus, for example, passing off led the way in protecting packaging get-up and product appearance well before these were recognised as registrable trade marks.

Second, some care is needed when encountering claims (sometimes made by US commentators) that prevention of 'consumer confusion' is what underpins trade mark law. This might be a broadly accurate way of characterising passing off: even though the tort is designed to safeguard a trader's property interest in its trading reputation, the essence of passing off is that the defendant has engaged in conduct that misleads consumers. However, the history of Anglo-Australian registered trade mark law reveals that the interests it seeks to protect are far more diverse. Registered trade mark law at times serves a broad regulatory function in that it sets limits on what can be registered for reasons unrelated to consumer confusion, as well as regulating the conduct of competing traders in the marketplace. For example, the core actions for trade mark infringement under Australian law do not ultimately turn on the existence of consumer confusion, even though they might have the incidental *effect* of preventing consumers from being deceived. In addition, similar marks can sometimes coexist on the Register, or defendants may have defences to infringement, in circumstances where consumer confusion does exist. As the High Court recognised in *Campomar Sociedad Limitada v Nike International Ltd* [2000] HCA 12; (2000) 202 CLR 45, Australian registered trade mark statutes have always tolerated some degree of consumer confusion, and can best be seen as attempting to balance sometimes conflicting interests in regulating the conduct of competing traders, as well as safeguarding consumers.

JUSTIFICATIONS FOR PROTECTING TRADE MARKS AND INDICIA

Unlike the fields of copyright and patent law, in trade mark law it is unusual to see attempts to justify the legal protection of trade marks and indicia on the basis that they are the product of creativity on the part of an 'author' or 'inventor'. Similarly, although the argument is sometimes made that legal intervention is needed to provide incentives for the creation of and investment in new brands, that tends not to be the primary justification for trade mark law. Rather, the orthodox view is that trade marks receive legal protection for largely economic reasons, based primarily on the signalling functions that they serve.

TRADE MARKS AND INDICIA AS SOURCES OF INFORMATION

The principal justification for the legal protection of trade marks and trade indicia is that they communicate valuable information that allows consumers to make informed choices about their purchases. The very essence of a trade mark is that it operates as an *indication of origin*—that is, it indicates that the goods or services bearing the mark come from a particular trade source (more accurately, that they are produced under the overarching control of a particular entity). A consumer seeing or hearing the word 'Samsung' used in relation to tablets will know that they are Samsung brand machines; a consumer seeing four interlocking circles on the grille of a car will recognise those cars to be a particular make (which many will know to be Audi).

Trade marks fulfil various other functions that help to provide additional information to consumers, each dependent on that primary 'origin' function. One is a *product differentiation* function. Trade marks help traders to differentiate their goods and services from those of others. Imagine a rack of seemingly identical but branded white T-shirts in a sports clothing store: the 'swoosh' symbol marks out Nike's shirts, while the 'three stripes' logo would signal Adidas, and a leaping puma would distinguish Puma's goods. A further, related function is the *quality guarantee* function: a trade mark indicates that the goods are of a similar quality to other goods bearing that mark. If consumers are satisfied (or dissatisfied) with a particular product, they can purchase (or avoid) products of similar quality by reference to their trade marks.

In all the above ways, trade marks help to reduce consumer search costs and increase the economic efficiency of markets.

A useful statement about the relationship between the three related functions identified above and the justification for protecting trade marks is contained in the Opinion of the Advocate General of the then Court of Justice of the European Communities in Case C-10/89, *SA CNL-SUCAL NV v HAG GF AG* [1990] ECR I-3711:

> Whereas patents reward the creativity of the inventor and thus stimulate scientific progress, trade marks reward the manufacturer who consistently produces high-quality goods and they thus stimulate economic progress. Without trade mark protection there would be little incentive for manufacturers to develop new products or to maintain the quality of existing ones. Trade marks are able to achieve that effect because they act as a guarantee, to the consumer, that all goods bearing a particular mark have been produced by, or under the control of, the same manufacturer and are therefore likely to be of similar quality. The guarantee of quality offered by a trade mark is not of course absolute, for the manufacturer is at liberty to vary the quality; however, he does so at his own risk and he—not his competitors—will suffer the consequences if he allows the quality to decline. Thus, although trade marks do not provide any form of legal guarantee of quality—the absence of which may have misled some to underestimate their significance—they do in economic terms provide such a guarantee, which is acted upon daily by consumers.

On the basis of these rationales, the scope of both trade mark and passing off laws has always been limited. Owners do not have absolute rights to stop other traders or parties from using their marks or indicia in all commercial circumstances. Rather, a trader's rights are generally restricted to preventing use of that trader's marks or other indicia that would cause a degree of deception among consumers and thus impair the origin identification, product differentiation and quality guarantee functions identified above. For example, in classic cases of passing off, the defendant must have engaged in a misrepresentation as to the origin of its goods or services that damages the plaintiff's reputation: one aspect of this damage will be that the defendant's conduct adversely impacts on the information provided by the plaintiff's sign or indicia. Similarly, the core zone of protection provided by the law of registered trade marks covers situations where a defendant uses an identical or similar mark in relation to identical or similar goods. In both cases, such protection can be contrasted with the much broader rights given to copyright and patent owners.

PREVENTING MISAPPROPRIATION AS A STAND-ALONE JUSTIFICATION?

A different justification for trade mark protection is based on the idea that misappropriation of the brand owner's labour, investment and reputation ought to be prevented. Most commonly this is framed as a form of natural rights argument that a party should not be allowed to reap the benefits of another trader's labour.[6] Sometimes this argument can be used to explain the traditional contours of the passing off action and registered trade mark law. That is, it is said that someone should not be allowed to take advantage of another trader's goodwill by using that trader's mark, such that traders ought to be granted rights to prevent the use of their marks by rivals in relation to the same or similar goods as those provided by the mark owner. However, the justification is sometimes said to extend beyond this form of protection to encompass situations where the user can be said to be taking advantage of or otherwise harming the trade mark's reputation, even in the *absence* of consumer confusion.

This latter argument is often made on the basis that the traditional functions of trade marks no longer represent market reality and that the law ought to intervene to safeguard a different function that marks are said to serve—the *advertising function*. It is sometimes said that consumers no longer care about the origin or quality of goods and services, but instead, often as a result of advertising, see trade marks as symbols that are desirable commodities in their own right. This involves a recognition that trade marks form the outward manifestation of a company's 'brand', and that many businesses invest vast amounts of money in the construction and maintenance of 'brand image', which involves attempting to communicate their corporate ethos or certain feelings and aspirations their goods or services are intended to inspire in consumers and to locate this symbolism within the company's marks. It is argued that in light of this advertising function, which at least *some* trade marks serve, owners should have legal protection against conduct that somehow 'dilutes' the value of their marks, irrespective of whether any consumer deception is caused. An early advocate of such legal protection was US scholar Frank Schechter, who in 'The Rational Basis of Trademark Protection' (1927) 40 *Harvard Law Review* 813 considered that the real value of a trade mark lay in its 'selling power' and its 'psychological hold upon the public' (at 831), and complained of 'the gradual whittling away or dispersion of the identity and hold upon the public mind of the mark or name by its use upon non-competing goods' (at 825). As such, he suggested that the only rational basis for protecting a mark was to preserve its 'uniqueness', in effect giving traders a monopoly over the use of the mark in question in relation to non-competing goods or services.

DILUTION

In many jurisdictions around the world, including the EU and the USA, some legal protection is available against the 'dilution' of trade marks. This tends to be limited to particularly 'famous' marks or marks with a reputation. The following extract provides a succinct summary of the various forms of trade mark dilution that might be said to exist.

---

6   For an examination of this argument, see D Scott et al, 'Trade Marks as Property: A Philosophical Perspective' in L Bently et al, eds, *Trade Marks and Brands: An Interdisciplinary Critique*, Cambridge University Press, Cambridge, 2008.

CASE EXTRACT: COMPARATIVE LAW

Ty, Inc v Perryman

306 F 3d 509 (7th Cir, 2002)
United States Court of Appeals, Seventh Circuit

Posner J (at 510–511): But what is 'dilution'? There are (at least) three possibilities relevant to this case, each defined by a different underlying concern. First, there is concern that consumer search costs will rise if a trademark becomes associated with a variety of unrelated products. Suppose an upscale restaurant calls itself 'Tiffany.' There is little danger that the consuming public will think it's dealing with a branch of the Tiffany jewelry store if it patronizes this restaurant. But when consumers next see the name 'Tiffany' they may think about both the restaurant and the jewelry store, and if so the efficacy of the name as an identifier of the store will be diminished. Consumers will have to think harder—incur as it were a higher imagination cost—to recognize the name as the name of the store. *Exxon Corp v Exxene Corp*, 696 F 2d 544, 549–50 (7th Cir 1982); cf. *Mead Data Central, Inc v Toyota Motor Sales, USA, Inc*, 875 F 2d 1026, 1031 (2d Cir 1989) ('The [legislative] history [of New York's antidilution statute] disclosed a need for legislation to prevent such 'hypothetical anomalies' as 'Dupont shoes, Buick aspirin tablets, Schlitz varnish, Kodak pianos, Bulova gowns'); 4 *McCarthy on Trademarks and Unfair Competition*, supra, §24:68, pp 24–120 to 24–121. So 'blurring' is one form of dilution.

Now suppose that the 'restaurant' that adopts the name 'Tiffany' is actually a striptease joint. Again, and indeed even more certainly than in the previous case, consumers will not think the striptease joint under common ownership with the jewelry store. But because of the inveterate tendency of the human mind to proceed by association, every time they think of the word 'Tiffany' their image of the fancy jewelry store will be tarnished by the association of the word with the strip joint. *Hormel Foods Corp v Jim Henson Productions, Inc*, 73 F 3d 497, 507 (2d Cir 1996); 4 *McCarthy on Trademarks and Unfair Competition*, supra, §24:95, pp 24–195, 24–198. So 'tarnishment' is a second form of dilution. Analytically it is a subset of blurring, since it reduces the distinctness of the trademark as a signifier of the trademarked product or service.

Third, and most far-reaching in its implications for the scope of the concept of dilution, there is a possible concern with situations in which, though there is neither blurring nor tarnishment, someone is still taking a free ride on the investment of the trademark owner in the trademark. Suppose the 'Tiffany' restaurant in our first hypothetical example is located in Kuala Lumpur and though the people who patronize it (it is upscale) have heard of the Tiffany jewelry store, none of them is ever going to buy anything there, so that the efficacy of the trademark as an identifier will not be impaired. If appropriation of Tiffany's aura is nevertheless forbidden by an expansive concept of dilution, the benefits of the jewelry store's investment in creating a famous name will be, as economists say, 'internalized'—that is, Tiffany will realize the full benefits of the investment rather than sharing those benefits with others— and as a result the amount of investing in creating a prestigious name will rise.

Clearly, anti-dilution laws that are designed to prevent 'blurring', 'tarnishment' or mere 'free riding' represent an attempt to provide a degree of protection for certain brands (Posner J's choice of 'Tiffany'—a name representing not merely a jewellery store but a brand many would immediately associate with prestige, conspicuous consumption and Hollywood glamour—is no accident).

It is trite to note that brands can be enormously valuable commercial assets and that firms invest substantial sums in creating and maintaining their 'brand image'. And clearly, many brands do carry significant semiotic freight—they become social signifiers and cultural reference points as much as mere indications of trade origin. However, the fact that *some* brands might have such commercial or symbolic value does not necessarily mean that the law ought to intervene by providing anti-dilution protection.[7]

The main concern with extending trade mark protection in this way is that it is not clear why advertising expenditure or investment in the creation of ever-greater brand value should necessarily be rewarded with stronger legal rights. By protecting and rewarding such investment alone, in the absence of other justifications, such laws have the potential to impose undue limits on free competition in markets.

Further, such laws tend to give trade mark owners control over the associations and expressive qualities that their marks develop when such associations and qualities are ultimately more to do with social responses to the brand than the owner's actions. In natural rights terms, it is not at all clear how much of the value of the resulting brand is the result of the mark owner's 'labour'. As Jessica Litman noted:

> The argument that trade symbols acquire intrinsic value—apart from their usefulness in designating the source—derives from consumers' investing those symbols with value for which they are willing to pay real money ... It may well increase the total utils in our society if every time a guy drinks a Budweiser or smokes a Camel, he believes he's a stud. We may all be better off if, each time a woman colors her hair with a L'Oreal product, she murmurs to herself *'and I'm worth it.'* If that's so, however ... Anheuser-Busch, RJ Reynolds, and L'Oreal can hardly take all the credit. They built up all that mystique with their customers' money and active collaboration. If the customers want to move on, to get in bed with other products that have similar atmospherics, why shouldn't they? It's not very sporting to try to lock up the atmospherics.[8]

Anti-dilution laws also tend to be based on the problematic assumption that marks, particularly famous marks, have uniformly positive associations which might be 'diluted' by a secondary use. While brand owners have an obvious interest in proclaiming that their brands stand for certain values and have clear meanings, consumer reaction to owners' practices will often mean that brands take on different, more complex meanings. It is because of this fluidity of meaning that brands often make good targets for parody or criticism through appropriation. Providing brand owners with rights that could stifle what Sonia Katyal terms 'semiotic disobedience' puts trade mark law in potential conflict with free speech rights.[9]

As we will see in the following chapters, Australia does not have specific anti-dilution laws, although the outcomes of certain decisions might suggest a desire to protect certain aspects of

---

7   See further R Burrell and M Handler, 'Dilution and Trademark Registration' (2008) 17 *Transnational Law and Contemporary Problems* 713.

8   J Litman, 'Breakfast with Batman: The Public Interest in the Advertising Age' (1999) 108 *Yale Law Journal* 1717 at 1730.

9   See S Katyal, 'Semiotic Disobedience' (2006) 84 *Washington University Law Review* 489. For careful arguments explaining how stronger trade mark rights might be justified on speech grounds, see M Spence, 'The Mark as Expression/The Mark as Property' (2005) 58 *Current Legal Problems* 491.

'brand value'. It is therefore important to keep in mind that the core focus of Australian law is on conduct that impacts on the origin or quality guarantee function of trade symbols.

JUSTIFICATIONS FOR TRADE MARK REGISTRATION

While much has been written about justifications for trade mark laws generally, relatively little has been said about why we should have trade mark *registration*.[10] The main justification is that the Register acts as a valuable source of public information as to the signs that are protected in a given commercial sphere, and matters such as initial ownership and subsequent assignments of marks. Thus for a trade mark register to perform its function effectively it must reflect as accurately as possible the marks that enjoy legal protection so that those consulting the register can rely on the information it conveys. The problem, however, is that not requiring the registration of marks—that is, allowing passing off and the registered trade mark system to operate side by side—undermines the information function of the Register. A trader consulting the Register will only ever gain a partial sense of what signs are protected. Under Australian law, attempts are made to deal with conflicts between applications for registration of marks on the one hand and rights in unregistered marks on the other, although, as we will see in Chapter 17, there are some problems with the current approach.

CURRENT CONTEXT
SOURCES OF LAWS PROTECTING BUSINESS REPUTATION

As we have seen, the tort of passing off allows a trader to take action against a party whose adoption of that trader's distinctive sign or indicia constitutes a misrepresentation. Since the mid-1970s this has been supplemented in Australia by provisions of state, territory and Commonwealth consumer protection legislation, the most important of which were contained in the *Trade Practices Act 1974* (Cth) (*TPA*). With effect from 1 January 2011, the *TPA* was renamed the *Competition and Consumer Act 2010* (Cth) (*CCA*), and the consumer protection and remedies provisions that had been used to afford protection for trade signs and indicia were moved (in amended form) from the body of the *TPA* to Sch 2 of the *CCA*, titled the 'Australian Consumer Law' (ACL). The ACL also replaced a large number of state and territory consumer protection laws. It operates as Commonwealth law by virtue of Part XI of the *CCA* and as state/territory law by virtue of Part XIAA of the *CCA*.

Before the ACL, the most important consumer protection provision used to protect trading reputation was s 52(1) of the *TPA*, which provided:

> A corporation shall not, in trade or commerce, engage in conduct that is misleading or deceptive or is likely to mislead or deceive.

Section 52 was used to catch conduct broadly in the nature of passing off and was almost always pleaded alongside passing off (a key advantage being that actions for passing off could then be brought before the Federal Court).

Section 18(1) of the ACL is in the same terms as s 52 of the *TPA*, except that the prohibition applies to 'a person' rather than 'a corporation'. However, the ACL only applies as a law of the

---

10 For a detailed consideration, see R Burrell, 'Trade Mark Bureaucracies' in G Dinwoodie and M Janis, eds, *Trademark Law and Theory: A Handbook of Contemporary Research*, Edward Elgar, Cheltenham, 2008.

Commonwealth to the extent the conduct is by a corporation,[11] and only actions for contravention of s 18(1) by corporations can be brought in the Federal Court.[12]

Remedies for contravention of s 18 of the ACL include interim or final injunctions,[13] damages,[14] or other orders as the Court sees fit.[15]

SOURCES OF TRADE MARK LAW

Australian registered trade mark law has also been shaped by a number of international agreements.

The earliest of these is the *Paris Convention on the Protection of Industrial Property* (1883), as revised. This Convention requires member states to ensure equal treatment for both foreign and domestic nationals (Art 2(1)), to afford a six-month right of priority for applications first filed in another member state (Art 4A(1)), and to register certain marks that have been registered in another member state (Art 6*quinquies*). In addition, it requires members to have specific protections in place for well-known marks (Art 6*bis*). Australia is also a member of the *Nice Agreement Concerning the International Classification of Goods and Services for the Purposes of the Registration of Marks* (1957), which regulates the way goods and services are to be specified in applications for registration.

At a substantive level, the most important treaty has been the *Agreement on Trade-Related Aspects of Intellectual Property Rights* (the 'TRIPS Agreement') (1994). The TRIPS Agreement not only requires WTO members to comply with Arts 1–12 and 19 of the Paris Convention (Art 2.1), but also imposes further obligations relating to trade marks. These concern the definition of trade marks (Art 15), the scope of rights in registered marks (Arts 16–17) and requirements as to use (Arts 20–21). In addition, members can bring dispute resolution proceedings at the WTO against other members in the event of alleged non-compliance with TRIPS obligations. At the time of writing, five tobacco-producing countries have brought disputes against Australia in relation to the *Tobacco Plain Packaging Act 2011* (Cth), which prohibits tobacco companies from using trade marks, other than brand names presented in a tightly prescribed manner, on the retail packaging of tobacco products. Among other things it is claimed that the Act puts Australia in contravention of its obligations under Art 20 of the TRIPS Agreement to ensure that the use of a trade mark in the course of trade is not 'unjustifiably encumbered by special requirements'.[16]

It is important to note that neither the Paris Convention nor the TRIPS Agreement aims to harmonise substantive trade mark law or establish a 'supra-national' trade marks registration scheme.

In the early 1990s a Working Party was set up by the Commonwealth government to consider reforming Australian registered trade mark law, particularly in light of Australia's imminent WTO obligations. In 1992 the Working Party released its report titled *Recommended Changes to the Australian Trade Marks Legislation*. Many of its recommendations were adopted by Parliament,

---

11 *CCA*, s 131(1), and see the definition of 'corporation' in s 4(1) and see also ss 5–6 on the ACL's extended application.

12 *CCA*, s 138(1).

13 ACL, ss 232, 234; cf *TPA*, s 80.

14 ACL, s 236; cf *TPA*, s 82.

15 ACL, s 238; cf *TPA*, s 87.

16 See generally S Frankel and D Gervais, 'Plain Packaging and the Interpretation of the TRIPS Agreement' (2013) 46 *Vanderbilt Journal of Transnational Law* 1149; M Davison and P Emerton, 'Rights, Privileges, Legitimate Interests, and Justifiability: Article 20 of TRIPS and Plain Packaging of Tobacco' (2014) 29 *American University International Law Review* 505.

which enacted the *Trade Marks Act 1994* (Cth) (which never commenced) and subsequently the nearly identical *Trade Marks Act 1995* (Cth). The *Trade Marks Regulations 1995* (Cth) set out many of the procedural requirements relating to registration.

Although the 1995 Act and Regulations brought about a number of significant changes to Australian law, particularly in relation to registrability, infringement and exploitation, many of the concepts underpinning the current law are derived from earlier Anglo-Australian legislation. Importantly, however, in adopting the new Act in 1995 Australia did not closely follow current UK law. The UK's *Trade Marks Act 1994* had been designed to implement the European Trade Marks Directive (now codified as Directive 2008/95/EC) and, as we will see in Chapters 17 and 18, some aspects of European trade mark law differ significantly from current Australian law.

Since the coming into force of the 1995 Act and Regulations there have been a number of international developments, some of which have required changes to Australian law. The most important of these was Australia becoming a party to the *Protocol Relating to the Madrid Agreement Concerning the International Registration of Marks* (1989) ('Madrid Protocol'). This serves a similar function to the *Patent Cooperation Treaty* (1973) (discussed in Chapter 9) by streamlining the procedures for obtaining registration of the same trade mark in other Madrid Protocol countries. Australia has also become a member of both the *Trademark Law Treaty* (1994) and the *Singapore Treaty on the Law of Trademarks* (2006), both of which are designed to harmonise trade mark registration procedures. Australian has also entered into free trade agreements with countries including the USA, Singapore, Chile, Korea and Japan, each containing obligations concerning trade marks, although such obligations have reflected pre-existing Australian law and practice.

There have also been a number of domestic reviews and inquiries on the operation of the 1995 Act and Regulations. These included IP Australia's three *Trade Marks Legislation Review* Papers (2003–04) and the Advisory Council on Intellectual Property's *Review of Enforcement of Trade Marks* (2004), which led to legislative changes in 2006, and IP Australia's *Options Paper on Review of Penalties and Additional Damages* (2008) and its report titled *Toward a Stronger and More Efficient IP Rights System* (2009), which led to legislative changes that took effect in 2013. Notwithstanding these reforms, the essential elements of the registered trade mark system have remained largely unchanged since the commencement of the 1995 Act.

OTHER DIMENSIONS

Before turning to consider the substance of Australian registered trade mark law and laws protecting business reputation, it is worth mentioning some other forms of regulation of marks and related trade signs.

Under the TRIPS Agreement, Australia is required under Arts 22–24 to protect 'geographical indications' or GIs. These are terms used to indicate not only that a product originates in a certain region or country, but also that a quality or characteristic or the reputation of that product is attributable to its geographical origin—terms such as 'Proscuitto di Parma', 'Scotch' whisky, 'Colombian' coffee and 'King Island' cheese.[17] Unlike some countries or regions that have *sui generis* schemes in place for the registration and protection of GIs, Australia complies with its TRIPS

---

17   See generally D Gangjee, *Relocating the Law of Geographical Indications*, Cambridge University Press, Cambridge, 2012.

obligations, as well as other obligations as a result of bilateral treaties with the EU and the USA, through a range of measures including passing off, registered trade mark laws, consumer protection statutes and specific laws regulating the labelling of wine and foodstuffs.

'Event specific' legislation is also used to regulate the use of names and indicia associated with particular sporting events. For example, the *Olympic Insignia Protection Act 1987* (Cth) regulates the use of the Olympic rings and various 'Olympic'-related words, symbols and expressions. More recently, the *Major Sporting Events (Indicia and Images) Protection Act 2014* (Cth) was passed, to set up a framework for the prevention of the unauthorised commercial use of indicia and images associated with major events (currently limited to the 2015 Asian Cup, the 2015 Cricket World Cup and the 2018 Commonwealth Games). These and similar Acts are examples of somewhat controversial attempts to prevent what is loosely known as 'ambush marketing', which refers to activities that attempt to leverage off the goodwill surrounding an event by suggesting the existence of some association with that event, and may weaken the perceived value of official event sponsorship.

Finally, there are separate, *sui generis* laws regulating internet domain names. Since many domain names, such as those ending in .com and .net, are allocated on a first-come, first-served basis, there is potential for conflict between licensees of domain names and the rights of trade mark owners. Some of these conflicts can be resolved through the operation of traditional doctrines, such as the tort of passing off or consumer protection legislation. However, the problem of 'cybersquatting' (the registration of a domain name containing another's trade mark or a similar variation in order to frustrate the mark owner's attempt to secure the domain name, often with the purpose of selling the name to the mark owner at a profit), as well as issues with jurisdiction, were thought to present a number of novel challenges to the law. One response was the establishment by the Internet Corporation for Assigned Names and Numbers of the *Uniform Domain Name Dispute Resolution Policy* (UDRP) in 1999. The UDRP forms part of every contract between a domain name registrant and licensee, and para 4(a) obliges the licensee to submit to mandatory arbitration where a third party complains that:

- the domain name 'is identical or confusingly similar to a trademark or service mark in which the complainant has rights';
- the licensee has 'no rights or legitimate interests in respect of the domain name'; and
- the domain name 'has been registered and is being used in bad faith'.

Over its 15 years of operation the UDRP has proved to be an effective tool for trade mark owners to reclaim domain names from cybersquatters, although many arbitrators' interpretations of para 4(a) have been controversial.[18] There are also similar dispute resolution procedures in place for .au domain names.[19]

---

18 For detailed consideration, see D Lindsay, *International Domain Name Law: ICANN and the UDRP*, Hart Publishing, Oxford, 2007.
19 See 'auDA auDRP Overview 1.0' (July 2014), at www.auda.org.au/policies/audrp/audrp-overview.

—16—

PASSING OFF AND CONSUMER PROTECTION LEGISLATION

INTRODUCTION

In this chapter we look at the operation of the tort of passing off and provisions of related consumer protection legislation that prohibit corporations from engaging in 'misleading or deceptive conduct' in trade or commerce—in particular, s 18 of the Australian Consumer Law (ACL),[1] which replaced s 52 of the *Trade Practices Act 1974* (Cth) (*TPA*) with effect from 1 January 2011.

As we saw in the previous chapter, the tort of passing off is ostensibly designed to safeguard a trader's goodwill or reputation, while the statutory prohibition on engaging in misleading or deceptive conduct is supposed to operate as a consumer protection measure. Having said this, they both play a nearly identical role in the particular context we consider in this chapter. Both provide certain traders with a degree of protection against other traders using trade marks (whether registered or unregistered), or similar indicia, in a manner that would mislead consumers in various ways. Although there are some differences between the two causes of action, the prevailing approach in Australia is to treat the two as having a largely 'merged' operation. Accordingly, we treat the two causes of action as being broadly coterminous.

We start this chapter by looking at the essential elements of the tort of passing off and the action for contravention of s 18 of the ACL. We then turn to look at those elements in detail.

TESTS FOR PASSING OFF AND CONTRAVENTION OF CONSUMER PROTECTION LEGISLATION

Although passing off is a flexible tort that is incapable of precise definition, two tests that attempt to set out in general terms the essential elements of the passing off action have emerged. Both derive from House of Lords decisions.

---

1   The ACL is Sch 2 to the *Competition and Consumer Act 2010 (Cth)* (*CCA*). As explained in Chapter 15, the ACL can also operate as state/territory law and can catch misleading or deceptive conduct other than by 'corporations' (as that term is defined in the *CCA*).

THE *ADVOCAAT* TEST

CASE EXTRACT: CURRENT LAW

Erven Warnink BV v J Townend & Sons (Hull) Ltd ('Advocaat')

[1979] AC 731
House of Lords

[In this case, makers of the spirit drink 'advocaat', which is made in accordance with a traditional Dutch recipe, brought an action against a trader selling as 'advocaat' a drink not made in accordance with that recipe.]

Lord Diplock (at 742): My Lords, *AG Spalding & Bros v AW Gamage Ltd*, 84 LJ Ch 449 and the later cases make it possible to identify five characteristics which must be present in order to create a valid cause of action for passing off: (1) a misrepresentation (2) made by a trader in the course of trade, (3) to prospective customers of his or ultimate consumers of goods or services supplied by him, (4) which is calculated to injure the business or goodwill of another trader (in the sense that this is a reasonably foreseeable consequence) and (5) which causes actual damage to a business or goodwill of the trader by whom the action is brought or (in a *quia timet* action) will probably do so.

THE *RECKITT & COLMAN* TEST

CASE EXTRACT: CURRENT LAW

Reckitt & Colman Products Ltd v Borden Inc

[1990] 1 WLR 491
House of Lords

[This case involved a dispute between a trader that had for over 30 years packaged its lemon juice in a yellow, lemon-shaped container and a trader that had started selling its differently named lemon juice in similar packaging.]

Lord Oliver (at 499–500): The law of passing off can be summarised in one short general proposition— no man may pass off his goods as those of another. More specifically, it may be expressed in terms of the elements which the plaintiff in such an action has to prove in order to succeed. These are three in number. First, he must establish a goodwill or reputation attached to the goods or services which he supplies in the mind of the purchasing public by association with the identifying 'get-up' (whether it consists simply of a brand name or a trade description, or the individual features of labelling or packaging) under which his particular goods or services are offered to the public, such that the get-up is recognised by the public as distinctive specifically of the plaintiff's goods or services. Secondly, he must demonstrate a misrepresentation by the defendant to the public (whether or not intentional) leading or likely to lead the public to believe that goods or services offered by him are the goods or services of the plaintiff. Whether the public is aware of the plaintiff's identity as the manufacturer or supplier of the goods or services is immaterial, as long as they are identified with a particular source which is in fact the plaintiff. For example, if the public is accustomed to rely upon a particular brand name in purchasing goods of a particular description, it matters not at all that there is little or no public awareness of the identity of the proprietor of the brand name. Thirdly, he must demonstrate that he suffers or, in a *quia timet* action, that he is likely to suffer damage by reason of the erroneous belief engendered by the defendant's misrepresentation that the source of the defendant's goods or services is the same as the source of those offered by the plaintiff.

Thus the three issues in the instant case ... were and are as follows:

(i) Have the respondents proved that the get-up under which their lemon juice has been sold since 1956 has become associated in the minds of substantial numbers of the purchasing public specifically and exclusively with the respondents' (or 'Jif') lemon juice?

(ii) If the answer to that question is in the affirmative, does the get-up under which the appellants proposed to market their lemon juice ... amount to a representation by the appellants that the juice which they sell is 'Jif' lemon juice?

(iii) If the answer to that question is in the affirmative, is it, on a balance of probabilities, likely that, if the appellants are not restrained as they have been, a substantial number of members of the public will be misled into purchasing the defendants' lemon juice in the belief that it is the respondents' Jif juice?

Australian courts have tended to find greater guidance in the *Reckitt & Colman* test, which restates what is known as the 'classical trinity' of passing off. These are the requirements of:

1 goodwill or reputation;
2 misrepresentation; and
3 damage, or the likelihood of damage.

We will consider each of these elements of the classical trinity in turn, but before doing so, four preliminary comments need to be made.

First, it is important to heed Gummow J's statement in *ConAgra Inc v McCain Foods (Aust) Pty Ltd* (1992) 33 FCR 302 at 356 that despite the utility of the above tests, the tort 'contains sufficient nooks and crannies to make it difficult to formulate any satisfactory definition in short form'. As we will see, in some circumstances courts have been prepared to find that the plaintiff has protectable goodwill, or that a misrepresentation has occurred, in broader circumstances than those set out by Lord Oliver in *Reckitt & Colman*, and that the requirement of damage is more complex than as described by Lord Oliver. Notwithstanding these qualifications, the classical trinity remains a useful device to understand the operation of the passing off action.

A second preliminary point about the classical trinity concerns the interrelationship between the three elements. Reputation is not a concept that can be assessed in isolation from the other elements: assessing whether the plaintiff has a sufficient reputation is not an 'all or nothing' question. The *extent* of a plaintiff's reputation will significantly impact on the question of whether the defendant's conduct involves a misrepresentation that causes damage to the plaintiff's interests. As we will see, the same factors and evidence are often relevant in establishing all three elements of what is ultimately a single enquiry.

Third, recognising the interconnected nature of the elements of the passing off action helps to explain why passing off and actions for contravention of consumer protection legislation in the present context can be seen as broadly coterminous. On a superficial reading of s 18 of the ACL and its predecessor, s 52 of the *TPA*, it might seem that the plaintiff only needs to establish one element: misleading or deceptive conduct (i.e. a misrepresentation) by the defendant. However, it has been recognised in numerous cases that conduct involving the use of a trader's sign or similar indicia will only constitute misleading or deceptive conduct if that trader has a protectable reputation that attaches to the sign or other indicia. For instance, in *Mars Australia Pty Ltd v Sweet Rewards Pty Ltd* [2009] FCA 606; (2009) 81 IPR 354, Perram J held at [22] that in the passing off action it is:

> necessary to identify the features of the applicant's packaging in which a reputation is said to inhere for it is the existence of that reputation which [passing off] protects. So too, in the context of the corresponding claim under s 52 it is the reputation in those features which is the springboard for the argument that consumers are deceived by a particular imitation. Thus although the interests protected by the two actions are different both indispensably require the identification of features known to the public mind. The expression 'get-up' is a convenient shorthand for that concept but can be apt to mislead if one loses sight of the necessary connexion between the get-up and reputation. For that reason the identification of a get-up by an applicant in a passing off action or a claim under s 52 is both coherent and necessary.

In addition, while establishing damage or the likelihood of damage is not a formal element of s 18 of the ACL, a plaintiff seeking an injunction to restrain the defendant from engaging in misleading or deceptive conduct (under ACL, ss 232 or 234), or damages for the defendant's contravention (under ACL, s 236), is likely to need to show likely or actual damage to its trading reputation.[2]

Fourth, despite the breadth of the passing off action and the consumer protection legislation, neither can be said to extend to catch all types of 'copying' of names and images that might be said to be 'unfair'. Even though Australian courts have interpreted the requirements of misrepresentation and misleading or deceptive conduct flexibly and in accordance with changing business practices, conduct which might intuitively be considered 'unfair' but does not involve a misrepresentation will not be actionable. Courts have resisted calls for the adoption of a common law tort of 'unfair competition' to plug any perceived gaps left by the passing off action and consumer protection legislation. Most notably, in *Moorgate Tobacco Co Ltd v Philip Morris Ltd [No 2]* (1984) 156 CLR 414, Deane J held at 445–446:

> The rejection of a general action for 'unfair competition' involves no more than a recognition of the fact that the existence of such an action is inconsistent with the established limits

---

2   For a detailed consideration of the relationship between passing off and consumer protection legislation, see R Burrell and M Handler, *Australian Trade Mark Law*, 2nd ed, Oxford University Press, Melbourne (forthcoming 2016), ch 13.

of the traditional and statutory causes of action which are available to a trader in respect of damage caused or threatened by a competitor. Those limits, which define the boundary between the area of legal or equitable restraint and protection and the area of untrammelled competition, increasingly reflect what the responsible Parliament or Parliaments have determined to be the appropriate balance between competing claims and policies. Neither legal principle nor social utility requires or warrants the obliteration of that boundary by the importation of a cause of action whose main characteristic is the scope it allows, under high-sounding generalizations, for judicial indulgence of idiosyncratic notions of what is fair in the market place.

REPUTATION

The first element of the classical trinity is that of 'goodwill' (described in *Inland Revenue Commissioners v Muller & Co's Margarine Ltd* [1901] AC 217 at 224 as 'the attractive force that brings in custom'). Under Australian law, 'goodwill' and 'reputation' are treated as being synonymous.

There is no fixed minimum level of reputation that a plaintiff needs to establish in order to maintain a passing off action. Instead, much will depend on the relationship between the factors that will be explored in this section. That is, whether a plaintiff has sufficient reputation will turn on such factors as: the nature of the sign or other indicia to which the reputation is said to attach (in particular, the degree of distinctiveness or descriptiveness of that sign); the geographical area in which the plaintiff is claiming to enjoy the reputation; the length of time the trader has been trading; and the intensity of that trade. Establishing this last factor often involves the plaintiff adducing evidence of the volume of sales of its products, the extent of its advertising and its expenditure on advertising.

TO WHAT DOES THE REPUTATION ATTACH?

As Lord Oliver held in *Reckitt & Colman* at 499, the tort of passing off is concerned with protecting a trader's reputation 'attached to the goods or services which [the trader] supplies in the mind of the purchasing public by association with the identifying "get-up"' of those goods or services. This get-up can take a variety of forms. Most commonly, it will consist of one or more 'trade marks', such as a brand name, a logo, and/or various features of labelling or packaging of a product. However, this branch of the law is not concerned with protecting 'trade marks' (whether registered or unregistered) as such, but rather the plaintiff's reputation, as manifested in its get-up. Thus passing off can also be used where a defendant has adopted indicia such as images, characters or advertising themes that cannot be classified as 'trade marks'.

The following extracts explore the signs and other indicia in which reputation might exist. They also highlight some of the difficulties plaintiffs might face in establishing reputation in certain aspects of their get-up, such as descriptive words, aspects of packaging or features of shape that other traders might legitimately wish to use (e.g. for descriptive or decorative purposes).

REPUTATION IN DESCRIPTIVE WORDS

CASE EXTRACT: PRECEDENT

Reddaway v Banham

[1896] AC 199
House of Lords

[Since 1879 Reddaway had manufactured belting, made chiefly from camel hair, which it sold as 'Camel Hair Belting'. In the early 1890s, Banham started making a similar product, which it also called 'Camel Hair Belting'. At trial, a jury found that Banham had engaged in passing off, leading to Collins J granting an injunction restraining Banham's use of the words 'Camel Hair' in such a way as to deceive purchasers into the belief that they were purchasing Reddaway's belting. This decision was overturned by the Court of Appeal. Reddaway appealed to the House of Lords.]

Lord Herschell (at 208–211): For many years belting made of camel hair yarn had been known in the markets of the world. It had been sold under a variety of names. But there was ample evidence to justify the finding, that amongst those who were the purchasers of such goods, the words 'camel hair' were not applied to belting made of that material in general; that, in short, it did not mean in the market belting made of a particular material, but belting made by a particular manufacturer. It is impossible, I think, to read the correspondence which passed between the defendants, and those who were ordering goods of, or procuring orders for them, without seeing that this was the case ...

The name of a person, or words forming part of the common stock of language, may become so far associated with the goods of a particular maker that it is capable of proof that the use of them by themselves without explanation or qualification by another manufacturer would deceive a purchaser into the belief that he was getting the goods of A when he was really getting the goods of B. In a case of this description the mere proof by the plaintiff that the defendant was using a name, word, or device which he had adopted to distinguish his goods would not entitle him to any relief. He could only obtain it by proving further that the defendant was using it under such circumstances or in such manner as to put off his goods as the goods of the plaintiff. If he could succeed in proving this I think he would, on well-established principles, be entitled to an injunction.

In my opinion, the doctrine on which the judgment of the Court of Appeal was based, that where a manufacturer has used as his trade-mark a descriptive word he is never entitled to relief against a person who so uses it as to induce in purchasers the belief that they are getting the goods of the manufacturer who has theretofore employed it as his trade-mark, is not supported by authority, and cannot be defended on principle. I am unable to see why a man should be allowed in this way more than in any other to deceive purchasers into the belief that they are getting what they are not, and thus to filch the business of a rival.

Lord Halsbury (at 204–205): If I had been sitting as a juryman in this case I confess (but for a circumstance I am about to mention) I should have had great difficulty in acquiescing in the contention that a person was making his goods pass as the goods of somebody else by simply describing the subject of sale by these words. It is partly made or substantially made of camel hair, and it is belting.

PRECEDENT

To me or to other persons not familiar with the trade this undoubtedly does seem simply a description of the article sold, and not a representation of its being made by a particular manufacturer. But then I should not know, what persons engaged in the trade would know, how far particular words, even though descriptive of the article sold, may have acquired a kind of technical signification which would give to them in the trade as impolitely the character of being made by a particular manufacturer as if they were stamped with his trade-mark.

The circumstance to which I referred is to be found in the letter of June 12, 1891. The writer, who doubtless knew what he was doing, specially desires that the thing which he is ordering should bear no other stamp than 'Camel Hair Belting,' and if he gets that he adds 'I think I can take this order from Reddaways.'

My Lords, I think with this letter before them the jury were perfectly right, and that my prima facie impression from the words being only descriptive of the article sold would have been wrong. The result is, in my mind, that the proof is satisfactory, and that one man's goods are being sold as if they were the goods of the other ...

[Lords Macnaghten and Morris also concluded that Reddaway's appeal should be allowed.]

CURRENT LAW

CASE EXTRACT: CURRENT LAW

Hornsby Building Information Centre Pty Ltd v Sydney Building Information Centre Ltd

(1978) 140 CLR 216
High Court of Australia

[The Sydney Building Information Centre, which had been trading for approximately 30 years, sought and obtained from the Industrial Court an interim injunction under the *TPA* to restrain the Hornsby Building Information Centre (based in the Sydney suburb of Hornsby) from trading under that name on the basis that the Hornsby Centre's conduct contravened s 52. The Hornsby Centre appealed to the High Court.]

Stephen J (with whom Barwick CJ, Jacobs and Aickin JJ agreed) (at 228–231): When, as in s 52(1), the focus is upon the misleading of others rather than upon the injury to a competitor, it becomes of particular importance to identify the respect in which there is said to be any misleading or deception. The particular feature of the Hornsby Centre's conduct of which the Sydney Centre complains as being misleading and deceptive is not simply the use of its corporate name, so similar in part to its own name, but rather that by that use others are led to believe that the Hornsby Centre is a branch of, or is otherwise associated with, the Sydney Centre.

The Sydney Centre tendered some evidence that persons had been misled in this way and for present purposes I will assume that this has occurred. But to determine whether there has been any contravention of s 52(1) it is necessary to inquire why this misconception has arisen in the minds of others. This necessarily leads one to examine the name of the Sydney Centre. The name which it adopted as its own consists of three descriptive words, prefixed by a word of locality, the whole of which it uses as its trade and corporate name. Having done so it cannot, as it acknowledges, claim any monopoly in the descriptive words; yet it does in fact seek to impose conditions upon another's use of those words, the condition being that an explanatory disclaimer should accompany that use. The Court, of course, has gone much further, it has granted to the applicant an interim monopoly in those words, despite the fact that the Sydney Centre neither claimed that monopoly nor now seeks to retain in that extreme form the injunctive relief which it has now obtained below.

The use by the Sydney Centre of the three descriptive words was no doubt convenient. It thereby acquired a name which at the same time very clearly described its activities. That it has, over the years, appreciated their value as descriptive of its business is shown by the fact that some of the signs on its premises have been confined to the two words 'Building Centre' and that the large illuminated signs and the like which it has displayed on its premises, and which are perhaps more in the nature of advertising material then mere identification, have omitted the word 'Ltd', using all three descriptive words prefixed by 'Sydney'.

There is a price to be paid for the advantages flowing from the possession of an eloquently descriptive trade name. Because it is descriptive it is equally applicable to any business of a like kind, its very descriptiveness ensures that it is not distinctive of any particular business and hence its application to other like businesses will not ordinarily mislead the public. In cases of passing off, where it is the wrongful appropriation of the reputation of another or that of his goods that is in question, a plaintiff which uses descriptive words in its trade name will find that quite small differences in a competitor's trade name will render the latter immune from action (*Office Cleaning Services Ltd v Westminster Window and General Cleaners Ltd* (1946) 63 RPC 39, at p 42, per Lord Simonds). As his Lordship said at p 43, the possibility of blunders by members of the public will always be present when names consist of descriptive words—'So long as descriptive words are used by two traders as part of their respective trade names, it is possible that some members of the public will be confused whatever the differentiating words may be.' The risk of confusion must be accepted, to do otherwise is to give to one who appropriates to himself descriptive words an unfair monopoly in those words and might even deter others from pursuing the occupation which the words describe.

If this be so in the case of passing off actions the case of s 52(1), concerned only with the interests of third parties, is *a fortiori*. To allow this section of the *Trade Practices Act* to be used as an instrument for the creation of any monopoly in descriptive names would be to mock the manifest intent of the legislation. Given that a name is no more than merely descriptive of a particular type of business, its use by others who carry on that same type of business does not deceive or mislead as to the nature of the business described. Thus both the Hornsby and the Sydney Centres are building information centres and no one is being deceived as to the nature of the service which is available there. Any deception which does arise stems not so much from the Hornsby Centre's use of the descriptive words as from the fact that the Sydney Centre initially chose descriptive words as its title and for many years thereafter was the only centre in Sydney which answered the description which those words provide. In consequence members of the public have come to associate its particular business with that type of activity. Evidence of confusion in the minds of members of the public is not evidence that the use of the Hornsby Centre's name is itself misleading or deceptive but rather that its intrusion into the field originally occupied exclusively by the Sydney Centre has, naturally enough, caused a degree of confusion in the public mind. This is not, however, anything at which s 52(1) is directed ...

CURRENT LAW

There was evidence before the Industrial Court about the antecedents and activities of the Hornsby Centre from which it could have concluded that those concerned with that Centre's activities were intent to benefit from the good repute which the Sydney Centre had, over the years, created for the particular kind of services, unique of their kind, which it had offered as the only building information centre in the Sydney area. However to say this is not to suggest any wrongdoing on their part. Neither the concept of such a centre nor its conduct is anything for which a monopoly can be claimed, any more than it could be claimed for, say, an art gallery. If the first commercial art gallery in a city meets with an enthusiastic response from the public, competitive galleries are likely to be attracted to the field. They will be free to enter it and to describe themselves as art galleries, that being the descriptive name appropriate to their business; and this despite the fact that the pioneer gallery might have chosen also to style itself 'art gallery', prefixed by a regional name. For competitors' conduct to be misleading and deceptive they would have to have adopted as their names the same or a similar regional prefix followed by 'art gallery'. A quite distinct regional prefix, followed by 'art gallery' would neither mislead nor deceive. The opposite view would involve treating this provision of the trade practices legislation as the source of a newly created monopoly heretofore unknown to the law and likely to deter new entrants into a field which ought to be open to legitimate competition. It is difficult to contemplate any less likely legislative source of such a consequence. The present case of building information centres is, I think, no different in principle.

Although passing off was not in issue in *Hornsby*, the above approach is entirely consistent with that which would be taken in a passing off action. For instance, in *Apand Pty Ltd v The Kettle Chip Co Pty Ltd* (1994) 52 FCR 474 the Full Federal Court accepted that The Kettle Chip Co had acquired secondary meaning in the word 'Kettle' as a term distinctive of its brand of kettle-cooked chips. For other recent examples of the difficulties involved in bringing passing off/consumer protection actions in relation to descriptive names, see *Vendor Advocacy Australia Pty Ltd v Seitanidis* [2013] FCA 971; (2013) 103 IPR 1 (involving 'Vendor Advocacy') and *Kosciuszko Thredbo Pty Ltd v ThredboNet Marketing Pty Ltd* [2014] FCAFC 87; (2014) 223 FCR 517 (involving 'Thredbo').

It will also be hard to establish secondary meaning in aspects of get-up such as the packaging or appearance of goods, or advertising images and themes, as seen in the next section.

REPUTATION IN PACKAGING, PRODUCT SHAPE AND OTHER INDICIA

PRECEDENT

CASE EXTRACT: PRECEDENT

Reckitt & Colman Products Ltd v Borden Inc

[1990] 1 WLR 491
House of Lords

[The basic facts of the case are set out at p 619 above. Reckitt & Colman's lemon-shaped container had the brand name 'Jif' embossed on the side and bore a green paper label also featuring the word 'Jif'. Borden's three types of container each bore a yellow paper label featuring the brand name 'ReaLemon'.

The trial judge found for Reckitt & Colman and ordered that Borden be restrained from selling its product without making it clear that its goods were not those of Reckitt & Colman. The Court of Appeal agreed. Borden appealed to the House of Lords.]

Lord Oliver (at 504–507): [T]here is, to my mind, a fallacy in the argument which begins by identifying the contents with the container and is summarised in the central proposition that 'you cannot claim a monopoly in selling plastic lemons.' Well, of course you cannot any more than you can claim a monopoly in the sale of dimpled bottles. The deception alleged lies not in the sale of the plastic lemons or the dimpled bottles, but in the sale of lemon juice or whisky, as the case may be, in containers so fashioned as to suggest that the juice or the whisky emanates from the source with which the containers of those particular configurations have become associated in the public mind ... It is, no doubt, true that the plastic lemon-shaped container serves, as indeed does a bottle of any design, a functional purpose in the sale of lemon juice. Apart from being a container *simpliciter*, it is a convenient size; it is capable of convenient use by squeezing; and it is so designed as conveniently to suggest the nature of its contents without the necessity for further labelling or other identification. But those purposes are capable of being and indeed are served by a variety of distinctive containers of configurations other than those of a lemon-sized lemon. Neither the appellants nor the respondents are in the business of selling plastic lemons. Both are makers and vendors of lemon juice and the only question is whether the respondents, having acquired a public reputation for Jif juice by selling it for many years in containers of a particular shape and design which, on the evidence, has become associated with their produce, can legitimately complain of the sale by the appellants of similar produce in containers of similar, though not identical, size, shape and colouring.

So I, for my part, would reject the suggestion that the plastic lemon container is an object in itself rather than part of the get-up under which the respondents' produce is sold. But it is argued that that is not the end of the matter, for the get-up which is protected is not just a plastic lemon-shaped container, but the container plus the respondents' labelling, and it is not open to the respondents to argue that, though the labels themselves could not, fairly regarded, possibly be confused, a part, albeit perhaps a dominant part, of the get-up can, as it were, be separated and made the subject matter of protection in its own right. I confess that I do not see why not, given that the respondents establish a right to the protection of their get-up as a whole. The question is whether what the appellants are doing constitutes a misrepresentation that their juice is Jif juice, and whether that results from the similarity of their get-up to the whole of the respondents' get-up or to only the most striking part of it is wholly immaterial if—and of course this is critical—it is once established as a matter of fact that what they are doing constitutes a misrepresentation which effectively deceives the public into an erroneous belief regarding the source of the product.

Then it is said—and again there is no disagreement as to this—that the mere fact that the produce of the appellants and that of the respondents may be confused by members of the public is not of itself sufficient. There is no 'property' in the accepted sense of the word in a get-up. Confusion resulting from the lawful right of another trader to employ as indicative of the nature of his goods terms which are common to the trade gives rise to no cause of action. The application by a trader to his goods of an accepted trade description or of ordinary English terms may give rise to confusion. It probably will do so where previously another trader was the only person in the market dealing in those goods, for a public which knows only of A will be prone to assume that any similar goods emanate from A. But there can be no cause of action in passing off simply because there will have been no misrepresentation. So the application to the defendants' goods of ordinary English terms such as 'cellular clothing' (*Cellular Clothing Co Ltd v Maxton and Murray* (1899) 16 RPC 397) or, 'Office Cleaning' (*Office Cleaning Services Ltd v Westminster Window and General Cleaners Ltd* (1946) 63 RPC 39) or the use of descriptive expressions or slogans in general use such as 'Chicago Pizza' (*My Kinda Town Ltd v Soll* [1983] RPC 407) cannot entitle a plaintiff to relief simply because he has used the same or similar terms as descriptive of his own goods and has been the only person previously to employ that description.

All this is accepted by the respondents. The appellants, however, starting from this undoubted base, argue that what the respondents are asking the court to protect is no more than the use by them of a descriptive term, embodied in a plastic lemon instead of expressed verbally, which is common to the trade ...

In the instant case, what is said is that there was nothing particularly original in marketing lemon juice in plastic containers made to resemble lemons. The respondents were not the first to think of it even though they have managed over the past 30 years to establish a virtual monopoly in the United Kingdom. It is, in fact, a selling device widely employed outside the United Kingdom. It is a natural, convenient and familiar technique ... If and so far as this particular selling device has become associated in the mind of the purchasing public with the respondents' Jif lemon juice, that is simply because the respondents have been the only people in the market selling lemon juice in this particular format. Because there has been in fact a monopoly of this sale of this particular article, the public is led to make erroneous assumption that a similar article brought to the market for the first time must emanate from the same source. This has been referred to in the argument as 'the monopoly assumption.' The likelihood of confusion was admitted by the appellants themselves in the course of their evidence, but it is argued that the erroneous public belief which causes the product to be confused arises simply from the existing monopoly and not from any deception by the appellants in making use of what they claim to be a normal, ordinary and generally available selling technique.

The difficulty about this argument is that it starts by assuming the only basis upon which it can succeed, that is to say, that the selling device which the appellants wish to adopt is ordinary and generally available or, as it is expressed in some of the cases, 'common to the trade' ... In one sense, the monopoly assumption is the basis of every passing off action. The deceit practised on the public when one trader adopts a get-up associated with another succeeds only because the latter has previously been the only trader using that demonstrates nothing in itself. As a defence to a passing off claim it can succeed only if that which is claimed by the plaintiff as distinctive of his goods and his goods alone consists of something either so ordinary or in such common use that it would be unreasonable that he should claim it as applicable solely to his goods, as for instance where it consists simply of a description of the goods sold. Here the mere fact that he has previously been the only trader dealing in goods of that type and so described may lead members of the public to believe that all such goods must emanate from him simply because they know of no other. To succeed in such a case he must demonstrate more than simply the sole use of the descriptive term. He must demonstrate that it has become so closely associated with his goods as to acquire the secondary meaning not simply of goods of that description but specifically of goods of which and he alone is the source.

[After quoting from Lord Herschell's judgment in *Reddaway v Banham* at 210, Lord Oliver continued:]

The trial judge here has found as a fact that the natural size squeeze pack in the form of a lemon has become so associated with Jif lemon juice that the introduction of the appellants' juice in any of the proposed get-ups will be bound to result in many housewives purchasing that juice in the belief that they are obtaining Jif juice. I cannot interpret that as anything other than a finding that the plastic lemon-shaped container has acquired, as it were, a secondary significance. It indicates not merely lemon juice but specifically Jif lemon juice.

Lord Jauncey (at 517–519): The appellants submitted that the respondents' plastic lemon was merely the exemplification of the descriptive word 'lemon.' It was impossible to acquire a monopoly in the use of a word which accurately described the relevant goods, from which it followed that the appellants were not entitled to establish that the plastic lemon had acquired the secondary meaning of Jif lemon juice ...

I do not consider that it is legitimate to equiparate a plastic lemon of natural shape and size, which is unique in the market, to a word in ordinary use. Indeed I can see no reason why a trader should not obtain protection for a get-up whose shape and colour ingeniously alluded to its contents but not for a phrase containing ordinary words which described them. I agree ... that the proper way to regard a plastic lemon is as a fanciful and attractive variant of the get-up of the ordinary plastic squeeze bottle lemon container and I can see no reason why the fact that this get-up is allusive of its contents should deprive it of protection to which it would otherwise be entitled ...

The decisions in the courts below and in this House do not have the effect of conferring on the respondents a monopoly right to sell lemon juice in plastic lemons. They merely decide that on the facts as found the appellants in seeking to enter the plastic lemon market have not taken adequate steps to differentiate their get-up from that of the respondents so that consumers will not be deceived.

Lord Bridge (at 494–495): My Lords, when plastic containers made in the shape, colour and size of natural lemons first appeared on the market in the United Kingdom as squeeze packs containing preserved lemon juice the respondents were astute enough to realise their potential and to buy up the businesses of the two companies who first marketed preserved lemon juice in this way. They thereby acquired a de facto monopoly which, by the periodical threat or institution of passing off actions over the years, they have succeeded in preserving ever since. This is the first such action to come to trial.

The idea of selling preserved lemon juice in a plastic container designed to look as nearly as possible like the real thing is such a simple, obvious and inherently attractive way of marketing the product that it seems to me utterly repugnant to the law's philosophy with respect to commercial monopolies to permit any trader to acquire a de jure monopoly in the container as such. But ... the order made by the trial judge in this case does not confer any such de jure monopoly because the injunction restrains the appellants from marketing their product 'in any container so nearly resembling the plaintiffs' Jif lemon-shaped container as to be likely to deceive *without making it clear to the ultimate purchaser that it is not of the goods of the plaintiff.*' (Emphasis added.) How then are the appellants, if they wish to sell their product in plastic containers of the shape, colour and size of natural lemons, to ensure that the buyer is not deceived? The answer, one would suppose, is by attaching a suitably distinctive label to the container. Yet here is the paradox: the trial judge found that a buyer reading the labels proposed to be attached to the appellants' ... containers would know at once that they did not contain Jif lemon juice and would not be deceived; but he also enjoined the appellants from selling their product in those containers because he found, to put it shortly, that housewives buying plastic lemons in supermarkets do not read the labels but assume that whatever they buy must be Jif. The result seems to be to give the respondents a de facto monopoly of the container as such which is just as effective as de jure

PRECEDENT

monopoly. A trader selling plastic lemon juice would never be permitted to register a lemon as his trade mark, but the respondents have achieved the result indirectly that a container designed to look like a real lemon is to be treated, per se, as distinctive of their goods.

If I could find a way of avoiding this result, I would. But the difficulty is that the trial judge's findings of fact, however surprising they may seem, are not open to challenge …

With undisguised reluctance I agree with my noble and learned friends that the appeal should be dismissed.

[Lords Brandon and Goff agreed that the appeal should be dismissed.]

CURRENT LAW

CASE EXTRACT: CURRENT LAW

Nutrientwater Pty Ltd v Baco Pty Ltd

[2010] FCA 2; (2010) 84 IPR 452
Federal Court of Australia

[From October 2006, the applicant (NW) sold its 'NutrientWater' flavoured water in 575 mL bottles as set out below and at [12] of the judgment (the 'NW Product Range'):

It was established that the NW Product Range had copied elements of the get-up of another company's 'vitaminwater' flavoured water, which at the time was only available overseas. In February 2008, 'vitaminwater' entered the Australian market and proved to be highly successful. Other parties also entered the flavoured water market in 2007 and 2008. In May 2009, the respondent (Baco) started selling its 'Grassroots' flavoured water as set out below and at [53] of the judgment:

NW sued Baco for passing off and contravention of the *TPA*.]

Kenny J: 91. .... [I]n order to establish passing off, or breach of ss 52 or 53 of the TPA, NW had to show that it had, as at May 2009, the requisite reputation in the feature or features of packaging or get-up that Baco had allegedly appropriated: compare *Natural Waters [of Viti Ltd v Dayals (Fiji) Artesian Waters Ltd* (2007) 71 IPR 571] at 585 per Bennett J. As to this, Baco argued that NW's claim failed because NW had not established any discrete reputation in those features as opposed to its overall get-up or packaging. This was because NW had not shown that Baco had appropriated any features that were distinctive of the NW Product Range within the enhanced water market. Absent the requisite reputation in these specific features, then, so Baco said, NW's passing off claim must fail. Further, without a showing of reputation, so Baco said, there could be no finding of relevant misrepresentation in breach of ss 52 or 53 of the TPA.

92. *Natural Waters* is illustrative of the difficulty of establishing reputation in get-up alone. The case concerned competitors in the bottled water market and, like this case, involved claims in passing off and under ss 52 and 53 of the TPA. The claimant argued that the respondent's bottled water shared the following features with its product: (1) use of a clear bottle with a recessed central body portion defined by protruding shoulders and base portions, with the label positioned in the recessed body portion; (2) use of a blue cap; (3) use of a colourful, tropical motif featuring tropical plants and other vegetation; (4) a three-dimensional effect created by having a partially transparent label on the front panel of the bottle revealing the inner side of the back label; and (5) prominent use of the word 'Fiji': see *Natural Waters* at 575.

93. In dismissing the claims, Bennett J found that the claimant had failed to establish that these features had become individually distinctive of its product, or had come to be associated by consumers with it or its product: see *Natural Waters* at 579, 586. Her Honour explained (at 583):

> The fact that Natural Waters may establish reputation in the Fiji Water get-up does not mean that it has a monopoly over each aspect of that get-up. The goods are ordinary articles of consumption. By their nature, goods of different manufacturers will bear some resemblance to each other. Water is sold in bottles, frequently in transparent bottles and commonly with blue caps. The marks, brands and labels play an important part in distinguishing the goods of one manufacturer from those of another: *Parkdale Custom Built Furniture Pty Ltd v Puxu Pty Ltd* (1982) 149 CLR 191 at 200 ... per Gibbs CJ. Whether the reason for the distinctiveness of Fiji Water is one or more particular aspects of its packaging or the totality of its get-up, the offending product will only mislead or deceive consumers where it has taken the distinctive aspect(s) or so much of the totality of the get-up that the overall impression or the 'gestalt' of the Fiji Water brand ... is adopted.

94. Her Honour added (at 585):

> The reputation which must be proved in a case such as this is that the get-up, packaging, shape, or trade dress relied upon is associated by consumers with the applicant's product. It takes a strong case to establish a reputation of this nature (*Interlego [AG v Croner Trading Pty Ltd* (1992) 22 IPR 65] at 103–4) as consumers will not necessarily associate a get-up with the applicant's product ... The requisite reputation will more readily be found where the get-up is unique or striking rather than descriptive, mundane, merely functional, or *in common use*. (Emphasis added.)

95. In *Natural Waters* Bennett J accepted (at 590) that the applicant had sufficient reputation in the overall effect of its get-up to found an action in passing off or under s 52 (or s 53) of the TPA,

but her Honour considered that, despite the similarities between the claimant's and the respondent's products, no reasonable consumer would be mislead or deceived into believing they were from the same manufacturer.

96. ... I accept that, as at May 2009, NW had a reputation in the NW Product Range, but NW has not established that its reputation lay in the features it seeks to protect as opposed to its overall packaging or get-up, including its distinctive name and logo, which Baco has not sought to appropriate. NW has relied on a combination of features, which are said to be distinctive of the NW Product Range. Most of these features are shared with other competitors in the enhanced water market, particularly with vitaminwater, and, to a lesser extent, Smart Water. Most of the brands of the enhanced water products in evidence produced a rainbow-like effect of brightly coloured beverages when arranged appropriately. Most, if not all, enhanced water products presented their beverages in similarly bright colours. The numbers of variants in most brand ranges were similar. All enhanced water products were presented in clear plastic bottles and the principal traders used comparatively large wrap-around labels, with colour and white horizontal banding—the bright colour on the label complementing the colour of the beverage variety. The three principal traders each used light-hearted quirky comments on their labels too. All the enhanced water products in evidence had a 'wellness' theme. I am unable to accept that NW established such a degree of distinctiveness in the colours of the NW Product Range or any other feature, alone or together, that might have justified the proposition that it had a discrete reputation in those colours or some other feature.

97. As stated above, in the design of its own products, NW had copied many of the distinctive features of the US version of vitaminwater. By May 2009, a similar Australian version of vitaminwater had been on the market for well over a year and had become the market leader in terms of sales volume. It is, therefore, unsurprising that the features that might have been seen as distinctive of the NW Product Range in the Australian market before vitaminwater entered the market were no longer distinctive after vitaminwater had established itself there. This had clearly happened by May 2009. Other traders ... had, moreover, by then entered the market and adopted many of the features that might previously have been thought characteristic of vitaminwater and NW.

98. In the circumstances of this case, the sales and marketing evidence adduced by NW cannot justify the conclusion that the features that Baco allegedly appropriated were, as at May 2009, associated by consumers with NW in particular as opposed to competitors in the enhanced water market generally. There is no room in such a case as this for a finding that NW has the requisite reputation in the features of the get-up on which it relies, because, when it first entered the market, NW substantially adopted the 'look and feel' or the 'gestalt' of the US version of the vitaminwater product and a local version of vitaminwater has since entered the Australian market.

99. On this analysis, NW's case fails from the outset, because it has not established the reputation, which is the first element in the tort of passing off; nor has it established the foundation upon which the misrepresentations referred to in ss 52 and 53 might be proved.

Cases involving the shape or appearance of the goods themselves, such as the shape of a piece of furniture (*Parkdale Custom Built Furniture Pty Ltd v Puxu Pty Ltd* (1982) 149 CLR 191), or the appearance of a shoe (*Dr Martens Australia Pty Ltd v Rivers (Australia) Pty Ltd* [1999] FCA 1655; (1999) 95 FCR 136), or the shape of a three-headed rotary shaver (*Koninklijke Philips Electronics*

NV v Remington Products Australia Pty Ltd [2000] FCA 876; (2000) 100 FCR 90) have shown how difficult it is to demonstrate 'secondary meaning' in such features. A case in which the plaintiff was successful is extracted below.

CASE EXTRACT: CURRENT LAW

Peter Bodum A/S v DKSH Australia Pty Ltd

[2011] FCAFC 98; (2011) 92 IPR 222
Federal Court of Australia, Full Court

Greenwood J (with whom Tracey J agreed): 1. The first appellant, Peter Bodum A/S ('Bodum'), is a Danish company founded in 1944. It is the holding company for the Bodum group of companies. It designs, manufactures and sells throughout the world, and in Australia, a range of household products including coffee plungers ...

...

4. The respondent DKSH Australia Pty Ltd ('DKSH') ... imports into Australia and sells by wholesale, homewares and kitchen products including a coffee plunger the subject of Bodum's suit before the trial judge.

5. Bodum's case, put simply, at trial against DKSH involved these contentions.

6. Since 1958, Bodum or its predecessors in title have manufactured and sold a coffee plunger exhibiting particular features embodied in a coffee plunger described as the Bodum Chambord Coffee Plunger. From at least April 1986, Bodum made substantial sales in Australia of the Bodum Chambord Coffee Plunger exhibiting those features. The Bodum Chambord Coffee Plunger has been promoted and advertised widely in Australia in many ways ...

7. Bodum further contended that the Bodum Chambord Coffee Plunger is packaged for sale in packaging that prominently depicts a photograph of the coffee plunger thus giving prominence and emphasis to the design features of the plunger within, rendering, it is said, the packaging, in a practical sense, transparent to the consumer. At the point of sale, the coffee plunger might be exhibited in its packaging or, for ease of examination of the plunger by a potential consumer, standing outside and near its packaging or independently of its packaging.

8. Bodum contended that by reason of these matters Bodum has acquired a substantial and valuable reputation in the features of the Bodum Chambord Coffee Plunger and the distinctive shape of the Bodum Chambord Coffee Plunger with the result that the sale in Australia of coffee plungers which embody those features or a significant number of them and the shape of the Bodum Chambord Coffee Plunger, signifies or is likely to signify to consumers in Australia, that such a coffee plunger is the Bodum Chambord Coffee Plunger or is made, promoted or sold by or with the licence, sponsorship or approval of Bodum (that is, relevantly associated with Bodum).

9. Bodum contended that independently of the hierarchy of trade marks a manufacturer uses in connection with a product in the course of the owner's trade, such as the trade marks Bodum or Chambord, a secondary meaning or independent reputation can, as a matter of law, subsist in the features and shape of an article or the get-up for a product which operates to associate products of that shape or those features in the mind of consumers with a particular trader although it is not necessary

that the consumer knows the name of that trader. An iconic example of secondary meaning is said to be the independent reputation subsisting in the shape of the Coca-Cola bottle which associates carbonated cola sold in a bottle of that shape with a particular trader. The presence of the Coca-Cola trade mark on every bottle of that product sold, does not diminish, it is said by way of example, the secondary or independent reputation in the shape (or features) of the bottle itself, signifying to consumers that the product is the product of that particular company. Whether a secondary meaning or independent reputation exists in the features or shape of a particular product or its get-up is, it is said, a question of fact to be determined having regard to all the relevant contextual circumstances.

10. ... A brief observation should be made about the terms 'secondary meaning' or 'secondary reputation'. The question to be determined is whether the features or shape of the Bodum Chambord Coffee Plunger have acquired a reputation and have become distinctive in the minds of consumers or potential purchasers of its maker. The reputation, if made out on the facts, is only 'secondary' in the sense that it subsists in the features of the product itself rather than a reputation that may or may not be isolated to a brand, label, mark, trade mark or house mark.

11. Bodum contended that DKSH from July 2004 began to distribute and sell in Australia a coffee plunger described as the Euroline Coffee Plunger which embodies each of the features, or features that closely resemble the features, of the Bodum Chambord Coffee Plunger ...

12. Bodum further contended that DKSH adopted, like Bodum, packaging ... giving prominent emphasis to a photographic representation of its coffee plunger; the Euroline Coffee Plunger is displayed at the point of sale either in its packaging or, for ease of examination by a potential consumer, outside (and away from) its packaging or, alongside the Bodum Chambord Coffee Plunger; the Euroline Coffee Plunger is not marked or engraved with any branding or labelling visible on the coffee plunger ... so as to distinguish it from the Bodum Chambord Coffee Plunger; and DKSH intended to mislead consumers by importing and selling a coffee plunger it knew to contain the features of the Bodum Chambord Coffee Plunger ...

...

REPUTATION AND THE ADVERTISING MATERIAL

184. There is no point of departure in a case based on the features of a product, as a matter of principle, from the 'one short general proposition—that no man [trader] may pass off his goods as those of another' (Lord Oliver, *Reckitt & Colman Products Ltd* [v *Borden Inc* [1990] RPC 341] at p 406), or get-up goods in a way that is misleading or deceptive or likely to be mislead or deceive consumers.

185. The questions are ultimately questions of fact in each case. More fundamentally however, the cases recognise that a trader's goods may, as a question of fact, become distinctive of and associated with a particular trader by reason of the get-up or design of the goods even though other labelling or brand names are also present ... Get-up or features can acquire a reputation independently of trade names used in connection with the product.

186. In this case, the primary judge, correctly with respect, described the many years of greatly diversified and extensive advertising of the Bodum Chambord Coffee Plunger as 'vast'. Short of evidence of an extensive television campaign directed to consumers generally (rather than those consumers of products in the housewares market), there is little more, one imagines, Bodum could have done to reach out to the cohort of consumers (potential purchasers) interested in coffee-drinking,

coffee-making or particular homeware appliances to hold out the Bodum Chambord Coffee Plunger as a product exhibiting a particular distinctive look by reason of the pleaded combination of features ... The primary judge also correctly, with respect, described at [90] the reputation so established as a 'significant reputation in Australia' giving rise to 'well-known and appreciated' products with a 'separate and distinct identity': [121]. However, with respect, the facts do not support the findings of the primary judge that that reputation subsists simply in the Bodum brand ([90]) or that in the absence of the Bodum brand (or logo) there is no independent or secondary reputation in the features or shape of the product ([92]). This seems to me to deny the overwhelming force of the advertising of the product itself.

187. It is true that much of the advertising of the features of the Bodum Chambord Coffee Plunger, depicting the plunger in large images either in use or in a stand-alone depiction, is associated or connected with the use of the Bodum trade mark or name.

188. Some consumers in their responses to the images might well strongly identify the features of the Bodum Chambord Coffee Plunger with the name Bodum and learn to describe the product as 'a Bodum' with the result that when such a consumer engages in the sequence of steps and thought processes involved in a potential consumer transaction, he or she will look for the Bodum Chambord Coffee Plunger by name, astute to precisely what they want, and conscious that any plunger not bearing the name Bodum is not what they want. However, such a realisation simply speaks to the success of the advertising campaign in associating a distinctive product in the mind of purchasers with its manufacturer. The very point of the advertising material is to associate the features or get-up of the Bodum Chambord Coffee Plunger with Bodum as the point of origin of the product. The trade mark or brand name reinforces the link to the particular trader/manufacturer of the product which is otherwise distinctive and associated in the mind of consumers by reason of the product's distinctiveness. The distinctive features of the product in that sense are reinforced by the use of the trade mark. The secondary reputation is not lost by the association of the images with the manufacturer's trade marks.

189. Those consumers that retain a recognition of the trade mark and the distinctive features of the Bodum product are prima facie likely to think that a product exhibiting those features is a Bodum Chambord Coffee Plunger unless something about the rival product tells the consumer—'You are not looking at a Bodum Chambord Coffee Plunger here'—which goes to the question of labelling and the differentiation factors applicable to the rival product. The absence of the Bodum mark or name from the rival product, exhibiting the Bodum features of significant secondary distinction, does not diminish the attractive force of the secondary reputation in the features associated with the particular trader/ manufacturer. The reputation for the shape and distinction of the Bodum Chambord Coffee Plunger does not dissolve in the absence of the trade mark.

190. Some consumers might not recall the Bodum name or trade mark and they might well seek out—'that distinctive coffee plunger' recognising that the distinctive coffee plunger is the product of a particular trader although unrecalled by name. Those consumers might seek out the Bodum Chambord Coffee Plunger because of the distinctive features they have seen and, acting reasonably, treat a coffee plunger exhibiting those features as a Bodum Chambord Coffee Plunger in the absence of something about the rival product (having regard to the relevant differentiation factors) which tells them that—'You are not looking at a Bodum Chambord Coffee Plunger here' ...

192. The advertising material is vast. It has endured over a long period. It is reinforced by substantial sales of the product. The reputation for the product by reason of its aesthetic features reflected in the pleaded elements of the shape of the product, is very significant. The presence of the bodum® trade

mark operates to reinforce the association in the mind of consumers or potential purchasers between the distinctive product and its maker which is established by the reputation subsisting in the features of the product itself …

194. Two examples (among many) speak loudly to the independent or secondary reputation in the features of the product at approximately each end of the chronological spectrum. The first is the feature article as early as 17 June 1986 addressing the coffee-drinking behaviours and coffee preferences of consumers, in the Good Living section of *The Sydney Morning Herald* which depicts as the signature image for the article a large Bodum Chambord Coffee Plunger standing next to a mound of coffee beans. Presumably, the publishers of the article in that section of the newspaper thought that consumers would immediately identify with the image. The second is the front page of the 2008 Myer Christmas Catalogue. In that catalogue Myer placed the Bodum Chambord Coffee Plunger at the apex of the Christmas tree of products presumably on the footing that consumers ready to engage in purchase transactions in the Christmas retail cycle would identify and associate with the products on the cover of the catalogue including, for present purposes, the Bodum Chambord Coffee Plunger.

195. What further evidence could be needed of a significant independent reputation in the features of the product itself connecting consumers with the maker of the product (even if the name of the maker may not readily be called to mind) although, in fact, the promotional material is, as found, vast.

196. As to the distinctiveness of those features, there is no evidence which suggests that the features of the Bodum Chambord Coffee Plunger are simply generic features. There are many different coffee makers which exhibit many different shapes. The evidence within the advertising material contains many images of different styles of coffee makers. Moreover, the primary judge found at [120] that although copyists had entered the market from time to time, the presence of copyists had not diluted Bodum's reputation. Rather, it 'would have had the inverse effect' having regard to the factors mentioned by the primary judge at [120].

THE REPUTATION IN THE FEATURES OF THE BODUM CHAMBORD COFFEE PLUNGER

197. I am satisfied that the evidence establishes a very significant secondary reputation in the features of the Bodum Chambord Coffee Plunger associated in the mind of consumers with Bodum as the manufacturer of the product and, with respect to the primary judge, that reputation is not 'distinctly tied' to Bodum in the sense that in the absence of the name Bodum there cannot be a secondary reputation in the features of the product …

198. The real question to be determined in the proceeding is whether DKSH has done enough having regard to all the relevant differentiation factors to distinguish its rival product from the Bodum product.

[Buchanan J dissented, holding at [286] that the 'conclusion that Bodum had no "secondary reputation" in the features of the plunger and the findings from which the respective conclusions proceeded were clearly open on the evidence before the trial judge'.]

As has already been mentioned, the reputation does not necessarily need to attach to a 'trade mark'. It can also attach to indicia such as the image of famous personalities: parties such as a pair of famous ballroom dancers, swimmer Kieren Perkins and pop star Rihanna have all had success restraining the unauthorised use of their images in passing off and/or *TPA* cases.[3] Passing off and consumer protection legislation can also be used to prevent the unauthorised marketing of goods associated with film characters or famous television shows or advertisements. For example, in *Hogan v Koala Dundee Pty Ltd* (1988) 20 FCR 314, Pincus J considered at 323:

> the inventor of a sufficiently famous fictional character having certain visual or other traits may prevent others using his character to sell their goods and may assign the right so to use the character; furthermore, the inventor may do these things even where he has never carried on any business at all, other than the writing or making of the work in which the character appears.

Reputation may even attach to something as broad as advertising concepts and themes although, again, this may prove difficult to demonstrate. A useful illustration is *Cadbury Schweppes Pty Ltd v Pub Squash Co Pty Ltd* [1980] 2 NSWLR 851. In the 1970s Cadbury started selling a lemon drink called 'Solo' which, as Lord Scarman recounted at 854, Cadbury promoted 'as a man's drink, fit for, and a favourite with, rugged masculine adventurers. The advertising campaign was to stress its masculinity and at the same time to awaken happy memories of the sort of squash hotels and bars in the past used to make'. A series of television and radio advertisements featuring these themes and certain slogans were aired in the mid-1970s. In 1975 the Pub Squash Co started making a similar lemon drink called 'Pub Squash' which was advertised on television using similar 'heroically masculine' and 'nostalgic' themes (at 856). Lord Scarman held at 858 that the passing off action:

> is wide enough to encompass other descriptive material, such as slogans or visual images, which radio, television or newspaper advertising campaigns can lead the market to associate with a plaintiff's product, provided always that such descriptive material has become part of the goodwill of the product. And the test is whether the product has derived, from the advertising, a distinctive character which the market recognizes.

On the facts, however, it was held that Cadbury had not established exclusive reputation in its advertising themes, and its action failed.

We will return to some of these issues, and see further examples of the signs and indicia in which reputation can subsist (see 'Misrepresentation, or misleading or deceptive conduct' below, p 645).

LOCATION OF REPUTATION

In actions for passing off and contravention of consumer protection legislation the plaintiff must establish a reputation in the area in which the defendant is trading. This does not require the plaintiff to have a trading presence in the same suburb, town or even state in which the defendant is trading. Rather, it is enough that consumers who are encountering the defendant's operations are aware of the plaintiff's business. In cases where the defendant is trading in a local area and the plaintiff enjoys significant trade in other parts of Australia, the existence of a sufficient reputation will often be relatively easy to establish. For example, in the High Court case *BM Auto Sales Pty Ltd v Budget Rent A Car System Pty Ltd* (1976) 12 ALR 363, Budget (the well-known car hire company) was able to demonstrate it had a reputation in the term 'Budget' in the Northern Territory primarily through the presence of travellers there who were aware of Budget's business elsewhere in Australia.

---

3   See, respectively, *Henderson v Radio Corp Pty Ltd* [1960] NSWR 279, *Talmax Pty Ltd v Telstra Corp Ltd* [1997] 2 Qd R 444 and *Fenty v Arcadia Group Brands Ltd* [2015] EWCA Civ 3.

SPILLOVER REPUTATION

A more difficult question is whether it is sufficient for a foreign trader merely to have a reputation in Australia, or whether it is also necessary for that trader to have an Australian trading presence. The question of whether mere 'spillover' reputation is sufficient to found a passing off action is a controversial one in the UK, where in some cases courts have found against foreign plaintiffs that did not have a trading presence in the UK. However, Australian courts have taken a more liberal approach to this question.

CASE EXTRACT: CURRENT LAW

ConAgra Inc v McCain Foods (Aust) Pty Ltd

(1992) 33 FCR 302
Federal Court of Australia, Full Court

[ConAgra was incorporated in the USA and sold frozen foods under a number of brand names including 'Healthy Choice'. It had a substantial reputation in this name in the USA but had never traded in Australia. McCain, an Australian company, applied for trade mark registration for the same name, and ConAgra sued in passing off and for contravention of s 52 of the *TPA*.]

Lockhart J (at 342–346): In my opinion, the 'hard line' cases in England conflict with the needs of contemporary business and international commerce. A trader's reputation may be injured locally by many means. A trader may have a famous and well-known commodity, yet a person, totally unconnected with him, may in a country where the trader's goods are not sold and where he has no place of business nevertheless cause confusion in the marketplace and lead the consumers to believe that a business connection exists between the two. The local person may produce a product inferior in quality to the product of the overseas trader and this may taint irreparably the reputation of the original product and of its maker. The reality of modern international business is that contemporary consumers are not usually concerned about the actual location of the premises of a company or the site of its warehouse or manufacturing plant where the goods are produced, but they are concerned with maintenance of a high level of quality represented by internationally known and famous goods.

The requirement in some of the cases that a very slight form of business activity is sufficient is really a somewhat artificial concept. The real question is whether the owner of the goods has established a sufficient reputation with respect to his goods within the particular country in order to acquire a sufficient level of consumer knowledge of the product and attraction for it to provide custom which, if lost, would be likely to result in damage to him. This is essentially a question of fact.

As I outlined in more detail earlier, it is still necessary for a plaintiff to establish that his goods have the requisite reputation in the particular jurisdiction, that there is a likelihood of deception among consumers and a likelihood of damage to his reputation. But reputation within the jurisdiction may be proved by a variety of means including advertisements on television or radio, or in magazines and newspapers within the forum. It may be established by showing constant travel of people between other countries and the forum, and that people within the forum (whether residents there or persons simply visiting there from other countries) are exposed to the goods of the overseas owner ...

CURRENT LAW

Certainly the law of passing off does not confer protection on the owners of goods who have no reputation in a particular jurisdiction, otherwise they would have an international monopoly with respect to the name, get-up or mark applied to their goods (and services) and may never intend to exploit it in the particular jurisdiction. It is the likelihood of deception among consumers and of damage to reputation that are the critical requirements to establish a case of passing off and they prevent any such unauthorised international monopoly being granted to a plaintiff. A *quia timet* injunction is a good illustration of this point for, in most cases, while such an injunction will be granted where the plaintiff has at the time of action no relevant business connection with the particular jurisdiction but has a reputation there and has established a likelihood of deception amongst consumers, he must go on to establish a likelihood of damage to his reputation and that he intends to establish in some way his business or sell his goods in that jurisdiction ...

For these reasons, I am of the opinion that it is not necessary in Australia that a plaintiff, in order to maintain a passing-off action, must have a place of business or a business presence in Australia; nor is it necessary that his goods are sold here. It is sufficient if his goods have a reputation in this country among persons here, whether residents or otherwise, of a sufficient degree to establish that there is a likelihood of deception among consumers and potential consumers and of damage to his reputation ...

[On the question of the extent of the plaintiff's reputation, Lockhart J subsequently held:]

In my opinion the plaintiff must prove that there are within the jurisdiction in which the defendant is carrying on business a substantial number of persons who are aware of the plaintiff's product: see *Saville Perfumery Ltd v June Perfect Ltd* (1941) 58 RPC 147 at 176, per Viscount Maugham ... This was the test adopted by the primary judge ... and in my opinion correctly. Further, it does not matter whether the persons within the relevant jurisdiction who are aware of the plaintiff's product are resident or visitors from anywhere in the world.

The reason for the requirement of a substantial number of persons is in my opinion that the reputation of a plaintiff in the forum is the source of his potential business there; his goods are known to people there who are his potential customers. For him to have in a practical and business sense a sufficient reputation in the forum requires something more than a reputation among a small number of persons, although the size and extent of the class may vary according to the circumstances of the case. Also, the law seeks to promote local competition and innovation and does not extend its protection to persons whose goods are not sufficiently known in the forum.

Gummow J (at 372): In my view, where the plaintiff, by reason of business operations conducted outside the jurisdiction, has acquired a reputation with a substantial number of persons who would be potential customers were it to commence business within the jurisdiction, the plaintiff has in a real sense a commercial position or advantage which it may turn to account. Its position may be compared with that of a plaintiff who formerly conducted business within the jurisdiction and has retained a reputation among its erstwhile customers, and with that of a plaintiff with a reputation which arises from its trade in the jurisdiction, but extends to goods or services which are not presently marketed by him. If the defendant moves to annex to itself the benefit of such a reputation by attracting custom under false colours, then the defendant diminishes the business advantage of the plaintiff flowing to it from the existence of his reputation.

[French J agreed with both Lockhart and Gummow JJ.]

In the above case, ConAgra was unable to show that it had in fact acquired a sufficient reputation in Australia: evidence of its reputation in the USA, occasional spillover magazine advertisements and the frequency of travel to the USA by Australians were considered to be inadequate. The case remains important in an age of internet commerce, demonstrating that a mere internet presence will not be sufficient unless further evidence shows that a substantial number of (potential) Australian consumers are aware of the plaintiff's goods or services.

TEMPORAL CONSIDERATIONS

Two temporal issues are important in assessing whether sufficient reputation can be shown to found an action for passing off or contravention of consumer protection laws. The first is whether the plaintiff can bring the action based on a reputation acquired by virtue of pre-trade advertisements and publicity alone. The second related issue is what happens once a trader ceases trading. Does the trader lose the ability to bring an action at this time, or can the plaintiff rely on residual, post-trade reputation?

PRE-TRADE REPUTATION

CASE EXTRACT: CURRENT LAW

Fletcher Challenge Ltd v Fletcher Challenge Pty Ltd

[1981] 1 NSWLR 196
Supreme Court of New South Wales

[On 22 October 1980 it was announced in New Zealand that as a result of the amalgamation of three New Zealand companies (two of which were called Challenge Corporation Ltd and Fletcher Holdings Ltd), the plaintiff company, to be called Fletcher Challenge Ltd, was to be incorporated in Australia. This announcement was widely publicised in Australia. On 23 October the unrelated defendants reserved the corporate name 'Fletcher Challenge Pty Ltd' in Australia and this company was incorporated in Australia in December 1980. In January 1981 the plaintiff company commenced business in New Zealand. In February 1981 it sought an interlocutory injunction requiring the defendants to change the name of their company, on the basis that the defendants were engaging in passing off.]

Powell J (at 204–205): The first question thus is, has the plaintiff, at this interlocutory stage, established a sufficient prima facie case of a reputation in this State? The defendants would deny that it has, either at all, or at either of what are submitted to be the relevant dates—the date of reservation of name, or the date of incorporation. This, so the defendants submit, flows from the [fact] that, at the date of reservation of name, the plaintiff did not exist ...

[I]t seems to me that even if—which, since this is a *quia timet* proceeding, I do not necessarily accept—the relevant date is the date of reservation of name, where, as here, the plaintiff has, as it were, risen Phoenix-like from the amalgamation of the three holding companies, it is not illegitimate for it to be treated as entitled to the combined goodwill of all three; but, if something more directly related to the plaintiff's corporate name must be shown it is, I think, not illegitimate to hold, at least at this stage of the proceedings, that the announcement of the proposed amalgamation and of the proposed new corporate name created a new reputation, which reputation preceded, albeit, perhaps, by only a few hours, the lodgment of the application of reservation of company name: see, for example, *Turner v General Motors (Australia) Pty Ltd* (1929) 42 CLR 352.

POST-TRADE REPUTATION

CASE EXTRACT: CURRENT LAW

Ballarat Products Ltd v Farmers Smallgoods Co Pty Ltd

[1957] VR 104

Supreme Court of Victoria

[The plaintiff, Ballarat Products, and its predecessor in title had for many years traded under the mark 'Farmers' for smallgoods. Seven years after the plaintiff ceased trading it sought to prevent the defendant producing the same foodstuffs under the name 'Farmers Smallgoods Company Ltd'.]

Hudson J (at 107–108): On behalf of the defendant Mr Phillips contended that the plaintiff must fail in its action because the evidence does not establish that it has any goodwill to which the trade name 'Farmers' is attached or with which the acts of the defendant will interfere. Clearly, he said, the plaintiff has not for over six years used the name 'Farmers' in connexion with the production or sale of goods such as the defendant intends to produce and a mere intention on the part of the plaintiff to resume this branch of its business and exploit the use of the name, even if this were taken to have been established, which he contended it had not, would be insufficient to entitle the plaintiff to any of the relief claimed.

On behalf of the plaintiff Mr Mann contended that the evidence established that there had been built up a valuable reputation attaching to the use of the word 'Farmers' in connexion with goods such as the defendant intends to manufacture; that this represented a commercial advantage which the plaintiff had acquired and enjoyed as part of its business and had never abandoned; that such reputation still subsists so that goods sold under that name would still be regarded by the public and persons in the trade as the products of the plaintiff; and that though it may be true that the probability of damage is a necessary element in the cause of action, this is satisfied by evidence establishing the likelihood of the plaintiff, or an assignee in the form of the proposed company the subject of its negotiations, resuming business under the name 'Farmers'.

… I am satisfied not only that there still subsists a valuable reputation in the name 'Farmers' when used in connexion with ham, bacon and small goods, but also that the plaintiff has never decided to abandon the advantage which it represents. Having regard to the evidence to which I have already referred, as to the retention and maintenance of the premises, plant, etc, as to the improvement in conditions in the trade, and as to the negotiations for the formation of a new company, I consider it to be probable that the plaintiff, either directly or indirectly, will in the not too distant future again commence to exploit the use of the name. The question is whether this is sufficient to justify the Court in interfering to prevent the defendant from using the name and by doing so depriving the plaintiff of what appears to be a valuable right.

> The gist of the plaintiff's action is that the course of conduct upon which the defendant intends to embark—the carrying on of business as a manufacturer and distributor of ham, bacon and small goods under the name of Farmers Smallgoods Pty Ltd—is calculated to represent to the public and persons in the trade that the goods of the defendant are the goods of the plaintiff or that the business of the defendant is a branch or subsidiary of the plaintiff.
>
> In my opinion the mere fact that the plaintiff is not for the time being producing or marketing any goods under the name does not present any obstacle to the plaintiff establishing that the defendant's conduct will amount to such a representation. For any one of a number of reasons a trader whose goods have acquired a favourable reputation may be compelled temporarily to cease production. His premises or plant may be totally destroyed or his supplies of raw materials may be completely cut off. But the reputation of his goods under his trade name will survive for some period depending no doubt upon how firmly it has become established and what steps he takes to keep it alive. In such circumstances may a rival trader lawfully appropriate the trade name and enjoy the reputation which it has earned despite the fact that in so doing he is making a false representation to the public and is using a name which the owner has not abandoned but intends to use and probably will use again in the course of his trade? In my opinion the law does not permit the appropriation of a trade name by a rival trader in such circumstances.

The requirement that the plaintiff intends to recommence trading in order to bring a passing off action is controversial, and tends to be explained on the basis that without such an intention, the plaintiff cannot be said to suffer any damage.[4] However, as we will see, this argument is problematic given that loss of the ability to expand into a new market is a recognised head of damage (see 'Damage' below, p 670). In actions under consumer protection legislation it has been held there is no such requirement of an intention to recommence trading,[5] and it has been suggested that the same approach should be taken both under consumer protection legislation and in passing off: *WMC Ltd v Westgold Resources NL* (1997) 39 IPR 319 at 324.

OWNERSHIP OF GOODWILL

A final point that needs to be considered relates to the question of the 'ownership' of goodwill. Generally, in order to make out a passing off action, the plaintiff needs to show it has an exclusive reputation in the indicia in question. There are some limited exceptions. Courts have been prepared to accept that two or more traders who have honestly and concurrently used the same sign or indicia have a protectable reputation, and may be able to obtain remedies against third parties, but not against each other.[6]

COLLECTIVE GOODWILL

UK courts have also been prepared to recognise and protect 'collective' goodwill, as outlined in the following case.

---

4   See for example *Pete Waterman Ltd v CBS UK Ltd* [1993] EMLR 27.
5   *Mark Foy's Pty Ltd v TVSN (Pacific) Ltd* [2000] FCA 1626; (2000) 104 FCR 61.
6   See for example *Habib Bank Ltd v Habib Bank AG Zurich* [1982] RPC 1; *Colorado Group Ltd v Strandbags Group Pty Ltd* [2007] FCAFC 184; (2007) 164 FCR 506 at [221] (Allsop J). Whether this applies under the ACL is uncertain.

CASE EXTRACT: COMPARATIVE LAW

Erven Warnink BV v J Townend & Sons (Hull) Ltd ('Advocaat')

[1979] AC 731
House of Lords

[One of the key issues in this case (also extracted above, p 643) was whether a passing off action could be brought by one member of a class of traders, all of which have a reputation in a sign that describes some quality or characteristic of the goods provided by them (in this case, the product description 'advocaat'), where a third party falsely represents by the adoption of that name that its goods have those relevant qualities or characteristics.]

Lord Diplock (at 739–745): [T]his is an action for 'passing off', not in its classic form of a trader representing his own goods as the goods of somebody else, but in an extended form first recognised and applied by Danckwerts J in the champagne case (*J Bollinger v Costa Brava Wine Co Ltd* [1960] Ch 262). The ratio decidendi of that case was subsequently adopted as correct by Cross J in the sherry case (*Vine Products Ltd v Mackenzie & Co Ltd* [1969] RPC 1) and by Foster J in the Scotch whisky case (*John Walker & Sons Ltd v Henry Ost & Co Ltd* [1970] 1 WLR 917) ...

[Lord Diplock turned to consider the 'Champagne' case, and quoted the following assumptions of fact in that case (set out at [1960] Ch 262 at 273):]

(1) The plaintiffs carry on business in a geographical area in France known as Champagne;

(2) the plaintiffs' wine is produced in Champagne and from grapes grown in Champagne;

(3) the plaintiffs' wine has been known in the trade for a long time as 'champagne' with a high reputation;

(4) members of the public or in the trade ordering or seeing wine advertised as 'champagne' would expect to get wine produced in Champagne from grapes grown there; and

(5) the defendants are producing a wine not produced in that geographical area and are selling it under the name of 'Spanish champagne.

These findings disclose a factual situation (assuming that damage was thereby caused to the plaintiff's business) which contains each of the five characteristics which I have suggested must be present in order to create a valid cause of action for passing off. The features that distinguished it from all previous cases were (a) that the element in the goodwill of each of the individual plaintiffs that was represented by his ability to use without deception (in addition to his individual house mark) the word 'champagne' to distinguish his wines from sparkling wines not made by the champenois process from grapes produced in the Champagne district of France, was not exclusive to himself but was shared with every other shipper of sparkling wine to England whose wines could satisfy the same condition and (b) that the class of traders entitled to a proprietary right in 'the attractive force that brings in custom' represented by the ability without deception to call one's wines 'champagne' was capable of continuing expansion, since it might be joined by any future shipper of wine who was able to satisfy that condition.

My Lords, in the champagne case the class of traders between whom the goodwill attaching to the ability to use the word 'champagne' as descriptive of their wines was a large one, 150 at least and probably considerably more, whereas in the previous English cases of shared goodwill the number of traders between whom the goodwill protected by a passing off action was shared had been two, although in the United States in 1898 there had been a case, *Pillsbury-Washburn Flour Mills Co v Eagle* (1898) 86 Fed R 608, in which the successful complainants to the number of seven established their several proprietary rights in the goodwill attaching to the use of a particular geographical description to distinguish their wares from those of other manufacturers.

It seems to me, however, as it seemed to Danckwerts J, that the principle must be the same whether the class of which each member is severally entitled to the goodwill which attaches to a particular term as descriptive of his goods, is large or small. The larger it is the broader must be the range and quality of products to which the descriptive term used by the members of the class has been applied, and the more difficult it must be to show that the term has acquired a public reputation and goodwill as denoting a product endowed with recognisable qualities which distinguish it from others of inferior reputation that compete with it in the same market. The larger the class the more difficult it must also be for an individual member of it to show that the goodwill of his own business has sustained more than minimal damage as a result of deceptive use by another trader of the widely-shared descriptive term. As respects subsequent additions to the class, mere entry into the market would not give any right of action for passing off; the new entrant must have himself used the descriptive term long enough on the market in connection with his own goods and have traded successfully enough to have built up a goodwill for his business.

For these reasons the familiar argument that to extend the ambit of an actionable wrong beyond that to which effect has demonstrably been given in the previous cases would open the floodgates or, more ominously, a Pandora's box of litigation leaves me unmoved when it is sought to be applied to the actionable wrong of passing off.

I would hold the champagne case [1960] Ch 262 to have been rightly decided and in doing so would adopt the words of Danckwerts J where he said, at pp 283–284:

> There seems to be no reason why such licence [sc. to do a deliberate act which causes damage to the property of another person] should be given to a person, competing in trade, who seeks to attach to his product a name or description with which it has no natural association so as to make use of the reputation and goodwill which has been gained by a product genuinely indicated by the name or description. In my view, it ought not to matter that the persons truly entitled to describe their goods by the name and description are a class producing goods in a certain locality, and not merely one individual. The description is part of their goodwill and a right of property. I do not believe that the law of passing off, which arose to prevent unfair trading, is so limited in scope.

In the champagne case the descriptive term referred to the geographical provenance of the goods, and the class entitled to the goodwill in the term was accordingly restricted to those supplying on the English market goods produced in the locality indicated by it. Something similar was true in the sherry case (*Vine Products Ltd v Mackenzie & Co Ltd* [1969] RPC 1) where the word 'sherry' as descriptive of a type of wine unless it was accompanied by some qualifying geographical adjective was held to denote wine produced by the solera method in the province of Jerez de la Frontera in Spain and the class entitled to the goodwill in the word was restricted to suppliers on the English market of wine produced in that province. In the Scotch whisky case (*John Walker & Sons Ltd v Henry Ost & Co Ltd* [1970] 1 WLR 917) the product with which the case was primarily concerned was blended whisky and the class entitled to the goodwill in the descriptive term 'Scotch whisky' was not restricted to traders who

COMPARATIVE LAW

dealt in whisky that had been blended in Scotland but extended to suppliers of blended whisky wherever the blending process took place provided that the ingredients of their product consisted exclusively of whiskies that had been distilled in Scotland. But the fact that in each of these first three cases the descriptive name under which goods of a particular type or composition were marketed by the plaintiffs among others happened to have geographical connotations is in my view without significance. If a product of a particular character or composition has been marketed under a descriptive name and under that name has gained a public reputation which distinguishes it from competing products of different composition, I can see no reason in principle or logic why the goodwill in the name of those entitled to make use of it should be protected by the law against deceptive use of the name by competitors, if it denotes a product of which the ingredients come from a particular locality, but should lose that protection if the ingredients of the product, however narrowly identified, are not restricted as to their geographical provenance.

Advocaat has been followed in a number of UK cases (discussed on pp 660–661 below) which, in recognising 'collective' reputation, have become known as cases of 'extended passing off'. While these cases have not been directly applied in Australia, Lord Diplock's statement of the elements of the passing off action in *Advocaat* has been approved in numerous Australian decisions. In any event, an affected trader could always bring an action under the ACL.

MISREPRESENTATION, OR MISLEADING OR DECEPTIVE CONDUCT

The second element of the classical trinity is that of misrepresentation, or, in the context of s 18 of the ACL, misleading or deceptive conduct.

Whether conduct conveys a misrepresentation or is misleading or deceptive is to be determined in all the circumstances of the case. Courts will not only assess the similarity between the signs or indicia used by the plaintiff and defendant (including surrounding content such as disclaimers), but will also take into account the extent of the plaintiff's reputation, the nature of the goods or services in question, the context in which those goods or services are sold or provided, and the nature of the consumers of such goods or services and how they would respond in making purchasing decisions, in making an overarching assessment as to the likelihood of consumers being deceived. As will become clear in Chapter 18, this is a broader assessment from that undertaken in determining whether a registered trade mark has been infringed.

Various types of misrepresentation have been recognised by the courts. These range from misrepresentations as to origin (that the defendant's goods or services are those of the plaintiff) to misrepresentations as to quality (that the defendant's goods or services have certain qualities or characteristics that they do not in fact have), cases of 'inverse passing off' (where the *plaintiff's* goods or services are misrepresented as being those of the *defendant*), and misrepresentations as to the existence of a sponsorship arrangement or some form of commercial association between the parties.

Before looking at these types of misrepresentation in more detail, a number of preliminary issues need to be addressed.

THE RELEVANT STANDARD: IS MERE CONFUSION SUFFICIENT?

Clearly, a 'misrepresentation' or 'misleading or deceptive conduct' must lead consumers into error—it must cause a response among consumers that is capable of influencing their purchasing behaviour. A difficult issue is determining how definite the consumer's view must be of the link between the plaintiff's and defendant's goods or services. Under Australian law conduct that causes consumers to be misled is often contrasted with that which causes 'mere confusion'. Most notably, in the *TPA* case of *Parkdale Custom Built Furniture Pty Ltd v Puxu Pty Ltd* (1982) 149 CLR 191, Gibbs CJ held at 198 that:

> to prove a breach of s 52 it is not enough to establish that the conduct complained of was confusing or caused people to wonder whether two products may have come from the same source, and ... *Southern Cross Refrigerating Co v Toowoomba Foundry Pty Ltd* (1954) 91 CLR 592 ... is distinguishable.

In *Southern Cross* the High Court was interpreting the phrase 'likely to deceive' in the *Trade Marks Act 1905* (Cth) (the equivalent provision under the *Trade Marks Act 1995* (Cth) (*TMA*) now reads 'likely to deceive or cause confusion'). The effect of *Parkdale* is that conduct that merely causes a consumer to wonder as to a particular state of affairs may have certain consequences under the *TMA* (as we will see in Chapters 17 and 18) but will not be sufficient to constitute 'misleading or deceptive conduct'. Although this distinction was also made in passing off cases that pre-dated the *TPA*, the difficulties involved in making such a distinction—and a different way of looking at this issue—can be seen in the following extract.

CASE EXTRACT: COMPARATIVE LAW

Phones4u Ltd v Phone4u.co.uk Internet Ltd

[2006] EWCA Civ 244; [2007] RPC 5
Court of Appeal of England and Wales

Jacob LJ (with whom Carnwath and Tuckey LJJ agreed): 16. ... Sometimes a distinction is drawn between 'mere confusion' which is not enough [for passing off], and 'deception', which is. I described the difference as 'elusive' in *Reed Executive v Reed Business Information* [2004] RPC 767 at 797. I said this, [111]:

> Once the position strays into misleading a substantial number of people (going from 'I wonder if there is a connection' to 'I assume there is a connection') there will be passing off, whether the use is as a business name or a trade mark on goods.

17. This of course is a question of degree—there will be some mere wonderers and some assumers—there will normally (see below) be passing off if there is a substantial number of the latter even if there is also a substantial number of the former.

COMPARATIVE LAW

18. The [2005] edition of *Kerly* contains a discussion of the distinction at paragraphs 15-043–15-045. It is suggested that:

> The real distinction between mere confusion and deception lies in their causative effects. Mere confusion has no causative effect (other than to confuse lawyers and their clients) whereas, if in answer to the question: 'what moves the public to buy?', the insignia complained of is identified, then it is a case of deception.

19. Although correct as far as it goes, I do not endorse that as a complete statement of the position. Clearly if the public are induced to buy by mistaking the insignia of B for that which they know to be that of A, there is deception. But … [a] more complete test would be whether what is said to be deception rather than mere confusion is really likely to be damaging to the claimant's goodwill or divert trade from him. I emphasise the word 'really.'

That is, the real nature of the distinction might be said to rest on whether the public would be more likely to be 'moved to buy' the defendant's product as a consequence of the representation. If so, there will be deception and not mere confusion. Yet (as we will see under 'Types of misrepresentation: Sponsorship, endorsement, affiliation' below, p 663) this may occur where consumers conclude that there is some 'business association' between the plaintiff and the defendant and are more likely to purchase the defendant's goods as a result. Although in theory this remains a higher standard than asking whether consumers would be given 'cause to wonder' whether goods were produced under licence or with the sponsorship of the plaintiff, the very nature of a business association is such that there may be little difference in practice between the two standards. Indeed, the relationship between these standards was recognised in some *TPA* cases: for example in *Telmak Teleproducts (Australia) Pty Ltd v Coles Myer Pty Ltd* (1988) 84 ALR 437 Gummow J indicated that although mere confusion is not sufficient to establish liability under the *TPA*, it is evidence from which a likelihood of deception can be inferred.

OTHER PRELIMINARY ISSUES

Three further preliminary points should be made. The first relates to the question of who must be misled in order for an action for passing off or contravention of the consumer protection regime to be made out. In passing off cases it has long been held that a 'substantial number' of consumers of the defendant's goods must be misled, with such consumers being taken largely as they are found.[7] For s 52 of the *TPA*, the High Court held in *Campomar Sociedad Limitada v Nike International Ltd* [2000] HCA 12; (2000) 202 CLR 45 at [102]–[103] that whether conduct is misleading or deceptive is to judged by reference to a representative 'ordinary' or 'reasonable' member of the class to which the representation has been made. In cases since then, the Full Federal Court has asked whether a 'not insignificant' number of prospective consumers have been misled.[8] The precise relationship between these tests has not yet been articulated, although in *Optical 88 Ltd v Optical*

---

7   *Saville Perfumery Ltd v June Perfect Ltd* (1941) 58 RPC 147.
8   *National Exchange Pty Ltd v Australian Securities and Investments Commission* [2004] FCAFC 90; (2004) 61 IPR 420; *Hansen Beverage Co v Bickfords (Australia) Pty Ltd* [2008] FCAFC 181; (2008) 171 FCR 579; *Peter Bodum A/s v DKSH Australia Pty Ltd* [2011] FCAFC 98; (2011) 92 IPR 222.

88 Pty Ltd (No 2) [2010] FCA 1380; (2010) 89 IPR 457, Yates J appeared to suggest that there was little difference between them.

The second issue relates to the evidence on which the parties can rely to establish that a misrepresentation has occurred. While evidence from experts in fields such as marketing and consumer behaviour is potentially admissible (provided it otherwise meets the requirements of the *Evidence Act 1995* (Cth)), courts will not give much weight to such evidence in determining whether a misrepresentation has occurred if such evidence is not based on systematic research going directly to the facts in issue.[9] Survey evidence of consumer responses can also be useful, and the Federal Court has provided guidance as to how surveys should be run.[10] Surveys not run in accordance with such guidance may well be excluded under s 135 of the *Evidence Act*, which gives the court discretion to refuse to admit evidence if its probative value is substantially outweighed by the danger it might be unfairly prejudicial to a party, misleading or confusing, or result in undue waste of time.[11] Evidence from consumers that they have been misled might also be helpful, but such evidence is often treated with scepticism, and courts have developed techniques to filter out the responses of consumers on the basis that such responses are 'erroneous' or 'fanciful'.

A third point is that that there is no requirement that the plaintiff and defendant be engaged in a 'common field of activity' (i.e. that they be direct competitors). Instead, this is treated as a relevant factor in assessing whether the defendant has engaged in a misrepresentation.[12]

TYPES OF MISREPRESENTATION: ORIGIN

Turning to the types of actionable misrepresentation, or the types of conduct that have been held to be misleading or deceptive, the paradigmatic case involves a defendant misrepresenting that its goods are those of the plaintiff. Establishing such misrepresentations as to origin tends to be most difficult in cases involving descriptive words or non-textual get-up, as discussed in the following cases.

MISREPRESENTATIONS INVOLVING DESCRIPTIVE WORDS

CASE EXTRACT: PRECEDENT

Reddaway v Banham

[1896] AC 199
House of Lords

[The basic facts of the case are set out at p 623 above.]

Lord Macnaghten (at 218–219): The learned counsel for the respondents maintained that the expression 'camel hair belting' used by Banham was the 'simple truth.' Their proposition was that

---

9   *CA Henschke & Co v Rosemount Estates Pty Ltd* [1999] FCA 1561; (1999) 47 IPR 63; *Cadbury Schweppes Pty Ltd v Darrell Lea Chocolate Shops Pty Ltd (No 8)* [2008] FCA 470; (2008) 75 IPR 557.

10   Practice Note *CM 13—Survey Evidence*, 1 August 2011, available at www.fedcourt.gov.au/law-and-practice/practice-documents/practice-notes/cm13.

11   *Cadbury Schweppes Pty Ltd v Darrell Lea Chocolate Shops Pty Ltd (No 2)* [2006] FCA 364.

12   See *Henderson v Radio Corp Pty Ltd* [1960] NSWR 279, affirmed by the High Court in *Campomar Sociedad Limitada v Nike International Ltd* [2000] HCA 12; (2000) 202 CLR 45.

PRECEDENT

'where a man is simply telling the truth as to the way in which his goods are made, or as to the materials of which they are composed, he cannot be held liable for mistakes which the public may make.' That seems to me to be rather begging the question. Can it be said that the description 'camel hair belting' as used by Banham is the simple truth? I will not call it an abuse of language to say so, but certainly it is not altogether a happy expression. The whole merit of that description, its one virtue for Banham's purposes, lies in its duplicity. It means two things. At Banham's works, where it cannot mean Reddaway's belting, it may be construed to mean belting made of camel's hair; abroad, to the German manufacturer, to the Bombay mill-owner, to the up-country native, it must mean Reddaway's belting; it can mean nothing else. I venture to think that a statement which is literally true, but which is intended to convey a false impression, has something of a faulty ring about it; it is not sterling coin; it has no right to the genuine stamp and impress of truth.

[The importance of this point can also be seen in the form of injunction that was granted. Banham was not restrained from using the words 'camel hair' at all, but rather from using them in a manner that would deceive the public as to the origins of its belting. That is, it was always open to Banham to assert, for example, that 'our belting is made from the finest camel hair'.]

MISREPRESENTATIONS INVOLVING COPYING DESCRIPTIVE GET-UP

Misrepresentations as to origin can occur even if the plaintiff and defendant are using different primary brand names. *Reckitt & Colman* is one example of this—there, it was considered that Borden had not done enough to distinguish its packaging from that of Reckitt & Colman. A key factor in that case was the low-cost nature of the goods in question, which would be purchased in a hurry. This is explored further in the following case, which is also useful in showing the importance courts attach to evidence of an intention to mislead—sometimes known in this context as 'fraud'—on the part of the defendant.

CURRENT LAW

CASE EXTRACT: CURRENT LAW

Red Bull Australia Pty Ltd v Sydneywide Distributors Pty Ltd

[2001] FCA 1228; (2001) 53 IPR 481
Federal Court of Australia

[Red Bull, whose energy drinks are sold in the get-up set out below, left, brought an action in passing off and for contravention of s 52 of the *TPA* in relation to Sydneywide's sale and distribution of 'LiveWire' energy drinks in the get-up set out below, right. In both cases, the darker markings are the same dark blue, the lighter markings are the same silver, and the brand names 'Red Bull' and 'LiveWire' are in red. The images below are set out as annexures to the Full Federal Court's judgment on appeal: *Sydneywide Distributors Pty Ltd v Red Bull Australia Pty Ltd* [2002] FCAFC 157; (2002) 55 IPR 354.]

Conti J: 61. … Particularly when one stands back from the Red Bull and LiveWire cans when placed together, such steep line or thrust, which runs diagonally from the top of the Red Bull can to the bottom thereof, provides a telling impression of similarity to the equally strong feature of the so-called lightning bolt of the LiveWire can, which comprises a similarly diagonal angle from the top to the bottom thereof. No matter how often one casually picks up the Red Bull and LiveWire cans contemporaneously, or places the same together on a horizontal plane in alternative positions, one is impressed with an instantaneous perception of the similarity of get-up of the two packagings. Colour and colour combinations, particularly of cans such as those of the 250ml size here involved, tends to attract attention before brand names embossed thereon … These conclusions leave remaining for decision whether the critical factor of the differing brand names of Red Bull and LiveWire should nevertheless cause the litigation to prevail in Sydneywide's favour …

   …

   63. … The evidence which I have reviewed in detail leads to the conclusion that Sydneywide intentionally, if not also carefully and skilfully, set about the adaption of the most prominent features and characteristics of Red Bull's packaging get-up in the ways and to the extent postulated by Dr Beaton [Red Bull's expert], though not of course the trade mark or brand name of Red Bull and the associated portrayal of the two charging bulls …

   64. That is not to deny that the actual appearance of packaging to prospective consumers is ultimately the determining factor, rather than the alleged infringer's intention per se. Whether or not the packaging of LiveWire is deceptively similar to that of Red Bull is of course essentially a question of fact for the Court to determine, with the assistance of any available expert evidence of value … The obvious difference between the brand names of 'LiveWire' and 'Red Bull' appearing on the packaging is thus not decisive, even given that the latter is portrayed in an attractive context of the two charging bulls …

   65. The circumstances of the present complaint … bear some material similarity to those summarised by Burchett J at first instance in *Kettle Chip Co Pty Ltd v Apand Pty Ltd* (1993) 46 FCR 152, whose judgment was upheld by a Full Court … At 161, his Honour commenced his discussion of the applicable approach to the circumstances in that litigation as follows:

> Of course, a person who places the packets before him, side by side, can also see differences. But that is not how passing off by the imitation of another trader's mark or get-up is to be tested.

CURRENT LAW

In general, and more particularly in the case of an item likely to be purchased for a small price without long consideration, the comparison which must be made is between the impression of the applicants goods retained in a customer's mind and the impression made by the sort of consideration he is likely to give to the respondent's product before purchasing it. Only a rare potato chip consumer, who has previously studied the applicant's packet, is likely to go through that exercise again upon seeing a packet, some time later, on display in a service station or a corner shop. If, as he passes it, it appears to him to be the 'Kettle' product he liked before, or another flavour put out by the same people, he is very likely to purchase it without further examination …

…

69. I would infer that Sydneywide identified distinct advantages for the launch and establishment of LiveWire in a broadly dispersed marketplace for its manufactured energy drink, by [using] a packaging get-up which would likely be of significant advantage in the retail market-place for a newly emerging product in the form of LiveWire, without the need moreover for costly advertising and promotion, being an advantage available for exploitation as a consequence of the very substantial promotional and marketing activities which had been undertaken by Red Bull Australia in relation to the Red Bull product over the preceding three years or thereabouts … Sydneywide would have been able to readily identify the implications of such an advantage, particularly by reason of its substantial existing involvement in the energy drink trade as a distributor, and in particular as a major distributor of Red Bull as one of the two leading energy drink brands. Sydneywide would have appreciated the further advantage it held, as an already established distributor of the Red Bull product, to merchandise its LiveWire product in at least some of the places where it had been already distributing Red Bull. The temptation to market a product with packaging, which potential consumers would identify as similar in get-up presentation or 'general characteristics' … to the already heavily publicised Red Bull product, was something which I would infer was too great a temptation for Sydneywide to resist. Sydneywide would have doubtless perceived that from the normal or usual standing distance of potential retail customers of energy drink products from the shelves and refrigerated containers of retailers, there was scope for such customers to mistake the LiveWire product for the Red Bull product, particularly if no Red Bull product was also on display, or where both products were on display in circumstances where either or both brand names were not readily discernible …

…

71. It is material to the conclusion which I have reached that the market for energy drinks is in the nature of an impulse market … [S]uch [a] market is distinguishable in that context from for instance, furniture and clothing retail markets, where potential buyers will customarily tend to first identify brand names before making their commitments to purchasing … The following passage in Wadlow, *The Law of Passing Off* (2nd ed, 1995) at 429–430 is apposite to the present circumstances:

It is probably quite normal for customers selecting goods from supermarket shelves to go by some aspect of the overall appearance as much by the name. What is more difficult is to identify the precise visual clues on which the customer relies. Despite the fact that many of the brands of any particular commodity often bear an overall resemblance to one another, the eye seems to be able to distinguish them and select one without any conscious reference to the brand names as such. Unfortunately, there has been no objective analysis of this effect in the reported cases, and self-serving assertions of what is or is not distinctive do not help.

CURRENT LAW

I think that Dr Beaton's comprehensive evidence came to grips with the marketing phenomena, which the author is here speaking, more effectively than Ms Strachan [Sydneywide's expert]. I do not think that she addressed, or addressed sufficiently, the significance of the circumstance … as to the manner in which a retailer's presentation of both the LiveWire and Red Bull cans at a given point of sale, particularly when placed together without both brand names being distinctively visible, may add to their respective similarities in a context of a few seconds decision-making. Especially would that be so where the decision-making relates to a product such as an energy drink having a retail price of the order spoken of in the evidence … In *de Cordova v Vick Chemical Co* (1951) 68 RPC 103 at 106, Lord Ratcliffe said:

> [I]n most persons the eye is not an accurate recorder of visual detail, and … marks are remembered rather by general impressions or by some significant detail than by any photographic recollection of the whole.

[Conti J thus found in favour of Red Bull. Sydneywide's appeal to the Full Court was dismissed.]

In *Red Bull*, the defendant's intention to deceive was treated as an important factor in establishing the existence of passing off and contravention of s 52 of the *TPA*. However, it is important to remember that the mere copying of aspects of another trader's get-up might not demonstrate an intention to deceive, especially if the defendant takes adequate steps to differentiate its goods from those of the plaintiff. In addition, if the plaintiff does not have a protectable reputation in Australia the defendant's intention to deceive will be irrelevant.[13]

MISREPRESENTATIONS INVOLVING COPYING PRODUCT APPEARANCE

Because it will be extremely difficult for a plaintiff to establish it has a reputation in the appearance of the *actual goods* that it sells, the copying of such product appearance, even if deliberate, is unlikely to constitute a misrepresentation. This is demonstrated in the first extract below (which is also useful in showing how the courts construe the way 'reasonable' consumers of the defendant's goods would behave). The second extract provides a rare illustration of where a misrepresentation involving the copying of product appearance was established.

PRECEDENT

CASE EXTRACT: PRECEDENT

Parkdale Custom Built Furniture Pty Ltd v Puxu Pty Ltd

(1982) 149 CLR 191
High Court of Australia

[Puxu had since late 1976 designed and sold a range of lounge suites of distinctive appearance under the name 'Contour'. In June 1978 Parkdale started selling a range of 'Rawhide' furniture, which was virtually identical in appearance to Puxu's 'Contour' range. A small label was sewn onto each piece

---

13   See for example *ConAgra Inc v McCain Foods (Aust) Pty Ltd* (1992) 33 FCR 302 at 344–345 (Lockhart J) and 365 (Gummow J).

of Parkdale's furniture indicating it was 'Parkdale Custom Built Furniture' of the 'Rawhide' range, this being the customary manner in the industry of labelling such furniture. This label could be tucked under the upholstery of the furniture. Puxu sought an injunction under the *TPA* on the basis of a contravention of s 52. Its action was dismissed at trial but upheld by the Full Federal Court. Parkdale appealed to the High Court.]

Gibbs CJ (at 199–200): Section 52 does not expressly state what persons or class of persons should be considered as the possible victims for the purpose of deciding whether conduct is misleading or deceptive or likely to mislead or deceive. It seems clear enough that consideration must be given to the class of consumers likely to be affected by the conduct. Although it is true, as has often been said, that ordinarily a class of consumers may include the inexperienced as well as the experienced, and the gullible as well as the astute, the section must in my opinion by regarded as contemplating the effect of the conduct on reasonable members of the class. The heavy burdens which the section creates cannot have been intended to be imposed for the benefit of persons who fail to take reasonable care of their own interests. What is reasonable will of course depend on all the circumstances. The persons likely to be affected in the present case, the potential purchasers of a suite of furniture costing about $1500, would, if acting reasonably, look for a label, brand or mark if they were concerned to buy a suite of particular manufacture.

The conduct of a defendant must be viewed as a whole. It would be wrong to select some words or act, which, alone, would be likely to mislead if those words or acts, when viewed in their context, were not capable of misleading. It is obvious that where the conduct complained of consists of words it would not be right to select some words only and to ignore others which provided the context which gave meaning to the particular words. The same is true of acts ... [I]n my opinion, the conduct of the appellant did not contravene s 52. Speaking generally, the sale by one manufacturer of goods which closely resemble those of another manufacturer is not a breach of s 52 if the goods are properly labelled. There are hundreds of ordinary articles of consumption which, although made by different manufacturers and of different quality, closely resemble one another. In some cases this is because the design of a particular article has traditionally, or over a considerable period of time, been accepted as the most suitable for the purpose which the article serves. In some cases indeed no other design would be practicable. In other cases, although the article in question is the product of the invention of a person who is currently trading, the suitability of the design or appearance of the article is such that a market has become established which other manufacturers endeavour to satisfy, as they are entitled to do if no property exists in the design or appearance of the article. In all of these cases, the normal and reasonable way to distinguish one product from another is by marks, brands or labels. If an article is properly labelled so as to show the name of the manufacturer or the source of the article its close resemblance to another article will not mislead an ordinary reasonable member of the public. If the label is removed by some person for whose acts the defendant is not responsible, and in consequence the purchaser is misled, the misleading effect will have been produced, not by the conduct of the defendant, but by the conduct of the person who removed the label.

For these reasons I have reached the conclusion that the conduct of the appellant was not of the kind to which s 52 refers ...

Brennan J (at 219–226): [T]his is a case where common law principles are relevant to a true understanding of the scope and operation of s 52. The relevant principles prescribe the protection to

PRECEDENT

which a manufacturer is entitled against the marketing of copies of his goods and the correlative (albeit incidental) protection of consumers who might be led by the appearance of a copy into believing that it is made by that manufacturer.

The protection afforded by the common law stops short of according to a manufacturer a monopoly right to the manufacture and sale of goods of a particular design unless he is the owner of a design validly registered under the *Designs Act 1906* (Cth) in respect of goods of that kind. The relevant principles in a passing off action were stated by Graham J in *Benchairs Ltd v Chair Centre Ltd* [1974] RPC 429, a case in which the plaintiffs' claim in passing off depended solely on the fact that the shape and design of the defendants' chair was so close to the shape and design of the plaintiffs' chair that its mere existence on the market would lead to confusion with the plaintiffs' chair ... Graham J held at p 435:

> the mere copying of the shape of the plaintiffs' article is not in itself such a representation [i.e. a representation by the defendant that his goods are those of the plaintiff]. Anyone is entitled, subject to some monopoly or statutory right preventing him, to copy and sell any article on the market, and false representation and passing off only arise when a defendant does something further which suggests that the article which he is selling is that of the plaintiff. This he may do by a direct representation to that effect such as by the use of the plaintiffs' name or mark, or by an indirect representation such as by imitation of get-up by enclosing the article in a distinctive package which is similar to that used by the plaintiff ...

The design of the 'Contour' suite was not registered under the *Designs Act* ... Therefore Parkdale was free to apply the design of the 'Contour' suite to suites of its own manufacture. Of course, Parkdale was not free to pass off the 'Rawhide' suite as a 'Contour' suite, but there is no evidence that it did so. It used its own trade name; it affixed its own distinguishing label. Nor did Parkdale get up the 'Rawhide' suite for sale in a way which would induce anybody to think that it was the 'Contour' suite ...

If s 52 of the *Trade Practices Act* authorized or required the granting of such an injunction [restraining Parkdale in these circumstances], it would run counter to the intention of Parliament implied in the statutes which create or provide for the creation of monopolies. Those statutes define the conditions governing the creation of monopolies and thus chart the limits of the contemporary reservations from the freedom to manufacture and sell which the *Statute of Monopolies* assured ...

It would be surprising if s 52 of the *Trade Practices Act* were to alter the 'careful balance' of the *Patents Act* ... and the *Designs Act* by a side-wind and, after four centuries, open the way to the creation of prescriptive monopolies for the manufacture of goods. In my view, it does not have that effect ...

Conduct cannot be held to fall within s 52 unless a consumer, not labouring under any mistake or imperfection of understanding of law, would be or would be likely to be misled or deceived by that conduct. Section 52 operates in a milieu of the external legal order, so that the character of conduct which falls for consideration under s 52 is to be determined by reference to the external legal order as it exists when the conduct is engaged in. Therefore, a manufacturer who exercises his freedom to manufacture goods according to a design which is not protected by valid registration does not engage in conduct which is misleading or deceptive or which is likely to mislead or deceive. If consumers or potential consumers believe that all goods of a particular design are manufactured by him who first establishes a market reputation as a manufacturer of those goods, that belief is or may be erroneous ...

PRECEDENT

Of course, where identical or similar goods are on the market, it may take very little evidence of conduct additional to the mere manufacture and sale of the goods to establish a case under s 52. The degree of risk of confusion is material to an appreciation of the conduct of a trader in marking or getting up his goods for sale in competition with the goods of another trader. In the present case, however, where Parkdale labelled the 'Rawhide' suite in accordance with the practice of the trade and the label clearly distinguished that suite from the 'Contour' suite, there was no misleading or deceptive get-up. If customers mistook the 'Rawhide' suite for the 'Contour' suite the mistake was not induced by Parkdale's conduct. It was not misleading or deceptive conduct merely to manufacture and sell a lounge suite similar to the Contour suite—or, for that matter, a suite identical with the Contour suite. Something more was needed to show conduct inducing a mistaken belief that the 'Rawhide' suite was manufactured by Puxu, but only additional evidence, the label, showed conduct which was calculated to correct any confusion as to source.

The appeal should be allowed and the injunction dissolved.

[Mason J agreed that the appeal should be allowed.]

CASE EXTRACT: CURRENT LAW

CURRENT LAW

Peter Bodum A/S v DKSH Australia Pty Ltd

[2011] FCAFC 98; (2011) 92 IPR 222
Federal Court of Australia, Full Court

[The basic facts of the case are set out at pp 633–634 above.]

Greenwood J (with whom Tracey J agreed): 231. The DKSH rival product has no branding on the product itself. The word Pyrex is on the glass beaker. There is no other differentiating symbol, name or logo on the product.

232. However at [94], the primary judge found that the accused's products were 'clearly packaged' to distinguish them from Bodum and the packaging for the rival product contained 'no reference to the distinctive name or logo of Bodum'. There are two aspects to the significance of the packaging. The first concerns the importance the primary judge attributed to the branding on the packaging for the Bodum Chambord Coffee Plunger. The primary judge noted Mr Bodum's evidence that Bodum placed its trade mark on the packaging and the product itself. The various application[s] of the Bodum name to the product and the packaging has already been described. The primary judge noted that from the year 2000 Bodum also gave emphasis to the phrase 'the original French press' and the use of the word 'original'. At [98], the primary judge noted Mr Perez's evidence that this was done to draw attention to the product's French heritage and to educate consumers to watch out for look-alikes.

233. The primary judge regarded the use by Bodum of its trade mark in this way as part of its education of consumers to look for and seek out the Bodum Chambord Coffee Plunger by name with the result that in the absence of the combination of names and descriptions, consumers would readily identify and understand that such a product was not associated with or a product of Bodum. The primary judge found at [113] that a purchaser would be 'left in no doubt about the provenance of the Bodum Chambord Coffee Plunger'.

234. The second aspect of packaging concerns the distinction or differentiation evident in the DKSH packaging. At [111], the primary judge found that the packaging of the various products is 'different' and has 'a significant role to play in informing the consumer of the different brands by reference to each product'. The primary judge found at [111] that all the packaging is 'clearly labelled and sufficiently distinctive to distinguish the various products'.

235. The brand name for the rival product selected by DKSH is 'EURO LINE'. The primary judge found at [176] that the Euroline brand is 'not well known' and further described that brand as an 'unknown brand'. Those findings are not surprising since at least so far as 2008 and 2009 is concerned there had been no advertising of the brand Euroline and sales of the Bodum product had dwarfed sales of DKSH's product.

236. Ultimately, these questions are matters of impression against the background of all of the factors identified in seeking to answer the questions postulated above. Having regard to these factors I find it difficult to accept that DKSH has distinguished its product as found by the primary judge … The rival product is, as to the front and back sections of the box, two thirds white. It also displays a large image of the rival product which for all practical purposes is substantially the same product by appearance which is not surprising having regard to the findings of the primary judge at [182] and [155]. It is marked with a trade name 'EURO LINE**TM**' at the base of the box on the left-hand side of the front and back of the box. The name 'Euroline' is not distinctive and at July 2004 was very likely to be regarded as an abbreviated description of a product having a provenance as a product within a line of European products.

237. What else could EUROLINE possibly mean other than a product in a line of European products, especially in the absence of pronounced advertising or sales which might have rendered such a description distinctive in some way?

238. The box for the rival product is not prominently marked with the name of the respondent although at the base of the box in small print is the following text: 'EUROLINE**TM** is a registered trade mark of DKSH Australia Pty Ltd. Packaging designed in Australia. Made in Taiwan'.

239. The consumer seeks out the product not the box.

240. The product is often removed from the box and displayed outside the box. The DKSH product has no Euroline marking on the product itself. It may or may not contain an instruction leaflet. In 2008, DKSH attached a sticker to the rival product to mark it Euroline. That sticker may or may not be easily detachable and may or may not represent a fixed method of differentiating the product in a way which would guarantee an enduring representation to a consumer that the rival product is something different from Bodum's product or Bodum. In any event, the sticker was not present from July 2004 to October 2008. Presumably, DKSH thought it necessary in 2008 to put a product name on the Euroline Coffee Plunger itself.

241. The products are offered for sale by Bodum and DKSH to retailers and then by retailers to consumers. As to consumers, the primary judge found at [105] that in most shops the packaging as well as the products are on display in varying ways. The packaging is most commonly displayed behind the plungers. In almost all cases there will be some products displayed out of the packaging but corresponding packaging will be present. The primary judge found at [106] that in most cases different brands are sold together with different packaging on display indicating different brands. The primary judge found at [106] that where the Bodum product is sold alone it is sold in conjunction with

the Bodum name or logo and where DKSH's product is sold alone, these sales 'seemed to occur in the context of the packaging alongside'.

242. At [110]–[111], the primary judge recognised that 'obviously' the product will be available for the consumer to 'actually examine' and the practice of displaying the products out of their packaging is adopted because consumers will want to see and touch the product they are buying and the main reasons why the product is displayed outside its packaging are that retailers want to simulate the impression of the 'home environment' ...

244. It seems to me that the adoption on the box of a non-distinctive and descriptive trade mark Euroline for a rival product which for all practical purposes embodies all of the features (that is, copies those features) of the product exhibiting the pronounced and substantial reputation at July 2004 of the Bodum Chambord Coffee Plunger, is not sufficient to distinguish the rival product from the distinctive product sought to be copied. This is especially so as the rival product and the Bodum product are regularly displayed outside the packaging for each product notwithstanding that it may be that the products are ... proximately located to the packaging and in some locations in front of the boxes. It would have been a simple matter for DKSH to mark its name prominently on the box or mark its trade mark and product name prominently on the rival product itself (or at least as prominently as Bodum marks its product) or both. A plainly distinctive differentiating trade mark might also have been selected for use on the box and on the product.

245. An inference is open that at July 2004 DKSH's get-up of its product was such as to lead consumers to believe, or be likely to lead consumers to believe, that when they engaged with the rival product they were actually engaging with Bodum's product or a product in the Bodum line of products even if they saw the words Euroline on the box when engaging in the sequence of steps leading up to selection and purchase of a coffee plunger. If they did not see the box and were drawn to the rival coffee plunger by reason of the distinctive features of the Bodum product, a consumer might well pick up the rival product and handle and examine it, and if a potential purchaser did so, there is no indication from DKSH on the product itself that the consumer was not looking at a Bodum product or a product in the Bodum line of products, but looking at a DKSH product.

246. The references in the primary judgment to the association between the distinctive features of the Bodum product and the use of Bodum's name and logo inverts the real question to be addressed. A consumer looking specifically for the Bodum Chambord Coffee Plunger by reference to the name Bodum could pick up the Bodum product as displayed out of its box, hold it ... and see the Bodum name and trade mark. That might well be so for a consumer looking for the product specifically by name because they know the product by name. They may be replacing a Bodum product they already own; or they may have seen the product closely in particular settings at a restaurant, in a home or in many other settings which attracted their attention to its features and the Bodum name as well as the features. The real question is what impression is made on the mind of the reasonable or ordinary member of the class of consumers seeking to buy a coffee plunger (rather than sophisticated members of the class, which applies a more stringent and incorrect test) drawn to the rival product by reason of the copying of the distinctive features of the Bodum product and conscious of the reputation associating the product distinctly with Bodum (although the name might not be immediately recalled), when such a consumer examines the rival product without any differentiating name, title or logo on the product at all to signify that it is not actually a Bodum product.

247. As a matter of impression, it seems to me entirely rational to conclude that such a member of the class is very likely to think that the largely indistinguishable product embodying those features (as DKSH chose to do) is the Bodum product, a version of the Bodum product or in some way sponsored or approved by Bodum ...

...

264. I am satisfied on the evidence that Bodum established at July 2004 a contravention of s 52 and s 53 of the *Trade Practices Act 1974* (Cth) by reason of DKSH's adoption of the features of the distinctive Bodum Chambord Coffee Plunger in circumstances where DKSH failed to adopt distinguishing or differentiating indicia for its rival product which made it plain to consumers attracted to the rival product by reason of the distinctive reputation and secondary meaning subsisting in the features of the Bodum Chambord Coffee Plunger that the rival product was not a Bodum Chambord Coffee Plunger or a coffee plunger promoted and sold with the licence, sponsorship or approval of Bodum. I am also satisfied that such conduct involved DKSH passing off its product as that of Bodum's product or a product sold with the licence, sponsorship or approval of Bodum.

265. Placing 'EURO LINE' on the box was not enough. Nor was placing the small sticker in the following small text 'MADE IN TAIWAN' ... on the base of the beaker sufficient to distinguish DKSH's rival product from that of the Bodum Chambord Coffee Plunger.

Buchanan J (dissenting): 294. To the extent that the claimed reputation (or 'secondary meaning') in the features alone might actually exist, the relevant enquiry is whether it has been made sufficiently clear to a consumer at the point of sale that the product they are about to purchase is not a Bodum plunger. In that connection the trial judge made the following findings (at [171]–[174] and [176]):

> 171. The Euroline packaging features the prominent use of DKSH's trade mark, EUROLINETM. EUROLINETM is printed on all six panels of the packaging. It is printed in large, stylised type on the bottom left-hand side of the front, back, top and two side panels. It is printed in smaller capital letters on the bottom panel in the statement, EUROLINETM is a registered trade mark of DKSH.
>
> 172. The EUROLINETM trade mark on DKSH's packaging is at least as large as the BODUM trade mark on Bodum's packaging. The photographs of in-store displays demonstrate that the EUROLINE trade mark is not concealed when the glass plunger is displayed in front of the packaging. Even if it was concealed, anyone interested in purchasing the plunger would reveal the packaging when they picked up the plunger.
>
> 173. A prominent photograph of the Euroline Coffee Plunger appears on the front and back panels of the packaging. A smaller photograph of the plunger appears on the side panels. As I have already indicated, it is common practice in the housewares industry for products to be displayed and sold in packaging that features a photograph of the product that is inside the packaging. When the plunger is displayed outside its packaging, the photograph and the name Euroline enables consumers to match the product and its packaging.
>
> 174. In context, I do not accept that the branding with the name 'Euroline' as it appears on the box does little to distinguish the DKSH product.
>
> ...
>
> 176. I do accept that the Euroline brand is not well known. However, that is not to say that a potential customer will assume that this 'unknown brand' is connected in someway to Bodum, particularly whether Bodum goes out of its way to use its own name and logo, and the features

CURRENT LAW

of the product are different. In any event, I consider the use of 'Euroline' on the packaging does indicate clearly a different brand.

295. ... [T]he findings were clearly open to the trial judge as a matter of impression, making the judgment for himself once the relevant matters had been sufficiently identified for him if necessary. In addition, the trial judge recorded at [163(e)] that 'at all times the Euroline plunger has had a gold "Made in Taiwan" sticker on its base'. That appears to me to be substantially destructive of a claim of a 'secondary meaning' arising simply from the features shared between the Bodum and Euroline plungers, even if the sticker seems not wholly consistent with the name 'Euroline'.

296. However the matter is examined, therefore, there is no basis to conclude that the trial judge made any error in the evaluation of the evidence, or in the application of relevant principles, which might provide a ground to uphold the appeal.

297. Finally, the trial judge observed that there was no evidence of any consumer being actually misled. That was a relevant, even though not determinative, matter. It provided a practical touchstone against which to test what was otherwise a debate concerned with possibilities and competing versions of available impressions.

TYPES OF MISREPRESENTATION: QUALITY

It has long been established that actionable misrepresentations are not confined to those as to origin. Another key type of misrepresentation is that the defendant's goods have certain qualities or characteristics associated with the plaintiff's goods, where the defendant's goods do not have such qualities.

PRECEDENT

CASE EXTRACT: PRECEDENT

AG Spalding & Bros v AW Gamage Ltd

(1915) 32 RPC 273
House of Lords

[In 1910 and 1911 the plaintiffs, Spalding, sold three varieties of moulded 'Orb' footballs. In 1912 Spalding advertised an 'Improved Sewn Orb' football, with its advertisements featuring a picture of the ball stamped with the words 'Orb' and 'specially tested', and referring to the patent under which the balls had been made. Spalding also withdrew from sale much of its stock of moulded 'Orb' balls, which it considered defective. The defendant, Gamage, legitimately acquired a batch of the 1910 and 1911 line of withdrawn footballs, which it then advertised for sale as 'Improved Orb' balls, with the statement that they were 'a great improvement on the old moulded ball', and featuring the same picture used in Spalding's advertisements for its 1912 line and the reference to the same patent number. Gamage offered these balls for sale at less than half the price of Spalding's 'Improved Sewn Orb'.]

Lord Parker (with whom Lord Atkinson agreed) (at 284–287): The proposition that no one has a right to represent his goods as the goods of somebody else must, I think, as has been assumed in this case, involve as a corollary the further proposition that no one who has in his hands the goods of another of a particular class or quality has a right to represent these goods to be the goods of that other of a different quality or belonging to a different class. Possibly, therefore, the principle ought to be restated as follows: 'A cannot, without infringing the rights of B, represent goods which are not B's goods or B's goods of a particular class or quality to be B's goods or B's goods of that particular class or quality.'

[After setting out the facts of the case in detail, Lord Parker continued:]

It appears to me to be quite certain that anyone comparing any of these advertisements with the catalogue, or anyone with a knowledge of the catalogue and seeing the advertisements, would be led to conclude that the respondents were offering for sale at 4s 9d the identical ball catalogued by the appellants in their 1912 catalogue at 10s 6d. Indeed, I find it difficult to imagine that the advertisements were not deliberately framed so as to convey this impression. The respondents' counsel sought to justify the advertisements on the ground that the statements therein contained were only a repetition of what the appellants had themselves said in former catalogues of the moulded ball described as the 'Improved 1910 Orb,' or the 'Improved Orb,' but this, unfortunately, is not so. No ball had been theretofore catalogued by the plaintiffs as made under patent No 15,168. No ball had in any preceding catalogue of the plaintiffs been illustrated as stamped with the words 'Specially tested.' Even when we come to the words 'better than the old moulded ball,' I can find no justification for their use in the advertisements. The appellants in their catalogue were contrasting the new sewn variety with the old moulded variety theretofore sold by them.

Even if the respondents say that they intended to contrast one moulded ball with another their statement would be untrue, for the balls they were selling were old moulded balls of the 1910 and 1911 varieties. But, after all, the question whether any particular statement was true or otherwise is not a pertinent question; the really pertinent question is whether the advertisements as a whole were calculated to deceive, and it seems to me that they were so calculated … In my opinion, therefore, the misrepresentation on which the appellants rely may be taken as fully established. Further, the misrepresentation so established was, in my opinion, of such a nature as to give rise to a strong probability of actual damage to the appellants in both their retail and wholesale trade. I refrain, however, from amplifying this point so as not to prejudice any question which may arise on any inquiry as to damages which your Lordships may direct. It is sufficient to say that the misrepresentation being established, and being in its nature calculated to produce damage, the appellants are prima facie entitled both to an injunction and to an inquiry as to damage, the inquiry, of course, being at their own risk in respect of costs …

[Lords Sumner and Parmoor wrote separate concurring judgments.]

This type of misrepresentation has more recently been recognised in UK cases involving 'extended passing off'. For example, in *Advocaat* [1979] AC 731 the House of Lords held that the defendant had engaged in a misrepresentation that its 'Old English Advocaat', made from fortified wine, was made from the traditional Dutch recipe for advocaat which included brandewijn. Similarly:

- in *Taittinger SA v Allbev Ltd* [1993] FSR 641, a French Champagne maker was able to prevent the distributor of a non-alcoholic carbonated drink from selling it as 'Elderflower Champagne';

- in *Chocosuisse Union des Fabricants Suisses de Chocolat v Cadbury Ltd* [1998] RPC 117 (substantially affirmed on appeal at [1999] RPC 826), two Swiss chocolate makers were able to prevent Cadbury from marketing a UK-made 'Swiss Chalet' chocolate;
- in *Diageo North America, Inc v Intercontinental Brands (ICB) Ltd* [2010] EWCA Civ 920; [2011] RPC 2, Smirnoff was able to prevent the sale in the UK of a white spirit called 'Vodkat' marketed in get-up reminiscent of vodka bottles; and
- in *Fage UK Ltd v Chobani UK Ltd* [2014] EWCA Civ 5; [2014] FSR 29, a Greek yoghurt manufacturer was able to prevent the sale of US-made thick and creamy 'Greek Yoghurt'.

'Extended passing off' is an important mechanism by which the law might provide protection against the misuse of geographical indications (GIs). GIs are terms that indicate not only that a good comes from a particular country or region, but also that it has certain qualities, characteristics or a reputation attributable to that geographical origin. As we saw in Chapter 15, members of the World Trade Organization (WTO) are under obligations to provide interested parties with the means to prevent the misleading use of other members' GIs. Australia complies with these obligations through a patchwork of laws. These include: passing off; provisions of consumer protection legislation; provisions of the *TMA* dealing with the registration of certification of trade marks and the denial of registration as trade marks of 'false' GIs (discussed in Chapter 17); provisions of the *Australian Grape and Wine Authority Act 2013* (Cth) regulating the labelling of wine; and the *Australia New Zealand Food Standards Code*, compliance with which is mandatory under state and territory food legislation.

TYPES OF MISREPRESENTATION: INVERSE PASSING OFF

A third type of misrepresentation occurs where the defendant misrepresents that the *plaintiff's* goods or services are in fact those of the *defendant* (the inverse of the usual form of misrepresentation as to origin).

CASE EXTRACT: CURRENT LAW

Testro Bros v Tennant

(1984) 2 IPR 469
Supreme Court of New South Wales

[The plaintiff, Testro Bros, produced tailored directories for hospitals which listed each hospital's facilities, services, rules and information for patients and visitors. The defendants (a former employee of and a former commission agent for Testro Bros) wished to produce different directories to compete with Testro Bros. In the course of pitching their idea to various hospitals that had not been approached by Testro Bros it was alleged that the defendants relied on samples of Testro Bros' directories (which did not feature any reference to Testro Bros) as the defendants' own work and represented that the hospitals referred to those directories were the defendants' clients. Testro Bros sought an interlocutory injunction to restrain the defendants' continuing conduct.]

Holland J (at 473–474): The defendants contend that because the evidence does not show the plaintiff's name, business or trademark or other identification of the plaintiff was used by them and they were expressly offering to supply under their own business name goods to be produced by themselves, there is no basis on which the court may or should interfere to protect the plaintiff.

The question, as I see it, is whether it is a passing off or otherwise unfair trading that the law will restrain, to represent to a prospective customer that you have been successful in the market with goods the equivalent of which you are offering to supply when the success has not been yours but that of another unidentified supplier whose goods you are then displaying to the prospective customer as your own and as an example of your success? Can the unidentified supplier of whose success advantage is thus being taken have such conduct restrained in the absence of any suggestion to the customer of some relationship between the representor and the original supplier?

In my opinion, it is strongly arguable that the answer to these questions is affirmative. Here there is a misrepresentation in the course of trade made to a prospective customer calculated to injure the plaintiff's goodwill and business and likely to do so: see *Erven Warnink BV v J Townend & Sons (Hull) Ltd* [1979] AC 731, per Lord Diplock at 740, 742 for the elements generally to be found in a passing off case. The defendants' use of the plaintiff's publications as samples of their own work makes a number of false representations, namely, that having produced that work they have a proven capacity to produce more of the same quality and standard, the product is a success in the market achieved by them, their business reputation or reliability as a producer and supplier of this kind of product is already proved by the fact that this example of it has been approved, accepted, supplied to and distributed by the administration of leading and reputable public hospitals. By this means the defendants seek to appropriate to themselves the success of the plaintiff both in producing a quality product and finding a market for it amongst responsible authorities. If the defendants succeed in obtaining the business, and the evidence shows they seek five year contracts, they thereby deprive the plaintiff of the opportunity of using its own success to obtain that business from that potential customer. As the defendants expect to get the business by displaying a false sample of their work one may readily infer that the plaintiff would have got it by displaying a true sample. As Powell J said in *Fletcher Challenge Ltd v Fletcher Challenge Pty Ltd* [1981] 1 NSWLR 196 at 204: 'The object of the law's intervention into the arena of trade or business is preservation of a trader's or businessman's goodwill from appropriation by another trader or businessman.'

Whilst this is not the more common case of misuse of a trader's name, trademark, trade description or get-up, the categories of passing off and unfair trading are not closed because attempted appropriation of another trader's success may take as much variety in form as the ingenuity of man: see Lord Diplock in the case above cited at 740–42 and Powell J in the *Fletcher Challenge* case at 204 ...

I think that the plaintiff is entitled to [an] interlocutory order restraining the defendants in appropriate terms from using the plaintiff's publications for the purpose of obtaining business for themselves without at the same time clearly stating that such publications have not been produced, printed or published or indeed supplied by the defendants. That form of order does not require the defendants to advertise the plaintiff by stating whose publications they are, but at the same time it is designed to ensure that if the defendants persist in using the plaintiff's publications to attract business to themselves they do so in such a way that they do not misrepresent to the prospective customer that the publication is their own and that the business by which it is being supplied presently to hospitals is their business.

TYPES OF MISREPRESENTATION: SPONSORSHIP, ENDORSEMENT, AFFILIATION

In *Campomar Sociedad Limitada v Nike International Ltd* [2000] HCA 12; (2000) 202 CLR 45 the High Court was prepared to maintain an injunction restraining a Spanish manufacturer from marketing its 'Nike Sports Fragrances' on the basis that this would misrepresent that such products were 'in some way promoted or distributed by Nike International *itself or with its consent and approval*' (at [107], emphasis added). This is an example of a situation where the conduct of a defendant supplying different goods or services from those of the plaintiff could be characterised as a misrepresentation as to (1) origin (i.e. that the plaintiff has engaged in brand extension) or (2) the existence of a sponsorship agreement or some other form of commercial association between the parties. In relation to the latter type of misrepresentation, much will depend on the extent of the plaintiff's reputation, whether that reputation is in relation to a variety of goods and services, and the way consumers would respond in seeing the defendant's use of the plaintiff's indicia, in determining whether a misrepresentation is established.

In contrast to *Campomar*, in *McIlhenny Co v Blue Yonder Holdings Pty Ltd* (1997) 39 IPR 187 the maker of 'Tabasco' sauce was refused an injunction to restrain the defendant from using the word 'Tabasco' as the name of its company and in advertisements for its exhibition design services. Although Lehane J accepted that the defendant had clearly sought to take advantage of a well-known characteristic of the plaintiff's product, namely, its reputation for being 'hot', his Honour held that there was no misrepresentation because consumers would not conclude that there was any commercial connection between the parties. This case is also interesting because of the contrast it offers with the anti-dilution protection available in other jurisdictions, discussed in Chapter 15. That the defendant might have been 'free-riding' on the plaintiff's reputation, or had possibly even engaged in 'tarnishment' (because the advertisement for its 'Tabasco Design' services contained the slogan 'Tabasco. Lousy on your tie, great on your exhibit'), were irrelevant to the passing off inquiry.

A misrepresentation as to sponsorship or commercial association can also be made out where the defendant has adopted an aspect of 'secondary branding' in advertising its unrelated goods, even in the absence of the adoption of any primary branding. Again, as the following extract demonstrates, much will depend on what indicia have been adopted and how such indicia have been used by the defendant.

CASE EXTRACT: CURRENT LAW

Telstra Corporation Ltd v Royal & Sun Alliance Insurance Australia Ltd

[2003] FCA 786; (2003) 57 IPR 453
Federal Court of Australia

[Telstra ran a popular television advertisement in the 1990s for the Yellow Pages. This involved the actor Tommy Dysart playing a Scottish-accented character known as 'Mr Goggomobil' who used the Yellow Pages in a series of attempts to find a mechanic who recognised his rare Goggomobil car, finally finding some success in doing so. In 2002 Shannons, a car insurance company, ran a series of television and radio advertisements for its car insurance products. All of these featured Tommy Dysart reprising his

'Mr Goggomobil' character. The first television advertisement involved the character ringing a number of insurers in an attempt to obtain insurance for his green Goggomobil, finally finding success with Shannons. The other television advertisements and the radio advertisement featured the character and made reference to the Goggomobil, but did not involve the character using the phone to solve a problem. Telstra unsuccessfully argued that the Shannons' advertisements infringed Telstra's copyright in its scripts for the original Goggomobil advertisement. Telstra also argued that Shannons and its advertising agent, Wilson Everard, had engaged in passing off and had contravened s 52 of the *TPA*.]

Merkel J: 57. Secondary branding or suggestive brand advertising occurs when a word, character, symbol or image creates, on its own, instant recognition or association with a particular product or business. The adoption of such characters, symbols or images by another advertiser will usually raise the question of whether that advertiser is representing that it, or its goods or services, have an affiliation, association or connection they do not have. In *R & C Products Pty Ltd v SC Johnson & Sons Pty Ltd* (1993) 42 FCR 188 at 194 Davies J observed:

> if advertising or get-up has acquired special signification, then the adoption of elements of the advertising or get-up by another trader may give rise to a misrepresentation. Then the question will be whether other steps have been taken which sufficiently distinguish the one trader and its products from the other trader and its products.

58. *Twentieth Century Fox Film Corporation v South Australian Brewing Co Ltd* (1996) 66 FCR 451 ('the *Duff Beer* case') was concerned with the name 'Duff', which had acquired a powerful secondary meaning in relation to 'Duff Beer' as a result of the use of the name 'Duff Beer' in the television program 'The Simpsons'. Tamberlin J concluded (at 470) that the use by the respondents of the term 'Duff Beer' was misleading and deceptive as it [was] likely to lead to an assumption by consumers that permission had been given by 'The Simpsons' to the respondents to produce 'Duff Beer'. His Honour found (at 467) that the respondents' intention was 'to "sail as close as possible to the wind" in order to "cash in" on the reputation of 'The Simpsons' without stepping over the line of passing off or deceit' ...

59. Of course each case must depend on its own particular facts. In the present case the evidence establishes that as a result of the first Yellow Pages advertisement Dysart's 'Mr Goggomobil' had become a form of secondary branding for Yellow Pages when employed in the manner and context set out in the first Goggomobil advertisement ...

...

69. The real question for the Court in the present case is whether the manner and context in which Dysart and the Goggomobil were used by Shannons in the first Shannons advertisement represented that Yellow Pages had some association or connection with that advertisement or had endorsed or approved the services offered in it. It is to that question that I now turn.

70. The first Shannons advertisement was intended to 'overhaul the Shannons brand', 'broaden' Shannons appeal and to 'generate immediate telephone responses' by 'grab[bing] the attention of consumers very quickly'. Although the new advertisement was to look 'completely different' to the first Goggomobil advertisement those objectives would only be achieved if the new advertisement drew on the features of the first Goggomobil advertisement that provided 'instant recognition, understanding and high memorability'. Wilson Everard exercised considerable skill in reproducing those features and was thereby able to 'cut through the "clutter" of advertising' because of the memorability of the Yellow Pages Goggomobil advertising campaign. The features reproduced relate essentially to the similar manner and context in which Dysart and the Goggomobil are used in each advertisement. Both advertisements

feature the likeable and memorable character who would be instantly recognised as 'Mr Goggomobil', his unusual and distinctive motor vehicle ('the Goggomobil'), the use of the telephone to help solve a unique problem in relation to the Goggomobil and tell their similar stories in a humorous manner which is heavily reliant on Dysart's Scottish brogue and his pronunciation of 'Goggomobil' and some of the letters in that name ...

...

74. As observed above, whether the use of Mr Goggomobil and his Goggomobil vehicle to solve a problem by use of the telephone would result in secondary or suggestive brand advertising for Yellow Pages depends upon the manner and context in which that subject matter is employed. The extensive and significant contextual similarities between the first Goggomobil advertisement and the first Shannons advertisement and the manner in which Dysart and his Goggomobil have been used to ensure 'instant recognition' have led me to conclude that the first Shannons advertisement constitutes such secondary advertising. The difficulty that confronted Shannons is that it needed to appropriate the features that made the first Goggomobil advertisement both famous and popular, if it were to 'cut through the 'clutter' of advertising and gain the instant recognition and attention of the viewing public that it was seeking. Thus, the features that Shannons most desired to retain, and did retain, in the advertisement that was broadcast were the features that were most likely to result in the first advertisement being perceived by the relevant class of the public to be another Yellow Pages advertisement or to be in some other way connected or associated with Yellow Pages. Of course, the further Shannons moved away from those features (such as the other Shannons advertisements) the less likely its advertisement would be seen to have a connection with Yellow Pages. However, the problem for Shannons with that outcome is that it would lose the advantage of the instant recognition and response it was seeking from its first advertisement. That recognition and response was gained by Shannons recreating in its advertisement the features that gave the first Goggomobil advertisement the 'warmth, humour and familiarity' that made that advertisement so well-known, popular and memorable ... In particular, Shannons relied on re-creating the character of 'Mr Goggomobil' in a similar problem solving context ...

...

76. ... I am satisfied that the overall impression created by the showing of the first Shannons advertisement upon a significant portion of ordinary and reasonable members of the relevant class of the public was that Yellow Pages is in some way associated or connected with the advertisement or with locating the services offered in it. Accordingly, I am satisfied that the advertisement made a representation to that effect. While there would be doubt as to the precise form of the association or connection a significant segment of the relevant public would also be likely to conclude that the first Shannons advertisement is another Yellow Pages 'Mr Goggomobil' advertisement, but that he is now using his telephone to look for Shannons insurance, rather than a repairer, for his vehicle. The representations of association or connection I am satisfied were conveyed by the first Shannons advertisement 'cause more than mere wonderment or confusion [as to whether an association or connection exists] and travel into the areas of positive misrepresentation': see *Mark Foys Pty Ltd v TVSN (Pacific) Ltd* (2000) 104 FCR 61 at 77.

77. The most compelling argument of the respondents against a connection or association between the first Shannons advertisement and Yellow Pages is the absence of any Yellow Pages branding, and the presence of Shannons' branding, in the advertisement. It was argued that those features would leave the public in little doubt that this was an advertisement for Shannons insurance and not for Yellow Pages. There may be force in that argument if the viewing public consisted solely of persons

who had insured with Shannons or were aware of its specialised products. Those persons might have responded to the advertisement by regarding it as a clever use of the Yellow Pages advertisement in an advertisement by Shannons insurance. That view, however, is predicated upon those persons being well aware of Shannons and the unique role it plays in insuring 'special' vehicles. The problem with that view is that such persons only constitute a small segment of the viewing public and therefore their likely response to the advertisement provides no answer as to how the larger section of the relevant viewing public, which would not have an awareness of Shannons, might view it. Indeed, the advertisement was primarily targeting a section of the viewing public that was not aware of Shannons.

78. There is a further difficulty with the respondents' argument. While a viewer would appreciate that the policies of a particular insurer, Shannons, are being offered in the advertisement, that is not inconsistent with it also being a Yellow Pages advertisement or an advertisement with which Yellow Pages is in some way associated or connected. Yellow Pages customers are all businesses throughout Australia. There would be nothing anomalous about Yellow Pages advertising its services together with one of those businesses. The situation might be analogous to a restaurant directory entering into joint advertising with a restaurant which is an advertiser in that directory. Thus, the fact that the advertisement might be seen to have Shannons branding is not inconsistent with the secondary or suggestive branding that it is also a Yellow Pages advertisement or an advertisement with which Yellow Pages is in some way connected or associated.

79. For the above reasons I have concluded that the first Shannons advertisement misrepresents that it is also an advertisement by Yellow Pages or that Yellow Pages is in some way associated or connected with that advertisement or with locating the services offered in it. As Yellow Pages had no association or connection whatsoever with the advertisement or with those services, the making of the representation:

- contravened s 52 of the *TPA* because it was misleading or deceptive or likely to mislead or deceive; [and]
- established a critical element of the applicants' claim of passing off.

80. However, I do not regard the first Shannons advertisement as representing that the insurance services offered by Shannons are sponsored or approved by Yellow Pages. There is nothing in the context of the advertisement or in the secondary or suggestive brand advertising that I have found to exist that would constitute a representation by Yellow Pages relating to the quality of the services offered in the advertisement: cf *Mark Foys* at 77–78.

81. The reasons that led me to conclude that the first Shannons advertisement contains a secondary or suggestive brand connection or association with Yellow Pages are absent in respect of the second Shannons television advertisement and the Shannons radio advertisements. Those advertisements lack the context of the first Shannons advertisement which has given rise to a secondary or suggestive brand association with Yellow Pages. Although the advertisements rely upon 'Mr Goggomobil', his Scottish pronunciation and the insurance of a Goggomobil, they do not do so in the humorous and entertaining problem solving context of the first Shannons advertisement. As explained above, that problem solving context is an integral aspect of the first Shannons advertisement that has led me to conclude that there is a representation of connection or association with Yellow Pages. Accordingly, I am of the view that no representation has been made in the Shannons advertisements, other than the first Shannons advertisement, as to a connection or association with Yellow Pages. That conclusion, however, does not lead to the consequence that the other advertisements are irrelevant. It is clear that the first

CURRENT LAW

Shannons advertisement was a springboard for the introduction of the other advertisements with the consequence that their role might be relevant to the question of loss and damage (if any) suffered by the applicants by reason of the broadcast of the first Shannons advertisement. However, the other Shannons advertisements do not involve a misrepresentation and therefore the claims in relation to them must fail.

82. The respondents argued that the applicants' claims are misconceived insofar as they seek to claim some proprietary rights or goodwill in the character of 'Mr Goggomobil'. As explained above, I have not founded my decision in respect of the first Goggomobil advertisement on any such rights or goodwill. Indeed, my rejection of the applicants' claims in respect of the other Shannons advertisements is based upon my acceptance of the respondents' argument that the applicants do not have proprietary rights or goodwill in the character of 'Mr Goggomobil'. However, a different outcome attended the first Shannons advertisement because the context and the manner in which 'Mr Goggomobil' was used in that advertisement resulted in a representation of association or connection that does not exist.

Further difficult issues can also arise in cases where a defendant uses the image or likeness of a celebrity or a fictitious character, divorced from any commercial context in which that image or character has been or is normally employed, in order to advertise or sell the defendant's non-competing goods or services. In these cases of 'character' or 'personality' merchandising the only type of potential misrepresentation involved is that the defendant's activities have been approved or endorsed by the plaintiff. Australian courts (unhampered by a 'common field of activity' requirement for liability) have been prepared to find for plaintiffs in such circumstances in a number of cases. However, the precise basis on which this has been done has sometimes been elusive.

In *Hogan v Koala Dundee Pty Ltd* (1988) 20 FCR 314, actor Paul Hogan brought an action against the operator of a Gold Coast store called 'Dundee Country', whose marketing and merchandise featured a drawing of a koala wearing a sleeveless vest and a bush hat with teeth in the band and carrying a knife, such features being reminiscent of Hogan's Crocodile Dundee character. Pincus J was dismissive of the argument that the misrepresentation was that there was a licensing or sponsorship agreement between Hogan and the store, on the basis that consumers did not ordinarily think about such matters. Rather, his Honour thought that there had been a 'wrongful appropriation of a reputation or, more widely, wrongful association of goods with an image properly belonging to the applicant' (at 325), and accordingly found in favour of Hogan. The breadth of Pincus J's approach was criticised by Fisher J in *Tot Toys Ltd v Mitchell* [1993] 1 NZLR 325, who said at 362–363:

> It is not easy to see how the 'association of goods with an image properly belonging to the applicant' could be wrongful on any basis other than either a property right or the misrepresentation that the defendant had some form of association with those who stood behind the image. It cannot be false for the defendant to assert that his goods have some form of association with the image itself, divorced from its proprietors and their other property, if the association amounts to nothing more than joint appearance of the image and the defendant's product in the same advertisement. If it is a property right instead of a deception, where did it come from? It cannot be suggested that it came from passing off, since passing off requires deception ...

> It is not easy to escape the conclusion that on occasion the result in Australia may have sprung not so much from a finding of actual deception or independent damage as

the tacit assumption that there should be a right of property in names, reputations and artificial images for character-merchandising purposes. If the latter is the real aim, it might be questioned whether passing off is the best vehicle for achieving it. What of the obvious satirist, the obvious backyard copyist, or the advertiser who expressly disowns any association with the originator of the image? And what of the credibility of Courts if they are seen to strain towards a particular finding of fact in order to adapt an ill-fitting cause of action? Is it really necessary to force the square peg of character merchandising into the round hole of passing off?

Later Australian character merchandising cases have, however, shied away from the *Koala Dundee* approach and tended to focus more on consumer responses (i.e. whether consumers believed the plaintiff had consented to or authorised the use of the character or image, and whether they might change their behaviour as a result) in finding the existence of a misrepresentation.

CURRENT LAW

CASE EXTRACT: CURRENT LAW

Pacific Dunlop Ltd v Hogan

(1989) 23 FCR 553
Federal Court of Australia, Full Court

[Pacific Dunlop ran a 30-second television advertisement for its shoes, featuring a parody of the famous 'That's Not a Knife' scene in the 1986 movie *Crocodile Dundee*. The advertisement involved an actor who did not look like Paul Hogan but was dressed somewhat like the Crocodile Dundee character. Hogan sued in both passing off and for breach of s 52 of the *TPA*. At first instance, Gummow J found in favour of Hogan.]

Beaumont J (at 581–582): On behalf of the appellant, it was strongly submitted that, although the attention of consumers may have been 'grabbed' by reference to the film 'Crocodile Dundee', consumers were induced to buy by reason of the subsequent 'sales pitch', which, it was said, was a different thing. In my view, the distinction sought to be drawn is unlikely to be made by viewers. The thrust of the advertising is to identify the image of 'Crocodile Dundee' with the product to be sold. That image and [Pacific Dunlop]'s product are not portrayed as separate. On the contrary, the image is put forward as endorsing the product. The message conveyed is that Dundee is recommending the shoes.

It is true that the Dundee figure in the advertising does not appear to be the first respondent. But it does not follow that the image of 'Crocodile Dundee' is not projected as sponsoring the product. Viewers are given the impression that a variant of the Dundee figure is endorsing the shoes. The question for the judge was whether this impression would be seen as connected with the first respondent in a commercial context.

It was further argued on behalf of the appellant that the effect of [Gummow J's] decision would be to proscribe the use of parody in advertising or, indeed generally. But the essential question is whether the appellant has conveyed the message that the first respondent has agreed to an advertisement for the appellant's goods in which an image identified with the respondents is seen to endorse the goods … [T]here is a real distinction to be drawn between a 'mere' caricature on the one hand and a caricature 'embedded' in an advertisement on the other. The former is innocent because viewers would receive the impression that the person caricatured would not have agreed. The latter carries with it a different impression, favourable to the subject of the caricature, in which he or she is perceived as endorsing the object of the advertising … The Dundee figure, albeit a variant of the original image, is seen as sponsoring the appellant's shoes. The advertising is not a 'mere' caricature.

Burchett J (at 583–584): Character merchandising through television advertisements should not be seen as setting off a logical train of thought in the minds of television viewers. Its appeal is nothing like the insistence of a logical argument on behalf of a product, which may persuade, but also may repel. An association of some desirable character with the product proceeds more subtly to foster favourable inclination towards it, a good feeling about it, an emotional attachment to it. No logic tells the consumer that boots are better because Crocodile Dundee wears them for a few seconds on the screen … but the boots *are* better in his eyes, worn by his idol. The enhancement of the boots is not different in kind from the effect produced when an alpine pass makes a grander impact on the tourist whose mind's eye captures a vision of Hannibal urging elephants and men to scale it.

To ask whether the consumer reasons that Mr Hogan authorised the advertisement is therefore to ask a question which is a mere side issue, and far from the full impact of the advertisement. The consumer is moved by a desire to wear something belonging in some sense to Crocodile Dundee (who is perceived as a persona, almost an avatar, of Mr Hogan). The arousal of that feeling by Mr Hogan himself could not be regarded as misleading, for then the value he promises the product will have is not in its leather, but in its association with himself. When, however, an advertisement he did not authorise makes the same suggestion, it is misleading; for the product sold by that advertisement really lacks the one feature the advertisement attributes to it.

Sheppard J (dissenting) (at 571–572): I have reached the conclusion that viewers of the advertisement could not reasonably conclude that Mr Hogan had consented to or authorised the advertisement. In reaching this conclusion I have been much influenced by the very different advertising style used in the advertisements from the style used by Mr Hogan himself. That style or stamp is, in a sense, an essential part of his case, because, as I have endeavoured to show, it is that which in effect is claimed to have been damaged as a result of the showing of the advertisements. I have been influenced also by the weakness, from the respondents' point of view, of the lay evidence. It crossed the mind of only two of the seven members of the public who were called that Mr Hogan must, in some way, have approved of the advertisements. The three witnesses called in the appellant's case were firmly of the view that the showing of the advertisements did not imply consent. Two of the respondents' witnesses did not think about the matter until they were asked to do so by the solicitor who interviewed them. It seems to me that their reactions to his question reflected a vagueness and an uncertainty which militated against the evidence establishing that they were deceived or confused about the matter. I bear in mind that this evidence is by no means conclusive and that I have an obligation to reach my own conclusions about the matter. But the reactions of the seven witnesses called, although varied, accord with my own general reactions. The witness who expressed my own views closely was Mr Jedlin who thought the advertisement was terrible and that it could not have had anything to do with Mr Hogan.

One can understand the indignation which the respondents and their own advertising agents must have felt when they saw one of the well-known scenes from this most successful film adapted in this way. But the question is whether what was done constituted a misrepresentation. There being no question of copyright, no right of property is involved. The only question is whether the use made of the advertisements caused a significant number of people to be misled or at least confused.

As can be seen from the differences in opinion in *Pacific Dunlop*, not every use of a celebrity image or famous character (or variant) will necessarily constitute passing off: much will depend on the nature of the use and how consumers might be expected to respond. For example in *Newton-John v Scholl-Plough (Australia) Ltd* (1986) 11 FCR 233 the court accepted that consumers would understand the defendant's magazine advertisement (which used a model who looked like Olivia Newton-John, together with the prominently placed words: 'Olivia? No, it's Maybelline') to be referencing Olivia Newton-John's appearance, but would not understand the advertisement to be in any way authorised by her, such that no misrepresentation had occurred.

DAMAGE

The final element of Lord Oliver's classical trinity is damage to the plaintiff's reputation or goodwill as a result of the misrepresentation.

TYPES OF DAMAGE

The most obvious form of damage, particularly when the defendant's misrepresentation is as to origin, will be loss of business through diversion of trade. For example, in *Reckitt & Colman Products Ltd v Borden Inc* [1990] 1 WLR 491 the damage was the lost sales of the plaintiff's Jif lemon juice as a result of the defendant's conduct. Another recognisable head of damage is harm to reputation, in the sense that consumers might think less of the plaintiff's goods or services as a result of the defendant's misrepresentation (cases such as *AG Spalding & Bros v AW Gamage Ltd* (1915) 32 RPC 273 or *Testro Bros v Tennant* (1984) 2 IPR 469 are useful illustrations). A third type of damage is the loss of the ability to exploit reputation. For example, the plaintiff might be denied the opportunity to expand its business by providing new goods or services, or a foreign plaintiff might be pre-empted from trading in Australia under the name in which it has established a reputation (in which case there is an ongoing question about whether the plaintiff needs to establish an intention to commence trading in order to obtain a remedy: see *ConAgra Inc v McCain Foods (Aust) Pty Ltd* (1992) 33 FCR 302 at 343 (Lockhart J) and 372 (Gummow J)). Particular care is needed in the character and personality merchandising contexts. In *Henderson v Radio Corp Pty Ltd* [1960] NSWR 279, which involved the defendant having used a photo of the plaintiffs (who were famous ballroom dancers) on the cover of one of its dance music records, Evatt CJ and Myers J held at 285:

> Without the permission of the respondents, and without any other right or justification, the appellant has appropriated the professional reputation of the respondents for its own commercial ends. It claims that a court of equity has no power to restrain the appellant from falsely representing that the respondents recommend its products, unless the respondents can prove that their professional reputation has thereby been injured, or that in some other way their capacity to earn money by the practice of their profession has thereby been impaired. We do not think that is the law.
>
> It is true that the coercive power of the court cannot be invoked without proof of damage, but the wrongful appropriation of another's professional or business reputation is an injury in itself, no less, in our opinion, than the appropriation of his goods or money. The professional recommendation of the respondents was and still is theirs, to withhold or

bestow at will, but the appellant has wrongfully deprived them of their right to do so and of the payment or reward on which, if they had been minded to give their approval to the appellant's record, they could have insisted. In our opinion it is idle to contend that this wrongful appropriation is not an injury to the respondents. It is as much an injury as if the appellant had paid the respondents for their recommendation and then robbed them of the money. That injury, and the acknowledged intention to continue to inflict it, is ample justification for the injunction which was granted.

Given that a misrepresentation or misleading or deceptive conduct always needs to be established, this should be taken to suggest that once it is concluded that consumers are likely to change their behaviour as a consequence of the defendant's conduct (e.g. because they are more likely to purchase the defendant's goods because of the unauthorised endorsement), the loss of a licensing opportunity follows axiomatically.

A remaining question is the extent to which 'dilution' of the plaintiff's mark (i.e. where some diminution in the value of the mark might occur, but where no change in consumer behaviour can be established) might be recognised as a stand-alone head of damage under Australian law. This issue has proven to be controversial in the UK, as discussed in the extract below.

CASE EXTRACT: COMPARATIVE LAW

Harrods Ltd v Harrodian School Ltd

[1996] RPC 697
Court of Appeal of England and Wales

[The owners of the Harrods department store sought to restrain the defendants from operating a preparatory school under the name 'The Harrodian School' (famous alumni of which have since included Robert Pattinson and Tom Sturridge). The trial judge and a majority of the Court of Appeal held that there was no misrepresentation, with Millet LJ holding (at 713) that it is not sufficient 'to demonstrate that there must be a connection of some kind between the defendant and the plaintiff, if it is not a connection which would lead the public to suppose that the plaintiff has made himself responsible for the quality of the defendant's goods or services'. The Court of Appeal also considered the issue of damage.]

Millet LJ (with whom Beldam LJ agreed) (at 715–718): In *Taittinger SA v Allbev Ltd* [1993] FSR 641 the [Court of Appeal] appears to have recognised a different head of damage. If the defendants were allowed to market their product under the name Elderflower Champagne

> there would take place a blurring or erosion of the uniqueness that now attends the word 'champagne', so that the exclusive reputation of the champagne houses would be debased ...

It is self-evident that the application of the plaintiff's brand name to inferior goods is likely to injure the plaintiff's reputation and damage his goodwill if people take the inferior goods to be those of the plaintiff. That is a classic head of damage in cases of passing off. But Peter Gibson LJ may have had more in mind than this. He referred without disapproval to the submission of Counsel for the plaintiffs that if the defendants were allowed to continue to call their product Elderflower Champagne the effect would be to demolish the distinctiveness of the word champagne, and that would inevitably damage the goodwill of the champagne houses.

This is a reference to the debasement of the distinctiveness of the name champagne which would occur if it gradually came to be used by the public as a generic term to describe any kind of sparkling wine. Erosion of the distinctiveness of a brand name has been recognised as a form of damage to the goodwill of the business with which the name is connected in a number of cases ... but unless care is taken this could mark an unacceptable extension to the tort of passing off. To date the law has not sought to protect the value of the brand name as such, but the value of the goodwill which it generates; and it insists on proof of confusion to justify its intervention. But the erosion of the distinctiveness of a brand name which occurs by reason of its degeneration into common use as a generic term is not necessarily dependent on confusion at all. The danger that if the defendant's product was called champagne then all sparkling wines would eventually come to be called champagne would still exist even if no one was deceived into thinking that such wine really was champagne. I have an intellectual difficulty in accepting the concept that the law insists upon the presence of both confusion and damage and yet recognises as sufficient a head of damage which does not depend on confusion. Counsel for the Plaintiffs relied strongly on the possibility of damage of this nature, but it is in my opinion not necessary to consider it further in the present case. There is no danger of 'Harrods' becoming a generic term for a retail emporium in the luxury class, and if such a danger existed the use of a different name in connection with an institution of a different kind would not advance the process ...

[E]ven if there is scope for some limited confusion to linger in the public mind, the Plaintiffs have not discharged the heavy burden of establishing a real likelihood of more than minimal damage to the Plaintiffs' goodwill. I ask myself what would happen if the Defendants' school were to go bankrupt or suffer a drug or sex scandal. The attendant publicity might temporarily tarnish Harrods' good name; but I cannot see any real danger that a material number of Harrods' customers would withdraw their custom. Anyone who was under the mistaken impression that Harrods was responsible for the school would surely say to himself: 'They obviously have no idea how to run a school. I always thought they were foolish to try; a cobbler should stick to his last. But they run an excellent store. This won't stop me shopping there.' Damage to goodwill is not confined to loss of custom, but damage to reputation without damage to goodwill is not sufficient to support an action for passing off.

Since we reserved judgment on this appeal [the director of the school] has dismissed his wife as headmistress and accused her of having committed adultery with the English Master, who has resigned. The affair has been widely reported. We allowed the plaintiffs to put the press reports in evidence. The publicity must at least temporarily have damaged the reputation of the school and may cause it some loss of custom. But the evidence does not affect my conclusion, since I have already considered the possibility that there might be a sex or drug scandal at the school and dismissed the suggestion that the attendant publicity would be likely to cause damage to Harrods' commercial goodwill.

Sir Michael Kerr (dissenting) (at 724–726): In the great majority of cases the relevant damage will not be measurable in pounds and pence, but consist in the probability of damage to the plaintiff's reputation and goodwill which is ultimately liable to lead indirectly to a reduction in trade. Loss of distinctiveness causes damage to a reputation for excellence, and loss of trade will ultimately follow. The authorities show two relevant propositions in this regard. First, a debasement or dilution of the plaintiff's reputation, as the result of the action of the defendant, is a relevant head of damage. Secondly, if the act which constitutes the passing-off has the effect of raising in people's minds the mistaken belief of a connection between the defendant and the plaintiff, but which is in fact non-existent, then the court will have regard to the fact that the plaintiff has, to that extent, lost control of his reputation, and that he has therefore suffered damage to his goodwill by a potentially injurious association with the defendant against which the court will protect him by injunction …

[I]f the continued use of the name by the defendants is permitted in the present case, then it seems highly likely that it would proliferate. There would then be nothing to prevent [the director of the school] from also giving this name to his school in Putney and thereafter perhaps to other schools as well. The free use of the name might then spawn Harrodian garages, newsagents and other businesses, and even a moneylender might emerge under this name …

DAMAGE AND REMEDIES

To obtain an award of more than nominal damages a plaintiff must show it has suffered actual damage by reason of the erroneous belief engendered by the defendant's misrepresentation.[14] Similarly, a person seeking damages for contravention of s 18 of the ACL will only be entitled to an award of damages under s 236 of the ACL (formerly s 82 of the *TPA*) if that person has in fact suffered loss or damage by reason of the defendant's conduct. If the plaintiff seeks injunctive relief for passing off, it will need to show at least the likelihood of such damage as a result of the defendant's actual or proposed conduct. A court can grant an injunction under ss 232 and 234 of the ACL to restrain conduct in contravention of s 18 even where there is no 'imminent danger of substantial damage', but it would be rare for a defendant to engage in a misrepresentation which did not result in even a likelihood of one of the forms of damage outlined above.

We have already seen that 'fraud'—in the sense of an intention to deceive—can be important in establishing whether a misrepresentation has occurred. It appears to be the case that a plaintiff seeking either an award of damages or an account of profits for passing off will also need to show 'fraud' on the part of the defendant (there is no such requirement where the plaintiff seeks injunctive relief). What 'fraud' might involve in this context is set out below.

CASE EXTRACT: CURRENT LAW

ConAgra Inc v McCain Foods (Aust) Pty Ltd

(1992) 33 FCR 302
Federal Court of Australia, Full Court

[The basic facts of the case are set out at p 638 above.]

Gummow J (at 363–364): A defendant originally may have adopted a mark honestly and innocently, either in ignorance of the existence of the plaintiff's mark or in the belief that his mark was so different

---

14 See for example *Henderson v Radio Corp Pty Ltd* [1960] NSWR 279.

from that of the plaintiff as not to be calculated to mislead purchasers. But the authorities establish that, in such a case, the continuing use of the mark after awareness that its use does cause the goods of the defendants to be mistaken for those of the plaintiff is no less fraudulent in the eye of the court than user with an original fraudulent intent …

It may be that even after notice of the plaintiff's rights the defendant does not intend to deceive purchasers of his goods by representing those goods to be the goods of the plaintiff. Nevertheless, if the defendant shuts his eyes as to the reasonable consequences, upon facts known to him, of what he is doing, then there would be grounds upon which a jury might make a finding of fraud in the full sense …

I have referred to the evolution in the 19th century of the doctrine that in a passing-off case equity would intervene by injunction in aid of the plaintiff's proprietary rights. At that time and thereafter, it was generally accepted that where legal (as distinct from equitable) rights were at stake, 'the foundation of the jurisdiction to grant an injunction is the existence of some civil right of a proprietary nature proper to be protected': *Cameron v Hogan* (1934) 51 CLR 358 at 377 … So it is not surprising that as regards the passing-off action which at law was a variant of a claim in deceit, Chancery strove to put its intervention on a proprietary basis …

The result of these developments in the law is that in a passing-off suit a successful plaintiff may elect for his pecuniary remedy between an account of profits and an inquiry as to damages; if the defendant embarked upon his activities fraudulently, these remedies run from that time. But in any event, even if the defendant was at that stage innocent, pecuniary remedies will be available for the period of the defendant's persistence after notice of the plaintiff's rights, in the manner described in the authorities.

This has the consequence that in circumstances where damages would be available for contravention of s 52 of the *Trade Practices Act 1974*, nevertheless in passing-off no pecuniary remedy may be available. Section 82 of the statute operates to give a remedy in damages for what in substance may be an innocent and non-negligent misrepresentation. As Gibbs CJ pointed out in *Parkdale Custom Built Furniture Pty Ltd v Puxu Pty Ltd* (1982) 149 CLR 191 at 197, the statutory liability is unrelated to fault. An appreciation of this may underlie some essays into restrictive interpretations of s 52.

[Lockhart J agreed that, historically, fraud needed to be shown for an award of more than nominal damages, but chose not to express an opinion as to whether this remained the case (at 345). French J expressed no view on the issue.]

In the UK there no longer appears to be an 'innocence defence' to an award of more than nominal damages in an action in passing off: *Gillette UK Ltd v Edenwest Ltd* [1994] RPC 279.

As a separate and final point, s 230(2) of the *TMA* provides that in a passing off action damages may not be awarded against a defendant who uses its own registered trade mark, was unaware at the time of the action that the plaintiff's mark was in use, and who, when it became aware of the plaintiff's mark, immediately ceased using the mark. This 'defence' is not, however, available to actions for contravention of consumer protection legislation and is thus, in practice, largely redundant.

——17——

REGISTERED TRADE MARKS: PROCEDURAL AND SUBSTANTIVE REQUIREMENTS FOR REGISTRATION

INTRODUCTION

In this chapter we consider the requirements for registering a trade mark under Australian law. This involves a detailed consideration of various provisions of the *Trade Marks Act 1995* (Cth) (*TMA*) and *Trade Marks Regulations 1995* (Cth) (*TMR*), as well as cases that have interpreted those provisions or similar provisions under former legislation such as the *Trade Marks Act 1955* (Cth) and *Trade Marks Act 1905* (Cth).

TYPES OF TRADE MARKS

Under s 17 of the *TMA*:

> A *trade mark* is a sign used, or intended to be used, to distinguish goods or services dealt with or provided in the course of trade by a person from goods or services so dealt with or provided by any other person.

As French CJ, Gummow, Crennan and Bell JJ explained in *E & J Gallo Winery v Lion Nathan Australia Pty Ltd* [2010] HCA 15; (2010) 241 CLR 144 at [42]:

> Whilst that definition contains no express reference to the requirement, to be found in s 6(1) of the *Trade Marks Act 1955* (Cth), that a trade mark indicate 'a connexion in the course of trade' between the goods and the owner, the requirement that a trade mark 'distinguish' goods encompasses the orthodox understanding that one function of a trade mark is to indicate the origin of 'goods to which the mark is applied'. Distinguishing goods of a registered owner from the goods of others and indicating a connection in the course of trade between the goods and the registered owner are essential characteristics of a trade mark. There is nothing in the relevant Explanatory Memorandum to suggest that s 17 was to effect any change in the orthodox understanding of the function or essential characteristics of a trade mark.

In other words, a trade mark is something that operates as a 'badge of origin', allowing consumers to recognise that the goods or services in respect of which the mark is used are produced by or under the control of a particular trader. The requirements that a trade mark be a 'sign', and that it be 'used' for the purpose of 'distinguishing' goods and services, are key elements of trade mark law, and will be discussed in more detail in both this and the following chapter.

It is worth briefly mentioning that three other types of trade mark can potentially be registered under the *TMA*.

First, *collective trade marks* are signs that are used, or intended to be used, in relation to goods or services provided in the course of trade by *members of an association* to distinguish those goods or services from goods or services provided by persons who are not members of the association (see Part 15 of the *TMA*).

The second category consists of *certification trade marks*. These are signs used, or intended to be used, to distinguish goods or services provided in the course of trade that have been *certified* by a person or organisation in relation to such things as quality, accuracy or some other characteristic, including origin, material or mode of manufacture, from goods or services that have not been so certified. Famous examples include the 'Australia Made' kangaroo-within-a-triangle logo and the Heart Foundation 'tick' (see Part 16 of the *TMA*).

The third category consists of *defensive trade marks*. Where a mark is registered in relation to certain goods and services, and the owner can show that if that mark were to be used on other goods or services such use would indicate a connection between those other goods or services and the owner, such a mark may be separately registered in relation to those other goods or services as a defensive trade mark. Unlike standard trade marks, there is no requirement that defensive trade marks be used in relation to those other goods or services (see Part 17 of the *TMA*).

In this and the following chapter, we will focus on the law relating to standard trade marks.

THE REGISTRATION PROCESS
APPLICATION FOR REGISTRATION

The application process for registration of a standard trade mark starts with ss 27–29 of the *TMA* and Part 4 of the *TMR*. Applications are made to the Australian Trade Marks Office, a division of IP Australia. The Office sets out detailed guidelines concerning the application process in its *Trade Marks Office Manual of Practice and Procedure*.[1]

Under s 27(1), a person may apply for registration of a trade mark in relation to particular goods and services if:

(a) the person claims to be the owner of the trade mark; and

(b) one of the following applies:

(i) the person is using or intends to use the trade mark in relation to the goods and/or services;

(ii) the person has authorised or intends to authorise another person to use the trade mark in relation to the goods and/or services;

(iii) the person intends to assign the trade mark to a body corporate that is about to be constituted with a view to the use by the body corporate of the trade mark in relation to the goods and/or services.

---

1   Available at www.ipaustralia.gov.au/pdfs/trademarkmanual/trade_marks_examiners_manual.htm.

The application must be in approved form (see s 27(2) and regs 4.1–4.2). It must contain a *representation* of the mark and must specify the goods and services in respect of which registration is sought, in accordance with the regulations (known as the *specification*) (s 27(3)). The representation and the specification are crucial aspects of the application because, in large part, they determine the scope of the application and of any resulting rights in the registered mark.

Regulation 4.3 sets out further requirements as to the form of the representation (including special provisions where the mark is a shape, colour, sound or scent). Regulation 4.4 provides further detail about the specification, including the following two requirements:

(3) The goods and/or services must be grouped according to the appropriate classes described in Schedule 1.

(4) The applicant must nominate the class number that is appropriate to the goods or services in each group.

The Office uses the International Classification of Goods and Services, which was agreed to at the Nice Diplomatic Conference, for this purpose. Under the Nice system, all goods and services are classified in one of 45 classes (set out in Sch 1 to the *TMR*). Each class covers a different category of (often related) goods or services. The system is primarily an administrative tool that simplifies searching for trade marks.

For most applications, the filing date of the application becomes the *priority date* (see ss 6(1), 12 and 72). This date is crucial in determining, among other things, the marks against which the application is assessed. For applications based on an earlier application in a 'Convention country' (i.e. a member of the *Paris Convention for the Protection of Industrial Property* (1883)), the priority date becomes the date of the earlier application (s 29).

EXAMINATION

Under s 31, a delegate of the Registrar (known as an examiner) will examine and report on the application as to whether:

- it has been made in accordance with the *TMA*; for the most part this involves considering whether the application complies with the requirements in ss 27–28 and the associated regulations; most commonly, this involves determining whether the goods and services have been correctly classified (see also s 32), but might also involve a consideration of whether the application is in fact for a 'trade mark' as defined in s 17; and
- there are any grounds for rejecting the application; the grounds for rejection are set out in ss 39–44 and reg 4.15A; in short, these are that the trade mark:
  - contains or consists of certain prescribed or prohibited signs (s 39);
  - cannot be represented graphically (s 40);
  - is not capable of distinguishing the owner's goods or services from those of other traders (s 41);
  - contains or consists of scandalous matter (s 42(a));
  - would, if used, be contrary to law (s 42(b));
  - contains a connotation such that its use is likely to deceive or cause confusion (s 43); or
  - is substantially identical with or deceptively similar to an earlier registered mark or application in relation to similar or closely related goods and/or services (subject to questions of honest

concurrent use of the two marks, or whether the applicant can show prior continuous use of its mark) (s 44 and reg 4.15A)).

If the examiner does not form a 'reasonable belief' that one of the above grounds for rejection exists or that the application has not been made in accordance with the Act, it must accept the application for registration (reg 4.8 and s 33(1)). If the examiner does form such a belief, the applicant has a period of time (initially 15 months) in which to respond, otherwise its application will lapse (s 37). The applicant may seek to argue its case informally (i.e. through correspondence with the examiner) or put in evidence to overcome a ground of objection (reg 4.9). If the examiner continues to maintain its belief, the applicant can try again. If an impasse is reached, the examiner will issue a Notice of Intention to Reject. The applicant then has two months to make a further response or to request either a decision on the written record or a hearing before a delegate of the Registrar (s 33(4)). If the applicant does not respond, or makes further unpersuasive submissions but does not request a hearing, or is unsuccessful at the hearing, the application must be rejected (s 33(3)). The applicant may appeal the Registrar's decision to the Federal Court (s 35).

ACCEPTANCE AND OPPOSITION

If the application is accepted under s 33(1):

- that fact is advertised in the *Official Journal of Trade Marks* (s 34); and
- a third party has two months from the date of advertisement in which to file a notice of intention to oppose the registration (s 52(2) and reg 5.6) and a further month within which to file a statement of grounds and particulars (reg 5.7); the grounds on which an opposition can be made are:
  - any of the grounds on which the application could have been rejected, except for s 40 (i.e. the grounds set out in ss 39, 41–44 and reg 4.15A) (s 57);
  - that the applicant is not the owner of the mark (s 58);
  - that where the application was accepted on the basis of the applicant's prior continuous use under s 44(4), the opponent can show earlier continuous use of the mark (s 58A);
  - that the applicant does not intend to use or authorise the use of the mark in Australia or to assign the mark to a body corporate for use in Australia (s 59);
  - that an earlier mark had acquired a reputation in Australia before the applicant's priority date and for that reason the applicant's use of its mark would be likely to deceive or cause confusion (s 60);
  - that the trade mark contains a false geographical indication (s 61);
  - that the application was amended contrary to the *TMA* (s 62(a));
  - that the application was accepted on the basis of false evidence (s 62(b)); or
  - that the application was made in bad faith (s 62A).

Both parties have certain periods of time within which to lodge evidence in support of their positions (see regs 5.14–5.15), and both are afforded the opportunity to be heard on the opposition before a delegate of the Registrar, called a hearing officer (see s 54). At the end of the opposition proceedings, the hearing officer must decide whether to refuse to register the mark or to register it (s 55). Either party may appeal this decision to the Federal Court (s 56).

At any time before registration, under s 38 the Registrar can revoke acceptance if satisfied that the application should not have been accepted and it is reasonable to revoke the acceptance. The consequence of such revocation is that the application must be re-examined.

REGISTRATION, RENEWAL AND LOSS OF RIGHTS

Once the opposition period expires, or if an opposition is unsuccessful, the Registrar must register the mark (s 68). This is done by entering certain particulars in the Register (s 69). The Office provides a searchable online database of registered marks (as well as applications for registration and many marks taken off the Register) called ATMOSS (the Australian Trade Mark Online Search System).[2]

Trade mark protection takes effect from the earliest priority date (s 72(1)–(2)) and lasts for 10 years from the filing date (s 72(3)). Registered trade marks can be renewed under s 75 on the payment of renewal fees. Thus, trade mark protection is potentially perpetual.

However, the registration of a mark can be amended or cancelled, or the mark removed from the Register, in a range of circumstances set out in Parts 8 and 9 of the *TMA*. Three provisions are worth emphasising here:

- under s 84A, the Registrar may *revoke* the registration of a mark within one year from registering that mark on much the same basis that acceptance of the mark could have been revoked under s 38; this, in effect, allows the Registrar in limited circumstances to reconsider whether the application was made in accordance with the Act (see s 31(a)) and whether any of the grounds of rejection at the examination stage should have been raised (see ss 39–44 and reg 4.15A), as well as any unsuccessful grounds of opposition (see ss 58–62A).
- under s 88(2), on the application of an 'aggrieved person' a registration may be *cancelled* on a number of grounds, including:
  - any of the grounds on which the registration of the mark could have been opposed (s 88(2)(a)); and
  - the further ground that because of the circumstances applying at the time when the application for cancellation is filed, the use of the trade mark is likely to deceive or cause confusion (s 88(2)(c)).
- under s 92(4) a trade mark can be *removed* from the Register on the basis of non-use. This can occur either where the applicant did not intend to use the mark at the time of the application and has never in good faith used the mark, or where the owner has not made good faith use of the mark in a particular three-year period.

These grounds will be considered in more detail in Chapter 18.

THE DEFINITION OF A TRADE MARK: A 'SIGN'

As indicated above, under s 17 of the *TMA* a 'trade mark' is 'a sign used, or intended to be used, to distinguish goods or services dealt with or provided in the course of trade by a person from goods or

---

2   Online at www.ipaustralia.gov.au (select menu tab 'Trade Marks', then 'Search for a trade mark', then the ATMOSS link).

services so dealt with or provided by any other person.' What then is meant by a 'sign'? This is defined in s 6(1) of the *TMA* as including:

> the following or any combination of the following, namely, any letter, word, name, signature, numeral, device, brand, heading, label, ticket, aspect of packaging, shape, colour, sound or scent.

The vast majority of signs that make up trade marks are either words (which can be used in any format) or what are known as 'devices'. The latter might be words represented in a particular stylised manner (such as 'Coca-Cola', represented in its famous script), combinations of text and graphic elements (such as the BMW logo), or logos without any textual elements (such as the Nike 'swoosh'). However, the definition of a sign encompasses other indicia, such as shapes, colours, sounds and smells, which when used in relation to goods and services might be recognised as indicating the trade origin of those goods and services. For example, the Coca-Cola Co has registered the 'contour' shape of its Coke bottle, and Cadbury has secured registration for the colour purple for chocolate, while Intel has obtained a trade mark over the five-note jingle that plays in its advertisements. Indeed, the definition of a 'sign' in s 6 is open-ended: indicia such as tastes, textures, moving images and gestures can potentially be registered as trade marks. The concept does have some limits: for example a mere concept or idea would be unlikely to constitute a 'sign' under Australian law. In Case C-321/03, *Dyson Ltd v Registrar of Trade Marks* [2007] ECR I-693, the Court of Justice of the European Communities held that Dyson's application for trade mark registration of 'a transparent bin or collection chamber forming part of the external surface of a vacuum cleaner', not limited to any particular shape or form, could not be registered because there was no 'sign' described in the application.

The relatively recent acceptance of shapes, colours and other more exotic indicia as being potentially registrable trade marks raises a number of difficult issues. The most important relates to the possible effects on competition in a market if one trader is allowed to monopolise a shape (either of aspects of packaging, or of the goods themselves), or a particular colour that has certain associations. A related issue is whether a distinction needs to be drawn between the 'mark' and the 'goods' to which the mark is applied, in order to ensure that the 'natural' or 'inherent' form of goods, or a feature of the goods that performs a particular function, cannot be the subject of a trade mark registration.

How some of the above issues intersect can be seen in the following extract.

CASE EXTRACT: CURRENT LAW

Kenman Kandy Australia Pty Ltd v Registrar of Trade Marks

[2002] FCAFC 273; (2002) 122 FCR 494
Federal Court of Australia, Full Court

[This case involved an attempt to register a 'bug' shape of a piece of confectionary, set out on p 702.]

Stone J: 129. Nothing in this definition [of 'sign' in s 6] in any way detracts from the crucial requirement that the 'sign', be it shape, colour or anything else, must have the capacity to distinguish one trader's goods from another's; see Burchett J in *Koninklijke Philips Electronics NV v Remington Products*

Australia Pty Ltd (2000) 100 FCR 90 at [15] ('*Philips v Remington (Aust), FC*'). Similarly, the Act does not distinguish between the criteria that apply to determine whether a shape has the requisite capacity and those that apply to any other element referred to in the definition of sign.

130. Despite this, the current state of the authorities suggests that there is a particular problem concerning the registrability of a shape trade mark, namely whether it is necessary that a trade mark be able to be described and depicted as something separate and apart from the goods in relation to which it is to be used and, if so, whether this is possible for a shape which is the whole shape of a good (the 'separation issue'). This issue sometimes appears to be quite separate from the issue of inherent adaptation and sometimes an element of that issue.

SEPARATION OF TRADE MARK FROM GOODS

131. The separation issue was articulated by Windeyer J in *Smith Kline and French Laboratories (Australia) Ltd v Registrar of Trade Marks* (1967) 116 CLR 628 ('*Smith Kline*'). This was an appeal from a decision of the Registrar of Trade Marks refusing to accept for registration certain applications relating to medicinal capsules, one half of which was opaque and coloured and the other half, transparent and colourless. The capsules contained different coloured granules or pellets that gave a speckled appearance to the transparent part of the capsule. According to Windeyer J, the applicant wanted to register 'the total appearance of its capsules' and thus obtain a monopoly for the sale of 'parti-coloured capsules containing pellets of different colours'. In an ex tempore judgment his Honour said this (at 639–640):

> A trade mark is defined in the [*Trade Marks Act 1955*] as 'a mark used or proposed to be used in relation to goods' for the purposes stated. This definition assumes, it seems to me, that the mark is something distinct from the goods in relation to which it is used or to be used. It assumes that the goods can be conceived as something apart from the mark and that the mark is not of the essence of the goods. The goods are assumed to have an existence independently of the mark … A thing can always be described and distinguished in appearance by any visible characteristic which it has, its shape, colour or any mark which it bears. But the test is not—Can the goods be described or depicted without reference to their markings? As I see it, a mark for the purposes of the Act must be capable of being described and depicted as something apart from the goods to which it is to be applied, or in relation to which it is to be used … It accords … with the various things included in the definition of 'mark'. That list is not expressed as exhaustive but it is certainly illustrative. I do not think that a mere description of goods simply by shape, size or colour can be a trade mark in respect of those goods.

132. It would seem from Windeyer J's subsequent comments that his Honour regarded the separation issue as distinct from the issue of capacity to distinguish. In the context of legislation that, at the time, did not permit the registration of shape trade marks this is not surprising.

133. In *Philips v Remington (Aust), FC* the separation issue was also taken up by Burchett J (with whom Hill and Branson JJ agreed) although in this case it seems to have been seen, at least in part, as an element of capacity to distinguish. Unlike *Smith Kline*, *Philips v Remington (Aust), FC* was decided under the provisions of the 1995 Act, that is after the definition 'trade mark' was amended to refer to a 'sign' rather than a 'mark' and after the word 'shape' was included in the definition of 'sign'. The case concerned trade marks registered by Philips in relation to a rotary shaver, the design of which involved

three cutters in a triangular head. Philips claimed these trade marks had been infringed by a Remington shaver that used a similar triple head configuration.

DID THE 1995 ACT EFFECT A RADICAL CHANGE TO TRADE MARK LAW?

134. Burchett J stated, at [15], that the changes in the 1995 Act were not intended to effect a radical change in trade mark law and concluded that a shape that goods possessed 'because of their nature' or because of the need for a 'particular technical result' could not function as a trade mark because such a shape could not distinguish the trade source. His Honour went on to say, at [16], that he did not regard this as precluding the shape of goods being registered as a trade mark where the shape is the whole or part of the relevant goods, but added,

> But that is not to say that the 1995 Act has invalidated what Windeyer J said in *Smith Kline*. The special cases where a shape of the goods may be a mark are cases falling within, not without, the principle he expounded. For they are cases where the shape that is a mark is 'extra', added to the inherent form of the particular goods as something distinct which can denote origin. The goods can still be seen as having, in Windeyer J's words, 'an existence independently of the mark' which is imposed upon them.
>
> The conclusion of this discussion is not that the addition of the word 'shape' to the statutory definition calls for some new principle, or that a 'shape' mark is somehow different in nature from other marks, but that a mark remains something 'extra' added to distinguish the products of one trader from those of another, a function which plainly cannot be performed by a mark consisting of either a word or shape other traders may legitimately wish to use.

135. In considering Burchett J's views it is important to appreciate the context in which those views were formed and the policy concerns expressed by his Honour. In the opening words of his judgment Burchett J made this comment:

> A fundamental issue of trade mark law is involved in this appeal. Under the new *Trade Marks Act 1995* (Cth), can a permanent monopoly for a product be obtained by the registration as a mark of a representation of one of its *vital* features? If a shield against all competition can be raised in that way, the proprietor of the mark will be in a better position than a patentee or the proprietor of a registered design, each of whom has a protection limited to the span of a relatively short time. [emphasis added]

His Honour then quoted from *Philips Electronics NV v Remington Consumer Products* (1997) 40 IPR 279 ('*Philips v Remington (Eng)*') in which Jacob J, considering a similar dispute between Philips and Remington, expressed the same concern. Jacob J, at 290, stated that the case involved:

> the extent to which trade mark law, conferring a perpetual monopoly, can interfere with the freedom … of manufacturers to make an artefact of a desirable and good engineering design.

136. The issue of function was of great significance in the dispute between Philips and Remington that surfaced in a number of jurisdictions. In *Philips v Remington (Eng)*, Jacob J was quite explicit about this aspect. His Honour accepted that it was possible to make an effective rotary shaver that would be outside the scope of the trade mark protection but stated, at 287–288:

> However, it is also the case that the engineering scope for variation outside the trade mark is very limited. Moreover the three-headed shape of the present Philips design is one of the best ways possible of making a rotary shaver …

So, if Philips are right, they will have obtained a permanent monopoly in respect of matters of significant engineering design by virtue of a trade mark registration.

137. The concerns expressed in both *Philips v Remington (Aust), FC* and *Philips v Remington (Eng)* about the prospect of trade marks creating monopolies related only to the registration of trade marks that would restrict access to functional features or innovations, and for this reason were well founded. It is this concern that finds expression in the requirement that a trade mark be something added to the inherent form of goods. The 'inherent form' of goods, in my view, can only refer to those aspects of form that have functional significance. Were the 1995 Act to enable the registration of a trade mark that would give the owner a monopoly over functional features it would indeed have made a radical change to trade mark law. There is nothing in the 1995 Act or in the discussions that preceded it to suggest that this was intended ...

138. In *Philips v Remington (Aust), FC* Burchett J noted, at [15], that the trial judge, Lehane J had expressed a similar view concerning the impact of the 1995 Act (see *Koninklijke Philips Electronics NV v Remington Products Australia Pty Ltd* (1999) 91 FCR 167). It is useful to consider the whole of the passage, at [26], in which Lehane J expressed his opinion:

> One clear impression left by [the history of the 1995 amendments] is that it was not thought that the inclusion of 'shape' in the definition of 'sign' would effect a radical change in trade mark law. Undoubtedly, however, the Working Party recommendation proceeded on the basis that 'shape' included the shape of goods, or of part of them ... The 1994 Act plainly proceeded on the basis that 'shape' was to include the shape of the goods. And nothing in the explanatory memorandum or in the Minister's speech suggests that substantially the same definition of 'sign' in the 1995 Act was intended to operate differently. In short, the legislative history, I think, suggests nothing to the contrary of, but rather offers some support for, what I think is the natural meaning of the word 'shape' included in the definition of 'sign': it includes the shape of goods, or of part of them, in relation to which a sign of that kind is used.

139. Earlier in his reasons his Honour, referring to the views expressed by Windeyer J in *Smith Kline* said (at [19]):

> But if 'shape' does not include the shape of goods, or of a part of goods, within the class for which a trade mark is registered, it is not easy to see what 'shape' adds to 'device'; it hardly seems a sensible construction to limit 'colour' or 'scent' to a colour or scent used in relation to goods, but not as the colour or scent of the goods, or part of the goods, themselves; and if that is so in relation to 'colour' and 'scent', why should 'shape' be construed in a more limited way? One possible limitation, perhaps, might be to read 'shape' as limited to the get-up of the goods, not extending to the goods themselves ... but to limit 'shape' in that way would give it no field of operation not already covered by 'aspect of packaging'.

140. I agree that the 1995 Act was not intended to make the radical change of providing for registration of a trade mark that would have the effect of restricting access to functional features or innovations. The policy concerns expressed by Burchett J were relevant to the issues considered in *Philips v Remington (Aust), FC*, because that case was concerned with functional features.

[The outcome of this case is considered in detail in a later extract (see p 702) on the issue of 'distinctiveness' under s 41 of the *TMA*, which has also been used to prevent the registration of 'functional' marks.]

In other jurisdictions a more direct approach is taken to ensure that 'functional' marks cannot be registered. For example, the *European Trade Marks Directive 2008/95/EC* excludes from registrability shapes 'which result from the nature of the goods themselves', which are 'necessary to achieve a technical result' or which give 'substantial value to the goods' (Art 3(1)(e)). US law goes further in excluding from protection *all* signs that perform a technical or aesthetic function (15 USC §1052(e)(5) and (f)). This 'functionality' doctrine has been used not only in relation to functional shapes but also to deny protection for a flavour used to disguise the taste of medicine (*In re NV Organon*, 79 USPQ 2d 1639 (TTAB, 2006)) and to prevent registration of the sound emitted by a personal attack alarm (*In re Vertex Group LLC*, 89 USPQ 2d 1694 (TTAB, 2009)).[3]

EXAMINATION, OPPOSITION AND CANCELLATION GROUNDS: AN OVERVIEW

We now turn to the grounds on which an application for registration of a standard mark may be rejected (either at the examination stage and/or on the basis of a successful opposition), or on which the registration of a mark may be cancelled. These can be grouped into two broad categories.

One category consists of what can be called *relative grounds*. These are grounds involving potential conflicts between the applicant's mark and an earlier registered or unregistered mark, or where another party has better title to the applicant's mark. There are seven such grounds. These are contained in ss 44 (read with s 58A), 60, 42(b), 43, 58, 62A and 61. The other category consists of *absolute grounds*—that is, grounds that do not involve such conflicts, but where there is some other inherent problem with the mark or application. We consider 10 such grounds, contained in ss 41, 39, 40, 42(a), 42(b), 43, 59, 62A, 62(a) and 62(b). This latter category will be considered first.

ABSOLUTE GROUNDS OF REFUSAL
DISTINCTIVENESS

As we have seen, a trade mark by definition is a sign that is used to distinguish goods and services from those of other traders. Whether a mark has the capacity to fulfil this function is assessed under s 41 of the *TMA*.

Section 41 sets up what can be described as the test of 'distinctiveness'. The key concern here is to ensure that parties are not able to register marks that lack such distinctiveness. The sorts of marks likely to raise such concerns will consist of signs that tend to describe the goods or services in question, or contain other desirable significations that other traders would legitimately wish to use. Taking words as an example, if one chocolate maker were allowed to register CHOCOLATE, or DARK, or SWISS it is not hard to imagine the problems this would cause rival traders or the consumer confusion that would be generated. What makes the assessment of distinctiveness difficult is that there is no straightforward dichotomy between 'distinctive' and 'descriptive' signs. Rather, a mark's distinctive character in relation to the specified goods or services can be thought of as falling somewhere along a *continuum*. Wholly generic or descriptive marks will fall at one end

---

3   For further consideration, see R Burrell and M Handler, *Australian Trade Mark Law*, 2nd ed, Oxford University Press, Melbourne (forthcoming 2016), ch 3.

(e.g. attempts to register words such as CHOCOLATE or DARK for chocolate). Invented or arbitrary marks will fall near the other end (examples in relation to chocolate might include made up names such as KIT KAT, or words having no direct reference to the goods, such as BOOST or DREAM). More suggestive or partially descriptive marks fall somewhere in the middle (examples might include MALTESERS or CRUNCHIE). A further issue is that even where the mark is highly descriptive, it might have been *used* in the marketplace to such an extent that consumers have come to recognise it as indicating a particular trader's goods or services (DAIRY MILK being a good example). Section 41 attempts to manage these issues.

Section 41 was repealed and re-enacted by the *Intellectual Property Laws Amendment (Raising The Bar) Act 2012* (Cth). The new version applies to all applications for registration made on or after 15 April 2013. Section 41(1) provides:

> (1) An application for the registration of a trade mark must be rejected if the trade mark is not capable of distinguishing the applicant's goods or services in respect of which the trade mark is sought to be registered (the *designated goods or services*) from the goods or services of other persons.

How this is to be determined is set out in s 41(2)–(4):

> (2) A trade mark is taken not to be capable of distinguishing the designated goods or services from the goods or services of other persons only if either subsection (3) or (4) applies to the trade mark.
> (3) This subsection applies to a trade mark if:
>   (a) the trade mark is not to any extent inherently adapted to distinguish the designated goods or services from the goods or services of other persons; and
>   (b) the applicant has not used the trade mark before the filing date in respect of the application to such an extent that the trade mark does in fact distinguish the designated goods or services as being those of the applicant.
> (4) This subsection applies to a trade mark if:
>   (a) the trade mark is, to some extent, but not sufficiently, inherently adapted to distinguish the designated goods or services from the goods or services of other persons; and
>   (b) the trade mark does not and will not distinguish the designated goods or services as being those of the applicant having regard to the combined effect of the following:
>   (i) the extent to which the trade mark is inherently adapted to distinguish the goods or services from the goods or services of other persons;
>   (ii) the use, or intended use, of the trade mark by the applicant;
>   (iii) any other circumstances.

Working out whether a mark passes the s 41 hurdle is a two-step process. The first step involves assessing the *extent* to which the mark is 'inherently adapted to distinguish' the applicant's goods or services from those of other traders: that is, where along the continuum of distinctive character the mark falls. In making this assessment the decision-maker will need to classify the mark in one of three ways. One possibility is that the mark is not inherently adapted to distinguish the applicant's goods or services to any extent: such marks (many of which are likely to be wholly descriptive of the designated goods/services) fall to be considered under s 41(3). A second possibility is that the mark has a slight degree of inherent adaptation to distinguish, but not enough for it to be able to do the job of distinguishing the applicant's goods or services on that basis alone: such partially descriptive marks fall to be considered under s 41(4). A third possibility is that the mark is inherently adapted to distinguish the designated goods or services to such an extent that it will do the job of distinguishing on that basis alone: such 'prima facie distinctive' marks pass the s 41 hurdle at the first step of the inquiry.

For a mark that is not prima facie distinctive (i.e. it falls to be considered under s 41(3) or (4)), we need to apply the second step of the distinctiveness test. Such a mark can still pass the s 41 hurdle, but the applicant will need to put forward sufficient evidence of *factual distinctiveness*—that is, that because of the extent to which the mark has been used (and possibly other circumstances), consumers have come to recognise it as, in fact, being a badge of origin and thus capable of distinguishing the applicant's goods or services from those of other traders.

THE FIRST STEP: INHERENT ADAPTATION TO DISTINGUISH— GENERAL PRINCIPLES

The following three extracts set out how Australian courts go about determining whether a mark is inherently adapted to distinguish the designated goods or services.

CASE EXTRACT: PRECEDENT

Clark Equipment Co v Registrar of Trade Marks

(1964) 111 CLR 511
High Court of Australia

[The case involved an attempt to register MICHIGAN for earth-moving equipment.]

Kitto J (at 513–514): That ultimate question [of whether a mark is adapted to distinguish] must not be misunderstood. It is not whether the mark will be adapted to distinguish the registered owner's goods if it be registered and other persons consequently find themselves precluded from using it. The question is whether the mark, considered quite apart from the effects of registration, is such that by its use the applicant is likely to attain his object of thereby distinguishing his goods from the goods of others. In *Registrar of Trade Marks v W & G Du Cros Ltd* [1913] AC 624, at pp 634, 635 Lord Parker of Waddington, having remarked upon the difficulty of finding the right criterion by which to determine whether a proposed mark is or is not 'adapted to distinguish' the applicant's goods, defined the crucial question practically as I have stated it, and added … 'The applicant's chance of success in this respect (ie in distinguishing his goods by means of the mark, apart from the effects of registration) must, I think, largely depend upon whether other traders are likely, in the ordinary course of their businesses and without any improper motive, to desire to use the same mark, or some mark nearly resembling it, upon or in connexion with their own goods. It is apparent from the history of trade marks in this country that both the Legislature and the Courts have always shown a natural disinclination to allow any person to obtain by registration under the Trade Marks Acts a monopoly in what others may legitimately desire to use.' The interests of strangers and of the public are thus bound up with the whole question,

PRECEDENT

as Hamilton LJ pointed out in the case of *RJ Lea Ltd* [1913] 1 Ch 446, at p 463; (1913) 30 RPC 216, at p 227; but to say this is not to treat the question as depending upon some vague notion of public policy: it is to insist that the question whether a mark is adapted to distinguish be tested by reference to the likelihood that other persons, trading in goods of the relevant kind and being actuated only by proper motives—in the exercise, that is to say, of the common right of the public to make honest use of words forming part of the common heritage, for the sake of the signification which they ordinarily possess—will think of the word and want to use it in connexion with similar goods in any manner which would infringe a registered trade mark granted in respect of it.

CASE EXTRACT: CURRENT LAW

CURRENT LAW

Kenman Kandy Australia Pty Ltd v Registrar of Trade Marks

[2002] FCAFC 273; (2002) 122 FCR 494
Federal Court of Australia, Full Court

Stone J: 144. The authorities give very little guidance as to what is necessary for inherent adaption either generally or with respect to shapes. It is clear that words (ordinary or technical) which are descriptive of the character or quality of the goods are not inherently adapted to distinguish; *Burger King Corporation v Registrar of Trade Marks* (1973) 128 CLR 417 ('Whopper' as descriptive of large hamburgers); *Eutectic Corporation v Registrar of Trade Marks* (1980) 32 ALR 211 ('eutectic' as descriptive of machines and tools used in welding); *FH Faulding & Co Ltd v Imperial Chemical Industries of Australia and New Zealand Ltd* (1965) 112 CLR 537 ('Barrier' in respect of hand cream). This is so even if the word or words are contractions or corruptions of ordinary words; *Tastee Freez's Application* [1960] RPC 255 ('Tastee Freez' used in connection with ice cream and water ices); *Registrar of Trade Marks v Muller* (1980) 144 CLR 37 ('Less' in respect of pharmaceutical products); *Bausch & Lomb Inc v Registrar of Trade Marks* (1980) 28 ALR 537 ('Soflens' in respect of contact lenses); *Advanced Hair Studio of America Pty Ltd v Registrar of Trade Marks* (1988) 12 IPR 1 ('hairfusion' in respect of a service for fixing hairpieces to the head). The same principle applies to pictorial descriptions of goods; *Eclipse Sleep Products Inc v Registrar of Trade Marks* (1957) 99 CLR 300 (a six-sided border having circular ends, as in the shape of a spring, used in connection with a 'Springwall Mattress'). It is also well established that the name of a geographical location is not inherently adapted to distinguish goods because another trader may legitimately wish to use the name in connection with goods made in or associated with that place; *Thomson v B Seppelt & Sons Ltd* (1925) 37 CLR 305 (use of the words, 'Great Western' in respect of still and sparkling wines produced from grapes grown in the Great Western region of Victoria); *Clark Equipment* (use of the name 'Michigan' in respect of earthmoving and the like equipment); *Blount Inc* [*v Registrar of Trade Marks* (1998) 83 FCR 50] (use of name 'Oregon' inside an oval device in respect of power tool accessories); *Oxford University Press v Registrar of Trade Marks* (1990) 24 FCR 1 (use of name 'Oxford' in respect of printed publications); *A Bailey and Co Ltd v Clark, Son and Morland* [1938] AC 557 (use of name 'Glastonburys' in connection with sheepskin slippers).

145. Signs that are descriptive of the character or quality of the relevant goods or which use a geographical name in connection with them cannot be inherently distinctive because the words have significations or associations that invite confusion and because registration of a trade mark using such

words would preclude the use by others whose goods have similar qualities or which have a connection with the relevant areas. This concern is to any of the elements referred to in the definition of sign and involves the courts in policy considerations inherent in trade mark law. In *Registrar of Trade Marks v W & G Du Cros Ltd* [1913] AC 624 at 635 Lord Parker said,

> It is apparent from the history of trade marks in this country that both the Legislature and the Courts have always shown a natural disinclination to allow any person to obtain by registration under the Trade Marks Acts a monopoly in what others may legitimately desire to use.

[Stone J then quoted from *Clark Equipment* at 514 and continued:]

146. ... Kitto J was referring to word trade marks because that was the issue before him, but there can be no doubt that his Honour's test would equally apply to shapes or other signs forming 'part of the common heritage'.

147. In my opinion it is the absence of these associations and significations that makes a sign inherently adapted to distinguish one trader's goods from those of another. In other words the concept is negative not positive ...

148. It is the absence of association and signification that accounts for invented words often being found to be inherently adapted to distinguish a trader's product ...

CASE EXTRACT: CURRENT LAW

Cantarella Bros Pty Ltd v Modena Trading Pty Ltd

[2014] HCA 48; (2014) 109 IPR 154
High Court of Australia

[The issue before the High Court was whether Cantarella's registration of two trade marks in relation to coffee, ORO and CINQUE STELLE (the Italian words for 'gold' and 'five stars', respectively), should be cancelled on the basis that the marks were insufficiently inherently adapted to distinguish at their filing dates.]

French CJ, Hayne, Crennan and Kiefel JJ (some footnotes omitted): 26. ... [I]n *Clark Equipment*, Kitto J explained that whether a trade mark consisting of a word is 'adapted to distinguish' certain goods is to be tested:

> by reference to the likelihood that other persons, trading in goods of the relevant kind and being actuated only by proper motives—*in the exercise, that is to say, of the common right of the public to make honest use of words forming part of the common heritage, for the sake of the signification which they ordinarily possess*—will think of the word and want to use it in connexion with similar goods in any manner which would infringe a registered trade mark granted in respect of it. (emphasis added)

27. The purport of the emphasised parenthesis was a particular focus of dispute before the Full Court, which dispute was reiterated in this Court.

28. Cantarella relied on the emphasised passage to support the proposition that the inherent adaptability of a trade mark consisting of a word (including a foreign word) is to be tested by checking

the ordinary meaning (that is, the 'ordinary signification') of the word to anyone ordinarily purchasing, consuming or trading in the relevant goods, characterised by Cantarella as 'the target audience'.

29. Modena asserted that the emphasised language was not essential to the test because Lord Parker of Waddington in *Registrar of Trade Marks v W & G Du Cros Ltd* [[1913] AC 624 at 635] stated the test in terms of the likelihood that other traders might legitimately desire to use the word in connection with their goods.

30. ... Cantarella's submissions are correct and must be accepted.

...

70. ... [D]etermining whether a trade mark is 'inherently adapted to distinguish' ... requires consideration of the 'ordinary signification' of the words proposed as trade marks to any person in Australia concerned with the goods to which the proposed trade mark is to be applied.

71. As shown by the authorities in this Court, the consideration of the 'ordinary signification' of any word or words (English or foreign) which constitute a trade mark is crucial, whether (as here) a trade mark consisting of such a word or words is alleged not to be registrable because it is not an invented word and it has 'direct' reference to the character and quality of goods [*Howard Auto-Cultivators Ltd v Webb Industries Pty Ltd* (1946) 72 CLR 175; *FH Faulding & Co Ltd v Imperial Chemical Industries Ltd* (1965) 112 CLR 537], or because it is a laudatory epithet [*Burger King Corporation v Registrar of Trade Marks* (1973) 128 CLR 417] or a geographical name [*Thomson v B Seppelt & Sons Ltd* (1925) 37 CLR 305; *Clark Equipment* (1964) 111 CLR 511], or because it is a surname [*Mangrovite Belting Ltd v JC Ludowici & Son Ltd* (1938) 61 CLR 149], or because it has lost its distinctiveness [*James A Jobling & Co Ltd v James McEwan & Co Pty Ltd* [1933] VLR 168], or because it never had the requisite distinctiveness to start with [*Faulding* (1965) 112 CLR 537]. Once the 'ordinary signification' of a word, English or foreign, is established an enquiry can then be made into whether other traders might legitimately need to use the word in respect of their goods ...

As can be seen from the extracts above from *Kenman Kandy* at [144] and *Cantarella* at [71], certain kinds of words, when used in relation to certain goods, are unlikely to pass the first step of the distinctiveness enquiry. Extracts from cases considering whether certain types of work mark are inherently adapted to distinguish, as well as cases addressing other types of sign (such as logos, colours and shapes) are set out in the next section.

One feature of the Australian cases (as seen in the three extracts above, and in the extracts below) is that they often seem to be asking a binary question: that is, whether or not the mark is 'inherently adapted to distinguish'. This is somewhat problematic, given that the test under s 41 contemplates a tripartite classification: whether the mark is not to *any extent* inherently adapted to distinguish; whether it is to *some* extent, but not sufficiently, inherently adapted; or whether it is *sufficiently* inherently adapted to distinguish such that the mark is capable of distinguishing on that basis alone. It is not, therefore, immediately obvious how the tests articulated by the High Court in *Clark Equipment* and *Cantarella* map on to this tripartite structure of s 41. The best way of reading *Clark Equipment* and *Cantarella* is as follows. Once the 'ordinary signification' of the mark is determined, and once it is asked whether other traders would wish to use that sign for the sake of its ordinary signification, it is only if it can be said that there is *little or no likelihood or possibility* that other traders would wish to use the sign (because the only signification of the sign is that it is, for example, invented, arbitrary or allusive) that the mark will be *sufficiently* inherently adapted to distinguish. (When courts ask whether a mark is 'inherently adapted to distinguish', they are often using this as shorthand for 'sufficiently inherently adapted to distinguish'.) If applying the *Clark Equipment* and *Cantarella* test results in the answer that there *is* a likelihood that other traders would wish to use the sign for the sake of its ordinary signification, this does not necessarily mean that the mark is not 'inherently adapted to distinguish'. Rather, there is a further issue that needs to be addressed: what is the *degree* of that likelihood? The greater the degree of likelihood, the more likely it is that the mark will fall to be considered under s 41(3) (as a mark that is not to any extent inherently adapted to distinguish). A lesser degree means that the mark is more likely to fall to be considered under s 41(4) (as a mark that is not sufficiently inherently adapted). In either case, the non-prima facie distinctive mark can still be registered on the basis of factual distinctiveness (see below, p 708).

As can be seen from some of the extracts below, evidence of use of the mark will often be lacking (e.g. because the mark had not been used at the filing date), making the decision as to whether or not the mark is prima facie distinctive of crucial importance.

ASSESSING INHERENT ADAPTATION TO DISTINGUISH: PARTICULAR EXAMPLES
Descriptive and geographical terms

PRECEDENT

CASE EXTRACT: PRECEDENT

Clark Equipment Co v Registrar of Trade Marks

(1964) 111 CLR 511
High Court of Australia

Kitto J (at 514–517): It is well settled that a geographical name, when used as a trade mark for a particular category of goods, may be saved by the nature of the goods or by some other circumstance from carrying its prima facie geographical signification, and that for that reason it may be held to be adapted to distinguish the applicant's goods. Where that is so it is because to an honest competitor the idea of using that name in relation to such goods or in such circumstances would simply not occur: see per Lord Simonds in the *Yorkshire Copper Works Case* (1953) 71 RPC 150, at p 154. This is the case, for example, where the word as applied to the relevant goods is in effect a fancy name, such as 'North Pole' in connexion with bananas: *A Bailey & Co Ltd v Clark, Son & Morland Ltd* (the *Glastonbury Case* (1938) AC 557, at p 562; (1938) 55 RPC 253, at p 257) (see also the *Livron Case* (1937) 54 RPC 327, at p 339), or where by reason of user or other circumstances it has come to possess, when used in respect of the relevant goods, a distinctiveness in fact which eclipses its primary signification. Cf. in the case of a descriptive word: *Dunlop Rubber Co's Application* (1942) 59 RPC 134. But the probability that some competitor, without impropriety, may want to use the name of a place on his goods must ordinarily increase in proportion to the likelihood that goods of the relevant kind will in fact emanate from that place. A descriptive word is in like case: the more apt a word is to describe the goods, the less inherently apt it is to distinguish them as the goods of a particular manufacturer ...

The consequence is that the name of a place or of an area, whether it be a district or a county, a state or a country, can hardly ever be adapted to distinguish one person's goods from the goods of others when used *simpliciter* or with no addition save a description or designation of the goods, if goods

PRECEDENT

of the kind are produced at the place or in the area or if it is reasonable to suppose that such goods may in the future be produced there. In such a case, the name is plainly not inherently, ie in its own nature, adapted to distinguish the applicant's goods; there is necessarily great difficulty in proving that by reason of use or other circumstances it does in fact distinguish his goods; and even where that difficulty is overcome there remains the virtual if not complete impossibility of satisfying the Registrar or the Court that the effect of granting registration will not be to deny the word to a person who is likely to want to use it, legitimately, in connexion with his goods for the sake of the geographical reference which it is inherently adapted to make ...

The principles to which I have referred appear to me to conclude the present case against the appellant. Michigan is the name of a State of the United States of America. The appellant produces there goods of the kind for which it uses the name as its mark in Australia as well as in America. It is true that there is no evidence before me that any other manufacturer produces similar goods in Michigan at present, but it is a matter of common knowledge, of which I take judicial notice, that in the State there are important manufacturing centres, and it is well within the bounds of reason to suppose that persons other than the appellant may in the future produce there goods similar to some or all of the goods comprised in the category for which the appellant now seeks trade mark registration. There are only two circumstances which may be considered as tending to diminish the normal likelihood that another manufacturer of (for example) power cranes in Michigan, sending his goods to Australia, may fairly wish to use the word Michigan in respect of them in this country in a manner which a trade mark registration would prevent. One circumstance I have mentioned already: it is that the word has at present a reputation here as referring specifically to the appellant's goods. The other I have not mentioned: it is that in the United States the appellant has obtained registration of the word MICHIGAN as a trade mark in respect of such goods as those described in its present application. No evidence has been tendered as to the effect of trade mark registration according to United States law, but I shall assume for the purposes of the case that apart from the appellant no manufacturer of the relevant goods, not even a Michigan manufacturer, is free to use the word Michigan in the manner of a trade mark for his goods in the United States. The appellant submits that for that reason no such manufacturer will be very likely to want the word for use in Australia in any manner which would infringe a registered trade mark consisting of the word, especially if he knows, as he almost certainly will, of the distinctiveness the word has come to have in this country. But even allowing for the cumulative effect of these considerations it seems to me impossible to conclude that there is no likelihood of other traders, in the ordinary course of their businesses and without any desire to get for themselves a benefit from the appellant's reputation, wishing in advertisements and otherwise to describe (eg) their power cranes from Michigan as Michigan power cranes. They may well wish by such means to take legitimate advantage of a reputation which they believe or hope that the State of Michigan possesses among Australians for the quality of its manufacturing products, and it would be contrary to fundamental principle to grant a registration which would have the effect of denying them the right to do so by using the name of the State. It is no answer to say that if registration be granted such a manufacturer may nevertheless describe his goods as 'made in Michigan' or in some other ways indicate that Michigan is their place of origin. He is not to be excluded by the registration of a trade mark from any use of the word Michigan that he may fairly want to make in the course of his business.

Kitto J's statement at 515 that 'the probability that some competitor, without impropriety, may want to use the name of a place ... must ordinarily increase in proportion to the likelihood that goods of the relevant kind will in fact emanate from that place' is well illustrated by two recent cases. In *Yarra Valley Dairy Pty Ltd v Lemnos Foods Pty Ltd* [2010] FCA 1367; (2010) 191 FCR 297, Middleton J considered PERSIAN FETTA to be not to any extent inherently adapted to distinguish. Even though 'Persia' is not the current name of a geographical area, it was thought that its ongoing geographical significance is such that other traders would have a legitimate interest in wanting to describing their Iranian-sourced cheese, or a style of cheese derived from cheese produced in Iran, by reference to such a term. In contrast, in *Clearlight Investments Pty Ltd v Sandvik Mining and Construction Oy* [2013] ATMO 50 the delegate of the Registrar considered SANREMO for remote control devices to be to some extent, but not sufficiently, inherently adapted to distinguish, on the basis that San Remo is 'a sizeable place in its own right and somewhere the designated goods and services might be made or offered' (at [27]).

Similarly, Kitto J's statement in *Clark Equipment* at 515 that 'the more apt a word is to describe the goods, the less inherently apt it is to distinguish them as the goods of a particular manufacturer' helps explain why certain descriptive or laudatory marks have been classified as they have under the 1995 Act. For example, the word YELLOW for goods and services including print and online phone directories, and APP STORE for retail store services, were both held to lack any inherent adaptation to distinguish (see *Phone Directories Company Australia Pty Ltd v Telstra Corporation Ltd* [2014] FCA 373; (2014) 106 IPR 281 and *Apple Inc v Registrar of Trade Marks* [2014] FCA 1304; (2014) 109 IPR 187). In contrast, TENNIS WAREHOUSE for the online retailing of tennis equipment was held to have a slight degree of inherent adaptation to distinguish, albeit not enough for it to be prima facie distinctive (see *Sports Warehouse Inc v Fry Consulting Pty Ltd* [2010] FCA 664; (2010) 186 FCR 519).

Neologisms, word combinations and foreign words

CASE EXTRACT: CURRENT LAW

Cantarella Bros Pty Ltd v Modena Trading Pty Ltd

[2014] HCA 48; (2014) 109 IPR 154
High Court of Australia

[The facts of this case are outlined at p 688 above. At trial, Emmett J was not persuaded that Italian was so widely spread that 'cinque stelle' and 'oro' would be generally understood in Australia as meaning 'five stars and 'gold', and found the marks to be prima facie distinctive. The Full Federal Court overturned this decision, stating that the test should focus on the interests of traders in the market who might wish to take advantage of language in the 'common heritage'. Taking into account: (1) the laudatory meanings of 'oro' and 'cinque stelle' when translated from Italian to English; (2) the fact that in Australia coffee is commonly associated with Italy; (3) the number of people in Australia who speak or have some knowledge of Italian; and (4) evidence that both 'oro' and 'cinque stelle' had been used by other traders in Australia as words descriptive of the quality of the coffee products, the Full Court found the two marks to lack any inherent adaptation to distinguish. Cantarella appealed to the High Court.

In discussing whether the two marks were inherently adapted to distinguish, the High Court drew substantially on case law on distinctiveness under former Anglo-Australian trade marks legislation. This legislation required that in order to be registrable, the applicant's mark had to consist of an 'invented' word or words, or be a 'word having no direct reference to the character or quality of the goods'. Implicit in the High Court's reasoning (at [22]–[23]) is that the sort of words that would have been considered registrable under these former provisions would be sufficiently inherently adapted to distinguish under s 41 of the current Act].

French CJ, Hayne, Crennan and Kiefel JJ (some footnotes omitted):

FOREIGN WORDS

45. Establishing the 'ordinary signification' of a trade mark consisting of a word is just as critical if the word is to be found in a dictionary of a foreign language. This is particularly so when an objection to registrability is based on an assertion that the mark is not an invented word because it makes direct reference to the character or quality of the goods in question. The *Solio Case* [*Eastman Photographic Materials Co v Comptroller-General of Patents, Designs, and Trade-marks* [1898] AC 571] concerned the registrability of 'SOLIO' for photographic papers. It had been contended that 'solio' (a word in Italian and Latin) was not an invented word and moreover was a word containing a 'reference' to the goods. Lord Macnaghten stated the principle to be applied to a word put forward as an invented word [at 583]:

> If [a word] is an invented word, if it is 'new and freshly coined' (to adapt an old and familiar quotation), it seems to me that it is no objection that it may be traced to a foreign source, or that it may contain a covert and skilful allusion to the character or quality of the goods. I do not think that it is necessary that it should be wholly meaningless.

46. That was followed by Parker J (as his Lordship then was) in *Philippart v William Whiteley Ltd* [[1908] 2 Ch 274] ('the *Diabolo Case*') when he found a trade mark consisting of the Italian word 'diabolo' unregistrable, because it applied to a well-known game in England called 'the devil on two sticks', for which reason it could not be treated as an 'invented word'. Parker J explained [at 279]:

> To be an invented word, within the meaning of the Act, a word must not only be newly coined in the sense of not being already current in the English language, but must be such as not to convey any meaning, or at any rate any obvious meaning, to ordinary Englishmen.

47. In *Howard Auto-Cultivators Ltd v Webb Industries Pty Ltd* [(1946) 72 CLR 175] ('*Howard*'), Dixon J stated what was required for a word to qualify as an invented word. Citing Lord Macnaghten in the *Solio Case*, his Honour said that although a word should be [at 181]:

> substantially different from any word in ordinary and common use ... [it] need not be wholly meaningless and it is not a disqualification 'that it may be traced to a foreign source or that it may contain a covert and skilful allusion to the character or quality of the goods.

These authorities show that it is not the meaning of a foreign word as translated which is critical, although it might be relevant. What is critical is the meaning conveyed by a foreign word to those who will be concerned with the relevant goods.

48. In *Kiku Trade Mark* [[1978] FSR 246], the Supreme Court of Ireland approved Parker J's speech in the *Diabolo Case* and held that the Japanese word 'kiku', meaning chrysanthemum, was registrable for perfume because the word had no 'direct reference' to the character or quality of the goods. The Court considered that a word which required translation could not be said to have any signification to ordinary people living in Ireland who see and hear it. That approach accords with Dixon J's statement of principle in *Howard*.

. . .

WORDS CONTAINING A REFERENCE TO GOODS

50. The practical difference between a word making some 'covert and skilful allusion' to the goods (prima facie registrable) and a word having a 'direct reference' to goods (prima facie not registrable) is well illustrated in two Australian cases decided under the 1905 Act. Understanding the distinction is the key to resolving this appeal.

51. In *Howard*, this Court was considering whether a trade mark consisting of the word 'rohoe' was registrable as an invented word in respect of agricultural implements. Parker J's reference in the *Diabolo Case* to a word (in that case a foreign word) having an 'obvious meaning' to 'ordinary Englishmen' was considered by Dixon J. Because of the special nature of the goods to which 'rohoe' was to be applied, Dixon J said the question was whether the word 'rohoe' would appear as an obvious contraction of 'rotary hoe' and be so understood by 'a farmer, a horticulturist, a trader in agricultural and horticultural implements or a person otherwise concerned with them' [at 185].

52. By comparison, in *Mark Foy's* [*Ltd v Davies Coop & Co Ltd* (1956) 95 CLR 190], the trade mark 'TUB HAPPY' was found registrable by a majority in this Court as a trade mark having no direct reference to the character or quality of cotton garments. In agreeing with Williams J, Dixon CJ described the test for a word having 'direct reference to the character or quality of the goods' as lying 'in the probability of ordinary persons understanding the words, in their application to the goods, as describing or indicating or calling to mind either their nature or some attribute they possess' [at 195]. His Honour considered 'TUB HAPPY' to be allusive such that it did not convey a meaning or idea 'sufficiently tangible' to amount to a 'direct reference' to the character or quality of the goods [at 195]. Citing with approval Lord Macnaghten in the *Solio Case* and Parker J in the *Diabolo Case*, Williams J illustrated why a covert and skilful allusive reference to goods does not render a word directly descriptive of goods as that expression is used in trade mark law [at 201]. His Honour said the registration of 'TUB HAPPY' for cotton goods did not prevent others from describing their cotton goods as having the characteristics or qualities of 'washability, freshness and cheapness' [at 201–202].

. . .

'ORDINARY SIGNIFICATION' AND 'INHERENTLY ADAPTED TO DISTINGUISH'

. . .

59. The principles settled by this Court (and the United Kingdom authorities found in this Court to be persuasive) require that a foreign word be examined from the point of view of the possible impairment of the rights of honest traders and from the point of view of the public. It is the 'ordinary signification' of the word, in Australia, to persons who will purchase, consume or trade in the goods which permits a conclusion to be drawn as to whether the word contains a 'direct reference' to the relevant goods (prima facie not registrable) or makes a 'covert and skilful allusion' to the relevant goods

(prima facie registrable). When the 'other traders' test from [*Registrar of Trade Marks v W & G Du Cros Ltd* [1913] AC 624] is applied to a word (other than a geographical name or a surname), the test refers to the legitimate desire of other traders to use a word which is directly descriptive in respect of the same or similar goods. The test does not encompass the desire of other traders to use words which in relation to the goods are allusive or metaphorical. In relation to a word mark, English or foreign, 'inherent adaption to distinguish' requires examination of the word itself, in the context of its proposed application to particular goods in Australia.

...

71. ... Once the 'ordinary signification' of a word, English or foreign, is established an enquiry can then be made into whether other traders might legitimately need to use the word in respect of their goods. If a foreign word contains an allusive reference to the relevant goods it is prima facie qualified for the grant of a monopoly [*Howard* (1946) 72 CLR 175 and *Mark Foy's* (1956) 95 CLR 190 approving the *Solio Case* [1898] AC 571]. However, if the foreign word is understood by the target audience as having a directly descriptive meaning in relation to the relevant goods, then prima facie the proprietor is not entitled to a monopoly of it [*Howard* (1946) 72 CLR 175 and *Mark Foy's* (1956) 95 CLR 190 approving the *Diabolo Case* [1908] 2 Ch 274] ...

72. Because coffee is a commodity and a familiar beverage consumed by many, the consideration of the 'ordinary signification' of the words 'oro' and 'cinque stelle' in Australia undertaken by the primary judge accorded with settled principles ...

73. Both Modena in argument and the Full Court in its reasons misunderstood Lord Parker's reference in *Du Cros* to the desire of other traders to use the same or similar mark in respect of their goods. Lord Parker was not referring to the desire of traders to use words, English or foreign, which convey an allusive or metaphorical meaning in respect of certain goods. What Lord Parker's 'other traders' test means in practice is well illustrated by the fate of the marks considered in *Faulding*, *Clark Equipment* and *Burger King*. Like 'TUB HAPPY' in respect of cotton goods, 'ORO' and 'CINQUE STELLE' were not shown to convey a meaning or idea sufficiently tangible to anyone in Australia concerned with coffee goods as to be words having a direct reference to the character or quality of the goods.

74. The evidence, relied on by Modena at trial, did not show that 'ORO' and 'CINQUE STELLE' should not be registered as trade marks (and should be removed from the Register as trade marks) because their registration would preclude honest rival traders from having words available to describe their coffee products either as Italian coffee products or as premium coffee products or as premium blend coffee products.

75. The evidence led by Modena purporting to show that rival traders used (or desired to use) the word 'oro' to directly describe their coffee products showed no more than that the word 'oro' or the form 'd'oro' had been employed on internet sites and coffee product packaging in respect of coffee products in a range of composite marks featuring Italian words which ostensibly were distinguishable aurally, visually and semantically. Further, the presence on the Register, before Cantarella's trade mark 'ORO' was registered, of another proprietor's composite mark 'LAVAZZA QUALITA ORO plus device' and Cantarella's own composite mark 'MEDAGLIA D'ORO' in respect of coffee products fell well short of proving that the word 'oro', standing alone, is understood in Australia by persons concerned with coffee products to be directly descriptive of the character or quality of such goods.

CURRENT LAW

76. The evidence led by Modena to show that some traders in Australia used the expression 'five star' on packaging of coffee and many traders used 'five star' in respect of a range of services including restaurant and accommodation services also fell well short of proving that 'cinque stelle' is understood in Australia by persons concerned with coffee products to be directly descriptive of the character or quality of such goods.

77. Modena's complaint that the primary judge insufficiently considered the desires of rival traders to use the words 'oro' or 'cinque stelle' to directly describe their coffee goods was premised on a misconception that such was demonstrated by the evidence. The primary judge was right to reject Modena's submission, based on the evidence, that honest traders might legitimately wish to use the words to directly describe, or indicate, the character or quality of their goods.

Logos and devices

CURRENT LAW

CASE EXTRACT: CURRENT LAW

Bavaria NV v Bayerischer Brauerbund eV

[2009] FCA 428; (2009) 177 FCR 300
Federal Court of Australia

[Bayerischer Brauerbund (BBA) sought to oppose Bavaria NV's registration of the following device mark in relation to beer and other beverages:]

Bennett J: 70. I make the following preliminary observations in relation to the trade mark and to the question whether other persons may legitimately wish to use the word 'Bavaria' in connection with their goods because of its geographical reference and whether the trade mark is capable of distinguishing Bavaria NV's goods from the goods of other traders:

* The trade mark is not just the word 'Bavaria' or, put another way, it is not used simpliciter or with no addition save for a description or designation of the goods.
* The use of the trade mark for beer does not save the word 'Bavaria' from carrying its prima facie geographical signification.

- This is not a case where the goods for which the trade mark is used are remote from the geographical location where those goods are produced and with which the goods are associated (cf. discussion in *Colorado* [*Group Ltd v Strandbags Group Pty Ltd* [2007] FCAFC 184] at [29] per Kenny J).
- Bavaria is a place in Germany where beer is produced. This is likely to continue in the future. As at 2005, there were 623 breweries in operation in Bavaria.
- Other beer makers in Germany may want to use the word 'Bavaria' or 'Bavarian', on or in connection with their beer, either to signify the brewing style or to indicate that their beer comes from Bavaria.
- Bavaria NV does not suggest that the word 'Bavaria' alone would be registrable for beer. It is unlikely that it would be as, for the reasons given in *Clark Equipment*, *Colorado* and *University of Oxford* [(1990) 24 FCR 1], it would not be capable of distinguishing or acquiring distinctiveness for beer.
- Bavaria NV's beer was named partly in recognition of the fact that there is a style of beer-making associated with, or originating from, Bavaria.
- Bavarian breweries produce a wide variety of beers, for example blonde and dark beers, pilsener and export beers, wheat beers and diet beers. There is no uniform type of Bavarian beer.
- The word BAVARIA is prominent in the trade mark ...
- Many of the elements of the trade mark, namely the non-word elements such as the heraldry, would not, to the average consumer, indicate a particular country. A coat of arms and old-world emblems evoke Europe.
- Other brewers in Bavaria use the word 'Bavaria' across a label with sprigs of barley and a crest ...
- Although BBA's evidence is that some such labels are for the export market, BBA has not established that any such labels are used on beer sold into the Australian market.
- None of the examples in evidence use all of the elements of the trade mark, although the impression is of a similar use by some brewers of devices and symbols to give a European or medieval, bucolic impression ...

72. Are other traders likely to wish to adopt the same trade mark or symbols or features resembling that trade mark? Bavaria NV emphasises that there was no evidence that any other trader wishes to use, or would wish to use, the word 'Bavaria' in Australia together with heraldic material as in the trade mark. BBA says that the heraldic devices used by Bavaria NV are themselves broadly generic and thereby incapable of adding distinctiveness to the word BAVARIA or distinguishing Bavaria NV as the source of the beer ...

...

74. This case is not about whether Bavaria NV can register a trade mark for the word 'Bavaria'. It is whether the trade mark, which contains BAVARIA, is capable of distinguishing Bavaria NV's goods from those of other traders, including traders who sell beer from Bavaria. On the assumption that traders of beer from Bavaria may wish to use 'Bavaria' on their labels or in their trade marks, the way to distinguish their goods is to create a distinctive trade mark or label by the use of other words and devices. Bavaria NV has utilised the Swinkels family crest and other devices, repeated references to 'Holland' and the prominent placing of HOLLAND below BAVARIA to draw attention to the fact that BAVARIA HOLLAND BEER is a specific product, the source of which is Lieshout, Holland.

75. Although the matter is not without difficulty, I have come to the view that the trade mark is inherently adapted to distinguish Bavaria NV's goods. Accordingly, the ground of opposition based on s 41 of the Act is not made out.

Colours

CASE EXTRACT: CURRENT LAW

Philmac Pty Ltd v Registrar of Trade Marks

[2002] FCA 1551; (2002) 126 FCR 525
Federal Court of Australia

[Philmac sought to register 'The colour TERRACOTTA as applied to the connecting insert of polypipe fittings'.]

Mansfield J: 50. The Registrar correctly submitted that under [s 41], there are no special rules which apply to colour marks compared to other features of goods which come within the definition of 'sign'. Nevertheless, the application of the test in *Clark Equipment* [*Co v Registrar of Trade Marks* (1964) 111 CLR 511] to the context of colour marks itself raises difficulties peculiar to the application presently before the Court. The test for inherent adaptability to distinguish set out in *Clark Equipment*, and followed since in a body of cases pertaining to the registration of word marks, provides that (at least) a word mark may be inherently capable of distinguishing an applicant's goods if it is not purely descriptive ... or geographical in origin (as in *Clark Equipment* itself).

51. In the present case, the test in *Clark Equipment* demands consideration of the likelihood that other traders actuated only by proper motives might think of the sign applied for, namely the colour terracotta, and want to use it in connection with similar goods in a manner which would infringe a registered mark granted in respect of it. The concept of a properly motivated competing trader was discussed by Buckley J in *Blue Paraffin Trade Mark* [1977] RPC 473 at 500:

> Speaking for myself, I should describe the duty of the Registrar as this: that examining the facts he has also to survey the possible confusions or difficulties and the possible impairment of a right of innocent traders to do that which apart from the grant of the mark would be their natural mode of conducting their business.

52. There are, in my view three obvious respects in which the right referred to in that passage might be impaired by the registration of a mark of the type contemplated in the present case.

53. First, a trader might legitimately choose a colour to apply to goods to denote a meaning that that colour might ordinarily possess. For example, the concepts of hot, cold, environmentalism, danger, stop, go, communism, mourning and femininity are universally conveyed as colours. Accordingly, an application for the colour mark red applied to taps might fail to satisfy the test in *Clark Equipment* because the registration of such a mark would impair the right of other traders in taps from legitimately using that colour to convey the meaning it ordinarily possesses. The application would, in my judgment, be analogous to an application for registration of a purely descriptive word and the mark applied for would therefore not be inherently adapted to distinguish. That conclusion is consistent with international jurisprudence in respect of the registration of trade marks comprising colour applied to goods or parts of goods. The colour blue in relation to fertiliser pellets was precluded from trade mark protection by the United States [District] Court because it had the utilitarian function of identifying the presence of nitrogen, and was therefore ornamentally functional: *Nor-Am Chem Co v OM Scott & Sons Co*, 44 USPQ 2d (BNA) 1316 at 1320 ...

CURRENT LAW

54. Secondly, a trader might legitimately choose a colour for its practical utility. That is, the colour may be a feature of a product that serves to improve the functionality or durability of the product. The function of visibility is, for example, served by the colour yellow; heat absorption by the colour black; light reflection by the colour white; military camouflage by a combination of khaki, brown and green. In the present case Philmac's evidence was that the colour black was ordinarily applied to polymer piping to serve the function of protecting the product from degradation through exposure to ultraviolet light. The shape mark cases properly indicate a reluctance to permit, by virtue of a trade mark registration, a permanent monopoly of matters of engineering design: *Kenman* [*Kandy Australia Pty Ltd v Registrar of Trade Marks* [2002] FCAFC 273] per French J at [45]; *Koninklijke Philips Electronics NV v Remington Products Australia Ltd* (1999) 91 FCR 167; *Philips Electronics NV v Remington Consumer Products* (1997) 40 IPR 279 per Jacob J; *British Sugar Plc v James Robertson & Sons Ltd* [1996] RPC 281. In my view there is no reason why the functionality principles applied to the registration of shape marks should not also apply to the consideration of the application of colour marks.

55. Thirdly, a product may be produced in a particular colour being the naturally occurring result of the manufacturing process. Terracotta is a case in point. Were the applicant to apply for the registration of the colour terracotta to terracotta roof tiles or garden pots, the effect of granting the registration would be to force on other traders a method of manufacture that would involve a departure from the 'natural mode' of conducting the business of manufacturing those terracotta products.

56. Whilst those are considerations that might preclude the registration of particular colours applied to particular goods under the test set out in *Clark Equipment*, in my view, they do not have any direct application to the present case. There is no suggestion that the colour terracotta conveys a particular meaning, nor does it serve any functional purpose in respect of fittings for rural B or imperial polyethylene irrigation piping. Nor is the colour a naturally occurring result of the manufacturing process of the goods in respect of which the application of the mark is sought.

57. Nevertheless, I have reached the conclusion that the Philmac mark is not inherently adapted to distinguish the goods of Philmac in respect of which the Philmac application is sought from the goods or services of other persons. I have reached that conclusion having regard to the fact that the range of colours available to an honestly motivated trader is in fact limited and that the colour terracotta the subject of application, or any shade of terracotta that might be deceptively similar to that colour, might naturally and legitimately occur to another trader as a choice of colour for application to goods in the same class.

58. In a scientific context, the range of colours available to traders for application to goods is in fact infinite. However, in the context of trade mark law that is not the case. In *Oxford University Press v Registrar of Trade Marks* (1990) 24 FCR 1 Gummow J said at 18:

> The concept … of adaption to distinguish is less difficult to grasp once it is appreciated that the statute is looking forward to the consequences of a grant of registration …

> …

60. In the present application, the consequence of a grant of registration would be to prevent any other trader in goods of the same description from using not only that shade of terracotta specifically described and visually represented in the application in respect of the goods to which the application relates, but all other shades of colour that might be described as deceptively similar to that colour. That conclusion, in my judgment, is relevant to the legitimate or honest use test set out in *Clark Equipment*. That is, (to superimpose the words of the test to the context of colour marks) the limited palate of

colours available to a trader at the very least renders it more likely that other persons trading in goods of the relevant kind and being actuated only by proper motives—in the exercise, that is to say, of the common right of the public to make honest use of the colours forming part of the common heritage, for the sake of the signification which they ordinarily possess—will think of a colour and want to use it in connection with similar goods in a manner which would infringe a registered trade mark granted in respect of it. Stating the proposition in that way equates it with what has become known in international jurisprudence as the 'colour depletion' argument.

61. The United States [Court of Appeals] in *Re Owens-Corning Fiberglas Corporation*, 774 F 2d 1116 ([Fed Cir,] 1985) (*Pink Batts*) rejected a 'colour depletion theory' asserted in an earlier case. In *Campbell Soup Co v Armour & Co*, 175 F 2d 795 [(3rd Cir, 1949)] the applicant was denied registration of labels that were half red and half white. The Court held that if the applicant were to 'monopolize red in all its shades the next manufacturer [could] monopolize orange in all its shades and the next yellow in the same way. Obviously, the list of colours would soon run out'. The Court in *Pink Batts* considered that approach inconsistent with the legislative framework that provided that colour was capable of registration as a trade mark. It stated at 1122 that 'where there is no competitive need for colors to remain available, the color depletion argument is an unreasonable restriction on the acquisition of trademark rights'.

62. I consider the qualification in that statement to be of critical importance in this matter. In my view, it is not inconsistent with the conclusion in *Pink Batts* that in circumstances where there is a proven competitive need for colours to remain available, it is not an unreasonable restriction on the acquisition of trade mark rights to have regard to that competitive imperative and preclude the granting of a monopoly in a colour applied to goods.

63. In the present application I have concluded on the evidence that colour has been and continues to be applied to irrigation fittings and related products by manufacturers as a means of coding their products for measurement compatibility and other purposes. That evidence includes the evidence of Philmac that its products manufactured for export to overseas markets are coloured so as to identify them as products manufactured for that purpose, and evidence of the Registrar that Philmac's most significant market competitor Plasson has applied the colours red, burgundy and 'red-pink' to its rural compression fittings since 1998. I note also the use by the manufacturer Iplex of the colour blue on the nuts of its metric compression fitting so as to identify it as a metric product. The use of colour as a means of distinguishing between products with different measurement and performance specifications is also evident in the broader irrigation market. In that context I have had regard to brochures or catalogues from several manufacturers including the following: James Hardie Irrigation Pty Ltd depicting the use of colour as a means of distinguishing between many ranges of products and individual products within each range, Netafim Australia depicting colour as a means of distinguishing between precipitation performance of sprinklers and Amiad Irrigation depicting colour as a means of indicating the flow rate of regulated drippers.

64. Having regard to that evidence, I have reached the conclusion that in the narrow class of goods in respect of which the Philmac application relates, and less relevantly in the wider irrigation market, there is indeed a competitive need for colours to remain available. That conclusion is relevant, in my view, to the test in *Clark Equipment*. The proven existence of a competitive need for colours to remain available in my view places the present application in the same class as an application for registration of a purely descriptive word. That is because the existence of that competition renders it more likely in fact that 'other traders are likely, in the ordinary course of their business and without any improper motive to desire to use [it] in connection with their goods ...

65. By approaching the matter in that way, despite what the ... Court in *Pink Batts* defined as a 'colour depletion argument', I do not mean to suggest that a single colour applied to goods may never be inherently adapted to distinguish an applicant's goods from those of other traders. Such a conclusion would be inconsistent with the provisions of the Act that contemplate that a colour may serve as a trade mark. The definition of a sign in the Act provides that a colour may be a sign in its own right, and not merely as an element of another species of sign such as a logo or aspect of packaging. It would therefore not be in accordance with the Act to reject a trade mark purely on the basis that rejection would secure a monopoly over part of what is in reality a limited resource. However, having regard to the above principles and the test in *Clark Equipment*, I consider that the circumstances in which a colour applied to goods will be inherently adapted to distinguish are limited to the following:

- the colour does not serve a utilitarian function: that is, it does not physically or chemically produce an effect such as light reflection, heat absorption or the like;
- the colour does not serve an ornamental function: that is, it does not convey a recognised meaning such as the denotation of heat or danger or environmentalism;
- the colour does not serve an economic function: that is, it is not the naturally occurring colour of a product and registration of that colour in respect of that product would not thereby submit competing traders to extra expense or extraordinary manufacturing processes in order to avoid infringement;
- the colour mark is not sought to be registered in respect of goods in a market in which there is a proven competitive need for the use of colour, and in which, having regard to the colour chosen and the goods on which it is sought to be applied, other properly motivated traders might naturally think of the colour use it in a similar manner in respect of their goods.

66. I have concluded that the mark applied for does not serve the functions set out in the first three of those points. The fourth point raises two considerations. First, whether there is a competitive need for the use of colour. I have concluded that on the present application there is such a need. Second, the likelihood of properly motivated traders naturally thinking of the relevant colour and wishing to apply it to their goods should be considered in the context of both the colour the subject of the application and the goods in respect of which registration of the trade mark is sought. It is to that second consideration that I now turn.

67. In cross-examination, the Managing Director of Philmac Pty Ltd, Mr Paul Haysman, gave evidence as to how Philmac determined that the colour terracotta should be applied to its goods. The following exchange is pertinent:

Q: So putting aside for a moment the extent of the use made by your company in sales—you say, do you, that there's nothing particularly distinctive about the terracotta colour compared with pink or red or yellow or any other colour. Is that right?

A: It was chosen because my marketing team believed that it had some affinity to the earth but, beyond that, there's nothing magical about it. I mean, it doesn't have any particular properties. It doesn't glow in the dark or anything like that. It's just a colour that was—no pun intended— deemed to be fitting for the purpose and we've stuck with it.

Q: Given the farm usage of these fittings, terracotta as you describe it [in the application] is particularly an apt colour for use on these compression fittings?

A: We believe it to be for marketing purposes.

CURRENT LAW

I conclude from that evidence that Philmac struck on the colour terracotta not because it was an unnatural and unusual choice for application to compression fittings for irrigation piping, but because it was an obvious and apt choice for application to that type of goods. It follows that at the time of the Philmac application, another honest trader might also legitimately desire to apply the colour to the same class of goods. Were the colour chosen a lilac purple (a colour chosen by way of example only) the application might give rise to different considerations. While I am not prepared to hypothesise on such an application, in my view counsel for the Registrar correctly identified that in some circumstances the choice of a colour with respect to particular goods might on rare occasions amount to an 'out of left field choice' and therefore assist the registrability of a colour mark, notwithstanding the competitive need for the use of colour in the relevant market. It was submitted, and I am inclined to agree, that the application of the colour pink to insulation batts is such a case: see *Pink Batts.* In my view such an application might lead the Court to consider that the mark applied for was, *to some extent*, inherently adapted to distinguish and therefore cause the application to fall for consideration under the less stringent test set out in [what is now s 41(4)] of the Act. Those considerations do not arise on this application. The colour terracotta, or any shade of colour deceptively similar to it, applied either to rural compression fittings or more generally to farming irrigation products is, in my view, a combination that an honest trader in those products might legitimately desire to use.

68. Applying the test in *Clark Equipment*, the Philmac mark is, therefore, not inherently adapted to distinguish Philmac's goods from those of other traders.

[In the result, Philmac was able to establish that, because of the extent of its pre-filing date and use of terracotta before the filing date, its mark had come to distinguish its designated goods, and its application was thus accepted for registration.]

Shapes

CURRENT LAW

CASE EXTRACT: CURRENT LAW

Kenman Kandy Australia Pty Ltd v Registrar of Trade Marks

[2002] FCAFC 273; (2002) 122 FCR 494
Federal Court of Australia, Full Court

[Kenman Kandy sought to register the following shape of its 'millennium bug' for confectionary:]

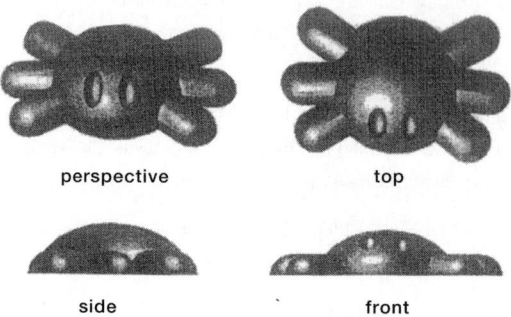

perspective   top

side   front

French J: 46. The present case turns upon whether the shape of the subject goods is inherently adapted to distinguish them from the goods or services of other persons. No issue of distinctiveness based on use arises … [T]he established test must be construed so as to be applicable to shapes. To say that a shape cannot ever pass the test of being 'inherently adapted to distinguish' would be to read into the statute a limitation not warranted by its terms. In considering pre-1995 cases, generalisations must not be drawn based on the narrower range of signs to which those cases related. Such generalisations might not give effect to the legislative intent that from 1995 'shapes' were to be capable of registration as trade marks.

47. The ultimate question in applying this test is whether the mark, considered apart from the effects of registration, is such that by its use the applicant is likely to attain its object of thereby distinguishing its goods from the goods of others—*Clark Equipment Co v Registrar of Trade Marks* [(1964) 111 CLR 511] at 513. This does not involve adventures in the Aristotelian taxonomy of form and substance. It requires a practical evaluative judgment about the effects of the relevant mark in the real world …

…

49. Lindgren and Stone JJ have considered the authorities dealing with inherent adaptation at greater length. As indicated, in my opinion, it is largely a matter of evaluative judgment within the broad principles laid down by those authorities. In determining whether or not his Honour erred in holding that the trade mark is not inherently adapted to distinguish the appellant's confectionary from that of others, due weight must be given to his assessment and that of the Registrar. I agree however, for the reasons given by Stone J, that in this case the learned primary judge erred in concluding that the shape of the millennium bug was not inherently adapted to distinguish.

50. The shape of the millennium bug involves a symmetrical disposition of projections ('legs') and recesses ('eyes'). Theoretically it may be the case that the number of possible symmetrical arrangements of projections and recesses is not infinite. Assuming that to be so, it is speculative, absent evidence, to draw conclusions about that number and whether the particular arrangement has any significant impact upon the access of other traders to the use of insect like shapes as trade marks. In that connection it is necessary to bear in mind that this trade mark is still at the registration stage. It enjoys the benefit of the presumption of registrability mandated by s 33. To the extent that critical criteria upon which registration might be rejected are in doubt, the application should be accepted. Closer adversarial scrutiny may occur in opposition—*Registrar of Trade Marks v Woolworths* [(1999) 93 FCR 365] at 377 …

Stone J:

[After referring to Dixon CJ and Williams J's judgments in *Mark Foy's Ltd v Davies Coop & Co Ltd* (1956) 95 CLR 190 (discussed at [52] in the second extract from *Cantarella*, above p 694), her Honour continued:]

155. A similar approach was taken by Lehane J in *Wella Aktiengesellschaft v Registrar of Trade Marks* (1995) 33 IPR 374 ('*Wella*'). The applicant had been refused registration of a trade mark comprised of the words, 'perfectly you' in respect of, inter alia, a range of cosmetics and hair care products. His Honour stated that the phrase, 'perfectly you', unlike the phrase, 'tub happy', had some currency in ordinary use and, in some contexts, an accepted meaning. His Honour concluded at 377, however, that when applied to the relevant goods the phrase was,

> a use of words which is purely emotive; an employment of words for no purpose but to evoke in the reader or hearer some feeling, some mood, some mental attitude.

156. In the above examples the trade marks were held to be inherently adapted not because of any positive content but because they had no associations or significations that prevented them from being inherently adapted to distinguish a trader's goods. In addition they show, especially in the comments made in *Mark Foy's* and *Wella*, that, at least in relation to word trade marks, it is not an obstacle to inherent adaptation that the trade mark is also designed to elicit a positive emotional response. The fact that the 'sign' that comprised the trade mark in those cases had a dual function was not seen to be inconsistent with the sign acting as a trade mark in respect of certain goods. I see no reason why the attractiveness of a shape should be considered differently. Moreover, I also see no reason why an invented shape should be regarded as different from an invented word in terms of assessing its inherent capacity to distinguish a trader's goods.

THE DECISIONS OF THE RESPONDENT'S DELEGATE AND THE PRIMARY JUDGE

157. It was accepted by the respondent's delegate that the bug shape was not a shape in common use. The delegate stated:

> It is a stylised six-legged 'creature'. It does not represent a recognisable animal or insect or other living or mythical thing of which I am aware, and no ready descriptive word comes to mind in viewing it. It is, in my view, an invented shape. It strikes the eye as distinguishable from other shapes, being not so amorphous or ordinary as to be unmemorable, even though no name readily attaches it. It could be said that it carries the stamp of an individual imagination.

158. The delegate distinguished such an invented shape from ordinary well-known shapes which, in relation to confectionery, could include:

- easily recognisable shapes that occur in nature (eg animals, flowers, insects, people, teeth);
- reproductions of common man-made objects (eg pillows, buildings);
- shapes familiar to everyone because they are commonplace solid geometric forms (eg cubes, globes, rectangular solids); and
- shapes neither natural nor geometric that form part of our common mythologic heritage (eg mermaids, angels, dragons).

159. Despite the delegate accepting that the bug shape did not fall into any of these categories but was an invented shape and was not a shape that others need to use, he ultimately rejected the claim that it was inherently adapted to distinguish the appellant's confectionery because their shape did not appear, at first instance, to have trade mark significance.

160. The learned primary judge took a slightly different approach. While he appeared to accept, or at least did not dispute, the delegate's description of the bug shape, his Honour accepted the respondent's submissions that registration of the trade mark with the consequent grant of exclusive use of that trade mark to the appellant would narrow the 'great common' of shapes available to traders generally. His Honour stated, at [33],

> I have reached the conclusion that the subject mark is not inherently adapted to distinguish Kenman's confectionery from that of others. I agree that the mark is concocted; so far as I am aware,

no real insect has this shape. However, the shape is reminiscent, to a greater or lesser degree, of a variety of insects. That fact is important, especially when it is remembered that the mark is intended to be registered in respect of confectionery. Children constitute a significant part of the confectionery market; and children relate spontaneously and strongly to animals and animal-like creatures. Moreover, confectionery is highly malleable. Taken together, these factors make it likely that confectionery manufacturers will, from time to time, wish to put out products in shapes reminiscent of animals. To allow registration, for confectionery, of the shape of a real or readily-imagined animal would be to commence a process of 'fencing in the common' which would speedily impose serious restrictions upon other traders.

CONCLUSION

161 … [I]t is my opinion that the test propounded by Kitto J in *Clark Equipment* [at 514] sets out the necessary and sufficient criteria to determine whether a mark is adapted to distinguish one trader's goods from those of another. Applied here, the question is whether, if the bug shape were to be registered as a trade mark, other persons trading in confectionery and 'being actuated only by proper motives' would think of this shape and want to use it in connection with their goods in any manner that would infringe the appellant's trade mark. That question must be answered bearing in mind that infringement would include using as a trade mark in relation to confectionery, not only the bug shape but also any 'sign that is substantially identical with, or deceptively similar to' the bug shape; s 120 of the 1995 Act. A subsidiary and difficult question is whether the appellant's bug shape, by virtue of it being recognisable as a 'bug', has associations that deprive it of the inherent capacity to distinguish the appellant's confectionery from that of other traders.

162. A shape (or word) that is entirely concocted does not have the associations that would lead to confusion. I do not regard such a shape as being part of the 'great common' any more than does a concocted word or a novel combination of common words; see for example *Mark Foy's* and *Wella*. The learned primary judge drew a distinction between concocted words, which, he said, were possibly infinite in number and the possibilities for concoction of animal-like shapes, which, he said were finite. With respect, I do not see the justification for this distinction. If there is any distinction I would have thought the advantage of greater variety lay with the category of three dimensional shapes which may involve any number of combinations of planes, arcs, angles and so forth.

163. Although the bug shape is suggestive of insect life it is not the shape of any specific insect or bug. Indeed, were it not for the description given by the appellants, it might as easily be seen as some extra-terrestrial object or space equipment such as a modified lunar landing module. Registration of the bug shape as a trade mark would not give the appellant a monopoly over all bug or insect shapes—only this particular shape and any substantially identical or deceptively similar shape. I see no reason in principle or policy why this should not be so.

The problematic nature of the majority's approach in *Kenman Kandy* was noted by Lindgren J in dissent (especially at [107]–[111]). It can also be seen by a comparison with the approach taken to such marks under US law.

CASE EXTRACT: COMPARATIVE LAW

Wal-Mart Stores, Inc v Samara Brothers, Inc

529 US 205 (2000)
Supreme Court of the United States

[The case concerned the question of whether a product's design (in this case, the design of children's garments) could be prima facie distinctive. In this context, s 2 of the *Lanham Act 1946* (US) requires that registration be granted to any trademark 'by which the goods of the applicant may be distinguished from the goods of others'.]

Scalia J (delivering the opinion of the Court) (at 210–214): In evaluating the distinctiveness of a mark under §2 [of the *Lanham Act 1946*], courts have held that a mark can be distinctive in one of two ways. First, a mark is inherently [i.e. prima facie] distinctive if '[its] intrinsic nature serves to identify a particular source.' [*Two Pesos, Inc v Taco Cabana, Inc*, 505 US 763, 768 (1992)]. In the context of word marks, courts have applied the now-classic test originally formulated by Judge Friendly, in which word marks that are 'arbitrary' ('Camel' cigarettes), 'fanciful' ('Kodak' film), or 'suggestive' ('Tide' laundry detergent) are held to be inherently distinctive. See *Abercrombie & Fitch Co v Hunting World, Inc*, 537 F 2d 4, 10–11 (CA2 1976). Second, a mark has acquired distinctiveness, even if it is not inherently distinctive, if it has developed secondary meaning, which occurs when, 'in the minds of the public, the primary significance of a [mark] is to identify the source of the product rather than the product itself.' *Inwood Laboratories, Inc v Ives Laboratories, Inc*, 456 US 844, 851, n 11 (1982) ...

... Nothing in §2, however, demands the conclusion that every category of mark necessarily includes some marks 'by which the goods of the applicant may be distinguished from the goods of others' without secondary meaning—that in every category some marks are inherently distinctive.

Indeed, with respect to at least one category of mark—colors—we have held that no mark can ever be inherently distinctive. See *Qualitex* [*Co v Jacobsen Products Co*], 514 US [159 (1995)], at 162–163. In *Qualitex*, petitioner manufactured and sold green-gold dry-cleaning press pads ... We held that a color could be protected as a trademark, but only upon a showing of secondary meaning. Reasoning by analogy to the *Abercrombie & Fitch* test developed for word marks, we noted that a product's color is unlike a 'fanciful,' 'arbitrary,' or 'suggestive' mark, since it does not 'almost *automatically* tell a customer that [it] refer[s] to a brand,' *ibid*, and does not 'immediately ... signal a brand or a product "source",' *id*, at 163. However, we noted that, 'over time, customers may come to treat a particular color on a product or its packaging ... as signifying a brand.' *Id*, at 162–163. Because a color, like a 'descriptive' word mark, could eventually 'come to indicate a product's origin,' we concluded that it could be protected *upon a showing of secondary meaning. Ibid*.

It seems to us that design, like color, is not inherently distinctive. The attribution of inherent distinctiveness to certain categories of word marks and product packaging derives from the fact that the very purpose of attaching a particular word to a product, or encasing it in a distinctive packaging, is most often to identify the source of the product. Although the words and packaging can serve subsidiary functions—a suggestive word mark (such as 'Tide' for laundry detergent), for instance, may invoke positive connotations in the consumer's mind, and a garish form of packaging (such as Tide's squat, brightly decorated plastic bottles for its liquid laundry detergent) may attract an otherwise

COMPARATIVE LAW

indifferent consumer's attention on a crowded store shelf—their predominant function remains source identification. Consumers are therefore predisposed to regard those symbols as indication of the producer, which is why such symbols 'almost automatically tell a customer that they refer to a brand,' *id*, at 162–163, and 'immediately ... signal a brand or a product "source",' *id*, at 163. And where it is not reasonable to assume consumer predisposition to take an affixed word or packaging as indication of source—where, for example, the affixed word is descriptive of the product ('Tasty' bread) or of a geographic origin ('Georgia' peaches)—inherent distinctiveness will not be found. That is why the statute generally excludes, from those word marks that can be registered as inherently distinctive, words that are 'merely descriptive' of the goods, §2(e)(1), 15 USC §1052(e)(1), or 'primarily geographically descriptive of them,' see §2(e)(2), 15 USC §1052(e)(2). In the case of product design, as in the case of color, we think consumer predisposition to equate the feature with the source does not exist. Consumers are aware of the reality that, almost invariably, even the most unusual of product designs–such as a cocktail shaker shaped like a penguin—is intended not to identify the source, but to render the product itself more useful or more appealing.

The fact that product design almost invariably serves purposes other than source identification not only renders inherent distinctiveness problematic; it also renders application of an inherent-distinctiveness principle more harmful to other consumer interests. Consumers should not be deprived of the benefits of competition with regard to the utilitarian and esthetic purposes that product design ordinarily serves by a rule of law that facilitates plausible threats of suit against new entrants based upon alleged inherent distinctiveness. How easy it is to mount a plausible suit depends, of course, upon the clarity of the test for inherent distinctiveness, and where product design is concerned we have little confidence that a reasonably clear test can be devised. Respondent and the United States as amicus curiae urge us to adopt for product design relevant portions of the test formulated by the Court of Customs and Patent Appeals for product packaging in *Seabrook Foods, Inc v Bar-Well Foods, Ltd*, 568 F 2d 1342 (1977). That opinion, in determining the inherent distinctiveness of a product's packaging, considered, among other things, 'whether it was a "common" basic shape or design, whether it was unique or unusual in a particular field, [and] whether it was a mere refinement of a commonly-adopted and well-known form of ornamentation for a particular class of goods viewed by the public as a dress or ornamentation for the goods.' *Id*, at 1344 (footnotes omitted). Such a test would rarely provide the basis for summary disposition of an anticompetitive strike suit. Indeed, at oral argument, counsel for the United States quite understandably would not give a definitive answer as to whether the test was met in this very case, saying only that '[t]his is a very difficult case for that purpose.' (Tr of Oral Arg 19)

... Competition is deterred ... not merely by successful suit but by the plausible threat of successful suit, and given the unlikelihood of inherently source-identifying design, the game of allowing suit based upon alleged inherent distinctiveness seems to us not worth the candle. That is especially so since the producer can ordinarily obtain protection for a design that is inherently source identifying (if any such exists), but that does not yet have secondary meaning, by securing a design patent or a copyright for the design—as, indeed, respondent did for certain elements of the designs in this case. The availability of these other protections greatly reduces any harm to the producer that might ensue from our conclusion that a product design cannot be protected under §43(a) without a showing of secondary meaning.

THE SECOND STEP: FACTUAL DISTINCTIVENESS

If a mark falls to be considered under either s 41(3) or (4), it can still pass the s 41(1) test by virtue of a showing of factual distinctiveness. The precise circumstances that can be taken into account in assessing factual distinctiveness differ according to whether the mark falls to be considered under s 41(3) (for marks with no inherent adaptation to distinguish) or s 41(4) (for marks that are to some extent, but insufficiently, inherently adapted to distinguish).

If the mark falls under s 41(4), the examiner must consider the combined effect of:

- the extent of the mark's inherent adaptation to distinguish (is it borderline prima facie distinctive? Is it only inherently adapted to distinguish to a very slight extent?);
- the applicant's or a predecessor in title's use of the mark, including the post-filing date, or its intended use of the mark; and
- any other circumstances.

Unless the examiner is satisfied that the mark has not or will not come to distinguish the applicant's goods or services after considering the above, the mark will pass the s 41 hurdle.

If the mark falls under s 41(3), then only one factor is relevant: the extent of the applicant's or a predecessor in title's use of the mark *before* the filing date. Unless the examiner is satisfied that the mark had not acquired distinctiveness by the filing date on the basis of such use, the mark will pass the s 41 hurdle.

Importantly, the assessment of factual distinctiveness does not involve any consideration of whether other traders would wish to use the term in question. Rather, the question is one of fact: has (or will) the mark come to distinguish the applicant's goods and services from those of others? In showing this, the applicant will need to provide evidence of how it has used and promoted its mark.[4] For marks falling under s 41(4), 'other circumstances' that an applicant might point to include use of the mark on related goods or services to those specified and, more controversially, overseas registrations of the same mark in relation to the same goods or services.[5]

Some of the difficulties involved in assessing factual distinctiveness are set out in the following extract.

CURRENT LAW

CASE EXTRACT: CURRENT LAW

Chocolaterie Guylian NV v Registrar of Trade Marks

[2009] FCA 891; (2009) 180 FCR 60
Federal Court of Australia

[This case involved Guylian's attempt to register its well-known seahorse shape for pralines and chocolate. Sundberg J held that the mark was to some extent, but not sufficiently, inherently adapted to distinguish, and thus turned to consider whether the mark did or would distinguish the designated goods. This extract also contains a useful summary of *Woolworths Ltd v BP Plc (No 2)* [2006] FCAFC 132;

---

4   See *Blount Inc v Registrar of Trade Marks* (1998) 83 FCR 50 at 60–62.
5   This factor appears to be taken into account by the Office, but is difficult to reconcile with *Burger King Corporation v Registrar of Trade Marks* (1973) 128 CLR 417 at 422.

(2006) 154 FCR 97, in which BP was unable to demonstrate factual distinctiveness in the colour green as the predominant colour applied to external surfaces of petrol stations: in that case the Full Federal Court held that BP's evidence only showed that it had used green *in conjunction with yellow* as its trade mark.]

Sundberg J: 83. ... [What is now s 41(4) involves] a balancing exercise in that, for example, a mark that is inherently adapted only to a small degree is thereby likely to require greater evidence that it has been (or will be) used in such a way as to distinguish the relevant goods ...

84. ... [A]n applicant relying on use prior to the priority date will need to point to evidence that the mark has been used *as a trade mark*, so as to have acquired the requisite capability to distinguish the applicant's goods: see ... *Woolworths Ltd v BP Plc (No 2)* (2006) 154 FCR 97 at [72] and [77] (*BP (No 2)*); *Ocean Spray* [*Cranberries Inc* v *Registrar of Trade Marks* (2000)] 47 IPR 579 at [38]–[41], in particular [40].

GUYLIAN'S SUBMISSIONS

85. In short, Guylian contends that its long standing and extensive sales and promotion of its sea shell range with the seahorse shape—beginning in 1980 and continuing up to the priority date (16 April 2002) and beyond—demonstrate that the shape itself has been used as a trade mark and was therefore capable of distinguishing Guylian's chocolate goods as at the priority date ... Guylian emphasises that its sales, advertising and promotion of the sea shell range with the seahorse shape has been not only significant in scope but continuous over a long period of time. It refers to its promotional material, including its chocolate box packaging, and placed particular reliance on its seahorse shaped boxes, which it commenced selling in 1999, together with their related point of sale display units ...

86. As has become common in trade mark registration appeals, Guylian seeks to rely on the ACNielsen survey results as evidence of an association by consumers of the seahorse shape with Guylian, an association it says is 'clear' and 'strong' and demonstrates that Guylian has been, and is, using the shape as a badge of origin. Particular reference was made to the survey responses being 'unprompted' (ie respondents were not, for example, provided with brand names and asked to choose between them), as well as the fact that the Registrar did not ... controvert any of [Guylian's expert] Mr Callaghan's evidence, most notably his conclusions (1) that consumers' association of the shape with Guylian was of a 'very high level', and (2) the strength of the association with Guylian, when compared to associations made with other brands, was statistically 'very significant' ...

REGISTRAR'S SUBMISSIONS

87. The Registrar contends that Guylian's evidence of use fails to demonstrate that the shape has been used as a trade mark. The Registrar referred to the observations of Jacob J in *British Sugar* [*Plc v James Robertson & Sons Ltd*] [1996] RPC 281 at 303, where his Lordship dealt with evidence of the use of the word 'Treat' by the applicant in relation to its dessert sauce and syrup products:

> There is an unspoken and illogical assumption that 'use equals distinctiveness'. The illogicality can be seen from an example: no matter how much use a manufacturer made of the word 'Soap' as a purported trade mark for soap the word would not be distinctive of his goods ... I do not consider that the evidence filed to support the registration was anywhere near enough to support the conclusion that when the mark was registered, it was distinctive. Yes it had been used for

about 5 years in conjunction with Silver Spoon, but it was not proved that the public regarded it as a trade mark—a reliable badge of trade origin—on its own.

88. In the case of a three dimensional shape mark, the Registrar said, the necessity to show clear evidence that consumers have been educated to perceive the shape as a trade mark, an indicator of origin, is all the more important. While the shape of goods might distinguish the goods as goods, the shape will not necessarily distinguish the goods as originating from one trade source rather than another. In this case, says the Registrar, the shape has been used not as a badge of origin but rather as simply one of the chocolate shapes out of a number of sea shell/marine shapes that Guylian sells and markets as one collection. Where Guylian uses the shape on its packaging and promotional material, it is more often than not displayed alongside the other sea shell shapes. It is not given such a prominence as to educate the public that it is being used as a trade mark. Rather, it is used in a descriptive or informative manner, identifying to the public examples of the novelty shapes included in Guylian's sea shell chocolate range.

89. … [T]he Registrar says that one should take into account the extent to which the mark applied for has been used in conjunction with any other distinctive marks. Here, there are two: (1) the 'Guylian' trade mark … and (2) the letter 'G', which Guylian uses as a logo on each of its chocolate pieces. The image of the seahorse shape on Guylian's packaging, it said, is overwhelmed by the use of the highly distinctive 'Guylian' trade mark, which serves as the true indicator of origin. Similarly, the 'G' logo, appearing on each chocolate piece and the pictures of the chocolates on the boxes, plays a dominant role in indicating the origin of the goods, particularly when they are out of the box.

90. The Registrar makes two main submissions about the survey evidence. First, it says the results fail to establish that consumers see the seahorse shape as a badge of origin. It referred to *BP (No 2)* … and *British Sugar* … where surveys indicating 85% and 60% recognition of the mark in suit nevertheless failed to demonstrate distinctiveness. Those cases, it said, show that there is a difference between mere association and the perception of a sign as a trade mark. Evidence of an association between a sign and a manufacturer, even a high one, will not necessarily mean that consumers rely on the sign to identify the origin of the goods. Here, the survey question tested association and no more. It did not test whether consumers have in fact come to perceive and understand the seahorse shape as a trade mark, by, for example, asking whether or not respondents believed that the shape belonged to one particular manufacturer and, if so, whether they could identify the manufacturer. Secondly, the Registrar relied on the survey results themselves, referring to the fact that (1) less than half of the respondents associated the shape with Guylian … and, (2) of those that did associate it with a particular manufacturer, approximately 25% associated it with someone other than Guylian. While the degree of association with an applicant's goods may in itself be relevant to the overall assessment whether the mark has acquired a capacity to distinguish, the results here, said the Registar, are manifestly insufficient so as to be satisfied that the shape alone distinguishes Guylian's goods in the minds of the chocolate buying public.

RESOLUTION

91. In *Unilever plc's Trade Mark Applications* [2003] RPC 35 (*Unilever*) (the Walls' 'Viennetta' case), Jacob J considered survey evidence which demonstrated a 'high degree of association' (approximately 67% of ice cream eaters) between an image of the 'Viennetta' ice cream and its manufacturer, Walls.

(Respondents were shown four ice cream products and asked if they recognised them). At 662, his Lordship said:

> Putting the other products on one side for the moment, there can be no doubt that the product appearance has achieved considerable recognition on its own as denoting Walls' 'Viennetta'—the product of a particular manufacturer. Is that enough to give it a 'distinctive character' ... ? For what has not been proved is that any member of the public would rely upon the appearance alone to identify the goods. They recognise it but do not treat it as a trade mark.
>
> There is a bit of sleight of hand going on here and in other cases of this sort. The trick works like this. The manufacturer sells and advertises his product widely and under a well-known trade mark. After some while the product appearance becomes well-known. He then says the appearance alone will serve as a trade mark, even though he himself never relied on the appearance alone to designate origin and would not dare to do so. He then gets registration of the shape alone. Now he is in a position to stop other parties, using their own word trade marks, from selling the product, even though no-one is deceived or misled.
>
> I do not think that is what the European Trade Mark system is for. It is a system about trade marks, badges of trade origin. For that reason I think that in the case of marks consisting of product shapes it is not enough to prove the public recognises them as the product of a particular manufacturer. It must be proved that consumers regard the shape alone as a badge of trade origin in the sense that they would rely upon that shape alone as an indication of trade origin, particularly to buy the goods. If that cannot be proved, then the shape is not properly a trade mark, it does not have a 'distinctive character' for the purposes of trade mark law.

92. Notably, his Lordship also considered it relevant that a not insignificant proportion of the survey respondents (approximately 15%) identified one or more of the other ice creams as the 'Viennetta', as this showed the potential for infringement by other traders seeking to sell a similar product.

93. In *BP (No 2)* ... [BP] failed to establish ... that it had used a particular shade of green as a trade mark, either by itself or as the predominant colour in its branding. Two aspects of their Honours' reasoning are instructive. First, the Court took into account survey evidence indicating, on a weighted basis, that 85% of respondents identified BP when they were asked to look at a picture of a building (a service station) which was coloured substantially in green and were asked to describe what they saw. In considering an expert's conclusion that this showed a 'strong association' between green and BP, the Court stated at [117]:

> This conclusion is hardly surprising. Green had been one of BP's company colours since at least 1956. After 1989 it had been used as the predominant colour with yellow. In particular, in circumstances where there were only a few oil companies, where all have used colour historically to distinguish themselves, where BP has been the only company before 1995 to use green in that way, it is hardly surprising that people shown this stimulus would associate the green service station with BP service stations which have been coloured with a predominant green and accompanying yellow. That association does not lead to the conclusion that the use of colour from 1989 has included use, as a trade mark, of either green alone, or green as the predominant colour accompanied by any other colour. The mere fact that consumers associate green with BP does not, in our view, satisfy the test of distinctiveness ... Evidence of promotion and use does not, without more, demonstrate distinctiveness: see *Blount Inc v Registrar of Trade Marks* at 61G,

citing with approval Jacob J in *British Sugar Plc v James Robertson & Sons Ltd* at 286 and 302; and *Koninklijke Philips Electronics NV v Remington Products Australia Pty Ltd* (2000) FCR 90 … at [13]. *It is necessary for BP to establish that the association is referable to the use of the mark as a trade mark.* The learned authors of *Kerly's Law of Trade Marks and Trade Names* (14th ed, Sweet & Maxwell Ltd, UK, 2005, at [8–025]) state, albeit in the European context, that *to establish distinctiveness through use the proprietor must have done something in its use to identify the sign as being a trade mark; the use of a sign, without more, does not necessarily create the perception that the products originate from a particular trade source:* compare *Unilever Plc's Trade Mark Applications* [2003] RPC 35 at [31] (Emphasis added)

94. Ultimately, their Honours concluded at [118] that:

These responses are consistent with a recognition that green has always been part of the BP colour scheme; however, they do not lead to the conclusion that green alone, or green predominantly with other unspecified colours, has been used as a trade mark.

95. … [T]heir Honours' observation that associations must be 'referable to the use of the mark as a trade mark' is apt to describe the problem confronting Guylian in this case. The survey evidence here plainly shows an association between the seahorse shape and Guylian. This is no doubt due in large part to the substantial sales of Guylian's sea shell chocolates with the seahorse shape over a considerable period of time. However, even assuming that the association in this case is strong enough, the anterior question is whether the association is referable to Guylian having used the shape as a trade mark. In other words, is the fact that a relatively large proportion of consumers may think of Guylian when they see the shape a consequence of Guylian having educated the public to recognise it as a badge of origin. When the evidence of use is considered as a whole, I am not satisfied that Guylian has done so, for the following reasons.

96. First, my impression is that the seahorse shape (or, more correctly, an image of the shape) is used on Guylian's packaging to attract consumers and provide an example of the box's contents. It is by no means the only shape that features on Guylian's packaging. Many of the other sea shell shapes are displayed with equal prominence and on the back of most boxes, almost all of the shapes are shown, some sitting inside a picture of the box and others outside. As an example, [one box] shows the seahorse shape with two others on the front in a triangular arrangement, positioned closely to the words '44 Finest Belgian Chocolate Sea Shells'. Eight of the other 'Sea Shells' are displayed across the four sides of the box and all of the shapes shown are the same size and colour. On these boxes, the seahorse shape does not in my view function as a trade mark. It is not used in any sense to identify Guylian but to illustrate some examples of the elegance of the chocolates and the contents of the box more generally. The sales sheets, brochures and website extract tendered by Guylian confirm this … [I]t does not seem to me likely that consumers would conceive of the seahorse shape on Guylian's boxes as a trade mark, so much as simply an example of the novelty shapes that Guylian manufactures. I also note that there is a lack of precision in the evidence as to the timing, duration and location of much of the packaging, advertising and point of sale material. Most of the evidence (in particular, the sales sheets, magazine catalogues and website extract) appeared to be quite recent, in the two to three years leading up to the priority date and beyond. Absent, for example, was any evidence about how the seahorse shape had been used between the time it entered the market in 1980 and the end of the 1990s. It is not at all clear what use, in a trade mark sense, was made of the seahorse shape by Guylian over that period.

CURRENT LAW

97. Secondly, I agree with the Registrar's submission that the 'Guylian' trade mark printed on Guylian's packaging has the effect of diluting any trade mark significance that might otherwise attach to the seahorse shape. On all of the boxes, the 'Guylian' trade mark is prominently displayed and acts as the key, distinctive identifier of the products. In addition to the 'Guylian' trade mark, Guylian engraves a stylised letter 'G' into each piece of chocolate. The 'G' itself appears to be a registered trade mark, as recorded on the back of Guylian's boxes, and its function is described in Guylian's marketing material: 'Every Guylian chocolate creation bears the letter "G", indicating the outstanding quality and consumer assurance that it is a genuine Guylian praline'. I also observe that the images of the various shapes pictured on Guylian's boxes, including the seahorse shape, clearly reveal the 'G' logo and the shapes appear to be orientated in almost all cases so that the 'G' is upright and readable. In my view, the presence of these other distinctive marks makes it difficult to conclude that the seahorse shape has by itself become distinctive of Guylian's products ... I accept, as Guylian contends, that a sign may be registrable as a trade mark even though it is used together with other trade marks. However, where an application for registration relies on use the question is whether the particular sign for which registration is sought has itself been used as a trade mark so as to become capable of distinguishing the relevant goods. Each case turns on its own facts and here my impression of the packaging and promotional material as a whole is that it is the 'Guylian' trademark, together with the 'G' logo', that does the work of distinguishing the goods, not the seahorse shape ...

98. Thirdly, I have taken into account Guylian's use of seahorse shaped boxes. These to some extent show a trade mark use of the shape, with the box approximating an outline of the shape and displaying an enlarged image of the seahorse across the entire front side of the box. The shape of the boxes is unique and has some ability to catch the eye, particularly when they are presented in rows in an upright position on Guylian's display stands. However, once again, both the 'Guylian' trade mark and the 'G' trade mark feature significantly on the front of the boxes, which diminishes the trade mark significance the image of the seahorse shape might otherwise have ... I also think it relevant that the seahorse shaped boxes have only been on the Australian market since 1999, that is, only 3 years prior to the priority date. Beyond the sales figures provided, the extent to which the boxes have actually been used in Australia is unclear ... [I]t would appear that only a comparatively small amount of each of the small and large boxes have been sold in Australia between 1999 and 2003, assuming equal sales of the two sizes ... The retail brochures state that the boxes are 'Only available as limited edition—Christmas'. It thus appears that the seahorse shaped boxes have been sold on a fairly limited basis prior to the priority date, and this must be taken into account in assessing the impact their use might have on consumers ...

...

100. Finally, I have had regard to the survey evidence, and the expert evidence of Mr Callaghan, which indicates that a significant proportion of the survey respondents were able to identify Guylian when they were shown the seahorse shape. However I am of the view that this association on the whole is likely to be referable to Guylian's sale of the sea shell and seahorse shaped chocolates, over a long period of time, under the banner of the distinctive 'Guylian' and 'G' trade marks, rather than to the shape itself being used as a trade mark. The cases confirm that association evidence on its own does not prove distinctiveness; the evidence must establish that the public has been educated to understand the sign as an identifier of the origin of the goods: see *BP (No 2)* ... and *Unilever* ... In essence, the survey

in this case tested respondents' ability to recognise a shape and associate it with a manufacturer or brand. It tested 'brand recognition', as Mr Callaghan suggested; 'the ability of a consumer to confirm prior exposure to a brand when presented with one of the brand's identity elements'. When regard is had to the way the shape has been used, the survey results do not in my view confirm that consumers actually understand the shape as an indicator of the origin of the goods. The results plainly show a large degree of public recognition of the shape, but as Jacob J said in *Unilever* ... at 662: '[W]hat has not been proved is that any member of the public would rely upon the appearance alone to identify the goods. They recognise it but do not treat it as a trade mark'. In any event, I agree with the Registrar's submission that the results tend to confirm the view I have already come to that the shape has not been used as a trade mark, because almost half the respondents were in fact unable to identify the shape with any particular brand or manufacturer ... Further, Mr Callaghan also attributed the association to more than just the shape itself. He said it was likely that many associations would have been based on recognition of the overall image and not simply its shape, for example colour and a perception of the texture of the object ... This is important, because it is the shape alone over which Guylian seeks a monopoly. In the circumstances as described by Mr Callaghan, it seems to me that the probative value of the association evidence is to some extent diminished by the way many of the respondents are likely to have made their association.

CONCLUSION

101. Having regard to Guylian's use of the shape and the extent to which it is inherently adapted to distinguish, I am not satisfied that the shape does or will distinguish the designated goods as being Guylian's ...

Recent Federal Court decisions show how difficult it can be to demonstrate factual distinctiveness, even when what might appear to be extensive evidence of use is provided. For example, in *Phone Directories Company Australia Pty Ltd v Telstra Corporation Ltd* [2014] FCA 373; (2014) 106 IPR 281, involving Telstra's application for the word mark YELLOW, Murphy J, having found the mark to lack any inherent adaptation to distinguish, was unpersuaded that the impact of Telstra's use of the word 'yellow' in various forms since the mid-1970s meant that the mark had acquired distinctiveness by its 25 July 2003 filing date. Notwithstanding Telstra's extensive use of the 'Yellow Pages' brand, both as a word mark and in conjunction with the famous 'walking fingers' device, dating back to the 1970s, Murphy J considered that the term 'yellow' remained descriptive of the colour and nature of Telstra's directories when used in that manner. Telstra's brief 'Hello Yellow' advertising campaign in the early 1980s was considered not to have involved trade mark use of 'yellow', but rather use as a 'shorthand reference' to the 'Yellow Pages' mark. In any event, Murphy J thought if Telstra's use of 'yellow' since the 1970s was to be taken to be use as a trade mark, any such use was diluted by the fact the word was almost invariably used as part of larger word marks or composite marks, and was not used extensively enough to distinguish Telstra's goods and services from those of other traders. Murphy J also considered that if YELLOW was in fact inherently adapted to distinguish to a slight extent, Telstra's evidence of post-filing date use was insufficient to demonstrate that the mark had or would become factually distinctive. His Honour thought that a 'Find It In Yellow' campaign, run in 2005–06, still used 'yellow' as a shorthand reference to 'Yellow Pages', and that despite the $20 million rebranding of Telstra's entire product and service from 'Yellow Pages' to 'Yellow' from

2006–09, there was only negligible evidence indicating strong consumer recognition that 'Yellow' had become factually distinctive.

PROHIBITED OR PRESCRIBED SIGNS

Turning to the remaining absolute grounds, s 39 sets out a ground of rejection if the mark contains or consists of certain prescribed signs. More particularly, s 39(1) provides that an application *must* be rejected if the mark contains or consists of a sign that, under regulations made for the purposes of s 18, is not to be used as a trade mark. No such regulations have yet been made. Section 39(2) provides that an application *may* be rejected if the trade mark contains or consists of a prescribed sign, or a sign so nearly resembling a prescribed sign as to be likely to be taken for it. The list of prescribed signs is set out in reg 4.15 and Sch 2, and contains an eclectic mix of signs including the words 'Registered', 'Copyright', 'Austrade', 'Olympic Champion' and 'Returned Soldier', as well as representations of the Arms, flag or seal of the Commonwealth, a state or a territory.

GRAPHICAL REPRESENTATION

Section 40 provides for a ground of rejection 'if the trade mark cannot be represented graphically'. This cannot be raised as a ground of opposition or cancellation (although the Registrar can decide to revoke acceptance or registration on the basis of non-compliance with s 40 (see ss 38 and 84A)). The requirement appears designed to ensure that what ends up on the Register conveys sufficiently clear and precise information about what the mark is, and to help to delineate the scope of rights in the mark. It might appear that there is a tension between s 40 and the definition of 'sign' in s 6(1) that include non-visual phenomena such as sounds and signs (and that the definition would presumably cover things such as tastes and gestures). However, it appears that compliance with s 40 only requires the applicant to represent its mark in accordance with the Office's instructions as set out in the *Manual of Practice and Procedure* and on the Office's application forms. For example, for scent and sound marks the Office has been prepared to accept that a precise verbal description of the scent or sound will be a sufficient graphic representation. Consequently, this is an issue that is unlikely to cause significant problems in Australia, despite the fact that it has caused controversy in the EU where, following the decision of the Court of Justice in Case C-273/00, *Sieckmann v Deutsches Patent- und Markenamt* [2002] ECR I-11737, it is unlikely that certain non-visually perceptible marks such as scents and tastes can ever be adequately graphically represented.

SCANDALOUS MARKS

Section 42(a) states that an application must be rejected if the mark 'contains or consists of scandalous matter'. While the precise rationale for the prohibition remains uncertain, it would seem that the ground is motivated by a desire not to give a form of state-sanctioned imprimatur, through the act of trade mark registration, to subject matter such as obscene, profane, abusive or racist terms or images, and to help ensure that the trade marks registry is not discredited by creating a suggestion that the Office approves of or sanctions the applicant's choice of mark (see *Hanlon* [2011] ATMO 45).

While no clear consensus has emerged as to how the term 'scandalous' is to be interpreted, it is clear that it requires more than the sign being merely indecent, crude or in bad taste, or that it merely alludes to or suggests an obscene term (French Connection's FCUK mark being perhaps the best-known example). A scandalous mark must at least be 'shameful, offensive or shocking' (according to the *Manual of Practice and Procedure*) and possibly even cause a 'significant degree of disgrace, shock or outrage' (see *Cosmetic, Toiletry and Fragrance Association Foundation v Fanni Barns Pty Ltd* (2003) 57 IPR 594, where LOOK GOOD + FEEL GOOD = ROOT GOOD was accepted for registration). This assessment is to be made on the basis of contemporary social values and mores. It is, however, unclear whether the mark must be scandalous to an 'ordinary person' (as indicated by the *Manual of Practice and Procedure*) or whether it can be highly offensive to a particular class, where the significance of the use might not be appreciated by others outside that class.

CONTRARY TO LAW

Section 42(b) provides that an application must be rejected if 'its use would be contrary to law'. At times, this will involve a consideration of whether the use of the sign would be contrary to a specific legislative prohibition (e.g. those contained in the *Olympic Insignia Protection Act 1987* (Cth) on the use of 'protected Olympic expressions' such as 'Olympics' and 'Olympic Games', or those in the *Australian Grape and Wine Authority Act 2013* (Cth) regulating the use of GIs and other protected expressions in relation to wine). However, the scope of s 42(b) is broader than this, as can be seen from the following extract.

CASE EXTRACT: CURRENT LAW

Advantage Rent-A-Car Inc v Advantage Car Rental Pty Ltd

[2001] FCA 683; (2001) 52 IPR 24
Federal Court of Australia

[An application for registration of a device mark featuring the words 'Advantage Car Rental' underneath a star shape was opposed by the owner of a similar mark featuring the words 'Advantage Rent-A-Car', also underneath a star shape.]

Madgwick J: 22. … [B]ased on the evidence before the Court, in my opinion, use by the respondent of its trade mark would be contrary to the *Copyright Act* and accordingly contrary to law. Therefore, the ground for opposing the registration of a trade mark provided for by s 42(b) is made out by the [opponent]. It should however be noted, that this is but the expression of opinion upon a hypothesis and does not amount to a finding of any actual breach of the *Copyright Act* by the [applicant for registration].

ROLE OF THE REGISTRAR

23. Issue was taken as to the appropriateness of the Registrar determining issues of law outside the area of his or her expertise, namely trade marks. It was submitted by counsel for the Registrar that it was not within the competence of the Registrar to determine at the stage of opposition proceedings whether a mark would be contrary to law if it involved issues beyond those set out in the Act. It was submitted that the proper administration of the Act requires that the Registrar only make determinations under s 42(b) where there is a clear finding that the Registrar can apply, such as a decision of a court

CURRENT LAW

of competent jurisdiction that a mark infringes the law and not when it involves complex considerations of legal matters going beyond those specifically set out in the Act.

...

25. The contrary to law ground can fall for consideration at three different stages. Firstly, under s 42(b) itself, the Registrar is to reject an application for registration if it is contrary to law. Secondly, at the opposition stage a person may challenge registration of a trade mark on the basis that it is contrary to law. Thirdly, the court can rectify the Register by removing a trade mark if it is contrary to law. The first two are determinations made by the Registrar, which are judicially reviewable by this Court, whilst the third is a determination made by this Court.

26. However, in my opinion the fact that the existence of any contrariety to law is to be exercised in some circumstances by an administrative body and, in other circumstances, by a judicial body does not mean that the phrase 'if its use would be contrary to law' should have an ambulatory meaning, depending upon what kind of tribunal is to apply it. Nor can any reticence on the part of an administrative decision-maker to express an opinion on a matter of law be encouraged. The idea that 'contrary to law' in the context of judicial proceedings means contrary to all laws, whilst in the context of proceedings before the Registrar it means contrary to laws which are easy for the Registrar to determine or which are 'clear cut', is not sustainable. As a matter of practice, delegates of the Registrar have in some cases determined that a trade mark submitted for registration is contrary to law as a result of its being in breach of other legislation: see *Re Application by Slaney* (1985) 6 IPR 307 at 309 where a trade mark was found to be in breach of the *Health Legislation Amendment Act* 1983 (Cth) and *Re Application by Athol Thomas Kelly* (1987) 8 IPR 667 at 672 where it was found that the trade mark would infringe the *Advance Australia Logo Act 1984* (Cth). I see no reason why some legislation should be able to be relied on before the Registrar to establish contrariety to law and other legislation such as the *Copyright Act*, albeit more complex, should not. Further, it is well-settled that a power granted to the Registrar and to a court can be at once administrative and judicial depending on who was exercising the power. The High Court so held in *R v Quinn; Ex parte Consolidated Foods Corporation* (1977) 138 CLR 1, of a power to remove a trade mark from the Register.

...

28. I acknowledge the claim made by counsel for the Registrar that such an approach requires the Registrar to look at questions of law outside his or her expertise and that this can be difficult and may place a large and onerous responsibility upon the Registrar. However, the Registrar has the comfort that the criterion is that the use 'would' not 'could' be contrary to law. Further, there is no reason why the Registrar could not seek legal advice before forming his/her opinion. It should also be noted that what is required is that the Registrar form a view as to whether the use of a trade mark would be contrary to law. Such opinion does not have a similar effect to say, a judicial conclusion of law as to breach of copyright in copyright proceedings; the effect is limited to the refusal of registration. In any case, an appeal de novo lies from the Registrar's decision to this Court where any error of the Registrar may be corrected.

We will return to the broader consequences of the *Advantage* decision in the context of considering the relative grounds of refusal (see below, p 746).

DECEPTIVE OR CONFUSING CONNOTATION

Section 43 provides that:

> An application for the registration of a trade mark in respect of particular goods or services
> must be rejected if, because of some connotation that the trade mark or a sign contained in
> the trade mark has, the use of the trade mark in relation to those goods or services would be
> likely to deceive or cause confusion.

The language of 'likely to deceive or cause confusion' is one that also appears in ss 44, 60 and 120 of the *TMA* and is discussed in detail in extracts below on ss 44 (see p 725) and 60 (see p 739). It is a different standard from that of 'misrepresentation' in the tort of passing off and 'misleading or deceptive conduct' under s 18 of the ACL (considered in Chapter 16). In the context of s 43 of the *TMA*, a likelihood of deception or confusion requires the existence of a 'real, tangible danger' of consumers at least entertaining a 'reasonable doubt', or being 'caused to wonder', about the existence of a particular state of affairs as a result of the use of the mark.[6]

Perhaps the most difficult issue specific to s 43 is determining what is meant by 'connotation'. As seen from the two extracts below, s 43 can be used to catch marks that are inherently confusing, for example because they are 'misdescriptive' as to certain qualities or characteristics or the geographical origin of the specified goods or services.

PRECEDENT

CASE EXTRACT: PRECEDENT

Re The Registered Trade Mark 'Yanx'; Ex parte Amalgamated Tobacco Corporation Ltd

(1951) 82 CLR 199
High Court of Australia

Williams J (at 200–206): This is an application ... to rectify the register of trade marks by expunging therefrom registered trade mark 88717 on the ground that the entry of this trade mark was wrongly made on the register. The date of registration is 30th September 1946. The registration is in class 45 in respect of cigarettes. The trade mark consists of a label suitable for printing on packets or other containers of cigarettes comprising the word 'Yanx' in very prominent letters in combination with stars and stripes, the same word in less prominent letters, and also the words 'Yanx Cigarettes' followed by a statement that the cigarettes are manufactured from the finest Macedonian and choicest American tobaccos blended proportionately to bring out the flavour of each tobacco and ending with the words 'Made in England,' the letters of the words 'Yanx Cigarettes' and 'Made in England' being of about the same size as the letters of the word 'Yanx' where it secondly appears. The words Menzala and Menzala Cigarette Co Ltd, London, EC, also appear on the label ...

... [The grounds of rectification] raise the question whether the use of the word 'Yanx' is deceptive as suggesting to persons buying the goods, contrary to fact, that they are American cigarettes or that

---

6   See *McCorquodale v Masterson* [2004] FCA 1247; (2004) 63 IPR 582.

they are in some definite way connected with the United States ... The question is essentially one of fact. The respondent has not used trade mark 88717 in Australia so that the applicant could not be expected to produce evidence of actual confusion. The words on the label 'Made in England' assist the respondent to the extent stated by the Assistant Comptroller in *Green's Case* (1946) 64 RPC, at p 17: 'They are a factor which might reduce the possibility of deception but would not entirely remove it.' There is no doubt that in its ordinary signification the word 'Yankee' or 'Yank' has come to mean a citizen of the United States of America and that 'Yanx' means such citizens in the plural. The word 'Yanx', which is simply a mis-spelling of 'Yanks', is so conspicuously displayed on the label that its use alone would suggest to persons buying the cigarettes that they were American cigarettes, and this suggestion would be heightened by its combination with the stars and stripes which are emblematic of the national flag and song of the United States. The words 'Made in England' are not very conspicuous on the label and could easily be overlooked. On the whole I think that the label is likely to cause such deception and that in the public interest it should be expunged on this ground also.

CASE EXTRACT: CURRENT LAW

Scotch Whisky Association v De Witt

[2007] FCA 1649; (2007) 74 IPR 382
Federal Court of Australia

[This case involved an opposition by the Scotch Whisky Association (referred to below as 'the applicant') to the registration of the stylised words 'GLENN OAKS' for goods including 'bourbon'.]

Sundberg J: 48. The applicant's case was put in two ways: in a broad sense and in a more specific sense. The latter is dealt with at [57]. The broad submission was that the words GLENN OAKS (particularly GLENN) convey a clear connotation of Scottish origin, and their use in relation to bourbon products is likely to deceive or cause confusion. This submission went to the real difference between the parties, namely whether bourbon should be listed in the statement of goods.

49. In order to succeed under s 43 of the Act, an opponent must show that there is a connotation in the proposed trade mark, and that because of that connotation, the use of the mark would be likely to deceive or cause confusion. See *McCorquodale* [*v Masterson* [2004] FCA 1247] at [25] and [26].

50. The word 'connotation' is defined in the Oxford English Dictionary as:

1   The signifying in addition; inclusion of something in the meaning of the word besides what it primarily denotes; implication.

 b   That which is implied in a word in addition to its essential or primary meaning.

51. In *Dunn's Trade Mark* (1890) 7 RPC 311 at 318–319 Lord Macnaghten said that a tribunal should refuse to register 'words which involve a misleading allusion or suggestion of that which is not strictly true, as well as words which contain a gross and palpable falsehood'. His Lordship's comments were referable to the principle underlying a predecessor of s 43. In two Trade Mark Office decisions which applied Lord Macnaghten's observations, connotation was said to be more than a mere 'allusion'

PRECEDENT

CURRENT LAW

or 'suggestion': see *Aktion Zahnfreundlich v Suntory Ltd* (1998) 42 IPR 593 and *Effem Foods Pty Ltd v Star-Kist Foods, Inc* (2000) 50 IPR 121.

52. Whether there is a likelihood of deception or confusion is to be answered 'not by reference to the manner in which the applicant for registration has used its mark in the past, but by reference to the use to which it can properly put the mark if it becomes registered': *Berlei v Hestia Industries Ltd* (1973) 129 CLR 353 at 362. Here, the GLENN OAKS mark is the relevant mark in suit. The surrounding circumstances provide guidance as to what is proper, normal and fair use of the respondent's mark and whether confusion exists: *McCorquodale* at [52]–[53] and [60] in particular. See also, *Southern Cross Refrigerating Co v Toowoomba Foundry Pty Ltd* (1954) 91 CLR 592 at 494–495, *Registrar of Trade Marks v Woolworths (Woolworths Metro)* (1999) 45 IPR 411 at [50] and *Johnson & Johnson v Kalnin* (1993) 26 IPR 435 at 438.

[Sundberg J then set out a number of principles on assessing deception and confusion, and continued:]

56. The applicant's specific case under s 43 was put as follows:

- Glen is an anglicised spelling of the Scottish Gaelic word 'Gleann' or 'Ghlinne' which means narrow valley, dale or glen. Scotland is renowned for whisky. 'Glen' is evocative of Scotland and in particular of Scotch whisky.
- Use of GLENN OAKS on bourbon products labelled 'bourbon', 'bourbon whiskey' or 'Tennessee whiskey' that do not originate in Scotland would be likely to deceive or cause confusion because of that connotation.
- Alternatively, in the hypothetical case of a bourbon product being labelled solely as 'whiskey', the use of the GLENN OAKS mark would unequivocally evoke Scotland as the source of the product.

57. The applicant also placed emphasis on the fact that bourbon is a form of whiskey albeit one made in the United States.

58. In the circumstances described, the applicant submitted that consumers would be led into confusion if the GLENN OAKS mark could be applied to bourbon products as indicated on the statement of goods listed in the application. I am not persuaded by this submission.

59. First, for both involved and uninvolved purchasers of bourbon products, the words Glen or Glenn [are] more likely to be associated with a person's name than with a place denoting Scottish origin. Most uninvolved scotch whisky consumers, particularly those of pre-mixed drinks, would also think of a person's name before thinking of a Scottish place. The LMMA Report indicates that scotch whisky drinkers prefer pre-mixed drinks. There was no evidence of any pre-mixed drinks with the name Glen or Glenn. Involved scotch whisky consumers are in the same position. Consumers in the involved malt whisky class are discerning in their choice and are very knowledgeable about the products they purchase. Purchasing habits are more refined, which lessens the chance of confusion. Glen or Glenn, as a person's name, overshadows the connotation propounded by the applicant. Accordingly, that connotation is not strong enough to cause 'enough persons in the relevant public to be deceived or confused': *Carlton & United Breweries v Royal Crown* (2001) 53 IPR 599 at 606; *The Kendall Co v Mulsyn Paint and Chemicals* (*Kendall*) (1963) 109 CLR 300 at 305.

60. Second, involved and uninvolved purchasers of bourbon and scotch whisky products review product labels. This is the fair and normal way in which consumers behave. In this case, confusion is

mitigated by the circumstances in which such products are bought and sold. Bourbon products are typically labelled as bourbon, bourbon whiskey or Tennessee whiskey. Importantly, a consumer of these products must be 18 years of age. Bourbon products are much more expensive than impulse products such as soft drinks and confectionary … Purchasers of alcohol generally tend to be discerning in their purchasing habits … Where goods are denoted as being from a particular country, this constitutes another factor that reduces the possibility of confusion: *Green's Application* (1946) 64 RPC 14.

61. Both involved and uninvolved purchasers of bourbon and scotch whisky products will inspect labels and see that the product is in fact bourbon, made in the USA or the states Kentucky or Tennessee. A label indicating bourbon, bourbon whiskey and/or made in the USA clearly connote an origin of a place other than Scotland. Labels indicating 'Tennessee Whiskey' again connotes an origin in a place other than Scotland. For a mark to be rejected under s 43 there must be a 'real tangible danger of deception or confusion'. That exceptionally stupid or careless consumers might be confused does not suffice.

62. Third, there is no evidence that the GLENN OAKS mark would be used or would be likely to be used on a bottle of bourbon labelled solely as 'whisky' or 'whiskey'. While that does not limit the prospective use of a label of this nature, I infer from the absence of such evidence that such use would not be in the fair and normal course … In my view, the hypothetical scenario that the applicant proffers is one that will not, in all likelihood, eventuate. It cannot, therefore, lead to consumer confusion for the purposes of the Act. However, to cover this hypothetical case, the Court's order will state that bourbon in the statement of goods does not include bourbon which is labelled only as 'whiskey' or 'whisky'.

63. The applicant's case on s 43 of the Act fails.

The issue of whether s 43 extends beyond cases of this type (i.e. inherently misdescriptive marks) to cover situations where the applicant's mark is in conflict with a mark or sign in which another party has rights is less clear, and will be considered in the context of the relative grounds of refusal (below, p 747).

NO INTENTION TO USE

Section 59, which can only be raised in opposition proceedings, provides that registration may be opposed on the basis:

> that the applicant does not intend:
> (a) to use, or authorise the use of, the trade mark in Australia; or
> (b) to assign the trade mark to a body corporate for use by the body corporate in Australia;
> in relation to the goods and/or services specified in the application.

The opponent bears the onus of proving a negative state of affairs (i.e. a *lack* of intention), although the Full Federal Court confirmed in *Food Channel Network Pty Ltd v Television Food Network GP* [2010] FCAFC 58; (2010) 185 FCR 9 that the opponent only needs to make out a prima facie case to shift the onus to the applicant to rebut an allegation of a lack of intention to use. How s 59 applies is considered further in the following extract.

CASE EXTRACT: CURRENT LAW

Suyen Corporation v Americana International Ltd

[2010] FCA 638; (2010) 187 FCR 169
Federal Court of Australia

Dodds-Streeton J:

PRESUMPTION OF INTENTION

193. Historically, an application for registration of a trade mark has given rise to a presumption that the requisite intention to use the mark exists. In *Aston v Harlee Manufacturing* (1963) 103 CLR 391 ('*Aston*'), Fullagar J stated at 401 that:

> I do not regard his Honour [Dixon J in *Shell Co*] as meaning that an applicant is required, in order to obtain registration, to establish affirmatively that he intends to use it. There is nothing in the Act or the Regulations which requires him to state such an intention at the time of application, and the making of the application itself is, I think, to be regarded as *prima facie* evidence of intention to use.

...

196. A number of recent authorities have ... endorsed [*Aston*'s] continuing application. Most significantly, in *Food Channel* [*Network Pty Ltd v Television Food Network GP* [2010] FCAFC 58], the Full Court affirmed, in reliance on *Aston,* that 'the very act of making the application is, without more, sufficient to establish the requisite intention' ([67]) ...

197. ... [N]othing in the language of s 27 or any other relevant provision of the present Act suggests a legislative intention to depart from the long-established presumption of intention to use recognised under previous legislation. To the contrary, as possession of the requisite intention is a pre-condition of entitlement to apply, it may readily be presumed from the fact of application.

NATURE OF THE INTENTION

198. In *Ritz Hotel Ltd v Charles of Ritz Ltd* (1988) 15 NSWLR 158 ('*Ritz Hotel Ltd*') at 203E–F, McClelland J stated that: '[i]n my opinion the correct view is that an unused mark is not "proposed to be used" by an applicant for registration unless that applicant has, at the time of the application, a real and definite intention to use the mark publicly in Australia as a trade mark, although not necessarily immediately or within any limited time'.

...

201. McLelland J also referred to *Re Ducker's Trade Mark* [[1929] 1 Ch 113] at 121 where Lord Hanworth MR stated that 'I think that the words "proposed to be used" mean a real intention to use, not a mere problematical intention, not an uncertain or indeterminate possibility, but a resolve or settled purpose which has been reached at the time when the mark is to be registered'.

...

205. In *Aston*, Fullagar J also discussed the nature of the intention. His Honour stated at 401 that:

> A manufacturer of (say) confectionary would, I should suppose, be entitled to register three trade marks in relation to confectionary, though he intended only to use two of them and had not made up the mind as to which two he would use.

206. Fullagar J's frequently reiterated observation qualifies the absolute requirement for a real and definite intention to use each particular mark, at least in the context of multiple related applications in respect of the same goods.

ABSENCE OF INTENTION NOT INFERRED FROM NON-USE PER SE

207. There is long standing recognition that the absence of the requisite intention to use cannot be inferred from lack of use *per se*, particularly as there may be good reason to defer use until the protection of registration is secured.

...

211. Although non-use does not, in itself, imply a lack of the intention, the intention would usually accompany genuine use in Australia, which accordingly may constitute evidence of its existence. As confirmed by the Full Court in *Food Channel* ... use of the mark after the date of filing the application may also throw light on the existence of the intention at that earlier time.

212. Because the intention concerns the applicant's state of mind, it is, as the authorities make clear, difficult for an opponent to discharge the onus it bears under s 59 of the Act. Opposition has nevertheless succeeded in a number of cases. The intention has been held to be contra-indicated where the applicant company was not operating and failed to provide evidence, had no capacity to trade in the relevant goods or services or was subject to a relevant contractual restraint: see *Daimaru Pty Ltd v Kabushiki Kaisha Daimaru* (1990) 19 IPR 129. In other cases, opposition has succeeded because the evidence established the existence of only illegitimate purposes, including the use of registration defensively, speculatively, to gain competitive advantage or to sell the trade mark. See also *John Batt* [& Co's Registered Trade Marks [1898] 2 Ch 432] at 439–440.

213. In *Food Channel*, the Full Court observed that 'only a low threshold has been set with regard to intention to use' (at [67]). Their Honours referred to *Michael Sharwood & Partners Pty Ltd v Fuddruckers Inc* (1989) 15 IPR 188 (in which the applicant companies appeared not to carry on business, their location was illegal for a restaurant for which service the trade mark was to be registered and they adduced no evidence in answer to the opponent's material) and to *Danjaq LLC v Resource Capital Australia Pty Ltd* (2004) 61 IPR 651 (in which the applicant had made a large number of applications that were subsequently permitted to lapse, had a history of 'cybersquatting' and advanced the evidence of an unreliable sole witness. It was therefore inferred that the applicant was trading in registrations and had neither the capacity nor means to use the trade mark.).

214. Opposition has also succeeded where the applicant advances no or no credible evidence of the intention or concedes its absence; or where documents or the circumstances indicate an intention which is, for example, not sufficiently definite, or not directed at use as a trade mark.

215. In *Health World* [*Ltd v Shin-Sun Australia Pty Ltd* [2008] FCA 100], Jacobson J at first instance concluded that there was no intention to use the mark where the applicant's principal witness did not make the final decisions on such matters, and did not distinguish between the applicant company and another company in relation to steps said to evidence an intention to use the mark. The person who did constitute 'the controlling mind' of the applicant company gave limited evidence which disclosed no positive intention to use the trade mark on goods of the relevant class. Rather, he testified that 'we wanted to widen our business' to use the mark on any goods or products the company might make ...

CURRENT LAW

216. In *Food Channel*, the Full Court upheld the appeal on grounds, *inter alia*, that the primary judge erred in finding that the applicant had no intention to use the trade mark where its sole director (and 'controlling mind') gave unchallenged (and not inherently improbable) evidence of intention to use the mark, and there was 'some evidence not found to be unreliable' that the assignor company (controlled by the same person) had used the mark in respect of the relevant class of goods ([82]). The Full Court concluded that 'in this state of the evidence, the judge could not reasonably conclude that [the opponent] had discharged its onus on the s 59 issue': [83].

Notwithstanding the above, it is possible to point to a large number of Office decisions where opponents have struggled to make out a prima facie case to shift the onus to the applicant to make out an intention to use the mark.

BAD FAITH

Section 62A allows registration to be opposed on the basis that the application was made in bad faith. When s 62A was introduced in 2006, it was suggested that this ground might deal with situations involving applicants making speculative applications (e.g. for foreign marks, or misspelled variations of other marks) with no intention of using such marks and primarily to disrupt the businesses of other traders. It is, however, difficult to see what this ground was intended to add to s 59. It is possible that it was thought necessary because opponents had often struggled under s 59 to establish that the applicant had an absence of intention to use the mark. However, in cases where 'bad faith' is to be established from the fact that the applicant has no intention of using the mark, the evidentiary burden must be the same, and it is possible to point to Office decisions where opponents have failed under both s 59 and s 62A because they could not shift the onus to the applicant to justify its intentions.

Section 62A has come to have a greater role to play in cases involving conflicts between marks, and we will return to the provision in the context of the relative grounds of refusal (see below, p 755).

PROBLEMS WITH THE APPLICATION PROCESS

Section 62(a) provides for a ground of opposition where the application, or a document filed in support of the application, was amended contrary to the Act (see ss 63–66 on the procedural requirements for making such amendments). In contrast, s 62(b) provides that registration may be opposed on the ground 'that the Registrar accepted the application for registration on the basis of evidence or representations that were false in material particulars'. Falsity here simply requires a material misrepresentation by the applicant, rather than dishonesty.

RELATIVE GROUNDS OF REFUSAL

We now turn to the seven relative grounds of refusal, contained in ss 44, 60, 42(b), 43, 58, 62A and 61, which manage conflicts between the mark whose registration is being sought and other marks. These grounds overlap to some extent, but each one has a slightly different sphere of operation.

CONFLICTS WITH EARLIER REGISTERED MARKS OR APPLICATIONS UNDER S 44

The most important relative ground is set out in s 44, which provides in part:

(1) Subject to subsections (3) and (4), an application for the registration of a trade mark (*applicant's trade mark*) in respect of goods (*applicant's goods*) must be rejected if:

    (a) the applicant's trade mark is substantially identical with, or deceptively similar to:

        (i) a trade mark registered by another person in respect of similar goods or closely related services; or

        (ii) a trade mark whose registration in respect of similar goods or closely related services is being sought by another person; and

    (b) the priority date for the registration of the applicant's trade mark in respect of the applicant's goods is not earlier than the priority date for the registration of the other trade mark in respect of the similar goods or closely related services.

(2) Subject to subsections (3) and (4), an application for the registration of a trade mark (*applicant's trade mark*) in respect of services (*applicant's services*) must be rejected if:

    (a) it is substantially identical with, or deceptively similar to:

        (i) a trade mark registered by another person in respect of similar services or closely related goods; or

        (ii) a trade mark whose registration in respect of similar services or closely related goods is being sought by another person; and

    (b) the priority date for the registration of the applicant's trade mark in respect of the applicant's services is not earlier than the priority date for the registration of the other trade mark in respect of the similar services or closely related goods.

The grounds for rejection in s 44(1) and (2) are subject to two qualifications:

1 Section 44(3) gives the Registrar the discretion to accept an application on the basis of honest concurrent use of applicant's marks and the earlier mark, or 'other circumstances'; and

2 Section 44(4) provides that the Registrar *must not* reject the application if the applicant can show that it has made prior continuous use of its mark before the priority date of the earlier mark. Where an application has been accepted on the basis of s 44(4), registration can be opposed under s 58A on the basis that the owner of the earlier mark in fact made continuous use of the mark from before the applicant's first use.

In determining whether an application will be caught by s 44(1) and/or (2), three broad issues potentially fall for consideration:

1 Are the applicant's mark and the earlier registered mark/application 'substantially identical' with or 'deceptively similar' to each other? The former term is undefined. In relation to the latter, s 10 provides that 'a trade mark is taken to be deceptively similar to another trade mark if it so nearly resembles that other trade mark that it is likely to deceive or cause confusion'.

2 Do the specifications of the two marks cover 'similar goods' (for s 44(1)) or 'similar services' (for s 44(2))? 'Similar' here is defined as being the 'same' or 'of the same description' (s 14).

3 Are the applicant's goods 'closely related' to the services covered by the earlier mark (for s 44(1)) or the specified services 'closely related' to the goods covered by the earlier mark (for s 44(2))?

These issues are explored in greater detail in the following seven extracts (some of which are infringement cases because, as we will see in the following chapter, the concepts of 'substantial identity', 'deceptive similarity' and similar goods/services are also relevant to the question of whether a registered trade mark has been infringed).

'SUBSTANTIALLY IDENTICAL' AND 'DECEPTIVELY SIMILAR' MARKS

CASE EXTRACT: PRECEDENT

Shell Co of Australia Ltd v Esso Standard Oil (Australia) Ltd

(1961) 109 CLR 407
High Court of Australia

[Esso argued that Shell had infringed its registered trade mark for an anthropomorphic 'oil-drop' character. One of the issues to be decided for this purpose was whether Esso's mark and Shell's sign were substantially identical with or deceptively similar to each other.]

Windeyer J (at 414–416): In considering whether marks are substantially identical they should, I think, be compared side by side, their similarities and differences noted and the importance of these assessed having regard to the essential features of the registered mark and the total impression of resemblance or dissimilarity that emerges from the comparison. 'The identification of an essential feature depends', it has been said, 'partly on the Court's own judgment and partly on the burden of the evidence that is placed before it': *de Cordova v Vick Chemical Co* (1951) 68 RPC 103, at p 106. Whether there is substantial identity is a question of fact: see *Fraser Henleins Pty Ltd v Cody* (1945) 70 CLR 100, per Latham CJ at pp 114, 115, and *Ex parte O'Sullivan; Re Craig* (1944) 44 SR (NSW) 291, per Jordan CJ at p 298, where the meaning of the expression was considered. Judging by the eye alone, as I think is proper for the determination of substantial identity, my opinion is that in each film there are one or more moments when the personified figure of the oil-drop appears in a form that is substantially identical with the registered mark. If the films were arrested at these moments and the image displayed in still form, I consider that use of a substantially identical mark would be established. But that is not what happens. The figure does not stand still. It does not hold its pose or expression for long enough, nor is it sufficiently isolated from its surroundings for long enough to establish infringement by the use of a substantially identical mark. That is my conclusion. But these fleeting glimpses of substantial identity are, I think, significant when one comes to consider deceptive similarity. To that I now turn.

On the question of deceptive similarity a different comparison must be made from that which is necessary when substantial identity is in question. The marks are not now to be looked at side by side. The issue is not abstract similarity, but deceptive similarity. Therefore the comparison is the familiar one of trade mark law. It is between, on the one hand, the impression based on recollection of the plaintiff's mark that persons of ordinary intelligence and memory would have; and, on the other hand, the impressions that such persons would get from the defendant's television exhibitions ... I must assume that among the viewers of the television advertisements there will be motorists, accustomed to buying petrol and capable of being influenced by suggestions that one brand of petrol may be superior to another. The advertisements are directed to them, not to those who are obstinately content to fill their tanks at any convenient station without caring which oil company supplied its wares. And I must assume them to be persons of ordinary intelligence acquainted with the plaintiff's marks, and that they will watch the films with some degree of attention, whether that springs from enjoyment of the pantomime activities of the oil-drop man or from irritation and impatience at the interruption of the programme. When the Act speaks of marks being 'deceptively similar' to the registered mark, it propounds, I think, the same test as in the former Act was expressed by the phrase 'so nearly resembling it as to be likely to deceive'. The deceptiveness that is contemplated must result from similarity; but the likelihood of deception must be judged not by the degree of similarity alone, but by the effect of that similarity in all the circumstances. Doing the best I can to estimate what would be the impression created by the films on viewers of the sort that I have postulated, I am of opinion that the oil-drop man in each of the films is at various times so similar in body, build and expression to the plaintiff's mark that confusion is likely to arise. There is thus, I consider, a deceptive similarity.

[Windeyer J's reasoning was not disturbed on appeal to the Full Court.]

CASE EXTRACT: CURRENT LAW

Registrar of Trade Marks v Woolworths Ltd ('Woolworths Metro')

[1999] FCA 1020; (1999) 93 FCR 365
Federal Court of Australia, Full Court

[Woolworths had sought to register a device mark featuring the word 'metro' below the much smaller word 'WOOLWORTHS' and with a background of wavy lines in relation to 'Retailing and wholesaling services in the nature of supermarkets, department stores, variety stores, boutiques, specialty products stores, liquor outlets and discount stores'. The application was rejected by the Office on the basis of the mark being deceptively similar to 13 earlier registered marks and one earlier application for registration, all featuring the word 'Metro', in relation to closely related goods. Woolworths successfully appealed that decision to the Federal Court, and the Registrar subsequently appealed that decision to the Full Court.]

French J (with whom Tamberlin J agreed): 49. The question of fact for the Court on an appeal from the Registrar in a case of alleged deceptive similarity between marks was posed by the High Court in *Australian Woollen Mills Ltd v FS Walton & Co Ltd* [(1937) 58 CLR 641] at 658: 'whether in fact there is such a reasonable probability of deception or confusion that the use of the new mark and title should be restrained.' The reference to 'restrained' reflects the fact that unlike this case the *Australian Woollen Mills Ltd* case was an appeal in an infringement action. The judgment of the likelihood of deception or confusion is a very practical one and what has long been accepted as the proper approach to making that judgment was set out in *Australian Woollen Mills Ltd*. It requires assessment of the effect of the challenged mark upon the minds of potential customers. Impression or recollection taken away from the point at which the challenged mark is observed will be the basis of any belief about a connection between the new and the old marks. The effect of spoken description must be considered. What confusion or deception may be expected is to be based upon the behaviour of ordinary people.

As potential buyers of goods they are not to be credited with high perception or habitual caution. Exceptional carelessness or stupidity may be disregarded. The question ultimately is not susceptible of much discussion (at 659):

> It depends on a combination of visual impression and judicial estimation of the effect likely to be produced in the course of the ordinary conduct of affairs.

50. In *Southern Cross Refrigerating Co v Toowoomba Foundry Pty Ltd* [(1954) 91 CLR 592] at 594–595, which concerned the 1905 Act, Kitto J set out a number of propositions which have frequently been quoted and applied to the 1955 Act. The essential elements of those propositions continue to apply to the issue of deceptive similarity under the 1995 Act. Applied also to service marks and absent the imposition of an onus upon the applicant they may be restated as follows:

(i)   To show that a trade mark is deceptively similar to another it is necessary to show a real tangible danger of deception or confusion occurring. A mere possibility is not sufficient.

(ii) A trade mark is likely to cause confusion if the result of its use will be that a number of persons are caused to wonder whether it might not be the case that the two products or closely related products and services come from the same source. It is enough if the ordinary person entertains a reasonable doubt.

It may be interpolated that this is another way of expressing the proposition that the trade mark is likely to cause confusion if there is a real likelihood that some people will wonder or be left in doubt about whether the two sets of products or the products and services in question come from the same source.

(iii) In considering whether there is a likelihood of deception or confusion all surrounding circumstances have to be taken into consideration. These include the circumstances in which the marks will be used, the circumstances in which the goods or services will be bought and sold and the character of the probable acquirers of the goods and services.

(iv) The rights of the parties are to be determined as at the date of the application.

(v)   The question of deceptive similarity must be considered in respect of all goods or services coming within the specification in the application and in respect of which registration is desired, not only in respect of those goods or services on which it is proposed to immediately use the mark. The question is not limited to whether a particular use will give rise to deception or confusion. It must be based upon what the applicant can do if registration is obtained.

In respect of the last proposition, Mason J observed in *Berlei Hestia Industries Ltd v Bali Co Inc* (1973) 129 CLR 353 at 362:

> the question whether there is a likelihood of confusion is to be answered, not by reference to the manner in which the respondent has used its mark in the past, but by reference to the use to which it can properly put the mark. The issue is whether that use would give rise to a real danger of confusion.

[French J then turned to consider whether the first instance judge had erred in finding that Woolworths' mark was not deceptively similar to the earlier cited marks.]

57. ... [I]t was said that in comparing the mark in suit with each of the cited marks his Honour gave undue emphasis to the word 'WOOLWORTHS' in the mark in suit and failed to give proper emphasis to the word 'METRO'.

58. The evaluative decision which his Honour was called upon to make is not one which this Court should review unless satisfied that it was informed by some error of principle … On the facts of this case, he would have ample ground for not being satisfied as required for the application of s 44(2). This limb of the Registrar's attack upon the decision therefore also fails.

59. Then it was said that his Honour erred in another way in saying:

> I do not think the mere fact that an item branded with the word 'metro' is displayed in a Woolworths
> Metro store would cause a shopper to believe in a common origin.

This indicated, it was said, a higher threshold for deceptive similarity than that required by law. For a mark will be deceptively similar to another if it is likely to cause confusion. A likelihood of confusion exists if, as a result of the use of the mark, there is a real probability that some people will wonder or be left in doubt about whether the products and services in question come from the same source—see the propositions extracted from the *Southern Cross Refrigerating* case (supra).

60. Counsel for Woolworths pointed out that this sentence in his Honour's judgment occurs in context of a consideration of the relationship between the services covered by the applicant's mark and the goods covered by thirteen of the cited marks. There is some force in the Registrar's concern that his Honour did not expressly address the wider issues of confusion. However the strength of his findings about the impact of the word WOOLWORTHS in the proposed mark negatives that wider possibility. This is particularly apparent in that passage in the judgment in which his Honour said:

> Although I take [counsel for the Registrar's] point about imperfect recollection, I cannot accept
> that viewers of the mark would overlook or forget that it refers to 'Woolworths metro', not merely
> 'metro'. The word that is unique to this mark, as against each of the cited marks, constitutes a
> major feature of it. Applying the *Australian Woollen Mills* test, the impression or recollection of the
> subject mark a viewer would carry away and retain is quite different from that which he or she
> would retain in respect of any of the cited marks.

61. In respect of the fourteenth cited mark which is an accepted application pending opposition, his Honour found that there is likely to be some similarity between the services in respect of which registration of this mark is sought and the services offered by Woolworths. However in that respect he said:

> As the name would not be displayed on goods, the aural impression may here be more
> important than the manner of visual presentation. But it is only possible to say the oral use of
> the term 'Woolworths metro' is deceptively similar to 'metro' if one ignores or discounts the word
> 'Woolworths'. In comparing the marks, it is not legitimate to ignore a major element in one of
> them; and, for the reasons I have given, I do not think that word should be discounted. On the
> contrary, having regard to its aural prominence and familiarity to Australians, it is the element of
> the mark most likely to be noticed and remembered.

His Honour's reference to the familiarity of the name 'Woolworths' in Australia was appropriate. Where an element of a trade mark has a degree of notoriety or familiarity of which judicial notice can be taken, as is the present case, it would be artificial to separate out the physical features of the mark from the viewer's perception of them. For in the end the question of resemblance is about how the mark is perceived. In the instant case the visual impact of the name 'Woolworths' cannot be assessed without a recognition of its notorious familiarity to consumers.

Branson J (dissenting as to the outcome): 83. … The proper approach to the question of whether one trade mark so resembles another as to be likely to deceive was said by the High Court in *Cooper Engineering Co Pty Ltd v Sigmund Pumps Ltd* (1952) 86 CLR 536 at 538 to be well settled and summed-up by Parker J, as he then was in *In the Matter of An Application by the Pianotist Co Ltd for the Registration of a Trade Mark* (1906) 23 RPC 774 at 777 in the following passage:

> You must take the two words. You must judge of them, both by their look and by their sound. You must consider the goods to which they are to be applied. You must consider the nature and kind of customer who would be likely to buy those goods. In fact, you must consider all the surrounding circumstances; and you must further consider what is likely to happen if each of those trade marks is used in a normal way as a trade mark for the goods of the respective owners of the marks. If, considering all those circumstances, you come to the conclusion that there will be a confusion—that is to say, not necessarily that one man will be injured and the other will gain illicit benefit, but that there will be a confusion in the mind of the public which will lead to confusion in the goods … you must refuse the registration, or rather you must refuse the registration in that case. (citations omitted)

The High Court (Dixon, Williams and Kitto JJ) then went on to say:

> It is sufficient if persons who only know one of the marks and perhaps have an imperfect recollection of it are likely to be deceived.

84. The High Court indicated in the *Cooper Engineering* case, at 539, that the question of whether one trade mark so resembled another trade mark as to be likely to deceive is, in substance, a two stage test. First, do the marks really look alike or sound alike? Secondly, if they do, is the resemblance likely to deceive? The court rejected a contention that it would be sufficient that the two marks conveyed the same idea (see also, *Southern Cross Refrigerating Co v Toowoomba Foundry Pty Ltd* (1954) 91 CLR 592 at 607).

85. Nothing in the *Cooper Engineering* case, in my view, is inconsistent with the notion that the test of whether a trade mark is 'deceptively similar' to a registered trade mark within the meaning of ss 10 and 44(2) of the Act is a test concerned with the inherent qualities of the two marks seen in the light of the proper uses that may be made of them.

86. The decision of the Full Court of the High Court in the *Southern Cross Refrigerating Co* case is, in my view, supportive of the above approach …

88. It is not in dispute on this appeal that in applying the test provided for by s 44(2) of the Act, consideration is not to be given to the actual use made by the owners of the trade mark cited against the applicant for registration. The test to be applied is that proposed by Evershed J in *Re An Application by Smith Hayden & Co Ltd* (1945) 63 RPC 97 at 101. That test may be paraphrased for the purposes of this appeal as follows. Assuming use by the proprietor of the cited trade marks in a normal and fair manner for any of the goods or services covered by the registrations of trade marks, is the Court satisfied that there is a reasonable likelihood of deception or confusion among a substantial number of persons if the applicant for registration also uses its mark normally and fairly in respect of services covered by the proposed registration. See also *Berlei v Hestia Industries Ltd* (1973) 129 CLR 353 per Mason J at 362.

89. In deciding whether there is a reasonable likelihood of deception or confusion such that the application for registration must be rejected the marks are not to be compared side by side but rather:

> [a]n attempt should be made to estimate the effect or impression produced on the mind of potential customers by the mark ... The impression or recollection which is carried away and retained is necessarily the basis of any mistaken belief that the challenged mark or device is the same. The effect of spoken description must be considered. If a mark is in fact or from its nature likely to be the source of some name or verbal description by which buyers will express their desire to have the goods, then similarities both of sound and of meaning may play an important part. The usual manner in which ordinary people behave must be the test of what confusion or deception may be expected

(*Australian Woollen Mills Ltd v FS Walton & Co Ltd* (1937) 58 CLR 641 per Dixon and McTiernan JJ at 658).

The following two extracts provide useful illustrations of how the assessment of 'deceptive similarity' is undertaken.

CASE EXTRACT: CURRENT LAW

Starr Partners Pty Ltd v Dev Prem Pty Ltd

[2007] FCAFC 42; (2007) 71 IPR 459
Federal Court of Australia, Full Court

[The owner of the registered 'Starr Partners' device mark, below left, brought infringement proceedings against the user of the 'Star Realty' device mark, below right. The trial judge held that the marks were not deceptively similar.]

Lindgren, Emmett and Finkelstein JJ: 22. The first step in the analysis is to identify the impression produced by the registered mark considered in its entirety. Similarity is not based on only part of the registered mark. On the other hand, when one decides upon the impression produced by that mark it is not improper to give more or less weight to particular features of it, provided the ultimate conclusion is based on a consideration of the mark in its entirety. This approach does no more than recognise that one word or feature of a mark can be more striking and memorable than another ...

23. It may also be appropriate when comparing the registered mark with the allegedly infringing mark to have regard to the pronunciation of words in the mark or any verbal translation of devices. But a comparison based on sounds is likely to be important only if the goods or services to which the mark relates are acquired by reference to words based on the mark. For example, one might commonly hear a person say 'Can I have a Coke?' but not 'We need to find a new tenant, let's call Star Realty'. Put in another way, phonetic similarities and differences will not have a large role to play if words in the mark are not usually spoken or devices in the mark are not usually orally conveyed.

...

25. ... [W]e think that the respondent's mark so nearly resembles the appellant's registered mark that it is likely to deceive or cause confusion.

26. Because the likelihood of deception or confusion must be assessed in the light of the imperfection of human recollection, where a trade mark includes both common and uncommon words, the uncommon words (such as 'Star' or 'Starr') will be the more memorable, and therefore significant for infringement purposes, than the common words (such as 'Partners' or 'Realty').

27. The hypothetical person will have seen both marks. He or she may have seen both of them some time before the hypothetical moment at which the likelihood of deception or confusion is to be assessed, or he or she may have seen one or both of them only a short while before that moment. For some people the spelling of the family name 'Starr' with its double 'r' ending and the associated play on the 'star' idea will be more striking than it will be for other people. Sensitivity to such matters differs widely in the community.

ESSENTIAL FEATURES

28. The essential features of the two marks are the star device, its close relationship with the initial capital letter 'S', and the idea or concept of a star. One does not expect to encounter such features as a matter of course in the advertising of a real estate agency, whereas the word 'realty' is unremarkable in that context, and the word 'partners' almost equally so.

29. The appellant has taken advantage of the association between the family name 'Starr' and the idea of a star. By doing so, and juxtaposing the word 'Starr' and the star device, it has drawn attention away from the double 'r' ending of 'Starr' as signifying a family name in favour of the star device and the capital letter 'S'.

INESSENTIAL FEATURES

30. While the word 'Partners' differs from 'Realty', the question is whether the two words would make such a lasting impression on the hypothetical reader's mind that he or she would not be likely to be deceived or confused. We do not think they would do so.

31. It must be remembered that both marks would be used in relation to real estate services. This consideration reduces the effect of the presence of the word 'realty' in the respondent's mark: the reader knows from the context that the business entity in question is engaged in 'realty' business.

32. Similarly, the word 'Partners' in the appellant's registered mark is not distinctive. While it is encountered less frequently than 'Pty Ltd' of 'and Company', it is far from arresting and is certainly not calculated to cause the reader to ponder the form of business structure adopted by the appellant. The word 'Partners' would not be remembered as indicating one form of business structure as distinct from another. Indeed, the respondent is a proprietary company, not a partnership. The word 'Partners' is a fairly non-descript term that does not seriously convey much meaning more than 'and Company'. It would be forgotten very soon after being read.

33. In sum, a reader would gloss over the words 'Partners' and 'Realty', and would be likely to remember only the star device and a 'star kind of word' associated with it as the mark of a real estate agency.

CASE EXTRACT: CURRENT LAW

Vivo International Corporation Pty Ltd v Tivo Inc

[2012] FCAFC 159; (2012) 99 IPR 1
Federal Court of Australia, Full Court

[Tivo Inc is the registered owner of the word mark TIVO for a wide range of goods including televisions, remote controls, transmitters and receivers, with a registration date of 10 November 1999. It sought the cancellation of the registration of a device mark, owned by Vivo, prominently featuring the word 'Vivo', for 'apparatus for use in audio visual communication' and 'transmission of data by audio-visual apparatus', which had been applied for on 18 February 2008. At trial, Jagot J held that the marks were deceptively similar, and ordered the cancellation of Vivo's registration].

Nicholas J (with whom Dowsett J agreed): 153. ... [T]he primary judge's finding of deceptive similarity was based upon phonetic similarity and ... her Honour's rejection of TiVo's case based upon visual similarity was not challenged on appeal. This creates an element of complexity in what some might otherwise regard as a relatively straightforward case. The way in which the appeal has been conducted has prevented me from concluding that the Vivo trade mark is deceptively similar to the [TiVo] trade mark based upon a visual comparison of the marks.

154. The Vivo trade mark is a composite word and device mark. The word 'Vivo' is the dominant element of the mark. I doubt that the device that forms part of the mark would make any lasting impression on the mind of most consumers. Consumers who wish to refer to Vivo products in written or oral communications will almost certainly do so using only the word component of the mark.

155. The present case is unlike those involving goods usually sold over the telephone or from behind a counter where there is often a heightened risk of confusion stemming from aural similarity. Nevertheless, the primary judge's finding (at para [176]) that in a significant number of cases both TiVo products and Vivo products would be identified, requested or ordered orally is of considerable importance in this case.

156. In my view, the risk of confusion is most apparent if it is assumed that TiVo applies its mark not only to DVRs but also to televisions and other goods covered by the TiVo trade mark registration, which may or may not be expensive when compared to the Vivo branded products, and which may or may not be sold in the same retail outlets.

157. There is another matter I consider particularly relevant in this case. The word 'TiVo' is an invented word without any ordinary meaning. The word 'Vivo' may have an ordinary meaning, but it is not a meaning that would be likely to enter most consumers' minds when shopping for audio-visual products. I think most consumers would regard Vivo as an invented word. In those circumstances, it cannot be said that either word conveys any distinctive meaning or impression of its own that might diminish the effects of imperfect recollection.

158. In my opinion there was, as at 18 February 2008, a real danger that consumers who might know of the [TiVo] trade mark because they had seen products to which it had been applied, or because they had seen or heard advertising which made reference to it, would confuse it with the Vivo trade mark in the course of spoken communications with sales staff engaged in selling audio-visual products.

CURRENT LAW

159. My decision on the s 44(1) point turns not on any risk that the two marks might be confused as being related, but on the basis that they exhibit a strong phonetic similarity, and that consumers of ordinary memory and intelligence who had an imperfect recollection of one or other of the marks might not appreciate that the brand name referred to in the course of discussions taking place prior to sale was different to that which the consumer had previously seen or heard.

SIMILAR GOODS AND SERVICES

CURRENT LAW

CASE EXTRACT: CURRENT LAW

E & J Gallo Winery v Lion Nathan Australia Pty Ltd

[2008] FCA 934; (2008) 77 IPR 69
Federal Court of Australia

[One issue in this case was whether radler beer ('radler' being a particular style of citrus-flavoured beer) and wine were goods 'of the same description' for the purposes of s 120(2).]

Flick J: 67. ... [I]t is a question of fact and impression whether goods are 'of the same description': *Rowntree plc v Rollbits Pty Ltd* (1988) 10 IPR 539 at 545 per Needham J.

68. In resolving this question, the fact that goods serve different purposes is not conclusive; nor is any one particular consideration conclusive. Assistance, however, has been provided as to those matters which may be taken into account: *Southern Cross Refrigerating Co v Toowoomba Foundry Pty Ltd* (1954) 91 CLR 592. Dixon CJ, McTiernan, Webb, Fullagar and Taylor JJ there, at 606–7, gave content to the task to be undertaken as follows:

> The fact that examination of the nature of the applicant's goods may, by itself, induce an observer to conclude that they are different in character from those of an opponent, and designed to serve different purposes, is by no means conclusive. Nor is the fact that the applicant's goods are not specified by the regulations as being within the same class of goods ... There may be many matters to be considered apart from the inherent character of the goods in respect of which the application is made and some indication of what matters are relevant to this inquiry was given by Romer J in *In re Jellinek's Application* [(1946) 63 RPC 59]. Romer J thought it necessary to look beyond the nature of the goods in question and to compare not only their respective uses but also to examine the trade channels through which the commodities in question were bought and sold. Shortly after the decision in *Jellinek's Case* the Assistant-Comptroller elaborated on the observations of Romer J in the following manner: 'In arriving at a decision upon this issue the reported cases show that I have to take account of a number of factors, including in particular the nature and characteristics of the goods, their origin, their purpose, whether they are usually produced by one and the same manufacturer or distributed by the same wholesale houses, whether they are sold in the same shops over the same counters during the same seasons and to the same class or classes of customers, and whether by those engaged in their manufacture and distribution they are regarded as belonging to the same trade. In the case of *Jellinek's Application* [(1946) 63 RPC 59], Romer J classified these various factors under three heads, viz,

CURRENT LAW

the nature of the goods, the uses thereof, and the trade channels through which they are bought and sold. No single consideration is conclusive in itself, and it has further been emphasized that the classifications contained in the schedules to the Trade Marks Rules are not a decisive criterion as to whether or not two sets of goods are "of the same description"': *In re an Application by John Crowther & Sons (Milnsbridge) Ltd* [(1948) 65 RPC 369 at 372]. Much the same considerations are evident in the observation of Dixon J (as he then was) in *Reckitt & Colman (Australia) Ltd v Boden* [(1945) 70 CLR 84 at 94] when he said: 'What forms the same description of goods must be discovered from a consideration of the course of trade or business. One factor is the use to which the two sets of goods are put. Another is whether they are commonly dealt with in the same course of trade or business. In the present case, the goods are quite different, their uses are widely separated and they are not commonly sold in the same kinds of shops or departments.

69. In *McCormick & Co Inc v McCormick* (2000) 51 IPR 102, Kenny J also identified some of the factors to be taken into account when determining whether goods were of the same description. Her Honour there observed:

[18] The authorities establish that there are three principal factors to be considered in this regard. They are: (1) the nature of the goods, including their origin and characteristics; (2) the uses made of them, including their purpose; and (3) the trade channels through which the goods are bought and sold.

[Flick J held that radler beer and wine were not similar goods. This decision was overturned by the Full Federal Court:]

E & J Gallo Winery v Lion Nathan Australia Pty Ltd

[2009] FCAFC 27; (2009) 175 FCR 386
Federal Court of Australia, Full Court

Moore, Edmonds and Gilmour JJ: 72. The primary judge accepted that there were a number of factors which supported the view that Lion Nathan's beer and wine were goods at the same description. They were both alcoholic beverages and generally distributed by this same major wholesale distributors. The beer was intended to be an appealing alternative to wine and in developing the product, Lion Nathan deliberately set out to attract people who did not drink beer. Indeed it was developed with the deliberate objective of enticing consumers who previously drank wine but not beer. Producers of alcoholic beverages are no longer confined to the production of beer, as opposed to wine, and large producers of alcoholic beverages now produce a range of products and market themselves as doing so. Companies which were once brewers now market and distribute a range of products including beer, wine, spirits, cider and non-alcoholic drinks. Wine and beer are now frequently distributed by the same retailers. We agree that these matters point, and in our opinion point convincingly, to Lion Nathan's beer and wine being goods of the same description.

73. The considerations which led his Honour to reach the opposite conclusion are, in our opinion, of materially less significance. The first, which concerned the origin of the goods, focused on the manner of manufacture of beer on the one hand and wine on the other. While this clearly establishes that they

are not the same goods, it is unlikely that this difference would be significant to the consuming public if, as his Honour found, large producers of alcoholic beverages produce a range of products. Additionally it is important to bear in mind that this issue is being considered in the more general context of whether consumers might see the goods as having the same trade origin: *Southern Cross* at 606. The same can be said of the next consideration relied on by his Honour, namely the specific manner of sale in restaurants on the one hand and retail outlets on the other. If large producers of alcoholic beverages are producing a range of products then the fact that the wine might be sold in a slightly different way would not be a difference of significance to the consuming public who may come to consider the trade origins of Lion Nathan's beer. The next consideration was the manner in which beer is consumed, that is drunk for its refreshing qualities, and not, like wine, consumed in a "sipping fashion". For our part, we doubt this is a relevant consideration. Nor do we think the last consideration, the detailed corporate structure of Lion Nathan, is of any real significance.

In *MID Sydney Pty Ltd v Australian Tourism Co Ltd* (1998) 90 FCR 236 the Full Federal Court held that in determining whether services are similar, the same principles used to determine whether goods are similar should apply. In that case it was held that 'property management services' were not similar to 'hotel management services'. Although it was recognised that running a hotel might involve the performance of some services that unquestionably fall under the rubric of 'property management', as when a large hotel leases out, maintains and manages retail space, such activities were considered to be purely incidental to the principal activity of running a hotel, and were thus discounted.

'CLOSELY RELATED' GOODS AND SERVICES

CASE EXTRACT: CURRENT LAW

Registrar of Trade Marks v Woolworths Ltd ('Woolworths Metro')

[1999] FCA 1020; (1999) 93 FCR 365
Federal Court of Australia, Full Court

French J (with whom Tamberlin J agreed): 37. ... The term 'closely related' recognises that goods and services are different things. There will be classes of goods which are similar to each other. There will also be classes of services which are similar to each other. But the word 'similar' does not apply as between goods and services. So there must be some other form of relationship between the services covered by one mark and the goods covered by another to enable the goods or services in question to be described as 'closely related'. As its use in the Mathys Committee Report indicated however, it is a term of wider import than 'similar' and can apply to the relationships between competing services as well as between goods and services: Cmnd 5601, par 70.

38. The range of relationships between goods and services which may support the designation 'closely related' will be limited by the requirement in s 44(2) that there be a substantial identity or deceptive similarity between the potentially conflicting trade marks which attach to them.

The relationships may, and perhaps in most cases will, be defined by the function of the service with respect to the goods. Services which provide for the installation, operation, maintenance or repair of goods are likely to be treated as closely related to them. Television repair services in this sense are closely related to television sets as a class of goods. A trade mark used by a television repair service which resembles (to use the language of s 10) the trade mark used on a prominent brand of television sets could be deceptively similar for suggesting an association between the provider of the service and the manufacturer of the sets. Similar examples were suggested in *Caterpillar Loader Hire (Holdings) Pty Ltd v Caterpillar Tractor Co* (1983) 77 FLR 139; 48 ALR 511 by Lockhart J who saw service marks as potentially giving rise to problems of confusion with goods marks and other service marks 'of greater difficulty and subtlety than has previously been experienced in the case of goods marks alone'. His Honour observed that (at 150; 522):

> Confusion is more likely to arise where services protected by service marks necessarily involve the use or sale of goods or where services (for example, consultancy services) involve goods but can be provided either with or without the sale or promotion of goods.

39. In *Rowntree plc v Rollbits Pty Ltd* [(1988) 90 FLR 398] registration was sought for a trade mark in respect of foods which included biscuits, cakes and pastry goods. The same applicant also sought registration of a service mark with respect to services rendered or associated with restaurants, take-away food stores and other retail food outlets which sell and promote prepared food and drinks for consumption. Both applications were accepted but opposed. On appeal by the opponent from the decision of the Registrar, Needham J found the applicant's mark in respect of goods to be deceptively similar to the opponent's registered mark as covering goods 'of the same description' under s 33(1). His Honour also concluded that the goods covered by the opponent's registered mark were 'closely related' to the services in respect of which registration of the applicant's service mark was sought. While accepting that it was not a logical necessity that the relevant question under s 33(2) of the 1955 Act must be answered in the same way as the question under s 33(1), his Honour said (at 405):

> I think, in the present case, that the conclusion that the goods are goods of the same description requires a conclusion that the services contemplated by the defendant, which would feature the goods already held to be goods of the same description as those of the plaintiff, are services closely related to the plaintiff's goods.

Apposite to the present case is the question whether a retailer of various classes of goods provides a service to customers which warrants the description of the goods for sale as 'closely related goods' in respect of that service. The characterisation of the relationship between services and goods in this way is evaluative. The logic of s 44(2) suggests that the determination whether goods are closely related to the services in question is logically antecedent to the determination whether the trade mark in respect of the services is deceptively similar to that in respect of the goods. Wilcox J at first instance in this case saw the questions as 'conceptually distinct' but accepted that one could not be addressed in isolation from the second: 'The closer the relationship between the services and particular goods, the more likely any similarity in marks will prove deceptive.' This approach is not greatly assisted by the language of s 10 which, like s 6(3) of the 1955 Act, defines deceptive similarity solely in terms of the degree

CURRENT LAW

of resemblance of the trade marks in question and whether that degree of resemblance is 'likely' to deceive or cause confusion. But that definition must, in the context of s 44, be applied to the case of 'closely related' goods and services.

40. In the end there is one practical judgment to be made. Whether any resemblance between different trade marks for goods and services renders them deceptively similar will depend upon the nature and degree of that resemblance and the closeness of the relationship between the services and the goods in question. It will not always be necessary to dissect that judgment into discrete and independent conclusions about the resemblance of marks and the relationship of goods and services. Consistently with that proposition, the Registrar or a judge on appeal from the Registrar could determine in a particular case that, given the limited degree of resemblance between the relevant marks he or she could not be satisfied, no matter how closely related the goods and services concerned, that the use of the applicant's marks would be likely to deceive or to cause confusion.

COMPARISON OF MARKS: A GLOBAL APPROACH?

As can be seen from *Woolworths Metro* at [40], Australian judges have at times blended some of the issues under s 44 going to the similarity of marks and the similarity of the goods and services. This 'global' approach is more explicitly taken under European law.

COMPARATIVE LAW

CASE EXTRACT: COMPARATIVE LAW

Case C-342/97, Lloyd Schuhfabrik Meyer GmbH v Klijsen Handel BV

[1999] ECR I-3819
Court of Justice of the European Communities

[Article 4(1)(b) of the *European Trade Marks Directive* provides for a ground of refusal where, because the applicant's mark is identical with or similar to an earlier mark and the goods or services covered by the two marks identical or similar, there exists a likelihood of confusion. Article 5(1)(b), which applies at the infringement stage (and was considered in this case), is expressed in the same way.]

The Court: 18. ... [The] likelihood of confusion on the part of the public must be appreciated globally, taking into account all factors relevant to the circumstances of the case ...

19. That global assessment implies some interdependence between the relevant factors, and in particular a similarity between the trade marks and between the goods or services covered. Accordingly, a lesser degree of similarity between those goods or services may be offset by a greater degree of similarity between the marks, and vice versa. The interdependence of these factors is expressly mentioned in the tenth recital in the preamble to the Directive, which states that it is indispensable to give an interpretation of the concept of similarity in relation to the likelihood of confusion, the appreciation of which depends, in particular, on the recognition of the trade mark on the market and the degree of similarity between the mark and the sign and between the goods or services identified ...

20. Furthermore, the more distinctive the earlier mark, the greater will be the likelihood of confusion ... and therefore marks with a highly distinctive character, either per se or because of the

recognition they possess on the market, enjoy broader protection than marks with a less distinctive character …

21. It follows that, for the purposes of Article 5(1)(b) of the Directive, there may be a likelihood of confusion, notwithstanding a lesser degree of similarity between the trade marks, where the goods or services covered by them are very similar and the earlier mark is highly distinctive …

22. In determining the distinctive character of a mark and, accordingly, in assessing whether it is highly distinctive, the national court must make an overall assessment of the greater or lesser capacity of the mark to identify the goods or services for which it has been registered as coming from a particular undertaking, and thus to distinguish those goods or services from those of other undertakings …

…

25. In addition, the global appreciation of the likelihood of confusion must, as regards the visual, aural or conceptual similarity of the marks in question, be based on the overall impression created by them, bearing in mind, in particular, their distinctive and dominant components. The wording of Article 5(1)(b) of the Directive—'… there exists a likelihood of confusion on the part of the public …'—shows that the perception of marks in the mind of the average consumer of the category of goods or services in question plays a decisive role in the global appreciation of the likelihood of confusion. The average consumer normally perceives a mark as a whole and does not proceed to analyse its various details …

26. For the purposes of that global appreciation, the average consumer of the category of products concerned is deemed to be reasonably well-informed and reasonably observant and circumspect … However, account should be taken of the fact that the average consumer only rarely has the chance to make a direct comparison between the different marks but must place his trust in the imperfect picture of them that he has kept in his mind. It should also be borne in mind that the average consumer's level of attention is likely to vary according to the category of goods or services in question.

27. In order to assess the degree of similarity between the marks concerned, the national court must determine the degree of visual, aural or conceptual similarity between them and, where appropriate, evaluate the importance to be attached to those different elements, taking account of the category of goods or services in question and the circumstances in which they are marketed.

While s 44 only deals with conflicts with earlier registered marks or applications for registration, the remaining six relative grounds deal with conflicts with earlier registered or unregistered marks. These are considered below.

CONFLICT WITH AN EARLIER MARK WITH A REPUTATION

The second relative ground to be considered is s 60, which can only be raised in opposition proceedings. This provides:

The registration of a trade mark in respect of particular goods or services may be opposed on the ground that:

(a) another trade mark had, before the priority date for the registration of the first-mentioned trade mark in respect of those goods or services, acquired a reputation in Australia; and

(b) because of the reputation of that other trade mark, the use of the first-mentioned trade mark would be likely to deceive or cause confusion.

We have come across the concept of 'likely to deceive or cause confusion' in relation to both ss 43 and 44. In French J's decision on s 44 in *Woolworths Metro* at [50] (extracted at p 728 above), his Honour set out a number of propositions from Kitto J's judgment in *Southern Cross Refrigerating Co v Toowoomba Foundry Pty Ltd* (1954) 91 CLR 592 at 594–595 on whether the use of a mark would be likely to deceive. These propositions are equally applicable under s 60.

Section 60 overlaps with s 44 to some extent, but it also applies where the earlier mark is not registered or is not the subject of an application for registration: the mark only needs to have 'acquired a reputation in Australia'. In addition, there is no requirement that the earlier mark be substantially identical with or deceptively similar to the applicant's mark, or that it acquired its reputation in relation to similar or closely related goods or services (although, logically, these factors are likely to be relevant in assessing whether the use of the applicant's mark is likely to deceive or cause confusion). Section 60 has its origins in the more broadly worded s 28(a) of the *Trade Marks Act 1955* (Cth), which prevented from registration a mark whose use 'would be likely to deceive or cause confusion' (this provision was itself based on s 114 of the *Trade Marks Act 1905* (Cth), which simply referred to the use being 'likely to deceive'). Case law on those earlier provisions is useful in interpreting the scope of s 60 of the current Act (although it needs to be remembered that under the current Act, the opponent must be able to point to the existence of an earlier trade mark that has acquired a reputation in Australia as the cause of any likely deception or confusion).

CASE EXTRACT: PRECEDENT

Radio Corporation Pty Ltd v Disney

(1937) 57 CLR 448
High Court of Australia

[Australian company Radio Corporation applied for registration of the word marks MICKEY MOUSE and MINNIE MOUSE in respect of radio receiving sets. Disney had used these names and the images of these characters in films and books and had licensed their use on various goods (not including radios), but had not applied for registration of the marks in Australia. Disney opposed Radio Corporation's application under s 114 of the *Trade Marks Act 1905*.]

Dixon J (at 456–459): The applications for the trade marks now before us are made by complete strangers to the opponents. The applicants have obtained no licence, and have acquired from the opponents no right of any sort, actual or supposed. Their case is that the words 'Mickey Mouse' and 'Minnie Mouse' are simply the well-known names of highly popular characters in the fiction of the cinema and its adjuncts and that no one possesses an exclusive right to their use and no objection can exist to applying the names to goods unconnected with films or their exhibition …

The registrar thought radio receiving sets and films for talking pictures were so much mixed up in the interests and modes of dealing of people as to raise a sufficient doubt whether the use of the words 'Mickey Mouse' on a receiving set would not lead to a belief that it had the same origin as the films for talking pictures produced by the opponents. In connection with such films it seems that the words are used by the opponents as a trade mark, a fact which apparently entered into the decision of the registrar.

I find it hard to believe that the use of the words on or in connection with a radio receiving set would produce any other impression than in the case of most of the other almost innumerable classes of articles to which the name or the representation of Mickey Mouse has been applied. That impression does not, I think, primarily relate to the origin, selection or treatment of the goods. The reason for using the names is to attract the attention of members of a public that has found pleasure and amusement in the grotesque forms and absurd antics of Disney's creatures, and at the same time to give to the goods a name or means of description at once familiar and pleasing or interesting to the possible buyer. No doubt this means that the trader makes use of elements which belong to the reputation and fame of Disney's creations and it may be that in some vague way the buyer supposes that Disney must have sanctioned it.

To my mind the question upon which the matter turns is whether because of this kind of unauthorized diversion to the applicant's use and advantage of part of the public reputation and interest which Disney has created for himself and his figures, registration can be refused under sec 114. It was not argued that the words were incapable of distinguishing the goods. And for the reasons I have stated I am unable to regard the possibility of a belief arising that Disney or any other of the opponents has produced or distributed the goods as a probability. I think it is most unlikely that anyone would suppose it.

In the well-known case of *Eno v Dunn* (1890) 15 App Cas, at p 263, an important statement is made by Lord Macnaghten. Dunn had applied to register as a trade mark a label representing a woman holding up a dish of cakes with the words 'Dunn's Fruit Salt Baking Powder. The Cook's Best Friend.' The proprietor of Eno's fruit salt objected. The objection failed before the Court of Appeal, but in the House of Lords it was upheld by Lord Watson, Lord Herschell and Lord Macnaghten against the dissent of Lord Halsbury and Lord Morris. The passage in Lord Macnaghten's opinion is as follows:—'The learned judges who were in favour of Mr Dunn in the court below seem to have come to the conclusion that Mr Dunn's object was to obtain the benefit of the celebrity which the name adopted by Mr. Eno has acquired, but that it was not his object to steal Mr Eno's trade. So far I am disposed to agree; but I do not think that those propositions cover the real question. The question is one between Mr Dunn and the public, not between Mr Eno and Mr Dunn. It is immaterial whether the proposed registration is or is not likely to injure Mr Eno in his trade. Equally immaterial, as it seems to me, is the fact that for a considerable time Mr Eno had on the register, as his trade mark, the words "Fruit Salt." Mr Eno may have gained some advantage to which he was not properly entitled; but that is hardly a reason for permitting Mr Dunn to practice a deception upon the public': at pp 263–264.

In the present case it is the same intangible advantage arising from public celebrity, widespread fame and interest, that the applicants seek. It is not a diversion of trade, custom or profit.

Except for the refusal to pay licence fees, the continued use of the trade mark by the applicants will not affect any of the commercial operations of the opponents. It is clear, I think, that the opponents could on their part obtain no injunction for the protection of such an interest as that arising from the mere celebrity or reputation of Disney's productions. Further, in selling, so to speak, the advantage of that celebrity to traders as the opponents have done under their licensing system, they have done much to destroy the significance which they now seek to ascribe to it, namely, the significance of trade reputation based upon a mark. But these are matters which do not make it less right to keep off the register a mark improperly adopted by the applicants. If the circumstances are such that its adoption will give the applicants no right to protection by injunction or other remedy under the general law, then it should be kept off the register. This is what Lord Macnaghten means. Further, the burden of establishing that the mark is free from this disqualification lies on the applicants.

On the whole, I think there are present elements which leave them unable to discharge this burden. Those elements are, first, the belief which many people are not unlikely to hold that in some way or another Disney, or one of his companies has permitted, if not procured, the application of the name Mickey Mouse to the radio sets in connection with which it is used and, second, the unauthorized diversion to their own purposes on the part of the applicants of the celebrity and reputation obtained by the various activities of the opponents in relation to Mickey Mouse. The latter may give no cause of action but I think that, at any rate in conjunction with the former element, it would be enough to deprive the proposed mark of protection.

I think the appeal should be dismissed.

[Latham CJ, Rich and McTiernan JJ each agreed that Radio Corporation's appeal should be dismissed.]

CASE EXTRACT: CURRENT LAW

McCormick & Co Inc v McCormick

[2000] FCA 133; (2000) 97 FCR 218
Federal Court of Australia

[Mary McCormick applied for registration of the word marks MCCORMICK'S and MCCORMICK'S INSTANT BATTER SIMPLY ADD WATER in relation to instant batter. The priority date of these marks was 9 March 1992. The marks were opposed by McCormick & Co, the owner of earlier registered device marks prominently featuring the word 'McCormick' in relation to goods such as spices, condiments and seasonings (referred to in the judgment as 'the MCCORMICK marks'). Kenny J found that although Mary McCormick's application was caught by s 44(1), that ground of rejection did not apply because of Mary McCormick's honest concurrent use of her marks with those of McCormick & Co (see s 44(3)). Kenny J then considered McCormick & Co's further ground of opposition under s 60.]

Kenny J: 81. What is intended by the word 'reputation' in s 60? The word is defined in *The Macquarie Dictionary* as follows:

> reputation … 1. the estimation in which a person or thing is held, esp. by the community or the public generally; repute … 2. favourable repute; good name … 3. A favourable and publicly recognised name or standing for merit, achievement, etc … 4. The estimation or name of being, having done, etc, something specified.

Cf. *The Oxford English Dictionary*. In s 60, the word is, I think, apt to refer to 'the recognition of the McCormick & Co marks by the public generally'.

82. Does the evidence establish that in Australia before 9 March 1992 the McCormick & Co marks were recognised by the public generally and, because of that, the use by Mary McCormick of her marks would be likely to cause the public confusion, as for example, by the public's mistakenly attributing a business connection between the two or attributing her product to the company?

CURRENT LAW

83. ... In *ConAgra Inc v McCain Foods (Aust) Pty Ltd* (1992) 33 FCR 302 at 343, Lockhart J said:

> [R]eputation within the jurisdiction may be proved by a variety of means including advertisements on television or radio, or in magazines and newspapers within the forum. It may be established by showing constant travel of people between other countries and the forum, and that people within the forum (whether residents there or persons simply visiting there from other countries) are exposed to the goods of the overseas owner ...

In this case McCormick & Co relied on the following evidence to establish the reputation of its marks: ... (2) extensive sales under the marks; (3) considerable expenditure on advertising; and (4) the use of promotional material.

84. As I have said, McCormick & Co directly or through its subsidiary, McCormick Australia, had sold products in Australia since 1962, ie, for thirty years before March 1992. There was evidence that in 1991 (and thereafter until 1995) the value of McCormick & Co's retail gross sales across Australia was very large. (The precise details were the subject of a confidentiality order.) Further, the sales were substantial in every state, save perhaps for Tasmania. There was evidence that in 1998 the company marketed its products to about 1400 supermarkets throughout Australia. The evidence supports the inference that the company was marketing its products to a large number of supermarkets in 1992, including major supermarket chains. Use of the McCormick & Co marks has been extensive. Very many of the McCormick & Co's products bore one or other of the McCormick & Co marks. The products ranged from herbs and spices to condiments, sauces and food flavourings. Notwithstanding the large value of the company's retail gross sales, the company's products were commonly relatively inexpensive. There was also evidence that in 1991 (and thereafter until 1998) the company spent a very large amount (about 1.5% in 1991 and about 3% of its gross retail sales in 1995) on advertising and promotion. There was extensive use made of the MCCORMICK marks in that advertising and promotional material. Officers of McCormick & Co, including Mr RW Skelton (the company's chief legal officer and an honest and credible witness) believed that the MCCORMICK marks were well known ... I infer from these facts, when taken together, that consumers would recognise with relative ease the McCormick & Co marks as indicative of the food products made and supplied by the company.

85. It may be correct to say, as counsel for Mary McCormick did, that the volume of the company's sales does not directly establish that a significant number of people held the McCormick & Co marks, as distinct from the company's products, in favourable regard. It does not follow, however, that the volume of sales and promotional expenditures are irrelevant. As Hearing Officer Thompson observed in *Hugo Boss AG v Jackson International Trading Co Kurt D Bruhl GmbH & Co KG* (1999) 47 IPR 423 ('*Hugo Boss*') at 436:

> [I]t is true that the assessment of the reputation of a trade mark goes far beyond mere examination of sales or turnover of goods sold under that trade mark and contemplation of the advertising and promotional figures.
>
> As regards a trade mark, its reputation derives both from the quantum of sales under that mark and also the esteem, or image, projected by that trade mark. The quantum of sales, advertising and promotion contributes to the 'recognition' component of the trade mark's reputation. The credit, image and values projected by a trade mark attaches to the 'esteem' component of the reputation as do the public events and other trader's marks with which [the] owner of the trade

marks in question chooses to associate the trade marks via sponsorships, cross-promotions, 'contra deals' and so forth.

It follows that a trade mark used in relation to goods with comparatively low sales may have a high and strong reputation by virtue of the high credit or esteem in which it is held or, conversely, that a trade mark which has very high sales may have a strong reputation notwithstanding the lack of esteem that attaches to it. The particular popular images, or sets of values, that attach to the trade mark are also, therefore, important parts of the reputation of the trade mark and may be as strong an associative force in the minds of the public as the association of the trade marks with the goods or services themselves.

86. In practice, it is commonplace to infer reputation from a high volume of sales, together with substantial advertising expenditures and other promotions, without any direct evidence of consumer appreciation of the mark, as opposed to the product: see, eg, *Isuzu-General Motors Australia Ltd v Jackeroo World Pty Ltd* (1999) 47 IPR 198; *Marks & Spencer plc v Effem Foods Pty Ltd* (2000) AIPC ¶91-560; *Photo Disc Inc v Gibson* (1998) 42 IPR 473; and *RS Components Ltd v Holophane Corp* (1999) 46 IPR 451. This Court has followed this approach as well, acknowledging that public awareness of and regard for a mark tends to correlate with appreciation of the products with which that mark is associated, as evidenced by sales volume, amongst other things. Thus, in *Toddler Kindy Gymbaroo Pty Ltd v Gymboree Pty Ltd* [2000] FCA 618 ('*Gymboree*'), Moore J accepted at [94] that the applicant had established a reputation for the purposes of s 60 solely on the basis of use and promotion of the relevant mark. Another example of this approach is *Nettlefold Advertising Pty Ltd v Nettlefold Signs Pty Ltd* (1997) 38 IPR 495 ('*Nettlefold*'), in which Heerey J relied upon the public visibility of the applicant's marks over approximately two decades as well as a $100 000 promotional campaign in finding that a reputation for the purposes of s 28 of the 1955 Act existed.

87. It is true, as Mary McCormick's counsel points out, that the evidence does not establish what proportion of sales was made under or by reference to any particular mark. It is also true, as he points out, that, apart from the evidence as to sales and advertising expenditure, there is little or no evidence about the effect of advertising upon consumers. There were no consumer surveys in evidence, nor was there evidence about the marketing of McCormick & Co's products. There was also no evidence to connect whatever international reputation McCormick & Co might have with the reputation of the McCormick & Co marks in Australia.

88. I accept that those were important omissions and, in another case, might have proved fatal. Still, none of the factors pointed to by counsel for Mary McCormick are essential requirements for a finding of reputation under s 60. The sales and advertising of the order of magnitude involved in this case are, in my view, a sufficient basis for establishing reputation along the lines of the approach indicated in *Gymboree* and *Nettlefold* and other relevant authorities ... Without speculating on what the threshold level of sales or promotional expenditures might be (if, indeed, one exists), McCormick & Co have clearly passed it. Bearing in mind all the circumstances to which I have referred, I am satisfied that McCormick & Co have established that the McCormick & Co marks had acquired a reputation in Australia before March 1992.

89. I am also satisfied that because of the reputation of the McCormick & Co marks, the use of Mary McCormick's marks would be likely to cause confusion. Briefly, not only are Mary McCormick's marks deceptively similar to those of McCormick & Co, the name 'McCormick' is a prominent element

of the marks in question. As I have said, Mary McCormick seeks the registration of her marks for a product (instant batter) that is sold in the same channels of trade, to the same kind of customers, as the products sold by McCormick & Co under its marks. Mary McCormick's instant batter is sold in supermarkets. So too are McCormick & Co's spices, herbs and like products. Mary McCormick's instant batter is ordinarily located in close proximity to the herbs, spices and like products of McCormick & Co. The dollar value of Mary McCormick's 150g instant batter packet is low and broadly commensurate with many of McCormick & Co's supermarket products.

90. The ultimate question is whether s 60 is subject to s 44(3) of the Act. The delegate decided that it was upon the basis that ss 44(3) and 60 were the equivalent of ss 34(1) and 28 of the 1955 Act respectively ...

...

93. As counsel for McCormick & Co observes, the structure of the [*TMA*] and the provisions with which this appeal is concerned differ markedly from the 1955 Act. Parts 4 and 5 of the [*TMA*] relate to separate stages in the registration process ... Within Division 2 of Part 4, s 44(1) provides for a ground for rejecting an application before acceptance by the Registrar. Subsection 44(1) expressly states that it is subject to s 44(3), the honest concurrent user provision. The whole of s 44 is expressed as an interlocking series of subsections. Section 60, which is part of a Division specifically setting out the grounds for opposing registration, is directed to the position after acceptance. Section 60 is not expressed to be subject to s 44(3), any analogous limitation, or even the Act generally: contrast s 89(1). On its face, it is a stand-alone provision. Furthermore, s 60 is apparently intended to afford a ground of opposition that is additional to the grounds set out in Part 4. Section 57 expressly states that the grounds of opposition may be 'any of the grounds on which an application for the registration of a trade mark may be rejected under Division 2 of Part 4' (which includes s 44). Sections 58 to 62 add further grounds for opposition. On its face, there is no honest concurrent user exception to s 60.

94. Further, there are pertinent differences between s 44(1) and s 60. Subsection 44(1) requires a comparison of the applicant's mark with the mark of another person and the goods to which they both apply. If the Registrar concludes the marks are deceptively similar and the goods to which they apply are goods of the same description (and par 44(1)(b) is satisfied), then the registration application must be rejected; that is, of course, unless, in an exercise of discretion under s 44(3), the Registrar determines to permit the registration. Section 60 also requires a comparison, this time between the accepted mark and a mark that, before the relevant date, had acquired a reputation in Australia ... [T]he question is whether the use of the mark, which has been accepted, would be likely to deceive or cause confusion, because of that reputation ...

95. These differences may reflect the different stages of the registration process at which the questions of deceptive similarity and confusion arise. In this connection the observations of Branson J in [*Registrar of Trade Marks v*] *Woolworths* at 389–390 are apposite. Her Honour said:

> The broad provision contained in s 28(a) of the 1955 Act is now reflected in two separate sections of the Act: ss 43 and 60. Section 43, which is a ground for the rejection of an application for registration of a trade mark, looks to the inherent qualities of the trade mark of which registration is sought for the purpose of identifying whether the use of the trade mark would be likely to deceive or cause confusion. Section 60, which is a ground of opposition to registration, is concerned with

whether the use of the trade mark of which registration is sought would be likely to deceive or cause confusion by reason of the reputation in Australia of another trade mark.

The fact that s 43 is found in Pt 4, Div 2 of the Act, whilst s 60 is found in Pt 5, Div 2, reflects, in my view, an appreciation of the practical reality that before the acceptance for registration and advertising of an application for registration of a trade mark, the information available to the Registrar touching on issues of likely deception and confusion will be limited. The Registrar will be in a position to assess the extent to which the trade mark for which registration is sought resembles a registered trade mark. He or she will also be in a position to appreciate the proper uses which may be made of the registered trade mark on the one hand, and of the trade mark for which registration is sought, should it be registered, on the other. However, the Registrar cannot reasonably be expected to be cognisant of the reputation of registered and unregistered trade marks generally or, indeed, of the extent, for example, to which all Australians, whose circumstances and geographic locations are diverse, may be assumed to be familiar with particular words. As French J has pointed out, the acceptance stage is not the time for detailed adversarial examination of an application.

The position will change following the filing of a notice of opposition to registration. An opponent is entitled to rely on evidence in support of the opposition and the applicant for registration may rely on evidence in answer to the opposition. By this means, material which could not ordinarily be expected to be available to the Registrar for the purpose of determining whether an application for registration of a trade mark should be accepted, may become available to him or her for the purpose of determining whether the trade mark should be registered ...

96. Whilst I accept, as counsel for Mary McCormick contends, that the doctrine of honest concurrent user is derived from the common law and pre-dates trade mark legislation, I am of the view that s 44(3) of the Act does not provide an exception to s 60. Accordingly, I would order that the appeal pursuant to s 56 of the Act be allowed and the cross appeal be dismissed. I would set aside the delegate's decision and in lieu refuse registration. I would hear the parties on the question of costs once they have had an opportunity to consider these reasons.

CONTRARY TO LAW, AND DECEPTIVE AND CONFUSING CONNOTATIONS

We have already seen how ss 42(b) and 43 operate as absolute grounds of refusal. However, they both have a potential role to play as relative grounds, and are discussed here as the third and fourth relative grounds.

In relation to s 42(b), it follows from *Advantage Rent-A-Car Inc v Advantage Car Rental Pty Ltd* [2001] FCA 683; (2001) 52 IPR 24, extracted above at p 716, that the Registrar, at the examination stage as well as in opposition proceedings, is obliged to consider whether the use of the mark would be contrary to *any* law. This would include consideration of whether the applicant's use of its mark would contravene the ACL as well as consideration of common law actions such as the tort of passing off. In this way, s 42(b) can be used to deal with situations involving conflicts between marks. This has the potential to put the Office in a difficult position, given that it would be hard for it to determine whether an application contravenes a third party's rights in an unregistered sign. In practice (and notwithstanding the breadth of *Advantage*), the Office does not examine marks on this basis, and instead leaves it to third parties to raise s 42(b) as a relative ground in opposition proceedings.

Section 43, as Kenny J indicated in *McCormick*, extracted immediately above, was based in part on s 28(a) of the *Trade Marks Act 1955* (Cth), which provided: 'A mark ... the use of which would be likely to deceive or cause confusion ... shall not be registered as a trade mark'. Given that some of the work of the former s 28(a) is now done by s 60, this raises the question of the extent to which the current s 43 can be raised in situations involving conflicts between marks. In *TGI Friday's Australia Pty Ltd v TGI Friday's Inc* [2000] FCA 720; (2000) 100 FCR 358 the Full Federal Court held that where the alleged confusion or deception is said to result from the similarity between two marks, this does *not* depend on any 'connotation' in the first mark, meaning that such matters fall outside the scope of s 43. Notwithstanding this, a line of cases has emerged in which it has been held that s 43 *does* have a role to play where the applicant's mark suggests endorsement by, approval from or a licensing relationship with a well-known person or commercial entity. This can be seen in *McCorquodale v Masterson* [2004] FCA 1247; (2004) 63 IPR 582 (where an application for a device including the words 'Diana's Legacy in Roses' under a floral wreath was thought to suggest endorsement or approval by the estate of Diana, Princess of Wales, and thus fell foul of s 43), and also in the following extract.

CASE EXTRACT: CURRENT LAW

Twentieth Century Fox Film Corporation v Durkan

[2000] ATMO 5; (2000) 47 IPR 651
Australian Trade Marks Office

HR Hardie (Deputy Registrar of Trade Marks) (at 651–656): Trade mark application No 740114 is an application to register the words 'Braveheart the Musical' for T-shirts and caps in class 25, and for theatre musical production in class 41. The application was filed on 28 July 1997 (the relevant date) by Michael F Durkan ...

Fox Corporation oppose the application on the ground that, due to the existence of Fox Corporation's trade marks, the use of No 740114 by Mr Durkan is likely to deceive or cause confusion. The operation of s 43 does not, however, depend on the existence of a conflicting trade mark. The purpose of the section is to exclude from registration any trade mark which, in respect of the nominated goods or services, conveys a meaning which, in respect of those goods or services, is likely to deceive or confuse. This does not require the existence of a conflicting trade mark.

I have been shown no evidence that Fox Corporation used the word 'Braveheart' as a trade mark ... For the purpose of the s 43 ground, however, this finding is of no great consequence. What I need to consider for the purpose of s 43 is simply the question of whether, as a consequence of some connotation conveyed by the words 'Braveheart the Musical', that trade mark, when used in relation of T-shirts and caps (in class 25), and theatre musical productions (in class 41) is likely to deceive or cause confusion.

SUBMISSION, EVIDENCE, AND CONSIDERATION

Mr Yates constructed his submissions on the presumption of Fox Corporation's trade mark use of the word 'Braveheart'. That line of argument, I think, fails on the basis that so far as the evidence shows, Fox Corporation has no trade mark use of that word.

The facts in evidence are, however, that the term 'Braveheart' was coined as a fictional sobriquet for the historical figure of William Wallace. The expression 'brave heart' is an ordinarily descriptive term used as a salute to an heroic attitude. The 'coining' claimed by Fox Corporation is therefore nothing more than the conjunction of two ordinary words which, in their normal usage, constitute a laudatory and well recognised expression. Nevertheless, before Fox Corporation merged these two words into one, there is no evidence that the word 'Braveheart' had any currency, any presence in English dictionaries, or any attachment to the Scottish hero, William Wallace. I do note, under Ms Gillies' Ex MG-2, a cutting from the Sunday Mail newspaper, Adelaide, 28 May 1995, which headlines an article about a football team, the 'Adelaide Crows', with the words:

> Week of trauma ends in triumph as the Crows go from being 'No-Hearts' to … 'Bravehearts'.

I treat this, however, as an article which merely reflects and picks up on the publicity which at that time was surrounding the first release of the film in Australia.

Since the release of the *Braveheart* film, however, the word 'Braveheart' no longer remains unknown. On the undisputed evidence, 'Braveheart' now has significant currency as the name of one of the most successful films of late 1990s.

That film has had exceptional critical and popular success and the publicity associated with its acclaim has also been exceptional. On this basis, I think it is very clear that the trade mark 'Braveheart the Musical', dominated as it is by the word 'Braveheart', will openly give rise to a connotation of the film *Braveheart*. The remaining words—'the Musical'—do not detract from that connotation. On the contrary, it seems to me that the overall connotation likely to be imparted to a substantial portion of the Australian public by the trade mark 'Braveheart the Musical' is that the makers of the film *Braveheart* are now presenting (by way of a musical production) or promoting (by way of T-shirts or caps) a musical version of the story previously unfolded in the film.

The test for deception or confusion is recently dealt with in the judgment of French J in *Registrar of Trade Marks v Woolworths* (1999) 45 IPR 411 at 426; AIPC 91-499 at 39,695 (at [43]) (the *Metro* case). In considering the phrase likely to deceive or cause confusion, his Honour says:

> The use of the word 'likely' in this context does not import a requirement that it be more probable than not that the mark has that effect. The probability of deception or confusion must be finite and non-trivial. There must be a 'real tangible danger of its occurring'.

In my view a real and tangible danger of deception and confusion does attach to use of the trade mark 'Braveheart the Musical', by Mr Durkan, in respect of theatre musical productions and T-shirts and caps. Use of this sign, dominated as it is by the name 'Braveheart', will connote the celebrated *Braveheart* film and therefore give rise to expectations that the theatre musical productions and the T-shirts and caps are associated with the maker of the *Braveheart* film.

In respect of the s 43 ground, I find in favour of the opponent, Fox Corporation.

OWNERSHIP

The fifth relative ground is s 58, which provides that 'registration of a trade mark may be opposed on the ground that the applicant is not the owner of the trade mark'. In essence, the owner of a mark (known as the 'proprietor' under former legislation) will be the first user of the mark, as a mark, in Australia. If the mark is unused, then ownership is determined by the combined effect of 'authorship' of the mark (which refers to the first adoption of the sign as a trade mark, rather than any copyright law sense of 'creation' of the mark), an intention to use it in relation to the goods and services, and an application for registration (see *Shell Co of Australia Ltd v Rohm & Haas Co* (1949) 78 CLR 601 at 627–628 per Dixon J).

What this means is that an opposition under s 58 will, in almost all cases, only be successful if the opponent can show that it or another party had made prior use of the mark (or a substantially identical mark: see *Carnival Cruise Lines Inc v Sitmar Cruises Ltd* (1994) 31 IPR 375), in relation to the same goods or services as those specified in the application for registration. In addition, the prior use must have been use in Australia: in a number of cases where foreign traders have made extensive use of their marks overseas but have not used their marks in Australia they have been unable to prevent an unrelated party from registering the mark in Australia (see *Aston v Harlee Manufacturing Co* (1960) 103 CLR 391). Having said this, the extent of use that needs to be demonstrated for a trader to become the owner of a mark is generally slight, although there are some limits, as can be seen in the following extract.

CASE EXTRACT: CURRENT LAW

Shahin Enterprises Pty Ltd v Exxonmobil Oil Corporation

[2005] FCA 1278
Federal Court of Australia

[Exxonmobil applied for registration of ON THE RUN for a range of goods and services, including service station and restaurant services. The priority date was 18 June 1999. Shahin opposed registration on the ground that it was the owner of the mark. Shahin owned four unbranded convenience stores in South Australia as at January 1999. In February and March 1999 Shahin applied for registration of the business name 'On the Run' in South Australia and New South Wales, stating its intention to operate convenience stores and fuel outlets under that name by May 1999. Promotional material featuring the words 'On the Run' and 'Opening Soon On The Run' was prepared and distributed in May and early June 1999, and an A-frame sign with the words 'On The Run' was placed on the footpath near one of its convenience stores in early June 1999.]

Lander J: 67. Trade mark use is not any use. It must be public use in the course of trade so as to distinguish one trader's goods from another. In *Moorgate Tobacco Co Ltd v Philip Morris Ltd* (1984) 156 CLR 414 at 432 ('*Moorgate*'), Deane J said:

> The prior use of a trade mark which may suffice, at least if combined with local authorship, to establish that a person has acquired in Australia the statutory status of 'proprietor' of the mark, is public use in Australia of the mark as a trade mark, that is to say, a use of the mark in relation to

goods for the purpose of indicating or so as to indicate a connexion in the course of trade between the goods with respect to which the mark is used and that person.

...

69. It is not necessary to establish an actual dealing of in the goods to which is attached the mark. There must, however, be more than a subjective intention to use a mark in the course of trade in the future. There must be goods to which the mark can attach. In *Moorgate*, Deane J said at 433:

> The cases establish that it is not necessary that there be an actual dealing in goods bearing the trade mark before there can be local use of the mark as a trade mark. It may suffice that imported goods which have not actually reached Australia have been offered for sale in Australia under the mark (*Re Registered Trade Mark 'Yanx'; Ex parte Amalgamated Tobacco Corporation Ltd* (1951) 82 CLR at 204-205 or that the mark has been used in an advertisement of the goods in the course of trade: *Shell Co of Australia v Esso Standard Oil Australia Ltd* (1963) 109 CLR at 422. In such cases, however, it is possible to identify an actual trade or offer to trade in the goods bearing the mark or an existing intention to offer or supply goods bearing the mark in trade. In the present case, there was not, at any relevant time, any actual trade or offer to trade in goods bearing the mark in Australia or any existing intention to offer or supply such goods in trade. There was no local use of the mark as a trade mark at all; there were merely preliminary discussions and negotiations about whether the mark would be so used.

70. However, the subjective intention must be accompanied by some evidence of objective proof of that intent. In *Woolly Bull Enterprises Pty Ltd v Reynolds* (2001) 51 IPR 149, Drummond J said at 155, speaking of dicta of Deane J in *Moorgate*:

> Deane J did not say that a subjective intention of the owner of the mark to use the mark in trade at some time in the future was, without more, sufficient to show use of a mark. What he said was that such an intention, if accompanied by objective proofs of that intention in the form of evidence of action by the mark owner to commit goods bearing the mark to actual trade in Australia, would suffice to show use of the mark here at the time in question, though no marked goods had yet been offered for sale in this country.

McGarvie J understood Deane J's dictum as being to this effect in *Settef*. One issue there was whether an Italian company, Settef, had used its 'Riv-Oland' word mark in Australia before 1978 so as to become the proprietor of the mark here and thus entitled to the registration of the mark which it obtained in 1978. McGarvie J said at 417–18:

> I consider that it follows from the authorities that a mark is used as a trade mark only if it is used with a view to facilitating or promoting the operation of a trading channel which in a business sense had already been opened to Australia. The mark must be used for the purpose of trade ... The forwarding of samples and brochures [in 1967] is not sufficient to indicate that Settef was ready and willing to fulfil such orders as it received from Australia. The purpose of these items may well have been to ascertain whether there was a market in Australia sufficient for it to be worthwhile for Settef to export here. Use of the mark in such preliminary activities would not be a use in the course of trade: *Moorgate Tobacco Co Ltd v Philip Morris Ltd* (1984) 156 CLR 414 at 432–3; 56 ALR 193; 3 IPR 545 at 556.

71. Drummond J's explanation is consistent with the passage which I have cited above. A mere claim of intention to use a mark could never be enough. It would mean an intention by itself could give

rise to personal property: s 21. In *Moorgate* and *Settef SpA v Riv-Oland Marble Co (Vic) Pty Ltd* (1987) 10 IPR 402 (the authority to which Drummond J referred), there was evidence that the mark had been applied to the goods. There is no such evidence in this case.

72. The applicant contended that the flyer which was handed to customers in early June 1999 was evidence of the public use of the mark. It also said that the A-frame which had the words 'On the Run Coming Soon' was also evidence of the public use of the mark. I reject that contention. In my opinion, the flyer and the A-frame are both evidence of an intention of the applicant to conduct a business under the name of 'On the Run' in the future. That is consistent with the application to register the business names at that time. There is no evidence that there was ever any intention to use that 'sign' to distinguish goods or services dealt with or provided by the applicant in the course of trade for goods or services dealt with or provided by any other person. The other dealings with the marketing firm, the shopfitters, the builder and the graphic designer are not evidence of the public use of a mark.

73. The applicant has established that it intended to use the title 'On the Run Convenience Store' in its various stores. The applicant has established, in my opinion, an intention to conduct a business under the name 'On the Run' or 'On the Run Convenience Store'. That intention has been established by the registration of the business names both in South Australia and in New South Wales. It has not, however, established any intention it intended to deal with or provide goods using the 'On the Run' mark. There is a clear distinction, in my opinion, between conducting a business under a particular name and using a mark in respect of goods or services. The intention which the applicant needed to establish was an intention to use a mark to distinguish goods or services in the course of the applicant's trade from goods or services provided by any other person. Because it has established that it intended to use the name to brand its businesses, that does not mean, however, it has established that it has used a mark or a sign to distinguish goods or services in the course of trade ...

...

75. There is no proof that the sign has been used or intended to be used to distinguish goods or services provided by the applicant in the course of trade from goods or services provided by any other. Even if it might be said that the use was in the course of trade that does not establish that the description 'On the Run' or 'On the Run Convenience Store' is a mark. That is not enough by itself.

The following extract discusses the circumstances in which a party can be said to be the owner of a mark for certain goods by having used the mark in relation to similar goods.

CASE EXTRACT: CURRENT LAW

Colorado Group Ltd v Strandbags Group Pty Ltd

[2007] FCAFC 184; (2007) 164 FCR 506
Federal Court of Australia, Full Court

[One issue in this case was whether the appellant Colorado's ownership of COLORADO for backpacks by virtue of first use in relation to those goods meant that it was also the owner of the mark in respect of goods 'of the same kind', which was argued to include handbags, wallets, purses and belts.]

Kenny J: 6. .... Ownership by first use is therefore ownership (or proprietorship) in relation to the goods or classes of goods on which the mark has first been used. The owner's right to registration in this circumstance is not limited to the identical goods or classes of goods but extends to goods or classes of goods 'of the same kind': see *Jackson & Co v Napper* (1886) 35 Ch D 162 at 178 and *In re Hick's Trade Mark* (1897) 22 VLR 636 at 640.

...

11. I agree with Allsop J that there is no error in the finding made by the primary judge ... that bags, wallets, purses and belts are not goods of the same kind as backpacks. The parties invited the Court to elucidate the phrase 'of the same kind' in this context.

12. Counsel for the appellants contended that whether goods were of the same kind for this purpose should be determined 'with the same degree of liberality that one approaches the matter when one is dealing with goods of the same description' elsewhere in the 1995 Act: see, eg, ss 14 and 44(1); and ss 120(2) and (3). The authorities that have considered the phrase goods 'of the same description' are numerous: see, eg, *Re Jellinek's Application* (1946) 63 RPC 59 at 69–72 per Romer J; and *Southern Cross Refrigerating Co v Toowoomba Foundry Pty Ltd* (1954) 91 CLR 592 at 606–607 per Dixon CJ, McTiernan, Webb, Fullagar and Taylor JJ. These authorities indicate that, depending on the goods, there are various factors that may be important in determining whether goods are of the same description as other goods, including their nature and uses, and the trade channels or markets in which they are sold. The appellants' counsel submitted that the primary judge concentrated unduly on the fact that their backpacks were predominantly for use by school children and failed to pay sufficient attention to the evidence that backpacks were in some instances fashion items too. He argued that handbags, purses and wallets were the same kind of thing as backpacks because they were 'receptacles which ordinary people carry around with them every day for transporting their things'.

13. The respondent's counsel argued for a narrow approach to the notion of goods of 'the same kind'. He contended that appropriate approach was necessarily constrained by s 27 of the 1995 Act, which required that the applicant for registration be the owner of the mark 'in relation to the goods and/or services'. This entailed, so the respondent's counsel argued, a more refined approach to the problem of characterization than that mooted by the appellants. I accept that the respondent's approach is to be preferred, although I do not consider the authorities to be especially helpful in this regard.

14. As we have seen, generally speaking, the prior public use in Australia of a mark as a trade mark—that is, the use of the mark in relation to goods or services in order to show a connection between the goods and the user of the mark—may support the user's claim to be the 'owner' of the mark for the purpose of s 27 of the 1995 Act: see *Moorgate Tobacco Co Ltd v Philip Morris Ltd [No 2]* (1984) 156 CLR 414 at 432 per Deane J (with whom Gibbs CJ, Mason, Wilson and Dawson JJ agreed). For this purpose, too, the owner's right to registration extends to goods 'of the same kind' as the goods that have already borne the mark: see *Jackson & Co v Napper* (1886) 35 Ch D 162 at 178 per Stirling J and *In re Hick's Trade Mark* (1897) 22 VLR 636 at 640 per Holroyd J. Authoritative discussions show that this extension to goods of the same kind is confined to goods that are essentially the same, though they may differ in size, shape and name. This point is emphasised in *Jackson v Napper* where Stirling J gave some attention to this question in considering the difference between an axe and a hatchet. He said (at 177–178):

[The Respondents] said there was a little difference in the size, as I understand, and a little difference in the shape; but can it be, that a man having made goods of a particular size, which might be designated as small axes—which in fact is the definition given in Johnson's Dictionary of a hatchet—is to be precluded from putting his mark upon things of the same description or belonging to the same class of goods, but of a different size and a different shape? The objection of course is founded on *Edwards v Dennis* [(1885) 30 Ch D 454], in which it was held that a man having registered a mark for iron goods and having manufactured, I think, sheet-iron, and applied his mark to that, was not entitled to stop another man from using the same mark in respect of iron wire which he had never used at all. That to my mind is a totally different thing from saying that a man who has used a mark on hatchets of a particular size and shape is not entitled to use a trade-mark as applied to an axe, *which is a thing of the same kind but a little different in size and a little different in shape.* No doubt at first the classes of goods under the Trade Marks Act were drawn too wide, and that has led to difficulty, but if I were to accede to this notion and say that because a man had merely manufactured small axes, he was not to be allowed to register in respect of axes, the logical consequence would be that he would have to register the shapes and sizes of everything to which he attached his mark. That was an inconvenience that was never intended to be imposed on an applicant, and *I hold that a man who has manufactured and applied his mark to small axes is entitled to register it in respect of axes generally.*

...

16. In identifying whether or not goods or a class of goods are essentially the same as other goods or classes of goods, a decision-maker will have regard to a range of factors, depending on the goods in question. Physical and functional differences may be relevant. Other matters may be as well. There is no bright line that marks out the factors for a 'same kind' inquiry from the factors for a 'same description' inquiry, although these inquiries may differ in the answers they yield. Goods that are properly regarded as 'essentially the same' may well cover a narrower field that goods 'of the same description'.

17. ... [T]his approach conforms to the approach in the Trade Mark Office in opposition proceedings based on prior use ... In *Howe Laboratories Inc v Daemar* (1996) 36 IPR 638 the services of the opponent—the treatment of motors and engines—were held not to be the same kind of thing as the applicant's lubricant conditioning agent. In *Coleman Co Inc v Igloo Products Corporation* (1999) 48 IPR 158 the opponent's insulated containers were held not to be the same kind of thing as the applicant's insulated thermoelectric containers. In *The Hoyts Corporation Pty Ltd v Hoyt Food Manufacturing Industries Pty Ltd* (2003) 61 IPR 334, the opponent's service of providing food and drink refreshments to cinema patrons was not the same kind of thing as the applicant's food goods. In *Nissan Jidosha Kabushiki Kaisha v Woolworths Ltd* (1999) 45 IPR 649 the clocks mounted in the opponent's vehicles were not the same kind of thing as the applicant's clocks and watches. In *Cantarella Bros Pty Ltd v Novadelta-Comercio E Industria De Cafes LDA* (1998) 42 IPR 265 olive oil and olive products were held not to be the same kind of thing as coffee.

18. This approach best serves the purposes of the 1995 Act. It may be borne in mind that an applicant for registration may apply for registration in respect of as broad a range of goods and services as desired. Whilst the application does not confer a right to registration, a right to registration arises once certain conditions are met, including that the mark is free from objection: see s 68. As the High Court observed in *Moorgate Tobacco Co Ltd v Philip Morris Ltd* (1980) 145 CLR 457 at 478, in relation to the *Trade Marks Act 1955* (Cth) ... :

Even so, a critical question, if not the critical question, for the Registrar to decide is whether the applicant is the proprietor in the statutory sense. If the applicant is the proprietor and there are no lawful grounds of objection, then the Registrar is bound to accept the application.

19. The Register is a public document in so far as it is open to inspection when the Trade Mark Office is open for business: see s 209. Whilst the Register may be altered or amended from time to time, it is at the heart of the statutory regime for trade mark regulation: see Pts 8 and 9 of the 1995 Act. If the acquisition of ownership of a mark by prior user were to extend to a broad ill-defined set of goods, this would have the capacity to undermine the efficiency of the registration system.

20. For these reasons and for the reasons stated by Allsop J, I agree that backpacks used predominantly by school children are not essentially the same as handbags. For largely utilitarian purposes, backpacks such as these are designed to be worn on the back and to hold the articles schoolchildren ordinarily carry between home and school, some of which may be quite heavy or bulky. Handbags are ordinarily smaller than backpacks. Handbags are generally held in the hand or worn over the shoulder. They are intended to carry the small everyday articles that an adult requires to move around the community (such as money or keys), as well as small items for personal use (such as a comb). They are also an everyday fashion item for use by women of all ages and, on occasions, by men. Plainly enough, a purse or wallet is even less like a school child's backpack than a handbag.

21. The appellants conceded that, if backpacks and handbags were not goods of the same kind, then the respondent's predecessor Edgarlodge made first use of the mark 'Colorado' in respect of handbags. A further issue of proprietorship arose, however, in relation to wallets and purses. The parties approached this question on the basis that purses and wallets were goods of the same kind. On this basis, the primary judge stated his view that purses and wallets were goods of the same kind as handbags. The appellants contested this on their appeal. His Honour reached this conclusion because he considered that handbags and purses were 'intended as fashion items and are used to carry small, everyday items such as money, credit cards, keys and like objects': see *Colorado Group Ltd Strandbags Group Pty Ltd (No 2)* (2006) 69 IPR 281 at [31]. Allsop J states the contrary view, observing that handbags often have a wider purpose than purses and wallets. There is something to be said for both points of view. Indeed, the difference of opinion highlights that the matter is essentially one of impression about which reasonable minds might well differ.

22. For my own part, I am reminded of Stirling J's comments in *Jackson v Napper* at 178 (set out above). A purse is usually (though not always) smaller than a handbag and often (though not always) holds only money or credit cards. A purse or wallet can be as much a fashion item as a handbag. Viewed in this way, there is no clear, generally valid, distinction to be made between handbags and purses (and therefore wallets). This supports the view, expressed by the primary judge, that handbags, purses and wallets should be regarded as goods of the same kind. In any case, I do not think it can be said that the primary judge was wrong in this conclusion, even if the Court on appeal preferred the contrary view ...

23. Having reached this conclusion, it is unnecessary for me to express a view as to whether, as the appellants assert, they made first use of the word mark 'Colorado' on wallets and purses. I would add, however, that, for the reasons stated by Allsop J, I agree that it was open to the primary judge to find that Edgarlodge (the respondent's predecessor) used swing tags with the word 'Colorado' on wallets and purses from before 1993.

BAD FAITH

The sixth relative ground of refusal, contained in the opposition ground in s 62A, is that the application was made in bad faith. This can also be raised as a relative ground where both the applicant and opponent are using the contested mark. While in many cases s 62A will duplicate the work of other relative grounds such as s 60, the following case demonstrates that it does have an independent sphere of operation.

CASE EXTRACT: CURRENT LAW

DC Comics v Cheqout Pty Ltd

[2013] FCA 478; (2013) 212 FCR 194
Federal Court of Australia

[Cheqout's application for registration of the word mark 'superman workout' was opposed by DC Comics. Bennett J held that the s 60 ground of opposition was not made out, on the basis that use by the applicant without any reference to the indicia associated with DC Comics 'Superman' superhero would not generate confusion. Bennett J then turned to consider s 62A, which the Registrar had held was not established. There was evidence that before the filing date, the applicant had used the words 'superman workout' in conjunction with a 'BG Shield Device'. This device, as well as DC Comics' 'S Shield Device', are set out at [70] below.]

Bennett J: 54. DC Comics submits that the use of the Trade Mark together with the BG Shield Device … which, it says, mimics the S Shield Device, demonstrates that the application for the Trade Mark was made in bad faith.

55. The Registrar accepts that it may be inferred that Cheqout intended to strengthen an allusion to the Superman character by use of the BG Shield Device but submits that, even so, DC Comics's 62A argument adds little to the other grounds of opposition. He accepts that it is relevant that ordinary people would think of the superhero when they see the Trade Mark, but repeats the conclusion (at [74]) of his reasons that they would not be confused or deceived by the use of that mark.

56. However, this conclusion was reached with respect to the notional use of the Trade Mark (in the context of s 60) and therefore was based, at least in part, in the absence of the associated indicia present in DC Comics' trade marks. The Registrar submits that the link between DC Comics' trade marks (Agreed Facts at [22]) and their associated indicia is so strong that use of the words without those indicia would not cause confusion and, in the context of s 62A, that such use is within normal commercial use.

57. The Registrar seems to rely … on the fact that, as at the date of the hearing before him, Cheqout had removed the BG Shield Device from its website. The Registrar did not, in his decision, accept that the previous use of the BG Shield Device, together with the Superman word mark, amounted to bad faith. Rather, he said, obvious or even deliberate use of, or allusion to, well known trade marks has been considered unobjectionable. He submits that s 62A establishes a 'high bar' in situations where there is no deception or confusion. He submits that *Fry Consulting v Sports Warehouse Inc (No 2)* (2012)

201 FCR 565 (*Fry*) should be viewed as deciding that 'conduct designed to acquire a springboard or advantage is not for that reason alone of an unscrupulous, underhand or unconscientious character'.

CONSIDERATION

58. In the absence of Australian judicial authority, Dodds-Streeton J recently considered s 62A in *Fry*. The relevant facts were:

- The director of Fry Consulting, Mr Fry, was well aware of the online retail store, Tennis Warehouse, as run by Sports Warehouse, the opponent to the application, and the fact that it sold goods to Australia through that website.
- His visits to the online store run by Sports Warehouse led him to register the business name Tennis Warehouse and the domain name www.tenniswarehouse.com.au and to set up an online retail store in competition.
- Mr Fry adopted the name 'Tennis Warehouse' knowing that it would cause confusion between the stores.
- The potential for confusion was at least partly why he chose the name.
- In developing his website, Mr Fry took images from the Sports Warehouse website.
- After complaints by Sports Warehouse, Mr Fry changed the name on the website from 'Tennis Warehouse' to 'Tennis Warehouse Australia' but did not change the business name or domain name.
- In the earlier factual proceedings before Kenny J (*Fry Consulting Pty Ltd v Sports Warehouse Inc (No 1)* [2011] FCA 1417 (*Fry (No 1)*), Mr Fry's explanation regarding the change to 'Tennis Warehouse Australia' was rejected and his credibility was criticised (at [67]) ...

59. Justice Dodds-Streeton rejected Sports Warehouse's submission that an application could be in bad faith if, as in that case, the applicant for the mark knew or intended that its use would cause confusion, or was aware that an overseas company which owned the mark was already operating or intending to operate in Australia (at [139]) ...

60. Her Honour considered (at [144]) the Explanatory Memorandum relating to s 62A, which stated:

> ... current opposition grounds do not cover instances in which a person has deliberately set out to gain registration of a trade mark, or adopted a trade mark in bad faith. There have been several instances in which trade mark applicants have deliberately set out to gain registration of their trade marks, or have adopted trade marks, in bad faith. Some examples of these include:
>
> - a person who monitors new property developments; registers the name of the new property development as a trade mark for a number of services; and then threatens the property developer with trade mark infringement unless they licence or buy the trade mark;
> - a pattern of registering trade marks that are deliberate misspellings of other registered trade marks; and
> - business people who identify a trade mark overseas which has no market penetration in Australia, and then register that trade mark with no intention to use it in the Australian market and for the express purpose of selling the mark to the overseas owner.

When such situations occur, there is very little third parties can do to prevent registration of this type of trade mark, because existing grounds for rejection and opposition do not allow the Registrar to take these facts into account.

61. Justice Dodds-Streeton observed (at [163]) that the examples of bad faith given in the Explanatory Memorandum are predominantly, but not exclusively, manifestations of blocking or holding to ransom a party which is, at least in conscience, entitled to a mark. However, her Honour noted that the illustrations are merely inclusive and do not limit the breadth of the concept of bad faith …

62. Given limited Australian authority, her Honour (at [145]–[166]) also considered relevant authorities from the United Kingdom. These cases stated, relevantly:

- Bad faith is a serious allegation and the more serious the allegation, the more cogent the evidence required to support it.
- Bad faith does not require dishonesty.
- Bad faith is a combined test that involves subjective and objective elements. The subjective element refers to the knowledge of the relevant person at the time of making the application. The objective element requires the decision-maker to decide whether, in the light of that knowledge, the relevant person's behaviour fell short of acceptable commercial standards.
- The question is whether the conduct falls short of the standards of acceptable commercial behaviour observed by reasonable and experienced persons in the particular area. It is whether the knowledge of the applicant was such that the decision to apply for registration would be regarded as in bad faith by persons adopting proper standards.
- It is difficult to see how a person who applies to register, in his own name, a mark he has previously recognised as the property of a potential overseas principal can be said to be acting in accordance with acceptable standards of commercial behaviour. Combining the mark with the applicant's own name is no answer to that criticism.
- The registration of a trade mark is designed to enable bona fide proprietors to protect their proprietary rights without having to prove unfair trading.
- All the circumstances surrounding the application to register the mark are relevant.
- An act of bad faith cannot be cured by an action after the date of application.

63. Justice Dodds-Streeton concluded (at [164]) that bad faith in the context of s 62A does not require (although it includes) dishonesty or fraud and that it is a wider notion, potentially applicable to diverse species of conduct. Her Honour rejected the proposition that mere awareness that an overseas company owning the mark operated or intended to operate in Australia would amount to bad faith, concluding that this would be unduly absolute. Justice Dodds-Streeton instead adopted as a touchstone the United Kingdom formulation of conduct falling short of the standards of acceptable commercial behaviour observed by reasonable and experienced persons (at [165]). Her Honour observed that the applicant's mental state is also relevant, and stated (at [166]) that:

… mere negligence, incompetence or a lack of prudence to reasonable and experienced standards would not, in themselves, suffice as the concept of bad faith imports conduct which, irrespective of the form it takes, is of an unscrupulous, underhand or unconscientious character.

64. Justice Dodds-Streeton accepted that certain aspects of the behaviour described in *Fry* may well have been regarded as being in bad faith. Her Honour also accepted (at [171]–[172]) that

subsequent modifications to a mark or name appropriated in such circumstances would not necessarily negate improper motivation and noted that Kenny J had previously held that the use of the trade mark, although including a subsequently added device, did not evidence use actuated only by proper motives.

65. Her Honour did not conclude, contrary to the Registrar's submission, that exploitative conduct alone cannot ground a finding of bad faith.

66. Her Honour said (at [170]) that:

> Mr Fry's conduct was exploitative and designed to acquire a springboard or advantage for his fledgling business. While it is unnecessary to decide the question, given his knowledge as at September 2004, an attempt to register the words 'TENNIS WAREHOUSE' at that time may well have been regarded as in bad faith according to proper or ordinary commercial standards.

67. Her Honour's finding that the 'exploitative' conduct was not sufficient to establish the requisite bad faith was grounded in the facts of that case, and in particular, on the fact that Mr Fry's application for the relevant trade mark was not lodged until November 2006, more than two years after the exploitative conduct. Furthermore, her Honour's statement regarding unscrupulous behaviour was made in the context of her conclusion [quoted in [63] above].

68. Justice Dodds-Streeton concluded that Sports Warehouse had not successfully discharged its onus of proof in regards to s 62A. Pivotal to her Honour's reasoning (at [174]) was the correspondence between Mr Fry and Sports Warehouse prior to Fry Consulting's application for the mark. It established that:

- In December 2004, Mr Fry had unequivocally indicated his willingness to cease using 'Tennis Warehouse' if Sports Warehouse provided evidence of its entitlement and sought a prompt response so that he could change the name prior to expanding his business any further.
- Mr Fry did not acknowledge Sports Warehouse's ownership or rights in Australia.
- Despite undertaking to do so, Sports Warehouse did not provide any documentation or evidence to Mr Fry of its entitlement or rights to the 'Tennis Warehouse' mark in Australia, and their later attempt to register this mark was ultimately unsuccessful.
- In the period from December 2004 to November 2006 (in which Sports Warehouse did not attempt to correspond with Fry) Fry developed his business using the words 'Tennis Warehouse Australia' and commissioned a tennis ball logo that formed the composite mark which he sought to register in December 2006.

69. No such facts are present here. In the present case, there is no dispute that Superman, his strength and the indicia with which he is associated, including the S Shield Device, were very well known. There is no dispute that DC Comics has licensed the use of its registered Superman marks in Australia in relation to an array of goods, but has not licensed the use of these marks with respect to gyms or personal training.

70. It is an agreed fact that Cheqout used the Trade Mark together with the BG Shield Device in relation to its personal training and film and entertainment services and in titles to video clips appearing on its website. The triangular shape of the BG Shield Device is of a similar shape and style of lettering to the S Shield Device in DC Comics' trade marks. This similarity can be observed through the side to side comparison of the devices:

CURRENT LAW

71. The evidence as to the use of the BG Shield Device as at the Priority Date of 2 June 2009 is not clear. What is clear is that Cheqout's website displayed the BG Shield Device at the time the images in the Statement of Agreed Facts were captured on 15 December 2009. It only removed the BG Shield Device after receipt of a 'cease and desist' letter sent on behalf of DC Comics on 17 December 2009.

72. The Registrar's decision sets out evidence adduced in the statutory declaration of Mr Gabrielle, the sole director and company secretary of Cheqout. Mr Gabrielle stated that the use of the words 'superman workout' was designed to:

> ... convey to potential users of my exercise program the potential of changing yourself into a muscularly powerful athletic superman ... not to associate my exercise program with the Opponent's comic book character.

73. That assertion is, in my view, at odds with the use of the BG Shield Device, to which Mr Gabrielle's evidence did not refer. It was Mr Gabrielle's decision to use the words 'superman workout' together with the BG Shield Device. As the sole director of Cheqout, that mental element is attributable to the company. In my view, the inference is clear, from the immediate use of the Trade Mark together with the BG Shield Device that, in making the application to register the Trade Mark, Mr Gabrielle (and therefore Cheqout) intended to use it in combination with the BG Shield Device in order to strengthen the allusion to Superman. The inference can also be drawn that this use was designed to gain a benefit by appropriating Superman indicia and the reputation of the DC Comics superhero, so as to further the viewer's association between the Trade Mark and the Superman word mark.

74. This is a 'relevant circumstance' in a consideration of bad faith for the purposes of s 62A (*Fry* at [167]).

75. The Registrar submits that if the fair use of the mark is unlikely to deceive or cause confusion, then this should 'undercut' any argument that the application to register the trade mark was in bad faith. However, an important factor in both the Registrar's decision and my conclusion as to whether the Trade Mark is likely to deceive or cause confusion is the absence of any of the indicia associated with Superman. The relevant use of the Trade Mark for s 60 purposes is the notional use of the mark itself, which properly excludes the appropriation of indicia associated with Superman.

76. Conversely, s 62A was introduced into the Act as a separate ground of opposition to the registration of a trade mark. Section 62A does not require the opponent to establish that the trade mark's use would result in deception or confusion. That aspect is the subject of other grounds of opposition, such as ss 43 and 60. Such a requirement would, in my view, contradict the legislative

intent in introducing a new ground of opposition by limiting its application to circumstances provided for by existing grounds. Evidence that the use of a mark is likely to cause confusion or deception may be persuasive in considering whether the application to register a mark was in bad faith. However, it is neither determinative of that finding, nor a prerequisite for it.

77. I am satisfied that DC Comics has established that Cheqout made the application for the Trade Mark in bad faith. This is evidenced by the use, soon after the application, of the word Superman together with the BG Shield Device, in the context of male fitness and strength. I note also that the red, white and blue colours traditionally used in conjunction with the Superman character were used by Cheqout together with the BG Shield Device. The design of the BG Shield Device closely resembles the insignia closely associated with the DC Comics character and the DC Comics registered trade marks. I am satisfied that at the date of application for the Trade Mark, Cheqout's conduct fell short of the standards of acceptable commercial behaviour observed by reasonable and experienced persons.

78. For the above reasons, I conclude that DC Comics has discharged its onus of proof with respect to the ground of opposition provided for in s 62A of the Act ...

CONFLICT WITH A GEOGRAPHICAL INDICATION (GI)

The final relative ground of refusal is contained in s 61(1), which states that:

> The registration of a trade mark in respect of particular goods (*relevant goods*) may be opposed on the ground that the trade mark contains or consists of a sign that is a geographical indication for goods (*designated goods*) originating in:
>
> (a) a country, or in a region or locality in a country, other than the country in which the relevant goods originated; or
>
> (b) a region or locality in the country in which the relevant goods originated other than the region or locality in which the relevant goods originated;
>
> if the relevant goods are similar to the designated goods or the use of a trade mark in respect of the relevant goods would be likely to deceive or cause confusion.

'Geographical indication' is defined in s 6(1) as a sign that identifies goods as originating in a country, or in a region or locality in that country, where a given quality, reputation or other characteristic of the goods is essentially attributable to their geographical origin. That is, it is designed to provide a degree of protection for producers of goods such as 'Parmigiano Reggiano' or 'Swiss' watches that have certain qualities or reputations attributable to their geographical origin. While s 61(1) overlaps to some extent with s 43, it also applies simply where the application is for a 'false' GI (i.e. where the relevant and designated goods are similar), irrespective of the issue of deception or confusion. A range of exceptions to s 61(1) are set out in s 61(2)–(4), dealing with situations such as where the applicant has made earlier use of its trade mark, or where the GI has ceased to be used in its country of origin.

—18—

REGISTERED TRADE MARKS: INFRINGEMENT, DEFENCES, LOSS OF RIGHTS AND EXPLOITATION

INTRODUCTION

In this chapter we consider trade mark infringement and defences. We then turn to consider the ways in which trade mark rights might be lost, and the ways in which trade marks may be commercially exploited.

INFRINGEMENT

Once a trade mark has been registered, the registered owner has the exclusive rights under s 20 of the *Trade Marks Act 1995* (Cth) (*TMA*) to use and authorise the use of the mark. It also has the right to obtain relief if the trade mark has been infringed.

Section 120 of the *TMA* is the main infringement provision, and relevantly provides as follows:

(1) A person infringes a registered trade mark if the person uses as a trade mark a sign that is substantially identical with, or deceptively similar to, the trade mark in relation to goods or services in respect of which the trade mark is registered.

(2) A person infringes a registered trade mark if the person uses as a trade mark a sign that is substantially identical with, or deceptively similar to, the trade mark in relation to:

    (a) goods of the same description as that of goods (registered goods) in respect of which the trade mark is registered; or

    (b) services that are closely related to registered goods; or

    (c) services of the same description as that of services (registered services) in respect of which the trade mark is registered; or

    (d) goods that are closely related to registered services.

However, the person is not taken to have infringed the trade mark if the person establishes that using the sign as the person did is not likely to deceive or cause confusion.

(3) A person infringes a registered trade mark if:

    (a) the trade mark is well known in Australia; and

    (b) the person uses as a trade mark a sign that is substantially identical with, or deceptively similar to, the trade mark in relation to:

        (i) goods (unrelated goods) that are not of the same description as that of the goods in respect of which the trade mark is registered (registered goods) or are not closely related to services in respect of which the trade mark is registered (registered services); or

(ii) services (unrelated services) that are not of the same description as that of the registered services or are not closely related to registered goods; and

(c) because the trade mark is well known, the sign would be likely to be taken as indicating a connection between the unrelated goods or services and the registered owner of the trade mark; and

(d) for that reason, the interests of the registered owner are likely to be adversely affected.

Subsections (1), (2) and (3) operate as three *alternatives* for establishing infringement. None of these overlap. However, they contain a number of common elements. In each case the registered owner must establish that:

- the defendant is 'using' a sign;
- the defendant's use of that sign is 'as a trade mark'; and
- the defendant's sign is 'substantially identical with, or deceptively similar to' the registered mark.

These three issues will be considered below. Determining which of subs (1), (2) or (3) applies turns on the *nature* of the goods and/or services in relation to which the defendant is using its sign. Thus, s 120(1) applies where the defendant's goods/services are covered by those goods/services specified by the owner in its registration. Section 120(2) applies where the defendant's goods/services are of the same description as, or closely related to, those covered by the specification. Section 120(3) applies where the defendant's goods/services are not of the same description as, or are unrelated to, those covered by the specification.

Conceptually, s 120 sets up something of a hierarchy of rights. Section 120(1) applies in the narrowest set of circumstances (in that there must be identity between the registered owner's and defendant's goods/services), but otherwise is, in effect, a strict liability provision. Section 120(2) applies in broader circumstances, given that the defendant's goods or services only need to be similar to those of the registered owner, but contains a proviso, namely that the defendant will not infringe if it establishes that using the sign as it did 'is not likely to deceive or cause confusion'. Section 120(3) applies in the widest set of circumstances, potentially giving the owner rights against providers of non-competing goods or services. However, the owner must prove that its mark is 'well known in Australia' (as to which, see also s 120(4)), as well as the existence of a particular 'connection' (as set out in s 120(3)(c)) and an adverse impact on its interests (s 120(3)(d)). We will consider both the proviso under s 120(2), and the precise scope of s 120(3), below.

Before doing so, it is important to note that 'confusion' plays a somewhat unusual role in the Australian infringement action. While under passing off and the Australian Consumer Law much depends on whether the defendant's conduct constitutes a misrepresentation or is misleading in all the circumstances, a quite different assessment takes place under the *TMA*. In the infringement context, particularly in relation to s 120(1) and (2), the key questions relate to the similarity of the two marks and the similarity of the goods and services, both of which are assessed in a manner that is largely divorced from how the registered owner is using its mark (if it is using the mark at all) and the full context of the defendant's use of its sign. Further, while the absence of any consumer confusion appears to be a 'defence' to an infringement action under s 120(2), this proviso has a highly circumscribed role (and does not replicate how the existence of a misrepresentation would be assessed in passing off proceedings). Having said this, evidence of consumer confusion does have something of a role to play in determining whether the defendant has used its sign 'as a trade mark' and whether the two marks are deceptively similar. But while it might be said that confusion is the touchstone of liability for infringement under some systems of trade mark law (such as in the USA), the same cannot be said for Australian law.

'USE' OF A SIGN

The first issue that needs to be explored is what is meant by 'use' of a sign for the purposes of s 120. While 'use' is not specifically defined, s 7(4) provides that 'use of a trade mark in relation to goods' means use of the mark upon, or in physical or other relation to, the goods (including second-hand goods), and s 7(5) provides that 'use of a trade mark in relation to services' means use of the mark in physical or other relation to the services. Section 9 also provides guidance as to when a mark is to be taken to be applied to goods, or applied in relation to goods or services (see generally *Brother Industries Ltd v Dynamic Supplies Pty Ltd* [2007] FCA 1490; (2007) 163 FCR 530 at [53]–[54]).

The defendant's use must be in Australia. This raises potentially difficult questions in the internet context. In *Ward Group Pty Ltd v Brodie & Stone Plc* [2005] FCA 471; (2005) 143 FCR 479, Merkel J held at [43] that:

> the use of a trade mark on the Internet, uploaded on a website outside of Australia, without more, is not a use by the website proprietor of the mark in each jurisdiction where the mark is downloaded. However ... if there is evidence that the use was specifically intended to be made in, or directed or targeted at, a particular jurisdiction then there is likely to be a use in that jurisdiction when the mark is downloaded.

It was also held at [37] that merely having 'Australia' included in a drop-down menu of countries to which goods could be shipped was not sufficient in that case.

The following case provides a detailed examination of when use on a foreign website will be considered use in Australia, and deals with the common situation where the ownership of a mark is split between multiple entities around the world.

CASE EXTRACT: CURRENT LAW

International Hair Cosmetics Group Pty Ltd v International Hair Cosmetics Ltd

[2011] FCA 339; (2011) 218 FCR 398
Federal Court of Australia

[International Hair Cosmetics Ltd (IHC UK) was a UK company and the registered owner in the UK and a number of other countries of the mark AFFINAGE for hair care products. It operated the www.affinage. com website, which provided only corporate information and from which no goods were sold. Until

2010, IHC UK sold its products in Australia through a local distributor, International Hair Cosmetics Group Pty Ltd (IHC Aust), the owner of the Australian-registered AFFINAGE mark. IHC Aust had been established in the 1980s by Mr Bailey, a director of IHC UK, and Mr and Mrs Jolly. In 2002 the Jollys bought Mr Bailey's shares in IHC Aust and the parties entered what is described in the judgment as a 'gentlemen's agreement' in respect of the territorial allocation of rights for the distribution of AFFINAGE products worldwide. IHC Aust was allocated those rights for a group of countries in Asia and Oceania, including Australia, with IHC UK retaining the remaining rights. As part of a dispute between IHC UK and IHC Aust in 2010, that gentlemen's agreement was formalised as a deed of settlement, under which IHC UK undertook not to use AFFINAGE 'in connection with the importation, marketing, sale or manufacture in Australia of hair care products'.

In 2011, Mr Bennett of IHC Aust's lawyers accessed www.affinage.com. The landing page contained the word 'Affinage' as a large banner with 'Salon Professional' in smaller subscript, and various statements about Affinage. The page contained UK, US and Australian 'country box' options and the statement 'Select Australia for information on Australasia and Asian Pacific countries'. Clicking on 'Australia', the lawyer was taken to a page promoting 'A.S.P.'-brand hair care products ('A.S.P.' being the brand name IHC UK had started to use in Australia).]

Logan J: 21. Shortly after Mr Bennett conducted this search, IHC Aust filed a notice of motion [seeking that]:

    1   the Respondents be permanently restrained from using AFFINAGE ... as a sign in connection with the importation, marketing, sale or manufacture in Australia of hair care products including hair colours and dyes.

    2   In relation to the website www.affinage.com the Respondents forthwith:

        (a) Delete from the home or landing page of the website the sentence *Select Australia for information on Australasia and Asian Pacific countries;*

        (b) Remove Australia from the list of countries able to be displayed and selected in the country box on the said website;

        (c) Remove the A.S.P. pages from the said website;

        (d) Remove any references to Australia from the said website; and

        (e) Remove any link from the said website to any website marketing or promoting hair care products including hair colours and dyes for sale within Australia.

    ...

30. In a letter dated 15 February 2011 ... it was put that IHC UK was prepared to make further modifications to the global landing page of the website www.affinage.com. As there stated, these were:

    (a) Only maintain the drop-down links to the UK site and the US site under the sign AFFINAGE Salon Professional;

    (b) Insert the sign A.S.P. in the same font size as AFFINAGE;

    (c) Providing a drop-down link to the Australian site only under the sign A.S.P.

    ...

32. This offer was not accepted by IHC Aust. Instead, by a letter dated 16 February 2011, it was put on behalf of IHC Aust that the proposed revised page would still amount to a use of AFFINAGE (and AFFINAGE SALON PROFESSIONAL) in connection with the marketing and sale of hair care products in

Australia. Concern was also voiced by the solicitors that the proposed revised page continued to include 'Facebook and Twitter links which operate to persons visiting the site to link their personal Facebook or Twitter accounts with the Facebook or Twitter accounts maintained by [IHC UK]. These in turn use the Affinage Trade Marks.'

33. By way of response ... IHC UK [advised that it] intended in any event to implement the website changes proposed in their letter of 15 February 2011 and to draw this fact to the attention of the Court in the event that the matter proceeded to hearing.

...

44. Thus the questions are ... whether it has been shown that IHC UK and the other named respondents have failed to fulfil the undertaking, properly construed, and, if so, whether the relief claimed should be granted?

...

58. When, in the manner of the Treaty of Tordesillas (1494, between Spain and Portugal, dividing, by a fixed meridian, the newly discovered lands outside Europe), the parties to the deed of settlement divided what one might describe as the world of Affinage, thereby confirming earlier arrangements struck between Mr Bailey (and entities he controlled) and Mr and Mrs Jolly (and entities they controlled), they divided, as between them, all of that world including, as to targets of marketing, cyberspace. That division is locally buttressed by the trade marks owned by IHC Aust just as much as it is, for example, on the other part buttressed in the United Kingdom by trade marks owned by IHC UK.

59. Yet the internet knows no such physical limits and may be accessed, for example, from either and each of Australia and the United Kingdom. It seems to me, by analogy with the *Ward Group Case* ... that the reconciliation to which I have just referred is achieved, in terms of the undertaking given in this case, by an approach that finds a use of the nominated words in connection with 'marketing' in Australia if the words as so used are downloaded in Australia *and* there is evidence that the use was specifically intended to be made in, or directed or targeted at Australia.

60. ... A person seeking information concerning, 'Affinage' can readily access from Australia and download here the global 'affinage.com' web site maintained by IHC UK. As accessed by Mr Bennett this year, that global web site is, *inter alia*, directed to or targeted at Australia. That is the whole purpose of the 'Australia' option in the drop down box selection offered on the global landing page.

...

62. An internet [user] coming to the global landing page www.affinage.com, as did Mr Bennett, is immediately confronted with the bold type banner, 'AFFINAGE' and with the further reference to that word immediately below it as 'one of the world's fastest growing haircare [sic] companies using cutting edge technology to produce market leading hair products'. That, in my opinion, is a 'use' of a sign ... The use of the word Affinage in the setting presented has trade mark significance. As so used the word has the character of a device or brand. IHC UK is perfectly entitled to engage in such a use in the United Kingdom, for it holds the registered trade mark there. It is not so entitled when it targets or directs its presentation at Australia for IHC Aust, not IHC UK, holds the trade mark registration here. That Australian targeted use on the global landing page controls all that follows when one selects, as did Mr Bennett, the 'Australia' option in the drop down box.

63. The qualification in the undertaking of use in connection with, materially, 'marketing' does not remove this use from the scope of the undertaking. The web site is patently a means of marketing.

64. A like conclusion does not follow in respect of the Facebook and Twitter links displayed on the global landing page in that neither of these is not specifically targeted or directed at Australia.

65. Following the 'Australia' link on the global landing page, as did Mr Bennett, leads one to the 'company profile' statement, detailed above. Here, the 'AFFINAGE brand' is twice mentioned. Products of this brand are said to have been 'enthusiastically embraced by consumers and the hairdressing industry worldwide'. Then follows a reference to the launch of the new brand ASP. Under the heading 'Word Class, Wordwide' [sic] it is said that '*our products* are sold in over 50 countries' (emphasis added). The 'Asia Pacific' region is one location mentioned. It is then stated that, '*Our brands* are marketed globally by IHC UK and through its associated companies in the USA and Australia' (emphasis added).

66. As a matter of history, it is true that IHC UK created the Affinage brand. It is also true that it holds trade mark rights in respect of that brand there and in may other places in the world, but not in Australia. The undertaking was one means by which a compromise in the deed of settlement, which included the division of the Affinage world, was given effect. As used on this Australia specific profile page the purpose is to create a connection with a brand which, in Australia, is not that of IHC UK or Salon. That, in terms of the undertaking, is the use of a sign in Australia. It is patently a use in connection with marketing. Having divided the Affinage world and IHC Aust having the registered trade mark in Australia, IHC UK and its Australian distributor, Salon cannot, in terms of the undertaking, use that brand as a sign in Australia in connection with, materially, marketing. Representations which did not constitute a 'use' as described in *Shell v Esso* would not transgress, but that is not this case.

67. When one reads the language of the 'Profile' page in context, the repetition of AFFINAGE and the repeated use of 'our brands' in conjunction with 'worldwide' and 'are marketed globally by IHC UK and through its associated companies in the USA and Australia', the reference to Affinage is not just to a matter of foreign history but part of a current promotion that our goods worldwide, including those offered in Australia, include goods with the AFFINAGE brand. The end to which the profile is directed is to persuade those reading the profile to purchase or seek information as to how to purchase the goods of IHC UK and, materially, its Australian distributor, Salon, and to distinguish those goods from those of others partly because of an affiliation with the AFFINAGE brand … The respondents have not, in this manner, made it clear, since giving the undertaking, that the current commercial origin *in Australia* of goods with the AFFINAGE mark is neither IHC UK nor Salon.

68. In my opinion, and though the issue is not without difficulty, even after taking into account the modification of the global landing page, which IHC UK proposed to implement in any event and which became Exhibit 1 on the hearing of the notice of motion, there remains a use contrary to the undertaking.

69. The modification divides the global landing page as between an AFFINAGE Salon Professional banner and an 'A.S.P.' banner with the latter appearing in the lower half of the page. AFFINAGE and A.S.P. appear in equally large type but A.S.P., being the lower, in this sense strikes the viewer as being subordinate. Under the AFFINAGE banner the following appears, 'Affinage is one of the world's fastest growing haircare [sic] brands using cutting edge technology to produce market leading hair products.' In turn, under this the 'International Sites' portion contains drop down boxes and directions only in respect of the United Kingdom and the USA. The 'Australia' drop down box has been removed. Instead,

CURRENT LAW

it appears as a discrete, fixed link under the 'A.S.P.' banner in the lower half of the landing page. 'Australia' is thus immediately visible on the global landing page. Also under the A.S.P. banner is the following statement, 'products formulated by [IHC UK] are now marketed in Australasia & Asian Pacific countries under the ASP brand.'

70. The 'setting' for the viewer of this global landing page has undoubtedly changed and changed in a way that seeks to create a discrete Australian 'target'. What remains though is a determined endeavour to place AFFINAGE in the mind of the viewer who has an interest in reading further in relation to Australia. The Australian 'target' remains on the global landing page as a fixed feature. A connection between the AFFINAGE brand product and the ASP brand, each formulated by IHC UK is promoted and promoted to an Australian viewer. What the global landing page does not say is that IHC UK has no connection with the AFFINAGE brand in Australia. Instead, the overall 'setting' is that there is an Affinage world brand in which the Australian province is known as 'A.S.P.'. This, in my opinion, remains a use of that sign in Australia in connection with marketing contrary to the terms of the undertaking.

71. It follows that the respondents have failed and continue to fail to comply with the terms of the undertaking ...

72. IHC Aust is entitled to an order in terms of paragraph 1 of the notice of motion. Further, in light of the events which have transpired since that undertaking was given and in order to prevent an undermining by the respondents of the Court's authority, there is a need for the addition of more prescriptive orders directed to the respondents in respect of the website, www.affinage.com. The additional orders sought in paragraphs (b) (modified to take account of the modification of the global landing page), (c), (d) and (e) of paragraph 2 of the notice of motion are necessary to achieve this ...

USE 'AS A TRADE MARK'

The next issue to be determined is what is meant by the requirement that the defendant's use be 'as a trade mark'. The following case sets out some general principles in determining this issue.

PRECEDENT

CASE EXTRACT: PRECEDENT

Shell Co of Australia Ltd v Esso Standard Oil (Australia) Ltd

(1963) 109 CLR 407
High Court of Australia

Kitto J (with whom Dixon CJ, Taylor and Owen JJ agreed) (at 420–426): This appeal is from a judgment given in favour of [Esso] upon the trial of an action brought in this Court for infringement of two trade marks. The trade marks are registered in respect of 'products and preparations for lubricating, heating, illuminating, and fuel and power generating purposes'. One mark consists of a grotesque drawing of a person with a head in the shape of a drop of oil which has just fallen from a container and by reason of its viscosity is drawn out to an asymmetrical peak at the top. A face is suggested by lines indicating eyebrows, eyelids and mouth (but no nose or ears), all so curved and disposed as to give the impression that the being depicted is immensely pleased with himself. There is no neck. The

PRECEDENT

body is about as long as the head but narrower; and it is bifurcated to create a suggestion of short legs, each with a foot turned outwards. Arms and hands are indicated, and they assist the impression of self-satisfaction by being drawn as if the thumbs were hooked into braces near the armpits, though no braces, and indeed no indications of clothes, are to be seen. The other trade mark is identical, save that the figure displays an oval badge suspended immediately below the head and bearing the word 'Esso', which is a name used by the respondent for some of its products ...

The conduct of the appellant which the learned primary Judge held to have constituted infringement consisted in causing two advertising films, of the animated cartoon variety, to be exhibited to the public in the course of television programmes ... In each film a 'humanized' oil drop is made to personify the appellant's 'Shell' petrol, and to perform a series of exuberant antics designed, in conjunction with some letterpress and the spoken word, to create in the minds of viewers a feeling of pleasure at recognizing desirable attributes in Shell petrol. In the course of his merry pranks, the Shell Eulenspiegel constantly changes in shape and expression. He always has a head the shape of an oil drop drawn to a peak at the top, and generally the head is supported, without a neck, by a body bifurcated to indicate short legs with feet turned outwards. Arms and hands take up varying positions, and what passes for a face expresses varying emotions. On some occasions the figure, in the course of its mutations, approaches fairly closely in appearance to the respondent's trade marks; but the name 'Esso' is never seen, and the changes of appearance follow one another so swiftly that the viewer can hardly gain more than a general impression of a Protean creature who could be, having regard to some of his manifestations at least, the man whom the respondent has registered as its trade mark, but could equally be another member of the same tribe. It may be assumed for present purposes, however, that in the course of each film the figure takes on, at least for a moment or two now and then, an appearance substantially identical with that of the trade marks.

The question, then, is whether such a user of the oil drop figure as takes place by the exhibition of the films on television involves infringement of the trade marks. It is a question not to be answered in favour of the appellant merely by pointing to the brevity of the occasions when substantial identity is achieved. The assumption I have made means, of course, that if the oil drop figure as appearing in some of the individual frames of the films were transferred as separate pictures to another context the use of the pictures in that context could be an infringement. But the context is all-important, because not every use of a mark which is identical with or deceptively similar to a registered trade mark infringes the right of property which the proprietor of the mark possesses in virtue of the registration ...

[Kitto J then considered that infringement under s 62(1) of the *Trade Marks Act 1955* (Cth) required the defendant's use of the mark to be as a trade mark, and continued:]

The crucial question in the present case seems to me to arise at this point. Was the appellant's use, that is to say its television presentation, of those particular pictures of the oil drop figure which were substantially identical with or deceptively similar to the respondent's trade marks a use of them 'as a trade mark'?

With the aid of the definition of 'trade mark' in s 6 of the Act, the adverbial expression may be expanded so that the question becomes whether, in the setting in which the particular pictures referred to were presented, they would have appeared to the television viewer as possessing the character of devices, or brands, which the appellant was using or proposing to use in relation to petrol for the

PRECEDENT

purpose of indicating, or so as to indicate, a connexion in the course of trade between the petrol and the appellant. Did they appear to be thrown on to the screen as being marks for distinguishing Shell petrol from other petrol in the course of trade?

Clearly they were used so that the figure in all its varying forms would be understood as representing Shell petrol for the purposes of the disjointed tale that is told. But the connexion in the films between the oil drop man and the petrol he symbolizes is a connexion limited by the purpose of the occasion. At every point of the exhibition, whether the resemblance to the respondent's trade marks be at the moment close or remote, the purpose and the only purpose that can be seen in the appearance of the little man on the screen is that which unites the quickly moving series of pictures as a whole, namely the purpose of conveying by a combination of pictures and words a particular message about the qualities of Shell petrol. This fact makes it, I think, quite certain that no viewer would ever pick out any of the individual scenes in which the man resembles the respondent's trade marks, whether those scenes be few or many, and say to himself: 'There I see something that the Shell people are showing me as being a mark by which I may know that any petrol in relation to which I see it used is theirs.' And one may fairly affirm with even greater confidence that the viewer would never infer from the films that every one of the forms which the oil drop figure takes appears there as being a mark which has been chosen to serve the specific purpose of branding petrol in reference to its origin. No doubt if, later, the viewer were to come across the respondent's trade mark used in relation to petrol his recollection of the films might lead him to think that the appellant, taking advantage of a reputation created for the oil drop figure by means of the films, had adopted the figure, in one of its forms, as a mark for its petrol. But that would be quite a different matter from inferring, while sitting in front of his television set, that the figure in one or more, some or all, of its exhibited forms was being placed before him there as a trade mark for Shell petrol.

In my opinion this case is covered in principle by the English decisions I have cited. One or two may be particularly mentioned.

In *JB Stone & Co Ltd v Steelace Manufacturing Co Ltd* (1929) 46 RPC 406, a registered trade mark which consisted of the word 'Alligator' was held infringed by a use of the expression 'alligator pattern'; but the judgments make it plain that if the second word had been clear enough in meaning to make the whole expression signify only that the goods were of a type of which 'Alligator' goods were an example there would have been no infringement, because the context would then have shown that the word 'alligator' was being used otherwise than as a trade mark. The *Yeast-Vite Case* (1933) 50 RPC 139; (1934) 51 RPC 110 is a striking example of a context precluding a conclusion that a use complained of as an infringement was a use as a trade mark. The case of *Edward Young & Co Ltd v Grierson Oldham & Co Ltd* (1924) 41 RPC 548 is perhaps the case most usefully to be compared with the present. There the use complained of was a use of a static picture; here it is of a series of pictures. The only purpose served by the use of the single picture there was, as the only purpose of the use of all the pictures here is, to convey a particular message to those who should see it. There the purpose became apparent when the single picture was considered in the light of a usage common in the relevant trade; here it appears when each picture is considered in the light of all the other pictures amongst which it has a place in the sequence and of the accompanying letterpress and spoken word. There the message was simple: that the goods came from Portugal; here it is simple also, though the method of conveying it is complicated and incoherent; it is that the chemical composition of Shell petrol gives it advantages over its rivals. There, once the 'purpose and nature' of the use were understood—that is the expression of Sargant LJ (1924) 41 RPC, at p 579—the action for infringement failed. In my opinion the purpose and nature of the use complained of in the present case are such that this action should fail also.

Shell v Esso makes it clear that the defendant's use must be as a badge of origin, and that whether the sign is being used as a trade mark is to be judged objectively by reference to the perspectives of consumers of the defendant's goods or services. It is also clear that certain types of use of another's mark—such as descriptive, decorative, or nominative uses—will not constitute use 'as a trade mark' and will therefore not infringe. Determining whether or not such uses are for such purposes can be a difficult task, and a range of policy factors are often accommodated within the use 'as a trade mark' requirement, as the following three extracts demonstrate.

DESCRIPTIVE OR DECORATIVE USE

CASE EXTRACT: CURRENT LAW

Top Heavy Pty Ltd v Killin

(1996) 34 IPR 282
Federal Court of Australia

[Killin (the respondent) was the registered owner of a device mark prominently featuring the words 'Chill Out', in relation to clothing. Top Heavy (the applicant) manufactured T-shirts that bore a stylised representation of the phrase 'Chill Out' in which a Coca-Cola bottle appeared as the letter 'I'. Killin demanded that Top Heavy cease using the phrase 'Chill Out' on its T-shirts, following which Top Heavy sought an injunction restraining Killin from representing that Top Heavy's actions were infringing.]

Lehane J (at 285–287): Plainly the applicant's stylised 'Chill Out' is a 'sign' as defined in s 6 of the 1995 Act; T-shirts are, of course, goods in respect of which the mark is registered. The kind of use referred to in s 120(1) is, no doubt, use of the kind contemplated by s 17 of the 1995 Act, the provision which tells us what a trade mark is ...

It was clear, in relation to s 62(1) of the 1955 Act, 'that the use which is there referred to is limited to use of a mark as a trade mark': *Shell Co of Australia Ltd v Esso Standard Oil (Australia) Ltd* (1963) 109 CLR 407 at 422 per Kitto J ... Section 120(1) of the 1995 Act expressly provides that the relevant use is 'use as a trade mark'. What was meant by use as a trade mark for the purposes of the 1955 Act was clear enough. Phrases such as 'badge of origin' were used to summarise what was meant: *Johnson & Johnson Australia Pty Ltd v Sterling Pharmaceuticals Pty Ltd* (1991) 30 FCR 326; 21 IPR 1 per Lockhart J at FCR 335; IPR 12 and per Gummow J at FCR 347; IPR 24. The concept thus summarised was described by Williams J in *Mark Foys Ltd v Davies Coop & Co Ltd* (1956) 95 CLR

CURRENT LAW

190 at 205 in connection with the use by the defendants, in relation to their 'Exacto' garments, of the plaintiff's mark tub happy. His Honour said:

> The public are not being invited to compare the 'Exacto' goods of the defendants with the 'Tub Happy' goods of the plaintiff. They are being invited to purchase goods of the defendants which are to be distinguished from the goods of other traders partly because they are described as 'Tub Happy' goods.

The same 'badge of origin' notion is plainly to be seen in the definition of 'trade mark' in s 17 of the 1995 Act.

'CHILL OUT': USE AS TRADE MARK

It is common ground that, in contemporary usage, the phrase 'Chill Out' has a well understood meaning, similar to the perhaps more dated 'Cool It' or the rather more evergreen 'Relax'. Two dictionary definitions were brought to my attention. The *Concise Oxford Dictionary of Current English*, 1995, says that the phrase is especially in North American colloquial use as meaning 'relax; become less tense'. The *New Shorter Oxford English Dictionary*, 1993, tells us that the phrase is slang, 'chiefly US', meaning 'calm down, relax'. Both deponents for the applicant asserted that they understood the phrase in that sense. It was put to me that 'Chill Out' is a phrase of the same nature as 'Tub Happy'. This related, I think, not to a suggestion that 'Chill Out', like—as the majority held—'Tub Happy', was substantially meaningless, but to an argument that the phrase, as used on the T-shirts, was to be regarded as 'purely emotive' and 'employed for no purpose but to evoke in the reader or hearer some feeling, some mood, some mental attitude': at 194 per Dixon CJ. The difference, however, is that whereas the majority held that 'Tub Happy' had no particular meaning, it is clear that 'Chill Out' has a meaning and the question is whether, used in the way the applicant has used it, it indicates the trade origin of the T-shirts rather than (or at least as well as) conveying some other message to the reader.

Questions of this sort commonly arise where a word or phrase, claimed to be used as a trade mark, is capable of being read as descriptive of a characteristic, quality or function of the goods in relation to which it is used. *Mark Foys* itself was such a case. So too were *Johnson & Johnson* ('Caplets') and *Pepsico Australia Pty Ltd v Kettle Chip Co Pty Ltd* (1996) 33 IPR 161 ('Kettle Cooked' in relation to potato chips). The same question can, however, and does arise in other contexts. In *Shell* ... the question was whether an 'oil drop man' was used in television advertisements so as to distinguish Shell petrol from other petrol or merely (as the court held) for the purpose of uniting 'the quickly moving series of pictures as a whole, namely the purpose of conveying by a combination of pictures and words a particular message about the qualities of Shell petrol': at 425 per Kitto J. The oil drop man himself, of course, was not descriptive of character or quality. Similarly, in ... *Wrigley's (A'asia) Ltd v Life Savers A'asia Ltd* (1936) 37 SR(NSW) 9 the use of a new device, claimed and held to be trade mark use and an infringement, was not in any sense descriptive of the goods or their character or quality ...

In the end, the question here is whether the applicant's use of the designs incorporating the phrase 'Chill Out' is use as a badge of the trade origin of its T-shirts or, in the statutory language, use to distinguish goods dealt with or provided in the course of trade by a person from goods so dealt with or provided by another person. In my view it is not. It is relevant that there was no evidence that 'Chill Out' has acquired a secondary meaning of a kind which the full court had recently to consider in *Pepsico*.

CURRENT LAW

In my view the designs are not indications of the provenance of the T-shirts. The message which they convey may, not surprisingly, be one of less than complete clarity; but in general terms the message is, I think, an exhortation to the reader, reinforced by the slightly tilted picture of the drink in each case and, in the case of the more elaborate design, by the image of enjoyable winter sport, to relax; and this is combined with an advertising message that Coca Cola is a suitable medium or accompaniment of relaxation.

.... I should perhaps mention only that there were tendered on behalf of the respondent three other T-shirts, two of the applicant's manufacture, one not, which were said to be evidence of a practice of embellishing the fronts of T-shirts with designs incorporating trade marks. That may in a sense be right, though it is not by any means clear that the specimens tendered do so in a way that is relevant for present purposes: ie it is not clear to me that the matter emblazoned on them is indicative of the trade origins of the T-shirts themselves. Whether that is so or not, however, the question here is, what is the message conveyed by the two T-shirts carrying designs including the phrase 'Chill Out'? As I have said, I do not think it is a message about trade origin.

It is possible for a defendant to make 'descriptive' use of a trade mark that is an invented word: see *Australian Health & Nutrition Association Ltd t/as Sanitarium Health Food Co v Irrewarra Estate Pty Ltd t/as Irrewarra Sourdough* [2012] FCA 592; (2012) 292 ALR 101 (use of labels featuring 'ALL NATURAL HANDMADE GRANOLA' under an 'Irrewarra Sourdough' device held not to constitute trade mark use of the applicant's registered GRANOLA mark).

In the online context, use of a trade mark in a domain name, without any further activity, will not constitute use as a trade mark. However, where that domain name is used in the course of operating a website from which goods or services are offered, this will amount to trade mark use: see *Solahart Industries Pty Ltd v Solar Shop Pty Ltd* [2011] FCA 700; (2011) 92 IPR 165 at [50]. Use of a mark that is imperceptible, such as use as a 'metatag', hidden in the code of a website so as to assist in search engine optimisation, is unlikely to constitute use as a trade mark: see *Complete Technology Integrations Pty Ltd v Green Energy Management Solutions Pty Ltd* [2011] FCA 1319 at [62].

USE OF SHAPES OR DESIGN FEATURES

CURRENT LAW

CASE EXTRACT: CURRENT LAW

Global Brand Marketing Inc v YD Pty Ltd

[2008] FCA 605; (2008) 76 IPR 161
Federal Court of Australia

[Diesel, the owner of two registered marks for footwear, brought infringement proceedings against YD, the retailer of two styles of (non-Diesel) shoes called 'Photon' and 'Cube'. Diesel's marks, as reproduced at [4] of the judgment, are set out below:]

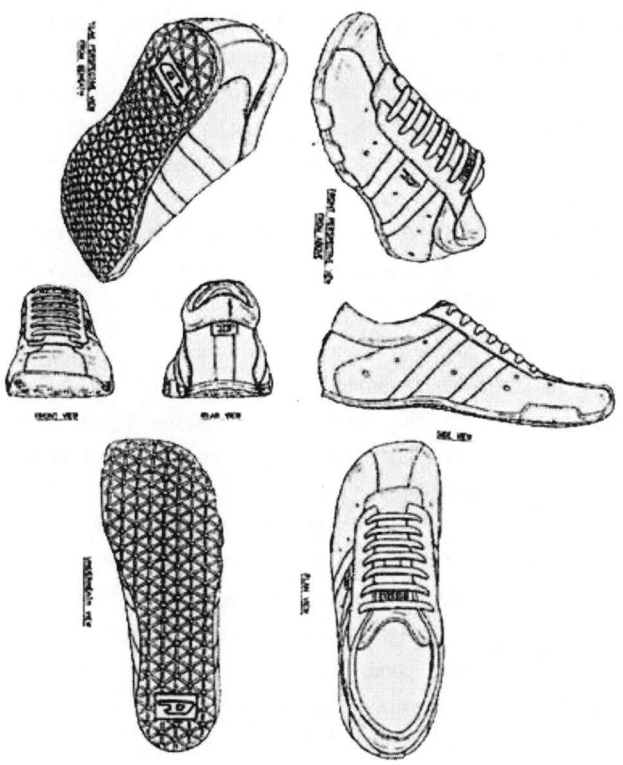

Sundberg J:

SUMMARY OF PRINCIPLES

61. The principles relevant to use of shape as a trade mark are now set out.

(a) A special shape which is the whole or part of goods may serve as a badge of origin. However the shape must have a feature that is 'extra' and distinct from the inherent form of the particular goods: *Mayne* [*Industries Pty Ltd v Advanced Engineering Group Pty Ltd* [2008] FCA 27] at [67], [*Koninklijke Philips Electronics NV v*] *Remington* [*Products Australia Pty Ltd* [2000] FCA 876] at [16] and *Kenman Kandy* [*Australia Pty Ltd v Registrar of Trade Marks* [2002] FCAFC 273] at [137].

(b) Non-descriptive features of a shape point towards a finding that such features are used for a trade mark purpose. Where features are striking, trade mark use will more readily be found. For example, features that make goods more arresting of appearance and more attractive may distinguish the goods from those of others: [*Coca-Cola Co v*] *All-Fect* [*Distributors Ltd* [1999] FCA 1721] at [25].

(c) Descriptive features, like descriptive words, make it more difficult to establish that those features distinguish the product. For example, the word COLA or an ordinary straight walled bottle are descriptive features that would have limited trade mark significance: *All-Fect* at [25] and *Mayne* at [61]–[62].

(d) Where the trade mark comprises a shape which involves a substantial functional element in the goods, references to the shape are almost certainly to the nature of the goods themselves rather than use of the shape as a trade mark: *Mayne* at [63]. For example, evidence that a shape was previously patented will weigh against a finding that the shape serves as a badge of origin: *Remington* at [12] and *Mayne* at [69].

(e) If a shape or a feature of a shape is either concocted compared to the inherent form of the shaped goods or incidental to the subject matter of a patent, it is unlikely to be a shape having any functional element. This may point towards the shape being used as a trade mark: *Kenman Kandy* at [162] and *Mayne* at [69].

(f) Whether a person has used a shape or a feature of a shape as a trade mark is a matter for the court, and cannot be governed by the absence of evidence on the point: *All-Fect* at [35].

(g) Context 'is all important' and will typically characterise the mark's use as either trade mark use or not: *Remington* at [19] and *Mayne* at [60]–[62].

62. As is apparent from the foregoing propositions, a shape mark case may require consideration of different types of features in determining whether the mark is used as a trade mark for the purposes of the Act. At one end of the spectrum are shapes or features thereof that are purely functional. The features may have derived substantially from a patented product, such as the S-shaped fence dropper, or go to the usefulness of the product: *Remington* at [3] and [12]. Cases such as *Mayne* and *Remington* show that such features point away from trade mark use.

63. At the other end of the spectrum are those features of a mark that are non-descriptive and non-functional. They ordinarily make the shape more arresting of appearance and more attractive, thus providing a means of distinguishing the goods from those of others. *All-Fect* and *Remington* show that non-functional features add something extra to the inherent form of the shape. A concocted feature will typically be considered non-functional: *Kenman Kandy*.

64. Finally, there will be cases, such as the present, that fall between the ends of the spectrum. These cases are not black and white. They involve consideration of whether one set of features supersedes, submerges or overwhelms the other.

YD'S USE OF THE SOLE PATTERN

65. In my view the sole pattern of the Photon and Cube shoes is used as a trade mark. In each case the sole acts as a badge of origin in that it indicates a connection in the course of trade between the goods and YD ...

66. The context in which the characterisation issue is to be resolved supports this conclusion. The shoes were displayed in profile in YD's stores, out of their boxes, in circumstances where customers could inspect them. Metro-shoppers handle and inspect the shoes. Metro-shoppers are not impulse buyers. They take time over their purchase of relatively expensive goods. Typically, the price and size of the shoes appeared on the sole.

67. The patterns on the soles are distinctive. The combined distinctive features of the sole pattern of the shoes are:

Photon: a blank rectangular space at the base of the sole; a rubber cross-hatched pattern; indentations from the rubber panels coming from outer side of the sole to the upper of the shoe (also known as the lugs).

Cube: a rubber cross-hatched pattern; indentations from the rubber panels coming from outer side of the sole to the upper of the shoe; small circular dimples in between the triangles formed by the cross-hatched pattern.

68. YD's submission that the sole patterns are applied to provide grip, and are thus for a functional and not for a trade mark purpose, is pitched at too high a level of generality to be helpful in the present context. All soles provide some grip. The sole is inherent in the shoe itself and provides traction when a person is walking or running. Saying that the grip is functional is like saying that the shoe protects the foot from cuts and abrasions. In each case it is too broad a proposition. The position might have been different had there been evidence that the grip pattern provided a special quality leaving little or no room for choice. When choice is limited, it is likely that the goods or an important feature thereof will reflect the product or feature itself, as in *Mayne* and *Remington*. In such a case function will overwhelm a trade mark purpose. In the absence of evidence to this effect, grip is in my view but a broad functional requirement. As Mr Vickery's evidence indicated, this function can be achieved by use of a variety of different patterns. In my view any functionality of the grip offered by the sole is overwhelmed by the non-descriptive aspects of the marks ...

...

YD'S USE OF THE SHAPE OF THE OVERALL SHOE

70. The features of the Photon and Cube shoes are set out below:

(a) a stylised YD label stitched to the inside sole of each shoe;
(b) a sole comprising a rubber cross-hatched pattern with dimples between the triangles in the Cube shoe, and without dimples in the case of the Photon, which also has a blank rectangular shape at the base of the sole;
(c) two oblique stripes on either side of the Cube shoes, and two stripes on the Photon shoe with the front stripe turning back to overlap the other;
(d) the Cube shoe has a 'small rounded piece' at the back of the shoe and the Photon has a stripe on the back that is parallel to the base of the sole;
(e) each shoe has a squarish toe cap or toe panel incorporating a strip of material flowing from the bottom of the laces to the point where the toe cap or toe panel joins the sole;
(f) each shoe has small dots carved into its side;
(g) the Cube shoe has a flat sole with two rubber panels coming from the outer side of the sole to the upper of the shoe. The Photon has a flat sole and three such panels;
(h) each shoe has one large rubber panel coming from the inner side of the sole to the upper of the shoe;
(i) each shoe has a facing;
(j) each shoe has a padded collar ...

71. In my view the Photon and the Cube shoe are used as trade marks where the features listed in [70], especially features (a), (b), (d), (g) and (h), are combined in the shape of a shoe. The most important of these features for present purposes are the stitched YD label on both shoes, the small rounded piece at the back of the Cube shoe, and the Photon's stripe running parallel to the base of the sole. Neither the Cube's rounded piece nor the Photon's parallel strip is found on any of the shoes in evidence other than YD's shoes. Mr Vickery described the rounded piece as 'quite distinctive' and not a feature commonly used in the shoe industry. It can I think be considered a striking feature given its lack of commonality in the trade: cf *All-Fect* at [25].

72. Features (c), (e), (i) and (j) in the list at [70] are either functional or in common use. Common features are like descriptive words.

73. In my view the non-functional and non-descriptive features referred to in [71] overwhelm the functional features and common features referred to in [72] and give the Cube and Photon shoes a trade mark purpose.

74. This case is not as clear cut as *Kenman Kandy* on the one hand (use) or *Mayne* and *Remington* on the other (no use). It is towards the middle of the spectrum referred to at [62] to [64], neither black nor white, but just on the use side of the grey in the middle.

[In the result, Sundberg J held that the Photon and Cube shapes and soles were not 'deceptively similar' to the registered marks.]

See also *Coca-Cola Co v PepsiCo Inc (No 2)* [2014] FCA 1287; (2014) 109 IPR 429, where Besanko J held that PepsiCo had used as a trade mark the shape of its 'Carolina' bottle (sold in Australia since 2007), on the basis that this shape was 'distinctive and consumers would associate it with the Pepsi brand' (at [213]) (this bottle shape was not, in the result, held to be deceptively similar to any of Coca-Cola's registered marks). His Honour was not, however, prepared to find that PepsiCo had used the outline or silhouette of its 'Carolina' bottle shape as a trade mark, because these would not be seen by the consumer as being used to indicate a trade connection between the goods and PepsiCo (at [215]–[216]).

NOMINATIVE USE

CASE EXTRACT: CURRENT LAW

Musidor BV v Tansing

(1994) 52 FCR 363
Federal Court of Australia, Full Court

[At issue was whether the respondent's sale of unauthorised but lawful CDs of live performances of concerts by The Rolling Stones, bearing the name of the group on the cover, infringed the appellant's registered word mark THE ROLLING STONES for compact discs and recording media.]

Gummow and Heerey JJ (at 376–377): On the question of infringement, one asks whether in the setting of the packaging and on the discs themselves in which the words 'THE ROLLING STONES' are depicted, that phrase appears as an expression which the manufacturer of the disc is using for the purpose of indicating or so as to indicate a connection in the course of trade between him and the disc contained within the packaging.

Turning to the discs first released for sale, in our view the use on the packaging and on the discs themselves of the words 'THE ROLLING STONES' would convey to the prospective purchaser that if that person purchased the disc and put it on a compact disc player there would emerge music of the well known group 'The Rolling Stones'. It is of fundamental importance to the purchaser to be able to identify, before purchasing the disc, the particular musicians whose performance or whose music is recorded.

Trade marks for compact discs and other forms of sound recordings will often be of importance to a purchaser, but for reasons unconnected with the identity of the performer or the music. Trade marks such as 'His Master's Voice' or 'Decca' may be important as indicating the technical quality of reproduction to be expected, but do not say anything about the music or the performer. In the present case the respondent's own Banana Label fulfils a like function. Indeed the use of the respondent's mark in a way that a mark would be used for goods of this type is in itself some indication that the words 'The Rolling Stones' are used for a different purpose.

We accept the submission for the respondent that the words 'The Rolling Stones' are not used for the purpose of indicating a connection in the course of trade between him and the discs or any other goods in respect of which the trade marks are registered. Rather, they are used here to identify a recording made many years ago of a live performance by those persons in the United States, which has been reproduced and embodied in the discs manufactured by the respondent. That is not a trade mark use by the respondent ... If it matters, there is force also in the further submission, that, as a practical matter, there is no other way in which identification readily can be made of the group, a sound recording of whose performance is embodied in the discs.

In determining whether there has been use as a trade mark, it is proper to have regard to the whole of the packaging. That was not disputed. Even if the discs contained within the packaging are examined in isolation, the same conclusion follows. Indeed, from the face of the discs the impression is stronger that the term 'The Rolling Stones' identifies the group who perform the 13 tracks which are then identified, the disc having been made in Australia under the Banana Label.

If regard is had to the subsequent and second version of the respondent's cover and discs, the conclusion which we have reached is, if anything, stronger. The use of the expression 'SONGS PERFORMED LIVE BY THE ROLLING STONES GROUP' on the cover of the second version only makes more explicit that which is conveyed by the first version. Indeed, the awkward supererogation of the second version emphasises how natural is the meaning conveyed by the first.

In the present context there is no significance in the words 'The Rolling Stones' being a coined or fancy name. In one sense, all names of human beings are coined or fancy, usually originating historically from personal characteristics, trade or occupation and the like. In the entertainment industry, celebrated performers are often known by a stage name which they have adopted. Marilyn Monroe and Cary Grant are familiar to us in a way that Norma Jean Mortenson and Archie Leach are not. The term 'The Rolling Stones' is a name which has been adopted by a particular group and serves an identification function which, in essence, for the purposes of this case serves a function no different from that of 'Melbourne Symphony Orchestra'.

The appellant's case is an attempt to obtain a monopoly over words used to describe a lawful product. Consistently with the appellant's argument, the maker of a film on the Rolling Stones entitled 'The Story of the Rolling Stones' would be infringing the mark. The producer of a compact disc called 'John Farnham Sings the Music of the Rolling Stones' would suffer a like fate.

Moreover, the protection of a registered trade mark may extend indefinitely in time and, if the appellant is right, protection would be obtained which extended far beyond the rights of a copyright owner, rights which (for the reasons already explained) the appellant does not have.

Davies J (dissenting) (at 369): The respondent's description does not suggest that the actual transcription onto the CDs was carried out by the Rolling Stones organisation or that the producer of the CDs was part of the Rolling Stones organisation. However, the use of the name 'Rolling Stones' identifies the musicians and the music with the Rolling Stones group. The value of the product lies in that connection. This is not a case such as *Irving's Yeast-Vite Ltd v Horsenail* (1934) 51 RPC 110 where the allegedly infringing product was distinguished as 'a substitute for Yeast-Vite'. Here the words 'The Rolling Stones group' are used in relation to the goods themselves.

To exemplify the infringement, assume that 'Pierre Cardin' and 'Gucci' are registered marks and that the Pierre Cardin organisation or the Gucci organisation manufactured goods but declined to put them on sale being not satisfied with their quality. It would, in my opinion, be an infringement for some other person without authority to put the goods on the market with the description that they were manufactured by Pierre Cardin or by Gucci but that the sale had not been authorised. Yet that is what the respondent seeks to do in the present case. It seeks to avail itself of the goodwill in the name 'Rolling Stones' by using that name to identify the goods and it seeks to defend the infringement by stating that the release was not authorised by the Rolling Stones.

In my opinion, the owner of a trade mark is entitled to protection against such a use of the mark.

OTHER CONCEPTIONS OF 'USE'

By way of contrast to s 120 of the *TMA*, under European law a registered owner is given the right 'to prevent all third parties not having [the owner's] consent from using in the course of trade' identical or similar signs in relation to identical, similar or dissimilar goods or services (see Art 5(1) and (2) of the *European Trade Marks Directive 2008/95/EC*). This raises a question about what sort of 'use' will constitute infringement, and whether such use must be 'as a trade mark', or otherwise.

CASE EXTRACT: COMPARATIVE LAW

Case C-206/01, Arsenal Football Club Plc v Reed

[2002] ECR I-10273
Court of Justice of the European Communities

[Arsenal FC, the owner of trade marks including the word mark ARSENAL, brought infringement proceedings against Mr Reed, who sold unofficial Arsenal merchandise from a stall outside Arsenal's home ground. The English Court asked the European Court of Justice whether a defendant could be taken not to infringe where its use does not indicate trade origin, notwithstanding the language of Art 5(1)(a) of the Directive, which simply refers to infringing use being use 'in the course of trade'.]

The Court: 43. ... [I]t must be determined whether Article 5(1)(a) ... presupposes the existence of a specific interest of the proprietor as trade mark proprietor, in that use of the sign in question by a third party must affect or be liable to affect one of the functions of the mark ...

...

47. Trade mark rights constitute an essential element in the system of undistorted competition … In such a system, undertakings must be able to attract and retain customers by the quality of their goods or services, which is made possible only by distinctive signs allowing them to be identified …

48. In that context, the essential function of a trade mark is to guarantee the identity of origin of the marked goods or services to the consumer or end user by enabling him, without any possibility of confusion, to distinguish the goods or services from others which have another origin. For the trade mark to be able to fulfil its essential role … it must offer a guarantee that all the goods or services bearing it have been manufactured or supplied under the control of a single undertaking which is responsible for their quality …

…

50. For that guarantee of origin, which constitutes the essential function of a trade mark, to be ensured, the proprietor must be protected against competitors wishing to take unfair advantage of the status and reputation of the trade mark by selling products illegally bearing it … In this respect, the 10th recital of the preamble to the Directive points out the absolute nature of the protection afforded by the trade mark in the case of identity between the mark and the sign and between the goods or services concerned and those for which the mark is registered. It states that the aim of that protection is in particular to guarantee the trade mark as an indication of origin.

51. It follows that the exclusive right under Article 5(1)(a) … was conferred in order to enable the trade mark proprietor to protect his specific interests as proprietor, that is, to ensure that the trade mark can fulfil its functions. The exercise of that right must therefore be reserved to cases in which a third party's use of the sign affects or is liable to affect the functions of the trade mark, in particular its essential function of guaranteeing to consumers the origin of the goods.

52. The exclusive nature of the right conferred by a registered trade mark on its proprietor under Article 5(1)(a) … can be justified only within the limits of the application of that article …

…

54. The proprietor may not prohibit the use of a sign identical to the trade mark for goods identical to those for which the mark is registered if that use cannot affect his own interests as proprietor of the mark, having regard to its functions. Thus certain uses for purely descriptive purposes are excluded from the scope of Article 5(1) … because they do not affect any of the interests which that provision aims to protect, and do not therefore fall within the concept of use within the meaning of that provision …

55. … In the present case, the use of the sign takes place in the context of sales to consumers and is obviously not intended for purely descriptive purposes.

56. Having regard to the presentation of the word 'Arsenal' on the goods at issue in the main proceedings and the other secondary markings on them … the use of that sign is such as to create the impression that there is a material link in the course of trade between the goods concerned and the trade mark proprietor.

57. That conclusion is not affected by the presence on Mr Reed's stall of the notice stating that the goods at issue in the main proceedings are not official Arsenal FC products … Even on the assumption that such a notice may be relied on by a third party as a defence to an action for trade mark infringement, there is a clear possibility in the present case that some consumers, in particular if they come across

the goods after they have been sold by Mr Reed and taken away from the stall where the notice appears, may interpret the sign as designating Arsenal FC as the undertaking of origin of the goods.

58. Moreover, in the present case, there is also no guarantee ... that all the goods designated by the trade mark have been manufactured or supplied under the control of a single undertaking which is responsible for their quality.

59. The goods at issue are in fact supplied outside the control of Arsenal FC as trade mark proprietor, it being common ground that they do not come from Arsenal FC or from its approved resellers.

60. In those circumstances, the use of a sign which is identical to the trade mark at issue in the main proceedings is liable to jeopardise the guarantee of origin which constitutes the essential function of the mark ... It is consequently a use which the trade mark proprietor may prevent in accordance with Article 5(1) ...

61. Once it has been found that, in the present case, the use of the sign in question by the third party is liable to affect the guarantee of origin of the goods and that the trade mark proprietor must be able to prevent this, it is immaterial that in the context of that use the sign is perceived as a badge of support for or loyalty or affiliation to the proprietor of the mark.

62. In the light of the foregoing, the answer to the national court's questions must be that ... where a third party uses in the course of trade a sign which is identical to a validly registered trade mark on goods which are identical to those for which it is registered, the trade mark proprietor is entitled, in circumstances such as those in the present case, to rely on Article 5(1)(a) ... to prevent that use. It is immaterial that, in the context of that use, the sign is perceived as a badge of support for or loyalty or affiliation to the trade mark proprietor.

SUBSTANTIALLY IDENTICAL OR DECEPTIVELY SIMILAR MARKS, AND SIMILAR OR CLOSELY RELATED GOODS OR SERVICES

We saw in the previous chapter how the concepts of 'substantially identical' and 'deceptively similar' marks have been interpreted under s 44 of the *TMA*. Much of that law applies in the same way in the infringement context. Similarly, although s 120(2) refers to goods and services 'of the same description', this phrase is defined in s 14 to mean the same thing as 'similar' goods or services under s 44. However, there are some differences between the assessments undertaken in ss 44 and 120.

First, while under s 44 the comparison is between the applicant's mark (which will have been represented in the application) and an earlier registered mark or application for registration, under s 120 the comparison is between the registered mark and a sign that the defendant has used in relation to a particular set of goods and services. One issue that will arise exclusively in the infringement context is determining what the defendant's sign actually is. This is particularly the case where the defendant might be using multiple signs or a 'compound' sign. Much will depend on the defendant's *actual* use in the marketplace. See, for example, *Wellness Pty Ltd v Pro Bio Living Waters Pty Ltd* [2004] FCA 438; (2004) 61 IPR 242, where the defendant sold bottled water branded as 'Pro Bio Living Waters' and the components 'Pro Bio' and 'Living Waters' were presented in a different form and sometimes used in isolation, such that it could be said that the defendant was using them as separate signs. This finding significantly impacted on the question of whether the defendant had used a sign substantially identical with or deceptively similar to the registered owner's LIVING WATER mark for the purposes of s 120.

A second difference relates to the assessment of 'deceptive similarity'. The issue under both ss 44 and 120 is whether the marks are 'likely to deceive or cause confusion'. This is predominantly a comparison between the registered mark and the mark used by the defendant/applicant for registration, and in neither case does the tribunal need to go as far as determining whether the use would cause actual confusion or result in passing off. Some aspects of actual use in the market, such as (in the case of word marks) the get-up or colours used by the plaintiff and defendant would not be relevant. Nevertheless, in a number of infringement cases courts have been prepared to take into account a slightly broader set of factors in determining whether marks are deceptively similar. One reason is that in the infringement context both the registered owner and the defendant will be likely to have used their marks, and evidence of consumer reaction is more likely to be forthcoming, whereas at the s 44 stage only notional use of the two marks is contemplated. As a result, the Full Federal Court has said that certain marketplace factors can be taken into account in assessing deceptive similarity in infringement proceedings. These include the commercial use made by a sign contained in the trade mark by third party traders[1] and the extent to which third party traders also make use of particular themes (such as the names of topographical features for wine).[2] Such an approach shows the tension between trying to keep the owner's monopoly within reasonable bounds (by taking account of factors that make it less likely that consumers will be confused if confronted with the two marks) and trying to preserve the essential nature of the registered trade mark right (as something determined by the scope of the registration rather than by the nature of the owner's actual trade).

A further issue relates to the relevance of the reputation of the registered owner's mark. We saw in *Registrar of Trade Marks v Woolworths Ltd* [1999] FCA 1020; (1999) 93 FCR 365 in the previous chapter that, under s 44, the Full Federal Court was prepared to take account of the notoriety of 'Woolworths' in the applicant's mark in finding that it was not deceptively similar to the earlier 'Metro' marks. This reasoning has also been used in the infringement context.

CASE EXTRACT: CURRENT LAW

CURRENT LAW

Mars Australia Pty Ltd v Sweet Rewards Pty Ltd

[2009] FCA 606; (2009) 81 IPR 354
Federal Court of Australia

[Mars, the registered owner of the 'Maltesers' device trade mark set out below, left, as reproduced at [83] of the judgment (the top representation is red), argued that Sweet Rewards had infringed by selling a 'Malt Balls' product set out below, right, as reproduced at [3] of the judgment (the lid and the background to the label are red).]

---

1   See *MID Sydney Pty Ltd v Australian Tourism Co Ltd* (1998) 90 FCR 236.
2   See *CA Henschke & Co v Rosemount Estates Pty Ltd* [2000] FCA 1539; (2000) 52 IPR 42.

Perram J: 95. In this area it is impermissible to take into account any matter added to the respondent's mark or any differences in get-up. The marks must be understood in their entirety. Both parties placed reliance upon the reasons given by Lord Radcliffe in *de Cordova v Vick Chemical Co* (1951) 68 RPC 103 at 105–106 [which] were examined by a Full Court of this Court in *Crazy Ron's Communications Pty Ltd v Mobileworld Communications Pty Ltd* (2004) 61 IPR 212 at 231 [84]. For present purposes *Crazy Ron's* establishes a number of principles:

1 The question of deceptive similarity is not to be judged by a side by side comparison. Instead what is involved is a comparison, on the one hand, of the impression based on recollection of an applicant's mark that persons of ordinary intelligence would have and the impression such persons would get from the respondent's mark (at 227 [73]). In that regard it is important to consider the 'idea of the mark' (at 228 [74]).

2 In assessing deceptive similarity, questions of aural impression may be important (at 228 [75]). In that context I regard the aural similarity between Malt Balls and Maltesers as negligible.

3 The risk of deception must be tangible but it is enough if an ordinary person entertains a reasonable doubt (at 228 [76]).

4 Allowance must be made for imperfect recollections in considering whether a mark so nearly resembles another mark that it is likely to cause confusion or deception (at 228–229 [77]–[78]).

5 That principle extends even to marks which are not just invented words. If a registered trade mark includes words which can be regarded as an essential feature of the mark, another mark that incorporates those words may well infringe the registered trade mark (at 229–230 [79]).

96. It is likewise established that, generally, reputation is irrelevant to the question of infringement. Despite the apparent breath of that proposition, however, it is also accepted that if a particular word or words has come to signify exclusively the goods of the proprietor of a mark (the mark including those words) then the use of that or those words by another would be an infringement. No doubt this involves some apparent departure from the general principle that reputation is irrelevant but it is sanctioned by authority: *Crazy Ron's* at 232 [88]–[89]. A corollary appears to be that in assessing the notion of a

consumer's imperfect recollection of a mark, the fact that a mark is notoriously so ubiquitous and of such long standing that consumers generally must be taken to be familiar with it and its use in relation to particular goods or services is a relevant consideration: *Crazy Ron's* at 232–233 [90].

97. The application of these principles is, so it seems to me, relatively straightforward. The Maltesers marks are very famous. Consumers generally must be taken to be familiar with them. That is relevant to assessing a consumer's imperfect recollection of the mark. So viewed, a comparison between the impression held in the consumer's mind and the direct impression of Sweet Rewards' mark is one which, in this case at least, occurs in a context in which the chances of the average consumer having forgotten the Maltesers mark are vanishingly small.

98. So too, an aural examination leads to the same result. 'Maltesers' does not sound like 'Malt Balls'. In particular, the pronunciation is phonetically different: 'mal-tesers' is syllabically distinct from 'malt balls'. I do not think that the colour red would cause confusion but even if there was such a risk such risk is clearly overcome by the effect of the other matters to which I have referred. My conclusions are therefore that … even if the trade mark use by Sweet Rewards were as Mars alleges, consumers are so familiar with Maltesers that they could not possibly be confused by the Malt Balls packaging—more formally, there is no likelihood of imperfect recollection by them of the Maltesers mark leading to confusion …

[Perram J's decision was not disturbed on appeal to the Full Court.]

THE PROVISO TO S 120(2)

Even if it is found that under s 120(2) the defendant is using as a trade mark a sign that is substantially identical with or deceptively similar to the registered mark, in relation to similar or closely related goods or services, the defendant may still avoid liability. This is because of the final sentence of s 120(2), which reads: 'However, the person is not taken to have infringed the trade mark if the person establishes that using the sign as the person did is not likely to deceive or cause confusion'. The meaning of this proviso is considered in the following extract.

CASE EXTRACT: CURRENT LAW

E & J Gallo Winery v Lion Nathan Australia Pty Ltd

[2009] FCAFC 27; (2009) 175 FCR 386
Federal Court of Australia, Full Court

[Gallo, the registered owner of BAREFOOT for wine, sued Lion Nathan, which had started selling radler beer under the mark BAREFOOT RADLER, under s 120(2). Having found that the marks were deceptively similar, and that radler beer was 'of the same description' as wine, the Court turned to consider the proviso to s 120(2).]

Moore, Edmonds and Gilmour JJ: 76. The last issue is Gallo's challenge to the primary judge's conclusion that Lion Nathan cannot be taken to have infringed Gallo's trade mark because using its sign as it did was not likely to deceive or cause confusion. This issue is raised by the concluding words of s 120(2) which have received only limited judicial consideration: see *Coca-Cola Co v All-Fect Distributors Ltd* (1999) 96 FCR 107 at [43]. The words 'as the person did' direct attention to the way in which, as a matter of fact, the alleged infringer has used the allegedly infringing trade mark. These concluding words pose a different question to that raised by the opening words of s 120(2) which, in the context of deceptive similarity, direct attention only to a comparison of the marks in the way already discussed. However, any conclusion about deceptive similarity would usually inform consideration of whether the actual use was likely to deceive or cause confusion. In a sense, an affirmative answer to the question of whether the alleged infringing mark was deceptively similar would be the starting point. If it was, then it would, in many instances, render it more likely (though not inevitable) that the actual use of the allegedly infringing mark was likely to deceive or cause confusion. Also relevant, in our opinion, would be the matters considered in determining whether the alleged infringer's goods are of the same description as the goods in respect of which the registered mark is registered.

77. In the present case, Lion Nathan pointed to the fact that its sign was used on beer. The beer was packaged in a beer bottle, packaged in six packs which, in turn were packaged in cartons. The beer was sold in retail stores in the section devoted to beer. It also pointed to the fact that its sign was used in conjunction with the image of a bare foot. However, in our opinion, these matters do not advance Lion Nathan's defence. The use of the image of a bare foot with the words 'BAREFOOT RADLER' would be more likely to reinforce the significance or prominence of the word 'BAREFOOT'. The fact that the allegedly infringing mark was on beer packaged in the way described does not, in our opinion, tell against the likelihood that a person looking at beer packaged in this way would think that the beer originated from Gallo. If, in a retail liquor outlet, there was beer bearing the trade mark 'BAREFOOT RADLER' where the word 'RADLER' was the description of a type of beer and also wine with the trade mark 'BAREFOOT' immediately followed by a description of the type of wine (by reference to grape type), then there is, in our opinion, little room to doubt that it is likely many would view the former as originating from the producer of the latter.

78. We should add that neither party suggested that the consideration of the way in which Lion Nathan actually used its trade mark also raises for consideration the way in which, in the period during which infringement might have arisen, Gallo actually used its registered mark as well. This analysis proceeds on that basis and it can be assumed that the registered mark might have been used by Gallo in any of a variety of ways on wine. This is important because we were not taken to evidence demonstrating how in the period after Lion Nathan launched its beer, Gallo was deploying its registered mark ...

SECTION 120(3) AND TRADE MARK DILUTION

Section 120(3) is the most unusual of the three infringement provisions in s 120, because it only applies where:

- the registered owner's mark is 'well known in Australia';
- the defendant's goods and services are *unrelated* to those covered by the registration; and
- the owner can show that because its mark is well known, the defendant's sign 'would be likely to be taken as indicating a connection between the unrelated goods or services and the registered

owner of the trade mark' and that 'for that reason, the interests of the registered owner are likely to be adversely affected'.

The fact that s 120(3) operates in such circumstances raises the question about whether it is intended to provide a degree of protection for certain marks that goes beyond safeguarding their function as 'badges of origin'. To return to some of the themes raised in Chapter 15, arguments have long been made that certain marks (namely, famous or well-known marks) deserve an even broader sphere of protection against conduct that might be said to 'dilute' their distinctive qualities, even in the absence of any consumer confusion as to origin. As we saw, three types of 'dilution' are said to exist: 'blurring', 'tarnishment' and 'free-riding'. Specific anti-dilution laws have been adopted in a number of jurisdictions. For example, in the USA, 15 USC §1125(c) (as amended by the *Trademark Dilution Revision Act 2006* (US)) provides owners of 'famous' marks with protection against dilution by 'blurring' (defined as 'association arising from the similarity between a mark or trade name and a famous mark that impairs the distinctiveness of the famous mark') and dilution by 'tarnishment' (defined as 'association arising from the similarity between a mark or trade name and a famous mark that harms the reputation of the famous mark'). Defences are available for various fair uses, including for parody. In Europe, Art 5(2) of the *European Trade Marks Directive* provides that a registered owner shall be entitled to prevent third parties from using in the course of trade identical or similar signs where the registered mark 'has a reputation in the Member State and where use of that sign without due cause takes unfair advantage of, or is detrimental to, the distinctive character or the repute of the trade mark'. 'Detriment to distinctive character' has been held to be akin to blurring, 'detriment to repute' has been held to be akin to 'tarnishment', while 'unfair advantage' has been held to be akin to 'free-riding'.

While the scope of s 120(3) of the Australian Act has yet to be interpreted by the courts, it would appear that it cannot be interpreted as an anti-dilution provision whose operation does not depend on the existence of consumer confusion. This is not only because of the possibility that the defendant's sign could be 'deceptively similar' to that of the registered owner (requiring the marks to resemble each other such that they are 'likely to deceive or cause confusion'). The main reason relates to the 'connection' requirement in s 120(3)(c). Whereas anti-dilution laws look only to whether the consumer would make a mental association between the defendant's *sign* and the well-known *mark* (such that 'blurring' might then be said to occur), s 120(3)(c) requires the existence of a different sort of connection. That connection must be between the defendant's *unrelated goods or services* and the *registered owner*. In other words, what is contemplated here is that consumers seeing the sign on the defendant's goods or services would think the registered owner was providing those goods or services, or at least had some commercial association with them. In light of these factors, s 120(3) can be said to be closer to a statutory enactment of the passing off action, in that both require some degree of confusion, or a misrepresentation, to be established.

Nevertheless, debate is likely to continue about whether Australia *ought* to adopt explicit anti-dilution protection along the lines of that which exists elsewhere. In this regard, it is instructive to see how the broader anti-dilution provisions under US and EU law have been interpreted. In the extract from *Ty, Inc v Perryman*, 306 F 3d 509 (7th Cir, 2002) in Chapter 15 Posner J provided examples of what he thought would constitute dilution by blurring (use of 'Tiffany' by an upscale restaurant) and dilution by tarnishment (use of 'Tiffany' by a striptease joint). These examples are, however, problematic, not least because they beg the question as to how exactly the restaurant's use 'impairs the distinctiveness' of the famous Tiffany mark, and how use by the striptease joint 'harms the reputation' of that mark. In cases where blurring or tarnishment has been found, most attention has been paid to the issue of the 'fame' of the plaintiff's mark, and establishing the similarity of the marks, and relatively little to the fundamental question of whether the defendant's use causes the harm required by the statute. A notorious recent example is *V Secret Catalogue, Inc v Moseley*, 605 F 3d 382 (6th Cir, 2010), where it was held that the use of any mark semantically associated with a famous mark to sell sex-related products creates a rebuttable presumption of tarnishment. This meant that the owner of the 'Victoria's Secret' mark was able to restrain a shop selling sex toys called 'Victor's Little Secret', notwithstanding the absence of any evidence as to how such use affected the reputation of the 'Victoria's Secret' mark. Such an approach raises real questions about the free speech implications of the anti-dilution cause of action (which were raised in Chapter 15). The extract from *Louis Vuitton Malletier SA v Haute Diggity Dog, LLC*, 507 F 3d 252 (4th Cir, 2007), below, shows a more cautious approach to assessing blurring and tarnishment taken by a different Circuit Court of Appeals. The second extract, from the Court of Justice of the European Communities in *Case C-487/07, L'Oréal SA v Bellure NV* [2009] ECR I-5185, shows how the 'free-riding' cause of action has been interpreted under European law, revealing that this cause of action has the potential to go further than dilution by blurring and tarnishment, and raises even greater concerns for free commercial competition.

COMPARATIVE LAW

CASE EXTRACT: COMPARATIVE LAW

Louis Vuitton Malletier SA v Haute Diggity Dog, LLC

507 F 3d 252 (4th Cir, 2007)
United States Court of Appeals, Fourth Circuit

[The appellant, LVM, argued that the respondent Haute Diggity Dog's advertising and sale of 'Chewy Vuiton' dog toys diluted its LOUIS VUITTON, LV and monogram canvas marks.]

Niemeyer J (for the Court) (at 264–270): LVM ... argues, 'Before the district court's decision, Vuitton's famous marks were unblurred by any third party trademark use.' 'Allowing defendants to become the first to use similar marks will obviously blur and dilute the Vuitton Marks.' It also contends that 'Chewy Vuiton' plush dog toys are likely to tarnish LVM's marks because they 'pose a choking hazard for some dogs.'

Haute Diggity Dog urges that, in applying the TDRA [*Trademark Dilution Revision Act 2006* (US)] to the circumstances before us, we reject LVM's suggestion that a parody 'automatically' gives rise to 'actionable dilution.' Haute Diggity Dog contends that only marks that are 'identical or substantially similar' can give rise to actionable dilution, and its 'Chewy Vuiton' marks are not identical or sufficiently similar to LVM's marks. It also argues that '[its] spoof, like other obvious parodies,' 'tends to increase public identification' of [LVM's] mark with [LVM],' ... rather than impairing its distinctiveness, as the TDRA requires. As for LVM's tarnishment claim, Haute Diggity Dog argues that LVM's position is at best based on speculation and that LVM has made no showing of a likelihood of dilution by tarnishment.

... Creating causes of action for only *dilution by blurring* and *dilution by tarnishment*, the TDRA defines 'dilution by blurring' as the 'association arising from the similarity between a mark or trade name and a famous mark that impairs the distinctiveness of the famous mark.' [15 USC] §1125(c)(2)(B). It defines 'dilution by tarnishment' as the 'association arising from the similarity between a mark or trade name and a famous mark that harms the reputation of the famous mark.' *Id.* §1125(c)(2)(C). Thus, to state a dilution claim under the TDRA, a plaintiff must show:

(1) that the plaintiff owns a famous mark that is distinctive;
(2) that the defendant has commenced using a mark in commerce that allegedly is diluting the famous mark;
(3) that a similarity between the defendant's mark and the famous mark gives rise to an association between the marks; and
(4) that the association is likely to impair the distinctiveness of the famous mark or likely to harm the reputation of the famous mark.

In the context of blurring, distinctiveness refers to the ability of the famous mark uniquely to identify a single source and thus maintain its selling power. In proving a dilution claim under the TDRA, the plaintiff need not show actual or likely confusion, the presence of competition, or actual economic injury. *See* ... §1125(c)(1). The TDRA creates three defenses based on the defendant's (1) 'fair use' (with exceptions); (2) 'news reporting and news commentary'; and (3) 'noncommercial use.' *Id.* §1125(c)(3) ...

We address first LVM's claim for dilution by blurring.

The first three elements of a trademark dilution claim are not at issue in this case. LVM owns famous marks that are distinctive; Haute Diggity Dog has commenced using 'Chewy Vuiton,' 'CV,' and designs and colors that are allegedly diluting LVM's marks; and the similarity between Haute Diggity Dog's marks and LVM's marks gives rise to an association between the marks, albeit a parody. The issue for resolution is whether the association between Haute Diggity Dog's marks and LVM's marks is likely to impair the distinctiveness of LVM's famous marks ...

LVM suggests that any use by a third person of an imitation of its famous marks dilutes the famous marks as a matter of law. This contention misconstrues the TDRA.

The TDRA prohibits a person from using a junior mark that is likely to dilute (by blurring) the famous mark, and blurring is defined to be an impairment to the famous mark's distinctiveness. 'Distinctiveness' in turn refers to the public's recognition that the famous mark identifies a single source of the product using the famous mark.

To determine whether a junior mark is likely to dilute a famous mark through blurring, the TDRA directs the court to consider all factors relevant to the issue, including six factors that are enumerated in the statute:

(i) The degree of similarity between the mark or trade name and the famous mark.
(ii) The degree of inherent or acquired distinctiveness of the famous mark.
(iii) The extent to which the owner of the famous mark is engaging in substantially exclusive use of the mark.
(iv) The degree of recognition of the famous mark.

(v)   Whether the user of the mark or trade name intended to create an association with the famous mark.

(vi) Any actual association between the mark or trade name and the famous mark.

15 USC §1125(c)(2)(B). Not every factor will be relevant in every case, and not every blurring claim will require extensive discussion of the factors ... [A]fter we apply the factors as a matter of law, we reach the same conclusion reached by the district court.

We begin by noting that parody is not automatically a complete *defense* to a claim of dilution by blurring where the defendant uses the parody as its own designation of source, ie, *as a trademark*. Although the TDRA does provide that fair use is a complete defense and allows that a parody can be considered fair use, it does not extend the fair use defense to parodies used as a trademark. As the statute provides:

> The following shall not be actionable as dilution by blurring or dilution by tarnishment under this subsection:
>
> (A)   Any fair use ... other than as a designation of source for the person's own goods or services, including use in connection with ... parodying ...

15 USC §1125(c)(3)(A)(ii). Under the statute's plain language, parodying a famous mark is protected by the fair use defense only if the parody is *not* 'a designation of source for the person's own goods or services.'

The TDRA, however, does not require a court to ignore the existence of a parody that is used as a trademark, and it does not preclude a court from considering parody as part of the circumstances to be considered for determining whether the plaintiff has made out a claim for dilution by blurring ...

Thus, it would appear that a defendant's use of a mark as a parody is relevant to the overall question of whether the defendant's use is likely to impair the famous mark's distinctiveness. Moreover, the fact that the defendant uses its marks as a parody is specifically relevant to several of the listed factors. For example, factor (v) (whether the defendant intended to create an association with the famous mark) and factor (vi) (whether there exists an actual association between the defendant's mark and the famous mark) directly invite inquiries into the defendant's intent in using the parody, the defendant's actual use of the parody, and the effect that its use has on the famous mark. While a parody intentionally creates an association with the famous mark in order to be a parody, it also intentionally communicates, if it is successful, that it is *not* the famous mark, but rather a satire of the famous mark ... That the defendant is using its mark as a parody is therefore relevant in the consideration of these statutory factors.

Similarly, factors (i), (ii), and (iv) ... are directly implicated by consideration of the fact that the defendant's mark is a successful parody. Indeed, by making the famous mark an object of the parody, a successful parody might actually enhance the famous mark's distinctiveness by making it an icon. The brunt of the joke becomes yet more famous ...

In sum, while a defendant's use of a parody as a mark does not support a 'fair use' defense, it may be considered in determining whether the plaintiff-owner of a famous mark has proved its claim that the defendant's use of a parody mark is likely to impair the distinctiveness of the famous mark.

In the case before us, when considering factors (ii), (iii), and (iv), it is readily apparent, indeed conceded by Haute Diggity Dog, that LVM's marks are distinctive, famous, and strong. The LOUIS VUITTON mark is well known and is commonly identified as a brand of the great Parisian fashion house, Louis Vuitton Malletier. So too are its other marks and designs, which are invariably used with the LOUIS VUITTON mark. It may not be too strong to refer to these famous marks as icons of high fashion.

While the establishment of these facts satisfies essential elements of LVM's dilution claim, *see* 15 USC §1125(c)(1), the facts impose on LVM an increased burden to demonstrate that the distinctiveness of its famous marks is likely to be impaired by a successful parody. Even as Haute Diggity Dog's parody mimics the famous mark, it communicates simultaneously that it is not the famous mark, but is only satirizing it … And because the famous mark is particularly strong and distinctive, it becomes more likely that a parody will not impair the distinctiveness of the mark. In short, as Haute Diggity Dog's 'Chewy Vuiton' marks are a successful parody, we conclude that they will not blur the distinctiveness of the famous mark as a unique identifier of its source …

[On factor (i)] Haute Diggity Dog mimicked the famous marks; it did not come so close to them as to destroy the success of its parody and, more importantly, to diminish the LVM marks' capacity to identify a single source. Haute Diggity Dog designed a pet chew toy to imitate and suggest, but not *use*, the marks of a high-fashion LOUIS VUITTON handbag. It used 'Chewy Vuiton' to mimic 'LOUIS VUITTON'; it used 'CV' to mimic 'LV'; and it adopted *imperfectly* the items of LVM's designs. We conclude that these uses by Haute Diggity Dog were not so similar as to be likely to impair the distinctiveness of LVM's famous marks.

In a similar vein, when considering factors (v) and (vi), it becomes apparent that Haute Diggity Dog intentionally associated its marks, but only partially and certainly imperfectly, so as to convey the simultaneous message that it was not in fact a source of LVM products. Rather, as a parody, it separated itself from the LVM marks in order to make fun of them.

In sum, when considering the relevant factors to determine whether blurring is likely to occur in this case, we readily come to the conclusion, as did the district court, that LVM has failed to make out a case of trademark dilution by blurring by failing to establish that the distinctiveness of its marks was likely to be impaired by Haute Diggity Dog's marketing and sale of its 'Chewy Vuiton' products …

LVM's claim for dilution by tarnishment does not require an extended discussion. To establish its claim for dilution by tarnishment, LVM must show, in lieu of blurring, that Haute Diggity Dog's use of the 'Chewy Vuiton' mark on dog toys harms the reputation of the LOUIS VUITTON mark and LVM's other marks. LVM argues that the possibility that a dog could choke on a 'Chewy Vuiton' toy causes this harm. LVM has, however, provided no record support for its assertion. It relies only on speculation about whether a dog could choke on the chew toys and a logical concession that a $10 dog toy made in China was of 'inferior quality' to the $1190 LOUIS VUITTON handbag. The speculation begins with LVM's assertion in its brief that 'defendant … admitted that "Chewy Vuiton" products pose a choking hazard for some dogs. Having prejudged the defendant's mark to be a parody, the district court made light of this admission in its opinion, and utterly failed to give it the weight it deserved,' citing to a page in the district court's opinion where the court states:

> At oral argument, plaintiff provided only a flimsy theory that a pet may some day choke on a
> Chewy Vuiton squeak toy and incite the wrath of a confused consumer against LOUIS VUITTON.

… The court was referring to counsel's statement during oral argument that the owner of Woofie's stated that 'she would not sell this product to certain types of dogs because there is a danger they would tear it open and choke on it.' There is no record support, however, that any dog has choked on a pet chew toy, such as a 'Chewy Vuiton' toy, or that there is any basis from which to conclude that a dog would likely choke on such a toy.

We agree with the district court that LVM failed to demonstrate a claim for dilution by tarnishment.

CASE EXTRACT: COMPARATIVE LAW

Case C-487/07, L'Oréal SA v Bellure NV

[2009] ECR I-5185

Court of Justice of the European Communities (First Chamber)

[L'Oréal is the registered owner of word marks including ANAÏS ANAÏS, TRÉSOR and MIRACLE, as well as marks for packaging for these perfumes. Three companies, Bellure, Malaika and Starion, sold cheap perfumes in the UK that were intended to smell like L'Oréal's perfumes, and used packaging (but not names) designed to call L'Oréal's packaging to mind for their products. L'Oréal sued these companies in the UK for trade mark infringement under the provision implementing Art 5(2) of the *European Trade Marks Directive*, arguing that the companies' use of similar packaging took 'unfair advantage' of the well known L'Oréal packaging marks. The UK Court referred a number of questions on the interpretation of Art 5(2) to the Court of Justice, the concern being that although the defendants might have taken 'advantage' of the famous marks, it was not clear how the national court was to go about assessing whether that advantage was 'unfair'.]

The Court: 32. ... [T]he referring court is essentially asking whether Article 5(2) ... must be interpreted as meaning that a third party who uses a sign similar to a trade mark with a reputation can be held to take unfair advantage of the mark, within the meaning of that provision, where such use gives that party an advantage in the marketing of his goods or services, without, however, giving rise, as far as the public is concerned, to a likelihood of confusion or causing or risking causing detriment to the mark or to its proprietor ...

...

36. The infringements referred to in Article 5(2) ... where they occur, are the consequence of a certain degree of similarity between the mark and the sign, by virtue of which the relevant section of the public makes a connection between the sign and the mark, that is to say, establishes a link between them without confusing them. It is thus not necessary that the degree of similarity between the mark with a reputation and the sign used by the third party is such that there exists a likelihood of confusion between them on the part of the relevant section of the public. It is sufficient for the degree of similarity between the mark with a reputation and the sign to have the effect that the relevant section of the public establishes a link between the sign and the mark (see *Adidas-Salomon and Adidas Benelux* [[2003] ECR I-12537], paragraphs 29 and 31, and *adidas and adidas Benelux* [[2008] ECR I-2439], paragraph 41).

37. The existence of such a link in the mind of the public constitutes a condition which is necessary but not, of itself, sufficient to establish the existence of one of the types of injury against which Article 5(2) ... ensures protection for the benefit of trade marks with a reputation (see, to that effect, *Intel Corporation* [[2008] ECR I-8823], paragraphs 31 and 32).

38. Those types of injury are, first, detriment to the distinctive character of the mark, secondly, detriment to the repute of that mark and, thirdly, unfair advantage taken of the distinctive character or the repute of that mark (see, to that effect, *Intel Corporation*, paragraph 27).

39. As regards detriment to the distinctive character of the mark, also referred to as 'dilution', 'whittling away' or 'blurring', such detriment is caused when that mark's ability to identify the goods or services for which it is registered is weakened, since use of an identical or similar sign by a third party leads to dispersion of the identity and hold upon the public mind of the earlier mark. That is particularly the case when the mark, which at one time aroused immediate association with the goods or services for which it is registered, is no longer capable of doing so (see, to that effect, *Intel Corporation*, paragraph 29).

40. As regards detriment to the repute of the mark, also referred to as 'tarnishment' or 'degradation', such detriment is caused when the goods or services for which the identical or similar sign is used by the third party may be perceived by the public in such a way that the trade mark's power of attraction is reduced. The likelihood of such detriment may arise in particular from the fact that the goods or services offered by the third party possess a characteristic or a quality which is liable to have a negative impact on the image of the mark.

41. As regards the concept of 'taking unfair advantage of the distinctive character or the repute of the trade mark', also referred to as 'parasitism' or 'free-riding', that concept relates not to the detriment caused to the mark but to the advantage taken by the third party as a result of the use of the identical or similar sign. It covers, in particular, cases where, by reason of a transfer of the image of the mark or of the characteristics which it projects to the goods identified by the identical or similar sign, there is clear exploitation on the coat-tails of the mark with a reputation.

42. Just one of those three types of injury suffices for Article 5(2) ... to apply (see, to that effect, *Intel Corporation*, paragraph 28).

43. It follows that an advantage taken by a third party of the distinctive character or the repute of the mark may be unfair, even if the use of the identical or similar sign is not detrimental either to the distinctive character or to the repute of the mark or, more generally, to its proprietor.

44. In order to determine whether the use of a sign takes unfair advantage of the distinctive character or the repute of the mark, it is necessary to undertake a global assessment, taking into account all factors relevant to the circumstances of the case, which include the strength of the mark's reputation and the degree of distinctive character of the mark, the degree of similarity between the marks at issue and the nature and degree of proximity of the goods or services concerned. As regards the strength of the reputation and the degree of distinctive character of the mark, the Court has already held that, the stronger that mark's distinctive character and reputation are, the easier it will be to accept that detriment has been caused to it. It is also clear from the case-law that, the more immediately and strongly the mark is brought to mind by the sign, the greater the likelihood that the current or future use of the sign is taking, or will take, unfair advantage of the distinctive character or the repute of the mark or is, or will be, detrimental to them (see, to that effect, *Intel Corporation*, paragraphs 67 to 69).

45. In addition, it must be stated that any such global assessment may also take into account, where necessary, the fact that there is a likelihood of dilution or tarnishment of the mark.

46. In the present case, it is a matter of agreement that Malaika and Starion use packaging and bottles similar to the marks with a reputation registered by L'Oréal ... in order to market perfumes which constitute 'downmarket' imitations of the luxury fragrances for which those marks are registered and used.

COMPARATIVE LAW

47. In that regard, the referring court has held that there is a link between certain packaging used by Malaika and Starion, on the one hand, and certain marks relating to packaging and bottles belonging to L'Oréal ... on the other. In addition, it is apparent from the order for reference that that link confers a commercial advantage on the defendants in the main proceedings. It is also apparent from the order for reference that the similarity between those marks and the products marketed by Malaika and Starion was created intentionally in order to create an association in the mind of the public between fine fragrances and their imitations, with the aim of facilitating the marketing of those imitations.

48. In the general assessment which the referring court will have to undertake in order to determine whether, in those circumstances, it can be held that unfair advantage is being taken of the distinctive character or the repute of the mark, that court will, in particular, have to take account of the fact that the use of packaging and bottles similar to those of the fragrances that are being imitated is intended to take advantage, for promotional purposes, of the distinctive character and the repute of the marks under which those fragrances are marketed.

49. In that regard, where a third party attempts, through the use of a sign similar to a mark with a reputation, to ride on the coat-tails of that mark in order to benefit from its power of attraction, its reputation and its prestige, and to exploit, without paying any financial compensation and without being required to make efforts of his own in that regard, the marketing effort expended by the proprietor of that mark in order to create and maintain the image of that mark, the advantage resulting from such use must be considered to be an advantage that has been unfairly taken of the distinctive character or the repute of that mark.

50. In the light of the above ... Article 5(2) ... must be interpreted as meaning that the taking of unfair advantage of the distinctive character or the repute of a mark, within the meaning of that provision, does not require that there be a likelihood of confusion or a likelihood of detriment to the distinctive character or the repute of the mark or, more generally, to its proprietor. The advantage arising from the use by a third party of a sign similar to a mark with a reputation is an advantage taken unfairly by that third party of the distinctive character or the repute of the mark where that party seeks by that use to ride on the coat-tails of the mark with a reputation in order to benefit from the power of attraction, the reputation and the prestige of that mark and to exploit, without paying any financial compensation, the marketing effort expended by the proprietor of the mark in order to create and maintain the mark's image.

When the case returned to the UK, the Court of Appeal felt that it was left with no choice but to find that the defendants' packaging took 'unfair advantage' of the L'Oréal marks. Jacob LJ was at pains to say that this outcome was regrettable, on the basis that it unduly restricted free and honest commercial speech, in circumstances where no harm was caused to the plaintiff brand owner (other than the harm 'of letting the truth out—that it is possible to produce cheap perfumes which smell somewhat like a famous original'): *L'Oréal SA v Bellure NV* [2010] EWCA Civ 535; [2010] RPC 23. For further, sustained criticism of the Court of Justice decision, see D Gangjee and R Burrell, 'Because You're Worth It: *L'Oréal* and the Prohibition on Free Riding' (2010) 73 *Modern Law Review* 282.

DEFENCES

A number of defences to infringement are set out in ss 122–124. These apply where the defendant:

- uses in good faith its name or the name of its place of business (or that of a predecessor) (s 122(1)(a));
- uses a sign in good faith to indicate the kind, quality, quantity, intended purpose, value, geographical origin, time of production or rendering, or some other characteristic, of goods or services (s 122(1)(b));
- uses the trade mark in good faith to indicate the intended purpose of goods or services (e.g. as accessories or spare parts) (s 122(1)(c));
- uses the trade mark for comparative advertising purposes (s 122(1)(d));
- exercises a right to use a trade mark given to it under the Act (e.g. as a registered owner) (s 122(1)(e));
- would obtain registration of the trade mark in its own name if it were to apply for registration of it (s 122(1)(f) and (fa));
- does not (because of a condition or limitation subject to which the trade mark is registered) infringe the exclusive right of the registered owner to use the trade mark (s 122(1)(g));
- is using a trade mark in relation to goods that are similar to goods to which the trade mark has been applied, by or with the consent of the registered owner (s 123(1));
- is using a trade mark in relation to services that are similar to services to which the trade mark has been applied, by or with the consent of the registered owner (s 123(2)); and
- made prior continuous use of the trade mark (s 124).

The s 122(1)(a) and 123 defences are considered in more detail below.

USE OF PERSON'S PLACE OF BUSINESS

CASE EXTRACT: CURRENT LAW

Angoves Pty Ltd v Johnson

(1982) 43 ALR 349
Federal Court of Australia, Full Court

[The appellant was the registered owner of ST AGNES for wine and brandy. Many years after the appellant started trading, a new suburb near the appellant's vineyards was named St Agnes. The respondents opened up a business in that suburb called ST AGNES LIQUOR STORE. The Court accepted that the respondent had prima facie infringed, and then turned to consider whether the respondent could make out the defence in s 64(1)(a) of the 1955 Act that covered 'the use in good faith by a person of his own name or the name of his place of business'.]

Fitzgerald J (with whom Deane J agreed) (at 373–375): The appellant submitted that the mark used by the appellants was 'St Agnes Liquor Store', which is the name of the respondents' business, not the name of their place of business. The submission assumes that the name of a shop may not be the name of the place of the business which is conducted in that shop. In *Hy-Line Chicks Pty Ltd v Swifte* (1965) 115 CLR 159, Windeyer J said at 161 that, notwithstanding that a trade mark 'Hy-Line' was registered in relation to chickens and all other bred poultry, a partnership of poultry breeders were entitled to describe their premises as the 'Hy-Line Poultry Farm and Hatchery', 'for it is the name of their place of business'.

In any event, in my opinion, the appellant's submission seeks to distort the statutory scheme against the respondents. Their need to rely upon s 64(1)(a) arises because, according to the appellant, although 'St Agnes Liquor Store' is the name of the respondents' business, their use of their business name as a mark in connection with the goods in which they trade constitutes or involves a use of the appellant's registered trade mark 'St Agnes'. It is their use, therefore, of 'St Agnes' which must be tested against s 64(1)(a).

The next question is whether, that being so, 'St Agnes' is the name of the respondents' place of business within the meaning of s 64(1)(a) ...

Reference has already been made to *Hy-Line Chicks v Swifte*, supra. Windeyer J did not elaborate the reasons for his conclusion. Nor did Higgins J do so in *Thomson v B Seppelt & Sons Ltd* (1925) 37 CLR 305 in which he seems to have expressed the opinion at 315 that the name of a wine growing district was not the name of the place of business of the vignerons producing wine in that district. In *RJ Reuter & Co Ltd v Mulhens* [1954] 1 Ch 50, Evershed MR, with whom Birkett and Romer LJJ agreed, said at 83 that 'No 4711' in connection with the city of Cologne might fairly be said to be the name of the defendant's place of business which was located in Bell St Cologne. The number '4711' was the address of the business and had been acquired when, after Napoleon's invasion of Germany, the houses in Cologne were each given a number without regard to street names. It was further held, however, that an embellishment of the number with a bell and a scroll prevented it from being the name of the place of business of the defendant.

For some purposes, perhaps income tax, one's place of business may be sufficiently defined by reference to whether it is in Australia or overseas. For others, eg a State stamp duty, the place of business may be designated by reference to the State, eg South Australia. In descending order, a place of business may be named by reference to the city or town, suburb, street, street number, or even a particular location such as a shopping centre. The name of each of these may be for one purpose or another the name of a place of business. The context must determine which is appropriate.

Section 64(1)(a) does not speak of the address of a business and I can perceive no reason why it should be so read down. It seems to me that the protection which it gives to the use of the name of the user's place of business is an aspect of the same policy which generally prohibits registration of a geographical name as a trade mark (s 24(1)(d)). In my opinion it would give effect to that policy to hold that, provided only that the name of the place chosen is apt and accurate in its application to the business in question, the section does not require that the location of the business be described in either the fullest or the most precise terms. In any particular case the aptness and accuracy of the name chosen must be approached as one of fact and degree. In the case of a suburban liquor store in a suburban shopping centre the name of the suburb can, in my opinion legitimately be considered to be the name of the place of business for the purposes of s 64(1)(a).

CONSENT OF REGISTERED OWNER

The s 123 defence has an important sphere of operation. The Full Federal Court recently held in *Paul's Retail Pty Ltd v Lonsdale Australia Ltd* [2012] FCAFC 130; (2012) 294 ALR 72 that the importation of goods bearing a trade mark will constitute trade mark use, and therefore potentially infringing conduct under s 120, irrespective of who applied the mark to the goods (at [64]–[68]). Section 123 of the *TMA* therefore functions as a defence to allow for the 'parallel importation' of legitimately branded goods, as well as the sale of second-hand goods bearing an owner's mark. The defence only applies where the mark was originally applied by or with the consent of the registered owner. Proving consent by the registered owner of the *Australian* mark can be difficult in two key scenarios: (1) where the Australian mark is owned by a different company (perhaps within the same corporate group) to the owner of the mark in the country where goods were manufactured and the mark applied; and (2) where the mark was applied overseas with the Australian owner's consent but subject to a contract that prohibited sale of the goods into Australia. The situation is made more complex by the fact that it is the parallel importer who must prove consent.

The notion of 'consent' is discussed in more detail in the following extract.

CASE EXTRACT: CURRENT LAW

Brother Industries Ltd v Dynamic Supplies Pty Ltd

[2007] FCA 1490; (2007) 163 FCR 530
Federal Court of Australia

[Brother Japan was the registered owner of the word mark BROTHER. It manufactured a printer drum unit called the DR-200, which it sold around the world branded with the BROTHER mark, including to its US subsidiary Brother America and its Australian subsidiary Brother Australia. Brother Japan also made and sold unbranded 'original equipment manufacturer' (or OEM) printer drum units, which were sent exclusively to Company X. Dynamic Supplies obtained from a US company called Discover Group quantities of printer drum units bearing the BROTHER mark (known as the Sample Units) which it imported into Australia. It turned out that these were in fact OEM units to which the BROTHER mark had subsequently been applied (and not by Brother Japan). Brother Japan sued Dynamic Supplies for infringement under s 120(1). Dynamic Supplies argued that it had a defence under s 123(1).]

Tamberlin J: 72. The onus is on Dynamic Supplies, raising the defence, to establish it. Dynamic Supplies contends that the application of Brother's Australian trade marks was done with licence or authority. Although the evidence indicates that Discover Group did not source all of its Brother DR-200 units from Brother America (via All Day Trading), Dynamic Supplies says the evidence establishes that, on the balance of probabilities, the Sample Units it imported from Discover Group were sourced originally from Brother America. It also argues that, as a matter of reasonable inference, Brother America must have unwittingly sourced these products from Brother Japan or Brother International, which had erroneously sent Brother America rather than Company X the Sample Units. This is said to be sufficient to discharge Dynamic Supplies' onus under s 123 of the Act. Dynamic Supplies maintains that it cannot, and is not obliged to, trace the provenance of the Sample Units and Sample Packaging back to Brother

Japan because any such evidence, particularly where it may involve Company X, is within the exclusive knowledge of the applicants.

73. Brother's case is that they did not licence or authorise any third party to apply the 'BROTHER' trade mark to the Sample Packaging. It says that Dynamic Supplies did not establish the chain of supply of the Sample Units back to Brother America, and relies on the acknowledgement by Mr Piccinini [the managing director of Dynamic Supplies] in cross-examination that it would be unlikely that Brother America would receive OEM products from Company X and sell them in counterfeit packaging with the wrong bar code and with false stickers. Brother notes that in cross-examination Mr Blackman [a director of Discover Group] was unable to demonstrate that all of the Brother DR-200 units which he told Mr Piccinini had been obtained from Brother America was supported by Discover Group's records. Several purchases which Mr Blackman in his affidavit stated were made from All Day Trading were not shown to be sourced from Brother America, therefore demonstrating that the chain of supply is not established back to Brother America and that Brother cannot be deemed to have impliedly consented to the application of its trade mark to the Sample Packaging. Brother also submits that, even if the evidence did establish a chain of supply with Brother America, any such link would not, of itself, be sufficient to avail Dynamic Supplies of the defence under s 123 because it still had not obtained the consent of the registered owner of the infringed trade mark, namely Brother Japan ...

...

75. Dynamic Supplies has not established that Brother Japan expressly or implicitly licensed or authorised the application of the 'BROTHER' trade mark to the Sample Units. Its submissions fail on two counts.

76. The first is that it has not established on the evidence that the chain of supply of the Sample Units and Sample Packaging traces back to Brother America, let alone to Brother Japan. Although the evidence shows that Brother America imports Brother DR-200 units only from Brother Japan or Brother International and on-sells them with little or no inspection, the evidence does not go so far as to demonstrate that the specific Sample Units and Sample Packaging were sold by Brother America to Discover Group. Without establishing this essential link in the supply chain, Dynamic Supplies has not shown any consent, express or implied, by Brother America or Brother Japan for the purposes of s 123 of the Act.

77. I do not accept that a reasonable inference is available that Discover Group sourced the Sample Units from Brother America. The records of Discover Group indicated that some of the Brother DR-200 units which it said it acquired from Brother America could have come from another source. Mr Blackman's evidence on this point was less than satisfactory. Simply because it is shown that Discover Group purchases some Brother DR-200 units from Brother America does not necessarily mean that there is a proper inference or a balance of probabilities that these particular trap purchases were originally sourced from Brother America. Nor do I accept the inference that Brother America must have accidentally received the products from Brother Japan or Brother International. The evidence that the Sample Units were made by Brother Japan for Company X and that Brother America only sources its Brother DR-200 units from Brother Japan or Brother International does not support such an inference.

78. The second ground on which Dynamic Supplies' submissions fail is that even if Brother America was part of the supply chain, it has not demonstrated that Brother Japan, the registered owner of the relevant trade marks, expressly or impliedly consented to the application of its trade mark to or

CURRENT LAW

in relation to the goods in question. Although the Full Court of this Court in [*Transport Tyres Pty Ltd v Montana Tyres Rims and Tubes Pty Ltd* (1999) 93 FCR 421] at 440 found that the sale of the goods in question constituted a 'use', which was excused by s 123 of the Act, that decision is distinguishable. In that case the registered owner of the trade mark applied it to the goods which were subsequently sold. The chain of supply could be traced back from the retailer of the goods to the registered owner of the trade marks which were applied to or in relation to those goods. The registered owner's consent for the purpose of s 123 was, in the opinion of the Full Court, necessarily implied in those circumstances. No such chain of supply exists in the present case. The Sample Units were not branded by Brother with its mark, and the Sample Packaging was counterfeit. No consent, whether express or implied, was given by Brother to any person or entity to apply its registered trade mark to the products. To the contrary, Brother has distanced itself from the OEM products, manufacturing them only as unbranded products and selling them only through a confidential arrangement with Company X.

79. In any event, a finding that Brother America was part of the supply chain of the impugned products would not allow Dynamic Supplies to rely on s 123 of the Act because it is the consent of the registered owner which must be acquired. Here, Brother Japan is the registered owner of Brother's Australian trade marks. There is no evidence, and Dynamic Supplies submitted that it should not be expected to adduce such evidence, that Brother Japan (rather than Brother America) consented to the application of its mark to or in relation to the products in question. The fact that Brother America and Brother Japan are related entities within the same corporate group does not affect the clear and ordinary meaning and operation of s 123 of the Act. The consent to apply Brother's Australian trade marks to or in relation to a product must be acquired from Brother Japan. The situation where consent is not acquired from the registered owner of the trade mark but from a related entity in its corporate group has not, so far as I am aware, been considered in Australian law ... I am of the view that Brother Japan's consent for the purposes of s 123 of the Act is not to be implied from the fact that another member of the Brother corporate group may have, contrary to my finding, given its consent.

Two recent cases involving the Australian sporting goods retailer Paul's show how difficult it can be for parallel importers to establish the s 123 defence. In *Paul's Retail Pty Ltd v Sporte Leisure Pty Ltd* [2012] FCAFC 51; (2012) 202 FCR 286, Paul's imported clothing bearing 'Greg Norman' and 'shark' device marks that were registered in Australia. The evidence was that GNC, an Indian licensee of the registered Australian marks, had granted BTB, an Indian company, a licence to apply the marks to clothing in India. BTB in fact applied the marks on clothing for the purpose of fulfilling an order from a company in Pakistan. This company then sold the goods to a Singaporean company, from which Paul's acquired the goods for sale in Australia. The Full Federal Court held that because BTB had breached the territorial restriction in its licence with GNC it could not be said that the marks had been applied with the consent of the registered owner, making Paul's liable for infringement.

In *Paul's Retail Pty Ltd v Lonsdale Australia Ltd* [2012] FCAFC 130; (2012) 294 ALR 72 a number of Australian-registered 'Lonsdale' marks were originally owned by a UK company, LSL, which licensed a German company, Punch, to sell goods bearing 'Lonsdale' trade marks within Europe. Under the terms of the licence, Punch was able to have such goods manufactured in China. In June 2011 LSL assigned ownership of the Australian marks to Lonsdale Australia. Two months later, Punch entered an agreement with a Cypriot company, Unicell, to sell Lonsdale-branded goods to it, and Punch arranged for such goods to be manufactured in China to meet this contract. The goods were sold to Unicell in China, then onsold to a US company, TMS, from which they were acquired and sold in Australia by Paul's. The Full Federal Court held that Paul's could not rely on the s 123 defence because the Lonsdale-branded goods had been *sold* to Unicell in China, this being outside the terms of the LSL–Punch licence (which only allowed Punch to sell goods in Europe). The Court did not explain why LSL's consent, rather than Lonsdale Australia's, was relevant for the purposes of s 123.

The fact that in both cases Paul's would not have had the ability to assess whether the marks had been applied in accordance with the conditions of the original licence shows the challenges involved in seeking to rely on the s 123 defence.

The potentially anti-competitive effects of laws that suppress parallel importation were acknowledged in the Competition Policy Review Panel's *Draft Report* (2014), where it was noted that 'trade mark owners are able to prevent parallel imports of trade marked goods into Australia by limiting trade mark licences to specific territories' (p 89). The Panel's view (at p 93) was that:

> removal of parallel importation restrictions would promote competition and potentially lower prices of many consumer goods, while the concerns raised about parallel imports (such as consumer safety, counterfeit products and inadequate enforcement) could be addressed directly through regulatory and compliance frameworks and consumer education campaigns.

LOSS OF RIGHTS

As we saw in the previous chapter, there are a number of ways in which a registered mark is vulnerable to being amended, cancelled or removed from the Register.[3]

CANCELLATION OF REGISTRATION

Sections 85–88 deal with circumstances in which the registration of a mark may be cancelled, or an entry in the Register amended, upon application to a prescribed court by an 'aggrieved person' (or, for ss 86–88, by the Registrar). The 'aggrieved person' requirement was considered by the High Court in *Health World Ltd v Shin-Sun Australia Pty Ltd* [2010] HCA 13; (2010) 240 CLR 590. French CJ, Gummow, Heydon and Bell JJ held that, given that there is a clear public interest in maintaining the 'integrity' of the Register (in ensuring that it reflect only those marks that ought to be protected), the 'aggrieved person' requirement should be interpreted liberally. The majority held that it was inappropriate to set up an exhaustive test for when a party would be 'aggrieved', but noted at [27] that the requirement was intended to prevent applications being made by busybodies or 'common informers or strangers proceeding wantonly' or persons without any interest in the Register or the functions it serves beyond gratifying an intellectual concern or reflecting 'merely

---

3   For detailed consideration, see R Burrell and M Handler, *Australian Trade Mark Law*, 2nd ed, Oxford University Press, Melbourne (forthcoming 2016), chs 9–10.

sentimental motives'. On the facts in *Health World* it was enough that the party seeking rectification of the Register and the owner of the registered mark were in the same trade, and that each traded in the same class of goods in respect of which the mark was registered to make the first party 'aggrieved'.

Two of the rectification provisions merit particular attention.

First, under s 88(1), an application for cancellation of a registration can be made on any of four grounds, which are set out in 88(2). These are as follows.

1   Under s 88(2)(a), an application may be made on any of the grounds on which the registration of the mark could have been opposed. That is, ss 58–62A, as well as ss 39 and 41–44 and reg 4.15A of the *Trade Mark Regulations 1995* (Cth) (by virtue of s 57 and reg 5.18) also become potential grounds of cancellation of a registered mark. In most cases this will require the court to look at the state of affairs at the filing date or priority date of the registered mark. For example, if the s 41 ground is raised in cancellation proceedings, the court will assess the distinctiveness of the mark as at the filing date, not at the time of the cancellation proceedings. Similarly, if a s 42(b) ground is raised, the court will assess whether the use of the mark was contrary to law as at its filing date: the fact that the ongoing use of the mark would no longer be contrary to law is not a relevant consideration under s 88. The registration of certain marks that were registered under previous legislation can only be cancelled on the opposition grounds if a number of 'gateway conditions' set out in s 234(2)(c)–(e) are first satisfied.

2   Under s 88(2)(b), an application may be made if an amendment of the application for the registration of the trade mark was obtained as a result of fraud, false suggestion or misrepresentation.

3   Under s 88(2)(c), an application may be made if, because of the circumstances applying at the time when the application for rectification is filed (i.e. post-filing), the use of the trade mark is likely to deceive or cause confusion (this is discussed in more detail in the extract from *Health World Ltd v Shin-Sun Australia Pty Ltd* [2008] FCA 100; (2008) 75 IPR 478 below, p 806).

4   Under s 88(2)(e), an application may be made if it is in respect of an entry in the Register, and the entry was made, or has been previously amended, as a result of fraud, false suggestion or misrepresentation.

Second, under s 87 a registration can be cancelled on the basis that either ss 24 or 25 of the *TMA* applies.

•   Section 24 deals with situations where the registered mark has become generic. More particularly, it applies where the registered mark consists of or contains a sign that, after the date of registration, 'becomes generally accepted within the relevant trade as the sign that describes or is the name of an article, substance or service'. This is a narrow ground—many marks might be used generically by consumers (such as 'kleenex' for tissues, 'band-aid' for sticking plasters, or 'google' for conducting an internet search), but provided these are still understood *within the relevant trade* as serving a trade mark function, they will not fall foul of ss 24 or 87.

•   Section 25 deals with situations where a registered trade mark consists of or contains a sign that describes or is the name of an article or substance that was formerly exploited under a patent, or a service that was formerly provided as a patented process, and it is at least two years since the patent has expired or ceased, and the sign is the only commonly known way to describe or identify the article, substance or service. This section applies to the trade marked names of formerly patented articles, but has also been applied in the case of the trade marked shape of such articles.[4]

Where the application for rectification is made under s 87 or on the grounds contained in either s 88(2)(a) (based on ss 43, 44, 60 or 61) or s 88(2)(c), the court has the discretion under s 89 to refuse to cancel or amend the registration if the registered owner 'satisfies the court that the ground relied on ... has not arisen through any act or fault of the registered owner'.

REMOVAL ON THE BASIS OF NON-USE

The rationale for protecting trade marks is dependent on them being used in the marketplace to distinguish goods or services. Part 9 of the Act therefore sets up a mechanism under which certain unused marks can be removed from the Register.

A person may apply to the Registrar to have a trade mark that is or may be registered removed from the Register (s 92(1)). Under s 92(4), this application can be made on either or both of two grounds. The first is:

> (a) that, on the day on which the application for the registration of the trade mark was filed, the applicant for registration had no intention in good faith:
>   (i) to use the trade mark in Australia; or
>   (ii) to authorise the use of the trade mark in Australia; or
>   (iii) to assign the trade mark to a body corporate for use by the body corporate in Australia;
> in relation to the goods and/or services to which the non-use application relates and that the registered owner:
>   (iv) has not used the trade mark in Australia; or
>   (v) has not used the trade mark in good faith in Australia;
> in relation to those goods and/or services at any time before the period of one month ending on the day on which the non-use application is filed;

The second ground is:

> (b) that the trade mark has remained registered for a continuous period of 3 years ending one month before the day on which the non-use application is filed, and, at no time during that period, the person who was then the registered owner:
>   (i) used the trade mark in Australia; or
>   (ii) used the trade mark in good faith in Australia;
> in relation to the goods and/or services to which the application relates.

Use by an 'authorised user' of the mark will be sufficient to defeat a non-use action (see s 7(3) and our discussion below).

An application under s 92(4)(b) can only be brought after five years from the filing date of the application for registration (s 93(2)).

Where an application for removal is made under either ground, any person can oppose removal (usually this is the registered owner). The procedural requirements relating to removal proceedings

---

4 See *Mayne Industries Pty Ltd v Advanced Engineering Group Pty Ltd* [2008] FCA 27; (2008) 166 FCR 312, [71]–[99].

are set out in ss 95–99. In a reversal of the usual onus under the *TMA*, the *opponent* has the burden of rebutting any allegation of non-use made under s 92(4) (see s 100). At the conclusion of proceedings, if the Registrar is satisfied that a ground has been made out he or she may order the removal of the mark from the Registrar in relation to any or all of the specified goods or services (s 101(1), with a residual discretion not to order removal contained in s 101(3)).

CASE EXTRACT: CURRENT LAW

E & J Gallo Winery v Lion Nathan Australia Pty Ltd

[2010] HCA 15; (2010) 241 CLR 144

High Court of Australia

[Lion Nathan sought removal of Gallo's registered mark BAREFOOT for wine under s 92(4)(b) on the basis of non-use. Gallo argued that the owner of the mark at the relevant time, Mr Houlihan, had authorised Californian company Barefoot Cellars to apply the mark to wine in California, which was then sold to a German wholesaler. Unbeknown to Mr Houlihan or Gallo, a small quantity of this wine was then imported into Australia and sold by a retailer called Beach Avenue. At first instance and on appeal to the Full Federal Court, it was held that since Barefoot Cellars had not consciously projected its goods into the Australian market, there was no use of the mark by the owner sufficient to prevent the mark from being removed from the Register under s 92(4)(b). Gallo appealed to the High Court.]

French CJ, Gummow, Crennan and Bell JJ (some foonotes omitted): 45. In *Estex [Clothing Manufacturers Pty Ltd v Ellis and Goldstein Ltd* (1967) 116 CLR 254], Windeyer J and then the Full Court considered whether an overseas manufacturer (who was a registered owner of the trade mark in question) uses a trade mark in Australia when the manufacturer sells goods to Australian retailers for delivery in Australia and those retailers import the goods into Australia and sell them.

46. In considering what 'use' meant under s 23 of the *Trade Marks Act 1955* (Cth), a provision similar to, but not identical with, s 92(4)(b), Windeyer J said:

> [W]hen it is said that a trade mark is used to distinguish the goods of one man from those of another, that abbreviated statement obviously does not refer to the goods of the owner of the mark in the sense of goods which he owns or possesses. After the goods have been sold by him his mark may still, using the definition of trade mark in the Act, be used in relation to those goods for the purpose of indicating a connexion in the course of trade between them and him, the registered proprietor of the mark. The manufacturer who sells goods, marked with his mark, to a warehouseman, wholesaler or retailer does not, in my view, thereupon cease to use the mark in respect of those goods. The mark is his property although the goods are not; and the mark is being used by him so long as the goods are in the course of trade and it is indicative of their origin, that is as his products. Goods remain in the course of trade so long as they are upon a market for sale. Only when they are bought for consumption do they cease to be in the course of trade.

47. His Honour distinguished the facts in *Estex* from those in *WD & HO Wills (Australia) Ltd v Rothmans Ltd* [(1956) 94 CLR 182], where the consumers of certain goods concluded their purchases overseas, with the result that the trade mark in question was not used 'in the course of trade' in Australia.

48. In dismissing appeals from the judgment of Windeyer J, the Full Court said nothing to detract from Windeyer J's analysis of use. The Full Court stated that the denotation of use in s 23 was 'not limited by any concept of the physical use of a tangible object'. The Full Court went on to state:

> [W]hen an overseas manufacturer projects into the course of trade in this country, by means of sales to Australian retail houses, goods bearing his mark and the goods, bearing his mark, are displayed or offered for sale or sold in this country, the use of the mark is that of the manufacturer.

49. This passage and a similar passage led to Lion Nathan's contention that it was a necessary condition to establish a use in Australia that an overseas manufacturer knowingly 'projects' his goods into the course of trade in Australia. This misreads the judgment. In *Estex*, the facts described in the passage set out above were sufficient for establishing a use in Australia. There was no suggestion that what was sufficient in that case was necessary in every case. As Aickin J observed in *Pioneer Kabushiki Kaisha v Registrar of Trade Marks* [(1977) 137 CLR 670], Estex was authority for 'the proposition that the foreign owner of an Australian mark uses it in Australia when he sells goods for delivery abroad to Australian retailers and those retailers import them into Australia for sale and there sell them'.

50. On the facts of this case, there was use of the registered trade mark on vendible products offered for sale and sold in Australia by the trader Beach Avenue to consumers. There was no issue about the registered trade mark's capacity to distinguish the goods to which it was attached. The goods had been on the market for sale under the registered trade mark in the United States of America and had arrived in Australia via Germany. The then registered owner, Mr Houlihan, through Barefoot Cellars, had sold the goods to a German trader for resale without any limitation as to their destination.

51. The capacity of a trade mark to distinguish a registered owner's goods from those of others, as required by s 17, does not depend on whether the owner knowingly projects the goods into the Australian market. It depends on the goods being in the course of trade in Australia. Each occasion of trade in Australia, whilst goods sold under the trade mark remain in the course of trade, is a use for the purposes of the *Trade Marks Act*. A registered owner who has registered a trade mark under the provisions of the *Trade Marks Act* can be taken, in general terms, to have an intention to use that trade mark on goods in Australia. It is a commonplace of contemporary international trade that prior to consumption goods may be in the course of trade across national boundaries.

52. An overseas manufacturer who has registered a trade mark in Australia and who himself (or through an authorised user) places the trade mark on goods which are then sold to a trader overseas can be said to be a user of the trade mark when those same goods, to which the trade mark is affixed, are in the course of trade, that is, are offered for sale and sold in Australia. This is because the trade mark remains the trade mark of the registered owner (through an authorised user if there is one) whilst the goods are in the course of trade before they are bought for consumption. As affirmed by Gummow J in *Wingate Marketing Pty Ltd v Levi Strauss & Co* [(1994) 49 FCR 89 at 136], 'whilst a trade mark remains on goods, it functions as an indicator of the person who attached or authorised the initial use of the mark'. During the trading period, the trade mark functions as an indicator of the origin of the goods, irrespective of the location of the first sale.

53. Provided Barefoot Cellars was an authorised user, the facts and circumstances of this case are sufficient to constitute a use of the registered trade mark by the registered owner for the purposes of the relevant sections of the Trade Marks Act set out above ...

[Having found that Barefoot Cellars was an authorised user, Lion Nathan separately argued that Gallo's use was not 'in good faith'.]

60. ... Lion Nathan contended that the requirement that use of a trade mark be 'use in good faith' involved consideration of the volume of use, which it was suggested should be substantial, and also involved consideration of the state of mind of the registered owner in respect of the use. Lion Nathan's position was that the use of the registered trade mark was neither substantial nor genuine. In terms of volume, Lion Nathan described the sales in Australia as minuscule. It was also submitted that a registered owner should not be taken to have used a trade mark in good faith when the owner was unaware that such use was occurring. The primary judge rejected these arguments and the Full Court did not consider them.

61. Gallo responded with a submission that the use which was proven to have occurred was sufficient to constitute use in good faith.

62. In *Electrolux Ltd v Electrix Ltd* [(1953) 71 RPC 23] ('*Electrolux*') a question arose of bona fide use within the meaning of s 26 of the *Trade Marks Act 1938* (UK). It was held that bona fide use must be ordinary and genuine use judged by commercial standards. In *Imperial Group Ltd v Philip Morris & Co Ltd* [[1982] FSR 72] ('*Imperial Group*'), it was held that use of a trade mark for a purpose other than deriving profit and establishing goodwill is not use as required by the legislation. It has also been held that contriving use for the purpose of defeating a trade rival's plans will lack the necessary quality of genuineness. However, a use does not cease to be genuine even if it only occurs after an appreciation that a registration was vulnerable to an attack on the grounds of non-use. In deciding that a use is not genuine, a court may be influenced by the quantum of sales. In *'Concord' Trade Mark* [[1987] FSR 209] ('*Concord*'), Falconer J relied on Lawton LJ's summary of the findings in the *Electrolux* case in *Imperial Group*:

> According to the judgments given in this court in that case [*Electrolux*] a bona fide use should be 'ordinary and genuine' (per Lord Evershed MR at p 36), 'perfectly genuine', 'substantial in amount', 'a real commercial use on a substantial scale' (per Jenkins LJ at p 41) and not 'some fictitious or colourable use but a real or genuine use' (per Morris LJ at p 42).

63. Lion Nathan relied on a passage in *New South Wales Dairy Corporation v Murray-Goulburn Co-operative Co Ltd* [(1989) 86 ALR 549] in which Gummow J noted that in *Concord*, Falconer J held that, for a use to be bona fide within the meaning of s 26 of the *Trade Marks Act 1938* (UK), the use should be 'substantial and genuine judged by ordinary commercial standards considered in relation to the trade concerned'. Concord concerned the launch of cigarette products under a trade mark which had not been in use for some years. Falconer J found that the sales, in the context of cigarette sales, were 'negligible' and therefore could not be regarded as substantial.

64. Whilst a single act of sale may not be sufficient to prevent removal, in the case of genuine use, a relatively small amount of use may be sufficient to constitute 'ordinary and genuine' use judged by commercial standards. It has been recognised by the Court of Justice of the European Communities, dealing with the expression 'genuine use' as used in Arts 10 and 12 of [the *European Trade Marks*

Directive], that use of a mark 'need not … always be quantitatively significant for it to be deemed genuine'. On the facts here, it is not necessary to decide whether a single use of the registered trade mark in good faith would have been sufficient to resist removal.

65. A commercial quantity of wine, some 144 bottles, was … offered for sale under the registered trade mark by Beach Avenue during the [alleged period of non-use]. Some 41 sales during that time were proven by reference to invoices and tax paid. There was no suggestion in the evidence that the offering for sale and selling either overseas or in Australia was for any purpose other than making profit and establishing goodwill in the registered trade mark. It was not contended that the use was fictitious or colourable. In all the circumstances the use was genuine and sufficient to establish use in good faith for the purposes of Lion Nathan's application for removal.

CASE EXTRACT: COMPARATIVE LAW

Case C-40/01, Ansul BV v Ajax Brandbeveiliging BV

[2003] ECR I-2439
Court of Justice of the European Communities

[Article 12(1) of the *European Trade Marks Directive* provides that '[a] trade mark shall be liable to revocation if, within a continuous period of five years, it has not been put to genuine use in the Member State in connection with the goods or services in respect of which it is registered'. One issue in this case was the meaning of 'genuine use'.]

The Court: 36. 'Genuine use' must therefore be understood to denote use that is not merely token, serving solely to preserve the rights conferred by the mark. Such use must be consistent with the essential function of a trade mark, which is to guarantee the identity of the origin of goods or services to the consumer or end user by enabling him, without any possibility of confusion, to distinguish the product or service from others which have another origin.

37. It follows that 'genuine use' of the mark entails use of the mark on the market for the goods or services protected by that mark and not just internal use by the undertaking concerned. The protection the mark confers and the consequences of registering it in terms of enforceability vis-à-vis third parties cannot continue to operate if the mark loses its commercial raison d'être, which is to create or preserve an outlet for the goods or services that bear the sign of which it is composed, as distinct from the goods or services of other undertakings. Use of the mark must therefore relate to goods or services already marketed or about to be marketed and for which preparations by the undertaking to secure customers are under way, particularly in the form of advertising campaigns. Such use may be either by the trade mark proprietor or … by a third party with authority to use the mark.

38. Finally, when assessing whether there has been genuine use of the trade mark, regard must be had to all the facts and circumstances relevant to establishing whether the commercial exploitation of the mark is real, in particular whether such use is viewed as warranted in the economic sector concerned to maintain or create a share in the market for the goods or services protected by the mark.

39. Assessing the circumstances of the case may thus include giving consideration, inter alia, to the nature of the goods or service at issue, the characteristics of the market concerned and the scale and frequency of use of the mark. Use of the mark need not, therefore, always be quantitatively significant for it to be deemed genuine, as that depends on the characteristics of the goods or service concerned on the corresponding market.

EXPLOITATION

A final issue in this chapter relates to the exploitation of registered trade marks. Section 21(1) of the *TMA* provides that a registered trade mark is personal property. One of the consequences of this is that a trade mark can be dealt with much like other forms of personal property, and Part 10 of the *TMA* deals with the exploitation of registered marks and applications for registration. However, exploitation of trade marks is a more complex matter than exploitation of other forms of IP. This is because trade marks are protected to the extent that they operate as 'badges of origin'. There may be some circumstances in which use of a trade mark by an assignee or a licensee will disrupt the origin function of the mark, which will leave the registration of the mark vulnerable to being cancelled.

On the issue of *assignment*, s 106 provides that a registered trade mark, or mark whose registration is being sought, may be assigned (s 106(1)). That assignment may apply to some of the specified goods or services. However (unlike in copyright law), an assignment cannot be made in relation to the use of a trade mark in a limited area (s 106(2)). Importantly, there is no requirement that the assignment be in conjunction with the sale of the goodwill of the business in relation to which the mark has been used (s 106(3))—unlike the situation with unregistered marks. However, there may be circumstances where the assignment of a mark without the underlying goodwill might result in the registration of the mark being cancelled on the grounds that its use has become deceptive.

The *licensing* of marks is a more complicated matter. In the early twentieth century it was thought that the inevitable result of licensing would be deception of the public, since the mark's function as a badge of origin would be compromised. Such a view failed to reflect emerging marketing and merchandising practices and consumer perceptions as to how marks functioned. Following the UK's lead, the *Trade Marks Act 1955* (Cth) contained provisions to allow for 'registered users' of trade marks, which required the Registrar to be satisfied as to the 'degree of control' that the owner exercised over a licensee's use of the mark. More importantly, the Anglo-Australian courts came to recognise that a valid trade mark licence did *not* require the licensee to be a registered user. In *Pioneer Kabushiki Kaisha v Registrar of Trade Marks* (1977) 137 CLR 670 at 683, Aickin J considered in the context of a licensing arrangement that:

> the essential requirement for the maintenance of the validity of a trade mark is that it must indicate a connexion in the course of trade with the registered proprietor, even though the connexion may be slight, such as selection or quality control or control of the user in the sense in which a parent company controls a subsidiary. Use by either the registered proprietor or a licensee (whether registered or otherwise) will protect the mark from attack on the ground of non-user, but it is essential both that the user maintains the connexion of the registered proprietor with the goods and that the use of the mark does not become otherwise deceptive.

The *TMA* takes a more permissive view of licensing: the 'registered user' system has been abolished, and the Act instead contemplates that an 'authorised user' can make an 'authorised use' of a mark. A person will be an 'authorised user' if it 'uses the trade mark in relation to goods or services *under the control of the owner* of the trade mark' (s 8(1)). Authorised use is similarly defined as only such use by an authorised user under the control of the owner (s 8(2)). 'Quality control' (s 8(3)) or 'financial control' (s 8(4)) will suffice for these purposes, although the concept of 'control' in s 8(1)–(2) is at large (s 8(5)).

AUTHORISED USE

The understanding of 'control' as set out in the *Pioneer* decision has continued to be influential in interpreting the requirement of 'authorised use' under the *TMA*. That is, the licensee's use must indicate a connection in the course of trade with the registered owner. This can be seen in the following extract, which is also relevant to the question of when the registration of a licensed mark might nevertheless be cancelled under s 88(2)(c) on the grounds that its use has become deceptive, or the mark removed from the Register on the grounds of non-use under s 92(4)(b), because the use in question falls outside the scope of being 'authorised use'.

CASE EXTRACT: CURRENT LAW

Health World Ltd v Shin-Sun Australia Pty Ltd

[2008] FCA 100; (2008) 75 IPR 478
Federal Court of Australia

[Shin-Sun was the registered owner of the mark 'Health*Plus*'. Health World sought the removal (under s 92) and/or cancellation (on the s 88(2)(c) ground) of that mark, on the basis that to the extent that the mark had been used, it was to identify the goods of a related company called Nature's Hive, and not Shin-Sun. This issue turned on whether Nature's Hive could be said to have been an 'authorised user' of the 'Health*Plus*' mark.]

Jacobson J:

SHIN-SUN AND NATURE'S HIVE

60. Shin-Sun was incorporated in 1993. The directors of the company are Mr James Shin and his wife, Mrs Anna Shin. Mr and Mrs Shin are the sole shareholders of the company.

61. Ms Theresa Shin is the general manager of Shin-Sun. She is the daughter of Mr James Shin and Mrs Anna Shin. She has held this position since 2000.

62. Shin-Sun's principal place of business is … a retail outlet. It is also the principal place of business of Nature's Hive. The retail outlet is known as Shin-Sun Natural Health Products.

63. Ms Shin describes the companies Shin-Sun and Nature's Hive as family businesses, managed principally by her and her parents. She is the General Manager of both companies but they have different shareholders.

64. Nature's Hive was incorporated in 1995. Mr and Mrs Shin are directors but they were appointed only as at May 2006 and July 2006 respectively. Ms Theresa Shin owns twenty of the twenty-one issued shares. Her uncle owns the remaining share.

65. Nature's Hive operated a store in Chatswood from 1996 to 1999. Ms Shin's evidence is that Nature's Hive ceased to trade in May 1999, except for its role as sponsor of listings for HealthPlus products under the *Therapeutic Goods Act 1989* (Cth).

66. Nature's Hive did not have a bank account from May 1999 to December 2006. In December 2006 it commenced to operate a retail outlet in Pitt Street, Sydney under the name HealthPlus …

NATURE'S HIVE'S USE OF THE HEALTH*PLUS* TRADE MARK

…

184. In summary, the effect of the evidence was that Shin-Sun's name has never appeared on the packaging and Nature's Hive procured the manufacture of the products.

185. The function of a trade mark is to give an indication to a purchaser as to the manufacture or quality of the goods and an indication of the trade source from which the goods come or through which they pass on their way to market: *Aristoc Ltd v Rysta Ltd* (1944) 62 RPC 65 at 74, 79.

186. Here, whatever the subjective intentions of the Shin family may have been, the public face of the Health*Plus* trade mark was that of Nature's Hive. It was the only name that appeared publicly as part of the 'badge of origin' of the product.

187. In *Pioneer Kabushiki Kaisha v Registrar of Trade Marks* (1977) 137 CLR 670 at 686, Aickin J recognised that a mark may be used to indicate a connection with an unidentified person. His Honour said that in those circumstances it must indicate a connection with both the proprietor and the user.

188. In my opinion, that requirement is not satisfied as a matter of fact because the evidence does not demonstrate any connection between the actual use of the mark and the registered proprietor, Shin-Sun.

189. Nevertheless, Shin-Sun contends that s 88(2)(c) is not enlivened because Nature's Hive's use of the mark was under the control of Shin-Sun so that Nature's Hive was an 'authorised user' within the meaning of s 8(1) of the Act.

WHETHER SHIN-SUN CONTROLLED NATURE'S HIVE'S USE OF THE MARK

190. Section 8(3) refers to the exercise by the owner of quality control over the goods dealt with in the course of trade by another. Section 8(4) refers to the exercise by the owner of financial control over the other person's trading activities.

191. However, s 8(3) and s 8(4) do not limit the meaning of the expression 'under the control of' the owner of the trade mark in s 8(1): see s 8(5). It is therefore necessary to deal with the question of whether Shin-Sun exercised quality or financial control over Nature's Hive's use of the mark, or whether it controlled the use in the broad sense referred to by Aickin J in *Pioneer* at 683.

192. There is no evidence before me that Shin-Sun has exercised quality control over the Health*Plus* products manufactured for Nature's Hive and supplied under Nature's Hive's packaging.

193. Indeed, in my view, the evidence establishes that Nature's Hive has the relevant obligations of quality control under the *Therapeutic Goods Act*. Nature's Hive is the sponsor and the certificate of listing for the goods imposes the obligation of quality control on Nature's Hive.

194. Ms Shin accepted in cross-examination that the conditions on the certificate of listing were binding on Nature's Hive. I reject Ms Shin's evidence that the conditions were also binding on Shin-Sun. There was no evidence to support such a finding.

195. The only written agreements dealing with the manufacture of the goods were the Good Manufacturing Practice Agreements which are entered into by Nature's Hive. There are no written agreements between Nature's Hive and Shin-Sun relating to the manufacture of the goods or covering any other topic.

...

197. Nor did Shin-Sun exercise 'financial control' over Nature's Hive's trading activities within the meaning of s 8(4). This is because, in my view, the financial control to which the subsection is directed is a legally enforceable power of control which did not exist between Shin-Sun and Nature's Hive.

198. Ms Shin's evidence was that Nature's Hive did not have a bank account. I accept this evidence but it does not follow that Shin-Sun exercised financial control within the meaning of s 8(4). What that subsection requires is evidence of the exercise of financial control over trading activities, perhaps in the way in which a parent company may exercise control over a wholly owned subsidiary. Here, there was no such relationship and any control by Shin-Sun was revocable: [CA] Henschke [& Co v Rosemount Estates Pty Ltd [2000] FCA 1539] at [69].

199. Nature's Hive and Shin-Sun have different shareholders. They have common directors but that has only been the position since July 2006. Of course, in a practical sense, it may be unlikely that Ms Shin would remove her parents as directors of Nature's Hive. But that is not an answer to the separate corporate identity of Shin-Sun and the power of Ms Shin as the majority shareholder to revoke any exercise of control flowing from common directorships.

200. The 'control' which is contemplated by s 8(5) would seem to be as wide as the 'connection in the course of trade' to which Aickin J referred in *Pioneer* at 683. His Honour said that the connection may be slight, such as selection or quality control or control of the user in the sense in which a parent company controls a subsidiary ...

201. However, Aickin J observed in *Pioneer* at 683 that it is essential that the user maintains the connection of the registered proprietor with the goods. That connection is not established on the facts of the present case.

202. It follows in my view that Nature's Hive was not an authorised user of the mark. It also follows that the use of the Health*Plus* trade mark was likely to deceive or cause confusion within the meaning of s 88(2)(c) of the Act.

[Jacobson J also held that the mark was liable to be removed from the Register on the grounds of non-use by Shin-Sun. In the result, however, Jacobson J considered that Health World did not have standing to bring the removal and cancellation proceedings, a decision overturned by the High Court: *Health World Ltd v Shin-Sun Australia Pty Ltd* [2010] HCA 13; (2010) 240 CLR 590.]

—19—

INTELLECTUAL PROPERTY LITIGATION AND REMEDIES

INTRODUCTION

This chapter provides a brief overview of some of the key aspects of IP litigation and remedies. Previous chapters have demonstrated the huge diversity in IP laws. The type of law governing a particular IP right will have an impact on the way litigation relating to that right is conducted and the remedies available to successful parties. This chapter is not intended to provide a comprehensive account of all of the provisions in the IP statutes, common law and equitable principles, and associated case law relating to IP litigation and remedies. Rather, it provides illustrative examples of these matters from the statutes and case law.

As a general rule, equitable and common law causes of action will be instituted in state and territory courts, whereas causes of action arising from federal legislation (such as for infringement of copyright, designs, patents and registered trade marks) are commonly, but not exclusively, instituted in federal courts. Where causes of action are instituted concurrently—for example for passing off and for contravention of s 18 of the Australian Consumer Law (ACL)[1], or for breach of confidence and copyright infringement—parties initiating litigation need to decide on the most appropriate forum.

Most IP laws fall within the civil jurisdiction, although some criminal offences are created in the IP statutes, particularly in relation to infringement of copyright on a commercial scale. A brief summary of some of the key criminal offences is presented at the end of this chapter.

LITIGATION

CAUSES OF ACTION

As illustrated in the previous chapters, the bulk of IP litigation relates to the establishment and enforcement of IP rights. In many instances litigation commences when an IP rights holder alleges that its rights have been infringed. Infringement proceedings are often accompanied by counterclaims challenging the validity of the right sought to be enforced. The reported cases therefore tend to cover the whole gamut of legal principles associated with the establishment and enforcement of IP rights.

Legal actions are also frequently initiated relating to ownership of such rights. Statutory and contract law principles are both relevant in this regard, particularly in the employment context. Contract law principles also apply to litigation relating to the licensing and assignment of IP rights.

---

1   The ACL is Sch 2 to the *Competition and Consumer Act 2010* (Cth).

The IP legislation also provides for various administrative proceedings. For example, opposition proceedings under ss 59–60 of the *Patents Act* are heard by the Commissioner of Patents and opposition proceedings under ss 52–55 of the *Trade Marks Act 1995* (Cth) (*TMA*) are heard by the Registrar of Trade Marks. Appeals to a federal court are available in both cases.

The Copyright Tribunal is established under Part VI of the *Copyright Act 1968* (Cth). The main tasks of the Tribunal relate to the determination of remuneration payable for copying, public performance and broadcasting of copyright works and other subject matter, and royalties payable for making recordings of musical works. The Tribunal also deals with various matters relating to the operation of collecting societies, including but not limited to distribution of equitable remuneration, remuneration for government copies and remuneration by educational institutions and other licence schemes. The rules relating to Tribunal procedures and evidence are provided in ss 163–169 of the *Copyright Act*, and procedures relating to alternative dispute resolution are provided in ss 169A–169G.

JURISDICTION OF THE COURTS

As the IP statutes are federal laws, the Federal Court of Australia and, in some cases, the Federal Circuit Court of Australia, are vested with original jurisdiction to hear and determine matters if prescribed under those IP statutes and related regulations (see *Federal Court of Australia Act 1976* (Cth), s 19, and *Federal Circuit Court of Australia Act 1999* (Cth), s 10, respectively). The Federal Court also has appellate jurisdiction (*Federal Court of Australia Act*, s 24). Common law and equitable actions are matters of state and territory jurisdiction. However, if such causes of action are joined with federal matters, they can be initiated in a federal court. In practice most IP litigation is instituted in the Federal Court.

The IP statutes themselves include provisions relevant to the civil jurisdiction of the courts. For example, s 154(1) of the *Patents Act* provides the Federal Court with broad jurisdiction over matters arising under the Act (including infringement proceedings: s 120(1)). Section 155 also provides the state and territory Supreme Courts with original jurisdiction to hear matters under the Act, but appellate jurisdiction is not provided to these courts. Section 154(2) specifies that the Federal Court has the exclusive jurisdiction (aside from the jurisdiction of the High Court under s 75 of the Constitution) to hear and determine appeals from decisions or directions of the Commissioner of Patents, including such matters as opposition proceedings under s 59 and re-examination proceedings under s 97.

Broadly similar provisions are found in ss 73(2) and 83–89 of the *Designs Act 2003* (Cth) and in s 125 and ss 190–198 of the *TMA*. The key difference is that the Federal Circuit Court also has jurisdiction with respect to matters arising under both Acts, as well as the exclusive jurisdiction (aside from the jurisdiction of the High Court and Federal Court) to hear and determine appeals against decisions of the Registrar of Designs or the Registrar of Trade Marks. Jurisdiction in actions for breach of s 18 of the ACL is conferred on the Federal Court, the Federal Circuit Court and on the 'several courts' of the states and territories (i.e. inferior courts as well as Supreme Courts) (*Competition and Consumer Act 2010* (Cth), s 86).

Similar civil jurisdictional provisions are found in the *Copyright Act* but, as with most other aspects of copyright law, the provisions are more complex and are scattered through the Act. For example, ss 131A–131D include provisions relating to copyright infringement, technological protection measures and electronic rights management information; ss 135AP–135AS relate to broadcast decoding devices; s 195AZGH relates to infringement of moral rights; and ss 248K–248MA relate to unauthorised use of performances. In summary, these provide that the Federal Court, Federal Circuit Court, and state and territory Supreme Courts have jurisdiction to deal with relevant actions, but they also provide a right of appeal from the state and territory courts to the Federal Court and, by special leave, to the High Court.

STANDING

As a general rule the owner of an IP right will be the person who institutes an action to enforce that right, since this is the person who suffers the relevant detriment. However, in some circumstances an exclusive licensee of the relevant IP right may suffer greater loss than the owner as a result of the infringing acts by other parties, and may be in a better position to enforce that right. This is generally reflected in the standing rules in the IP statutes. For example, s 120(1) of the *Patents Act* states that 'infringement proceedings may be started in a prescribed court, or in another court having jurisdiction to hear and determine the matter, by the patentee or an exclusive licensee'. Section 119 of the *Copyright Act* similarly provides that exclusive licensees can bring actions for infringement, and s 26 of the *TMA* provides authorised users with the right to bring infringement proceedings, subject to any agreement between the registered owner and authorised user. The *Designs Act* does not include like provisions.

There are no standing requirements relating to opposition and revocation proceedings or applications for compulsory licensing under the *Patents Act*, or to revocation proceedings under s 93 of the *Designs Act*. There are no standing requirements for opposition or removal proceedings under the *TMA*, but applications to rectify the Register under ss 85–88 must be made by an 'aggrieved person' (see Chapter 18).

INTERLOCUTORY REMEDIES

Interlocutory remedies play a vital role in IP disputes. In fact, the outcome of hearings relating to interlocutory applications will often have the practical effect of bringing litigation to an end. The three main interlocutory remedies that are made use of in IP disputes are:

- *interlocutory injunctions*, which can be used to prohibit or mandate particular conduct;
- *search orders* (also known as Anton Piller orders), which require one party to allow the other party onto their premises to search, seize and make copies of evidence relevant to the case in issue; and
- *freezing orders* (also known as Mareva orders), which have the effect of freezing a party's assets.

Equity is the jurisdictional basis for each of these interlocutory orders.

In addition to these types of orders, the *representative order* under the *Federal Court Rules 2011* (Cth) is another important interlocutory tool for IP rights holders. Where a representative order is made by the courts against a particular party, if that party is representative of a class of other unknown parties, the order is enforceable against the whole class.

Each of these orders can have a significant impact on the business of the affected party. For example, an interlocutory injunction in a patent infringement dispute could prohibit the alleged infringer from selling products alleged to infringe the patent. One of the difficulties for judges hearing these interlocutory applications is that they must make their decisions before the evidence is fully tested. In addition, proceedings are often ex parte by necessity, particularly for search and freezing orders, because a party against whom the order is being sought would be likely, if forewarned, to destroy evidence or remove assets from jurisdiction, undermining the point of the application. To some extent, concerns about the oppressive nature of such orders can be ameliorated by affording the party against whom the order is made a right of appeal and ensuring that such appeals are heard as soon as practicable. In addition, the party seeking the order generally has to give an undertaking to pay damages to the other party for losses suffered as a consequence of compliance with the order if its cause of action turns out to lack foundation. Nevertheless, the risk remains that interlocutory orders can impact on a party in a way that cannot be fully compensated by a simple award of damages.

INTERLOCUTORY INJUNCTIONS

An interlocutory injunction 'aims to keep matters in status quo until the final hearing of the action or determination of the dispute, so as to avoid irreparable harm to the parties' rights prior to the trial or order. Such an injunction is merely provisional in nature and does not conclude or determine any rights.'[2] As recently reiterated by Gleeson CJ and Crennan J in *Australian Broadcasting Corporation v O'Neill* [2006] HCA 46; (2006) 227 CLR 57 at [19], and recently applied in *Samsung Electronics Co Ltd v Apple Inc* [2011] FCAFC 156; (2011) 217 FCR 238, there are three factors an applicant must establish. First, there must be a 'serious question to be tried'. Second, the plaintiff must be likely to suffer injury for which damages will not be an adequate remedy. Third, the 'balance of convenience' must favour the grant of the interlocutory injunction.

In the past, Australian and UK courts articulated seemingly opposing standards with regard to the first factor ('serious question to be tried') in determining applications for interlocutory injunctions. In Australia the language of 'prima facie case' was adopted by the High Court in *Beecham Group Ltd v Bristol Laboratories Pty Ltd* (1968) 118 CLR 618, but this was rejected by Lord Diplock in the House of Lords in *American Cyanamid v Ethicon* [1975] AC 396. Both cases related to patent disputes, where traditionally the courts had been reluctant to grant interlocutory injunctions whenever validity was in issue.

PRECEDENT

CASE EXTRACT: PRECEDENT

Beecham Group Ltd v Bristol Laboratories Pty Ltd

(1968) 118 CLR 618
High Court of Australia

Kitto, Taylor, Menzies and Owen JJ (at 623–624): It is as well to begin consideration of the appeal by recalling the principles to be observed in dealing with applications for interlocutory injunctions in patent cases. The jurisdiction is discretionary, being a part of the jurisdiction under s 31 of the *Judiciary Act 1903–1965* (Cth) to make all such orders as are necessary for doing complete justice in the cause. The Court addresses itself in all cases, patent as well as other, to two main inquiries. The first

---

2   G Dal Pont, *Equity and Trusts in Australia*, 5th ed, Lawbook Co, Sydney, 2011, p 942 [31.90].

PRECEDENT

is whether the plaintiff has made out a prima facie case, in the sense that if the evidence remains as it is there is a probability that at the trial of the action the plaintiff will be held entitled to relief: *Preston v Luck* (1884) 27 ChD 497 at p 506; *Challender v Royle* (1887) 36 ChD 425 at p 436. How strong the probability needs to be depends, no doubt, upon the nature of the rights he asserts and the practical consequences likely to flow from the order he seeks. Thus, if merely pecuniary interests are involved, 'some' probability of success is enough: *Attorney-General v Wigan Corporation* (1854) 5 De GM & G 52 at pp 53, 54 (43 ER 789) and in general it is right to say, as Roper CJ in Eq said in *Linfield Linen Pty Ltd v Nejain* (1951) 51 SR (NSW) 280 at p 281:

> There are disputes of fact as to a number of matters ... but this being an application for an interlocutory injunction I look at the facts simply to ascertain whether the plaintiff has established a fair prima facie case and a fair probability of being able to succeed in that case at the hearing.

Thus where the defendant goes into evidence on the interlocutory application the Court does not undertake a preliminary trial, and give or withhold interlocutory relief upon a forecast as to the ultimate result of the case ...

The first of these inquiries [as to prima facie case] in the present case is not complicated by the special considerations which generally arise in a patent action where there is a substantial issue to be tried as to the validity of the patent. In such an action the plaintiff's prima facie case must be a strong one so far as the question of validity is concerned, for he asserts a monopoly and must give more proof of the right he claims than is afforded by the mere granting of the patent: *Smith v Grigg Ltd* (1924) 1 KB 655 per Atkin LJ (1924) 1 KB at p 659; *Bonnella v Espir* (1926) 43 RPC 159. The general practice in that kind of case has long been to refuse an interlocutory injunction unless either the patent has already been judicially held to be valid or it has stood unchallenged for a long period: *Smith v Grigg Ltd* (1924) 1 KB 655 at p 658. Even if the patent is an old one—which for this purpose is generally taken to mean more than six years old—it has been said that an interlocutory injunction will generally be refused provided that the defendant shows by evidence 'some ground' for supposing that he has a chance of successfully disputing the validity of the patent at the trial ...

CASE EXTRACT: COMPARATIVE LAW

COMPARATIVE LAW

American Cyanamid Co v Ethicon Ltd

[1975] AC 396
House of Lords

Lord Diplock (at 407–408): The use of such expressions as 'a probability', a 'prima facie case', or 'a strong prima facie case' in the context of the exercise of a discretionary power to grant an interlocutory injunction leads to confusion as to the object sought to be achieved by this form of temporary relief. The court no doubt must be satisfied that the claim is not frivolous or vexatious; in other words, that there is a serious question to be tried. It is no part of the court's function at this stage of the litigation to try to resolve conflicts of evidence on affidavit as to facts on which the claims of either party may ultimately depend nor to decide difficult questions of law which call for detailed argument and mature considerations. These are matters to be dealt with at the trial ... So unless the material available to the court at the hearing of the application for an interlocutory injunction fails to disclose that the plaintiff has any real prospect of succeeding in his claim for a permanent injunction at the trial, the court should go on to consider whether the balance of convenience lies in favour of granting or refusing the interlocutory relief that is sought.

CURRENT LAW

CASE EXTRACT: CURRENT LAW

Australian Broadcasting Corporation v O'Neill

[2006] HCA 46; (2006) 227 CLR 57
High Court of Australia

[The High Court was given the opportunity to address the apparent conflict in the threshold requirements for interlocutory injunctions between *Beecham* and *American Cyanamid* in this defamation case. All members of the Court agreed that there are no special rules for defamation cases, but that general equitable principles apply, taking into account the nature of the rights asserted and the practical consequences likely to flow from the interlocutory order sought.]

Gummow and Hayne JJ (footnotes omitted): 65. ... By using the phrase 'prima facie case', their Honours [in *Beecham*] did not mean that the plaintiff must show that it is more probable than not that at trial the plaintiff will succeed; it is sufficient that the plaintiff show a sufficient likelihood of success to justify in the circumstances the preservation of the status quo pending the trial. That this was the sense in which the Court was referring to the notion of a prima facie case is apparent from an observation to that effect made by Kitto J in the course of argument. With reference to the first inquiry, the Court continued, in a statement of central importance for this appeal:

> How strong the probability needs to be depends, no doubt, upon the nature of the rights [the plaintiff] asserts and the practical consequences likely to flow from the order he seeks.

...

67. Various views have been expressed and assumptions made ... respecting the relationship between the judgment of this Court in [*Beecham*] and the speech of Lord Diplock in the subsequent decision, *American Cyanamid Co v Ethicon Ltd*. It should be noted that both were cases of patent infringement and the outcome on each appeal was the grant of an interlocutory injunction to restrain infringement. Each of the judgments appealed from had placed too high the bar for the obtaining of interlocutory injunctive relief.

68. Lord Diplock was at pains to dispel the notion, which apparently had persuaded the Court of Appeal to refuse interlocutory relief, that to establish a prima face case of infringement it was necessary for the plaintiff to demonstrate more than a 50 per cent chance of ultimate success ...

69. In *Beecham*, the primary judge, McTiernan J, had refused interlocutory relief on the footing that, while he could not dismiss the possibility that the defendant might not fail at trial, the plaintiff had not made out a strong enough case on the question of infringement. Hence the statement by Kitto J in the course of argument in the Full Court that it was not necessary for the plaintiff to show that it was more probable than not that the plaintiff would succeed at trial.

70. When *Beecham* and *American Cyanamid* are read with an understanding of the issues for determination and an appreciation of the similarity in outcome, much of the assumed disparity in principle between them loses its force. There is then no objection to the use of the phrase 'serious question' if it is understood as conveying the notion that the seriousness of the question, like the strength of the probability referred to in *Beecham*, depends upon the considerations emphasised in *Beecham*.

71. However, a difference between this Court in *Beecham* and the House of Lords in *American Cyanamid* lies in the apparent statement by Lord Diplock that, provided the court is satisfied that the plaintiff's claim is not frivolous or vexatious, then there will be a serious question to be tried and this will be sufficient. The critical statement by his Lordship is '[t]he court no doubt must be satisfied that the claim is not frivolous or vexatious; in other words, that there is a serious question to be tried'. That was followed by a proposition which appears to reverse matters of onus:

> So *unless* the material available to the court at the hearing of the application for an interlocutory injunction *fails to disclose* that the plaintiff has any real prospect of succeeding in his claim for a permanent injunction at the trial, the court should go on to consider whether the balance of convenience lies in favour of granting or refusing the interlocutory relief that is sought. (emphasis added)

Those statements do not accord with the doctrine in this Court as established by *Beecham* and should not be followed. They obscure the governing consideration that the requisite strength of the probability of ultimate success depends upon the nature of the rights asserted and the practical consequences likely to flow from the interlocutory order sought.

[Gleeson CJ and Crennan J at [19] explicitly agreed with this explanation of the organising principles.]

The following extract sets out an example of how an Australian court will apply the test for whether an interlocutory injunction should be granted in the context of patent infringement proceedings.

CASE EXTRACT: CURRENT LAW

Interpharma Pty Ltd v Commissioner of Patents

[2008] FCA 1498; (2008) 79 IPR 261
Federal Court of Australia

[This case involved a fairly complex set of claim and cross-claims. The relevant matter in issue involved a cross-claim made by the pharmaceutical company Eli Lilly, alleging infringement of its Australian compound and process patents relating to its drug Gemzar by Interpharma (the cross-respondent). Interpharma countered with claims that both patents were invalid. Eli Lilly sought an interlocutory injunction to prevent Interpharma from engaging in further allegedly infringing conduct. In the process of deciding whether or not to issue interlocutory injunctions relating to the compound and process patents, Jessup J set out the equitable principles to be applied. This case illustrates how the courts interpret and apply these equitable principles in IP matters.]

Jessup J: 15. The parties are in agreement that the questions which arise in an application for an interlocutory injunction such as the present are—

(a) whether there is a serious question to be tried, or the cross-claimants have made out a prima facie case in the sense that, if the evidence remains the same, there is a probability that at trial they will be entitled to relief;

(b) whether the cross-claimants will suffer irreparable harm, for which damages will not be adequate compensation, unless an injunction is granted; and

(c) whether the balance of convenience favours the granting of an injunction.

...

16. With respect to the first question, in *Australian Broadcasting Corporation v O'Neill* (2006) 227 CLR 57, 82–83, [65] and [70] Gummow and Hayne JJ (with the assent of Gleeson CJ and Crennan J—at 68 [19]) pointed out that the requisite degree of seriousness of the question to be tried, or the strength of the probability of success at trial (which their Honours seemingly regarded as effectively two ways of saying the same thing) depended on 'the nature of the rights [the plaintiff] asserts and the practical consequences likely to flow from the order he seeks' (227 CLR at 82 [65], quoting from *Beecham Group Ltd v Bristol Laboratories Pty Ltd* (1968) 118 CLR 618, 622). Further, the issue whether there is a serious question (or a probability of success) should not be considered in isolation from the issue of the balance of convenience: *Tidy Tea Ltd v Unilever Australia Ltd* (1995) 32 IPR 405, 416 ... At base, the decision whether to grant an interlocutory restraint is a discretionary one, and it is traditionally at the point of considering the balance of convenience that the court takes into account every circumstance that has the rational capacity to assist in answering the question whether it would be in the interests of justice to do so. The apparent strength of the parties' substantive cases, to the extent that it is possible to assess such things provisionally, will usually be one of those circumstances: often an important one.

17. Another layer of complication is added to the deliberative exercise in cases in which the respondent (ie the non-moving party) goes further than a denial of the applicant's case for relief, and pleads a positive point of defence. In such a situation, it will not be enough to ask whether the applicant has shown a serious question, or a probability of success, on his or her own case. While the answer to that question may be in the affirmative, it will then be necessary to consider whether that answer should be qualified by the apparent strength of the defence. In a patent case, the fact of registration constitutes prima facie evidence of validity: *AB Hassle v Pharmacia (Australia) Pty Ltd* (1995) 33 IPR 63, 69–70, *GenRx Pty Ltd v Sanofi-Aventis* (2007) 73 IPR 502, 503–504. It has been said that it is for the respondent to show that want of validity is a triable question: *AB Hassle* 33 IPR at 69. This seems clear enough, but, in my opinion, the analysis needs to be taken a step further. Is it sufficient that the respondent does show a triable question on validity? In my view, if that is as far as the respondent goes, then, assuming always that the applicant has shown a triable issue on infringement, absent questions of validity, the conclusion would remain that the latter had a triable question. That is to say, as a matter of analysis, unless the case for invalidity is sufficiently strong (at the provisional level) to qualify the conclusion that, overall, the applicant has a serious question, or a probability of success, the court should move to consider the adequacy of damages, the balance of convenience and other discretionary matters. It is the applicant's title to interlocutory relief which is under consideration, and the bottom-line question, as it were, is whether the applicant has a serious question, or a probability of success, not whether the respondent does in relation to some point of defence raised or foreshadowed.

...

[Jessup J then considered issues relating to each of the three questions: serious question to be tried, adequacy of damages and balance of convenience. On the first issue, Jessup J examined the application of the legal principles relevant to infringement and validity to the facts in issue, concluding that Eli Lilly had a stronger case with regard to validity and infringement in respect of its process patent than its compound patent. Jessup J's analysis of the other two questions also favoured an interlocutory injunction in respect of the process patent but not the compound patent.]

83. In summary with respect to the compound patent, a significant consideration is that the patent expires on 7 March 2009. If an injunction is not granted, the maximum period during which the cross-respondent might be infringing the patent is three months and one week. Calculation of the damages suffered by the cross-claimants over that period is unlikely to present any real difficulties. To those considerations I add what I consider to be the apparent strength of the cross-respondent's case on validity. On balance, I am not persuaded to grant the interlocutory restraints sought by the cross-claimants.

84. In summary with respect to the process patent, the patent itself is still within term by some years. If an injunction is refused, but the cross-claimants succeed at trial, it seems to me that there are likely to be all manner of difficulties restoring them to the position of advantage that they now occupy. Had the cross-respondent shown a conscientious concern to discover whether its plans to market a gemcitabine product might be compromised by an Australian patent, it must surely have encountered the process patent. The cross-claimants have the advantage of the status quo. Finally, if anything I consider, provisionally, that the cross-claimants may have the better of the argument on the question of infringement. On balance, I think that the cross-claimants have shown enough to entitle themselves to an interlocutory injunction with respect to the process patent.

...

85. For the reasons set out above, I propose to grant such interlocutory relief as is relevant to the cross-claimants' case for infringement of the process patent. I am provisionally of the view that restraints of the kind sought in the cross-claimants' Notice of Motion are appropriate, but there may be a complication arising from the fact that it will be the process patent alone that sustains them. I do not intend that the cross-respondent be restrained from dealing in a gemcitabine product made by a process other than that referred to in the evidence. I shall give the parties the opportunity to address me on the terms of the interlocutory orders that would be appropriate, particularly in the light of the considerations to which I have just referred.

In *Sigma Pharmaceuticals (Australia) Pty Ltd v Wyeth* [2009] FCA 595; (2009) 81 IPR 339, *Alphapharm Pty Ltd v Wyeth* [2009] FCA 945; (2009) 82 IPR 71 and *Otsuka Pharmaceutical Co Ltd v Generic Health Pty Ltd* [2012] FCA 239; (2012) 291 ALR 763, patent holders alleging infringement of their pharmaceutical patents by generic manufacturers were also successful in obtaining interlocutory injunctions. In all three cases it was thought that the entry of generic equivalents into the market, which would result in the patent owners losing significant market share and being forced to reduce their own prices, would cause irreparable harm. However, much will depend of the facts of each case. For example, in *Interpharma Pty Ltd v Aventis Pharma SA* [2011] FCA 32 it was thought that damages would be an adequate remedy, because the patent in question was due to expire within 18 months, meaning that the price at which the patent owner would sell its product (but for the entry of the generic competitor) would be relatively fixed. In *Samsung Electronics Co Ltd v Apple Inc* [2011] FCAFC 156; (2011) 217 FCR 238, the fact that an interlocutory injunction to prevent sale of Samsung's Galaxy 10.1 tablet would effectively cause the loss of the Australian market for that device was an important factor weighing against an injunction.

SEARCH ORDERS (ANTON PILLER ORDERS)

A search order is another form of equitable interlocutory remedy commonly used in IP litigation. These orders have been likened to police search warrants, although the courts take great care to distinguish them, as illustrated in the extract below from *Anton Piller KG v Manufacturing Processes Ltd* [1976] 1 Ch 55.

A search order requires the person against whom the order is made to allow the plaintiff/ applicant onto their premises to inspect and remove items specified in the order. The justification for such orders is to ensure that justice will be done when there is a real risk that evidence will be removed from jurisdiction or destroyed prior to trial. Given the potential for such orders to be used oppressively, stringent preconditions for the grant of an order have been formulated by the courts in all jurisdictions and orders will contain detailed conditions for the protection of the party subject to the order (e.g. requiring that any search be conducted in business hours, with an independent solicitor present to advise the party).

As to preconditions, rule 7.43 of the *Federal Court Rules 2011* (Cth) provides that:

> The Court may make a search order if the Court is satisfied that:
>
> (a) an applicant seeking the order has a strong prima facie case on an accrued cause of action; and
>
> (b) the potential or actual loss or damage to the applicant will be serious if the search order is not made; and
>
> (c) there is sufficient evidence in relation to a respondent that:
>
>   (i) the respondent possesses important evidentiary material; and
>
>   (ii) there is a real possibility that the respondent might destroy such material or cause it to be unavailable for use in evidence in a proceeding or anticipated proceeding before the Court.

PRECEDENT

CASE EXTRACT: PRECEDENT

Anton Piller KG v Manufacturing Processes Ltd

[1976] 1 Ch 55
Court of Appeal of England and Wales

[Anton Piller KG were German manufacturers of frequency converters for computers. Manufacturing Processes Ltd (MPL) was their UK agent. Anton Piller claimed that secret information was being provided to their German competitors and applied for interlocutory injunctions to prevent MPL from infringing copyright and disclosing confidential information. They also applied for permission to enter MPL's premises to inspect documents and remove them into the custody of their solicitor. The injunction was ordered, but the application for entry and inspection was refused. An ex parte appeal was made to the Court of Appeal.]

Lord Denning MR (at 60–61): [N]o court in this land has any power to issue a search warrant. But the order sought in this case is not a search warrant. It does not authorise the plaintiffs' solicitors or anyone else to enter the defendants' premises against their will. It does not authorise the breaking down of any doors, nor the slipping in by a back door, nor getting in by an open door or window. It only authorises entry and inspection by the permission of the defendants. The plaintiffs must get the defendants' permission. But it does do this: it brings pressure on the defendants to give permission. It does more. It actually orders them to give permission—with, I suppose, the result that if they do not give permission, they are guilty of contempt of court … This may seem to be a search warrant in disguise.

…

It seems to me that such an order can be made by a judge *ex parte*, but it should only be made where it is essential that the plaintiff should have inspection so that justice can be done between the parties; and when, if the defendant were forewarned, there is a grave danger that vital evidence will be destroyed, that papers will be burnt or lost or hidden, or taken beyond the jurisdiction, and so the ends of justice be defeated; and when the inspection would do no real harm to the defendant or his case.

Nevertheless, in the enforcement of this order, the plaintiffs must act with due circumspection. On the service of it, the plaintiffs should be attended by their solicitor, who is an officer of the court. They should give the defendants an opportunity of considering it and of consulting their own solicitor. If the defendants wish to apply to discharge the order as having been improperly obtained, they must be allowed to do so. If the defendants refused permission to enter or to inspect, the plaintiffs must not force their way in. They must accept that refusal, and bring it to the notice of the court afterwards, if need be on application to commit.

Ormerod LJ (at 62): There are three essential pre-conditions for the making of such an order, in my judgment. First, there must be an extremely strong prima facie case. Secondly, the damage, potential or actual, must be very serious for the applicant. Thirdly, there must be clear evidence that the defendants have in their possession incriminating documents or things, and that there is a real possibility that they may destroy such material before any application inter partes can be made.

Ormerod LJ's list of preconditions has been widely accepted in subsequent judgments and has been incorporated into the *Federal Court Rules* (extracted above).

CASE EXTRACT: CURRENT LAW

Stirling House (Guildford) Pty Ltd v Coghlan

[2005] FCA 1623
Federal Court of Australia

[This case concerned alleged infringement of copyright and breach of confidence by Coghlan, an employee of Stirling House.]

French J: 21. The claim for interlocutory relief by way of an Anton Piller order was brought before this Court yesterday on an ex parte basis. Stirling House seeks an order under which Mr Coghlan and his company would be required to permit a group of up to six persons to enter his offices in the Australian Capital Territory. He would be required to permit them to search for, inspect, test and examine, copy, photograph or videotape all electronic equipment and computers, software, files, papers or any documents relating to materials or documents originating from the applicant or the means by which they were obtained. It would also require him to allow the applicant's representatives to remove into the possession and safety of the applicant's solicitors and/or the applicant's computer expert all or any electronic equipment computers, forensic disc, images or other data copies, files, papers or any documents relating to materials or documents originating from the applicant or the means by which those things were obtained.

22. The persons to be so empowered by the order would comprise:

(a)   not more than three (3) representatives of the applicant which will include two (2) computer experts;

(b)   not more than two (2) partners or employees of the applicant's solicitors Hammond King Touyz or appointed agents;

(c)   a solicitor other than a member of Hammond King Touyz ('independent solicitor').

23. The Court is empowered by s 23 of the *Federal Court of Australia Act 1976* (Cth) to make an Anton Piller order. However such orders are exceptional and established criteria for their grant require that:

(a)   There must be an extremely strong prima facie case.

(b)   The damage, potential or actual, must be very serious for the applicant; and

(c)   There must be clear evidence that the respondents have in their possession incriminating documents or things and that there is a real possibility that they may destroy such material before any application inter partes can be made.

These criteria are accepted by Stirling House in its submissions in support of the grant of such an order.

24. The causes of action relied upon by Stirling House are somewhat elusive. They are said to be 'breach of copyright' and 'breach of confidence'.

25. No infringement of copyright is identified on the written submissions put on behalf of Stirling House. It is said that the brochure was an original literary work for the purposes of the *Copyright Act 1968* (Cth) (the Act) and so much may be accepted for the moment. Beyond that however, it is not said how Mr Coghlan or his company infringed copyright in the brochure. It was submitted by counsel, upon questioning, that the supply of the brochure to Match Point constituted publication in infringement of the relevant copyright.

...

28. It may be that the transmission by email of the brochure to a third party could involve reproduction amounting to infringement but this was not argued. Nor was it pleaded. Nor, indeed, was infringement by way of publication pleaded ...

29. In my opinion the case as pleaded and explained on affidavit does not make a strong prima facie case for infringement of Stirling House's copyright in the brochure.

30. In relation to the alleged asserted cause of action in breach of confidence, counsel for the applicant submitted that there are three elements:

(a)   the information itself must have the necessary quality of confidence about it;

(b)   the information must have been imparted in circumstances purporting an obligation of confidence; and

(c)   there must be an unauthorised use of that information to the detriment of the party communicating it.

It was submitted that the brochure was a draft promotional brochure provided only to Mr King at a related company and clearly not something which was public property or public knowledge and not intended to be provided to a competitor.

31. It was submitted that the clear inference from the evidence is that the brochure was not lawfully obtained. The timing of the obtaining of the brochure the same afternoon after it was created by Mr Moyle supports, it was said, an inference that it was somehow obtained electronically by Mr Coghlan. This, it was submitted, was sufficient to meet the circumstances importing an obligation of confidence. Passing the brochure on to Match Point, a competitor of the applicant led, it was submitted, to an unauthorised use to the detriment of the applicant.

32. The quality and duration of the confidentiality of the brochure and the way in which its supply to Match Point could lead to damage to the applicant did not emerge from the affidavit evidence. It is plain that the brochure was intended to be made public for the purpose of marketing corporate hospitality packages. It was therefore not going to remain confidential for very long. It seems unlikely that it would simply have been copied and used by a competitor. Such a use would have been immediately obvious. The format of the brochure was not confidential to Stirling House as it was based upon a template provided by Telstra Dome. The only suggestion that was made from the bar table as to the way in which the brochure could have been misused was to provide information as to the proposed pricing of the applicant's package to a competitor in a way that might disadvantage the applicant. This was not pleaded expressly albeit it is at least plausible. It was not the subject of evidence which might enable any confident judgment to be made about the sensitivity of pricing information and therefore a judgment as to the period of its confidentiality and the damage which the applicant might suffer by its disclosure to a competitor.

33. In my opinion, the first condition for the grant of an Anton Piller order, namely that there must be a very strong prima facie case, is not made out on the materials put before me. Nor am I satisfied that on the basis of the materials relating to the obtaining of the relevant brochure that an inference can be drawn that absent the Anton Piller order the applicant would suffer serious damage.

34. The evidence does support a seriously arguable case that Mr Coghlan obtained unauthorised access to information held electronically by Stirling House. If he did obtain such access, it is unlikely to have been lawful. Moreover there is enough to indicate an arguable case of misuse of that information which, so far as it related to pricing, was at least for a time likely to have been confidential. That case is sufficient, in my opinion, to support the grant of the lesser interlocutory relief claimed by the applicant. On the materials before me at present the balance of convenience favours the grant of that relief. It will however be open to the respondents to apply on short notice to vary or discharge the orders.

35. I propose to refuse the claim for an Anton Piller order. As indicated however to counsel for the applicant, I am prepared to grant interlocutory injunctive relief in the alternative form sought by Stirling House. This is on the basis that there is an arguable case of misuse of confidential information and a balance of convenience in favour of the grant of the relief sought. It is subject to the usual undertaking as to damages which has been offered by Stirling House and, as indicated, liberty to the respondents to apply to vary or discharge it.

Search orders are usually only ordered where there is reason to believe the respondent will destroy evidence if ordinary court processes apply. One unusual case of a search order is *Universal Music Australia Pty Ltd v Sharman License Holdings Ltd* [2004] FCA 183; (2004) 59 IPR 299, where the evidence consisted of dynamic data regarding the operation of the respondent's peer-to-peer filesharing software and network. The inherently transitory nature of that information meant that it was likely to be destroyed and justified the grant of the search order.

FREEZING ORDERS (MAREVA ORDERS)

Asset preservation or freezing orders are another form of interlocutory remedy designed to prevent a party to litigation from removing assets from the jurisdiction, or from disposing of or dealing with them within the jurisdiction, so as to frustrate execution under proceedings to be brought by the other party. They are also known as Mareva orders (or, in early cases, Mareva injunctions).

As with search orders, the broad power in s 23 of the *Federal Court of Australia Act* has been held to empower the court to grant freezing orders. In addition, the *Federal Court Rules* include specific jurisdiction to make freezing orders in rule 7.32:

(1) The Court may make an order (a *freezing order*), with or without notice to a respondent, for the purpose of preventing the frustration or inhibition of the Court's process by seeking to meet a danger that a judgment or prospective judgment of the Court will be wholly or partly unsatisfied.

(2) A freezing order may be an order restraining a respondent from removing any assets located in or outside Australia or from disposing of, dealing with, or diminishing the value of, those assets.

PRECEDENT

CASE EXTRACT: PRECEDENT

Mareva Compania Naviera SA v International Bulkcarriers SA

[1975] 2 Lloyd's Rep 509
Court of Appeal of England and Wales

[Mareva Compania Naviera SA were shipowners who had let their vessel to International Bulkcarriers SA. Two instalments had been paid but none thereafter. Mareva proceeded to treat the conduct as repudiation of the contract and sued for unpaid hire and damages for repudiation. International Bulkcarriers had received funds for sub-charter, deposited in a London bank. Mareva applied ex parte for an injunction to restrain International Bulkcarriers from removing or disposing of the moneys.]

Lord Denning MR (at 510–511): If it appears that the debt is due and owing, and there is a danger that the debtor may dispose of his assets so as to defeat it before judgment, the court has jurisdiction in a proper case to grant interlocutory judgment so as to prevent him disposing of those assets. It seems to me that this is a proper case for the exercise of this jurisdiction. There is money in a bank in London which stands in the name of these charterers. The charterers have control of it. They may at any time dispose of it or remove it out of this country. If they do so, the shipowners may never get their charter hire. The ship is now on the high seas. It has passed Cape Town on its way to India. It will complete the voyage and the cargo will be discharged. And the shipowners may not get their charter hire at all. In face of this danger, I think this court ought to grant an injunction to restrain the charterers from disposing of these moneys now in the bank in London until the trial or judgment in this action. If the charterers have any grievance about it when they hear of it, they can apply to discharge it. But meanwhile the shipowners should be protected. It is only just and right that this court should grant an injunction. I would therefore continue this injunction.

CASE EXTRACT: CURRENT LAW

Cardile v LED Builders Pty Ltd

[1999] HCA 18; (1999) 198 CLR 380
High Court of Australia

[This case related to infringement of copyright in building plans owned by LED Builders by Eagle Homes. Shares in Eagle were held by a married couple, the Cardiles. The Cardiles had received a dividend from the company and formed a new company (Ultra Modern). Judgment was given in favour of LED against Eagle, and LED elected for an account of profits, but quantum had not yet been determined by the Court. Hence, the case was still on foot, although unusually the application for relief came after final determination of the cause of action. LED successfully applied for a Mareva order against the Cardiles and Ultra Modern restraining them from disposing of or dealing with their money, property or other assets other than for specified purposes. This extract relates to an appeal to the High Court by the Cardiles and Ultra Modern.

It should be noted in the extract from Lord Denning's judgment in the *Mareva* case above that he used the word 'injunction' to describe the order he made. The majority decision in this case included a long discussion of the doctrinal basis of the injunction and the Mareva order at [27]–[42]. The majority concluded that a Mareva order is a paradigm example of an order to prevent the frustration of a court's process and that because of the distinct doctrinal bases of the two orders, the words 'Mareva order' rather than 'Mareva injunction' should be used. The majority then went on to consider the requirements for Mareva orders.]

Gaudron, McHugh, Gummow and Callinan JJ: 50. As LED submits, the development of this ancillary jurisdiction to grant Mareva orders has been an evolving process and the courts have approached the different factual situations as they have arisen 'flexibly'. There is a temptation to use the term 'flexible' to cloak a lack of analytical rigour and to escape the need to find a doctrinal and principled basis for orders that are made. There are significant differences between an order protective of the court's process set in train against a party to an action, including the efficacy of execution available to a judgment creditor, and an order extending to the property of persons who are not parties and who cannot be shown to have frustrated, actually or prospectively, the administration of justice. It has been truly said that a Mareva order does not deprive the party subject to its restraint either of title to or possession of the assets to which the order extends [*Re Ling; Ex parte Enrobook Pty Ltd* (1996) 142 ALR 87 at 92; affd (1997) 74 FCR 19 at 29]. Nor does the order improve the position of claimants in an insolvency of the judgment debtor [*Jackson v Sterling Industries Ltd* (1987) 162 CLR 612 at 618, 639]. It operates in personam [*Mercedes Benz AG v Leiduck* [1996] AC 284 at 300] and not as an attachment. Nevertheless, those statements should not obscure the reality that the granting of a Mareva order is bound to have a significant impact on the property of the person against whom it is made: in a practical sense it operates as a very tight 'negative pledge' species of security over property, to which the contempt sanction is attached. It requires a high degree of caution on the part of a court invited to make an order of that kind. An order lightly or wrongly granted may have a capacity to impair or restrict commerce just as much as one appropriately granted may facilitate and ensure its due conduct.

51. We agree with the tenor of what was said with particular respect to Mareva relief before judgment by the Court of Appeal of New South Wales (Mason P, Sheller JA, Sheppard AJA) in *Frigo v Culhaci* [Unreported, 17 July 1998 at 10–11 ...]:

> [A Mareva order] is a drastic remedy which should not be granted lightly ...
>
> A [Mareva order] is an interlocutory order which, if granted, imposes a severe restriction upon a defendant's right to deal with his or her assets. It is granted at the suit of a plaintiff whose status as a creditor is in dispute and who need not be a secured creditor. Its purpose is to preserve the status quo, not to change it in favour of the plaintiff. The function of the order is not to [*Abella v Anderson* [1987] 2 Qd R 1 at 2–3 per McPherson J]:
>
> provide a plaintiff with security in advance for a judgment that he hopes to obtain and that he fears might not be satisfied; nor is it to improve the position of the plaintiff in the event of the defendant's insolvency ...
>
> Many authorities attest to the care with which courts are required to scrutinise applications for [Mareva orders]. The leading decision in this State is *Patterson v BTR Engineering (Aust) Ltd* (1989) 18 NSWLR 319.

52. Another reason, unfortunately rarely adverted to in the cases, for care in exercising the power to grant a Mareva order is that there may be difficulties associated with the quantification and recovery of damages pursuant to the undertaking if it should turn out that the order should not have been granted. These matters were the subject of discussion by Aickin J in *Air Express Ltd v Ansett Transport Industries (Operations) Pty Ltd* [(1979) 146 CLR 249 at 260 et seq (affd (1981) 146 CLR 306)]. A further question to which a Mareva order gives rise is the identification of the events to trigger its dissolution or an entitlement to damages. So far as this is possible, some attention to that question should be given at the time that the order is framed in the first instance.

53. Discretionary considerations generally also should carefully be weighed before an order is made. Has the applicant proceeded diligently and expeditiously? Has a money judgment been recovered in the proceedings? Are proceedings (for example civil conspiracy proceedings) available against the third party? Why, if some proceedings are available, have they not been taken? Why, if proceedings are available against the third party and have not been taken and the court is still minded to make a Mareva order, should not the grant of the relief be conditioned upon an undertaking by the applicant to commence, and ensure so far as is possible the expedition of, such proceedings? It is difficult to conceive of cases where such an undertaking would not be required. Questions of this kind may be just as relevant to the decision to grant Mareva relief as they are to a decision to dissolve it. These are matters to which courts should be alive. As will appear, they are matters which should have been considered by the Full Court in this case.

REPRESENTATIVE ORDERS

The representative order is provided for in rule 9.21(1) of the *Federal Court Rules*:

> A proceeding may be started and continued by or against one or more persons who have the same interest in the proceeding, as representing all or some of the persons who have the same interest and could have been parties to the proceeding.

The important role of representative orders in IP litigation is encapsulated in the extract below.

CASE EXTRACT: PRECEDENT

Tony Blain Pty Ltd t/as Acme Merchandising v Jamison

(1993) 41 FCR 414
Federal Court of Australia

[This case related to the sale of unofficial T-shirts outside a rock concert.]

Burchett J (at 414–416): [The relevant Federal Court Rule] authorizes the Court to appoint a particular respondent to represent other persons against whom orders are sought in a proceeding. Under the equivalent rule in England, the Court of Appeal, in a judgment delivered by Sir John Donaldson MR, made an Anton Piller order against a represented class of defendants: *EMI Records Ltd v Kudhail* (1983) 11 FSR 36. Sir John Donaldson said (at 37):

> The only problem which has concerned us is the second ground which concerned the learned judge, namely whether, if he was entitled to grant an injunction in a representative action, there was sufficient identity of interest amongst those who were engaged in the trade of selling cassette tapes bearing the trade name 'Oak Records'.

I interpolate that the case was concerned with the sale of what might be called pirate cassettes. The Master of the Rolls, a little later, went on to say, at the same page:

> The evidence also discloses that there is a link between all those who are dealing in these cassettes in the sense that they have a common interest in preventing anybody finding out where the cassettes come from and each must know some of the other members of the group otherwise they would not be able to obtain the cassettes. The secrecy of the organisation has been such that the plaintiffs have been quite unable to find out the source of the goods or, indeed, anything about the group. But prima facie there is here a group, and prima facie there is a sufficient common interest between the members of the group at least to justify the grant of ex parte relief. It will of course be open for any member of the group to come forward and ask for the order to be modified if he can provide evidence which would justify that course.

The present case is not identical with that. However, the evidence shows, prima facie, that a group of persons, apparently acting within at least fairly close ties of co-ordination, have been selling at a series of concerts articles of merchandise involving the unauthorized use of trade marks and other intellectual property of the applicants. These concerts, which featured a well known figure in popular music, a Mr Paul McCartney, share a generic likeness with a further series of concerts, to take place very shortly,

PRECEDENT

expected to feature a band known as Metallica. An individual has been identified with the group, who is known as Michael Jamison.

I propose to make a representative order. There would plainly be, in the nature of open-air selling activities at and in the vicinity of concerts of this kind, a great difficulty in identifying and naming all respondents.

The orders which are sought are not Anton Piller orders in the normal sense; they do not involve requiring a defendant to consent to entry upon his real estate. But they do have features which make them analogous to Anton Piller orders; they do involve orders requiring persons selling merchandise bearing the trade marks, for instance, of an applicant to deliver up such merchandise upon service of the order, and the making of a demand for compliance with it. That being so, I think that some of the observations, at least, made by Sir Donald Nicholls VC, as his Lordship then was, in *Universal Thermosensors Ltd v Hibben* [1992] 1 WLR 840 at 860–861 are applicable. I have, accordingly, required the applicants to give an undertaking designed to ensure that independent legal advice will be available, on the spot, to persons required by the terms of the order to deliver up what may be, at least in some sense, their own property.

Other undertakings, of the kind which are common in matters of this nature, have been offered, and are relevant to my decision that a sufficient case has been made out, upon the well known principles which govern the grant of ex parte interlocutory injunctions, to justify the making of the orders which I propose to make in this case. In particular, the undertakings will include an undertaking to provide a receipt for all merchandise which is handed over pursuant to the orders, and to provide safe custody for all such merchandise, and there will be liberty to apply on twenty-four hours notice. Accordingly, I propose to make the orders for ex parte relief.

I note the undertakings as to damages, as to an explanation in plain language of the orders, and to provide an answer to any bona fide inquiry. I note, in particular, an undertaking to make available the services of three independently instructed solicitors, with experience in intellectual property matters, to provide independent advice and assistance to any respondent served with a copy of the orders, at or about the time of service, and to arrange for those solicitors to provide a written report to the Court concerning the manner and circumstances of the service and execution of the orders. I note also an undertaking to provide to any respondent served with a copy of the orders, who delivers up merchandise, a signed receipt in respect of it; to ensure that all such merchandise is properly and securely stored, packed and labelled, and delivered up to the Court on the next return date—I note that I would not expect actual delivery up to the Court, but rather that the merchandise should be held available for delivery if required or otherwise to be disposed of as the Court may order; and, finally, to have their solicitor make and file an affidavit in the nature of a report concerning the manner and circumstances of the service and execution of the orders. I make the orders contained in the document submitted, on the grounds appearing in the affidavit accompanying the applicant's claim.

FINAL REMEDIES

At common law, the primary remedy available to wronged parties is damages, although some other remedial options do exist. In contrast, equity has a far more extensive array of options for remedial relief. Courts operating in the equitable jurisdiction have power to grant monetary relief, including both compensation for the harm suffered and an account of the profits obtained as a result of wrongful acts (discussed further below, p 830). However, the other remedial options available in this jurisdiction can be more powerful weapons. In particular, injunctions can be used to restrain people from doing particular acts or to require them to do particular acts. Courts may grant injunctions in equity's exclusive jurisdiction (e.g. to stop a person from using confidential information) and also in equity's auxiliary jurisdiction (e.g. to stop a person from engaging in passing off by misusing another's brand name). Other relevant remedies in the equitable jurisdiction include orders for specific performance of contractual obligations and for equitable rescission of contracts; orders for specific restitution of chattels, and for delivery up and destruction of documents; and declarations as to the parties' respective rights. The constructive trust is another significant equitable remedy, albeit one that is rarely awarded. This chapter focuses on monetary remedies and injunctions.

Each of the IP statutes includes its own remedial provisions. To a large extent, these statutory remedies reflect their common law and equitable counterparts. For example, s 115(2) of the *Copyright Act* provides for injunctions, damages and accounts of profit for infringement of copyright. Section 122(1) of the *Patents Act*, s 126(1) of the *TMA* and s 75(1) of the *Designs Act* provide the same set of remedies for patent, trade mark and design infringement respectively.

Ongoing concerns about infringement of copyright in the electronic environment prompted the introduction in 2006 of new subsections into s 115 of the *Copyright Act*, allowing for recovery without proof of the full extent of the loss suffered in certain limited circumstances:

(5) Subsection (6) applies to a court hearing an action for infringement of copyright if the court is satisfied that:

    (a) the infringement (the *proved infringement*) occurred (whether as a result of the doing of an act comprised in the copyright, the authorising of the doing of such an act or the doing of another act); and

    (b) the proved infringement involved a communication of a work or other subject-matter to the public; and

    (c) because the work or other subject-matter was communicated to the public, it is likely that there were other infringements (the *likely infringements*) of the copyright by the defendant that the plaintiff did not prove in the action; and

    (d) taken together, the proved infringement and likely infringements were on a commercial scale.

(6) The court may have regard to the likelihood of the likely infringements (as well as the proved infringement) in deciding what relief to grant in the action.

(7) In determining for the purposes of paragraph (5)(d) whether, taken together, the proved infringement and the likely infringements were on a commercial scale, the following matters are to be taken into account:

    (a) the volume and value of any articles that:

        (i) are infringing copies that constitute the proved infringement; or

        (ii) assuming the likely infringements actually occurred, would be infringing copies constituting those infringements;

    (b) any other relevant matter.

(8) In subsection (7):

article includes a reproduction or copy of a work or other subject-matter, being a reproduction or copy in electronic form.

Section 116 of the *Copyright Act* also provides the copyright owner with the right to bring actions for conversion or detention in relation to infringing copies of works and other subject matter, entitling the copyright owner to all the remedies that are available in such actions as if they were the owner of the infringing copy or the owner of the device used or intended to be used to make infringing copies.

The ACL has its own set of remedial provisions: see particularly s 236 (damages), s 232 (injunctions) and s 237 (other orders as the court thinks appropriate).

PERMANENT INJUNCTIONS

Superior courts in Australia are vested with jurisdiction to grant injunctions. For example, s 23 of the *Federal Court of Australia Act* provides:

> The Court has power, in relation to matters in which it has jurisdiction, to make orders of such kinds, including interlocutory orders, and to issue, or direct the issue of, writs of such kinds, as the Court thinks appropriate.

As noted above, the IP statutes also expressly state that injunctions can be awarded. The equitable nature of the injunction means that the courts apply discretionary considerations rather than the more concrete rules of the common law. Hence, injunctions will be awarded when it is 'just and convenient' to do so. The courts will consider whether the wronged party would suffer irreparable harm if the injunction were refused. For common law actions the issue is whether damages provide adequate relief. Futility (in the sense that there is no likelihood that the infringing actitivy will continue), the need for continuing curial supervision, and existence of equitable defences such as laches and unclean hands are all relevant considerations in the exercise of the discretion.[3]

The issue of whether these equitable principles apply in relation to applications for injunctions under the statutory IP provisions was considered by the US Supreme Court in the case extracted below. The position had been that if a party succeeded in a patent infringement action, they almost automatically were awarded a permanent injunction. The Supreme Court was given the opportunity to reconsider this issue and in doing so reminded the lower courts that general equitable principles apply.

COMPARATIVE LAW

CASE EXTRACT: COMPARATIVE LAW

eBay, Inc v MercExchange, LLC

547 US 388 (2006)
Supreme Court of the United States

[MercExchange held business method patents which were held to be valid and infringed by eBay. MercExchange sought a permanent injunction against eBay, which was denied by the District Court at first instance but allowed by the Court of Appeals. The Supreme Court noted (at 391) that in equity, four principles apply in determining the right of an applicant to permanent injunctive relief:

   (1) that [the applicant] has suffered an irreparable injury;

   (2) that remedies available at law, such as monetary damages, are inadequate to compensate
for that injury;

---

3 See generally G Dal Pont, *Equity and Trusts in Australia*, 5th ed, Lawbook Co, Sydney, 2011 at pp 938–940 [31.60]–[31.70].

(3) that, considering the balance of hardships between the plaintiff and defendant, a remedy in equity is warranted; and

(4) that the public interest would not be disserved by a permanent injunction.

The Court went on to explain that these principles apply with equal force in patent law and copyright law.]

Thomas J (delivering the opinion of the Court) (at 393–394): Neither the District Court nor the Court of Appeals below fairly applied these traditional equitable principles in deciding respondent's motion for a permanent injunction. Although the District Court recited the traditional four-factor test, 275 F Supp 2d, at 711, it appeared to adopt certain expansive principles suggesting that injunctive relief could not issue in a broad swath of cases. Most notably, it concluded that a 'plaintiff's willingness to license its patents' and 'its lack of commercial activity in practicing the patents' would be sufficient to establish that the patent holder would not suffer irreparable harm if an injunction did not issue. *Id*, at 712. But traditional equitable principles do not permit such broad classifications. For example, some patent holders, such as university researchers or self-made inventors, might reasonably prefer to license their patents, rather than undertake efforts to secure the financing necessary to bring their works to market themselves. Such patent holders may be able to satisfy the traditional four-factor test, and we see no basis for categorically denying them the opportunity to do so. To the extent that the District Court adopted such a categorical rule, then, its analysis cannot be squared with the principles of equity adopted by Congress. The court's categorical rule is also in tension with *Continental Paper Bag Co v Eastern Paper Bag Co*, 210 US 405, 422–430 (1908), which rejected the contention that a court of equity has no jurisdiction to grant injunctive relief to a patent holder who has unreasonably declined to use the patent.

In reversing the District Court, the Court of Appeals departed in the opposite direction from the four-factor test. The court articulated a 'general rule,' unique to patent disputes, 'that a permanent injunction will issue once infringement and validity have been adjudged.' 401 F 3d, at 1338. The court further indicated that injunctions should be denied only in the 'unusual' case, under 'exceptional circumstances' and 'in rare instances ... to protect the public interest.' *Id*, at 1338–1339. Just as the District Court erred in its categorical denial of injunctive relief, the Court of Appeals erred in its categorical grant of such relief. Cf. *Roche Products v Bolar Pharmaceutical Co*, 733 F 2d 858, 865 (CA Fed, 1984) (recognising the 'considerable discretion' district courts have 'in determining whether the facts of a situation require it to issue an injunction').

Because we conclude that neither court below correctly applied the traditional four-factor framework that governs the award of injunctive relief, we vacate the judgment of the Court of Appeals, so that the District Court may apply that framework in the first instance. In doing so, we take no position on whether permanent injunctive relief should or should not issue in this particular case, or indeed in any number of other disputes arising under the Patent Act. We hold only that the decision whether to grant or deny injunctive relief rests within the equitable discretion of the district courts, and that such discretion must be exercised consistent with traditional principles of equity, in patent disputes no less than in other cases governed by such standards.

As part of their inherent jurisdiction, Australian courts have power, in order to perfect an injunction restraining intellectual property infringement, to order delivery up of infringing items for either the obliteration of the infringement (for example, removal of a trade mark) or for destruction of the items: see for example *Corby v Allen & Unwin Pty Ltd* [2013] FCA 370; (2013) 101 IPR 181.

MONETARY REMEDIES

The principles of compensation are fairly straightforward at common law, although assessment of damages can take up a considerable period of court time and involve complex factual arguments. For tort, the principle is, as far as possible, to put the plaintiff in the position they would have been in if the tort had not occurred. For contract, the aim is to put the plaintiff in the position they would have been in if the breach had not occurred. In IP cases, this may be calculated by reference to lost licence fees (i.e. the fee that would have been charged for authorised use of the relevant IP) or, especially in cases where the plaintiff and defendant are competitors, by reference to the plaintiff's lost profits as a result of lost sales. Exemplary damages are also available in some circumstances.

CASE EXTRACT: PRECEDENT

General Tire & Rubber Co v Firestone Tyre and Rubber Co Ltd

[1976] RPC 197
House of Lords

Lord Wilberforce (at 212): As in the case of any other tort (leaving aside cases where exemplary damages can be given) the object of damages is to compensate for loss or injury. The general rule at any rate in relation to 'economic' torts is that the measure of damages is to be, so far as possible, that sum of money which will put the injured party in the same position as he would have been in if he had not sustained the wrong ... There are two essential principles in valuing that claim (in damages): first, that the plaintiffs have the burden of proving their loss: second, that the defendants being wrongdoers, damages should be liberally assessed but that the object is to compensate the plaintiffs and not punish the defendants.

In the equitable jurisdiction, various forms of monetary remedies have emerged over time.

1   Equitable compensation, which is available in equity's exclusive jurisdiction, is somewhat akin to common law damages, with the aim of compensating a plaintiff for their loss. Equitable compensation has been made widely available by the courts for breaches of fiduciary duty. While there has been some doubt about the issue, the Court of Appeal of the Supreme Court of Victoria confirmed in *Giller v Procopets* [2008] VSCA 236; (2008) 24 VR 1 that equitable compensation is available for breaches of confidence.

2   Equitable damages are made available by the courts in substitution for or in addition to other equitable remedies, including specific performance and injunctions. Equitable damages are available in equity's exclusive and auxiliary jurisdiction. In *Giller v Procopets*, the court confirmed that equitable damages may be awarded provided that the other equitable remedies would be available. It is not a requirement for the plaintiff to apply for an injunction or an order for specific performance prior to the award being made.

3   Accounts of profits focus on the defendant's gains instead of looking at the plaintiff's loss. The general principle of damages still applies: to restore the plaintiff to the position they would have been in had the infringement not occurred. Although accounts of profits are available for actions in equity's exclusive jurisdiction, they are generally not available for actions at common law, in equity's auxiliary jurisdiction. However, accounts of profits are available for IP actions. There are express statutory provisions in the IP legislation, but the remedy has also been made available by the courts for the common law tort of passing off (see e.g. *Conagra Inc v McCain Foods (Aust) Pty Ltd* (1992) 33 FCR 302). There is some indication that in the UK accounts of profit may be more widely available for common law causes of action. For example, in *Attorney-General v Blake* [2000] UKHL 45; [2001] 1 AC 268 the House of Lords held that there was no reason in principle why an account of profits should be ruled out as a remedy for breach of contract. It is for the plaintiff/applicant to elect whether to seek monetary award based on damages or an account of profits, and the election has to be made before any assessment is made by the courts. The wrong decision could have significant financial consequences.

In addition to the availability of compensatory damages and accounts of profit, the four key IP statutes also provide for additional damages in certain circumstances. For example, s 115(4) of the *Copyright Act* provides:

> Where, in an action under this section:
>
> (a) an infringement of copyright is established; and
> (b) the court is satisfied that it is proper to do so, having regard to:
>> (i) the flagrancy of the infringement; and
>> (ia) the need to deter similar infringements of copyright; and
>> (ib) the conduct of the defendant after the act constituting the infringement or, if relevant, after the defendant was informed that the defendant had allegedly infringed the plaintiff's copyright; and
>> (ii) whether the infringement involved the conversion of a work or other subject-matter from hardcopy or analog form into a digital or other electronic machine-readable form; and
>> (iii) any benefit shown to have accrued to the defendant by reason of the infringement; and
>> (iv) all other relevant matters;
>
> the court may, in assessing damages for the infringement, award such additional damages as it considers appropriate in the circumstances.

The jurisdiction to award additional damages is also provided in s 122(1A) of the *Patents Act*, s 75(3) of the *Designs Act* and, with effect from 15 April 2013, s 126(2) of the *TMA* (see *Halal Certification Authority Pty Ltd v Scadilone Pty Ltd* [2014] FCA 614; (2014) 107 IPR 23). Additional damages are usually ordered to mark the court's disapproval of the infringing (and other) behaviour of the defendant and to deter infringement. In one case relating to infringement of copyright in indigenous artistic works, *Milpurrurru v Indofurn Pty Ltd* (1994) 30 IPR 209, additional damages were awarded in recognition of the cultural harm suffered by the Indigenous artists as a result of being exposed to embarrassment and contempt within their communities after spiritually significant designs were used by the defendant on carpets.

ASSESSMENT OF COMPENSATORY AND ADDITIONAL DAMAGES IN IP MATTERS

CURRENT LAW

CASE EXTRACT: CURRENT LAW

Aristocrat Technologies Australia Pty Ltd v DAP Services (Kempsey) Pty Ltd (in liq)

[2007] FCAFC 40; (2007) 157 FCR 564
Federal Court of Australia, Full Court

[Aristocrat was a designer and manufacturer of electronic gaming machines. This matter related to Aristocrat's copyright in artistic works and literary works associated with the gaming machines. The trial judge held that there had been infringement of copyright by Vidtech (which later changed its name to DAP Services) and its directors, Mr and Mrs Parry. The issue on appeal was the quantification of compensatory damages under s 115(2) of the *Copyright Act* and of additional damages under s 115(4).]

Black CJ and Jacobson J: 1. The essential issue raised on this appeal is what degree of certainty is required for an applicant to prove its loss in a claim for damages for infringement of copyright.

2. It is almost trite to say that, in such a case, an applicant bears the onus of proof. But as Bowen LJ said over a century ago, as much certainty is required as is reasonable, having regard to all the circumstances; to require more 'would be the vainest pedantry'; *Ratcliffe v Evans* [1892] 2 QB 524 at 532–533; see also *Placer (Granny Smith) Pty Ltd v Theiss Contractors Pty Ltd* (2003) 196 ALR 257 at [37].

3. This appeal does not arise because of any pedantry on the part of the respondents. Rather, it arises because the primary judge found, in our view correctly, that he lacked the evidence necessary for him to calculate the value of lost sales, if any; see *Aristocrat Technologies Australia Pty Ltd v Vidtech Gaming Services Pty Ltd* (2006) 68 IPR 229 at [118]. His Honour then said that the 'only feasible course' was to calculate damages on an accounting for profit approach. He proceeded on that basis to award $80 000 damages against Vidtech, Mr Parry and Mrs Parry and $40 000 (ie 50%) additional damages against Vidtech and Mr Parry. Both sides agree that his Honour was in error in adopting this approach because the applicants had elected to claim damages rather than an account of profits.

. . .

DAMAGES UNDER S 115(2)

23. The remedies that may be granted to a copyright owner in an action for infringement include an injunction and either damages or an account of profits; s 115(2).

24. The authorities are clear that an applicant cannot claim both damages and an account; an election must be made before judgment; *Dr Martens Australia Pty Ltd v Bata Shoe Co of Australia Ltd* (1997) 75 FCR 230 (Goldberg J). It would be inconsistent with this principle, and contrary to the notions of fairness upon which it is founded, to proceed contrary to the election. Here, Aristocrat elected to claim damages, perhaps because additional damages under s 115(4) do not lie where an account of profits is claimed; McGregor on Damages, 17th ed [40,039].

25. The purpose of an award of damages for breach of copyright 'is to compensate the plaintiff for the loss which he has suffered as a result of the defendant's breach'; see *Interfirm Comparison (Aust)*

Pty Ltd v Law Society of New South Wales (1975) 6 ALR 445 at 446 (Bowen CJ); *Bailey v Namol Pty Ltd* (1994) 53 FCR 102 at 111 (Burchett, Gummow and O'Loughlin JJ).

26. In some cases, a royalty may provide the appropriate measure of damages; *Interfirm* at 446; *Bailey* at 111–112. Aristocrat argued that damages could be assessed on that basis as an alternative to its primary claim for loss of the value of sales.

27. However, a royalty does not provide the appropriate measure of damages where the copyright owner would not have granted a licence; *Columbia Pictures Industries Inc v Luckins* (1996) 34 IPR 504 at 509 (Tamberlin J); *Autodesk Australia Pty Ltd v Cheung* (1990) 94 ALR 472 at 476–477 (Wilcox J); *Microsoft Corporation v Goodview* (2000) 49 IPR 578 at [55].

28. In the present case, Aristocrat did not seek to establish that it would have granted a licence to Vidtech. The plain inference was that it would not have been prepared to do so. A royalty does not therefore provide an appropriate measure of damages.

29. In any event, Aristocrat did not lead evidence that licences were granted to users at any particular rate of royalty, let alone that which was claimed as a royalty in the present case. In those circumstances, where the quantification of royalties charged by a copyright owner is entirely within its own knowledge, a court should not speculate as to what royalty might have been foregone; *Paramount Pictures Corporation v Hasluck* (2006) 70 IPR 293; cf *Microsoft Corporation v Ezy Loans Pty Ltd* (2005) 63 IPR 54 at [88].

30. The gravamen of Aristocrat's claim for substantial damages was that the chartered accountant's report provided a clear 'ready reckoner' for the computation of the value of its lost sales. Senior Counsel submitted that the report 'stripped out' the intellectual property value of the units referred to by the Financial Controller, ie the initial game kits and the conversion kits.

31. The difficulty with this approach is that it rests upon assumptions that were not established. There was nothing to suggest that initial game kits were sold independently of the sale of new machines. Indeed, it would appear that they are part of each new machine. Thus, the position in respect of initial game kits is no different from the argument rejected by the primary judge. His Honour found, correctly in our view, that it could not be assumed, and was not established, that each sale by Vidtech was at the expense of a new Aristocrat machine.

32. His Honour found that there was no evidence of the price or volume of sales of conversion kits made to overseas customers. Moreover, during the hearing of the appeal, counsel for Mr and Mrs Parry pointed out that evidence had also been given at trial, during cross-examination, that Aristocrat itself sold second-hand machines. No evidence of their price or the volume of sales of second-hand machines by Aristocrat was led, and those figures were excluded from the information that the accountant used to estimate Aristocrat's loss. In our view, the accountant's 'intellectual property value' does not fill this evidentiary hole in Aristocrat's case.

33. In short, the suggested intellectual property value of each 'unit' cannot provide a basis for a finding that Aristocrat lost a sale of each item of intellectual property for each sale of an infringing copy made by Vidtech.

34. That is not to say that Aristocrat could not have discharged the onus of proving its loss. As Vidtech and Mr and Mrs Parry were found to be wrongdoers damages should be liberally assessed, in the sense that inferences will be more readily drawn against them, but the object remains to compensate Aristocrat, not to punish the respondents; *Bailey* at 110–111; *General Tire and Rubber Co v Firestone Tyre & Rubber Co Ltd* [1976] RPC 197 at 212 (Lord Wilberforce).

35. If a court finds that damage has occurred it must do its best to quantify the loss, even if some degree of speculation and guess work is involved; *Enzed Holdings Ltd v Wynthea Pty Ltd* (1984) 57 ALR 167 at 183 (Sheppard, Morling & Wilcox JJ). But, as their Honours emphasised, this principle applies only where a court finds that loss or damage has occurred; it is not enough merely to show wrongful conduct by a defendant. See also the observations of Mason CJ and Dawson J in *Commonwealth v Amann Aviation Pty Ltd* (1991) 174 CLR 64 at 83.

36. In *Placer* at [37]–[38] Hayne J pointed to the stricter approach taken by the courts in assessing damages where a plaintiff has not adduced evidence that was apparently available to prove the loss. Rares J has set out the relevant passages from *Placer* at [101] of his reasons for judgment. We agree with Rares J that it was open to Aristocrat to prove the volume and prices of sales in overseas markets. We also agree that it was artificial to suggest that Aristocrat lost the value of a sale for each of the 400 infringing sales by Vidtech.

37. Nevertheless, it may have been open to Aristocrat to contend that it lost some proportion of the sales made by Vidtech which would otherwise have been made by Aristocrat or a relevant member of the Aristocrat Group. This approach was adopted by Emmett J in *Sony Computer Entertainment Aust Pty Ltd v Stirling* [2001] FCA 1852 at [8]. His Honour did so notwithstanding that the respondent in that case sold counterfeit games for $15 whereas the sale price for the genuine article was $45–$50.

38. But the difficulty in adopting that approach here is that it was not adopted by Aristocrat. Its case was founded solely on the proposition that it lost the value of 400 sales and that proposition cannot be sustained.

39. It follows in our view that only nominal damages should be awarded. Such an award can be made, even though Aristocrat has not proved loss, because damages are not the gist of the action. The cause of action for infringement is conferred by s 115(1). Damages are merely one form of relief that the Court may order under s 115(2).

ADDITIONAL DAMAGES UNDER S 115(4)

40. Where an infringement of copyright is established the Court may, in assessing damages, award additional damages if it is satisfied that it is proper to do so having regard to the flagrancy of the infringement and the other matters referred to in s 115(4)(b).

41. Flagrancy is not an essential prerequisite for an award of additional damages. It is sufficient if the Court is satisfied that any one or more of the circumstances set out in s 115(4)(b) is established; *Raben Footwear v Polygram Records Inc* (1997) 75 FCR 88 at 93 (Burchett J), 103 (Tamberlin J), 104 (Lehane J); see also *Polygram Pty Ltd v Golden Editions Pty Ltd* (1997) 76 FCR 565 at 575 (Lockhart J); *Sony Entertainment (Australia) Ltd v Smith* (2005) 215 ALR 788 at [158].

42. Additional damages under s 115(4) may be awarded on principles that correspond to those governing awards of aggravated and exemplary damages at common law; *Autodesk Inc v Yee* (1996) 68 FCR 391 at 394 (Burchett J) ...

43. The objectives of an award of additional damages include deterrence; s 115(4)(b)(ia). An element of penalty is an accepted factor in the remedy; *Autodesk v Yee* at 384.

44. One of the factors referred to in s 115(4)(b) is any benefit shown to have accrued to a defendant by reason of the infringement; see 115(4)(b)(iii). In construing the English equivalent provision, Brightman J said that 'benefit' implies that the defendant has reaped a pecuniary benefit in excess of the damages otherwise payable; *Ravenscroft v Herbert* [1980] RPC 193 at 208. It is possible, however, that the benefit need not be confined to a pecuniary one; *Polygram v Golden Editions* at 576.

45. There need not be any proportionality between the amount of compensatory damages awarded under s 115(2) and the amount of additional damages ordered under s 115(4); *Raben* at 93, 103, 104; see also *Microsoft Corporation v PC Club of Aust Pty Ltd* (2005) 148 FCR 310 at 409–410 (Conti J).

46. In the present case the infringements were flagrant and Mr Parry sought to cover up his involvement and that of Vidtech. He was undeterred by the threat of legal proceedings.

47. The primary judge determined that Vidtech had obtained a pecuniary benefit of at least $80 000. His Honour found at [113] that there were significant unexplained cash transactions and that money had been directed to places such as the Isle of Man where tracing was difficult. He also found that money had been muddled between Vidtech's corporate accounts and personal accounts of Mr and Mrs Parry. It would therefore seem likely that Mr and Mrs Parry received substantial pecuniary benefits.

48. One of the purposes of an award of additional damages must be to strip the infringer of all pecuniary benefits received from the infringement but that is not the limit of the statutory objective which, as we have said, includes an element of penalty.

...

53. ... [T]he evidence before the primary judge demonstrated a cynical and flagrant exploitation of Aristocrat's copyright by Vidtech and Mr Parry ... $40 000, the amount awarded by the primary judge as additional damages, is not an appropriate figure to reflect the flagrancy of the infringements, the need to deter similar infringements and the need to mark the Court's disapproval of the conduct. The starting point, to reflect in a broad way the benefit obtained is, as we have said, $105 000. There should be added to this sum a substantial amount for the other factors we have identified. We should also take into account the fact that Vidtech failed to keep adequate records of its financial dealings so as to make proof of loss more difficult. We consider that a further amount of $95 000 should be added to the sum of $105 000 so as to arrive at $200 000 by way of additional damages against Vidtech and Mr Parry.

54. The fact that we have awarded only nominal damages under s 115(2) does not preclude a substantial award of additional damages, where, as here, the circumstances call for such an award. As Conti J said in *Microsoft v PC Club,* in an appropriate case, the quantification may well exceed the amount of compensatory damages under s 115(2) ...

ASSESSMENT OF ACCOUNTS OF PROFITS IN IP MATTERS

CASE EXTRACT: CURRENT LAW

Dart Industries Inc v Decor Corporation Pty Ltd

(1993) 179 CLR 101
High Court of Australia

[This case related to a patent owned by Dart for press button seals on the lids of kitchen containers, which had been infringed by Decor and Rian.]

Mason CJ, Deane, Dawson, Toohey JJ (at 109–121) (some footnotes omitted): Dart having elected between damages and an account of profits, the trial judge, King J, ordered an account of profits by Decor and Rian. In giving directions, King J dealt with two questions, the first of which falls to be determined upon this appeal and the second of which is raised in an application by Decor and Rian for special leave to cross-appeal. The first is whether any part of general overhead costs is allowable as a deduction to Decor or Rian in the determination of the profits made by them from the infringement. The second is whether Decor and Rian must account for profits arising from the manufacture and sale of the composite product, consisting of both the body of the canister and the press button seal, or merely for those profits attributable to the manufacture and sale of the press button seal alone, that being the patented invention.

...

Damages and an account of profits are alternative remedies. An account of profits was a form of relief granted by equity whereas damages were originally a purely common law remedy. As Windeyer J pointed out in *Colbeam Palmer Ltd v Stock Affiliates Pty Ltd* [(1968) 122 CLR 25 at p 34] ... an account of profits retains its equitable characteristics in that a defendant is made to account for, and is then stripped of, profits which it has dishonestly made by the infringement and which it would be unconscionable for it to retain. An account of profits is confined to profits actually made, its purpose being not to punish the defendant but to prevent its unjust enrichment. The ordinary requirement of the principles of unjust enrichment that regard be paid to matters of substance rather than technical form is applicable.

But it is notoriously difficult in some cases, particularly cases involving the manufacture or sale of a range of products, to isolate those costs which are attributable to the infringement from those which are not so attributable [See *Siddell v Vickers* (1892) 9 RPC 152 at pp 162–163; *My Kinda Town Ltd v Soll* [1983] RPC 15 at pp 57–58]. Whilst it is accepted that mathematical exactitude is generally impossible, the exercise is one that must be undertaken, and some assistance may be derived from the principles and practices of commercial accounting [See *Odeon Associated Theatres Ltd v Jones* [1973] Ch 288 at pp 294, 299, 305; *Federal Commissioner of Taxation v St Hubert's Island Pty Ltd (In Liq)* (1978) 138 CLR 210 at p 228]. Unfortunately, neither the Australian nor the English authorities contain any precise analysis of the problem.

...

Dart's argument, based on incremental costing as the proper method for taking an account of profits of infringing activities, is as follows. The profit should be calculated by taking the gross revenue received from the manufacture and sale of the infringing product and deducting from it direct costs, such as materials or labour, solely due to the manufacture or sale of the infringing product, and also deducting overheads, but only to the extent that they were increased by the manufacture or sale of the infringing product. Otherwise, the defendant would be able to deduct expenditure which it would have incurred in any event. This should not be allowed because if any of the revenue from the sale or manufacture could be set off against general overheads which would have been incurred without the infringing activities, the defendant would profit from the infringing activities. The defendant would gain by reducing the cost of its overheads, but would not have to account to the plaintiff for this gain.

...

But there was no evidence in this case that Decor or Rian had unused or surplus capacity. There was evidence that the infringing canisters were an integral part of one consistent product range produced, marketed and sold according to a common system. From this it might be inferred that, had those companies not been engaged in the manufacture and marketing of the infringing press button seal canisters, their capacity for those activities would have been taken up in the manufacture and marketing of alternative products.

Thus the cost of manufacturing and marketing the press button seal canisters may have included the cost of forgoing the profit from the manufacture and marketing of alternative products. The latter cost is called an opportunity cost. 'Opportunity cost' can be defined as 'the value of the alternative foregone by adopting a particular strategy or employing resources in a specific manner ... As used in economics, the opportunity cost of any designated alternative is the greatest net benefit lost by taking an alternative.' [*Kohler's Dictionary for Accountants*, 6th ed (1983) pp 362–363.] The practical reality of this concept was recognized in *Schnadig Corp v Gaines Manufacturing Co Inc* [(1980) 620 F 2d 1166 at p 1175], where the Court stated: 'The alternative available uses of the facilities devoted to the infringement must be considered, and these too will vary.'

In calculating an account of profits, the defendant may not deduct the opportunity cost, that is, the profit forgone on the alternative products. But there would be real inequity if a defendant were denied a deduction for the opportunity cost as well as being denied a deduction for the cost of the overheads which sustained the capacity that would have been utilized by an alternative product and that was in fact utilized by the infringing product. If both were denied, the defendant would be in a worse position than if it had made no use of the patented invention. The purpose of an account of profits is not to punish the defendant but to prevent its unjust enrichment.

Where the defendant has forgone the opportunity to manufacture and sell alternative products it will ordinarily be appropriate to attribute to the infringing product a proportion of those general overheads which would have sustained the opportunity. On the other hand, if no opportunity was forgone, and the overheads involved were costs which would have been incurred in any event, then it would not be appropriate to attribute the overheads to the infringing product. Otherwise the defendant would be in a better position than it would have been in if it had not infringed. It is not relevant that the product could not have been manufactured and sold without these overheads. Nor is it relevant that absorption method accounting would attribute a proportion of the overheads to the infringing product. The equitable principle of an account of profits is not to compensate the plaintiff, nor to fix a fair price for the infringing product, but to prevent the unjust enrichment of the defendant.

...

In the present case, the trial judge accepted that the manufacture and sale of the infringing goods was not a side line. He found that Decor's range of canisters with press button seals formed part of a much larger range of container systems, storage systems and canisters. On the evidence, the share of sales of the canisters with press button seals varied from 3.1 per cent to 1.3 per cent over a six-year period after they were added to Decor's existing range, and that percentage was similar to the percentage of sales of other types of containers in Decor's range.

Decor contends that it is possible to identify some overheads as direct costs which may be attributed to the press button seal canisters as actually incurred in respect of them, namely, the cost of product development/royalty expenses, media advertising, industrial design registration, legal fees and tooling expenses. It seeks to allocate all remaining overheads which are indirect costs by reference to the proportion which sales of canisters with press button seals bear to total sales.

Whether Decor and Rian should succeed in their contentions depends upon whether, as a matter of fact and substance, the overheads which they seek to have deducted are attributable to the manufacture and sale of the infringing product. In arriving at an answer, the Court must consider such questions as whether the overheads in any particular category were increased by the manufacture or sale of the product, whether they represent costs which would have been reduced or would have been incurred in any event, and whether they were surplus capacity or would, in the absence of the infringing product, have been used in the manufacture or sale of other products. Dealing with the last of these questions may require the use of the concept of opportunity cost. If any of the categories are to be brought into account, the proportion to be allocated to the infringing product must be determined and it is here that approximation rather than precision may be necessary. But such an approach has long been accepted. As was said in *Colburn v Simms* [(1843) 2 Hare 543 at p 560; 67 ER 224 at p 231]:

> The Court, by the account, as the nearest approximation which it can make to justice, takes from the wrongdoer all the profits he has made by his piracy, and gives them to the party who has been wronged.

It follows that we consider that King J was in error in directing that 'no part of general overhead costs is allowable as a deduction' and that the Full Court was substantially correct in directing, as it did, that 'the appellants are at liberty to show that various categories of overhead contributed to the obtaining of the relevant profit, and to show how and in what proportion they should be allocated in the taking of the account of profits'. But it would be better, we think, if the word 'contributed' were replaced by the words 'are attributable'.

The application by Decor and Rian for special leave to cross- appeal may be dealt with more shortly. In considering whether the profits for which an account was ordered should include those arising from the manufacture and sale of the canisters as well as the press button seals which were fitted to them, the trial judge correctly identified the problem when he said [(1990) 20 IPR at p 152]:

> The basic legal principle is that the relevant profits are those accruing to the defendants from their use and exercise of the plaintiff's patented invention. Where the defendants' products are, as here, composites of the invention and other features the determination of such a question is one of fact.

In answering the question which he posed, King J found that 'sales of press button canisters are for present purposes attributable to use of the patented invention' and for that reason directed that the profits for which Decor and Rian had to account included the profits from the containers to which the press button seals were fitted [ibid at p 154].

The Full Court identified the same question in somewhat different terms [(1991) 104 ALR at pp 630–631]:

> The respondent cannot gainsay that it is only entitled to the profits obtained by the infringement. If, for example, a patented brake is wrongfully used in the construction of a motor car, the patentee is not entitled to the entire profits earned by sales of the motor car. He must accept an appropriate apportionment. But the question is how that principle shall be applied to a situation where the patent relates to the essential feature of a single item … it seems to us that it was open to the judge to find, and he correctly found, that what characterised the infringing product was the press button lid, without which this particular container would never have been produced at all.

The questions posed by the trial judge and the Full Court concerning the apportionment of a total profit both accurately reflect the correct principle which was expressed in this Court by Windeyer J in *Colbeam Palmer Ltd v Stock Affiliates Pty Ltd* [(1968) 122 CLR at pp 42–43] as follows:

> The true rule, I consider, is that a person who wrongly uses another man's industrial property— patent, copyright, trade mark—is accountable for any profits which he makes which are

attributable to his use of the property which was not his ... If one man makes profits by the use or sale of some thing, and that whole thing came into existence by reason of his wrongful use of another man's property in a patent, design or copyright, the difficulty disappears and the case is then, generally speaking, simple. In such a case the infringer must account for all the profits which he thus made.

It is true that there is some divergence between King J and the Full Court in relation to whether, in the circumstances of this case, primary emphasis should be placed on reason for sale or reason for production. Nonetheless, the overall approach of both accurately reflects the application of the correct general principle in the resolution of what is ultimately a question of fact.

[The outcome was that the appeal was dismissed and the application for special leave to cross-appeal refused. The order of the Full Federal Court was varied by replacing the word 'contributed' with the words 'are attributable'.]

CONVERSION DAMAGES

CASE EXTRACT: CURRENT LAW

Sony Entertainment (Australia) Ltd v Smith

[2005] FCA 228; (2005) 64 IPR 18
Federal Court of Australia

[Section 116 of the *Copyright Act* provides the copyright owner with the right to recover damages for conversion or detention of infringing copies of works and other subject matter. This case related to infringement of copyright in various sound recordings by the sale of infringing CDs. Sony claimed compensatory and additional damages, as well as conversion damages under s 116. The assessment of conversion damages was complicated by the fact that the CDs included both infringing and non-infringing tracks.]

Jacobson J:

DAMAGES FOR CONVERSION

113. As Burchett J observed in *Autodesk v Yee* (1996) 139 ALR 735 at 739–740, the modern form of the copyright owner's right to bring an action for conversion under s 116(1) of the Act has been the subject of considerable criticism; see also *Polygram Pty Ltd v Golden Editions Pty Ltd* (1997) 38 IPR 451 ('*Polygram*') at 454–455 (Lockhart J).

...

116. In *Autodesk* at 738–740, Burchett J traced the history of s 116 of the Act. His Honour observed that an element of penalty is an accepted feature of copyright legislation, the infringer being treated as a 'pirate'. The effect of s 116(1) is to create a statutory fiction under which the copyright owner is treated as the owner of the infringing article with the consequent entitlement to sue for conversion or detinue; see *Autodesk* at 740–741 and Polygram at 454.

117. As Lockhart J said in *Polygram* at 454, the measure of damages in conversion is generally the value of the infringing copy at the date of conversion. Provision is made in s 116(1D) of the Act for the value to be assessed having regard to, inter alia, the expenses of the infringer in manufacturing the infringing copy.

118. Under s 116(1C) of the Act, the Court is not to grant relief in damages for conversion if the relief it has granted or proposes to grant under s 115 is, in the opinion of the Court, a sufficient remedy.

119. In the present case, I do not consider that relief under s 115(2) is sufficient. There are two reasons for this. The first is that the applicants' evidence establishes that the respondents have failed to give proper discovery of their records. It is plain that the respondents have not produced documents which contain details of the number of compact discs pressed or sold by them. The records that were produced by Tower showed the pressing of a much smaller number of discs than was revealed in documents obtained by the applicants from Technicolor.

120. It follows in my view that the respondents have not put before the Court the necessary documents to enable me to calculate the quantum of pecuniary relief under s 115(2) of the Act.

121. The second reason is that I am satisfied on the evidence before me that it is unlikely that the relevant applicants would have granted licences to any of the respondents to reproduce the copyright sound recordings or compilation CDs. It is true that Mr Kearney gave preliminary and informal approval for a few tracks. But the overall effect of the evidence is that the respondents would not have met the applicants' detailed requirements for the grant of licences. It is therefore inappropriate to assess damages under s 115(2) on the basis of assumed licences; see *Universal Music Australia Pty Ltd v Miyamoto* [2004] FCA 982 (Wilcox J).

WHETHER DAMAGES FOR CONVERSION OUGHT TO BE APPORTIONED

...

136. Section 116(1E) states three factors to which the Court may have regard in deciding whether to grant relief 'and in assessing the amount of damages payable'. I refer to the factors below. Thus, s 116(1E) relates both to the discretion to award damages for conversion and the quantum of any award.

...

139. Thus it seems to me that the effect of s 116(1E) is to give the Court a discretion to award an amount of damages in conversion which, having regard to the stated factors, provides a fair measure of damages in the particular case. The sub-section is directed at an assessment which strikes a fair balance between the compensatory aspect of the remedy and the acknowledgment of the copyright owner's domain over infringing copies.

140. It must be a matter for the exercise of the discretion of the Court in each case to determine where the proper balance lies.

...

[His Honour then proceeded to list the number of infringing tracks on each CD and took into consideration the fact that the infringing and non-infringing tracks could not be severed.]

149. It seems to me that in striking the appropriate balance, the starting point should be the proportion of the infringing tracks to the whole but an amount should be added to recognize the impossibility of severance. I therefore propose to increase the proportion by 100%, that is to say, I will double the percentage which would otherwise flow from the proportion of the infringing tracks on each CD.

CURRENT LAW

150. In my view, this provides a proper measure of damages in light of the rule that conversion damages are compensatory ... There is usually a punitive element in an award of conversion damages because the verdict operates as a forced sale but any further punitive aspect should be determined in the application for additional damages under s 115(4).

151. I do not consider that on its proper construction s 116(1C) prevents the Court from awarding conversion damages under s 116 and additional damages under s 115(4). I would only be precluded from doing so if I were of the opinion that additional damages of themselves would be sufficient. I am not of that opinion because the conversion damages I will award are to be compensatory whilst the additional damages to which I refer below are of the nature of exemplary damages.

INNOCENT INFRINGEMENT AND SAFE HARBOURS FOR CARRIAGE SERVICE PROVIDERS

Although 'innocence' is not a defence to infringing acts, it may disentitle the IP rights owner to a damages award. For example, s 115(3) of the *Copyright Act* provides that:

> Where, in an action for infringement of copyright, it is established that an infringement was committed but it is also established that, at the time of the infringement, the defendant was not aware, and had no reasonable grounds for suspecting, that the act constituting the infringement was an infringement of the copyright, the plaintiff is not entitled under this section to any damages against the defendant in respect of the infringement, but is entitled to an account of profits in respect of the infringement whether any other relief is granted under this section or not.

Similar provisions are found in s 123 of the *Patents Act* and s 75(2) of the *Designs Act*, although the provisions state that the court *may* refuse damages, and focus on whether the defendant knew that the plaintiff's rights *existed*, not whether the defendant knew or ought to have known they were *infringing*. Relief for 'innocent' infringement is not provided in the *TMA*.

Sections 116AA–116AJ of the *Copyright Act*, introduced in 2005, create 'safe harbours' protecting 'carriage service providers' (defined in accordance with s 87 of the *Telecommunications Act 1997* (Cth)) from specific types of liability. Essentially, these provisions provide that there is no liability to pay damages, accounts of profits or additional damages, or to make other monetary relief, where infringement occurs during transmitting, routing, providing connections, caching, storing or referring users to an online location using information location tools or technology. The safe harbour only applies subject to certain conditions, which are set out in table format in s 116AH. The major requirements are that the carriage service provider must implement a policy that provides for the termination of accounts of persons who repeatedly infringe copyright, and must comply with the provisions of any relevant industry code relating to accommodation and non-interference with technical measures that are used to identify and protect copyrighted material. In some cases, the carriage service provider must implement a system for the expeditious take-down of alleged infringing material. There is no obligation to monitor for infringing activity unless required to do so under an industry code. These provisions were considered in detail in *Roadshow Films Pty Ltd v iiNet Ltd* [2011] FCAFC 23; (2011) 194 FCR 285, but were not the subject of Roadshow's appeal to the High Court. The Attorney-General's Department is considering whether the 'safe harbour' regime ought to be expanded to encompass the activities of all online service providers, such as independent search engines or web hosts (as it does under US law): see *Revising the Scope of the Copyright 'Safe Harbour Scheme': Consultation Paper* (2011) and *Online Copyright Infringement: Discussion Paper* (2014).

UNJUSTIFIED THREATS OF INFRINGEMENT PROCEEDINGS

All of the major IP statutes have provisions allowing a party to bring an action for unjustified threats of infringement proceedings. For example, s 128(1) of the *Patents Act* states:

> Where a person, by means of circulars, advertisements or otherwise, threatens a person with infringement proceedings, or other similar proceedings, a person aggrieved may apply to a prescribed court, or to another court having jurisdiction to hear and determine the application, for:
>
> (a) a declaration that the threats are unjustifiable; and
> (b) an injunction against the continuance of the threats; and
> (c) the recovery of any damages sustained by the applicant as a result of the threats.

Similar provisions are found in s 202 of the *Copyright Act*, s 129 of the *TMA* and s 77 of the *Designs Act*. These provisions are designed particularly to protect businesses in cases where they or their competitors are threatened by an IP owner. A party accused of engaging in unjustified threats can defend the action by commencing infringement proceedings.

Actions for unjustified threats are rare and there are few relevant judgments. One example is *U and I Global Trading (Australia) Pty Ltd v Tasman-Warajay Pty Ltd* (1995) 32 IPR 494, which relates to the interpretation of s 128 of the *Patents Act*. The key test as expounded by Cooper J at [19] was:

> whether the language would convey to any reasonable person that the author of the letter in the present case intended to bring proceedings for infringement against the person said to be threatened. It is not necessary that there be direct words that action would be taken.

CRIMINAL OFFENCES

Article 61 of the *Agreement on Trade-Related Aspects of Intellectual Property Rights* (the 'TRIPS Agreement') (1994) requires World Trade Organization (WTO) members to 'provide for criminal procedures and penalties to be applied at least in cases of wilful trademark counterfeiting or copyright piracy on a commercial scale', and more detailed criminal measures are required under various bilateral agreements, notably the *Australia–US Free Trade Agreement* (2004). To this end, the *Copyright Act* and *TMA* both contain extensive criminal measures.

Part V Div 5 of the *Copyright Act* provides for a range of criminal offences relating to infringement of copyright, technological protection measures and electronic rights management. Part VAA Div 3 sets out criminal offences relating to broadcast decoding devices. These provisions apply where a person has engaged in such acts as: substantial infringement on a commercial scale; dealings with infringing copies; airing of works, sound recordings and films; dealings with technological protection measures (including circumventing access control technological protection measures and manufacture of circumvention devices for technological protection measures, and providing circumvention services for technological protection measures); and dealings with electronic rights management (including removing or altering electronic rights management information, and distributing, importing or communicating copies after removal or alteration of electronic rights management information). A range of criminal offences relating to performers' rights is provided in ss 248P–248QH. Other criminal offences can be found in ss 203A–203H (including for conduct as inconsequential as failing to arrange certain declarations chronologically) and 248R. The copyright legislation makes distinctions between summary, strict liability and indictable offences, largely based on the scale of the infringing acts and the state of mind of the person committing those acts.

A range of trade mark offences is contained in Part 14 of the *TMA*, and can be grouped into three categories. The first covers 'counterfeiting' offences, targeting those who are producing or selling infringing products, or assisting in the production of such products (ss 146–148). The second group relates to the removal or alteration of the trade mark from goods without the owner's permission (ss 145, 147–148). The third group is aimed at trade mark owners, making it an offence to falsely represent that a trade mark is registered (s 151), or to intentionally make a false entry in the Register (s 152).

The other IP statutes contain less extensive criminal provisions, more akin to the third group of trade mark related offences. Chapter 18 of the *Patents Act* and Ch 11 Part 3 of the *Designs Act* list a number of offences, including for making certain false representations and for failure to comply with various requirements of the Commissioner of Patents or Registrar of Designs.

In terms of jurisdiction, s 133A of the *Copyright Act* provides that prosecutions for summary and strict liability offences relating to copyright infringement, technological protection measures and electronic rights management may be brought in the Federal Court and other courts with competent jurisdiction, but denies the Federal Court jurisdiction to hear and determine prosecutions for indictable offences. In contrast, s 154(3) of the *Patents Act*, s 83(3) of the *Designs Act* and s 191(3) of the *TMA* provide that prosecutions under those Acts must not be started in the Federal Court, while s 83A(3) of the *Designs Act* and s 191A(3) of the *TMA* provide that prosecutions under those Acts must not be started in the Federal Circuit Court.

INDEX